Elizabeth Compton
(da. of 7th Earl of
Northampton) (1760–1835)

William Brabazon, 1st
Baron Ponsonby (b.1744)
m.1769
Louisa Molesworth
(1749–1824)

Horatio Walpole
Earl of Orford
(1752–1822)
m.1781
Sophia Churchill
(d. 1797)

Mary Walpole (1754–1840)
m.1777
Thomas Hussey of
Galtrim

George Walpole
(1758–1835)

Horatio Walpole
Earl of Orford
(1723–1809)

George Augustus Cavendish
(1728–94)

Frederick Cavendish
(1729–1803)

Daughter (d. 1731)

John Cavendish
(1732–96)

Sir William Lowther
(1727—56)

Elizabeth Lowther
(b. 1728)

Son (b. 1733)

Henry Cavendish
(1731–1810)

Frederick Cavendish
(1733–1812)

Anne Cavendish
(d.1780)

Diana Cavendish
(d.1722)

John Cavendish
(d.1720)

Mary Cavendish
(1699–1778)
m.1716
John Fane, 7th Earl
of Westmorland
(1686–1762)

William Cavendish
(1709?–1751)
m.1731
Barbara Chandler
(d. 1786)

Elizabeth Cavendish
(1701–79)
m.1732
Richard Chandler-
Cavendish (1703?–1769)

Sir Butler Cavendish
Wentworth of Crambe
(d.1741)

Two more sons

Henry Cavendish
(1673–1700)
m.
Rhoda Cartwright
(d.1730)

James Cavendish
(d.1751)
m.1708
Anne Yale
(d.1734)

Elizabeth Cavendish
(d.1741)
m.
Sir John Wentworth
of Broadsworth

D1160064

Cavendish

Cavendish

by

CHRISTA JUNGNICKEL

and

RUSSELL McCORMMACH

THE AMERICAN PHILOSOPHICAL SOCIETY

Philadelphia, Pennsylvania

1996

Memoirs of the American Philosophical Society
Held at Philadelphia
For Promoting Useful Knowledge
Volume 220

Front leaf: Cavendish Family; back leaf: Grey family.

Library of Congress Cataloging in Publication Data:

Jungnickel, Christa
McCormmach, Russell

Cavendish

Illustrations, bibliography, index, charts
1. Cavendish, Henry, and Lord Charles Cavendish
2. Science, history of 3. British science 4. Biography

ISBN:0-87169-220-1   95-79391

For
Albert L. McCormmach
and
Marie Peetz McCormmach

TABLE OF CONTENTS

LIST OF FIGURES
(Between pages 218–219)

LIST OF PLATES: DIAGRAMS, DRAWINGS, AND MAPS

INTRODUCTION

Problem of Cavendish

Henry Cavendish, 1731–1810, is described in superlatives. Regarding matters of intellect and fortune, he has been called the "the wisest of the rich and the richest of the wise."[1] In his dedication to science, he has been compared with "the most austere anchorites," who were "not more faithful to their vows."[2] His accomplishment has been likened to the highest example: since the death of Newton, England had suffered "no scientific loss so great as that of Cavendish."[3] He is described by superlatives of another, darker kind as well. Cavendish had a "most reserved disposition," which was seen as "bordering on disease."[4] Cavendish was, indeed, one of the greatest scientists of his century, one of the richest men of the realm, a scion of one of the most powerful aristocratic families, a scientific fanatic, and a neurotic of the first order. These things being the case, it would seem that Cavendish's biographers are called upon to construct a psychological portrait of a tormented genius.

We have taken a different approach (though in concluding this biography we discuss a psychological point). Cavendish's scientific achievement depended upon his talent, a given, but it depended no less on his dedication to science, and about this we, his biographers, can say something useful. Until we looked closely at the life of his father, Lord Charles Cavendish, 1704–83, we did not have a firm understanding of Henry's. Coming from a family of politicians, Lord Charles predictably entered public life as a politician. It so happened that while he was active in politics, he also pursued science as a side interest, and indeed at a certain point he left politics to devote himself increasingly to science. His example was constantly before his son Henry while Henry was a student and later while he was giving direction to his life, and it is clear that Henry followed Lord Charles's scientific path. The public expression of the scientific calling of Lord Charles and Henry was their dedication to the work of the Royal Society of London.

From the perspective of the larger society, Lord Charles could have been regarded as overstepping the bounds of his station in life. Drawn to experiment and especially to the instruments of experiment, he was a type of technical man. His aristocratic contemporary Lord Chesterfield made a sound judgment for the time when he censored the architectural expert Lord Burlington for having more technical competence than his rank permitted.[5] Within the Royal Society, however, both rank and scientific competence were honored, and Lord Charles and his son Henry are the outstanding example of their union in the eighteenth century. By the time Henry joined Lord Charles in the Society, it had been in existence for a century, and it had its hallowed traditions, but it still retained a measure of its revolutionary potential in English society. Lord Charles Cavendish definitely found support in the Royal Society for his move from a traditional aristocratic career in politics to an uncommon life of an aristocrat in science.

Lord Charles Cavendish's attention to the affairs of the Royal Society was extraordinary by any standard: no member of the Society, including any of its presidents, gave as much of himself to the organization of science as he did. It is critical to the nature of this biography that the next member of the Royal Society to do the same was his son Henry. In this respect, of the two, father and son, the father was the more original. At a time when science did not yet offer itself as a profession, Lord

[1] J. B. Biot, "Cavendish (Henri)," *Biographie Universelle*. Vol. 7 (Paris, 1813), 272–73, on 273.

[2] Georges Cuvier, "Henry Cavendish" This biographical writing of 1812 is translated by D. S. Faber in *Great Chemists*, ed. E. Faber (New York: Interscience Publishers, 1961), 227–38, on 236.

[3] Humphry Davy, quoted in John Davy, *Memoirs of the Life of Sir Humphry Davy, Bart*, 2 vols. (London, 1836) 1:222.

[4] Henry, Lord Brougham, "Cavendish," in his *Lives of Men of Letters and Science Who Flourished in the Time of George III*, 2 vols (London, 1845–46) 1:429–47, on 444. Thomas Thomson, *The History of Chemistry*, 2 vols. (London, 1830–31) 1:337.

[5] Quoted in Dorothy Marshall, *Dr Johnson's London* (New York: John Wiley & Sons, 1968), 219.

Charles Cavendish turned to science, as he had done earlier to politics, thereby crafting a version of an acceptable profession for himself, the evidence for which is as undramatic as it is indisputable, a change of location of his committee work from the House of Commons to the Royal Society. Lord Charles and his son Henry were the great councillors and committeemen of the Royal Society. Councils and committees are not ordinarily places of high endeavor, and their members often feel impatient, irritated, and stupefied; nevertheless, they are the level of organization in scientific and learned institutions in which necessary tasks get done, and they are where colleagues get to know one another well and find out who has good judgment and who takes responsibility.[6] The importance of Lord Charles Cavendish for the history of science lies not in any one achievement but in his forty years of organizational work in science. Having made no great discovery, he has entered the history of science as, at most, a footnote, but in a biography of the discoverer Henry Cavendish, Lord Charles Cavendish necessarily appears with nearly equal importance. Lionel Trilling's stricture "Every man's biography is to be understood in relation to his father"[7] may not be a practical guide for all biographers, but for biographers of Henry Cavendish, it is indispensable. We have written this book as a biography of father and son.

Historians of science know of Cavendishes earlier than Lord Charles and Henry Cavendish. Richard Cavendish, one of the Cavendishes of Suffolk from whom the Devonshires descended, was an Elizabethan politician and professional student— for twenty-eight years he was a student at Cambridge and Oxford—who translated Euclid into English and wrote poems including (and in spirit foreshadowing our Henry Cavendish) "No Joy Comparable to a Quiet Minde," which begins, "In lothsome race pursued by slippery life."[8] The namesake of one of our Cavendishes, Charles Cavendish, a seventeenth-century politician, was an important man in science: a solver of mathematical problems, a maker of experiments, an improver of telescopes, he corresponded with the inventors of new world systems, René Descartes and Pierre Gassendi. This Charles was "small and deformed," but he had a beautiful mind. In a time of violent controversy, he

advocated cooperation as the way to truth. He subscribed to Descartes's maxim, "to strive to vanquish myself rather than fortune and to change my desires rather than the order of the world. . . ."[9] This Charles and his older brother William, duke of Newcastle, who had a scientific laboratory, were friends of Thomas Hobbes, the philosopher who envisioned a state of war of each against all, and who also wrote the most original scientific philosophy in England. Hobbes tutored and influenced three generations of the other main branch of the Cavendishes, the earls (not yet dukes) of Devonshire. He moved in the great houses of the Cavendishes, Chatsworth and Hardwick Hall (both of which our Lord Charles and Henry Cavendish knew well), in the libraries of which he found the true university that he had not found in Oxford.[10] By Charles Cavendish's time, science was not exclusively a male preserve: a case in point, Margaret Cavendish, duchess of Newcastle, wrote a number of good popular books on the microscope and other scientific novelties. She demanded to be, and was, admitted as a visitor to the Royal Society. She dressed like men and, in general, behaved like a George Sand of science. For that, this original and independent first scientific lady in England was called Mad Madge.[11] In Henry Cavendish's time, Margaret Cavendish Bentinck, duchess of Portland, also of the Newcastle branch of the family, was a correspondent of Rousseau and a passionate collector; at her death, the sale of her natural history collection, second only to that of the pre-

---

[6]Lewis Thomas, a redoubtable committeeman of science, has remarked in various places on the indispensability and value of committees and on the inescapable disruptiveness of human individuality in the work of committees. E.g., in *The Youngest Science: Notes of a Medicine-Watcher* (New York: Viking, 1983), 171; "On Committees," in *The Medusa and the Snail: More Notes of a Biology Watcher* (New York: Bantam, 1980), 94–98. Thomas's appreciation is not incompatible with Alvin Weinberg's widely held opinion that "committees… can no more produce wisdom than they can design a camel." *Reflections on Big Science* (Cambridge, Mass.: MIT Press, 1967), vi.

[7]From Lionel Trilling's introduction to *The Portable Matthew Arnold*, ed. L. Trilling (New York: Viking, 1949), 15.

[8]"Cavendish, Richard," *DNB* 3:1266–67.

[9]Jean Jacquot, "Sir Charles Cavendish and His Learned Friends. A Contribution to the History of Scientific Relations between England and the Continent in the Earlier Part of the 17th Century. I. Before the Civil War. II. The Years of Exile," *Annals of Science* 8 (1952): 13–27, 175–91, on 13, 187, 191.

[10]Samuel I. Mintz, "Hobbes, Thomas," *DSB* 6:444–51, on 444–45.

[11]Gerald Dennis Meyer, *The Scientific Lady in England 1650–1760* (Berkeley: University of California Press, 1955), 1–15.

sident of the Royal Society, Hans Sloane, took thirty-eight days.[12] As if handing on the torch, in the year Henry Cavendish was born, 1731, Charles Boyle, the earl of Orrery died. This earl, whose mother was Anne Cavendish, sister of the first duke of Devonshire, was related to the great seventeenth-century chemist Robert Boyle, and it was after this earl that the instrument-maker George Graham's invention of the machine to show the motions of the heavenly bodies, the "orrery," was named.[13] (The Cavendishes would make another connection with the family of Robert Boyle in the year that Henry Cavendish began university study, when Henry Cavendish's first cousin, the fourth duke of Devonshire, married Charlotte Boyle.) Other early scientifically inclined Cavendishes include three important Fellows of the Royal Society: the third earl of Devonshire, the first duke of Devonshire, who was tutored by the famous secretary of the Royal Society Henry Oldenburg,[14] and the youngest son of the first duke, Lord James Cavendish. English aristocrats who actively pursued science were few indeed, and if a titled family was destined to distinguish itself in the eighteenth century, it was surely the house of Cavendish. Lord Charles and Henry Cavendish's lineage was remarkable scientifically as it was politically.

Our Cavendishes descended from two revolutions, one political and the other scientific. The Cavendish who became the first duke of Devonshire took a leading part in the Glorious Revolution of 1688, which deposed one king and sat another. When compared with subsequent political upheavals, the Glorious Revolution may not seem all that revolutionary[15] (in part because it was bloodless, hence glorious), but to the British of the eighteenth century, it was the embodiment of a radical change in human affairs. Joseph Priestley, a scientific colleague of Henry Cavendish and also a friend of revolutions, said of this "revolution under king William" that before the French and American "revolutions," it "had perhaps no parallel in the history of the world," and for support he cited the philosopher David Hume's view that this revolution "cut off all pretensions to power founded on hereditary right; when a prince was chosen who received the crown on express conditions, and found his authority established on the same bottom with the privileges of the people."[16]

The Glorious Revolution coincided with the publication of Newton's magisterial *Mathematical Principles of Natural Philosophy*, or *Principia*, an event which has often been singled out as the culmination of the scientific revolution. By the middle of the eighteenth century, the new political notion of a revolution as a radical change, rather than a cyclical return, was being applied to science, and with specific reference to Newton's *Principia*.[17] Today, we often still speak of *the* scientific revolution, but when we do, we recognize it as a long, complex historical development and one that did not consist solely in a preparation for the principles of mechanics and the gravitational system of the world as laid down in the *Principia*. Human understanding of the vastly more complex operations of chemistry and of life underwent profound reinterpretations as well, and the subtle art of experiment was immensely enriched by advances in techniques and instruments. That ingenious master of experimental apparatus Robert Hooke was not less important than Newton in preparing the way for Lord Charles and Henry Cavendish. The same can be said of that preeminent model of experimental persistance and perspicacity Robert Boyle (who as an aristocrat working in experimental science and shaping the Royal Society was the preeminent model for them in another sense). Together, the scientific power revealed to the world by Boyle, Hooke, and Newton and the political settlement of the Glorious Revolution go far to make intelligible the remarkable careers of Lord Charles and Henry Cavendish.

The Royal Society of London facilitated the transition from politics to science in our branch of the Cavendish family. Itself a legacy of the scientific revolution, the Royal Society looked upon scientific knowledge as public knowledge, thereby opening up a new avenue of public service

---

[12]David Elliston Allen, *The Naturalist in Britain: A Social History* (London: Allen Lane, 1976), 29.

[13]"Boyle, Charles, Fourth Earl of Orrery," *DNB* 2:1017.

[14]A. Rupert Hall, "Oldenburg, Henry," *DSB* 10: 200–3, on 200.

[15]In reaction to the whiggish interpretation of the Glorious Revolution, a recent generation of historians has given it a tory bias, emphasizing its conservative aspects. This trend is discussed in Mark Goldie's review of Lois G. Schwoerer, *The Declaration of Rights 1689* (Baltimore: The Johns Hopkins University Press, 1981), in *Parliamentary History, a Yearbook* 2 (1983): 242–44.

[16]On this point, Joseph Priestley's *Lectures on History and General Policy* (London, 1826) are quoted and discussed in I. B. Cohen, "The Eighteenth-Century Origins of the Concept of Scientific Revolution," *Journal of the History of Ideas* 37 (1976): 257–88, on 263–64.

[17]Ibid, 264.

for the Cavendishes. The scientific lives of Lord Charles and Henry Cavendish were public careers and, moreover, careers built upon an idealism worthy of those idealistic elements that did enter the Glorious Revolution. The Royal Society, to which the Cavendishes devoted themselves unstintingly, upheld the utopian dream of the scientific revolution: scientific knowledge improves human life.

Since our subjects are eighteenth-century men of science, and since we have made Newton's *Principia* a prominent marker in this introduction, we can envision the brickbats flying. For thirty years now, historians of science have argued that the eighteenth century should be regarded as a time of originating scientific energies of its own and recognized, as it was at the time, as another century of scientific revolution. Historians have reacted against the idolatry of Newton.[18] We concede the point; nevertheless, in following the tracks of our Cavendishes, we repeatedly confront Newton. With Lord Charles Cavendish we are less certain about this point than we are with his son. Lord Charles was drawn mainly to instruments and to their use in the new experimental fields, but his early scientific associates were mathematically accomplished colleagues of Newton. Lord Charles entered the Royal Society the year Newton died. Henry Cavendish was educated at Cambridge at a time when Newton's *Principia* dominated the curriculum. Although his greatest contributions to science were experimental, he was also a mathematical scientist whose objective was to grasp the new experimental fields in Newton's "mathematical way."[19] New instruments, apparatus, and experimental techniques were invented in the eighteenth century, but not everything about science had to be invented anew. The *Principia* was Henry Cavendish's luminous if ever-receding ideal; for his purposes, it was still, after a century, science at its best. It had introduced the mathematical physics of forces, which made intelligible the world as an orderly system; and the physics of forces was Henry Cavendish's physics, as it still is the physics of today. Cavendish incorporated a living Newton, not an icon. By the measure of his ambition, Cavendish failed, but he did marvelous research in the process. For the record, we do not subscribe to the view (if it was ever held) that science of the eighteenth century consisted in filling in the blanks left by Newton's uncompleted natural philosophy.

In the accepted usage of his time, Henry Cavendish was a "Newtonian philosopher," but to call him that does little more than place him in the eighteenth century. That ambiguity was implied by the eminent mathematician Charles Hutton at the close of the eighteenth century, in his *Mathematical and Philosophical Dictionary*, where he identified five meanings of "Newtonian philosophy," each held by numbers of subscribers, to which we could add several more meanings. We prefer to call Cavendish a "natural philosopher"; namely, one whose study of nature is founded on reason and experience or, to draw again on Hutton's *Dictionary*, one whose study of nature is characterized by an "enlarged comprehension, by which analogies, harmonies, and agreements are described in the works of nature, and the particular effects explained; that is, reduced to general rules."[20]

In one generation, roughly from the 1680s to the 1720s, science had come to dominate educated thought in Western Europe. Science was discussed in sermons, journals, coffee-house clubs, and societies newly established for the purpose.[21] This was the time when Lord Charles Cavendish was educated and introduced to politics and to science. Not long after he was elected to parliament, he was elected to the Royal Society, and although he continued as an M.P. for many years, he was drawn to science. Cavendish was caught up in the new currents of thought, which ultimately led him to think of a new way of living, one that would be continued by his son. Henry Cavendish would find a completely fulfilling life within science.

In eighteenth-century Britain, people in different stations of life attached their fortunes to science in different ways. The Cavendishes' way

———

[18]This by now historiographic commonplace once had some freshness; eg., R. W. Home, "Out of a Newtonian Straitjacket: Alternative Approaches to Eighteenth-Century Physical Science," in *Studies in the Eighteenth Century. IV: Papers Presented at the Fourth David Nichol Smith Memorial Seminar, Canberra 1976*, eds. R. F. Brissenden and J. C. Eade (Canberra: Australian National University Press, 1979), 235–49.

[19]Newton's expression, quoted and discussed in Henry Guerlac, "Where the Statue Stood: Divergent Loyalties to Newton in the Eighteenth Century," in *Aspects of the Eighteenth Century*, ed E. R. Wasserman (Baltimore: The Johns Hopkins University Press, 1965), 317-34, on 323.

[20]Entries for "Newtonian Philosophy" and "Philosophy" in Charles Hutton, *Mathematical and Philosophical Dictionary*, vol. 2 (London, 1795), 157 and 227.

[21]Margaret C. Jacob, *The Cultural Meaning of the Scientific Revolution* (Philadelphia: Temple University Press, 1988), 105.

did not have long-term consequences, since in the next century access to science became regular, as science came to be organized in the manner of the established professions. Indirectly, their way made the point: for unlike the Cavendishes, persons drawn to science were not rich aristocrats, and for them to make a life in science, a new career had to be invented. There did, of course, continue to be the occasional wealthy scientific aristocrat, but wealth and rank were then incidental, as they had not been to the Cavendishes. The Cavendishes did have direct consequences in science, but these were based on Henry Cavendish's example as an exacting experimental and mathematical investigator. When Cavendish died in 1810, a distinguished French scientist wrote to a colleague that Cavendish was a "model for those who cultivate the physical sciences."[22] This "model" was not of the occupant of the particular niche that Charles and Henry Cavendish had made for themselves in the society of scientific practitioners but of the man of precision who had recently weighed the world. Henry Cavendish contributed to advances in experimental precision, a leading development in the physical sciences in the second half of the eighteenth century. His example of technique carried over from the earlier setting of scientific practice to the modern one.

Lord Charles and Henry Cavendish present their biographers with a difficult problem. The acquisitive habit of their family ensured that every scrap of paper having to do with property was saved for the record but that almost nothing else was. We have Lord Charles Cavendish's business correspondence, but his large private correspondence is all gone. Henry Cavendish's business correspondence is preserved too, but other than that, for such a prominent man, his surviving correspondence is meager in the extreme. To judge from what we have seen, it would appear that he never recorded a feeling or a thought about life. He had a professional correspondence, which was never large but which is invaluable to his biographers, and a portion of this has survived.

Virginia Woolf approached her biography of Roger Fry with the question, "How can one make a life of six cardboard boxes full of tailors's bills, love letters, and old picture postcards?"[23] The answer is, as she went on to show, that it is not easy

but that it is not impossible either. Henry Cavendish, whose cardboard boxes contain nothing so personal as even tailors' bills, let alone love letters, presents his biographers with an even harder task. How can they make a life from a fifty-year record of observations of thermometers and magnetic needles? It is not easy or straightforward, but once again, as we hope to show, it can be done. Cavendish's scientific writings are revealing of his individuality; in a way, they are his love letters.

When Cavendish died his scientific papers passed to his principal heir, Lord George Cavendish. They evidently remained with Lord George's family until his grandson became the seventh duke of Devonshire in 1858, at which time they were removed to the ancestral house of the Devonshires, Chatsworth, where they remain.[24] The papers, which consist of experimental and observational data, calculations, and studies in various stages of writing, are voluminous, an embarrassment of riches which pose a biographical hazard of their own. We have heeded Henry Adams's advice to biographers, "proportion is everything,"[25] while at the same time we have accepted that Cavendish's life *was* his science. The distinction between biography and history of science can be fine, and in the case of Cavendish, we have had to do a balancing act. This biography could not have been written without Cavendish's unpublished papers, and we have relied extensively on them. At the same time we have tried not to lose a sense of proportion and with it the man.

Some of Cavendish's manuscripts have been published, though only one group of them, the electrical, with anything approaching completeness. His electrical papers were examined by a series of experts in that branch of physics, first by William Snow Harris, who borrowed them from the earl of Burlington and included extracts from them

---

[22]Claude Louis Berthollet to Charles Blagden, 21 May 1810, Blagden Letters, Royal Society, B138.

[23]Quoted in Susan Sheets-Pyenson, "New Directions for Scientific Biography: The Case of Sir William Dawson," *History of Science* 28 (1990): 399–410, on 399.

[24]*Treasures from Chatsworth, The Devonshire Inheritance*. A Loan Exhibition from the Devonshire Collection, by Permission of the Duke of Devonshire and the Trustees of the Chatsworth Settlement, Organized and Circulated by the International Exhibitions Foundation, 1979–1980, p. 67.

[25]Quoted in John A Garraty, *The Nature of Biography* (New York: Knopf, 1957), 247.

in a revision of his textbook on electricity.[26] In 1849 William Thomson visited William Snow Harris and examined Cavendish's manuscripts.[27] Thomson thought that Cavendish's electrical manuscripts should be published in their entirety, and he together with several other men of science put the case to the duke of Devonshire. In 1874 the duke placed the manuscripts in the hands of the first Cavendish Professor of Experimental Physics, James Clerk Maxwell. For the next five years, Maxwell repeated Cavendish's experiments, transcribed the manuscripts, and prepared a densely annotated and nearly complete edition of Cavendish's unpublished electrical papers together with his two published electrical papers. This extraordinary edition was published by Cambridge University Press only a few weeks before Maxwell's death in 1879, as *The Electrical Researches of the Honourable Henry Cavendish*.[28] Cavendish's unpublished chemical papers came to the attention of chemists in the context of a resurrected priority dispute over the discovery of the composition of water. To document his defense of Cavendish's claim, in 1839 Vernon Harcourt appended a selection of Cavendish's chemical manuscripts to his published presidential address to the British Association for the Advancement of Science. Harcourt believed that an edition of Cavendish's papers was then being planned.[29] In fact, there had been intermittent discussion of such a plan from the time of Cavendish's death, but for one reason or another it had been put off, as it would continue to be long after Harcourt. In due course, with further delays caused by World War I, in 1921 Cambridge University Press reprinted Maxwell's edition of the electrical papers and published a new, companion volume containing the rest of Cavendish's published papers from the *Philosophical Transactions* along with a small selection of scientific manuscripts from outside the field of electricity, the two volumes appearing as *The Scientific Papers of the Honourable Henry Cavendish, F.R.S.*[30] The selection this time was made by the general editor and chemist Edward Thorpe, together with four other experts from physics, astronomy, and geology.

The bulk of Cavendish's scientific manuscripts remain unpublished. We might assume that every scrap of writing by Cavendish about science has been preserved if we did not

have conclusive evidence to the contrary. A case in point is *the* Cavendish experiment, his weighing of the world: if as with so many of his researches, he had not published it, we would know nothing of its existence, as his scientific papers, as they have come down to us, reveal no trace of it. Or to take an example of another kind: Richard Kirwan, a colleague of Cavendish, wrote to foreign scientist that Cavendish had made a discovery about magnetism that "merits great attention."[31] The surviving manuscripts on magnetism by Cavendish, which are primarily about earth-magnetic instruments, give no hint of what this discovery might have been. In recent years important new scientific manuscripts of Cavendish have been made public, and we have no doubt that many others once existed and, we hope, may one day come to light.

As needed, we refer to the several obituaries and brief early accounts of Cavendish, a number of which were written by persons who knew him. There are two book-length biographies of Cavendish, both by chemists. The recent biography by A. J. Berry provides a readable summary of Cavendish's papers but gives little more than what the editors of the collected papers do, and it does not present anything new about Cavendish's life.[32] Berry would seem to have

---

[26] William Snow Harris, *Rudimentary Electricity*, 4th ed. (London, 1854). In the preface, he says that Lord Burlington has loaned him Cavendish's manuscripts to use as he sees fit. He gives a fair sense of the scope of Cavendish's electrical researches with the object of showing how much of the modern subject Cavendish has anticipated.

[27] S. P. Thomson, *The Life of William Thomson, Baron Kelvin of Largs*, 2 vols. (London, 1901) 1:218.

[28] *The Electrical Researches of the Honourable Henry Cavendish, F.R.S.*, ed. J. C. Maxwell (Cambridge, 1879; London: Frank Cass, 1967).

[29] W. Vernon Harcourt, "Address," *British Association Report*, 1839, pp. 3–45, on p. 45. The address is followed by an "Appendix," pp. 45–68, containing extracts of Cavendish's papers on heat and chemistry, which in turn is followed by sixty pages of lithographed facsimiles of Cavendish's papers.

[30] *The Scientific Papers of the Honourable Henry Cavendish, F.R.S.*, 2 vols. (Cambridge: Cambridge University Press, 1921). The subtitle of the first volume edited by Maxwell and revised by Joseph Larmor is *Electrical Researches*. The subtitle of the second volume under E. Thorpe's general editorship is *Chemical and Dynamical*. Hereafter, this work is cited as *Sci. Pap.* 1 and 2.

[31] Richard Kirwan to Louis-Bernard Guyton de Morveau, 28 Feb 1786, in Louis-Bernard Guyton de Morveau and Richard Kirwan, *A Scientific Correspondence During the Chemical Revolution: Louis-Bernard Guyton de Morveau and Richard Kirwan, 1782–1802*, ed. E. Grison, M. Sadoun-Goupil, and P. Bret (Berkeley: Office for the History of Science and Technology, University of California at Berkeley, 1994), 142–47, on 146.

[32] A. J. Berry, *Henry Cavendish: His Life and Scientific Work* (London: Hutchinson, 1960).

confirmed what the editor-in-chief of the collected papers, Thorpe, said: Little is known about the "personal history" of Cavendish, "nor is there much hope now that more may be gleaned," since it is doubtful that "there is much more to learn" about this "singularly uneventful" life.[33] Cavendish's earlier biographer, George Wilson, however, wrote an original account of his subject in a highly unusual form of biography.[34]

If ever a biography violated Adams's advice about proportion, it was Wilson's *The Life of the Honourable Henry Cavendish*. Cavendish's "life," in the ordinary sense of the word, occupies only two chapters, the first and the fourth, which comprise fifty pages out of a total of nearly five hundred pages. The "life" in the *Life* was stuck onto a book with a different purpose; namely, to put to rest the priority dispute that had prompted Harcourt's intervention. The dispute, which had simmered briefly in Cavendish's lifetime, was fanned to white heat in the middle of the nineteenth century by a French éloge of James Watt, which advanced Watt's claims over Cavendish's. Dealing almost exclusively with the water controversy, Wilson's account has elements of a detective story and legal drama; his principal subject was, after all, not Cavendish but a fight for prize and honor. Apart from the polemics, the book is a useful work in the history of chemistry, though it does not seem to have been used that way. What it has been used for is the "life" of Cavendish, little longer than some of the character sketches it drew on.

Wilson's biography was published by and at the request of the Cavendish Society. Founded in 1846, the Society was one of a number of early nineteenth-century subscription printing clubs, this one for chemical works and named after Henry Cavendish no doubt because of the furor going on then.[35] In addition to the water controversy and the subscription printing club, there was one other reason for Wilson's *Life*. In the middle of the nineteenth century, a call went out for biographies of scientists, presumed to be a neglected category of eminent Britons. Believing that scientists and men of letters gave their age "greater glory than the statesmen and warriors,"[36] in 1845 Lord Brougham published biographical sketches of Cavendish and several other scientists. In 1848 the historian of the Royal Society Charles Richard Weld condemned the lack of a biography of the

late president of the Society Joseph Banks as a "reproach to scientific England." If Banks had been a military man or a romantic hero, his biography would long since have been written, Weld said.[37] In 1843 Wilson began collecting materials for a book on the lives of the British chemists. He never did publish this book, but in the life of the chemist he did publish, Cavendish's, in 1851, he regretted that "no other European nation has so imperfect a series of biographies of her philosophers, as Britain possesses." There was not even a good biography of Newton, Wilson said, let alone biographies of Thomas Young, William Hyde Wollaston, and John Dalton, and only now was there a biography of Cavendish.[38] That Wilson included a "life" at all in his book on Cavendish was due to his sympathy with the general desire for biographies of scientists.

When Wilson applied to the Cavendish family for the loan of Henry Cavendish's manuscripts, he said he had delayed asking because he understood that Lord Burlington was going to write an account of Cavendish's discoveries. (We start here with esoterica about British titles: the earl of Burlington, an extinct title, was resurrected by William IV as a courtesy title for Henry Cavendish's heir, Lord George Cavendish; thereafter it went to the eldest son of the eldest son of the duke of Devonshire.) This Lord Burlington was the forty-eight-year-old William Cavendish, who would go on to become the seventh duke of Devonshire. A scientifically gifted man who placed second wrangler in the competitive mathematical examinations at Cambridge and first Smith's Prizeman, the duke returned to Cambridge in 1861 to succeed Prince Albert as chancellor. The richest of all the dukes, in 1870 he drew on his wealth to build a laboratory for experimental physics at Cambridge (where its first professor, Maxwell, would repeat Cavendish's experiments for his edition of Cavendish's electrical papers). The laboratory was going

[33] From Thorpe's "Introduction" to Cavendish, *Sci. Pap.* 2:1.

[34] George Wilson, *The Life of the Honourable Henry Cavendish* (London, 1851).

[35] W. H. Brock, "The Society for the Perpetuation of Gmelin: the Cavendish Society, 1846–1872," *Annals of Science* 35 (1978): 599–617, on 604–5.

[36] Brougham, *Lives of Men of Letters and Science* 1:xi.

[37] Charles Richard Weld, *A History of the Royal Society, . . .*, 2 vols. (London, 1848) 2:116–17.

[38] Wilson, *Cavendish*, 15.

to be called the Devonshire Physical Laboratory after the seventh duke, but it was named the Cavendish Laboratory instead, after Henry Cavendish.[39] The seventh duke did not write an in-house biography after all, but he established one of the world's greatest physical laboratories and saw to it that it was named after the greatest representative of his family, Henry Cavendish. Wilson told the future duke that he had been studying Cavendish's works for ten years, that he admired Cavendish's character, and that he intended to do him justice in the water controversy.[40] Burlington let Wilson see the manuscripts.

Wilson drew his conclusions about Cavendish largely from stories he collected, many of them from old timers at the Royal Society and former neighbors of Cavendish. The stories conflict and often contain things that could not be true, yet taken together they are suggestive. Like the hundreds of unverifiable stories about Lincoln, they are most revealing of the time in which they were told, but they also tell something about the man.[41] The stories illustrate two rather forbidding traits of Cavendish, a pathological fear of strangers that could render him speechless, and a clockwork regularity in all his transactions with life. Wilson tried to understand his man: he tried to "become for the time Cavendish, and think as he thought, and do as he did." But as he closed on his subject, Wilson conflated Cavendish with the remorse he felt on devoting so much time and effort to "so small a matter." Like all his past efforts, this effort Wilson saw as "bleak and dark," and the image of the man he distilled from the Cavendish stories corresponds.[42]

Wilson kept his promise to Burlington to portray Cavendish as a man of exemplary probity. But there is more to character than honesty, and Wilson did not admire the rest of what he saw. A deeply religious man, Wilson at the time he wrote his life of Cavendish was contemplating writing a "Religio Chemici" along the lines of Sir Thomas Browne's "Religo Medici," and in the year following the publication of his life, he published a biography of the physician John Reid, a man of "Courage, Hope, and Faith," whom he greatly admired. Wilson tried to penetrate to where Cavendish's courage, hope, and faith lay, his heart, only to discover that Cavendish was a "man without a heart."[43] In the *Life*, Wilson said that Cavendish

was "passionless," "only a cold, clear Intelligence, raying down pure white light, which brightened everything on which it fell, but warmed nothing." Wilson's striking judgment has been uncritically repeated. Francis Bickley, chronicler of the Cavendish family, concluded from Wilson's *Life* that "there is something pathetic about such an existence as Henry Cavendish's, so fruitful and yet so utterly barren."[44] Edward Thorpe, general editor of Cavendish's *Scientific Papers*, wrote to a fellow editor that Cavendish was "not a man as other men are, but simply the personification and embodiment of a cold, unimpassioned intellectuality."[45] Cavendish's recent biographer, A. J. Berry, quoting Wilson, speaks of Cavendish's "striking deficiencies as a human being."[46] Wilson is entitled to his image of Cavendish, but we should point out that in addition to being his conviction, it is a mid nineteenth-century Romantic cliché. It is Keats's Appolonius, whose cold mathematical philosophy denies the imagination by subjecting the rainbow and all other mysteries to its "rule and line," emptying them of charm by conquering them. We have dwelled this long on Wilson's biography because it has provided the portrait of Cavendish for nearly a hundred and fifty years. We have consulted a much wider range of sources than Wilson did, and so our account naturally shows differences from the original. And times have changed and biographies with them.

We can, it would seem, at least agree on the appearance of Henry Cavendish, since there is only one portrait. The original was a graphite and gray-wash sketch, from which Wilson had an engraving made for his biography. Cavendish was an immensely wealthy man, but one would not know it from this portrait, which shows him in his rumpled coat and long wig, both long out of date, and with

[39] John Pearson, *The Serpent and the Stag: The Saga of England's Powerful and Glamourous Cavendish Family from the Age of Henry the Eighth to the Present* (New York: Holt, Rinehart and Winston, 1983), 214.

[40] George Wilson to Lord Burlington, 15 Mar 1850, Lancashire Record Office, Miscellaneous Letters, DDCA 22/19/5.

[41] Garraty, *Biography*, 216–17.

[42] The quotations are from a letter Wilson wrote at the time, included in his sister's biography, Jessie Aitken Wilson, *Memoir of George Wilson* (London, 1862), 340–41.

[43] Ibid., 338, 342–43.

[44] Francis Bickley, *The Cavendish Family* (London: Constable, 1911), 207.

[45] Edward Thorpe to Joseph Larmor, 7 Feb. 1920, Larmor Papers, Royal Society Library, 1972.

[46] Berry, *Cavendish*, 22.

his slouching walk. The latter was a family trait: of the Cavendishes, Horace Walpole observed that a "peculiar awkwardness of gait is universally seen in them."[47] The physical scientist Thomas Young, who knew Cavendish in his late years, said that he always dressed the same way, presumably as in this picture.[48] (Young also described Cavendish as tall and thin, which is where agreement ends; another contemporary, the chemist Thomas Thomson, described Cavendish as "rather thick" and his neck as "rather short."[49]) The circumstances under which this picture was executed make one of the best stories about Cavendish, and one there is no reason to doubt. Whenever he was approached to sit for a portrait (probably for the meeting room of the Royal Society), Cavendish always gave a blunt refusal. But William Alexander, a draughtsman from the China embassy, succeeded by subterfuge; with the help of an accomplice, John Burrow, he was invited as a guest to the Royal Society Club, at which Cavendish dined once a week. As advised, Alexander sat at one end of the table close to the peg on which Cavendish invariably hung his green coat and three-cornered hat, both of which he surreptitiously sketched. He then sketched Cavendish's profile, which he inserted between the hat and coat at home where he finished the portrait. Cavendish, of course, was not shown it, but people who knew him were, and they recognized it as Cavendish. The artist left the sketch at the British Museum, where Wilson obtained it.[50] It is a wonderful sketch, and part of the wonder is that it ever came into existence in the first place.

"I desire" was one of Cavendish's favorite expressions. His life was filled with desire, and to a greater extent than most persons, what he desired he could have. For he was perfectly placed: born an aristocrat when the aristocracy was in high tide, he could expect his desires to be taken seriously. Because he was not a peer, he escaped the meaningless aspects of privilege, the time-consuming duties, rituals, and display; he was free to choose inherently more rewarding pursuits, while at the same time he could feel as confident of his place in society as the duke of Devonshire. (As far as his place was concerned, Henry Cavendish had absolute confidence; his lack of confidence in particular social groups was an entirely different matter.) What he desired more than anything else,

we know, was to understand the natural world. Given his enviable position, he could separate the rewards of scientific work from those of society at large, which were in any event given to him without having to desire them. That advantage lent his life its peculiar direction and intensity.

Owing to the nearly total absence of biographical materials of a personal sort, we have had to rely upon other kinds of evidence. To get to know Cavendish and form our image of him, to draw the human face between the three-cornered hat and the crumpled great-coat, we have placed him in all the human settings in which we know he appeared. The result is a long book. Critical readers will say that Cavendish is again unfortunate in his biographers, who do not know when to stop. Sympathetic readers will see our predicament and consider our worst fault to be the common lot of biographers, an overenthusiasm for their subject. We have handled the Cavendish "problem" in the way a sculptor works with a resistant material like stone. To give form to it, the sculptor is condemned to work constantly from the outside inward. No matter how much material he works, the visible product of his labors is never anything but an outer surface, though the viewer may think of the sculpture as being solid as well. This analogy gives us a little courage, but it does not go very far; the sculptor's intention is art, and the form we have given this biography is intentionally artless (in one of its meanings).

The period we consider in this biography covers just over a century, from the end of the seventeenth century to the beginning of the nineteenth. It was an extraordinary time in science, when great new fields of investigation were laid down. Lord Charles Cavendish, a master of scientific instruments and experimental art, took up challenging problems in these fields, and his son Henry Cavendish explored them systematically with exacting experimental technique and mathematical theory. The time of Lord Charles and

[47]Horace Walpole to Horace Mann, 4 June 1749, in *Horace Walpole's Correspondence*, ed. W. S. Lewis et al., 48 vols. (New Haven: Yale University Press, 1937–83) :15:317.
[48]Thomas Young, "Life of Cavendish," *Encyclopaedia Britannica*, Supplement, 1816–24; in Cavendish, *Sci. Pap.* 1:435–47, on 444.
[49]Thomson, *The History of Chemistry* 1:339.[50]John Burrow, *Sketches of the Royal Society and Royal Society Club* (London, 1849), 146–47.
[50]John Burrow, *Sketches of the Royal Scoiety and Royal Society Club* (London, 1849), 146–147.

Henry Cavendish was (as all times are) one of transition, in this instance from the passing era of the scientific "virtuosi" to the dawn of our own era of scientific professionals. In terms of the Cavendish family, the period begins when the rooms of the great Cavendish house, Chatsworth, resounded with the pugnacious first duke of Devonshire's clanking sword, and it ends when the tone of those same rooms was set by the Proustian languor of the fifth duke of Devonshire. Where the first duke saw worlds to conquer, the fifth duke saw only the already conquered world in which his comfort was well secured. The fifth duke was no fool. He saw that his cousin Henry Cavendish existed in another world, though he may not have recognized it as a new world to conquer, one which demanded of Henry what had been demanded of

the first duke, hard work. (By "conquer," in the borrowed sense, we mean to understand the workings of nature, ruled by the authority of natural laws.) The fifth duke got it nearly right when he ordered his wife Georgiana, duchess of Devonshire to stay away from Henry Cavendish (she did not obey) on the grounds that "He is not a gentleman—*he works*."[51] In this biography, we show what it meant for two gentlemen, first, Lord Charles Cavendish and, then, Henry Cavendish to work in science.[52]

---

[51] Bickley, *Cavendish Family*, 202

[52] *Work* in the setting of professional science is our theme in Christa Jungnickel and Russell McCormmach, *Intellectual Mastery of Nature: Theoretical Physics from Ohm to Einstein*, 2 vols (Chicago: University of Chicago Press, 1986).

PART 1

The Dukes

The Dukes

In the spring of 1691, two young English aristocrats on the grand tour on the Continent met in Venice and apparently liked one another well enough to begin a correspondence after they parted.[1] The older of the two was Henry de Grey, Lord Ruthven, then not quite twenty, the younger the nineteen-year-old William, Lord Cavendish. Forty years later, in 1731, they were to become the grandfathers of Henry Cavendish, although William did not live long enough to know of this grandson.

The eldest sons of propertied English earls, the two young men, accompanied by tutors and servants, met as seasoned travelers despite their youth. William Cavendish had already been abroad for over two years, Henry de Grey for over a year.[2] William was on his way to Rome, Henry returning from there. Both of them were no doubt acquiring the rudiments of their later great interest in the arts and architecture, but letters about their travels do not show any youthful ardor for the beauties of Italy, Switzerland, or The Netherlands. In Rome, William Cavendish and his younger brother Henry did "little or nothing . . . that was worth giving your Lordship an account of."[3] From Padua, Frankfurt, or The Hague they reported seeing friends or missing them, as they crisscrossed the Continent, but not a word about the finer things of classical civilization these young English barbarians had been sent abroad to experience.

What did interest them was the war threatening between England and its allies and France and the dynastic quarrels that were giving rise to it. The war might affect their travel plans, as it did Henry de Grey's, but, more important, it was to be fought to secure the rights to power and property of certain European ruling *families*, the usual purpose of wars then, and understandably a matter of concern to aristocrats of high rank like young Cavendish and Grey.

The Elector of Brandenburg has declared, that he will fullfill the Promise he made to the Duke of Lorrain, at the siege of Bonn, *to maintain the interests of his children* and to contribute to their restoration. The Emperor and all the allys have declared the same thing,

William Cavendish reported to Henry de Grey in the summer of 1691.[4] The concern for the dynastic interests of the ruling family that an aristocrat chose to ally himself with was very much a concern for the interests of his own family. That was why William Cavendish was ready to risk his life in battle in 1691 and why his father, the earl of Devonshire had risked *his* life only three years earlier to secure the interests in England of the Protestant branch of the Stuarts.

In 1688, William Cavendish's father, the earl of Devonshire, had joined six other English aristocrats in the risky business of inviting William of Orange to the British throne, even though that throne was then rightfully occupied by James II and could some day be legally claimed by James's son, who had just been born. If their scheme of deposing James had misfired, they might have suffered the fate of traitors. But luck was with them, and with the succession of William and his Stuart wife, Mary, to the crown, the earl ensured abundantly the survival of the Cavendish family in political power and in the enjoyment of their property. In 1691, in the spring of which William

---

[1]William Cavendish to Henry de Grey, 30 May/9 June 1691 and 23 December 1691 Bedfordshire Record Office, Wrest Park Collection, L 30/8/14/1–2.

[2]One of William Cavendish's first stops on the Continent was at Brussels, from where he wrote to his mother-in-law, Lady Russell. He was about to continue on his tour, and she approved, "for to live well in the world; 'tis for certain most necessary to know the world well." *Letters of Lady Rachel Russell; from the Manuscript in the Library at Woburn Abbey*, 5th ed. (London, 1793), 415–16. Henry de Grey, as Lord Ruthven, had been issued a pass on 16 April 1690 "to travel abroad for purposes of study." G. E. C. (George Edward Cokayne), *The Complete Peerage of England Scotland Ireland Great Britain and the United Kingdom: Extant, Extinct, or Dormant*, vol. (3) (Gloucester: Alan Sutton, 1982), 176–78. The Cavendish and Grey families were connected through marriage, in 1601. Ibid., 173–74.

[3]Henry Cavendish to Henry de Grey, 7/19 May 1691, Bedford County Record Office, Wrest Park Collection, L 30/8/21/1.

[4]William Cavendish to Henry de Grey, 30 May/9 June 1691, Bedfordshire Record Office, Wrest Park Collection, L 30/8/14/1.

and Henry met in Venice, the earl of Devonshire outshone "most of the Princes," including the elector of Brandenburg, with his "magnificent" establishment at the royal congress at The Hague, to which he had accompanied King William as lord steward. Three years later, in 1694, the royal couple rewarded his services by raising the earl to duke of Devonshire, the highest rank short of royalty.[5]

Traditionally the number of dukes in the land was extremely small, one or two. That changed during the Restoration with Charles II's spate of peer-making, especially of dukedoms, which he gave to his mistresses and six bastard children. At the beginning of the eighteenth century there were about 160 English peers and among them about 20 dukes, figures which remained pretty constant thereafter into the twentieth century. After acquiring the throne, between 1688 and 1694 the new king, William III, created a group of new noble titles including seven dukedoms,[6] and Devonshire had profited from this brief, post- Revolution beneficence.

The Cavendishes rose to their title relatively quickly, in not much more than a century, and they prepared for it by a steady accumulation of landed property until they were among the richest landowners in England. Along the way, they used some of their money to buy first a baronetcy and then an earldom when the political shifts of the seventeenth century from monarchy to commonwealth and back to monarchy prompted the granting of royal favors. They remained loyal to the Stuarts—being prudent enough to make their peace with the commonwealth as well—until under Charles II such loyalty was no longer in their financial and political interest.[7]

If the dynastic concern of the Cavendishes was to further strengthen their newly found hold on the top rung of the social ladder, the Greys' was to reclaim their former footing. The Greys had been earls of Kent since the fifteenth century, Henry de Grey's father the eleventh of the line. But Henry's branch of the family had succeeded to the title and estates only in the middle of the seventeenth century, beginning with a country rector with a very large family who was too poor and too old to take his seat in the House of Lords. His successor, Henry's grandfather, did enter politics, but on the wrong side, as it turned out, adopting the cause of parliament against the king. After the restoration of the Stuarts, the Greys prudently kept their distance from court and parliament. In any case, their most pressing need was still to secure their estate and finances; at court or in government in those troubled years, they would only have risked making enemies or spending money that they could not afford. Taking big chances, as the earl of Devonshire had on behalf of William of Orange, was acceptable to a prudent man only if he had power, and power then derived from landed property. In that regard, the Greys were not the Cavendishes' betters or even equals. Nor would they take chances with the life of their heir. Instructing Henry to leave Holland before the king arrived there for his campaign, Henry's father wrote to him: "It would be expected you should go to the campaign with him, and not to do it would be took ill both from your father and you." So Henry traveled on to Geneva, and from there, against his cautious parents' wishes, into Italy.[8]

Personal Characteristics

If Henry had any brothers, they died young, for soon the love and hope of his family focused on him. He responded by developing into an affectionate young man, good natured, easygoing. Once he had a family of his own, his concern for his wives—after his first wife died, he remarried—and his children was reflected in their letters to him, full of warmth and appreciation. He was not especially gifted in anything, but he had sufficient intelligence and curiosity to inform himself on a wide range of subjects, including science, as his substantial library attests. One of his contemporaries in 1707 credited him with "good sense" and with always being "very moderate."[9] Be that as it may, he had dynastic ambitions for his family and enough vanity to aspire to important positions at court, only he lacked the drive to work for such

[5]John Pearson, *The Serpent and the Stag: The Saga of England's Powerful and Glamourous Cavendish Family from Age of Henry the Eighth to the Present* (New York: Holt, Reinhart & Winston, 1983), 68–71 Francis Bickley, *The Cavendish Family* (London: Constable, 1911), 170–74.

[6]J. V. Beckett, *The Aristocracy in England, 1660–1914* (Oxford: Basil Blackwell, 1986), 27–28.

[7]Pearson, *Serpent and Stag*, 61.

[8]Joyce Godber, *Wrest Park and the Duke of Kent, Henry Grey (1671–1740)*, 4th ed. (Elstow Moot Hall: Bedfordshire County Council Arts and Recreation Department, 1982), 2–3.

[9]G. E. C., *The Complete Peerage* 3(7):178.

positions by seeking political power. "A quiet mind is better than to embroil myself amongst the knaves and fools about either Church or State," he wrote at a moment of disappointment.[10] He sought offices in the courtier's way, through gaining favor with influential people and then using his connections to request honors and positions. The offices he accepted were administrative rather than political, requiring abilities well within his reach and skills he was already exercising in the running of his estates. He attended the House of Lords dutifully even when he came to dislike the burden in his middle years.[11] He displayed the same level-headed estimate of his abilities in his later years, when his chief occupation came to be his estate at Wrest Park, its agriculture and its gardens, informing himself thoroughly on those subjects and planning and directing the work with considerable and lasting success. His enemies at court—political opponents who wanted the positions he held, or rivals for royal favors—gave Henry de Grey the name "The Bugg";[12] they meant to ridicule him, implying in this way that he was pompous and proud, but their description must be admitted to have some truth to it. A good-looking man, he spent the money necessary to cut a fine figure, his annual clothes bills running higher than those of his wife and several daughters combined, not only while he held high office at court and needed expensive formal apparel, but long before, as a young man about town. On his tomb, he had himself sculpted wearing a Roman toga over a strong, muscular body, his curly hair cropped close to the head, resembling in face and attire Laurent Delvaux's statue of George I, undeniably betraying a certain vanity. A large family portrait painted about five years before his death shows him to be, on the contrary, a relatively short, slender man whose simple velvet coat is decorated only with what appears to be the garter and ribbon. Far from posing as the patriarch in his own home, he has yielded center stage to his mother-in-law, the countess of Portland, who was governess of the royal children; he stands rather meekly by her side, receiving from her a cup of tea.[13] His pride lay in his "ancient and noble" family, as he called it, which he hoped, in vain, as it turned out, to continue through his five sons. Not one of them survived him.[14] He achieved a dukedom for his family in 1710, but he ended up without an heir to inherit it;

he could only look forward to its extinction with his death. All that remained for him to do was to build an ostentatious marble mausoleum, which although pompous, also evokes his struggle against so much disappointed hope.

For at least ten years, beginning in 1736, the Kent estate served as a lecture theater in the physical sciences and an observatory. In those years the duke of Kent and, after his death in 1740, the duchess of Kent employed Thomas Wright as a scientific teacher. This is the famous astronomer who was first to delineate the structure of the Milky Way, which he published in 1750, as *An Original Theory or New Hypothesis of the Universe*. Born into an artisan family, self-taught in astronomy, Wright made his living by teaching science, mathematics, and surveying, publishing on these subjects, and surveying the estates of the aristocracy. His pupils included Jemima, duchess of Kent and Kent's daughters Ladies Sophia de Grey and Mary de Grey (but not Lady Anne de Grey, who married Lord Charles Cavendish), his son-in-law Lord Glenorchy, and his granddaughter Jemima, the future Marchioness de Grey. He taught the Kent women geometry, navigation, surveying, and no doubt other subjects from his ambitious curriculum. Residing for months at a time at Wrest Park, Wright probably did surveying there as well as teaching, for the duke was always building, and the duchess, Wright noted in his diary, surveyed all the garden and made plans for it. Wright also carried out his own astronomical studies at Wrest, in 1736, for example, communicating to the Royal Society from there his observations of the eclipse

---

[10]Duke of Kent to Prior, 26 July 1710, quoted in Ragnhild Hatton, *George I, Elector and King* (Cambridge, Mass: Harvard University Press, 1978), 121.

[11]"Memoir of the Family of De Grey," Bedfordshire Record Office, Wrest Park Collection, L 31/114/22,23, vol. 2, p. 99.

[12]The earl of Godolphin to the duchess of Marlborough, /24 Apr. 1704/, *The Marlborough-Godolphin Correspondence*, 3 vols., ed. H. L. Snyder, vol. 1 (Oxford: Clarendon Press, 1975), 284.

[13]*Conversation Piece at Wrest*, around 1735. Illustration opposite p. 40 in Joyce Godber, *The Marchioness Grey of Wrest Park*, vol. 47 (Bedfordshire Historical Record Society, 1968).

[14]G. E. C., *Complete Peerage* 3:(7):47.

[15]What is known of Thomas Wright's life is based mainly on his journal. Entries telling of his contacts with the Kent family are reproduced in Edward Hughes, "The Early Journal of Thomas Wright of Durham," *Annals of Science* 7 (1951): 1–24, on 13–22. His observations at Wrest Park are reported in Royal Society, JB 15:371 (28 Oct. 1736).

of Mars by the moon.[15] Lord Charles and Henry Cavendish may well have got acquainted with Thomas Wright at Wrest Park with his telescope or in London on tutorial visits to the Grey side of the family. Wright was still teaching the Kents when Henry Cavendish was fifteen.

An even more fitting monument to the duke of Kent than the family vault at Flitton is Wrest Park in Bedfordshire, with its vast and elegant garden, one hundred and twenty acres bounded by a two-mile gravel walk. Here and there inside the garden the duke set out mementos of friends and of princes he had served or admired, which included statues of King William (put up because the duke was a "good Whig") and of Queen Anne (put up because he was a "good Servant"). Standing in a corner of the garden was a pyramid inscribed with the years of the beginning and end of the duke's proud improvements. The larger setting, the park, was eight hundred acres with a grass walk around it, with exotic plantations, oak woods, canals containing carp and pike, an obelisk eighty-six feet high, extensive lawns, a pavilion, a greenhouse, a bowling green, statues, vases, a temple of Diana, falls, and herds of deer. In the distance cottages and churches could be seen, including a church that resembled a ruined castle. The grand house of the estate was approached by a straight, broad, mile-long, tree-flanked avenue. This description is from a letter written at Wrest Park three years after the duke's death, in 1743, by Thomas Birch. A literary man, Birch thought that the best room in the house was the library. We reflect that the legacy of this combination of grandeur and learning included the man of science Henry Cavendish.

Growing up in the shadow of the "Great Duke of Devon"—his contemporaries spoke of the first duke of Devonshire as if he were already a legend—Henry Cavendish's other grandfather, William Cavendish, the future second duke of Devonshire, could have been crushed completely. His father was a willful, flamboyant man who defied and created kings, picked violent quarrels at the drop of a hat,[16] and built one of England's finest great houses, Chatsworth. In the event, the son grew up to be more mature, better balanced, more reasonable, and on the whole a much more solid and, one suspects, more intelligent man than

the father—and, of course, a much less exciting man. About William there are none of the stories about duels and mistresses, street fights and defiance of all authority that make the first duke such fascinating reading. Up to a point, William, reasonably enough, allowed his life to be directed by his father: at sixteen, he was married to fourteen-year-old Rachel Russell, the daughter of Lord William Russell, Devonshire's former political ally and friend and now "martyr" to the whig cause.[17] As soon as William came of age, he followed his father into politics. In his early years as a member of parliament, he even imitated his father's boldness, taking initiatives and speaking frequently for his principles in the House of Commons, on one occasion going so far as to challenge an opponent. But when he spoke up, he spoke his own mind, not his father's, and to tackle conflicts, he was much more likely to use reasoning, persuasion, and compromise than the sword. "His mansion was not a rendezvous for the assemblies of foppery," it was said of him: "none were permitted to partake of the . . . refined . . . pleasures of his house . . . but the ingenious, the learned, the sober, the wise."[18] He was not really that proper, but he did value learning and cool judgment, and in an environment of courtly intrigue and political passions, he impressed the duke of Marlborough as a "very honest man" and a man who "governs himself by reason."[19] George I, according to Lady Cowper, thought so, too: he was one of only two men in the kingdom whom the king had found "very honest, disinterested" men.[20]

Of his relationship with his family we get a glimpse only now and then. As a newly married boy, too young yet to be allowed to live with his wife, on his continental tour, he wrote considerate letters to his mother-in-law, Lady Rachel Russell,

[16]Great Britain, Historical Manuscripts Commission, *Report on the Manuscripts of the Marquess of Downshire, Preserved at Easthampstead Park, Berks* Vol. 1: *Papers of Sir William Trumbull.* Part 1 (London: His Majesty's Stationary Office, 1924), 60, 240, 268–69, 271–72, 276.

[17]Lois G. Schwoerer, *Lady Rachel Russell: "One of the Best of Women"* (Baltimore: The Johns Hopkins University Press, 1988), 161–63.

[18]From Hiram Bingham, *Elihu Yale: The American Nabob of Queen Square* (New York: Dodd, Mead, 1939), 308.

[19]The duke of Marlborough to the earl of Godolphin, 14/25 June 1708, in *Marlborough-Godolphin Correspondence* 2:1011.

[20]George I quoted by Lady Cowper, 10 July 1716, in Mary, Countess Cowper, *Diary of Mary Countess Cowper, Lady of the Bedchamber to the Princess of Wales, 1714–1720,* ed. C. S. Cowper (London, 1864), 115.

to which she replied: "I can have no better content in this world than to have your Lordship confirm my hope that you are pleased with your so near relation to us here, that you believe us kind to you, and value our being so."[21] The boy's thoughtfulness and good breeding made his high expectations all the more agreeable. Writing about William and Rachel's marriage, Lady Russell sensibly remarked: "We have all the promising hopes that are (I think) to be had: of those I reckon riches the least, though that ingredient is good if we use it rightly."[22] William and Rachel Cavendish used their riches responsibly and tried to teach their children to do the same. Rachel apparently was the one to deal with the children. "I must needs tel you yᵗ yʳ father can by noe means allow you to goe on in this way," she admonished their second son James for gambling while on tour abroad, "& soe he bids me tel you, yᵉ expences of yʳ travels have been very great already without yˢ addition, more I believe then is allow'd to most elder brothers, & tho I hope yʳ father is able to make you very easy in yʳ fortunes yet you may consider yᵉ more you spend aboard soe much yᵉ less you will have at home whare it wou'd doe you more credit & I should think be more for yʳ owne satisfaction to spend yʳ money amongst yʳ friends then strangers."[23] Lord James never learned the value of careful husbandry of his means, but, as we shall see, his younger brother Lord Charles, accompanying him on this trip, learned it very well. Like many of his well-to-do contemporaries, William, duke of Devonshire did spend some of his fortune on works of art; however, even as a collector he managed to enrich the family fortune. Whether out of frugality or good taste, he avoided the more expensive but often second-rate large works and instead acquired one of the finest collections of old master drawings, including works by Raphael, Dürer, Holbein, Rubens, Van Dyck, and, above all, Rembrandt.[24]

William's reliance on reason and integrity, a quality apparently shared by his wife, also is reflected in their family life. "I have always taken you to have a very good understanding," Rachel wrote to James; "if you make but a right use of that, you will know what is most for yʳ owne good."[25] They encouraged their children to think for themselves. In the matter of an allowance, for example, Rachel twice asked James what he might need while he was abroad, his parents reserving the right to disagree with him: "I thought I was right to ask yʳ opinion as to yᵉ sum, concluding I knew you soe well yᵗ if I shou'd happen to think it too much, you wou'd not take it ill yᵗ I told you soe."[26] Their difference of opinion resulted in a compromise, with James sending pleasing reports of his economy to his parents. With regard to the boys' travels, too, "yʳ father in that wo'd be willing to do what he thought was most agreeable to yʳ own inclinations . . . you may let me know what yʳ own thoughts are."[27] In a future son-in-law, William and Rachel valued that he was said to be "very sober & of an extreem good character wᶜʰ is above every thing elce."[28] This sensible family life not only nurtured love and respect but also the clear thinking and the level-headed assumption of responsibility of Lord Charles Cavendish.

Career of the Duke of Devonshire

From the time he returned from his continental tour until his death in 1729, William Cavendish, from 1707 the second duke of Devonshire, continuously devoted much of his life to public service at the highest level of government.[29] This is not the place to discuss all the details of his public life, but some aspects of it are indispensable to our understanding of his son Lord Charles and his grandson Henry Cavendish. First, *his* public position determined *theirs*; for both of them, and for all those with whom they came into contact, their being a Cavendish was no small matter. Second, the *nature* of his public life reveals much about his understanding of his public role and obligations. Whether in politics or in science, Lord

[21]Lady Russell to William, Lord Cavendish, 5 Oct. 1688, in *Letters of Lady Rachel Russell*, 410.

[22]Lady Rachel Russell to Dr. Fitzwilliam, 29 June 1688, *Letters of Lady Rachel Russell*, 399.

[23]Rachel, duchess of Devonshire to Lord James Cavendish, /late 1722 or early 1723/, Devon. Coll.

[24]John Pearson, *Serpent and Stag*, 87–88.

[25]Rachel, duchess of Devonshire to Lord James Cavendish, /late 1722 or early 1723/.

[26]Rachel, duchess of Devonshire to Lord James Cavendish, 20 Mar. 1723, Devon. Coll.

[27]Rachel, duchess of Devonshire to Lord James Cavendish, 13 Feb. 1724, Devon. Coll.

[28]Rachel, duchess of Devonshire to Lord James Cavendish, /late 1722 or early 1723/.

[29]Many details on the positions and actions of the second duke of Devonshire and, in the next section, of the duke of Kent are reported in the annual volumes of *The Historical Register, Chronological Diary*, published in London.

Charles Cavendish brought the same attitudes to public service, and we see them in his son Henry as well. Without our knowledge of their way of viewing themselves in their society, we may easily misinterpret—as has been done by earlier biographers—Henry Cavendish's life in science. Although Henry Cavendish would not have had in mind specifically his family's political principles, there is nonetheless a similarity of aspirations; if the Cavendishes secured the ancient rights and laws of the kingdom, why should not a Cavendish aim as high in any other endeavor, including the search for the fundamental ruling laws of nature?

William, second duke of Devonshire, brought to whig politics not only his own political but also his wife's strong personal interest. Rachel Russell had been brought up not to forget the injustice done her family by her father's execution in 1683 at the hands of the Stuarts. Nine years old at the time of her father's trial and execution, she had been taken by her mother to see her father imprisoned at the Tower.[30] Her mother had later written about her: "Those whose age can afford them remembrance, should, methinks, have some solemn thoughts for so irreparable a loss to themselves and family."[31] Attending the proclamation of William and Mary as king and queen, Rachel pronounced herself "very much pleased" to see them take the place of "King James, my father's murderer."[32] Lady Russell tried to turn the family's suffering for the whig cause to her son-in-law's political advantage. Soon after William Cavendish's return in 1691, his "friends," including Lady Russell, exerted their influence to have him stand for member of parliament for Westminster. Lady Russell warned off other potential whig candidates, reminding them of their political debts: "I believe the good his father did in the House of Commons . . . will be of advantage to this /William Cavendish's candidacy/. And it will not hurt his interest that he is married to my Lord Russell's daughter."[33] The Russell name was then thought so great a guarantee of political success that in 1695 two of the principal government whigs unsuccessfully tried to talk Lady Russell into letting her fifteen-year-old son stand for parliament, certain that he would be elected and bring in another whig with him.[34]

The services of the Cavendishes and the Russells received official recognition in 1694, when not only William's father was raised to a dukedom, but also Rachel's grandfather William Russell became the first duke of Bedford, an honor that would have gone to her father if he had lived. Devonshire already held the office of lord high steward in the royal household. In 1695, when William III was about to go to the Continent for half a year, Devonshire was appointed by him to be also one of seven lord justices to serve as regents during the king's absence, in charge of the army and navy, the economy, and public order. Devonshire continued in that function during the king's absences in succeeding years as well, joined in 1697 by Rachel's uncle Edward Russell, the man who had smuggled the whigs' invitation to the English throne to William of Orange in 1688, and who was now a member of the governing whig "Junto."[35]

Of the principles the second duke of Devonshire promoted, none was so important as the strict limitation of the power of the monarch. In that century two kings had been deposed for their absolutist practice, and no sensible politician wished for a repetition. There had been more than enough political and religious turmoil for a century if not for forever; the century ended by entering upon a new age, one committed to tolerance instead of fanaticism, in which political power was invested in reasonable men from the propertied classes, who were thought to have most at stake in ensuring order and responsibility in the public realm. Power, Devonshire and like-minded fellow politicians believed, was properly located in parliament, which represented the power of the landed aristocracy, and they strove to increase the power of parliament as a defense against any resurgence of royal absolutism. Since the Glorious Revolution, parliament was no longer a body that met occasionally to raise new taxes but a body that met regularly as part of ongoing government. It did not serve the executive but checked it; it served the

[30]Mary Berry, *Some Account of the Life of Rachael Wriothesley Lady Russell* . . . (London, 1819), 36.

[31]Lady Rachel Russell to her daughter Rachel Russell, /1687/, in *Some Account . . . Lady Russell*, 81.

[32]Rachel, Duchess of Devonshire to a friend, Feb. 1689, in *Some Account of . . . Lady Russell*, 93–96, on 95.

[33]Lady Rachel Russell to Mr Owen, 23 Oct. 1691, in *Letters of Lady Russell*, 532–34, on 533.

[34]William L. Sachse, *Lord Somers: A Political Portrait* (Manchester: Manchester University Press, 1975), 107.

[35]Geoffrey Holmes, *British Politics in the Age of Anne* (London: Macmillan, 1967), 235.

aristocracy, who dominated it.[36] Devonshire could, however, act to temper the power of parliament in the name of a higher authority, the laws of the land, the constitution, when he saw parliament behaving like earlier monarchs, infringing on the rights of the greater "commons," the people of England. Devonshire defended the constitutional distribution of authority with ringing appeals to rights and liberties. The assertion of parliamentary power, the continuing resistance to royal prerogative, and the call to constitutional responsibility were, in effect, Devonshire's public career. In making political alliances to this end, he was serving the interests of his family and caste and, he was convinced, the people of England. He was, in his eyes, a man of principle.

Although William and Mary had come to the English throne with the support of the whigs, William would not govern with that party only. William and Mary had accepted the English crown on conditions dictated by the Declaration of Rights (made into a statute known as the Bill of Rights) of a governing convention; these conditions constituted a reduction of royal power which, to no one's surprise, annoyed the king and made him suspicious of any further encroachments in the following years. Also to no one's surprise, the king sought his friends elsewhere than among the whigs, namely, among politically neutral men or tories.[37] However, by 1695, several whig leaders had maneuvered themselves into positions at court with power to set policy for the next few years. In parliament, on the other hand, they faced opposition not only from the tories but also from the so-called country whigs, loyal to the interests of England above those of their foreign monarch, and they needed all the votes they could muster to carry their program.[38] Devonshire could provide them with at least two that year: both of his elder sons, William and Henry, were now of age and duly elected.

William Cavendish, now marquess of Hartington (we cannot avoid a proliferation of titles: the duke of Devonshire had a subsidiary, lesser title, marquess, which his eldest son was allowed to borrow as a courtesy title), began his parliamentary career in the winter of 1695 as member for Derbyshire, his home county. He was elected as a whig when whigs, including his own father, made up the greater part of the court party, but this court was soon to learn—as others had before and would again in the future—that

Cavendishes were no slavish followers of any one party in parliament or ruling group at court. They acted out of what has been described as the "deep consciousness of rank" of the aristocracy of the time, the Cavendishes with better reason than some others. They "possessed a sense of themselves as a caste apart which gave them an arrogance, a panache, and an almost unconscious egoism which allowed them to live and to die with little thought of any standards or loyalties but their own."[39] Their loyalties they identified with the good of the country.

The principle that Hartington applied with annoying regularity to the issues most important to the court was, as we have pointed out, that of vesting as much power as possible in parliament, and away from the crown. The Declaration of Rights had left open to dispute the exact relationship between king and parliament, and Hartington stood guard over the gaps.

Almost immediately after his arrival in parliament, an issue of royal prerogative arose over the establishment of a council of trade. Factions in parliament were dissatisfied with the lack of protection for trading vessels during these years of war and wanted to set up a commission. But the king, who had procrastinated on the problem until the Commons lost patience and acted on its own, rejected the parliamentary establishment of such a commission as an encroachment upon his prerogative. When the question was put to a vote, Hartington (and his brother, an earlier Henry Cavendish) voted that the members of the proposed commission should be appointed by parliament, not the crown.[40]

Another serious dispute between parliament and the crown was over the size of the army that William wanted to retain after the peace of Ryswick in 1697, as many as 30,000 men, constituting a standing army. The king's request met with the

---

[36]M. L. Bush, *The English Aristocracy: A Comparative Synthesis* (Manchester: Manchester University Press, 1984), 199–200.

[37]*The Divided Society, Parties and Politics in England 1694–1716*, eds. Geoffrey Holmes and W. A. Speck (New York: St. Martin's Press, 1968), 98. Stephen B. Baxter, *William III and the Defense of European Liberty 1650–1702* (New York: Harcourt, Brace & World, 1966), 256.

[38]Holmes and Speck, eds, *Divided Society*, 16–17. Sachse, *Somers*, 113.

[39]J. H. Plumb, *Sir Robert Walpole*. Vol. 1, *The Making of a Statesman* (London: Cresset, 1956). Vol. 2, *The King's Minister* (London: Cresset, 1960), 9–10.

[40]Henry Horwitz, *Parliament, Policy and Politics in the Reign of William III* (Newark: University of Delaware Press, 1977), 165.

strong objection that such an army had been forbidden by the Bill of Rights because of the threat it posed to English liberty. Parliament settled instead on a much smaller force of 8,000 men, and that bill was so vigorously supported by Hartington and his brother that they drew a reprimand from the king. Loyal first of all to Cavendishes, even above the king, Devonshire took his son's part and threatened to resign his office at court. He felt the attack, he said, as if it had been directed against himself, "for he believed their reasons were sensible, as the king was forbidden to maintain a large establishment."[41]

During Hartington's second term in parliament, from 1698 to 1700, the composition of the Commons was such that the whigs found it difficult and often impossible to control it. Encouraged by the king's growing rejection of his whig ministers, the Commons was in a mood to break the junto by wearing down its members in a series of politically motivated attacks, especially over the royal grants of crown lands in England and Ireland since 1685. In these debates the question came up, at least implicitly, of the king's right—or lack of it—to choose his own advisors. The Commons argued that they needed to guard against "an ill ministry, and the influence of foreigners." The reference to foreigners was part of a more general resolution aimed at removing the lord chancellor John Somers from office. It would have been put aside along with the rest of the resolution when the Commons voted against it, if Hartington, who voted in favor of Somers with the majority, had not insisted on the question of foreign influence. He introduced one more resolution, which called for the exclusion of all foreigners except Prince George, the future queen Anne's Danish husband, from the king's councils in England and Ireland. After giving a vote of support to a minister whom the king wanted to be rid of, the Commons now supported without contest Hartington's resolution against councillors whom their foreign king might want.[42] The implication was that it was the Commons, not the king, who would make or break ministers. But the king had not yet come around to that view: a few weeks later he dismissed Somers.

By 1701 the whigs had lost control of the Commons altogether, yielding it to a combination of tories and the so-called country party. As the first item of business in importance, this coalition was

confronted once again with the task of settling the Protestant succession to the English throne, for Anne's last surviving child had died the previous summer. Hartington moved to take up the question in committee. When the committee of the whole house met a few days later, it resolved that in addition to "a further Declaration . . . of the Limitation and Succession of the Crown in the Protestant Line" it would make "further Provision . . . for Security of the Rights and Liberties of the People." The latter was taken up first: in nine resolutions, the Commons placed further restrictions on the crown, including a definition of the role of the privy council, the exclusion of foreign-born persons from holding office or from receiving land grants from the crown, and the requirement that the king seek the consent of parliament for waging wars in defense of other than British territories.[43] Britain then had a foreign monarch and was about to settle its crown on yet another foreign royal family, that of Hanover. Past experience and common sense dictated that the protection of the "Rights and Liberties of the People" be carefully set down in law.

Hartington's constant concern with questions of rights extended to the "Rights and Liberties" of individuals, or, as he put it, "of all the Commons of England," and not merely of the House of Commons as a body. In the parliamentary session of 1701–1702, a particular case raised the question of the right to initiate a dissolution of parliament. The suggestion by the tories that that right rested exclusively with the king caused Hartington to move a resolution asserting the subject's right to address the king for "the calling, sitting, and dissolving" of parliaments. In reaction to the protracted impeachment proceedings against the whig ministers Somers and Orford (Hartington voted for the acquittal of both, the latter his relative Edward Russell), Hartington moved another resolution asserting the rights of individuals, this one even more fundamental than the first, namely,

———————
[41] Horwitz, *Parliament*, 250. Sachse, *Somers*, 130–32.
[42] Horwitz, *Parliament*, 265–68. Sachse, *Somers*, 160–64.
[43] *Journal of the House of Commons* 13:375 (3 Mar. 1701). Horwitz, *Parliament*, 283–84. Hartington's wish to exclude foreigners from high office did not prevent him from welcoming them into the army. When in 1702 a tory member of the House proposed to deny foreign-born military men commissions in the British army, Hartington, leading the whigs, objected vigorously. George Macaulay Trevelyan, *England under Queen Anne*, vol. 1: *Blenheim* (London: Longmans, Green, 1930), 205.

the subject's right to "a speedy trial" of "any accusation," including impeachment, against him. The Commons approved both resolutions without debate.[44] In 1704 yet another case caused Hartington to defend an individual's right to vote as standing above the privileges of the Commons. "As long as I live, I shall be as tender of the privileges of this house as any body," he said in the Commons, but he added, "I must confess, I think the liberty of a cobler ought to be as much regarded as of any body else; that is the happiness of our constitution." In this case of Ashby and White, an elector who claimed that he had been denied his right to vote had taken his complaint to the courts. The Commons insisted that the actions following from this infringed on the privileges of the Commons, that the matter should have been brought before them. Hartington saw the question as "a matter of great consideration." "For when a person offers his vote at an election, and is not admitted to give it, and upon such refusal brings his action in the courts in Westminster-hall, (which I take to be the present case), if giving judgment upon it be contrary to the privileges of this House, then it is pretty plain, that our privileges do interfere with the rights of the people that elected us." The aggrieved party in Hartington's opinion had no recourse but to the law. His careful reasoning was wasted on his colleagues, but he persisted. When the matter was moved from committee to the whole house, he spoke up again: "I do not expect the House will be of a different opinion from the Committee; but I think it is my duty, when I apprehend what you are doing will be of ill consequence to the constitution, to give my dissent in every step. I think it will be dangerous to the very being of this House." The argument was simple: if the Commons could affirm or deny an individual's right to vote, then "by the influence of officers they might have filled this House with what members they had pleased, and then they could have voted themselves duly elected."[45] He was defending—in vain, as far as his colleagues in the Commons were concerned—what a supporter of his called the "birthright" of the people of England. Lord Somers, trained in the law, agreed with Hartington and gave a scholarly defense of their position in the House of Lords when the Lords considered the outcome of the case in the Commons. Somers carried the conclusion one step

further than Hartington. Denying an elector his right to vote, Somers concluded, was equivalent to denying him his right to his estate, since the law had "annexed his Right of voting to his Freehold."[46] Somers was speaking as a lawyer, citing precedent; Hartington, not referring to the connection between landed property and the right to vote, may have supported a more liberal view, but, given the base of Hartington's power, we have no reason to think he had any serious disagreement with Somers's legal position.[47]

Acting often independently of party and almost constantly in opposition to the court was no route to high office or political power. Hartington did not want a place as courtier at William's court, as he demonstrated when he declined a sought-after "Bedchamber place" offered him in the summer of 1700.[48] Court posts at that level always went to peers; if Hartington had accepted the post, he would probably have been elevated to the peerage, which would have forced him to move from the Commons to the Lords. He would have had to leave a sphere of political action where he was most needed, where the whigs required additional strength. (The duke of Kent's eldest son, Anthony, in 1720 accepted a post as gentleman of the bedchamber to George I and was prematurely, i.e., in his father's lifetime, elevated to the peerage and the House of Lords as Lord Harold.) Hartington may have been holding out for a political post—in 1701 rumor had it he was being considered for secretary of state—but that the king denied him.

Possible disappointment along with the influence of new associates may have changed Hartington's political activities, if not his principles, after 1700. He became part of a group of politicians and friends that included Robert Walpole, all

[44]Horwitz, *Parliament*, 302–3. *The Manuscripts of the House of Lords*, vol. 4 (New Series), *1699–1702* (London: His Majesty's Stationery Office, 1908), 300.

[45]*Cobbett's Parliamentary History of England. From the Norman Conquest, in 1066, to the Year 1803*, vol. 6: *Comprising the Period from the Accession of Queen Anne in 1702, to the Accession of King George the First in 1714* (London, 1810), cols. 256–57, 301.

[46]Sachse, *Somers*, 225.

[47]An important precipitant of the Revolution of 1688 was James II's interference with the privileges of the traditional ruling class. The Cavendishes along with their kind "combined to create, in the Revolution Settlement, government of the property-owners, for the property-owners, by the property-owners." W. A. Speck, *Tory & Whig. The Struggle in the Constituencies 1701–1715* (New York: St. Martin's Press, 1970), 3.

[48]Horwitz, *Parliament*, 276.

associated with the well-known political club known as the Kit-Cat Club of whigs.[49] Walpole enjoyed the political support of Orford, Hartington's relative, and in 1702 Walpole had an opportunity to return the family favor by ensuring Hartington's re-election to the Commons. A strongly High-Church-oriented electorate, including the bulk of the gentry, had just turned Hartington out of his seat as Member of Parliament for his home county of Derbyshire, a seat that must have seemed to him as though it ought to have been his birthright. The details of the election suggested fraud. Six different polling places had been designated for the election, one for each hundred, but in the end, they were all set up in the oppositions' bastion of Derby, in booths and on tables in and around the same hall, and well away from the country places of the Cavendishes and the Manners, the two leading aristocratic families of the shire whose respective eldest sons were the whig candidates for the county.[50] Hartington petitioned the Commons to review the Derbyshire election. The opposition quickly retaliated with a petition of their own, charging that Hartington's brother Lord James Cavendish had been illegally elected for the borough of Derby.[51] Before any further action was taken on either case, Walpole's fellow Member of Parliament for Castle Rising declined to sit, and Walpole secured the seat for Hartington. Returning to the Commons as the second member from Walpole's own constituency meant that Hartington now, albeit only for a few months, owed his seat in parliament not to family interest and local power, but to political loyalty, circumstances that his father Devonshire found "humiliating,"[52] but which speak for the common sense of the son. The accession of Anne to the throne in 1702 brought new general elections; this time Hartington accepted the patronage of the duke of Somerset and was returned for Yorkshire,[53] a more distinguished county seat, which he retained until, at his father's death in 1707, he moved to the House of Lords as the second duke of Devonshire.

During the five years remaining to him in the Commons, Hartington became firmly associated with Walpole and the whigs. In those years the whig junto regained its influence and even some of its power. A minority in the Commons, the whigs controlled the Lords and shared the ministries with moderate tories willing to compromise. That the

five junto lords were all in the upper house left room in the Commons for their juniors to lead whig issues through the debates. The opening was filled especially by Walpole and Hartington, who were becoming leaders among the younger whigs in the Commons.[54] Hartington and Walpole acted with a few men of like mind as well as close family and political ties such as Hartington's brother-in-law John Manners, marquess of Granby, Walpole's brother-in-law Sir Charles Turner, their fellow Norfolk whig Sir John Holland (holding "sentiments & principles [that] are the same together with my Ld Hartington, yrself [Walpole] . . ." and voting "according to yr wishes").[55]

Hartington's activities in the Commons in these years give us a good idea of the political role he chose for himself. He rarely participated in the committee work on so-called private bills, which dealt with local problems such as bridge repairs or with questions of individual estates. He preferred to take up general questions, such as the Protestant succession and the rights of non-conformists.[56] Hartington and his associates in the Commons battled unsuccessfully against the bill to prevent "occasional conformity." Hartington and Walpole acted as liaison to the whigs in the Lords, who on this issue were led by the duke of Devonshire and who killed off the bill every time the Commons sent it up. The bill, one of the measures of greatest priority for the queen and the tories, was aimed at the practice of non-conformists occasionally to take

―――――

[49]Holmes, *British Politics . . . Anne*, 297.

[50]*The Victoria History of the Counties of England, Derbyshire*, ed. W. Page, vol. 2 (London: Constable, 1905), 142.

[51]3 Jan. 1702, *House of Commons Journal* 13:649.

[52]Dennis Rubini, *Court and Country 1688–1702* (London: Rupert Hart-Davis, 1967), 245.

[53]*Collins's Peerage of England; Geneological, Biographical, and Historical*, 9 vols, ed. E. Brydges (London, 1812) 1: 354. Holmes and Speck, eds., *Divided Society*, 47. Bickley, *Cavendish*, 186.

[54]Plumb, *Walpole* 1:112.

[55]Holmes, *British Politics . . . Anne*, 233.

[56]The committees he was on in 1792, after Anne had succeeded to the crown, for example, were the committee to reformulate the oath of loyalty to the queen and the Protestant succession, and three committees to draw up addresses to the queen, the first an address of condolence to the queen on the death of William III, the second, in March 1702, a reply to her address to the Commons, and, most important, the third, in May 1702, an address to assure her that the Commons "will, to the utmost, assist and support her" following her declaration of war on France. (One of the committees on which he served in 1702—"for the better Discovery of all Lands, and other Revenues, given to Poppish superstitious Uses, and for applying the same for the Support of the Royal Hospital of Greenwich"—brought Hartington together with Isaac Newton.) 8 Mar. 1702, and following, *HCJ* 13:782, 808–11, 830, 870.

communion in an Anglican church to avoid the legal disabilities placed upon them.[57] To the whigs, non-conformists were important supporters, a good practical reason, aside from questions of political principle or religious conscience, to fight a bill that aimed at depriving them of the franchise.[58] In 1706 Hartington was appointed to the English commission, headed by Somers and other members of the junto, working for a union with Scotland. With a Scottish commission, they worked out the Act of Union, filling the last gap in the agreements that ensured the Hanoverian succession. Always much more a party man than his Court-oriented father, Hartington in his last years in the Commons went out of his way to assume political responsibility and a clearly defined political identity.[59] Nobody, not even the junto or the queen, would in the future find it easy to ignore him.

The year 1707 was to add the aura of power to Hartington's political activities. Already during his father's lifetime, Hartington was on occasion called upon to take his place at the great ceremonial events of the court. In August of 1705, for example, the queen proclaimed a "general thanksgiving throughout this kingdom" for a military victory. In the procession from St. James's palace to St. Paul's cathedral, as the eldest son of a duke, Hartington ranked right below the dukes, and ahead of the earls (among them the then still earl of Kent), the queen's ministers, and the bishops. "The streets were lined by the citty train'd bands, and at Temple Barr by our lord mayor, aldermen, and sherifs, who conducted her to church. . . ."[60] Among his fellow Members of Parliament, Hartington moved almost as if he were royalty himself; Robert Molesworth, a whig M.P. but not an adherent of the junto, wrote to his wife in 1704:

> Yesterday being Sunday, the Marquis of Hartington sent me word about 8 that he intended to dine with me. I entertained him and his company as well as I could at so short warning and sent for several gentlemen of the neighbourhood to wait on him, who came and dined with him, and after dinner (about 5 or 6) we all of us conducted His Lordship a mile or two of his way towards the Earl of Kingston's, whither he was a-going.[61]

He was prepared to take over from a father who was powerful enough even to stand up to royalty. "Here lies William duke of Devonshire, a faithful subject of good princes, and an enemy to tyrants," the first duke had ordered inscribed on his tomb. Two

weeks after his death in August of 1707, his body was sent off in princely fashion, "carried in great state thro' this citty . . . followed by about 80 coaches, the lord James Cavendish, his youngest son, was cheif mourner; the officers of the queen's household attended with the heralds at arms, who carried the ensigns of honour belonging to the family," on the long, final journey from London to Derby that many Cavendishes took. Two days later, Hartington, now duke of Devonshire, was called to the queen "to receive the white staffe as steward of the household, vacant by the death of his father"; a week later he was sworn of the privy council; and in October he took his father's seat in the House of Lords.[62]

The court position that the second duke more or less inherited from his father[63] was still a politically important position during Anne's reign, because it placed its holder among her constant political advisors in the cabinet. Altogether, Devonshire held high office at Anne's and the subsequent Hanoverian court for more than ten of the next twenty-two years; that is, from the time from his succession to the title until his death.

Whereas while he was at court, half of the time he found himself out of office, in parliament Devonshire always remained one of the leaders of his party, judged "a very honest man" and "a very usefull man."[64] The House of Lords, rather than the court, was the politically more rewarding scene for the whigs—and for Devonshire—where their aim was the same as at court, to retain or to return to power.

---

[57]Narcissus Luttrell, *A Brief Historical Relation of State Affairs from September 1678 to 1714*, 6 vols. (Oxford, 1857) 5:258–59, 264, 273, 362–64, 369, 490–98. Sachse, *Somers*, 220–22. Plumb, *Walpole* 1:112.

[58]Henry L. Snyder, "The Defeat of the Occasional Conformity Bill and the Tack: A Study in the Techniques of Parliamentary Management in the Reign of Queen Anne," in *Peers, Politics and Power: The House of Lords, 1603–1911*, eds. C. Jones and D. L. Jones (London and Ronceverte: Hambledon Press, 1986), 111–31, on 111.

[59]Holmes, *British Politics . . . Anne*, 232.

[60]Luttrell, *Brief Historical Relation* 5:585.

[61]Great Britain, Historical Manuscripts Commission, *Report on Manuscripts in Various Collections*, vol. 8: *The Manuscripts of the Hon. Frederick Lindley Wood; M. L. S. Clements, Esq.; S. Philip Unwin, Esq.* (London: His Majesty's Stationery Office, 1913), 232.

[62]Luttrell, *Brief Historical Relation* 6: 204, 207, 209, 211, 226. House of Lords Manuscripts, vol. 7 (New Series): *The Manuscripts of the House of Lords, 1706–1708* (London: His Majesty's Stationary Office, 1921), 97.

[63]"My Lord Steward /i.e., the first duke/ dyed yesterday. The Queen seems resolved that his son shall succeed to his employment," the earl of Godolphin wrote to the duke of Marlborough on 19 Aug. 1707, in *Marlborough-Godolphin Correspondence* 2:887.

[64]The duke of Marlborough to the duchess of Marlborough, /28 Aug.//8 Sep. 1707, *Marlborough Godolphin Correspondence* 2:895.

The accession of George I in 1714 must have seemed to the whigs like the morning of a long day of reaping the rewards for their labor on behalf of the Hanoverian succession. Probably as a matter of course, Devonshire was on the list of eighteen regents sitting in for the king until his arrival in England. (Also on the list were Kent and Orford.) Soon after, he received back his old positions of lord steward and lord lieutenant of Derbyshire and was sworn to the privy council (as was Kent). With him, most of his junto colleagues as well as Walpole and his friends returned to high office.[65]

Success, however, allowed rifts among the whigs themselves to emerge. Although eager to reach a final peace with France, George, England's latest foreign king, had continental wars of his own to fight. Not all of his whig ministers were still willing to support royal demands toward that end before the war-weary English people. For a while, despite disagreements, events further strengthened the whig hold on the government. The Jacobite uprising of 1715/16, for example, resulted in the dismissal of the remaining tories in the ministry, and in the summer of 1716 Devonshire resigned his court office of lord steward to the duke of Kent to assume the political office of lord president of the council, the one top-ranking office that since 1714 had still been held by a tory.[66] His new duties required him to make decisions on all issues before the government.

During the next ten years, Devonshire, sometimes in office and sometimes out, was concerned with a broad range of proposals, such as reduction of the army, reduction of taxes (for the landed men), trade with Spain (for city men), building of Whitehall and hospitals (for the poor, who were to be put to work), pardon for the Pretender's followers, supremacy of state over church, and so on. In 1725, when Walpole had a sensitive task for someone with the access to government policy and who also had good sense, he turned to his trusted old whig ally Devonshire. When the prince and princess of Wales had been thrown out of the royal residence after the prince's quarrel with the king, Devonshire was one of the first to offer the prince and princess his own house as residence. Eventually they settled at Leicester House where Devonshire became a frequent guest. Walpole had the tricky job of being the king's minister and at the same time keeping the goodwill of the heir to the throne who had been alienated by the king and removed from official business. He managed it by secretly keeping the prince informed of state affairs through their mutual friend Devonshire. Thus, when George I died suddenly in 1727, Walpole maintained himself in power under the new king. Devonshire had once more contributed to stability and an orderly transition of power. Appropriately the first session of the inner ministerial circle held to draw up the new king's speech to parliament met at Devonshire House.[67]

Career of the Duke of Kent

Whereas Devonshire sought and acquired political power and served the whig cause (in his view) with a fierce loyalty, Kent stood for neither power, party, nor principle. His political career had only this in common with Devonshire's: great ambition, which in Kent's case took the form of self-interested maneuvering at court. His legacy to Lord Charles and Henry Cavendish was great pride in the standing of his family and a breadth of cultural interests outside politics.

On his return from the Continent in 1691, Henry de Grey lived the life of a well-to-do private gentleman for the next ten years, taking up neither of the usual two occupations of young aristocrats, the military or parliament.[68] His public life began almost simultaneously with the reign of Queen Anne. At her coronation, Henry's father carried one of the swords of state; four months later, in August of 1702, his father died suddenly in the middle of a game of bowls, leaving Henry, his heir, on his way to the House of Lords as earl of Kent.

Kent took his seat in the Lords with the opening of parliament in October. From the beginning he took a safe, middle-of-the-road position in politics, which, given what is known about his character, seems to have reflected his personal attitude as much as any design to acquire office. On the important issue of the occasional

---

[65]Plumb, *Walpole* 1:197, 201–4. *Collins's Peerage*, 355.

[66]Henry Horwitz, *Revolution Politicks The Career of Daniel Finch Second Earl of Nottingham, 1647–1730* (Cambridge: Cambridge University Press, 1968), 250, 252.

[67]Plumb, *Walpole* 2:165. Pearson, *The Serpent and the Stag*, 86.

[68]Thomas Wentworth, *The Wentworth Papers, 1705–1739. Selected from the Private and Family Correspondence of Thomas Wentworth, Lord Raby, Created in 1711 Earl of Strafford, of Stainborough, Co. York*, ed. James J. Cartwright (London, 1883), 134.

conformity bill taken up during that session of parliament and the next, for example, he voted for the bill in accordance with the queen's wishes.[69] For that reason, he is said to have been a tory in the early part of his career, but his early voting is of a piece with his later voting even though he then voted with the whigs: he was almost always, certainly while he held office, the queen's man. From a conversation with a friend during Sacheverell's trial in 1710 it is clear that Kent, still undecided on how he should vote on the doctor's guilt, was more concerned to guess correctly the queen's opinion in the matter than to formulate his own.[70] In politics, Anne wished for moderation, and Kent by temperament agreed with her wishes.

In the spring of 1704, party pressures of the sort the queen so greatly disliked caused her to dismiss three high-ranking tory officeholders, among them her lord chamberlain. Kent was at Newmarket at the races in April, suffering a fall from his horse that at first seemed to threaten his life.[71] Three weeks later he had not only recovered, but he had been appointed the queen's new lord chamberlain and a member of the privy council.[72] This sudden and very high leap into a career at court has been ascribed to the efforts of the duchess of Marlborough, then Anne's groom of the stole and friend, and Kent's neighbor in Bedfordshire.[73] The duchess was never Kent's friend, although she may have promoted him because she hoped to dominate him. Other factors would have recommended Kent to the queen as well. Anne, who had only just rid herself of one political group trying to dictate their views to her, was not about to turn for replacements to strong party whigs of whose party fervor she was equally suspicious. Kent was a relatively new face at court, without disturbing political associations, and already of proven loyalty. In his political views, Kent's also fit those of the queen's lord treasurer, Godolphin, who was involved in appointments. Robert Harley, appointed secretary of state in the same shakeup, wrote to him at the time: "I am glad that My Lord Treasurer will choose moderate men to carry on his Ministrye, which is approved by all people hithertoe, but those who are very much inclined to passion, and Selfe Interest."[74] They agreed that service to the queen should come before party loyalty, undoubtedly the reason why Kent allowed himself "always" to be "governed by

Lord Treasurer and that party whilst he was Chamberlain."[75]

Kent's office of lord chamberlain was that of "greatest honour and dignity" at court, awarded as a sign of royal favor and always to a person of very high rank (after Kent's tenure it was always held by a duke).[76] He received emoluments of over £1,000 in the form of money or plate, a pension, lodgings, and, because of his daily access to the queen, the opportunity to gain whatever he could through the sale of offices. The office of lord chamberlain controlled by far the largest department of the four highest administrative, as opposed to political, offices at court (the others being the lord steward's department consisting of the household "below stairs," the stables under the master of the horse, and the royal private apartments or bedchamber under the groom of the stole). As lord chamberlain, Kent found himself in charge of all appointees and employees as well as of all daily and ceremonial affairs associated with the public rooms of the royal residence "above stairs"; his department also included personnel and functions not directly a part of the royal household, such as the physicians, surgeons, and apothecaries to the court, the court's mathematical instrument-maker or the court poet (in all, at the time of George I, over 600 persons, and not many fewer before) and the general supervision over theaters. The annual budget of the lord chamberlain's department was well over £50,000.

An earl or duke was not expected personally to carry out the many duties of the office; "dukes did not open doors for themselves."[77] Most of the work was left to the vice chamberlain and members of the staff. But the lord chamberlain did supervise the overall coordination of the work and had to be

---

[69] Holmes, *British Politics . . . Anne*, 102.

[70] *The Wentworth Papers*, 146. Kent voted for conviction, as the queen wished, but against her opinion on the severity of the penalty, which he may have come to regret. Geoffrey Holmes, *The Trial of Doctor Sacheverell* (London: Eyre Methuen, 1973), 116, 210, 285.

[71] Luttrell, *Brief Historical Relation* 5:410.

[72] Ibid. 417–18.

[73] Holmes, *British Politics . . . Anne*, 211.

[74] Sheila Biddle, *Bolingbroke and Harley* (New York: Knopf, 1974), 103.

[75] *The Wentworth Papers*, 134.

[76] John M. Beattie, *The English Court in the Reign of George I* (Cambridge: Cambridge University Press, 1967), 24. Much of our information about the office of lord chamberlain below is derived from Beattie's chapter on this office: "The Departments of the Household. 1. The Chamber and the Bedchamber," 23–65, and elsewhere in this book.

[77] Ibid. 40.

in attendance practically year round. On the Sunday after his appointment, Kent for the first time "handed her majestie to chappel."[78] He arranged any public ceremony the queen desired, and he acted as her escort. In her exchanges with the House of Lords, it was Kent as her lord chamberlain who acted as go-between, a responsibility attended by a great deal of ceremony. When, early in his tenure, Kent on one occasion sent a message to the Lords by another peer, informing them of the time the queen had fixed for them to attend her, his messenger—and by implication Kent himself— was immediately reprimanded by one of the dukes, "a man jealous of the Orders of the House," for so "irregular" a procedure.[79] Greatly devoted to his gardens at his country estate of Wrest in Bedfordshire but kept in the city by his office, he could do no better late in May than to have his wife's account of the work he was having done there and learn that "the country is very pleasant and sweet for the Honeysuckles are in perfection." "I desire you in return to lett me heare from you & tell me what politicks goes forward," she added, sympathetic to his plight.[80] Another part of his duties was that he frequently had to entertain at his own expense. He inaugurated his tenure as lord chamberlain in style: a month after his appointment he "treated her majestie and the court upon the river Thames, where were near 1000 barges and boats, with all sorts of musick and eatables" on what one hopes was a lovely day late in May.[81]

The office of lord chamberlain had at one time included what was by the early eighteenth century a separate department of the royal bed-chamber under the groom of the stole. There were still areas where the lines of authority of the two departments were not clearly sorted out, and there was a certain amount of rivalry between the holders of the top offices. The difficult duchess of Marlborough, holding office alongside Kent, made his tenure especially hard and tarnished his reputation. She apparently thought that he would be easy to control. Godolphin's remark to her about Kent's appointment that the "whole town was thoroughly disappointed about Bugg" would not have been made if Godolphin had known her to be holding Kent in high esteem.[82] Godolphin himself and the duke of Marlborough, Anne's chief ministers then, certainly did not, for they never invited Kent into the cabinet, which was highly unusual

behavior toward one of such high office.[83] Within a few years, the duchess's influence with the queen began to wane, while Kent proved to be less malleable than the duchess may have expected, creating tension and eventually downright hostility— at least on the Marlboroughs' side—between them. When Kent, for example, ignored the duchess's recommendation in making an appointment, she sent him a message "of a very rude nature."[84] Kept informed of the duchess's complaints while with the army on the Continent, Marlborough was angered for months by Kent's wish for the Garter in 1707: "I think it should not be given til the Queen is sensible of the sham it would be to let so worthless a creature . . . /as Kent/ so much as expect itt," he wrote to his wife, no doubt hoping that his wife would make the queen "sensible" of the worthlessness she herself apparently did not perceive.[85] Kent quickly learned to guard his interests and not to trust the duchess. Settling a theater dispute in 1706, Kent "was big of the plot," reported the theater's manager who worked with him, "and was afraid if any body shou'd let it be known at Court before him, he shou'd be Robbed of the glory of Establishing the Stage upon a foot of going on." When the plot succeeded, "he told it at the Dutchesse of Marlbro's" (who tried to influence the theater as well although she had no jurisdiction over it), no doubt with a note of triumph.[86] The duchess absented herself from the court after 1708 because of a bitter quarrel with the queen. Kent, linked to the more reasonable

---

[78]Luttrell, *Brief Historical Relation* 5:417.
[79]William Nicholson, *The London Diaries of William Nicholson Bishop of Carlisle 1702–1718*, ed. C. Jones and G. Holmes (Oxford: Clarendon Press, 1985), 257–58.
[80]Jemima, duchess of Kent to Henry, duke of Kent, 18 May /probably 1708/, Bedford Record Office, Wrest Park Collection, L 30/8/35/3.
[81]Luttrell, *Brief Historical Relation* 5:429.
[82]*The Marlborough-Godolphin Correspondence* 1:284.
[83]Holmes, *British Politics . . . Anne*, 227.
[84]*Papers of Sir William Trumbull*, part 2, p. 866.
[85]The duke of Marlborough to the duchess of Marlborough, 14 May 1708, in *The Marlborough-Godolphin Correspondence* 2:895, 972. Toward Godolphin, Marlborough was more restrained, suggesting that he was either humoring his wife or aware that Godolphin thought somewhat better of Kent than he. On the same day on which he wrote to his wife that "it would be scandelous to give it /the Garter/ him /Kent/, since he has no one quallity that deserves itt," he wrote to Godolphin, not mentioning Kent's name, "I wish for the service of the Queen, that she may have no thoughts of disposing of the blew ribons, til she may find the giving of them be a satisfaction to herself, or of some use to her business." Letters of 8 Sep. 1707, ibid., 894–95.

Godolphin, was safe for another two years, and then the queen waited until Godolphin was out of town before she asked Kent to resign.[87]

That Kent's hold on his office after 1707 was at times only tenuous had much to do with the constant political shifts between tories and whigs in their struggle for power during Anne's reign. Any high court office was a potential foothold for political domination. Kent was not a political man, and to those of either party who were, his office must have seemed to be a wasted opportunity. In 1708, when the whigs were trying to force their way back into government, Kent feared for his office: "My Ld Chamb: is in a Tottering way, I know he expects to be out which he has not a mind to," someone who knew him wrote in July.[88] In December gossip had it that "So many think themselves fit for Chamberlain that the fear of disobliging a multitude still keeps in Lord Kennt."[89] It may also have been the queen's stubbornness with which she was opposing the rest of the whigs' demands for office then that kept Kent in. Only in 1710, when party politics had brought the tories into the ascendancy again, the queen yielded to Harley and gave Kent's office to a tory duke, dismissing Kent, as he said, "with all the marks of kindness."[90] Kent, Godolphin reported to Marlborough, "is extreamly nettled, and is not shie of expressing a good deal of resentment" against Harley and Somerset, "who he thinks have been the chief occasion of it."[91] Sparing the queen was wise: for sacrificing him, she made him duke of Kent.

In the last four years of her reign, Kent at times acted the party man, voting with the whigs in the House of Lords. But the queen could still sway him, too: "I am told that the night before the Parliament meet the Queen sent for the D. of Kent and talked to him a good while, and the next day he voted with the Tories," a lady at court reported in 1711.[92] Along with receiving further honors from the queen after his dismissal, Kent was one of only a few whigs who still held positions of honor (if not of profit) after the queen had turned her government over to an unabashedly tory administration.[93]

Kent's appointment to lord chamberlain coincided with the beginning of an important cultural development in which he was to play an official part; namely, the introduction of Italian opera at English theaters. The lord chamberlain's supervision of theaters was only a small part of his

official domain and need hardly have involved him personally at all. As it was, he left much of the day-to-day business of singers' and actors' complaints over contract terms or disagreements with the theater managers to his vice chamberlain Thomas Coke.[94] But Kent had long taken an interest in music in his private life, which he could indulge in his official capacity as well.

Kent and his wife Jemima Crewe from the beginning of their marriage had a common love of music. Every month, sometimes several times a month, they attended "musick meetings," the then fashionable subscription concert series arranged by music lovers such as Thomas Britton who could present Handel. At times they spent more money on "a Musick book and Italian songs" than on all books on other subjects combined.[95] Away from London, the "Nightingale" had to "supply yᵉ want of Margarita" (Françoise Marguérite de l'Epine, one of the leading singers of the day) for Jemima.[96]

The principal theaters over which Kent's new office gave him control in 1704 were those at Drury Lane and Lincoln's Inn Fields, to which the Haymarket was added in 1705. Lincoln's Inn Fields was closed for most of Kent's tenure. Drury Lane was then performing both plays and English operas, which were not operas in the modern sense, but spoken plays with musical numbers and masques. When the Haymarket opened it followed suit. All-sung or "Italian" operas had until then been produced only abroad, but in the season of 1704/5, the owner-manager of Drury Lane, Christopher Rich, successfully staged the first

---

[86] Judith Milhous and Robert D. Hume, eds., *Vice Chamberlain Coke's Theatrical Papers 1706-1715* (Carbondale and Edwardsville: Southern Illinois University Press, 1982), 12.

[87] The earl of Godolphin to the duke of Marlborough, 17 Apr., 1710, in *The Marlborough-Godolphin Correspondence* 3:1463.

[88] Milhous and Hume, *Coke's Theatrical Papers*, 113.

[89] Thomas Butler to Sir William Trumbull, 28 Dec. 1708, in *Papers of Sir William Trumbull*, 867.

[90] Letter by Peter Wentworth to a friend, end of Sep. 1710, in *The Wentworth Papers*, 146.

[91] The earl of Godolphin to the duke of Marlborough, 17 Apr. 1710, in *The Marlborough-Godolphin Correspondence*, 1464.

[92] *The Wentworth Papers*, 222.

[93] Holmes, *British Politics . . . Anne*, 436–39.

[94] Milhous and Hume, *Coke's Theatrical Papers*, xxi–xxii, xxvii, 106.

[95] Accounts from 1692 to 1697, p. 84 and passim. Bedfordshire Record Office, Wrest Park Collection, L 31/129.

[96] Jemima Kent to the marquis of Kent, Wrest, 18 May /probably 1708/, Bedfordshire Record Office, Wrest Park Collection, L 30/8/35/3.

Italian opera in London. The Haymarket immediately put on Italian operas of its own.[97]

From the start, Italian operas appealed primarily to fashionable society: "the Great chiefly incourage them," a contemporary periodical reported, perhaps because "the Expence of that Diversion is a little too great for such as declare for exact Oeconomy."[98] Nevertheless, theater managers, along with their official patron, Kent, and other aristocratic supporters expected Italian operas to become popular and a great financial success, especially if they could induce the best Italian singers to accept engagements at the London theaters. For a short time, their expectations were met, but at a price. Rich, at Drury Lane, by putting on both operas and plays, profited despite staging expensive operas because he did not pay the actors whom he had under contract for plays. The Haymarket's venture into Italian opera was a financial failure. Both actors and singers complained to the lord chamberlain, without whose permission they could not leave their engagements to earn money elsewhere. Kent's solution to their problems was a ruling, which became known as the Order of Union; by it, one theater, Drury Lane, would perform only plays, and the other, Haymarket, only operas, and they would avoid competing with one another by not both playing the same night. Kent's ruling earned him warm gratitude from the actors, even the dedication of a play by the actor-playwright Colley Cibber.[99] But it was to create problems for opera, even though it was meant to strengthen it: opera was set on a financial course it has had to follow ever since, sustaining itself through philanthropic or state support. The foreign singers brought in as the star attractions, intended to keep opera profitable, asked for very high salaries, several times those of actors, the English "Climate being much wors than any other for voices"[100] and, no doubt, English aristocrats wanting the novelty of their singing. When they could not get the salaries they asked for, they sang at "musick meetings," threatening the existence of the opera, which could not get singers at "reasonable sallarys" if they could earn more elsewhere. To protect the opera, Kent tried several means. He stopped competing concerts; with the owner-manager of the Haymarket, Sir John Vanbrugh, he organized an opera company including a full, regular orchestra; and he thought of creating year-round opportunities for singers to earn money, during the summer as well as during the regular opera season. "Voices are the things at present to be got," Vanbrugh wrote to the English envoy at Venice, who was to negotiate with the Italian singers; "if these Top ones come over, 'twill facilitate bringing the Queen into a Scheme, now preparing by my Ld Chamb: and Others, to have Concerts of Musick in the Summer at Windsor, twice a Week in the /queen's/ Appartment. There is no doubt, but by some such way as this, if the best Singers come, they will tast of the Queens bounty." Within two or three seasons it had become clear that opera could not support itself, and Vanbrugh appealed to Kent to "move the Queen . . . to give a Thousand Pounds a year towards the opera support."[101] With an enterprise so new it took longer than Kent's term in office to put it on a regular footing, but he kept it alive, even when managers like Vanbrugh were driven off by their financial losses."[102]

After being out of court office during the last four years of Queen Anne's reign, Kent's reputation as a "staunch court man" earned him a place on George I's list of eighteen regents who were to govern in his place until the king's arrival in England.[103] Under an administration of clear political orientation such as the whigs's immediately after the accession of George I, a politically lukewarm, if not disinterested, courtier such as Kent had to be

---

[97]Our discussion of opera at London theaters at this time is based primarily on Milhous and Hume, *Coke's Theatrical Papers*.

[98]Ibid, 81.

[99]*Colley Cibber: Three Sentimental Comedies*, ed. M. Sullivan (New Haven: Yale University Press, 1973), 177–79. The play was Cibber's *The Lady's Last Stake or, the Wife's Resentment*. The dedication, which describes the actors' difficulties that Kent was trying to end by decree, also describes Kent as the mild-mannered man he was: "My Lord," Cibber wrote, "there is nothing Difficult to a Body of *English* People, when they are unanimous, and well commanded: And tho' your Lordship's Tenderness of oppressing is so very just, that you have rather stay's to convince a Man of your good Intentions to him, than to do him ev'n a Service against his Will: Yet since your Lordship has so happily begun the Establishment of the separate Diversions, we live in Hope, that the same Justice and Resolution will still persuade you to go as successfully through with it." On p. 178.

[100]Milhous and Hume, *Coke's Theatrical Papers*, 45.

[101]Ibid, 74, 100, 107.

[102]Kent was no doubt helped in preserving Italian opera in London by his shutting down of Rich's exploitative operation at Drury Lane in 1709. He reunited the actors with the singers at the Haymarket, which for a time—apparently profitably—put on plays alongside Italian operas as Drury Lane had in 1704/5.

[103]Ragnhild Hatton, *George I, Elector and King* (Cambridge, Mass: Harvard University Press, 1978), 120–21.

satisfied with less than first-rank offices. In the fall of 1714 the king appointed him to a bewildering assortment of positions: member of the privy council; gentleman of the bedchamber; constable, governor, and captain of Windsor Castle as well as "Keeper of the Parks, Forests, and Warrens there, and Lieutenant of the said Castle and Forest"; and lord lieutenant and Custos Rotulorum of Bedfordshire (positions which could have been set to music by Gilbert and Sullivan).[104] It meant that Kent was back at court, with regular access both to the king during his weeks of "waiting" and to court society for emoluments nearly as large as those he had enjoyed as lord chamberlain.[105] Two years later, when the duke of Devonshire moved from the office of lord steward to that of lord president, Kent succeeded him as lord steward, reaching once again the top of the royal household. In 1719 the king found it politically expedient to reward another peer with that office, and Kent moved on to lord privy seal. As in 1710, in 1720 a political shakeup, this time in favor of the whigs, brought to an end Kent's career as a courtier.

His many years of service, however, and his rank created an unofficial but well-understood obligation toward him at court that continued after he left office. The royal favors that he claimed were now for his children. His eldest son Anthony de Grey, Earl of Harrold, elevated to the House of Lords as Baron Lucas of Crudwell as early as 1718, was appointed a gentleman of the bedchamber in the year in which his father lost his own office at court.[106] Kent was being rewarded just as Queen Anne had wanted to reward him in 1710, when she promised him any favor he might wish to ask in return for his resignation, and Kent could think of none but a place for his wife as one of the queen's ladies.[107] A week after his son's appointment, his son-in-law John Campbell, Lord Glenorchy, profited as well by becoming envoy to the Danish court.[108] That such an obligation was perceived not only by Kent but was generally accepted as a fact of political life is illustrated by a court conflict over a post in 1723. Kent's eldest son died that summer in an accident, leaving vacant his post as gentleman of the bedchamber. This left Kent with a "particularly strong claim" to the post because, one assumes, it had been given to his son in acknowledgment of his own service or possibly even in return for his relinquishing of his office.[109] Kent wanted the post

for his son-in-law John Campbell, Lord Glenorchy. Glenorchy was a Scot, who as a young man had been expected to follow his kinsmen in their Jacobite politics. At the time of his marriage to Lady Amabell de Grey in 1718, he was considered a "youth of good sense" and "as to the young lady," a tory relative wrote, "I think it more probable he may turn her than she him, and, if he be a hawk of the right nest, as I think he is, he will turn her to purpose and wants not an argument that may be a good means to make her a very early convert, and as to his father-in-law, I have no great fear of him, for I hope *Lord Glenorchy* has too much sense to be brought over by him."[110] Glenorchy *was* a man of good sense who realized that his future was better served by the ruling king of England and a father-in-law in high office than by the pretender in exile on the Continent. By 1723 Glenorchy was ready to return to England from his Danish post, and in August, the king's secretary for the south, John Carteret, who had been Kent's fellow gentleman of the bedchamber in 1714–16 and who was now acting for Kent because he was then with the king in Hanover, applied to the king to secure the position for Glenorchy. The king delayed the decision. In October Amabell wrote to her father: "My Lord has no longer any hopes of going to Hanover, which is the greater mortification to him, because he has yᵉ less reason to expect to succeed, in what your Grace is so good as to sollicit for him."[111] But Walpole acknowledged Kent's claim when he proposed that the duke ought to be compensated for the post with a pension of £3,000 a year if the post did not go to Glenorchy.[112] By 1725, Kent was

---

[104]*The Historical Register*, vol. 2, *Chronological Diary*, 9, 18, 21 October 1714, pp. 15–16.

[105]His salary as gentleman of the bedchamber alone was £1,000 a year. Beattie, *The English Court . . . George I*, 211.

[106]*The Historical Register*, vol. 5, *Chronological Diary*, 6 June 1720, p. 24.

[107]*The Wentworth Papers*, 146–47.

[108]*The Historical Register*, vol. 5, *Chronological Diary*, 11 June 1720, p. 25.

[109]Beattie, *The English Court . . . George I*, 151–52.

[110]Colin Campbell to the duke of Marlborough, 22 Apr., 1718. Great Britain. Historical Manuscripts Commission, *Calendar of the Stuart Papers Belonging to His Majesty the King Preserved at Windsor Castle*, vol. 6 (London: His Majesty's Stationery Office, 1916), 348–50, on 349–50.

[111]Lady Amabell Glenorchy to the duke of Kent, 2 October N.S. /1723/, Bedfordshire Record Office, Wrest Park Collection, L 30/8/8/27.

[112]Beattie, *The English Court ... George I*, 151–52.

receiving an annual pension of £2,000, suggesting that others had recognized his claim as well.[113]

Out of political office, except for his lord lieutenancy of Bedfordshire and the few occasions when he was called upon to act as lord justice while the king was out of the country, Kent nevertheless remained close to court life, and he continued to attend the House of Lords.[114] Walpole, who never overlooked anyone who might produce votes for his party, sought his support as late as 1733. Kent was still proud even if bitter: "I . . . am very much obliged to you for thinking I have any interest in this county worth being desired . . . . I have no fear that the country will goe at any time against my inclination, having never lost any ellection here these 30 years but I have been thought of late a person of so little consequence that I think the less I have to doe in any of these matters the better, and only desire to live well with all my neighbours."[115] In his and the second duke of Devonshire's lifetime a change had taken place in the criteria of a person of political "consequence": the high court office and a relationship of trust with the monarch had at one time signified great importance; but with the shift of power from the king to parliament and political parties, the

courtier's real importance was slight unless he represented party more than the monarch. The first time Kent had lost high court office, he lost it to the interest of a royal favorite more than to that of party; the second time, ten years later, he had lost it purely to party interest. In 1711 court wits could still jest that Kent thought himself "the head of the Whigg Party."[116] But when power came to be identified more with politics than position, Kent parted company with political men like Walpole.

With that attitude Kent was akin to his third son-in-law, Lord Charles Cavendish, and to his grandson Henry Cavendish. They, too, sought and found "consequence" along paths other than political. In their choice, science, they found opportunity to exert their Devonshire legacy of political principle.

---

[113]18 May 1725, *HCJ* 20:536.

[114]Great Britain, Historical Manuscripts Commission, *Report on the Manuscripts of the Earl of Egmont Diary of Viscount Percival Afterwards First Earl of Egmont.* Vol. 1: *1730–1733* (London: His Majesty's Stationery Office, 1920), 189, for example. In August of 1732 Kent was at "a great Court, being Council day" and was "saluted" by Egmont, Walpole, and other chief ministers. Ibid. 1:290.

[115]The duke of Kent to Robert Walpole, 15 Dec. 1733, in Plumb, *Walpole* 2:297.

[116]*The Wentworth Papers*, 219.

PART 2

Lord Charles Cavendish

CHAPTER 1

❧❧❧

Politics

Early Years and Education

Lord Charles Cavendish was born in July or August of 1704.[1] He joined three sisters and two brothers in the nursery of William and Rachel Cavendish, Lord and Lady Hartington. At least three more girls and one more boy were born into the family in the next few years; Charles grew up probably not very much noticed in the middle of his siblings.

When Charles was three, his paternal grandfather, the first duke of Devonshire, died, and his father took possession of the title and of the extensive properties of the Devonshires. The new Devonshire House at Piccadilly, the grand house at Chatsworth in Derbyshire, Hardwick Hall in Nottinghamshire, and several other houses could now all be called home by the Cavendish children, even if they did not live in all of them. For a while their homes also included Southampton House, the London residence of their maternal grandmother, Lady Rachel Russell. They visited the homes of their other Russell relatives, particularly Woburn Abbey in Bedfordshire, their mother's girlhood home, Stratton House in Hampshire, their grandmother Russell's country estate, and Belvoir Castle in Leicestershire.[2]

We pause to consider the architectural setting into which Lord Charles Cavendish was born, and which he would have taken for granted as rightfully *his*. Lord Charles coincided with the great age of English domestic building, the enthusiasms of which did not play themselves out until the end of his son Henry's life. The moving of earth and the piling of stones were ubiquitous sounds of the gentle English landscape in this period. By whatever manner the aristocracy and their imitators managed to raise money, they knew what to do with it: build, expand, and then rebuild. On the same scale as their palaces were the parks they set them in, with their artificial lakes, waterfalls, forests, and picturesque details such as

villages (or their removal). Servants came cheap and were employed at these houses in numbers far beyond what was needed to keep them running. The public display expressed the raison d'etre of a caste: wealth, power, and title. Ostentation sometimes led a peer to ruin but in a good cause, since overspending on developing an estate was not regarded as a disgrace. The Devonshires did not overreach, but they did not hold back either; they simply got richer with each passing generation, and as they did, they added more rooms and filled them with more statuaries and libraries and gilt.[3]

Devonshire House in London was rebuilt for the third duke of Devonshire by William Kent in 1733. Likened by an unfriendly critic of the time to an East India Company warehouse, its exterior was indeed plain, but that together with the rich interior could be taken as a kind of family portrait of the Cavendishes.[4]

Chatsworth, the family house in Derbyshire, with its splendid rooms kept in readiness for visits

---

[1]We deduce his probable birthdate from several facts: he became a member of the House of Commons in 1725, and the standard practice for the son of an aristocratic family was to enter an election right after his majority. Corresponding to the assumption that he was therefore born in 1704, we have a remark in a letter by the duchess of Queensberry to Lady Hartington, Lord Charles's mother, dated 4 July /1704/, Devon. Coll., no. 94.1: "I believe before now the wedding is over in your family and I hope the next news we hear from it will be your having follow'd my example in bringing a son," which suggests that Lady Hartington was expecting a child soon. The order of births of the other Cavendish children, for some of whom the birthdates are known, make an earlier date not very likely. Neither does the fact that Charles received independent means of support from his father only a week before his election to Parliament in April 1725, since if he had been 21 already, he would have already been receiving a regular annuity. Devon. Coll., L/19/31.

[2]Lois G. Schwoerer, *Lady Rachel Russell, "One of the Best of Women"* (Baltimore: The Johns Hopkins University Press, 1988), 222. Schwoerer lists the Russell family homes and refers to Lady Russell's closeness to her children. Various family letters from this period and later refer to members of the family visiting one another.

[3]J. H. Plumb, *Men and Centuries* (Boston: Houghton Mifflin, 1963), 69–70, 74–75, 79.

[4]Hermione Hobhouse, *Lost London* (New York: Weathervane Books, 1971), 29.

by the royalty, held, and still holds, pride of place among the Devonshire properties. The first duke of Devonshire made great additions to the existing Tudor house as a testimony to two inseparable facts: his own greatness and the successful outcome of the Glorious Revolution. The interior of the redone house and the gardens outside it were inspired by Versailles (the duke instinctively hated Louis XIV but saw no contradiction in emulating his taste), but the feature for which the house was most famous was probably not the lofty ceilings painted with scenes of classical mythology but the ten or more flush toilets.[5] These unlikely conveniences were a touch of modern practicality, which we imagine made a technical impression on young Lord Charles Cavendish.

The next frenzy of rebuilding at Chatsworth left the house pretty much as it was but totally transformed the park. The fourth duke of Devonshire brought in the great landscape gardener Lancelot "Capability" Brown to remove the Euclidean geometry of the first duke's version of the gardens of Versailles and to replace it with the type of English garden that was then coming into fashion, one not set apart from the natural landscape but arranged in harmony with it. The Swiss scientist Horace Bénédict De Saussure visited Chatsworth in the 1760s, after the fourth duke's changes, and called it a "fairy palace in a beautiful wilderness."[6] With its acres of lawns and clusters of elms and oaks, this was the park described by Jane Austin. The new response to nature coincided with Henry Cavendish's entry into the world of science. Unlike Lord Charles, Henry did not live at Chatsworth, so far as we know, but he was certainly familiar with it from visits. The two superposed styles of the Chatsworth park, which might be called the geometrical and the natural, would seem to prefigure Henry Cavendish's calling.

Chatsworth would undergo other major changes, such as the landscaping of Joseph Paxton, who went on to design the famous, prefabricated glass-and-iron Crystal Palace for the 1851 international exhibition in London, but to describe these would take us beyond our subject. To this day, Chatsworth House reveals to the world the good sense of the rebuilding undertaken by the first duke of Devonshire, a respectable amateur architect. The good sense did not belong to that

extravagant man so much as to the architecture he inherited. For all of its grandeur, the house has the harmonious proportions and classical elegance of the period. What Lord Charles and his son Henry seem to have extracted from the material setting of their family was the core of reason expressed in the graceful architecture.

In Henry Cavendish's day, as today, the great country houses of the nobility were semipublic tourist stops. There was, as the tourist Saussure said, a fairyland quality about Chatsworth, for it was only fifteen miles from Sheffield, a rising industrial center. The owner of Chatsworth, the duke of Devonshire, was also the very sensible owner of income-producing mines. In its best days, the duke's copper and lead mine at nearby Ecton brought in 30,000 pounds a year. Two hundred fathoms deep, a Boulton steam engine worked it from the top, a tourist noted.[7]

Inside their substantial four walls, in town and in the country, the Cavendish family enjoyed warm, informal relationships. Unlike many another aristocratic family, for example, the duke of Kent's, Charles's family did not use their formal titles for one another. In their letters, even after they were adults, Charles's sisters referred to their mother as "mama," not "her Grace," the title appropriate for a duchess, and they wrote of "brother Charles" rather than "Lord Charles" and of "Granmama Russell" rather than "Lady Russell." Charles's sister Elizabeth looked back with sadness on their childhood when, in 1721, after the deaths of their eldest sister, Mary, and their youngest brother, John, she wrote to another brother James abroad about Charles, who was about to join him: "It was some comfort to have one of you, but when both are gone I shall find /a/ great change when I consider I was once happy in yᵉ company of so many brothers and sˢ; but it is a thought I cannot bear to think of."[8]

---

[5]John Pearson, *The Serpent and the Stag...* (New York: Holt, Reinhart and Winston, 1983), 72–79.

[6]Douglas W. Freshfield and H.F. Montugnia, *The Life of Horace Bénédict De Saussure* (London: Edward Arnold, 1920), 114.

[7]The tourist was Henry Cavendish's colleague Charles Hatchett, whose "expectations" for Chatsworth were disappointed. *The Hatchett Diary. A Tour through the Counties of England and Scotland in 1796 Visiting Their Mines and Manufactures*, ed. A. Raistrick (Truro: D. Bradford Barton, 1967), 64–66.

[8]Lady Elizabeth Cavendish to Lord James Cavendish, 13 Feb. /1721/ and 24 April /1721/, and Lady Rachel Morgan to Lord James Cavendish, 26 September /1723/. Devon. Coll., nos. 166.0, 166.1, and 167.0, respectively.

Of his siblings, two brothers, William and James, and four sisters, Mary, Rachel, Elizabeth, and Anne, survived into adulthood with Charles. Their earliest education was probably under the care of tutors and governesses. Their grandmother Lady Rachel Russell, who on her mother's side was of Huguenot origins, in the 1680s had advocated using the French refugees as tutors.[9] Later, she entertained some negative views of the instruction offered by French tutors, but she nevertheless took considerable trouble to find a French tutor for her grandchildren by another daughter.[10] The Cavendishes may have followed her advice, too, especially since the whole family continued the close connection with their Ruvigny relatives, now settled in Greenwich and parts of Hampshire.[11] At any rate, when James and Charles toured the Continent in 1721–24, they did so under the care of a Frenchman, a Mr. Cotteau.[12] The Cavendish daughters were educated to interests as commonsensical as their brothers. On her honeymoon, Rachel reported to her brother James on a visit to the Derby silk mills, "thought to be one of the finest inventions that ever was seen of the kind."[13] Elizabeth was even more impetuous and independent than Rachel, if we can judge from her few letters. Seeing her life as "idle," she wrote to James: "I only wish I was your brother instead of your sister and then I would have bin partaker with you in your travels." Forced to remain behind, she informed her brothers of the politics of the day. Looking at it from the heights of her father's positions in the House of Lords and in Walpole's government, she approved of a minister who did not enrich himself by his office, and she reported the birth of a prince causing "very great" joy amongst the people as a political advantage, the birth coming "very seasonably to stir up ye spirit of loyalty in yᵉ people who are in a general dissatisfaction with yᵉ king and parliament who they think don't go yᵉ way to redrys their grivances caus'd by yᵉ south sea."[14] There are no girlish frills. The Cavendish boys received only the beginnings of their education at home. Their grandmother Lady Rachel Russell was of the opinion that "our nobility should pass some of their time" at a university; "it has been for many years neglected."[15] The view was shared by her daughter and son-in-law Devonshire who sent their eldest son, William, the first to attend a university, to Oxford in 1715,

when he was sixteen, entering him at New College. As a member of a whig family in a tory citadel, William joined with others of whig persuasion, only to find their group the target of the mob. Two months later, in 1717, he was granted the degree of Master of Arts and left Oxford. The family biographer comments on how quickly a duke's son could attain that degree; considering Cavendish prudence, which was an especially characteristic trait of his parents, Lord William's political adventures and his leaving Oxford may not have been unconnected.[16] Lord James and Lord Charles in any case were not sent to a university.

They began their formal schooling at Eton, where they were entrusted to Dr. Andrew Snape, headmaster from 1711 to 1720, on the recommendation of Robert Walpole, their father's friend and political ally. In 1718, for which there exists a "Bill of Eton Schole," Charles, then fourteen, was in the fifth year, a grade in the Lower School known as Lower Greek. James was two years ahead of him.[17] Neither boy finished the entire course, which for Charles would have required

---

[9]Mary Berry, *Some Account of the Life of Rachael Wriothesley Lady Russell, . . . Followed by a Series of Letters . . . .* (London, 1819), 73.

[10]Schwoerer, *Lady Rachel Russell*, 227.

[11]Ibid., passim. Samuel Smiles, *The Huguenots: Their Settlements, Churches, and Industries in England and Ireland* (New York, 1868), 208–11, 314.

[12]Rachel Cavendish, duchess of Devonshire, to Lord James Cavendish, about 1722, 20 March, 12 July, and 11 Nov. 1723, and 13 Feb. 1724. Devon. Coll., nos. 30.10, 30.11, 30.12, 30.13, and 30.14, respectively.

[13]Lady Rachel Morgan to Lord James Cavendish, 26 September /1723/.

[14]Lady Elizabeth Cavendish to Lord James Cavendish, 24 April /1721/.

[15]Lady Rachel Russell, *Letters of Lady Rachel Russell; from the Manuscript to the Library at Woburn Abbey. . . .* 5th ed. (London, 1793), 550.

[16]Joseph Foster, *Alumni Oxonienses: The Members of the University of Oxford, 1715–1886. . .*, 4 vols. (London, 1891) 1:231. Francis Bickley, *The Cavendish Family* (London: Constable, 1911), 189–90.

[17]R. A. Austen Leigh, *Eton College Lists 1678–1790* (Eton College: Spottiswoods, 1907), xxiv–xxvii, 14–18. J. H. Plumb, *Sir Robert Walpole*. Vol. 1: *The Making of a Statesman* (London, The Cresset Press, 1956), 253. H. C. Maxwell Lyte, *A History of Eton College 1440–1884* (London, 1889), 286–87. The "lower master" of the lower school in 1718 was Francis Goode, who held that position from 1716 to 1734, succeeding Thomas Carter. There were four lower school assistants that year, Thomas Thackeray, Adam Elliot, John Burchett, and Charles Willats, most of whom were drawn from King's College, Cambridge, but Burchett was from Peterhouse. *Eton College Lists*, xxxv. It was customary at Eton for the "sons of wealthy persons to have private tutors," who were not the same as the assistant masters. Lyte, *History of Eton College*, 4th ed. (London, 1911), 284.

another five years. By 1721 both were heading in a direction other than the university, for which they probably were not prepared in their knowledge of ancient languages in any case. Young noblemen, as the advice given to the father of one of them in 1723 shows, had other options: "Tho' he does not ply his book close," this father was told about his son, it may not proceed from the want of capacity and inclination

> but rather from his studying in the dead languages, which he has not been well grounded in. I have knowen severall instances of this and if it be the case or perhaps his being too much indulged in sloth when younger, I do not see why either of them should be a reason for breaking off his studies. He can read in Italian and French most of the things that are necessary for a gentleman, and tho' he should not give a very close application, something usefull will stick; and who knows but by degrees he may come to like what he now has ane aversion to. Were he mine, I would make him spend some time at Geneva in the studie of the law, should it be only to keep him from being imposed upon by pettyfoggers. Historie and geometry are accomplishments fitt for a gentleman and surely he can never serve his country or famely without knowledge, and geometry, if he give in to it, will at all times be ane amusement when he cannot be more profitably imploy'd. When he has made a tolerable progress in these, it will not be amiss that he make a tour in France and Italy that he may learn from observation what he has not gote by reading.[18]

The reference was to the by now obligatory grand tour that began in France, perhaps passed through Holland and Switzerland, and then settled down to a residence in Italy, home of Rome and the Renaissance. No Englishman could pretend to an education or any degree of sophistication or any defense against a sense of inferiority without it. Two or three years abroad were the rule, a just compensation for having been born in backwater England.[19] Some formal study might be combined with the sightseeing and cultural exposure. Lords Anthony and Henry de Grey, the sons of the duke of Kent and the brothers of Lord Charles's future wife, Lady Anne, had followed this course several years earlier. Now their sons were doing their duty: in 1716 Lord Henry was planning to go to Geneva, and Lord Anthony sent him advice from Venice:

> Att Geneva you will find several persons that will be very helpful to you I don't doubt, and I shall send a letter or two to some of the best I knew there who are of the best familys, men who are

pretty well acquainted with the world and whose conversations will be agreble as well as instructive, that shall wait upon you and do any service that lies in their power as soon as ever you arrive; there are like wise some of the young men I was acquainted with who will be ready enough to introduce you into any other company you shall like or care for. I suppose you intend to study a little of the Civil Law there; the person I had and who is accounted one of the best is Mr Guip a diligent and Studious man and likewise understanding in History and Chronology.

Having followed his own stay at Geneva by travels in Italy, Lord Anthony displayed in the remainder of his letter that he had profited from the lessons in history and become a careful observer of "antiquities."[20] Lord James Cavendish, whose later exploits suggest an early interest in horsemanship and an active life, was probably, and quite appropriately, intended for the military. By 1721, he had gone from Eton to the "Academy" at Nancy and then Lunéville in Lorraine. Lord Charles was then about to join him, and two years later he was writing to his mother from Geneva.[21] Hence there is the likelihood that both places contributed to his education.

The "académie d'exercices" at Nancy, the capital of Lorraine, had been established in 1699, soon after Lorraine had been taken back from the French and reconstituted a duchy by the Treaty of Ryswick of 1697. Although the dukes of Lorraine were allowed no army of their own, their military academy attracted young foreign aristocrats, some carrying "the greatest names of Europe." By 1713 the academy had added a course in public law to its curriculum, and Duke Leopold himself established one in natural law. The academy had the purpose of educating the cadets for the court guards, the only military body (aside from a civilian militia) still remaining to the dukes, creating a close association with the court, which affected its location. In 1702, for example, at the start of the War of the Spanish Succession, the French had

---

[18]Great Britain. Historical Manuscripts Commission, *Report on the Manuscripts of Lord Polwarth, Preserved at Mertoun House, Berwickshire*, vol. 3 (London: His Majesty's Stationary Office, 1931), 287–88.
[19]Plumb, *Men and Centuries*, 55–60.
[20]Anthony de Grey, earl of Harrold, to Lord Henry de Grey, about 1716, Bedford County Record Office, Wrest Park Collection, L 30/5.
[21]Lady Elizabeth Cavendish to Lord James Cavendish, 13 Feb. and 24 April /1721/. Rachel Cavendish, duchess of Devonshire, to Lord James Cavendish, 11 Nov. /1723/.

reoccupied Nancy, forcing Leopold to withdraw with his court to his castle at Lunéville, a building then too ancient to be suitable for an eighteenth-century ducal residence. Leopold replaced the old structure with a large, new residence, which gradually became the official capital of the dukedom even after Nancy had been freed of the French again in 1714. In 1719 a fire temporarily set back this development by destroying the ducal apartments at Lunéville, apparently forcing the court back to Nancy for a short time. It was during this period that Lord James Cavendish joined the academy. Duke Leopold, seeing an opportunity for further building, added a "cabinet des herbes" to his Lunéville residence, a good library, and a physical cabinet. Under the influence of Newton's physics and determined to do his own experimenting, he constructed some of the necessary instruments himself and bought the rest, a beautiful and expensive collection from London. In the spring of 1721, just before Lord Charles joined his brother in Lorraine, the duke moved his military academy from Nancy to Lunéville,[22] bringing it into the immediate neighborhood of the scientific facilities he had assembled there.

Lord Charles Cavendish left London for his education and tour abroad in March 1721, undoubtedly with another party traveling to Paris, since he was to be met by his brother Lord James's valet there, and as the seventeen-year-old son of a duke he would not have been sent off alone.[23] Expected to be with James by mid-April, he instead stayed on in Paris for three weeks longer than planned. As Lord Anthony de Grey had informed his brother a few years earlier, at Paris there were "many things" to be "observed."

> You will not stay long there perhaps the first time only see a little of the Town. . . . You wont ommitt however the sight of the most principal things, as the Louvre, the Tuilleries, Place Vendosme & Victoire, Place Royal, the Luxemburg, the Church of Notre dam, L'hotel des invalides, Versailles, Trianon. . . .[24]

Both his initial visit to Paris and his and Lord James's stay there for several months in 1723–24 came at a favorable stage in English-French relations, during the regency of the duke of Orleans and immediately after. The friendly climate toward England at court was accompanied by a resurgence of cultural life in Paris as, following the death of Louis XIV in 1715, the French

aristocrats returned from Versailles to Paris.[25] The flourishing arts, operas, theater, and other entertainments lured so many of the British to Paris in these years that the resident at Paris, Thomas Crawford, complained in 1723 that "we . . . should have had the halfe of the people of England" there if it had not been for the unsafe conditions of the roads; "this town began to be full of London apprentices that came running over here with their superfluous money instead of going to Tunbrige," an English resort.[26] The regency was also marked by another interest of the duke of Orleans, much closer to Lord Charles's eventual concerns; this was the duke's interest in the natural sciences and his attention to the "improvement of the implements and appliances of the mechanical arts."[27] René Antoine Réaumur, the regent's protégée at the academy, published his important study of the iron and steel industry in Paris in 1722, which may well have come to Lord Charles's attention, given the practical bent of his family and their ownership of Derbyshire lead mines.[28] As a Cavendish, he may have enjoyed even more direct exposure to the Parisian scientific world, but we have no evidence for that.

After about a month in Paris in 1721, if he proceeded as planned, Lord Charles joined Lord

---

[22]Michel Parisse, Stéphane Gaber, and Gérard Canini, *Grandes Dates de L'Histoire Lorraine* (Nancy: Service des Publications de l'Université de Nancy II, 1982), 43 Michel Antoine, "La cour de Lorraine dans l'Europe des lumières," 69–76, and Claude Collot, "La faculté de droit de l'Université de Pont-à-Mousson et de Nancy au XVIIIe siècle," 215–26, both papers in *La Lorraine dans l'Europe des lumières. Actes du colloque organisé par la Faculté des lettres et des sciences humaines de l'Université de Nancy, Nancy, 24–27 octobre 1966.* Series *Annales de l'Est.* Mémoire 34. (Nancy: Faculté des lettres et sciences humaines de l'Université, 1968), 70–72, 218. Edmond Delorme, *Lunéville et son arrondissement* (Marseilles, Lafitte Reprints, 1977), 3, 17, 18, 111. Pierre Boyé, *Les Chateaux du Roi Stanislas en Lorraine* (Marseille, Laffitte Reprints, 1980), 3–4.

[23]Lady Elizabeth Cavendish to Lord James Cavendish, 13 Feb. /1721/. One party bound for Paris that Lord Charles might have joined was that of the English ambassador in France, Sir Lucas Schaub, a young man of thirty-one, who was to leave London for Paris on 23 Feb./7 March. That plan, given that the trip took four to five days if all went smoothly, would have put him in Paris in the second week of March, the time when Lord James was to send his valet to meet Lord Charles. In the event, Schaub did not leave London until March 1/12, which may account for the delay in Lord Charles's plans, too. *Manuscripts of Lord Polwarth* 3:49, 52.

[24]Anthony de Grey, earl of Harrold, to Lord Henry de Grey, about 1716.

[25]James Breck Perkins, *France under the Regency with a Review of the Administration of Louis XIV* (Boston and New York, 1892), 374–96, 554–57, 559–62.

[26]*Manuscripts of Lord Polwarth* 3:309.

[27]Perkins, *France under the Regency*, 556.

[28]J. B. Gough, "Réaumur, René-Antoine Ferchault de," *DSB* 11:327–35, on 328.

James at Lunéville. For nearly two years after that, until late in 1722 or early in 1723, Lord Charles's activities and whereabouts can only be conjectured. Given the pattern of his brother's stay abroad, Lord Charles may very well have spent a year at Lunéville. During the winter of 1722–23, the brothers, together with a tutor, were traveling, probably in the south. James had been tempted into gambling, prompting his mother to point out to him that the "right use" of their travels should be "seeing what is most curious in yᵉ places you pass thru & making yʳ observations upon 'em." The following March, James was staying with a prince and princess, an "expensive enuff" way of life, as his mother comments, discussing his allowance. Neither the duchess's letter to James in March nor another one in the middle of July refer to Lord Charles, making it likely that Charles spent some time on his own at Geneva, from where he had written to his mother that summer or fall.[29]

The Académie de Calvin in Geneva had attracted not only the sons of the duke of Kent, but the sons of several great English and Scottish families, including the Cavendishes. In 1723, four professors at the academy offered courses in civil and natural law and in philosophy, including, apparently, natural philosophy, since one of its students, the later mathematician Gabriel Cramer, had only recently completed a thesis on sound and would the next year compete for the chair of philosophy, receiving a share in the chair of mathematics instead, with the assignment of teaching algebra and astronomy.[30] If Lord Charles did not meet Cramer at the academy that year, he may have become acquainted with him through Cramer's brother Jean, the new professor of civil and natural law, only twenty-two at the time himself. At any rate, when Gabriel Cramer visited London sometime in 1727–29, he was easily received into the circle of mathematicians and Fellows of the Royal Society connected with Lord Charles.[31]

In November of 1723 Lords James and Charles Cavendish were together again, having only just arrived in Paris. Their stay in France required a doubling of their allowances, each now getting £100 annually, and advice about greater caution on the roads: "be very carefull now you are in France," their mother wrote, "how you travel, & also of being out late in yᵉ streets wᶜʰ they tel me is very dangerous, murthers being there soe common."[32] They spent the winter there, still under the care of Mr. Cotteau, with their mail reaching them through the banker Jean Louis Goudet. In February 1724 when the end of the their tour was in sight, they appealed to their parents for a few months more. "Relating to yʳ return into England," the duchess wrote,

> I believe yʳ father in that wo'd be willing to do what he thought was most agreeable to yʳ own inclinations, Mr Cotteau writs word you imploy yʳ time so well, that he thinks it might be for yʳ advantage if you stay'd in France some months longer, but in yʳ next you may let me know what yʳ own thoughts are, yʳ coming back by Holland is what I believe my Lᵈ designes if you like it.[33]

Charles and James had their way. They also followed their father's plan of returning home by way of Holland, a detour that very nearly cost Charles his life. On 24 September that year, in "blowing Stormy weather," Captain Gregory of the Katherine Yacht at Ostend

> about Three in the afternoon was unhappily Surprized by a Passage Boat oversetting just under my Stern, in which were Two of his Grace the Duke of Devonshire's Sons, viz the Lord James and Charles, with their Governor and Servants, who by the assistance of my People were all most miraculously Saved, particularly Lord Charles, who Sunk under my Counter, and was carried by a very Strong Tide between me and another Ship

---

[29]Letters from the duchess to Lord James Cavendish above.

[30]Charles Borgeaud, *Histoire de l'Université de Genève. L'Académie de Calvin 1559–1798* (Genève: Georg, 1900), 442, 641–42. According to the registers of students, the Cavendishes who attended the Geneva academy were Charles Cavendish's great-grandfather William Cavendish, who was accompanied there by his tutor Thomas Hobbes, the philosopher, and Charles's grandfather William Cavendish, the later first duke of Devonshire. However, the registers are not complete, particularly not on foreign noblemen, who might have stayed in Geneva only a few months. Anthony de Grey, earl of Harrold, who studied law in Geneva for a while, for example, does not appear in the register; the absence of Charles's name there is no indication that he did not attend the academy or study with a private teacher in Geneva for a while. Sven Stelling-Michaud and Suzanne Stelling-Michaud, eds., *Le Livre du Recteur de l'Académie de Genève*, vols. 1–3 (Geneva: Droz, 1959–72). On the registers: Michael Heyd, *Between Orthodoxy and the Enlightenment. Jean-Robert Chouet and the Introduction of Cartesian Science in the Academy of Geneva* (Boston: Martinus Nijhoff, 1982), 245–47.

[31]Cramer and Lord Charles Cavendish were exact contemporaries. Cramer's travels were a part of his appointment at Geneva and intended for his further education. The scientists he met in England included Nicholas Saunderson, Halley, Sloane, De Moivre, and Stirling. Phillip S. Jones, "Cramer, Gabriel," *DSB* 3:459–62, on 459.

[32]Rachel Cavendish, duchess of Devonshire, to Lord James Cavendish, 11 Nov. /1723/.

[33]Rachel Cavendish, duchess of Devonshire, to Lord James Cavendish, 13 Feb. /1724/.

under water, till he got as far forward as my Stern, where he arose, and got hold of my Shoar fast, from whence we Saved his Lordship, though almost Spent.

Lords James and Charles had been on their way to Calais, which suggests that they were coming from The Netherlands, probably The Hague. After losing "most of their Baggage and Apparel, except what they had Ordered to Calais," in the accident, the Cavendish brothers decided to stay with Captain Gregory for the crossing. The captain's report of the accident reached their father by courtesy of the admiralty on 5 October.[34] Lords Charles and James undoubtedly followed close behind, Charles having been abroad for three and a half years.

House of Commons

Technically speaking, despite his courtesy title (although courtesy, the title was not optional), Lord Charles Cavendish was a commoner, but he was nevertheless a member of the highest circle of the British aristocracy, and as such he had been brought up to the values of the aristocracy, which included the principal one of "duty of service."[35] To a member of the aristocracy, especially at the very top, the only acceptable form of occupation (aside from administrating, but definitely not farming, his property) was public service, usually in government or in the military. It came down to a narrow but attractive choice of occupations. The Cavendishes had served in some of the highest offices at court and in the government for almost half a century, and Lord Charles Cavendish followed suit as soon as he reached maturity by becoming a member of the House of Commons at a by-election in the spring of 1725. Other interests, in the arts, architecture, belles lettres, various areas of scholarship, or natural science, no matter how expertly pursued, had to keep the outward appearance of an aristocrat's private indulgence, at best to be shared with friends. To carry out any such work to earn money or recognition, that is, in the case of scholarship and science, to publish the product of one's work for income, for someone of Lord Charles Cavendish's rank would have been out of the question.

The occupational limitations that British society imposed on its aristocrats guided Lord Charles Cavendish's work in science (and probably determined his reputation as a scientist, or rather

the lack of it). For many years he carried on scientific investigations that were valued and used by other scientists—he even won the Royal Society's Copley Medal—but as befitted someone of his rank, he published nothing except the one piece of work for which he received the prize. But he could and did contribute publicly to science in the same manner in which he had served in government, as a "parliamentarian" of science: as a member of the Royal Society, on its councils and committees, and on the boards and committees of other institutions. He became one of the most important of the official representatives of science of his time in Britain and its untiring servant; he achieved that by scientific talent, practical ability, and long parliamentary experience, and not least of all also by being a Cavendish.

Lord Charles Cavendish is a good example of a kind of scientific practitioner who played a useful role in eighteenth-century British science but did not survive into the later professional organization of science. He also offers us the understanding of science that he himself arrived at, which was a general and new understanding of the time; namely, that science was becoming an area of public concern, with an increasing number of connections to practical problems; he took this understanding futher, seeing in science an activity of sufficiently general importance to constitute an appropriate area for the service of an aristocrat.

When Lord Charles Cavendish took his seat in the House of Commons as Member of Parliament for Heytesbury, Wiltshire, in the 1725/26 parliamentary session,[36] he joined there all but two of the adult males of his immediate family: his eldest brother, Lord Hartington, his uncle Lord James Cavendish, his two brothers-in-law, Sir Thomas Lowther and Sir William Morgan, and a first cousin. The two exceptions were his father, who as duke of Devonshire sat in the House of Lords and was then lord president of the privy council, and his brother Lord James Cavendish, who was in the military,

---

[34] J. Burchett to William Cavendish, duke of Devonshire, 5 Oct. 1724, with the enclosure of a "Copy of a Letter from Captain Gregory of the Katherine Yacht to Mr Burchett dated the 25th of September 1724 O. S. from Ostend," Devon. Coll., no. 179.0.

[35] John Cannon, *Aristocratic Century. The Peerage of Eighteenth-Century England* (Cambridge: Cambridge University Press, 1984), 34.

[36] Romney Sedgwick, *The House of Commons 1715–1754*, 2 vols. (New York: Oxford University Press, 1970) 1:536.

putting off his brief stint in the Commons by fifteen years, until just before his death. Lord Charles Cavendish could have had no doubt about what was expected of him. (To get a proper picture of the inevitability of that particular blueprint for an aristocrat's life it should be noted that except for his uncle, Lord Charles and his relatives in the Commons were all under thirty, he being the youngest then at twenty-one.) This dense representation in the Commons of an aristocratic family such as the Cavendishes was only partly due to politics; beyond his father's close association with Robert Walpole, the head of the current whig administration, Lord Charles was in the Commons as a representative of his family's private interest. Very suitably, therefore, he made his first appearance in the Journal of the House of Commons in April of 1726 in connection with a private bill (which we discuss below), drawn up by his brother, concerning the estate of his brother-in-law Sir Thomas Lowther.

During the years 1725–41, the period Lord Charles Cavendish was to spend in parliament, the Commons had 558 members who met usually in the second half of January and remained in session usually until May or June, the precise beginning and end of each session being subject to political manipulation by the administration. Attendance— the Commons met five or six days a week, usually from around the middle of the day until late afternoon and at times late into the night—was similarly a matter of politics: usually fewer than half of the members attended, but for important issues the House had means of coercing attendance, tactics that were more easily brought into effect by the party in power, which by this time could elect one of its own speaker of the house, than by the opposition. With an acceptable excuse, a member could avoid attending the House altogether.[37]

The business of the Commons divided into three parts. First, the House had the "public" tasks of levying taxation and supplying the government for its operation and for the military; of considering foreign policy (which was the monarch's prerogative but took up much of the Commons' time, anyway); and indeed of acting on every public issue the administration or other members chose to put before it. The second task of the Commons, in importance if not in order of attention, for it was always taken up before anything else, was to hear grievances concerning the privileges of the members of the House and concerning election improprieties. The third task of the Commons was the enactment of so-called private bills. They would more appropriately have been described as bills of local—as opposed to national—concern. These bills, which covered everything from road and canal building to labor disputes and manufacturing regulations to legal settlements of private estates, took up less time than the national issues in the sessions of the whole House, but they did require extensive committee work. They were assigned to select committees usually of between thirty and sixty members, first to consider the petition for legislation on the matter, and then to draw up and discuss a bill before the House voted on it. Having the right to conduct hearings, the committees brought in witnesses and material evidence. They met when the House as a whole was not in session, unless the committee was constituted of the whole House, in the mornings, for example, often for several weeks, greatly extending the hours of attendance to the parliamentary duties of a conscientious M.P.[38]

Given that Lord Charles Cavendish was so very young, completely inexperienced, and relatively unknown (more than once in those early years he was mistaken for his brother James, who was older but not as serious a young man), it is not surprising that he entered only slowly into the work of the Commons. Re-elected in 1727, but from the large constituency of Westminster instead of small Heytesbury,[39] his involvement in the House's activities immediately picked up in 1728 and 1729, only to be followed by four years of personal problems arising especially from his wife Anne's struggle with tuberculosis that kept him away from his duties much of the time. When, in 1733, his wife died, Cavendish immersed himself in his duties in the Commons.

In his first years there, Cavendish was often brought into committees by members of his family on family matters, the natural way for him to be

[37]P. D. G. Thomas, *The House of Commons in the Eighteenth Century* (Oxford: Clarendon Press, 1971), 2, 92, 123–26, 157–57.

[38]Thomas, *House of Commons*, 13, 45–46, 51–59, 264–70.

[39]Sedgwick, *House* 1:285. 21 July 1727, St. Margaret's Vestry, Minutes 1724–1733, Westminster City Archives, E 2419.

introduced to committee work. His family first enrolled his services in March 1726, in a case that would benefit his sister Lady Elizabeth and her husband Sir Thomas Lowther. Here is how it went. Lowther had petitioned the Commons that his family be granted the inheritance of Furness monastery in Lancashire, trying to establish permanently an old family claim. Lord Charles Cavendish's brother Hartington was ordered, along with two others, to draw up a bill to that effect, which was then handed over to a committee that included all the Cavendishes in the House, including Charles. The bill was passed, and as was the custom, the chairman of the committee, Hartington, was ordered to carry it to the House of Lords for their "concurrence." When two weeks later this still had not been done, Lord Charles was sent to the Lords with it in his brother's place.[40] In 1727 he was on a committee approving a bill from the House of Lords settling estate matters for the daughters of Elihu Yale, one of whom was married to his uncle Lord James Cavendish;[41] in 1729 he dealt with the selling of two parts of the manor of Steane, the duke of Kent's property and therefore a matter having to do with the inheritance of Lord Charles Cavendish's wife, Lady Anne;[42] in 1730 he dealt with an estate sale for his brother Lord James, who needed money to pay gambling debts.[43] Even more distant relatives could claim his support on committees: he was involved in settling the estate of one Thomas Scawen,[44] for example, the husband of his mother's first cousin, or in the legal change of name of two of his Manners cousins.[45] In 1736 his relatives could serve him in turn, when he sold the Hertfordshire estates he had bought shortly after his marriage as an investment of his wife's dowry and as a country seat for his family.[46]

In the spring of 1726, Cavendish was involved in work on a private bill that offers us a good example of a family matter which is also of public importance.[47] It was also Cavendish's first parliamentary exposure to certain technical problems. The bill was the latest of a long series of parliamentary acts beginning in the seventeenth century providing for the draining of the Bedford Level fens, over 1,600 square miles of marshland to the south and west of The Wash in eastern England. In the seventeenth century, Francis Russell, fourth earl of Bedford, and his son and successor William, later first duke of Bedford (Lord Charles Cavendish's

direct ancestors), had organized about eighty landowners into a corporation of "adventurers" to finance the draining of these plains, which were still common land, in return for 83,000 acres of the resulting farmland. The Russells and their adventurers undertook also to maintain the resulting drainage system, for which the corporation was entitled by law to tax the landowners. Having invested more in this undertaking and also profited more than any of the other members of the corporation, the Russells were still at the head of it in 1726, but the present duke then was a minor and the project was in the hands of his uncle and guardian the duke of Devonshire. For Lord Charles Cavendish it was also of even more immediate concern, since as a younger son he derived income from his mother Lady Rachel Russell's interest in the Russell estates.[48]

The methods used to drain the Bedford Level in the seventeenth and early eighteenth centuries had succeeded only in part. Of the various factors that soon brought back frequent flooding of the new farmland, the most important was the lowering of the level as a result of shrinkage and wastage of the peat surface after draining. Before long, the water levels in many of the drainage channels were higher than the land on either side of them. To add to the problem, the rivers fell toward the sea so gradually that their estuaries silted up, further obstructing drainage. One way of dealing with the flooding was to shorten the courses of the rivers by constructing new, steeper "outfalls." This was proposed by the bill of 1726 with which the Cavendishes were connected. With the consent of the duke of Bedford and other landowners, the duke of Devonshire proposed to finance a new outfall for the Bedford Level, which had become "choked by the Sands thrown up by the Tides" and where thousands of

[40]Great Britain Parliament, *House of Commons Journals (HCJ)* 20:600–70. Entries from 4 Mar. 1726/27 to 19 Apr. 1726.
[41]29 Mar. 1727, *HCJ* 20:822.
[42]18, 23 Apr. and 6 May 1729, *HCJ* 21:327, 343, 360.
[43]17, 19, 25 Mar. and 3 Apr. 1730, *HCJ* 21:500, 505, 515, 531.
[44]12, 21 Mar. 1729 (1728), *HCJ* 21:263, 284.
[45]20, 26, Feb. and 7 Mar. 1735 (1734), *HCJ* 22:385, 392, 406.
[46]17, 18, 23 Mar. and 7 Apr. 1736, *HCJ* 22:635, 644–45, 675.
[47]10 May 1726, *HCJ* 20:697.
[48]Samuel Wells, *The History of the Drainage of the Great Level of the Fens, Called Bedford Level: With the Constitution and Laws of the Bedford Level Corporation*, 2 vols. (London, 1830) 1:424–25, 661–62. 4 Mar. 1726 (1725), *HCJ* 20:599.

acres were again frequently flooded if not, as after the "great Rains and Floods' of 1725/26, "totally drowned." However, his surveyors could find no suitable location for the new drainage canal but through lands lying outside the Bedford Level proper, and although the Cavendishes organized strong support for the bill in the affected areas in Lincolnshire, Hartington and his committee (which eventually was the whole House of Commons) failed to bring their negotiations with opposing Lincolnshire landowners and local commissioners of sewers (who feared for their autonomy and authority) to a successful conclusion before the end of the parliamentary session.[49]

The next year the Haddenham Level, an area in the southern part of the fens as far inland as the lands involved in the debates of 1726, tried another method. Moving water to the sea could also be done by pumping it up into drainage canals and into embanked rivers. Windmills had been tried earlier but had met with opposition. The Haddenham Level bill called for "Mills, or some other Engine," a plan which was approved.[50] Although he was not on the Haddenham committee, Cavendish attended the Commons while the bill was discussed, and he was in fact working on another committee on a similar problem; namely, to make navigable again a river whose channels had been destroyed by the tide.[51]

When the next petition for a drainage bill was filed, in 1729, this time by landowners of the Waterbeach Level, also in the southern part of the fens, Cavendish was elected (or had himself elected) to the committee to consider it,[52] even though he had no family connection or known personal interest, such as property in the area. Waterbeach Level is in Cambridgeshire. The petition was brought by the Member of Parliament for the county Thomas Bacon, a lawyer and wealthy landowner, unlike Cavendish a tory, but like Cavendish a Fellow of the Royal Society with a great interest in books and a valuable collection.[53] He apparently could depend on Cavendish's interest in the technical problem, returning the favor seven years later, when he served on the committee that saw through the Commons Cavendish's private bill for the sale of his country estates in Hertfordshire.[54] As to the Waterbeach drainage petition, the Commons ordered a bill but never acted on it. Truly effective draining of the fens had to await the steam engine and an administrative reorganization into small local units.

The obligation to attend to estate matters of family and other associates on House committees remained with Cavendish throughout his sixteen years in the Commons; in all he was on thirty-five such committees. Landed property, under British law, could not be sold or "alienated" from the designated line of descent without specific authorization by parliament. Since bills of this type originated in the House of Lords, they usually needed only to be confirmed, or at most amended, by the Commons and took up little time.

Lord Charles Cavendish's official constituencies, Westminster from 1727 until 1734, and Derbyshire from 1734 until 1741, involved him in many fewer committees, even though, when he did work on a bill for them, he and his fellow Member of Parliament (every constituency except for London was represented by two members) were in charge of it, had to chair the committees considering the petitions and the bills, report on their findings to the House, draw up the bill, and finally see to it that it was passed. The regular problems of Westminster were the usual ones for cities: repairing streets in "ruinous Condition," clearing them of the "Filth and Dirt" that covered them, and keeping them safe at night.[55] In 1729, for example, Cavendish and his colleagues worked out a bill designed to correct the ill effects of having several different privately owned "waterworks" lay water lines and cover them with pavement that was neither level nor strong and lasting enough.[56] A few weeks later he and his fellow Member of Parliament William Clayton were ordered "to bring in a Bill for appointing a better nightly Watch, and regulating the Beadles . . . and for better enlightening the Streets, and publick Passages. . . ."[57]

[49]Wells, *Bedford Level*, 1:426, 744–45 H. C. Darby, "The Draining of the Fens, A.D. 1600–1800," in *An Historical Geography of England Before A.D. 1800*, ed. H. C. Darby (Cambridge: Cambridge University Press, 1936), 444–64, on 456–59. 4 Mar. 1726 (1725), *HCJ* 20:599.
[50]Wells, *Bedford Level* 1:437–39.
[51]14, 23 Feb. 1727 (1726), *HCJ* 20:740, 769.
[52]19, 28 Feb. 1729 (1728), *HCJ* 21:229, 244.
[53]Sedgwick, *House* 2:411.
[54]23 Mar. 1736 (1735), *HCJ* 22:645.
[55]4 Feb. 1729 (1728), *HCJ* 21:208.
[56]19 Feb. 1729 (1728), *HCJ* 21:229.
[57]10 Apr. 1729, *HCJ* 21:313.

He worked on such problems for Westminster again in 1736 and 1737, after he had switched to Derbyshire.[58] In 1736 he had been appointed to the commission for the new bridge to be built at Westminster. The commission had authority to acquire and condemn the real property needed to provide for broad carriage approaches—in fact, for wide streets and regularly aligned new houses—which eventually transformed the old tangle of dark alleys that made up Westminster in that area. But the initial result of their control was a worsening of the conditions there as property owners moved away, leaving undone what little they had contributed toward maintaining the streets, and as squatters moved in. But even aside from such special circumstances, Westminster was at times difficult to represent because it was the seat of parliament and because it was contiguous with London and large (its electorate was larger than London's), the two together containing the biggest concentration of population in all of England. Popular dissatisfaction with local or national matters there often took on tangible forms. The streets bills in 1729, for example, brought out thousands of angry people, whose complaints the Commons refused to hear. London during these years was in vehement opposition to much of Walpole's administrative program. In 1733, Walpole's handling of the proposed excise on tobacco brought not only local opponents but also the London mob to Westminster: members of the Commons complained of a "tumultuous Crowd" who "menaced, insulted, and assaulted" them as they left the House. By order of the Commons, Cavendish and Clayton had to notify the high bailiff of Westminster that such actions constituted a crime and an infringement of the privileges of the Commons.[59]

Like his Westminster predecessors for years, Lord Charles Cavendish had been elected with government support, that is, with whig support. Derbyshire, on the other hand, had been in the hands of the tories for just as long; Cavendish was the first whig to be elected for the county since his father had lost the seat over thirty years before, and his election was close.[60] His fellow Member of Parliament there was in fact still a tory, Nathaniel Curzon, a lawyer and land- and mine-owner who voted consistently against the administration.[61] Other counties in the area such as Lancashire, Cheshire, and Yorkshire were also represented by

tories, even ardent Jacobites. As a result, Cavendish was often not nominated to committees dealing with matters of concern to Derbyshire, although, as its representative, he could not be excluded from such committees, since the speaker of the house had the obligation to add to a committee any member who had a legitimate interest in the matter in question.[62] As a result, Cavendish was very actively engaged in only a few private acts initiated by his constituency in Derbyshire, altogether drawing up only four bills for them. But he worked on a number of private acts that benefited Derbyshire even if they did not deal with the county directly.

The subject of these private acts was road repair. From the beginning of the century, the administration and maintenance of English roads had been undergoing an important change: as the uses of the roads were converted from mainly local, foot and animal, traffic to through traffic for carriages and wagons, the roads were gradually changed into turnpikes to make the principal users contribute to their maintenance. At the initiative of the local parishes responsible for road maintenance and other interested parties, parliament passed private acts establishing trusts that were given the responsibility of setting up, financing, and maintaining the new turnpikes. The earliest turnpikes had been along the main roads leading to London. By the 1730s two of these, the so-called Great North Road and the road from London to Manchester, both of which were important links between Derbyshire and the metropolis, had already been turnpiked over considerable distances immediately north of London and immediately south of Yorkshire and of Manchester. In some areas, the original turnpike trusts were already up for renewal. For Derbyshire coal trade, industry,

---

[58] 16, 25 Mar. 1736 (1735) and 14, 21 Feb. 1737 (1736), *HCJ* 22:633, 652, and 22:746, 756.

[59] 12, 13 Apr. 1733, *HCJ* 22:115–16. Plumb, *Walpole* 2:262–71.

[60] Sedgwick, *House* 1:223. In his first run for a seat from Derbyshire, Cavendish's vote was 2081, the runner-up tory Curzon's 2044, and the third candidate, the loser, Harper's 1795. Places where the Cavendishes owned property such as Normanton gave almost all their votes to Cavendish. Other places such as Thornhill and Pilsley (just outside Chatsworth, it is interesting to note) gave him virtually no votes. *A Copy of a Poll Taken for the County of Derby, The 16th, 17th, 18th, and 20th Days of May, 1734 before George Mower, Esq.; High-Sheriff for the Said County* (Derby, n.d.).

[61] Sedgwick, *House* 1:599.

[62] Thomas, *House of Commons*, 58.

and agriculture, it was of great importance to complete the turnpiking of these roads and the east-west roads lying between them as well.[63]

The first such committee that Cavendish had himself assigned to, in 1735, was formed to examine the turnpike acts dealing with the part of the London-Manchester road closest to London.[64] Three years later he and Curzon drew up the act that was to close the longest stretch of the London-Manchester road yet to be turnpiked, thirty-nine miles of it between Loughborough and Hartington in Leicestershire and Derbyshire, respectively.[65] Altogether he worked on twelve private acts for turnpikes either on or near these two important highways. In addition he worked on five turnpike bills for roads west and southwest of London.[66] To no other subject did he devote as much work, and his interest in this area is strongly confirmed by his committee work on repairing bridges, and, above all, by the decade of work he devoted to the building of Westminster Bridge.

The one local legislative matter Cavendish took charge of for Derbyshire was typical of these road bills. In February 1739, he brought a petition to the Commons from the inhabitants of several parishes in Derbyshire and Nottinghamshire, particularly in the area of Bakewell (the town closest to Chatsworth, the country house of the dukes of Devonshire), requesting the repair of some of the major roads linking their towns. Cavendish was put at the head of a committee of forty-five plus. Five days later he reported the committee's findings and the testimony of his two witnesses. The roads in question had become so deep that they were all but impassable to carriages and coaches, especially in the winter. Neither the repair work required by local statute nor any taxes raised locally for the purpose were enough any longer to maintain the roads. The Commons ordered that Cavendish and Curzon and the two members for Nottinghamshire draw up a bill, which Cavendish presented in the middle of March. By the end of March, people from a town in Nottinghamshire were petitioning against the bill, claiming it would be a "burden" to them, and persons connected with a "Company of Cutlers" in a town in Yorkshire protested that the bill's provisions for a tollgate near the north-south route would increase the price of goods for people in the north. After another forty-five members had been added to Cavendish's committee early in

April, the opposing petitioners were heard, and when Cavendish reported the outcome of that action in the middle of April, the whole House amended the bill to prevent the undesirable turnpike. The bill was passed by the House in early May and became law in June.[67]

The interest of the Commons in turnpike construction and repair was organizational. Turnpike acts made no technical provisions but instead named the administrative body, the trust, that was to bear the financial and the—as yet rather undeveloped—technical responsibility. The turnpikes rationalized and improved the network of English roads, particularly those parts of it centered on London (and later on the growing industrial centers such as Manchester) without removing the roads from control of the local landowners in rural areas such as Derbyshire and Nottinghamshire, where Cavendish had most of his landed property.[68]

Only rarely did legislation dealing with mining or manufacturing draw Cavendish's interest. There was an instance in 1738, when British ironmongers asked the Commons for a bill that would protect their market in the American colonies against competition from the colonies' own manufactures of iron wares.[69] The decline in the ironmongers' trade, they argued, threatened not only the livelihood of a "multitude of Poor" but the woodlands, whose timber was needed for the royal navy, the leather manufacturers using bark, and the balance of trade. During the same session Cavendish heard the case of button manufacturers asking for enforcement of a law against buttons made from woven materials.[70] The law was meant to protect the cottage industry of buttons and buttonholes made with silk and wool thread using a needle. This industry employed the "poor" in large numbers, nearly 30,000, and it protected native textiles such as wool, encouraging, as the report put it, the consumption of raw silk

---

[63]Sidney and Beatrice Webb, *English Local Government: The Story of the King's Highway* (London: Longmans, Green and Co, 1920), 70. William Albert, *The Turnpike Road System in England 1663–1840* (Cambridge: Cambridge University Press, 1972), 31–43.
[64]18 Apr. 1735, *HCJ* 22:469.
[65]9, 20 Mar. 1738 (1737), *HCJ* 23:73, 107.
[66]Information from *HCJ*.
[67]21 Feb.–14 June 1739, *HCJ* 23:242–380.
[68]Albert, *Turnpike*, 22–24.
[69]1 Feb.–21 Mar. 1738 (1737), *HCJ* 23:15, 109.
[70]9, 14 Mar. and 10, 18 Apr. 1738, *HCJ* 23:73, 88 and 142, 156.

and wool yarn. The industry was now "much decayed." Fabric-covered buttons were the reason, because one person with a loom could do the work of eight to ten needle workers.

For the entire sixteen years Cavendish served in parliament, Walpole was prime minister. Cavendish stepped down in 1741, Walpole in 1742. In addition to whatever family loyalty Cavendish may have felt toward Walpole, he would have been drawn to him for his similarity of outlook. Walpole preferred the "mathematical, provable side of administration." Since the Revolution, political arithmetic had been energetically implemented by the administrators, who were often Fellows of the Royal Society who believed that similar methods applied to government and nature. English government, Walpole's biographer says, was "revolutionized" by these professional public servants.[71] Their quantitative approach agreed well with Walpole's penchant for exacting detail.

Cavendish did not always vote with Walpole, however. In 1725, the year Cavendish entered parliament, William Pultney broke with Walpole,[72] and there is at least the suggestion that Cavendish sympathized with Pultney's opposition whigs. In any event, Cavendish had other important interests to serve, his family's of course but also London's and Westminster's. He continued to serve Westminster even after he stopped representing it in parliament, as we will see. His interests would seem to have been closer to the commercial and financial ones of the city than to those of the country (he sold his own country home in 1736) and the colonies. The episode of Walpole's excise tax on tobacco in 1733 brings this out. Walpole almost fell from power because of it, and Cavendish did nothing to help him. Walpole's excise tax on tobacco was in the interest of Virginia growers, who had long resented the dominion over their business of the London tobacco brokers. There was violent opposition to this tax in the city, which nearly prevailed. When Walpole got his bill passed, by a narrow vote, the city raised a petition against it. Walpole's majority melted away, but he did manage to get the Commons to refuse to hear the petition. Walpole survived, but barely, and not without a riot outside the Commons. Cavendish supported the bill in the beginning, then he voted with the opposition on the city's petition against it. The king, who was strongly with Walpole on this

bill and regarded opposition to it as treason, called Cavendish "half mad" and Lord James Cavendish, who voted exactly as Charles did, a "fool."[73]

Cavendish's political career as a Member of Parliament ended in 1741, not by defeat but by choice. If he sensed it or not, he left politics at about the time his family could dispense with his services. To the mid 1740s but not beyond, the outcome of the Glorious Revolution remained in question; for up to then the tories were predominantly a Jacobite party ready to ally itself with France to restore the Stuart dynasty. Thereafter, the vigilance of the Devonshires could be relaxed. Lord Charles Cavendish could, with clear conscience, consider another path in life.

Cavendish was elected to the Royal Society about two years after he was elected to the Commons. In 1736 he served on the council of the Royal Society for the first time, though not again until the year after he left parliament, thereafter serving on the council almost without interruption for twenty-five years. His work on the council and on the committees of the Royal Society would take the place of his complementary work in parliament.

In the course of his sixteen years in the Commons, Cavendish associated with about two hundred Members of Parliament on parliamentary committees. Very few of them were Fellows of the Royal Society, at most a dozen, with maybe another half dozen becoming Fellows after he had left the Commons, and none of them were to become close scientific associates of his.[74] Of candidates for membership in the Royal Society, Cavendish signed the certificates of only two men with whom he had served on committees in parliament: a

[71]Plumb, *Walpole* 2:234.
[72]Plumb, *Walpole* 2:122–24, 127.
[73]Plumb, *Walpole* 2:250–71. Thomas, *House of Commons*, 68–71. John, Lord Hervey, *Memoirs of the Reign of George the Second from His Accession to the Death of Queen Caroline*, ed. J. W. Croker, vol. 1 (London, 1884), 200. Sedgwick, *The House* 1:537.
[74]Members of the House of Commons associated with Lord Charles Cavendish who were also Fellows of the Royal Society: Thomas Sclater Bacon, F.R.S. 1722; Benjamin Bathurst, F.R.S. 1731; Charles Calvert, Lord Baltimore, F.R.S. 1731; Thomas Cartwright, F.R.S. 1716; Lord James Cavendish, F.R.S. 1719; John Conduitt, F.R.S. 1718; James Dawkins, F.R.S. 1755; Thomas, Lord Gage, F.R.S. 1728; Edward Hooper, F.R.S. 1759; Robert Hucks, F.R.S. 1722 (or possibly his father, William); Sir James Lowther, F.R.S. 1736; Henry Pelham, F.R.S. 1746; Hugh Hume Campbell, Lord Polwarth (until 1740, then earl of Marchmont), F.R.S. 1753; Sir Hugh Smithson (after 1750 earl of Northumberland, after 1766 duke of Northumberland) F.R.S. 1736; Charles Stanhope, F.R.S. 1726; Sir John Brownlow, Lord Tyrconnel, F.R.S. 1735; Thomas Walker [?], F.R.S. 1730; and Edward Wortley Montagu, F.R.S. 1750.

distant relative, Sir James Lowther of Whitehaven, who had communicated experiments to the Royal Society, and Edward Hooper.[75]

Gentleman of the Bedchamber

The duke of Kent was gentleman of the bedchamber to George I, and in 1728 his future son-in-law Lord Charles Cavendish was appointed to the same position, only to the prince of Wales, Frederick. Cavendish was indeed a "gentleman," though as son of the duke of Devonshire he was referred to as "lord" of the bedchamber to the prince.[76] With this position Cavendish was now a man both of parliament and of the court-in-waiting. He was a consort to the man who stood next in line for the throne, required to be in attendance for much of the day when it came his turn. The appointment presumably was made by the king but not against the wishes of the prince. In any case, the relations between Cavendish and the prince were good; Cavendish's second son would be named Frederick after the prince, who would stand in as his godfather.

As it turned out, this prince did not live long enough to become king but long enough to be a political force in his own right and the occasion of the scandal of the reign. Frederick was born in Hanover in 1707 and remained there until December 1728, when he was brought suddenly to England because word was received at court that he was about to marry the princess royal of Prussia. The marriage had been negotiated and sanctioned by George I, but in 1727 his father came to the throne, and George II did not see eye to eye with the king of Prussia and called off the marriage. In submitting, the prince detested his father for keeping him dependent. He later married Princess Augusta, daughter of Frederick, duke of Saxe-Gothe, with his father's approval, but the prince turned this marriage into a weapon against his father. Competing with his father for popularity in the country, the prince formed an opposition court, welcoming into his household ambitious young men like Pitt, Lyttleton, and the Grenvilles, and he developed an intense dislike for Robert Walpole, his father's favorite minister. Fond of music and literature, he sought the company of men of wit and learning, such as Chesterfield, Carteret, Pulteney, Cobham, and Wyndham. He associated with persons who had an interest in science too, for

which there was a precedent in the family. When Frederick's father had been prince of Wales, his secretary was the astronomer Samuel Molyneux, who was a close friend and colleague of James Bradley; he had his own instrument-maker as well. Later, as George II, his master of mechanics was the very competent Robert Smith, professor of astronomy and natural philosophy at Cambridge.[77] John Theophilus Desaguliers, demonstrator of experiments in the Royal Society, was chaplain to Frederick, prince of Wales, to whom Desaguliers dedicated his *Course of Experimental Philosophy*.[78] So was Thomas Rutherforth, Fellow of the Royal Society and professor of divinity at Cambridge, where he lectured and wrote on natural philosophy.[79] The princess's chaplain, Caspar Wetstein, was a correspondent of the great mathematical scientist Euler.[80] In 1731, we know, the prince was pleased to be seen in the company of men of science, for he attended a meeting of the Royal Society at which experiments on electricity, magnetism, phlogiston,

---

[75]Sir James Lowther was elected in 1736 on the strength of a proposal in which Cavendish's signature was only preceded by that of the president of the Royal Society; we discuss this relative and wealthy land and mine owner in another place On the proposal in 1759 of Edward Hooper, Cavendish's signature was less prominent, seventh out of twelve. Hooper was introduced to the Society as "one of the commissioners of his Majesties customs, a gentleman of great merit, & well versed in various branches of usefull learning." Royal Society Certificates, vol. 1, no. 5, f. 118 (Lowther), and vol. 2, no. 10, f. 177 (Hooper). Cavendish had first joined a committee with Hooper, a lawyer and opposition whig, over twenty years before his election to the Royal Society. Hooper had been on Cavendish's committee for the turnpiking of the Derbyshire roads around Bakewell, and in turn Cavendish had sat on Hooper's committee for naturalizing Andrew (then Adrian) Coltee Ducarel, D.C.L. and later F.R.S. Sedgwick, *House* 2:147.

[76]John Edward Smith and W. Parkinson Smith, *The Parliamentary Representation of Westminster from the Thirteenth Century to the Present Day*, vol. 2 (London: Wightman, 1923), 272. James Douglas, earl of Morton, who became president of the Royal Society while Cavendish was a member, had held a parallel position at court, as lord of the bedchamber. "Douglas, James, Fourteenth Earl of Morton," *DNB* 5:1236–37, on 1236.

[77]Frederick Louis, Prince of Wales," *DNB* 7:675–78. E. G. R. Taylor, *Mathematical Practitioners of Hanoverian England, 1714– 1840* (Cambridge: Cambridge University Press, 1966), 10, 135–36.

[78]J. T. Desaguliers, *A Course of Experimental Philosophy*, vol. 2 (London, 1744). Like many subscription books, this one was long in the making; among its subscribers were Newton, George I, George II, and Queen Caroline, all but George II then dead.

[79]Thomas Rutherforth later became chaplain to the princess dowager as well. "Rutherforth, Thomas," *DNB* 17:499–500. In 1748 he published his lectures at Cambridge as *A System of Natural Philosophy*, a well-known text which we discuss when we take up scientific teaching at Cambridge.

[80]"Extract of a Letter from Professor Euler, of Berlin, to the Rev. Mr. Caspar Wetstein, Chaplain to Her Royal Highness the Princess Dowager of Wales," *PT* 47 (1751): 263–64.

and phosphorous were performed.[81] He was thought to have a certain special interest in astronomy. Filial competition, we suspect, if not native interest, would have drawn Frederick, prince of Wales, to the scientifically knowledgeable Lord Charles Cavendish. (Frederick's son, George III, would be the first British monarch to be tutored in science.[82])

There may also have been a political sympathy between Charles and Frederick, but in personality this studious gentleman of the bed-chamber would seem to have had little in common with this rakehell-living prince. Confronted with the prince's passionate rebellion, the king drew the line in 1738; thereafter no one who paid court to the prince of Wales or his wife was admitted to the king's presence at any of the royal palaces.[83] But by the year of the prince's banishment, Lord Charles

Cavendish had long before left his service, having resigned in October 1730.[84]

---

[81]Charles Richard Weld, *A History of the Royal Society*, 2 vols. in 1 (New York: Arno Press, 1975) 1:465–66.

[82]George III was tutored by George Lewis Scott, a mathematical colleague of Charles Cavendish. Leonard Weiss, *Watch-Making in England, 1760–1820* (London: Robert Hale, 1982), 21–22. This king had a number of other connections with science: he had an instrument-maker provide him with a set of demonstration apparatus; he had a private observatory; Lord Bute, another tutor and his principal advisor, was a botanist; he provided an income for the astronomer William Herschel; and he gave large sums to the Royal Society for its projects.

[83]Duke of Grafton to /Theophilus, Earl of Huntington/, 27 Feb. 1738, in Great Britain, Historical Manuscripts Commission, *Report on the Manuscripts of the Late Reginald Rowden Hastings, Esq., of the Manor House, Ashby de la Zouche*, 4 vols. (London: His Majesty's Stationary Office, 1928–47) 3:22.

[84]Entry on 17 Oct. 1730 in *The Historical Register*, vol. 15: *The Chronological Diary* (London, 1730), 64.

⤝⤞

CHAPTER 2

Science

De Moivre Circle

Families of the landed aristocracy in England settled their estates on their eldest sons and turned out their younger, such as Lord Charles Cavendish, with the expectation that they would contribute to their upkeep by entering one of a highly restricted number of suitable professions. We can say with confidence that Cavendish's options did not include science, regardless of how great an interest he might have had in it. He entered politics, as we know.

If not as a profession, how then would science have appeared to Lord Charles Cavendish? We should point out here that science did already show some of the essential characteristics of a profession, though they had not been brought together, and they were probably less apparent (and less interesting) in his time than they are to us looking back. Scientific instruction was widely available on a catch-as-catch-can basis, often taking the form of self-instruction from books or tutoring or apprenticeship. Lectures on science could be heard in the universities, certain kinds of schools, shops of instrument-makers, coffee houses, and private homes. In the middle of the eighteenth century, a father educating his son in law, pointed out that in London, in addition to reading books on law, his son could attend a "variety of lectures both of mathematics & experimental philosophy."[1] There were various circles avid for knowledge of the new science, and they made possible a variety of livelihoods, which were often combined, but which hardly ever paid for scientific research. Practitioners of science, in addition to teaching, could earn money by consulting,[2] publishing popular books on science, making and selling scientific instruments, or serving a wealthy patron. There were only a very few government scientific jobs such as astronomer royal. Public recognition in science took the form of membership in, honors bestowed by, and approval of work for publication by a mixed group such as the members of the Royal Society. Such standards as existed were neither very rigorous nor uniform. The practitioner of science worked in science for himself, largely on his own initiative, whether it earned him a living, a distinction, or simply personal satisfaction.

If by comparison with the professions, science in the time of our Cavendishes is found wanting in certain ways, it is nonetheless true that the professions themselves were then loosely organized and regulated, and that they, like science, were undergoing change. Physicians, for example, acquired a positional status through professionalism in the nineteenth century, but in our eighteenth century "individual and personal characteristics were of greater consequence"; for one thing, formal licensing laws did not yet exist.[3] By the same token, the clergy was an extraordinary mix by any standard. Much of it was impoverished, yet intellectually inclined, and to this portion of the clergy science owes a large debt. The bishops of the church, who were well to do, were sometimes highly qualified men of learning and ability but often men of rank and ease and little else to recommend them.[4] In law, the inns of court had abandoned their original function of teaching students, and Oxford took little interest in them, which left them to study on their own and attend courts at Westminster or work in an attorney's office. Administration was another mix of the able and the indifferent; English government, apart from the central government in London, consisted of practically autonomous local units, which did not form a system but a "hotch-potch of authorities and con-

---

[1]Sollom Emlyn to John Ward, 8 Jan. 1758, "Letters of Learned Men to Professor Ward, BL Add Mss 6210.

[2]Larry Stewart, "Public Lectures and Private Patronage in Newtonian England," *Isis* 77 (1986): 47–58, on 55–56.

[3]W. F. Bynum, "Health, Disease and Medical Care," in *The Ferment of Knowledge: Studies in the Historiography of Eighteenth Century Science*, ed. G. S. Rousseau and R. Porter (Cambridge: Cambridge University Press, 1980), 221–53, on 234.

[4]L. B. Namier, *Crossroads of Power: Essays on Eighteenth-Century England* (London: H. Hamilton, 1962), 185–86.

flicting institutions," whose officials were not professional bureaucrats but were, at least nominally, unpaid and were drawn from a "half-educated" class.[5] Science, to Lord Charles Cavendish, would have seemed like a disorganized enterprise, but then so would have the activities of the lawyer and doctor, the surgeon and apothecary, the merchant and manufacturer, many of whom began with little formal schooling, underwent apprenticeship, and then set up practice where they found clients, largely unhampered by restrictions.

It was, of course, unthinkable for Lord Charles Cavendish to enter *any* of the learned professions or administration or business—or science, even if it had been regarded in the same light as the learned professions. *If* his social circumstances had been radically different, given his talents and inclinations, we suspect that he would have been happy as an instrument-maker, associating with men of science, and earning three or four pounds a week. What he *did* do was to pursue science on the side, the only course open to him, and on his own initiative, in one way or another, he got a good foundation in science.

In his twenties, Lord Charles Cavendish enjoyed several years of relative freedom from the duties of family and public office. Circumstantial evidence leads us to think that during these years he continued his education in London. His teacher, or one of his teachers, may have been the great mathematician Abraham De Moivre.

Fifty years De Moivre's junior, Matthew Maty was his close friend and the author of a valuable biographical piece on him. To Maty we owe a list of De Moivre's eminent mathematical friends: Newton, Edmond Halley, James Stirling, Nicholas Saunderson, Martin Folkes, and, on the Continent, Johann I Bernoulli and Pierre Varignon. (To this list of mathematical friends we add from other sources William Jones[6] and Brook Taylor,[7] and there were still others.) Maty also named De Moivre's pupils or, to use the exact French word, *disciples:* Lord Macclesfield, Charles Stanhope, George Lewis Scott, Peter Davall, James Dodson, and Cavendish.[8] (John Colson should be included among his pupils, and no doubt others.[9])

Since Maty gave only last names, we are forced to speculate about whom he meant by "Cavendish." Writing in the late 1750s, Maty

would unlikely have meant Henry Cavendish, who had only recently come down from Cambridge and was not yet a Fellow of the Royal Society. Nor, we think, is it likely that he would have had in mind William Cavendish, duke of Devonshire; for the judgment Maty wished his readers to make of De Moivre was of his standing among accomplished mathematicians and not within society at large, and so far as we know, none of the early dukes of Devonshire had a mathematical reputation, though it is conceivable the first duke, a man of many reputations, had something of one. The likeliest possibilities narrow down to two, Lord Charles Cavendish and his uncle Lord James Cavendish.[10] Both were active in the Royal Society, and both were proposed for membership in the Society by the good friend of De Moivre, the eminent mathematician William Jones. Both subscribed to De Moivre's *Miscellanea analytica de seriebus et quadraturis*, which was published in 1730, and which was the first mathematical or scientific book to which Lord Charles subscribed. The duke of Devonshire was also a subscriber to this book, and it is just conceivable that Lord Charles and Lord James were both pupils of De Moivre and that various Devonshires were as well. (De Moivre called at the Devonshire house in London, very possibly in the capacity of mathematical tutor; see below.) Because of the reasonable possibility that by "Cavendish," Maty meant Lord Charles Cavendish, and, in any event, because of the evidence it provides of the mathematical culture of the close-knit Cavendish family, we include the following brief discussion of De Moive.

---

[5]Basil Williams, *The Whig Supremacy, 1714–1760*, 2d rev. ed. by C. H. Stuart (Oxford: Clarendon Press, 1962), 44–45, 62–63.

[6]De Moivre called William Jones his "intimate friend" in the preface to his book *The Doctrine of Chances; or, a Method of Calculating the Probability of Events in Play* (London, 1718), x.

[7]De Moivre called Brook Taylor his "worthy Friend" in his *Doctrine of Chances*, 101. He had a correspondence with Brook Taylor, described in Ivo Schneider, "Der Mathematiker Abraham de Moivre (1667–1754)," *Archive for History of Exact Sciences* 5 (1968): 177–317, on 196–97.

[8]Matthew Maty, *Mémoire sur la vie et sur les éscrits de Mr. Abraham de Moivre* (The Hague, 1760), 38–39.

[9]In the foreword to his first book, *Animadversiones*, De Moivre referred to John Colson as one of his pupils, noted by Schneider, "Abraham de Moivre," 189.

[10]Lord James Cavendish was proposed for membership in the Royal Society by William Jones on 19 Mar. 1718/19, and was admitted on 16 Apr. 1719. Royal Society, JB 11: 311 and 326. The other Lord James Cavendish, Lord Charles's brother, is not a likely a candidate for Maty's "Cavendish."

The friends and pupils of De Moivre spanned two generations: De Moivre was Newton's junior by twenty-five years and Cavendish's senior by about the same number of years. Many of them were prominent in the Royal Society: Newton, Folkes, and Macclesfield were presidents, Cavendish, Jones, Davall, Scott, and Stanhope members of the council, Halley a paid corresponding secretary and also editor of the *Philosophical Transactions,* and Taylor, like Maty himself, a secretary. De Moivre's pupils, in part through De Moivre, had a living connection with the great scientists of the recent past. To judge by their work, De Moivre encouraged in them a wide-ranging response to the problems of quantity, both scientific and practical, of the early eighteenth century. There was a social connection too: Cavendish, for example, met privately as well as publicly with Folkes, Macclesfield, Jones, Davall, and Stanhope. There is reason to believe that De Moivre fostered a sense of connection between his pupils, as he evidently brought them together at social evenings and later kept them "together as a kind of clique." Maty, De Moivre's friend and biographer, contributed by noting every work published by De Moivre's pupils in his *Journal Britannique.*[11] They appear together in other connections as well.[12] If we leave aside the foreigners named by Maty, we are directed by him to a select few within the larger group of British mathematicians in the early eighteenth century with whom Cavendish came to be closely connected. For convenience, we will speak of a "De Moive circle," whose members will give us an idea of the mathematical world in which Lord Charles Cavendish may have completed his (other than self-) education.

De Moivre is not an English name, and Maty wrote about him in French; we now explain. The learned world of London was greatly enriched by Protestant refugees, Huguenots, forced to leave France after the revocation of the edict of Nantes. Within the Cavendish family, as we have seen, the Huguenot Ruvignys settled in Greenwich (a prophetic location) and encouraged other refugees to follow their example.[13] De Moivre's father was one of a large number of Huguenot surgeons and physicians to seek asylum, in 1686, in England, where he and his son were naturalized.[14] De Moivre was then nineteen and a student of mathematics.

In De Moivre's mind, his arrival in England

became so closely identified with his discovery of Newton's work that although two or three years elapsed between the two events, to him they seemed simultaneous. For biographers of Charles and Henry Cavendish, it is gratifying that the meeting between De Moivre and Newton's work occurred in the house of the earl of Devonshire. It was probably in 1689, when Newton spent a good deal of time in London as a member for Cambridge of the Convention Parliament, and when Devonshire enjoyed the fruits of the revolution as a prominent member of parliament and of the court of William and Mary. De Moivre first saw Newton as Newton was leaving Devonshire's house after presenting a copy of his *Principia.* Shown into the antechamber where Newton had just left his book, De Moivre picked it up expecting to read it without difficulty. He found that he understood nothing at all. Whether it was on that first encounter or later, when he studied his own copy of the work, he felt that all of his mathematical studies so far, which he had considered entirely up to date, had really taken him only to the threshold of a new direction.[15] De Moivre's confidence in his own gifts proved to be well founded, however, for he promptly mastered

---

[11] Uta Janssens, *Matthieu Maty and the Journal Britannique, 1750–1755* (Amsterdam: Holland University Press, 1975), 17. Augustus De Morgan, "Dr. Johnson and Dr. Maty," *Notes and Queries* 4 (1857): 341.

[12] They appeared together, for example, with a much larger number of like-minded persons in the following context. De Moivre republished his mathematical papers from the *Philosophical Transactions* in a book, mentioned above, *Miscellanea analytica de seriebus et quadraturis* (London,1730). As was customary with technical books, it was sold by subscription and listed the names of the subscribers; this list could serve as a guide to British mathematics and its patrons in the early eighteenth century. The Cavendishes, as noted, are subscribers, and the book is dedicated to Folkes. With an exception or two, the friends and pupils of De Moivre, as given by Maty, are all there.

[13] Mary Berry, *Some Account of the Life of Rachael Wriothesley Lady Russell . . . Followed by a Series of Letters . . .* (London, 1819), 73.

[14] Father and son, "Abraham and Daniel de Moivre," are listed as being in England as of 16 Dec. 1687, in a request to the Attorney or Sollicitor Generall to prepare a bill for royal signature making them free denizens of the kingdom. *Lists of Foreign Protestants, and Aliens, Resident in England 1618–1688*, ed. W. Durrant Cooper (London, 1862), 50. Samuel Smiles, *The Huguenots: Their Settlements, Churches, and Industries in England and Ireland* (New York, 1868), 235–38.

[15] Maty, *Mémoire.* 6–7. Although the *Principia* was published in the summer of 1687, there is no evidence that Newton came to London to distribute copies of it at that time. Moreover, it would have been of no advantage to either Newton or De Moivre that summer to seek the earl of Devonshire's patronage, since he was then so much out of favor at court; in 1688 the earl took refuge at Chatsworth to avoid being arrested by the king. By 1689, however, James II had been displaced by William and Mary, at whose court Devonshire had a great deal of influence.

the new mathematics, with the result that Newton is said to have referred persons asking him about his work to De Moivre, who knew it better than he did.[16] Through the astronomer Edmond Halley, De Moivre was introduced to Newton properly and as well to the scientific society of London, which led to his election to the Royal Society. He made himself available to Newton in a variety of capacities: he sent news and results of Newton's work to colleagues abroad;[17] he translated and took charge of Newton's publications;[18] he defended Newton;[19] and he kept philosophical company with Newton at the Rainbow coffee-house and elsewhere.[20] De Moivre's own work drew heavily on Newton's, which he acknowledged by dedicating his masterwork, a treatise on probability, *Doctrine of Chances*, to Newton. This friend of Newton, Halley, and other prominent Fellows of the Royal Society and correspondent of leading mathematicians on the Continent was, we speculate, Lord Charles Cavendish's teacher in advanced mathematics.

De Moivre just might have been Cavendish's teacher in natural philosophy too. He gave lectures on the subject but without much success, since his English was not good and neither were his skills as an experimental demonstrator.[21] It was otherwise with his teaching of mathematics, which has its own language, though this is not to say that he made a good living at it. He barely subsisted. In just what setting he taught mathematics, we are uncertain. We know only that he tried most of the ways that a person could make money through mathematics short of writing popular manuals. In 1689 a committee in the Commons considered how to raise funds to establish a royal military "Academy" in or near London or Westminster and to aid "French and Irish Protestants, who are fled from France and Ireland for their Religion."[22] The project apparently did not die, for three years later we find another reference to a "Royal Academy," this time linking it to De Moivre. Richard Sault, who published a mathematical proof in the *Philosophical Transactions*, and De Moivre were to be its mathematics teachers. Later on Sault ran a so-called mathematical boarding school, calling himself a "professor of mathematics,"[23] and De Moivre may have taught at this or at similar schools. Twice he presented himself as a candidate for the Lucasian professorship of mathematics at Cambridge. Well connected in mathematical circles

and highly regarded for his work, he still could not get a good job. Even his conversion to the Church of England in 1705 could not alter the fact that he was an alien. Toward the end of his (long) life, he worked out of Slaughter's Coffee House in St. Martin's Lane, solving problems of games and lives for a fee and, perhaps, for a handout.[24]

De Moivre had a philosophical viewpoint, which he believed was close to Newton's.[25] Probability is useful for gamblers, De Moivre wrote in *Doctrine of Chances*. It is for fun and gain, but it is also for the reasoning mind: it clarifies the world through the paradoxes it exposes, since chance is the denial of luck, of which there is no such thing in "nature." The doctrine of chance, De Moivre said, supports the doctrine of design: probability can grow until it becomes demonstration, and so the order and constancy of nature express design.[26] And so from whist to God, mathematics applies and illuminates, and bright young men like Lord Charles Cavendish were caught up in its charms, as revealed by De Moivre.

In the seventeenth and eighteenth centuries, mathematical tutoring was a common finishing school for "gentlemen." It provided a useful skill

---

[16]Ian Hacking, "Moivre, Abraham de," *DSB* 9:452–55, on 452.

[17]For example, concerning copies of Newton's *Principia* promised by De Moivre: letters from Pierre Varignon to Newton, 24 Nov. 1713, and from Johann Bernoulli to Leibniz, 25 Nov. 1713; in *The Correspondence of Isaac Newton*, vol. 6: *1713–1718*, ed. A. R. Hall and L. Tilling (Cambridge: Cambridge University Press, 1976), 42–43, 44–45.

[18]David Brewster, *Memoirs of the Life, Writings, and Discoveries of Isaac Newton*, 2 vols. (Edinburgh, 1855) 1:248. Schneider, "Abraham de Moivre," 212–13.

[19]In Newton's dispute with Leibniz over the invention of the calculus. Hacking, "Moivre," 452.

[20]Frederick Charles Green, *Eighteenth-Century France. Six Essays* (New York: D. Appleton, 1931), 31.

[21]Schneider, "Abraham de Moivre," 208.

[22]The funds were to be raised by licensing hackney coaches, the subject of the bill under consideration. 22 Apr. 1689, *HCJ* 10:97.

[23]The project was advertised in the short-lived *Athenian Mercury*. E. G. R. Taylor, *Mathematical Practitioners of Tudor and Stuart England* (Cambridge: Cambridge University Press, 1954), 289.

[24]For a long time Slaughter's was De Moivre's mailing address. Bryant Lillywhite, *London Coffee Houses. A Reference Book of Coffee Houses of the Seventeenth, Eighteenth, and Nineteenth Centuries* (London: George Allen & Unwin, 1963), 421–22.

[25]O. B. Sheynin, "Newton and the Classical Theory of Probability," *Archive for History of Exact Sciences* 7 (1970–71): 217–43, on 230.

[26]De Moivre, *Doctrine of Chances*, iii–vi. Until the nineteenth century random events were unthinkable: De Moivre is called one of the "deterministic probabilists" in Lorraine Daston, *Classical Probability in the Enlightenment* (Princeton: Princeton University Press, 1988), 10.

for men who sought public office and lacked the advantage of rank.[27] It also prepared men who intended to make a living directly from mathematics, especially teachers. In becoming a pupil of De Moivre, Lord Charles Cavendish was on a path that was uncommon for anyone and especially for someone whose career and opportunity were so clearly marked out; for it would lead him to scientific research and administration.

Of De Moivre's friends, as opposed to pupils, James Stirling and Brook Taylor were mathematicians of the first order. Stirling, an Oxford-educated Scot, taught mathematics privately and later in a successful school in London, the Little Tower Street Academy. His first paper, in 1718, dealt with Newton's differential method, the subject of his major work, in 1730, *Methodus differentialis*. With Newton's help, he was elected to the Royal Society in 1726, shortly before Cavendish's election. Stirling spent the last half of his life in Scotland surveying, administering mining enterprises, and teaching mathematics.[28] Brook Taylor came from a well-to-do family with strong interests in music and art. To these interests Taylor added mathematics and experimental natural philosophy, which led to his election to the Royal Society in 1712. His most important work was a treatise in 1715 on the method of increments and its relationship to Newton's fluxions, *Methodus incrementorum directa and inversa*. With De Moivre, he joined the Royal Society's defense of Newton's claims in the priority dispute over the invention of the calculus.[29] Edmond Halley had very broad interests and competences including mathematical ones, but his outstanding work was in astronomy. He was educated at Oxford, to which he returned as Savilian professor of geometry; and from 1720 he was astronomer royal.[30] The Lucasian professor of mathematics Nicholas Saunderson we will discuss when we take up scientific education at Cambridge. Of De Moivre's friends, that leaves only William Jones and Martin Folkes, both of whom Cavendish came to know very well.

William Jones was another mathematics teacher under whom Cavendish may well have studied.[31] Early on, Jones published a book on navigation and another, a syllabus of mathematics, which drew the attention of Halley and Newton, both of whom became his friends. He settled in London where he taught and then tutored in

mathematics. With one of his pupils Philip Yorke, later earl of Hardwicke and lord chancellor, he became friends and later traveled with him on his circuit. Another pupil was George Parker, later earl of Macclesfield, with whom he had an especially close and enduring association. For years he lived at Macclesfield's home, Shirburn Castle, where he served as secretary to Macclesfield's father. Through this connection he was appointed deputy teller to the exchequer, a position similar to Macclesfield's own there. Jones published a number of original papers in the *Philosophical Transactions*, edited important tracts of Newton, and served with De Moivre on the committee of the Royal Society on the discovery of the calculus. He intended to write an introduction to Newtonian philosophy but died before he completed it. His library of mathematical books and manuscripts was reputed to be the largest in the country. Jones was an important figure in the Royal Society, to which he was elected in 1712, and he was an important personal and scientific link between Newton and the science of his day and Lord Charles Cavendish.[32]

Martin Folkes studied at Cambridge under one of the first Newtonian mathematical teachers there, Richard Laughton, of Clare College. At the age of twenty-three, in 1714, he was elected Fellow of the Royal Society. He published several papers in the *Philosophical Transactions* dealing with astronomy and with the proportions of English weights and measures to the French and on those of the Royal Society to those in the exchequer and

---

[27]A. J. Turner, "Mathematical Instruments and the Education of Gentlemen," *Annals of Science* 30 (1973): 51–88, on 51–54.

[28]E. G. R. Taylor, *Mathematical Practitioners of Hanoverian England, 1714–1840* (Cambridge: Cambridge University Press, 1966), 144–45. P. J. Wallis, "Stirling, James," *DSB* 13: 67–70.

[29]Phillip S. Jones, "Taylor, Brook," *DSB* 13: 265–68. L. Feigenbaum, "Brook Taylor and the Method of Increments," *Archive for History of Exact Sciences* 34 (1985): 2–140, on 6–7.

[30]Colin A. Ronan, "Halley, Edmond," *DSB* 6:67–72.

[31]It was Jones's practice to hand out transcripts of Newton's mathematical writings to his pupils; that is the likely way Lord Charles Cavendish came to make a copy of Jones's transcript of Newton's *Artis Analyticae Specimina sive Geometria Analytica*. Cavendish later loaned his copy of the transcript to the mathematician Samuel Horsley, who was preparing a general edition of Newton's papers. Isaac Newton, *Mathematical Papers of Isaac Newton*, ed. D. T. Whiteside, 8 vols. (Cambridge: Cambridge University Press, 1967–81) 1:xxiii; 8:xxiv, xxvii.

[32]"Jones, William," *DNB* 10:1061–62. Taylor, *Mathematical Practitioners of Tudor and Stuart England*, 293–94. "Jones (William)," in Charles Hutton, *Mathematical and Philosophical Dictionary* vol. 1 (London, 1796), 643–44. Thomas Birch to Jemima Grey, 5 Aug. 1749, BL Add Mss 35397, ff. 198–99.

elsewhere in England. Picked by Newton as his vice president, Folkes went on to become president both of the Royal Society and of the Society of Antiquaries. Thomas Birch wrote in his memoir of Folkes that he brought to antiquities the "philosophical spirit, which he had contracted by the cultivation of the mathematical sciences . . . These talents appeared eminently upon the subjects of coins, weights and measures . . ." Folkes's *Table of English Silver Coins*, giving the grains and carats and physical descriptions of all the coins, reign by reign, was a showpiece of quantitative work in historical scholarship.[33]

As we have seen, De Moivre counted among his friends a good many eminent men of science. By and large, his "pupils," as opposed to his "friends," did not do work of the same distinction, but they hold an interest of another kind. That has to do with the diversity of their lives in mathematics: some made a living from it, some made it an avocation, some took jobs that required a grasp of numbers, and some, like Cavendish, took quantitative reasoning in directions of research in fields outside of mathematics.

James Dodson, the youngest of De Moivre's pupils, earned a good living through mathematics as an accountant, a teacher, and a writer of practical books. At the end of his life, he was master of the Royal Mathematical School at Christ's Hospital, in London, a coveted job (decided by interest as much as by merit; William Jones was passed over for it); his pupils—"Mathematicall children," Newton, one of the governors of this school, called them—were intended for the navy or trading companies.[34] Dodson extended his teaching and his income through books, dedicating the first volume of his *Mathematical Repository* to De Moivre and the third volume to a fellow pupil, Macclesfield. The *Repository* was a collection of questions and answers for "beginners," which meant that it was concerned with those problems of quantity that could be solved without the need of fluxions. The questions, some five hundred in all, reflect the practical concerns of the time, the unknowns in the algebraic expression of the questions standing for miles traveled, yards of cloth, wages, charitable contributions, gallons of beer, sizes of regiments, quantities of wheat, anhuities computed by compound interest, and numbers of fowl, sheep, servants, and gentlemen. The second volume of *Mathematical*

Repository (dedicated to David Papillon, of Huguenot descent, Fellow of the Royal Society, who confronted numbers in practice as one of the nine commissioners of the excise for England and Wales) introduces the doctrine of chances, the author of which (rather, of the first system of this doctrine in English), Dodson pointed out, was still living and was, of course, De Moivre. Of the many problems addressed by Dodson none was so interesting to his British readers as the problem of annuities and their reversions. That was understandable given the "great property invested in them": the "values of the possessions, and the reversions, of much the greatest part of the real estates in these kingdoms, will, one way or other, depend on the values of lives." In the year before, in a paper in the *Philosophical Transactions*, Dodson observed that the determination of property was of too great a practical importance to be left to "custom" and was properly the business of "calculation." The problem had been treated by Halley and soon after by De Moivre with his "truly admirable hypothesis, that the decrements of life may be esteemed nearly equal, after a certain age." Another of Dodson's publications was the *Anti-Logarithmic Canon*, designed to assist the serious calculator, a table of eleven-place anti-logarithms together with examples of its uses in interest, annuities, mensuration, and so forth. Mathematics was indeed useful, and logarithms were the greatest modern discovery in the "useful sciences,"[35] according to Dodson, one of the most active proponents of the mathematics-of-life of the first half of the eighteenth century.

---

[33]Thomas Birch, "Memoirs of the Life of Martin Folkes Esq. Late President of the Royal Society," BL Add Mss 6269, ff. 292–301, quotation on f. 300; Martin Folkes, *A Table of English Silver Coins from the Norman Conquest to the Present Time. With Their Weights, Intrinsic Values, and Some Remarks upon the Several Pieces* (London, 1745).

[34]Newton to Nathaniel Hawes, Treasurer to Christ's Hospital, 25 May 1694, in *The Correspondence of Isaac Newton*, vol 3, ed. H. W. Turnbull (Cambridge: Cambridge University Press, 1961), 357–67, on 358.

[35]James Dodson, *The Mathematical Repository. Containing Analytical Solutions of Five Hundred Questions, Mostly Selected from Scarce and Valuable Authors. Designed to Conduct Beginners to the More Difficult Properties of Numbers*, 3 vols. (London, 1748–55), quotation on 2:viii; James Dodson, "A Letter … Concerning an Improvement of the Bills of Mortality," *PT* 47 (1752): 333–40, on 335; *The Anti-Logarithmic Canon. Being a Table of Numbers Consisting of Eleven Places of Figures, Corresponding to All Logarithms under 100000* (London, 1742), quotation from the dedication. Various letters and editorial notes in *The Correspondence of Isaac Newton*, ed. H. W. Turnbull, vol. 2 (Cambridge: Cambridge University Press, 1960), 373–77. Taylor, *Mathematical Practitioners of Hanoverian England*, 174.

The next youngest of De Moivre's pupils, George Lewis Scott, was, like Papillon, one of the commissioners of excise and so a man of quantity and, as well, a barrister. Scott is remembered for his mathematical skill and his advice to his friend, the future author of *Decline and Fall of the Roman Empire*. Early in life, Edward Gibbon formed a new plan of study, hesitating between mathematics and Greek; upon consulting Scott ("a pupil of De Moivre," Gibbon noted in his autobiography), he gave his preference to Greek; Scott's "map of a country," by which Gibbon meant mathematics, "which I have never explored may perhaps be more serviceable to others." Upon reading the proofs of the first volume of *Decline and Fall*, Scott reassured Gibbon that when the book came out its readers would not be shocked, but they were. From his election in 1737, Scott was active in the Royal Society, and though he did not publish any mathematics in the *Philosophical Transactions*, he kept up his interest in mathematics privately. Naturally, he was drawn to the doctrine of chances: in a letter to Folkes, Scott wrote that "Matters of Chance are fertil in paralogisms," and the question Folkes had "mentioned the other Day about Whist has furnished me with examples enough." Scott provided Folkes with two sheets of probability calculations[36] and by that gift paid an implicit compliment to De Moivre.

The De Moivre pupils Charles Stanhope and Peter Davall were elected to the Royal Society in 1726 and 1740, respectively. Stanhope served as a Member of Parliament from a number of constituencies, and he held offices accountable for money (and was held accountable, being charged and nearly convicted during the South Sea bubble of using his office to make money on stock): under George I he was treasurer of the chamber and secretary to the treasury.[37] Davall published three papers in the *Philosophical Transactions* dealing with the sizes of cities, the distance of the sun, and an extraordinary rainbow; he seems to have made his mathematical services available to the Royal Society.[38] John Colson published three mathematical papers in the *Philosophical Transactions*, but his importance lies in his teaching; like Saunderson, he was Lucasian professor of mathematics, and as such he enters our discussion of science at Cambridge.

Two of De Moivre's pupils were especially important to the advance of science, the two aristocrats, George Parker, second earl of Macclesfield, and Lord Charles Cavendish. Macclesfield's father, as lord chancellor, was impeached by the House of Lords under a long list of articles, which taken together specify practically all the ways money can be misused. Before that, at the time he was installed, he was given a pension for his son until his son was old enough to become a teller for life of the exchequer, which he became in 1719. Like his father, Macclesfield studied law and became an M.P., but his first love was always the mathematical sciences. In addition to studying under De Moivre, he studied under William Jones, and he may have profited from still another Newtonian teacher, since he, like Folkes, studied at Clare Hall when Richard Laughton was there. He was elected to the Royal Society at age twenty-five, and he was promptly elected to the council, serving while Newton was still president. In 1752, the year he succeeded Folkes as president of the Royal Society, Macclesfield was instrumental in bringing about a famous practical application of astronomy, a change in the reckoning of history, the calendar. Friends and fellow pupils of De Moivre assisted him: Davall drew up the bill and made most of the tables, and Folkes examined the bill. In the calendar then in use, the new year began on 25 March, in the new style calendar, on 1 January; and it corrected for the accumulated errors in the calendar owing to the precession of the equinoxes by a one-time elimination of eleven days in September. Anyone who doubts the emotional power, as well as the power to bewilder, of numbers, has only to recall Macclesfield's unpopularity, which was visited upon the next generation; when running for a seat in Oxfordshire, his son was met by a mob crying, "Give us back the eleven days we have been robbed of." Macclesfield's private astronomical observatory was reputed to

[36] Joseph Timothy Haydn, *Book of Dignities: Continued to the Present Time (1894)*. . . , 3d ed., ed. N. and R. McWhirter (Baltimore: Geneological Publishing Co, 1970), 280–81. "Scott, George Lewis," *DNB* 17:961–62. *The Autobiography of Edward Gibbon*, ed. John Murray (London, 1896), 191. D. M. Low, *Edward Gibbon, 1737–1794* (London: Chatto & Windus, 1937), 262–63. Letter from George Lewis Scott to Martin Folkes, 25 Apr. 1744, Royal Society, Folkes Corr., Ms. 250, f. IV, 26.

[37] Ragnhild Hatton, *George I, Elector and King* (Cambridge, Mass: Harvard University Press, 1978), 255–56, 413.

[38] Davall evidently refereed mathematical papers for the Royal Society: Peter Davall to Thomas Birch, 11 Dec. 1754, BL Add Mss 4304, p. 128.

have the best equipment of any. He published three papers in the *Philosophical Transactions*, one on finding the time of Easter, one on an eclipse of the sun, and one on the temperature of Siberia; his importance for science was as an administrator and patron.[39] Lord Charles Cavendish's quantitative bent found its main outlet in experimental natural philosophy. His importance for science was primarily as an administrator, like Macclesfield, and as mentor to his son Henry Cavendish.

Royal Society

Early in June 1727, De Moivre's friend William Jones proposed the twenty-three year old Lord Charles Cavendish for fellowship in the Royal Society. Two weeks later, on 22 June, Cavendish was formally admitted.[40] At a meeting of the executive council of the Society on that same day, its president, Hans Sloane, raised the question of qualifications for admission of new members. By statute, as a son of a peer, Cavendish was treated as if he were a peer and had to furnish no proof of scientific achievement, ability, or even interest. Under English law, however, the sons of peers were commoners until they inherited the family title. To raise the standards of membership of the Society and reduce the exceptions to the general rules of admission, Sloane proposed to treat all commoners the same way with respect to requirements. The issue came to a head a few months later, in February 1728, when William Jones proposed yet another son of a peer. The members at large engaged in "Debates arising upon the sense of the Statute with Relation to peers Sons and privy Councellors whether any other Qualifications of such Gentlemen are required to be mentioned or not. . . ."[41] In the end, the Society changed some of its requirements for membership, but it let stand those for peers and sons of peers.[42]

Election to the Royal Society was the most important event in Lord Charles Cavendish's public life. For his son Henry it was decisive, for without his father in the Royal Society, it is hard to imagine the shy Henry entering science in any public way and, perhaps, doing science at all.

Cavendish may have been a pupil of De Moivre then, and he probably knew others of the circle who were elected at about this time, such as De Moivre's

friend Stirling, who was proposed in late 1726, and his pupil Stanhope who was admitted then.[43]

In 1727 Newton was still president of the Royal Society, and when he was absent, Folkes or Sloane took the chair in his place. Several members of the governing council were Newton's friends and, as we have noted, De Moivre's friends too. Halley, one of them, was especially active in the scientific discussions at the meetings. Folkes, Jones, and Bradley were on the council, as were the two secretaries of the Society, the physician and polymath James Jurin, a pupil of Newton's, and John Machin, an astronomer who Newton thought understood his *Principia* best of anyone, and who with Halley and Jones had been appointed to the committee on the discovery of the calculus. Other council members who had a close association with Newton were Richard Mead, physician and author of a Newtonian doctrine of animal economy, Thomas Pellet, a physician who with Folkes brought out an edition of Newton's *Chronology of Ancient Kingdoms* in the year after Newton's death, Henry Pemberton, who edited the third edition of Newton's *Principia*, and John Conduitt, husband of Newton's niece. Hans Sloane was a physician, natural historian, and good friend of Newton and Halley. Like Sloane, several members of the council were physicians with scientific interests: John Arbuthnot, Paul Bussiere, James Douglas, and Alexander Stuart. Roger Gale was a commissioner of excise. The one peer, Thomas Foley, who was repeatedly elected to the council, had an observatory at his country seat near Worcester, from which observations were sent to the Royal Society from time to time. Two members of the council repre-

———
[39]"Parker, Thomas, first Earl of Macclesfield," *DNB* 15: 278–82, on 280. "Parker, George, second Earl of Macclesfield," *DNB* 15: 234–35. *Collins's Peerage of England; Geneological, Biographical, and Historical*, 9 vols., ed. E. Brydges (London, 1812) 4:192–94. Macclesfield, then George Parker, was at Clare Hall apparently under the care of Francis Barnard, who reported to his father in 1716 on his progress; in the same year, Richard Laughton reported to Macclesfield's father about a college election. *Catalogue of the Stowe Manuscripts in the British Museum*, vol. 1 (London, 1895), 548–49. Charles Richard Weld, *A History of the Royal Society*, . . ., vol. 1 (New York: Arno Press, 1975), 432. In addition to Davall, James Bradley also examined the calendar bill and made some of the tables for it. *Miscellaneous Works and Correspondence of the Rev. James Bradley, D.D. F.R.S.*, ed. S. P. Rigaud (Oxford: Oxford University Press, 1832), lxxx–lxxxii.
[40]Royal Society, JB 13:103 and 107 (8 and 22 June 1727).
[41]Royal Society, JB 13:175 (8 Feb. 1727/28).
[42]Weld, *History* 1:461.
[43]Royal Society, JB 13:1 (27 Oct. 1726).

sented a distinctive British contribution to science in the eighteenth century, the making of scientific instruments. They were John Hadley, who was first to develop the reflecting telescope that Newton had introduced and who later introduced a reflecting octant (based on a proposal by Newton), and George Graham, to whom Bradley later said that his own success in astronomy had " principally been owing."[44] The governance of the Royal Society was entrusted to the makers of scientific instruments as well as to their users and to a good number of able mathematicians. This diversified and, by and large, eminent group of scientific men on the council enlarged Cavendish's world in 1727.

That year was an auspicious year to enter science. *Vegetable Staticks*, published by Stephen Hales in 1727, was the most impressive demonstration yet of the promise of Newton's philosophy to elucidate a new domain of facts. Educated at Cambridge, where he began experimenting on animal physiology, Hales continued his scientific studies while earning his living as a provincial cleric. Hales's great inspiration was Newton's *Opticks*, to which Newton appended his speculations about forces of attraction and repulsion between particles, with the help of which Hales investigated the composition of plants and the air "fixed" in plants. In early 1727 the chapter of his book on air was read to the Royal Society, after which Newton's handpicked experimenter Desaguliers repeated many of Hales's experiments before the Society. Hales had gone beyond his original enquiry into plants to conclude that air is in "all Natural Bodys" and is "one of the Principal Ingredients or Elements in the Composition of them." His experiments on fixed air laid the foundations of pneumatic chemistry, the field in which Lord Charles Cavendish's son Henry would make his greatest reputation. The full importance of *Vegetable Staticks* could not have been foreseen— it was to encourage a generation of experimental philosophers—but it was already appreciated, and Hales was made a member of the council of the Royal Society at the next election, at the end of 1727. Newton, who had presided during the final reading of Hales's chapter on air, died five weeks later, just shortly before Desaguliers' demonstration of experiments from that chapter.[45] The new member of the Society Lord Charles Cavendish was attracted to the physical sciences, to which

Hales's experiments on air came to be attached (and detached from their origin in plant physiology).[46]

Meetings of the Royal Society varied greatly in content and level of interest. On 8 June 1727, the day Cavendish was elected to the Society, Desaguliers performed another of Hales's experiments. Two weeks later, on the day he was admitted to the Society, Folkes brought in, and read about, tusks.[47] To appreciate Lord Charles's continuing education in science, we turn to matters that came up in the meetings at the time he began attending.

We begin with practical schemes. In 1627, exactly one hundred years before Lord Charles Cavendish entered the Royal Society, Francis Bacon's scientific utopia, *New Atlantis*, was published. Salomon's House, Bacon's projected cooperative scientific college, was the original inspiration for the Royal Society, which adopted the goal of Salomon's House, the "effecting of all things possible." The expectation was that the Royal Society, like Salomon's House, would advance human welfare through knowledge. That one hundred years after *New Atlantis* the claims for the utility of a scientific society could still be seen as belonging to the realm of utopia is shown by a savage satire on the Royal Society. Just two years before Cavendish was elected to the Royal Society, Jonathan Swift wrote the third book of *Gulliver's Travels*, in which the Royal Society, renamed the Academy of Lagado, labors to extract sunbeams from cucumbers to warm the air on cold days. The source of this ridicule was, evidently, Hales's recent

---

[44]Bradley's words, from 1747, in Taylor, *Mathematical Practitioners of Hanoverian England*, 120–21.

[45]Stephen Hales, *Vegetable Staticks: Or, an Account of Some Statical Experiments on the Sap in Vegetables. . . Also, a Specimen of an Attempt to Analyze the Air . . .* (London, 1727). Henry Guerlac, "Hales, Stephen," *DSB*: 6: 35–48, on 35–36, 41–43. References to the reading of Hales's discourse on air and to Desaguliers' repetition of experiments from it, in Royal Society, JB 13:44 (2 Feb. 1726/27), 45 (9 Feb. 1726/27), 48–50, quote on 48–49 (16 Feb. 1726/27), 70 (13 Apr. 1727), 74 (20 Apr. 1727), 83 (4 May 1727), 103 (8 June 1727), 144 (16 Nov. 1727). Newton's death caused the cancellation of the Society's meeting on 23 March 1726/27: Royal Society, JB 13:62.

[46]Insofar as publication in the *Philosophical Transactions* is a measure, the physical sciences were a serious but not dominating concern of the Royal Society at the time Cavendish was elected to it. What we might call *greater physics*, including mechanics, meteorology, and various border subjects of our modern physics, accounted for about a third of the papers appearing in the *Philosophical Transactions*. The absolute numbers of papers are very small. John L. Heilbron, *Physics at the Royal Society During Newton's Presidency* (Los Angeles: William Andrews Clark Memorial Library, 1983), 43.

[47]Royal Society, JB 13:103 and 107 (8 and 22 June 1727).

experiments on plant and animal respiration. To Swift, who was disgusted by everything the Royal Society stood for, Bacon's optimism, projects, experiments, the Newtonian philosophy, the disparity between a utopian faith and the reality of life was self-evident. Whatever its logic, however, Swift's satire was lost on the world of science. At a meeting three months before Cavendish entered the Royal Society, a letter was read from the secretary of the newly founded academy at Petersburg, giving the plan of the academy, which largely followed that of the academies at Paris and Berlin, which in turn had profited from that of the original, the Royal Society of London. Moreover, like its predecessors, the Petersburg academy would be interested in cultivating learning and as well in improving medicine and encouraging inventions.[48] Observers as intelligent as Swift could disagree with Bacon. To us, looking back, it seems doubtful that Bacon's inspiration did anything directly to advance technology, but it seems equally likely that it did stimulate scientific activity. The proceedings of the Royal Society would seem to bear this out.

The Royal Society did not distinguish between basic scientific understanding and its applications, as is evident from the examples that follow. The first is from medicine and public health. Inoculation against smallpox, which had long been practiced in the East, had just been introduced in Britain when Cavendish entered the Royal Society. The eminent London physician and secretary of the Royal Society James Jurin enthusiastically supported it in the face of opposition from doubting physicians and clerics. The operation did carry risk to the community as well as to the patient, but so did this disfiguring and killing epidemic disease, and Jurin argued with figures that the risk of inoculation was less than that of exposure. In the second year, the royal children were inoculated (after the operation had been tried, at royal request, on several condemned criminals, without loss of any). In time inoculation came to be widely practiced in Britain, if more so in the countryside than in the cities. (Deaths by smallpox continued to figure large in London bills of mortality throughout the century; it is not known if Lord Charles and Henry Cavendish were inoculated but only that they escaped or survived this scourge. At the time Lord Charles left London for his first

visit to Paris, his sister Lady Elizabeth wrote that "the small pox continues here very fatal."[49])

Inoculation was based on an empirical observation—a mild form of smallpox often prevented a serious infection—which insured that it would become a topic of interest in the Royal Society. From far and near, Jurin received reports of inoculations written up methodically in columns, like weather reports, with which they had a connection. The cause engaged other Fellows of the Royal Society too, such as the physician who inoculated the seven condemned criminals, Richard Mead, who in 1727 was appointed physician to the king and reelected to the council of the Royal Society. The subject of smallpox inoculation recurred in the meetings of the Society in 1727, and controversial as it was at the time, it offered a glimpse into Baconian paradise to those who believed. Despite Jurin's best efforts, in Britain inoculation fell into disfavor owing to deaths in prominent families. It revived in the 1740s as a remunerative surgical practice, but the true paradise began to be realized only at the end of the eighteenth century, when the English physician Edward Jenner introduced cowpox vaccination, the safe method of controlling smallpox, which he came upon in the course of his practice of giving original smallpox inoculations. (George III, who was roughly Henry Cavendish's age, was given Jenner's cowpox vaccination.) Medicine was a large concern of Lord Charles Cavendish's Royal Society, and although it did not happen to be one of his own, he was an active and long-time governor of the Foundling Hospital where his good friend William Watson regularly gave smallpox inoculations and where he made an important scientific investigation of competing methods of inoculation.[50]

Technology too was a concern of the Royal Society in the early eighteenth century. For industry

---

[48]Francis Bacon, *New Atlantis*, published 1627. Jonathan Swift, *Gulliver's Travels and Other Writings*, ed. M. K. Starkman (New York: Bantam Books, 1962), 177. Royal Society, JB 13:52 (2 Mar. 1726/27).

[49]Lady Elizabeth Cavendish to Lord James Cavendish, 24 Apr. /1721/, Devon. Coll., no. 166.1.

[50]Royal Society JB 13: 148 (7 Dec. 1727), 191 (7 Mar. 1727/28), 198 (21 Mar. 1727/28), 210 (11 Apr. 1728). "Jurin, James," *DNB* 10: 1117–18, on 1118. Leonard G. Wilson, "Jenner, Edward," *DSB* 7: 95–97, on 96. William H. McNeill, *Plagues and Peoples* (New York: History Book Club, 1993; first published 1976), 249–50. After 1800, smallpox mortality in London fell to one half of what it had been in the eighteenth century. Charles Creighton, *A History of Epidemics in Britain*. Vol. 2: *From the Extinction of the Plague to the Present Time*, 2d ed. (London: Frank Cass, 1965), 479–81, 504, 568.

and for domestic heating, coal was increasingly essential, since the forests were becoming depleted and with them the alternative to coal, namely, wood and charcoal. Mining was hazardous because of the accumulation of unbreathable and inflammable air in the pits. Two weeks before Cavendish's election to the Royal Society, its curator of experiments, Desaguliers, reported on his invention to remove unhealthy air from mines. With a working model of it, one inch to the foot, he gave a demonstration, which he called the Sir Godfrey Copley's Experiment.[51] (This was the annual experiment named after a benefactor of the Society; four years later, in 1731, Copley's legacy would be used to fund the Copley Award, which both Lord Charles and Henry Cavendish would receive for their scientific work.)

Britain was a maritime country, to which fact the Royal Society was constantly being recalled. Ships were lost or delayed because navigators did not know their position relative to the neighboring land. Nicolas Fatio de Dullier, Newton's close friend, presented the Society with a theorem for calculating latitude at sea and a copy of his book on the subject, *Navigation Improved*. Latitude could be known by taking the altitude of the sun or a star, but longitude was not that simple. The Greenwich Observatory was founded in 1675 to perfect astronomical tables for finding longitude, but the tables did not work for ships. To secure the safety of ships and to promote trade, in 1714 parliament passed an act providing rewards for improvements in taking longitude at sea proportional to their accuracy. The ultimate reward, 20,000 pounds, a fortune, was to be paid to the discoverer of a method that could, on a six-week journey to the West Indies, give the longitude upon arrival within an accuracy of thirty miles. To evaluate proposals, the Board of Longitude was established, with Newton on it. The Board was quickly innundated; before a parliamentary committee, Newton rejected all of the proposals, which added glory to fortune as an incentive to future inventors. The Royal Society was brought in as a source of expert opinion on proposals, and Lord Charles Cavendish advised on the marine clocks submitted by the man who eventually won (nearly) the jackpot, John Harrison. Joining science, invention, and utility, the problem of longitude at sea made an ideal subject for the Royal Society, where it came up repeatedly around

the time of Cavendish's election. Halley, for example, a commissioner of the Board of Longitude and champion of an astronomical method of determining longitude at sea, criticized a book on longitude referred to him by the Society: the author, Halley said, made two mistakes, one in thinking his method was original, the other in assuming what did not yet exist, "a true Theory of the Moons Motion." For Halley, what was needed for the astronomical solution of the problem was more science. There were as well other practical problems of the sea, such as measuring its depth and mapping its coasts, and the Royal Society heard about them all.[52]

The atmosphere of the earth was another kind of sea, with problems as daunting. In 1724, in the name of the Royal Society, James Jurin had invited meteorological observations kept according to a plan, and around the time of Cavendish's election, the Society was receiving weather journals from abroad in considerable numbers. These systematic observations of everyday weather were in addition to the usual occasional observations of the spectacular events of the atmosphere, great cold spells, aroras, and the like.[53] The weather was one of Lord Charles Cavendish's major scientific interests, as it would be Henry's later.

Like Hales's fixed air, electricity at the beginning of the eighteenth century was a relatively new field of experimental study. Electricity had no immediate utility, but it did pose scientifically intriguing questions. Desaguliers alternated his demonstrations of Hales's experiments on air with experiments on the communication of electrical virtue to a glass tube as shown by the attraction and repulsion of fibers of a feather and of gold leaves. Within a year of Cavendish's election, Desaguliers announced that Stephen Gray intended to bring before the Society experiments showing that rubbed glass communicates its electrical

[51]Desaguliers published the experiments on his model pump for damps: "An Attempt Made Before the Royal Society, to Shew How Damps, or Foul Air, May Be Drawn Out of Any Sort of Mines, etc. by an Engine Contriv'd by the Reverend J. T. Desaguliers, L.L.D. and F.R.S.," *PT* 34 (1727): 353–56.
[52]Royal Society, JB 13:168–69 (25 Jan. 1727/28), 84 (11 May 1727), 113 (29 June 1727), 302 (4 May 1727), 214 (2 May 1728), 232 (20 June 1728), 287 (23 Jan. 1728/29). Humphrey Quill, *John Harrison: The Man Who Found Longitude* (London: John Baker, 1966), 1–6.
[53]Royal Society, JB 13:34–36 (12 Jan. 1726/7), and many other places.

quality to any body connected to it by a string.[54] It is indicative of the state of electrical knowledge that Gray was the first to describe explicitly electrical conduction and to distinguish between conducting and non-conducting bodies. Lord Charles Cavendish would take up this new field of electrical conduction, and Henry Cavendish would work out its basic laws.

The full range of topics discussed at the Royal Society around 1727 was, of course, much greater than these examples suggest. From the side of medicine, there were reports on stones, cataracts, and aneurisms. There were accounts of coconuts, cinnamon, and poison snakes from the side of natural history (and from the far-flung British colonies). Fossils and other natural collectibles and curious specimens were displayed at the meetings. Two-headed calves and various other monstrous productions were as common at the Royal Society as they were uncommon in nature. Fellows travelling abroad wrote home or brought back information about everything having to do with science. Investigative natural reporting of singular disasters such as earthquakes was given as often as opportunity permitted. Correspondence was read, books were received, guests were introduced, and, in general, the Society served its members as a great clearing house for scientific news. Except for the formalities, the meetings were kept lively by the variety of their proceedings. Here is a typical offering. John Byrom, Fellow of the Royal Society and frequent attender, noted in his journal persons and topics at the meeting on 27 February 1728/29: "Vernon there from Cambridge; Dr. Ruty read about ignis fatuus; humming bird's nest and egg, mighty small; Molucca bean, which somebody had sent to Dr. Jurin for a stone taken out of a toad's head; Desaguliers made some experiments about electricity."[55] That night there was something for just about everybody, and Byrom ran it all together in his journal. Within the Society there was a kind of democracy of interests. When one interest was perceived to be systematically favored, allegations could fly; Henry Cavendish would be caught up in them.

When Lord Charles Cavendish became a Fellow, the Society wore two crowns, one scientific, one royal. We begin with the scientific. Newton had just died, but he lived on in the causes that continued to be championed in his name. Thomas Derham wrote to the Society from Rome about a

book by an Italian that "pretends" to refute propositions in Newton's *Opticks*; Desaguliers responded to the perceived danger. The dispute over whether the measure of force is the velocity, as Newton said, or the square of the velocity, as foreign mathematicians said, was settled by Desaguliers (he thought) by experiment and was adjudicated by Jurin, who regarded it as a mere dispute arising from an ambiguity in the meaning of the word force. Andrew Motte presented to the Society his English translation of Newton's *Principia*, and William Jones was asked to look it over and give the society an account of it.[56] As to the royal crown, in the year Newton died and Cavendish entered the Society, King George I died, and his successor to the throne, George II, agreed to succeed him as well in the role of patron of the Royal Society. The change in monarchs entailed considerable ceremony and protocol, the carrying of the charter book to St. James's for the royal signature, the making of an address, the paying of compliments to the queen. There was also a change of heir to the crown. The new prince of Wales, Frederick, became a member of the Royal Society, an honor which was commemorated by the dedication to him of the volume of the *Philosophical Transactions* for 1728. That year Lord Charles Cavendish became gentleman of the bedchamber to Frederick.[57]

Below the rank of royalty, but not far, within the dukedom of the Devonshires, another succession was about to occur. But for the time being, as Charles Cavendish entered the Royal Society, his father, the second duke of Devonshire, was still alive and the owner of a great loadstone, supported in a fine mahogany case and raised by screws, which came up in discussion at the Royal Society a few months after Cavendish was elected. This magnet had prodigious force, as Folkes bore witness, having seen it lift "more than its own weight."[58] In 1730 the magnet was produced again, this time by

[54]Royal Society, JB 13: 307 (27 Feb. 1728/29), 316 (13 Mar. 1728/29), 330 (1 May 1729).

[55]John Byrom, *The Private Journal and Literary Remains of John Byrom*, ed. R. Parkinson, 2 vols. in 4 parts (Manchester, 1854–57), vol. l, part l, p. 334 (27 Feb. 1728/29).

[56]Royal Society, JB 13:175–76 (8 Feb. 1727/28), 242 (4 July 1728), 251 (24 Oct. 1728), 252 (31 Oct. 1728), 257 (7 Nov. 1728), 262 (14 Nov. 1728), 339–40 (22 May 1729), 341 (5 June 1729).

[57]Royal Society, JB 13:86 (11 May 1727), 114 (6 July 1727).

[58]Royal Society, JB 13:314 (13 Mar. 1728), 18:400 (25 Apr. 1745). William Dugood, F.R.S., who built this magnet for the duke, built an even bigger one for the king of Portugal.

Desaguliers, who showed the Society experiments with it including lifting 175 pounds.[59] With this, the "famous Great Loadstone of his Grace the Duke of Devonshire," we conclude our account of Lord Charles Cavendish's introduction to the Royal Society. This magnet, with its remarkable powers, might be taken here to have a double meaning, physical and political, and to imply, if fancifully, a third and prophetic scientific meaning through the duke's son and grandson, Lord Charles and Henry Cavendish.

Later we take up Lord Charles Cavendish's work in science, but here we should mention his earliest recorded observations and their circumstances. More or less coinciding with his election to the Royal Society, they foretell the kind of member he will be.

Although the experimental fields of pneumatic chemistry and electricity were under-way around the time Lord Charles Cavendish joined the Royal Society, the incontrovertible achievements in the physical sciences continued to be in the exact sciences. Cavendish began his scientific work in conjunction with James Bradley, a practicing astronomer of world renown, who was on the eve of his momentous discovery of the aberration of light from the stars.

In June 1728 Cavendish made zenith observations at Bradley's observatory at Wansted with a telescope for detecting the parallax of the fixed stars.[60] The instrument had been in place for less than a year, and after Bradley himself, and then Halley, Cavendish was the next person to observe with it. Later that year, in the course of looking for the parallax, Bradley made his discovery of the aberration of light.

This was a great discovery. With his new instrument Bradley observed the small motions of stars passing nearly through the zenith, motions which he knew were too large and in the wrong direction to be caused by the parallax of the fixed stars. In 1729 Bradley had found the answer: the motion of the zenith stars was the resultant of two motions, that of the orbital motion of the earth and that of light. In his announcement of Bradley's

discovery of the aberration of light to the Society, Halley remarked that the "three Grand Doctrines in the Modern Astronomy do receive a Great Light and Confirmation from this one Single Motion of the Stars Vizt. The Motion of the Earth. The Motion of Light and the immense distance of the Stars." Bradley had, in fact, provided the first direct evidence of the motion of the earth, i.e., of the Copernican theory, and twenty-four year-old Lord Charles Cavendish had had a connection, however slight, with this great work of observation and reasoning in astronomy.[61]

Cavendish's observations at Wansted are only the first of his many connections with Bradley. This is the appropriate place to cite another, since it brings together Cavendish, Bradley, and members of the De Moivre circle, the starting point of our discussion of Cavendish in London science. Macclesfield, father and son—the lord chancellor and the president of the Royal Society—were patrons and friends of Bradley throughout his life. In 1732 Bradley moved from Wansted to Oxford, which was only a few miles from Macclesfield's home at Shirburn castle. There, in Macclesfield's observatory, he and Macclesfield regularly made observations together. When Bradley became a candidate to succeed Halley as astronomer royal, Macclesfield exerted his influence, only he had to do it indirectly, since his voting had put him out of favor with the court. To build scientific support for Bradley, Macclesfield wrote to William Jones to ask him to enlist Folkes and Lord Charles Cavendish. Here, at this important juncture in Bradley's career, we come across a constellation of De Moivre's friends and pupils, now all prominent figures in the Royal Society.[62]

---

[59] Royal Society, JB 13:454 (9 Apr. 1730). The magnet remained within the family, passing from the second duke to his brother Lord James Cavendish, F.R.S.

[60] Bradley, *Miscellaneous Works*, 237.

[61] Royal Society, JB 13:260–62, quotation on 262 (14 Nov. 1728).

[62] Lord Macclesfield to William Jones, 13 Jan. 1741/42; Lord Macclesfield to Lord Hardwicke, 14 Jan. 1741/42, in Bradley, *Miscellaneous Works*, xlvi and xlvii, respectively.

CHAPTER 3

❧

*F*amily and Friends

Marriage and Money

In January 1728/29, Lord Charles Cavendish married Lady Anne de Grey, daughter of the duke of Kent. Cavendish was very young, in his middle twenties instead of in his middle thirties, a much commoner age for younger sons of nobility to marry.[1] He could afford to take this step in life early because he was a son of the duke of Devonshire and a son-in-law of the duke of Kent, who had a lesser estate than the duke of Devonshire, but who was ambitious for his family and, in particular, for advantageous marriages for his daughters. We know nothing of the affection between Charles and Anne, but in any case, wealth, rank, and respectability were probably the governing considerations in this match.

Financial arrangements made at the time of marriages within the nobility in eighteenth-century England took a standard form. In each generation the essential provisions for the family were settled on the occasion of the eldest son's marriage, and these were always directed to ensuring that the family estate descended to him for his life. The supreme object of favoring the eldest son was to prevent the dispersal of the estate owing to whim, greed, enmity, or debauchery, which meant that the daughters and younger sons had to be helped financially in ways other than by inheritance of the family estate. In 1723 the lord chancellor, Macclesfield, ruled that under the law, equity placed younger children "on a level with creditors, taking it to be a debt by nature from a father to provide for all his children."[2] In practice, the otherwise complete freedom of parents in providing for the younger children was constrained only by the assumption that the settlement would be sufficient to allow the younger sons to live independently and the daughters to marry well. The independence of Lord Charles Cavendish and his brother Lord James, the other younger son, was securely established by the second duke of Devonshire.[3]

It was standard for younger sons at the time of their marriage or coming of age to receive capital sums and often also annuities or rent charges. Daughters at the time of their marriage were given dowries, or portions, and in the event of their husbands' deaths, widows were supported by annual incomes, or jointures. Marriage settlements also specified the fortunes that would go to the eventual children of the marriage. Numbers of children and combinations of sexes and possible orders of deaths were all taken into account, as nothing in matters of such importance was left to chance.

Like their parents' marriage settlement, that of Lord Charles and Lady Anne conformed to the pattern. It was customary for wives to provide for their younger sons. Lady Anne's father, the duke of Kent, at his death left 12,000 pounds to her and through her to her children, 2,000 pounds to the oldest child and 10,000 pounds to the others, in this case, to the only younger child, Frederick. Lord Charles's mother, Rachel, duchess of Devonshire, had left the bulk of her personal estate to him and to her other younger son, Lord James. Lord Charles's marriage portion was 6,000 pounds in Bank of England stock, 2,000 pounds in South Sea stock, and 4,000 pounds in South Sea annuities, a total of 12,000 pounds on paper. From her father, Lady Anne acquired her portion, 10,000 pounds. The two portions of 12,000 and 10,000 pounds, in the form of securities, were transferred to trustees of the marriage settlement, who raised 17,000 pounds by the sale of the securities for the purchase of the estate of George Warburton. This estate consisted of three manors, Putteridge, Lilley, and Hackwellbury, together with several farms,

---

[1]Lawrence Stone, *The Family, Sex and Marriage in England 1500–1800*, abr. ed. (Harmondsworth: Penguin Books, 1982), 42.

[2]Quoted in Randolph Trumbach, *The Rise of the Egalitarian Family: Aristocratic Kinship and Domestic Relations in Eighteenth-Century England* (New York: Academic Press, 1978), 87.

[3]Ibid., 89–90.

located directly north of London, at about half the distance of Cambridge, in the adjacent counties of Bedford and Hertford. Putteridge Manor would become the first and only home of Lord Charles and Lady Anne. From her father, Lady Anne, as one of four sisters, also received one quarter part of his estate at Steane, the rents from which were vested in trustees for Anne's separate use during her marriage. She was also given the power to leave these rents as she willed, and she left them (or their equivalent in stock, as it turned out, since the Steane estate was sold in 1744) to Frederick. The married couple would have a home, Lady Anne's personal expenses would be provided for, and the children's needs anticipated.[4]

What remained was for Lord Charles to be assured an income that would enable him and his family to live in appropriate comfort; this was seen to by Lord Charles's father. Younger sons of the aristocracy customarily received 300 pounds a year, which is what Lord Charles had been receiving from his father since 1725.[5] His father intended for the annuity to be raised to 500 pounds at his death, but he moved the plan ahead: starting in 1728, with his marriage, Lord Charles would receive 500 pounds annually. In addition his father granted him the interest on 6,000 pounds and eventually the capital itself.[6]

That was not all. In eighteenth-century society, in which "men were measured by their acres,"[7] nothing could compare with ownership of land for imparting a sense of independence. Following a practice that had been commoner in the seventeenth century than in the eighteenth, the second duke of Devonshire devolved property (a crumb, relatively speaking) on Charles Cavendish and his heirs. These were tithes, rectories, and lands in Nottinghamshire and in Derbyshire. Having been promised them in 1717, Lord Charles received the rents in 1728 and the inheritance the following year; the marriage settlement directed that from these rents Lady Anne was to receive one hundred pounds a year for their joint lives. At the beginning the rents brought in over a thousand pounds a year, and after the enclosures of the 1760s and 1770s they increased considerably. Since for some years to come, these rents would provide an important contribution to Lord Charles's income, he took good care of this property. There was one last provision of the marriage settlement from

which Lord Charles would benefit: after the duke of Kent died, in 1740, Lord Charles received interest on 12,000 pounds left to Lady Anne's trustees. From his mid twenties, Lord Charles Cavendish could count on a disposable annual income of between 2000 and 3000 pounds, and this income grew steadily. To give an idea of what this meant: Samuel Johnson, a professional man, who rarely made above 300 pounds, thought that 50 pounds was "undoubtedly more than the necessities of life require"; and a gentleman lived comfortably on 500 pounds and a squire on 1000 pounds. Cavendish's income enabled him to live very well indeed, invest in stock, and acquire books and instruments and generally support his scientific pursuits. It permitted his son Henry to do the same, and, at the same time, it laid the foundation of Henry's fortune.[8] Within the conventional financial arrangements of wealthy English families of the time, the Cavendishes and the Greys combined to create what was in effect a scientific endowment for Lord Charles and Henry Cavendish.

Before his marriage, Cavendish evidently kept a residence in Westminster.[9] Immediately upon his marriage, as we have seen, in February 1729 he

---

[4]Devon. Coll., L/19/33 and L/5/69.

[5]This financial detail would seem to settle the birthdate or, at least, the year of birth of Lord Charles Cavendish, on which we were indefinite earlier. On 6 April 1725 his father gave him the annuity; we think he was twenty-one on this occasion, which would suggest that his birthdate was on or near 6 April 1725. But that is not right, since, as we have pointed out, his mother was expecting a baby in July 1725. Lord Charles needed an income in April because he was about to be returned as M.P. for Heytesbury on 13 April that year.

[6]The 500 pounds and 6,000 pounds were determined by a much earlier family settlement, of 1678.

[7]J. H. Plumb, *Men and Centuries* (Boston: Houghton Mifflin, 1963), 72.

[8]Devon. Coll., L/5/69, L/13/8, L/19/20, L/19/31, L/19,33, L/78/2, L/114/32. Charles Cavendish also received a legacy of 1,000 pounds from his father: Chatsworth, 86/ comp 1. There is some discrepancy between the description of the marriage settlement we give from the legal documents and what Charles Cavendish jotted down in a short abstract of the settlement, but it is minor: Devon. Coll., L/114/74. H. J. Habakkuk, "Marriage Settlements in the Eighteenth Century," *Transactions of the Royal Historical Society* 32 (1950): 15–30, on 15–16, 18, 20–24. George Rudé, *Hanoverian London, 1714–1808* (Berkeley: University of California Press, 1971), 48, 61.

[9]We know nothing about this residence other than that it was probably substantial. Cavendish appeared on the poor rolls of Westminster Parish of St. Margaret's in 1728; he paid 5.5.0 annually, which is what the duke of Kent paid and a quarter of what the duchess of Devonshire paid. Westminster Public Libraries, Westminster Collection, Accession no. 10, Document no. 343.

acquired the country manor of Putteridge and the other manors and farms that came with it, from which he would have received rents. In 1730 he sold a rectory, which was appended to one of these manors, Lilley, to the master and fellows of St. John's College, Cambridge (with which college he would later have scientific connections). There is every reason to believe that he planned to stay at Putteridge and raise his family there, in which case if it had not been for his wife's early death, the still countrified site of Putteridge would be hallowed ground in the history of science.

When Lord Charles and Lady Anne moved to Putteridge, Charles had an active life in the city, in court, in politics, and in science; in 1729, the year of his marriage, he had already begun to serve on committees of the Royal Society.[10] A portrait of Lord Charles Cavendish shows a handsome young man of slender build and medium dark complexion, with a long, narrow face, a long nose, full lips, prominent eyes, and an alert expression. We have two portraits of Lady Anne, one of her together with two of her sisters, and one of her by herself and somewhat older. She is slender with a round face, wide-set, intelligent eyes, high, rounded eyebrows, and straight nose. At the time of these portraits she was evidently in good health, which was not to last.

There is evidence that Lady Anne was not strong before her marriage,[11] and in any case, in the winter one year later, she was ill. Sophia, duchess of Kent, her step-mother, wrote to her father, the duke, that she had just dined at the Cavendishes: "Poor Lady Anne does not seem so well as when I saw her last. Her spirits are mighty low and she has no stomach at all. She has no return of spitting blood nor I don't think she coughs more than she did so that I hope this is only a disorder upon her nerves that won't last."[12] The next winter, 1730/31, was bitterly cold, colder—William Derham, F.R.S., wrote to the president of the Royal Society—than the winter of 1716, when the Thames froze over.[13] That winter, we believe, Lord Charles and Lady Anne went abroad. From Paris Lady Anne wrote to her father that in Calais she had been very ill with a "great cold" and that she had been blooded and kept low to prevent fever. She did not expect to see much of Paris for fear of being cold, and in any case they were about to leave the city for Nice.[14] Nice (where the yearly mean temperature is 60

degrees, in winter 49 degrees and in summer 72 degrees) was much milder than London, where—to use Lord Charles's own, later twenty-year averages—the mean minimum temperature in January is 34.7 degrees and the mean minimum temperature in July is 55.6 degrees (and the mean temperatures, not minimums, are 37 degrees and 63.5 degrees, respectively). The combination of sun and sea has given Nice a reputation for being especially suited for people convalescing from acute lung ailments.[15] In all likelihood, Lord Charles and Lady Anne went there for the weather and the waters because of Anne's health. They definitely did not go as conventional tourists, for although Nice did become popular with English tourists, that did not happen until the second half of the eighteenth century. In 1731 Charles Cavendish was the only Englishman to stay in Nice who did not have commercial or diplomatic ties there. The only permanent English resident was the consul, who did double service as an English spy on the French.[16] About three months after leaving Paris, Lady Anne conceived. In Nice, on Sunday, 31 October 1731, she gave birth to her first child, named after her father, Henry de Grey. No birthplace could be less predictive: beginning life in a sleepy Mediterranean town of about 16,000 inhabitants situated amongst olive groves, Henry

---

[10]On 17 July 1729 Cavendish was appointed to a committee to inspect the library and the collections and deliver reports; it met every Thursday from 24 July until 6 November 1729, and on 11 December it was ordered to continue its work. Royal Society, Minutes of Council 3:28–30, 34–36, 39, 55–56, 114–16.

[11]In the summer before Lady Anne's marriage, the house accounts for the duke of Kent repeatedly record "Chair hire for Lady Ann." None of the duke's other daughters required chairs then. "July 1728. House Account. To yᵉ 28 December 1728," Bedfordshire Record Office, Wrest Park Collection, L 31/200/1.

[12]Sophia, duchess of Kent to Henry, duke of Kent, 21 Feb. 1729/30, Bedfordshire Record Office, Wrest Park Collection, L 30/8/39/3.

[13]William Derham, "A Letter . . . Concerning the *Frost* in *January*, 1730/1," *PT* 37 (1731; published 1733): 16–18.

[14]Lady Anne Cavendish to Henry, duke of Kent, 4 Nov. /1730?/, Bedfordshire Record Office, Wrest Park Collection, L 30/8/11/1.

[15]"Nice," *Encyclopaedia Britannica* (Chicago: William Benton, 1962) 16:414–15. Lord Charles Cavendish's twenty-year averages of his readings of nighttime lows in London are included in William Heberden, "A Table of the Mean Heat of Every Month for Ten Years in London, from 1763 to 1772 Inclusively," *PT* 78 (1788): 66.

[16]Henri Costamagna, "Nice au XVIIIᵉ siècle: présentation historique et géographique," *Annales de la Faculté des Lettres et Sciences Humaines de Nice*, no. 19, 1973, pp. 7–28, on p. 26. Daniel Féliciangeli, "Le développement de Nice au cours de la seconde moitié de XVIIIᵉ siècle. Les anglais à Nice," ibid., pp. 45–67, on pp. 55–56. Anon., *Les Anglais dans le Comté de Nice et en Provence depuis le XVIIIᵐᵉ siècle* (Nice: Musée Masséna, 1934), 72.

Cavendish grew up to be one of the most confirmed Londoners ever.

The next stage of Lord Charles and Lady Anne's marriage is short and ends sadly. A year and a half had passed since they had left England, and they were now back in France, in Lyon, from where in the summer of 1732 she wrote to her father about her health and happiness. It was with her usual perfected penmanship, the letters large, uniform, and inclined at precisely the same angle, but her hand was unsteady, like that of an elderly person. Nevertheless, her letter home begins with reassurances: her fever had not returned, and she was so far recovered that she and Lord Charles were going to Geneva the next day, a three-day trip. If she handled that well, they would stay there only two or three days and then go directly to Leyden. She did not know when they could return to England. Lady Anne closed the letter with word of her baby, Henry. "I thank God," she wrote, "my boy is very well and his being so very strong and healthy gives me a pleasure I cannot easyly express."[17]

The Cavendishes were going to Leyden to see the great teacher and healer Hermann Boerhaave. Although Boerhaave was nearing the end of his career at the University of Leyden, where he taught medicine and, until recently, botany and chemistry alongside it, in 1732 he was still lecturing on the theory and practice of medicine and giving clinical instruction. He had written influential treatises on medicine and was, by many accounts, the most famous physician in the world, if not the most famous scientist since Newton. His ties with British medicine and, in general, with British science were particularly close. From all parts of the world but especially from Britain, students came to Leyden to attend his lectures: of the nearly two thousand students enrolled in Leyden's medical faculty, fully one third were English-speaking. British physicians who had studied under Boerhaave consulted him when their treatment of aristocratic or otherwise important patients had not worked. Prominent British travelers went to Leyden to see Boerhaave, often but not always about their health.[18] For his part, Boerhaave was a tremendous admirer of British experimental philosophy and one of the first exponents of Newtonianism in Europe. He was elected to the Royal Society in 1730. For all these reasons, it was natural for the well-informed Lord

Charles Cavendish to seek out Boerhaave's services for his wife. Lady Anne told her father that they thought it would be right for Dr. Boerhaave to "see me pretty often in order to make a right judgment of my illness." No other letters by her have been found, so we do not know what Boerhaave said and prescribed.[19] Tuberculosis was a common disease for which medicine then, of course, had no cure.

At some point Lord Charles and Lady Anne returned to England. Three months after her consultation with Boerhaave, Lady Anne was well enough to conceive again, and on 24 June 1733 she delivered another son, Frederick, named after his sponsor, the prince of Wales. The next we hear is that Lady Anne Cavendish died at Putteridge on 20 September 1733.[20] She was twenty-seven. Henry was not quite two years, Frederick was three months, and Lord Charles was around twenty-nine. In Lord Charles's station, remarriage was uncommon, and he would live for fifty years as a widower.

Although for someone like Lady Anne Cavendish who lived into her twenties, life expectancy was over sixty in the eighteenth century, life then at any age was precarious. Hygiene was unknown, medicine was helpless, and death was indifferent to privilege. Henry and Frederick Cavendish grew up with one parent, which was a common fate under the prevailing conditions of life.[21]

Great Marlborough Street

In 1738 Lord Charles Cavendish sold Putteridge together with the rest of the estate purchased by his trustees at the time of his marriage. The deal was not straightforward though it was not uncommon either. For the trustees to be empowered to make the sale, an act of parliament had to be passed, and for that, a reason had to be given for wanting it. Putteridge, Cavendish said,

---

[17]Lady Anne Cavendish to Henry, duke of Kent, 22 June /1732/, Bedfordshire Record Office, Wrest Park Collection, L 30/8/11/2.

[18]A typical example from this time: Bolingbroke wrote to his half-sister Henrietta from Totterdam: "I was yesterday at Leyden to talk with Doctor Boorehaven, and am now ready to depart for Aix-la-Chapelle . . ." Letter of 17 Aug. 1729, in Walter Sichel, *Bolingbroke and His Times: The Sequel* (New York: Greenwood, 1968), 525.

[19]G. A. Lindeboom, *Boerhaave and Great Britain* (Leiden: E. J. Brill, 1974), 18; "Boerhaave, Hermann," *DSB* 2:224–28. .

[20]Four days later, on 24 Sep. 1733, Lady Anne Cavendish was buried in the Kent family vault at Flitton. "Extracts from the Burial Register of Flitton," Bedfordshire Record Office, Wrest Park Collection, L 31/43.

[21]Stone, *Family*, 46–48, 54, 58–59.

was too remote from the rest of his estate, whatever he meant by that. No doubt he wanted to move into the city, where his political and scientific life lay. Parliament directed the trustees to sell the estate for the best price possible.[22]

It would seem that Cavendish got about what was paid for the estate,[23] which was 17,000 pounds, and the house he bought in its place that same year, 1738, cost only one tenth that: for the absolute purchase of a freehold in Westminster, he paid 1,750 pounds. The location was near Oxford Road, at the corner of Great Marlborough and Blenheim, both streets named to commemorate a military action of the duke of Marlborough in 1704. Victories like the one at Blenheim had, in fact, assured the conditions of life for the kinds of persons who lived on Great Marlborough Street, namely, gentlemen and tradesmen, evenly balanced. In appearance Great Marlborough Street was, and is, an atypical London street, long, straight, and broad. Admired for its Roman-like grandeur, it had its drawbacks too. The street opened onto no vistas, and its houses, though solid, were undistinguished. Now all demolished, the houses gave the street a uniform appearance, though the house that Cavendish bought, number 13, was unusual in one respect. It was, in fact, *two* houses (the setting for this dual biography), which had been joined around 1710 when John Richmond, who had actually fought at Blenheim and had risen to the rank of general, leased the then two separate houses. Following the general's death in 1724, the house went on the market as two houses-in-one. From a newspaper advertisement the next year, we get an idea of its size and layout. The property extended forty-five feet to the front, and in depth two hundred feet, accommodating a spacious garden, at the end of which an apartment had been built with a communication to the house. There is reason to think that later on Henry Cavendish made use of this apartment, which had a kitchen underground and living quarters, consisting of four rooms, on the one floor above. To some degree Lord Charles and the adult Henry maintained separate establishments in the same house; they had separate silver, for example.[24] Naturally, the property also had stabling and coach houses. The spaciousness of the buildings and of the garden were important for the life of science that was lived there; for like the house, the life of science was double too. Here, on Great

Marlborough Street, Lord Charles Cavendish would live the rest of his life and Henry Cavendish most of his, and here they, together and singly, would carry out experimental, observational, and mathematical researches in all parts of natural philosophy.[25]

Two years after Lord Charles Cavendish bought the house on Great Marlborough Street, in 1740 an opening was created by death on the local governing body of the parish, the vestry of St. James, Westminster. Cavendish was elected to fill it. His father-in-law, the duke of Kent, who had been a vestryman in the parish, had just died, and he too was replaced at the same time, by another duke. The vestry dealt with every kind of practical problem of civil life: road repair, paving, night watch, workhouses, petitions for the commons, rates, levies, grants, and accounts. No detail was too small; the vestry approved a new umbrella for ministers attending burials in the rain. It was characteristic of Cavendish to turn up faithfully at vestry meetings, held as needed, roughly once a month. A few other members attended as regularly too, and these he was either related to, such as Philip Yorke, or met with on boards of other institutions, such as Macclesfield from the Royal Society. Cavendish served his parish for thirty-three years, attending his last meeting in early 1783, just before he died.[26] The wider setting for the scientific drama that took

---

[22] "An Act for Discharging the Estate Purchased by the Trustees of Charles Cavendish . . . from the Trusts of his Settlement, and for Enabling the Said Trustees to Sell and Dispose of the Same for the Purposes Therein Mentioned," Devon. Coll.

[23] Devon. Coll., L/114/32.

[24] In the year before his father died, Henry Cavendish took a house in Hampstead. That year he made an inventory of silverware, plates, pans, coffee pots, lamps, and so on; beside many entries, he wrote "CC," and beside other entries "H," standing, we suppose, for Charles Cavendish and for Henry. "An Inventory of Silver Plate Belonging to the Honble Henry Cavendish Delivered to the Care of Geo. Dobson Feby the 7th 1782," Chatsworth, 86/comp. 1.

[25] "Assignment of Two Messuages in Marlborough Street from the Honorable Thomas Townshend Esq to His Right Honble Lord Charles Cavendish," 27 Feb. 1737/38, Chatsworth, L/38/35. London County Council, *Survey of London*, vol. 31: *The Parish of St. James Westminster. Part 2: North of Piccadilly*, gen. ed. F. H. W. Sheppard (London: Athlone, 1963), 251–56.

[26] Minutes of the Vestry of St. James, Westminster, D 1760–1764, Westminster City Archives, from his election to the vestry on 26 Dec. 1740 (D 1760, p. 145) to his last meeting on 13 Feb. 1783 (D 1764, p. 518). With the vestrymen, Cavendish had other duties in the parish; he was a trustee, for example, of the King Street Chapel and its school and met with other trustees at the end of year to pass the accounts. Great Britain. Historical Manuscript Commission, *Manuscripts of the Earl of Egmont. Diary of the First Earl of Egmont, Viscount Percival*, vol. 3 (London: His Majesty's Stationary Office, 1923), 270 (4 Jan. 1742/3), 306 (4 Jan. 1744/5). King Street Chapel was also known as Archbishop Tenison's Chapel, King St.

place on Great Marlborough Street was greater London, which included Westminster. At around the time Cavendish bought his Westminster house, one sixth of the people of England either lived or had once lived in greater London. In his son Henry's lifetime, owing to an influx from the provinces and from abroad, its population swelled to nearly a million. Whereas the filth, poverty, and drunkenness of eighteenth-century London are faithfully depicted in Hogarth's prints, the city's lure is equally well depicted in Boswell's London journals. London was wealth, power, and patronage, an opportunity to rise in the world. London was the seat of national government, a great port city, the commercial center of a colonial system, headquarters of great trading companies, and the financial capital of the world. Whether a Londoner was rising or was, like a Cavendish, already at the top, he was in the presence of every convenience known to civilization. Westminster could boast of almost four hundred distinct trades, among which were trades of special interest to Lord Charles and Henry Cavendish, such as the instrument and book trades. The resident of London was in the center of the world; yet whenever he felt that the world was too much with him, he had only to step back out of the street to find himself inside his own house, his castle "in perfect safety from intrusion." For a man who was interested in the great world and yet was a shy homebody like Henry Cavendish, it was no small recommendation of London that there "a man is always *so near his burrow.*"[27]

London was the principal center of science in Britain for most of Lord Charles Cavendish's life and for a good part of Henry's. Even though in the second half of the eighteenth century, when much of the important scientific activity took place elsewhere, in the Scottish university towns and in the industrial midlands, in the rising towns of Birmingham, Manchester, and others, still London remained "intellectually pre-eminent," a "magnet for men with scientific and technical interests" and the "Mecca of the provincial mathematical practitioner."[28] Over half of the British scientific practitioners of the eighteenth century who enter the *Dictionary of Scientific Biography* worked mainly in or near London.[29] The city was large enough to be home to numbers of experts in every part of science, yet small enough for persons of common interests to meet frequently in societies, coffee houses, and private homes. Scientifically interested and interesting visitors from the provinces and from abroad were warmly welcomed into these circles. To paraphrase Johnson, as Lord Charles and Henry Cavendish might have done: anyone who was tired of London was tired of science.

Family of the Greys

After Lady Anne Cavendish's death, Lord Charles kept in touch with the Greys, insuring that although Henry Cavendish was brought up without a mother, he knew his maternal as well as paternal family. We have Thomas Birch to thank for our knowledge of Lord Charles Cavendish's visits with his wife's family.

Birch owed his patronage to a branch of the Greys, the Yorkes. Philip Yorke, first earl of Hardwicke, engaged Birch as tutor to his oldest son, who was also named Philip. He then kept Birch on, from 1735, as a kind of secretary with light duties, which left Birch plenty of time for his writing.[30]

In 1740, the younger Philip married Jemima Campbell, granddaughter of the duke of Kent. That same year the duke died; thereupon Jemima became Marchioness de Grey and Baroness Lucas of Crudwell. In the years to come, in the off-season Philip and Jemima lived at the duke of Kent's great estate at Wrest Park in Bedfordshire, and the rest of the time they lived in London at St. James Square. No match for his self-made father the lord chancellor, Philip rejected his ample opportunities for high political office, withdrawing into his chief pleasure in life, literature. In temperament he was personable, languid and reserved, and in health he was not robust. He spent much of the day dressing, visiting, and reading long letters from Birch.[31]

[27]Quoting an acquaintance on the importance of living in London: James Boswell, *The Life of Samuel Johnson LL.D.*, vol. 3 (New York: Heritage, 1963), 73. George Rudé, *Hanoverian London, 1714–1808* (Berkeley: University of California Press, 1971), 4–7, 25, 28, 32–33.

[28]A. E. Musson and Eric Robinson, *Science and Technology in the Industrial Revolution* (Toronto: University of Toronto Press, 1969), 55, 57, 66–67, 119, 138. E. G. R. Taylor, *The Mathematical Practitioners of Hanoverian England 1714–1840* (Cambridge: Cambridge University Press, 1966), 14.

[29]*Dictionary of Scientific Biography*, ed. C. C. Gillispie, 15 vols. (New York: Charles Scribner's Sons, 1970–78).

[30]Albert E. Gunther, *An Introduction to the Life of the Rev. Thomas Birch D.D., F.R.S., 1705–1766.* (Halesworth: Halesworth Press, 1984), 8, 35.

[31]Gunther, *Birch*, 41. L. B. and John Brooke, *The House of Commons 1754–1780*, vol. 3: *Members K-Y* (London: Her Majesty's Stationary Office, 1964), 681.

Birch was personally close to the younger Philip Yorke, serving as his secretary, literary assistant, and eyes and ears in London when Yorke was at Wrest Park. Although Wrest Park appears frequently at the head of Birch's letters, Birch's principal assignment was London, from which watch he kept his patron informed on literary affairs and also on scientific affairs. Given Yorke's friends and membership in the Royal Society, Birch expected him to take an interest in, for instance, the test of John Harrison's chronometer for determining longitude on a journey to Jamaica. Philip Yorke's wife, Jemima, also took an interest in science, for we find Birch writing to her about the contents of the *Philosophical Transactions.*[32] When Philip and Jemima Yorke were in London, Birch would join them for weekly breakfasts at the Kent family house on St. James Square.[33] The duchess of Kent was usually there along with Mary and Sophia de Grey and other members of the Grey family, including male in-laws Lords Glenorchy and Ashburnham. Lord Charles Cavendish visited the Greys often in 1741 and 1742 and less often over the next ten years, and sometimes he brought along his son Henry to visit with his maternal grandmother and aunts and uncles.[34] Henry Cavendish may not have had a memory of his mother who died when he was two, but his father made certain that he knew the other dukedom from which he descended.

Friends and Colleagues

Lord Charles Cavendish's friends and colleagues tended to be one and the same. Apart from those within his family, his friendships were based not on aristocratic ties but on mutual interests. His birth was no impediment to his association with persons from other walks of life.

Many of Cavendish's friends belonged, as he did, to the Royal Society Club. Originally named the Club of the Royal Philosophers, its members referred to it simply as "the Society." It undoubtedly had a predecessor, but if Cavendish had been a member then, it remains that he was not elected to the Royal Society Club until eight years after its founding in 1743.[35] From the beginning of its records, the Club included close friends of Cavendish, such as William Watson, William Heberden, and Birch, and members of the De Moivre circle, such as Folkes, Davall, Scott, and

Stanhope. The occasion of Cavendish's election was the fatal illness of the president of the Club, who was also the president of the Royal Society, Folkes. This was at the end of 1751, when the regular time for electing new members to the club was many months off. As vice president, Cavendish had already taken Folkes's place in the Royal Society, and the Club wanted Cavendish to take Folkes's place there too. Cavendish's election was therefore made an exception, and in January 1752 he assumed the chair at the Royal Society Club.[36]

For convenience the Club met on the afternoon of the same day the Royal Society met, Thursday. Members of the Club did not also have to be members of the Royal Society, but normally they were, and the president of the Club was the president of the Society. Its membership was fixed at forty, though members could bring guests; when Cavendish was admitted, the usual number of members and guests was about twenty in the winter and fourteen in the summer. The dinners, which were heavy (fish, fowl, red meat, pudding, pie, cheese, and alcohol), were held for the first three years at Pontack's and then, throughout Cavendish's membership, at the Mitre Tavern on Fleet Street. The Club provided a fuller opportunity than did the formal meetings of the Royal Society for members to talk about science. Cavendish belonged to the Club for twenty years and dined with it often, but he did not attend the yearly business meetings with any particular regularity, unlike Watson, Birch,

---

[32]There are many letters from Thomas Birch to Philip Yorke reporting on scientific news between 1747 and 1762 in the Birch correspondence in the British Library, Add Mss 35397 and 35399. Thomas Birch to Jemima, Marchioness de Grey, 12 Aug. 1749, BL Add Mss 35397, ff. 200–1.

[33]Gunther, *Birch*, 35–39.

[34]We have no idea of the frequency of Lord Charles Cavendish's visits to his wife's family. We do know that he *and* Birch were at the Grey's together twenty-six times between 1741 and 1751. On two of the occasions Henry Cavendish came with Lord Charles; Henry was nine and ten at the time. Thomas Birch Diary, BL Add Mss 4478C.

[35]T. E. Allibone argues that the Royal Society Club was continuous with "Halley's Club," for which he has a few pieces of evidence. His assertion that Lord Charles Cavendish was probably a member of "Halley's Club" has none, however, so this lead we are unable to follow up. . . T. E. Allibone, *The Royal Society and Its Dining Clubs* (Oxford: Pergamon Press, 1976), 45, 97. An opposing view of Halley's part in the origins of the Club is given by Archibald Geikie, *Annals of the Royal Society Club: The Record of a London Dining-Club in the Eighteenth & Nineteenth Centuries* (London: Macmillan, 1917), 6–9. Lord Charles Cavendish was elected to the Club on 25 July 1751 and became a member on 9 January 1752.

[36]Allibone quotes from the Club's Minutes for 28 Nov. 1751, *Royal Society and Its Dining Club*, 44–45.

Heberden, and several other friends, and for that matter, unlike his son Henry later.[37]

The Royal Society Club was the most prestigious and probably the largest of the learned clubs in eighteenth-century London, of which there were many. Meeting to discuss science, literature, politics, business, or whatever interests drew men together, London clubs often had a more or less formal membership, with rules and dues, but often too they were informal; certain persons simply formed the habit of being found at particular hours at certain coffee-houses. Folkes, president of the Royal Society, dined not only at the Royal Society Club but as well at a club of his own, which met at the Baptist Head in Chancery Lane. Birch met with groups at Tom's Coffee House and at Rawthmell's Coffee-House on Henrietta Street, Covent Garden, later the place of origin of the Society of Arts. Another society of scientific and literary men met at Jack's Coffee House on Dean Street, Soho, and later at Old (or Young) Slaughter's Coffee House on St. Martin's Lane, where De Moivre solved problems of games of chance.[38] We do not know at which coffee houses other than the Mitre Lord Charles Cavendish might be found, but we do know some of those where Henry Cavendish could be, a subject we come to later.

Coffee houses and taverns provided clubs with a measure of privacy in their supper rooms, but these were noisy places at best. Private houses provided quieter, more intimate settings for small groups. Lord Willoughby, a prominent Fellow of the Royal Society, presided both over a club that met at a tavern—a life insurance society based on the principles of the De Moivre student and mathematician James Dodson, which met at the White Lion Tavern—and over a club that met in his and Birch's houses, alternately.[39] Another group met at Macclesfield's.[40] Cavendish too dined with his friends in houses, in particular, at his own house on Great Marlborough Street. We have a record of fifteen dinners he hosted between 1748 and 1761, to which a total of thirty-two guests came, and to which Charles's son Henry may be added. Birch was at all of these dinners, necessarily, for our knowledge of Cavendish's circle of friends comes from Birch, who kept a social calendar in the form of a diary. Cavendish's first mention in Birch's diary was in 1730, as if it were public news: "Ld Ch

Cavendish resigns."[41] The reference is clearly to Cavendish's resignation as gentleman of the bed-chamber to the prince of Wales. Birch's first mention of any personal contact with Cavendish was six years later, in 1736. Their connection then was probably rather formal, since in that entry, and in an entry a year later, Birch identified Cavendish as the brother of the duke of Devonshire.[42] The occasion for this early contact was Birch's scholarship, for Birch recorded that Cavendish gave him original papers concerning his grandfather William Russell, who, Birch notes, was beheaded in Charles II's reign.[43] Here Charles was acting as a representative of the great Cavendish family, but he and Birch did become personal friends.

In August 1750 Cavendish invited Birch and six other "Bretheren of the Royal Society" to a "small Party," at which he offered a "philosophical Entertainment of an artificial Frost by a Solution of Sal Ammoniac in common Water," after which he provided "what was equally relish'd, a very good Dinner."[44] If Cavendish performed experiments at his other dinners, we do not know, but it was not an unheard of entertainment at the time. (This particular experiment on artificial frost foreshadows Henry Cavendish's later researches on freezing solutions.) Earlier that same year, 1750, Cavendish agreed to come to dinner at Martin Folkes's house, to which John Canton was invited along with his

---

[37]Royal Society Club, Minute Books, in the Royal Society Library. Cavendish resigned from the Club at the annual meeting in 1772, though he continued to take an interest in it, making it a gift of venison five years later. Royal Society Club, Minute Book, no. 7 (9 Sep. 1779).

[38]Thomas Birch, Diary, BL Add Mss 4478C, 19 Oct. 1736. W. Warburton to Thomas Birch, 27 May 1738, in John Nichols, *Illustrations of the Literary History of the Eighteenth Century*, 8 vols. (London, 1817–58) 2:86–88, on 88. Bryant Lillywhite, *London Coffee Houses. A Reference Book of Coffee Houses of the Seventeenth, Eighteenth, and Nineteenth Centuries* (London: George Allen and Unwin, 1963), 280–81, 369–70, 421–23, 595.

[39]Lillywhite, *London Coffee Houses*, 745. Beginning in 1754, a group met every Sunday at Willoughby's house until spring, when it moved to Birch's house; this alternation was kept up for years. The regular members of this group were Watson, Heberden, Israel Maudit, James Burrow, Daniel Wray, and several other Fellows of the Royal Society whom Cavendish saw socially; he might be expected to have belonged, but he did not. Birch Diary, passim.

[40]Rodolph De Vall-Travers to Thomas Birch, n.d. /April 1757/, BL Add Mss 4320, f.9.

[41]Birch Diary, 12 Oct. 1730.

[42]Birch Diary, 29 June 1736 and 1 Aug. 1737.

[43]Birch Diary, 1 Aug. 1737.

[44]Thomas Birch to Philip Yorke, 18 Aug. 1750, BL Add Mss 35397. The guests were Birch, Folkes, Heberden, Watson, Thomas Wilbraham, and Nicholas Mann.

magnetic bars. Cavendish, Folkes told Canton, was "very curious" to see Canton perform his magnetic experiment, which Cavendish could do "more at ease" at Folkes's house than he could at the Society. The next year, when Folkes was ill, Cavendish presided at the Royal Society and gave an undoubtedly well-prepared, "excellent discourse" on Canton's artificial magnets, for which Canton received the Copley Medal.[45]

Let us look at who came to dinner at Cavendish's house. For example, on 21 October 1758 Cavendish had eight dinner guests, all professional men out on the town, all but one middle aged, some but not all married. They were mutual friends, not people Cavendish brought together for introductions. Besides Birch, two other men at that dinner, Watson and Heberden, also came to most of the other dinners at Cavendish's. The guests were all Fellows of the Royal Society, though with the exception of Birch, who was secretary of the Society, they were not then on the council. Cavendish, the only aristocrat, at fifty-four was the next-to-oldest member of the party. Two years older than Cavendish, Thomas Wilbraham had long been practicing medicine in London and was physician to Westminster Hospital. Birch was fifty-three, like Cavendish a long-time widower, with an adult daughter about thirty. Watson was forty-two and married, or at least he had been married, with a son about fourteen and a daughter. Having started out as an apothecary, Watson now had a mail-order doctorate from Germany and was practicing as a physician; in the minutes of the meetings at the Royal Society, he had just begun to be listed as "Dr. Watson." Heberden was forty-seven, another widower, with a son about five who was probably living at home. Earlier Heberden had lectured on and practiced medicine in Cambridge, but for the past ten years he had been practicing in London. Israel Maudit was fifty, a rich bachelor, who liked to entertain at home himself. Like a good number of men who entered Cavendish's scientific life—De Moivre, Desaguliers, Matthew Maty—Maudit was of Huguenot descent and, it stands to reason, a writer on religious freedom (from having to subscribe to the Thirty-Nine Articles of the Church of England, for example) and politics. Samuel Squire was about forty-five, married and probably with children by now (he had three). Indebted to the duke of Newcastle for

advancement, this ambitious clergyman was about to rise higher, to bishop. Gowin Knight was forty-four and apparently unmarried. He was then devoted to the mariner's compass and to his new duties as principal librarian at the British Museum, with a meager income of two hundred pounds a year. The only young man in the company was John Hadley, twenty-seven, who only that year had been elected to the Royal Society. Hadley was still trying to find his place in the world, dividing his time between Cambridge, where he was professor of chemistry, and London, where he was soon to settle and become physician to St. Thomas's Hospital. These were men of liberal outlook and where their political leaning is known, whig. Some of them were university men, some—including the accomplished Birch and Watson, and the host, Cavendish himself—were not. This dinner was not a high-powered scientific gathering, though there were some very good scientific men there. Only the year before Cavendish had been awarded the Copley Medal, as had earlier two of his guests, Watson and Knight. Several of Cavendish's guests were primarily interested in antiquities, which made the party a mix like the Royal Society itself, which was so obviously satisfying to Cavendish. Only Watson had published extensively in the *Philosophical Transactions*, on a variety of subjects, including his professional field, medicine, but also including electricity, on which he had important papers. Knight too had published important papers, his on magnetism, which just that year he was bringing out in a collection. Heberden had published four papers on miscellaneous topics, one, a human calculus, falling within his professional field, medicine. Birch too had published four papers, one on Roman inscriptions belonging to his field, history. Half of the guests were, like Cavendish himself, one-paper men. Wilbraham had published a medical account of an hydrophobia. Hadley's one paper was yet to come, on a mummy examined in London. Maudit's paper was on a wasp's nest. Squire's was on a person who had been dumb for four years and had recovered his tongue upon experiencing a bad dream. Since the dinner guests were all men of learning, some, like Birch, had substantial publications outside of the *Philosophical Transactions*.

[45] Royal Society, JB 20:571–73 (30 Nov. 1751).

Cavendish and Birch dined together at houses other than Cavendish's in the period for which we have a record, 1748 to 1762: at Heberden's and Stanhope's houses as often as at Cavendish's, and at Watson's, Macclesfield's, and Yorke's half as often. Dinners at Macclesfield's were often business meetings for the auditors too. Stanhope we have met before as a pupil of De Moivre, who had worked in the treasury and had served as a Member of Parliament to 1741, the same year that Cavendish had stepped down as Member of Parliament; he was elected to the Royal Society in 1726, two years ahead of Cavendish. Stanhope never married. Philip Yorke, now Viscount Royston and about to become, in two years, the second earl of Hardwicke, was a patron of Birch, as we have seen, and an in-law of Cavendish; he held political offices, and in 1741 he was elected a Fellow of the Royal Society.[46] With Birch, together with other men of science and learning, Cavendish dined two hundred times, often at the Mitre with the Royal Society Club.[47]

Lord Charles Cavendish (and Henry Cavendish) belonged to a circle that met in a private house located in the Strand. Nothing is known about it except that Cavendish's good friends Heberden, Watson, and Maudit also belonged, along with several others. Most of the members were physicians: in addition to Heberden and Watson, they were George Baker, Richard Huck Saunders, and John Pringle. Two others, John Ross and Peter Holford, completed the circle, insofar its membership is known.[48] The interest that brought these men together was probably science, though in general outlook, there would seem to have been a commonality too, which might be called a spirit of enlightened protest. Upon becoming Bishop of Exeter, the antiquarian John Ross advocated the extension of toleration to dissenters in the House of Lords.[49] We have already noted Maudit's writings on religious freedom. John Pringle, president of the Royal Society from 1772, made it his lifework to reform medicine and sanitation in the military.[50] George Baker determined that in his county, Devonshire, drinkers of cider were being poisoned by lead; denounced as a faithless son, Baker nevertheless got his fellow Devonians to stop using lead vats, and he went on to clarify the whole subject of lead poisoning.[51] Watson and Huck Saunders were among the twenty-nine

"rebel Licentiates" who joined John Fothergill in urging the Royal College of Physicians to admit more readily as Fellows physicians who did not have an M.D. from Cambridge or Oxford.[52] Heberden, from within the College of Physicians, sided with, and lost with, Fothergill, Watson, and Huck Saunders. Heberden had already been a thorn in the side of the College of Physicians with his denunciation of mithridatum, a presumed antidote to poisons, as an ineffective farrago; the College nonetheless kept it in their pharmacopeia until late in the century, until his former pupil George Baker took over the presidency. Like Birch, Heberden was a fervid whig, a Wilkite, and a supporter of petitioning clergy.[53] Science, we see, provided Cavendish not only an outlet for his intellectual and administrative energies but also provocative company committed to progress.

What brought Cavendish together with Birch and the others was, apart from conviviality, a common public world. Birch had recommended several of Cavendish's dinner guests in 1758 for membership in the Royal Society: Maudit, Heberden, and Hadley.[54] Birch and Cavendish worked together in the Royal Society year in and year out. During the nine years centering on the date of this sample dinner at the end if 1758, Cavendish attended 81 meetings of the council of the Royal Society, considerably more than did the president, Macclesfield, with 63. Only two persons came more times, necessarily, the secretaries:

----

[46]Birch's Diary records dinners in which Cavendish was present at the homes of fourteen persons, all but one of whom were Fellows of the Royal Society. The names are familiar: in addition to those mentioned above, they include Josiah Colebrooke, Samuel Squire, Mark Akenside, Philip Yorke, Daniel Wray, and William Sotheby.

[47]This count of two hundred is from Birch's Diary. It is a minimum number, since Birch made his entries hastily, usually not giving the names of everyone he dined with.

[48]Andrew Kippis's life of the author published in John Pringle, *Six Discourses, Delivered by Sir John Pringle, Bart. When President of the Royal Society; on Occasion of Six Annual Assignments of Sir Godfrey Copley's Medal. To Which Is Prefixed the Life of the Author. By Andrew Kippis, D.D. F.R.S. and S.A.* (London, 1783), lxiii–lxiv. Kippis says that the group met at Mr. Watson's. This Watson he identifies as a grocer, so he cannot be William Watson. Of the group, Peter Holford is a relative unknown; he was elected Fellow of the Royal Society in 1747 and, much later, in 1783, a member of the Royal Society Club.

[49]"Ross or Rosse, John," *DNB* 17:266–67.

[50]"Pringle, Sir John," *DNB* 16:386–89, on 388.

[51]"Baker, Sir George," *DNB* 1:927–29, on 928.

[52]Dorothea Waley Singer, "Sir John Pringle and His Circle—Part I. Life," *Annals of Science* 6 (1949): 127–80, on 161–62.

[53]Humphry Rolleston, "The Two Heberdens," *Annals of Medical History* 5 (1933):409–24, 566–83, on 412–13, 567–68.

[54]From Royal Society, Certificates.

Davall 86 times and Birch, the record-holder, 96 times. Only one other Fellow came close, Burrow, who was frequently a vice-president, with 76 attendances.[55] Little happened in the Royal Society that Birch and Cavendish did not know about, which was an important tie. Birch was an historian who met the scientific and medical men more than halfway. He was not a member of the College of Physicians, but he was its chaplain,[56] and he became a member of the Royal Society in 1735, soon after embarking on his first great literary work. When Pierre Bayle's biographical dictionary was translated into English in 1710, London publishers planned a patriotic revision that would do more justice to English notables. Birch, at age twenty-six, was invited to be one of the three editors of the *General Dictionary, Historical and Critical*, which appeared in ten volumes between 1734 and 1741, three volumes of which were dedicated to presidents of the Royal Society. Nearly all of the roughly nine hundred new lives were written by Birch, who in writing about English scientists such as Flamsteed and Newton consulted the scientists who had known them, Halley, Bradley, and Jones, who were the same scientists from whom Cavendish also got his start. Halley signed Birch's recommendation at the Royal Society, which read that Birch was "well versed in Mathematics and Natural Philosophy,"[57] indicating that he was recognized for his scientific knowledge as well as his literary attainments. Birch's literary contributions to science continued, his most important being his biography of the seventeenth-century chemist Robert Boyle, to whom he was drawn for his religious and scholarly interests as well as for his scientific, a combination of interests Birch himself had. Birch wrote enthusiastically of Boyle's mastery of Greek, which enabled him to read the New Testament in the original, of Hebrew, which led him to the Rabbinical writings, of Chaldee and Syriac and Arabic, of the vast collection of commentaries on controversies in religion, of the mathematical sciences, of geography, history, medicine, natural history, natural philosophy and, above all, chemistry.[58] Birch wrote of, or implied, the importance for one's scholarly work of living near other scholars, as Boyle did at Oxford, and as Birch himself did in London, meeting with them in its coffee houses, salons, and institutions of learning.[59] In 1757, he completed a history of the

Royal Society. He had intended to bring it up to date, to 1750, but in four volumes he did not get past the seventeenth century, which is where he left it. He wrote his history from the original journals, registers, letters, and council minutes of the Society, documents which he largely reproduced; his method of history was the method of science, as he understood it, the bringing together of facts. "No fact has been omitted," Birch said, and he might have said that no analysis was included: dense with footnotes, his history is a chronicle of the Royal Society, meeting by meeting.[60] Birch, who depended on clerical living, presented his sermons in the same spirit, citing chapter and verse, Newton as well as the Scriptures.[61] An historian who wrote of science to praise it, a man of learning, convivial and energetic, Birch was a natural for scientific society.

Like Birch, Heberden was both an intimate friend of Cavendish and a participant in Cavendish's public world. Like Birch again, Heberden, a physician, met the men of science more than halfway; if Birch brought the method of science to history, Heberden brought it to medicine. Heberden's goal was to make the College of Physicians a medical version of the Royal Society, a proper scientific body. He used his influence in the College—in which he took on the duties of councillor, censor, and elect, one of the powerful senior fellows who chose the president from among themselves—to get it to establish a committee of papers and a journal modeled and named after the Royal Society's *Philosophical Transactions*, the *Medical Transactions*. Consistent with his belief that until "a Newton appears in the science of the animated world" to discover the "great principle of life," medicine had only one recourse, experience, he regarded his job as the patient and laborious assembling of facts. He was a painstakingly accurate observer who made no large generalizations (or

[55]From Royal Society, Minutes of Council.
[56]C. Barton to Thomas Birch, 19 Sep. 1754, BL Add Mss 4300, f. 174.
[57]Gunther, *Birch*, 13–19.
[58]Thomas Birch, *The Life of the Honourable Robert Boyle* (London, 1744), 304–7.
[59]Birch, *Boyle*, 113–14.
[60]Thomas Birch, *The History of the Royal Society of London for Improving of Natural Knowledge, from Its First Rise . . .*, vol. 1 (London, 1756), quotation from the preface.
[61]Quotations from Newton's *Opticks* in notes to his sermons: Thomas Birch's Sermons, vol. 7, f. 188, BL Add Mss 4232C.

discoveries). Despite his admonitions to physicians to publish, he himself was reluctant to do so. His high reputation was based on his practice and his knowledge of the classics, a combination in irreversible decline. Upon being asked what physician he wanted in his final illness, Johnson called for Heberden, "the last of our learned physicians."[62]

Watson, a friend and colleague regularly to be found in Cavendish's company, kept the Royal Society abreast of the major developments in science. For his role as informant, he was well equipped, equally capable of giving the Society a thorough exposure of Franklin's work in electricity and Linnaeus's work in botany. More than any other member, he made the meetings of the Society scientifically rewarding. He also entered energetically into the administration of the Royal Society as he did into that of the other institutions he served, which were more or less the same ones that Birch, Heberden, and Cavendish served.[63]

In personality and appearance, Heberden, Watson, Birch, and Cavendish were as different as their public endeavors were similar. Heberden was tall, extremely thin, short-sighted, with a florid countenance.[64] Watson gave an impression of solidity, with his massive face, arched eyebrows, and large eyes; in conversation he was forceful, exact (because of his remarkable memory, his friends called him "the living lexicon of botany"), and a good judge of men.[65] What people thought of when they thought of Birch was not his appearance, which was unremarkable except perhaps for an alertness of expression, but his conversation, which was irrepressible, "brisk as a bee," according to Johnson, a connoisseur of conversation.[66] This was the company Cavendish kept.

We learn more about Cavendish's friendships and associations by looking at his activity in the Royal Society. Like every member, he could vote on everyone who was considered for admission, though there is no record of how he voted. There is, however, a record of which candidates he recommended and of the members with whom he signed recommendations.

Even before a candidate was proposed for membership, he was usually canvassed by the council. The candidate then had to be formally recommended by three or more members, who drew up a sheet with their signatures, the candi-

date's name, address, and profession, and a brief description of his qualifications for membership. This sheet would be dated and posted by one of the secretaries in the meeting room for the period of several ordinary meetings before the candidate was put to the vote. An exception was made for peers and their sons and various dignitaries, for whom only one recommender was required.[67] To further a candidate's chances, other members could add their signatures to the sheet. Ten, not an uncommon number, signed Henry Cavendish's certificate in 1760. Occasionally, there was a groundswell of enthusiasm for a candidate, as there was for Captain James Cook, whose certificate was signed by twenty-six members. Certain members were constantly putting up candidates, and on them falls a good share of responsibility for the Society's early accelerated growth. In the first forty years the number of ordinary members tripled to three hundred, and the number of foreign members grew even faster, rising to almost half the number of ordinary members.[68] During the twenty-five years that Lord Charles Cavendish recommended candidates, the growth of the Society had slowed to one or two a year. Cavendish's own contribution was moderate: between 1734 and 1766, he recommended twenty-seven candidates, fewer than one a year.

Birch signed recommendations with Cavendish more often than any other member, nineteen times. Birch, it should be pointed out, recommended a large number of candidates, a half dozen a year.[69] Next came Folkes with ten recommendations in common with Cavendish, then Watson and Wray each with nine. This agreement is probably not surprising, since Birch, Watson, and Wray, as

---

[62]Humphry Rolleston, "The Two Heberdens," 414, 417. Audley Cecil Buller, *The Life and Works of Heberden* (London, 1879), 16, 21–22. William Munck, *The Roll of the Royal College of Physicians of London. Comprising Biographical Sketches of All the Eminent Physicians Whose Names Are Recorded in the Annals*, 2d ed., 4 vols. (London, 1878) 2:159–64. William Heberden, *Commentaries on the History and Cure of Diseases*, 2d ed. (London, 1803), 483, and appendix, "A Sketch of a Preface Designed for the Medical Transactions, 1767," 486–94.

[63]"Watson, Sir William," *DNB* 20:956–58.

[64]Rolleston, "The Two Heberdens," 416.

[65]"Watson," *DNB* 20:957.

[66]"Birch," *DNB* 2:531.

[67]Royal Society, Minutes of Council 3:51, 77 (20 Aug. 1730).

[68]Henry Lyons, *The Royal Society 1600–1940: A History of Its Administration under Its Charters* (Cambridge: Cambridge University Press, 1944), 125–26.

[69]In 1748–60, Birch recommended seventy-six candidates Royal Society, Certificates.

we have seen, were good friends of Cavendish. Then came Jones, of the De Moivre circle, Cavendish's own recommender; then Burrow; then Willoughby. There was only one person who signed often with Cavendish with whom he does not seem to have had outside connections, John Machin, professor of astronomy at Gresham College and secretary of the Royal Society; Machin died in 1751, early in this account, and he was in poor health in his last years, which may explain his absence. It should be noted that Cavendish joined Sloane in his early recommendations until Sloane retired as president in 1741. Among Cavendish's ninety-three co-signers, most of the other familiar names appear too, though with less frequency: Heberden, Bradley, Stanhope, De Moivre, Macclesfield, Scott, Jurin, Davall, and Richard Graham, to name several.

If we turn now from Cavendish's co-signers to the candidates he recommended, we get another indication of his associations. In 1753 the council resolved that candidates were to be known "personally" to their recommenders, a practice that in the past had usually been followed though not invariably.[70] We can be reasonably certain that Cavendish was on a personal basis with most if not all of the persons he recommended. Seventeen of the certificates he signed said that the candidates were proficient in the sciences (designated variously as natural philosophy, experimental philosophy, natural knowledge, natural history, philosophical knowledge, philosophy, and different branches of science); six certificates mentioned mathematics, three useful learning, two mechanics, and another two astronomy. Seven of the candidates were distinguished in literature or polite learning, though never that alone. There were a few other accomplishments: antiquities, architecture, medicine, anatomy, musical theory, and (not very helpful) learning and knowledge. Two candidates were professors at Cambridge and Oxford, about whom nothing more needed to be given than the names of their professorships, which in their cases were astronomy and experimental philosophy. For one other candidate no explanation was given other than his position, under-librarian at the British Museum, an institution in which Cavendish was an officer. Recommenders of foreign members of the Society did not have to know the candidates personally but they did have to know their work. Cavendish

recommended two French candidates, one an astronomer, the other known as the author of a commentary on Newton's *Principia*. It is clear that the persons Cavendish helped gain entry into the Royal Society favored the physical sciences and mathematics, as might be expected, but they were not narrowly identified with particular fields or, in most cases, even with particular sciences. This dimension of generality is to be expected, given the composition of the Society. Every candidate Cavendish recommended was elected, with the exception of his first; in 1734 Cavendish joined Sloane and John Stevens, one of the surgeons to the prince of Wales, and two others in a recommendation of John Wreden, another surgeon to the prince of Wales. As a recent gentleman to the bedchamber of the prince of Wales, Cavendish would have known these surgeons; and because of the highly political nature of this prince of Wales, politics as much as qualifications may have led to the rejection of Cavendish's candidate. That, in general, it helped a candidate for Cavendish to recommend him there can be no doubt. When Joseph Priestley, who unlike Cavendish had to make his living, which he did in part by the sale of his books, heard that membership in the Royal Society would encourage sales of his history of electricity, he discussed his prospects and strategy with his friend John Canton. Priestley expected that not only Canton but Watson and Richard Price would support his candidacy, and "If L. C. Cavendish could be prevailed upon to join you," he told Canton, " I should think the rest would be easy." (Canton, it would seem, refused to approach Lord Charles Cavendish on the technical ground that Priestley was not a "personal acquaintance" of his.)[71]

Sorrows and Riches

Frederick Cavendish—Fredy, his family called him[72]—followed in his older brother Henry's footsteps, at a two-year interval. He first went to Hackney Academy and then as a fellow-commoner

[70]Royal Society, Minutes of Council 4:118–19 (10 May 1753).

[71]Joseph Priestley to John Canton, 14 Feb. 1766, Canton Papers, Royal Society, 2:58. Priestley was elected that year without the help of Cavendish; Benjamin Franklin joined the other three instead. Joseph Priestley to Richard Price, 8 Mar. 1766, in *A Scientific Autobiography of Joseph Priestley (1738–1804)*, ed. R. E. Schofield (Cambridge, Mass.: M.D.T. Press, 1966), 17–19, on 19.

[72]Henry Cavendish referred to "Fredy's" letters and expenses in "Papers in Walnut Cabinet," Cavendish Mss, Misc.

to Peterhouse, Cambridge. In the year after Henry Cavendish came down from Cambridge, and in his next to final year at Cambridge, Frederick Cavendish had a bizarre accident, falling from an upper window in one of the courts and striking his head. There is no indication of what he was doing in that window. Riotous behavior at Cambridge was common enough, prompting Thomas Gray to change his living quarters and affiliation, from Peterhouse, Frederick's college, to Pembroke. Or maybe Frederick was in his window trying Franklin's experiment on lightning. Whatever the cause, the fall was serious, leaving Frederick's life in the balance for a time and his head with a deep indentation as a reminder of it.[73] The accident happened in late July or early August 1754. By mid August Frederick was "mending, but not out of danger."[74] That summer Charles Cavendish had been dining frequently with his scientific friends; then for four and a half months he dropped out, due in part to Frederick's condition.[75] In mid October Thomas Birch wrote to Charles Cavendish to say that his friends hoped that "Mr. Frederick Cavendish's Recovery" would soon allow him to join them "in town."[76] Frederick did not return to the university, and although he gradually regained his health, his brain was permanently impaired.

Of how Frederick occupied himself in the years after his accident, there is no account. However, thanks to the legal and financial ties that bound in the eighteenth century, we have his father's view of Frederick's mental "state." As we have pointed out, as the younger son of the marriage, Frederick's eventual prosperity was looked after by his mother, who at her death in 1733 left him her one quarter share of the duke of Kent's Steane estate, which was sold and converted into stock. Also through her, after the duke of Kent's death in 1740, Frederick received 12,000 pounds. Finally, from the proceeds from the sale of the Putteridge estate in 1738 and its aftermath, Frederick received another roughly 17,500 pounds.[77] While still a minor, then, Frederick became independently wealthy. Only he was not independent according to the argument his father made to justify his management of Frederick's wealth, which, as it turned out, was legally questionable if otherwise understandable. The Steane estate and, after its sale, the equivalent in stocks were placed in the hands of trustees. In 1772, the last surviving trustee, Lord William Manners, died, and his son, John, did not want the inherited trusteeship. This meant that Lord Charles Cavendish had to choose new trustees, who would have to be persuaded of the legality of the way the trust had been used in the past. Cavendish wrote up a case for this practice and submitted it for a legal opinion, which went against his wishes. He had been receiving first the profits from the Steane estate and after its sale the dividends from stock. His explanation was that because of Frederick's accident, "it was manifestly improper to pay the money to him" during his minority and even after; Frederick was then thirty-nine, and "even now," Cavendish said, "it appears to be doubtful whether it is prudent to do it." The earnings from the trust Cavendish had spent on the "maintenance & education" of Frederick, the "expense of which greatly exceeded the income of the estate, except in some of the first years of F's life." The legal opinion he solicited was that the trustees had no power to permit him to receive that money for the purpose he gave, for it was a father's duty to support his child. In the eyes of the law, then,—although it was not put this way—Cavendish had been stealing from his disabled son, and he and his heirs (who would be Henry Cavendish) were accountable to Frederick for the money taken from him. Despite this ruling, the new trustees chosen by Cavendish, all members of the family, agreed to let him continue to accept all dividends and interest from the funds in their name. Henry Cavendish as well as Lord Charles was a party to the new but, in effect, old financial arrangements for Frederick's support. Several lawyers got involved, but in the documents we have seen, there is no suggestion that Frederick himself was unhappy with his father. What we have learned from them is that in Lord Charles's judgment, his son Frederick was incompetent.[78]

[73]Lord Charles's Cavendish's legal case involving his marriage settlement and Frederick's expenses, 30 Apr. 1773. Devon. Coll., L/114/32. "Memoirs of the Late Frederick Cavendish, Esq.," *Gentlemen's Magazine* 82 (1812): 289–91, on 289.

[74]Lord Hartington to the duke of Devonshire, 17 Aug. 1754 Devon. Coll., no. 260.119.

[75]Lord Charles Cavendish hosted a dinner at his house on 17 July 1754; the next time he dined with this circle was at Stanhope's house, on 2 December of that year. Birch Diary.

[76]Thomas Birch to Lord Charles Cavendish, 17 Oct. 1754. BL Add Mss 4444, f. 180.

[77]Devon. Coll., L/114/32.

[78]"Copy Case Between Father and Son with Mr. Perryn," 30 Apr. 1773. Lord Charles Cavendish to S. Seddon, 27 and 29 July

If Henry Cavendish's biographer Wilson was accurately informed, Henry and Frederick made a visit to Paris at some time or other, probably early, before Henry was well known. Travel abroad after leaving the university was the standard way for a young man to complete his education, and it would seem that Henry combined this course with an effort to include Frederick in the world. This possible journey by the two brothers is the occasion of the earliest anecdote about Henry Cavendish. At a hotel in Calais, the brothers passed a room in which a corpse was laid out for burial; neither said anything, but the next day on the road to Paris, this conversation supposedly took place. " 'Fred. C., *loq.*—Did you see the corpse?' Henry C., *res.*—I did.' "[79] This (Pinteresque) fragment is one of many anecdotes that are meant to show Henry's taciturnity. Beyond that, the possible truth in it is the reserve between the brothers, for which there is other, better evidence. Frederick and Henry's relationship was cordial but distant.

Frederick was in effective retirement. Henry's mother, Lady Anne, had been dead for many years, of course, and his grandparents, Cavendishes and Greys alike, were all dead. Henry, now of age and home from the university, would be truly close only to his father. Henry had a good many nominally close relatives. At the time he was born, he had fourteen first cousins, to which seven more were later added. At the time he came of age, all but two of the twenty-one first cousins were still living. He had contact with many or all of them, but he does not seem to have been particularly close to any of them. None of them, it might be noted, had any accomplishment in science.[80]

Lord Charles was evidently close to his brother Lord James, with whom he had traveled abroad as a youth. James was the older of the two, but he deferred to Charles in family affairs: he asked Charles to dispose of his mother's estate and gave him power of attorney in all matters of their joint executorship.[81] James's military life took him away, for example, to Ireland;[82] later he was a Member of Parliament for Malton. In 1741, at age thirty-eight he died.[83]

Lord Charles's only surviving brother, William, may have had an interest in science and was at least sympathetic to persons with a scientific interest. Belatedly, he was elected to the Royal Society in 1747, and he subscribed to a number of scientific books to which Charles also subscribed; e.g., De Moivre's in 1730, Roger Long's in 1742, and Colin Maclaurin's in 1748.[84] William, however, cared much more about paintings than he did about science. The brothers saw one another from time to time, at Chatsworth usually. Charles kept accounts with William,[85] and he served him as a political go-between,[86] but they led very different lives, due in part to temperament and in part to their order of birth. William and Charles started out the same way, as Members of Parliament, only Charles left politics and William did not and realistically could not. After his father's death in 1729, William, as third duke of Devonshire, sat in the House of Lords, where he rarely spoke, and when he did it was with such a soft voice that no one could hear him. Not a leader of the party and not a fighter, William accepted high office without high ambition. Like his father, he was a friend of Walpole and did well by the friendship. Walpole made him lord privy seal, then lord lieutenant of Ireland, a responsible, highly lucrative job because of its immense patronage. Local government was the

1772. "Discharge from the Right Honourable Lord Charles Cavendish to John Manners Esqr as to Trusts for his Lordship and the Honourable Henry Cavendish & Frederick Cavendish His Sons." Devon. Coll., L/14/32. The new trustees were Philip Yorke, earl of Hardwicke and Lord Charles's nephews Lords Frederick and George Augustus Cavendish.

[79] George Wilson, *The Life of the Honble Henry Cavendish* (London, 1851), 18, 173. Wilson was told about Henry and Frederick's trip abroad by his informant in London, Tomlinson, who was told it by an unspecified Fellow of the Royal Society.

[80] Of the cousins alive when Henry Cavendish was born, two died young: Rachel Morgan and Edward Morgan. Omitting their titles, the others were Elizabeth Morgan, William Morgan, Carolina Cavendish, William Cavendish, Elizabeth Cavendish, Rachel Cavendish, George Augustus Cavendish, Frederick Cavendish, William Lowther, John Cavendish, Jemima Campbell, and John Ashburnham. The cousins born after Henry were Henry Gregory, David Gregory, George Gregory, Jemima Gregory, Amelia Egerton, John William Egerton, and Francis Henry Edgerton.

[81] Lord James Cavendish to Lord Charles Cavendish, 25 Mar. 1727 and 23 Aug. 1732, Devon. Coll., no. 34/2.

[82] J. Potter to the duke of Devonshire, 3 July 1739, Devon. Coll., no. 252.1.

[83] *Gentleman's Magazine* 11 (1741): 609.

[84] Subscriber lists in Abraham De Moivre, *Miscellanea analytica de seriebus et quadraturis* (London, 1730); Roger Long, *Astronomy, In Five Books*, vol. 1 (Cambridge, 1742); Colin Maclaurin, *An Account of Sir Isaac Newton's Philosophical Discoveries* (London, 1748).

[85] Charles Cavendish, "Account between my br. Devonshire & me. June 18. 1733," Devon. Coll., 86/comp 1.

[86] In a dispute over appointments between the duke of Devonshire and the duke of Newcastle. Duke of Devonshire to Hartington, 8 and 20 May, 15 and 24 June 1755. Devon. Coll., nos. 163.51. 163.52, 163.60, and 163.62.

basis of political power in the eighteenth century, and the lord lieutenant of a county was the highest local official, though the lord lieutenancy of Ireland had a trace of derogation. In any event, William carried out his job competently for seven years. William did favors for Walpole in kind, helping to keep him in office.[87] William was a hard drinker, a gambler, not overly smart, and distinctly lazy. He was also cautious and duty-bound, family traits, which could be regarded as strengths. Johnson, who rarely saw anything he could admire in a whig, saw in William a man who was "unconditional . . . in keeping his word," a man of honor.[88] The record we have of Charles's relationship with his brother William has entirely to do with money. That was so even during the second Jacobite rebellion of 1745 (the first had been thirty years before, in 1717), when the pretender, Prince Charles Edward Stuart, landed in Scotland from France with seven followers, raised an army, and after initial military victory advanced south a good ways into England. (If by discussing in detail the political career only of the second duke of Devonshire, who died in 1729, we have given the impression that after the second duke the dynastic future of the kingdom had been settled in the Revolution, we again correct it: until this rebellion, the tories remained by and large Jacobites, who schemed to restore the Stuart dynasty with foreign intervention.[89]) The rebels reached as far as Derby, from where they menaced Chatsworth. By subscription William raised a regiment in Derbyshire to stop the invasion, marching here and there, and generally keeping out of the way until danger was past. In London, Charles was William's surrogate banker and advisor on how to save William's medals then at Chatsworth; unless the medals were "sent out of the Kingdom" (which speaks of the peril of the dynasty, as Lord Charles saw it), he did not think they could be saved if the French landed, since there would be a rising right there.[90] Nothing, as it turned out, had to be done, as the prince was forced to retreat, and the revolt ended in 1746.

William had great confidence in his youngest brother. Two years after succeeding to the dukedom, William made out his will, in which he left to William Manners and others his horses but named twenty-seven year-old Charles Cavendish and his wife, Anne, and Robert Walpole trustees for his children,[91] of which he had seven. Of the

four sons, three entered politics, all staunch whigs and allies of Fox, and one entered the military, which by then was an uncommon career for a Cavendish. The youngest son, Lord John, who was Henry Cavendish's age and went through school with Henry, held cabinet posts and of the sons was by far the most determined in politics. But the oldest son, William, was the most determined in love, and in so being, he knitted the two greatest aristocratic families in science, Robert Boyle's and Henry Cavendish's. When he was twenty-eight, William picked for his wife the sixteen-year-old Charlotte Boyle, a distant relation of the seventeenth-century chemist. From the point of view of the Cavendish fortune, she was a prize, the sole heir of the immensely rich Lord Burlington. (There is a story that Henry Cavendish was brought up in Burlington House in Piccadilly, but it seems rather improbable.[92]) But the Burlington family was talked about not because of its wealth but because of its scandals, which decided William's mother, herself a commoner before becoming duchess of Devonshire, against the match. The duke supported his son, the marriage took place, the duchess became unhinged, and the third duke's marriage fell apart. The practical result of all this

---

[87]Plumb, *Walpole* 1:42–43, 235–36, and 2:280.

[88]Pearson, *The Serpent and the Stag*, 89–91; quotation from Johnson on 90.

[89]Romney Sedgwick, *The House of Commons 1715–1754* (New York: Oxford University Press, 1970), 2:ix.

[90]William, Lord Hartington to Dr. Newcome, 14 Dec. 1745; Lord Charles Cavendish to the duke of Devonshire, undated, Devon. Coll., nos. 260.58 and 211.3. John Whitaker to Dickenson Knight, undated /1745/; R. Knight to Dickenson Knight, undated /Dec. 1745/; John Holland to Ralph Knight, undated /1745/, in Great Britain. Historical Manuscripts Commission, *Report on the Manuscripts of Sir William Fitzherbert, Bart., and Others* (London: Her Majesty's Stationary Office, 1893), 164–65. William, duke of Devonshire to Robert Wilmot, 25 Oct. 1745, in Great Britain. Historical Manuscripts Commission, *Report on the Liang Manuscripts Preserved in the University of Edinburgh*, vol. 2 (London: His Majesty's Stationary Office, 1925), 349. Richard Burden to /Viscount Irwin/, 7 Dec. 1745, Great Britain. Historical Manuscripts Commission, *Report on Manuscripts in Various Collections*. Vol. 8: *The Manuscripts of the Hon. Frederick Lindley Wood; M. L. S. Clemens, Esq.; Philip Unwin, Esq.* (London: His Majesty's Stationary Office, 1913), 138.

[91]Duke of Devonshire, "My Will," 1 Oct. 1731. Devon. Coll., no. 163.95.

[92]Royal Society, *The Record of the Royal Society of London*, 4th ed. (London: Royal Society of London, 1940), 65. By the time the Boyles and the Cavendishes became in-laws (for the second time) and the Cavendishes thereby acquired Burlington House, Henry Cavendish was about to begin his university studies. We have not been able to follow up this suggestion that Henry Cavendish lived in that house, but, of course, it could be true, since we know very little about his early years.

turmoil was that the already fabulous Cavendish estate nearly doubled in value.[93] To William's sorrow, his wife did not live long enough to become duchess, and he himself did not live many years after becoming the fourth duke. Lord Charles Cavendish was the responsible family intermediary once again; he met several times with the third duke's lawyer in connection with Hartington's marriage to Charlotte Boyle.[94]

The third duke of Devonshire died in 1755, and for a time his will was lost; it was Lord Charles who found it, on a sheet of letter paper, almost worn out (and not showy, in keeping with everything else about the plain third duke), which clarified the disposition of property and enabled life to go on.[95] The third duke's daughters made notable marriages too. Rachel married Horace Walpole's (the gossip Walpole's) cousin and name-sake, which might have been the reason why Horace Walpole eventually visited Chatsworth and changed his mind; before seeing the estate, he had always run it down, but no longer.[96] Another daughter of the third duke, Lady Carolina, married William Ponsonby, second earl of Bessborough, who at the time was secretary to the third duke as lord lieutenant of Ireland. To their son, the third earl of Bessborough, Henry Cavendish would leave a sixth of his great fortune in his will.[97] The third duke's third daughter, Lady Elizabeth, married into the same family, John Ponsonby, and to make up her dowry the duke borrowed from Lord Charles Cavendish. The duke was rich in property but, typically, short of cash.[98]

For the women in his family, Lord Charles Cavendish assumed various obligations. When he was in his mid thirties, he together with his uncle Lord James served as executors of the estate of his aunt Lady Elizabeth (Cavendish) Wentworth.[99] Property was commonly assigned for raising dowries, and in 1723, just after his daughter Diana died in childhood, the second duke of Devonshire set aside lands to raise 6,000 pounds for each of his three surviving daughters, Ladies Rachel, Elizabeth, and Anne. Rachel and Elizabeth were about to be married at the time, and their brother Charles was named representative for Anne, who was without prospect and, in the event, never did marry. In time everyone was paid off in cash with interest to keep the properties within the Cavendish estate,[100] but Charles had to talk hard to

bring Anne around to the logic of the family's investments, she being "extreamly jealous, & fearful of being injured."[101] Like all of the second duke's daughters who did not die prematurely, Anne lived a long life, dying in 1780 at age seventy. Rachel, who married Sir William Morgan of Tredegar of a family of big landowners and country whigs, had four children, and lived upwards of eighty.[102] Charles kept in touch with Rachel's family: when her daughter Elizabeth married William Jones of Llanarthy in 1767, Lord Charles was a party to the settlement.[103] In 1723 Charles's sister Elizabeth married the Member of Parliament for Lancaster Sir Thomas Lowther, whose family together with the Musgraves "controlled the nerve centre of political

---

[93]Pearson, *The Serpent and the Stag*, 93–103.

[94]Lord Charles Cavendish's involvement is reflected in the statement of expenses rendered to the third duke by Hutton Perkins, the duke's lawyer, on 13 May 1748. Devon. Coll., no. 313.1.

[95]R. Landaff to the fourth duke of Devonshire, 6 Dec. 1755; Thomas Heaton to the fourth duke of Devonshire, 6 Dec. 1755. Devon. Coll., nos. 356.5 and 432.0. Theophilus Lindsey to Earl of Huntington, 24 Dec. 1755. Great Britain, Historical Manuscripts Commission, *Report on the Manuscripts of the Late Reginald Rawdon Hastings, Esq., of the Manor House Ashby de la Zouche*, 4 vols. (London: His Majesty's Stationary Office, 1928–47) 3:111–14, on 113.

[96]Pearson, *The Serpent and the Stag*, 102–3.

[97]Entries for the second and third earls of Bessborough, in *Collins's Peerage of England* 7:266–67. Francis Bickley, *The Cavendish Family* (London: Constable, 1911), 207.

[98]The third duke of Devonshire created a bond to Lord Charles Cavendish for 12,000 pounds, the purpose of which was to give the duke power to raise 6,000 pounds for the dowry of Lady Elizabeth. Lord Charles advanced the 6,000 pounds for this use, and the duke agreed to take out a mortgage on his properties to repay Lord Charles with interest. "Bond from His Grace the Duke of Devonshire to the Rt Honble Lord Charles Cavendish," 22 Sep. 1743, Devon. Coll., L/44/12.

[99]"Probate of the Will of Ly Eliz. Wentworth 1741," Devon. Coll., L/43/13. Lady Elizabeth was the widow of Sir John Wentworth of Northempsall. Seven years later, Lords Charles and James Cavendish were released from any further claim on them as executors by another Lady Wentworth, Dame Bridget of York: "Ly Wentworths Release to Lady Betty Wentworths Executors March 5 1748." But Lord Charles kept a notebook for Lady Betty Wentworth's personal estate for twenty years, from 1741 to 1761. After 1748 Lords Charles and James received a small dividend from two hundred shares of South Sea stock regularly. After Lord James's death, his part went to Richard (Chandler) Cavendish and, eventually, to Lord Charles.

[100]"Deed to Exonerate the Estate of the Duke of Devonshire from the Several Portions of Six Thousand Pounds . . . to be Directed to Be Raised for Lady Rachel Morgan, Lady Elizabeth Lowther and Anne Cavendish the Three Surviving Daughters of William Second Duke of Devonshire . . . ." 28 July 1775. Devon. Coll., L/19/67.

[101]Lord Charles Cavendish to Heaton, 18 Aug. 1775, draft, and "Account of Deeds to Be Executed by Lord Charles Cavendish." Devon. Coll., 86/comp. 1.

[102]*Collins's Peerage of England* 1:356. Holmes, *British Politics . . . Anne*, 222.

[103]Articles on the marriage of William Jones and Miss Morgan, daughter of Lady Rachel Morgan, to which Lord Charles Cavendish is a party, 4 July 1767: Devon. Coll., L/43/16.

power in the two border counties of Cumberland and Westmorland."[104] The Lowther connection drew Charles into a legal fog worthy of Dickens.

Frequently Lord Charles saw his sister Lady Elizabeth at Chatsworth or at Holker, the great Lowther house in Lancashire, edged with magnificent gardens, set on a wooded, hilly park on Morecambe Bay.[105] Charles was named godfather to Elizabeth's second child.[106] Then the troubles began. The spunky Elizabeth, who wished she had been a brother so she could have gone abroad with Charles and James, went insane. In 1737 she was placed in the hands of physicians "to try what effect it will have upon her to make her of better behaviour."[107] (It evidently had none; it may be that she was placed in Saint Luke's Hospital for Lunaticks, since Sir James Lowther left a bequest to it in his will.[108]) Sir Thomas, her husband, a kind but improvident man, lapsed into heavy drinking and debt. In 1745 Thomas died at Holker without a will, and his and Elizabeth's one surviving child, William, was placed under the guardianship of Lord Charles Cavendish, the duke of Devonshire, and Lord Lonsdale.[109] Charles pursued every possibility of turning the encumbered Lowther property into cash; e.g., Thomas had been a hunter and had dogs, which Charles wanted to sell, as he explained to the agent on the scene: "people are more inclineable to beg than to buy, but my business is to sell & not to give." Charles wanted to sell the beer too, since it would not be "worth the Guardians while" to buy it for Sir Williams use when he came of age.[110] Soon after Thomas had died, another Lowther died, his cousin John, leaving most of his estate to Thomas and Elizabeth's single child, William, and Charles had now to sort out the details of this property as well. Charles made notes of 120 letters in one of the books he kept on the Lowther business. Young William Lowther, in the meantime, was now at Cambridge desiring books from his father's library and money for his tutor and tailor, and contemplating a political life. Debters were on Charles's back. For Elizabeth, "Lady B." (Lady Betty), his insane sister and now widow, he paid a fee to the best doctors in London, Drs. Richard Mead and Edward Wilmot, another to her apothecary, and still other bills to other persons. She did not live long after he took charge of the estate.[111] Charles kept on friendly terms with William, his former ward, now of age, inviting him

to dinner at his house with scientific friends in 1753.[112] That year William was appointed lord lieutenant of Westmorland,[113] and two years later he was elected a Member of Parliament. Then suddenly, in 1756, while attended by Drs. Heberden and Shaw, Sir William died of scarlet fever. Sir William in the meantime had acquired immense riches from his distant uncle Sir James Lowther of Whitehaven, who died in 1755.[114] This Lowther was the fourth mainly rich Lowther to die in just over ten years. There was a funneling effect, with the wealth piling up. Sir William brought a fortune close to the bosom of the Cavendishes, which was seen as a kind of family coup.[115] He was only twenty-eight when he died, and he had no son to succeed him. His will directed his estate to go to certain people and the work of distributing it to Lord Charles Cavendish, who was entitled to residual plunder.[116]

According to an acquaintance of Henry Cavendish, the Lowther estate at Holker was owned by Lord Charles Cavendish and then by

---

[104]*The London Diaries of William Nicolson Bishop of Carlisle 1702–1718*, ed. C. Jones and G. Holmes (Oxford: Clarendon Press, 1985), 3.

[105]Sir Thomas Lowther to Sir James Lowther, 12 Aug. and 5 Sep. 1726, and 11 July 1734. Cumbria County Record Office, Carlisle, D/Lons./W. Bundles 30 and 37. *The Victoria History of the County of Lancaster*, ed. W. Farer and J. Brownbill, vol. 8 (London: Constable, 1914), 270–72.

[106]Thomas Lowther to James Lowther, 8 Aug. 1728, Cumbria County Record Office, Carlisle, D/Lons/W, Letters, 39: Misc. Letters & Papers, 1728–39.

[107]Sir James Lowther to John Spedding, 16 June 1737; quoted in J. V. Beckett, "The Lowthers at Holker: Marriage, Inheritance and Debt in the Fortunes of an Eighteenth-Century Landowning Family," *Transactions of the Historic Society of Lancashire and Cheshire* 127 (1977): 47–64, on 51.

[108]Sir James Lowther's will, 1754. Devon. Coll., L/31/17.

[109]Court appointment of Lord Charles Cavendish as administrator of Sir Thomas Lowther's estate: Devon Coll., L/11/31. Lord Charles Cavendish to John Fletcher, 18 July 1745; Edward Butler to John Fletcher, 16 May 1745. Lancashire Record Office, DDca 22/5 and 22/3/1.

[110]Lord Charles Cavendish to John Fletcher, 27 July 1745; Lord Charles Cavendish to William Richardson, 29 Mar. /1746/. Lancashire Record Office, DDca 22/5 and 22/7.

[111]Lord Charles Cavendish, third notebook, in Devon. Coll., L/43/14. Elizabeth Lowther died in 1747, according to Beckett, "The Lowthers at Holker," 51.

[112]Birch Diary (5 June 1753).

[113]Beckett, "The Lowthers at Holker," 51.

[114]Sir James Lowther's will of 1754, Devon Coll., L/31/17.

[115]Henry Fox wrote to Hartington, who in two months would become the fourth duke of Devonshire, "I must wish yr Lordship Joy of the very great Acquisition made by your near Relation Sr. W. Lowther, which I am credibly informed, is 4,000 pounds a year in Land, Coal Mines bringing in 11,000 pounds a year, & not less than 400,000 pounds in Money. Sr. James Lowther has 100,000 pounds & an Estate in Middlesex, not a great one." Letter of 4 Jan. 1755. Devon. Coll., no. 330.30.

[116]What was not specified in the will went to Lord Charles Cavendish, the sole executor. "Inventory of Wrought Plate from

Henry, but this account puzzles us and can hardly be right. Holker and another nearby estate, Furness, were devised by Sir William to his maternal cousins Lords George Augustus and Frederick Cavendish, sons of the third duke of Devonshire.[117] This is not to say that Lord Charles would not have liked to own the valuable and beautiful estate of Holker.

The great portion of the wealth of the deceased Sir William was reverted by the will of the deceased Sir James Lowther to another James Lowther, the future first earl of Lonsdale, who was not yet of age. The sudden fortune of this young man prompted Horace Walpole to fear that England was becoming the "property of six or seven people."[118] Cavendish, as Sir William's executor, was soon in conflict with young James Lowther. His overseeing of the Lowther properties—manors, farms, collieries, iron pits, lead mines, fire engines, timber, even a fishery—was an immense job, which now became compounded by a law suit. Katherine Lowther, James's mother, thought that Cavendish was unreasonable and hard. She had a point, though both parties appear grasping. It is clear that Cavendish hoped to profit from a technicality arising from the close deaths of Sir James and Sir William Lowther. Cavendish was not only William's sole executor, he was also sole executor of James, since the original executor, William, had died almost immediately after James. Charles claimed that Sir James's residual estate, consisting of collieries, land, and buildings, passed through Sir William to him. He also claimed 30,000 pounds in New South Sea Annuities, which were put in trust to finance the transfer of Sir William's estate to young James. Charles argued that these funds were his because the transfer of estates could not take place in the specified time for the reason that James was not of age.[119] Charles, that is, claimed property that fell through the legal net; for in neither will was he the intended beneficiary. The case was debated, council on both sides was heard, and the judge declared that the collieries and so forth belonged to young James and that the 30,000 pounds did too and that Cavendish was to pay over to young James the interest on those annuities. Charles lost completely.[120] As the biographers of Lord Charles Cavendish, we are partial and take satisfaction in what young James Lowther, earl of Lonsdale, made of his great

wealth. He proved to be a successful politician, who insured his own elections and commanded those in several other seats by means of lavish expenditure. He owned nine Members of Parliament, who were called "Sir James's Ninepins." In part because of the way he used his wealth to exercise power and in part because of his character, he was known in his counties as the "bad earl." In boasting that he owned the land, fire, and water of Whitehaven, he was referring to the collieries and so on that came to him from Sir James Lowther's estate instead of going to Lord Charles Cavendish.[121]

The Lowther affair occupied as many pages of notation and probably as much time as Lord Charles Cavendish's scientific experiments. Throughout, Cavendish exercised the hereditary instinct of his family to acquire property. The

----

Holker" is a long list of flatware and hollowware. The numbers alongside the items are in Henry Cavendish's hand. Devon. Coll., 86/comp. 1.

[117]John Burrow, who knew Henry Cavendish from the Royal Society Club, recalled that Cavendish told him that Lord George Cavendish left Holker Hall to his father and that his father left it to him. Cavendish told him that he wanted to do with this what the iron-founder John Wilkinson had done with his property across the bay from Holker, expand it into the water. John Barrow, *Sketches of the Royal Society and Royal Society Club* (London, 1849), 146–47. But that Lord George (Augustus) died in 1794, after Lord Charles. In the year Sir William Lowther died, Lord Charles Cavendish learned that Katherine Lowther (see below) had "thoughts of making over the estate /of Holker/ to Lord George for a consideration." Charles Cavendish to William Richardson, 28 Dec. 1756, Lancashire Record Office, DDca, 22/7. Lord George (Augustus) Cavendish acquired Holker and went there frequently, and as late as around 1788 he was making alterations in the gardens. *Victoria History of the County of Lancaster,* 271. Holker eventually went to Henry Cavendish's heir Lord George (Augustus Henry) Cavendish, but not through Henry Cavendish. A confusion may have arisen from the rectory of Cartmet, near Holker, which Lord Charles Cavendish and after him Henry held in trust. There is a long series of leases in the Cavendish estate papers, beginning with "Copy of the Lease of the Rectory & Tythes of Cartmell from the Bishop of Chester to Lord Charles Cavendish for the Lives of Sir James Lowther, Mrs. Katherine Lowther & Lord George Augustus Cavendish." Devon. Coll., L/36/62. The trust took over the payments that the Lowthers earlier had paid directly to the bishop of Chester for the rectory of Cartmel. Beckett, "The Lowthers at Holker," 54.

[118]Horace Walpole to Montague, 20 Apr. 1756, *Horace Walpole's Correspondence,* ed. W. S. Lewis, vol. 9 (New Haven: Yale University Press, 1941), l83–87, on 185.

[119]Katherine Lowther to James Lowther, 8, 11, 15, 19 July 1756; "Heads of What Is Agreed on between Ld Charles Cavendish & Sir James Lowther," n.d. Cumbria Record Office, Carlisle, Archive, D/Lons/L1/61 and 62.

[120]"Sr. W. & Sr. J. Lowthers' Wills & Papers Relating to Law Suit between L.C.C. & Sr. J. Lowther." Devon. Coll., no. 31/17. Cavendish appealed the decision concerning the 30,000 pounds.

[121]"Lowther, James, Earl of Lonsdale," *DNB* 12:217–20. We have referred only to Lowther's flaws. He was capable of exercising good political judgment: during the American Revolution, for example, he was active on the side of Lord John Cavendish and the other whigs who opposed the war and George III.

dispute was entirely impersonal on Cavendish's part, and precisely for that reason, it gives us an insight into his person. His involvement came about because of his mad sister, who had married a Lowther, but it became more than a family duty; it became an unexpected opportunity. Without question, at a certain point Cavendish thought that he was going to become a very rich man into the bargain. He was aware that he was in a delicate position, since any worldly goods that came to him did not go to another, the last in this sequence of Lowthers, the still-living (and still minor) James. The Lowther riches were intended to go to a Lowther, as was right and proper. Lord Charles Cavendish had been invited in as an administrator, but because he was also something of an interloper too, he took pains to make clear that his claim on William's personal estate did not arise out of greed: "I do not desire to have a farthing more than I have a right to." We have to take this man of principle at his word: what was his was his by *right*, and so by "law as well as from the principles of justice," he was "intitled" to a full disclosure of the extent and value of the estate. In this matter he believed he had not been treated with "strict justice." For his part in this dispute over interests, he intended to "act with perfect openness & candour."[122] The expressions that Lord Charles Cavendish used, "strict justice" and "perfect openness," are those, as we will see, that his son Henry would use. They applied equally to personal conduct, politics, and science.

Try as hard as he might, Lord Charles did not grow rich through the Lowthers. He did become rich, but it was to be from another line of the family. Elizabeth Cavendish, another Elizabeth—Elizabeth was one of the often repeated Cavendish names, starting with the impressive founder of the family's riches, Bess of Hardwick—was a younger first cousin of Charles. Her father was Lord James Cavendish (Lord Charles's uncle, not his brother of the same name), a Fellow of the Royal Society, who had an interest in mathematics and natural philosophy,[123] and her mother was Anne Yale, daughter of Elihu, a rich diamond merchant and governor of Fort St. George in Madras, after whom an Ivy League university is named. In 1732 Elizabeth married the politician Richard Chandler, son of Edward Chandler, bishop of Durham, just a year after Lord James's other child, William, had married another Chandler, Barbara. Richard

Chandler was a man of wide learning, with a very substantial library; he and Lord Charles Cavendish would seem to have had interests in common.[124] In 1751 Elizabeth's father and brother both died, and her mother had died earlier, leaving only her and Richard Chandler to continue that branch of the family. That year, 1751, Richard took his wife's name and was known from then on as Richard Cavendish. Richard Cavendish died before Elizabeth, leaving her sole owner of a house in Piccadilly, and a great deal more real estate and, in addition, a large sum in securities and mortgages.[125] Having no children, she originally intended to leave her real property to the duke of Devonshire and the rest of her estate to her only living male first cousin on the Cavendish side, Charles. Shortly before her own death, however, she changed her will, cutting off the duke (her second cousin) and naming as co-executor with Lord Charles Cavendish the prominent lawyer and politician Lord Charles Camden. The two executors were to hold the Piccadilly house in trust, but otherwise, as far as Cavendish was concerned, the will was practically the same. Cavendish took upon himself the task of executing the will, which, except for the land and specific requests, left everything to him.[126]

To begin with relative trifles: as residuary legatee, Lord Charles Cavendish was entitled to Lady Elizabeth's diamond earrings, pearls, solitaire, coins, Oriental stories, and so on, but in so avaricious a family as the Cavendishes, his right to these things did not go unchallenged. This time Charles prevailed.[127] The main point was the

---

[122]Lord Charles Cavendish to William Richardson, 26 and 29 June and 27 July 1756. Lancashire County Record Office, DDca, 22/7.

[123]Lord James Cavendish and Lord Charles Cavendish together recommended Gowin Knight for fellowship in the Royal Society for his "mathematical and Philosophical knowledge," 24 Jan. 1745, Royal Society, Certificates, vol. 1, no. 14, f. 297.

[124]Richard Chandler's library was evidently on all subjects, including science; it contained books by Newton, Boyle, Hooke, and a good many eighteenth-century scientific writers. *A Catalogue of a Large, Valuable, and Elegant Collection of Books; Including the Libraries of the Late Richard Cavendish, Esq.; the Rev. Dr. Jortin; and Several Other Curious Parcels Lately Purchased . . . The Sale Will Begin in February 1771 . . . By Benjamin White, at Horace's Head, in Fleet Street, London.*

[125]The round figure of 30,000 pounds turned up again, this time in a promise by the duke of Devonshire to repay that amount to Lady Elizabeth. The duke's promise is in a formal letter enclosed in the document, "The Duke of Devonshire to Lord Charles Cavendish and Mr. /Dudley/ Long, Lease for a Year, 15 June 1772." Devon. Coll., L/19/64.

[126]Lady Elizabeth Cavendish's will, 26 Feb. 1778. Devon. Coll., L/31/37. In a codicil of 31 Jan. 1779, she removed her real property from the duke of Devonshire, substituting Dudley Long.

wealth on paper: 75,000 pounds in three percent consolidated bank annuities (consols), 22,000 pounds in three percent reduced bank annuities, and 47,000 pounds in mortgages. Elizabeth Cavendish's will was brought to court in May 1780, and three and a half years later the fortune it had bequeathed to Charles Cavendish became the property of his son Henry.[128]

[127] "Copy Case with Mr. Att^y General's Opinion," 1780, Devon. Coll., L/114//74. The judge, in coming down on Lord Charles's side, declared that the jewels were personal ornaments, not part of a "collection" to be preserved for posterity. This was not the end of the matter: "Lord Geo. Cavendish & Lord Camden Bill," 1782, ibid.

[128] "Lord Camden and the Honourable Henry Cavendish Assignment and Deed of Indemnity," 31 Dec. 1783, Devon. Coll., L/31/37. Also "Copy of Mr Pickerings Letter to Mr Wilmot," 26 Apr. 1780, ibid., 86/comp. 1.

CHAPTER 4

❧

Public Activities

Public Life

Lord Charles Cavendish was a man of reason, whose manifest administrative skills were valued in arenas outside of politics and science, in the founding and working of new institutions. The people he worked with were, in many cases, the same people he worked with in politics and science.

For twenty years Robert Walpole kept the country in peace and prosperity, during which time London acquired several new institutions. They included hospitals, Westminster in 1720, Guy's in 1724, and several more by 1740. These were hospitals in the usual sense of the word, and in addition there was a new charitable hospice for unwanted children, the Foundling Hospital. Inspired by foundations for this purpose on the Continent, in Amsterdam, Paris, and elsewhere, the Foundling Hospital was the culmination of an arduous and heartfelt campaign by Thomas Coram on behalf of "great numbers of Helpless Infants daily exposed to Destruction," as he put it in a memorial addressed to the king. The Hospital was incorporated by royal charter in 1739, in a ceremony attended by bankers and merchants from the city and by six dukes, eleven earls, and assorted lesser peers, who set the tone of the endeavor. The charter was received by the president of the Foundling Hospital, the duke of Bedford, a relative of Cavendish. Cavendish's brother the duke of Devonshire and his father-in-law the duke of Kent were named in the charter as original governors. Lord Charles Cavendish himself was elected governor later that year.[1] The Foundling Hospital was first located in a leased house, but soon, by 1752, it had acquired a new building, set in the fields, like the buildings of most other new institutions in eighteenth-century London. This building, a pair of Georgian brick blocks flanking a deeply recessed entrance, was in its way an imposing structure, almost palatial. Because the Foundling Hospital was financed by private wealth, with some help from parliament, its new building was architecturally elaborated, unlike, say, the new London hospitals, which were financed by annual subscription. The interior of the Hospital was adorned with paintings; elegant concerts were held there.[2]

This fashionable charity needed administrators who were both able and hardened to the task, for conditions of life in an eighteenth-century foundling hospital were, at best, appalling. During the first four years, the Hospital admitted children indiscriminately, whether true foundlings—exposed and deserted children who would otherwise die—or not, nearly a hundred a week at times. Of the roughly 15,000 children received then, over 10,000 did die, a mortality rate of seventy percent. An unanticipated traffic sprang up. Infants from the provinces were brought to London under barbaric conditions and dumped at the Hospital, thereby sparing parish officials the trouble and expense of maintenance. Parents exploited the Hospital too by abandoning their children there, more dead than alive, to avoid the cost of burial. The administrators of the Hospital had to deal with the consequences of and, ultimately, with their policy.

Public attitude favored the Hospital. There were practical as well as humanitarian reasons why children should be saved if possible; e.g., to keep the kingdom from running out of soldiers after the high casualties in the recent war with France. The best medical opinion in London was made available to the institution. Hans Sloane, president of the Royal Society, and Richard Mead, both of whom were named in the charter, were among the leading physicians who volunteered their expensive services. Cavendish's good friend and colleague at the Royal Society William Watson, an expert on

---

[1]R. H. Nichols and F. A. Wray, *The History of the Foundling Hospital* (London: Oxford University Press, 1935), 16, 19.

[2]John Summerson, *Georgian London*, rev. ed. (Harmondsworth: Penguin Books, 1978), 119–20.

infectious childhood diseases, was appointed physician to the Foundling Hospital. Watson distinguished himself in the crusade of the Hospital to prevent the devastations of smallpox, which was then a disease that primarily struck children under three.[3]

At about the same time that Cavendish was elected governor, the next two presidents of the Royal Society, Folkes and Macclesfield, were elected governors too, and all three went on to become vice-presidents of the Hospital. The job of vice-president was not a ceremonial but a working job, the only kind Cavendish ever took on.[4] Cavendish spent endless hours at the Hospital every week, over decades.

With the desire to put its children to work, the Foundling Hospital turned for help to the white-herring industry. The Society of Free British Fisheries, having encouraged the setting up of the famous Ropeyard in the Colonnade, in 1753 agreed to buy as much Yarmouth Shale as the foundlings could braid. It turned out to be considerable; a workshop for the purpose was laid out in a converted kitchen in the Hospital and was proudly opened to the public so that it could observe the children at work.[5] Lord Charles Cavendish was active at both ends of this arrangement; he was not only a governor of the Foundling Hospital but also a member of the council of the Society of Free British Fisheries.[6]

Incorporated by an act of parliament in 1750, the Society was a London-based company modeled after the great chartered trading companies. Like the British East India Company, it was formed in response to competition from the Dutch, who then dominated the trade in cod and herring. Called "white fish," the herring, about a foot long, was silver sided, the cod, two to over three feet in length, was white on the belly. These fish were known to be nutritious, and the fresh head of cod was thought delicious. Moreover, they were believed to be inexhaustible. By studying the melt, the great microscopist Antoni van Leeuwenhoek estimated that there were more animalcules in a single codfish than there were people on earth. If only two males and two females were left in the sea, in the next season there would be as many cod as ever. The promoters of the Society reasoned that since Britain was situated in the "midst of one continuous Herring Shoal," all that was needed to

revive British fisheries was the "Power and united Strength" of a trading company. *Flourish the Herring-Fishery!*, a new ballad, was sung to the tune of *The Charming Month of May* in meetings halls across London. A good white-fish industry, the argument went, would empower the kingdom against France (by insuring a supply of seamen), improve its moral character (by eliminating the barbaric practice of impressing seamen), rebuild the economy in depressed regions like the Highlands, and provide work for the unemployed and for children in charity schools (the Society and the Hospital were made for one another). The Society was permitted to own ships, build warehouses and wharves, carry naval staples, regulate trade, and raise a capital sum for these purposes in the form of joint stock paying three percent.[7]

The officers of the Society, elected for three years, included a governor, a president, and a council. We do not know when Charles Cavendish was elected to the council, but we can imagine why he would have been interested. First, there was the connection with the Foundling Hospital, to which Cavendish, as governor, gave conscientious service. Then, as usual, there was a family connection. When the Society was founded, Cavendish was overseeing the Lowther estates. Sir James Lowther

---

[3]Ruth K. McClure, *Coram's Children: The London Foundling Hospital in the Eighteenth Century* (New Haven: Yale University Press, 1981), 205–18. William Watson, *An Account of a Series of Experiments Instituted with a View of Ascertaining the Most Successful Method of Inoculating the Smallpox* (London, 1768). Charles Creighton, *A History of Epidemics in Britain*, vol. 2: *From the Extinction of the Plague to the Present Time*, 2d ed. (London: Frank Cass, 1965), 500, 514.
[4]Nichols and Wray, *Foundling Hospital* , 298, 354, 413.
[5]Ibid., 131.
[6]*Collins's Peerage of England Geneological, Biographical, and Historical*, 9 vols., ed. E. Brydges (London, 1812) 1:356.
[7]Francis Grant, *A Letter to a Member of Parliament, Concerning the Free British Fisheries* (London, 1750), 37. Anon., *The Fisheries Revived: or, Britain's Hidden Treasure Discovered* (London, 1750), 13, 46, 50–52. By a Trader in Fish, *The Best and Most Approved Method of Curing White-Herrings, and All Kinds of White–Fish* (London, 1750). Anon., *The Vast Importance of the Herring Fishery, etc. to These Kingdoms: As Respecting the National Wealth, Our Naval Strength, and the Highlanders. In Three Letters Addressed to a Member of Parliament* (London, /1750/). Mr. Horsley, *A Translation of the Dutch Placart and Ordinance for the Government of the Great Fishery* (London, 1750). Anon., *Britannia's Gold-Mine; or, the Herring-Fishery for Ever. A New Ballad, to the Tune of, There Was a Jovial Beggar, etc. Sung at Draper's-Hall, by the Anti-Gallacians; at Merchant-Taylor's Hall, by the Sons of the Clergy; and at the Spring-Gardens, Vauxhall. To Which Is Added Another New Ballad, on the Same Subject*, 2d ed. (London, 1750). Britain had three sorts of fishing, "free," "common," and "several." A person with the right of free fishing could take possession of fish without title; a free fishery implied the freedom of fishing with others. William Nelson, *The Laws Concerning Game . . .*, 4th ed. (London, 1751), 97– 101.

had owned a fishery and a fleet of fifteen ships, which, Cavendish was convinced, were now lawfully his. Sir James had belonged to the Society of Free British Fisheries; in fact, in the list of nearly seventy charter members, his name came second, following that of the Lord Mayor of London. Cavendish was not a charter member but he may well have become a member when, and because, Sir James (and Sir William) Lowther died.[8] As a councillor of the Society, Cavendish would have been performing a duty, as usual looking after his and everyone else's interests.

Readers of books lacked a public institution in London. The Universities of Oxford and Cambridge had libraries, cathedrals had them, wealthy individuals did too, and there were a few specialized libraries such as the one for law at the Inns of Court and the one for science at the Royal Society. In addition a few small public libraries had been established in London in the seventeenth century, but in general, people who were not rich enough to own their own libraries or did not have a rich patron or did not belong to a learned profession did not have access to books. There was a good deal of borrowing among ordinary persons with small holdings of books, but what books an interested person could lay his hands on was up to chance. In the matter of public libraries England was a poor cousin to European countries. Italy had had important public libraries since the fifteenth century; in Prussia Berlin had had a great public library since the late seventeenth century; in France the royal library in Paris had been open to the public since 1735, and the Mazarin library there was nearly as large; and other great European cities such as Vienna and Munich had their major public libraries.[9] London, the late-comer, in the middle of the eighteenth century, acquired its own in the form of the British Museum.

The British Museum was not primarily a library, though in the eighteenth century that became its principal use. Its benefactor was Hans Sloane, a great collector of natural history objects, various of which he would bring to meetings of the Royal Society. So identified was Sloane with his collection that when he stepped down from the presidency in 1741, the secretary Cromwell Mortimer dedicated a volume of the *Philosophical Transactions* to him and his "noble and immense Collection."

His natural history collection together with his large library of books on the subject and on medicine, inflated by Mortimer to the "most complete in the Universe,"[10] lived on after him as an institution.

By Sloane's will, at his death in 1753, the nation was offered his collection and books, for a price. Parliament accepted and decided on a way of raising the necessary money, a (mildly corrupt, as it turned out) lottery. In 1754, the trustees bought Montague House and moved into it Sloane's collection and in addition the Cottonian Collection and the Harleian Manuscripts. Montague House, which was open and free to "all studious and curious Persons,"[11] was sometimes referred to at first as Sloane's Museum, but it would be known as the British Museum.

Cavendish was not named in Sloane's will as one of the original trustees, but he was included in it in a long list of dignitaries, designated "visitors," starting with the king and the prince of Wales, who were charged with watching over Sloane's collection.[12] To get from these important people to the working people, the librarian and under-librarians, parliament approved a complicated plan. A manageable but still large number of persons selected from the larger number of trustees and visitors was directed to elect fifteen persons. These so-called "elected trustees" were then to name a standing committee to meet regularly with the staff and be responsible for the actual management of the Museum.

The elected trustees were joined by the president of the Royal Society, then Macclesfield, as an ex officio member. The connection with the Royal Society was and would remain close: eleven of the fifteen elected trustees were Fellows of the

---

[8]Sir James Lowther died five years after the founding of the Society. The original members of the Society are listed in *A Bill Intitled an Act for the Encouragement of the British White Herring Industry* (London, 1750). The third member listed, after Sir James Lowther, was Nathaniel Curzon, Lord Charles Cavendish's earlier fellow Member of Parliament from Derbyshire, the county of the duke of Devonshire. The duke from time to time was party to legal cases involving fisheries, evidently fisheries of the "several" kind, in which the owner is the owner of the soil where the water flows. Stuart A. Moore, *A History of the Foreshore and the Law Relating Thereto . . .*, 3d ed. (London, 1888), 720–21.

[9]Edward Miller, *That Noble Cabinet: A History of the British Museum* (London: Deutsch, 1973), 25.

[10]Dedication on 31 Dec. 1741, just a month after Sloane's resignation: *PT*, vol. 41. for 1739 and 1740, published in 1744. .

[11]Arundell Esdaile, *The British Museum Library: A Short History and a Survey* (London: George Allen & Unwin, 1946), 18.

[12]Sloane's printed will: BL Add Mss 36269, ff. 39–54. A handwritten list in 1753 of additional trustees includes Cavendish, f. 57.

Royal Society, one of whom was Cavendish, who was also named to the standing committee, which met regularly with the staff. Cavendish was among friends on the standing committee, his brother-in-law Philip Yorke and his colleagues Watson, Birch, and Macclesfield.[13]

Cavendish was involved in every stage of preparation for the opening of the Museum in 1759. He and his committee went to Sloane's house, where they found the insects in good condition but some of the birds and animals in an expected state of decay. They compared the contents of the cabinets with the catalogues in forty-nine volumes, and they made comparable inspections of the books of the several collections. There were endless, tedious meetings about repairs, insurance, contracts, finances, and the like. By 1755 Cavendish's name sometimes headed the list of trustees at the general meetings, despite the number of peers who could come but often did not, and whose names would have preceded his. Attendance at the weekly committee meetings dropped to five or so, but Cavendish was always there, and when Macclesfield was not, which was often, Cavendish presided.[14] Cavendish was a man of public affairs with broad intellectual interests and administrative skill, who could be counted on absolutely. That was not the least of the reasons why his services were valued at the British Museum and, in general, in the affairs of the learned world of London.

Montague House, which earlier had almost been grabbed up by the Foundling Hospital, was situated at the north end of town, on one of the first of the London squares, Bloomsbury, beyond which lay open fields and then Hampstead. Bloomsbury Square was then highly fashionable, home to rich and famous physicians such as Sloane and Mead. The original house, designed in the French style for Ralph, later first duke of, Montagu by the versatile curator of experiments of the Royal Society Robert Hooke, had burned down, and the duke had replaced it by a new but similar house resembling a contemporary Parisian hôtel. With its imposing facade, colonnades, an entrance topped by a cupola, and wings extending to the front to form a grand courtyard, and with an interior of spacious and lofty apartments and wall paintings, this mansion was in itself an expression of the grandeur of the idea of a great library and scientific collection in the British metropolis. Given the load it was to bear, of equal significance was the sober evaluation by the standing

committee, to which Cavendish belonged, of the house as a "Substantial, well built Brick Building." Seven and a half acres of garden came with it, to which Cavendish's friend and fellow trustee William Watson devoted a great deal of care.[15]

Montagu House had been unoccupied for several years and was generally run down; in the end, no expense was spared to restore the house to its former glory. Countless times Cavendish went up the elegant main staircase to the upper floor where the trustees met and where the manuscripts were housed. Less imposing was the reading room in the basement, a dark space containing a wainscot table and twenty chairs.[16]

The collections of the British Museum were dedicated to the "Advancement and Improvement of Natural Philosophy and Other Branches of Speculative Knowledge." If the Museum sounded like the Royal Society, it was not by accident. Its scientific ambition is evident in the high, if not actually incredible, qualifications desired of the head of staff (who was, however, called Principal Librarian rather than Keeper of the Collections, the title of a book man rather than a man of science). He was to be studious, learned, educated as a physician, versed in mathematics, a judge of inventions, able to carry on conversation with the learned in their fields, and competent to write and speak French and Latin and correspond with foreigners.[17] There were disqualifying criteria too, which were not mentioned.[18] Plenty of persons believed they fit

———————

[13]A. E. Gunther, "The Royal Society and the Foundation of the British Museum, 1753–1781," *Notes and Records of the Royal Society of London* 33 (1979): 207–16, on 209–10.

[14]Thomas Birch's minutes of the meetings of the Trustees of the British Museum: BL Add Mss 4450, ff. 1 and following. Minutes of the General Meetings and the Standing Committee Meetings of the Trustees of the British Museum, ibid., 4451, ff. 3 and following.

[15]Miller, *Noble Cabinet*, 50–54.

[16]Esdaile, *The British Museum Library*, 38–40. Edmund William Gosse, *Gray*, new ed. (London: Macmillan, 1906), 141–42.

[17]"Qualifications and Duty Required in the Principal Librarian," BL Add Mss 4449, f. 108. "Rules Proposed to Be Observed in Making the Collections of Proper Use to the Publick by Way of Resolutions in a General Meeting of the Trustees," ibid., f. 115.

[18]Emanuel Mendes da Costa applied for an under-librarian's job at the British Museum, with these credentials: he was a long-time Fellow of the Royal Society, an expert on fossils, and fluent in all of the main languages. Letter to Lord Hardwicke, 4 Feb. 1756, BL Add Mss 36269, f. 100. William Watson considered da Costa to be eminently qualified, but his "religion is an unsurmountable object." Letters to Archbishop of Canterbury, 21 June 1756, and Lord Hardwicke, 22 June 1756, BL Add Mss 36269, ff. 139–42, 144–45. Da Costa could not have been surprised. A few years later he asked Thomas Birch if it was "obnoxious to the Society that I (as by Profession a Jew) can put up for Hawksbee's place" in the Royal Society. Letter of 17 Jan. 1763, BL Add Mss 4317, f. 113.

the bill and offered credentials to prove it. Gowin Knight, who was chosen principal librarian, presented himself as a physician who had devoted the greatest part of his life to the "pursuit of natural Knowledge"[19] (the evidence, his powerful artificial steel magnets, he brought with him to the British Museum.)[20] Matthew Maty, De Moivre's friend, who was appointed an under-librarian, had accomplishments equally impressive. He had taken an M.D. under Boerhaave at the University of Leyden; he had studied natural philosophy, and he had been taught mathematics by his father; he had wide-ranging foreign connections as editor of the *Journal Britannique*, and he spoke French and Dutch.[21] Soon after joining the staff of the British Museum, Maty was elected secretary of the Royal Society. Another of the under-librarians was Charles Morton, physician to the Middlesex and Foundling Hospitals, who also had taken his M.D. at the University of Leyden and who too was a secretary of the Royal Society, and like Maty he too one day would become principal librarian.[22] A third under-librarian, James Empson, was in charge of Sloane's natural history collection. As each under-librarian had an assistant, the staff was sizable and "unexceptionable." That was William Watson's opinion on its competence; its "disposition," however, was another matter. Librarians and assistants were not on speaking terms; insubordination was rampant; ill-will persisted for years. Watson analyzed the conflict in terms of turf,[23] and the poet Thomas Gray, one of the first users of the library of the British Museum, compared the rebellious factions to fellows of a college: "The whole society, trustees and all, are caught up in arms."[24] The scientific use of the collections was not great at first.[25] People came to the Museum to read, and for a time, a two-month reservation was required even to secure a seat, but before long the reading room proved ample; after the Museum had been open a few months, Thomas Gray found himself one of only five readers, the others being the antiquarian William Stukeley and three hacks copying manuscripts for hire.[26] Readers were admitted for six months at a time, upon recommendation; members of the Royal Society and other learned bodies were admitted without recommendation. In 1759, the first year, beside men of historical and literary interests, such as Gray and David Hume, men of science, such as Watson,

Heberden, and John Hadley, visited the reading room too.[27] The library became the national library, and the natural history collection evolved into a great research center. This successful institution had no more assiduous early administrator than Lord Charles Cavendish.

Westminster Bridge

The early eighteenth century saw both the rapid improvement of roads through turnpiking and the beginning of bridge building on a large scale. The urgency was due to London, far and away the largest city in the world, the demands of which on the still largely agricultural nation were vast and insatiable. Herds of cattle and flocks of geese were driven down the turnpikes to feed the concentrated mass of humanity on the banks of the Thames. The streets of the city were filled with mud or dust depending on the weather, and to riders of carriages they were bone-jarring. Here and there stairs led down to the river, where cursing boatmen ferried paying passengers to the opposite bank. London Bridge, the one bridge in the city, was medieval, dangerous, and congested, built up with houses. Ideas for improving transportation in London by a second, modern bridge had been around since Elizabethan times, successfully resisted by impecunious monarchs, fierce watermen defending their traffic from ruin, and parties

---

[19]Gowin Knight to Lord Hardwicke, 22 Sep. 1754, BL Add Mss 36269, ff. 29–30.

[20]For placing his magnetic apparatus, Gowin Knight requested that a passage five feet wide be taken from two rooms in the British Museum. BL Add Mss 36269, f. 134.

[21]J. Jortin to Lord Hardwicke, n.d. and 12 Feb. 1756, BL Add Mss 36269, ff. 104–7.

[22]"Morton, Charles," *DNB* 13:1047–48.

[23]The under-librarians were naturalists, and their assistants were antiquarians, an unworkable combination. The different parts of the British Museum required different talents, which had to be properly assigned. Watson pointed out: "We have an extensive collection of the productions of nature & of art; a very large medical & philosophical library; as well as one relating to antiquities, & a vast collection of coins. . . ." The friction among the staff was rooted in this fact: "it must require a great length of time for any person to have a competent knowledge of any one branch of the museum & unless he be acquainted with it, he will be but little qualified to instruct others." The proper persons had to be matched up with the proper subjects. Typical good sense from William Watson to the Archbishop of Canterbury, 21 June 1756.

[24]Gosse, *Gray*, 142.

[25]A. E. Gunther, *The Founders of Science at the British Museum, 1753–1900* (Halesworth: Halesworth Press, 1980), 10–11.

[26]Gosse, *Gray*, 142.

[27]"Persons Admitted to Reading Room Jan. l2. 1759 to May ll. 1763," BL Add Mss 45867.

expressing a variety of fears, such as commercial competition, armed rebellion, and the falling down of London Bridge once it was neglected for a rival.[28]

Nobody knows why Lord Charles Cavendish left politics to immerse himself in scientific and learned affairs. It is, of course, not hard to imagine that after so many years in parliament he had grown tired of politics. He was, after all, politically unambitious and only dutiful. Whatever his reasons for desiring a change, he lived in a time and place that invited experiment in life as well as in the laboratory; England in the eighteenth century encouraged individual self-expression and personal autonomy.[29] For Cavendish, Westminster Bridge proved to be, in effect, a bridge between his earlier political career and his later one outside of politics.

Renewed energy behind the proposal of a new bridge at Westminster took the form of two petitions to parliament in 1721, presented by Westminster and the Home Counties. James Thornhill, Member of Parliament and Fellow of the Royal Society, produced a plan for a bridge at Westminster and enough support for a parliamentary committee to recommend proceeding.[30] A bridge bill was drawn up by William Pulteney, chairman of the committee, and Samuel Molyneux, Fellow of the Royal Society, astronomer, and secretary to the prince of Wales. Molyneux spoke for the prince's interest when he pointed out to the Commons that the "building of the bridge would be agreeable to his highness and be convenient for his family's passing and re-passing to his country house."[31] On the advice of Lord Burlington, architectural innovator and Fellow of the Royal Society, the committee commissioned the architect Colin Campbell to design the bridge. Burlington then consulted "two eminent mathematicians" and prominent Fellows of the Royal Society Edmond Halley and John Arbuthnot, who gave the bridge the go-ahead. The House of Commons debated the bridge bill but then dropped it, probably for political reasons, since Walpole, who favored the bridge and was on the committee, was well hated by then.[32]

The project was revived, this time for good, in 1733, when a "Society of Gentlemen," businessmen and the like who could afford the large expense of a petition, began meeting at Horn Tavern in New Palace Yard, Westminster. The promoters ordered the river "measured and sounded,"

and they solicited maps and surveys from Charles Labelye, the future engineer of the bridge. They asked the architect Nicholas Hawksmoor to prepare a design, and in 1735 a stone model of the bridge was shown to the prince of Wales and the House of Commons.[33] (Vying for the commission was Batty Langley, who at about this time was employed by Cavendish's father-in-law, the duke of Kent; turned down, Langley gleefully published a pamphlet at the time when the construction of the bridge was having its worst problems, in 1748, *A Survey of Westminster as 'Tis Now Sinking into Ruin*.[34])

In February 1736 a renewed petition for the bridge was submitted to the House of Commons, which again appointed a committee. This committee, which could hear testimony of any kind, chose J. T. Desaguliers on the subject of the "proper Instruments for boring the Soil under the River Thames," undoubtedly hoping this way to avoid the commercial controversy that had upset bridge plans in the past. They had to decide several matters: if a bridge was technically feasible; if its foundations and piers would affect the flow of the river and its traffic; and, finally, which site would be best. All of these matters were fraught with complications.[35]

The Westminster Bridge bill in May 1736 set up a large body of commissioners, about 175 in number. They were not necessarily Members of Parliament, although a good proportion of them were. They included such obviously useful persons as the director of the Bank of England and the Members of Parliament from Westminster. They included as well dukes, bishops, and admirals, who were useful in other, more or less obvious ways. And there were a good many Fellows of the Royal Society, such as Cavendish and Macclesfield. The first meeting was held in June, with Lord Sundon

[28]R. J. B. Walker, *Old Westminster Bridge: The Bridge of Fools.* (Newton Abbot: David and Charles, 1979), 12–32.
[29]Lawrence Stone, *The Family, Sex and Marriage in England 1500–1800* (Harmondsworth: Penguin Books, 1982), 151–52, 179.
[30]Walker, *Old Westminster Bridge*, 45–47.
[31]Romney Sedgwick, *The House of Commons 1715–1754*, 2 vols. (New York: Oxford University Press, 1970) 2:263.
[32]Walker, *Westminster Bridge*, 47–49.
[33]Ibid., 27, 50–51, 61.
[34]Howard Montagu Colvin, *A Biographical Dictionary of British Architects, 1600–1840*, rev. ed. (London: J. Murray, 1978), 355. Walker, *Old Westminster Bridge*, 182–83.
[35]16 Feb. 1736 (1735), *HCJ* 22:569.

in the chair and about fifty commissioners attending. One of the two officers appointed at the meeting was another Fellow of the Royal Society, Sir Joseph Ayloffe. The commissioners viewed the models of the bridge that had been exhibited in the Commons, and they set up a lottery with the Bank of England to finance the construction.[36]

The lottery did not catch on at first. In July 1736 the Bank of England reported that so far only about one fifth of the tickets had been sold, leading knowledgeable observers to say that that was the "end of that scheme for raising money." Of the original, large body of commissioners, only one or two now came to the meetings, too few for a quorum, and for the likely reason that there was nothing for them to do. The upshot was a second bridge act, which added incentives to the lottery.[37]

Cavendish was present at the meeting of the commissioners in June 1737 to consider the reality, the actual bridge in design stage. Thomas Ripley, comptroller of the King's Works and protégé of Walpole, presented plans for a stone bridge at a cost of 75,000 pounds, a figure which got bigger with subsequent discussions, and he also gave an estimate of 35,000 pounds for an alternative timber bridge at the Horseferry. The commissioners liked the lower estimate of the timber bridge.[38]

Bridge-builders followed parliament's deliberations closely, eager for the commission for this remunerative project; it took only two weeks for the first plans to be submitted, probably pulled out of the drawer. The Royal Society was kept informed; Thomas Innys showed the Society a model of his invention of a machine for laying the foundation of the piers of the new bridge. To decide on technical matters of this sort, in June 1737 the bridge commissioners formed a committee of thirteen, the so-called committee of works. Cavendish was appointed to it, as were several other Fellows of the Royal Society, though William Kent, the famous architect, was perhaps the only member of the committee with obvious qualifications.[39] Now both a commissioner and a committeeman for the bridge, Cavendish took his duties with his customary seriousness.

The works committee resolved to consider economical wooden bridges only, but it and the commissioners took an interest all the same in the stone-bridge advocate Labelye, especially for his method of laying the foundations of the piers,

which would work for either a timber or a stone superstructure.[40] Labelye had credentials different from those of his competitors, the best known of whom all came from the side of architecture and seem to have had no engineering experience. Labelye, by contrast, was not an architect at all but evidently had some training in engineering and surveying. The Commons treated him as an expert "engineer," calling on him to testify on the bridge before their own petition committee along with J. T. Desaguliers, who claimed Labelye as his "disciple" and "assistant."[41] Like Desaguliers, Labelye was of Huguenot origins. Educated in Geneva, he had settled in England, where he became involved in such projects as draining the fens and improving harbors.[42] Not himself a Fellow of the Royal Society, he was a friend of a good number of scientists. In the midst of building the bridge (to get ahead of our story) he wrote from Westminster to the president of the Royal Society, Folkes, sending him a calculation having to do with the card game whist.[43] The prospect of a gambling bridge-builder could be upsetting, but Labelye's calculation was only an exercise in the doctrine of chances. Labelye was a good enough mathematician for Desaguliers to publish Labelye's mathematical investigation of the *vis viva* controversy in mechanics.[44]

An unusually large number of commissioners, fifty-four, met in February 1738 to decide where the bridge was to be built. A petition for locating it was then presented to the Commons, which acting as a committee decided that it should be at Woolstaple, a short distance from the original

---

[36]Walker, *Westminster Bridge*, 63–67.

[37]Westminster Bridge, Minutes of the Bridge Commissioners, vol. 1: June 1736–Feb. 1740. Walker, *Westminster Bridge*, 73–4.

[38]Walker, *Westminster Bridge*, 78–79.

[39]Besides Cavendish, three others on the committee had been Fellows of the Royal Society since the 1720s. They were the chairman of the committee, Joseph Danvers, M.P., a lawyer by training and now a landowner; David Papillon, M.P., practicing lawyer; Thomas Viscount Gage, M.P., from 1743 master of the household to the prince of Wales. Walker, *Westminster Bridge*, 79, 86 n.7.

[40]5 Aug. 1737, Minutes of the Committee of Works, vol. l: Aug. 1737–Sep. 1744, Public Record Office, Kew, Work 6/39. 31 Aug. 1737 and 3 May 1738, Bridge Minutes.

[41]16 Feb. 1736 (1735), *HCJ* 22:569. J. T. Desaguliers, *A Course of Experimental Philosophy*, vol. 2 (London, 1744), 506.

[42]Walker, *Westminster Bridge*, 83–86.

[43]Charles Labelye to Martin Folkes, 22 Mar. 1742/41, Folkes Correspondence, Royal Society.

[44]Charles Labelye to J. T. Desaguliers, 15 Apr. 1735, published in Desaguliers, *Course* 2:77, 89–91.

site at New Palace Yard. The third bridge act, fixing the location, became law in May.[45]

The commissioners hired the "foreigner," Labelye, to build stone foundations for a bridge that still could be made of wood or stone.[46] Wood was the material of choice because it was cheaper, but there was widespread feeling that a wooden bridge at Westminster would be ridiculous; the dignity of London and Westminster demanded a stone bridge. A formal decision would have to be made, but for the time being the commissioners busied themselves with appointments. Richard Graham, a maker of scientific instruments and Fellow of the Royal Society, was named surveyor and comptroller of the works.[47] Thomas Lediard, who was named surveyor and agent, would deal with the owners of the property condemned to provide approaches to the bridge.[48] Lediard was elected to the Royal Society in 1742.

In June 1738 the commissioners reappointed thirty of their number to the works committee. At the first meeting that month, only six attended, Cavendish one of them, along with a newcomer, the earl of Pembroke, who was to make himself the heart and soul of the project. Coming from a cultured family, Pembroke had a strong interest in architecture and considerable experience, having helped build houses for George II and the duchess of Marlborough. Pembroke was elected to the Royal Society in 1743. At another meeting of the commissioners that month, contracts were decided. The masonry contract for the center piers went to master masons Andrews Jeolfe and Samuel Tufnell; the former had worked on fortifications, and the latter was the latest representative of a prestigious family of Westminster masons. Jeolfe and Tufnell were guests at the Royal Society occasionally but never members, very knowledgeable practical men who were perhaps insufficiently "learned." None of the architects and builders on this project, even the best known, seems to have made it into the Royal Society, but perhaps none wanted to be there.[49]

Once construction began, opposition to the bridge turned violent. At a meeting of the commissioners in August 1738, Cavendish heard the report. Labelye was putting in place the pile-driving engine, a machine for lifting and dropping the heavy ram, powered by three horses (and designed by the watchmaker James Vauloue, a friend of

Desaguliers). Angered over the threat of losing their trade to the bridge, the watermen ran their barges into the boats moored beside the engine. The commissioners ordered Ayloffe to advertise the part of the bridge act that legislated the death penalty for anyone found guilty of sabotaging the bridge works. That done, the new engine was tried without incident and found to work. In December of that year, Richard Graham brought Vauloue and his model of the engine to a meeting of the Royal Society, which then invited Vauloue to write it up. He did not do it, but when Desaguliers published the second volume of his *Course of Experimental Philosophy* in 1744, he included a description and plate showing the mighty engine. Labelye too published an account of the engine. When in January 1739 the foundation for the first pier was finished, Pembroke laid the first stone "with great Formality, Guns firing, Flags displaying."[50] In 1750 the bridge was at last opened to traffic. Up to the final year, Cavendish attended the meetings of the commissioners. He had done much of the quiet work to bring off this wonder of the modern world.

Technical problems had dogged the construction all the way, the most damaging (in every sense) being the sinking of the bridge. The unhappy watermen burst into cheers as they watched the bridge start to go under, as many as four inches in a night.[51] People sat up to watch it and to be able say "What kind of a Night the Bridge has had."[52] The bridge was supposed to bear 1200 tons, but when it was loaded with only 250 tons of cannon, as a test, it sank.[53] It kept on sinking—"Westminster-Bridge continues in a most declining Way," Thomas Birch reported to Philip Yorke—as one of the piers subsided into the river bed.[54] Possibly it was

[45]Walker, *Westminster Bridge*, 80.
[46]Ibid., 82.
[47]E. G. R. Taylor, *The Mathematical Practitioners of Hanoverian England 1714–1840* (Cambridge: Cambridge University Press, 1966), 160.
[48]Walker, *Westminster Bridge*, 99.
[49]Colvin, *Dictionary*, 281, 318–19, 628. Walker, *Westminster Bridge*, 67–68, 88–91.
[50]Walker, *Westminster Bridge*, 91–95. Desaguliers, *Course* 2:417–18.
[51]Thomas Birch to Philip Yorke, 12 Sep. 1747, BL Add Mss 35397, ff. 72–73.
[52]Thomas Birch to Philip Yorke, 19 Sep. 1747, BL Add Mss 35397, ff. 74–76.
[53]Thomas Birch to Philip Yorke, 11 June 1748, BL Mss Add 35397, ff. 114–15.
[54]Thomas Birch to Philip Yorke, 18 June 1748, BL Add Mss 35397, f. 116.

sabotaged, but whatever the cause, the pier had to be rebuilt, which took extra years. The wait was worth it. There had not been a new bridge across the Thames in London since the London Bridge in the twelfth century. Spanning 1200 feet, the Westminster Bridge was a worthy successor: this bridge, built of Portland and Purbeck stone, heavily delicate, was a monument to both engineering and architectural grace.[55]

In a report on the bridge halfway through, Labelye wrote that the bridge commissioners "have nothing, and can expect nothing, but Trouble for their Pains," and he admired their selfless "publick Spirit" and "Patience."[56] Labelye was right about a few of the commissioners such as Cavendish. Cavendish devoted a tremendous effort to the bridge while at the same time carrying out his parliamentary duties. In 1739, in the third year of the bridge, for example, in the Commons he served on twenty-four committees; and he also went to nineteen meetings of the Westminster Bridge commissioners. In the middle years of the construction, he rarely missed a meeting of the commissioners or of its works committee. In addition he came fairly regularly to a third kind of meeting, that of a small committee of accounts for the bridge, often chairing the meeting.[57] In 1744, Cavendish attended 25 out of 26 meetings of the commissioners and 18 out of 19 meetings of the works committee; this was his most conscientious year, but other years came close to this one. By this time he was also active on the council of the Royal Society. He saw the Westminster Bridge through to the end, as he did any project he undertook. He worked well with all kinds of persons in this project. He brought the same combination of political, administrative, technical, and accounting skills to his organizational work for the Royal Society.

Scientific Administration

We begin this discussion of Lord Charles Cavendish's administrative work by recalling some basic facts about the running of the Royal Society at the time of his election. By a royal charter of 1663, the Society was constituted a self-governing corporation. Every St. Andrew's Day, November 30, the members elected from their own number a council of twenty-one, from whom they elected a smaller number of officers, president, treasurer, and two secretaries. The president chose one or more vice-presidents to sit in for him when he was absent. (Macclesfield was absent often and needed vice-presidents; in 1755 he appointed Cavendish, who joined the *four* he had already appointed.) To ensure that the council did not become fixed and at the same time to give it continuity, ten of its members were newly elected each year while eleven were kept on from the old council. The entire government of the Society was invested in the council and president, who were assisted by a person responsible for foreign correspondence and translations of foreign papers. New members were elected by two thirds of the members who were present at the meeting, and the election of officers was by simple majority.[58]

In 1736, eight years after his election to the Society, Cavendish was elected to its council for the first time. He was elected next in November 1741, and for the next twenty years he was on the council every year with the exception of 1753, when family business called him away. He served four more, non-consecutive terms on the council, his last in 1769, in which year he served on the council together with his son Henry. Henry would have an even longer record of service; combined, their membership on the council would span seventy-three years, with few interruptions. For many years Lord Charles was also a vice-president.

The Royal Society was now in its third home, in Crane Court, a quiet, central location. The front of the house faced a garden, the back a long, narrow court. Up one flight of stairs and fronting the garden was the meeting room, about the size of a modern living room.

The Society as a whole met weekly except during Christmas and Easter and the long recess in late summer, about thirty times a year in all. How often the council met depended on how busy the Society was and on the energy of the current officers. Ordinarily it met six or fewer times a year toward the end of Folkes's presidency in the late 1740s, and eight to ten times under Macclesfield in

[55]Summerson, *Georgian London*, 113–16.

[56]Charles Labelye, *The Present State of Westminster Bridge* (London, 1743), 24–25.

[57]Minutes of the Committee of Accounts, vol. 1: 1738–1744, Public Record Office, Kew, Work 6/41.

[58]This information is from the Royal Society's Minutes of Council. In connection with recovering arrears of members, the new statutes of the Society were drawn up: Minutes of Council 3: 50–61 (20 Aug. 1730).

the 1750s, but it met twenty-two times in 1760 during preparations for observing the transit of Venus the following year. The president presided over the meetings both of the council and of the ordinary membership. Presidents before Newton rarely came to council. Newton came all the time, even changing the day of the meetings of the council to accommodate his schedule. His precedent was followed, with decreasing rigor, by his successors: Sloane missed only 8 out of 105 council meetings in his fifteen years as president; his successor, Folkes, missed one quarter of his; and Folkes's successor, Macclesfield, missed about a third of his. Administrative continuity depended increasingly on a small number of council members, none of whom was more dependable than Cavendish. Cavendish's first term on the council was under Sloane's presidency, in 1736, and this time he missed a good many meetings, perhaps because he found work on the council difficult to accommodate to his political duties. He did not return to the council until six years later, the year he stepped down from parliament, which was also the beginning of Folkes's presidency. Now Cavendish's attendance picked up; for the next six years he came to two out of three meetings, and after that he was almost never to miss a meeting. Frequently only a half dozen members attended council meetings, a meager number considering that it included the two secretaries and usually the president; ten or so were a better turnout, but whatever the number, Cavendish was one of them. To give an idea of his commitment: in the five years from January 1748 through November 1752, he attended every one, in all twenty-seven meetings; in the eight years from December 1753 through November 1761, out of eighty-seven meetings, he attended seventy-eight (at least, since he may only have been late sometimes, and not listed). Only two Fellows came close to matching Cavendish's record of attendance at council, the two secretaries of the Society, who had no choice short of neglecting their duties: Peter Davall from 1747, and Thomas Birch from 1752. One other councillor came regularly over a long period, the eminent barrister James Burrow, who like Charles Cavendish was sometimes temporary president of the Society during a vacancy.[59]

Cavendish's contribution to the running of the Royal Society is more remarkable when his rank is considered. The minutes of the council always listed Cavendish first after the president, except on occasion when Macclesfield (before he was president) was there, and later Morton, both earls (this protocol ceased after 1760 when the councillors were listed alphabetically). Council members in the 1740s were professionals and gentlemen, not aristocrats. Macclesfield was a notable exception, but barely, since he was only the second earl, and his father was a lawyer. The duke of Richmond, Charles Lennox, attended one council meeting in 1741, the earl of Abercorn, James Hamilton, attended three times in 1743, and that is about it. At this time one seventh of the membership of the Royal Society was aristocratic, so Cavendish was not unusual for supporting science. What set him apart was his solicitous attention to the affairs of the Society.[60]

During his long service in the Royal Society, Cavendish never initiated an important change in the way things were done. He was rather the man to second a motion by a more assertive leader. Just as his family made rulers but were themselves not rulers, Cavendish was content with the job of vice-president. When Folkes was sick in 1752, Cavendish often took the chair,[61] and it was he who informed the Society that Folkes was stepping down.[62] Folkes's successor, Macclesfield, was an initiator of change, and Cavendish helped him to achieve his goals. Early in 1752 Macclesfield asked the council to consider the way papers were chosen for publication in the *Philosophical Transactions*. There had been a committee of papers, but it had not decided which papers were to be published.[63] One of the secretaries had run the journal, making the decisions on his own though probably taking

---

[59]Information from the Royal Society, Minutes of Council.

[60]From an inspection of persons attending council meetings during Cavendish's tenure: Royal Society, Minutes of Council 3. Bound with the Minutes of the Committee of Papers is a printed membership list for the Society in 1749. The total British membership then was around 340, and of these around 45 were aristocratic, counting bishops and persons like Cavendish with the courtesy title "Lord."

[61]In 1752 Cavendish chaired five meetings of the council and frequently the ordinary meetings of the Society, alternating with James Burrow, Lord Willoughby, James West, and Nicholas Mann. Royal Society, Minutes of Council 4 and JB 21.

[62]In this event, Cavendish was the one to make a motion, returning thanks to Folkes. Royal Society, JB 21:195–96 (30 Nov. 1752).

[63]Cavendish was present on 30 Oct 1749. "At a Committee for Reviewing the Papers." "Minutes of the Royal Society," vol. 2, Birch Collection, BL Add Mss 4446. The earlier Committee of Papers met annually to preserve the papers. A new kind of committee was called for by the natural historian John Hill's published criticism of the Society under Folkes in 1751.

into consideration requests by individual members. This one-man show was to end: for the "credit and honour of this society," henceforth decisions about publication were to be made by a committee. The committee had to be prestigious; the council declared that the president, vice-presidents, and the two secretaries were to be on it and that no decisions on papers could be made without a quorum of five. For advice on particular papers, authorities outside the committee could be brought in by request of a majority of the committee. In committee, any paper was to be read in full if a member desired it, and then without "debate or altercation." Finally a vote was to be taken, by ballot, so as to "leave every member more at liberty to fully declare his opinion." Since the decision to publish a paper was a recognition not every author received, the new committee had a sensitive assignment.[64] Macclesfield (correcting himself) said that the Society had not "usually meddled" in the selection of papers to be published. That it had meddled at various times in various ways, he now conceded; what was going to change was that it would meddle in a systematic and accountable way. Cavendish joined Macclesfield in proposing amendments, and on 26 March 1752 the new statutes were passed by the council.[65] With Cavendish in the chair, Philip Yorke proposed that for the time being the council be the "committee of papers," which was agreed to.[66] The *Philosophical Transactions* was now wholly under the direction of the council and for the "sole use and benefit of the Society, and the Fellows thereof."[67] The readers of the journal were informed of the takeover by the council in an advertisement. In April 1752, the committee convened for the first time, Charles Cavendish presiding. Macclesfield came to the first three meetings, but this mover and shaker dropped out once he saw that his plan was working; at the end of the year when he became the new president of the Royal Society, he started coming around again. Cavendish chaired all of the meetings but one through November 1752.

By mid century the time-consuming experimental demonstrations at the meetings were becoming a thing of the past, leaving more time for the reading of papers. The work of the papers committee was correspondingly demanding. In the years just before 1740 the number of papers reached a peak of well over a hundred per year on the average.

After that, the number fell off, but slowly, and the load remained great through Cavendish's years on the committee. It should be said that the number of papers is not a particularly good measure of the committee's work, since as the papers became fewer, they became longer, tending to the large, interpretative syntheses of facts of Henry Cavendish's time.[68] At the time the committee of papers was formed, there was a backlog. The committee went through the papers chronologically, beginning with January of the previous year, 1751, taking several meetings to get through that year. At the first meeting the committee approved 16 papers for publication, at the second meeting 15, and at the third 24, and so it was getting more efficient, though in some later meetings it got through fewer. Daniel Wray, who began coming at the second meeting, wrote to Philip Yorke of their "diligence, as members of the Committee of Papers,"[69] and we can believe it.

The committee of papers met four to six times a year. The usual attendance was about four persons in addition to the two secretaries, who were required to be there, and the president, when he came. In 1753 Cavendish was not on the committee, as he was not on the council owing to family affairs. When he was returned to the council in 1754, he attended every meeting of the committee, which remained his habit in the years following. He was by far the most faithful member of this committee. After Cavendish Burrow came most often to the meetings. Watson and Bradley came occasionally, and other members came and went. Cavendish's tenacity set an example for his son Henry, who was to be an unfailing laborer for this committee in his time.[70]

To evaluate critically every paper that came before the Royal Society was an excellent way to

---

[64]Macclesfield's motion on the publication of papers was made on 23 Jan. 1752 and spelled out on 15 Feb. 1752, Royal Society, Minutes of Council 4:49–53.

[65]Royal Society, Minutes of Council 4:55, 64 (20 Feb. 1752), 71–75 (19 Mar. 1752), 83 (26 Mar. 1752).

[66]Royal Society, Minutes of Council 4:64 (27 Feb. 1752) .

[67]Royal Society, Minutes of Council 4:76 (19 Mar. 1752).

[68]Raymond Phineas Stearns, *Science in the British Colonies of America* (Urbana: University of Illinois Press, 1970), 97–98.

[69]Daniel Wray to Philip Yorke, 5 July 1752, Hardwicke Papers, BL Add Mss 35401, f. 157.

[70]Rough notes of the meetings of the Committee of Papers taken by Thomas Birch, one of the secretaries, in "Minutes of the Royal Society," vols. 1 and 2, Birch Collection, BL Add Mss 4445 and 4446.

keep abreast of everything that went on in science, good and bad, but we believe that Cavendish's main motivation was service to the Society. In a variety of ways the Society rationalized its procedures at this time,[71] and those that applied to the *Philosophical Transactions* were especially important, since its contents were the public record of the Society. Because the external authority of the Society derived mainly from its journal, the selection of papers to publish was a high responsibility. Cavendish got the committee off to a conscientious start in its first year.

In connection with the transit of Venus in 1761, the minutes of the council recorded scientific matters for the first time. Halley had foretold the transit and with it the opportunity for measuring the distance of the earth from the sun, the standard by which the distances of the other bodies of the solar system were expressed. Preparations were made long in advance, since world-wide expeditions were needed to get the best view of Venus crossing the solar disc. From the summer of 1760 to early 1763, the council was almost exclusively occupied with the project, energized as never before by its complex planning. The East India Company and the admiralty were enlisted, the treasury was approached, and money was received from the king, instruments were specified, observers were selected, and sites of observation were determined. During the flurry of activity in 1760, Cavendish was sometimes in the chair. In addition to dealing with all of the council matters having to do with the expeditions, he was involved in the scientific work at every level from the examination of a faulty instrument[72] to the writing of a synopsis of the completed observations of the transit.[73] (The council was preoccupied with instruments at this time; while the project for observing the transit of Venus was in progress, John Harrison's clock for finding longitude at sea came before the council, which recommended a trial at sea, on a voyage to Jamaica.[74]) Soon after the transit of Venus, another expedition was planned: two of the observers of the transit, Charles Mason and Jeremiah Dixon, were commissioned by the Royal Society to measure a degree of latitude between Maryland and Pennsylvania, and Cavendish was on the committee to draw up their instructions.[75] There was little of significance done officially at the Royal Society in the middle of the

eighteenth century in which Cavendish was not fully involved.

Meetings of the council typically had to do with money: bills from printers, bookbinders, solicitors, and instrument-makers, payment of debts, insurance on the houses owned by the society, East India Company bonds, salaries; it was pretty much the same, and it was endless. Besides dealing with these matters routinely as they came up in council, Cavendish went over them all again as auditor; nearly every year he was appointed one of a committee of auditors of the treasurer's accounts, often together with William Jones until Jones's death in 1749. Cavendish was on call as the all-purpose, responsible Fellow of the Royal Society, as his son Henry would be after him.

As we have seen, Cavendish's first recorded scientific work was in astronomy, and we find him active in astronomical administration through the Royal Society's oversight of the Royal Observatory. He was involved in drawing up the regulations for the observatory, for one thing.[76] In 1765, by warrant from the king, the president of the Royal Society together with other Fellows of the Royal Society were charged with making regular tours of inspection of the instruments of the Royal Observatory[77] Cavendish was for several years one of a small number of Fellows who made the so-called

---

[71]On keeping records of all sorts: "Proposal Concerning the Papers of the Royal Society" /by Macclesfield, presumably/, BL Add Mss 4441. The Society eliminated unnecessary duplication and classification in its record keeping: it was found that papers presented before the Society ended up in two kinds of books, while only one, the minutes of ordinary meetings, was needed. Royal Society, Minutes of Council 3:285 (12 July 1742).

[72]Royal Society, Minutes of Council 4:333–34 (27 May 1762).

[73]Thomas Birch to Philip Yorke, Viscount Royston, 20 June 1761, BL Add Mss 35399, f. 207.

[74]Royal Society, Minutes of Council 4 (25 June 1761).

[75]Royal Society, Minutes of Council 4:45 (25 Oct .1764). .

[76]Lord Morton to Thomas Birch, 24 Sep. 1764, BL Add Mss 4444.

[77]From early in the century, Fellows of the Royal Society had been making visits to the Royal Observatory, but not until Maskelyne became astronomer royal in 1765 was the council designated as the visitors. H. S. John wrote to the president of the Royal Society on 12 Dec. 1710 that it would benefit astronomy and navigation if the Royal Society's "visitors" were to inspect the instruments of the Royal Observatory, direct the astronomer royal to make observations they thought proper, and require that the astronomer royal turn over his observations each year. This letter was attached to the "Regulations for the Astronomical Observer at Greenwich," of 1756. From Maskelyne's speech about Bradley's observations, made to the Society on 9 June 1763, Lord Charles Cavendish concluded that the council members were "not really visitors of the royal Astronomer; but upon Mr. Maskelynes being appointed to that office, they were made so." Lord Charles Cavendish to Joseph Banks, 19 May 1781, Greenwich Observatory Letters and Papers," Royal Society, vol. 2, Gh. 121.

visitations to Greenwich to decide on the repairs needed and to estimate the expense, and in this capacity again, his son Henry would follow in his footsteps. As late as 1781, two years before his death, Cavendish was still discharging the Royal Society's obligations, reminding the president of the Royal Society that the publication of the Greenwich observations was long overdue.[78]

Cavendish's private interest in books and manuscripts had a public outlet in the Royal Society, where he served as one of a committee of three inspectors of the library to report on the addition of the great Norfolk library of books and manuscripts. Having fallen into a state of neglect, the Society's library in general benefited from bookish types like Cavendish and his fellow inspector Thomas Birch. This valuable library was the size of a very good private library, around 10,000 volumes, which was just the size of Henry Cavendish's private library later in the century.[79]

Elected during Sloane's presidency, Cavendish served through Folkes's, Macclesfield's, and Morton's. In 1768, while the council was absorbed in preparations for a second transit of Venus the next year, Morton died. Like Macclesfield before him, Morton was an astronomer, thus an appropriate president under these circumstances. The next president turned out to be the antiquarian James West, who had been the Society's treasurer for thirty-two years and was currently a vice-president. West held the office for only four years, but it was long enough for Henry Cavendish to have formed a strong negative opinion of his presidency.[80] Ten days after Morton died, Daniel Wray wrote to Lord Hardwicke, F.R.S., that *Lord Charles is deaf to all our prayers; and will not preside over us.*[81] Wray may have meant that Cavendish would not preside over them as temporary president or he may have meant as permanent president. Since Cavendish was used to sitting in for absent presidents, the latter meaning seems more likely. Cavendish was in his early sixties and in good health and on the council. If he would not be elected president, it was in the first instance because he did not want to be.

Science

Lord Charles and Henry Cavendish's scientific work was of a kind that involved them in a great deal of measuring, weighing, and perfecting of standards. In these activities they were working in a direction that was increasingly prominent in the physical sciences. No other reason is required, but because of the Cavendishes' place in society, we note the following connection. Weights, measures, and standards are the preserve of central political authority in modern commercial society.[82] Within eighteenth-century science, in which exactness of reasoning was increasingly equated with quantitative reasoning, authority tended to be conferred on persons who were adept at measuring, weighing, calculating, and making mathematical theory (and, in part, because of that connection, rebellion against that direction of science was commonplace as well). With evident awe, William Henly, an early expert on electrical measuring instruments, wrote to a colleague that he had heard that Henry Cavendish had determined iron wire to conduct electricity 400,000 times better than rain water, adding: "I suppose this, is *mathematically demonstrated.*"[83]

That Lord Charles Cavendish's scientific work belonged to the best, we know from knowledgeable contemporaries, just as we know that it

[78] "Visitations of Greenwich Observatory, 1763 to 1815," Royal Society, Ms. 600, XIV.d.11. Cavendish to Banks, 19 May 1781.

[79] Andrew Coltee Ducarel to Thomas Birch, 13 Oct. 1763, Birch Correspondence, BL Add Mss 4305, 4:57. The library at this time was described by one of the Society's officials as unkempt but not negligible: "At present the books weigh less than the filth that covers them. I compute about 10000 vol to whit the Norfolk 500 MSS & 3000 printed. The Society Library about 6000 printed books only." Emanuel Mendes da Costa to William Borlase, 9 July 1763, E. Da Costa Correspondence, BL Add Mss 28535, 2:150.

[80] Henry Cavendish's opinion is reported in Charles Blagden to Joseph Banks, 22 Dec. 1783, original letter in Fitzwilliam Museum Library, copy in BM(NH), DTC 3. 171–72. We return to this point in the chapter dealing with Henry Cavendish's politics.

[81] Daniel Wray to Lord Hardwicke, 22 Oct. 1768, in George Hardinge, *Biographical Anecdotes of Daniel Wray* (London, 1815), 137. Next month, James West presided over them as president.

[82] Witold Kula, *Measures and Men*, trans R. Szreter (Princeton: Princeton University Press, 1986), 18.

[83] William Henly to John Canton, n.d., Canton Papers, Royal Society, Correspondence 2:86. What Henly heard was off by a factor of 1000. The figure 400,000 corresponds roughly to the experimental measurements Cavendish made on *saturated salt solution* in 1773. His experiments on *rain water* gave much higher figures, as he reported in his published paper on the electric torpedo in 1776: "Iron wire conducts about 400 million times better than rain or distilled water." *The Electrical Researches of the Honourable Henry Cavendish, F.R.S. . .*, ed. J. C. Maxwell (Cambridge, 1879; London: Frank Cass reprint, 1967), 195, 295, 359. Henly's observation that Cavendish's proof was no doubt *mathematical* derives from this fact: no one but Cavendish knew how to compare resistances experimentally, and he had not published his method. The first instrument capable of comparing resistances was the galvanometer, which was long in the future; Cavendish's method was, in effect, to use his body as a galvanometer, as we discuss later.

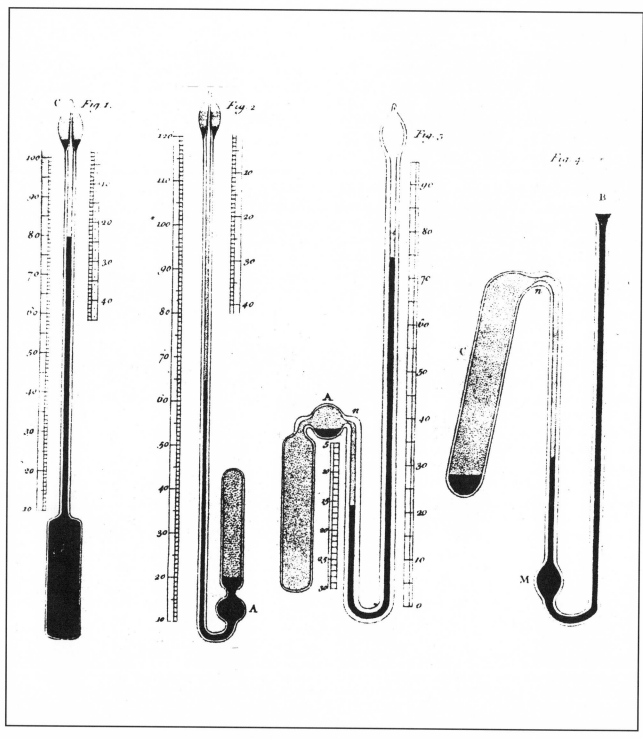

PLATE I. Lord Charles Cavendish's Thermometers. The thermometer in Figure I shows the greatest degree of heat. It differs from ordinary thermometers only in that the top of the stem is drawn into a capillary tube, which ends in a glass ball C. The cylinder at the bottom and part of the stem are filled with mercury (dark part of the figure), showing the ordinary degree of heat. Above the mercury is spirit of wine (dotted part of the figure), which also fills the ball C almost to the top of the capillary tube. When the mercury rises with temperature, some spirit of wine is forced out of the capillary tube into the ball. When the mercury falls with a fall in temperature, a space at the top of the capillary tube is emptied of spirit of wine. A scale laid beside the capillary tube measures the empty length, which is proportional to the greatest degree of heat that has been registered. Figure 2 is an alternative construction. Figure 3 shows a thermometer for giving the greatest degree of cold. Figure 4 shows how the instrument can be made more compact, as would be desirable if it were to be sunk to the bottom of the sea or raised to the upper atmosphere by a kite. "A Description of Some Thermometers for Particular Uses," *Philosophical Transactions* 50 (1757): 300.

was only little known to them, as it is to us. Cavendish's only publication was a paper on a meteorological instrument in 1757, by which time he had been working in science for thirty years. Macclesfield, then president of the Society, proposed Cavendish as the Copley Medalist, a choice which the council unanimously approved. In his address to the Society on the occasion, Macclesfield said that Lord Charles Cavendish was as conspicuous for "his earnest desire to promote natural Knowledge, and his Skill and abilities together with his continual Study and endeavour to accomplish that his desire" as he was for his "high Birth and eminent Station in life." Because of Cavendish's "excess of Modesty" and a seeming insensibility of "his own extraordinary Merit," the Royal Society, and consequently the public, had been deprived "of many important discoveries as well as considerable improvements made and contrived by his Lordship, in Several Instruments and Machines necessary for trying Experiments and deducing proper consequences from the Same; and also of the results of various useful and instructive Experiments that he has been pleased to make in private, with that accuracy and exactness which are peculiar to his Lordship, and which few besides himself have a just right to boast of."[84] Within their lofty phrasing, Macclesfield's remarks contain an accurate observation. In that age of aristocracy, Cavendish was, as Macclesfield said, an "Ornament" to the Royal Society, and he was an ornament too because he promoted natural knowledge, the purpose of the Royal Society. What Macclesfield called Cavendish's "modesty" could with equal right be called his "confidence." Given his rank and his competence, he did not need to (any more than Macclesfield needed to) publish his researches. It was enough that he made them available to his colleagues in the Royal Society. As Macclesfield said, Cavendish had not kept his work entirely to himself (otherwise how should Macclesfield know) and had communicated papers to the Royal Society not intended for publication. With greater ease than those who had to advance themselves in the world, Cavendish could live an approximation to the cooperative scientific life envisioned by the utopians of the previous century.

We know that Cavendish did good work in science because he was constantly in demand at the Royal Society, certain to be appointed to committees in which scientific skill, knowledge,

and exactitude were prized. His first scientific committee was concerned with longitude at sea. For over twenty years, the Board of Longitude had been unimpressed until the watchmaker John Harrison caught their attention. In principle, a well-known alternative to the lunar method of finding longitude at sea was a clock that is seaworthy and accurate. Harrison, at first with his brother, James, built a series of clocks and was granted several sums of money by the Board of Longitude as encouragement. The Royal Society reported favorably on an early clock in 1735, and in 1741 Cavendish was one of twelve Fellows of the Royal Society who recommended a perfected version of his second clock to the Board of Longitude as reason to continue to reward him. His first clock overcame the disturbing variations of heat and cold, moisture and dryness, friction, and fluidity of oil so perfectly that its error was less than one second a month for ten years running. This wonder was, however, a delicate pendulum clock. Harrison's second clock, built for shipboard, had kept good time under all kinds of violent motions simulating storms. Now Harrison planned a third, even better machine. What is of interest here are the persons Cavendish came together with on the committee, Fellows selected, in most cases, for their authority in matters of high precision. The other eleven members were mathematicians, astronomers, and instrument-makers: mathematicians De Moivre and his circle, Folkes, Jones, Macclesfield; astronomers Bradley and Halley; instrument-makers John Hadley and George Graham; the polymath James Jurin; and the Cambridge professors Robert Smith and John Colson. The Board of Longitude encouraged Harrison to continue to improve his clock but withheld the crowning glory. On the eve of a second trial run of Harrison's latest clock to the West Indies, in 1763 Cavendish was appointed by an act of parliament to another committee on the subject. From what became a lifework and legal battle, and with the help of Cavendish and other Fellows of the Royal Society, in the end Harrison got most of the money he deserved and along the way a Copley Medal, and

---

[84]The Copley Medal was awarded to Lord Charles Cavendish "on account of his very curious and useful invention of making Thermometers shewing respectively the greatest degrees of heat and cold during the absence of the observer." Royal Society *JB* 23:638–48, quotations on 638–39 (30 Nov. 1757).

British ships got a reliable instrument for determining longitude. Captain Cook used Harrison's clock on his voyage to the South Seas in 1772, justifying all the claims of precision made for it.[85]

Lord Charles Cavendish's next assignment two years later, in 1743, was again concerned with measurement. The object this time was to compare the Royal Society's weights and measures with those kept by the Academy of Sciences in Paris: measurements were becoming decisive in experimental work, and depending upon the country in which the work was done, measurements were expressed in the English foot or the Paris toise, lengths marked off on metal standards and deposited in various archives. Their comparison was an obligation of the London Society and the Paris Academy. The project expanded to include a comparison of the Royal Society's standards with other standards in England, with the original standards for the yard and the pound at the exchequer and as well with other copies located at various places in London. The instrument-maker George Graham carried out the experiments in the presence of a delegation from the Royal Society, which, other than being smaller, was almost the same as the committee that had investigated Harrison's clock. Of the delegation of seven, five we have discussed in connection with De Moivre: Folkes, who was president then, Macclesfield, Jones, Peter Davall, and Cavendish. The other two were the instrument-maker Hadley and the secretary Cromwell Mortimer. Cavendish was in his element, that of precision and accuracy.[86]

For our last example of Lord Charles Cavendish's scientific work in committee, we turn to his experiments on the compressibility of water. The originator of the experiments was John Canton, a schoolmaster best known for his experiments in electricity, for which he had earned a Copley Medal. His new experiments were highly exacting, and the interpretation he put on them contradicted a famous finding of the Florentine Accademia del Cimento a hundred years before. There arose, in a sense, a dispute between scientific societies, even if one was defunct; the honor of the Royal Society was at stake.

Canton's apparatus was transparently simple: a small, narrow glass tube was open at one end and closed at the other by a hollow glass ball an inch and a quarter across. The ball was placed in a water bath, and it and a few inches of the tube were filled with mercury. The bath was heated until the mercury rose to the top of the tube, then the tube was hermetically sealed. After the mercury had cooled to its original temperature, Canton observed that it stood about a half inch higher than before; he found the same when water was used instead of mercury, though the water rose slightly higher than the mercury. The only difference before and after the expansion of the liquid was the pressure of the atmosphere over it. Water, Canton concluded, is compressible. He published his experiments in the *Philosophical Transactions* in 1762, and two years later he published a sequel extending his experiments to other liquids. In the sequel Canton also reported his discovery of another "remarkable property" of water: its compressibility is less at summer temperatures than in winter, contrary to his expectation and to the behavior of other liquids.[87]

Doubts were raised about the accuracy of Canton's experiments and about his inference from them about the compressibility of water. The *Monthly Review*, which was not a scientific journal but which nevertheless reviewed *critically* the contents of the *Philosophical Transactions*, found

---

[85]The act of 1763 altered the original act of 1714 offering the prize. The other members of the new committee were Lord Morton, Lord Willoughby, George Lewis Scott, James Short, John Michell, Alexander Cumming, Thomas Mudge, William Frodsham, and James Green. Only the instrument-maker Short and the watch-makers Frodsham and Green were satisfied with Harrison's explanation. Cavendish was also appointed by the Board to another committee; John Bird deputized for him this time. Taylor, *Mathematical Practitioners of Hanoverian England*, 126, 170, 172. "Some Account of Mr. Harrison's Invention for Determining the Longitude at Sea, and for Correcting the Charts of the Coasts. Delivered to the Commissioners of the Longitude, January 16th 1741-2," given in / John Harrison/, *An Account of the Proceedings, in Order to the Discovery of the Longitude* (London, 1763), 7–8, 19, 21. Humphry Quill, *John Harrison: The Man Who Found Longitude* (London: Baker, 1966), 120–22, 139–46, 186, 221.

[86]"An Account of the Proportions of the English and French Measures and Weights, from the Standards of the Same, Kept at the Royal Society," *PT* 42 (1742): 185–88. "An Account of a Comparison Lately Made by Some Gentlemen of the Royal Society, of the Standard of a Yard, and the Several Weights Lately Made for Their Use; with the Original Standards of Measures and Weights in the Exchequer, and Some Others Kept for Public Use, at Guild-hall, Founders-hall, the Tower, etc.," *PT* 42 (1742): 541–56. *Select Tracts and Table Books Relating to English Weights and Measures (1100–1742)*, ed. H. Hall and F. T. J. Nicholas, Camden Miscellany, vol. 15 (London: Office of the Society, 1929), 40.

[87]John Canton, "Experiments to Prove that Water is not Incompressible," *PT* 52 (1762): 640–43; "Experiments and Observations on the Compressibility of Water and Some Other Fluids," *PT* 54 (1764): 261–62. John Canton to Benjamin Franklin, 29 June 1764, in *The Papers of Benjamin Franklin*, vol. 11, ed. L. W. Labaree (New Haven: Yale University Press, 1959), 244–46, on 245.

fault with the experiments in both of Canton's papers. The critic for the journal concluded that Canton's experiments would ultimately be judged as inconclusive as the Florentine they claimed to disprove. By the time the *Monthly Review* commented on Canton's second paper, the Royal Society had honored Canton with the Copley Medal; the journal hinted that this award was to the Society's dishonor.[88]

The question of awarding a second Copley Medal to Canton for his experiments on the compressibility of water was moved in council, but in "conversation" some Fellows of the Royal Society expressed objections. Concerned for the "honor of the Society," on 28 November 1764, the council appointed a committee to repeat Canton's experiments at the expense of the Society and to report back to the council.[89] The president was directed to inform the Society that any objections to Canton's experiments had to be submitted in writing if they were to be considered by the committee. On 17 June 1765 the council ordered the instruments by the committee,[90] and the committee selected the instrument-makers John Bird, James Ferguson, and Edward Nairne to assist it in carrying out the experiments.[91] It was summer, the Society was in recess, and many of the committee members were out of town. Those who remained—Lord Charles Cavendish, Franklin, Watson, Heberden, and Ellicott—met four times in July to perform experiments in the Musem of the Society. At the beginning of August the clerk of the Society, Emanuel Mendez da Costa, informed the president, Lord Morton, that the attending members of the Committee were convinced of Canton's conclusion, but since they were "all friends to the experiments," da Costa anticipated a "contest," especially since the experiments were of such "nicety."[92] In November, after the Society had resumed its meetings, some of the experiments were performed a second time before the larger committee.

This larger committee contained the principal skeptic of Canton's claims, Francis Blake, an Oxford mathematician who was an active, highly regarded member of the Society. Blake raised this and that question about Canton's experiments, but his essential concern appears to have rested on an appeal to authority backed up by what seemed to him commonsense. In the Florentine experiment, water was subjected to great pressure without,

evidently, causing any change in its bulk, whereas in Canton's experiment, an observable change was alleged to have resulted from a very slight pressure. Which account was Blake to credit? As requested, Blake put his question to the council in writing.[93]

Cavendish was a friend of Canton, and since his repetition of Canton's experiments was not private but judicial, he kept Canton well informed. He sent Canton his measures and computation to review. Everything was above board: throughout Cavendish wrote "by my measure," and he signed the bottom of every sheet. We have Canton's ordeal to thank for the only surviving record of Cavendish's experimental work, preserved in Canton's papers. The impression this work gives is one of great thoroughness and accuracy, characteristics that apply equally to the work of his son Henry, of which we have ample record.[94]

In a paper drawn up for the council, Cavendish stated and answered the objections to Canton's experiments that had come to his notice.[95] The first objection went to the heart of the matter, the conflict with the Florentine experiment. Experiment is authority, Cavendish said, in effect, and experiment can overrule experiment. In response to Blake's objections, Cavendish wrote a separate paper in response to

[88]*The Monthly Review* 29 (1763): 142–44, and 33 (1765): 455–56, quotation on 456.

[89]Besides Cavendish, the committee consisted of the president, Matthew Raper, John Ellicott, James Short, William Watson, Israel Maudit, and Charles Morton. 28 Nov. 1764, Royal Society, Minutes of Council 5:57. Francis Blake, Edward Delaval, Benjamin Franklin, and George Lewis Scott were added to the committee: 21 Feb. 1765, ibid., 62–63.[90]Royal Society, Minutes of Council 5:57 (28 Nov. 1764), and 109 (17 June 1765).

[91]John Bird is referred to in Cavendish's memoranda on the experiments. James Ferguson was paid for his time and trouble: 10 July 1766, Royal Society, Minutes of Council 5:161. Edward Nairne was also appointed according to Lord Morton: 30 Nov. 1765, Royal Society, JB 25:655.

[92]Emanuel Mendez da Costa to the earl of Morton, 1 Aug. 1765, in John Nichols, *Illustrations of the Literary History of the Eighteenth Century*, 8 vols. (London, 1817–58) 4:754.

[93]Blake was the only doubter to give the council anything in writing, and his paper was mislaid and came to the attention of the committee late in its deliberations. Francis Blake, "Remarks and Queries Recommended to the Consideration of the Right Honourable the Earl of Morton," Canton Papers, Royal Society, 3.

[94]The sheets in Cavendish's hand record his variations on Canton's experiments and include sketches of his apparatus. They give numbers for trials with glass balls of different sizes and thicknesses and a large number of glass tubes, and they give a table of the expansion of water with heat, from thirty degrees to fifty. Canton Papers, Royal Society, 2.

[95]Ibid. These objections are contained also in another, much longer (eleven-page) paper, which would also seem to have been written by Cavendish, though the copy in the Canton Papers is not in his handwriting.

Blake's objections, which he began by making the same point: "The authority of the most able experimenters /including the Florentine/ is of no weight, when it appears that their experiments were made in such a way, as could not possibly show so small a degree of compressibility as Mr Canton has discovered."[96] There had been progress in the art of experiment in the century since the Florentines; Canton's skill in showing "so small a degree of compressibility" was proof of that, as was, in its way, Cavendish's follow-up. On 28 November 1765 the council resolved that the hypothesis of the compressibility of water accounts for Canton's experiments and that no other appears to do so as satisfactorily, and it voted to award Canton the Copley Medal for 1764.[97] Two days later, at a general meeting of the Society, Lord Morton presented the Medal to Canton and gave an address, in which he brought up the controversy. He did not describe the ensuing experiments carried out at the Society, since Cavendish had written a "full and accurate Account" of them and of the "Theory deducible from them."[98] Cavendish's paper was read at the next general meeting of the Society.[99]

As the historian of the Royal Society Charles Richard Weld put it, Lord Charles Cavendish had given the Society a "warm and able" defense of Canton's exquisitely precise experiment.[100] In his address on the Copley Medal, Lord Morton referred to the extraordinary work on Canton's experiments by that "Noble Member of the Society," Lord Charles Cavendish, who was "eminent for his great Abilities, and deep knowledge in all the branches of science that come before them."[101]

"It were to be wished, that this noble philosopher would communicate more of his experiments to the world, as he makes many, and with great accuracy." This reference to Charles Cavendish is contained in a letter written in 1762 by one who knew, the able electrical experimenter Benjamin Franklin.[102] The occasion was Franklin's admiration for Cavendish's experiment on the conduction of electricity by heated glass. From this source and from several others, we know that Cavendish had a keen interest in electrical conduction. This new subject had been expanded by the discovery of the Leyden jar, or electrical capacitor, an instrument which delivered far greater quantities of electricity than did the unaided electrical machine. The insulating and con-

ducting properties of glass had acquired particular interest because of the behavior of the glass in the Leyden jar. Franklin had shown that the whole power of the Leyden jar is concentrated in the glass of the jar and not in the metallic foil coating it. Cavendish's apparatus consisted of a glass tube thickened to solid glass in the middle. It was, in effect, an ingenious Leyden jar, which he showed ceased to work like a Leyden jar when the solid, middle section of the glass was heated to 400 degrees or higher; the evident reason was that the glass at that heat ceased to be an insulator, as at lower temperatures it must be for a Leyden jar made of glass to work at all.

The man who best knew Cavendish's electrical work was William Watson, the leading electrical researcher in London. In 1747 Watson invited the Royal Society to join him in an experiment on electrical conduction, the scale of which, miles literally, was a measure of his enthusiasm for the subject. This inspired experiment was made possible by the new Leyden jar, the discharge, or "explosion," of which could communicate shocks over long distances. Nobody knew how long; Watson thought that a powerful Leyden jar might send a shock clear across the River Thames. To try that idea (Watson must have had a good idea that it would work), Watson and "many others" assembled at the new Westminster Bridge (to which Cavendish had recently devoted so much work). A wire connected to a Leyden jar was laid across the bridge, and with the river and the bodies of the experimenters completing the circuit, Watson and his associates

[96]Lord Charles Cavendish, "Observations on Mr Blake's Objections to Mr Canton's Experiments," Canton Papers, Royal Society, 3.

[97]Royal Society, Minutes of Council 5:141–42 (21 and 28 Nov. 1765).

[98]Lord Morton's address was given at the anniversary meeting, 30 Nov. 1765, Royal Society, JB 25:647–64. Quotation on 656. The award of the Copley Medal to Canton for his experiments on the compressibility of water did not bring the work of the committee to an end. Two and a half weeks later the council resolved that an experiment on the compressibility of water proposed by Lord Morton be resumed. 19 Dec. 1765, Minutes of Council, Royal Society, 5:148.

[99]Two papers by Cavendish, one an appendix to the other, were read: "A Paper Delivered to Mr. da Costa for the Use of the Committee on Mr. Canton's Experiments," dated 21 Oct. 1765, and "Appendix to the Paper on Mr. Canton's Experiments," dated 5 Dec. 1765, Royal Society, JB 25: 668–79. The material is also in the Canton Papers, Royal Society, 3.

[100]Weld, *Royal Society*, 2:32.

[101]30 Nov. 1765, Royal Society, JB 25:656.

[102]Benjamin Franklin to Ebenezer Kinnersley, 20 Feb. 1762, in *The Papers of Benjamin Franklin*, vol. 10, ed. L.W. Labaree (New Haven: Yale University Press, 1966), 37–53, on 42.

felt shocks in their wrists and elbows when the jar was discharged. The circuit was progressively lengthened until finally the experimenters moved from the river onto dry land, at Shooters' Hill. Using signals and watches in an attempt to quantify electrical conduction, they were forced to conclude that conduction is "nearly instantaneous." In these experiments, which went on for weeks, twenty-five Fellows of the Royal Society took part, Charles Cavendish, needless to say, one of them. Almost all the rest of the De Moivre circle was there too: Folkes, Stanhope, Davall, Jones, and Scott. Bradley was there, as were most of the leading instrument-makers. These outdoor experiments in the middle of summer were an outing as well as an enquiry into nature; Stanhope, for one, brought venison pastry and French wine.[103] The experiments were financed by and "made by the order and for the service of the /Royal/ Society,"[104] and Watson published an account of them in the *Philosophical Transactions*.[105] Of the phenomena produced by the equipment of the experimental philosopher, nothing could compare with Watson's experiment on the Thames for drama. In nature the only comparable phenomenon studied by the philosopher was lightning, which was understood to be a phenomenon of the same kind. Electricity was clearly the next great natural power to be subjected to the rule of law. We suspect that that is how Lord Charles Cavendish saw it, and we know it was the way his son Henry did.

Lord Charles continued to assist Watson in his researches on electricity. In a paper in 1752 Watson published an apparatus made by Cavendish for the conduction of electricity through a vacuum. Watson passed electricity from a machine and from a Leyden jar through a vacuum to learn if the vacuum transmits electricity; he found that it does, though not as freely as do metals and water. He had to make do with the imperfect vacuum obtained by an air pump until Cavendish solved the problem with an apparatus that achieved a Torricellian vacuum and an electrical circuit at once. Bending a narrow glass tube seven and a half feet long into a parabolic shape, Cavendish filled the tube with mercury and placed its ends in basins of mercury; the mercury in the two arms of the parabola descended until the level stood about thirty inches above the basins, leaving a Toricellian vacuum at the top of the tube. Cavendish brought

up a wire from an electrical machine, which caused electricity to pass through the vacuum in a "continued arch of lambent flame." The simplicity and ingenuity of Cavendish's apparatus are again striking to us, as they were to Watson. Cavendish, Watson observed, joined a "very complete knowledge" of science with that of making apparatus.[106]

Of Lord Charles Cavendish's apparatus, the ultimate in simplicity was his sealed vessel for converting water to vapor, though all we have to go on is his son Henry's admiring references to it.[107] From Henry, we also know that Lord Charles did experiments on the bulk of water over a very wide range of temperatures,[108] that he determined the expansion of steam with heat,[109] that he did experiments on the depression of mercury in glass tubes of different sizes,[110] that he determined the expansion of mercury with heat,[111] that he did chemical experiments,[112] and that he made astronomical observations together with Henry.[113] He computed

---

[103]Thomas Birch to Philip Yorke, 15 Aug. 1747, BL Add Mss 35397, ff. 70–711747, BL Add Mss 35397, ff. 70–71.

[104]Royal Society, Minutes of Council 4:15 (17 Oct. 1748).

[105]William Watson, "A Collection of the Electrical Experiments Communicated to the Royal Society," *PT* 45 (1748): 49–120.

[106]William Watson, "An Account of the Phaenomnena of Electricity in Vacuo, with Some Observations Thereupon," *PT* 47 (1752): 362–76, on 370–71.

[107]Henry Cavendish mentioned his father's experiment to various persons; e.g., to the instrument-maker Edward Nairne in 1776 for its bearing on the effect of moisture in an air pump, as reported by John Robison, *A System of Mechanical Philosophy*, ed. D. Brewster, 4 vols. (Edinburgh, 1822) 3:593.

[108]In connection with government taxes on spirits, Henry Cavendish supplied a table of the bulk of water at degrees of heat from 25 to 210 degrees. "From the Experiments of Lord Charles Cavendish, Communicated by Mr. Henry Cavendish. March 1790," Blagden Collection, Royal Society, Misc. Notes. In the same connection, Henry Cavendish communicated the weight of a cubic foot of water, "the result of my father's experiment." Henry Cavendish to Charles Blagden, undated /probably 1790/, Royal Society.

[109]Thomas Young, *A Course of Lectures on Natural Philosophy and the Mechanical Arts*, vol. 2 (London, 1807), 401.

[110]Henry Cavendish included his father's table of the depression of mercury in his report on the meteorological instruments of the Royal Society in 1776: "An Account of the Meteorological Instruments Used at the Royal Society's House," *PT* 66 (1776): 375–401; in *Sci. Pap.* 2:112–26, on 116.

[111]Young, *Natural Philosophy*, 2:391.

[112]Here and there Henry Cavendish referred to his father's chemicals; e.g., 16 June 1781, "Experiments on Air," Cavendish Mss II, 5:56.

[113]Packet of astronomical observations from 1774, in Lord Charles Cavendish's hand, with Henry Cavendish's observations interleaved, and kept by Henry in his own papers. Cavendish Mss, Misc. We know of Lord Charles Cavendish's interest in astronomy from sources other than his son, too; e.g., William Ponsonby, Viscount Duncannon to the duke of Devonshire, 24 Jan. 1744/43, Devon. Coll.: "I have not had an opportunity lately of seeing Lord Charles, but I make no doubt of his Lordship having made proper observations on the Comet, which appears here in great Splendor."

tables of errors of time for William Ludlam, an astronomer at Cambridge and unsuccessful candidate for the Lucasian professorship of mathematics.[114] He made meteorological observations with Heberden,[115] and he kept a meteorological journal, as we know from the correspondence of William Borlase.[116] But in the end, we have only a scanty and fragmentary record of Lord Charles Cavendish's experiments and observations. We know little more than that he made many and that his contemporaries knew of them and were impressed.

We conclude our discussion of Lord Charles Cavendish's public activities with his membership in a new society that, it would seem, more than any other body breathed the spirit of the times. Founded in 1754, the Royal Society of Arts enlisted in the cause of human progress, calling upon the ingenuity of the race to advance it. The hopeful application of empirical knowledge was to be stimulated by competition; persons with winning ideas for improvements were to be awarded prizes from money donated by public-spirited supporters of progress. Given its ambition, the Society predictably attracted a good many Fellows of the Royal Society, such as Franklin, Knight, Macclesfield, Heberden, and Watson. The latter proposed Lord Charles Cavendish, who was elected on 8 June 1757. Because the Society also attracted a strong aristocratic patronage, Cavendish found himself at home in it in another way. Its list of members included the dukes of Devonshire and Bedford, the earls of Besborough and Ashburnham, Viscount Royston, and Lord George Cavendish, members all of the Cavendish clan as well. It is indicative of Lord Charles's breadth of public interests that in 1760 he was appointed to special committees for judging competitions in the fine arts, industrial technology, and agriculture.[117]

In what follows, part 3 of this biography and beyond, our focus shifts from Lord Charles, a well-rounded representative of his age, to his son Henry, for whom we lack any such ready characterization. A child of the English Enlightenment Henry

Cavendish certainly was, but we would hesitate to call him one of its models, and yet neither would we comfortably apply to him our own designation *scientist*. Let us, then, get to know (more or less) without preconceptions this *wizard*, as he was known by his neighbors, a man who spoke rarely and when he did with tremendous difficulty and hesitation and into the void, who fought off any attempt to draw him into conversation, reacting in horror to a strange face, averting his eyes from the gaze of others, walking always down the middle of the road acknowledging no passersby, acting ever nervous, and caring nothing of how he appeared to the world. No less striking than these singularities was his self-assurance, his absolute confidence in his chosen path. He knew what mattered to him, science, and he pursued it with a singleminded will, relentlessly, as we will see. We should be surprised if at least some of our readers do not respond with wonder, as we do, and as his contemporaries did, to Henry Cavendish's forbidding integrity, strange dignity, and manifest genius.

––––––––––

[114]Lord Charles Cavendish, "Difference to Be Subtracted from Sidereal Time to Reduce It to Mean Time." This and two other tables of calculations on errors of time, in William Ludlam, *Astronomical Observations Made in St. John's College, Cambridge, in the Years 1767 and 1768: With an Account of Several Astronomical Instruments* (Cambridge, 1769), 145–48. Thomas Baker, *History of the College of St. John the Evangelist, Cambridge* (Cambridge, 1869), 1069–70.

[115]In 1769 Lord Charles Cavendish's good friend, the physician William Heberden published a paper in the *Philosophical Transactions* comparing the rainfall at the bottom of a tall building with that at the top. Benjamin Franklin had an explanation, which he put in a letter and in which he referred to the experiments of Heberden and Lord Charles Cavendish, both "very accurate experimenters." Franklin to Thomas Percival, undated /probably June 1771/, in *The Papers of Benjamin Franklin*, vol. 18, ed. W. B. Willcox (New Haven: Yale University Press, 1974), 155–57, on 156.

[116]Letters from William Borlase to Thomas Hornsby in 1766 and to Charles Lyttleton in 1767, quoted in J. Oliver, "William Borlase's Contributions to Eighteenth–Century Meteorology and Climatology," *Annals of Science* 25 (1969): 275–317, on 293.

[117]Entries for 26 Mar., 9 and 30 Apr. 1760, "Minutes of the Society," Royal Society of Arts, vol. 5. Derek Hudson and Kenneth W. Luckhurst, *The Royal Society of Arts 1754–1954* (London: John Murray, 1954), 6. There was a considerable overlap in the membership of the Society of Arts and that of the Royal Society: of the eleven founding members of the Society in 1754, four were Fellows of the Royal Society, and in 1768 the president and all of the ten vice-presidents of the Society were Fellows of the Royal Society.

PART 3

❧

The Honourable Henry and
Lord Charles Cavendish

CHAPTER 1

❧

Education of Henry Cavendish

Hackney Academy

Henry Cavendish no doubt received an early education from tutors. We know that one of his first cousins had a tutor who was paid one hundred pounds a year,[1] and we assume that a comparable investment was made in Henry's early education. Given that education limited to tutoring at home had disappeared in England by the early eighteenth century, Lord Charles had to make further arrangements; he had the choice of sending his sons, Henry and Frederick, either to a public school or to a private one. Lord Charles had been to a public school, and he might have been expected to educate his sons in one too, especially since that was increasingly the practice among the aristocracy. Public schools, the argument went, were the proper training ground for public lives, the destiny of the upper classes. Most of the English peerage, for example, were educated at Eton and Westminster, which gained a reputation as nurseries of statesmen.[2] Cavendish's sons may not have looked to him like statesmen; in any case, he chose to send them to a private school.

Cavendish had his pick of convenient private schools, since most of them were located in the suburbs of London.[3] There was a variety of types to choose from: certain schools were denominational, others were classical, others neither. The one selected by Lord Charles Cavendish was one of the so-called academies, which offered a modern curriculum that emphasized mathematics, natural sciences, vocational subjects, and the most important modern foreign language, French. Academies also taught the ancient languages for their educational value while de-emphasizing rote learning (their students' Latin being the less proficient for it). With an enrollment of about one hundred, Hackney Academy was the largest of these academies, and it was also the oldest, founded in 1685, and the most fashionable academy in eighteenth-century England. There Lord Charles Cavendish chose to educate his sons, first Henry and then Frederick.[4]

The Academy was located two miles northeast of London, in the village of Hackney, which at mid century numbered a thousand or so householders. The inhabitants included a few craftsmen, such as the well-known mathematical instrument-maker John Ellicott, who with Peter Dolland observed the transit of Venus there in 1761;.[5] but the village was best known for the rich Londoners who built country seats there. The traffic between London and Hackney was so heavy that "hackney" had become the general word for coaches of the type that plied the route. Hackney Academy, with its magnificent playing fields and clean air, enjoyed a reputation for healthy living.[6] Like other private schools, it was also thought to answer the standard complaint about the public schools, their rampant sexuality. Hackney, in sum, was modern, healthy, and safe.

Hackney attracted a certain kind of clientele. Whereas many academies took in day students from the lower middle class or the crafts, Hackney was strictly a boarding school for the upper middle

---

[1] Henry Cavendish's aunt Rachel Cavendish married Sir William Morgan of Tredgar; they had two sons, William and Edward, born a few years before Henry Cavendish, and one of these "Master Morgans" had a tutor who received one hundred pounds per annum. This is according to Lord Charles Cavendish in an account for his widowed sister, undated /1740/, Devon. Coll., no. 167.1.

[2] Of the peers about the same age as Lord Charles Cavendish, 46 attended Eton and 31 Westminster; of those about the age of Henry Cavendish, 53 attended Eton and 78 Westminster. From the count in John Cannon, *Aristocratic Century: The Peerage of Eighteenth-Century England* (Cambridge: Cambridge University Press, 1984), 40, 43–44.

[3] Randolph Trumbach, *The Rise of the Egalitarian Family...* (New York: Academic Press, 1978), 254, 265.

[4] Nicholas Hans, *New Trends in Education in the Eighteenth Century* (London: Routledge & Kegan Paul, 1951), 63–66, 70.

[5] E. G. R. Taylor, *The Mathematical Practitioners of Hanoverian England, 1714–1840* (Cambridge: Cambridge University Press, 1966), 156.

[6] William Thornton, *New, Complete, and Universal History, Description, and Survey of the Cities of London and Westminster. . . Likewise the Towns, Villages, Palaces, Seats, and Country, to the Extent of Above Twenty Miles Round*, rev. ed. (London, 1784), 481. Daniel Lysons, *Environs of London; Being an Historical Account of the Towns, Villages, and Hamlets, Within Twelve Miles of That Capital*, vol. 2: *County of Middlesex* (London, 1795), 450–51.

and upper classes, in particular, for wealthy whig families. The hard-headed Lord Hardwicke had sent his son Philip Yorke to Hackney to get a good modern education ten years before Lord Charles Cavendish sent his son Henry. The duke of Grafton, the earl of Essex, and the earl of Grey, whigs all, patronized Hackney. So did the duke of Devonshire, who sent his son Lord John Cavendish there at the same time that his brother Lord Charles sent Henry. Lord John and Henry were evidently the first Cavendishes to attend Hackney, soon to be joined by Henry's brother, Frederick. They in turn were followed by the sons of the next, the fourth, duke of Devonshire, Lord Richard and Lord George Henry Cavendish. Hackney became a Cavendish tradition.[7]

For most of the eighteenth century, Hackney was run by the Newcomes, a family of teachers, Anglican clergy, and Cambridge graduates with an interest in science. So identified with the school was the family that Birch referred to it as "Newcome's Hackney." The first of the Newcomes, Henry, who was said to be a good classical scholar and strict disciplinarian, was still headmaster when Henry Cavendish was there. There was a close connection between the Newcome family and Lord Charles Cavendish's own. Henry Newcome and his son Peter Newcome, who later became headmaster himself, were friends of the duke of Kent's family and dined with them at St. James Square.[8] Lord Charles Cavendish had a high opinion of Peter Newcome. In 1742, just as he entered his son Henry at Hackney, Lord Charles recommended Peter Newcome for membership in the Royal Society, identifying him as one who was well skilled in mathematics and polite literature. Co-signers of the certificate included the Hackney graduate Yorke, Birch, and Wray, strongly suggesting that Peter Newcome was one of Cavendish's circle.[9] Birch, Wray, and Yorke often visited the Newcomes at Hackney, and they went regularly to the Hackney Theater, where Shakespearean plays, for which the school was famous, were put on by the students every third spring.[10] While Henry Cavendish was at Hackney, Newcome joined Lord Charles Cavendish and others in participating in Watson's experiments on the conduction of electricity across the Thames, and a year after Henry had left Hackney, Newcome published his observations on an earthquake felt at Hackney in the

Philosophical Transactions.[11] Shortly before Henry Cavendish was elected to the Royal Society, Peter Newcome invited him to a meeting as his guest.[12] In 1763 and 1764 Newcome was a member of the council of the Royal Society.[13] We find clear connections between Lord Charles Cavendish's scientific interest and Hackney.

Students were admitted to Hackney at age seven, but Henry Cavendish did not enter until he was eleven, in 1742. The six-year advanced course that he took contained subjects that would apply to his later studies and work, mathematics, natural sciences, French, and Latin. In 1749, at age seventeen, the usual leaving age for students going on to the university, Henry Cavendish, like all of the other Cavendishes and like most of the other students at Hackney, proceeded directly to the university.

Peterhouse, Cambridge

From the fourteenth century to the time Henry Cavendish entered Cambridge, twenty Cavendishes had graduated from this university.[14] The first of the dukes of Devonshire to get a university education, however, was the third duke, who went to Oxford not Cambridge, though he sent his two sons to Cambridge. His only surviving brother, Lord Charles, likewise sent his two sons to Cambridge. The eldest, Henry, having just turned eighteen, entered St. Peter's College, or Peterhouse,

---

[7]Hans, *New Trends*, 72, 243–44.

[8]Thomas Birch Diary, BL Add Mss 4478C, frequent entries beginning in 1740.

[9]Royal Society, Certificates, vol 1. Nr. 12, f. 260 (25 Nov. 1742). The other signers were Jurin, Benjamin Hoadley, John Ward, and Thomas Walker. Newcome was elected on 24 Feb. 1743.

[10]Birch Diary. After dining at the Mitre in the afternoon, Wray and Lord Willoughby planned to go to the Hackney Theater, and they asked Birch to join them. Daniel Wray to Thomas Birch, 15 Apr. 1748, BL Add Mss 4322, f. 111. There were other occasions too: Newcome invited Birch to Christmas at Hackney, 24 Dec. 1744, BL Add Mss 4315, f. 222.

[11]William Watson, "A Collection of the Electrical Experiments Communicated to the Royal Society," *PT* 45 (1748): 49–120, on 62. Newcome reported the earthquake as it was felt by persons at his house in Hackney; these included the son of John Hadley, the great instrument-maker and vice-president of the Royal Society. "A Letter from Mr. Peter Newcome F.R.S. to the President, Concerning the Same Shock Being Felt at Hackney, Near London," *PT* 46 (1750): 653–54; read 29 Mar. 1750.

[12]Royal Society, JB 23: 711 (10 Jan. 1760).

[13]Royal Society, Minutes of Council, 5.

[14]John and J. A. Venn, *Alumni Cantabrigienses . . .*, pt. 1: *From the Earliest Times to 1751*, vol. 1 (Cambridge: Cambridge University Press, 1954).

Cambridge, on 24 November 1749.[15] He was the first Cavendish to go to that particular Cambridge college, where he remained in regular attendance for over three years.

Henry Cavendish was never far from evidences of family power. Two years before he arrived at the university, Philip Yorke, a relative on the Grey side, was elected to parliament from the county of Cambridge. In the next election he and John Manners, the marquess of Granby, a relative on the Cavendish side, were returned unopposed. These two Members of Parliament represented the two aristocratic whig families of Hardwicke and Rutland that vied for power in Cambridgeshire and dominated its politics.[16] The chancellor of the university was the duke of Newcastle, a whig, a minister of state, and distantly related to Cavendish. Newcastle did what was expected of him by securing for the university a bountiful share of crown livings, deaneries, and bishoprics. As it happened, in the year that Newcastle became chancellor, the master of Peterhouse died, and Newcastle promptly appointed a whig in his place, a fellow of Peterhouse, Edmund Keene. This was Newcastle's way of rewarding Keene for his active support of the whig interest in Cambridge. In 1750-51, while master of Peterhouse, Keene served as vice-chancellor of the university, the most important resident officer; usually the vice-chancellor served for only one year, but Newcastle got Keene to serve two years because he was so compliant. Horace Walpole put it more bluntly: Keene was "Newcastle's tool" in the university. As another contemporary put it, Keene was a "very sensible & agreeable man."[17] In any event, Keene went on to still higher things, becoming Bishop of Ely. While Keene was still at the university, especially through his brother, the distinguished diplomat Sir Benjamin, F.R.S., he was in touch with the larger world, including men of science.[18]

Lord Charles Cavendish helped see to that. A close shepherd of his sons' education, he was on familiar terms with Keene at Peterhouse, as he was with the Newcomes at Hackney. While Henry Cavendish was at Peterhouse, Keene dined with Cavendish's friends, Birch, Heberden, Wray, Mann, and Squire, and on one occasion Keene dined with Birch *and* Cavendish.[19] Keene is said to have had a preference for the privileged, and although Peterhouse was not a stronghold of the nobility, for a time

in the middle of the eighteenth century, it was fashionable with the upper classes.[20] Evidence of this is that the Cavendishes, Henry, Frederick, and their cousin Lord John, and soon after them, a distant relative James Lowther, all went to Peterhouse.

To a visitor entering Cambridge from the direction of London, the first college on the left on Trumpington Street was Peterhouse, the (then disputed) oldest college in Cambridge, dating from the thirteenth century. The buildings of the college formed two courts separated by a cloister and gallery. There was an impressive chapel with a painted glass window depicting Christ's crucifixion between two thieves; the most eminent alumni of Peterhouse were bishops.[21] According to a description from the time Cavendish was at Peterhouse, the college then had forty-three scholars and a total membership "of all Sorts" of about ninety.[22] These figures, however, give an exaggerated idea of the residential society of Peterhouse and of the university. When the poet Thomas Gray was a student at Peterhouse, not long before Cavendish, there were not a dozen undergraduates in residence at any given time, and in the entire university there were only about four hundred residential students and about an equal number of fellows.[23]

---

[15] The date, recorded in the Peterhouse books, is given in George Wilson, *The Life of the Honourable Henry Cavendish* (London, 1851), 17.

[16] *The Victoria History of the Counties of England. Cambridge and the Isle of Ely* (London: Dawsons of Pall Mall reprint, 1967) 2:412–13.

[17] Conyers Middleton to Thomas Birch, 16 Jan. 1748/49, BL Add Mss 4314, f. 30.

[18] Denys Arthur Winstanley, *Unreformed Cambridge* (Cambridge: Cambridge University Press, 1935), 13, 193. Horace Walpole, *Horace Walpole's Correspondence*, ed. W. S. Lewis, 48 vols. (New Haven: Yale University Press, 1937–83), vol. 2, pt. 4, p. 346. "Keene, Edmund," *DNB* 10:1191–92, on 1192. Keene, like the Hackney Newcomes, and like Lord Charles Cavendish, subscribed to an important scientific publication at this time, Colin Maclaurin, *An Account of Sir Isaac Newton's Philosophical Discoveries* (London, 1748).

[19] Birch Diary, 6 June 1747, 17 May 1751, 18 and 22 Feb. 1752.

[20] Winstanley, *Unreformed Cambridge*, 193. Of peers born in 1711–40, Henry Cavendish's period, only three went to Peterhouse. By contrast, nine went to Clare, eight to King's, seven to Trinity, and six to St. John's. In attendance at Cambridge, in 1740–59, when Henry Cavendish was there, out of twenty-seven peers' sons, only three were at Peterhouse. Cannon, *Aristocratic Century*, 48–51.

[21] *A Concise and Accurate Description of the University, Town, and County of Cambridge*, new ed. (Cambridge, n.d. /probably 1784/), 16. Joseph Wilson, *Memorabilia Cantabrigiae: or, an Account of the Different Colleges in Cambridge . . .*(London, 1803), 1–3.

[22] Edmund Carter, *The History of the University of Cambridge, from Its Original, to the Year 1753* (London, 1753), 29.

[23] Robert Wyndham Ketton-Cremer, *Thomas Gray; A Biography* (Cambridge: Cambridge University Press, 1955), 10.

Although at the time Henry Cavendish entered Cambridge, the overall attendance at the university was small and declining, the proportion of students who were aristocratic was rising.[24] Peterhouse reflected the hierarchical character of English society. Its foundation consisted of a master and fourteen fellows with an additional eight bye-fellows on special foundations. The master, who was elected from among the fourteen fellows, was entitled to a sizable estate, with considerable financial advantage and patronage, and he had autocratic power. He lived in a lodge across the street, Trumpington, which drew a line of demarcation between him and the other fellows. There were a dozen other annually elected officers in the college, who discharged their corporate duties in hierarchical order: before a fellow could become a lecturer, he had first to be a bursar, and so forth. Peterhouse students were classed roughly in accordance to their station in life: in ascending order, they entered as sizars, pensioners, fellow-commoners, or noblemen. Sizars, who were the poorest and were charged the lowest fees, and who were really a college charity, were sons of poor clergy, small farmers, petty tradesmen, and artisans. The majority of students were pensioners, who were better off, commonly sons of more prosperous clergy and professional men, but without distinction of birth. Noblemen paid the highest fees, and since they did not have substantial privileges beyond those of fellow-commoners, they often settled to be fellow-commoners.[25] In general, the university reinforced the order of society; that is, the political supremacy of the upper classes.[26]

Fellow-commoners were occasionally older men who simply liked university life, but most of them were young men of independent means, often of considerable wealth and rank, scions of nobility, country families, and commercial magnates. They were conspicuous, often extravagant, inclining to fine dress, sometimes appearing with their own servants, and in any case able to afford to hire poor students to wait on them. They were equivalent to the fellows of the college in that they were admitted to the fellows' table, common room, and cellar, where they smoked clay pipes and drank Spanish and French wine. Usually they were excused from performing the college exercises required of humbler undergraduates and of attending lectures by the college tutors.[27]

When Cavendish arrived, Peterhouse had twenty-four students, not all in residence, and during his three and a half years there, fifty-nine others were admitted. Of these, thirteen were fellow-commoners, most of whom later went into politics, with a sprinkling of nabobs and unclassifiables; and of the others, sizars and, the majority, pensioners, most became clerics. There were fourteen Peterhouse wranglers, ranking third through sixteenth, persons who did notably well on their examinations, indicating competent tutoring in mathematics. John Cuthbert and William Hirst became Fellows of the Royal Society, and the latter, as a naval chaplain, assisted in observations of the transits of Venus,[28] but there is nothing in any of this to suggest that this college might nurture a great scientist.

The same might be said of Cambridge in general. Thomas Gray described Cambridge fellows as sleepy and drunken and fellow-commoners as their imitators, and in his letters from Cambridge he constantly referred to the stupor of the place. There is a measure of truth in his observation, for fellows of a college had little to occupy them officially. They had given lectures at one time, but by the middle of the eighteenth century their teaching duties had largely fallen away, while their fellowships were becoming sinecures. Most of them took holy orders and waited in hope of attaining a college living, freeing them to leave Cambridge and to marry. While Cavendish was at Cambridge, college lecturers still performed, but the practice was on the way to extinction. The motivation to do any work had to come from within. While there were fellows who had a love of learning and teaching, even a few who were great scholars, most of them contributed nothing.[29]

The serious teaching that was done at Cambridge was done by fellows who were also tutors. Their job was enviable, entitling them to

[24]Cannon, *Aristocratic Century*, 45.

[25]Thomas Alfred Walker, *Peterhouse* (Cambridge: W Heffer, 1935), 76–78. Carter, *The History of the University of Cambridge*, 5, 29.

[26]Cannon, *Aristocratic Century*, 34–35, 54–55.

[27]Winstanley, *Unreformed Cambridge*, 198. Walker, Peterhouse, 78.

[28]Thomas Alfred Walker, *Admissions to Peterhouse or S. Peter's College in the University of Cambridge. A Biographical Register* (Cambridge: Cambridge University Press, 1912), 286–306.

[29]Winstanley, *Unreformed Cambridge*, 256–61. Thomas Gray to Horace Walpole, 31 Oct. 1734, in *Horace Walpole's Correspondence*, vol. 13, pt. 1, pp. 58–59.

fees from their students, and providing them with hard-to-order stimulation. Lecturing regularly, and ruling over their pupils as disciplinarians and financial advisers, tutors could make and break the reputation of a college. They had individual influence, since their numbers were few at any given time, only one or two in a college.[30] Peterhouse had two tutors, both formerly hard-working sizars at the college, Charles Stuart and Chapel Cox. Both had taken their M.A. seven years before Henry came up and had tutored off and on for the previous five years.[31] Both were vicars; neither left a mark as a scholar or teacher. They were everyone's tutor, and they tutored in everything, and since no one in the college except Cavendish took a scientific direction, we may suppose that they were not strong in science. Lord John Cavendish, Henry Cavendish's first cousin, was also assigned to the same pair of tutors, though he brought his own private tutor, and Henry might have brought his own too.

In the absence of accounts of Cavendish at Cambridge, we have to fall back on the usual life of a Peterhouse undergraduate at the time to give some idea of his. An undergraduate dined off pewter and ate mutton five times a week and at all meals drank ale and beer, which was brewed at a profit by the college butler. Service was spare but again hierarchical: for the relatively few fellows and fellow-commoners, the butler kept four tablecloths, whereas he kept only two for all the rest, pensioners and sizars combined.[32] It was cold indoors; in the year Cavendish came up, 1749, it was ruled that a fire was to be made in the combination room from noon to two o'clock. Prayers were given at six in the morning and again at six at night, supper was at eight, and at ten the college closed. Heads were barbered by a barber appointed by the college. When students ventured outside the college gates, they found themselves in a very small town, Cambridge, with shops that made money off them, selling them wine, candles, gentlemen's wear, books on law and medicine, and pens, pencils, and paper. Cambridge could be dark, chilly, and dreary. Fellow-commoners had extra money, which helped or hindered them depending on how they used it, in study or in idleness.[33]

The fellow-commoner was privileged in some ways but not in all ways. He was not excused from the acts, opponencies, Senate House Exami-

nation, and religious tests at the end of his studies, if he wanted a degree, but since a degree was unlikely to make any difference in his life, he usually left without taking one. That is what Henry Cavendish did, in February 1753. It has been suggested that he objected to the religious tests,[34] which were stringent, but if so there is no proof. A likely reason why he left without a degree was the exercises in Latin and the examination, which would have required him to sit in the Senate House for three days at the mercy of any M.A. who wanted to ask him questions, an unimaginable horror for the shy Cavendish.[35] An even more likely reason was that he did not even consider a degree but simply followed tradition. Of the thirteen fellow-commoners at Peterhouse during Cavendish's stay, only four took degrees, and three of these were pro forma Masters of Arts only.[36]

The examination that Cavendish did not take was on its way to becoming the famous Cambridge mathematical tripos. In fact, beginning in the year Cavendish would have taken it, 1753, the list of examinees was divided into wranglers and senior and junior optimes, and there was lively competition for a high position on it. Mathematics had become the main discipline and almost the sole subject of the examination, having taken the place in the curriculum once held by logic. Bolingbroke wrote to his son (who happened to be at Oxford, not Cambridge) in 1748: "I am glad to hear that you are at present applied to pure mathematics; they give a proper exercise to the mind, fix the attention of it, and create the habit of pursuing long trains of ideas, the benefit of which you will reap on subjects much more to your purpose."[37] Mathematics toughened the mind for entering the world of men, but it also illuminated the system of the physical world and with it the divine order.[38] This system was first and foremost

---

30 Winstanley, *Unreformed Cambridge*, 269–70.
31 Walker, *Admissions*, 269–72.
32 Walker, *Peterhouse*, 79–80.
33 Ibid. 79–85.
34 Wilson, *Cavendish*, 17, 181.
35 Winstanley, *Unreformed Cambridge*, 43–49, 199.
36 Walker, *Admissions*, passim.
37 Viscount Bolingbroke to his son, Frances, 10th earl of Huntington, 24 Oct. 1748. Great Britain. Historical Manuscripts Commission, *Report on the Manuscripts of the Late Reginald Rawden Hastings, Esq., of the Manor House, Ashby de la Zouche*, 4 vols. (London: His Majesty's Stationary Office, 1927–48) 3:65–66.
38 Winstanley, *Unreformed Cambridge*, 48–51, 132. John Gascoigne, "Mathematics and Meritocracy: The Emergence of the Cambridge Mathematical Tripos," *Social Studies of Science* 14 (1984): 547–84, on 568–72.

Newtonian. John Green, bishop of Lincoln, writing in 1750 while Cavendish was a student, observed that at Cambridge, "Mathematics and natural philosophy are so generally and exactly understood, that more than twenty in every year of the Candidates for a Batchelor of Arts Degree, are able to demonstrate the principal Propositions in /Newton's/ *Principia*; and most other Books of the first Character on those subjects."[39]

Given the mathematical emphasis at Cambridge, there were naturally some very able mathematical teachers there, such as John Lawson of Sidney Sussex College, who was mathematical lecturer and then tutor when Cavendish was a student.[40] Also given the very general purposes of mathematical education, students who distinguished themselves in mathematics would as a rule go on to careers that required no mathematics. If Cavendish *had* taken a degree, his competition in the examinations of 1753 would have included William Disney, Thomas Postlethwaite, and John Hadley. The first two became writers on religion and made their careers in Cambridge; the third became a physician and professor of chemistry at Cambridge. Disney, first wrangler, later regius professor of Hebrew, published against Gibbon's history of the Roman Empire and for the superiority of religious duties over worldly considerations.[41] Postlethwaite, third wrangler, later master of Trinity College, published only one work, a discourse on Isaiah, while retaining his reputation as one of the best mathematicians in the university.[42] Hadley, fifth wrangler, a good friend of Henry Cavendish, comes up later.

Whereas Lord Charles Cavendish learned mathematics by private lessons from mathematicians who were Newton's associates, Henry Cavendish learned mathematics at Cambridge, if not elsewhere too. Whether or not he had a mathematically adept tutor or attended lectures on mathematics, for over three years he was exposed to the mathematical tradition of Cambridge and to the books listed in the various editions of the student guide at Cambridge.[43]

Cavendish was the *only* major English experimentalist of the second half of the eighteenth century with a Cambridge mathematical education, and to that degree his work was markedly different than his contemporaries'. From his earliest researches, he demonstrated his mastery of mathematics, revealing a strong imprint of his Cambridge years.

The one record we have of Cavendish's thinking while he was at the university brings together education, politics, and science. Frederick, prince of Wales, after holding court in opposition to his father, George II, for nearly fifteen years, died while still waiting his chance. The royal misfortune was an excuse for academic exercises at Cambridge and with them Henry Cavendish's first publication. His "Lament on the Death of Most Eminent Frederick, Prince of Wales" was written in Latin, and as a poem it met the standard of the day, which was not high. Horace Walpole made a play on words: "We have been overwhelmed with lamentable Cambridge and Oxford dirges on the Prince's death. . . ."[44] The premature death of a prince was an appropriate occasion to reflect on the fragility and vanity of life.[45] Tears are fruitless, Cavendish wrote; the thistle and the lily alike flourish, death plays no favorites. The middle stanza, however, is not conventional. Here we hear the scientist speak, the "intimate" of nature: while nature may mock us, Cavendish wrote, it "does lay bare hidden causes, and the wandering paths of the stars."[46]

Learning Science

Very few eminent British scientists were like Cavendish upper class.[47] Philip Stanhope —

[39]John Green, *Academic*, 1750, p. 23; quoted in Christopher Wordsworth, *Scholae Academicae. Some Account of the Studies at the English Universities in the Eighteenth Century* (London: Frank Cass reprint, 1968), 73.

[40]Lawson published a number of books on mathematics in the 1760s and 1770s. "Lawson, John," *DSB* 11:736–37.

[41]Nichols, *Literary Illustrations* 6:737.

[42]"Postlethwaite, Thomas," *DNB* 42:204–5.

[43]Daniel Waterland, *Advice to a Young Student. With a Method of Study for the Four First Years*, 1706–40; reported in Wordsworth, *Scholae Academicae*, 78–81, 248–49, 330–37.

[44]Horace Walpole to Horace Mann, 18 June 1751, *Horace Walpole's Correspondence*, vol. 20, part 4, pp. 260–61.

[45]As did the future life scientist Erasmus Darwin, who was at Cambridge at this time: in Darwin's lament, Neptune tells people to stop mourning since the prince might be in Jove's court and wearing a smile. Darwin was admired for this writing. Desmond King-Hele, *Doctor of Revolution. The Life and Genius of Erasmus Darwin* (London: Faber and Faber, 1977), 27.

[46]Cavendish's verse appears in the collection: Cambridge University, *Academiae Cantabrigiensis Luctus in Obitum Frederici celsissimi Walliae Principis* (Cambridge, 1751).

[47]Hans, *New Trends*, 34, groups Delaval with Cavendish and Boyle as the three eminent scientists out of 680 British scientists, most chosen from the *Dictionary of National Biography*, who were "sons of peers." Cavendish was not, of course, the son of a peer, but the point is made of the rarity of aristocrats in this company.

not the mathematician Stanhope who was Charles Cavendish's friend, but the famous essayist, the earl of Chesterfield—advised his son on what to know and what not to waste his time knowing, in a letter written in 1751, when Henry Cavendish was at Cambridge. Stanhope had just brought the bill in the House of Lords to change the calendar from the Julian to the Gregorian. He knew nothing about astronomy but he gave a good speech anyway, one which was considered more effective than the accompanying speech by Macclesfield, who did know what he was talking about. The reason for his success, Stanhope told his son, was his words and periods, his eloquence. Reason and good sense made no impression in politics, he had observed. It was all right if his son learned a little astronomy and geometry so that he would not appear ignorant in conversation, but six months were all he needed for that. Stanhope said he would rather talk with captains in the military than with Newton or Descartes. Since manner *was* everything, Stanhope advised his son to read Bolingbroke on style.[48]

Henry Cavendish was set apart from most of his scientific colleagues by education as well as by class. The fraction of eminent British scientists in his time who had a Cambridge or Oxford education was small and steadily falling.[49] Still there were a few young men of future scientific achievement at Cambridge when he was there. One of them was Edward Delaval, younger brother of a peer from an ancient Northumberland family, who would become a chemist, a recipient of the Royal Society's Copley Medal and another gold medal from the Manchester Literary and Philosophical Society. Because of Delaval's scientific interest, his station, his residence (his college, Pembroke, was across the street from Peterhouse), and his voice (which was resounding, a family trait, earning him the local name of "Delaval the loud"), Cavendish could not have failed to know him or about him; he was to receive the Copley Medal of the Royal Society *with* Cavendish.[50] One year younger than Cavendish, Nevil Maskelyne, a student at Trinity College, would go on to a distinguished career in astronomy, first as assistant to James Bradley and then in Bradley's post of astronomer royal; he was also to become one of Cavendish's most valued colleagues. At Cambridge and also of about the

same age as Cavendish were the promising but short-lived chemist John Hadley, the capable practical astronomer Francis Wollaston, who graduated second wrangler, and the eccentric mathematician Francis Maseres, who graduated first wrangler and coveted the Lucasian chair that went instead to Edward Waring. Hadley was a guest in the Cavendish home, and Cavendish recommended both Wollaston and Maseres—and in both cases he was first to sign the certificate—for membership in the Royal Society.[51]

Of eventual importance to Cavendish as a friend and colleague was another young man at Cambridge, John Michell. Having graduated the year before Cavendish entered Cambridge, Michell was a fellow of Queen's College, where he gave lectures. Unprepossessing in appearance ("a little short man of a black Complexion, and fat"), Michell was described by a contemporary diarist as a "very ingenious Man and an excellent Philosopher," which he was.[52] While Cavendish was at Cambridge, Michell was doing research in natural philosophy and keeping in touch with the wider world. Having made a thorough investigation of the properties of the magnetic force and having published a method for making strong magnets artificially in 1750, that year he invited scientific men to Cambridge to observe his experiments.[53]

---

[48]Earl of Chesterfield to his son Philip, 18 Mar. and 7 Apr. 1751, and 19 Sep. 1752, in *Letters Written by the Late Right Honourable Philip Dormer Stanhope, Earl of Chesterfield, to His Son, Philip Stanhope, Esq; Late Envoy Extraordinary at the Court of Dresden: Together with Several Other Pieces on Various Subjects*, ed. E. Stanhope. vol. 2 (Dublin, 1774), 118–22, 127–30, 285–88.

[49]Hans, *New Trends*, 34, estimates that the proportion of scientific Oxford and Cambridge graduates dropped from 67 percent in the seventeenth century to 20 percent at the end of the eighteenth century. Hans's figures do not have much significance, since they are based on rather arbitrary definitions, but the large fraction of scientific practitioners in Henry Cavendish's time who were not Oxford or Cambridge graduates is significant.

[50]The name was given to Delaval by his friend Thomas Gray. Cremer, *Gray*, 142–43. Two years older than Cavendish, Delaval took his M.A. and became a fellow of Pembroke. "Delaval, Edward Hussey," *DNB* 5:766–67.

[51]Royal Society, Certificates 3:65 (Francis Wollaston's announced candidacy, 3 Jan. 1769) and 3:104 (Francis Maseres's announced candidacy, 31 Jan. 1771).

[52]The diarist William Cole is quoted in Archibald Geikie, *Memoir of John Michell* (Cambridge: Cambridge University Press, 1918), 8.

[53]Michell recalled this visit to Cambridge in 1750 by John Canton, John Ellicott, and another person in connection with a priority dispute: letter of 17 May 1785 to the editor of the *Monthly Review*, pp. 478–80, on p. 479.

In the introduction, we discussed Lord Charles and Henry Cavendish in relation to two revolutions, one political and one scientific. The education that Henry received at Cambridge can be related to those revolutions, too. By that time Newton's natural philosophy, as presented in the *Principia*, had come to be taught as an integral part of the curriculum at Cambridge, and it has been argued that one of the reasons for this curriculum is a change brought about in the university by the Glorious Revolution. After the Revolution, Cambridge became a stronghold of low-church latitudinarians and whigs, to whom Newtonianism had a particular appeal (for the support it gave to the argument from design).[54] It is certainly the case that Cavendish was indoctrinated in a scientific orthodoxy originating in the scientific revolution in an institution sympathetic to the Revolutionary Settlement. For some three odd years, Cavendish lived and breathed Newtonianism.

Just as the university was dominated by its colleges, its teaching was dominated by tutors in their colleges and not by the small number of professors of the university. In critical and historical accounts of the university in the eighteenth century, the professors have generally fared poorly, judged even less important than their numbers would suggest, and derogated if not treated as figures of fun. Professors sometimes deserved this treatment, but it can be said on their behalf that their teaching was becoming increasingly marginal as their subjects were being taken over by the tutors. They were deprived of the usual incentive to lecture, though some of them took this form of teaching seriously all the same, and almost all of them brought out textbooks. Of interest to us are certain professors whose subjects would have been of interest to Cavendish.

Whether or not Cavendish heard Cambridge professors lecture, he most certainly knew their textbooks and their common desire to build science on Newton's example. Just what a scientifically minded student like Cavendish made of it was, ultimately, up to him. Just as Cavendish had to start somewhere, so must we: in this chapter we examine some textbooks by professors used at Cambridge and in this way learn, as students in Cavendish's day learned, the approved way of studying nature.

The great influence of Newton on Cambridge

was through his physical theories, the mathematical theorems of which were the main study when Cavendish was there.[55] The philosophical power of the mathematical description of nature was demonstrated—once and for all time, his followers believed—by Newton in his treatise *Mathematical Principles of Natural Philosophy*, which appeared in three editions in Newton's lifetime, with changes in technical and philosophical content, between 1687 and 1726.[56] The complementary power of the experimental enquiry into nature was as persuasively demonstrated in Newton's optical researches, collected in his treatise *Opticks*, which also appeared in three editions, between 1704 and 1717/18. This latter book had a speculative part, "queries," which was enlarged in each edition. Its purpose being to stimulate others to carry forward the investigation of nature in Newton's mathematical and experimental way, it was regarded as the most important part of the book by Newton's followers in the eighteenth century.[57]

By contrast with his principal physical writings, Newton's published mathematical writings at the time of his death amounted to a few scattered tracts, which by no means revealed the extent of his researches. In the beginning of the *Principia*, he introduced the mathematical ideas needed for understanding what followed, and to the first edition of the *Opticks* he appended two Latin treatises on curves and their quadrature, which a few years later reappeared in English translation. It was left to others to bring out certain other of Newton's mathematical writings, the existence of which was known, since Newton lent

[54]John Gascoigne, *Cambridge in the Age of the Enlightenment: Science, Religion and Politics from the Restoration to the French Revolution* (Cambridge: Cambridge University Press, 1989), 145.
[55]W. W. Rouse Ball, *A History of the Study of Mathematics at Cambridge* (Cambridge, 1889), 74–76.
[56]The editors of the three editions of Newton's treatise (generally referred to by the short Latin title *Principia*) were early disciples of Newton: Halley in 1687, Roger Cotes in 1713, and Henry Pemberton in 1726. In 1729 an English translation was brought out by Andrew Motte: *Sir Isaac Newton's Mathematical Principles of Natural Philosophy and His System of the World*, rev. F. Cajori, 2 vols. (1934; Berkeley and Los Angeles: University of California Press, 1962). I. B. Cohen, *Introduction to Newton's Principia* (Cambridge: Cambridge University Press, 1971), vii, 7.
[57]The editions were the first, in 1704, in English; the second, in 1706, in Latin; and the third, in 1717/18, in English again. Isaac Newton, *Opticks; or a Treatise of the Reflections, Refractions, Inflections & Colours of Light*, based on the 4th ed. of 1730 (New York: Dover Publications, 1952). I. B. Cohen, "Newton, Isaac," DSB 10:42–101, on 59.

out his mathematical manuscripts. William Whiston, Newton's successor at Cambridge, published Newton's *Arithmetica Universalis* in 1707, and in 1711 he published short works by Newton on fluxions and infinite series, under the title *Analysis per Quantitatum Series, Fluxiones ac Differentias.* . . William Jones's copy of Newton's systematic account of the method of fluxions was published in English translation by John Colson, holder of Newton's Lucasian chair in Henry Cavendish's time. Roger Smith, the Plumian professor of astronomy and experimental philosophy then, discovered more mathematical manuscripts by Newton, though he did nothing with them.[58] Newton was gone but his works appeared as if he were still among the living. Other than in stature, Newton did not seem distant to people at Cambridge when Cavendish was there.

The *Principia* lays down the laws of matter in motion and the law of universal gravitation, with which Newton deduced the motions of the planets, comets, moon, and tides.[59] Its sweeping deductive power was the basis of its appeal.[60] The laws of motion were presumed to contain all relations between matter, motion, and force in the sense that all theorems of geometry are contained in the axioms of that subject. In addition to gravitation, other forces were known to exist, which had yet to be described, which defined for Newton the "whole burden of philosophy": it was to observe the motions of bodies and from them to deduce the forces acting and then to deduce from these forces the other phenomena of nature.[61]

For the phenomena, Newton drew mainly on known empirical laws and on available astronomical observations. He kept his discussion of experiments separate from the mathematical development, consigning them to "scholiums," the purpose of which was to make clear that the mathematical propositions were not "dry and barren."[62] Newton reported exacting experiments of his own on pendulums, but he revealed himself as the proven master of experimental enquiry as the author of the *Opticks*.

Like the *Principia*, the *Opticks* begins with definitions and axioms. However, a glance at its pages reveals that it contains an orderly progression of experiments and that it ends with a series of questions. It argues experimentally for a new understanding in optics, which Newton had earlier announced in the *Philosophical Transactions*: the white light of the sun is compounded of heterogeneous colored rays, and these colors are original and immutable qualities of light, and they are quantitatively distinguishable by their different degrees of refrangibility upon passing through bodies. For the explanation of the bending and reflecting of light by bodies, Newton looked to the subject of his earlier treatise, forces and motions. Between the rays of light and bodies, a force acts; the only uncertainty was "what kind of Force,"[63] and for that to be known, "both /light and bodies/ must be understood." Newton did a variety of experiments on the interaction of light and bodies: on the colors of thin, transparent bodies, and on the inflexion of light by a knife edge. The book ends inconclusively. Newton did not have a complete "Theory of Light," only the beginning of one. The sixteen queries of the first edition complete Newton's design insofar as they suggest how the science might look when completed, after the optical forces had been subsumed under mathematical law as had the force of gravitation. The *Opticks* returns to the *Principia*, to the ideal of the derivation of all motion from force, but the problem optics posed was obviously more difficult than the one astronomy had. The bodies of the solar system moved in regular ellipses and parabolas; in the queries, Newton spoke of light passing near bodies as having a "motion like that of an Eel."[64]

Heat, one of the consequences of the action of light on bodies, is the subject of nearly half of the first set of queries in Newton's *Opticks*. By the law of action and reaction, the third of Newton's laws of motion, the reflection, refraction, inflection, and emission of light by bodies induce an agitation of the small parts of the bodies. Heat, for Newton, is that agitation, an internal vibration.[65] The rest of

───────────

[58]D. T. Whiteside, in his edition of Isaac Newton, *Mathematical Papers of Isaac Newton*, vol. 1 (Cambridge: Cambridge University Press, 1967), xv–xvi, xxv, 33.

[59]The discussion that follows of Newton's *Principia* and *Opticks* is taken largely from the section "Newton's Science," in Russell McCormmach, "The Electrical Researches of Henry Cavendish," PhD. diss., Case Institute of Technology, 1967, on 5–29.

[60]C. Truesdell, "A Program Toward Rediscovering the Rational Mechanics of the Age of Reason," *Archive for History of Exact Sciences* 1 (1960): 1–36, on 6.

[61]Newton, *Mathematical Principles*, 1:xvii–xviii.

[62]Ibid, 2:397.

[63]Newton, *Opticks*, 82, 276.

[64]Ibid, 339.

[65]Ibid, 339.

the queries have to do with the action of bodies on light and on the optic nerve and the physiology of color vision.

In the second edition, Newton added seven more queries, which constitute the fullest statement of his expectations for the mechanics of the forces between particles of bodies and of light. A final set of eight queries on the ether was added to the third edition. Backed by Newton's authority, the queries of the *Opticks* proved to be a source of new science (and of dead ends) for readers throughout the eighteenth century.

Newton's *Principia* became a canonical text at Cambridge. Even if only the early propositions had to be mastered, students found it hard going, which gave their teachers something to do. They lectured, tutored, and wrote texts on Newton's work for the learners.

One of the first to lecture on it at Cambridge was William Whiston, who wrote several books still in use at Cambridge when Cavendish was there. An ambitious man of wide interests and fervid commitments, Whiston's discovery of Newton carried the force of a conversion. After he had studied mathematics at Cambridge and had taken holy orders, he returned to Cambridge, there to join the "poor wretches," as he recalled in his *Memoirs*, who were still studying Descartes's fictions. He had actually heard Newton lecture a time or two without understanding a word. It was upon reading a paper by the astronomer David Gregory that Whiston became aware that Newton's *Principia* was the work of a "*Divine Genius*." With "immense pains" and "utmost zeal," Whiston tackled the *Principia* on his own.[66] An early result of his discovery of Newton was his book *A New Theory of the Earth*, which he submitted and dedicated to Newton, "on whose principles it depended, and who well approved of it." Drawing upon Newton's triumphant reduction of comets to mathematical law and order in the *Principia*, Whiston demonstrated the book of Genesis. The earth, originally a sun-bound comet, was struck by another comet, which caused the Deluge and at the same time its present elliptical path and diurnal rotation. These cosmic events were the expression of God's will, but the physical agency was Newton's universal gravitation.[67] When Newton left Cambridge for his post at the mint in London, in 1701 he arranged for Whiston to

succeed him as Lucasian professor of mathematics. Whiston published his lectures at Cambridge on astronomy and on natural philosophy, the latter the first extensive commentary on Newton's *Principia*. And, as we said, with Newton's approval, he published Newton's lectures on universal arithmetic, or algebra, which presented the subject with intellectual grandeur and pedagogic practicality. Newton asserted that arithmetic and algebra make "one perfect science," with algebra distinguished by its "universal" character, allowing general theorems and giving it power over particular arithmetic for solving "the most difficult problems." The material is presented according to Newton's method in teaching: "in learning the sciences, examples are of more use than precepts."[68] Whiston eventually fell out of favor with Newton (and Cambridge), but Newton had done much for him, placing him at Cambridge as his successor and showing him his favor for many years, which Whiston reciprocated by implementing Newtonian studies at Cambridge.[69]

While he was Lucasian professor, Whiston let the young scholar Nicholas Saunderson lecture on the same material, Newton's *Universal Arithmetic*, *Principia*, and *Opticks*. Blind virtually from birth, Saunderson demonstrated, his publisher said, how far the faculties of the imagination and memory could compensate for the want of a sense. He was a kind of prodigy and living experiment of the

[66]William Whiston, *Memoirs* (London, 1749), 37.

[67]William Whiston, *A New Theory of the Earth* . . ., 5th ed. (London, 1737); *Memoirs of the Life and Writings of Mr. William Whiston* (London, 1749), 43. Jacques Roger, "Whiston, William," *DSB* 14:295–96.

[68]Whiston's edition of Newton's lectures appeared in Latin in 1707 and was translated by the mathematician Joseph Ralphson, *Universal Arithmetick; or, A Treatise of Arithmetical Composition and Resolution* . . . (London, 1720). Most of the problems Newton discusses are geometrical, but some are mechanical; e.g., problems 12 and 16, on elastic collisions and the position of a comet. References to the English edition, pp. 1–2, 80, 117, 191.

[69]Whiston was banished from Cambridge in 1710 for unorthodox religious beliefs, which he made public; this time he did not receive help from Newton, who held similar beliefs but kept them private. Whiston published his astronomical lectures in 1707: *Praelectiones Astronomicae*, translated in 1715 as *Astronomical Lectures, Read in the Publick Schools of Cambridge* . . .; these lectures speak of "attraction" and Newton's theory of the moon, but they are not so much a Newtonian text as the astronomical preparation for Newton's philosophy, which Whiston promised to give next term. He published his lectures on natural philosophy in 1710, *Praelectiones Physico-Mathematicae*, translated in 1716 as *Sir Isaac Newton's Mathematic Philosophy More Easily Demonstrated*. Maureen Farrell, *William Whiston* (New York: Arno, 1981), 200. Rouse Ball, *History*, 83–85, 94–95. "Whiston, William," *DNB* 21:10–14. Whiteside, Newton's *Mathematical Papers* 1:xvi.

Enlightenment. He definitely was a source of local wonder, able to distinguish a fifth part of a musical note, estimate the size of a room from the sounds in it, tell the difference between genuine and false medals by touch, and, most important, gain great proficiency in higher mathematics. Elected Whiston's successor in the Lucasian chair, Saunderson had good relations with the scientific circle associated with Newton: Cotes, Jones, De Moivre, Machin, John Keill, and others. Like Whiston, Saunderson's importance was not as an original mathematician but as an industrious teacher of the new mathematics and natural philosophy at Cambridge. Saunderson did not publish any books himself, but soon after his death, his lectures on fluxions and algebra were published. When Cavendish entered Cambridge, various of Saunderson's lectures in manuscript were still in circulation, parts of which had been published under others' names. Even several years after Cavendish had left Cambridge, Saunderson's lectures could still be promoted as the best presentation for university students.[70]

Saunderson was known to have revered Newton, whose work he made the basis of his teaching. Saunderson's *Method of Fluxions* begins abruptly with a proposition about triangles, the sides of which are identified with Newtonian forces. His subject, fluxions, was the new, powerful mathematics of the natural world. Like their inventor, Saunderson defined fluxions with reference to motion: fluxion $\dot{x}$ is the velocity of a flowing quantity x, the familiar wording and image. Saunderson referred to some experiments on air, but for the most part he treated only the mathematical part of natural philosophy, weaving together fluxions, algebra, geometry, and mechanics as one inseparable subject. Saunderson's way of teaching mathematics entailed a way of thinking about nature, the lesson a Cambridge student in the middle of the eighteenth century would have drawn from his lectures.[71]

Upon Saunderson's death in 1739, the aging De Moivre (who looked to one observer as if he were "fit for his coffin . . . a mere skeleton") and Whiston (who wanted to return but was not taken seriously) were passed over for the mathematical schoolmaster John Colson as the new Lucasian professor.[72] Besides teaching, Colson had taken a modestly active part in the science of his day; his principal claim to the Lucasian chair was his publication three years before of the tract Newton had wanted to publish but for which there was no market, *The Method of Fluxions and Infinite Series.* Long circulated in Cambridge, Newton's manuscript was translated from Latin into English by Colson, and as we said, for this purpose Colson used a copy owned by William Jones, to whom he warmly dedicated the publication.[73] The Cambridge diarist and antiquarian William Cole got it right when he described Colson as a "plain honest man of great industry and assiduity."[74] If he disappointed people at Cambridge, as Cole said he did, it was not by his lack of original mathematics but "by his lectures." In Colson, Cambridge had acquired a known quantity: he remained what he had always been, essentially a teacher.

Whatever might be said of Colson's accomplishments, his enthusiasm for his subject and its inventor cannot be faulted. His words in the annotated edition of Newton's *Method of Fluxions* stand out even among the most excessive Newtonian panegyrics. Mathematics was the greatest of all intellectual attainments, Colson said, and

---

[70] Rouse Ball, *History*, 86. "Saunderson or Sanderson, Nicholas," *DNB* 17:821–22. Roger Cotes to William Jones, 25 Nov. 1711, and Nicholas Saunderson to William Jones, 4 Feb. 1713/14, in Stephen Jordan Rigaud, ed., *Correspondence of Scientific Men of the Seventeenth Century*, vol. 1 (Hildesheim: Georg Olms reprint, 1965), 261–62, on 261, 264–65, on 265.

[71] Nicholas Saunderson, *The Method of Fluxions Applied to a Select Number of Useful Problems; . . . and an Explanation of the Principal Propositions of Sir Isaac Newton's Philosophy* (London, 1756), ix–x, 79, 81, and Advertisement. "Saunderson," *DNB* 17: 821. Like Newton's lectures, Saunderson's were a set of examples; that was how they were described by the Cambridge astronomer William Ludlam, who knew them firsthand, having been one of Saunderson's pupils engaged in reading sections of Newton's *Principia*. William Ludlam, *The Rudiments of Mathematics; Designed for the Use of Students at the Universities* (Cambridge, 1785), 6.

[72] Quotation about De Moivre's age and infirmity from William Cole's diary, quoted in "Colson, John," *DNB* 4:801–2, on 801. From 1709 until he was named Lucasian professor, John Colson taught at Sir Joseph Williamson's Mathematical School, in Rochester. He has been confused with a relative of the same name who headed a mathematical school in London from 1692; early on, the younger John Colson may have taught at that school too. R. V. and P. J. Wallis, *Biobibliography of British Mathematics and Its Applications.* Part 2: *1701–1760* (Newcastle upon Tyne: Epsilon Press, 1986), 35.

[73] In 1738 Colson translated from the French a theoretical paper by Alexis Clairaut on the figure of the planets for the *Philosophical Transactions.* Before that, he had published two mathematical papers of his own on algebra and another on spherical maps in the same journal, and one of the algebra papers had been translated into Latin and appended to the 1732 Leyden edition of Newton's *Arithmetica Universalis.* "Colson," *DNB* 4:801–2. Rouse Ball, *History*, 100–1. Whiteside, Newton's *Mathematical Papers* 1:xv, 8:xxiii.

[74] Quoted in "Colson," *DNB* 4:801.

Newton was the "greatest master in mathematical and philosophical knowledge, that ever appear'd in the world." The subject at hand, fluxions, in particular, was the "noblest effort that ever was made by the human mind." Newton's *Method*, unlike his other mathematical writings, "accidental and occasional," was intended as a text for "novices and learners," a goal which the teacher Colson could become enthusiastic about. Colson could not have made a clearer distinction between textbook and original work nor between a teacher like himself and the author of great works like Newton, yet he implied that the humble beginner could comprehend the work of the greatest thinker of all time— false encouragement perhaps for many of his auditors and readers but not for someone like Cavendish. Colson's edition of Newton was at once a textbook and an indoctrination into mathematical Newtonianism, and it was also a book of advocacy, as Colson eagerly enlisted in the ranks of Newton's supporters, defending Newton and attacking his critics.[75]

For the learner of fluxions and infinite series, there was Newton's own presentation, and then there was Colson's. If Newton's was terse, Colson's was prolix; Newton's treatment of infinite series occupies twenty pages, Colson's "perpetual comment" ninety-eight.[76] Colson assumed little of his reader, expanded freely on the text, gave copious examples, and wrote not as a mathematician but as an eternally patient teacher who repeated the obvious as well as the essential.[77] We cannot know if Cavendish read Colson's commentary as well as Newton's text; *but* if he did, he read two observations that might stimulate a beginning mathematical student. One was that Newton had not said the last work on the subject: improvements in the method of fluxions had been made since Newton, and the subject was capable of further perfection. The other observation had to do with Newton's general method, that of analysis. In his tract, Newton noted that modern mathematicians favored the "analytical" method over the "synthetical." Colson elaborated: by the ancient synthetical method, the mathematician proceeds from truths already known, proving them from axioms, whereas by the modern analytical method, he proceeds from the known to the *unknown*. Analytics is the "art of invention," a method of discovery.[78]

We turn now from the professors of mathematics to the professors of astronomy and experimental philosophy. Their chair was the more recent of the two, endowed in 1704 by the archdeacon of Rochester, Thomas Plume. Its appearance coincided with the beginning of the Newtonian school at Cambridge.

The acceptance of Newtonian teaching at Cambridge began in 1699, soon after Newton had left Cambridge for London, but before he had resigned his Lucasian professorship, when the mastership of Trinity fell vacant. The man elected to fill it in the following year was the king's librarian Richard Bentley, a classical scholar greatly impressed by the new science.[79] Not himself a man of science, Bentley was a good judge of men who were and also of their needs. Wanting to make

---

[75]Colson thought that the beginner's greatest difficulty was in understanding the notion of a vanishing quantity. His patient elucidation was intended to make this notion "rational." Colson had a second purpose beside instructing: it was to prove the superiority of Newton's vanishing quantity over the foreign, Leibnizian notion of indivisibles, and to answer Bishop Berkeley's criticisms of Newton's notion of quantity. To Colson, the resolution of the controversy over the nature of quantity had the utmost urgency, since it fostered distrust of science itself. To this end, Colson explained the two principles of quantity in Newton's mathematics: the first, taken from rational mechanics, is that mathematical quantity can be conceived of as generated by local motion; the second is that quantity is infinitely divisible. Newton, Colson says, is to be trusted over his foreign rivals, with their infinitesimal method, because Newton had a "compleat knowledge of the philosophy of quantity." Colson's comments in his edition of *Method of Fluxions*, ix–xii, xx, 335–36.

[76]Colson was a teacher of a familiar kind, one who once has hold of a subject cannot let go. His contemporary John Stewart, professor of mathematics at the University of Aberdeen, published a translation of two mathematical tracts by Newton with commentary. The two tracts occupy 54 pages of Stewart's book, and the rest of the 497 pages plus introductory matter is Stewart's commentary. His book, like Colson's, was intended for beginners. *Sir Isaac Newton's Two Treatises: Of the Quadrature of Curves, and Analysis by Equations of an Infinite Number of Terms, Explained . . .* (London, 1745).

[77]One of Colson's main points is that the idea of quantity as something generated by motion in time is not essential to Newton's *Method of Fluxions*. Time itself is a quantity and can be represented by symbols and lines, so that in the final analysis Newton's method does not depend upon time at all, only on geometry. Time, however, is heuristic, aiding the mind to grasp the idea of quantity, and it is because of the uniform flow of time that Newton called his method the method of "fluxions." Fluxions are a mathematical method conducive to discovery. A second main point is that fluxions are the proper mathematics for treating a pair of inverse "problems" that lie at the heart of the science of motion. These problems arise from the fact that the velocity of a point and the distance described by the point mutually determine one another. They are: given the distance continously described by a point at any time, the problem is to determine the velocity; and given its continuous velocity at any time, the problem is to determine the distance described. Corresponding to the two problems are, respectively, the *direct* method fluxions and the *inverse* method of fluxions (or in later terminology, differentiation and integration).

[78]Colson's edition of Newton's *Method of Fluxions*, 1, 144.

[79]Rouse Ball, *History*, 75.

Trinity a center of experimental and observational science, Bentley had a laboratory built there for Newton's friend John Francis Vigani, who had lectured on chemistry at Queen's and had been named the first professor of chemistry at Cambridge in 1702. Bentley succeeded in securing the new Plumian professorship for his colleague at Trinity, the young mathematician Roger Cotes. Bentley then raised a subscription for an observatory to be built over Trinity's entrance gate and for neighboring rooms to be assigned to Cotes and to his assistant, his cousin Robert Smith. To further his scientific ambitions for Trinity, Bentley arranged for Whiston, of Clare College, also to have rooms in Trinity next to the gate under Cotes's observatory.[80] Trinity set a precedent for other colleges; Bentley, more than any other person, was responsible for the eventual dominance of the Newtonian school of science and mathematics at Cambridge.

Bentley bore the expense of a new edition of Newton's *Principia* in 1713 and was himself going to edit it, but sensibly the task was reassigned to a proper mathematician, Cotes, who wrote a preface for it that became a cardinal document in the dissemination of Newtonian thought. Three years later, in 1716, Cotes died suddenly, at age thirty-three. He had published only two papers at the time of his death, one on logarithms, which Robert Smith included along with some theorems of his own in a posthumous edition in 1722 of Cotes's mathematical manuscripts, *Harmonia Mensurarum*. This publication testifies to Cotes's exceptional promise, for which we also have Newton's often quoted observation, "Had Cotes lived we might have known something." To be sure, had he lived, he might have inspired an enduring mathematical school at Cambridge, for he was one of the few British mathematicians capable of it and one of the last for a long time.[81]

Cotes left another record of his scientific activity in the form of lectures. With Whiston, in the observatory at Trinity, he gave experimental lectures in natural philosophy, among the first to be given in England. After Whiston's expulsion from Cambridge, Cotes continued to give the lectures by himself, and after Cotes's death, Robert Smith kept them going. In 1738 Smith published Cotes's lectures. Unlike Cotes's *Harmonia Mensurarum*, written tersely in Latin and intended for a select audience of skilled mathematicians, his *Hydrostatical and Pneumatical Lectures* was written expansively and popularly. Readers could take in the limited mathematics, his editor Smith said, "with as much ease and pleasure, as in reading piece of history." (Smith could not leave it at that but added mathematical notes of his own.)[82]

Cotes's lectures were mostly concerned with air but also with hydrostatics because the two subjects were so close. Hydrostatics and pneumatics were experimentally studied by that most precise of instruments, the balance. Gravitation, the new acquisition of science, the force to which the balance responds, gave Cotes's lectures their unity. Gravity, Cotes wrote, "is a property of so universal an extent" that even "air, which as I shall afterwards shew, may be weighed in the ballance." The elasticity of air Cotes explained by referring to the *Principia*, to the place where Newton derived Boyle's law (the proportionality of the density of air to the compressing force) by assuming that particles of air mutually repel with a force inversely proportional to their separation. To explain the phenomena of sound, the minute rapid waves in the air, Cotes again referred to the *Principia*, to Newton's a priori calculation of the velocity of sound from its causes, in agreement with measurements of the velocity by Halley and others. Cotes's principal inspiration came from Newton: the *Principia* for its mathematical demonstration of the subtle properties of air, and the *Opticks* for its rich insights into the working of the smallest parts of creation. He wrote of the fecundity of the final query of the *Opticks*: "Whoever will read those few pages of that excellent book, may find there in my opinion, more

---

[80]"Bentley, Richard," *DNB* 2:306–14, on 312. A. Rupert Hall, "Vigani, John Francis," *DSB* 14:26–27. James Henry Monk, *The Life of Richard Bentley*, 2d ed., 2 vols. (London, 1833) 1:202–4. Whiston, *Memoirs*, 133.

[81]J. M. Dubbey, "Cotes, Roger," *DSB* 3:430–33. Roger Cotes, *Harmonia Mensurarum, sive Analysis & Synthesis per Rationum & Angulorum Mensuras Promotae: Accedunt alia Opuscula Mathematica* , ed. R. Smith (Cambridge, 1722). Rouse Ball, *History*, 90.

[82]Cotes's intention was to exemplify the experimental philosophy, and his method was first to demonstrate by experiment and then to draw general conclusions, which meant reading his lectures. To convey his method, Smith added to the published lectures descriptions of experiments and drawings of apparatus. "The Editor's Preface," in Roger Cotes, *Hydrostatical and Pneumatical Lectures*, ed. Roger Smith (London, 1738). The second edition was published in Cambridge in 1747. For his joint course of experiments with Cotes, Whiston wrote half of the lectures, but he did not publish his. With Francis Hauksbee, Whiston gave experimental courses in London after leaving Cambridge. "Cotes," *DNB* 4:1029.

solid foundations for the advancement of natural philosophy, than in all the volumes that have hitherto been published upon that subject." Cotes concluded the four-week course with a lecture on Boyle's "factitious airs." These were airs, or gases, contained in bodies that could be freed from them artificially by fire, explosion, dissolution, putrefaction, and fermentation. At the time of the lectures—which was before Stephen Hales's work—Boyle's were the "best and almost only trials which have yet been made concerning factitious airs." Cotes told of Boyle's extraction of airs from a variety of substances, animal, vegetable, and mineral, and by a variety of means; for example, chemical, as in mixing iron with the acids aqua fortis and spirit of wine. Cotes presented factitious airs not as a closed subject for a textbook but as a new, hardly begun subject full of experimental challenge. Drawing on Boyle, Cotes extended the exact science of pneumatics beyond its origins to a vast, largely unknown field of gaseous phenomena attending chemical actions.[83] We know that Cavendish read Cotes's lectures, since he cited them in his first publication, which was on, as it happened, factitious air.

In 1716 Robert Smith was elected to succeed Cotes. Smith was twenty-seven, and for the next forty-four years he was the Plumian professor at Cambridge. He also became master of Trinity after Bentley, and like his predecessor he promoted science in Cambridge in every way he could think of. Before becoming master, he had lectured, and afterwards he took on able students. For example, to encourage Richard Watson, later professor of chemistry at Cambridge, Smith appointed him to a scholarship, urged him to read Saunderson's *Fluxions* and other mathematical books, and gave him, Watson said, "a spur to my industry, and wings to my ambition." Israel Lyons, who lived in Cambridge, showed such mathematical promise that Smith offered to put him through school.[84] When Cavendish studied at Cambridge, he would have been aware that the Plumian professor was one of the founders of Newton's science through his teaching at Cambridge.

With the strong Newtonian direction at Cambridge in the first half of the eighteenth century, the holders of the Lucasian and Plumian professorships might have been mathematical astronomers and developers of rational mechanics,

but this was not the case. The most important scientific publication to come out of Cambridge was strongly Newtonian but the subject was optics, Robert Smith's *A Compleat System of Opticks*, published in 1738. We know that this book was in the Cavendish library at Great Marlborough Street, since Lord Charles Cavendish was one of the men of science who subscribed to it.[85] The confidence implied by the subscription proved fully justified, for this book was probably the most influential optical textbook of the eighteenth century.[86]

When Smith published his *System of Opticks*, Newton's *Opticks* was nearly thirty-five years old. Newton's treatise was meant as a scientific work, and though the early experiments on the analysis of white light into colored rays were accessible to learners, the rest of the book addressed the most difficult problems of the interaction of light and

---

[83]Cotes, *Lectures*, 5, 187, 201–3.

[84]At Trinity College and in the university, Smith encouraged science in a variety of ways. He not only published Cotes's works, he gave the college money to erect a monument to Cotes, which carried an epithet by Bentley, and he gave the college library a bust of Cotes. Later Smith presented the college with the statue of Newton by Roubiliac. He completed the observatory Cotes had begun. He left a huge benefaction to the college, the university, and to science, which included funds for his own Plumian Professorship. He set up annual prizes to go to the two commencing bachelors of arts who had done the most promising work in mathematics and natural philosophy. These so-named Smith's Prizes were later used to encourage work on parts of higher mathematics not appearing in the examinations; they promoted distinguished mathematical work at Cambridge. "Smith, Robert," *DNB* 18:517–19. Winstanley, *Unreformed Cambridge*, 150. Gunther, *Cambridge Science*, 61. Rouse Ball, *History*, 91. Monk, *Life of Bentley* 2:168. Willis and Clark, *Architectural History of the University of Cambridge* 2:600. Richard Watson, *Anecdotes of the Life of Richard Watson, Bishop of Landaff . . .*, 2d ed., vol. 1 (London, 1818), 14. In 1758 Lyons dedicated to Smith his *Treatise on Fluxions*, which was used in teaching at Cambridge alongside texts on the same subject by Newton, Saunderson, and others.

[85]Robert Smith, *A Compleat System of Opticks in Four Books, viz A Popular, a Mathematical, a Mechanical, and a Philosophical Treatise. To Which Are Added Remarks upon the Whole*, 2 vols. (Cambridge, 1738). The 340 subscribers included members of Lord Charles Cavendish's mathematical circle, such as Macclesfield, De Moivre, and Folkes (who subscribed for twelve copies); Cambridge mathematicians and physical scientists, such as John Colson, Roger Long, Nicholas Saunderson, Charles Mason, John Rowning, and Richard Davies; Scottish professors of mathematics and physical science, such as Colin Maclaurin, Robert Simpson, John Stewart, and Robert Dick; and London instrument-makers, such as George Graham, James Short, and Jonathan Sissons. Ten years before its publication, in 1728, Smith first advertised for subscribers for his optical treatise, and if that was when Cavendish subscribed, it was the year he entered the Royal Society. He paid thirty shillings each for the two volumes of the book. Alice Nell Walters, "Tools of Enlightenment: The Material Culture of Science in Eighteenth-Century England" (Ph.D. diss., University of California at Berkeley, 1992), 7.

[86]E. W. Morse, "Smith, Robert," *DSB* 12:477–78. Smith's book was influential not only in Britain but abroad as well, where it was translated into German, Dutch, and French.

matter, accompanied by explanations that often lacked the conclusiveness expected of textbooks. Moreover, the treatise ended by raising questions and by suggesting not always consistent answers. As the reader progressed through Newton's account, the subject of optics widened rather than closed in on itself as a body of knowledge suitably prepared for learners.

By contrast, Smith's book on optics was a proper textbook, an example of Cambridge science teaching at its best, insofar as that teaching can be conveyed by a book. Smith gave a selective account of Newton's optics, overlooking Newton's second thoughts and hesitations, omitting what did not fit. He cited and quoted Newton's queries where they supported his system, ignoring their grammatical form and treating them as if they were assertions not questions.

Since Smith's purpose was to present optics as a *system*, he could not leave undecided the nature of light. On this question, he followed Newton but was more decisive than Newton had been. Although Newton was inclined toward the corpuscular view of light, he speculated freely on alternative, or supplementary, etherial forms of explanation. Smith acknowledged that Newton's ether could explain the phenomena of light equally well, but he used only Newton's streaming corpuscles and the intense forces with which they and the corpuscles of bodies interacted at intimate distances. In this interpretation, he had plenty of support, for by the second decade of the eighteenth century, the corpuscular theory of light was widely subscribed to in principle. Because Smith's *System of Opticks* came to be recognized as the main authority on Newtonian optics after Newton's own *Opticks*, in some respects supplanting it, it further entrenched the corpuscular theory as the dominant theory of light in eighteenth-century Britain.[87] Cavendish subscribed to the corpuscular theory; in all of his writings, published and unpublished, he never used the word that characterized the alternative theory, "ether."

Smith illustrated the indispensable role of instruments in optics by giving a history of astronomy, which he began with Galileo, from whom astronomy acquired its essential, modern instrument, the telescope, and he brought the history down to Bradley's great discoveries incidental to his work on the cosmological problem (the occasion for Lord Charles Cavendish's first recorded scientific observations). He told of the excellent London scientific instrument-makers, such as George Graham, a man of "extraordinary skill," whose help he had solicited in writing this book[88]. Smith included papers on refracting telescopes by Huygens and by his friend the astronomer Samuel Molyneux.[89] Smith gave over an entire chapter to Huygens's long, highly magnifying refracting telescopes, including his 123-foot telescope, which Huygens gave to the Royal Society, and which Henry Cavendish later borrowed and erected at his house. Smith treated the human eye as an optical instrument, constructing a "tolerable eye" from two hemispheres filled with water.[90] He appended an essay on indistinct vision by his friend and colleague at Trinity, the Bentley protégé James Jurin;[91] Jurin made scientifically precise the imprecision of the senses, the ultimate source of knowledge of the external world. Indistinct vision was of great interest to Henry Cavendish, as we will see.

Smith's presentation of optics was comprehensive. Not only were theory, mathematics, experiments, and the construction and use of instruments included, but so was the theory of knowledge. In discussing how we come by our ideas of things by sight, he took up the question Molyneux asked of Locke. Would a blind man who suddenly regained his sight be able to distinguish a globe from a cube by sight alone? To this question, the philosophers had answered in the negative and were apparently confirmed by the recent experience of just such a man reported in the *Philosophical Transactions*. This man did not know the shape of anything by sight; he did not know how to move

---

[87]Authors in the first half of the eighteenth century in Britain who held a corpuscular view of light are identified in Henry John Steffans, *The Development of Newtonian Optics in England* (New York: Science History Publications, 1977), 48, 50, 53; G. N. Cantor, *Optics after Newton: Theories of Light in Britain and Ireland, 1704–1840* (Manchester: Manchester University Press, 1983), 32–33.

[88]Smith, *Opticks*, 332.

[89]Smith, like Bradley, was a collaborator of Molyneux. When Molyneux was appointed to the admiralty, he gave Smith his papers and access to his house, which was fitted out with a complete set of instruments. The plan was for Smith to complete Molyneux's work on perfecting the methods of telescope-making. Molyneux died soon after his appointment. Smith did the next best thing by publishing Molyneux's papers in his book on optics. Smith, *Opticks*, 281.

[90]Smith, *Opticks*, 25.

[91]James Jurin, "An Essay upon Distinct and Indistinct Vision," on pp. 115–70 at the end of Smith's *Opticks*.

his eyes; and he thought that things touched his eyes as things touched his skin. Smith was not satisfied with this answer, since it overlooked the human capacity to reason about experience and compare experiences derived from our several senses. Smith had a ready subject at hand, his colleague the Lucasian professor, the blind mathematician Nicholas Saunderson. When approached on the subject by Smith, Saunderson agreed with him that by "reason," the blind man upon regaining his sight could tell the globe from the cube.[92] The answer Smith and Saunderson gave to the question about the blind man was an inference from the experimental philosophy. In knowing the world, experience is reflected upon by reason.

Smith published one other book while Plumian professor, this one concerned with the sense of hearing instead of sight, *Harmonics, or the Philosophy of Musical Sounds.* As in optics, in music Smith set out to make a system and to do it within the experimental philosophy. The book came out in 1749, the year that Henry Cavendish entered Cambridge, and given his interest in physics and music, it is likely that he read it. Like his book on optics, Smith's book on music was well received and became a standard text; George Lewis Scott, one of De Moivre's pupils, recommended it to Edward Gibbon as "the principal book of the kind."[93]

Like natural philosophy, music had recently undergone great change. The monodic idea had become well established, and with it came the harmonic, as opposed to the contrapuntal, approach to musical composition, with its emphasis on chords and the modern notion of key. By the use of a definite key and of modulation between keys, unity could be achieved in long expressive melodies, but there was a technical problem: although the modulation between closely related keys could be carried out satisfactorily, the same could not be said of the modulation between remoter keys, as demanded for greater contrast. The first workable solution came with the introduction of an octave scale of twelve tones, the half steps of which were precisely equal.[94]

These several, related innovations—the sense of key, modulation between keys, and equal temperament—made possible the extended musical forms of the early eighteenth century. Robert Smith enters musical history at this point; with his *Harmonics*, he intended to provide a full under-standing of temperament. Ancient musical theorists such as Ptolemy considered only perfect consonances, and the scales they built upon them necessarily contained imperfect consonances, disagreeable to the ear. By distributing the largest imperfections in certain concords over the others, the modern theorists improved upon, tempered, the ancient scales, with the result that the imperfect concords were less offensive although there were more of them. Smith did not adopt the well-tempered scale, as promoted by Bach in the *Well-Tempered Clavichord*, but addressed the problem starting with the "first principles of the science." He redistributed the imperfections of the ancient scales in such a way as to make the imperfect consonances all equally "harmonious." For this "scientific solution" of the artistic problem, Smith constructed a theory of imperfect consonances, the first ever (his acoustical version of indistinct vision in optics).[95]

As an experimental philosopher, Smith confirmed his mathematical theory by practice. One experiment was done by the Cambridge organist, another by the bass-viol-playing clockmaker, John Harrison, (who, Smith digressed, as we do, if encouraged would improve navigation "to as great exactness, in all probability, as need be desired"). Musical instruments and scientific instruments became one in Smith's investigation. His theory required that instruments be modified, and to this end he was helped by "two of the most ingenious and learned gentlemen in this University," John Michell, who would become a good friend of Henry Cavendish, and William Ludlam, to whom Lord Charles Cavendish would supply astronomical calculations.[96] Smith's was an improvement over

---

[92] Smith, *Opticks*, 42–43, and "The Author's Remarks upon the Whole," at the end of the book, on 28–29.

[93] Robert Smith, *Harmonics, or the Philosophy of Musical Sounds*, 2d ed. (Cambridge, 1759). First edition in 1749. "Smith," *DSB* 12:477. "Smith," *DNB* 18:519.

[94] Donald N. Ferguson, *A History of Musical Thought*, 2d ed. (New York and London: Appleton, Century, Crofts, 1935), 272–78.

[95] Smith's solution was based on an analysis of the musical interval, a "quantity" terminated by a higher and a lower sound. To be precise, the musical interval is proportional to the logarithm of the ratio of the freqencies of the terminal sounds, on which Smith cited Cotes's *Harmonia Mensurarum*. If the ratio of the frequencies of two sounds is not perfect, the interval they define, and the consonance, is called "imperfect" or "tempered." By using the idea of "arithmetical mean," Smith built a system in which the imperfect consonances "at a medium of one with another, shall be equally and the most harmonious." Smith, *Harmonics*, v–vii, 5–6, 8–9, 123.

[96] Smith, *Harmonics*, ix–xiv, 123.

other systems of temperament, but in the end the modification of instruments it called for made it impractical.

For many reasons it is understandable that the Cambridge natural philosopher Smith should write a scientific treatise on music. To start with, he loved music and was expert on the violin-cello, and his friends included musically talented scientific colleagues, who encouraged his interest and assisted him. He and his colleagues, after all, belonged to a tradition of musical scientists going back to Pythagoras and coming down to Huygens and Newton. The tradition of the university too worked in favor of this combination of interests: music had been grouped with astronomy and the parts of mathematics in the quadrivium, and there was much that was still medieval about Cambridge. Smith's *Harmonics* is filled with early writings on music, often quoted at length in Latin and Greek, and this too reflected the university with its emphasis on mathematics and the classics.[97]

In the ancient world, musicians no doubt followed their ear rather than the "theories of philosophers," Smith said, arriving at temperament "before the reason of it was discovered, and the method and measure of it was reduced to regular theory." But the ear was no longer sufficient, and the theory was insufficient too, which was Smith's starting point. Smith had a musical ear, but he did not need one in harmonics; he had to have only scientific theory, as he explained: a person without a musical ear could tune an organ to any temperament and to "any desired degree of exactness, far beyond what the finest ear unassisted by theory can possibly attain to." It was the same thing in optics: Smith's colleague the blind mathematician Saunderson taught Newton's theory of colors.[98]

Finally, we recall, Smith lived in the age of enlightenment, an image derived from sight but which referred generally to a felt need for clarity. Like musicians of "delicate ear," in listening to a performance, Smith preferred to listen to a single string rather than unisons, octaves, and multiple-part music. This he called a preference for "distinctness and clearness, spirit and duration" over "beating and jarring" and "confused noise." When he listened, for instance, to a harpsichord, he heard only single strings instead of the multiplicity of strings that most people heard. He quoted from his other book, *System of Opticks*, from Jurin's

account there of what happens when a person comes out of a strong light into a closed room: at first the room appears dark, but in time the eye accommodates to the darkness and the room appears light. Jurin's observation applied to sounds too. The discernment of clarity within a confusion of sound and the recovery of vision in darkness symbolized the natural philosopher's quest. In his primary capacity as a teacher of science, Smith was provided with an implicit image by his music. Musicians at first disliked Smith's retuned organ despite its improved harmony, but musicians, like scientists, could be educated; when the musicians persisted, in time they could no longer stand the "coarse harmony" of organs tuned the old way. Smith's esthetics was an esthetics *understood*, which meant by mathematics and experiment.[99]

Robert Smith was the complete natural philosopher, designer of instruments, experimenter, and mathematical theorist. Of all the persons teaching scientific subjects at Cambridge, with the exception of John Michell, he was closest to the kind of scientist Cavendish would become. We would like to think that Cavendish became acquainted with Smith at Cambridge, but that event seems unlikely. They were not in the same college, and Smith probably did not lecture then and was ill and reclusive.[100] It is, however, virtually certain that Cavendish knew Smith through his books on optics and music. Cavendish's theoretical views on optics were the same as Smith's, and, as we

---

[97]As in his book on optics, in his *Harmonics* Smith accorded Huygens a prominent place, referring often to his *Harmonic Cycle*, in which Huygens divided the octave into thirty–one equal intervals. Huygens assumed that mean tones provide the best system, but he erred, Smith said, in assuming that equal temperaments make all tones equally disagreeable. In the course of his book, Smith cited many scientific as well as musical authors on tempered musical systems, such as the mathematicians John Wallis, Cotes, and Leonhard Euler. He cited many works of science: Newton's *Principia* on the nature of air pulses constituting sound and on the velocity of sound, and Newton's *Opticks* on Newton's "happily discovered" proportionality between the breadths of the primary colors in the sun's spectrum and the differences of lengths of musical strings; Cotes's *Lectures upon Hydrostatics and Pneumatics* on the expansion of air with heat; De Moivre's *Doctrine of Chances* for the number of permutations of the elements of a system of sounds; and Colin Maclaurin's *Fluxions*. He cited the mathematician Brook Taylor, an associate of Newton, with whom Taylor had planed to write a work on music, and Jurin and Saunderson and other now familiar names. Phillip S. Jones, "Taylor, Brook," *DSB* 13:265–68, on 265. Smith, *Harmonics*, 8, 25–29, 44, 100, 228, 230.
[98]Smith, *Opticks*, ix, 33–35.
[99]Ibid., 171–72, 210.
[100]"Smith," *DNB* 18:518.

discuss later in this chapter, Cavendish was drawn to music.

Smith's professorship was designated for astronomy as well as for experimental philosophy, but Cambridge acquired another professorship for astronomy all the same, this one joining astronomy to mathematics, specifically to geometry, which made equally good sense. (Neither Smith nor his predecessor Cotes was an astronomer, though they did improve practical astronomy at Cambridge by building the Trinity observatory.) Thomas Lowndes left funds for establishing a salaried professorship of astronomy and geometry, an important recognition of astronomy at Cambridge during the time Cavendish was there. In 1750 Roger Long, a graduate, then fellow, and since 1733 master of Pembroke Hall, was named the first Lowndean professor. Long was an eccentric character, a tory in a predominantly whig Cambridge, an autocrat constitutionally destined to be at cross purposes with the people around him, constantly feuding with the fellows of his college, especially over the right of veto, which he exercised with willful frequency. Like his Plumian colleague, Smith, Long was a skillful musician, who presented the king and queen with a musical instrument of his own invention, the "lyrichord." Long was renowned as an inventor of fantastic machines in his scientific field, astronomy, immense, dramatic things never before seen in Cambridge, which actually served the purposes of education. Some of these Long described in his *Astronomy*, a standard text in the university when Cavendish arrived there. The frontispiece of the first volume illustrates an early construction, a glass celestial sphere known to a "great number of people" and, Long complained, imperfectly copied by several. The book describes another of his machines, a narrow ring twenty feet across on which the constellations of the zodiac and the ecliptic were inscribed. The viewer, who sat in the middle, was treated to a panoramic view of this bit of the heavens. Long wrote of his wish to build the ultimate apparatus, a "planetarium," which would rotate around a platform of spectators. He later built and installed at Pembroke the famous "great sphere," a revolving globe eighteen feet across, capable of holding thirty people. Designated the "Uranium," this consummate lecturer's planetarium provided the frontispiece of the second volume of Long's *Astronomy*. Long had an excellent

assistant,—formerly Long's footboy—Richard Dunthorne, who held the butlership at Pembroke, and who published a number of books and papers on the motions of the moon, comets, and the satellites of Jupiter; he promoted the building of an observatory over the gate of another college, St. John's, which he used to derive his lunar tables; this versatile astronomer also superintended the draining of the fens for the Bedford Level Corporation.[101] Long's own contribution to astronomy in Cambridge in Cavendish's time was his teaching, and his lecture-text was his main publication.[102]

In *Astronomy* Long used mathematics sparingly, but he was emphatic on the point that astronomy was a quantitative science, in observation and in theory, and his account of astronomy accordingly began with the subject of quantity in all of its manifestations in astronomy. His descriptive treatment of astronomy was, like his machines, grand if not grandiose; in contrast to the usual perfunctory single chapter on the fixed stars, his book devoted many chapters to their immense distances and so on. He placed astronomy within natural philosophy, the study of the bodies that comprise the universe. Since the gravitational force was known but the forces of light, magnetism, and electricity were not, gravitational astronomy was far more advanced than the other parts of natural philosophy. Newton's *Principia* "gave an entirely

[101]Wordsworth, *Scholae Academicae*, 249. "Dunthorne, Richard," *DNB* 6: 235–36.

[102]The first volume of Long's *Astronomy, In Five Books* was published in Cambridge in 1742. The second volume did not appear until twenty-two years later, in 1764, for reasons "it would be of no service to the public to be informed." These reasons had in part to do with his interest in music, as a letter from Cambridge noted: "Dr. Long advances, but slowly, in his astronomical work; tho' yᵉ larger part of his 2d vol. is I believe printed. But he keeps amusing himself. . . with alterations in musical instruments, of wᶜʰ he is very fond . . ." J. Green to Thomas Birch, 29 Jan. 1760, BL Add Mss 4308, ff. 192–93. Instead of an apology, Long gave his readers accounts of notable work in astronomy carried out since he began his text; e.g., Bradley's discovery of the aberration of light, the French measurements of the length of a degree to determine the shape of the earth, and observations of the 1761 transit of Venus across the sun. Only in 1784, after Long's death, was the remaining part of the book published. Long, *Astronomy* 1:ix–x, and 2:iii. "Long, Roger," *DNB* 12:109. Rouse Ball, *History*, 105. Gunther, *Early Science in Cambridge* , 164–67. Ketton-Cremer, *Gray*, 83–84. Long did do some observational astronomy, in which he was attracted to the great questions of the science, such as the distance of the fixed stars and their possible motion, concluding after "long and careful enquiry," but incorrectly as it happened, that stars do not move. He knew the active astronomers, such as Bradley, under whose vertical telescope he lay with his head on a cushion. Long, *Astronomy*, 2:637–38.

new face to theoretical astronomy"; it had been "raised, at once, to a greater degree of perfection than could have been hoped for from the united labours of the most learned men, for many ages, by the amazing genius of one man—the immortal *Newton*!"[103] The great instrument-makers, especially the British, supplied the observers who kept astronomy advancing after Newton. Because Lord Charles Cavendish was a subscriber to Long's *Astronomy*, Henry Cavendish is certain to have seen it at home if not at Cambridge, and he might have attended the flamboyant lectures on which it was based. After Cambridge, Cavendish built his own observatory, where he studied the heavens for the rest of his life.

At Cambridge, where religion and Newtonianism had formed an alliance, we find the regius professor of divinity, Thomas Rutherforth, teaching Newtonian natural philosophy and publishing on it as well as on religion, and using his membership in the Royal Society to promote sales of his books.[104] In 1748, the year before Cavendish entered Cambridge, Rutherforth published the lectures he gave at St. John's College, *A System of Natural Philosophy*.[105] God's presence was taken for granted; the divinity professor presented natural philosophy as subject to be studied entirely within its own scientific terms. Throughout his lectures Rutherforth used geometrical arguments, even managing to convey a notion of infinitesimal reasoning while at the same time not assuming the most rudimentary knowledge of quantity (he explained that a fraction decreases as its denominator increases[106]). He had an engaging, self-deprecating honesty, asking forgiveness for the errors and inexactitude in his efforts to communicate to persons unfamiliar with the profounder parts of mathematics.[107] Being no particular expert himself, he gave the impression that he was writing for persons not much below his own level of understanding. Wordy, full of asides and sarcasms, Rutherforth's text reads like the spoken popular lectures they were. It was not one of the best elementary texts on Newtonian natural philosophy, but it was competent at the level of its intended audience.[108] Its list of subscribers is long, numbering about a thousand, of whom about a third are identified with Cambridge. (That Lord Charles Cavendish did not subscribe to this book does not surprise us.) The text and its local support are testimony of the prestige of Newtonianism at Cambridge, and

according to William Heberden, it furthered the cause by stimulating lectures on science within other colleges at Cambridge.[109]

For completeness, we should point out that when Cavendish was at Cambridge, the Jacksonian professorship of natural philosophy had not yet been established. The Woodwardian professor of geology, Charles Mason (not the Charles Mason of the Mason-Dixon line, whom we will meet later), was a Fellow of the Royal Society and took an interest in a miscellany of scientific questions, but he would not have contributed in any way to Cavendish's education.[110] The professorship of chemistry was held by John Mickleborough, who like his predecessor Vigani was an ardent advocate of Newtonian chemistry. Twenty-five years before Cavendish became a student, Mickleborough could excuse his delay in answering letters on the grounds that he was "now engaged in a course of Chemistry here, I can think of no things but calcinations, sublimations, distillations, precipitations, etc." but after 1741 he evidently did no more lecturing on chemistry, and neither did anyone else (to our knowledge) until after Cavendish had left Cambridge.[111]

Before we leave the subject of the contribution of Cambridge to Henry Cavendish's educa-

---

[103]Long, *Astronomy* 2:717–18.

[104]Thomas Rutherforth to Thomas Birch, 30 Jan. and 6 Feb. 1742/43, BL Add Mss 4317, ff. 305–6, 308.

[105]Thomas Rutherforth, *A System of Natural Philosophy, Being a Course of Lectures in Mechanics, Optics, Hydrostatics, and Astronomy; Which Are Read in St. Johns College Cambridge*, 2 vols. (Cambridge, 1748). "Rutherforth, Thomas," *DNB* 17:499–500.

[106]Ibid., 23.

[107]Ibid., 199.

[108]Robert E Schofield, *Mechanism and Materialism: British Natural Philosophy in an Age of Reason* (Princeton: Princeton University Press, 1970), 97.

[109]Heberden had been a colleague of Rutherforth at St. John's. He later recalled that in his student days at Cambridge, around 1730, Professor Saunderson had lectured on Newton, geometry, and algebra while the college lecturers largely ignored these subjects. "The works however of Dr Smith and Dr Rutherford naturally introduced a greater attention to the subjects of which they treated in the two great colleges," Trinity and St John's; the teaching spread from these to other colleges. Christopher Wordsworth, *Scholae Academicae: Some Account of the Studies at the English Universities in the Eighteenth Century* (Cambridge, 1877), 66–67.

[110]Indicative of Mason's range of interests and of his few papers in the *Philosophical Transactions* are the "hints" about melting iron and about a burning well in a letter he sent to the president of the Royal Society at about the time Cavendish entered Cambridge: Charles Mason to Martin Folkes, 22 Jan. 1746/47, Wellcome Institute, Martin Folkes Papers, Ms.5403.

[111]John Mickleburgh to Dean Moss in 1725, in Nichols, *Literary Illustrations* 4:520. Wordsworth, *Scholae Academicae*, 188–89. L. J. M. Coleby, "John Mickelburgh, Professor of Chemistry in the University of Cambridge, 1718–56," *Annals of Science* 8 (1952): 165–74.

tion in science, we return briefly to John Colson. He probably did not lecture, but he went to a great deal of trouble to see that good scientific and mathematical texts were available to students. After becoming Lucasian professor, he translated into English several books from several languages, which included Peter van Musschenbroek's *Elements of Natural Philosophy*, the subtitle of which is *Chiefly Intended for the Use of Students in Universities*.[112] The reason Colson gave for making this translation was that there was a need for a "system" of natural philosophy in English (Musschenbroek used that word himself), and he thought that Musschenbroek's was the best. Musschenbroek drew on Continental sources such as Descartes and Leibniz (concerning whom Colson had a bone to pick with Musschenbroek), but the principal source he made clear: he embraced the "very many and great discoveries of the illustrious *Newton* (the glory of *England*, to whom no age has produced an equal)."[113]

Colson recognized a kindred spirit in Musschenbroek, who at the time of Colson's translation was professor of mathematics and astronomy at the University of Leyden, and whose main publications were extensions of his lectures in ever larger books. His predecessor at Leyden had been Willem Jacob 'sGravesande, another systematizer and writer of textbooks whose famous *Mathematical Elements of Natural Philosophy, Confirmed by Experiments: or, an Introduction to Sir Isaac Newton's Philosophy* had been translated from the Latin into English by J. T. Desaguliers, in 1720-21. Musschenbroek and 'sGravesande had both studied at the University of Leyden when its most successful teacher Hermann Boerhaave was lecturing there. These three professors made Leyden the capital of Newtonianism on the Continent, and they did so not through their research, which was minimal, but through their teaching, which was ample. Experiment had replaced stable certainty with ceaseless change, they said, and they encouraged their students to discover using the experimental way to truth. In his textbook, Musschenbroek said that the person who solved the problem of electricity would have his name struck on public monuments.[114] When Cavendish was a student, Leyden was probably a better place to learn natural philosophy than Cambridge, but it was not necessary to be in Leyden to learn from it. Texts by Musschenbroek,

'sGravesande, and Boerhaave were recommended reading at Cambridge, and texts by British writers were strongly influenced by them.[115] In both universities the emphasis was on Newtonian philosophy, and in both the professors were primarily teachers and not researchers. Colson, Smith, and Long may not have been as influential in their teaching as Musschenbroek, but they regarded their work in much the same way. For an avaricious and perceptive reader like Cavendish, the experimental approach of the Leyden authors supplemented the mathematical emphasis at Cambridge, and there would have seemed no contradiction; 'sGravesande, for example, taught by the experimental method, but he believed that mathematics was the true foundation of natural philosophy.

In broad outline we have sketched the scientific tradition at Cambridge insofar as it was represented by the texts of its early and mid eighteenth-century professors. When Cavendish entered the ranks of scientific researchers, he was a master of mathematical methods and concepts of science within a certain Newtonian framework, and the connections between this framework and Cambridge education are many, significant, and unlikely to be mere coincidence.

Giardini Academy

If there was a musical influence on Henry Cavendish, it came from his mother's side of the family. The duke and first duchess of Kent had a love of music, and the duke, we may recall, combined this interest with his political career when as lord chamberlain he worked to bring Italian opera to London. Later, in 1719, the duke was one of the original subscribers to the Royal Academy of Music, and he (but not the duke of

---

[112]From the Latin Colson translated Petrus van Musschenbroek's *Elements of Natural Philosophy* in 1744; from the French he translated Jean Antoine Nollet's *Lectures in Experimental Philosophy* in 1748; from the Italian he translated Maria Gaetana Agnesi's *Analytical Institutions* in 1801; and he edited the 3d edition of Brook Taylor's *Linear Perspective, or a New Method of Representing Justly All Manner of Objects as They Appear to the Eye* in 1749. We have already discussed his translation from the Latin of Newton's *Method of Fluxions*.

[113]Preface and translator's advertisement in Musschenbroek, *Elements of Natural Philosophy*, v, xi.

[114]Edward G. Ruestow, *Physics at Seventeenth and Eighteenth-Century Leiden: Philosophy and the New Science in the University* (The Hague: Martinus Nijhoff, 1973), 7–8, 115–21, 135–39.

[115]D. J. Struik, "Musschenbroek, Petrus van," *DSB* 9:594–97. A. Rupert Hall, "'sGravesande, Willem Jacob," *DSB* 5:509–11.

Devonshire) became one of its twenty directors.[116] There is a painting of the Kent family showing them being musically entertained,[117] and we know that the Yorkes and the Greys often attended concerts at the Rotunda.[118] Had Henry Cavendish shown any musical interest, he would surely have been encouraged. Many of his future scientific colleagues were accomplished musicians, as we have suggested in our discussion of science at Cambridge. In describing a "water-worm" that propagated after being cut to pieces, the French scientist René Antoine Réaumur said the worm was "of the Thickness of the Treble String of a Violin," a remark which suggests an intimate knowledge of music and its instruments in the eighteenth century, since lost.[119]

Evidence of Henry Cavendish's interest in music is sketchy. There is a mathematical study by him, "On Musical Intervals."[120] There is a reference to a musical event in, of all places, Cavendish's laboratory notes on pneumatic chemistry: in 1782 he used his eudiometer—the instrument for measuring the "goodness" of air—to compare the good air of Hampstead, one of the benefits of Hampstead, to which Cavendish had just moved, to the used "Air from Oratorio."[121] The auction catalogue of the contents of Cavendish's house at Clapham Common at the time of his death, listed a grand piano.[122] According to a story that on face value seems unlikely but which probably contains a core of truth, Cavendish came together with Michell, Herschel, Priestley, and others over musical entertainment.[123]

Given the limited evidence, in this discussion (as in the discussion of De Moivre), we proceed tentatively. The name Henry Cavendish appears on a list of subscribers to the musical academy of Felice de Giardini, and we think that this Henry Cavendish is our subject. Giardini, a musical entrepreneur, moved from Italy to England in 1750, and for ten years beginning in 1755 he adapted Italian operas for the King's Theatre. Later he composed quartets and concertos for strings and even a successful English oratorio, *Ruth*. Like Lord Charles Cavendish, Giardini was a governor of the Foundling Hospital, where Handel gave concerts; and in 1774 Giardini proposed establishing a musical academy in the Hospital. By the time Cavendish was (if we are right) in contact with him, Giardini was the preeminent violinist in

London.[124] Johnson sympathized with Giardini when he learned that the man did not make more than seven hundred pounds a year despite his superior ability.[125] To do even this well, Giardini had to combine activities, and one way he did was by running an academy by subscription on the side. In 1758 or 1759, Henry Cavendish along with sixteen others agreed to continue to meet as an "academy" in the coming year as they had in the last, only under new terms, obviously having to do with Giardini's finances. The members of the academy agreed to pay eight pounds, half up front and the rest when the academy had met twenty times. The academy seems to have met weekly. It would be up to the subscribers if they were to meet in the morning or the evening; if in the morning, as they had been meeting, breakfast would be provided, if in the evening, lighting.[126] Thirteen of the seventeen, including Cavendish, had already paid their advance, and if all paid up, Giardini would have earned around one hundred

[116]Otto Erich Deutsch, *Handel: A Documentary Biography* (New York: DaCapo Press, 1974), 91, 102.

[117]Illustration 1, in Joyce Godber, *The Marchioness Grey of Wrest Park*, vol. 47 of the Publications of the Bedfordshire Historical Record Society, published by the Society, 1968.

[118]Gunther, *Birch*, 62. Great Britain, Historical Manuscripts Commission, *Report on the Manuscripts of the Earl of Egmont. Diary of Viscount Percival Afterwards First Earl of Egmont*, vol. 1: *1730–1733* (London: His Majesty's Stationary Office, 1920), 93, 227; vol. 2: *1734–1738* (London: His Majesty's Stationary Office, 1923), 30.

[119]René Antoine Réaumur, "An Abstract of What Is Contained in the Preface to the Sixth Volume of Mons Réaumur's History of Insects . . .," *PT* 42 (1742/43): xii–xvii, on xv.

[120]Cavendish Mss VI(a), 28.

[121]This entry is unclear as to Cavendish's part. It begins with a comparison of "air caught by /the instrument-maker Edward/ Nairne in 2d gallery of Drury Lane playhouse Mar. 15 1782 with air of Hampstead of Mar. 16." It follows with "Air from Oratorio about same time." The oratorio may have been attended at Drury Lane by Nairne, or it may be a separate source of air collected by Cavendish at about the same time. "Experiments on Airs," Cavendish Mss II, 5:189.

[122]*A Catalogue of an Assortment of Modern Household Furniture. . . the Genuine Property of a Professional Gentleman Which Will Be Sold by Auction by Mr. Squibb, at His Great Room, Saville Passage, Saville Row, on Wednesday, December 5, 1810, and Two Following Days, at Twelve O'Clock.* Item 45 is a grand piano-forte, by Longman and Broderip, in a mahogany case.

[123]"Michell, John," *DNB* 13:333–34, on 333.

[124]R. H. Nichols and F. A. Wray, *The History of the Foundling Hospital* (London: Oxford University Press, 1935), 247. Roger Fiske, *English Theatre Music in the Eighteenth Century* (London: Oxford University Press, 1973), 284, 286.

[125]Johnson's exchange with Goldsmith on this point is quoted in Fiske, *English Theatre Music*, 285.

[126]Great Britain, Historical Manuscripts Commission, *Report on Manuscripts in Various Collections*, vol. 8: *The Manuscripts of the Hon. Frederick Lindley Wood; M. L. S. Clements, Esq.; S. Philip Unwin, Esq.* (London: His Majesty's Stationery Office, 1913), 188–89.

and thirty-five pounds, less out-of-pocket expenses, a good installment on his seven hundred or so pounds for the year.

The subscribers were young persons of both sexes, two of them relatives of Cavendish, George Manners and Lady Granby (Frances Manners). One subscriber was Cavendish's almost exact contemporary William Hamilton,[127] who is popularly known as the husband of Lord Nelson's mistress Emma but who is also known as a solid diplomat and a good student of volcanoes. In 1794 Sir Joseph Banks wrote to Sir William Hamilton in Naples to compliment him on his description of the recent eruption of Vesuvius. Everyone at the Royal Society thought it was excellent: "Cavendish in particular who you know is little given to talking & not at all to flattery says it is very valuable addition to the theory of volcanoes & that tho he

does not on any account wish to derogate from the merit of your former papers this is certainly the most valuable one we have receivd from you."[128] Just what transpired twenty-five years earlier when Hamilton and Cavendish were in Giardini's academy is unclear, but it undoubtedly had to do with listening together.[129]

———————

[127]Hamilton has helped us date the agreement between Giardini and the subscribers to his academy. By our reckoning, it was made after Hamilton's marriage in 1758 and before December 1759.

[128]Sir Joseph Banks to Sir William Hamilton, 30 Nov. 1794, BL,.Egerton Ms. 2641, pp. 155–56.

[129]In Italy a private concert by dilettantes was called an "accademia," which may have been Giardini's meaning. This information is given in a work from the time, Charles Burney, *Present State of Music in France and Italy* (London, 1771), quoted in *Horace Walpole's Correspondence*, vol. 18: *With Sir Horace Mann*, vol. 2, eds. W. S. Lewis, W. H. Smith, and G. L. Lam (New Haven: Yale University Press, 1954), 13, n. 16a.

CHAPTER 2

❧

Science

Introduction to Scientific Society

Early in 1753 Henry came down from Cambridge, and that summer he and his brother, Frederick, went with their father to dinner at Heberden's. The usual people were there, Birch, Watson, Wray, Mann, and the many-sided physician and poet Mark Akenside, whom Lord Charles had recommended for fellowship in the Royal Society for his knowledge of natural philosophy.[1] Frederick, whose accident occurred the following year, did not come to any more of these collegial dinners. Henry Cavendish came to twenty-six dinners with his father in the ten years after completing his studies at Cambridge.[2] By far the most common location was Heberden's house, though dinners often took place at Yorke's and occasionally at Watson's, Stanhope's, Wray's, and at Cavendish's own home.[3] Lord Charles went to lengths to ensure that Henry was known to his scientific friends.

In 1760 Henry Cavendish entered the Royal Society, where he spent the rest of his life as an unsalaried, almost full-time servant. Evidently he never considered a career in politics, even though in aristocratic families, sons and even sons of sons were practically duty-bound to enter the House of Commons.[4] The aristocracy was then in full flower in parliament: in 1760, the year George III was crowned, the Commons had five Manners, five Townshends, and four Cavendishes (including Richard Chandler after marriage and a name change). In not following this pattern, Henry Cavendish had before him the example of his father, whose public life was then devoted to learned affairs. Twenty years earlier Lord Charles Cavendish had left politics for a more fulfilling life in science. Henry Cavendish would enter science directly, and there he would experience an even fuller life there than the one his father had known. There is every reason to think his father backed him all the way; indeed, he had paved the way.

It was common for Fellows of the Royal Society to introduce their sons to the Society by bringing them as guests.[5] Lord Charles brought Henry to his first meeting of the Royal Society, in June 1758, by which time he had already introduced Henry to the leaders of the Royal Society at his many dinners. Henry came to eighteen meetings of the Royal Society as a visitor, the last in March 1760, and at fifteen of these meetings he came as a guest of his father. He came also as a guest of Birch, the friend of the family, and of Peter Newcome, teacher at Henry's school at Hackney.[6] The year before Lord Charles Cavendish introduced Henry to the Royal Society, he had received the Copley Medal, and as vice-president, he presided over almost half of the meetings to which he brought his son. Henry Cavendish could feel reassured in this new public world of the learned.

At a meeting Lord Charles Cavendish absented himself from, on 31 January 1760, Henry Cavendish was proposed for membership in the Royal Society. The original three proposers were Willoughby, Macclesfield, and Bradley, and Heberden wrote the certificate. Seven more Fellows of the Royal Society signed the certificate during the

---

[1] 25 Aug. 1753, Thomas Birch, Diary, BL Add Mss 4478C, f. 235.

[2] Again with the proviso that Birch also attended the dinners Birch Diary, passim.

[3] Henry Cavendish came with his father to dinner at Heberden's twelve times.

[4] L. B. Namier, *The Structure of Politics at the Accession of George III,* 2 vols. (London: Macmillan, 1929) 1:5.

[5] Examples from around this time: John Canton, jun., was a guest of John Canton, and Johnathan Watson, jun., was a guest of Johnathan Watson. Entries for 26 Mar. and 9 July 1767, Royal Society, JB 26.

[6] Royal Society, JB 23, 1757–60, passim. The third person to invite Henry Cavendish to the Royal Society as a guest was Michael Lort, an antiquarian, who in 1759 was appointed professor of Greek at Cambridge. Since he was not yet himself a Fellow of the Royal Society, he must have had the right to invite guests as a university professor. Lort was a good friend of the Cavendish in-law Philip Yorke, and he is also said to have been librarian to the duke of Devonshire.

three months it was posted: in addition to Heberden, they were Wray, Birch, Wilbraham, Hadley, Squire, and Watson, all, we note, members of Lord Charles Cavendish's dining circle, with whom Henry too had dined. With that endorsement, he was balloted and unanimously elected on 1 May 1760. The certificate read simply that Henry Cavendish was worthy, "having a great regard for Natural Knowledge, & being studious of its improvement."[7] The generality of the endorsement in this case was no doubt not an excuse, as it sometimes was; we suspect that from the beginning, Henry Cavendish's trademark was his knowledge in all parts of natural philosophy.

Just as at the Royal Society, at the Royal Society Club prospective members were customarily brought as guests before they were elected members. This was the case with Henry Cavendish, though he was proposed for, as opposed to elected to, membership before he had actually attended a dinner. There was no need for him to make himself known to the members, since he knew them already from his father's dinners. Those frequently attending were Watson, Birch, Heberden, Knight, Willoughby, Davall, Squire, Peter Newcome, Akenside, and the president of the Royal Society, who also presided over the dinners, Macclesfield.[8] Macclesfield recommended Henry Cavendish for membership on 10 November 1757, at a dinner at which Lord Charles Cavendish attended, which implied that his election was also a virtual certainty.[9] Cavendish was balloted according to his place in line, a two-year wait as it turned out, though that was a readily circumvented formality. Cavendish was repeatedly invited to dinners as a guest of his father and treated as if he were a member from the time of his proposal. As it so happened, the timing was perfect: he was elected to membership in the Royal Society Dining Club on 31 July 1760, two months after his election to the Royal Society. Henry Cavendish was then twenty-nine and certainly not a ward of his father; he continued to accompany his father to the club, but often he came on his own.

In 1760 Henry Cavendish also was elected to the Society of Arts, where his father was an active member. Henry was not active, but he kept up his subscription and received the journal, showing that much interest in the Society.[10] We will return to his relative indifference to this society later in this biography in connection with his highly active membership in the Royal Institution.

It has been alleged that Henry Cavendish's family was greatly disappointed that he did not pursue an ordinary public career and that as a result he was treated by his father in a niggardly fashion.[11] This speculation is plausible, but it also goes against certain known facts. Chief among them is that Lord Charles brought his son into his scientific circle, and at an early age, as we have seen. Given the harmony of interests of father and son, there is good reason to think that Henry wished to live with his father in the double house with separate living quarters on Great Marlborough Street. Lord Charles Cavendish, it would appear, raised his son in the manner that was then becoming established in England; that is, with respect for individual autonomy and with a show of sympathetic interest.[12] Henry was not coerced into attempting a public life for which he was not suited but was allowed to do what he wanted. As to the charge of niggardliness, we have little evidence to go on. Since Henry did not marry, there was no subsequent settlement, and we have nothing in writing between him and his father. Thomas Thomson said that he had an annuity of 500 pounds,[13] which sounds right; it was the annuity Lord Charles received from his father at the time of his marriage. Since Henry lived at home and did not gamble and carouse, he could have managed comfortably with that income.

Science at the Royal Society

We turn to the public world of science for Henry Cavendish's education in the practice of

---

[7]Royal Society, Certificates, vol 2, no. 10, f. 198.

[8]Royal Society Club, Minute Book, no. 4, 1760–64, Royal Society, passim.

[9]Archibald Geikie, *Annals of the Royal Society Club* (London: Macmillan, 1917), 63.

[10]On 9 January Henry Cavendish was proposed for membership by Mr. Cosheap; he was elected at the next meeting, on 16 Jan. 1760. Royal Society of Arts, Minutes, vol. 4. Henry Cavendish held no office in the Society, did not publish in its journal, and, it seems, did not belong to any of its committees. In 1786 he was summoned to attend-he did not attend-the Committee of Polite Arts to take part in an educational experiment. D. G. C. Allan, personal communication, and *Jnl. R.S.A.*, 1966, p. 1033, n. 11.

[11]George Wilson, *The Life of the Honourable Henry Cavendish* (London, 1851), 161.

[12]Stone, *Family*, 22, 151 Rudolph Trumbach, *The Rise of the Egalitarian Family: Aristocratic Kinship and Domestic Relations in Eighteenth-Century England* (New York: Academic Press, 1978), 292.

[13]Thomas Thomson, *The History of Chemistry*, vol. 1 (London, 1830), 336.

science, using as our source the papers appearing in the Royal Society's *Philosophical Transactions*, which came regularly into Lord Charles's house during the years Henry was a student at Cambridge. (When we say that Henry was a student at Cambridge, we suppose that he was away from home only during term, about six months out of each year; for the rest of the year, he probably was living with his father on Great Marlborough Street.) Beginning in the year Henry came home from Cambridge for good, Lord Charles was on the committee that passed judgment on every paper considered for publication in that journal.

Every issue of the *Philosophical Transactions* in the middle of the eighteenth century was an expression of confidence in the experimental philosophy. An account of an aurora borealis in that journal in 1750 makes the point: "The best description I can give of it /an aurora seen in Norwich/ is, to liken it to that light produced in a dark room, when one of the seven original colours is separated from the rest, after they have passed thro' a prism, and been collected together again by a convex lens."[14] By this time the direct experience of nature could be likened to an experiment on nature, not the other way around. The experiment was more familiar than nature.

The original strictures of the Royal Society against inflated language in reporting scientific findings were still professed. In an exchange of letters in the *Philosophical Transactions*, the foreign electrical experimenter George Matthias Bose conceded that by his "style and expressions" he had "embellished a little" the account of an experiment. Watson, his correspondent, took Bose to task: "The language of philosophers should not be tainted with the licence of the poets; their aim in the communicating their discoveries to the world, should be simple truth without desiring to exaggerate." The thing itself, nature, was cause enough for "admiration."[15] Spare writing can have an elegance and force of its own; Henry Cavendish had a gift for this kind of writing, which was not a small reason why he could make a life satisfactorily within science. Not all contributors to the journal wrote as plainly as he; descriptions of auroras, for example, that filled the pages of the *Philosophical Transactions* typically combined objective descriptions with expressions of awe. We make the obvious observation here that this journal does not read like a scientific journal of today.

Most of the papers in the *Philosophical Transactions* were in English, though papers in Latin from abroad were not uncommon and were almost never translated, a reflection of British education and the continuing use of Latin as a universal language of scholars. All of the papers in French, Spanish, and other modern European languages were translated, again reflecting British education and also British insularity.[16] Cavendish read Latin and wrote it passably, and he also read French, but that was about the extent of his competence in languages. There were Fellows of the Royal Society in London who could translate, and Cavendish like most other readers of the journal were in their debt.

Authors appearing in the *Philosophical Transactions* were identified by profession and title, if they had them, and sometimes by place. When they were referred to, it was often as experts, sometimes highly specialized ones, such as "electrician," sometimes less specialized ones, such as "chemist," and often very broad ones, such as persons who pursued "natural history" and "natural philosophy." Those interested in minerals were likely to be called not "mineralogists" but "naturalists" or "natural historians." These same terms applied to persons interested in, say, stones from a rhinoceros's stomach. "Philosopher" was an all-purpose term for the learned.[17] "Natural philosopher" was commoner. Cavendish is often called a "chemist," but that is because he is discussed primarily in connection with the chemical revolution. In his day he was usually called a "natural philosopher."

When Lord Charles Cavendish entered the Royal Society in 1727, the year Newton died, references to Newton in the *Philosophical Transactions* were usually to praise. Twenty years later, when Charles's son Henry was at college, references to Newton were respectful but tempered

[14]Henry Baker, "A Letter . . . Containing Abstracts of Several Observations of Aurorae Boreales Lately Seen," *PT* 46 (1750): 499–505, on 501.
[15]William Watson, "A Letter . . . Declaring That He as Well as Many Others Have Not Been Able to Make Odours Pass Thro' Glass by Means of Electricity . . .," *PT* 46 (1749/50): 348–56, on 355–56.
[16]There is one exception. A paper sent to the instrument-maker James Short was translated from the Latin: Joseph Steplin, "An Account of an Extraordinary Alteration in the Baths of Toplitz in Bohemia . . .," *PT* 49 (1755): 395–96.
[17]*PT* 46 (1750): 118, 126, 250–5, 362, 369, 589, and passim.

and occasionally critical. The author of a paper on tides said that Newton had discovered the cause of tides, but because tides were so complex they still had to be observed.[18] Great as he was, Newton had not done everything. Thomas Simpson, mathematics teacher at the Royal Military Academy at Woolwich and the principal contributor of mathematics to the *Philosophical Transactions*, solved a problem in inverse fluxions (integration); conscious that his solution differed from Newton's, Simpson said that it was "impossible to disagree without being under some apprehensions of a mistake."[19] In this case: Newton was great, but he made mistakes. If foreigners pointed out Newton's mistakes, it was a different matter; like the Italian who claimed he had discovered six errors in Newton's *Principia*, they would be attacked by the home guard.[20] Alexis Claude Clairaut, who had argued that Newton's inverse-square law of gravitation was inexact, made a public retraction, but that did not spare him. Having detected an absurdity in Clairaut's reasoning, Patrick Murdock wrote a paper to dispel the erroneous view that Newton's propositions on the moon's motions were "mere mathematical fictions, not applicable to nature"; on the contrary, Murdock said, Newton's work was "fully confirmed and verified."[21] Clairaut wrote a kind of apology for the *Philosophical Transactions*, in which he said that he had not intended to disparage Newton. Newton had not thought it impossible to be "opposed by experience," but in their zeal some people did not distinguish "between the different ways of opposing that great man's sentiments," but still, if the Royal Society wished, Clairaut would reword his disagreement with Newton.[22] (The disagreement hinged on assumptions about the density of the earth, and Clairaut's book on the figure of the earth stimulated Henry Cavendish's lifelong interest in the density of the earth.) Criticism of Newton was a touchy matter. Euler too had once believed that Newton's theory conflicted with observations of the motion of the moon but he did no longer; Clairaut's retracted claim, he said, had not been damaging but on the contrary had given "quite a new lustre to the theory of the great Newton."[23]

Euler did, however, have a quarrel with Newton, which had to do with the indistinctness of the image in refracting telescopes, which was thought to arise from two sources, the different refrangibility of different colors, and the shape of the eyeglass. The latter was a matter of craft, the former was thought to have no remedy; Newton was cited as the authority for this despairing conclusion on chromatic aberration, and though in principle Newton had more than one opinion on the subject, in practice he had given up on refracting telescopes in favor of reflecting ones.[24] Euler, who thought that Newton believed it was impossible to perfect refracting telescopes, said that Newton was wrong on this point, and to correct him he wrote letters to the *Philosophical Transactions* with his own prescription for making refracting telescopes free of chromatic aberration. The English optical instrument-maker John Dolland gave the rejoinder this time, deferring to Newton, "that great man," who had proved the elimination of aberration impossible.[25] Dolland went on to change his mind; the polemic with Euler led him to make experiments, the results of which differed "very remarkably" from those in Newton's *Opticks*.[26] By combining different kinds of glass, Dolland constructed achromatic lenses, which greatly improved refracting telescopes, and for this bold heterodoxy he was awarded the Copley Medal in 1758. (The problem of indistinctness of images in refracting telescopes was not completely solved, and Cavendish would investigate it thoroughly.) Thomas Melvil was more speculative in his rejection of an explanation given by Newton.

----

[18]Murdoch Mackenzie, "The State of the Tides in Orkney," *PT* 46 (1749): 149–60, on 149.

[19]Thomas Simpson, "Of the Fluents of Multinomials, and Series Affected by Radical Signs, Which Do Not Begin to Converge Till After the Second Term," *PT* 45 (1748): 328–35, on 333.

[20]James Short, "An Account of a Book, Intitled, P. D. Pauli Frisii Mediolanensis, etc. Disquisitio mathematica . . . printed at Milan in 1752 . . .," *PT* 48 (1753): 5–17, on 14–15.

[21]Patrick Murdock, "A Letter . . . Concerning the Mean Motion of the Moon's Apogee . . .," *PT* 47 (1751): 62–74, on 62–63, 74.

[22]Alexis Claude Clairaut, "A Translation and Explanation of Some Articles of the Book Intitled, *Théorié de la Figure de la Terre*," *PT* 48 (1753): 73–85, on 82–83.

[23]"Extract of a Letter from Professor Euler of Berlin, to the Rev Mr. Caspar Wetstein . . .," *PT* 47 (1751): 263–64.

[24]D. T. Whiteside, ed., *The Mathematical Papers of Isaac Newton* (Cambridge: Cambridge University Press, 1969) 3: 442–43.

[25]Leonhard Euler, "Letters Concerning a Theorem of His, for Correcting the Aberrations in the Object-Glasses of Refracting Telescopes," *PT* 48 (1753): 287–96. John Dolland, "A Letter . . . Concerning a Mistake in M. Euler's Theorem for Correcting the Aberrations in the Object-Glasses of Refracting Telescopes," *PT* 48 (1753): 289–91, on 289.

[26]John Dolland, "An Account of Some Experiments Concerning the Different Refrangibility of Light," *PT* 50 (1758): 733–43, on 736.

Newton had attributed the different refrangibilities of colors to the different sizes or densities of the particles of light of different colors; Melvil said that Newton had been misled by an "analogy" between the refraction of light and the gravity of bodies, for the true cause of different refrangibilities was the different velocity of the ether pulses (not particles) of different colors. This serious challenge to Newton had observational consequences, and James Short was ordered to make the observations and report on them to the Royal Society; Melvil's hypothesis did not stand up.[27] Henry Eeles's explanation of the ascent of vapors was accompanied by an even broader criticism of Newton. Eeles defended his "hypothesis" of the fluid of fire against the disapproval of "our great modern philosopher" of the use of hypotheses in general. Eels made the apt observation that Newton himself used hypotheses in his queries in the *Opticks*. Even gravitation, he thought, would not have come to Newton without an hypothesis. Since "supposition must always precede the proof," if an hypothesis is rationally founded, it should be tested; that is how science advances.[28] (Cavendish implicitly agreed with Eeles). Newton at mid century was still the immortal Newton, but attitudes were conflicting on his authority on this or that point. Newton's name was invoked to stand for correct practice in science, but of course much of the research reported in the *Philosophical Transactions* in the middle of the eighteenth century proceeded without any specific connection with Newton's writings.

Scientific results had to be supported by empirical evidence, of course, but on the question of whether greater trust was to be placed in theory or in observation, the answer was not always observation. The following discussion of the limits of observational accuracy in relation to instruments and theory is by the astronomical instrument-maker and astronomer James Short, who at the time was on the council of the Royal Society. Short's purpose was to clarify the disagreements over the observed shape of the earth and Newton's gravitational theory of its flattening at the poles. Critics of Newton's theory such as Clairaut had made a mistake in regarding their observations as absolutely exact (Clairaut denied that he placed too much certainty in observations), while other observers, such as Boscovich, had made a mistake in thinking that the observations were too inexact

to draw any conclusions. When theory and observation were compared, Short said, the theory could not be faulted until the disparity with observation was greater than the errors attributed to the instrument used and to its user, the observer. Newton had a just appreciation of such limits, Short said; Newton, for example, calculated the ratio of the two diameters of the earth to be 229 to 230, that is, to three figures, not to four or more figures, which would have been only a show of precision. It would be "absurd" for an observer to compute an angle to a second or a length to a part of an inch if the instrument could only measure to a degree or a foot. Mathematical results were rigorously true, but observations always had "certain limits." The error of the instrument was itself one of the "*data.*" Observers should follow the "judicious caution" of Newton and read Cotes's treatise on the subject of errors, Short advised.[29] There was a high degree of sophistication in the art of experiment and observation in the middle of the eighteenth century, which was thoroughly assimilated by Henry Cavendish, who routinely assessed the limits of observation and the consequent limits on theoretical calculations of physical phenomena. Cavendish's great reputation as an observer of precision depended on his mastery of the theory and practice of errors.

Errors implicit in instruments and in the sense organs of observers could be diminished by making repeated observations and taking their mean. The mathematician Thomas Simpson proved that it was better to take many observations than a few and that by taking a mean of them, the chances of small errors were reduced and the chances of great ones were almost eliminated. This method was used by astronomers, and Simpson urged all others who made experiments to adopt it.[30] Taking mean values was, again, standard practice for Cavendish.

---

[27]T. Melvil, "A Letter . . . Concerning the Cause of the Different Refrangibility of the Rays of Light," *PT* 48 (1753): 261–70.

[28]Henry Eeles, "Letters . . . Concerning the Cause of the Ascent of Vapour and Exhalation, and Those of Winds; and of the General Phaenomena of the Weather and Barometer," *PT* 49 (1755): 124–49, on 124–25.

[29]Short, "An Account of a Book," 5–7.

[30]Thomas Simpson, "A Letter . . . on the Advantage of Taking the Mean of a Number of Observations, in Practical Astronomy," *PT* 49 (1755): 82–93.

In addition to multiplying his observations, the observer was obligated to spell out their circumstances. To establish a scientific fact, it was not enough to report an experiment; unless others were able to repeat it, it did not become the public property of science.[31] A variant of this requirement of repeatability was the presence of multiple observers and witnesses at the scene of a given experiment. The *Philosophical Transactions* rarely contained a joint paper, other than those by committees,[32] but it was common for a paper to record observations by several persons. Peter Newcome of Hackney Academy reported that six persons in his house felt an earthquake upstairs but not downstairs. James Burrow said that the same experience was reported by another person in another house, though that report was not as valuable, since it "depends indeed upon the perception of a single person; whereas his /Newcome's/ is verified by the sensations of six different ones."[33] Papers often mentioned other persons, usually by name, who were there and who looked through the telescope or whatever. Testimonials were given, as if in a court of law: in a witness, intelligence counted, but so equally did profession, wealth, and rank.[34] In a paper on a bright rainbow, Peter Davall said that he heard about other bright rainbows from "intelligent persons."[35] James Burrow heard about an earthquake from "a very sensible Scotchman;"[36] he heard about another from a woman with "superior" judgment, accuracy, veracity, and a title.[37] The president of the Royal Society was assured that observers of an earthquake were not "mean, ignorant, or fanciful" but truthful, "rational and just."[38] When a great storm struck a village, the author of a report on it took two reliable men with him to the spot to observe, the local physician and clergyman.[39] The dimensions of an "extraordinary" young man, two feet seven inches tall and twelve or thirteen pounds, were confirmed by eight witnesses, all "of figure and fortune" in the neighborhood.[40] In the cases above, the importance of the reliability of witnesses arose, in part, from the uniqueness of the phenomenon, which unlike an experiment could not be reproduced, though the young man presumably could be measured again. But the character of witnesses came up in the accounts of experiments too: the French electrical experimenter Jean Antoine Nollet had used two servants who proved untrustworthy,

which, he said, "made me very delicate in the choice of the persons who I was desirous should be admitted to our experiments," and thereafter he was unwilling to use "either children, servants, or people of the lower class."[41] Henry Cavendish on occasion repeated his experiments before or with other experimenters, whom he selected from Fellows of the Royal Society, whose reliability normally was beyond question.

Observers often gathered to make concerted observations. For a repetition of J. H. Winkler's experiments on passing odors through electrified glass, one friend of Winkler and six Fellows of the Royal Society met at William Watson's house.[42] Joint examinations of instruments were common.[43] So were observations of astronomical events involving many observers working in coordination, including observers abroad.[44] No one was more active in

---

[31]William Watson, "A Letter . . . Declaring That He as Well as Many Others Have Not Been Able to Make Odours Pass Thro' Glass by Means of Electricity . . . ," *PT* 46 (1749): 348–56, on 348–49.

[32]The rare exception: John Bevis and James Short, "Astronomical Observations Made in Surry-Street, London," *PT* 48 (1753): 301–5.

[33]Peter Newcome, "A Letter . . . Concerning the Same Shock Being Felt at Hackney, near London," *PT* 46 (1750): 653–54. James Burrow, "A Letter . . . Concerning the Same Earthquake Being Felt at East Sheen, Near Richmond Park in Surrey," *PT* 46 (1750): 655–56.

[34]As in the seventeenth century, a gentleman's word was seldom questioned: Steven Shapin, "The House of Experiment in Seventeenth-Century England," *Isis* 79 (1988): 373–404, on 398–99.

[35]Peter Davall, "A Description of an Extraordinary Rainbow Observed July 15, 1748," *PT* 46 (1749): 193–95, on 195.

[36]James Burrow, "An Account of the Earthquake on Thursday Morning, March 8, 1749, as Seen in the Inner Temple Garden, by Robert Shaw (a Very Sensible Scotchman) Then at Work There," *PT* 46 (1749/50): 626–28, on 626.

[37]Lady Cornwallis told James Burrow how she experienced an earthquake: James Burrow, "Part of a Letter . . . Concerning an Earthquake Felt Near Bury St. Edmund's in Suffolk . . . ," *PT* 46 (1750): 702–5, on 703.

[38]William Barlow, "Concerning a Shock of an Earthquake Felt at Plymouth, about One O'Clock in the Morning, Between the 8th and 9th of Feb. 1749–50," *PT* 46 (1750): 692–95, on 693.

[39]William Henry, "An Account of an Extraordinary Stream of Wind, Which Shot Thro' Part of the Parishes of Termonomungen and Urney, in the County of Tyrone, on Wednesday October 11, 1752," *PT* 48(1753): 1–4, on 1.

[40]John Browning, "Extract of a Letter . . . Concerning a Dwarf," *PT* 47 (1751): 278–81, on 279.

[41]Abbé Nollet, "Extract of a Letter . . . Accompanying an Examination of Certain Phaenomena in Electricity . . .," *PT* 46 (1749): 368–97, on 377.

[42]William Watson, "An Account of Professor Winkler's Experiments Relating to Odours Passing through Electrified Globes and Tubes . . .," *PT* 47 (1751) : 231–41, on 237–38.

[43]John Smeaton, "An Account of Some Experiments upon a Machine for Measuring the Way of a Ship at Sea," *PT* 48 (1754): 532–46, on 535, 537, 539–40.

[44]The subject here is the parallax of Mars, determined by observations at two places on earth, in France and in England. "A Letter from Monsieur de L'Isle, of the Royal Academy of Sciences at Paris, to the Reverend James Bradley . . .," *PT* 48 (1754): 512–20.

cooperative scientific ventures in the middle of the eighteenth century than James Short. At his own house, Short with three others observed the occultation of Venus by the moon.[45] At Birch's house, he and two others observed the transit of Mercury, and at five other locations observations of this event were made by others.[46] To observe an eclipse of the sun, an excursion was made to Morton's castle north of Edinburgh by Short, Morton, and Pierre Charles Le Monnier who had come from Paris for the purpose. This excursion was only one part of a wider effort in Scotland to observe the eclipse, coordinated by cannon fired from Edinburgh Castle. Bad weather obscured this eclipse in Edinburgh, but observations were made at Morton's and at nine other locations in Scotland (with poor agreement owing, Short believed, to some observers' want of "sufficient practice").[47] Henry Cavendish often engaged in experimenting with others, sometimes in private but more often in committees of the Royal Society.

The occasional meteor or earthquake was experienced by the unaided sight or touch of the observer, who had no choice in the matter, but by the middle of the eighteenth century most scientific observations were made with the aid of instruments. The *Philosophical Transactions* at this time contained many papers describing new instruments, usually written by their makers, giving full details of their construction and use together with drawings. In his account of a new pyrometer, John Smeaton said that its construction and use were clearer from the drawing than "from many words."[48] What Smeaton said of his pyrometer was true in general: the elaborate, detailed, and scaled drawings, with charioscuro, were as integral to papers on instruments as drawings of specimens were to botanical papers. Apart from the occasional surgical instrument,[49] the instruments described in the journal were designed to aid in the production and observation of phenomena (e.g., air pumps)[50] or, as in most cases, to measure (e.g., micrometers, thermometers, and clocks). Users of instruments explained their principles and their use in experiments and, as a rule, sang their praises. In the case of Smeaton's pyrometer, for example, which was used to measure the expansion of metals, the point of contact of the piece of metal with the point of the micrometer screw was determined not by sight or touch but by hearing, the more discriminating sense. This pyrometer was capable of measuring an expansion to an accuracy of one four thousandth part of an inch, and repeated measurements with it differed by no more than one twenty-thousandth part of an inch. Its sensibility, Smeaton said, "exceeds any thing I have met with."[51]

The need for instruments was obvious—*almost*: from Norwich, a keeper of records of the weather complained that many people in his neighborhood judged the weather only by their "outward senses," without resorting to the thermometer, and accordingly they made mistakes such as putting the hottest day in June when it was in July.[52] In astronomy, the importance of exact instruments had long since been demonstrated, though the point was still thought worth making in the middle of the eighteenth century. James Bradley, for example, spelled out the case for instruments as the means of discovery: not long ago, he said, astronomy had seemed perfected and no further progress was expected, a conclusion based on the instruments at hand, the telescope and the pendulum clock, and on the theory of "our great Newton." But Bradley's own discoveries proved that this confidence was misplaced. He had first discovered the aberration of light, and now he had discovered another annual change in the place of the stars, perceptible only because, he said, "of the exactness of my instrument." Like his first, his second discovery was the result of his lifelong search—this guided by theory—for an annual

---

[45]The other observers at Short's were John Bevis, John Pringle, and the duke of Queensbury. John Canton observed it at his house too. John Bevis, "An Occultation of the Planet Venus by the Moon in the Day Time Observed in Surrey-Street," *PT* (1751): 159–63. Bradley also observed it, as written up by James Short, ". . . Bradley's Observation of the Occultation of Venus by the Moon," *PT* 47 (1751): 201–2.

[46]The other observers were Sisson, Bird, Smeaton, Canton, and Macclesfield.

[47]James Short, "An Eclipse of the Sun, July 14 1748 . . .," *PT* 45 (1748): 582–97.

[48]John Smeaton, "Description of a New Pyrometer, with a Table of Experiments Made Therewith," *PT* 48 (1754): 598–613, on 600, 605.

[49]The surgical instruments were knives, forceps, and puncturing instruments; e.g., translation of M. le Cat, "A New Trocart for the Puncture in the Hydrocephalus, and for Other Evacuations, Which Are Necessary To Be Made at Different Times," *PT* 47 (1751): 267–72.

[50]John Smeaton, "A Letter . . . Concerning Some Improvements Made by Himself in the Air-Pump," *PT* 47 (1752): 415–28.

[51]Smeaton, "Description of a New Pyrometer," 600.

[52]William Anderson, "Extract of a Letter . . . Concerning the Hot Weather in July Last," *PT* 46 (1750): 573–75, on 574.

parallax of stars arising from the earth's orbital motion. Bradley had made his discovery of the aberration of light at the time Lord Charles Cavendish entered the Royal Society; he made his discovery of the nutation of the earth's axis caused by the pull of the moon on the earth's equator while Henry Cavendish was at the university. The cause of nutation was understood theoretically, but the nutation Bradley discovered had not been foreseen. Here was an object lesson in science: theory did not predict everything but was indebted to observations and experiments, which pointed to the "great advantage of cultivating this, as well as every other branch of natural knowledge, by a regular series of observations and experiments." The "more exact the instruments are ... and the more regular the series of observations is ... the sooner we are enabled to discover the cause of any new phaenomenon." Bradley advised astronomers to begin by examining the correctness of their instruments, an injunction Henry Cavendish would carry out in every branch of physical science.[53]

It was not, of course, just in astronomy that quantitative work was done. It might appear anywhere: draughts given to, and the blood taken from, a patient;[54] bills of mortality;[55] the path of lightning;[56] the heat of a cave.[57] Henry Miles, a clergyman with a wide-ranging interest in quantities—he reported the "bigness" of a fungus, 210th part of an inch[58]—published an unusual paper for the *Philosophical Transactions*, a philosophical essay. The topic was quantity: prompted by a treatise by Thomas Reid, in which ratios were applied to virtue, Miles set out to determine what things were properly subject to mathematical proof, and thus beyond dispute. Miles, who believed that affections and appetites could not be reduced to quantity, identified quantity with "measures," which required a "standard," so that "all men, when they talked of it, should mean the same thing."[59] In the *Philosophical Transactions*, we see evidences of agreement on the importance of measures and standards. The physician and sophisticated experimentalist John Pringle, who would become president of the Royal Society, laid down "standards" in his quantitative ranking of salts by their power to resist putrefaction.[60] The introduction of standards in science was Henry Cavendish's goal as a quantitative experimentalist.

The balance and the thermometer acquired a new importance in science because of their use in

quantitative chemistry; by contrast, in the model quantitative science, astronomy, the thermometer played a very subordinate role and the balance none at all (until Cavendish, at the end of his life, weighed the world with a kind of balance). Pneumatic chemistry, as Cavendish would soon show, made use of specific gravities to distinguish different species of air; as if to point the way, the physician Richard Davies published a history of tables of specific gravities, with their "manifold applications ... in Natural Philosophy," including the recent work of his contemporaries George Graham, James Dodson, and John Ellicott with his "exquisite assay-scales," and to his own work with his sensitive hydrostatical balance built by Francis Hauksbee.[61] Cromwell Mortimer, secretary of the Royal Society and a physician who studied the effects of chemical remedies in diseases, set out the uses of the thermometer in chemistry. Chemistry, the "most extensive Branch of Experimental Philosophy," suffered from the unrepeatability of its experiments. The reason, Mortimer said, was the failure to record the heat: the chemist's laboratory should be equipped with "various Sorts of Thermometers, proportion'd to the Degree of Heat he intends to make use of," and the chemist should keep track of the time the heat is applied, observing "his Clock with as much Exactness as the Astronomer."[62] Cavendish's most important experimental work

[53]James Bradley, "A Letter . . . Concerning an Apparent Motion Observed in Some of the Fixed Stars," *PT* 45 (1748): 1–43, on 2–4.

[54]George Bayly, "A Letter . . . of the Use of the Bark in the Small-Pox," *PT* 47 (1751): 27–31.

[55]James Dodson, "A Letter . . . Concerning an Improvement of the Bills of Mortality," *PT* 47 (1752): 333–40.

[56]William Henry, "Account of an Extraordinary Stream of Wind in the Parishes of Thermonomungan and Urney, in the County of Tyrone," *PT* 48 (1753): 1–4.

[57]William Arderon, "An Account of Large Subteranneous Caverns in the Chalk Hills Near Norwich," *PT* 45 (1748): 244–47.

[58]Henry Miles, "A Letter . . . Concerning the Green Mould on Fire-Wood; With Some Observations of Mr. Baker's upon the Minuteness of the Seeds of Some Plants," *PT* 46 (1749/50): 334–38.

[59]Henry Miles, "An Essay on Quantity; Occasioned by Reading a Treatise, in Which Simple and Compound Ratios Are Applied to Virtue and Merit, by the Rev Mr. Reid," *PT* 45 (1748): 505–20, on 506.

[60]John Pringle, "A Continuation of the Experiments on Substances Resisting Putrefaction," *PT* 46 (1750): 525–34.

[61]Richard Davies, "Tables of Specific Gravities, Extracted from Various Authors, with Some Observations upon the Same," *PT* 45 (1748): 416–89.

[62]Cromwell Mortimer, "A Discourse Concerning the Usefulness of Thermometers in Chemical Experiments; and Concerning the Principles on Which the Thermometers Now in Use Have Been Constructed; Together with the Description and Uses of a Metalline Thermometer, Newly Invented," *PT* 44 (1746/47): 672–95, on 673. This paper was first read in 1735 and printed later with revisions.

was done in chemistry, in which he used the balance as an astronomer did his clock and micrometer, and in heat, in which his principal instrument was the thermometer.

Electricity was the liveliest experimental science at the time Cavendish was at the university. Stephen Hales observed on a visit to London, where he saw electrical experiments performed, that in this "new field of researches there are daily new discoveries made."[63] As we have seen, Cavendish's father was active in this field, a collaborator of Watson. It was Watson who introduced the Royal Society to the device that transformed the experimental field and guided Franklin to his understanding of electricity, the Leyden jar.[64] It was Watson too who gave the Society an account of Franklin's book on electricity, consisting of four letters to his English correspondent, Peter Collinson, all or parts of which had been read at the Royal Society. This book, Watson said, shows Franklin to have "a head to conceive, and a hand to carry into execution." Nobody, Watson said with characteristic candor and generosity, knows electricity better than Franklin.[65] There was a sense among investigators that they were no longer working on the periphery of the subject but on the "nature" of electricity and, as John Ellicott put it, on the "general principles" and the "laws of electricity."[66] Investigators were talking about "quantities" of electricity. Twenty years later Henry Cavendish would base his quantitative experimental and mathematical researches on the principles of electricity drawing on Watson's and Franklin's work.

The contents of the *Philosophical Transactions* reflected the great interest taken in electrical effects in the laboratory of nature. After Franklin had proposed experiments on lightning, Watson together with several Fellows of the Royal Society tried to draw electricity during a thunder storm; they failed, but others in London, such as John Canton and John Bevis, succeeded.[67] Daring experiments on lightning were reported from Philadelphia, Paris, and elsewhere around the world.

Lightning was a new phenomenon insofar as it was explained by an electrical hypothesis. Otherwise it belonged to the general category of violent events that were a staple of the *Philosophical Transactions* (as they were of life in the eighteenth century). Provided they were sufficiently devas-tating, incidents of thunder and lightning with their attendant "melancholy accidents" were reported in the journal independently of electrical science.[68] Lightning struck a ship in a "violent manner, disabling most of the crew in eye and limb."[69] The mainmast of another ship was shattered when a "large ball of blue fire" rolled over the water and exploded "as if hundreds of cannon had been fired at one time."[70] In a valley, in the "violence of the storm," a cloudburst and flash flood threw up "monstrous stones," which were "larger than a team of ten horses could move."[71] A meteor that looked like a "black smoky cloud" split an oak, and its "whirling, breaks, roar, and smoke, frightened both man and beast."[72] Clouds and auroras were seen to turn "blood-red."[73] Plagues of locusts "hid the sun," and undeterred by "balls & shot," they "miserably wasted" the land.[74] Victims of the "black vomit" experienced delirium "so violent" that they had to be tied down so that they did "not tear themselves in pieces."[75] Bitten

----

[63]Stephen Hales, "Extract of a Letter . . . Concerning Some Electrical Experiments," *PT* 45 (1748): 409–410, on 410.

[64]William Watson, "A Sequel to the Experiments and Observations Tending to Illustrate the Nature and Properties of Electricity," *PT* 44 (1747): 704–49, on 709 ff.

[65]William Watson, "An Account of Mr Benjamin Franklin's Treatise, Lately Published, Intituled, Experiments and Observations on Electricity, Made at Philadelphia in America," *PR* 47 (1751): 202–11, on 210.

[66]John Ellicott, "Several Essays Towards Discovering the Laws of Electricity . . . ," *PT* 45 (1748): 195–224.

[67]William Watson, "A Letter . . . Concerning the Electrical Experiments in England upon Thunder-Clouds," *PT* 47 (1752): 567–70. John Canton, "Electrical Experiments, with an Attempt to Account for Their Several Phaenomena; Together with Some Observations on Thunder-Clouds," *PT* 48 (1753): 350–58. There were many more papers at this time on lightning experiments.

[68]William Borlase, "An Account of a Storm of Thunder and Lightning in Cornwall," *PT* 48 (1753): 86–93.

[69]John Waddell, "A Letter . . . Concerning the Effects of Lightning in Destroying the Polarity of a Mariner's Compass," *PT* (1749): 111–12.

[70]Mr. Chalmers, "An Account of an Extraordinary Fireball Bursting at Sea," *PT* 46(1749): 366–67, on 366.

[71]"An Account of a Surprising Inundation in the Valley of St John's Near Keswick in Cumberland, on the 22d Day of August 1749, in a Letter from a Young Clergyman . . . ," *PT* 46 (1749/50): 362–66.

[72]Thomas Barker, "An Account of an Extraordinary Meteor Seen in the County of Rutland, which Resembled a Water-Spout," *PT* 46 (1749): 248–49.

[73]Henry Miles, "A Letter . . . Concerning an Aurora Borealis . . . ," *PT* 46 (l749/50): 346–48, on 348. William Stukeley, "The Philosophy of Earthquakes," *PT* 46 (1750): 731–50, on 743.

[74]"An Account of the Locusts, which Did Vast Damage in Walachia, Moldavia, and Transilvania, in the Years 1747 and 1748 . . . by a Gentleman Who Lives in Transilvania," *PT* 46 (1749): 30–37, on 30–31.

[75]"Extract of So Much of Don Antonio De Ulloa's F.R.S. Account of His Voyage to South America, as Relates to the

by a mad dog, a horse in its agony gave off breath "like smoke from a chimney-top."[76] Children were carried away by contagion— a five-year-old girl was observed as she coughed up a "large quantity of white rotten flesh."[77] Fright and misery would end only because the world was going to end, by astronomical calculation, when it spiraled toward the sun and would "necessarily be burnt."[78] In the laboratory the violence of nature was simulated, and if in the laboratory it was moderated, it was violence all the same, and dangerous; lacking apparatus with effective safety features, investigators sometimes had been "intimidated" and "deterred."[79] The Leyden jar manufactured a form of lightning and was itself the inspiration for the electrical understanding of lightning and, as well, of thunder.[80] The "violent explosion of glass drops" in the laboratory was likened to volcanoes.[81]

The *Philosophical Transactions* was, among other things, a sometimes lurid newspaper for the learned. Reading the journal was not a quieting experience. "Letters" from a participant or observer or victim at the scene would begin "I was much surprised," then go on to relate grisly details. Most of the medical papers described extreme pathologies and monstrous productions in more or less ordinary language, which did not spare the reader. The most frightening event of all was an earthquake.

The year 1750, one Fellow of the Royal Society observed at the time, "may rather be called the year of earthquakes, than of jubilee." These earthquakes occurred as if on command of the Royal Society: their center was thought to be London, "the place to which the finger of God was pointed."[82] Henry Cavendish was in his second year at the university when an entire issue of the *Philosophical Transactions* was given over to the subject. Presented as an appendix to the regular issues, it consisted of fifty-seven papers submitted to the Royal Society dealing with several, principally four, earthquakes in England and the Continent in 1750. The earthquakes that year were only a curtain raiser. The great earthquake of 1755 destroyed Lisbon and, what is important to us, prompted John Michell to explain earthquakes scientifically.

Half of the observers reporting on earthquakes in the *Philosophical Transactions* were Fellows of the Royal Society. Fellows also collected testimony and communicated letters from others

for publication in the journal. Fellows or otherwise, reporters of the earthquakes rarely observed the direction, time, and duration of the shock.[83] In this connection, it is noteworthy that none of the observations was made by an astronomer. As earthquakes go, those of 1750 were not severe— buildings did not come down, persons were not hurt—but witnesses nonetheless described them as "violent." People thought first of gunpowder, cannon, the explosion of a magazine or powder mill or a mine, or lightning.[84] At Martin Folkes's house, Folkes, Macclesfield, and two other visitors were "strongly lifted up, and presently set down again," while the coachmen standing outside Folkes's door feared that the house would come down on them.[85] Gowin Knight's house "shook violently," and the duke of Newcastle's servant came to Knight to tell him what had happened at his house, and a man from Greenwich told him that all the way from London Bridge the people were frightened.[86] Animals were frightened too: a cat was startled, a dog was terrified, cows and sheep were alarmed,

Distemper Called There Vomito Prieto, or Black Vomit," *PT* 46 (1749–50): 134–39, on 135.

[76]John Huxham, "A Letter . . . Containing an Account of an Horse Bit by a Mad Dog," *PT* 46 (1750): 474–78, on 478.

[77]John Starr, "An Account of the Morbus Strangulatorius," *PT* 46 (1750): 435–46, on 439.

[78]Leonard Euler, "Part of a Letter . . . Concerning the Gradual Approach of the Earth to the Sun," *PT* 46 (1749): 203–5, on 204.

[79]For this quotation, we go outside the time when Cavendish was at the university to the time when he began his electrical experiments at home: C. L. Epinasse, "Description of an Improved Apparatus for Performing Electrical Experiments, in Which the Electrical Power Is Increased, the Operator Intirely Secured from Receiving Any Accidental Shocks, and the Whole Rendered More Convenient for Experiments than Heretofore," *PT* 57 (1767): 186–91, on 188.

[80]Henry Eeles, "A Letter . . . Concerning the Cause of Thunder," *PT* 47 (1752): 524–29. Eeles took exception to the standard analogy between fired gunpowder and thunder; he had an up–to–date explanation based on the fire observed in electrical experiments.

[81]Claude Nicolas Le Cat, "A Memoir on the Lacrymae Batavicae, or Glass-Drops, the Tempering of Steel, and Effervescence, Accounted for by the Same Principle," *PT* 46 (1749): 175–88, on 187.

[82]William Stukeley, ". . . Concerning the Causes of Earthquakes," *PT* 46 (1750): 657–69, on 669; "The Philosophy of Earthquakes," *PT* 46 (1750): 731–50, on 732.

[83]As was noted by W. Cowper, Dean of Durham, ". . . Of the Earthquake on March 18, and of the Luminous Arch, February 16, 1749," *PT* 46 (1750): 647–49, on 648.

[84]Smart Lethieullier, ". . . Of the Burning of the Steeple of Danbury in Essex, by Lightning, and of the Earthquake," *PT* 46 (1749/50): 611–13.

[85]Abraham Trembly, "Extract of a Letter, Concerning the Same," *PT* 46 (1749/50): 610–11, on 611.

[86]Gowin Knight, "An Account of the Shock of an Earthquake Felt Feb. 8 1749–50," *PT* 46 (1749/50): 603–4, on 603.

fish were disturbed, a horse refused water, crows took flight.[87] Sensations were described variously, as "falling into a fit.[88] "Roger Pickering, a clergyman who was a close observer of the weather and natural curiosities, gave a detailed account of his sensations while lying in bed when the quake occurred; he also gave his reflections, which led him beyond the "secondary causes" of the quake to the grandeur and majesty of the "Lord of Nature."[89]

Just what these "secondary causes" were was the scientific question of the day, to which various answers were given, two of which were published together with the collected reports of the earthquake in the *Philosophical Transactions*. Stephen Hales, a clergyman, said that both the ordinary and the extraordinary events of nature were caused by God, but that they did not lie outside natural explanation for that reason. Hales first described his sensations while lying in bed during a tremor; then he explained them by referring to experiments from his *Statical Essays:* an earthquake is caused by the explosive lightning of a sulphurous cloud, which ignites the rising sulphurous vapors in the earth.[90] A further explanation of earthquakes was given by another clergyman, William Stukeley. After a perfunctory consideration of the religious view, Stuckley turned to the subject of interest in the *Philosophical Transactions*, the physical causes; rejecting subterranean vapors, he attributed earthquakes to "electrical shock, exactly of the same nature as those, now become very familiar, in electrical experiments." With reference to Franklin, Stukeley said that the "little snap, which we hear in our electrical experiments," is the same snap, only magnified, that we hear in thunderstorms. When a cloud rises from the sea and discharges its contents on the earth, an earthquake results. Having gotten to know the "stupendous powers" of electricity by experiment, he turned to electricity to explain the "prodigious appearance of an earthquake."[91] Stukeley's and Hales's causes of earthquakes, electricity and vapors (or gases), were the two main experimental subjects in Britain in the second half of the eighteenth century, and they were two of Henry Cavendish's great experimental fields (heat was a third).

The catastrophic Lisbon earthquake in 1755 filled the last roughly hundred pages of the volume of the *Philosophical Transactions* for that year and much of the next year's.[92] Unlike the accounts of the earlier earthquakes of 1750, these dwelled on loss of life and physical destruction. This earthquake would not be the last scourge of humanity to prove a stimulus to science. The most important response was John Michell's paper on the cause of the earthquake "So Fatal to the City of Lisbon" and on earthquakes in general, printed in the *Philosophical Transactions* for 1760.[93] We will move ahead in time to consider this paper, since it, more than any other work, set the standard just as Henry Cavendish joined the scientific circles of London.

Michell and Cavendish's acquaintanceship, if not their friendship, began no later than the year of Michell's paper on earthquakes in 1760. That year, at Cavendish's first dinner as a member of the Royal Society Club, Michell was present as a guest, and in later years Cavendish often brought Michell as his own guest.[94] In 1760, Michell and Cavendish were both elected Fellows of the Royal Society, and in that same year and before their elections, Michell's paper on the causes of earthquakes was read in five consecutive meetings of the Society. Cavendish was present at all of these meetings, three times as a guest of his father.[95] Michell's subject, the earth's interior, linked his and Cavendish's interests thereafter.

For most of his life Michell was a clergyman, but in his paper on earthquakes he made no reference to providence or any other religious idea. He disagreed with both Hales and

---

[87]*PT* 46 (1750): 618, 621, 651, 682, and passim.

[88]Thomas Birch, "An Account of the Same," *PT* 46 (1749/50): 615–16, on 616.

[89]Roger Pickering, ". . . Concerning the Same," *PT* 46 (1749/50): 622–25, on 625.

[90]Stephen Hales, "Some Considerations on the Causes of Earthquakes," *PT* 46 (1750): 669–81.

[91]William Stukeley, ". . . On the Causes of Earthquakes"; "Concerning the Causes of Earthquakes"; and "The Philosophy of Earthquakes," *PT* 46 (1750): 641–46, on 642–4; 657–69, on 663; 731–50.

[92]About the last hundred pages of volume 49, part l, 1755, and much of part 2, 1756.

[93]John Michell, "Conjectures Concerning the Cause, and Observations upon the Phaenomena of Earthquakes; Particularly of that Great Earthquake of the First of November, 1755, which Proved So Fatal to the City of Lisbon, and Whose Effects Were Felt as Far as Africa, and More or Less Throughout Almost All Europe," *PT* 51 (1760): 566–634.

[94]Entry for 14 Aug. 1760, Minute Book of the Royal Society Club, Royal Society, no. 4. In 1766 the minutes began to identify visitors with the members who invited them; in that way we learn that Cavendish repeatedly invited Michell when Michell was in town on visits.

[95]The meetings were on 28 Feb., 6, 13, 20, and 27 Mar. 1760. Royal Society, JB, 23: 782, 795, 800, 802, and 807.

Stukeley, who located the cause of earthquakes above the earth. Volcanoes were proof that fires could exist underground, without contact with the air, and by analogy Michell reasoned that volcanoes and earthquakes had the same cause. Pent-up water vapor falling into underground fires was the cause of earthquakes. The elastic force of heated vapor exceeded even gunpowder in producing "sudden and violent effects."[96] Conceiving of the earth not as "heaps of matter casually thrown together" but as "uniform strata," Michell developed a mechanical theory of the propagation of waves through the elastic substance of the earth. By the same principles that explained the motions of the heavenly bodies, the motions of the earth were explained: earthquakes were a dynamic phenomenon, explicable by the laws of motion. The elastic, stratified earth was set in motion by the expansive force of heat. What Michell proposed was more than a theory of earthquakes; it was an exact science of the earth.

When we look at the empirical support that Michell brought to his theory, we recognize in it a vindication of the motivating ideals of the Royal Society. The natural histories that Bacon expected from Salomon's House had been tried many times by the Royal Society, often without much benefit, but the natural histories of earthquakes led to science. Michell was able to derive the cause of earthquakes, he said, because of the bounty of facts of the earthquake of 1755, the world's best documented earthquake. Many of the facts were collected in volume 49 of the *Philosophical Transactions* and in a separate publication on the history and science of earthquakes. Michell's paper of 1760 is replete with references to the *Philosophical Transactions*, most from volume 49 but some earlier. Michell's use of histories was sophisticated; he acknowledged that observations were often carelessly made and reported, but the "concurrent testimonies" of so many persons established the main point. He selected accounts having the "greatest appearance of accuracy" and took a "mean" of them in computing the time, location, and depth of the Lisbon earthquake.[97]

Michell's paper has another connection with the Society's founding ideals through its references to the experiences of artisans, such as their disastrous experience in casting a cannon in a damp mold, resulting in an explosion of the "greatest violence."[98] The explosion of coal damp in mines was powerful but not enough for earthquakes, Michell said. For that, water had to be converted into steam, and the steam engine was Michell's example, taken from the world of artisans.

Like earthquakes, the weather was regarded as a great force of nature.[99] The atmosphere was a source of the most violent events, as Hales and Stukeley had argued in their theories of earthquakes. Its normal behavior was the occasion of endless reports to the Royal Society. The barometer reading, the rainfall, the temperature, usually including the mean and the highest and the lowest, were reported from far and near, Madeira, Dublin, Charles-Town, and Tooting. Jurin's method of recording temperature was still practiced, but standardization was a remote ideal. Temperatures could be given in Fahrenheit, Réaumur, and in relationship to the heat of human blood.[100] The clergyman Henry Miles wrote about the thermometer, an instrument which Newton had considered and which several others had tried to bring to "greater Perfection." This much agreement was now widespread, Miles said: thermometers made with mercury work the best. The credibility of the mercury thermometer was implicitly put to the test in the extreme climate of Siberia, in which Johann Georg Gmelin recorded temperatures as low as minus 120 degrees Fahrenheit, which he said was scarcely believable "had not experiments, made with the greatest exactness, demonstrated the reality of it."[101] William Watson used nearly the same words: Gmelin's observations, however "extraordinary," were "scarce to be doubted," since they were made with "all possible exactness" and agreed with readings made by others under his direction in different parts of Siberia.[102] Beginning with this remarkable weather report, Henry Cavendish would make a study of the contraction of mercury on freezing, thereby clarifying the behavior of

---

[96]Michell, "Conjectures," 594.

[97]Ibid, 629.

[98]Ibid, 595.

[99]Henry Miles, " . . . On the Same," *PT* 46 (1749): 607–9.

[100]The weather at the time of earthquakes was recorded; eg., William Arderon, "Extract of a Letter . . . Concerning the Hot Weather in July Last," *PT* 46 (1750): 573–75.

[101]John Fothergill's extracts from Gmelin, "An Account of Some Observations and Experiments Made in Siberia . . .," *PT* 45 (1748): 248–62, on 260.

[102]William Watson, "A Comparison of Different Thermometrical Observations in Siberia," *PT* 48 (1753): 108–9.

thermometers made with mercury. The naturalist William Arderon, who published frequently on the weather in Norwich, kept a record of the constant temperature in a cavern under nearby hills, which he compared with the mean of the hottest and coldest temperatures above ground, finding them almost identical, and noting that the temperature of the Norwich cavern was within a degree of that of the cave beneath the Paris Observatory.[103] This measure of the average climate Henry Cavendish would expand on a worldwide basis. George Graham noted that the magnetic variation at London was not regularly published,[104] and although Cavendish kept a regular record of it, he did not publish it either. Auroras were a regular feature of the journal,[105] and Cavendish would publish his observations of an aurora.

Some of the same persons who worked in natural philosophy worked at the same time in natural history. To William Watson the study of living nature had the same goal as the study of the physical world: "general laws" of nature.[106] A strong advocate of Linnaeus, Watson published on the sex of plants, the discovery of which, he thought, was as important as that of the circulation of the blood in animals. The Royal Society Croonian Lectures in 1747 were given by the physician Browne Langrish, who explained muscular motion by Newton's attracting and repelling forces, giving credit, and dedicating his lectures, to Stephen Hales for showing that particles of air are attracted to solids.[107] The physician Charles Morton published a paper on the same subject, muscular motion, which he, a professed "Newtonian," laid out in observations and experiments, lemmas, and scholia. As was traditional, Morton regarded his subject as belonging to "natural philosophy."[108] Nevertheless, in practice, for some men of science, there was a sharp difference: Cavendish did research in all parts of natural philosophy, as he accepted it, which was as physical science; he did no research on plants and animals to understand *their* laws.

The Royal Society continued to honor Bacon's ideal of a scientific society that worked to "relieve the necessities of human life." At the time Cavendish was studying at the university, the *Philosophical Transactions* contained a large number of papers that were at least partly directed to utilitarian interests; these dealt with mechanical power, manufactures, gunnery, navigation, medicine and health, and the prevention of disasters. John Smeaton showed the Royal Society a tackle of twenty pulleys small enough to fit into the pocket. With another block of twenty pulleys, he offered an Archimedean-like demonstration of one man lifting a gun and carriage aboard a naval ship.[109] William Brownrigg offered lemmas and propositions on salt-making, which William Watson hoped would do what the Royal Society's histories of salt-making had not, overcome Britain's disadvantage in this trade.[110] John Mitchell gave a Baconian history of potash-making, which in England, he said, was "practised only by the vulgar, and neglected and overlooked by the learned."[111] In Newgate prison, infectious fevers killed convicts and, worse, officers of courts of justice who were exposed to convicts during trials.[112] On Stephen Hales and Lord Halifax's recommendation, Captain Henry Ellis installed Hales's ventilators in his ship, which caused candles to burn better and bells to ring louder and slaves and other cargo to hold up better.[113] Electrical healing was more often the product of enthusiasm than of repeatable experiments, and claims for it were received with caution; but that electricity had some medical advantages seemed evident to everyone at the time.[114] Bills of

---

[103]Arderon also measured the temperature of a spring in the cavern, a method Cavendish would recommend as well. William Arderon, "An Account . . .," 247.

[104]George Graham, "Some Observations, Made During the Last Three Years, of the Quantity of the Magnetic Variation . . .," *PT* 45 (1748): 279–80, on 280.

[105]John Martyn, "A Letter . . . Concerning an Aurora Borealis Seen February l6. 1749–50," *PT* 46 (1749/50): 345.

[106]William Watson, "Some Observations upon the Sex of Flowers," *PT* 47 (1751): 169–83 on 179, 182–83.

[107]Browne Langrish, "Three Lectures on Muscular Motion," supplement to the *PT* 44 (1747).

[108]Charles Morton, "Observations and Experiments upon Animal Bodies, Digested in a Philosophical Analysis, or Inquiry into the Cause of Voluntary Muscular Motion," *PT* 47 (1751): 305–14, on 308, 314.

[109]John Smeaton, "A Description of a New Tackle, or Combination of Pulleys," *PT* 47 (1752): 494–97.

[110]William Watson's abstract and review: "An Account of a Treatise by Wm Brownrigg . . .," *PT* 45 (1748): 351–72.

[111]John Mitchell, "An Account of the Preparation and Uses of the Various Kinds of Pot-ash," *PT* 45 (1748): 541–63, on 541.

[112]Stephen Hales and John Pringle were consulted on how to achieve purity of air at Newgate, and it was decided that Hales should design a ventilator for the purpose. John Pringle, "An Account of the Gaol-Fever with Which Several Persons Were Seized in Newgate," *PT* 48 (1753): 42–54.

[113]Henry Ellis, "A Letter to the Rev Dr. Hales . . .," *PT* 47 (1751): 211–16.

[114]William Watson, "An Account of Dr. Bianchini's Recueil d'expériences faites à Venise sur le médicine électrique," *PT* 47 (1752): 399–406.

mortality documented the relative unhealthiness of various places, useful knowledge for calculating annuities on lives. Medical waters were analyzed for their contents. Improvements were made in navigation, such as in the mariner's compass, the invention of which, the improver Gowin Knight said, had "probably been of more general and important use to human society, than the invention of any one instrument whatsoever."[115] To celebrate the recent peace, six thousand rockets were fired without incident in Green Park, following Stephen Hales's recommendation for preventing fire by spreading a layer of dirt or fine gravel over the wood floor.[116] The *Philosophical Transactions* had countless papers on lightning rods, a direct application of science; this application Henry Cavendish became involved with through his work in the Royal Society.

A reflection of eighteenth-century education, frequently astronomy and classics were combined in the *Philosophical Transactions*. William Stukeley referred to Thales's account of a solar eclipse to remind historians that they could profit from astronomy.[117] There was a tradition of astronomical reasoning in history; just as in science, in chronology Newton now received gentle criticism.[118] The contemporary university education in mathematics and classics resulted in exacting studies of

antiquity.[119] From China a Jesuit who had worked out a chronology of ancient China proposed to do the same for Chinese astronomy.[120] Henry Cavendish contributed even to this field, as we will see, with his study of the Hindoo calendar.

Nearly all of the scientific problems Henry Cavendish worked on during his long career were problems that were addressed in the *Philosophical Transactions* at the time he was doing his university studies. His distinction was in carrying certain directions of this work further than others.

———

[115]Gowin Knight had a mariner's compass made to his specification by John Smeaton. Gowin Knight, "A Description of a Mariner's Compass," *PT* 46 (1750): 505–12, on 505. John Smeaton, "An Account of Some Improvements of the Mariner's Compass, in Order to Render the Card and Needle, Proposed by Doctor Knight, of General Use," *PT* 46 (1750): 513–17.

[116]Stephen Hales, "A Proposal for Checking in Some Degree the Progress of Fires," *PT* 45 (1748): 277–79. At the end of this volume of the journal, the secretary Cromwell Mortimer made an addition to Hales's paper, reporting that the engineers followed Hales's scheme in the building they erected for the fireworks.

[117]William Stukeley, "An Account of the Eclipse Predicted by Thales," *PT* 48 (1753): 221–26.

[118]Stukeley, "An Account of the Eclipse," p. 222; George Costard, "Concerning the Year of the Eclipse Foretold by Thales," *PT* 48 (1753): 17–26, on 19.

[119]For example, this study by an Oxford Fellow draws equally on scientific and classical texts: George Costard, "A Letter . . . Concerning the Ages of Homer and Hesiod," *PT* 48 (1753): 441–84.

[120]"Extracts of Two Letters from Father Gaubil, of the Society of Jesus, at Peking in China," *PT* 48 (1753): 309–17.

CHAPTER 3

❦

*F*irst Researches

Chemistry

Cavendish entered the scientific world gradually and methodically, with help from his father. The earliest date in his scientific manuscripts is 1764, twelve years after he had left the university and four years after he had been elected to the Royal Society. Cavendish was then well into his thirties.

Concerning that time of life, William James remarked in his *Principles of Psychology* in 1890: "In most of us, by the age of thirty, the character has set like plastic."[1] James's observation can be applied to Cavendish if we take "character" to imply a steadfast devotion to science. The ongoing development of our subject, of which we have any record, is of a life *within* science.

Cavendish's earliest work in chemistry dealt with arsenic; he wrote a paper on it to be read, only to be read not by the readers of the *Philosophical Transactions* but by an unnamed person.[2] (One commentator described it ominously as "Notes on some experiments with arsenic for the use of friends."[3]) We suspect that the reader Cavendish had in mind was John Hadley, nephew of the great instrument-maker John Hadley. Hadley and William Lewis were the only London chemists Cavendish referred to in his first chemical writings, and although Lewis began collecting information on the physical and chemical properties of air at the right time, 1765–70,[4] he could not have been his correspondent.[5] Cavendish's reference to Hadley was to an *unpublished* work by Hadley, which Cavendish learned about first hand.[6] This work had to do with the distillation of metals with salts, as did Cavendish's earliest work. Hadley's approach to chemistry was close to Cavendish's, as we will point out as we go along. Hadley and Cavendish were of the same age and had been at Cambridge together. The year Cavendish came down from Cambridge, Hadley stayed on as a fellow of Queen's and a colleague of John Michell.[7] In 1756,

on the recommendation of the regius professor of physick, Russel Plumtre, Hadley was appointed successor to Mickleburgh as professor of chemistry in 1756. What Hadley did as professor not all Cambridge professors did, he lectured.[8] Hadley wanted a proper profession and income, and in 1758 he got permission from his college to study medicine and hold a "Physick Fellowship." He came to London frequently, where Cavendish saw him at the Royal Society—Hadley recommended Cavendish for fellowship in the Society—and at

---

[1]Paul T. Costa, Jr., and Robert R. McCrae, "Set Like Plaster? Evidence for the Stability of Adult Personality," in *Can Personality Change?*, eds. T. F. Heatherton and J. L. Weinberger (Washington, D.C.: American Psychological Association, 1994), 21–40, on 21–22.

[2]This earliest chemical work by Cavendish for which we have an apparently complete record consists of the following: a bundle of fifty-nine numbered pages of laboratory notes with index, an unpaginated rough draft of an account of the experiments, and a carefully written, probably final, paginated, twenty-five page version of the account. These are designated, respectively, "Experiments on Arsenic," "Arsenic," and "Experiments on the Neut. Arsen. Salt," Cavendish Mss II, l(a); II, 1(b); and II, 1(c). A brief description and analysis of these papers is given by Edward Thorpe, in Henry Cavendish, *The Scientific Papers of the Honourable Henry Cavendish, F.R.S.*, vol. 2, ed. E. Thorpe (Cambridge: Cambridge University Press, 1921), 298–301. The date Dec. 1764 appears on p. 27 of the laboratory notes. The unnamed reader of the work is referred to as "you": "as you tell me you have tried yourself," and the "particulars of this exper. which I showed you before," II(b): 20, 25.

[3]Quoted in John Pearson, *The Serpent and the Stag...* (New York: Holt, Reinhart and Winston, 1983), 118.

[4]F. W. Gibbs, "A Notebook of William Lewis and Alexander Chisholm," *Annals of Science* 8 (1952): 202–20.

[5]That is evident from the way Lewis is referred to in Cavendish's letter to his chemical correspondent.

[6]Hadley's work appears in a footnote to part 4 of Cavendish's paper on factitious air in 1766. The first three parts were published, the fourth withheld. "Experiments on Factitious Air. Part IV. Containing Experiments on the Air Produced from Vegetable and Animal Substances by Distillation." In Cavendish, *Sci. Pap.* 2:307–16, on 313.

[7]Hadley planned to take several persons to the Royal Society for the reading of John Michell's paper on earthquakes, but he could not make it and asked Birch to take them instead. John Hadley to Thomas Birch, 13 Mar. /1760/, BL Add Mss 4309, f. 3.

[8]John Twigg, *A History of Queen's College, Cambridge, 1448–1986* (Woodbridge, Suffolk: Boydell Press, 1987), 212–13. "Hadley, John," *DNB* 8:879–80, on 879. John Hadley, *A Plan of a Course of Chemical Lectures* (Cambridge, 1758). Hadley gave lectures for two consecutive years; beyond the syllabus of his lectures, Hadley published nothing on chemistry.

the Royal Society Club. Hadley was elected to the council soon after his election to the Society, and one year later he offered himself as a candidate to succeed Davall as secretary, an asset in his profession. To this end he approached Lord Charles Cavendish.[9] Hadley enjoyed the patronage of Hardwicke, who started him on a promising career in medicine in London.[10] He became assistant physician at St. Thomas's Hospital in 1760, and in 1763 he became physician to the Charterhouse and a Fellow of the College of Physicians. When Hadley died suddenly of fever at the Charterhouse in 1764, at the age of thirty-three, Henry Cavendish lost a friend and very able scientific colleague. His early direction as a chemist may have owed something to this friendship.[11]

The Royal Society was the locus of activity for Lord Charles and Henry Cavendish, but it was not their entire scientific world, certainly not Henry's, whose first researches drew on another, equally important source, books and papers from abroad. His first researches were in chemistry, and in the seven years he had been coming to meetings of the Royal Society, there had been very few reports on chemistry and nothing of real substance. Of the chemical authors mentioned in Hadley's syllabus of his lectures on chemistry at Cambridge in 1758, with the exception of the Scottish chemist Joseph Black, they were all foreign, mostly German. The Londoner Henry Cavendish, who was just then setting out on his chemical researches, would have consulted foreign writings as a matter of course.

The gentleman's double house on Great Marlborough Street, with its elegant stairs leading off the entrance, and with its rooms used for entertaining, was unlikely to have been used also as a chemical laboratory reeking of fumes. Henry's chemical researches must have been done either in the stables or in the connected but separate apartment on the grounds, and it probably was done in the former. By the time Cavendish wrote his first known paper on chemistry, he had an elaborate chemical establishment. Since we know that his father had chemicals, a laboratory in some form was undoubtedly already in place for Henry. We have no description of the laboratory, but because of its completeness we know in general what it had to be like. It would not have been in the underground rooms of the separate building behind the Cavendish house, for in the dampness

there, metals would have rusted, furnaces collected mold, salts turned watery, and labels fallen off bottles. The ground-floor laboratory room needed openings to the outside at each end to admit fresh air and clear away poisonous vapors. The chimney needed to be high enough to walk under and wide enough to walk in front of. Located underneath the chimney were various furnaces and probably a double bellows to fan the flames from gentle heat to red hot. Ready at hand, suspended on hooks, were pokers, pincers, tongs, shovels, and pans, much as in a kitchen of the day. Near the chimney was an anvil along with hammers and a range of other tools. Lining the walls were shelves for chemicals and various other supplies. Bins were there to store bulk charcoal, sand, and quicklime. Since acids, alkalis, metals, and earths were as pure as possible, standing in a corner of the laboratory was a lead or stone "fountain" with a drain pipe, where vessels were cleaned after each use, no doubt by an "assistant." Housekeeping was of the essence of good chemical practice. In the center of the room there would have been a big table for chemical operations not requiring a high heat. On it, we suppose, were scales, mortars and pestles, filtration paper, corks, stirrers, and, not least, pencils, pens and ink, and a stack of small sheets of paper for keeping notes of what was done as it was done.[12] From Cavendish's manuscripts, we can be specific about what he required to carry out his researches on his first substance, arsenic. To make the chemical reactions go, he used heating lamps, a furnace-forge, and a reverberator furnace (designed

----

[9]Hadley's father asked for Birch's support. Henry Hadley to Thomas Birch, 13 Oct. 1759, BL Add Mss 4309, f.1. Hadley told Birch and Charles Cavendish of his desire to become secretary. Thomas Birch to Philip Yorke, 13 Oct. 1759, BL Add Mss 35399, f. 115.

[10]Hadley wanted Hardwicke's help in getting a job at St. Thomas's, recalling "so many advantages last year in a similar pursuit" he had received from Hardwicke. John Hadley to Lord Hardwicke, 1 Jan. 1760, BL, Add Mss 35596, f. 73.

[11]"Hadley," *DNB* 8:879. We cannot be certain, of course, that Cavendish's correspondent was Hadley. The next possibility is Lord Charles Cavendish, the next William Heberden. Lacking direct evidence, we still think it likely that the person was Hadley.

[12]We have been guided in our sketch of Cavendish's laboratory by the entry "Laboratory (Chemical)" in Pierre Joseph Macquer's chemical dictionary, the first of its kind, published in 1766, just after Cavendish began his experiments. *A Dictionary of Chemistry. Containing the Theory and Practice of That Science: Its Applications to Natural Philosophy, Natural History, Medicine, and Animal Economy*, trans. J. Kier, 2 vols. (London, 1771). Macquer's laboratory was intended for the "philosophical chemist," and with its list of reagents, it sufficed for performing "any chemical experiment."

to direct the flame back on the heated substance), which he placed high into the chimney because of the "obnoxious" fumes. There was a sand pot for distilling at "sand heat" and for holding bottles. Heat entered into most of his operations: roasting, calcining (changing a substance to a calx, or powder), dissolving, distilling, subliming, and evaporating. His other operations included precipitating, crystallizing, filtering, deliquescing, and weighing. We assume that from the start, Cavendish's scales were of good quality, since for him weighing was the method of chemical precision. Cavendish had at hand an elaborate collection of containers, some metal, some earthen, most glass. There were open flasks, Florence flasks (having long, narrow necks), retorts (having downward bending necks for distilling), receivers (flasks for retaining condensates and distillates), adaptors (for connecting retorts and receivers), bottles for holding everything, pipkins (small pots and pans), and copper pipes. There was a lead crucible for keeping the bottom of another crucible placed in it cooler than the top of it, a kind of inverted double-boiler. There was another crucible, designed and drawn by Cavendish, for use in the reverberator furnace, complete with a set of aludels (pear-shaped pots open at the bottom as well as the top and made to fit over one another for subliming). All of this apparatus was made for the purpose, to which Cavendish added a make-do, humble coffee cup for calcining. The reagents that Cavendish performed his operations with and filled his flasks with were many, mostly solvents, various acids, solutions of various metals in acids, testing solutions and treated papers for acids and alkalis, various alkalis, and a few neutral salts among other things.[13] Cavendish's experiments on arsenic depended on a sizable investment in chemical apparatus and supplies.

The incentive for Cavendish's researches on arsenic (arsenious oxide) is unknown, but we know that his starting point was Pierre Joseph Macquer's discovery and naming of "neutral arsenical salt" (potassium arsenate), which appeared in two papers of the Paris Academy of Sciences *Memoires* in 1746 and 1748.[14]

If, as we suggest, Cavendish wrote up his experiments on arsenic for John Hadley to read, we can point to Hadley's Cambridge lectures as proof of his interest in Macquer's experiments on the neutral arsenical salt.[15] In this the most important

of his early work, Macquer distilled arsenic with nitre (potassium nitrate) and analyzed the residue, a compact, white, soluble, and mild salt. He noted that arsenic itself behaved like an acid, but he did not discover the acid of arsenic, which was left for Cavendish to do. The discovery of the acid was important at the time, since few acids were known, and each was a valuable reagent for the chemist. The discovery of the new salt was important, too; it had obvious value for philosophical chemistry, and it had practical uses, though Macquer thought that these did not include medicine, despite its actual mildness, since the "name of arsenic is so terrible."[16]

Like electricity, chemistry carried risks. The expansive power of air occasioned violent explosions, putting life and limb in jeopardy. Spilled acids ate "away the skin." In 1767 a paper appeared in the *Philosophical Transactions* on a new distilling apparatus that spared the chemist's lungs from harmful fumes.[17] And there were deadly poisons, like arsenic, the agonizing symptoms and fatal consequences of which were noted in every book of chemistry.

---

[13]In his study of arsenic, Cavendish used a good many reagants, which were, in his words and spelling, and with modern names in parentheses: distilled vinegar, spirit of salt (hydrochloric acid), oil of vitriol (sulphuric acid), spirit of nitre (nitric acid), aqua fortis (concentrated nitric acid), nitre, syrup of violets (test), tournsol paper (test), blue vitriol (copper sulphate), green vitriol (ferrous sulphate), solutions of silver, mercury, copper, and iron in nitric acid, solutions of mercury, copper, and iron in concentrated nitric acid, solutions of tin in hydrochloric acid, solutions of gold and nickel in aqua regia (mixture of nitric and hydrochloric acids), solution of regulus of cobalt, sope leys (potassium hydroxide), pearl ashes (potash), a fixed alkali (potassium carbonate), calcareous earth (whiting, or carbonate of lime), volatile alkali (ammonia), magnesia, earth of alum, sedative salt (boric acid), white flux, sulphur, linseed oil, and charcoal. Cavendish also had at hand pure, "rain" water.

[14]Pierre Joseph Macquer, "Researches sur l'arsenic. Premier mémoir," and "Second mémoire sur l'arsenic," *Mémoirs de l'Académie Royale des Sciences*, 1746 (published 1751), pp. 233–36, and 1748 (published 1752), 35–50. Macquer later described this work in 1766 in his *Dictionary of Chemistry*. The article "Neutral Arsenical Salt" is in vol. 2, pp. 666–67. Shortly before Cavendish's researches on the subject, Macquer's work was described in English in an annotation by William Lewis to his translation of Caspar Neumann, *The Chemical Works . . . Abridged and Methodized. With Large Additions, Containing the Later Discoveries and Improvements Made in Chemistry and the Arts Depending Thereon* (London, 1759), 143.

[15]The full lectures for which Hadley published the syllabus are preserved in manuscript in the library of Trinity College. They are discussed in L. J. M. Coleby, "John Hadley, Fourth Professor of Chemistry in the University of Cambridge," *Annals of Science* 8 (1952): 293–301; Hadley's lecture dealing with Macquer's neutral arsenical salt is mentioned on 301.

[16]Macquer, *Dictionary*, 100, 666–67.

[17]Peter Woulfe, "Experiments on the Distillation of Acids, Volatile Alkalies, etc. Shewing How They May Be Condensed without Loss, and How Thereby We May Avoid Disagreeable and Noxious Fumes," *PT* 57 (1767): 517–34.

Arsenic, the great German chemist Caspar Neumann wrote, is a "most violent poison to all animals," so that the "utmost caution is necessary in all operations upon arsenic, to avoid its fumes," which have a "strong fetid smell resembling that of garlic"; its solution has a nauseous taste; arsenic, it seemed, had no redeeming features. It was little wonder that this mineral, as Neumann said, had been "so little examined" by the chemists. At the time Cavendish made his study of arsenic compounds, chemists still had not been able to "determine what it /arsenic/ really is, or to what class of bodies it belongs."[18] Independently of, but befitting, its noxious properties, arsenic, Macquer said, has other "singular properties, which render it the only one of its kind." Neither fish nor fowl, but something of a flying fish, arsenic behaves like a metal in some states and like a salt in other states. On the one hand, like every metallic calx, arsenic can be changed into a metallic form, a "true semimetal," or "regulus of arsenic." The means of doing this for Macquer is to combine the calx with "phlogiston," the all-important substance or principle in the chemistry of Cavendish. On the other hand, like salts, arsenic is soluble in water. Even when regarded as a salt, arsenic is an uncommon thing, neither acidic nor alkaline, yet, Macquer claimed, behaving as if it were an acid.[19] The "very singular and extremely different" properties of arsenic had led Macquer to his investigations of this little studied calx in the first place.[20] In other ways than by its dual nature, arsenic differs from other known calces: it is volatile with a strong smell, it is fusible, it unites with metals and semimetals, and—the difference that Macquer and Cavendish picked up on—it decomposes nitre when distilled with it.[21] From the standpoint of affinities (the readiness to unite with other substances), arsenic is exceptional too.[22]

Although Cavendish did not tell us why he investigated arsenic, from the state of chemistry at the time, we get an idea of its considerable interest for him. The substance was at once dangerous, difficult, unique, and scientifically puzzling.[23] Its study demanded manipulatory and analytical skills of a high order, a stiff challenge and testing ground for a young chemist of genius.

In practice, chemistry was a complicated art, since it dealt with all kinds of matter and with a large repertoire of operations. In principle, chemistry looked simple, though this appearance was changing. Chemicals were put in classes and the outcomes of their combinations were put in small, tidy tables. Neutral salts, Cavendish's starting point, are a case in point. These were salts composed of acids and other substances, mostly alkalis, that were without acidity. Not long before, all of the known neutral salts could be listed in a table of twelve entries, which corresponded to the possible combinations of the four known acidic salts and the three known alkaline salts. Just as Cavendish began to work with these salts—in his arsenic experiments, with the acidic salt "arsenic," the alkaline or vegetable salt "nitre," and Macquer's new neutral salt of arsenic—the tidy, manageable table of neutral salts was fast expanding.[24] The empirical field of salts was recognized as highly undeveloped, so many salts "little known, or not even thought of."[25] Cavendish procured Macquer's neutral salt using Macquer's method of distilling arsenic with nitre, producing copious red fumes and leaving behind a cake of neutral arsenical salt. He then tried another way, dissolving arsenic in spirit of nitre, then adding pearl ashes to it to obtain neutral arsenical acid. He had made a discovery: what combined with the alkali to form the neutral salt was an acid, but not any known acid, a new acid, "arsenical acid" ("if you will allow me to call it by that name").[26] The change that arsenic underwent in distilling and dissolving (and

---

[18]Neumann, *Chemical Works*, 140–41, 145. What Neumann, Macquer, Cavendish, and their contemporaries called "arsenic" is a dense, brittle substance with a crystalline or vitreous look; this substance, arsenious oxide, is a common by-product of roasting metallic ores. Another name for it then, as now, is "white arsenic," the calx of regulus of arsenic, the white, shiny semimetal.

[19]Macquer, *Dictionary* 2:634.

[20]Pierre Joseph Macquer, *Elements of the Theory and Practice of Chemistry*, trans A. Reid, 2 vols. (London, 1758) 1:96.

[21]Macquer, *Dictionary* 1:99–100.

[22]Arsenic has the least, or next to least, affinity of the soluble substances for the several acids, with the exception of aqua regia. Gellert's "Table of the Solutions of Bodies," at the end of vol. 2 of Macquer, *Dictionary*.

[23]Arsenic was soluble in acids, and the results had "not yet been sufficiently examined." Macquer, *Dictionary* l:103.

[24]The Scottish chemist William Cullen's table of twelve neutral salts was reproduced in Donald Monro, "An Account of Some Neutral Salts Made with Vegetable Acids, and With the Salt of Amber; Which Shews that Vegetable Acids Differ from One Another . . .," *PT* 57 (1767): 479–516. Monro, 483, pointed out that a table had been published in Germany giving three or four more of these salts, and that there were actually many more because vegetable acid was in reality many acids each with its own neutral salts.

[25]Macquer, *Dictionary* 2:642, 649.

[26]Cavendish, "Arsenic," Cavendish Mss II, 1(b): 10.

calcining) made it acidic: neutralizing alkalies and so on, this new substance had "all the properties of an acid," which conclusion Cavendish qualified with an implicit acknowledgment of the fatal reputation of arsenic, "unless perhaps it should fail in respect of taste which I have not thought proper to try."[27] This discovery was the high point of Cavendish's researches on arsenic.

In the history of science Cavendish is invariably remembered as the man of quantity. Although it is a caricature, he was that too, a man who frequently made quantitative observations in pursuit of scientific understanding. His laboratory notes are filled with numbers, standing for weights, expressed in ounces and their breakdown into drams and grains. Other numbers stand for specific gravities, the index of concentration. Other numbers stand for proportions of reactants; Cavendish spoke of "saturation," a term in use for the point at which acids in combination with other bodies lose their acidity, and also a term used to describe solutions in which a solvent has dissolved as much of a substance as it can. Cavendish's skill in quantitative work is fully evident in this early chemical research. He worked with uncommonly small quantities of substances, ounces instead of the familiar pounds, the mark of a skilled chemist. In doing an experiment, he usually began with carefully measured quantities of substances, which he then combined and performed operations on, and the products he obtained he would again weigh. Having once obtained the products, however, he would put them through a series of tests, "small experiments," as he called them, in which he did not record, and probably did not measure, the quantities involved. Quantity had the same place in this work as did any quality, perceived by sight, smell, or taste. In the detective work on neutral arsenical salt, measurements and descriptions alike gave Cavendish clues about what was going on in the fumings and the shootings of crystals; that is, about what went in and what came out.[28] To the extent that there was a difference between weighing and seeing, the former could be more accurate than the latter: "as well as could be judged by the eye," Cavendish wrote of one arsenic observation, a kind of qualification he did not make about weighing. In this chemical work, Cavendish's senses were fully engaged, and he described his sensations with a discriminating vocabulary. With colors, he made the most distinctions: milky, cloudy, yellow, pale straw, reddish yellow, pale madeira, red, reddish brown, dirty red, green, bluish green, pearl color, blue, and transparent, turgid, and muddy. By smell, he distinguished between the various acids and their products. He observed the degree of heat, the strength of effervescence, the speed of dissolution, the shape and size of crystals. He observed textures: dry, hard, thin jelly, gluey, thick, stiff mud, lump. No poet paid greater attention to his sensations than Cavendish did to his. His notes on arsenic were the journal of a complete man—whose whole being was, just then, concentrated on arsenic.

Under "complete," we include the thinking man, one whose final goal was experimental results *together* with understanding. In the final writing of Cavendish's researches on arsenic, the longest section by far, roughly half of the whole paper, consisted of a combination of conjectures and experiment. It is to be expected that they were combined, since by then, a priori theoretical conjectures in chemistry were not regarded as the way to advance knowledge of the various substances of which the world is made.[29] Cavendish presented his experiments first, but his theoretical ideas did not arise inductively from them. They came from the same place his problem of arsenic did, from the chemical literature of his day.

Chemistry in the middle of the eighteenth century was still closely tied to pharmacy, medicine, metallurgy, and manufactures. It also had a philosophical content, with two sources. One was German, associated above all with Georg Stahl and his predecessor Johann Becher. Stahl gave the name "phlogiston" to the oily earth given off in combustion and presumed present in every combustible body. Phlogiston was one of four elements of Stahl's chemistry (the other three being water, mercury, and another kind of earth), but because of its ubiquitous presence in chemical processes of interest, his chemistry came to be known by the name phlogiston.[30]

[27]Ibid. II. 1(b): 13.

[28]Henry Guerlac characterizes chemistry as a qualitative science using quantitative techniques in "Quantification in Chemistry," *Isis* 52 (1961): 194–214, on 196.

[29]A. M. Duncan, "Some Theoretical Aspects of Eighteenth-Century Tables of Affinity—I," *Ann. of Sci.* 18 (1962): 177–94, on 185.

[30]Stahl developed the explanation of combustion of J. J. Becher, who worked in the second half of the seventeenth century.

Phlogiston entered Stahl's explanation of not only combustion but of acidity, alkalinity, chemical combination, and even colors and smells. Matter is composed of aggregated particles according to Stahl, but his chemistry is distinctly chemistry, not physics. The other philosophical source was associated with Boyle, Newton, and Boerhaave, who regarded chemistry as a branch of physics. After Newton, those who approached chemistry in this way thought that chemical substances attracted one another in analogy with the mutual attraction of the earth and the moon. There were unsuccessful attempts to express this understanding mathematically, but for the most part, chemists used it only as a guide in their researches, which they conducted experimentally. Cavendish adopted the physical approach to chemistry, which by this time had incorporated the combustible principle, phlogiston, from Stahlian chemistry. It is understandable that it was Macquer who served as Cavendish's guide in chemical research, for Macquer was at once a proponent of phlogiston, a Newtonian, and an advocate of weighing in chemistry, who believed that weighing was a likely starting point for the ultimate mathematical development of chemistry. His text on theoretical chemistry in 1749 was one of the earliest to present chemistry as a science instead of recipes, and it was the principal publication in the adoption of the phlogiston theory in France.[31] It was customary for chemists to divide their science into a theoretical and a practical part; Stahl and Boerhaave had done it, so did Macquer. Macquer's down-to-earth, complementary text on practical chemistry in 1751 together with his earlier text on theoretical chemistry were brought out together in 1758 in an English translation, which found a receptive audience in Britain.[32] Macquer emphasized the leading concept of the physical approach, affinity, popularizing the term, in place of the earlier "attraction"; in his *Dictionary of Chemistry* in 1766, he suggested that affinities could be treated quantitatively, which they later were. In these several ways, Macquer was important in giving shape to the chemistry that Cavendish endorsed from the beginning and built upon thereafter.[33]

At the time Cavendish took up chemistry, the phlogiston theory had long been familiar in Germany, but in France and Britain it was just taking hold.[34] William Lewis's translation in 1759 of the writings of Caspar Neumann, one of Stahl's school of chemists in Berlin, was the first account of the phlogiston theory in English.[35] Neumann's book is practical, filled with straightforward descriptions of operations and reactions, with little that is quantitative, nothing about air, and short on theory; but phlogiston is there, the "inflammable principle," the unitary principle, the same in one metal as in another, in other bodies as in metals, in the vegetable and animal as well as the mineral kingdoms.[36] At the heart of the theory was a unified explanation of combustion and of the calcination of metals (their transformation to powder, with properties of an earth). Metals, like ordinary combustibles, contain phlogiston in combination with another part, and as when combustibles are burned their phlogiston separates from the other part and flies off, when metals are dissolved in acids they likewise lose their phlogiston. The evidence of phlogiston in flight was obvious to the senses: flame and fumes, sight and smell. The experimental proof of phlogiston seemed incontrovertible, which is why the physical school of chemistry needed it as well as the Stahlian: if a metal is deprived of its phlogiston by an acid and reduced to its calx, the pure metal can be restored, if sometimes with great difficulty, by combining the calx with an inflammable substance from which it extracts the lost phlogiston. Either by its presence or its absence, phlogiston determines most chemical reactions, and by keeping a balance sheet on phlogiston, the chemist could foresee the outcome of chemical processes. However, indispensable as phlogiston was as a chemical concept, the thing itself was elusive. Phlogiston could not be isolated and studied in itself (though for a time Cavendish believed that it could be); it was the

―――――

[31]Duncan, "Some Theoretical Aspects of Eighteenth-Century Tables of Affinity," 190.

[32]W. A. Smeaton, "Macquer, Pierre Joseph," *DSB* 8:618–24, on 619. Macquer's *Élémens de chymie théorique* (Paris, 1749) and *Élémens de chymie pratique* (Paris, 1751) were brought out in English translation by Andrew Ried in 1758 as *Elements of the Theory and Practice of Chemistry*.

[33]Smeaton, "Macquer," 620–21. Maurice Crosland, "The Development of Chemistry in the Eighteenth Century," *Studies on Voltaire* 24 (1963): 369–441, on 397–98.

[34]Thomas L. Hankins, *Science and the Enlightenment* (Cambridge: Cambridge University Press, 1985), 95.

[35]Nathan Sivin, "William Lewis (1708–1781) as a Chemist," *Chymia* 8 (1962): 63–88, on 73.

[36]Neumann, *Chemical Works*, 53.

"least accurately known" of all chemical substances or principles.[37]

Although within Stahlian chemistry affinity was a useful concept, by the time of Lewis's translation of Neumann's text, affinity was principally associated with Newtonian attraction and the physical school. "Affinity," Lewis wrote, is the name for chemical attraction, which takes place at insensible distances. The union of one chemical substance with another could be broken by bringing up a third substance with an affinity for one or the other substance greater than they have for one other. The concept of affinity provided chemistry both with a philosophical foundation in Newtonian attraction and an ordering at the practical level: it told if any particular chemical substitution did or did not take place. Tables of affinity had been introduced early in the century, but they were widely taken up only about the time of Cavendish's first researches. Ultimately, tables of affinity did not fulfill their early promise of leading to the general laws of chemistry; other avenues led to that, considerably later.[38]

The distinction between what Cavendish started with, arsenic, and what he ended with, arsenical acid, he understood with the aid of phlogiston. "The only difference" between the two, he said, is that the acid "is more thoroughly deprived of its phlogiston."[39] Identifying arsenic with other "metallic substances," which by the phlogiston theory are rich in phlogiston, he accounted for the changes arsenic undergoes in becoming the neutral salt and the acid by the readiness with which spirit of nitre unites with phlogiston.[40] So convincing was the phlogistic explanation to Cavendish—or, looked at another way, so dependent then was chemistry on phlogiston—that Cavendish bent the theory repeatedly to accommodate it rather than bring it into question.[41]

Cavendish's extensive researches in chemistry were carried out entirely within the framework of phlogistic arguments, which for most of that time were also subjected to critical and, ultimately, fatal examination by Lavoisier. Cavendish's junior by ten years though entering into his researches only slightly after Cavendish, Lavoisier denied the existence of phlogiston, and in its place he offered explanations in terms of oxygen. (Cavendish's later researches would contribute

substantially, if unintentionally, to Lavoisier's successful attack on phlogiston.) In Lavoisier's route to his understanding of the role of oxygen, he gave great attention to acidity, "oxygen" meaning acid-forming.[42] Acidity was a principal issue between the defenders and the opponents of phlogiston, and neither got it right. Before that issue was joined, Cavendish discussed the action of acids in what was to be his only theoretical writing on phlogistic chemistry. In it he showed the power of phlogistic reasoning without yet having to defend it, but his reasoning, while useful in his understanding of chemical reactions, was tentative, and he did not publish it. If he had, Lavoisier would have had to answer it, since it was by a chemist worthy of refutation. Ultimately, as we

---

[37]Thomas Thomson, *The History of Chemistry*, vol. 2 (London, 1831), 250–63. Macquer, *Dictionary* 2:516.

[38]William Lewis, *Commercium Philosophiae-Technicum; or, The Philosophical Commerce of Arts: Designed as an Attempt to Improve Arts, Trades, and Manufactures . . .* (London, 1763), iv–ix. Lewis was one of the first to advocate the use of affinity tables, including a modification of the original Geoffroy's table in his *New Dispensatory* in 1753. Duncan, "Some Theoretical Aspects of Eighteenth-Century Tables of Affinity," 178–79, 232.

[39]Cavendish, "Arsenic," Cavendish Mss II, 1(b):16. Cavendish made the acid or the same thing, in effect, the neutral arsenical salt, three ways: distilling arsenic with nitre, dissolving nitre in concentrated nitric acid, and heating arsenic with fixed alkali. All three methods had the same rational: the effect of exposing a metal (for that is how he regarded arsenic) to an acid or to heat and open air was to deprive it of its phlogiston.

[40]Macquer wrote: "Nothing can equal the impetuosity with which nitrous acid joins itself to phlogiston." *Dictionary of Chemistry* 1:11.

[41]Here are two examples. 1) Cavendish distilled the product of arsenic and aqua fortis, obtaining a residue, or "caput mortuum," which he weighed. By the standard phlogiston theory, the caput mortuum should weigh less than the arsenic because of the phlogiston driven off, but Cavendish found that his caput mortuum weighed more. He attributed the excess weight to water acquired by the arsenic from the aqua fortis. It is the kind of explanation Cavendish and fellow upholders of the phlogiston theory would give for this frequently encountered excess weight. The oxygen theory, of course, had an explanation for this excess, the addition of oxygen. 2) Cavendish's hypothesis that arsenic acid is arsenic deprived of phlogiston suggested to him another, simpler method for making the acid. He designed a crucible luted to aludels and placed it in the reverberator furnace, subliming arsenic exposed to a current of air. He expected that phlogiston would be driven off and attach to the air and that what remained behind would be arsenic deprived of phlogiston, namely, arsenical acid. But he found that the sublimed arsenic was nothing other than pure arsenic. This failure did not discourage him; it did not invalidate the hypothesis. To Cavendish it only meant that sublimation is less effective than the other methods in getting arsenic to part with its phlogiston. Cavendish's reasoning in both of these examples seems slippery, but it does only in retrospect, after the success of the oxygen theory.

[42]Historians of chemistry have recently come to appreciate the importance of the problem of acids in Lavoisier's work; earlier their attention was directed mainly toward Lavoisier's approach to the problem of combustion. This change is summarized in William H. Brock, *The Fontana History of Chemistry* (London: Fontana, 1992), 125.

know, it would only have strengthened Lavoisier's case. In brief, Cavendish's theory of the "solution of metals in acids" was that all metals are deprived of phlogiston by acids and that the reactions are the result of affinities. To encompass mercury and the noble metals alongside the ordinary ones within his general theory, Cavendish had to engage in some tangled reasoning.[43] What is of enduring interest here is that Cavendish, in his first researches, already revealed himself as the seeker of general laws.

Chemistry emerged as a science in the eighteenth century with the development of pneumatic chemistry and analytical chemistry.[44] Cavendish's place in the history of chemistry is in pneumatic chemistry, and although he came to it through analytical chemistry, in his analysis of arsenic, Cavendish had already revealed himself as a close observer of air. "Air," "effervescence," "vapors," and "fumes" are words that appear throughout his account. Air, as Stephen Hales and Joseph Black had shown, is a chemically active substance, and referring to "air" as just another constituent that passes from substance to substance and sometimes flies off, Cavendish took into account the weight of air in his quantitative analysis of neutral arsenical salt. Although air was an essential consideration in Cavendish's analysis, he did not yet collect it and study it in its own right.

If Cavendish had published his researches on arsenic, he would have come before the world as an accomplished analytical chemist. But, as we have said, he did not write up his researches for publication but for a friend, who was a chemist and working on related problems. In going from the draft to the actual letter, or a copy of it, Cavendish made revealing changes in wording. Whereas in the draft he expressed his opinions, such as his differences with Macquer forcefully, in the final draft he left much of the forcefulness out or toned it down. Even in the semi-privacy of a correspondence, this man of strong feelings was guarded.

As it was, arsenical acid became known to the chemical world at large through a publication in 1775 by the Swedish chemist Carl Wilhelm Scheele, who became celebrated for his discoveries of this and other acids. That Cavendish's work was unknown is borne out by Scheele's remark that he did not know of any work on arsenic since Macquer's. Scheele's numerous experiments were less quantitative than Cavendish's, but the reasoning

behind his experiments was much the same: arsenic contains the "inflammable principle," phlogiston, which can be separated from it by nitric acid, leaving behind arsenic acid.[45]

Before we discuss Cavendish's first publication in chemistry two years later, we need briefly to discuss the one other early chemical research of his, done probably about the same time as his research on arsenic. This research was on tartar,[46] a deposit found on the sides of casks of wine, a hard, thick crust, red or white depending on the color of the wine. When crystallized by evaporation, it forms another crust, "cream of tartar," an acid. Cavendish's interest seems to have been in determining the amount of alkali in this acid, cream of tartar (potassium hydrogen tartrate), and in the soluble tartar (normal potassium tartrate). The stimulus no doubt was a publication in 1764 by the German chemist Andreas Sigismund Marggraf, who showed that tartar, despite its reputation as an acid, contains an alkali.[47] Like arsenic, then, tartar had what seemed to be contradictory properties, and we suppose that Cavendish was drawn to investigate these specific substances for the similar problem they posed. He was drawn to the chemists who worked on these substances too for the kind of work they did in general. In the case of arsenic it was Macquer, in the case of tartar, Marggraf. Caspar Neumann's pupil, famous for his precision, Marggraf has been called the originator of chemical analysis.[48] Once again, John Hadley suggests himself as Cavendish's

---

[43]William Lewis, one other chemical author besides Macquer cited by Cavendish, in the previous year, 1763, had published a book on practical chemistry, in which he said that when gold is dissolved in aqua regia (nitric acid mixed with hydrochloric), the nitric acid flies off. *Commercium Philosophico-Technicum,* 99. This observation enabled Cavendish to include even gold in his general rule that nitric acid dissolves metal readiest and yet has least affinity to metals. Not gold but the phlogiston of gold unites with the nitric acid, which comes off as vapor. Like gold, arsenic is deprived of its phlogiston only by nitric acid.

[44]Crosland, "The Development of Chemistry," 371.

[45]Karl Wilhelm Scheele, *The Chemical Essays of Charles-William Scheele,* trans. with additions by T. Beddoes (London, 1786), 143–46.

[46]Cavendish did two sets of experiments, describing them on numbered sheets: "Old Expert on Tartar," 10 ff., and "New Exper. on Tartar," 24 ff. plus 6 more sheets. Cavendish, Sci Mss II, 2(a) and 2(b), respectively.

[47]Thorpe, in Cavendish, *Sci. Pap.* 2:301. Cavendish discovered the true nature of cream of tartar and its relationship to soluble tartar: J. R. Partington, *A Short History of Chemistry,* 2d ed. (London: Macmillan, 1951), 104.

[48]Called that by Thomas Thomson, quoted in J. R. Partington, *A History of Chemistry,* vol. 2 (London: Macmillan, 1961), 724.

correspondent. A great admirer of Marggraf, Hadley in his Cambridge lectures said that Marggraf was the master of his science, the "most uncommonly Eminent whether we consider his ingenuity in Contriving, his practical Skill in conducting his Experiments, or his Sagacity and judgment in the Conclusions he draws from them."[49] Like arsenic, tartar was a fantastic substance, though in its own, very different way. The spectacular effects of experimenting on tartar were remarked on by every chemist who wrote on the subject, including Hadley, who discussed Hales's production of "fixed air" from the action of acids of tartar;[50] according to Hales, fully a third of the weight of tartar was lost in the air it gave off.[51] So powerful was the release of air that the vessels used in the distilling burst into shivers.[52] It has been suggested that Marggraf gave Scheele the idea of making tartaric acid. In any case, Cavendish again did not publish his work but left the analysis to Scheele, who made tartar the subject of his first, memorable paper.[53] Given the conspicuous presence of air in tartar and its compounds, in his chemical analysis of tartar Cavendish was halfway to pneumatic chemistry.

Before Cavendish appeared in print under his own name, an example of his chemical analysis appeared in a paper by William Heberden. Heberden was himself highly knowledgeable in chemistry, having lectured on it in connection with medicine at Cambridge, but in this examination he deferred to a superior, if still unknown, chemist, Cavendish. Heberden's brother, Thomas, had collected a fossil alkali from the lip of a volcano, a place where brimstone might be expected but not a salt like this. From experiments "made and communicated to me by the Hon. Henry Cavendish," Heberden laid down, and set off in quotation marks, a set of propositions about the salt in question. Cavendish found that this salt differed from the vegetable alkali in that it crystallized without the addition of "fixed air," and here, in a footnote, he cited Black's experiments on magnesia alba, the famous experiments on fixed air, which together with Hales's earlier experiments on air released from bodies, provided the foundation of eighteenth-century pneumatic chemistry. In this chemical examination of a mineral for his friend Heberden, Cavendish may have been encouraged to begin, if he was not already set upon, his course as a pneumatic chemist.[54]

At this point we need to discuss Black's work. Cavendish's senior by three years, Black in 1756 published an enlarged, English version of his medical thesis at the University of Edinburgh, "Experiments upon Magnesia Alba, Quicklime, and Some Other Alcaline Substances." The origin of this, Black's only major publication, was practical, the medical problem of urinary-tract stones. In it Black dealt briefly with the medical virtues of magnesia but mostly with its chemistry. At age twenty-seven, already a master of the chemical art, Black had an advantage that Cavendish did not, a great teacher of chemistry in William Cullen, who regarded chemistry as a science with laws as fixed as those of mechanics. Black informed himself of the wider world of chemistry, and like Cavendish, he looked to Marggraf for inspiration, a reason for, or a reflection of, the closeness of Black's and Cavendish's work in general. Black told Cullen that he would rather have written what Marggraf had written than anything else in the library of chemistry. Black showed his knowledge of the chemist's standard practice, determining, for example, the place of magnesia in Geoffroy's table of affinities, but his originality in chemistry began with his observation that when subjected to fire, magnesia lost a great proportion of its weight and that the lost portion was air. His experiments on magnesia led him to the nature of quicklime, that most caustic of substances. The causticity is inherent in alkali, Black concluded, made manifest when the alkali is deprived of its air. He showed that this same air, "fixed air" (not an original term), is found in other alkalis and that it is different from common air. Like Hales, whom he acknowledged, (and like

[49]Coleby, "John Hadley," 295.
[50]Ibid. 298.
[51]Antoine Baumé, *Manual de chymie, ou exposé des opérations et des produits d'un cours de chymie. Ouvrage utile aux personnes qui veulent suivre un cours de cette science, ou qui ont dessein de se former un cabinet de chymie* (Paris, 1763), 392.
[52]Antoine Laurent Lavoisier, *Essays on the Effects Produced by Various Processes on Atmospheric Air; with a Particular View to an Investigation of the Constitution of the Acids*, trans T. Henry (Warrington, 1783), 7.
[53]Partington, *History* 2:729. Thomas Thomson, *The History of Chemistry*, 2 vols. (London, 1830), 2:63.
[54]William Heberden, "Some Account of a Salt Found on the Pic of Teneriffe," *PT* 55 (1765): 57–60. This paper was read at the Royal Society on 7 Feb. 1764. In his analysis, Cavendish mentioned vitriolated tartar, which connected with his independent study of tartar.

Cavendish), Black did not begin his investigation with air but concluded with it. Like Hales and other chemists, he had observed that in their operations, "part of a body has vanished from their senses," and he intended to study this vanishing part, air, in itself, but he did not, leaving it to Cavendish and others. More than anyone before him, Black used the chemical balance to advantage, and in this too Cavendish was to follow in Black's footsteps.[55]

Chemistry had its unifying concepts, one of which was phlogiston, the inflammable principle, and another was acid: it was thought that there might be only one acid, or Stahl's "saline principle," vitriolic acid, of which the others were modifications.[56] Likewise, there might be only one solvent, water.[57] There was definitely only one air: it was one of the four elements or principles, which cannot be resolved into others, the others being earth, water, and fire.[58] In the course of the eighteenth century, chemistry would become more complex before it would become simpler again. Cavendish's first publication would reject the notion of a single air.

Air is Cavendish's subject, as he made clear in the opening sentences of his first publication, in 1766, "Three Papers, Containing Experiments on Factitious Air." The usual meaning of "fixed air" was any sort of air (or "gas," a contemporary word Cavendish did not use) contained in bodies; Cavendish had a specific meaning for it, the air by that name, which Black had studied. Since it was only one species of "fixed air," to avoid confusion Cavendish replaced it by Robert Boyle's word, "factitious." By "factitious air," Cavendish understood "any kind of air which is contained in other bodies in an inelastic state, and is produced from thence by art."[59] The first factitious air he described was new, but the name he gave to it, "inflammable air," was not. "Inflammable air" is a descriptive term—for it is our inflammable gas hydrogen—and it also corresponds to Cavendish's identification of it with the "inflammable" principle or substance, phlogiston. Cavendish's discrimination between different factitious airs in this first paper was the beginning of a concerted search by chemists for new kinds of air (gases); over the next ten years, a dozen would be discovered, by Cavendish and by others who followed.[60]

Cavendish found that three metals (zinc, iron, and tin) when dissolved in either of two acids (spirit of salt and dilute vitriolic acid) give off an inflammable air. This air, he convinced himself, came entirely from the metals and not at all from the acids. He had good reasons for thinking this: first, the inflammable air was the same whether he used the one acid or the other, and second, the same air was generated from different substances, vegetable and animal. He saw no reason to think that this inflammable air was anything other than phlogiston. What is important about this probable identification for our understanding of Cavendish's chemistry is that he regarded phlogiston not as a "principle," as some chemists did, but as a substance insofar as it had determinable properties like any other. He collected this substance, inflammable air, in bottles inverted in water and suspended by strings, much as Hales had done, and he weighed it and measured its specific gravity and compared it with that of water and common air.

Cavendish's first published paper is, in fact, "three papers," which make them hard to discuss without introducing confusion; the first paper, on inflammable air, was read to the Royal Society in May 1766, the second and third six months later, after the summer recess, in November. The three papers are distinct but related studies. The second paper, or part two as it is usually called, is about Black's "fixed air," and it proceeds in the same

---

[55] Henry Guerlac, "Black, Joseph," *DSB* 2:173–83; "Joseph Black and Fixed Air. A Bicentenary Retrospective, with Some New or Little Known Material," *Isis* 48 (1957): 124–51. William Ramsay, *The Life and Letters of Joseph Black, M.D.* (London: Constable, 1918), 4–5, 14–15. The observation that inspired Black's and his followers' enquiry was that "chemists have often observed, in their distillations, that part of a body has vanished from their senses, notwithstanding the utmost care to retain it; and they have always found, upon further inquiry that subtle part to be air, which having been imprisoned in the body, under a solid form, was set free and rendered fluid and elastic by the fire." Joseph Black, *Experiments upon Magnesia Alba, Quicklime, and Some Other Alkaline Substances*, 1756 (Edinburgh, Alembic Club Reprints, No. 1, 1898), quotation on 16.

[56] The "universal acid," in Hadley, *A Plan of a Course of Chemical Lectures*, 5. Discussion of Stahl's "saline principle" in Macquer, *Dictionary* 2:634.

[57] Water, the "universal menstruum," dissolving all bodies either immediately or with the aid of acids or alkalis. Neumann, *Chemical Works*, 258.

[58] Macquer, *Elements*, 2. From author to author, there were variations on these principles. Baumé's *Manuel de chymie*, for instance, was divided into five sections, one for phlogiston as well as one each for the four elements of the Greek tradition; Baumé says it is difficult to determine the exact number of elements, p. 16. A. M. Duncan, "The Functions of Affinity Tables and Lavoisier's List of Elements," *Ambix* 17 (1970): 26–42, on 36–37.

[59] Cavendish, "Three Papers, Containing Experiments on Factitious Air," *PT* 56 (1766): 141–84; in *Sci. Pap.* 2: 77–101, on 77.

[60] Henry Guerlac, "Joseph Black and Fixed Air," 454–56.

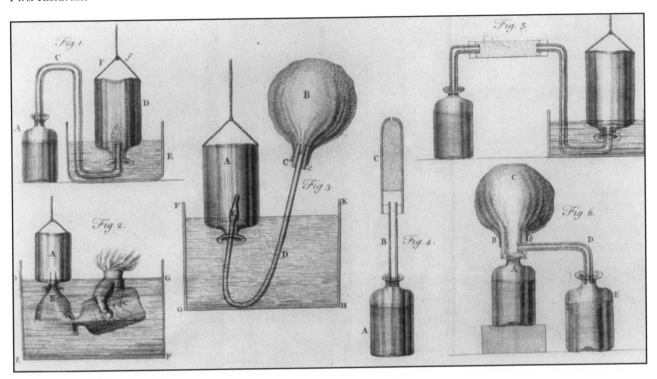

PLATE II. Factitious-Air Apparatus. Figure 1 gives Cavendish's technique for filing a bottle D with air. The bottle is first filled with water and inverted in the vessel of water E; the air to be captured is generated by dissolving metals in acids and by other means in bottle A. His measure of the quantity of air is the weight of the water it displaces in D. Figure 2 shows how he transfers air from one bottle to another. Figure 3 shows how he withdraws air from a bottle by means of a bladder. The speckled substance in Figures 4 and 5 is dry pearl ashes through which air is passed to free it from water and acid. "Three Papers, Containing Experiments on Factitious Air," *Philosophical Transactions* 56 (1766): 141.

manner as the first; what Cavendish did, in effect, was to set out and follow the form of a new kind of study, that of factitious airs. As he did for inflammable air, he examined the physical properties of fixed air, and as he did for the quantity of inflammable air in metals, he determined the quantity of fixed air in alkaline substances. In this part, he replaced the water in the collecting trough by mercury, since fixed air dissolves in water and not in mercury (as he determined by standing an inverted flask of it in mercury for "upwards of a year," which places the beginning of his research on air at least as far back as 1765).[61] He made the weights of fixed air in various alkalis meaningful by expressing their weights relative to the weights of the alkalis required to saturate an acid; he used as his standard one thousand grains of the alkali marble.

The point of departure of Cavendish's third paper, or part three, was the work on fermented and putrefied substances by David Macbride. Macbride, five years Cavendish's senior, a physician in Ireland, published a book of experiments in 1764 designed to show that fixed air is the cement of living bodies and that a putrefying body

falls apart because it loses this cement. Macbride took his understanding of fixed air from Hales, and he also cited Black, the first to do so in print.[62] Cavendish looked to see if fermentation and putrefaction yielded any factitious airs other than Black's fixed air. He compared the air from fermented sugar with that from marble in acid and found the two to be probably the same, fixed air. He also obtained air from putrefying gravy broth and raw meat, which he found to be a mixture of fixed air and inflammable air, neither pure.

There is a fourth paper in this group, which Cavendish carefully drafted for publication but then did not submit. If his third paper was less decisive than his first two, his fourth paper was even less so. It again was about vegetable and animal substances, this time about wood, tartar (his old friend), and hartshorn (bone) treated by distillation.[63] He obtained

---

[61]Cavendish, "Three Papers," 88.
[62]E. L. Scott, "The 'Macbridean Doctrine' of Air; an Eighteenth-Century Explanation of Some Biochemical Processes Including Photosynthesis," *Ambix* 17 (1970): 43–57, on 44–49.
[63]This unpublished paper is printed: "Experiments on Factitious Air. Part IV. Containing Experiments on the Air Produced

a mixture of gases, flammable and nonflammable, which he could not satisfactorily isolate.[64] He returned to this subject later, as we know from his laboratory notes, but with no more success. His unreachable goal was a comprehensive, systematic treatment of the new field of pneumatic chemistry, as it would he his goal in the other major experimental fields he addressed, electricity and heat.

There was one more paper, an addendum to his first, and written as if for publication. It was a fuller version of his discussion of the solution of metals in acids begun in his arsenic research, and it was just as tentatively expressed. It begins: "If it is not digressing too much," and goes on, "I have not indeed made sufficient experiments to speak quite positively as to this point."[65] He was not, however, tentative in his own conviction; at least, there is no indication he doubted that "no metallic substance . . . can dissolve in acids without being deprived of its phlogiston" and that the differences of behavior between different metals in acids are due to different affinities between the metals, the acids, and phlogiston. It is clear why he should have wanted this digression, since his discussion of inflammable air was incomplete in the first paper. There he identified this air with phlogiston, which by his theory is contained in all metals, and so for completeness, he should have discussed metals beyond the three of his first paper, zinc, iron, and tin. In the digression, he discussed experiments that gave signs of inflammable air, such as effervescence, but for the most part he had to fall back on theoretical arguments of affinities to give a systematic account of the phlogiston of all metals.

In any case, Cavendish's experiments on factitious air discredited the old notion of a single, universal air, and in so doing he laid out a new field of discovery. That work alone would entitle Cavendish to a memorable place in the history of science, but he was just beginning.

Cavendish has at the same time an important place in the history of the British contribution to science in the eighteenth century. His earlier chemical researches on arsenic and tartar began with foreign work, but his work on gases did not. In connection with gases, he cited seven authors, all British. Building on what was already a British tradition, he gave strong direction to the work of his British colleagues.[66]

From his early chemical studies, Cavendish published one more paper, in the following year, 1767.[67] This, an analysis of a mineral water, did not have the same significance as his first publication, but it further demonstrated his chemical skills. Mineral waters were a prominent subject in chemistry, as is evident from John Hadley's Cambridge lectures, which devote fifteen pages to this subject.[68] Cavendish's second paper was read to the Royal Society in February 1767, just three months after the last part of his first paper on factitious air was read. There was actually an overlap, since in the unpublished fourth part of his first paper, he referred to this second paper. His chemical researches of the 1760s, published and unpublished, were closely connected.

Cavendish's mineral water was not taken from the shelf, like arsenic. The substance occurred naturally, the water from a London pump, at Rathbone-Place. Produced by a spring, the water until "a few years ago" was raised by an engine for use by a part of London. Now a pump remained, from which Cavendish drew his sample, an evil looking water, "foul to the eye," on which a "scurf" formed upon standing. Cavendish chose this water to investigate for its unwholesomeness, or for a slightly more technical reason having to do with sediments.

Pump water was studied for practical reasons, for manufactures, drinks, medicine, and above all health. In the same year as Cavendish's paper, and probably related to it, a paper on London pump water was published by his friend William Heberden as the first paper in the first volume of the *Medical Transactions* of the College of Physicians. All of the waters Heberden examined had a "yellowish cast" and were distasteful and unhealthy, and yet some Londoners drank them. Heberden advised against that practice: Londoners,

from Vegetable and Animal Substances by Distillation," in Cavendish, *Sci. Pap.* 2:307–15.

[64]The mixture, we know, contained marsh gas, carbonic oxide, and hydrogen. Thorpe, in Cavendish, *Sci. Pap.* 2: 315–16.

[65]"On the Solution of Metals in Acids. Digression to Paper on Inflammable Air," in Cavendish, *Sci. Pap.* 2:305–7, on 305.

[66]The authors Cavendish cited are: Black, Cotes, Hadley, Hales, Hauksbee, Lewis, and Macbride. Three of these he cited in the unpublished part 4 and digression. There was one tangential reference to a foreign work, though no authors were given: the French publication in 1762 on the measurement of a degree in Peru.

[67]"Experiments on Rathbone-Place Water," *PT* 57 (1767): 92–108; in Cavendish, *Sci. Pap.* 2:102–11.

[68]Coleby, "John Hadley," 300–1.

he said, should not drink the pump waters but the purer Thames water, which gives us an indication of the foulness of London water in general. The best course, Heberden said, was to distill water, for example, by Hales's method.[69] In the 1760s London was an unhealthy place, but this was also the decade in which London began systematically to improve itself, beginning with the Westminster Paving Act of 1762. London was described a few years later:

> Beneath the pavements are vast subterraneous sewers arched over to convey away the waste water which in other cities is so noisome above ground, and at a less depth are buried wooden pipes that supply every house plentifully with water, conducted by leaden pipes into kitchens or cellars, three times a week for the trifling expence of three shillings per quarter.[70]

Lead pipes may not sound like an improvement, but under the circumstances they probably were. As we would expect, Cavendish's study of pump water was not motivated by a concern for the health of Londoners but by a scientific question. He wanted to know the cause of the suspended earth, which could not be neutralized by any acid.

The occasion for this research was evidently a paper in the *Philosophical Transactions* in 1765 by William Brownrigg, a physician in Whitehaven who studied the foul air from James Lowther's mines. Brownrigg wanted to know if the coal damps that caused the miners's misery were at the same time similar to the cause of the medicinal virtue of mineral waters. His paper of 1765 reported that spa water in Germany released fixed air when it was heated.[71] Looking to see if the same was true of Rathbone-Place water, Cavendish arrived at the answer to his question: the reason for the suspension of earth in Rathbone-Place water was its union with more than its normal amount of fixed air.[72] He concluded his study by looking at three other London waters, including water from a pump near his house on Great Marlborough Street. Cavendish did no more with the subject of mineral waters, but it was actively developed by other leading chemists of the time, such as Joseph Priestley, Torbern Bergman, and Bryan Higgens, and Cavendish followed their work.[73]

Writing about the analysis of waters a few years later, the Swedish chemist Torbern Bergman said that it was "one of the most difficult problems in chemistry" because the quantities were so small and there were so many impurities in the water.[74] For the same reasons, this was just the kind of problem to show off Cavendish's skills as a chemist. But these had already been shown and acknowledged: for his work the year before on factitious air, he had been awarded the Copley Medal of the Royal Society.

That year, 1766, two others shared the Copley Medal with Cavendish: Brownrigg for his analysis of mineral water, which we have discussed, and Edward Delaval for his study of the colors of metal films. Delaval, who had been Cavendish's contemporary at Cambridge, was now a fellow of his college there, Pembroke Hall, and a chemist. His experiments on thin metal deposits on glass showed that metals differ in color in the order of their density: the metal gold and the color red, the metal lead and the color orange, silver and yellow, copper and green, and iron and blue. Delaval regarded his work as an extension of Newton's on the relation of the dimensions of thin plates to the colors they produce.[75] His paper was a paper on chemical optics. The year 1766 was the year of the chemists.

Before we leave this discussion of Cavendish's first publications, we want to say something more about one of his sources, William Brownrigg. We have pointed out Brownrigg's connection with Sir James Lowther, an active member of the Royal Society and a relative of Lord Charles and Henry

---

69William Heberden, "Remarks on the Pump-Water of London, and on the Methods of Procuring the Purest Water," *Medical Transactions* 1 (1767): 1–22, on 2, 19.

70M. Dorothy George, *London Life in the Eighteenth Century* (Harmondsworth: Penguin Books, 1966), 110–11.

71William Brownrigg, "An Experimental Enquiry into the Mineral Elastic Spirit, or Air, Contained in Spa Water; as Well as into the Mephitic Qualities of this Spirit," *PT* 55 (1765): 218–35. J. Russell-Wood, "The Scientific Work of William Brownrigg, M.D., F.R.S. (1711–1800).—I," *Annals of Science* 6 (1950): 436–47, on 436–38, 441.

72Cavendish, "Experiments on Rathebone-Place Water," 107.

73Cavendish's papers contain a table comparing the analyses of seltzer, spa, and Pyrmont waters by Bergman and Higgens. Cavendish Mss, Misc. This table would have been prepared after Bergman's analyses of mineral waters in the 1770s, probably after 1778.

74Torbern Bergman, "Of the Analysis of Waters," in his *Physical and Chemical Essays*, trans. with notes by Edmund Cullen, vol. 1 (London, 1784), 91–192, on 109.

75Edward Delaval, "A Letter . . . Containing Experiments and Observations on the Agreement between the Specific Gravities of the Several Metals, and Their Colours When United to Glass, as Well as Those of Their Other Preparations," *PT* 55 (1765): 10–38.

Cavendish. In 1741 Lowther communicated a paper by Brownrigg to the Royal Society, entitled "Some Observations upon the Several Damps in the Coal Mines Near Whitehaven." Since that paper is found among Henry Cavendish's scientific manuscripts at Chatsworth, the suggestion is that Cavendish knew of this early work on air by Brownrigg and took an interest in it. British fascination with air had its origins in part in the violence of its mining industry. Brownrigg studied the two kinds of coal damps, the fire damp which catches fire explosively, and the choke damp which puts out fire (and life). If the fire damp is ignited deep inside a mine, "the Consequence is the most dreadful imaginable," with "an explosion equal to that of Gunpowder," killing "every living thing" near and far. After the explosion, the fire damp becomes choke damp, "a deadly Poison."[76] Brownrigg referred to Hales's recent experiments on elastic air, and in the next year, 1742, Hales addressed the same problem in the Royal Society, the foul air inside mines.[77] A sequel by Brownrigg to his paper on "mineral exhalations" was again presented by Lowther and read at several meetings in early 1742, and in it he addressed "Mineral Waters" as well.[78] This paper concluded with a discussion of the usefulness of a knowledge of mineral exhalations for "discovering the nature and properties of common Air."[79] Common air was the principal subject of interest to Henry Cavendish throughout his work in the chemistry of "airs." Through Lowther, a family connection may have become a scientific connection for Cavendish. Brownrigg's work was, in any case, a direct stimulus for Cavendish's work on mineral waters and perhaps too on the chemistry of air.

Heat

At about the same time that Cavendish performed his first dated chemical experiments, he began a series of experiments on specific and latent heats, which he recorded in an untitled, unindexed packet of 117 numbered small sheets.[80] The experiments are rarely dated; the first and earliest date, 5 February 1765, occurs only near the end of the record. But the few dates given are in order, and the sequence of experiments follows a natural progression of questions and answers. These sheets, in fact, make compelling reading, conveying the feel of experimental research leading to

important and unanticipated results. Although Cavendish did sometimes reorder the notes of his experiments for his own reference, the interruption of chronology is generally slight and obvious; for example, occasionally in a group of heat experiments, the "3rd exp." will be followed by the "1st exp." These sheets were not the original slips containing the measurements taken in the laboratory but an intermediate record, from which Cavendish later wrote a proper paper. Although this paper is still in rough draft, it is carefully worked out; Cavendish wrote it with an unidentified, specific reader in mind, "you."[81] This person too could have been John Hadley.[82]

Whereas we can speak with some confidence of what inspired Cavendish's earliest chemical experiments, the origin of his heat experiments is less clear to us. In a broad sense, however, these experiments are readily intelligible. Cavendish's father took great interest in thermometry, and others at the same time were working on the same subject. Then there is a matter of timing: just as Cavendish came forward as a scientist, in the 1760s, the experimental field of heat emerged as a quantitative science. Central to this development was the clear distinction between, and the relationship between, thermometer readings and quantities of heat. The quantitative concepts of specific and latent heats were the particular subject of Cavendish's researches. Although the immediate inspiration for Cavendish's heat experiments is probably unknowable, a reasonable speculation can be made about it.

Apart from Cavendish's own, the most important researches on heat and chemistry in Britain were not made in London. What Cavendish knew of them he learned from publications or by

[76]Royal Society, JB 17:239–43 (16 Apr. 1741).
[77]Royal Society, JB 17:403 (6 May 1742). Brownrigg's paper prompted Hales and Sloane to urge him to write a history of coal damps, which he did but did not publish.
[78]Royal Society, JB 17:394 (8 Apr. 1742).
[79]Royal Society, JB 17:405 (13 May 1742).
[80]Henry Cavendish Mss III(a), untitled bundle.
[81]Henry Cavendish, "Experiments on Heat," *Sci. Pap.* 2:327–47. Cavendish's experiments on heat are described in Vernon Harcourt, "Address," *British Association Report*, 1839, pp. 3–68, on pp. 45–50; and in Wilson, *Cavendish*, 446–54. Both of these commentators are concerned mainly with claims of priority in the discovery of specific and latent heats.
[82]In his chemical lectures, Hadley talked about heat, and it would seem that he held, as Cavendish did, the motion theory of heat. Coleby, "John Hadley," 298.

> **books**

The Scientist Who Weighed The World

"Cavendish: The Experimental Life," by Christa Jungnickel and Russell McCormmach, Bucknell University Press, 1999, 814 pages, **$34.50** (ISBN 0-8387-5445-7)

Reviewed by **George B. Kauffman**

It was during my early adolescence that I first encountered the name of Henry Cavendish, the 18th-century English chemist and natural philosopher whose family name graces the Cavendish Laboratory at Cambridge University. I was intrigued by the wealthy misogynistic recluse who communicated with his servants by means of notes and was said to have had a second set of stairs built at the back of his house after he had accidentally met a maid with a broom and pail on the existing stairs.

So I looked forward to reading Christa Jungnickel and Russell McCormmach's biography, "Cavendish: The Experimental Life," to learn more about one of chemistry's "greats," whom I had previously known only through a few anecdotes. I was not disappointed.

I learned that my youthful picture of Cavendish's character—the standard portrait of the man for almost a century and a half—was derived largely from the first book-length biography, "The Life of the Honourable Henry Cavendish," by George Wilson, published in 1851. This Victorian scholar depicted Cavendish as "a man lacking in piety, family, philanthropy, and poetry; estranged from humanity." A. J. Berry, in the second biography, "Henry Cavendish: His Life and Scientific Work," in 1960 repeated Wilson's phrase about Cavendish's "striking deficiencies as a human being."

In contrast, Jungnickel and McCormmach present a balanced, complete picture of the whole man from a variety of sources. The Cavendish who emerges is taciturn, solitary, awkward, and antisocial; not "without feelings, only without warmth." His strangeness, they conclude, "may have had less to do with his 'peculiarities' than with his single-minded scientific drive. . . . His life *was* his science." He was very reserved, but so were many of his contemporaries. Shy among strangers, he interacted fully with scientists he knew.

Wilson characterized Cavendish as a "confirmed woman-hater." Jungnickel

Henry Cavendish

and McCormmach present a milder picture, citing his saving a woman from the attack of a mad cow, his willingness to work with his close associate Charles Blagden in the presence of Blagden's wife, and his friendship with his cousin-in-law, Lady Georgianna Spencer, Duchess of Devonshire, to whom he may even have acted as a scientific tutor.

More than three decades in the making and over 800 pages in length, "Cav-

endish: The Experimental Life" is a thorough and extensive revision of the husband-and-wife team's earlier and shorter (414 pages) book, "Cavendish," published by the American Philosophical Society in 1996. Their earlier book received that society's John Frederick Lewis Award. Both books were published posthumously on the part of Jungnickel, who died in 1990.

McCormmach incorporated a large number of new primary and secondary sources (34 archives were consulted) into the new biography to correct previous errors and offer a more satisfying and, in some respects, new interpretation of Cavendish. Part 4, "Henry Cavendish's Scientific Letters," which, at 215 pages, represents one-quarter of the book, is entirely new. The 113 letters (six translated from French) to 37 correspondents and written from 1766 to 1805 reveal more of the taciturn scientist than his more widely studied publications do.

The authors have left no stone unturned in unearthing every conceivable piece of information in incredible—almost overwhelming—detail and in providing contextual background about almost every person, place, or thing mentioned in the narrative. Even the number of shelves in Cavendish's library and the names of guests at various dinners are recorded. On many pages the notes and references are far longer than the text itself.

Like a symphony by Mahler or Bruckner, the book is a monumental tour de force in richness, length, and development at a leisurely pace. It is actually a dual biography of both Henry Cavendish (1731–1810) and his less well-known father, Lord Charles (1704–83), a scientist in his own right, active member of the House of Commons, and, for 40 years, an important figure in the organization of science, particularly in the affairs of the Royal Society. The book begins with the 1680s, when science began to dominate educated thought in Western Europe, and concludes at the beginning of the 19th century.

Henry Cavendish has been called "one of the greatest scientists of his century . . . a scion of the most powerful aristocratic families, a scientific fanatic, and a neurotic of the first order." French scientist Jean-Baptiste Biot called him "the wisest of the rich and the richest of

(image credit, vertical:) AIP Emilio Segrè Visual Archives

Lab program includes deaf scientists

When Gina MacDonald, an assistant professor of chemistry at James Madison University, Harrisonburg, Va., saw a group of deaf teenagers in a local shopping mall, she was startled to realize that she never saw deaf students in her biochemistry classes.

Shortly afterward, MacDonald was recruiting high-school science teachers to be part of a summer research program in chemistry at James Madison sponsored by the National Science Foundation. MacDonald decided to contact Virginia School for the Deaf & Blind in nearby Staunton to see if a teacher there would be interested in doing summer research in her lab.

It wasn't very carefully thought out in advance, MacDonald admits, but her telephone call is reaping results. In 1998, Michael B. Marzolf, a science teacher at Virginia School for the Deaf & Blind who is deaf, spent five weeks in MacDonald's lab. Last summer, he returned for a second session, this time joined by Dorothy Wynne, who teaches science at the Model Secondary School for the Deaf in Washington, D.C., and by Jason Dietz, a deaf student from New York City who this fall entered Gallaudet University in Washington, D.C., a university primarily for students who are deaf and hard of hearing.

The idea, Marzolf explains, is to help high-school science teachers bring new ideas to their own students after the summer is over. The first summer, he worked with an undergraduate student from James Madison who was preparing to teach high-school chemistry. "I taught her what to expect from high-school students studying chemistry, and she taught me new and up-to-date lab techniques," Marzolf says.

One of the benefits of having deaf students and teachers in the James Madison program, MacDonald suggests, is that it gives the rest of the students an opportunity to realize how easy it is to interact with deaf people as colleagues. Marzolf, Wynne, and Dietz joined in all the activities of the summer research students, including parties, a canoe trip, and research presentations. A signing interpreter came to the university each morning to facilitate communication, but the rest of the time people communicated by using a few basic phrases of sign language and by writing things down.

Rebecca Rawls

Dietz (left) adds saline buffer to a chromatography column as Marzolf, MacDonald, and Wynne look on.

CIRCLE **2** ON READER SERVICE CARD

CIRCLE **12** ON READER SERVICE CARD

he wise," and the authors correctly consider him "the most important English scientist between Isaac Newton and James Clerk Maxwell."

A grandson of the Duke of Devonshire and the Duke of Kent, Henry was educated at Hackney Academy and Cambridge University at a time when Newton's "Principia," which had a lasting influence on his scientific work, dominated the curriculum. After leaving Cambridge without receiving his degree and spending some time on a tour of the Continent, he lived in London with his father until the latter's death, whereupon Henry became a millionaire.

Disdaining politics, "the lifeblood of the family," he became active in 1760 in the committees and councils of the Royal Society—in which he was the most scientifically eminent member—as well as a number of associated scientific social clubs, whose inside workings are vividly portrayed. He became a cautious theorist and master experimentalist who applied his painstaking quantitative technique to a variety of problems in chemistry, mechanics, theories of electricity and heat, mathematics, astronomy, geology, meteorology, and applied sciences. He published no books, only papers, and all in one journal, the *Philosophical Transactions of the Royal Society*.

In his last published article in 1798, he used a torsion balance to measure the force of gravitational attraction and from that calculated the value of the gravitational constant, G, and the mean density and mass of Earth. His value for Earth's density, 5.48 g per mL, is within 1% of today's accepted value. This so-called Cavendish experiment, popularly known as the weighing of the Earth, was recently called "the first modern physics experiment."

Cavendish left behind a large number of unpublished manuscripts, among them his hollow-globe experiment on the law of electrical attraction and repulsion, carried out before and independently of similar work by French physicist Charles Augustin de Coulomb. This experiment has been discussed perhaps more than any other unpublished scientific experiment.

A prominent contributor to pneumatic chemistry, Cavendish devised several types of eudiometers (instruments used to study gases) and thermometers, was the first to collect water-soluble gases over mercury, and investigated the composition of air. He is usually credited with discovering hydrogen, having been the first to describe systematically what he called "inflammable gas" and to distinguish it from other gases. He was the first to measure the densities of different gases. He demonstrated that hydrogen, on burning in air or "dephlogisticated air" (oxygen), produces water, thereby showing that water is a compound, not an element. He also discovered nitrous acid and, like Daniel Rutherford, is considered an independent discoverer of nitrogen.

Cavendish's virtually forgotten paper of 1785 reporting his inability to eliminate by oxidation or absorption a tiny residual bubble from atmospheric nitrogen is an excellent example of the value of the history of chemistry to practicing chemists. The work led Sir William Ramsay and Lord Rayleigh to discover argon, the first noble gas, more than a century later.

A defender of the phlogiston theory—the dominant 18th-century scientific view in which combustion was thought to release a substance called phlogiston—Cavendish at first opposed the new ideas proposed by French chemist Antoine-Laurent Lavoisier, including his rejection of phlogiston, theory of acids, and new systematic nomenclature. By 1787, however, Cavendish had renounced phlogiston, making him probably the first in Britain to do so.

Before Lavoisier's "new chemistry" was generally accepted, an earlier "new" chemistry, which involved quantitative exactness and an evaluation of errors, was brought into being largely through Cavendish's accurate work. (His balance was the earliest of the great precision balances of the 18th century.) From the very beginning of his chemical researches, he recorded equivalent weights, which prefigured such quantitative laws as the law of combining proportions, and he introduced the word "equivalent."

Copiously illustrated with 113 figures (portraits, maps, buildings, letters, handwritten manuscripts, and sketches and photographs of apparatus and instruments) as well as family trees, Cavendish's chronology and publications, officers of the Royal Society, and a 45-page bibliography, this book is the definitive biography of this enigmatic scientist.

George B. Kauffman is professor of chemistry at California State University, Fresno, and winner of the Dexter Award in the history of chemistry. ◄

Organic Thin Films: Structure and Applications. *ACS Symposium Series 695.* Curtis W. Frank, editor. xiv + 402 pages. American Chemical Society. Distributed by Oxford University Press, 198 Madison Ave., New York, NY 10016. (http://www.oup-usa.org). 1998. $135.

Pesticide Residues in Foods: Methods, Techniques, and Regulations. W. George Fong, et al. xiv + 358 pages. John Wiley & Sons, 605 Third Ave., New York, NY 10158. (http://wiley.com). 1999. $84.95.

Phosphoinositides: Chemistry, Biochemistry, and Biomedical Applications. *ACS Symposium Series 718.* Karol S. Bruzik, editor. xii + 298 pages. American Chemical Society. Distributed by Oxford University Press, 198 Madison Ave., New York, NY 10016. (http://www.oup-usa.org). 1999. $115.

Phosphorus Biogeochemistry of Sub-Tropical Ecosystems. K. R. Reddy, G. A. O'Connor, C. L. Schelske, editors. 448 pages. Lewis Publishers, 2000 N.W. Corporate Blvd., Boca Raton, FL 33431-9868. (http://www.crcpress.com). 1999. $69.95.

Plantwide Process Control. William L. Luyben, Björn D. Tyréus, Michael L. Luyben, editors. xii + 395 pages. McGraw Hill, 11 West 19th St., New York, NY 10011-4285. 1999. $69.95.

Pollution Prevention: Methodologies, Technologies, and Practices. Kenneth L. Mulholland, James A. Dyer. 214 pages. American Institute of Chemical Engineers, AIChExpress Service Center, 3 Park Ave., New York, NY 10016-5901. (http://www.aiche.org). 1999. $175.

Process Chemistry in the Pharmaceutical Industry. Kumar G. Gadmasetti, editor. xxi + 474 pages. Marcel Dekker, 270 Madison Ave., New York, NY 10016-0602. (http://www.dekker.com). 1999. $195.

The Self-Made Tapestry: Pattern Formation in Nature. *ACS Symposium Series 709.* Philip Ball. vi + 287 pages. American Chemical Society, Distributed by Oxford University Press, 198 Madison Ave., New York, NY 10016. (http://www.oup-usa.org). 1998. $37.50.

Sol-Gel Silica: Properties, Processing and Technology Transfer. Larry L. Hench. ix + 168 pages. Noyes Publications, 369 Fairview Ave., Westwood, NJ 07675. 1998. $64.

Solvent-Free Polymerizations and Processes: Minimization of Conventional Organic Solvents. *ACS Symposium Seris 713.* Timothy E. Long, Michael O. Hunt, editors. xii + 292 pages. American Chemical Society. Distributed by Oxford University Press, 198 Madison Ave., New York, NY 10016. (http://www.oup-usa.org). 1998. $113.◄

hearsay. Cavendish mentioned only one name in his experimental notes, "Martin." This reference comes at the end of the packet and probably has nothing to do with the origin of Cavendish's researches on heat.[83] He clearly meant the Scottish physician George Martine, who in 1740 published an account of rates of heating and cooling. In the approximately fair copy of his experiments, he mentioned three names, all in connection with latent heat. One reference was to the French physical scientist Jean Jacques Mairan and the production of heat by the freezing of water, but Mairan's work came twenty-five years earlier.[84] The other two references were to the Scottish chemists Cullen and Black.

Cullen, the older of the two, was professor of medicine and lecturer in chemistry at the University of Glasgow, in whose laboratory Black worked for a time, and whom Black succeeded later as lecturer in chemistry. Cullen moved to the University of Edinburgh as professor of chemistry in 1756, in which position Black again succeeded him ten years later. In 1755 Cullen published an account of the cooling produced by evaporation, which originated in the simple observation by a student that a thermometer cools when it is removed from a solution. Cullen recalled a similar observation by Mairan, and he suspected that evaporation was the cause and made experiments to find out. He evaporated some thirteen liquids, acidic and alkaline, producing cold of "so great a degree" that he thought it had not been observed before, and for this reason he thought this whole subject should be "further examined by experiments."[85] If not from the beginning, by the time Cavendish wrote up his heat experiments, he knew of this work by Cullen and thought well of it.[86] Going much farther than Cullen, Black made a thorough investigation of specific and latent heats, the first to do so.[87] Black published nothing of this work, but he did include it in his lectures.[88] In 1760, originally prompted by Cullen's experiments on the cold produced by evaporation, Black began his experiments on heat.[89] He realized that the commonly held opinion that bodies exchange heat in proportion to their mass was wrong: different kinds of matter communicate heat differently, "for which no general principle or reason" had been given. Black's own reason, based on the concept of specific heat, came to him after reading Martine's

essay on rates of heating and cooling and Hermann Boerhaave's *Elementa Chemiae*.[90] As it happened he came upon the idea of latent heats before that of specific heats, and his clue once again came from Boerhaave's text. Perhaps as early as 1758, before he had done any experiments, he lectured on the heat involved in changes of state of substances. To convey this concept, he gave this homely and effective example: if snow and ice were to melt immediately at the melting temperature, the commonly held view, then every spring the world would suddenly be overwhelmed by floods, which "would tear up and sweep away every thing, and that so suddenly, that mankind should have great difficulty to escape from their ravages." The reason why this did not happen is that it takes a long time for ice and snow to absorb the heat that originally is lost in the change of state of water to ice and snow. Black did experiments to confirm and quantify the "latent heat"—his term—of the liquefaction and solidification of water.[91] None of this information reveals when and what Cavendish knew of Black's work.[92] Both Cullen and Black were great teachers, and Black was a great investigator too, but neither published much research, even compared with the

[83]Cavendish Mss III(a), 9:114. His reference is probably to George Martine's *Essays Medical and Philosophical*, published in London in 1740.[84]Henry Cavendish, "Experiments to Show That Bodies in Changing from a Solid State . . .," *Sci. Pap.* 2:348. His source was probably J. J. d'Ortous de Mairan's *Dissertation sur la glace, ou Explication physique de la formation de la glace, & divers phénoménes* (Paris, 1749).

[85]Cullen's paper was first published in 1755 in the *Edinburgh Philosophical and Literary Essays* and was republished together with Black's essay, *Experiments upon Magnesia Alba, Quick-lime, and Other Alkaline Substances; by Joseph Black. To Which Is Annexed, An Essay on the Cold Produced by Evaporating Fluids, and of Some Other Means of Producing Cold; by William Cullen* (Edinburgh, 1777), 115–33, quotation on 132.

[86]Cavendish wrote: "Dr. Cullen has sufficiently proved that most if not all fluids generate cold by the first species of evaporation." By "first species," Cavendish meant evaporation by heating a liquid but not boiling it, in which case the evaporation was due to absorption by the air. Cavendish, "Experiments on Heat," *Sci. Pap.* 2: 344.

[87]The Swedish physicist Johan Carl Wilcke discovered latent heat independently of Black and later, in 1772, but unlike Black he published his finding. His work on latent and specific heats is discussed in detail in Douglas McKie and Niels H. de V. Heathcote, *The Discovery of Specific and Latent Heats* (London: Arnold, 1935), 54–121.

[88]Black's *Lectures on the Elements of Chemistry*, edited by his pupil John Robison, and published in two volumes in Edinburgh in 1803.

[89]Guerlac, "Black," 177.

[90]Quotation from Black's *Lectures* in McKie and Heathcote, *Discovery*, 13.

[91]Ibid., 16–20, quotation on 16.

[92]Douglas McKie, "On Thos. Cochrane's MS. Notes of Black's Chemical Lectures, 1767–8," *Annals of Science* 1 (1936): 101–10, on 103.

reserved Cavendish. When Cavendish wrote in his paper on heat that he was "informed" that Black had made observations on the heating of a worm tube by condensing water, he meant informed by word of mouth, and that could have happened anywhere at any time. As a regular attender of the meetings of the Royal Society and of the dinners of its club, Cavendish was well placed to learn of Black's work. We think that it was probably from his friend John Hadley that Cavendish heard about Cullen's work and with it Black's. Our evidence is a letter Benjamin Franklin wrote in 1762 in which he described the repetition of one of Cullen's experiments by John Hadley: "Dr. Cullen of Edinburgh, has given some experiments of cooling by evaporation; and I was present at one made by Dr. Hadley, then professor of chemistry at Cambridge, when, by repeatedly wetting the ball of a thermometer with spirit, and quickening the evaporation by the blast of a bellows, the mercury fell from 65, the state of warmth in the common air, to 7, which is 22 degrees below freezing."[93] This was one way that heat experiments in Scotland were learned of in London, and it was probably Cavendish's way, and for him the timing would have been just about right.

Cavendish knew about Black's work while he was still engaged in his own; this we know, because he said so. He had heard about Black's experiment on water in the worm tube of a still, but he did not know how the experiment came out, which is why he repeated it; by then Cavendish and Black were doing parallel researches on heat. It is likely that Cavendish came to his experiments on heat not directly through Black but by more or less the same route that Black took. Cavendish wrote of his findings on specific and latent heats as discoveries, as the theoretically unexpected; his laboratory notes on latent heat reinforce the impression of surprise. Boerhaave's text on chemistry, which guided Black, and which was recommended reading at Cambridge when Cavendish was there,[94] reported on Daniel Gabriel Fahrenheit's experiments on the hardening and melting of a substance, which showed that change of state involves a heat that does not register on the thermometer. Black called this heat "latent heat." Boerhaave also reported on Fahrenheit's comparison of the heating effects of mercury and water: mercury and water, Fahrenheit found, have

different heat capacities, or specific heats.[95] (Fahrenheit was an instrument-maker, a friend of Boerhaave, and a Fellow of the Royal Society, who published papers on meteorological instruments in the *Philosophical Transactions*. His most famous achievement was his thermometer scale, which was adopted in Britain.) Black began his own experiments on heat with an examination of the reliability of the thermometer as a measuring instrument.[96] (Like Cavendish, he did not think it was reliable, as he said in his lectures at about this time: "These /thermometers/ are very usefull in difft. Expts. but very fallacious seldom agreeing for they are liable to some variations."[97]) That concern with thermometers, we think, is the probable origin of Cavendish's experiments too. In addition to Fahrenheit and Boerhaave, Brook Taylor may be considered a source of Cavendish's work in this connection. In the *Philosophical Transactions* in 1721, Taylor published a study of thermometers, in the course of which he mixed given quantities of hot and cold water and measured the original and resulting temperatures.[98]

The instruments Cavendish needed for his heat experiments were few: lamps for heating mixtures in bottles made of glass or tin, thermometers, scales, and a watch. His method was that of mixtures, and he began his experiments with the simplest of mixtures, Fahrenheit's hot and cold water. He took three readings three minutes apart to determine the rate of cooling of the hot water and the warm mixture, and he did a separate experiment to determine the heating effect of the container. He found, as he expected, the "true heat" of the mixture to be the weighted mean of

[93]Benjamin Franklin to Ebenezer Kinnersley, 20 Feb. 1762, in Benjamin Franklin, *Benjamin Franklin's Experiments. A New Edition of Franklin's Experiments and Observations on Electricity*, ed. I. B. Cohen (Cambridge, Mass.: Harvard University Press, 1941), 359–75, on 360. Franklin was in London in 1762, as the agent of the Pennsylvania Assembly.
[94]Boerhaave's *A New Method of Chemistry* is listed in Christopher Wordsworth, *Scholae Academicae: Some Account of the Studies at the English Universities in the Eighteenth Century* (Cambridge, 1877), 79.
[95]Guerlac, "Black," 177–78.
[96]Ibid., 177.
[97]*Notes from Doctor Black's Lectures on Chemistry 1767/8*, ed. D. McKie (Cheshire: Imperial Chemical Industries, 1966), 8.
[98]Taylor's experiments were reported in the *Philosophical Transactions* for 1721; they are described in A. Wolf, *A History of Science, Technology, & Philosophy in the 18th Century*, 2d ed. by D. McKie, 2 vols. (New York: Harper & Bros., 1961) 1:189–90. Wilson, *Cavendish*, 447.

the temperatures of the hot and cold water before mixing: "It seems reasonable to suppose that on mixing hot and cold water the quantity of heat in the liquors taken together should be the same after the mixing as before; or that the hot water should communicate as much heat to the cold water as it lost itself."[99] Then, using the same procedure, but varying the apparatus somewhat, he mixed alternately hot water, mercury, and spirits with cold mercury, spirits, and any of a number of substances. These substances he took, in part, from his shelves of chemical reagants, oil of vitriol and solution of pearl ashes. Cavendish's heat and chemical researches crossed paths here in ways that would, as we will see, affect his fundamental theory of matter and motion.[100] The substances also included solids, such as sand, iron filings, shot, powdered glass, marble, charcoal, and brimstone, and other solids broken into lumps smaller than peas: tin, Newcastle coal, and spermaceti. He expressed his anticipated conclusion upon mixing different substances this way: "One would naturally imagine that if cold /mercury/ or any other substance is added to hot water the heat of the mixture would be the same as if an equal quantity of water of the same degree of heat had been added; or, in other words, that all bodies heat and cool each other when mixed together equally in proportion to their weights. The following experiment, however, will show that this is very far from being the case."[101] The "true explanation" is that "it requires a greater quantity of heat to raise the heat of some bodies a given number of degrees by the thermometer than it does to raise other bodies the same number of degrees."[102] Cavendish used water as the *standard* for calculating the "equivalent" weight of each substance in terms of its heating effect; he determined, that is, the specific heat of each substance. His experiments on specific heats proceeded smoothly until he came to spermiceti, whereupon he stopped to do a long series of experiments on this substance alone.[103] The minutes of the experiments suggest that spermiceti was a mess to handle and to measure. If the reported sequence of experiments corresponds roughly to the actual sequence, the minutes suggest that spermaceti was also the source of a major discovery, that of latent heats. In the first of the spermiceti experiments, Cavendish mixed cold lumps with hot water, in the next hot melted spermiceti with cold water, and he found that the

results disagreed. The only difference in the two trials was the condition of the spermaceti, solid in one trial, liquid in the other. That was Cavendish's clue; he concluded that when spermiceti hardens it gives off heat and when it melts it produces cold, and that this heat is characteristic of spermaceti. That is, there is a second heat in addition to the specific heat of a substance.[104] The next experiment was with a more tractable substance, water, for which Cavendish built a new apparatus. With it he measured the cold produced by boiling water; that is, by changing its state from liquid to vapor.[105] The conclusion he drew about latent heats was this: "As far as I can perceive it seems a constant rule in nature that all bodies in changing from a solid state to a fluid state or from a non-elastic state to the state of an elastic fluid generate cold, and by the contrary change they generate heat."[106] Then, evidently to achieve more accuracy, he began all over again with the simplest mixture, hot and cold water, but now with a new apparatus, a funnel into which the hot water was poured and which was tightly joined to a pan containing the cold water; stirrers and thermometers were inserted in both the funnel and the pan. The measured heat of the mixture and the theoretically computed heat now agreed to within a half degree, a realistic accuracy for experiments of this kind.[107]

It has been suggested that Cavendish did

[99]Cavendish, "Experiments on Heat," 327.

[100]The chemical mixtures generated an additional heat or cold, which Cavendish noted in these small sheets. He would later give an explanation for these heats in terms of a *change* in specific heats resulting from the reaction.

[101]Cavendish, "Experiments on Heat," 332.

[102]Ibid., 340.

[103]Cavendish Mss III(a), 9:22, 27–38.

[104]The heading of his experimental notes on p. 31, Cavendish Mss III(a), tells of this discovery: "Concerning Heat & Cold Produced by Hardening & Melting of Spermaceti." Cavendish measured the latent heat of spermaceti several times, obtaining only roughly consistent results; he found that the hardening of spermaceti was sufficient to raise an equal weight of water by about 64 to 75 degrees; the cold generated by the melting of it fell in that range, about 69 degrees. Cavendish returned to spermaceti using a different experimental arrangement and got higher values. Ibid., 78–81. His experiments on the change of state of water between solid, liquid, and vapor gave much more consistent results, and these he emphasized in his intended paper. He only just briefly mentioned there that he had found the same kind of phenomenon with hardening and melting spermaceti. This section Cavendish headed "Experiments to Show That Bodies in Changing from a Solid State to a Fluid State Produce Cold and in Changing from a Fluid to a Solid State Produce Heat," *Sci. Pap.* 2:348–50, on 349.

[105]Cavendish Mss III(a), 9:42–47. This experiment Cavendish wrote up in his paper "Experiments on Heat," and the apparatus is drawn there. *Sci. Pap.* 2:345–46.

[106]Cavendish, "Experiments on Heat," 343.

[107]Cavendish Mss III(a), 9:48–56. This apparatus, which Cavendish

not publish his experiments on heat because he did not want to enter into rivalry with Black in a field that Black had staked out for himself.[108] That may be correct, but it seems unlikely. There is rarely any worthwhile work in science that does not bring its author into rivalry, and in his first publication, on factitious air, Cavendish was not deterred by Black's prior work on fixed air; Black had even staked out a claim by saying that he intended to do more work on the subject. The only difference was that Black published his original experiments on fixed air and he did not his experiments on heat. We think that Cavendish refrained from publishing for a reason of a different kind: his experiments raised difficult problems for his theory of heat. Cavendish tried to resolve the theoretical problems, at first without success, and by the time he did succeed there was no point in publishing. Black's lectures were, in effect, a slow but sure publication; before 1780, a number of researchers in Britain were working with the concepts of heat that Black had communicated through his lectures. There also appeared work from abroad such as Johan Carl Wilcke's.

Cavendish did publish on heat, but it was not until 1783, when he invoked the rule of latent heat in a discussion of the freezing of water, and he gave neither an argument nor a citation for it but simply remarked that it was a "circumstance now pretty well known to philosophers."[109] Even though Cavendish did not publish his experiments on heat, his effort was not wasted. He had acquired a thorough familiarity with the phenomena of heat, which would serve him well in his researches over the next twenty years.

---

described and drew in his paper "Experiments on Heat," is reproduced in *Sci. Pap.* 2:328. Cavendish's readings and calculations were only as accurate as the experiments allowed. He kept minutes by a watch, read degrees of heat no finer than ¼ degree, and when estimating rates of cooling, he used comparably rough calculations, such as $(2 + 1¼)/3 = 1$. He repeated his experiments and took a mean of the readings, and if the mean should be, say, 90.1, in the paper he would round it off to 90.

[108] Wilson, *Cavendish*, 446. McKie and Heathcote agree with Wilson, in *Discovery*, 52.

[109] This "circumstance" is "that all, or almost all, bodies by changing from a fluid to a solid state, or from the state of an elastic to that of an inelastic fluid, generate heat; and that cold is produced by the contrary process." Henry Cavendish, "Observations on Mr. Hutchins's Experiments for Determining the Degree of Cold at Which Quicksilver Freezes," *PT* 73 (1783): 303–28; in *Sci. Pap.* 2:145–60, on 150.

CHAPTER 4

&ᔕ✦ᔕᔤ

*T*ools of the Trade

Instruments

Instruments, mathematics, and theory are principal tools of science, and like every good craftsman, Cavendish kept his tools sharp, giving at least as much attention to them in their own right as to their use in experiments with other ends. We begin this discussion with the instruments of science: Cavendish regularly compared his instruments, one with the other, and one after another, thermometer, barometer, hydrometer, electrometer, clock, compass, telescope, and eudiometer. His interest and skill were recognized by the Royal Society, which regarded him as its resident authority on all matters having to do with instruments.

Henry Cavendish varied and perfected existing instruments instead of inventing new ones. Beginning with his father's self-registering maximum and minimum liquid thermometers, the first of their kind, Henry Cavendish designed a convenient, self-registering, dial-type maximum and minimum thermometer, an all-in-one instrument. In it a mechanism registers a change in the height of mercury by a rotary movement of an axis; the instantaneous temperature is read by a large pointer, and the maximum and minimum temperatures are recorded by light pointers moved by the large one.[1] To take another example: like many meteorologists before and after him, Cavendish designed a better wind measurer. Having commissioned the firm of Nairne and Blunt to build it for him, Cavendish requested to meet with the employee who made the instrument on the premises, whereupon Cavendish "insisted upon his taking the whole apparatus to pieces, and then, by means of a file and a magnifying glass, he tested the pinions to see that they were properly hardened and polished, and of the right shape, according to his written directions."[2] We suppose that during this inspection of the pinions, the instrument-maker felt some anxiety, but since the anecdote ends here, we also suppose that the

outcome was favorable to all parties. At Nairne and Blunt, Cavendish was both a demanding customer and a frequent one, whose behavior, if tactless, would have been familiar and more than tolerated, since his patronage of the firm was an advertisement of a kind that money could not buy. The founder of the firm, Edward Nairne, a Fellow of the Royal Society, was Cavendish's all-purpose instrument-maker of choice and also an experimental collaborator of his.[3]

In the 1760s and 1770s, at about the time Cavendish began to do research, the experimental sciences were beginning to be supplied with instruments for making exact measurements. Aided by improvements in mechanics, in materials such as brass, steel, and glass, and in the graduation of scales, the makers of scientific instruments responded to the expanding demand for accurate instruments, and their product in turn stimulated the demand for ever greater accuracy.[4] Living in the same city with the instrument-makers, Cavendish could conveniently inspect, buy, and commission their wares.

----

[1]This instrument was calibrated at Chatsworth in 1779, which more or less dates it. Lord Charles Cavendish could have designed it, but at that late date the designer was more likely Henry Cavendish. The self-registering thermometer is one of two instruments (the other a metallic eudiometer) illustrated and described in an appendix in George Wilson, *The Life of the Honourable Henry Cavendish* (London, 1851), 477–78. Through Humphry Davy, this instrument was eventually given to the Royal Institution. William E. Knowles Middleton, *A History of the Thermometer and Its Use in Meteorology* (Baltimore: The Johns Hopkins University Press, 1966), 138–39. Related to this thermometer are undated experiments by Henry Cavendish, "Thermom. for Greatest Heat by Inverting the End of Tube into a Moveable Cyl. of Spt. & Water," Cavendish Mss III(a), 14(c).

[2]This anecdote about Cavendish originated with the instrument-maker John Newman, of Regent Street. Wilson, *Cavendish*, 179.

[3]Discussion of and entries for Edward Nairne and Thomas Blunt in E. G. R. Taylor, *The Mathematical Practitioners of Hanoverian England, 1714–1840* (Cambridge: Cambridge University Press, 1966), 62, 214, 256.

[4]Maurice Daumas, "Precision of Measurement and Physical and Chemical Research in the Eighteenth Century," in A. C. Crombie, ed., *Scientific Change; Historical Studies in the Intellectual, Social, and Technical Conditions for Scientific Discovery and Technical Invention, from Antiquity to the Present* (New York: Basic Books, 1963), 418–30, on 418, 426–30.

At some point his need for the services of instrument-makers became so constant that he employed one of his own.

Because he was wealthy, Cavendish could own any instrument he wanted, and because his scientific interests were wide-ranging, he owned a large number of instruments. In 1816, six years after his death, his collection was put up for sale. The catalogue of the auction[5] lists 91 numbered items, some of which are multiple; all told, it mentions about 150 instruments together with bottles, retorts, and maps, the lot selling for 159 pounds. The unnamed buyers of the instruments were probably persons who had use for them, since instruments used by Cavendish in the 1780s were still in use at the time of the sale, and Cavendish was not yet famous enough for his instruments to be collected as memorabilia; his name was not mentioned in the catalogue, only a "Gentleman Deceased." In some instances, an instrument is listed with the maker's name as a guarantee of quality; e.g., an air pump and a dipping needle by Nairne and Blunt, a thermometer by John Bird, and a theodolite and a thermometer by Jesse Ramsden. By the time of the auction, Cavendish's collection of instruments and related apparatus had been scavenged, stripped of all of its electrical measuring instruments and nearly all of the instruments for measuring gases, leaving mainly drawing instruments, telescopes, variation compasses, hygrometers, and thermometers (44 of them).[6] As we will see, the balance—or imbalance—of the collection is not too misleading; Cavendish devoted much of his life to the study of instruments of the earth's atmosphere and magnetism.

The probable reason why Cavendish commissioned the firm of Nairne and Blunt to build his wind-measurer was, apart from habit, the portable wind gauge for use at sea that Nairne and Blunt had recently built for James Lind, physician to George III.[7] It was the best instrument of its kind, which was the kind of nearly all early wind gauges. They were, in effect, pressure gauges, designed for "weighing the wind," used by seamen, who were interested in that property of the wind, its pressure.[8] Cavendish's wind measurer was of a different kind, one suited for meteorology, in the tradition of the vane-mill invented by Robert Hooke in the previous century.[9] The inspirer of Cavendish's earliest experiments would

have been Alexander Brice, who measured the velocity of the wind by observing the motion of the shadows of clouds, his answer to the irregularities in the velocity of wind as determined by light objects like feathers carried along in the breeze. Presumably the wind is unobstructed at the height of clouds.[10] Cavendish thought that Brice's experiments published in the *Philosophical Transactions* in 1766 were "ingenious" but incomplete, since Brice failed to measure the wind on the ground in an open place to discover if there is a difference in wind velocity at the surface of the earth and high above it, and Brice also failed to observe the angular velocity of the clouds at the same time as he observed their shadows, which would have determined their perpendicular altitude. "The most convenient way I know of measuring the velocity of the wind," Cavendish wrote to a correspondent, "is by a kind of horizontal windmill with rackwork like that used for measuring wheels to count the number of revolutions it makes. Such an instrument will make the same number of revolutions while the wind moves over a given space whether the wind moves fast or slow & it will be easy finding by experiment the actual number of revolutions which it makes while the wind moves over a given space."[11] Cavendish's apparatus in the 1760s was such a horizontal windmill and built nearly on the scale of a true windmill, the revolving arm measuring about eighteen feet long. Twenty years later, no doubt with the Nairne and Blunt instrument this time, he returned to these

---

[5]We are fortunate to have the catalogue of Cavendish's instruments, since few instrument catalogues from the eighteenth century have been preserved. Another surviving catalogue is that of John Stuart, earl of Bute, who had a large instrument collection rivaling that of his friend George III. The catalogue of its auction sale, listing 255 numbered items, has a large overlap with the catalogue of Cavendish's collection, especially in the category of "mathematical," or drawing, instruments. G. L'E. Turner, "The Auction Sales of the Earl of Bute's Instruments, 1793," *Annals of Science* 23 (1967): 213–42.

[6]*A Catalogue of Sundry Very Curious and Valuable Mathematical, Philosophical, and Optical Instruments, Electrifying Machines, Clocks, and Maps of a Gentleman, Deceased . . . Which Will Be Sold by Auction, by Mr. Willock, on the Premises, No. 21, in Sherrard-Street, Above-Mentioned, on Saturday the Fifteenth of June 1816, at Twelve O'clock.* Devon. Coll.

[7]Taylor, *Mathematical Practitioners*, 62–63.

[8]A. Wolf, *A History of Science, Technology, of Philosophy in the 18th Century*, 2d ed., ed. D. McKie, 2 vols. (New York: Harper & Bros., 1961) 1:320–23.

[9]William E. Knowles Middleton, *Invention of the Meteorological Instruments* (Baltimore: Johns Hopkins University Press, 1969), 203.

[10]Wolf, *History of Science*, 324.

[11]Henry Cavendish to "your Lordship," undated, Cavendish Mss, Misc.

experiments. Since his method was to count the number of revolutions corresponding to winds of different strengths,[12] the accuracy of the pinions that he insisted on testing on Nairne and Blunt's premises was the key to the accuracy of the instrument across a wide range of wind velocities.

To his correspondent Cavendish revealed his hope for the wind measurer: "By the help of such an instrument one might easily find the velocity of the wind at any time & if one had a mind keep a register of its velocity almost as easily as one can that of the thermometer."[13] Ideally, then, a complete weather journal would record the velocity of the wind in addition to its direction, which was then routinely observed by the weather vane. If that indeed was Cavendish's wish, it was not to be realized; complex and cumbersome wind measurers were invented and reinvented throughout the century, without leading to a standard practice. By the procedures recommended by Cavendish for recording the weather at the Royal Society, the strength of the wind was denoted numerically, but only conventionally: 1, 2, and 3 stood for "gentle," "brisk," and "violent or stormy."[14] The clerk was advised to look at how smoke was blown or how the wind sounded,[15] which was a far cry from reading the revolutions of a wind measurer. Like many other patient observers of the weather, Cavendish desired exactness and had to settle for less. There had long been instruments for the weather, the weather vane, the rain catch, and even a crude indicator of humidity, but these did not make the study of the weather exact. By Cavendish's time, it was understood that the science of the weather required instruments to *measure* it; above all, the thermometer and the barometer.[16] At the same time it was understood that these instruments were still primitive. The difference in rigor between an exact science and meteorology at the beginning of the eighteenth century can be appreciated by Newton's experiments on thermometry. The author of the system of the world used a linseed-oil thermometer and a scale fixed by two points, the heat of the air standing above water when it begins to freeze, and the heat of blood, from which Newton extrapolated freely to high temperatures.[17] Nearly forty years later, Robert Smith, who translated Newton's directions for making thermometers, observed that none of the thermometers he had seen had been tested for comparability,[18] which

was still pretty much the state of affairs when Cavendish took up the study of thermometers thirty years later.[19] There was a variety of scales in use and a wide variation in their adjustment; Britain and Scandinavia preferred the Fahrenheit scale while the nations on the Continent preferred the Réaumur scale.[20] When Cavendish received his first assignment from the Royal Society, to measure the boiling point of water, in 1766, thermometers were just then beginning to be calibrated for improved accuracy.[21] The boiling point of water was a problem basic to thermometry, and Cavendish's object was to determine if the boiling point is affected by the rapidity of boiling and by the thermometer's immersion either in the boiling water or in the steam above the water. The potential accuracy of a thermometer—the fractions of a degree to which it could be read—had little meaning in practice, since the results of different thermometers and of different users were wildly discordant, owing especially to an uncertainty regarding the upper point of the scale, the boiling point of water. Of the selection of excellent thermometers, built by Bird, Ramsden, Nairne, and George Adams, tried by Cavendish (probably with other Fellows) at the Royal Society in 1766, individual thermometers differed in their readings of the boiling point by two or three degrees.[22] While astronomical precision in meteorology was not regarded as important or obtainable,[23] a disparity of two or three degrees in the boiling point of water on

---

[12]Henry Cavendish, " No. 1. Measurer of Wind," Cavendish Mss, Misc. Dates are scattered through the trials: the spring of 1768 and of 1769, and twenty years later, in the fall of 1788, "Trial of Windgage."

[13]Cavendish, letter to "your Lordship."

[14]Henry Cavendish, "An Account of the Meteorological Instruments Used at the Royal Society's House," *PT* 66 (1776): 375–401; in *Sci. Pap.* 2:112–26, on 117.

[15]Royal Society, Minutes of Council 6:202 (9 Dec. 1773).

[16]Typical on this point is Richard Kirwan, *An Estimate of the Temperature of Different Latitudes* (London, 1787), iii.

[17]Middleton, *History of the Thermometer*, 57–58.

[18]Robert Smith, "The Editor's Preface," in Roger Cotes, *Hydrostatical and Pneumatical Lectures*, 2d ed. (Cambridge, 1747).

[19]There was, as we have noted, a general understanding that mercury was the best substance for a thermometer, though that did not diminish interest in thermometers using other substances: Henry Cavendish, "Thermometers of Different Fluids," Cavendish Mss III(a), 14.

[20]Middleton, *History of the Thermometer*, 65, 75, 115.

[21]Middleton dates the increase in accurate calibration from about 1770: *History of the Thermometer*, 127.

[22]Henry Cavendish, "Boiling Point of Water. At the Royal Society, April 18, 1766," in Cavendish, *Sci. Pap.* 2:351–53.

[23]Middleton, *History of the Barometer*, 132.

different thermometers was, to Cavendish's way of thinking, unacceptable and correctable. Instrument-makers might stress the accuracy attainable with a given instrument; Benjamin Martin, for example, claimed that with a vernier the barometer could be read to 1/100th of an inch (in a column of mercury of 28 inches),[24] and from the 1770s verniers and indices were used for reading the level of mercury in the barometer tube (on the mercury tubes of thermometers, verniers were not useful).[25] But Cavendish was not primarily concerned with accuracy in that sense; he was concerned with the consistency and compatibility of readings with instruments used by different observers.

Recently the atmosphere had taken on a new complexity and interest as an electrical medium, in which connection lightning, thunder, auroras, meteors, earthquakes, and other spectacular phenomena were studied, as were prosaic events such as fog and falling weather. William Henly, the inventor of a good electrometer, urged readers of the *Philosophical Transactions* to keep an "electrical journal" of the weather, as he did. "Let a large book be provided, and ruled in the manner of a bill-book, used by tradesmen . . . ." The entries in the columns were the same as in the usual weather journals except for a new measurement, the divergence of the balls of an electrometer, and a new observation, the kind of electricity. Henly recommended one other new standard meteorological measurement, taking the temperature of the upper air, for which Henly thought that Lord Charles Cavendish's self-registering minimum thermometer would serve, carried as high as possible by kites, frequently and in all kinds of weather.[26] At the time Henry Cavendish took up meteorology, the kind of record that Henly called for, journals[27] instead of isolated weather reports, began to appear more often in the *Philosophical Transactions*. It was a means to the end, if realizable, as the weather-journal enthusiast William Borlase put it, of "more perfect Theories of Wind and Weather in our Climate."[28] What Charles Hutton wrote in his scientific dictionary at the end of the eighteenth century could have been said at any time during the century:

There does not seem in all philosophy any thing of more immediate concernment to us, than the state of the weather . . . . To establish a proper theory of the weather, it would be necessary to have

registers carefully kept in divers parts of the globe, for a long series of years; from whence we might be enabled to determine the directions, breadth, and bounds of the winds, and of the weather they bring with them . . . . We might thus in time learn to foretell many great emergencies; as, extraordinary heats, rains, frosts, droughts, dearths, and even plagues, and other epidemical diseases.[29]

At once a challenge to science and a vital issue to humanity, the weather was the kind of problem that the Royal Society regarded as its reason for being. Meteorology supported the Society's early Baconian belief in the advancement of science through natural histories; the "journals," or "registers," of the weather submitted to the Royal Society and published in its *Philosophical Transactions* were *histories* of the weather at different locations. The model was the Royal Society's own new weather journal, with which Cavendish had much to do.

The Royal Society called on Cavendish's skill with meteorological instruments again in 1773, this time to draw up a plan for taking daily meteorological readings by the clerk of the Society.[30] The first thing in the morning and again at midday the clerk was instructed to read the barometer and nearby indoor and outdoor thermometers, and every morning he was to measure how much rain

[24]Benjamin Martin, *A Description of the Nature, Construction, and Use of the Torricellian, or Simple Barometer. With a Scale of Rectification* (London, 1778), 5.

[25]Middleton, *History of the Barometer*, 196–97; *History of the Thermometer*, 136.

[26]William Henly, "An Account of Some New Experiments in Electricity . . .," *PT* 64 (1774): 389–431, on 426–27.

[27]Charles Hutton, *Mathematical and Philosophical Dictionary*, 2 vols. (London, 1795–96) 2:667–68, listed the persons who published weather journals in the *Philosophical Transactions* from the late seventeenth century to the end of the eighteenth, and he gave an account of the Royal Society's own journal. His purpose was to encourage the keeping and printing of similar registers in other parts of the world. From the 1770s, for the next twenty years, there was a revival of interest in meteorology in Europe, owing to the presumed connections between weather and health and agriculture, and also to the connection with experimental science: according to Theodore S. Feldman, "Late Enlightenment Meteorology," in *The Quantifying Spirit in the Eighteenth Century*, eds. T. Frangsmyr, J. L. Heilbron, and R. E. Rider (Berkeley: University of California Press, 1990), 143–77, on 153, 161.

[28]J. Oliver, "William Borlase's Contribution's to Eighteenth-Century Meteorology and Climatology," *Annals of Science* 25 (1969): 275–317, on 291.

[29]Hutton, *Dictionary* 2:677.

[30]The council ordered that the clerk of the Society make daily observations of the weather "with the instruments to be procured for that purpose, & proper accommodations under the inspection of the Hon Henry Cavendish." Royal Society, Minutes of Council, 6:197 (22 Nov. 1773).

had fallen, every afternoon estimate the wind, and one fortnight a year consult the dipping needle four times a day. With regard to the thermometer readings, the clerk was also expected to calculate a rather complicated series of means of readings. Cavendish proposed that all of this information be printed at the end of the last part of the *Philosophical Transactions* for each year; this was done beginning with the weather for 1776.[31] So that the members did not have to wait to the end of the year to learn what the weather was, the clerk was ordered to post the previous week's weather in the public meeting room of the Society.[32] Three years later, at a time when the council was preoccupied with instruments, those of the Royal Observatory[33] and its own,[34] and expanding the instruments used for the Society's meteorological register,[35] Cavendish was named head of a committee to review the entire body of meteorological instruments of the Society. The committee included Heberden, who, as we have seen, kept a meteorological journal, Maskelyne and Aubert, who as astronomers necessarily concerned themselves with the weather and also constantly with instruments, Samuel Horsley, regarded by some as the "head of the English mathematicians"[36] and an astronomer and avid observer of the weather, the secretary of the Society Joseph Planta, and the most important member other than Cavendish, the meteorologist Jean André Deluc.[37] Deluc was a Swiss who had recently settled in London, where he took a position as reader to the queen. Just before his move, in 1772, he had published an influential work calling for the perfection of thermometers, *Recherches sur les modifications de l'atmosphère, ou Théorie des Baromètres et des Thermomètres*.[38] In the committee Cavendish took on Deluc by firmly endorsing the cistern barometer over the siphon type, which Deluc championed. Two important publications came out of this study of the Society's meteorological instruments, a paper by Cavendish alone in 1776 and one by the committee in 1777. The committee's paper was also written by Cavendish, at least in part, as we know from his manuscripts. What Cavendish said in his paper of 1776, in connection with the adjustment of the boiling point of water on thermometers, applies to his whole effort in meteorology:

It is very much to be wished, therefore, that some means were used to establish an uniform method

of proceeding; and there are none which seem more proper, or more likely to be effectual, than that the Royal Society should take it into consideration, and recommend that method of proceeding which shall appear to them to be most expedient.[39]

The recommendations followed in the paper of the committee the next year.[40] The study of the instruments of the Royal Society was a means to a greater end, the improvement of the accuracy of science through an agreement among practitioners on how to use them. Cavendish insured that the authority of the Royal Society was put behind this effort. Like every serious worker in meteorology, Cavendish would have agreed with Richard Kirwan that no other science required "such a conspiracy of nations,"[41] which entailed a uniformity of practice around the world.

The recommendations of the committee in 1777 for keeping the Society's meteorological journal were largely taken from Cavendish's report to the council in 1773. They repeated, for example, Cavendish's instructions to the clerk of the Society

---

[31] "Meteorological Journal Kept at the House of the Royal Society, by Order of the President and Council," *PT* 67 (1777): 357–84.

[32] "The Following Scheme Drawn up by the Hon. Henry Cavendish for the Regulating the Manner of Making Daily Meteorological Observations by the Clerk of the Royal Society . . .," Royal Society, Minutes of Council 6: 200–4 (9 Dec. 1773).

[33] In the mid 1770s Maskelyne and the Royal Observatory took up most of the time of the council. Cavendish was involved with the instruments of the Observatory as he would be with the Society's instruments. Cavendish, Maskelyne, Aubert, Shepherd, and Wollaston were appointed to a committee to examine two new equatorial sectors, which had imperfections due to the neglect of the instrument-maker. Royal Society, Minutes of Council, 6: 280 and 283 (14 Sep. and 12 Oct. 1775).

[34] Cavendish, Aubert, and Nairne were appointed a committee to "examine into the state of the Society's instruments." Royal Society, Minutes of Council, 6:313 (14 Nov. 1776).

[35] The council ordered that once-daily observations with John Smeaton's hygrometer be added to the Society's meteorological observations. Royal Society, Minutes of Council, 6:287 (16 Nov. 1775).

[36] This description is by John Playfair, *The Works of John Playfair*, ed. J. G. Playfair, 4 vols. (Edinburgh, 1822) 1:appendix no. l, "Journal," lxxix.

[37] Middleton, *History of the Thermometer*, 127.

[38] Middleton, *History of the Thermometer*, 116–17. Douglas W. Freshfield and H. F. Montagnier, *The Life of Horace Bénédict De Saussure* (London: Edward Arnold, 1920), 176–77.

[39] Cavendish, "An Account of the Meteorological Instruments," 115.

[40] Signed by Cavendish (listed first), Heberden, Aubert, Deluc, Maskelyne, Horsley, and Planta: "The Report of the Committee Appointed by the Royal Society to Consider of the Best Method of Adjusting the Fixed Points of Thermometers; and of the Precautions Necessary to Be Used in Making Experiments with Those Instruments," *PT* 67 (1777): 816–57.

[41] Kirwan, *An Estimate of the Temperature of Different Latitudes*, iv.

to consult the dipping and horizontal needles for a fortnight each year, but the clerk was now to make five observations a day instead of four. This kind of activity was incredibly tedious, though the maximum and minimum instruments made the routine somewhat less confining. Fully automatic clock-driven registers were the natural solution and already an old idea. Christopher Wren in the previous century had proposed a "weather clock," and Robert Hooke had developed it into a futuristic meteorograph using punches on rolled paper. But it would have been just as tedious to count the punches, and there were other reasons why a universal weather instrument was impractical.[42] Cavendish's thoughts turned in the direction of a clock-driven single instrument, a thermometer. He drew plans for an elaborate mechanical contrivance for recording the temperature every ten minutes on a rotating barrel.[43] It probably was built, but neither it nor anything like it was recommended for the Royal Society, where only the best of the tried and true instruments were used. In addition to the thermometer, they were the barometer, rain-gage, Smeaton's hygrometer, Gowin Knight's variation compass made by Nairne, and John Michell's dipping needle also made by Nairne. Cavendish discussed the "error of observation" and the "error of the instrument" in achieving "accuracy" in the recording of the weather. That was done in part by the indoor and outdoor placement of the instruments, the funnel collecting rain raised above the roof of the Society's house where there seemed "no danger of any rain dashing into it," the hygrometer sheltered from the rain but open to the wind "where the Sun scarce ever shines on it."[44] It was done too by taking the mean of observations and by applying corrections, such as Cavendish's corrections for the thermometer if the stem is cooler than the bulb, Deluc's rule for correcting the barometer by the thermometer, and by a table giving capillary depressions of the mercury standing in the tube of the barometer. That table, Cavendish pointed out, was made by his father, Lord Charles Cavendish.[45] Accuracy was achieved in still another way, by modifying instruments; the vibration of the needle of the variation compass was prevented from disturbing the observation of the needle, an improvement which Cavendish credited to his father.[46] The published paper on the meteorological instruments

of the Royal Society was, among other things, a display of the instrumental prowess of father and son. The unpublished papers of Henry Cavendish pertaining to the work on the Society's instruments are further testimony of the connection between the two. In 1776–77, Henry Cavendish made endless trials with "father's thermometer"; after his publication on the meteorological instruments of the Society, Henry Cavendish went right on with his trials of instruments at the Society, including his father's.[47] Experiments on the variation compass and the dipping needle were done far from the disturbing iron work of the Royal Society's house, in a "large garden" of a house on Marlborough Street, which had to be the house where the Cavendishes lived.[48] From various of Cavendish's records of observations, we conclude that whatever else Cavendish's garden might have contained, it was above all a garden of instruments.

The Cavendish garden is, in fact, the setting of our last example of Cavendish's work on instruments. Like the weather, the earth's magnetism varies complexly from place to place and from time to time, periodically and secularly. Cavendish observed the earth's magnetic variation and dip at regular intervals and calculated their mean yearly values. Before his study of the Royal Society's meteorological instruments, in the early 1770s, Henry and his father alternated in taking magnetical readings with a horizontal needle in the "garden." "Father" and "self" label two columns: on certain days, one would take a number of readings, on other days the other. Mixed in with Cavendish's readings

---

[42]Middleton, *Invention of the Meteorological Instruments*, 254–55.

[43]Henry Cavendish, "Clock for Keeping Register of Thermometer," Cavendish Mss IV, 1. He made a carefully ruled drawing to scale of this instrument, probably for his instrument-maker.

[44]Cavendish, "An Account of the Meteorological Instruments," 117.

[45]Cavendish, "An Account of the Meteorological Instruments," 116–17. Charles Cavendish's table gave the depression of mercury in inches corresponding to tubes of bores between 0.1 and 0.6 inches; for the largest bore, the depression was extremely small, 0.005 inches. This table had a long history after its publication by Henry Cavendish; in the theory of capillarity, it was cited by Thomas Young and by Laplace after the turn of the nineteenth century. Middleton, *The History of the Barometer*, 188–89.

[46]Cavendish, "An Account of the Meteorological Instruments," 120.

[47]Two packets of Henry Cavendish's papers are headed "Trial of Boiling Point with Father's Thermometer," one with 33 numbered pages, one with 4: Cavendish Mss III(a), 10 and 11. In addition, in packets labeled "Expansion of Steam" and Theory of Boiling," there are more readings taken with his father's thermometer in 1777 at the Royal Society, ibid. III(a), 5 and 13.

[48]Henry Cavendish, "Horizontal Needle," Cavendish Mss IX,4.

are others taken by Heberden at Heberden's house and also, it would seem, in Cavendish's garden.[49] Upon moving from his father's house, Henry Cavendish kept a record of variations of the magnetic compass at Hampstead from 1782 and then from Clapham Common until 1809, the year before he died. This record consists of more or less daily readings through the summer months.[50] The timing may have had to do with the weather, since Cavendish took several readings a day beginning before eight in the morning and ending about eleven at night; it may have had to do with his habits, too, since in the summer the Royal Society was not in session, and the summer was otherwise a good time to be constantly outside London. Cavendish did not place much weight on these readings, for when he was asked about the mean variation of his observatory at Clapham Common, he gave it for the past summer but not for past years, since, he said, many others there had observed the variation longer than he had.[51] (Cavendish's scientific company at Clapham Common included the Evangelicals who made that suburb famous in his time.) His interest centered on the instruments and their method of use. Because the magnetism of the earth draws the needle not only roughly north but also down, there are two kinds of instruments: in addition to the variation compass, there is the dipping needle, which Cavendish subjected to countless experiments and computations concerning suspensions, shapes, and sizes; he tried his father's dipping needle and Sisson's and Nairne's, and he designed his own, and he drew up directions for using the dipping needle on several voyages.[52]

We have chosen meteorology as our main source of examples to illustrate Cavendish's way of using instruments. Whoever reads through his papers on this subject must be impressed by the tenacity with which he compared his instruments among themselves and with those belonging to the Royal Society and to Nairne and other individuals. For ten years he compared the instruments for measuring the moisture of air, hygrometers, whose inventors disputed with their rivals so heatedly that Charles Blagden spoke of their "open war,"[53] and yet they and Cavendish all agreed on what one of the inventors J. A. Deluc called the "essential point" about the hygrometer; namely, that all "observers might understand each other, when mentioning degrees of humidity."[54] Another inventor John

Smeaton put it best: the goal was to construct hygrometers that, like the best thermometers, were "capable of speaking the same language."[55] Cavendish tried "Smeaton's" hygrometer used by the Royal Society, and other hygrometers labeled variously "Nairne's," "Harrison's," "Coventry's," "common," "old," "new," "4-stringed," and "ivory." The general type of instrument he studied was the hydroscopic hygrometer, which either weighed the water (he weighed the increase in weight of dry salt after moist air was passed over it) or measured the change in dimensions of a moistened substance such as the contraction of strings (he preferred this method, in contrast to our preference today for weighing). He roasted, salted, wetted, and stretched the moisture-absorbing strings, and he mixed vapors from acids and alkalis with the air to see if that made a difference. At times he made readings daily, morning and evening, as often as every twenty minutes, in warm rooms and cold rooms, often together with thermometer readings.[56] If this activity sounds obsessive, we need to remind ourselves that it went to the heart of the work of science. In any experimental investigation, the reliability and the errors of instruments and their method of use were an inseparable part of the scientific argument. It could be said, and Cavendish could have said it, that an unexamined instrument was not worth using.

---

[49]Cavendish, "Horizontal Needle." On p. 3, alongside Cavendish's readings taken in his garden, there is a list of readings by Heberden, who must have been there too. Cavendish's manuscripts also contain readings of the variation compass taken at Heberden's house: Cavendish Mss IX, 19, 21, 23.

[50]Henry Cavendish, "Observations of Magnetic Declination," Cavendish Mss IX, 1. The earliest observations in this manuscript of 256 numbered pages were made at Hampstead; those from p. 30 on were made at Clapham Common.

[51]Henry Cavendish to J. Churchman, n.d. /1793/, draft, Cavendish Mss, New Correspondence.

[52]Some of the manuscripts are Henry Cavendish's instructions to an instrument-maker, "Dipping Needle"; "Trials of Dipping Needles"; and "On the Different Construction of Dipping Needles," Cavendish Mss IX, 7, 11, and 40. He drew up directions for the use of the dipping needle for three voyages, by Richard Pickergill, James Cook and William Bayley, and Alexander Dalrymple: Cavendish Mss IX, 41, 42, 43.

[53]On Saussure and Deluc's disagreements: Charles Blagden to Henry Cavendish, 23 Sep. 1787, Cavendish Mss X(b), 14.

[54]Jean André Deluc, "Account of a New Hygrometer," *PT* 63 (1773): 404–60, on 405.

[55]John Smeaton, "Description of a New Hygrometer," *PT* 61 (1771): 198–211, on 199.

[56]Henry Cavendish, "Hygrometers," Cavendish Mss IV, 5. This manuscript consists of 77 numbered pages of laboratory notes and an index.

The work of the maker of scientific instruments and that of their user went hand in hand, in a complementary way.[57] Earlier it had been common for scientific researchers to make their own instruments, but in Cavendish's day it was common for researchers to build their apparatus but to buy or commission their instruments. Researchers still invented instruments and instrument-makers like Nairne still did experiments, but instrument-making was a business, and science for someone like Cavendish was pretty much full time. Virtually every one of Cavendish's instruments was made in London by a contemporary, highly skilled instrument-maker. This most precise of experimenters lived at the time of the world renown of London instrument-makers.[58] His achievement in science gives substance to the adage: being in the right place at the right time.

We close this discussion by paying tribute to British instrument-makers as it was then done. Cavendish's exhaustive work on instruments was an implicit form of tribute. His colleague George Shuckburgh made the tribute explicit, remarking on the "singular success with which this age and nation has introduced a mathematical precision, hitherto unheard of, into the construction of philosophical instruments."[59] In his living quarters at Greenwich Observatory, the astronomer royal Nevil Maskelyne exhibited in addition to a bust of Newton prints of the builder of the great eight-foot mural quadrant for Greenwich, John Bird, and of the inventor of the achromatic telescope used at Greenwich, John Dolland.[60]

Mathematics

Mathematics, the mathematical teacher and instrument-maker Benjamin Martin wrote, is "the science or doctrine of *quantity*."[61] It is a subject that we might expect Henry Cavendish to take an interest in, and we would not be wrong. His manuscripts on mathematics are as numerous as those on astronomy or magnetism or mechanics. He did not publish any of his work on mathematics, raising the question of why he did it.

Mathematics clearly held an interest of its own for Cavendish, as is shown by a paper on prime numbers[62] and by other papers on topics that interested mathematicians of that time. These include papers relating to De Moivre's work, such as the probability of winning more than losing in a

game, the probability of throwing a certain number with a certain number of dice, the possible ways of paying a sum with coins of different denominations, and annuities on lives.[63] There are papers on the binomial theorem, the multinomial theorem, infinite series, and the construction and solution of algebraic equations.[64] There are still other papers that have a direct bearing on Cavendish's scientific work; e.g., on Newton's rule of interpolating, on the accuracy of taking the mean of observations, on triangular forms that reduce the effects of errors of measurement, and on the errors of instruments.[65] The bulk of Cavendish's mathematical papers deal with problems relating to plane or spherical geometry. Some of these are purely mathematical in interest, for example, extremal problems (the greatest cube that can pass through a hole in another cube), and some have scientific implications (a curve drawn with reference to three points).[66] The next to longest of his mathematical papers deals with a geometrical problem of William Braikenridge, a London clergyman and Fellow of the Royal Society.[67] His longest mathematical paper is about the loci of equations of the third order (equations, like plants and animals, were classified into "orders," "classes," genera," and "species").[68] Both of these long papers, and many of the other mathematical papers, fall late in his life, when he

---

[57]The intimacy of instrument-makers and scientists of this time is remarked on in Taylor, *Mathematical Practitioners*, 43, 58.

[58]From 1760, when Cavendish entered the Royal Society, to 1780, the instrument-makers of London were at the height of their world fame, according to Taylor, *Mathematical Practitioners*, 43.

[59]George Shuckburgh, "On the Variation of the Temperature of Boiling Water," *PT* 69 (1779): 362–75, on 362.

[60]Visitations of Greenwich Observatory, 1763 to 1815, Royal Society, Ms. 600, XIV.d.11, f. 36 (29 July 1785).

[61]Benjamin Martin, *A New and Comprehensive System of Mathematical Institutions, Agreeable to the Present State of the Newtonian Mathesis*, 2 vols. (London, 1759–64) 1:1.

[62]Henry Cavendish, "On Prime Numbers," Cavendish Mss VI(a), 8.

[63]Cavendish Mss VI(a), 1, 23, 46, 48.

[64]Cavendish Mss VI(a), 15, 16, 21, 22, 24, 27.

[65]Cavendish Mss VI(a), 6, 34, 45. The paper on the probable error of instruments does not have a catalogue number. The problem it addresses is: to determine the probability of the sum of the errors of two instruments given the error of any one instrument.

[66]Cavendish Mss, VI(a) 17, 36.

[67]Braikenridge's problem has to do with a surface in three dimensions, generated by the line joining two points moving uniformly along two lines not in the same plane. Fifty-two-page manuscript: Henry Cavendish, "On Dr. Braikenridge's Surface," Cavendish Mss VI(a), 12.

[68]"On Some Properties of Lines of the 3rd Order & on the Loci of Equations of the 3rd Order." Seventy-page manuscript: Cavendish Mss VI(a), 19.

was doing less experimental work,[69] but some he clearly wrote much earlier. Doubtless solving mathematical problems gave him satisfaction, since he had mathematical abilities of a high order. We liken his exercising of these abilities to his constant handling and comparing of instruments.

A hard and fast line cannot be drawn between Cavendish's mathematical and scientific interests, given Cavendish's way of working in science and given the nature of eighteenth-century mathematics. Mathematics and science, particularly the theory of motion, were developed together and by the same people, so that one can speak of a "virtual fusion" of the two.[70] Hugh Hamilton offered his geometrical treatise on conic sections as an "Introduction to the Newtonian Philosophy."[71] Benjamin Martin's text on the "Present State of the Newtonian Mathesis" introduced fluxions, the "new geometry," in the first volume and "physical-mechanical mathesis" in the second volume.[72] William Emerson, in his text on the same subject, characterized fluxions as a method of calculation that "opens and discovers to us the secrets and recesses of nature."[73] The image of motion, a velocity, entered the understanding of the mathematical concept of fluxions.[74]

In the mathematics of Cavendish's time, algebra was dominant; in principle there was no distinction between algebra and fluxions, and the geometry was expressed algebraically.[75] Mathematicians were concerned with strengthening and extending the calculus, or fluxions,[76] and if some mathematicians concerned themselves with its logical foundations and related questions of metaphysics,[77] others simply applied fluxions with a kind of no-nonsense intuition and a confidence founded on results. Unlike their seventeenth-century predecessors, Cavendish and his contemporaries did not need to invent new mathematics to advance science. They needed only to be inventive with (and trust) the mathematics of their day.

Theory

Certain expressions of which Cavendish was particularly fond, such as, "as I know by experience," "by strict reasoning," "with tolerable certainty," and "according to the theory," when taken together, go far to characterize his scientific practice. He believed that the right combination of experience and reason led to theories of nature that

had a good likelihood of being true; these theories in turn led to experimental advances. Looked at in this way, theories were like instruments and mathematics, tools of investigation in the scientist's tool chest.[78]

To Cavendish, a theory rested upon a hypothesis about nature made credible by its experimental consequences, as drawn out by the theory. To propose a theory was a serious step, especially for a cautious man like Cavendish, and we should not be surprised that Cavendish proposed few theories. As in his experiments, in his theoretical work he strove for quantitative exactness. He preferred, but did not insist on, mathematical theory (there were very few mathematical theories in science then). In meteorology he had no general theory. He had a hypothesis about the location of the earth's magnetic poles, but he had no

---

[69] The mathematical manuscripts are never dated, but the watermarks on the paper give occasional indications. In the manuscripts on Braikenridge's surfaces and on the loci of third-order equations, some of the sheets bear watermarks from 1797 to 1804.

[70] Morris Kline, *Mathematical Thought from Ancient to Modern Times* (New York: Oxford University Press, 1972), 394–96.

[71] Hugh Hamilton, *A Geometrical Treatise of the Conic Sections* (London, 1773), xii.

[72] Martin's two volumes, *New and Comprehensive System . . . ,* appeared in 1759 and 1764.

[73] William Emerson, *The Doctrine of Fluxions: Not Only Explaining the Elements Thereof, But Also Its Application and Use in the Several Parts of Mathematics and Natural Philosophy* (London, 1768), iii.

[74] Typical of the statements to be found in books on fluxions in Cavendish's time: the method of fluxions, Emerson said, was founded on the simple and obvious principle that "any quantity may be supposed to be generated by continual increase, after the same manner that space is described by local motion." *Doctrine of Fluxions*, iv. Thomas Simpson differed from other authors who regarded fluxions as "meer velocities"; he regarded a fluxion as the magnitude a velocity would develop uniformly in a finite time, but the image of a velocity is still present. *The Doctrine and Application of Fluxions*, 2 vols. (London, 1750) 1:vi.

[75] Thomas Simpson used primarily the more extensive and direct "*analytic method of investigation*," only occasionally giving a "geometrical demonstration" for clarity and elegance. He was not one of those who disliked everything done "by means of *symbols* and an *algebraic* process." He was, in fact, typical in preferring algebraic to geometrical methods. *Miscellaneous Tracts on Some Curious, and Very Interesting Subjects in Mechanics, Physical-Astronomy, and Speculative Mathematics* (London, 1757), Preface.

[76] Kline, *Mathematical Thought*, 400.

[77] British mathematicians such as Maclaurin supplied logical foundations using the geometrical methods of the ancients for conclusiveness, but not everyone thought that it was necessary; Newton had given a logical, "new way of reasoning." William Ludlam, *The Rudiments of Mathematics; Designed for the Use of Students at the Universities . . .* (Cambridge, 1785), 45.

[78] These "tools" were, of course, all related. Mathematics and instruments had their "theory." The instrument-maker Benjamin Martin reminded any person who was using an instrument without knowing its rationale or theory that he was working "in the dark"; just as the "*Science* of any Profession consists in the Theory." *The New Art of Surveying by the Goniometer* (London, 1766), Preface.

theory of the cause of the magnetism of the earth. In chemistry, as we have seen, he worked out a general theory of metals within the framework of the phlogiston theory, but he did not make it public. He had theoretical notions about the cause of chemical reactions at the level of particles and forces, but he was far from being able to develop this approach sufficiently to give chemistry its general theory. In astronomy and optics, there were already successful general theories, that of gravitation and, though it was less complete, the corpuscular theory of light. In a subject that combined heat, gases, and vapors, Cavendish worked out a special theory to explain boiling. He worked out only two original, general theories, and only one of these he published. The theory he did not publish was on heat, which he developed from another, existing theory, that of motion. The theory he did publish was on electricity. We discuss Cavendish's early theory of heat and his early and mature theories of electricity below.

We need to clarify a point of mechanics at the start.[79] We assume that by the time Cavendish left Cambridge, in 1752, he was thoroughly at home with Newtonian mathematical principles of natural philosophy. For the purposes of this discussion it is sufficient to recall that in Newtonian mechanics, the measure of the quantity of motion of a body is the product of the body's mass and velocity, or momentum. At some point, undoubtedly at Cambridge, Cavendish became familiar with another formulation of mechanics, originating with Leibniz, in which the quantity of motion of a body is taken to be *vis viva*, the product of the mass and the square of its velocity (a quantity close to our kinetic energy). Leibniz and his followers regarded *vis viva* as a conserved quantity, incapable of disappearing without giving rise to a comparable effect, an equal quantity of potential motion. This understanding was well suited for the treatment of a range of mechanical problems, but it encountered difficulties in the treatment of collisions between bodies. It was known from experience that collisions are never perfectly elastic, which means that *vis viva* is lost. But because the belief in conservation was unshakable, the missing *vis viva* was regarded as only apparently lost, as continuing on in hidden forms such as the compression of bodies or the motion of parts internal to bodies.

Leibniz proposed the latter explanation, but he did not identify the hidden *vis viva* with heat, even though in his day heat was commonly believed to be the internal motion of bodies. It would seem that the conceptual problems of treating heat as a quantity made this identification difficult.[80]

By the time Cavendish began his independent studies, it was customary to assume that for isolated mechanical systems the sum of the actual and hidden *vis viva* is constant. To uphold the validity of the conservation law, various explanations for the lost *vis viva* were entertained, though experiments to measure the *vis viva* so transformed had not been proposed. (It would be nearly a century later, in the middle of the nineteenth century, before the identification was established between the mechanical motion lost or work performed and an equivalent quantity of heat. This became the first law of a new theory, the mechanical theory of heat, or thermodynamics, and it was extended to all forms of energy to become the completely general law of conservation of energy.[81])

We know from Cavendish's manuscripts that he intended to write a book largely dealing with the theory of motion. "Plan of a Treatise on Mechanicks" is the thirty-odd-page beginning, probably written in 1763 or soon after, making it one of the earliest of his surviving writings.[82]

---

[79]This account of Cavendish's theory of heat is taken from Russell McCormmach, "Henry Cavendish on the Theory of Heat," *Isis* 79 (1988): 37–67. See pt. 4, ch. 4, n. 24.

[80]Erwin N. Hiebert, *Historical Roots of the Principle of Energy Conservation* (Madison: State Historical Society of Wisconsin, 1962), 80–93; and P. M. Heimann, "'Geometry and Nature': Leibniz and Johann Bernoulli's Theory of Motion," *Centaurus* 21 (1977): 1–26.

[81]Hiebert, *Historical Roots*, 1, 5, 60, 95, 102. Larmor calls attention to Daniel Bernoulli's writings, which provide an exception to the general rule that *vis viva* was not identified with heat: in Cavendish, *Sci. Pap.* 2:408, 424.

[82]Henry Cavendish, "Plan of a Treatise on Mechanicks," Cavendish Mss IV(b), 45. The "Plan" is important for establishing the connections between Cavendish's various researches. No date is given in the manuscript, but Hugh Hamilton is mentioned in it for his discussion of the lever; Hamilton published on that subject in the *Philosophical Transactions* for 1763. The watermarks on the paper of the "Plan"—HF, GR, and ProPatria—point to an early date, not long after that year. HF, which rarely appears on the paper Cavendish used, appears on the paper of a theoretical manuscript, "Concerning Springs," which belongs to the subject of the "Plan," and again on the covering paper of the manuscript "Digression to Paper on Inflammable Air," which belongs to 1766. The other two watermarks appear in combination in the manuscript "Experiments on Factitious Air," which also belongs to 1766, and in experimental notes on the specific and latent heats, which bear the earliest date of 1765; these two watermarks are compatible with but do not demand an early dating, since they also appear in much later work. Taken together, the evidence argues for placing the "Plan" in the mid-1760s.

Concerned with the logical and empirical foundations of mechanics, the "Plan" is similar in nature to works that Cavendish read at Cambridge, and as such it reveals more about his formal education than about the original investigator he was to become.

The "Plan" is divided into two parts. The first treats the doctrine of pressures and mechanical powers, beginning with the lever. The second treats the theory of motion. There Cavendish argued that what Newton called the third law of motion is only a property of the doctrine of pressures and that all we know of the properties of matter in motion is contained in the first two laws. The foundation of Newton's third law of motion—to every action there is an equal and opposite reaction—was a deep question of mechanics, and there was a decided suggestion in Newton's applications of the law that it had for him a metaphysical, a priori foundation.[83] Cavendish's critical analysis of the logical foundations of mechanics and an enumeration of the experimental proofs of the laws of motion constitute the "Plan," so far as it goes.

Cavendish developed the theory in original directions in separate, unpublished papers, the most important of which is "Remarks on the Theory of Motion." Typical of his theoretical papers, this one is undated, but there is good reason to think that it too falls early in Cavendish's work, especially when it is compared with his datable experiments on heat, which would place it no later than 1765.[84] If the "Remarks" originated in the "Plan of a Treatise," they took another direction, leading to questions that only research outside of mechanics proper could answer. The purpose of the "Remarks" was to show the usefulness of *vis viva* as a "way of computing the force of bodies in motion." For most questions arising in "philosophical enquiries," Cavendish acknowledged that the usual and most convenient way of computing the forces was Newton's momentum and that *vis viva* was usually reserved for solving problems concerning machines for "mechanical" purposes. (The mechanical engineer John Smeaton wrote about *vis viva* for engineers, and he gave his writing on the subject to Cavendish for comment.[85]) But *vis viva* had "philosophical" uses, too, Cavendish said, as he went on to show, though instead of "*vis viva*" he preferred to speak of the "mechanical momentum" of bodies in motion. By this choice of terminology,

referring to both ways of computing the force as species of "momentum," Cavendish drew on his conviction that the choice of one way or the other was a matter of convenience, not of fundamentals.[86] Force itself was the fundamental thing, not the way it was measured.

---

[83]Roderick W. Home, "The Third Law in Newton's Mechanics," *British Journal for the History of Science* 4 (1968): 39–51, on 42, 51.

[84]In a theoretical discussion of heat in the "Remarks," Cavendish showed no awareness of specific and latent heats, which he began experimenting on no later than 1765.

Both the subject and the watermarks of "Remarks" favor an early date. The theory of motion continues the project of the "Plan," Cavendish's intended treatise on mechanics. One of the watermarks, LVG, appears on the earliest of Cavendish's extant papers, his calculations for the 1761 transit of Venus; its last datable appearance is on a paper of 1781. The other watermarks, GR without a circle and an emblem bearing the word "Eropa," appear also on the manuscript "Thoughts Concerning Electricity," which was written sometime between 1767 and 1771; on two manuscripts concerning pendulums; on three astronomical manuscripts, two of which are calculations for the transits of Venus of 1761 and 1769; and on three manuscripts on arsenic, which a given date places in and around 1764, the earliest of Cavendish's datable chemical researches. These correlations strongly suggest that "Remarks" was written in the 1760s and so is among Cavendish's earliest surviving scientific papers.

[85]John Smeaton published several papers in the *Philosophical Transactions* in which he argued that *vis viva* is a measure of mechanical power. He also argued that mechanical power can be lost, as in the turbulence of water in the working of a water wheel. Without specifying the circumstances of the problem at hand, he said, "the terms, quantity of motion, *momentum*, and force of bodies in motion, are absolutely indefinite." Smeaton, "An Experimental Examination of the Quantity and Proportion of Mechanic Power Necessary to Be Employed in Giving Different Degrees of Velocity to Heavy Bodies from a State of Rest," *PT* 66 (1776): 450–75, on 473. The paper Smeaton gave Cavendish to comment on was probably "New Fundamental Experiments upon the Collision of Bodies," *PT* 72 (1782): 337–54. John Playfair told Smeaton that foreign mathematicians already knew about *vis viva* in the way he was using it. Smeaton answered that it was not known by engineers, his intended audience, and that if his conclusion about collisions was not new, his experiments were. On one point, Playfair made Smeaton "very happy": he told Smeaton that "what he said was no way inconsistent with the Newtonian doctrine of motion." Playfair, *Works*, 1:lxxxiii–lxxxiv.

[86]There had been a protracted controversy over the true measure of force, Cavendish siding with the position taken by Jean d'Alembert and others. Momentum and *vis viva*, he said, are two ways of measuring the same thing, the force of bodies in motion: "It appears therefore that this famous controversy about the force of bodies in motion was merely a dispute about words the 2 sides meaning different by the expression force of bodies in motion, for if you measure the force of a body in motion by the time during which it will overcome a given resistance or by the degree of resistance which it will overcome during a given time then this force is directly as the velocity of the body. But if you measure this force by the space through which it will overcome a given resistance or by the degree of resistance against which it will move through a given space then its force is as the square of its velocity." This quotation forms the conclusion of an unnumbered four-page addition to "Remarks." It was not published with the "Remarks" in Cavendish's *Scientific Papers*, but it has since been published and analyzed in P. M. Heimann and J. E. McGuire, "Cavendish and the *Vis viva* Controversy: A Leibnizian Postscript," *Isis* 62 (1970): 225–27.

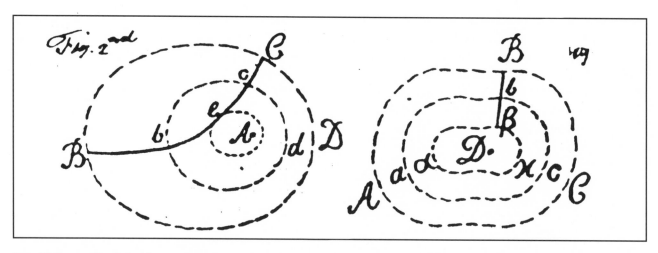

Plate III. Forces. The dashed lines represent forces of attraction and repulsion of constant intensity surrounding particles of matter, or force centers, A and D. BC in Figure 2 and Bb in Figure 3 are the paths of a second attracting and repelling particle. With the aid of these diagrams and a proposition from Newton's *Principia*. Cavendish argues for his general law of conservation of the sum of "real" and "additional" "mechanical momenta" (our kinetic and potential energy). It has been pointed out that Cavendish is struggling here with our concept of equipotential curves. "Remarks on the Theory of Motion," Cavendish Mss VI(b), 7:plate 3; *The Scientific Papers of the Honourable Henry Cavendish, F.R.S.*, vol. 2: *Chemical and Dynamical*. ed. E. Thorpe (Cambridge: Cambridge University Press, 1921), 430.

As in the "Plan of a Treatise," in the "Remarks on the Theory of Motion," Cavendish started with the lever and the motions of simple machines. He then examined, case by case, elastic and inelastic collisions, progressing to the more difficult problems involving any number of bodies attracting or repelling one another by forces. He concluded that, assuming the forces are "central" and act equally at equal distances from their centers, "whenever any system of bodies is in motion in such a manner that there can be no force lost by friction imperfect elasticity or the impinging of inelastic bodies, that then the sum of the mechanical momenta of the moving bodies added to the sum of the abovementioned additional momenta will remain constantly the same."[87] The "additional momenta," in contrast to the "real momenta," represented the hidden, or potential, mechanical momentum temporarily stored in elastic compression or gravitational elevation. Cavendish's statement of the conservation law had a most general character. It speaks of Cavendish's point of departure in mechanics that in reasoning to his law of conservation (of energy), he cited a proposition, number 40, from Newton's *Principia* and nowhere mentioned Leibniz or other Continental developers of the mechanics of *vis viva*.

Heat is identified in "Remarks on the Theory of Motion" with the vibrations of the particles of which the large bodies of our experience are composed. That much Newton and his contemporaries

had said. Cavendish went further by making the mechanical understanding of heat mathematically precise: heat, Cavendish said, is the mechanical momentum of the vibrating particles. He related his theoretical conservation law to an empirical one, the familiar rule that when two unequally heated bodies are placed in contact, the heat lost by one equals that gained by the other: one body receives "as much mechanical momentum or in other words as great an encrease of heat multiplied into its quantity of matter as the other loses so that the sum of their mechanical momenta may remain unaltered."[88]

Cavendish showed that mechanical momentum applies to other areas outside of mechanics in addition to heat. Representing air as a perfectly elastic, particulate fluid, he analyzed the motion constituting sound; and by analogy with sound waves in air, he analyzed waves in water. He discussed light, another particulate body, which communicates its mechanical momentum to absorbing bodies in the course of internal reflections, heating them. And so, over a range of problems belonging to mechanics, heat, acoustics, hydrodynamics, and optics, Cavendish in his "Remarks on the Theory of Motion" demonstrated the value of computing the forces by mechanical momentum when taken together with its conservation law.[89]

---

[87]Cavendish, "Remarks," 428.
[88]Ibid. 424–25.
[89]Ibid. 421, 426–27.

For all of its promise, however, the mechanical theory of heat was in itself incomplete. The explanation of the transfer of heat between bodies could not account for the generation of heat and cold accompanying certain chemical and physical changes in bodies. Cavendish observed that

> there is plainly both an encrease and loss of heat without receiving it from or communicating it to other bodies, as appears from the fermentations and dissolutions of various substances in which there is sometimes an encrease sometimes a loss of heat as well as from the burning of bodies in which there is a vast encrease of heat above what can reasonably be supposed to be produced by the action of emitting light.

Newton too had spoken of the emission of light and its internal reflections and refractions as causing bodies to heat, but Cavendish did not think that this source could account for the great heats observed in combustion. And Newton too had singled out fermentation, dissolution, and burning as evidence of the action of attractive forces, causing particles to collide with violence, manifesting heat. Newton had evidently been mistaken. Cavendish denied that the uncommon heats could arise from the approach or recession of the particles, increasing their motion at the expense of their "additional" momenta, which led him to consider other explanations:

> Particles must either not attract or repel equally at equal distances or must act stronger when placed in some particular situations than others or something else of that nature. One would be apt at first to explain this by supposing them to attract or repel some kind of bodies stronger than others; but then it should seem as if there should always ensue an encrease heat whenever 2 bodies are mixed which mix together with any degree of force whereas there is often produced a great degree of cold thereby as in mixing salt and water. There are other reasons too which seem to shew that this way of explaining it is insufficient.[90]

So even variable and asymmetrically acting forces, which violate the assumptions of the conservation law, could not answer for these heats. Cavendish had no answer.

Earlier we discussed Cavendish's experimental researches on specific and latent heats of the 1760s, pointing out that he wrote them up as a paper to be read, "Experiments on Heat." There is good reason to place this paper later than the "Remarks on the Theory of Motion," since it

contains a theoretical development originating in his experiments. Cavendish anticipated that it would not be obvious to his intended reader how specific and latent heats can be explained by Newton's theory of heat, and he concluded the "Experiments on Heat," with a section headed "Thoughts Concerning the Above Mentioned Phenomena." The section contains only one thought, an incomplete one at that: the foregoing experiments, Cavendish wrote, "at first seemed to me very difficult to reconcile with Newton's theory of heat."[91] The proposition to follow, which was to reconcile the experiments with Newton's theory, is not given.

The proposition Cavendish had in mind clearly had to do with specific heat and its relationship to the "additional" mechanical momenta of the theory. For at the time of the "Experiments on Heat," Cavendish regarded specific heat as fundamental and latent heat as derivative. The heat and cold produced during the change of state of a substance are explained entirely by differences in the specific heats of the substance in its three states. In Cavendish's words: "The reason of this phenomenon seems to be that it requires a greater quantity of heat to make bodies shew the same heat by the thermometer when in a fluid than in a solid state, and when in an elastic state than in a non-elastic state." Cavendish's reasoning enabled him to begin to resolve the theoretical difficulties he discussed in the "Remarks on the Theory of Motion." In a preliminary draft of the "Experiments on Heat," he referred to the cold produced by the mixture of salt and water, which in the earlier "Remarks" he spoke of as contradicting Newton's theory. Now he said of it that "I very much question indeed whether there is any real instance of cold being produced by the mixture of 2 bodies which have an affinity to each other," and he supposed that it "will be shown to be owing to another cause." In another experimental note he said that the "heat caused by mixing spirits & water is not caused by the commotion made by the particles of one uniting with those of the other but only that the mixture of spts & water requires a

---

[90] Ibid. 425–26.
[91] Henry Cavendish, "Experiments on Heat" This manuscript of 40 numbered pages and 10 more unnumbered sides on 3 folded sheets is in Cavendish Mss, Misc., and is published in entirely in *Sci. Pap.* 2:327–51, quotation on 351.

greater quantity of heat to make it raise the thermom. to a given degree than the 2 liquors separately do."[92] To account for the phenomena of heat, Cavendish now had another quantity to interpret mechanically in addition to the mechanical measure of the vibration of particles: the specific heats of substances and their combinations. The promised proposition was not given in "Experiments on Heat" because, we believe, Cavendish found that the explanation of his experiments required a full, new theoretical analysis of heat. Twenty years later he developed this proposition into a complete version of Newton's theory of heat; we discuss this theory in a later chapter.

Cavendish carried out fundamental theoretical studies on dynamics, heat, gases, and electricity more or less at the same time, in the 1760s,[93] and the relationships between these studies are many. Cavendish began working on his electrical theory at about the time of his first publication, on factitious air. This theory was based on the hypothesis of an electrical fluid, an elastic matter of electrical particles capable of being bound within the pores of ordinary bodies. The electrical fluid behaved, that is, like a factitious air, an analogy which Cavendish made explicit. Cavendish's electrical theory was a culmination of his previous theoretical work in the sense that he carried the theory of electricity, and that theory only, to a complete and published conclusion.

In the forty years before Cavendish took up electricity, the subject had been organized experimentally into broad classes of phenomena: attraction, induction, conduction, and so forth. To appreciate this progress, it is only necessary to recall the state of the subject when Newton took it up: to the Royal Society Newton described how glass rubbed on one side attracts and repels bits of paper to and from its opposite surface with an irregular and persisting motion.[94] By the 1760s electricians were beginning to associate electricity with a force acting over sensible distances according to a determinable law, the starting point of a systematically quantified field of electricity. The field was made for Cavendish, skilled manipulator of instruments and maker of mathematical theories.

If Newton observed only agitated bits of paper, he nevertheless sensed that electricity could play a great role in nature. In the *Principia* he speculated on an electrical ether, a "certain most subtle spirit which pervades and lies hid in all gross bodies." It might, Newton thought, account for the forces of electric bodies and beyond that for light and cohesion and animal sensation and will. To learn the laws of "this electric and elastic spirit," more experiments were needed.[95]

Through the early eighteenth century, as techniques were developed for detecting, generating, and accumulating electrical charges, Newton's prophesy of the importance of electricity in the great scheme of things seemed borne out (and, to some electricians, of his speculation about the electrical ether as well). The action of electricity promised to be as universal as that of gravitation and, as impressively demonstrated by the Leyden jar, far more powerful. Fifty years after Newton, the insightful student of the Leyden jar William Watson observed that electricity was an "extraordinary power" that "cannot but be of very great moment in the system of the universe."[96] On the eve of Cavendish's entry onto the scientific scene as an electrician, Joseph Priestley observed that electricity was "no local, or occasional agent in the theatre of the world," that it played a "principal part in the grandest and most interesting scenes of nature."[97] That was to repeat what Newton had said, only now with a good deal more evidence. Scientific expectations ran high. With the exception of his work for the Royal Society on its projects, for several years Cavendish devoted himself almost exclusively to a great work on electricity. He set out to treat a second force of nature after the model of the first, gravitation, and he planned a book about it after his model, Newton's *Principia*.

In accord with his idea of how theories are made, Cavendish began with a hypothesis, that of a

[92]Ibid. 343; four-page preliminary draft of the beginning of Part II of "Experiments on Heat"; and experimental notes on specific and latent heats. Cavendish Mss III(a), 9:39–40.

[93]The following discussion of Cavendish's electrical theory draws on Russell McCormmach, "The Electrical Researches of Henry Cavendish," PhD. diss., Case Institute of Technology, 1967, especially chapter 3, "Cavendish's Electrical Theory," 146–321.

[94]Reported in Joseph Priestley, *The History and Present State of Electricity with Original Experiments* (London, 1767), 13–14.

[95]Isaac Newton, *Sir Isaac Newton's Mathematical Principles of Natural Philosophy and His System of the World*, trans A. Motte, rev. F. Cajori, 2 vols. (Berkeley and Los Angeles: University of California Press, 1962), 2:547.

[96]William Watson, "An Account of the Phenomena of Electricity in Vacuo," *PT* 47 (1752): 363–76 on 375–76.

[97]Priestley, *The History of Electricity*, xii.

specialized matter of electricity, the electric fluid. This electric fluid, a common notion then, owed something to the older idea of electric effluvia but more to the later idea of a general or electric ether. Hermann Boerhaave's doctrine of elementary fire was an influential intermediary between the ether and the various imponderable fluids of the eighteenth century.[98] Particulate, active fluids were postulated for electricity, magnetism, light, and heat, which all bore the prime characteristic of Boerhaave's fire: they were bodies "*sui generis*, not creatable, or producible *de novo*."[99] For its unity, simplicity, and grandeur, the general ether held a strong appeal to experimental philosophers, though in the middle of the century in Britain, progress in the exact understanding electricity and heat did not depend on the concept of the ether directly but on the related concept of specific fluids of fixed quantity. Cavendish did not accept a fluid of heat but he did the fluid of electricity, for particulars of which he drew upon Watson's and Franklin's work.

Watson was the electrical experimenter with whom Lord Charles Cavendish worked closest. The leading British electrician before Franklin, Watson continued to be regarded as one of the Royal Society's leading electricians into the period of Henry Cavendish's researches twenty years later. His theory of electricity of 1748 was based on an electric fluid that permeated all bodies, giving no sign of its presence when the "degree of density" was everywhere the same; but when there was a local inequality in density, electrical effects were manifested as the electric fluid moved to adjust its density to the same "standard."[100] Watson's fluid invited the mathematization of electricity, and had he been a mathematician, he might have recognized that *two* quantities have to be specified to characterize electric phenomena.

In his *History of Electricity* in 1767, Priestley said that English electricians and most foreign ones too had adopted Franklin's theory of positive and negative electricity. Priestley's own opinion was that the basic features of the theory were as "expressive of the true principles of electricity, as the Newtonian philosophy is of the true system of nature in general."[101] Franklin defined a body to be "positively" electrified if it has more than its "normal" quantity of electric fluid, "negatively" electrified if is has less. The usefulness of his terminology is evident in his analysis of the Leyden jar: one side of the jar is electrified positively in exact proportion as the other side is electrified negatively. His theory requires that the amount of fluid that enters one side must flow out of the other. Franklin's analysis turns on the quantities of electric fluid, and although quantity alone is insufficient to explain all electrical phenomena, it nevertheless affords a reasonable understanding of the Leyden jar and of most instances of attraction and repulsion of electrified bodies.

"Thoughts Concerning Electricity," Cavendish's first electrical theory,[102] cannot be earlier than 1767, since Priestley's *History of Electricity* published in that year is cited in it. Here again, as in his writings from that time on chemistry and heat, there is mention of "the reader," who could be the same reader. Although the paper is carefully written, it is fittingly labeled "thoughts." It has a clumsy organization and conveys a sense of groping, and it certainly is not a final draft of anything. We learn from it that Cavendish rejected the commonly held idea of electric "atmospheres" surrounding bodies, an important element in Franklin's theory. We also encounter what would become the leading concept of Cavendish's final theory, the "compression," or "pressure" (as we would say), of the electric fluid (which, Maxell observed, means the same as our modern "potential"[103]). Pressure is an active concept borrowed from pneumatics. Cavendish used Franklin's terms "positive" and "negative"—like Watson's theory, Franklin's theory too, with his plus and minus terms borrowed from numbers, pointed toward the

---

[98] I. B. Cohen, *Franklin and Newton: An Inquiry into Speculative Newtonian Experimental Science and Franklin's Work in Electricity as an Example Thereof* (Philadelphia: American Philosophical Society, 1956), 214–34.

[99] Hermann Boerhaave, *A New Method of Chemistry; Including the Theory and Practice of That Art: Laid Down on Mechanical Principles, and Accommodated to the Uses of Life. The Whole Making a Clear and Rational System of Chemistry . . .*, trans. P. Shaw and E. Chambers, 2 vols. (London, 1727), 1:233.

[100] William Watson, "Some Farther Inquiries into the Nature and Properties of Electricity," *PT* 45 (1748): 93–120, on 95.

[101] Priestley, *History of Electricity*, 160, 455.

[102] Maxwell calls it the first "form of Cavendish's theory": *Sci. Pap.* 1:397–98. The paper, "Thoughts," is on 110–17.

[103] Maxwell, in Cavendish, *Sci. Pap.* 1:111. The fundamental concept of Cavendish's later electrical theory, the "compression," or as he renamed it, the "degree of electrification," was recognized by Maxwell as being equivalent to our electrical potential. We should recall here that in his "Remarks on the Theory of Motion," as Larmor pointed out, Cavendish introduced the equivalent of equipotential lines. Cavendish's original work in dynamics was a direct preparation for his original work in electricity.

mathematization of electricity—but with a different meaning, associating them not with quantity of electricity but with his new concept of compression: he called a body "positively" or "negatively" electrified according to whether the fluid in it is more or less compressed than it is in its natural state. Because Cavendish recognized the need for two quantitative concepts, he introduced another pair of opposing terms: a body is "overcharged" or "undercharged" if it contains more or less fluid than it does in its natural state. Two overcharged bodies repel one another, as do two undercharged bodies; an overcharged and an undercharged body attract. Cavendish would refine his theory, but already he had the theoretical basis for his extraordinary course of electrical experiments: that was the relationship between the two quantitative concepts, pressure or degree of electrification of a body and its charge.

To explain the attraction and repulsion of electrified bodies, Cavendish introduced local concentrations or deficiencies of electric fluid in a space initially filled with electric fluid of uniform density. He then showed that upon his hypothesis, two localized regions with more than their normal quantity of fluid would "appear" to be mutually repelled, one body receding from the other, just as a body of greater density than water "tends to descend in it." In Cavendish's first theory of electricity, the only true (as opposed to apparent) electrical force is the expansive force of the electric fluid. Developing his electrical thoughts at the same time that he carried out his researches on air, Cavendish gave a mathematical investigation of elastic fluids in general, and there he made reference to air as frequently as to the electric fluid, though electricity was his proper subject.[104] The paper "Thoughts," which was carefully drafted in the early parts, ends with a troubling thought: how far his hypothesis of an Watson-like electric fluid diffused uniformly throughout all bodies "will agree with experiment I am in doubt." The mathematical investigation accompanying "Thoughts" breaks off in mid sentence. Cavendish changed theories.

Cavendish's new, published theory of 1771 was based again on an expansive electric fluid but had a greater complexity of forces. He began with an "hypothesis," which reads: "There is a substance, which I call the electric fluid, the

particles of which repel each other and attract the particles of all other matter with a force inversely as some less power of the distance than the cube: the particles of all other matter also, repel each other, and attract those of the electric fluid, with a force varying according to the same power of the distance."[105] The hypothesis is close to Franklin's, but there are important differences. By Cavendish's but not Franklin's, there is an electric force of repulsion between the particles of ordinary matter, which explains the repulsion of undercharged bodies, the chief difficulty of Franklin's explanation. Cavendish's hypothesis also differs from Franklin's in that there is no mention of electric atmospheres, as we pointed out in connection with his earlier theory, and there is a statement about the mathematical form of the law of force. These differences facilitate the introduction of mathematical methods into electrical science; the forces between particles of the two kinds of matter explain everything, and the forces enter as quantifiable laws of force.

If the electric force varies with some power of the distance less than the cube, the force acts over sensible distances. Cavendish had grounds for thinking that the force varies inversely as the square of the distance, like gravitation; but the known phenomena were not conclusive on this point, and he had not completed his own experiments to decide it. In any case, the theory containing a range of possible laws of force and their consequences had to come first. Just as Newton had ultimately appealed to observations of the planets, Cavendish appealed to observations on electricity to decide between the alternative possibilities for the distance dependency of the real force.

In constructing his theory of the electric force, Cavendish's point of departure (in both senses) was the mathematical theory of air in Newton's *Principia*. Newton derived the physical properties of air by postulating a force between the particles of air that varies as the inverse first (not second, as in gravitation) power of the separation of

---

[104]Cavendish's first mathematical theory is reproduced in *Sci. Pap.* 1:398–404.

[105]Cavendish's paper was read at two meetings of the Royal Society, 19 Dec. 1771 and 9 Jan. 1772. "An Attempt to Explain Some of the Principal Phaenomena of Electricity by Means of an Elastic Fluid," *PT* 61 (1771):584–677; *Sci. Pap.* 1:33–81, on 33.

the particles. He derived from it Boyle's law relating the volume and the density or pressure of air, but this law was not as definitive as were Kepler's laws of the solar system for Newton's law of gravitation. Newton left it up to his followers to discuss if "elastic fluids do really consist of particles so repelling each other."[106] Before his electrical theory, Cavendish had already taken up Newton's invitation. Newton, in his upwardly revised derivation of the velocity of sound in air after William Derham's experiments, implied that the repulsion of air particles is inversely as the distance from their surfaces, whereas experiment, Boyle's law, requires it to be inversely as the distance from their centers. To explain the higher velocity, Newton also invoked the vapors in the air with their different "tone," which to Cavendish was not an explanation but an evasion. Newton's derivations of Boyle's law and of the velocity of sound both seemed right, and yet they were in contradiction. About the mathematical law of force of the particles of air, Cavendish was in uncertainty.[107] In his preliminary thoughts on electricity, Cavendish revisited this question, as we have seen, and in the published paper in 1771 he discussed it at length, at the end of his development of electrical theory. It is what Newton would have called a "scholium," an interesting nonsequitur in a paper that is otherwise entirely about electricity; the explanation for it is the closeness of Cavendish's thinking about the two subjects, electricity and air. It begins: "Sir Isaac Newton supposes that air consists of particles which repel each other with a force inversely as the distance."[108] Cavendish enumerated a range of laws of force for air, pointing out that each fails either to give Boyle's law relating pressure and density or to give the uniform distribution of the particles of air. Cavendish concluded that the only law that agrees with experiment is that of a force of repulsion that varies inversely as the distance but which terminates on the nearest particles, which, Cavendish said, "seems not very likely." Newton's law of force for air was regularly cited as a proven truth, a consequence both of Newton's authority and of the tendency of philosophy to follow where mathematics leads. The result was that investigators spoke of elastic fluids as though they were all of one species in their mathematical description. By contrast, Cavendish took up the question in

Newton's spirit, critically, and in the course of his study he drew a mathematical distinction between air and the electric fluid. Just as his experimental discrimination between several elastic, factitious airs helped discredit the notion that there was only one true, permanent air, his mathematical investigations showed that there were elastic fluids in nature that must be represented by different mathematical laws.

In his published theory of electricity, Cavendish made some changes in terminology. He spoke of "positive"' and "negative" electrification or "degree" of electrification instead of his earlier, more graphic "compression," but the concept was the same; namely, pressure. He introduced a term he was then using in his chemistry, "saturation," to describe what he had called the normal or natural state; in chemistry it meant that the affinities of particles were rendered inactive in a chemical union, and in electricity it meant that attractive and repulsive forces were equal and no net electrical activity was manifest. Cavendish spoke of electric and common matter as "contrary" matters, behaving in some respects like acids and alkalies or like factitious air and the bodies absorbing it; the main difference in these comparisons is that the electrical fluid is free to move inside conducting bodies and is prevented from running out of those bodies by the non-conducting air outside the bodies. Any departure from the saturated state causes a body to be "overcharged" or "undercharged," as before.

Cavendish presented his electrical theory in the form of Euclidean demonstration. This rigorously deductive model had been extended from the geometry of the ancients to the sciences; in antiquity by Archimedes, and in recent times by Galileo and Newton using modern mathematics. For British scientific authors in the eighteenth century, Newton's *Principia* was the standard of scientific exposition, and it was naturally adopted by Cavendish, who developed his electrical theory by definitions, propositions, lemmas, corollaries, problems, cases, and remarks. With these categories, he analyzed the electrical content of mathematically treatable bodies such as spheres, discs,

---

[106]Newton, *Mathematical Principles* 1:302.
[107]Henry Cavendish, "Concerning Waves," Cavendish Mss VI(b), 23:5.
[108]Cavendish, "An Attempt," 65.

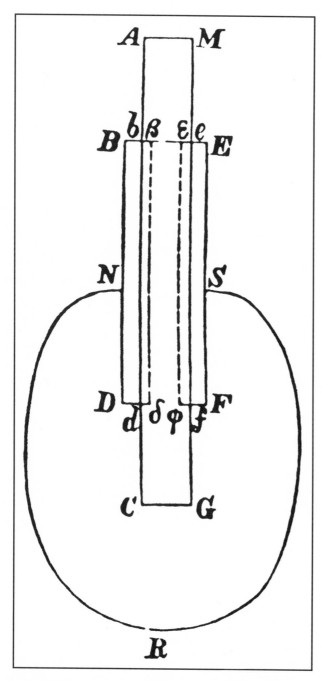

PLATE IV. Leyden Jar. Cavendish analyzes the the phenomena of the Leyden jar using this diagram; that the "jar" is not in the shape of a jar makes no difference to its working. ACGM stands for a plate of glass seen edgeways, on either side of which are plates of conducting matter, such as metal foil. The dotted lines indicate the possible penetration of the electric fluid into the glass from the conducting plates. To charge the Leyden jar, one conducting plate is electrified, the other grounded. If a canal (wire) NRS is connected to the two conducting plates, the redundant electric fluid passes from one to the other, "and if in its way it passes through the body of any animal, it will by the rapidity of its motion produced in it that sensation called a shock." "An Attempt to Explain Some of the Principal Phaenomena of Electricity, by Means of an Elastic Fluid," *Philosophical Transactions* 61 (1771): 623.

Newton's mathematics and mechanics. His theory was the single most impressive use of this education in the second half of the eighteenth century in Britain.

Cavendish's published paper of 1771 had two parts, the first theoretical, the second an application of the theory to experiments done by others. Given Cavendish's experimental skill and interest, it might seem odd that he used only experiments by others to confirm his theory. There were two reasons why he proceeded this way. First, the experiments he cited would be well known to his readers, being the work of Canton, Franklin, and other leading experimenters; they were the experiments on attraction, induction, the Leyden jar, and other phenomena that largely defined the experimental field. The other reason was that at the time his paper was read to the Royal Society, at the end of 1771, he had just begun his own experiments on a new class of phenomena predicted by his theory. Wanting to present these in completeness, he mentioned in his paper that he intended to follow this one with a publication of his own experiments. He also mentioned that these earliest experiments of his pointed to the inverse square law as the law of the electric force, which he also had not yet confirmed by experiments of his own. The paper of 1771 was only the beginning.

We have reserved to the end of our discussion of Cavendish's electrical theory our thoughts about its origins. This seemed to us the right order, since we wanted first to show how extensively his electrical theory was connected with his con-

and parallel plates, and he considered complicated systems of bodies in electrical equilibrium by connecting them with "canals," or wire-like threads of matter through which the electric fluid can freely move. Cavendish's theory of the electric fluid was an original essay in the difficult and still rudimentary science of fluid mechanics. Cavendish, we note, also worked on standard problems of fluid mechanics.[109] The foundation of Cavendish's electrical theory was again his mathematical education at Cambridge with its emphasis on

[109]The indispensable "canals" communicating (incompressible, he assumed here) electric fluid were derivative of the canals of fluid mechanics. Cavendish used "canals" in his work, for example on wave motion: "Concerning Waves," Cavendish Mss VI(b), 23.

temporary work in dynamics, heat, and chemistry. To this indigenous source we should recall that electricity was of particular interest to Cavendish's father. As for Cavendish's immediate incentive, we have little to go on, especially since in the decade or so before Cavendish's publication, relatively little was done on the subject of electricity in Britain. The fundamental researches of Watson, Franklin, and Canton belonged to an earlier time, the 1740s and 1750s. *The Philosophical Transactions* for the 1760s were particularly barren, and in the years immediately preceding Cavendish's paper, the only electrical publications in the journal were one by Giambatista Beccaria and several by Priestley on experiments originating in his *History of Electricity*. Cavendish's paper was the only one on electricity in the journal for 1771. New books in English on electricity in the years before 1771 were almost non-existent, and with two exceptions none was influential. One exception was Priestley's history in 1767, the full title of which is *History and Present State of Electricity with Original Experiments*. This book interested Cavendish not for the "history" but for the "present state" of the electrical research, of which Priestley gave a full account. Cavendish made six references to Priestley's book in his 1771 paper, and these six constitute a majority of his references. The book stimulated Cavendish for the wealth of experiments it brought together, though it definitely did not for what it had to say about the mathematical side of the subject. The deficiency was not Priestley's fault (with one exception, discussed below), since electricity had hardly begun to become mathematical. Priestley, who had no training in mathematics, could recommend electrical research because it required no "great stock" of knowledge, and "raw adventurers" like himself could make first-class discoveries. Priestley listed mathematics as one of the supplementary fields an electrician would be wise to cultivate, but he foresaw experiments as the expanding direction. With regard to mathematics, the one glaring weakness of the *History* was its account of F. U. T. Aepinus's theory, the first and only major attempt to make a mathematical theory of electricity.[110] Priestley dismissed Aepinus's theory (but not his experiments, which he admired) because he thought, incorrectly, that it was based on an incorrect law of electric force, one which led to

Boyle's law for air and not the facts of electricity, and that accordingly electricians would save themselves a "good deal of time and trouble" by not bothering with it.[111] One of Newton's legacies to science was his optical "queries," and Priestley offered his own in electricity, including this: by what law do the particles of the electric fluid repel one another?[112] It is not surprising that in the 1760s Priestley should ask this question but it is surprising that he should give a correct answer to it. From Franklin's observation that cork balls do not separate inside an electrified cup, Priestley inferred that the electric force varies inversely as the square of the distance. Cavendish did not mention this observation by Priestley, but the law of electric force was basic to his mathematical theory of electricity, and his own famous proof of the inverse-square law, his hollow-globe experiment, was an elaboration of the electrified cup. The other book that appeared right before Cavendish's paper was the fourth edition of Franklin's *Experiments and Observations on Electricity*. Published in 1769, a point halfway between Priestley's *History* and Cavendish's paper, this edition of Franklin was cited by Cavendish, and it may have contributed to his change of theories. Here Franklin included a letter to Ebenezer Kinnersely in which he spoke of the repulsion of negatively electrified bodies as a first principle. Franklin, who had rejected a repulsive force in the past, now was persuaded of it, and in its defense he recalled Newton's assertion of repelling forces throughout nature. This edition of Franklin could not be the cause of Cavendish's researches in electricity, but it could have helped reshape them.

The opening paragraph of Cavendish's paper refers to Aepinus's *Tentamen theoriae electricitatis et magnetismi*. Only after he first wrote his paper, he said, did he learn that Aepinus had used more or less the same hypothesis and had arrived at more or less the same results. Cavendish noted, correctly, that he had "carried the theory much farther" and "in a more accurate manner," and therefore he was going ahead with his own paper.

---

[110] R. W. Home, ed., *Aepinus's Essay on the Theory of Electricity and Magnetism*, trans. P. J. Connor (Princeton: Princeton University Press, 1979), 136.

[111] Priestley, *History of Electricity*, 463.

[112] Ibid. 488.

That was all Cavendish said about Aepinus. In recent times, Cavendish's remark has been subjected to historical scrutiny. A case has been made that Cavendish had his own copy of Aepinus in 1766, five and a half years before his paper on electrical theory was read to the Royal Society, and if that is so, Cavendish's assertion that he came across Aepinus only after completing his paper is bewildering. We know that his paper was not yet written in 1766. The argument for making 1766 the year of Cavendish's encounter with Aepinus depends upon a series of assumptions all having to do with Priestley. We need to explain how Priestley, Cavendish, and Aepinus came together, with Canton the middleman.

Aepinus, a leading member of the St. Petersburg Academy, published the *Tentamen* in 1759. On 23 June of an unspecified year, Cavendish wrote to John Canton to say that Canton need not ask Priestley for the book since he found a copy in a London bookstore.[113] The letter has been attributed to the year 1766 on the basis of a series of assumptions: that Priestley did not own the book; that Canton lent him his copy for his *History of Electricity*; that Priestley would not have kept the borrowed book after finishing his book in 1767; and that Priestley's interest had turned to other matters and he would not borrow Aepinus's book again.[114] All of the assumptions have a degree of plausibility, and they can all be reasonably doubted too. There was nothing, for example, to prevent Priestley from borrowing Canton's copy of the Tentamen again, if that is what had happened before. Priestley was still doing electrical research and, in fact, was the principal contributor on the to the *Philosophical Transactions* to 1770. As late as 1773 he was planning to write a continuation of his *History of Electricity*, and he consulted books on electricity for his revisions of the *History* in 1769 and 1775.[115]

The *Tentamen* is the only book Cavendish is known to have tried to borrow from someone. Given his shyness, he would not have made the request lightly, and once having gone to this considerable trouble to locate it, he would not have acquired it for the purpose of gathering dust on his shelf for five and a half years before opening it, while in the meantime he himself was working hard on precisely the same subject, the mathematical principles of electricity. Cavendish bought books not to bind in leather for display but

to read. On the basis of the fragmentary correspondence that has survived, Cavendish's letter informing Canton that he had found a copy of the *Tentamen* could have been written in any of the years between 1766 and 1771, and all things considered, especially from what we know of Cavendish's habits, we think that in all likelihood it was 1771, a few months before his paper was read to the Royal Society. In any case, that would have been about the time he first looked in Aepinus's book.

The main interest of the episode of Aepinus's book lies not in anything it tells us about Cavendish but in what it reveals about electrical work in Britain at the time. A related interest is in what it reveals about the communication of science at the time. In 1762, three years after Aepinus's *Tentamen* was published, a large shipment of publications from the St. Petersburg Academy was received in London. Thomas Birch, who was then secretary of the Royal Society, was sent a letter in late September 1762 alerting him to the shipment and also giving him a list of twenty-seven persons to receive Aepinus's publications. Canton is not on the list, nor is Priestley, nor, of course, either of the Cavendishes, but many friends of the Cavendishes are on it: Heberden, Watson, Macclesfield, Knight, Wray, and Willoughby, to name several. The parcels were addressed to the Royal Society, the British Museum, Cambridge, Oxford, and individuals.[116] We know that the Royal Society received its parcel in early November and that it contained the *Tentamen* among other publications by Aepinus, and we assume others on the list also received the *Tentamen*. The list contains some excellent experimentalists, notably Watson, but there is no one on it who could develop a mathematical theory of electricity or perhaps even follow one. Just as there would be no audience in Britain for Cavendish's mathematical theory in 1771, there was none in 1762 for Aepinus's. It

[113]Henry Cavendish to John Canton, 23 June, Canton Papers, Royal Society, correspondence, vol 2.
[114]R. W. Home, "Aepinus and the British Electricians: The Dissemination of a Scientific Theory," *Isis* 63 (1972): 190–204.
[115]Joseph Priestley to John Canton, 24 May 1768; Joseph Priestley to Alesssandro Volta, 10 Nov. 1773, in *A Scientific Autobiography of Joseph Priestley (1733–1804)*, ed. R. E. Schofield (Cambridge, Mass.: M.I.T. Press, 1966), 68 69, 144.
[116]Daniel Dumaresque to Thomas Birch, 25 Sep. 1762, BL Add Mss 4304, p. 79.

is entirely conceivable that Henry Cavendish would have heard no discussion of Aepinus's work in that direction, for there probably was none. Priestley's revisions of his *History of Electricity* left unchanged his discussion of Aepinus's mathematical theory[117] suggesting that none of his electrical colleagues recognized its error and corrected him. By the time Cavendish read the *Tentamen*, he saw that he had gone far beyond Aepinus, and that is what he told the readers of the *Philosophical Transactions* in 1771.

Aepinus's electrical theory was first discussed extensively in print in English only a half century later, by John Robison. Because of its mathematical nature, Robison said, Aepinus's theory was the first to tread in Newton's footsteps, and in this respect so it was.[118] Robison was a great admirer of Cavendish's electrical theory, too. His praise, of course, came too late to make any difference to Cavendish, Aepinus, or the science of electricity.

---

[117]Personal communication from Robert E. Schofield.
[118]John Robison, *A System of Mechanical Philosophy*, 4 vols, ed. with notes by D. Brewster (Edinburgh, 1822) 4:109.

CHAPTER 5

❧

Electricity

Electricity better than any other subject allowed Cavendish to make use of all of his skills as an improver of instruments, a constructor of mathematical theories, and a maker of experiments. In the last chapter we discussed the electrical theory he published; in this we discuss the electrical experiments that followed from it.

Cavendish's experimental precautions were legion. To give one example: he calculated the inductive influence on his apparatus of the experimental room itself, which he imagined to be a sphere sixteen feet in diameter, "about its real size."[1] (The precaution is analogous to that of the astronomer who considers the disturbing gravitational influence on his instruments by nearby mountains; it may not be a coincidence that Cavendish was working on the attraction of mountains for the Royal Society at the same.) There were very few electrical instruments, and Cavendish, as usual, did not invent new ones but adapted the best then in use, making endless comparisons of electrometers for measuring charge, Henley's, Lane's, and his own variants. His last experiments were on electrical conduction, for which there did not yet exist a measuring instrument, a limitation he overcame by using his body as an ingenious kind of galvanometer. His great battery of Leyden jars was similar to Priestley's, the first large battery.[2]

Capacity

When in his published paper of 1771 Cavendish supported his electrical theory with well-known experiments by others, he had just begun to do experiments of his own, of a new kind. The trials of the quantitative predictions of his theory turned out to be a work of several years.

Cavendish never delivered the experimental paper he promised in 1771, not because of disappointed hopes but because of unexpected riches. His theory pointed to a vast region of new

electrical facts, which, given his caution and his curiosity, he had to pursue to the last experiment. In this respect his theory was a success, which in a contrary way deflected him from publishing his experiments soon or, as it turned out, ever.

From the numbering of his experiments and other indications, we know that Cavendish's next paper would have given an experimental proof of the mathematical law of the electric force followed by the entirely new consequences he drew from this law together with the rest of the theory. Here Cavendish followed Newton, who deduced from the facts of planetary motions the inverse-square law of gravitation. Then, just as from the law of gravitation, Newton derived other planetary phenomena, from the law of electrical force Cavendish derived other phenomena of electricity. From his first experiments on electrical capacities, Cavendish anticipated that the electric force obeys the inverse-square law, but he needed an independent proof; two years passed before he came up with his famous hollow-globe experiment.[3]

Several attempts had been made to determine directly the law of electric force by experiment, for example, by Stephen Gray, Cromwell Mortimer, Daniel Bernoulli, and John Robinson. The latter two concluded that the law was the same as that of gravitation. There had also been an indirect inference of the law of electric force, Joseph Priestley's, as we have noted; according to a well-known theorem of the *Principia*, there is no force in the interior of a gravitating shell if the force

---

[1]Henry Cavendish, *The Scientific Papers of the Honourable Henry Cavendish*, vol. 1: *The Electrical Researches*, ed. J. C. Maxwell, rev. J. Larmor (Cambridge: Cambridge University Press, 1921), 169.

[2]William D. Hackmann, *Electricity from Glass: The History of the Frictional Electrical Machine 1600–1850* (Alphen aan den Rijn: Sijtoff & Noordhoff, 1978), 99–100.

[3]The discussion in this chapter is drawn from Russell McCormmach, "The Electrical Researches of Henry Cavendish," Ph.D. diss., Case Institute of Technology, 1967, especially chapter 4, "Cavendish's Electrical Experiments," and chapter 5, "Conclusion," 322–497.

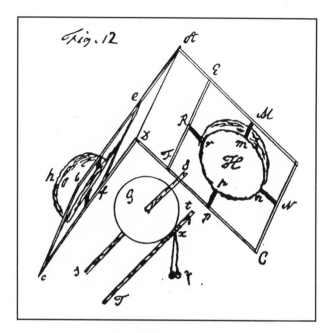

PLATE V. Hollow-Globe Apparatus. With this apparatus Cavendish demonstrates the law of the electric force. His drawing of it shows a hinged wooden frame that when closed brings together two hemispherical shells around but not touching an inner globe, which is 12.1 inches in diameter and suspended by a stick of glass. The hemispheres and the inner globe are covered with metal foil, and a metal connection is made between the two. When the frame is closed, the hemispheres are electrified with a Leyden jar. Then the metal connection is removed by a string from outside, and the frame is opened. A pair of pith-balls shown in the drawing is brought against the inner globe. Cavendish finds that the pith-balls do not separate, showing that no electricity has been communicated to the inner globe. By a theorem from Newton's *Principia*. Cavendish concludes that the electrical force obeys the inverse-square law of the distance. "Experimental Determination of the Law of Electric Force," Cavendish Mss I, 7(a); *The Electrical Researches of the Honourable Henry Cavendish*, ed. J. C. Maxwell (Cambridge, 1879), 104.

of gravitation obeys the inverse-square law. Other electricians gave different explanations of the electrified cup; Canton told Priestley that it contained "no mystery."[4] Only Cavendish, it seems, followed up Priestley's reasoning.

Cavendish demonstrated mathematically that if the intensity of the electric force falls off as the inverse-square of the distance from the electric source, the redundant electric fluid on an electrified sphere lies entirely on its outer surface. He made two conducting globes of slightly different sizes, placing one inside the other and connecting them electrically. Upon electrifying the outer globe, he found that the inner globe was not electrified, in agreement with the inverse-square law. The rough instrument he used for detecting any electricity on the inner globe—a simple pair of pith balls suspended by linen threads—he made into an instrument of relatively high precision by his method. By reducing the charge of the Leyden jar to one sixtieth of its original strength and applying it to the globe, he found that the pith balls barely separated. With that measure of the sensitivity of his apparatus, he knew that the quantity of redundant electricity communicated from the outer globe to the inner globe was less that one-sixtieth part of the redundant electricity, and he concluded that there was no reason to believe that any redundant electricity was communicated to the inner globe. He expressed this result in a more meaningful form: the electric force varies inversely as some power of the distance

between 2 + 1/50 and 2 - 1/50, from which he concluded that there is "no reason to think that it differs at all from the inverse duplicate ratio."[5] That is, if the inverse power of the distance of the law of electric force were 2 + 1/50 or 2 - 1/50, Cavendish would have detected a charge on the inner globe. Cavendish repeated the experiment replacing the globe within a globe by a parallelpiped within a parallelpiped. Then, just as the law of gravitation depends not only on the distance between two bodies but also on the quantities of matter in them, Cavendish did other experiments to show that electricity has the same kind of law: the electric force between two bodies depends also on the quantities of redundant electric fluids in them.[6] A hundred years later, in the laboratory named after him at Cambridge, Cavendish's hollow-globe experiment was repeated with refinements, using an electrometer capable of detecting a charge thousands of times smaller than Cavendish's, with this result: the electric force varies inversely as some power of the distance between 2 + 1/21600 and 2 - 1/21600.[7] We note that so compelling was the example of the law of gravitation that Cavendish did not consider the possibility that the distance dependency of the electric force could be anything but some inverse power of the distance. If

[4]John Canton to Joseph Priestley, 10 Jan. 1767, Canton Papers, Royal Society, Correspondence 2.
[5]Henry Cavendish, "Experimental Determination of the Law of Electric Force," *Sci. Pap.* 1:124.
[6]Henry Cavendish, "Whether the Force With Which Two Bodies Repel Is as the Square of the Redundant Fluid, Tried by Straw Electrometers," *Sci. Pap.* 1:189–93.
[7]The experiment was done by Donald MacAlister in 1877 and 1878 under Maxwell's direction. James Clerk Maxwell, "On the Unpublished Electrical Papers of the Hon. Henry Cavendish," *Proc. Camb. Phil. Soc.* 3 (1877): 86–89, on 87.

the null result of his hollow-globe experiment was compatible with a different kind of force, Cavendish did not regard it as a physically significant alternative.[8] Cavendish did not publish his indirect experimental determination of the inverse-square force; in the 1780s, Charles Augustin Coulomb established the law directly with a torsion balance, and with Coulomb's publication the law went into history.

Cavendish's plan for the published work was to follow the proof of the inverse-square law with experiments that confirmed his theory as a whole. The experiments were carried out on the charges of bodies of various sizes and shapes, connected by slender wires, the material embodiment of the canals of incompressible fluid of his theory. These were experiments on what came to be called the electrical "capacities" of bodies, a new activity in electrical science owing entirely to his theory. His method depended upon his leading, original idea in electrical theory, the "degree of electrification," which we can think of as equivalent to our electrical potential. Electrically connected bodies of various shapes and sizes carried different charges at the same degree of electrification; the ratio of these charges was therefore physically meaningful and, Cavendish showed, measurable. Repeating his approach in chemistry, to compare the electrical capacities of bodies, he introduced standard measures, here a conducting globe of 12.1 inch diameter, the same globe that he used in the hollow-globe experiment, and "trial plates," which were pairs of rectangular tin sheets that could be slid across one another to vary the area of the rectangle. Having shown that the charges of similar bodies are proportional to their linear dimensions, he could express his experimental results simply; his preferred way was to state the charge of a body as the charge of a globe of the same capacity at the same degree of electrification, as "globular inches" or "inches of electricity." By his extraordinarily careful technique, he obtained highly precise results for his capacities with the use of a simple pith-ball electrometer. For example, he found the ratio of the capacity of a circular disc to that of a sphere of the same diameter to be 1/1.57; today the theoretically calculated value is 1/1.570. . . .[9]

The "work," the electrical publication in progress, had another "Part," which was about experiments on the charges of plates of glass and other non-conductors coated in the manner of Leyden jars. For these experiments Cavendish again introduced trial plates, in this case plates that were themselves simple Leyden jars, plane glass plates with circular coatings of foil. The thickness of the glass he determined accurately with a Bird dividing engine.

This part of Cavendish's work has a decidedly unfinished quality to it. In fact, Leyden jars caused such difficulties for the theory that early on he feared that the "reader" might suspect that there was "some error in the theory."[10] He convinced himself that there was not, but it took a great many experiments and all his theoretical ingenuity.

In a qualitative way Cavendish's theory explained Leyden jars perfectly well, as he had shown in his published paper of 1771, but now Cavendish was doing quantitative electricity. The Leyden jar nearly ended his career as a mathematical electrician when he found that the measured charge of a glass Leyden jar was eight times greater than the charge predicted by his theory, a discrepancy which could not be written off as experimental error. "This is what I did not expect before I made the experiment," he said in the manner of understatement, and he then proposed an explanation of why the glass of the Leyden jar acted as if it were eight times thinner than it actually was. Glass, he reasoned, has an electrical structure according to which non-conducting and conducting parts are arranged in alternating layers, the thickness of any one conducting layer of glass being "infinitely small."[11] For the explanation to work, the total thickness of the non-conducting parts has to be one eighth the thickness of the conducting parts. Lest the explanation seem entirely ad hoc, Cavendish made an "analogy between this and the power by which

---

[8]Laplace gave the first proof that for there to be no force inside a uniform hollow globe, the only function of the distance it can have is the inverse square, as noted by Maxwell in *The Electrical Papers of the Honourable Henry Cavendish* (London, 1879), 422. Laplace's proof still does not rule out other possible forces consistent with Cavendish's experiment; the point is discussed in Jon Dorling, "Henry Cavendish's Deduction of the Electrostatic Inverse Square Law from the Result of a Single Experiment," *Studies in the History and Philosophy of Science* 4 (1974): 327–48, on 335–36, 341–42.

[9]R. J. Stephenson, "The Electrical Researches of the Hon. Henry Cavendish, F.R.S.," *The American Physics Teacher* 6 (1938): 55–58, on 56.

[10]Henry Cavendish, "Experiments on Coated Plates," *Sci. Pap.* 1:151–88, on 180.

[11]Ibid., 176.

a particle of light is alternately attracted and repelled many times in its approach towards the surface of any refracting or reflecting medium." He directed the reader to John Michell's explanation of Newton's so-called fits of easy reflection and transmission of light,[12] according to which each particle of a refractive or reflecting medium is surrounded by a great many equal intervals of attraction and repulsion, alternately succeeding one another; a particle of light either enters the medium or is deflected from it according to the pattern of these forces. In Cavendish's analogy, the particles of light are replaced by particles of the electric fluid, which are bound or repelled by forces of the particles of glass; where attractive and repulsive forces coincide, the electric fluid is free to move, constituting the infinitely thin conducting layer. By this appeal to the general theory of matter and forces that he accepted, Cavendish saved his electrical theory. He drew additional confidence in his explanation from experiments on Leyden jars made of air instead of glass. The air jar did not give an eightfold departure from the theory but agreed with it, and since air does not have a fixed structure like glass, the departure in the case of glass jars had to arise from the glass and not from the theory.[13] Cavendish made a thorough study of the electrical properties of glass, grinding the glass surfaces, subjecting the glass to intense electrical forces, and heating the glass of his Leyden jars in what was essentially a continuation of his father's experiments on the conductivity of hot glass.[14] In trying different kinds of glass and other non-conducting substances, Cavendish made a fundamental discovery, that of specific inductive capacities, which would be rediscovered by Faraday in the next century. He found that like the thermal properties of different substances, the electrical properties of different substances vary quantitatively and characteristically. In both fields, heat and electricity, Cavendish made this discovery by his quantitative experiments without any theoretical anticipation. Within the context of experiments undertaken to follow up the consequences of his electrical theory, his experimental technique was in itself a tool of discovery.

Conduction

Before we return to the nature and fate of Cavendish's "work," we will discuss the remainder of his electrical experiments, which went well beyond

his theory of 1771. Phenomena of conduction were only slightly represented among the "principal phaenomena" of electricity of his paper of that year. By 1773 he had changed his mind or at least his direction; from then on all of his electrical experiments were about conduction. He did a great many experiments on the new subject, in the course of which he revealed an ingenuity of experimental method unsurpassed in any of his other researches; he obtained results in very close agreement with modern ones, but his account of them remained in the form of rough notes, leaving us partially in the dark about his motivations. These experiments were, in his judgment, the most inconclusive of his electrical experiments.

One reason why Cavendish took up electrical conduction may have been his recent study of the Leyden jar in terms of conducting and non-conducting layers; moreover, it was generally understood at the time that there was no sharp division between conducting and non-conducting substances. Here we should recall the setting of his experiments on electricity, Great Marlborough Street, where he lived with his father, who had taken a great interest in electrical conduction in glass and in other substances and even in the vacuum. Henry Cavendish's work on conduction led him in new directions, but it was clearly related to his theoretical and experimental work in electricity up to that point; his experiments on the conduction of electricity closely paralleled the experiments he had just concluded on electrical capacities.

Since in the 1770s current electricity was still undiscovered, Cavendish studied conduction using transient discharges of Leyden jars, and to make the study accurate he made himself into his own principal instrument of measurement. In other kinds of experiments, Cavendish's primary sense was variously sight, hearing, and occasionally smell and taste, but in his experiments on electrical conduction, it was touch or, to be more specific, an electrically stimulated sensation in the skin of the hands and in the internal nerves of the wrists and

---

[12]Michell's account was reported in Joseph Priestley's *History and Present State of Discoveries Relating to Vision, Light, and Colours* (London, 1772), 1:309–11.

[13]Cavendish, "Experiments on Coated Plates," 180.

[14]As reported by Benjamin Franklin, in *Benjamin Franklin's Experiments: A New Edition of Franklin's Experiments and Observations on Electricity*, ed. with historical introduction by I. B. Cohen (Cambridge, Mass.: Harvard University Press, 1941), 363–64.

elbows. His technique was to insert himself into the electric circuit by holding a piece of metal in each hand and touching one piece to the knob of a Leyden jar and the other piece to one end of a tube containing a conducting solution; the other end of the conducting solution was connected by a wire to the other side of the Leyden jar. For containing his solutions, he used calibrated, glass tubes about a yard long with wires inserted at each end as electrodes. The resistance of a solution was varied by sliding one of the wires to vary the effective length of the solution. For the purpose of comparing one conducting solution with another, he prepared a series of six equally charged Leyden jars, which he then discharged alternately through the two solutions (and himself), adjusting the wire in one of the tubes until the shocks of the two solutions were as nearly equal as he could judge. In this way, with "truly marvelous" discrimination, he obtained conductivities consistent with one another and remarkably close to those obtained by later experimenters with their instrument for the purpose, invented forty years later, the galvanometer.[15]

As we would expect, Cavendish explained electrical conduction as he had electrical equilibrium, by the fluid mechanics of the matter of electricity. He attributed the shock he felt with his hands to the combined effect of the quantity of electric matter discharged and its velocity. He experienced the force of electricity in motion, the direct electrical analogue of momentum, the product of quantity of matter and velocity, the measure of the force of ordinary matter in motion. In passing through matter—wires, solutions, and flesh—the electric fluid encountered "resistance," and as in ordinary fluid mechanics, Cavendish assumed that the resistance varied as some power of the velocity.[16] His experiments to determine that power yielded the value 1 or values close to it; it has been pointed out that if Cavendish's velocity is interpreted as strength of current, or current per unit area, he came upon what would later be known as Ohm's law.[17] He arrived at a good many other results in electrical conduction that others after him would rediscover. (We make this observation about so many of Cavendish's researches that it becomes tiresome, but it is the truth all the same.)

By an oblique route, Cavendish revealed to the public his understanding of electrical

conduction. Long before Luigi Galvani's work at the end of the eighteenth century, animal electricity had been recognized and studied, but its identity with common electricity had yet to be experimentally demonstrated. With Cavendish's help, an electric fish called the "torpedo" was shown to be capable of delivering stupefying shocks with common electricity.

A number of species of fish belonging to more than one genus are known to use electricity as a weapon. The early experiences of our own species with electricity may well have been by this means, as Egyptian tombs portray fishermen with the electric catfish of the Nile. The electric ray is depicted in the ruins of Pompeii; Pliny wrote of it that "from a considerable distance even, and if only touched with the end of a spear or staff, this fish has the property of benumbing even the most vigorous arm, and of riveting the feet of the runner, however swift he may be in the race." Its numbing property gave rise to its Greek name, "narke," with the same root at *narcotic*, and its Roman name, "torpedo," from *torporific*. Biology subsequently made distinctions between electrical fish, rays, eels, and so on, naming them accordingly.[18]

Known in antiquity and in the Renaissance as a magical fish, defying natural explanation, the torpedo retained its occult aura even into the eighteenth century but not beyond the experiments of the 1770s.[19] In the decade before, it had been suggested that the most formidable of the electric fishes, a South American eel, the *Electrophorus electricus*, then called "Gymnotus," was indeed "electrical." This large, otherwise almost blind, weak-swimming fish with small teeth and no spines or scales was said to be able to kill men and horses. The identification of the singular power of the Gymnotus with electricity may be why John Walsh, with Franklin's encouragement, began to experiment on a nearby weaker electrical

[15]Maxwell's "Introduction," *Electrical Researches of the Honourable Henry Cavendish*, xxvii–lxvi, on lvii–lviii.

[16]In treating the motion of bodies in resisting mediums, Newton in the *Principia* assumed that the resistance is proportional to some power of the velocity.

[17]Maxwell made this observation in Cavendish, *Sci. Pap.* 1:25.

[18]R. T. Cox, "Electric Fish," *American Journal of Physics* 11 (1943): 13–22, on 13–14.

[19]Brian P. Copenhaver, "Natural Magic, Hermeticism, and Occultism in Early Modern Science," in *Reappraisals of the Scientific Revolution*, eds. D. C. Linberg and R. S. Westman (Cambridge: Cambridge University Press, 1990), 261–301, on 278–79.

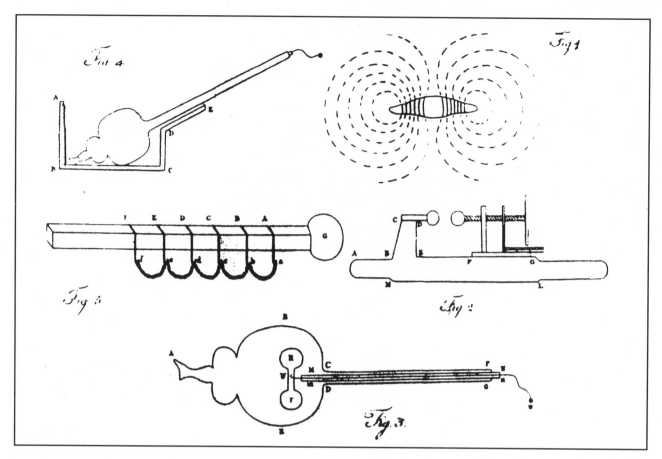

PLATE VI. Artificial Electric Fish. In Figure 1, the broken lines stand for the paths of the electric fluid, which passes from the electric ray, or torpedo (solid line), in water. Figure 2 is Cavendish's handheld modified version of Timothy Lane's electrometer, made of brass and wood, indicating the distance a spark flies. Not shown is the pitch-ball electrometer used to estimate the strength of a charge. Resembling a stringed musical instrument, the drawing in Figure 3 is the artificial torpedo. Cut to the shape of the fish, a piece of wood 16 3/4 inches long and 10 3/4 inches wide with a handle 40 inches long is fitted with a glass tube MNmn. A wire passing through the tube is soldered at W to a strip of pewter, which represents the electric organs. The other side of the apparatus is fitted exactly the same way, with tube, wire, and pewter. With the exception of the handle, the whole is wrapped with a sheet of sheep's skin leather. Figure 4 shows the apparatus immersed in a vessel of salt water. Through the wires and the body of the artificial fish, Cavendish discharges portions of his great battery of 49 extremely thin-walled Leyden jars. Figure 5 shows a device for testing if the shock of the artificial torpedo can pass through chain.

fish, the torpedo. Son of the governor of Fort St. George at Madras, Walsh had served in the East India Company, becoming paymaster to the troops at Madras and then Clive's private secretary in India. Now a nabob and a Member of Parliament, Walsh was well connected with men of science: he was Nevil Maskelyne's first cousin, a Fellow of the Royal Society, and a member of the Royal Society Club, to whom he introduced two Eskimos.[20] Drawn to exotica in science as in life, he was the sort of adventurous person whom Cavendish regularly sought out. It was no doubt through Walsh that Cavendish became involved with the torpedo.

In 1772 Walsh went on a torpedo hunt to La Rochelle and the Isle of Re, France. From La Rochelle he wrote to Franklin that he had found the torpedo's effect to be "absolutely electrical."[21] As in earlier experiments with the Leyden jar, only this time with the fish in place of the jar, several persons joined hands and felt the shock together. The back and breast of the fish have different electricities like the sides of a Leyden jar, leading Walsh to wonder if its effect could be exactly imitated by one. He enlisted the anatomist John Hunter to dissect a slablike specimen of a torpedo a foot and a half long, a foot wide, and two inches thick. Hunter was impressed by what he saw. Each

[20]Archibald Geikie, *Annals of the Royal Society Club* (London: Macmillan, 1917), 115–16, 121. "Walsh, John ," *DNB* 20:671–72.

[21]John Walsh to Benjamin Franklin, 12 July 1772, quoted in John Walsh, "Of the Electric Property of the Torpedo," *PT* 63 (1773): 461–80, on 462.

of the pair of electrical organs had about 470 prismatic columns, and each column was divided by horizontal membranes, 150 to the inch, forming tiny spaces filled with fluid.[22] Hunter presented the Royal Society with a pickled male and female example of this wonderfully structured animal.

Serious doubts were raised about the electrical nature of the torpedo, which could not produce a spark or separate pith balls. One of the doubters was the electrician William Henly, who (before Cavendish) made an "artificial torpedo," of conducting materials, which exhibited "no attraction or repulsion of light bodies, no snap, no light, nor indeed any sensation." Henly argued that the real torpedo was in the same predicament as his artificial torpedo, incapable of giving an *"electrical shock."*[23]

Moreover, if the torpedo did have ordinary electricity, it had to have a very great deal of it. The *Torpedo occidentalis* (a larger electrical fish than Walsh's torpedo) has been shown to deliver an instantaneous maximum voltage of 220 volts and a current of 60 amps.[24] How could a fish store all that electricity, and how did it deliver it? Walsh turned to Cavendish for the answers. Cavendish, he said, was the "first to experience with artificial electricity, that a shock could be received from a charge which was unable to force a passage through the least space of air."[25] Since Cavendish had published nothing from his electrical experiments, Walsh had got this information from him by request sometime early in 1773. In 1774 Walsh received the Copley Medal for his experiments on the electrical nature of the fish, on the significance of which the president of the Royal Society, John Pringle, had this to say: "between lightning itself and the Leyden Phial there is no specific difference, nay scarcely a variety, as far as is known, why then should we unnecessarily multiply species and suppose the torpedo provided with one different from that which is everywhere else to be found?"[26]

Cavendish went on to construct an artificial torpedo based on the anatomy and electricity of the fish, and in 1776 he published a paper on it.[27] A main objection to the idea that the torpedo possesses electricity was that its tremendous shock is delivered underwater where the electric fluid has easier channels than through the victim's (or the observer's) body. That criticism was based on the commonly held but incorrect view that all of the electric fluid flows along the "shortest and readiest" path. The paths it actually takes depend on the relative resistances of all of the paths available to it. The reason, Cavendish explained, why a person holding a wire with both hands, and thereby forming a parallel circuit with the wire, does not feel a shock when a discharge is sent along the wire is that the resistance of the body is so much greater than that of the wire that only an insensible fraction of the discharge passes through the body. To explain how a fish could throw a great shock and yet not produce a spark, Cavendish noted that the length of spark from a battery of Leyden jars varies inversely as the number of jars in the battery. He believed that the electric organs of the torpedo are equivalent to a great number of Leyden jars connected like a battery: these living jars are weakly electrified, but because of their great number, they can store a large quantity of electricity. Cavendish answered another common objection with this observation: the discharge of the torpedo is completed so quickly that a pair of pith balls in contact with the animal does not have time to separate. To prove the correctness of his explanations, Cavendish built his artificial torpedos. His first one was cut out of wood in the shape of the fish, but it did not conduct as well as Cavendish thought the real fish did; he built a second one by pressing together shaped pieces of thick leather like the "soles of shoes" to represent the body, and attaching thin plates of pewter to each side to imitate the electric organs. With glass-insulated wires he connected the pewter plates to a battery, and he encased the whole in sheep's skin soaked in salt solution, the stand-in for the skin of

---

[23]William Henly to William Canton, 14 Mar. 1775, Canton Papers, Royal Society, Correspondence 2:104.

[24]R. T. Cox, "Electric Fish," *American Journal of Physics* 11 (1943): 13–22, on 19. In one place among his notes on the torpedo experiments, Cavendish referred to an artificial Gymnotus. Cavendish, *Sci. Pap* 1: 304. This fish is an "electric eel" (though not truly an eel but related to the carp and catfish), and it is the most formidable of all electric fishes. Its electrical organs extend to the length of its tail, four-fifths of its body, and so its anatomy in this respect is entirely different from that of the torpedo.

[25]Walsh, "Torpedo," 476.

[26]John Pringle, *A Discourse on the Torpedo Delivered at the Anniversary Meeting of the Royal Society, November 30, 1774* (London, 1775). Quoted in Dorothea Waley Singer, "Sir John Pringle and His Circle.—Part III," *Annals of Science* 6 (1950): 248–61, on 251.

[27]Henry Cavendish, "An Account of Some Attempts to Imitate the Effects of the Torpedo by Electricity," *PT* 66 (1776): 196–225; in *Sci. Pap*.l:194–210.

the torpedo. Discharging different numbers of Leyden jars through the artificial torpedo and placing his hands on or near it, he found that the sensations agreed with descriptions of the shock of the real torpedo. With the artificial torpedo out of water, the shock was:

> very slight in fingers.
> only in hands, there seemed to be something wrong.
> brisk in elbows.
> briskish in elbows.

Under water it was:

> just sensible in hands.
> stronger.
> pretty strong Do.[28]

So that others could experience his artificial torpedo, Cavendish invited into his laboratory a number of interested persons: the torpedo anatomist Hunter, of course; Lane, whose electrometer Cavendish was using; Nairne, whose battery and coated glass plates he was using; Priestley, who was in London on a visit; and Thomas Ronayne.[29] The latter, a skeptic, had said of Walsh's electrical hypothesis of the torpedo that he would have to "give up his reason" to believe that the tissues of the fish could accumulate enough electricity to deliver a shock; he left Cavendish's laboratory a believer, we presume, since Cavendish recorded in his notes of the visit "Mr Ronayne felt a small shock."[30] For reason was with Cavendish, who pointed out that the battery of the real fish was superior to his, stupendous as his was for the time, seven rows of seven thin-walled jars each, equivalent in capacity in his units to a sphere 321,000 inches or 26,750 feet across.[31] From Hunter's observations Cavendish calculated that the torpedo had nearly fourteen times the electrical capacity of even this battery. He concluded that "there seems nothing in the phenomena of the torpedo at all incompatible with electricity."[32] Cavendish's was not to be the last word on this question, since the discovery of the Voltaic battery provided a better analog of the electric organs of fishes than the Leyden-jar battery. Davy, Faraday, and others did the definitive researches on the electrical character of the several kinds of electrical fish.[33] Although Cavendish thought that it was likely that the electric fish contained something "analogous" to the Leyden-jar battery, he also considered that there might be no such thing, and in envisioning the possibility that the electric fluid is not stored but gradually transferred by a small "force" through the substance and over the surface of the body of the fish, he anticipated (it has been pointed out) the Voltaic battery and the associated fundamental concept of electromotive force.[34]

Cavendish came to his conclusions about the torpedo entirely from scientific reasoning; for he certainly had never seen or touched a live torpedo. The significance of his paper on the subject was, above all, as a highly abbreviated treatise on the principles of electricity and a primer on laboratory technique. The main ideas and methods were all there, introduced by Cavendish as needed to support his arguments. This application, the torpedo, was, in fact, ideal for laying out the science. The question of the nature of the torpedo was tantamount to a series of related, fundamental questions: what is electricity, how is it produced, how is it stored, how is it conducted, how is it manifested, and how is it conceived, manipulated, and measured?

After his paper on the torpedo, Cavendish continued to experiment on conduction. Using a given salt solution as a standard measure, he determined the conductivities of solutions of fixed air, acids, and salts in water. Maxwell noticed this striking fact: the quantity of each acid and salt Cavendish used was proportional to its modern chemical equivalent weight. The explanation lies in Cavendish's use of standards and in coincidence. Cavendish expressed his equivalents in terms of his standard, 1000 grains of marble: his equivalent weights of various substances yielded the same volume of fixed air as did 1000 grains of marble. If Cavendish had taken as his standard 100 pennyweights of marble, then since the modern equivalent weight of marble happens to be 100, the equivalents of other substances, as we list them,

---

[28]Henry Cavendish, "Experiments with the Artificial Torpedo," Cavendish Mss I:20(a), in *Electrical Researches of the Honourable Henry Cavendish*, 310–20, on 312–13.

[29]The guests are named in Cavendish's laboratory notes for 27 May 1775. Ibid., 313.

[30]Ibid. Letter from William Henly, 21 May 1775, Canton Papers, Royal Society; quoted in *Electrical Researches of the Honourable Henry Cavendish*, xxxvii.

[31]Maxwell's note: *Electrical Researches of the Honourable Henry Cavendish*, 299.

[32]Cavendish, "Torpedo," 213.

[33]Maxwell's note: *Electrical Researches of the Honourable Henry Cavendish*, 435–37.

[34]Cox, "Electric Fish," 21–22.

would be exactly as Cavendish listed them.[35]

In his experiments on conductivities, Cavendish was painstaking as always. Maxwell made extensive comparisons between Cavendish's values and the values obtained with electrical instruments of precision a hundred years later. Typical of his wonder at Cavendish's accuracy is his opinion on Cavendish's comparison of the resistances of iron wire and salt water: "The coincidence with the best modern measurements is remarkable."[36] Cavendish carried out experiments on the conductivity of solutions through early 1777. Then, after a lapse of four years, in 1781 he returned briefly to the subject and then not again. Cavendish had at last, it seems, run out of original ideas he wanted to try in electricity, but by then he was deeply immersed in his experiments on air.

The Work

We close this account of Cavendish's electrical experiments with a discussion of the total "work," the book he intended to publish and did not, and of the response to what he did publish. When his paper on electrical theory was read to the Royal Society in 1771, Cavendish was immediately recognized as an authority in electricity. In the following year he was appointed to an ongoing committee of the Royal Society to protect the powder magazines at Purfleet from destruction by lightning. The government made the request, and the Royal Society responded by volunteering its best local electricians, Watson, Franklin, Wilson, and, its most recent arrival, Cavendish.[37] In 1773 this committee paid a visit to Purfleet to confirm that the lightning conductors were erected according to their instructions.[38] This work of oversight was ongoing, and Cavendish was always a part of it, though in his own research he was no longer working in electricity.[39] Many years later Cavendish and Charles Blagden were appointed a committee to reexamine the state of the conductors at Purfleet,[40] and in 1801 Cavendish was appointed to a committee with the related assignment of determining the proper floor covering to reduce frictional electricity at powder magazines and works.[41]

The remarkable fact about the response to Cavendish's electrical theory is that it was almost non-existent. Writers on electricity after 1771 showed no awareness of the need for two indepen-

dent quantities in electrical theory, and there is no evidence that Cavendish's publication stimulated an interest in mathematical electricity, nor that it led to any electrical experiments but his own. The fate of his published electrical theory hardly differed from that of his manuscripts: both were noticed only after most of his results had been rediscovered by others. His theory of electricity was not entirely unknown—it was published, after all—but it remained remote to, and little understood by, subsequent electrical researchers.

In 1812, the year of Simon Denis Poisson's great mathematical theory of electricity, and forty years after Cavendish's theory, Thomas Thomson wrote in his *History of the Royal Society:*

> The most rigid and satisfactory explanation of the phenomena of electricity, which has hitherto appeared in any language, is contained in a very long, but most masterly paper of Mr. Cavendish, published in the Philosophical Transactions for 1771. It is very remarkable, and to me an unaccountable circumstance, that notwithstanding the great number of treatises on electricity which have appeared since the publication of this paper, which is, beyond dispute, the most important treatise on the subject that has ever been published, no one, so far as I recollect, has ever taken the least notice of Mr. Cavendish's labours, far less given a detailed account of his theory. Whether this be owing to the mathematical dress in which Mr. Cavendish was obliged to clothe his theory, or to the popular and elementary nature of

---

[35]Maxwell, in Cavendish, *Sci. Pap.* 1:28, 321.

[36]Mawell's note: *Electrical Researches of the Honourable Henry Cavendish*, 444.

[37]Royal Society, Minutes of Council 6:146 (26 Aug. 1772). This was the second committee on the conductors; the first, in 1769, was without Cavendish, who had not yet published on electricity. The second committee, with Cavendish, gave a report and recommendations. Wilson dissented from the opinion of the report and did not sign it. Also on the committee was the clerk of the Royal Society, John Robertson, who was a skilled scientific investigator but had done no published work in electricity.

[38]Royal Society, Minutes of Council 6:195–96 (22 Nov. 1773).

[39]In 1777 there was a third committee with an almost entirely new membership, with the exception of Cavendish. On it were the specialists in electrical instruments Nairne, Henly, and Lane, and the other British scientist to bring forward a general, mathematical theory of electricity, Charles Stanhope, Lord Mahon, and also the experimenter and inspirer of much electrical experimentation, Priestley. This third committee reported on the dissident Wilson's recommendation for rounded instead of pointed lightning conductors, a controversy ideally suited for the talents of Swift, if he had been around to know of it. Henry Lyons, *The Royal Society, 1660–1940: A History of Its Administration under Its Charters* (New York: Greenwood, 1968), 193.

[40]Royal Society, Minutes of Council 7:314 (17 Mar. 1796).

[41]Cavendish had several friends on this committee, such as Sir Charles Blagden, Count Rumford, Charles Hatchett, Sir Joseph Banks. Royal Society, Minutes of Council 7:408–10 (11 June 1801).

the treatises which have been published, I shall not pretend to determine; but at all events it is a thing very much to be regretted.[42]

Thomson's impression is confirmed by one of the first nineteenth-century electricians to notice Cavendish's work, George Green, who came across it in a search of the literature after finishing his famous essay of 1828 on the electrical potential functions, noting that Cavendish's theory "appears to have attracted little attention."[43] In the forty years between Cavendish's work and Poisson's in 1812, Green said little had been done in the mathematical theory of electricity. That a profound, mathematical theory of electricity was for so long almost totally ignored is a striking comment on the decay of the mathematical tradition in late eighteenth-century Britain.

In the early eighteenth century, there had been a British circle of ardent admirers of Newton's mathematical philosophy, Roger Cotes, Colin Maclaurin, and others. They were not replaced. Newton had urged his followers to go out and discover the forces of nature the way he had done, but it had not happened. Newton himself had been the first to fail, in optics; his immediate followers failed in other parts of science. By Cavendish's time scarcely any investigator pursued Newton's end-in-view of natural philosophy; then, without warning, Cavendish presented British scientists with a mathematical theory of electricity modeled after the treatment of gravitation in Newton's *Principia*. There was not an electrician in Britain with the mathematical training to appreciate what Cavendish had done, let alone extend or criticize it. If Cavendish had belonged to a Continental scientific academy instead of to the British Royal Society, he might have had an appreciative audience,[44] but then Cavendish would have had to be a European and not a Briton whose family defied the power of the monarch. (On this point, Cavendish was at one with Joseph Banks, who wrote to a foreign colleague that the Royal Society "differs essentially" from its Continental imitators, which are "associations of learned men collected together by their respective monarchs"; speaking for the native membership of the Royal Society, Banks said that "our chief boast" is in maintaining the independence of the Royal Society.[45]) Cavendish's paper of 1771, the first work to have the substance of a genuine successor to Newton's *Principia* and not merely the surface and pretension of one, was passed by

almost without comment. Cavendish's experimental paper on the torpedo received more notice than did his paper on electrical theory.

There was another reason why Cavendish was ignored. The topics he addressed were no longer of central concern to electricians. In his paper of 1771 Cavendish limited his discussion to several "principal" matters: the attraction and repulsion of bodies, electric induction, the Leyden jar, and the electrification of air. These phenomena were generally thought to be adequately understood. Priestley's *History of Electricity* contained Priestley's own investigations of phenomena that were not adequately understood, and Priestley's queries suggest the nature of the problems that interested Cavendish's contemporaries; they had to do mainly with the connections between electricity and light, sound, heat, and chemistry. Typical of the thinking then was Henly's belief, in 1777, that light, fire, phlogiston, and electricity were "only different modifications of one and the same principle."[46] Although Cavendish's natural philosophy could accommodate connections between these subjects, his work was not directed to them.

Cavendish had begun his electrical researches right after his initial publication on factitious air, which earned him a Copley Medal. After his initial publication on electricity there was no sign that anyone comprehended that he might be on the track of a work that would stand beside Newton's. He never again published a theoretical paper. It was, in effect, ten years after he had given up the idea of publishing his comprehensive electrical experiments before he appeared in print again with original research; when he did, it was to return to the approach and subject of his original success, the experimental study of airs.

[42]Thomas Thomson, *History of the Royal Society from Its Institution to the End of the Eighteenth Century* (London, 1812), 455.
[43]George Green, *An Essay on the Application of Mathematical Analysis to the Theories of Electricity and Magnetism* (Nottingham, 1828), v.
[44]Thomas S. Kuhn's comparison of the "classical" mathematical sciences and the "Baconian" experimental sciences would suggest that had Cavendish been born a European instead of an Englishman, he would have had understanding colleagues in the Continental-type academies of science for his mathematical electricity: "Mathematical Versus Experimental Traditions in the Development of Physical Science," in Kuhn's *The Essential Tension: Selected Studies in Scientific Tradition and Change* (Chicago: University of Chicago Press, 1977), 31–65, on 58.
[45]Joseph Banks to Count W., 2 June /n.y./, Banks Correspondence, Kew, 3:3.
[46]William Henly, "Experiments and Observations in Electricity," *PT* 67 (1777): 85–143, on 135.

The reasons why Cavendish did not publish his electrical experiments are more complicated than neglect. What had begun as a second paper for the *Philosophical Transactions* became a large treatise on electricity.[47] He completed several of his subsequent electrical researches to his satisfaction, but he was not satisfied with the treatise. His discovery of the influence of chemical substances on the capacity of Leyden jars was, we think, what stopped him temporarily, then for good. His work on electricity took an inconclusive path similar to Newton's in the *Opticks*; before Newton could know the interaction of light with matter, every-thing else about matter had to be known, and so it seemed that in the field of electricity, too, everything else had to be known first.

---

[47]As an article the "work" would have been long: the material to be included occupies 104 pages of the Maxwell edition of Cavendish's electrical researches, and it would have expanded into nearly twice that number of pages in the *Philosophical Transactions*. The 1771 paper was itself long, taking up 49 pages in the Maxwell edition and ninety-four in the *Philosophical Transactions*, by far Cavendish's longest publication. It is likely that at some point Cavendish abandoned his original idea of publishing another article in the *Philosophical Transactions* and set out instead to write a book. Maxwell thought that Cavendish was working on a book, in Cavendish, *Sci. Pap.* 1:13.

CHAPTER 6

⚜

Learned Organizations

Royal Society

At the time Cavendish entered the Royal Society, in 1760, its membership was stable, as it had not been before and would not be after. During the twenty years centering on 1760, the average number of ordinary members was virtually constant, about 355, whereas it had grown by nearly one quarter in the thirty years after Cavendish's father had joined. The foreign membership was now at its maximum, at about 160, forty percent larger than it had been thirty years before; thereafter it slowly declined owing to a deliberate policy of the Society to stop the escalation of this honorary segment of its membership.[1]

Cavendish did his part to perpetuate, but not inflate, the membership of the Royal Society. In his first twenty years, he signed fourteen certificates for new members. The first time he signed one, he did so together with his father, whose name appears first on the certificate for the Plumian professor of astronomy and experimental philosophy at Cambridge, Anthony Shepherd. That was the only time father and son made a recommendation in common; Lord Charles Cavendish, in fact, made only four more recommendations altogether after 1760. Of the candidates recommended by Henry Cavendish, most were said to be proficient in natural philosophy (or an alternative term for it), astronomy, or mathematics. His preference of fields was clear, but it was not exclusive; polite literature, natural history, antiquities, and voyages of discovery were also cited. He welcomed as members persons who had been in India and the South Seas, who knew remote parts of the world firsthand. Some of the candidates, such as Francis Wollaston, Cavendish probably had known at Cambridge, but others do not seem to have been long-term friends, and he did not sign the certificates of a number of candidates who became his closest friends, such as Alexander Aubert, Alexander Dalrymple, and Charles Blagden. Of the almost one hundred names that appear together with his on the recommendations, only a few appear more than once; Nevil Maskelyne appears on half of them, and after him in decreasing frequency, come the keeper of the natural history department of the British Museum, Daniel Solander, William Watson, James Burrow, and William Heberden. Several of these persons are carry-overs from co-signers with Cavendish's father.[2]

In keeping with tradition, Cavendish invited some of his candidates to meetings of the Royal Society. Francis Wollaston was one, another was Timothy Lane, whom Cavendish brought to five meetings before his election.[3] Lane was an apothecary in London who took up the problem of mineral water where Brownrigg and Cavendish had left it, closely tying it to pneumatic chemistry. Before publishing his experiments on the solution of iron in water impregnated with fixed air in the *Philosophical Transactions* in 1769, he submitted them to Cavendish for judgment. Cavendish's papers of 1766 and 1767 were Lane's acknowledged starting point, and the learned world, he said, "had great reason to hope for many other new and useful experiments" from Cavendish.[4] Lane spoke of Cavendish's "known accuracy," which is what

---

[1] The council resolved on 19 Dec. 1765 to admit no more than two foreign members a year until their number fell to eighty. Excluded, however, from this limit were sovereign princes and their sons, ambassadors, and foreigners living in England. Into the next year the council passed a series of other resolutions about foreign members, the most important being that no foreigner could be admitted in shorter time than six months, and that he had to be recommended by three foreign and three domestic members. Royal Society, Minutes of Council, 5: 146–48 (19 Dec. 1765) and 153–54 (6 Feb. 1766).

[2] Royal Society, Certificates, vol. 2, ff. 242, 312, 343; vol. 3, ff. 65, 73, 79, 104, 161, 209, 237, 259; vol. 4, ff. 23, 24, 56.

[3] Cavendish brought Lane to meetings of the Royal Society on 9 Feb., 20 Apr., 4 and 11 May, 8 June, 9 Nov. 1769; Lane was elected the next year. Royal Society, JB 26 (1767–70).

[4] Timothy Lane, "A Letter . . . on the Solubility of Iron in Simple Water, by the Introduction of Fixed Air," PT 59 (1769): 216–27, on 216.

Lane was known for too, having recently published an account of an electrometer for introducing into electricity a "much greater degree of precision"; with "tolerable accuracy," his electrometer could measure the "quantity" of electric fluid stored in a Leyden jar.[5] In 1769, when Cavendish brought Lane repeatedly to the Royal Society, Lane's work in electricity probably interested him more than did Lane's work on mineral water. The Royal Society extended a scientific exchange that had already been established between Lane and Cavendish.

In November 1765 Henry Cavendish was elected to the council of the Royal Society,[6] the first of thirty-four times. Like his father, he almost never missed a meeting. In his first year on the council, other than for the two secretaries, Henry Cavendish attended with greater regularity than any other member. For the next twenty years he was on the council about half of the time; for the last twenty-five years, through 1809, he was on the council every year. His service on special committees appointed by the council was nearly as consistent.[7] He was extensively involved in the two big projects initiated by the Society during his time, the observation of the transit of Venus in 1769 and the experiment on the attraction of mountains in 1774. He drew up plans for a voyage of discovery to the Arctic. He worked on changes in the statutes of the Society and on the printing of the *Philosophical Transactions*. He was routinely appointed to committees concerned with the state of the instruments of the Royal Society and the Royal Observatory. And, as we have seen, he was on committees called into being by requests of the government. He was appointed to twenty-three committees, more or less,[8] and he took on many assignments for the Society that did not involve a committee but at most an instrument-maker to work with him. Altogether, on special committees Cavendish worked with sixty Fellows. Since the work of the Society was spread around, usually other Fellows appeared on only one committee with him. The exceptions were Nevil Maskelyne, the astronomer royal, and the astronomer Alexander Aubert, who was an expert on meteorological as well as astronomical instruments.[9]

In addition to serving on one-time committees, Henry Cavendish, like his father, was often elected one of the annual auditors of the treasurer's account. It happened the first time during his first year on the council, 1766; serving with two stalwart members James Burrow and George Lewis Scott, Cavendish reported to the council in the name of the three auditors.[10] He could accept that much prominence. The treasurer's balances were small, which did not diminish the responsibility of the auditors; Cavendish was joined in subsequent years by other members of impeccable reputation, such as Maskelyne and Benjamin Franklin.

Like his father again, Cavendish served regularly on the committee of papers.[11] This committee attracted the ablest scientific men, regardless of their own habits in the matter of publication; some of them, such as Maskelyne and William Herschel and Cavendish himself, were themselves authors of many papers in the *Philosophical Transactions*, but others, such as Aubert, published nothing or next to nothing there. In addition to attending the meetings of the committee, which took place monthly as needed, the members had homework. On any particular paper, the committee would make one of several decisions: to print, not to print, or to withdraw or postpone. If postponed, the paper might be referred to one or two members; this happened often to Cavendish, and among his papers we find a good many studies of his own that originated this way.

During Cavendish's first year, 1766, the council was occupied with John Canton's experiment on the compressibility of water, which his father had pretty much taken charge of. Cavendish's first work for the Society was on the subject for which his father had earned the Copley Medal, thermometers.

In June, 1766, the council began its painstaking preparations for observing the transit of Venus of 1769. This was the second of these rare, paired transits, which offered an accurate measure

---

[5]Timothy Lane, "Description of an Electrometer Invented by Mr. Lane; with an Account of Some Experiments Made by Him With It," *PT* 57 (1767): 451–60, on 451.

[6]Entry for 30 Nov. 1765, Royal Society, JB 25:663.

[7]From a survey of the Royal Society, Minutes of Council, vols. 5–7, 1763–1810.

[8]It depends on how one counts. Committees were often renewed becoming virtually new committees with the same or a redefined task.

[9]Cavendish served on eight committees with Maskelyne and as many with Aubert.

[10]Royal Society, Minutes of Council, 5:163 (24 Nov. 1766). One week later, on 30 Nov. 1766, p. 167, Cavendish reported for the auditors.

[11]From a survey of the bound volume of minutes of the Royal Society's committee of papers, vol. 1, covering 1780–1828.

of the sun's distance. It had been only four years since the Society had finished with the 1761 transit, with rather disappointing results. Instruments from the earlier transit were reassembled, and observers were selected, for example, Roger Joseph Boscovich, Fellow of the Royal Society and professor of mathematics at Pavia. For those involved, it was their last chance, since they would not be around for the next transit of Venus, a hundred years off. The first study of the transit of 1769 to be brought before the council was a letter by Henry Cavendish to Lord Morton, president of the Society, on the best places in the world to observe the transit.[12] Charles Cavendish had taken a leading part in the work on the first transit; Henry Cavendish would take a leading part in the work of the second.

We should point out that Cavendish had not yet published any research, though the first part of what would be his first publication, on factitious air, had just been read to the Society, at the end of May. He had been a Fellow for six years, and in this time he had obviously made known his talents and his willingness to serve.

Cavendish studied the observations of the earlier transit of Venus of 1761, and he did this while he was still in the middle of his experiments on air. There was a connection between these studies through the air, or atmosphere, of Venus, which affected the observed times of the external and internal contact of the limbs of Venus and the sun. At the time of the first transit, the effect of the atmosphere of Venus had not been considered, with the result that the reported times of contacts of Venus and the sun were wildly discordant.[13] By making different assumptions about the elastic fluid constituting the atmosphere of Venus, Cavendish computed the errors of observation owing to the refraction of light passing through it from the sun to the earth.[14] Before Cavendish was done with the transit of Venus of 1769, he had written over 150 pages, a large work of which nothing appeared in print.[15]

As it turned out, observations of the second transit did not result in an unambiguous figure for the distance of the sun, but they were a great achievement, and there were side benefits. The Society had been shown the work it could expect from Cavendish, for one. The second transit of Venus marked the beginning of his service as a committeeman of the Society, possibly its most called up and certainly its most versatile.

We turn next to the other great project of the Royal Society during Cavendish's membership, the experiment on the attraction of mountains.[16] This was an experiment on gravitation and on the earth, on a universal power and a particular body of the universe. Cavendish's work on this experiment foreshadows the most famous of his experiments twenty-five years later, the weighing of the earth. The experiment on the attraction of mountains came close upon the heels of the observation of the transit of Venus in 1769. In 1771 Maskelyne sent Cavendish a letter containing two theorems for calculating the gravitational attraction of mountain-like geometrical solids, a hyperbolic wedge and an elliptic cuneus; Cavendish wrote on the back of the letter his version of Maskelyne's two formulas.[17] This is our earliest evidence that the experiment on the attraction of mountains was underway, the object of which was to determine the average density of the earth. On the face of it, this experiment seems remote from the Society's recent concern, but the goals of the observation of the transits of Venus and the experiment on the density of the earth were much the same. They were to measure the earth in relation to its home in the universe, the solar system, by determining a standard in each case, a distance in the first and a quantity of matter in the second. The distances of the planets were expressed in terms of the distance of the earth from the sun; likewise, the densities of the sun and some of the planets were known only relatively, so that the density of the earth had first

---

[12]Royal Society, Minutes of Council 5:156 (5 June 1766) and 157 (19 June 1766). Cavendish would later be appointed to a committee of eight to consider places for observing the transit. Ibid., 5:184 (12 Nov. 1767).

[13]H. Spencer-Jones, "Astronomy through the Eighteenth Century," in *Natural Philosophy*, published by the *Philosophical Magazine* in 1948, pp. 10–27, on p. 16.

[14]Henry Cavendish, "On the Effects Which Will Be Produced in the Transit of Venus by an Atmosphere Surrounding the Body of Venus," Cavendish Mss VIII, 27.

[15]In addition to the above "Thoughts," letter to Morton, and "On the Effects . . . of an Atmosphere," Henry Cavendish wrote these studies: "Computation of Transit of Venus 1761, 1769," "Method of Finding in What Year a Transit of Venus Will Happen," "Computation of Transit of 1769 Correct," and "Computation for 1769 Transit," Cavendish Mss VIII, 30–33.

[16]The discussion of the attraction of mountains is based on Russell McCormmach, "The Last Experiment of Henry Cavendish," in `No Truth Except in Details': Essays in Honor of Martin J. Klein, eds. A. J. Kox and D. M. Siegel (Dordrecht: Klewer Academic Publishers, 1995), 1–30. See pt. 4, ch. 7, n. 1.

[17]Nevil Maskelyne to Henry Cavendish, 10 Apr. 1771, Cavendish Mss VIII, 4.

to be known to know the density of the other bodies.[18] It stands to reason that the same persons would work on the transits of Venus and the density of the earth.

We will briefly review some well-known historical facts about the attraction of mountains. Newton had concluded, as had Huygens, that owing to the attraction of the earth and to the centrifugal force of the earth's rotation, the shape of the earth was an ellipsoid of revolution; that is, a spheroid flattened at the poles. The Cartesian astronomer Jacques Cassini held the contrary opinion: on the basis of French measurements, he concluded that the earth is indeed a spheroid but one that is elongated at the poles, like an egg on end. The clear implication was that if Newton was right, the length of a degree of latitude is longer at the poles than at the equator, but if Casini was right, the length of a degree is longer at the equator. To settle this question, two expeditions were sent out, one in the direction of the north pole, the other in the direction of the equator. The question was answered in favor of Newton and his supporters, the "earth flatteners." This decision depended on the use of astronomical instruments, which is how mountains enter this study of the shape of the earth.

Peru is a land of mountains. If gravitation is a universal law, as Newton said, then a plumb bob in the vicinity of a mountain should be drawn aside by its gravitation. Newton calculated the effect: a hemispherical mountain of earth matter with a radius of three miles should deflect a plumb-line by a minute or two of arc. He thought that this effect was too small to measure, an opinion which was received by eighteenth-century precisionists as a challenge. Near the equator, the French party under Pierre Bouguer and D. M. de la Condamine did an experiment to see if the attraction of mountains did really exist. (It was a practical question for them, for they were measuring a degree of latitude, and astronomical instruments depend on a plumb-line to establish the vertical.) With a quadrant oriented by a plumb-line, they measured the distance between stars directly overhead in two places, one beside a mountain and one on a plain. They did observe a deflection, and in the expected direction, but they could not measure it with the instruments at hand. Upon his return from the expedition in 1744, Bouguer said

that he would like to see the experiment on the attraction of mountains repeated under proper conditions in Europe. His *La figure de la terre, determinée par les observations de Messieurs De la Condamine et Bouguer . . .*, published in 1749, was to be Cavendish's starting point in his work on the problem.[19]

The figure, density, and internal structure of the earth are connected properties, which in turn are connected to a seemingly remote phenomenon, the precession of the equinoxes. This precession is the slow movement of the earth's axis of rotation relative to the stars caused by the attraction of the sun and moon on the earth's equatorial bulge. In a carefully drafted but unpublished paper on the precession of the equinoxes, Cavendish tried to reconcile Bouguer's figure of the earth obtained by measurement with the figure that agrees with the variation of gravity with latitude, as determined by theory and tested by pendulums. He could not do it without assuming a "very improbable hypothesis of the density of the earth" or denying the well-founded gravitational theory. The explanation, he thought, lay with the gravitation of the high mountains in South America where the French made their equatorial observations.[20] Cavendish was inclined to favor theory over measurement in this case, as the French measurements were probably off owing to the attraction of mountains.

The transit of Venus in 1761 sent observers around the world with instruments that, as it turned out, recorded the presence of nearby mountains. Maskelyne, for example, was on St. Helena, where clouds prevented him from observing the transit, so the main point was lost. But while he was there he did another experiment

---

[18]Charles Hutton, "An Account of the Calculations Made from the Survey and Measures Taken at Schehallien, in Order to Ascertain the Mean Density of the Earth," *PT* 68 (1778): 689–788, on 784. B. E. Clotfelter, "The Cavendish Experiment as Cavendish Knew It," *American Journal of Physics* 55 (1987): 210–13, on 211.

[19]In his *System of the World*, Newton was discouraging on the prospect of detecting the attraction of mountains: "Nay, whole mountains will not be sufficient to produce any sensible effect. A mountain of an hemispherical figure, three miles high, and six miles broad, will not, by its attraction, draw the pendulum two minutes out of the true perpendicular. . . ." *Sir Isaac Newton's Mathematical Principles of Natural Philosophy and His System of the World*, trans. A. Motte, rev. F. Cajori, 2 vols. (Berkeley and Los Angeles: University of California Press, 1962) 2: 569–70. Derek Howse, *Nevil Maskelyne: The Seaman's Astronomer* (Cambridge: Cambridge University Press, 1989), 129.

[20]Henry Cavendish, "Precession of Equinoxes," Cavendish Mss VIII, 9:14–15.

to find the parallax of the brightest and supposedly closest star, Sirius; that would give not the distance of the earth from the sun but its distance from a fixed star, another measure of cosmological significance. Astronomers such as Bradley had looked hard for this parallax, using the earth's orbit as base line. St. Helena being mountainous, Maskelyne heeded the warning implied in Newton's calculation by taking into account the attraction of the mountains on the plumb-line of his zenith sector. His instrument proved defective, so nothing came of this attempt either. It had long been known that a pendulum beating seconds is shorter near the equator than at higher latitudes. Newton and Huygens and those who came after them recognized that comparative measurements of the lengths of a seconds pendulum at different latitudes could determine the shape of the earth. Experiments with pendulums had been made at various places, and Maskelyne made another experiment at St. Helena. Lord Charles Cavendish had approved of Maskelyne's experiment and pendulum clock, and Maskelyne communicated a paper to the Royal Society through Cavendish, which reported the lessened gravity on St. Helena compared to the gravity at Greenwich, but Maskelyne did not draw from it conclusions about the figure of the earth. As he explained to Cavendish, such conclusions depend not only on gravity but on the "internal constitution and density "of the earth. There had to be experiments of "other different kinds," which he did not specify but which he would soon pursue.[21] Charles Mason was another designated observer of the transit of Venus of 1761 who encountered the attraction of mountains. On his way home from the Cape of Good Hope where he had gone to observe the transit, Mason with his associate Jeremiah Dixon were hired to settle the old boundary dispute between the colonies of Pennsylvania and Maryland. During the five years they spent at this job, they also measured the length of a degree of latitude. In reviewing their measurement, Maskelyne said that he did not think it was flawed by the attraction of any mountain.[22] Cavendish took exception. By taking into consideration the Allegheny Mountains to the northwest and the deficiency of mountains in the Atlantic Ocean to the southeast, he calculated that Mason and Dixon's degree could fall short by sixty to one hundred Paris

toises. One toise equaling about two meters, this was a considerable error. Others, he pointed out, had made the same kind of error in measuring a degree.[23] The best way to determine the form of the earth, Cavendish thought, was not by measurement but by gravity.[24] The form of the earth, the length of a degree, the attraction of mountains, the density of the earth, and the precession of the equinoxes were a tangle of problems.

In 1771, as we have seen, Cavendish and Maskelyne consulted about the attraction of mountains. For Maskelyne, Cavendish worked out rules for finding the attraction of a particle at the foot of and at a distance from geometrical solids—slabs, wedges, and cones—generated by lines and planes and obeying the law of universal gravitation. Cavendish then turned to the subject of scientific interest, the real world of attracting bodies, which include the great irregular masses that the earth throws up. These masses distort astronomical observation but, as if in compensation, they also provide a means for measuring the density of the earth. Combining his geometrical representations of mountains with the French observations with pendulums on the real mountains of the equator, Cavendish made several estimates of the mean density of the earth, which fell between 2.72 and 4.44 times the density of water. These estimates, his earliest, required a correction, since the beating of pendulums depend not only on latitude and nearby mountains but also on the internal structure

---

[21]Nevil Maskelyne, "Observations on a Clock of Mr. John Shelton, Made at St. Helena: In a Letter to the Right Honourable Lord Charles Cavendish, Vice-President of the Royal Society," *PT* 52 (1762): 434–47, on 436, 442.

[22]Nevil Maskelyne, "Introduction to the Following Observations, Made by Messiers Charles Mason and Jeremiah Dixon, for Determining the Length of a Degree of Latitude, in the Provinces of Maryland and Pennsylvania in North America," *PT* 58 (1768): 270–73, on 273. Mason and Dixon's measurement, Maskelyne said, could not have been affected by mountains because the degree of latitude passes through level country. Maskelyne noted that Roger Joseph Boscovich was the first to take into account the effect of the attraction of mountains in his measurement of the length of a degree of latitude in Italy.

[23]Nevil Maskelyne, "Postscript by the Astronomer Royal," *PT* 58 (1768): 325–28, on 328. This postscript follows the paper by Mason and Dixon on the length of a degree. Maskelyne took back what he had said, the reason being that "Cavendish has since considered this matter more minutely" and demonstrated the effect of the mountains. Henry Cavendish, "Observations on the Length of a Degree of Latitude," Cavendish Mss VIII, 16.

[24]One reason he gave is the better fit with the precession of the equinoxes. Henry Cavendish, "Paper Given to Maskelyne Relating to Attraction & Form of Earth," Cavendish Mss VI(b), 1:18.

of the earth. To give Maskelyne an idea of this correction, Cavendish invoked an entirely different kind of evidence, Canton's experiment on the compressibility of water, which his father had confirmed. Supposing, he said, that even if the surface and the interior of the earth are of the same substance, the interior will be compressed. Beginning with Canton's demonstration that the density of water is increased 44/1,000,000 by the pressure of one atmosphere, and making a quantitative assumption about the compressibility of earth relative to that of water, Cavendish constructed a table of the densities of the earth at different distances from its center. He deduced that the mean density of the earth should be more than eleven times the surface density, a value much higher than the French (and the value he later measured). He did not comment on it, since the interior of the earth in his calculations was purely hypothetical. This and only this far could Cavendish go with his theoretical reasoning and observations made by others with the seconds pendulum. What were needed were new observations from a new experiment.[25] The new experiment was to be based on Cavendish's alternative, practical way of finding the density of the earth, which was to measure the "deviation of the plumb line at the bottom of a mountain by taking the meridian altitudes of stars." Although it was more difficult than the method of the seconds pendulum, it was "more exact," since it was less affected by irregularities in the internal parts of the earth. In the middle of 1772 Maskelyne proposed such an experiment to the Society. The council appointed a committee to consider it and to draw on the treasurer as needed.[26]

In a letter to Cavendish at the beginning of 1773, Maskelyne said that he had made a copy of Cavendish's rules, which were "well calculated to procure us the information that is wanted."[27] In a paper written for his fellow committeeman Benjamin Franklin, Cavendish explained what sorts of mountains are best. The want of attraction of a valley, he said, is as good as the attraction of a mountain and perhaps better.[28] In the middle of 1773 the council sent Charles Mason off on horseback into the Scottish Highlands to observe mountains and valleys suited for the experiment.[29] In early 1774, a year and a half after the committee had been formed, its mind was made up. From

Mason's survey, their choice was a 3547-foot granite mountain in Pershire, Maiden's Pap.[30] Its alternative and equally descriptive name, "Schiehallien," meaning "constant storm," was preferred by the Society. This mountain was made to Cavendish's order: big, regular, detached, with a narrow base in the north-south direction on either side of which observations could optimally be taken. Losing no time, the committee selected as their experimenter Charles Mason, who turned them down and with it unforseen glory. The committee next turned to Maskelyne's assistant Reuben Burrow. It was the dead of winter and the committee had time for second thoughts: the Greenwich assistant did not seem equal to this important experiment, the committee thought, so it turned to Maskelyne, who accepted the assignment.[31] Burrow determined the size and shape of the mountain, and Maskelyne observed forty-three stars from it. Cavendish supervised the repair of one of the instruments for the experiment. When the experiment was done, Cavendish and C. J. Phipps went over Burrow's scarcely legible papers from the field.[32] The attraction of Schiehallien proved measurable, if with not much to spare, as is evident from Cavendish's attempts to decide its likelihood in advance.[33]

---

[25] Ibid. 2–16, 19.

[26] Ibid. 19–20. Nevil Maskelyne, "A Proposal for Measuring the Attraction of Some Hill in This Kingdom by Astronomical Observations," *PT* 65 (1772): 495–99. Royal Society, Minutes of Council 6: 145 (23 July 1772). In addition to Cavendish, the committee to consider the experiment on the attraction of mountains contained Maskelyne, Benjamin Franklin, Samuel Horsley, and Daines Barrington. The king approved the use of money left over from observing the transit of Venus for the experiment on attraction.

[27] Nevil Maskelyne to Henry Cavendish, 5 Jan. 1773, Cavendish Mss X(b); published in full in Cavendish, *Sci. Pap.* 2:402. Having made his copy, Maskelyne returned Cavendish's "Rules for Computing the Attraction of Hills." The preliminary version of that paper is Henry Cavendish, "Thoughts on the Method of Finding the Density of the Earth by Observing the Attraction of Hills." Cavendish Mss VI(b), 2 and 6.

[28] Henry Cavendish, "On the Choice of Hills Proper for Observing Attraction Given to Dr Franklin," Cavendish Mss VI(b), 3:5.

[29] Royal Society, Minutes of Council 6:180 (24 June 1773) and 185–86 (29 July 1773).

[30] In Cavendish's papers is an untitled study of Maiden's Pap, Cavendish Mss, Misc.

[31] Royal Society, Minutes of Council, 6:210–11 (27 Jan. 1774) and 234 (5 May 1774).

[32] Royal Society, Minutes of Council, 6:218 (17 Feb. 1774), 242 (11 Aug. 1774), 244 (11 Oct. 1774), 255 (22 Dec. 1774), 260–61 (30 Mar. 1775), and 267–69 (27 Apr. 1775).

[33] Before the experiment, Cavendish prepared a table of deviations of the plumb-line in seconds of arc for mountains made of cones and spherical segments. If the observations on a steep slope could be made with the same accuracy as on level ground, Cavendish

On the basis of the experiment and Newton's "rules of philosophizing," Maskelyne told the Royal Society in July 1775 that "we are to conclude, that every mountain, and indeed every particle of the earth, is endued with the same property /attraction/, in proportion to its quantity of matter," and further that the "law of the variation of this force, in the inverse *ratio* of the squares of the distances, as laid down by Sir Isaac Newton, is also confirmed."[34] For this work, Maskelyne was awarded the Copley Medal in 1775. In his address on the occasion, John Pringle, the president of the Society, said that now the Newtonian system is "finished" and that every man must become a Newtonian.[35] Maskelyne's and Pringle's conclusions could have come as no surprise to Cavendish, who in any case was interested in the quantity the experiment addressed, the mean density of the earth. That quantity had to wait for the calculations of the mathematician Charles Hutton, who had been hired by Maskelyne. Not until 1778 did Hutton finished his paper of some hundred pages of "long and tedious" figuring. To explain why it took him so long, Hutton said that new methods of calculation had to be invented, and he also said that Cavendish had supplied him with some of these. It came down to this: the ratio of the mean density of the earth to the density of the mountain is 9 to 5. Hutton pointed out that the density of the mountain was unknown and only an empirical study of its internal structure could determine it. Nevertheless Hutton expressed the result in a more satisfying form: by assuming that the mountain is "common stone"; the density of common stone being 2½, the density of the earth is 4½ times the density of water. Newton's best guess was that the density of the earth is between 5 and 6 ("so much justness was even in the surmises of this wonderful man!"). Reminding his readers that this experiment was the first of its kind, Hutton hoped that it would be repeated in other places.[36]

Legend has it that Maskelyne threw a bacchanalian feast for the inhabitants around Shiehallion.[37] It is hard to picture the stodgy Maskelyne taking part in this affair and impossible to imagine Cavendish. But, of course, Cavendish was not there. Just as Cavendish did not travel to observe the transit of Venus, he did not go to Scotland but studied its mountains and valleys in his father's house on Great Marlborough Street in London. Cavendish had done the comprehensive planning of the experiment, but he did not make observations from the mountain or make final calculations of the earth's density. Others did these things and they published their results. In the landscape of the experiment, Cavendish may be likened to the valley as opposed to the mountain. As he demonstrated, the valley offers great accuracy, but the experiment was done on a mountain, a feature which draws the eye more than does the valley. Cavendish's work on the experiment went unseen except by others who worked on it. It was entirely characteristic of him. This work for the Royal Society was as important to him as his private researches and as hidden from the public eye.

Cavendish served on committees of the Royal Society for thirty-odd years after the experiment on the attraction of mountains. During that time the Society undertook nothing again so fundamental. There were, however, important domestic rearrangements. Crane Court, the meeting place of the Society, was cramped, and when Joseph Banks

---

reasoned that the observer should be able to determine the difference in the zenith distances of the stars on the two sides of the mountain with "tolerable certainty to 3"," and would not be "likely to err more than 1½"." Upon this estimate of accuracy, Cavendish further reasoned that "if the mean density of the Earth is not more than 7 times greater than that of the surface the effect of attraction must pretty certainly be sensible & it is an even chance that it will come out such that we may with tolerable certainty pronounce to be not owing to the error of observation & even if the mean density is 14 times greater than that of the surface the effect of attraction will most likely be sensible . . ." "Thoughts on the Method of Finding the Density of the Earth by Observing the Attraction of Hills," unnumbered sheet. There are a good many assumptions behind this cautious statement about tolerable certainty. To Franklin, Cavendish wrote: "It will be needless to send an account of any hill or valley if the sum of its deviations is less than 50" or 60" as I am in hopes some may be found nearer home near as good as that." "On the Choice of Hills Proper for Observing Attraction Given to Dr. Franklin," unnumbered sheet. Maskelyne's results fell just within Cavendish's estimated limits of *tolerable certainty*. The apparent difference in the position of the stars at the two sides of the mountain was 54.6", and the difference in latitude of the two stations, as determined by measuring, was 42.94"; so the difference, 11.6", was the true combined effect of the two attractions, or 5.8" was the effect of the attraction of Schiehallien on the plumb bob of the zenith sector.

[34] Nevil Maskelyne, "An Account of Observations Made on the Mountain Schehallien for Finding Its Attraction," *PT* 65 (1775): 500–42, on 532.

[35] John Pringle, *A Discourse on the Attraction of Mountains, Delivered at the Anniversary Meeting of the Royal Society, November 30, 1775* (London, 1775); the remark on the Newtonian system comes at the end of the discourse.

[36] Hutton, "An Account of the Calculations," 689–90, 750, 766, 781–83, 785.

[37] Howse, *Maskelyne*, 137–38.

became president in 1778 he approached the government for new quarters. These were decided to be in Somerset House, and Cavendish was appointed to a committee to meet with the architect about fitting up new apartments there.[38] Having examined the meteorological instruments of the Society a few years before, Cavendish was charged with seeing to the best placement of these instruments in the new location.[39] True to form, in his report to the council Cavendish was most concerned with the "error" arising from alternative placements, but he also watched for "any eye sore."[40] He was appointed to the committee to direct the keeping of the meteorological journal from its new location.[41] Somerset House was better located than Crane Court, and most important, it had more space though it was not exactly spacious.[42] In the meeting room, the president sat in a grand, high-backed chair, like a judge, well above the table at which the secretaries sat. The ordinary members sat on hard benches with rail backs resembling pews and like them discouraging sleep. For the last thirty years of his life, Cavendish came regularly to Somerset House, where he sat beneath the paintings of illustrious past members, crammed on the walls one above another. (By refusing to sit for a painting, he insured that he would not be exhibited on those walls exposed helplessly and forever after to the prying eyes of strangers.) The next move of the Society was not until 1857, when its new home was Burlington House in Piccadilly, which had belonged to the Cavendishes.

As we have seen in his work for the Royal Society on the transit of Venus and the attraction of mountains, Cavendish stayed at home, leaving it to other Fellows to make the necessary expeditions and observations in the field. A related activity from which Cavendish likewise stayed home was voyages of discovery, but he was fully involved in the scientific preparations for them in the Royal Society.

Persons who brought back scientific information from the ends of the earth had a particular appeal to Henry Cavendish, who recommended a good many of them for fellowship in the Royal Society. To give some examples: in 1774 Robert Barker, recent commander in chief in Bengal; in 1775 James Cook, the commander of two voyages of discovery and about to make his third; and in 1780

James King, captain in the royal navy recently returned from a voyage of discovery in the South Seas.[43] To dine at the Royal Society Club, Cavendish invited travelers such as the naval captain and voyager of discovery Constantine John Phipps.[44] His private physician, John Hunter (the "other" John Hunter), was a voyager as well as a pioneer in anthropology. Cavendish's library was stocked with books of voyages and travels and maps, in which department it was kept up to date.[45] Cavendish's interest in the wide world and in the people who knew it from experience is well documented. England was a seafaring nation and London was its capital, and the Royal Society offered an open invitation to any and all travelers who had a story to tell. For a homebody with a curiosity about the world, Cavendish was precisely located.

In the second half of the eighteenth century the world was still very incompletely explored by Europeans, and there were practical reasons, foremostly trade and power, why a country like Britain should know it better. In 1764 and again in 1766, the British admiralty sent ships to distant seas to make discoveries, with unimpressive results. This disappointment might have spelled the end of such voyages for a time, but for the Royal Society, which soon promoted a new justification, the second transit of Venus in 1769. The Society appealed successfully to the king for money again and to the admiralty for a ship for the purpose, the *Endeavour*. The admiralty appointed James Cook commander of the ship, and the Royal Society appointed Cook an observer of Venus. The

[38]Minutes of Council, Royal Society, 6:397 (16 Mar. 1780).

[39]Minutes of Council, Royal Society, 6:439 (6 July 1781).

[40]Minutes of Council, Royal Society, 6:440–42 (12 Aug. 1781). The concern for placing the meteorological instruments continued, leading to a committee of Cavendish, Alexander Aubert, William Heberden, Jean André Deluc, William Watson, and Francis Wollaston: ibid. 7:62 (12 Feb. 1784).

[41]Minutes of Council, Royal Society, 7:138 (19 Jan. 1786).

[42]D C. Martin, "Former Homes of the Royal Society," *Notes and Records of the Royal Society* 22 (1967): 12–19, on 16.

[43]Royal Society, Certificates, 3:209, 237, and 4:56.

[44]Archibald Geikie, *Annals of the Royal Society Club* (London: Macmillan, 1917), 234.

[45]The catalogue of Cavendish's library has 29 pages of entries on voyages and travels, 15 on geography, and 18 on maps. Taken together, these categories occupy more pages of the catalogue than astronomy or mathematics or any science other than natural philosophy. The catalogue is in the Devonshire Collection at Chatsworth. Examples of Cavendish's ongoing purchases are William Bligh's *Voyage to the South Sea in His Majesty's Ship the Bounty . . .* (London, 1792), and Thomas Forrest's *A Voyage from Calcutta to the Mergui Archipelago on the East Side of the Bay of Bengal* (London, 1792).

wealthy naturalist and future president of the Royal Society Joseph Banks, with a retinue, accompanied Cook, as did an assistant from the Royal Observatory together with scientific instruments from the Royal Society. After making observations of the transit on Tahiti, Cook went south to make geographical discoveries. It was commonly believed that for the earth's stability, the preponderance of the land masses in the northern hemisphere had to be balanced by a yet-to-be-discovered southern continent. There were firm believers in this continent such as Dalrymple (who had been turned down for the command of the *Endeavour*) and, on the voyage, Banks. There were also disbelievers on board, Cook among them. On this voyage, the question of the southern continent was not settled, but Cook made great discoveries, which persuaded the admiralty to send him on another in 1772, this time, at Cook's suggestion, definitely to prove or disprove that hypothetical continent; he disproved the existence of any continent other than a possible permanently frozen land.[46] In the wake of Cook's southern voyages, the Royal Society proposed, and the king agreed to, a voyage in the other direction, northward,[47] the primary object of which was to settle another practical question, that of the existence of a shorter route to the East Indies across the north pole, the hopefully designated Northwest Passage. The foremost champion in the House of Commons of the naval administration Constantine John Phipps was put in command of two frigates, and the astronomer Israel Lyons was appointed to accompany him. Cavendish was on the Royal Society's committee for drawing up instructions;[48] in Cavendish's papers there are several drafts of his instructions, parts of which are quoted in Phipps's account, *A Voyage Towards the North Pole.*[49] One instruction has to do with taking the temperature of the sea, since few observations had ever been made of it (or of its saltiness, and his instructions also say to bottle some sea water). That temperature was to be taken by two methods, one using Lord Charles Cavendish's self-registering thermometer, as recommended in his publication of 1757. Since that paper was written, Henry Cavendish pointed out, John Canton had shown that spirit of wine and other fluids are compressible, which would make the thermometer appear colder than it truly was. In light of this

source of error, and of another regarding the variable rate of expansion of spirit of wine with temperature, Cavendish provided Phipps with corrections, which he derived with the help of Deluc's experiments on the expansion of spirit of wine.[50] With Lord Charles Cavendish's thermometer, Phipps measured the temperature of the sea to an unprecedented depth, 780 fathoms, where the reading was 26 degrees. From repeated trials, the accuracy of the thermometer was found to be not greater than two or three degrees.[51] By the second method, buckets with valves were used to bring deep water to the surface, where its temperature was measured. Parties going ashore were instructed to make observations and measurements, which were spelled out by Cavendish. They were to measure the temperature of well and spring waters, for that was the "likeliest way of guessing at the mean heat of the climate." They were also to observe the corona of the aurora borealis in relation to the earth's magnetic pole and to note any irregularities of the dipping and horizontal needles." Cavendish had never seen an "ice mountain" (berg) and never would, but if Phipps's party could get close enough, they were to bore a hole in an ice mountain and insert a thermometer, and to melt a piece of it and bring it home in a bottle for Cavendish to examine, and at the same time they should observe the texture of the ice and see if

---

[46]Hector Charles Cameron, *Sir Joseph Banks, K.B., P.R.S. The Autocrat of the Philosophers* (London: Batchworth, 1952), 6–15, 18. I. Kaye, "Captain James Cook and the Royal Society," *Notes and Records of the Royal Society* 24 (1969): 7–18. J. C. Beaglehole, "Cook, James," *DSB* 3:396–97.

[47]After Daines Barrington, F.R.S., had spoken with the secretary Lord Sandwich, the council of the Royal Society formally wrote to him proposing a northern voyage with practical and scientific ends. Royal Society, Minutes of Council, 6:160–61 (19 Jan. 1773).

[48]Royal Society, Minutes of Council, 6:172–73 (22 and 29 Apr 1773). The instructions for Phipps's voyage were drawn up by Cavendish, Nevil Maskelyne, Samuel Horsley, and Matthew Maty. Charles Richard Weld, *A History of the Royal Society*, vol. 2 (London, 1848), 72.

[49]Henry Cavendish, "Rules for Therm. for Heat of Sea," 24 numbered pages of a draft, with much crossing out. Cavendish Mss, III(a): 7. "To Make the Same Observations on the Flat Ice or Fields of Ice as It Has Been Called," part of a 10-page manuscript, ibid., Misc. There is a second draft of the instructions about ice fields, found among Cavendish's Journals, ibid., X(a). Cavendish's instructions for the use of his father's thermometer are quoted in Constantine John Phipps, *A Voyage Towards the North Pole, Undertaken by His Majesty's Command, 1773* (London, 1774), 145.

[50]Phipps, *Voyage* 145–47 Jean André Deluc's experiments were given in his *Recherches sur les modifications de l'atmosphère . . .*, 2 vols. (Geneva, 1772) 1:252.

[51]Phipps, *Voyage*, 27, 32–33, 142.

roots of trees and plants were imbedded in it and try to determine where it was formed. "As a theory frequently enables people to make observations which would otherwise escape them," Cavendish said, "I will hint they /ice mountains/ may perhaps be formed on shores consisting of rocky islands with narrow channels between by the snow & ice falling from the sides of the rocks into the channels in the water & filling them up & that in the spring they are forced out by storms & the tides."[52] Cavendish's directions were clear and complete with rationale, including (in passing) one of the best arguments for the usefulness of theory in science; namely, as a stimulus to extraordinary observation.

Phipps's observations with a seconds pendulum by George Graham gave a figure for the earth that was the closest yet to Newton's calculation. He kept his two clocks for finding longitude, one by John Arnold and one of the Harrison type by Larcum Kendall, in boxes screwed down to shelves of the cabin, each with three locks, one key kept by the captain, one by the first lieutenant, and one by Lyons.[53] He brought back a befitting treasure chest of scientific information, though on the principal question of the Northwest Passage, the voyage proved inconclusive.[54]

The great trading companies, like the government, were, in effect, a part of the method of science in eighteenth-century Britain. Through Cavendish, scientific observations made on voyages between England and the East Indies were communicated to the Royal Society.[55] He drew up instructions for an observer in Madras, no doubt at Fort St. George, to take the temperature of wells. To become "better acquainted with the nature of those extraordinary phenomena," the typhoons, he wanted everything about the weather recorded while the storms were in progress. He wanted barometer readings made with a vernier scale to 1/100th of an inch and frequent corrections made of the height of the mercury in the cistern. He told the correspondent to remove his thermometer from under a shady tree, since evaporation from the leaves could cool it, as Cavendish had decided by observations of his own. Finally, he had heard that in Madras the usual way of cooling water was by placing it in porous earthen vessels, and he wanted his correspondent to try the method, as Cavendish had done.[56] Among his papers, in his own hand, is a copy of a weather journal from

Madras in 1777-78.[57] To nearly the end of his life, Cavendish received observations from East Indian companymen.[58] Whatever may be the larger legacy of the East India Company, it provided considerable opportunity for British science and to its gate-keeper in London in the 1770s and 1780s, Henry Cavendish. India might even be seen to have worked its spell on Cavendish as it did on many of his countrymen for another century and a half: one of his last papers was about the civil year of the Hindoos. This seemingly exotic irrelevance in the regular scientific concerns of Cavendish had its roots, in part, in the East India Company and its collaborations with the Royal Society of London.

Beginning in 1773 Cavendish incorporated the Hudson's Bay Company into his network of sources of an extended knowledge of the earth. Its northern remoteness offered Cavendish and science another and longer-lasting opportunity to study a cold climate after Phipps's voyage to the north. The

---

[52]Cavendish, "To Make the Same Observations on the Flat Ice."

[53]Phipps, *Voyage*, 229.

[54]The expedition reached 80 degree latitude before encountering ice, since it made was during good weather. It did not reach the pole, but if the pole were reachable by sea, Phipps said, the time would be after the solstice. Phipps, *Voyage*, 76.

[55]Robert Barker, "An Account of Some Thermometrical Observations Made at Allahabad in the East-Indies, in Lat. 25 Degrees 30 Minutes N. During the Y 1767, and Also During a Voyage from Madras to England in the Y 1774, Extracted from the Original Journal by Henry Cavendish," *PT* 65 (1775): 202–6. Alexander Dalrymple, "Journal of a Voyage to the East Indies, in the Ship Grenville, Capt. Burnet Abercrombie, in the Year 1775," Communicated by the Hon. Henry Cavendish, *PT* 68 (1778): 389–418. Dalrymple took measurements with thermometers and barometers made by Nairne and Blunt, and he made observations with a dipping needle, and in his report of them gave a long extract on the instrument by Cavendish (p. 390).

[56]These directions are in a draft of a letter to a person who has a "correspondent" in Madras. They are combined in the same manuscript with Cavendish's directions to Phipps on observing ice. Cavendish Mss, Misc. "Evaporation in Glazed and Unglazed Pans. Freezing Point of Pump & Rain Water Boiled and Unboiled," Cavendish Mss III(a), 12. This 22-page manuscript is wrapped in a notice to Cavendish of a meeting of the Royal Society's paper committee in 1775.

[57]"Journal of Weather at Madras," Cavendish Mss, Misc.

[58]James Horsburgh, captain of an East Indiaman, was introduced by Dalrymple to Cavendish in 1801. From Bombay, in 1805, Horsburgh sent a paper on meteorological readings to Cavendish to be read at the Royal Society. It was published, "Abstract of Observations on a Diurnal Variation of the Barometer between the Tropics," *PT* 95 (1805): 177–85. Dalrymple wrote to Horsborgh on 19 Sep. 1805 that he was going to propose to Cavendish, Maskelyne, and Aubert that they join him in recommending Horsborgh for Fellow of the Royal Society. It was done, as Dalrymple planned it, only Aubert did not sign the certificate as he died that year. Howard T. Fry, *Alexander Dalrymple (1737–1808) and the Expansion of British Trade* (London: Frank Cass, 1970), 253–55. Royal Society, Certificates, 6 (21 Nov. 1805).

connection again was the Royal Society. Hudson's Bay had just sent the Society a valuable collection of natural history specimens,[59] and in gratitude, of a sort, for this and other gifts, the Society sent the company a collection of meteorological instruments with instructions for its officers to measure the weather and report back to the Society.[60] What the Royal Society council had in mind is suggested by a letter from the secretary Matthew Maty to Cavendish three days after the council's motion. Maty acknowledged Cavendish's "hints" about the observations to be made at Hudson's Bay and asked where the instruments were to be placed in that frozen climate. Because the rain gauge, in particular, could only be used in summer, Maskelyne had proposed that the snow be collected on the frozen river, and Maty wanted to know what Cavendish thought about it all.[61]

From the outposts of science, Cavendish collected facts upon which a theory of the climates of the world could be based. He held out considerable hope for the method of the heat of wells and springs for measuring the mean heats of climates, and in connection with that method he wanted to test if the earth at some depth below the surface was permanently frozen.[62] He took the temperature on mountains and in the upper atmosphere, making use of a new kind of voyage, the manned balloon, a vertical outpost of his science. He encouraged the taking of the temperature of the sea, as we have noted. He calculated the time of the day when the heat of the air is equal to the mean heat,[63] and he calculated the heat at different latitudes of the earth assuming the sun is the source of the heat.[64] But for the most part, he could contribute only to the methods of meteorology, not to a general theory. For what he could do, he depended on the Royal Society and its connections with observers in far-away places and on accounts of travels, often published by other scientific societies.

One of Cavendish's few close friends in the Royal Society was a professional voyager, the first hydrographer for the East India Company and later the first such for the admiralty, Alexander Dalrymple. A man of great energy and versatility, he was an explorer, chart-maker, navigator, surveyor, commander, geographer, visionary of commercial expansion, policy maker, author of the first English book on nautical surveying, and moving spirit behind the "second British Empire."[65]

Thoroughly scientific in his approach to oceanic exploration, he had a keen interest in scientific instruments, indeed an obsession with chronometers. Although Dalrymple encouraged disappointed hopes in a southern continent and in a Northwest Passage, the voyages that disproved him made valuable scientific observations all the same. Dalrymple was a difficult person: Aubert got along well with him,[66] Blagden not well, and many not at all. Cavendish, who was always greeted warmly by Dalrymple in letters to him, had a good opinion of Dalrymple's character, naming him a trustee of his property, leaving him a legacy in his will, and repeatedly lending him money.[67] Cavendish no doubt thought he was amply rewarded in the news of the world Dalrymple regularly brought him.

British Museum

Henry Cavendish joined his father as a trustee of the British Museum in 1773, when he was elected to succeed Lord Lyttleton. For ten years he came to the biweekly meetings of the standing committee of the trustees with his father.

---

[59]The Society's committee of natural history reported on its examination of this collection (and another from another distant outpost, Cape of Good Hope): Royal Society, Minutes of Council, 6:208 (20 Jan. 1774).

[60]Royal Society, Minutes of Council, 6:206 and 208 (23 Dec. 1773 and 20 Jan. 1774).

[61]Matthew Maty to Henry Cavendish, 26 Dec. 1773, Cavendish Mss X(b), 2.

[62]He put this suspicion as a "Quere" in the draft of his sections of the Royal Society committee report on the fixed points of thermometers: "Whether the earth at considerable depths below the surface is constantly frozen or what comes to the same thing do they if they dig into the ground at the end of summer find the ground frozen & if they do at what depth they find it so. If they do not & they have any wells to observe the heat of the water in them at the end of summer & also at the end of winter & if they have any deep cellars to find the heat of the air or ground in them at the same time." Cavendish Mss, III(a), 3.

[63]Henry Cavendish, "Comput. at What Time Day Heat Is Equal to Mean Heat," Cavendish Mss, Misc.

[64]Henry Cavendish, "Comput. Heat in Diff. Parts of Earth," Cavendish Mss, Misc.

[65]W. A. Spray, "Alexander Dalrymple, Hydrographer," *American Neptune* 30 (1970): 200–216, on 200–l. Fry, *Alexander Dalrymple*, xiii–xvi, xx–xxi.

[66]"So valuable a friend," Alexander Aubert said of Dalrymple, in a letter to Joseph Banks, 28 Sept. 1785, BL Add Mss 33978, no, 35.

[67]Cavendish loaned Dalrymple 500 pounds in each of several years, 1783, 1799, 1800, and 1807. Dalrymple borrowed from Cavendish to pay off other debts due immediately: Alexander Dalrymple to Henry Cavendish, 2 July 1807. Upon Dalrymple's death, his administrator asked Cavendish for the amount owed him, which Cavendish provided. The matter was still pending a few years later when Cavendish died. "27 Dec. 1811 Principal Money and Interest This Day Received of Alex. Dalrymple Esq. Exctr. 2873.3.5." Devon. Coll., L/31/64 and 34/64.

Their commitment was substantial and unusual, since rarely as many as six trustees attended these meetings. The committee prepared reports for consideration at the general meetings of the trustees, which were held three or four times a year, and rarely were there a dozen in attendance at these, often not enough for a quorum. In addition to the Cavendishes, the few other trustees who attended frequently included their friends from the Royal Society and their relatives: Banks, Wray, Watson, Pringle, Yorke (now Lord Hardwicke), and Lord Bessborough.[68]

The standing committee had a wide range of responsibilities. It paid bills, made audits, and so on, but in much of its routine business there was great variety. The committee gave permission for visitors to copy documents and draw birds but also to examine human monsters under the inspection of an officer of the Museum. It heard complaints about the cold of the medals room and the damp of the reading room but also about the in-fighting of the several librarians (the committee ordered them to stop quarreling and be amicable[69]). It laid out money to buy or to subscribe to important works of science for the library, such as Robert Smith's *System of Opticks* and Samuel Horsley's edition of Newton's works.[70] It noted gifts of books and collectibles. No sooner had Henry Cavendish been elected a trustee than the committee ordered thanks to John Walsh and John Hunter for two specimens of the electric eel,[71] and two years later Walsh presented an electric eel the organs of which had been laid open by Hunter, and Hunter presented a transverse section of an electric eel.[72] Some gifts received by the British Museum were substantial; e.g., in 1773, Banks presented his large collection of Icelandic sagas, and Rockingham presented his large collection of animals preserved in spirit (in seventy-two glasses, to which he added seventeen more glasses the next year). Most gifts were isolated curiosities of the sort that were written about in the *Philosophical Transactions*, a six-legged pig, a frog preserved in amber, and the head of a sea horse. Stuffed birds from the Cape of Good Hope, serpents from the East Indies, shells from Labrador, insects from Jamaica, a gun and powder horn from Bengal, Captain Cook's artificial curiosities from the South Sea islands, and much else from Britain's colonial extremities piled up in the British Museum.[73]

First Lord Charles Cavendish, then Lord Charles and Henry Cavendish together, and then Henry Cavendish gave conscientious attention to the affairs of the British Museum for over fifty years. This central, public institution for books and collections expressed their interest in public service and learning.

Society of Antiquaries

In the same year that he became a trustee of the British Museum, 1773, Cavendish was elected a Fellow of the Society of Antiquaries of London. He was recommended by Heberden, Wray, Burrow, Josiah Colebrook, Daines Barrington, and Jean Louis Petit, all of whom were members too of the Royal Society.[74] Macclesfield, Birch, Banks, and other friends of Cavendish from the Royal Society were also members of the Society of Antiquaries, and in general the membership of the two societies had a large overlap.[75]

The Society, which originated with a group who met in a coffee house to discuss history and genealogy, was formally created, or re-created, in 1717. The leading spirit of the Society in its early years was the physician William Stukeley, an accomplished antiquarian, the "Archdruid of this age,"[76] who was also a prominent member of the Royal Society. Early on, there was an attempt to merge the Antiquarian Society and the Royal Society, but the stronger desire was for separateness and equality. In 1751 Martin Folkes, who was

---

[68]Henry Cavendish was elected trustee on 8 Dec. 1773. His record of attendance is recorded in the minutes of the British Museum: Committee, vols. 5 to 9; General Meeting, vols. 3 to 5.

[69]The order for amicable personal relations was made on 9 May 1777. British Museum committee minutes.

[70]Committee meetings on 31 July and 11 Sept. 1778, in vol. 6.

[71]Committee meeting on 23 Apr. 1773, vol. 5.

[72]Walsh's gift was in Jan. or Feb. 1775, and Hunter's was on 16 June 1775; "Diary and Occurrence-Book of the British Museum."

[73]Gifts during the first ten years of Henry Cavendish's tenure as trustee are listed in "Diary & Occurrence-Book of the British Museum, Ap. 2nd 1773 to April 1782 (Signed Dan. Solander)," BL Add Mss 45875.

[74]Cavendish was proposed on 21 Jan. 1773 and elected on 25 Feb. 1773. Society of Antiquaries, Minute Book 12: 53, 580.

[75]Of the twenty-one members of the council of the Society of Antiquaries in 1760, eleven were also Fellows of the Royal Society, and among its ordinary membership, there were forty-four more Fellows "A List of the Society of Antiquaries of London, April 23, MDCCLX," BL, Egerton 2381, ff. 172–75.

[76]"William Stukeley, MD.," in William Munk, *The Roll of the Royal College of Physicians of London. Comprising Biographical Sketches of All the Eminent Physicians Whose Names Are Recorded in the Annals*, 4 vols. (London, 1878), 2:71–74, on 74.

at this same time the president of the Society of Antiquaries and the president of the Royal Society, pushed through a reform, establishing a council and officers for the Society of Antiquaries in exact imitation of those for the Royal Society, and in that year the Society was granted a royal charter.[77] In other ways too it imitated the Royal Society, acquiring a dining club, a journal, and a committee of papers. Fellows of the Royal Society, it would seem, sometimes acted in concert in the politics of the other society.[78] Of the officers and council members of the Society of Antiquaries, an undue proportion were also Fellows of the Royal Society, who were often not the most productive scholars of antiquities. In an age so wondering of natural science, there was a distinct disadvantage in being *merely* an antiquary.[79]

At the time the Society of Antiquaries received its charter, a member wishing to make public new discoveries in antiquities might consider doing it through either the Royal Society or the Society of Antiquaries.[80] Even though the goal of the Royal Society was understood to be the "advancement of *natural* knowledge," just which topics were considered to belong to it and which to the antiquaries was unclear.[81] The duty of the Society of Antiquaries was uncontroversial: to record and where possible to collect "monuments," such as cities, roads, churches, statues, tombs, utensils, medals, deeds, letters, and whatever other ruins and writings supported the "History of British Antiquitys."[82] But just what was to be made of such objects and documents was a matter of judgment and strong feeling. By the time Cavendish joined the Society, its minutes recorded long papers, which reveal contemporary views on the direction of the field. There was, for instance, a paper on the history of Manchester, written on a "rational plan," which promised to rise above the parochialism of town histories to illuminate the general period in the entire kingdom and to lay open the causes of events. Antiquaries could already condemn antiquarianism in the later pejorative meaning of the term.[83] Other papers from this time made a moral point: a history of cockfighting corrected the errors of the modern writers, but its purpose was to show the perversion of cockfighting from a religious and political institution for instilling valor to the present-day pastime founded on cruelty, a disgrace to humanity.[84]

In 1770 the Society of Antiquaries introduced its own journal, the *Archeologia*, which was the occasion for a clear and forceful statement of the purpose of the Society. In the first volume of the journal, the director, Richard Gough, pointed out how things used to be done and how things were now done differently and better. At his own expense, Martin Folkes had published his *Tables of English Coins*, giving copies to some members. That was before the charter of 1751, which made the Society "a more respectable body," and according to which the Society moved to eliminate the remaining differences between it and the Royal Society: from then on, the council of the Society of Antiquaries, like that of the Royal Society, was empowered to print papers read before it, for which purpose the council constituted itself a standing committee. The chartered antiquaries had as their object not their "own entertainment" but the communication of their "researches to the public." Like science, antiquities had a duty to the public. Antiquaries belonged to the modern "age wherein every part of science is advancing to perfection." The proper use of antiquarian facts was "*history*," which was not a poetic narration but

[77] Joan Evans, *A History of the Society of Antiquaries* (Oxford: Oxford University Press, 1956), 442.

[78] Peter Davall to Thomas Birch, 22 Apr. 1754, BL Add Mss 4304, vol. 5, p. 126. Daniel Wray to Thomas Birch, 7 Mar. 1753, BL Add Mss 4322, f. 111.

[79] "You must know I am *a great Antiquary*," a correspondent of Thomas Birch wrote, "though I make no words of it; as half ashamed of my taste; like a man who has taken an odd fancy to an ugly mistress." W. Gloucester to Thomas Birch, 25 Oct. 1763, in John Nichols, *Illustrations of the Literary History of the Eighteenth Century*, 8 vols. (London, 1817–58) 2:144–45, on 145.

[80] Francis Drake told Charles Lyttleton (future president of the Society of Antiquaries) that he had had better success communicating discoveries of antiquities to the Royal Society than to the Society of Antiquaries and that he was inclined to do the same with his present subject, a Roman alter (which he did, publishing on it in the *Philosophical Transactions*). Francis Drake to Charles Lyttleton, 26 Jan. 1756, "Correspondence of C. Lyttleton," BL, Stowe Mss 753, ff. 288–89.

[81] James Burrow prepared a paper for the Society of Antiquaries and "never entertained the least thought of communicating it to the Royal Society." The Royal Society's committee of papers, however, changed his mind; it sent his paper to the secretary of the Royal Society, having drawn red lines through the passages directed expressly to the Society of Antiquaries. James Burrow to Thomas Birch, 18 June 1762, Birch Corr., BL Add Mss 4301, vol. 2, p. 363.

[82] In Stukeley's hand, in the first minute book of the Society, quoted in Evans, *History*, 58.

[83] The author of "The History of Manchester" was John Whitaker, an Oxford fellow. In Society of Antiquaries, Minute Book 11: entry for 6 Dec. 1770.

[84] Samuel Pegge, "A Memoir on Cockfighting . . .," in Society of Antiquaries, Minute Book 11: entries for 12 and 19 Mar. 1772.

a scientific, "regular" inquiry into the records and proofs of the past.[85]

Apart from their common cause, "science," "knowledge," and "truth," and their common membership, the Society of Antiquaries and the Royal Society had a common work. Because science had its own antiquities, both societies had a concern with the history and biography of science.[86] History and natural history were both collecting activities.[87] Between history and astronomy, both dating activities, there was a lively interaction.[88] Antiquaries were greatly interested in views of Pompeii and the like, and there was now a great interest in the Gothic as well as in the Classic, but there was also an interest in contemporary history, so strongly marked by science and technology, such as in the history of the Royal Society of Arts, to which Lord Charles and Henry Cavendish belonged.[89]

Henry Cavendish became a member of the Society of Antiquaries at a time when the membership was rapidly expanding, having nearly doubled in the ten years before his election.[90] The Society was becoming fashionable: many of the new members came from the upper classes including the nobility. A good number came from science too: in the same year as Cavendish, Benjamin Franklin and John Pringle were elected. There is the suggestion that the prosperous and the learned entered the Society to receive its new journal, *Archeologia*.[91] That may well have been the case with Cavendish, who became a member three years after the journal was founded, for we know that he was interested in the contents of the journal. Many Fellows of the Royal Society published in the antiquaries' journal, among them those who recommended Cavendish for Fellow of the Society of Antiquaries, Barrington, Colebrooke, and Wray. Cavendish took particular interest in papers in *Archeologia* having to do with India; his own paper on the Hindoo calendar fitted either that journal or the *Philosophical Transactions*, which was where he published it.

Henry Cavendish's membership in the Society of Antiquaries together with that in the Royal Society and his trusteeship in the British Museum were inscribed on the plate of his coffin, but to Cavendish the affiliations were not of comparable importance. He dedicated himself to the affairs of the Royal Society and the British Museum, whereas he took on no responsibilities in the Society of Antiquaries. He entered the record only once and then as an intermediary, submitting drawings of an Indian pagoda in the name of his scientific friend Alexander Dalrymple.[92]

There had been a plan to bring together in the same meeting place the Society of Antiquaries, the Royal Society, the British Museum, and the Royal Academy of Painting, Sculpture and Architecture, but it did not come off. The British Museum moved into Montagu House in 1754, and the year before the Society of Antiquaries took over a former coffee-house in Chancery Lane. Twenty years later, in 1773, the year Cavendish was elected to the Society of Antiquaries, the Royal Society began planning its apartments for its new location, Somerset House. Cavendish was much involved with that move, and with others on the council of the Royal Society that year, he agreed that it would be a "great inconvenience" to have any apartments in common with the Society of Antiquaries, or even a common staircase. The claim on all possible space was only consistent with

[85]Richard Gough on the purpose of the Society of Antiquaries' publication, in volume 1, 1770, of *Archeologia*.

[86]There was a broad use of "science." Birch, a writer of several biographies, received this compliment: he was said to be "curious in Biography as well as other Branches of Science." J. Owen to Thomas Birch, 1748, BL Add Mss 4316, f. 110. There are many letters from members of the Royal Society to John Ward, professor of rhetoric at Gresham College, F.R.S., who published frequently on antiquities in the *Philosophical Transactions* and was also president of the Society of Antiquaries. For example, Ward had a correspondence about collecting the scientist Robert Boyle's letters for the benefit of the Royal Society: Henry Miles, F.R.S., to Ward, 10 Feb. 1741/42 and 13 June 1746, in "Letters of Learned Men to Professor Ward," BL Add Mss 6210, ff. 248, 249–50.

[87]In connection with a natural history of fossils, Emanuel Mendes da Costa wrote to John Ward to ask if certain Roman vases were made of marble or porcelain. Letter of 13 Nov. 1754, "Letters of Learned Men to Professor Ward," BL Add Mss 6210.

[88]"My whole time has been employed in tedious and irksome calculations to adjust and settle the moons mean motion, in order to make a proper use of the eclipse at the death of Patroculus," John Machin wrote to John Ward. Machin was concerned with Homer's placement of Troy. Letter of 23 Oct. 1745, ibid., f. 230.

[89]This "history of the rise and progress of the Society for the Encouragement of Arts, Manufactures & Sciences" was read on the meetings of 1 and 8 June 1758. The paper was kept in a folio with the purpose of entering "occurrences of our own time." Emanuel Mendez da Costa, "Minutes of the Royal Society and the Society of Antiquaries," BL, Egerton Mss 2381, ff. 57–58.

[90]Membership was 173 in 1764 and 290 in 1774. Evans, *History*, 148.

[91]Evans, *History*, 150.

[92]Henry Cavendish to William Norris, undated. This letter is in the library of the Society of Antiquaries, and it has to do with an extract by Alexander Dalrymple from a journal in the possession of the East-India Company. It evidently refers to "Account of a Curious Pagoda Near Bombay . . .," drawn up by Captain Pyke in 1712, and communicated to the Society of Antiquaries on 10 Feb. 1780 by Dalrymple; published in *Archeologia* 7 (1785): 323–32.

the "external splendor" of the Royal Society.[93] The Society of Antiquaries did, in fact, meet in Somerset House from the beginning of the 1780s,[94] but in this vote of the council, Cavendish came down on the side of the Royal Society.

[93] Royal Society, Minutes of Council 6: 302–3 (10 May 1773).

[94] William Chambers, the architect, informed the Royal Society that no space could be allotted to it consistent with its "splendor" other than what it had in common with the Society of Antiquaries. Royal Society, Minutes of Council 6:304–6 (18 May 1776).

CHAPTER 7

❧

℘ersonal Life

Death of Lord Charles Cavendish

Lord Charles Cavendish was remarkably healthy. He experienced the almost universal malady of that time, gout, but he was not crippled by it,[1] and to judge by his attendance at meetings, he did not suffer from any protracted illnesses. He attended a meeting of the standing committee of the British Museum on 7 February 1783,[2] only a few weeks before his death. He died "on or about" 28 April 1783;[3] by our reckoning, he was probably seventy-nine. Not yet famous as the father of Henry Cavendish, his obituary notice in the *Gentleman's Magazine* identified him as the great uncle to the then present duke of Devonshire, who but for his title was a non-entity.[4]

For so rich a man, Cavendish's will was remarkably brief, as his son Henry's would be too. Unchanged since it was made out thirty years before, his will left to his younger son, Frederick, the money owed him from his mother's estate according to the marriage settlement. With the exception of a thousand pounds for charity, it left all the rest of his estate to his oldest son and sole executor, Henry.[5] That included real property, securities, and the recently inherited, combined estates of the three related Cavendishes Lord James, Richard (Chandler), and Elizabeth.[6]

Writing to Henry Cavendish a month after his father's death, John Michell apologized for imposing on him "so soon after the loss of Ld Charles."[7] What his death meant to Henry we can only surmise. Henry was now fifty-two, and no one in his life had had anything like his father's importance for him.

Besides his wealth, Lord Charles left all of his books and instruments to Henry, but then it would seem that these had always been common property. Henry made an inventory of his and his father's papers, which were kept in the same place, a tall walnut cabinet with an upper case, and which he now classified as *Fathers papers* and *Mine*. The occasion was probably Henry Cavendish's resettlement at Clapham Common and Bedford Square after his father's death. Like his father, Henry kept everything, even "begging letters" and crank science. All of the personal papers have, evidently, been destroyed, but it was unlikely Henry who destroyed them; rather he classified and stored them under lock and key. Spare as it is, Henry's inventory is an aid in understanding Lord Charles Cavendish's life. Papers belonging to his father that we do not have but that Henry Cavendish did include letters to and from his father and his family, letters to his wife, Lady Anne, Frederick's letters, letters from abroad,[8] poetry, and genealogy. Also lost are Lord Charles Cavendish's scientific papers, which include measurements (probably meteorological) taken at Chatsworth, mathematical papers, and other papers on meteorological instruments, refracting telescopes, crystals, artificial cold, specific gravities, and a

---

[1]Cavendish was hindered from writing by gout in his hand, he told his steward: letter to Thomas Revill, 2 Mar. 1765, Devon. Coll., L/31/20.

[2]Entry for 7 Feb. 1783, British Museum, Committee Minutes, vol. 7.

[3]Devon Coll., L/31/37.

[4]Entry in *Gentleman's Magazine* 53 (1783): 366 The notice put Lord Charles Cavendish's age at ninety, but it got this much right: he was "most amiable," and he was an "excellent philosopher."

[5]Lord Charles Cavendish's will was probated on 28 May 1783. "Special Probate of the Last Will and Testament of the Right Honble Charles Cavendish Esqr Commonly Called Lord Charles Cavendish Deceased," Devon. Coll., L/69/12.

[6]Upon Lord Charles Cavendish's death, Lord Camden became the sole surviving executor of the residue of Elizabeth Cavendish's estate. Henry Cavendish promptly applied to him, "being desirous of having" all the wealth in his own hands. "Lord Camden and The Honorable Henry Cavendish, Assignment and Deed of Indemnity, Dated Thirty-First of December 1783," Devon. Coll., L/31/37.

[7]John Michell to Henry Cavendish, 26 May 1783, Cavendish Mss, New Correspondence.

[8]Henry Cavendish lists among his father's papers the "Ruvigny papers" and "letters from abroad." We have not looked abroad for Charles Cavendish's letters, which the next biographers of Henry Cavendish will no doubt want to do. These may have been treated differently than the letters received by Charles Cavendish, which evidently suffered the fate of nearly all sentimental records in the Cavendish family.

pocketbook of experiments.[9] Papers that have survived include legal documents having to do with wills, annuities, titles, rents, dividends, suits, and his marriage settlement. With a few exceptions, Henry Cavendish's own papers in the combined classification have to do with the same things as his father's: properties and lawyers.[10]

What direct evidence we have of Lord Charles Cavendish's intimate life is meager. But we know this much: he died in the knowledge that his oldest son was in competent charge of his life and master of his chosen line of work, science. His son had followed his direction in life and had gone beyond him. Of all of his achievements, the example and assistance he gave Henry were his greatest and, we trust, his proudest.

Whatever Henry Cavendish felt about his father's death he kept to himself, as he did all private matters. To the rest of the world, there was one slight change, this a matter of protocol. Upon the death of *Lord* Charles, Henry Cavendish's name was no longer preceded by "*Hon.*" in his publications in the *Philosophical Transactions*. Strictly speaking Henry never had a right to the title;[11] "The Honourable" was a courtesy title once removed, and from 1783 on, he was Henry Cavendish "Esq." or simply, as he always put it, H. or Henry Cavendish.

Charles Blagden

At about the time his father died, Henry Cavendish acquired a close and lasting friend, Charles Blagden. Given Cavendish's habits of privacy, his willingness to allow a stranger to be close to him is remarkable in itself.

Blagden holds an interest of his own. A man of modest means and abilities (unlike his new friend Cavendish in both respects), he made for himself a life in science at a time when there was no such profession, and his friendship with Cavendish played a part in his plans.

Blagden received a good scientific education in the course of his medical studies at Edinburgh University, where he took his M.D. in 1768. While he was there, both William Cullen and Joseph Black lectured on chemistry, and he heard them both. Blagden became a friend of Cullen, whom he looked up to as his teacher; from his side, Cullen regarded Blagden as a "friend," with whom he had "particular intimacy," Blagden having been "very much in my family."[12] Blagden's manuscripts

contain a copy of Black's lectures, partly in his own hand,[13] and a testimonial by Black that Blagden attended his lectures.[14] In the year following his graduation, Blagden set up practice in Gloucester, where he kept an electrical machine made by Jesse Ramsden, which he evidently used on his patients. He acquired a good reputation in Gloucester, but he was restless.[15] His sights were set on London where, a friend told him, a physician like William Heberden could earn 2,000 to 4,000 pounds a year, maybe more. This friend also told him that he was still too young because no one in London took seriously a physician under thirty; he should stay in the provinces for four or five more years.[16] Another friend also tried to dissuade Blagden from leaving Gloucester, but he acknowledged that Blagden's happiness lay in the "great town."[17] By 1772 Blagden was living in London.

In London Blagden expanded his connections with science. Elected to the Royal Society, he carried out brave experiments in concert with a number of other Fellows. Guided (and protected) by a doctrine he attributed to Cullen, he tested the power of the human body to resist high temperatures, which became the subject of his first

[9]"Walnut Cabinet in Bed Chamber," "Papers in Walnut Cabinet," and "List of Papers Classed," Cavendish Mss, Misc.

[10]"List of Papers Classed."

[11]"The Honourable" followed by given name and surname was allowed the sons of earls and the children of viscounts and barons. Other than for a duke, who was called "His Grace," and a marquess, who was called "The Most Honourable," the title "The Right Honourable" was given to all peers as a courtesy. Henry Cavendish was none of these things. His father, however, was sometimes called "The Right Honourable Lord Cavendish," both parts of his title being by courtesy and proper. *Treasures from Chatsworth, The Devonshire Inheritance. A Loan Exhibition from the Devonshire Collection*, by Permission of the Duke of Devonshire and the Trustees of the Chatsworth Settlement, Organized and Circulated by the International Exhibits Foundation, 1979-1980, p. 24.

[12]William Cullen to William Hunter, 11 Feb. 1769; quoted in John Thomson, *An Account of the Life, Lectures, and Writings of William Cullen, M.D., Professor of the Practice of Physic in the University of Edinburgh*, 2 vols. (Edinburgh, 1859) 1:555-56, on 555.

[13]Blagden was in Edinburgh in 1765-69. Charles Blagden to William Cullen, 17 June 1784, draft, Yale, Blagden Letterbook. Joseph Black's lectures are in Box 71 of the Blagden Papers at Yale. Henry Guerlac, "Black, Joseph," *DSB* 2:173-83, on 173-74.

[14]Joseph Black to Charles Blagden, 5 Oct. 1769, Blagden Letters, Royal Society.

[15]J. Smart to Charles Blagden, 22 Sept. 1769; Henry Cumming to Charles Blagden, 7 Nov. 1769; Jesse Ramsden to Charles Blagden, 23 Nov. 1769; Thomas Curtis to Charles Blagden, 26 Dec. 1769 and 8 Feb. 1770. Blagden Letters, Royal Society, S.11, C.72, R.40, C.77, C.79.

[16]Thomas Curtis to Charles Blagden, 15 Jan. 1770, Blagden Letters, Royal Society, C.78.

[17]J. Smart to Blagden, 24 Feb. 1772, Blagden Letters, Royal Society, S.16.

paper in the *Philosophical Transactions*. He and his colleagues spent considerable time inside a room heated to temperatures above the boiling point, to nearly 260 degrees. Eggs hardened, beefsteak roasted, but Blagden and the other human subjects emerged unharmed, proof, to Blagden, of the ability of the human body to destroy heat.[18] In 1775, the year of the last of his experiments in a heated room, Blagden made a scientific connection with Cavendish. Now an army surgeon assigned to go to North America, he was instructed by Cavendish on how to serve science at the same time: on the voyage to America he was to compare the temperature of the sea with that of the air, and when he got there he was to make observations of the temperature of wells and springs. These directions, Blagden said, "led to my discovery of the heat of the gulf stream" and to a publication in the *Philosophical Transactions*.[19] Because of the war, Blagden had little opportunity to make the observations of wells and springs that Cavendish wanted. Blagden followed events in science as best he could at long distance, including its politics; he asked Banks why Cavendish was left off the council of the Royal Society in 1778.[20] He longed to resume his life in science, and in 1779 he got permission from Cornwallis to return from America to England.

By 1780 Blagden was settled in Plymouth, where he remained for two years, working in the military hospital there. He was back home but he was not in London; he was in Plymouth, which he characterized to Joseph Banks as "miserable exile."[21] In an ideal life, he would "live as much as I can among books," and he asked Banks if the Royal Society could make him "Inspector of the Library, or something of that sort," with apartments in or next to the Royal Society in Somerset Place. Banks said no,[22] leaving Blagden to explore other ways to escape his exile. The North Pole voyager Phipps, by then Lord Mulgrave, repeatedly offered his connections in the admiralty to help Blagden's career.[23]

In the summer of 1782 Blagden attended lectures by an "itinerant Philosopher," Dr. Henry Moyes, who was blind, and who was reputed to be a prodigy, but whose knowledge of recent developments Blagden found "extremely inaccurate & defective,"[24] at best scraps from Black's lectures on heat. Blagden scoffed at Moyes's claim that mercury freezes at minus 350 degrees. The day

after a lecture and apparently suggested by it, Blagden recorded in his diary "hints" for experiments on heat, "ideas which suggested themselves": in addition to experiments, he speculated "whether heat may not be the cause of all chemical attracting, the different bodies not attracting one another, but attracting the common medium, heat. . . ."[25] This way of thinking about heat was decidedly not Cavendish's, but that did not stand in the way; Blagden was soon making experiments on freezing mixtures, sometimes with Cavendish.

At some point Blagden moved from Plymouth to London to live with his brother and to make his fortune there. In early 1783 he went on half pay as a physician to the forces.[26] He was now again in regular personal contact with the leading men of science, at the Royal Society and its dining club, at the Monday Club that met at the George and Vulture, and at the homes of individuals, William Herschel, Alexander Aubert, and Banks. In the summer of 1782 Blagden began visiting the heads of the Cavendish family, the duke and duchess of Devonshire, often dining with them. In March of that year, he had breakfast at their cousin Henry Cavendish's house, and that fall he began

[18] During Blagden's stay in Edinburgh, "the idea of a power in animals of *generating cold* (that was the expression) when the heat of the atmosphere exceeded the proper temperature of their bodies, was pretty generally received among the students of physic, from Dr. Cullen's arguments." Blagden had done a simple experiment at the time that agreed with Cullen's idea. Charles Blagden, "Experiments and Observations in an Heated Room," and "Further Experiments and Observations in an Heated Room," *PT* 65 (1775): 111-23, 484-94, quote on 112.

[19] Blagden found the gulf stream to be several degrees warmer than the sea through which it ran. He thought that seamen ought to take a thermometer with them as an aid to navigation. Charles Blagden, "On the Heat of the Water in the Gulf-Stream," *PT* 71 (1781): 334-44, on 334, 341-44. The full quotation is: Cavendish in 1775 "recommended an attention to the temperature of the sea, as compared with that of the air, which led to my discovery of the heat of the gulf stream." Draft of a paper in Blagden Papers, Yale, box 2, folder 26.

[20] Blagden wrote to Banks about science, which interested him more than the war he was part of. He commented in the same letter about Cavendish's views on electricity. Charles Blagden to Sir Joseph Banks, 2 Mar. 1778, copy, BM(NH), DTC 3: 184.

[21] Charles Blagden to Sir Joseph Banks, 3 Nov. 1782, copy, BM(NH), DTC 3: 205.

[22] Charles Blagden to Sir Joseph Banks, 19 July 1782, draft; Sir Joseph Banks to Charles Blagden, 19 Aug. 1782, Blagden Letters, Royal Society, B.8a and 9.

[23] For example, Lord Mulgrave to Charles Blagden, 1 Mar. 1780, Blagden Letters, Royal Society, p. 35.

[24] Blagden to Banks, 19 July 1782.

[25] Entries for 16, 18, 19 July 1782, Blagden Diary, Royal Society.

[26] Letter from the war office: FitzPatrick to Charles Blagden, 7 May 1783, Blagden Letters, Royal Society, F10.

assisting Cavendish in experiments. In keeping with a promise he had made to Cavendish before he left for the war in America, Blagden collected Plymouth air in all kinds of weather, nine bottles worth, which he brought to Cavendish in his new house in Hampstead as, we imagine, a kind of house-warming present. Together they tested these samples of air with the eudiometer.[27] In December, with Cavendish, Blagden went over the experiments on extreme cold done at Hudson's Bay under Cavendish's direction, and, on "Cavendish's advice," he set about to learn what had been done on that subject "chiefly with a view to quicksilver,"[28] which would lead to his published history of the freezing of mercury the following year. In his enthusiasm for experimenting on freezing mixtures, he froze a finger white several times;[29] on 27 February 1783 he recorded that the day before Cavendish had frozen mercury. By 1785 Cavendish and Blagden's association was recognized: that year, for the first time, Banks in letters to Blagden asked him to give his compliments to Cavendish. Banks toasted them: "may success attend all your mutual operations."[30]

Blagden and Cavendish were both single and resettling, Cavendish in mid life at fifty-one, and Blagden in a change of career at thirty-four. They had much to offer one another. Blagden was interested in everything happening in science, eager to be found useful by men of science. He would give Cavendish unstintingly of his time; he would gladly be Cavendish's scientific assistant, secretary, eyes and ears, runner of errands, and companion in dining, meeting, and traveling. Blagden was knowledgeable in science, he could handle instruments, and at the same time he was definitely Cavendish's *assistant*. Blagden was a diligent correspondent, a linguist who cultivated connections with foreign scientists; he was eager to serve as a go-between, taking pride in his knowledge of persons and events, even of gossip. He would soon, in 1784, be secretary of the Royal Society, which would greatly extend his lines of communication. In that capacity, in 1786 he wrote to Benjamin Thompson in Germany: "It is scarcely possible that any ph/ilosophical/ discoveries can be made in England without coming to my knowledge by some channel or another."[31] With his extensive foreign connections, he could have said nearly the same about his knowledge of philosophical discoveries abroad. Blagden took on editorial work

for the *Philosophical Transactions*, and privately he did the same for Cavendish's papers published in that journal.[32] Blagden was boundlessly curious about the world, had an excellent memory, was a man of facts, and was reliable and loyal and always accessible when Cavendish had need for him.[33] It would be hard to invent a man better suited than Blagden to be Cavendish's right hand. What Blagden expected in return for his services to Cavendish is less clear. Some favors were simply mutual; Blagden could ask Cavendish to go to his house to look for things for him,[34] just as it worked the other way around. Cavendish supplied Blagden with any scientific information he wanted: on claims for a barometric tube made by George Adams, Blagden was skeptical but unsure: "but Mr Cavendish will be here presently, & then I will consult *him*."[35] Blagden's papers contain many letters from Cavendish on questions of science pertaining to Blagden's interests.[36]

During a stretch of Cavendish's most productive years, Blagden was closer to him than anyone else. Blagden assisted Cavendish in his researches, but then so did Cavendish assist him. Of ten papers Blagden published in the *Philosophical Transactions*, four originated with Cavendish and two others were done with Cavendish's help.[37]

---

[27]Charles Blagden to Sir Joseph Banks, 3 Nov. 1782, copy, BM(NH), DTC 3: 205. Entry for 28 Nov. 1782, Blagden Diary, Royal Society.

[28]Entries for 17 and 23 Dec. 1782, Blagden Diary, Royal Society.

[29]Entry for 25 Feb. 1783, Blagden Diary, Royal Society. There are many other entries on this subject around this time.

[30]Sir Joseph Banks to Charles Blagden, 28 July and 4 Aug. 1785, Blagden Letters, Royal Society, B.35 and 36.

[31]Charles Blagden to Benjamin Thompson, 7 Feb. 1786, draft, Blagden Letterbook, Yale.

[32]Blagden made changes in Cavendish's papers in manuscript and read and corrected their proofs. He always showed Cavendish the changes he made. In connection with Cavendish's paper on gases in 1785, for example, he sent Cavendish not only the revised proofs but the first proofs too so that Cavendish "may the more readily perceive some alterations which I thought it expedient to make." Charles Blagden to Henry Cavendish, n.d. /1785/, Cavendish Mss X(b), 4.

[33]Blagden told Cavendish he would be home that evening should Cavendish have any questions. Charles Blagden to Henry Cavendish, n.d. /1784 or 1785/, Cavendish Mss, New Correspondence.

[34]Charles Blagden to Henry Cavendish, 16 Sept. 1787, Cavendish Mss X(b), 13.

[35]Charles Blagden to Sir Joseph Banks, 12 Oct. 1786, BL Add Mss 33272, pp. 19-20.

[36]These Cavendish letters are in the Blagden Papers, Royal Society.

[37]In the ten papers, I omit two by Blagden in the *Philosophical Transactions*: an extract from a letter by Blagden on the tides at Naples in 1793, and an appendix to Ware's paper on vision in 1813. The repeated involvement of Cavendish in Blagden's scientific work is documented in Blagden's papers, both by what he writes and by the many sheets in Cavendish's handwriting intermixed with his. Blagden Papers, Yale, box 2, and elsewhere.

Blagden considered establishing a medical practice in London, but he lacked the desire or drive. He needed income, and it has been assumed that Cavendish answered his need. Given the social and financial mismatch of Cavendish and Blagden, the rumor mills were busy: the chemist Kirwan, who had a wicked pen, told a French colleague that Blagden only looked through Cavendish's telescope because Cavendish "is a near relation of the duke of Devonshire and has six thousand pounds sterling yearly income."[38] Cavendish is said to have settled an annuity of 500 pounds on Blagden, but we wonder if that is true.[39]

Blagden was drawn to persons of rank and of accomplishment and, in particular, to Cavendish who had both. Blagden kept an eye out for patronage, always, since that was how a person like himself advanced. Cavendish offered Blagden patronage but it was probably not financial, though Blagden probably calculated on that too one day. By placing his trust publicly in Blagden, Cavendish helped Blagden to realize a place in the world. Through Cavendish, Blagden had a small part in the great scientific developments of his time. In serving Cavendish, Blagden served a cause he believed in; what may sound like mutual exploitation is better described as mutual benefit and convenience. Their friendship probably was not that cold either, though the nature of it is elusive, as both men were reserved. Both lived by strict routines but were able to accommodate their routines to one another's; to what degree personal warmth made this possible, we can only wonder. When Blagden heard that Cavendish had died, he wrote in his diary that day, "felt much affected."[40]

The relationship between Blagden and Cavendish is said to have ended with a formal break, in 1789.[41] The break at that time, as we will see, was in the first instance not a break between Blagden and Cavendish but one between Blagden and Banks. After 1788 neither of them published any more experimental researches (with the exception ten years later of Cavendish's weighing of the world), but they continued to meet to perform experiments at Clapham Common,[42] and Blagden continued to dine at Cavendish's house.[43] When Blagden was out of the country, he continued to write to Cavendish with scientific news.[44] When Blagden wanted support in the Royal Society, Cavendish gave it, as in 1793 when Blagden wanted

to stay abroad another year and retain his secretaryship in the Royal Society.[45] And when Blagden fell ill while abroad, he had his doctor inform Cavendish, who in turn informed Banks.[46] Blagden would be known as an "intimate friend" of Cavendish.[47] The change in their friendship was one of degree not of kind, and as long as Blagden was in London he and Cavendish continued to meet regularly to the end of Cavendish's life. When Cavendish died, Blagden spoke of an earlier time when he was "intimate with him."[48]

In all of the correspondence we have seen, Blagden never said a word against Cavendish, as he did freely against persons who slighted him. Whatever their understanding had been, if it had ever been spelled out, Cavendish had treated Blagden justly by it, and Blagden never disappointed

------

[38]Richard Kirwan to Guyton de Morveau, 9 Jan. 1786, in *A Scientific Correspondence During the Chemical Revolution: Louis-Bernard Guyton de Morveau and Richard Kirwan, 1782-1802* ed. E. Grison, M. Sadoun-Goupil and P. Bret (Berkeley: Office for History of Science and Technology, University of California at Berkeley, 1994), 161-64, on 163.

[39]Lord Brougham, *Lives of Men of Science*, first series, pp. 445-46, cited in George Wilson, *The Life of the Honourable Henry Cavendish* (London, 1851), 133. There may have been such an annuity, but the evidence we have so far uncovered does not reveal it. In fairness to the rumor of a 500-pound annuity, however, we note that Blagden's income in 1785/86 was 511 pounds (he was in debt, since he paid out 726 pounds in the same time): Gloucester Record Office, D 1086, F 158. Blagden held securities, and he had a salary from the Royal Society. In the bundle of Blagden's papers labeled "Accounts, Bills, Insurance, and Copy of Will of S. Nelmes," we find that as executor and beneficiary of the will of his distant relative Sarah Nelmes, Blagden received over 2000 pounds in 1777, but there is no mention of Cavendish: Blagden Manuscripts, Royal Society. In Blagden's household records, we find two or three references to Cavendish but none to any income from Cavendish: Gloucestershire Record Office, D 1086. The Cavendish scientific and estate papers at Chatsworth do not refer to it either.

[40]Entry for 24 Feb. 1810, Blagden Diary, Royal Society.

[41]Wilson, *Cavendish*, 129.

[42]Charles Blagden to Henry Cavendish, 5 Oct. 1790, draft, Blagden Letterbook, Royal Society, 7.702.

[43]Charles Blagden to Captain Stirling, 4 Apr. 1791, draft, Blagden Letterbook, Royal Society, 7.511.

[44]Blagden told Banks to tell Cavendish to expect a letter from him on an excursion to Tivoli. Charles Blagden to Sir Joseph Banks, 11 May 1793, BL Add Mss 33272.

[45]Sir Joseph Banks to Charles Blagden, n.d. /after 11 May 1793/, draft, BL Add Mss 33272, p. 121.

[46]Cavendish had been informed of Blagden's illness a week before, but he did not tell Banks until he had something "more precise." Cavendish described the violent fever but reassured Banks that now there was the "utmost reason" to expect Blagden to recover. He was receiving the "utmost care," and his "head was perfectly clear." Henry Cavendish to Sir Joseph Banks, 23 Sept. 1793, copy, BM(NH), DTC 3:257.

[47]Lord Castlereagh to Sir Charles Stuart in the foreign office, 13 July 1819, copy, Blagden Letters, Royal Society, C6.

[48]Entry for 1 Mar. 1810, Blagden Diary, Royal Society, 5:back p. 428.

Cavendish in any important matter. It might seem odd that more cannot be said about the personal aspect of this unique friendship of Cavendish, since Blagden was a diarist, an untiring correspondent, and a fluid conversationalist. (He was known for his "copiousness and precision," Boswell said, and Johnson regarded Blagden as a "delightful fellow."[49] Lord Glenbervie found him "conceited and pedantic."[50] No one, however, accused him of ever being at a loss for words.) Blagden had an opportunity to see Cavendish on a daily, intimate basis for years on end. He might be expected to have left a personal account, since, after all, Cavendish was famous both as a great scientist and as an extremely eccentric character. The explanation may lie in a remark by Blagden on Boswell's account of his and Johnson's tour of the Hebrides: "Most people would be sorry to have a bosom friend, who kept a journal of their conversations, to publish as soon as they should be dead."[51] On principle, it would seem, Blagden did not become Cavendish's "Boswell." Nonetheless, it is from Blagden's letters and diary that we know much of what we do about Cavendish's life from the mid 1780s to the end. Perhaps not too much is lost because of Blagden's reserve, since Cavendish kept his thoughts about life to himself, and there were plenty of others who were glad to repeat anecdotes about Cavendish.

Monday Club

The setting of Henry Cavendish's social life was clubs. From the Restoration in the seventeenth century through the eighteenth century and beyond, men of science congregated in the coffee houses of London,[52] where they drank, ate, smoked, talked, and did experiments.[53] The Royal Society Club was the best known and is the best documented of Cavendish's clubs, but from letters to Cavendish and from Blagden's diary we know of other, less formal clubs, which kept no records. Clubs commonly went by the names of the coffee houses and taverns where their meetings took place, which is how we know Cavendish's. The earliest reference occurs in letters by Alexander Dalrymple, who sent greetings through Cavendish to their mutual friends at the Mitre and at the King's Head. The King's Head Tavern in Chancery Lane was where Robert Hooke and

other Fellows of the Royal Society gathered in the late seventeenth century, but King's Head was one of the commonest names for taverns.[54] The Royal Society Club met at the Mitre Tavern on Fleet Street, and later at the Crown & Anchor on the Strand. In the 1780s, in letters to Cavendish, John Michell repeatedly greeted their common friends at the Royal Society and at the Cat and Bagpipes. This latter sign is more original, but about all that is known is that the tavern was located on Downing Street and was popular.[55] There were many other scientific clubs, not always neatly separable. Cavendish did not belong to the club that met at the Chapter Coffee House and later at the Baptist Head Coffee House, even though persons he saw regularly such as Aubert, Nairne, and Kirwan belonged to it.[56] Nor did he belong to another club that met at Jack's Coffee House and later at Young Slaughter's Coffee House on St. Martin's Lane, though Blagden, Banks, Keir, Maskelyne, Ramsden, Smeaton, Schuckburgh, Phipps, and Cook, among others Cavendish knew, went there.[57] Other groups of scientific men met in houses; one, for example, met on Saturday evenings at Banks's,[58] another at Kirwan's.[59]

---

[49]Quoted in Frederick H. Getman, "Sir Charles Blagden, F.R.S.," *Osiris* 3 (1937): 69-87, on 73.

[50]Lord Glenbervie, *Diaries* (London, 1928), quoted in a footnote in "The Diary of Sir Charles Blagden," ed. G. R. De Beer, *Notes and Records of the Royal Society of London* 8 (1950): 65-89, on 76.

[51]Charles Blagden to Joseph Banks, 9 Oct. 1785, Banks Correspondence, Kew, l.210.

[52]A. E. Musson and E. Robinson, *Science and Technology in the Industrial Revolution* (Toronto: University of Toronto Press, 1969), 58.

[53]Bryant Lillywhite, *London Coffee Houses. A Reference Book of Coffee Houses of the Seventeenth, Eighteenth and Nineteenth Centuries* (London: George Allen & Unwin, 1963), 22-24. Joseph Banks described an unsuccessful experiment tried before the Royal Society Club at the Crown and Anchor: letter to Charles Blagden, 28 Sept. 1782, Royal Society, Blagden Letters, B10.

[54]Henry Lyons, *The Royal Society, 1660-1940: A History of Its Administration under Its Charters* (New York: Greenwood, 1968), 171. Many, seven, King's Head taverns are listed under signs of taverns in the Vade Mecum, and included in Walter Besant, *London in the Eighteenth Century* (London: Adean & Charles Black, 1902), 639-40.

[55]That much is known about the tavern, from *Notes and Queries*, 9 Nov. 1850, p. 397, quoted in Archibald Geikie, *Memoir of John Michell* (Cambridge: Cambridge University Press, 1918), 58.

[56]This club usually met twice a month. Its membership was about two dozen, and it was more formal than many of the associations then, keeping a minute book, of which there is a copy in the Museum of Science, Oxford. G. L'E. Turner, "The Auction Sales of the Earl of Bute's Instruments, 1793," *Annals of Science* 23 (1967): 213-42, on 220.

[57]Henry B. Wheatley, *London, Past and Present. A Dictionary of Its History, Associations, and Traditions*, 3 vols. (London, 1891), 2:484. Lillywhite, *London Coffee Houses*, 404.

[58]John Strange to Joseph Banks, 8 Aug. 1788, Banks Correspondence, Kew, l. 315.

[59]Musson and Robinson, *Science and Technology in the Industrial Revolution*, 123.

Besides the Royal Society Club, we know about only one other club to which Cavendish belonged, the Monday Club, named after the day of the week it met. The place was the George & Vulture, a coffee house located in George Yard, off Lombard Street.[60] This long-lived club went back at least to the 1760s,[61] and Cavendish came regularly to it for fifteen years or more. When John Pringle returned from Edinburgh to London in 1781, he rejoined the Monday Club, where he met with "such friends as Mr. Cavendish, Dr. Heberden, and Dr. Watson."[62] He also met with Blagden, who began coming to the Monday Club almost immediately after returning to London, as we know from his London diary.[63] Aubert, Dalrymple, and Franklin were also members, all friends of Cavendish.[64] The discussions at this club were, in part, continuous with those at the Royal Society and the Royal Society Club. For example: Aubert, who belonged to this club too, wrote to Herschel about a paper by the St. Petersburg academician Anders Johan Lexell (no doubt about Herschel's "comet" of 1781, which Lexell determined was not a comet but a new planet, Uranus), which he intended to communicate to the members of both the Royal Society and the Monday Club.[65] For another example: in 1789 Aubert read a paper by Peter Dolland to the Monday Club, who at that meeting consisted of Cavendish along with Blagden, Phipps, Nairne, Smeaton, John Hunter, and two others. The paper had to do with a disagreement between Dolland and his fellow instrument-maker Ramsden, and upon hearing the paper, the Monday Club agreed that it was temperate and clarifying, and as a result Aubert wrote to Banks to recommend that Dolland's paper be read at the Royal Society.[66] Blagden's diary reveals that through the mid 1790s, he and Cavendish often went together to dine at the Monday Club. Upon coming home from the George & Vulture one Monday night, Blagden wrote in his diary: "went with him /Cavendish/ to Club: I spoke of spirit & independence, & true friends."[67] He did not record what Cavendish said on the subject, if anything, but there can be no question that there was a friendship and that it was expressed in the setting of London's coffee houses and taverns.

---

[60]Lillywhite, *London Coffee Houses*, 160, 201, 699, 792.

[61]Verner W. Crane, "The Club of Honest Whigs: Friends of Science and Liberty," *William and Mary Quarterly* 23 (1966): 210-33, on 213.

[62]Quotation from the *Annual Register*, 1783, p 45; in James Sime, *William Herschel and His Work* (New York: Charles Scribner's Sons, 1900), 50.

[63]Entry for 1 Jan. 1782, Blagden Diary, Royal Society.

[64]On Franklin and Aubert: Crane, "Club of Honest Whigs," p. 213. On Dalrymple: 15 June 1795, Blagden Diary, Royal Society, 3:62, and elsewhere.

[65]Alexander Aubert to William Herschel, 7 Sept. 1782, Herschel Manuscripts, Royal Astronomical Society, W1/13, A 10.

[66]Alexander Aubert to Joseph Banks, 1 July 1789, BL Add Mss 33978, no 251.

[67]Entry for 25 Aug. 1794, Blagden Diary, Royal Society, 3:13.

Dukes, Duchesses, and Properties

FIGURE 1. *William Cavendish, Second Duke of Devonshire. By Charles Jervas. Devonshire Collection, Chatsworth. Reproduced by permission of the Chatsworth Settlement Trustees and the Courtauld Institute of Art.*

FIGURE 2. *Rachel Russell, Duchess of Devonshire. Wife of the Second Duke. By M. Dahl. Devonshire Collection, Chatsworth. Reproduced by permission of the Chatsworth Settlement Trustees and the Courtauld Institute of Art.*

FIGURE 3. *Henry de Grey, Duke of Kent. By Amiconi? Reproduced by permission of the Bedfordshire Record Office.*

FIGURE 4. *Jemima Crewe, Duchess of Kent. First Wife of the Duke. By Riley. Reproduced by permission of the Bedfordshire Record Office.*

FIGURE 5. *Kents. Conversation Piece at Wrest Park. By Silsoe, around 1735. Left to right:
Mary de Grey, William Bentinck, Barbara Godolphin, Lord Berkeley, Charles Bentinck, Earl of
Clanbrassil, Countess of Portland, Duke of Kent, Jemima Campbell (later Marchioness de Grey),
Sophia de Grey, Duchess of Kent, Elizabeth Bentinck, Countess of Clanbrassil, Viscountess
Middleton. Reproduced by permission of the Bedfordshire Record Office.*

FIGURE 6. *Chatsworth House. The country house in Derbyshire belonging to the dukes of Devonshire. Photograph by the authors.*

FIGURE 7. *Chatsworth House. Photograph by the authors.*

FIGURE 8. *Devonshire House. Picadilly. Demolished. Among aristocratic mansions in London, this townhouse of the dukes of Devonshire was uncommon for being detached instead of terraced. Reproduced by permission of National Monuments Record: RCHME © Crown Copyright.*

FIGURE 9. *Wrest Park. The duke of Kent's garden at his country house in Bedfordshire. Photograph by the authors.*

FIGURE 10. *No. 4 St. James Square. The duke of Kent's house in London. Reproduced by permission of the Greater London Record Office.*

The Scientific Branch of the Family

FIGURE 11. *Lord Charles Cavendish. By Enoch Seeman (c. 1694-1745). Devonshire Collection, Chatsworth. Reproduced by permission of the Chatsworth Settlement Trustees and by the Courtauld Institute of Art.*

FIGURE 12. *Lady Anne de Grey. Wife of Lord Charles Cavendish. By J. Davison. Reproduced by permission of the Bedfordshire Record Office.*

FIGURE 13. *The Honourable Henry Cavendish. Graphite and gray wash sketch by William Alexander. Beneath the sketch, in handwriting, it reads: "Cavendish Esqr. F.R.S. Trustee of the British Museum. 1812." The figure measures ten centimeters. Reproduced by permission of the British Museum.*

Places and Instruments of Science

FIGURE 14. *No. 13 Great Marlborough Street. Demolished. Lord Charles Cavendish's house from 1738 to the end of his life. Henry Cavendish lived here with his father, and after his father's death he leased the house. View of the back premises in Blenheim Street. From a watercolor sketch of 1888 by Appleton. Reproduced by permission of Westminster City Library.*

FIGURE 15. *Church Row, Hampstead. Henry Carendish lived in No. 34 Church Row for almost four years, from 1782 to 1785. But for the automobiles, this street with its church and terraced houses looks much as it did then. Photograph by the authors.*

FIGURE 16. *No. 11 Bedford Square. Henry Cavendish appears on the rate books for this townhouse from 1786 to the end of his life. Photograph by the authors.*

FIGURE 17. *The Cavendish House, Clapham. Demolished. Henry Cavendish 's country house from 1785 to the end of his life is shown here from the back, in a later, altered version.* Frontispiece to The Scientific Papers of the Honourable Henry Cavendish, *2 vols., ed. E. Thorpe (Cambridge, 1921). All rights reserved: Cambridge University Press. Reprinted with the permission of Cambridge University Press.*

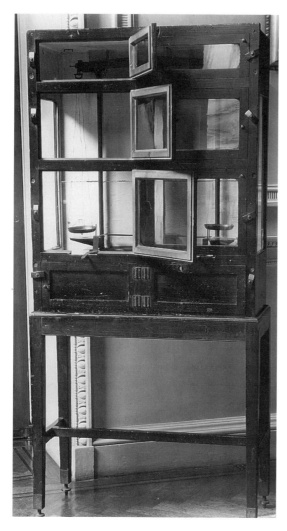

FIGURE 18. *Chemical Balance. Belonging to Henry Cavendish. Built by "Harrison, "probably Cavendish's private instrument-maker William Harrison, this instrument is the earliest of the great precision balances of the eighteenth century. Reproduced by courtesy of the Royal Institution of Great Britain.*

FIGURE 20. *Portable Barometer. Belonging to Henry Cavendish. The ingenious case opens into a tripod. Alongside the (now broken) barometer are two scales, one English and one French. There is a thermometer at the bottom with a correction scale. Cavendish may have used this instrument on his journeys outside London. Photograph by the authors. Devonshire Collection, Chatsworth. Reproduced by permission of the Chatsworth Settlement Trustees.*

FIGURE 19. *Battery of Leyden Jars. The box is labeled "JCM" [James Clerk Maxwell], "Electrical Apparatus belonging to Henry Cavendish." Photograph by the authors. Devonshire Collection, Chatsworth. Reproduced by permission of the Chatsworth Settlement Trustees.*

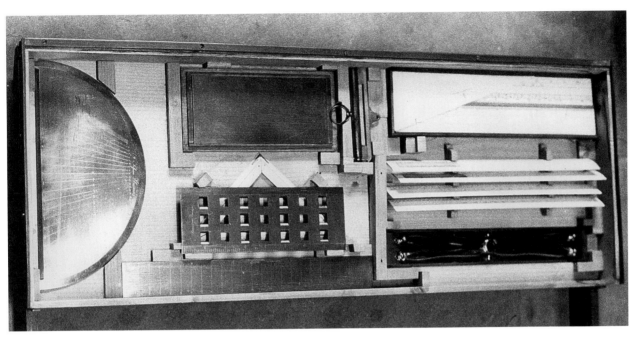

FIGURE 21. *Mathematical Instruments. Belonging to Henry Cavendish. The instrument cases in this and the next illustration are drawers that fit into a cabinet. There are many scales and rulers, a brass globe map projection, an ivory triangle, and so on, bearing the names of well-known instrument-makers: Jesse Ramsden, Jonathan Sisson, and Fraser, presumably, William Fraser. Photograph by the authors. Devonshire Collection, Chatsworth. Reproduced by permission of the Chatsworth Settlement Trustees.*

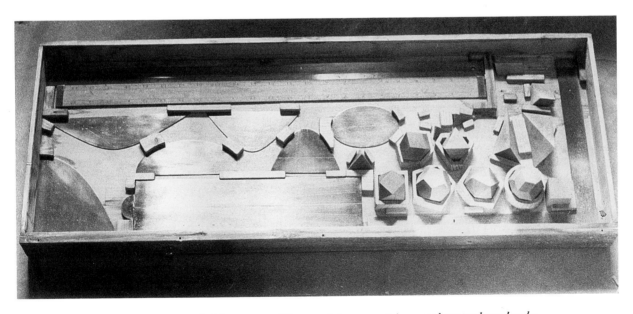

FIGURE 22. *Mathematical Instruments. The second drawer contains more brass and wood scales and rulers. The regular solids are made of hardwood. Cavendish's scientific papers contain many drawings made with these instruments, including drawings from which the plates accompanying his publications were made. Photograph by the authors. Devonshire Collection, Chatsworth. Reproduced by permission of the Chatsworth Settlement Trustees.*

Places of Public Service

FIGURE 23. *House of Commons, 1741-42. From an engraving by Benjamin Cole, after John Pine, 1749. Lord Charles Cavendish represented several successive constituencies in the Commons between 1725 and 1741. Frontispiece, Romney Sedgwick,* The History of Parliament: The House of Commons 1715-1754, *vol. 1 (New York: Oxford University Press, 1970).*

FIGURE 24. *Westminster Bridge.* Westminster from the North East. *By Samuel Scott.*
Westminster Bridge is shown in an early stage of construction. Lord Charles Cavendish was an
active bridge commissioner from 1736 to 1749, the eve of its opening. Reproduced by permission of
the Governor and Company of the Bank of England.

FIGURE 25. *Westminster Bridge.* Westminster Bridge, London, with the Lord Mayor's
Procession on the Thames, *1747. By Canaletto. Westminster Bridge is nearly finished; final*
construction can be seen at the far right. Reproduced by permission of the Yale Center for British
Art, Paul Mellon Collection.

FIGURE 26. *Royal Society.* The Meeting Room of the Royal Society at
Somerset House 1780-1857. *Painting by Frederick William Fairholt and
engraving by H. Melville. Henry Cavendish came regularly to meetings in this
room for the last thirty years of his life. Reproduced by permission of the Royal
Society of London.*

FIGURE 27. *Foundling Hospital. Demolished. Lord Charles Cavendish was a
governor of this institution from the year of its charter, 1739. From a contemporary print. Reproduced by permission of the Greater London Record Office.*

FIGURE 28. *British Museum.* Entrance to the Old British Museum, Montague House. *Lord Charles Cavendish became a trustee of the Museum at its first election, 1753. Henry Cavendish was elected a trustee in 1773. Watercolor by George Scharf the elder, 1845. Visitors are seen entering from the left; through one of the two arched gateways on the right can be seen visitors on the staircase and stuffed animals on the landing. The statue is of Sir Joseph Banks, former president of the Royal Society. Reproduced by permission of the British Museum.*

FIGURE 29. *British Museum.* Staircase of the Old British Museum, Montague House. *Watercolor by George Scharf the elder, 1845. Visitors are shown on the stairs and on the landing looking at stuffed animals. The giraffes seem to be outgrowing Montague House, which was in a sense the truth, for by the time this painting was made, most of the contents of the overcrowded and dilapidated Montague House had been removed to the new home of the Museum. Reproduced by permission of the British Museum.*

FIGURE 30. *Royal Institution.* Distinguished Men of Science Living in Great Britain in 1807-8. *Engraving by William Walker around 1862, taken from a drawing by Sir John Gilbert. The setting of this print is the library of the Royal Institution, but the group portrait is artificial. Henry Cavendish sits apart with eyes downcast, perhaps the artist's interpretation. Cavendish's profile and dress are drawn from William Alexander's sketch. Cavendish's hat has been removed, and he is seated and faced in the other direction. Henry Cavendish was a manager of the Royal Institution from 1800. Reproduced by permission of the National Portrait Gallery.*

PART 4

Henry Cavendish

CHAPTER 1

❧

Home

Propped in the corner of his carriage, Cavendish had himself conveyed through the streets of London to his many regular destinations, his clubs, for example, where by all accounts he cut a somewhat awkward figure. But he was not awkward at home, where everything was made to fit. Furnished in the taste of the scientific revolution, with instruments and laboratory, his home was the place of his most intense life. We give over this chapter to Cavendish at home.

Landlord

For over fifty years, Lord Charles Cavendish was responsible for farms and tithes primarily in Nottinghamshire but also in Derbyshire, which were his for life as a part of his marriage settlement. Living in London, he administered his estate by correspondence, delivered by the Nottingham coach, with his steward, who lived in the neighborhood. His steward was hired to keep an eye on the state of his properties, recommend to him repairs, improvements, and the proper rent to charge, inform him about the reliability of existing and prospective tenants and what to do when they caused problems, which included eviction, treat with other landlords and surveyors to settle disputes over enclosures, spend his money to influence voting in local elections, and, most important, collect his rents. He was a pleader, negotiator, spy, and enforcer, who was always caught in the middle between his distant employer and the tenants he met face to face. His job was not easy. This indispensable intermediary for Lord Charles Cavendish was a man named Cotes, who had come with a recommender whom Cavendish could not ignore, the "archbishop." Not further specified, he might have been the archbishop of Canterbury, a conscientious trustee of the British Museum, whom Cavendish saw regularly, but we suspect he was the archbishop of York, who received money from Cavendish for paying pensions due

from the rectory in the parish of Arnold. Cotes was healthy at the time, but he soon began to decline irreversibly. Cavendish "perceived the decay of his understanding for some years" without, however, taking any steps. "Out of tenderness," and perhaps also with due respect to the archbishop, Cavendish "could not dismiss him abruptly." He wanted Cotes to resign instead, which with the "assistance" of a confederate of Cavendish Cotes did in 1764. In his place, Cavendish hired Thomas Revill, a choice he almost immediately regretted but which he nonetheless lived with for almost twenty years.[1] Revill abused his predecessor, Cotes, and evidently abused Cavendish's tenants, and Cavendish came to regard him as a "peevish old man," who created more problems than he solved. Two words appear with striking frequency in Cavendish's half of their argumentative correspondence, "just" and "reasonable," positive words he never applied to his steward but to actions his steward did not take and should have taken.[2]

Lord Charles Cavendish introduced his eldest son to business as he had to science, turning over the management of his estate to Henry in the summer of 1782. Lord Charles did not yet formally make it over, and he continued to participate in its management,[3] but he allowed Henry to receive the income, which consisted of rents, tithes, and land taxes (the tithes were usually rented out), which amounted to a yearly net income of around £1,600. At age fifty-one, Henry Cavendish began his life of well-to-do independence as administrator of ancestral landed property. His life as an absentee landlord gives us insight into the man.

---

[1]Lord Charles Cavendish to Thomas Revill, 5 Sep. and 13 Dec. 1764, Devon. Coll., L/31/20.

[2]Lord Charles Cavendish to Thomas Revill, 31 Jan. 1765, 19 Sep. and 3 Dec. 1776, 12 Apr. 1777, 18 Mar. 1778, Devon. Coll., L/31/20 and 34/5.

[3]Henry Cavendish to W. Gould, draft, 30 Dec. 1782, Devon. Coll., L/34/7.

To master the business, like his father before him, Henry Cavendish had first to settle on a steward. Thomas Revill, the bad steward, was still steward, and with his father's support, Henry Cavendish was determined to replace him.

Unsatisfactorily as he had worked out, Revill had an extenuating circumstance. At the beginning of his employment, he had explained to Lord Charles Cavendish that because of a problem with his throat, he could scarcely speak and was reduced to communicating by writing, though he was helped in his work by a nephew.[4] Although Revill's attitude, a mix of servility and arrogance, was exasperating, it seems clear that his near inability to speak was part of his problem, explaining the roundabout way he went at his work. His new master, Henry Cavendish, who himself had such difficulty speaking that a defect was suspected, evidently felt no bond of sympathy. He neither made nor accepted excuses for Revill's lapses.

The duke of Devonshire was well served by his agent, J. W. Heaton, to whom Henry turned for advice. Heaton recommended William Gould for his steward, citing his "integrity and judgment on country business." Through Heaton, Gould let Cavendish know that he would accept the job.[5] Having lined up Gould, Cavendish turned to the unpleasant task of firing his father's steward of so many years. He told Revill, who had already written that he wanted to collect the next rents, to do nothing because he intended to replace him. Revill protested. In reply, Cavendish said that he would not have answered him at all but for Revill's concern that his reputation would suffer. There was no cause for such concern, Cavendish said, since it is "so natural" for someone taking over an estate to entrust it to a steward whose judgment "he can rely on." If, however, any doubts about his reputation were to arise on this account, Cavendish would set matters right. Cavendish had meant to end the letter here but changed his mind, adding that although he had no doubt of Revill's "fidelity & good intentions," he had good reasons for deploring his actions:

> the infirmity of your temper which has made you either quarrel or behave with petulance to so many of those you have had business with & the little information my father could ever get from you concerning the matters under your charge render you very unfit a person to take care of an estate without which cause I should never have thought of employing another steward.

To his new steward, Cavendish mentioned Revill's "angry letter," copying out part of his reply to Revill, only in place of "infirmity" of temper substituting his father's expression, "the peevishness of his temper." His judgment about Revill was confirmed by Revill's behavior after his firing: for a full year, Revill wrote repeatedly to Cavendish to complain of it. Cavendish neither answered Revill's letters nor entered them in the index of his correspondence. Revill had no understanding of this new landlord. The standard by which Cavendish judged Revill unfit he held up to his replacement: Gould was to give Cavendish's tenants no cause to complain, and he was readily to give Cavendish any information he desired. The first item of business was for Gould to make a complete examination "into the condition of the whole estate."[6]

In Nottinghamshire and Derbyshire, the Cavendishes had long counted among the big landlords who bought out the landed gentry and took over their manors.[7] Lord Charles and Henry Cavendish's properties were next door to the duke of Devonshire's, from which they had been separated off.[8] The duke of Devonshire's main country house was in the area, at Chatsworth, in Derbyshire. Nearby, in Nottinghamshire, was Hardwick Hall, where the family estate records were kept, and where Henry Cavendish directed his steward to examine documents concerning his properties.[9] In matters concerning their lands, the Cavendishes kept in touch, as a family. When one of Henry Cavendish's properties became available, for example, a prospective tenant approached him through his first cousin Lord John Cavendish.[10] Or

---

[4]Thomas Revill to Lord Charles Cavendish, 16 Dec. 1764.

[5]W. Gould to J. W. Heaton, 10 June 1782; this letter Heaton forwarded to Cavendish, adding his recommendation of Gould. Henry Cavendish to W. Gould, draft, 8 and 9 Aug. 1782, Devon. Coll., L/34/7.

[6]Henry Cavendish to Thomas Revill drafts, 16 and 28 Aug. and 5 Sep. 1782; Henry Cavendish to W. Gould, draft, 6 Sep. 1782, Devon. Coll., L/34/7.

[7]This practice was complained of in 1625, the earl of Devonshire being one of the guilty absentee landlords. J. D. Chambers, *Nottinghamshire in the Eighteenth Century: A Study of Life and Labour under the Squirearchy*, 2d ed. (London: Frank Cass, 1966), 7.

[8]For example, Cavendish received rent from the tithes of Marston in Derbyshire, the greater part of which parish was owned by the duke of Devonshire. W. Gould to Henry Cavendish, 28 Sep. 1782, Devon. Coll., L/34/7.

[9]Henry Cavendish to W. Gould, draft, 2 Dec. 1787, Devon. Coll., L/34/7.

[10]W. Gould to Henry Cavendish, 20 Aug. 1785; Lord Arundall Gallway to Henry Cavendish, 21 Aug. 1785; Milnes to Lord John Cavendish, 24 Aug. 1785; Lord John Cavendish to Henry Cavendish, 25 Aug. /1785/; Henry Cavendish to Lord John Cavendish, draft, n.d. /reply to letter of 25 Aug. 1785/. Devon. Coll., L/34/7.

when legislation pended that would affect his estate, Cavendish was assisted in parliament by his principal heir, Lord George Cavendish.[11] Legally, physically, politically, and otherwise, Henry Cavendish's properties were in the country of the Cavendishes. Property held them together as much as they held it together.

From the widely dispersed parts of his estate, in his first year as manager, in 1782, Cavendish received twenty-three separate rents of greatly varying amounts from as many persons, fifteen in Nottinghamshire and eight in Derbyshire. Taken altogether, Cavendish's properties were representative of productive lands in Nottinghamshire and Derbyshire. On them, depending on the kinds of soil, a range of crops were grown, wheat, oats, barley, hay, beans, and peas, and sheep and cattle were kept as well. The tilled land was rich in places and marginal in others; in addition, there was meadow, pasture, forest, and waste. Like his father, Henry Cavendish preferred to rent "to Farmers than to Gentlemen,"[12] and indeed most of his tenants worked the land themselves. In intelligence, energy, and responsibility, his tenants varied, and on occasion Henry Cavendish, like his father, had to concern himself with their affairs and character. Having learned that a tenant was in bad financial straits and in danger of failing, Cavendish instructed Gould to inquire if the problem was the tenant's fault, if he was overextended, extravagant, incompetent, or whatever and to tell Cavendish "what you think of him."[13] The disagreeableness arising from business of this kind Cavendish was usually spared by his go-between, his steward, although from time to time he received letters from tenants directly or even received them in person at his house. "I did not say much to him," Cavendish said of one of these uninvited personal encounters, which he clearly wished to avoid.[14] Fences, barns, stables, cowsheds, and houses all had to be maintained, but this routine business took up little of Cavendish's time.

This is not to say that Cavendish's estate did not cause him trouble and worry. It did, unavoidably; this was the late eighteenth century, and the enclosure movement in Britain was in full swing. To show how Cavendish's estate, and Cavendish with it, were caught up in the complex problems attending enclosure, we will take as an example one of his properties in Nottinghamshire. The problems with it went back to the time when Lord Charles Cavendish was in charge.

Under the old pattern of farming, tilled land was parceled into strips with mixed ownership; meadows, too, were parceled, and pastures were subject to common rights. To meet changing economic needs, this pattern was replaced by one in which strips were consolidated and common control and use of land were reduced; the device was enclosure.[15] The practical intent of enclosure, as Lord Charles Cavendish put it with his usual clarity, was to "lay each person's allotment together as much as can be."[16] Before the eighteenth century, most of the land suited for pasture in Nottinghamshire had already been enclosed, but it was only in the eighteenth century that most of the land used for grain was enclosed too, and a third of it was still unenclosed at the end of the century. Because substantial economic gains could be anticipated from enclosure, the big landlords and farmers were for it. If the landowners could not agree, as occurred in Nottinghamshire where small freeholders opposed enclosure, an act of parliament might be required to overcome local resistance. All but one of Cavendish's properties were in parishes enclosed by acts of parliament, most of them passed in the decades of the 1770s through the 1790s, when the greatest acreage was enclosed by this means in Nottinghamshire. Lord Charles and Henry Cavendish were not dominant landholders in favor of enclosure, and they could not avoid conflict.[17]

Enclosure by parliamentary act followed a regular procedure. With the support of three quarters or four fifths of the landholders, or of one sufficiently big landholder, a petition for permission to bring the bill was presented. If the petition was accepted, an interested member of parliament would draw up the bill, which was almost certain to pass without determined opposition. Commissioners

---

[11]George Bramwell to Thomas Dunn, n.d., enclosed in a letter from Thomas Dunn to Henry Cavendish, 14 Dec. 1790, Devon. Coll., L/34/10.

[12]Cavendish to Lord John Cavendish, draft, n.d. /reply to letter of 25 Aug. 1785/.

[13]Cavendish to Gould, draft, 6 Sep. 1782.

[14]Henry Cavendish to W. Gould, draft, 7 Mar. 1791, Devon. Coll., L/34/12.

[15]Chambers, *Nottinghamshire*, 141.

[16]Lord Charles Cavendish to Thomas Revill, draft, 8/9/ Dec. 1776, Devon. Coll., L/34/5.

[17]Chambers, *Nottinghamshire*, 148, 165, 171–73, 202.

were then appointed from among the big farmers and local landlords and one or two outside experts. Their job was to carry out a survey, place the owners' allotments in enclosed fields, see to it that the fences, drains, and roads specified in the act were built, and look into damage claims. Enclosure was a highly costly improvement: landowners were out the cost of passing the act, fees for lawyers, surveyors, and commissioners, and the very considerable capital expenses of building fences, drains, roads, and various farm structures.[18]

While Lord Charles Cavendish was still administering the estate, in 1776, the proprietors at the parish of Arnold in Nottinghamshire considered petitioning parliament to enclose their land. Cavendish did not want the petition but since he could not stop it either, with the help of his steward he decided what to insist on so that he would come out unharmed. He was entitled to tithes from the use of the land at Arnold; from his tithe tenant, he received rent twice yearly, the total of which, a little over £100, made Arnold intermediate in value among his properties. In the event of enclosure, Cavendish would be expected to forfeit his tithes in exchange for an allotment of land. Just how much and what kind of land were the question.

Roughly speaking, the parish of Arnold contained 1,600 acres of land already enclosed, 400 of open fields, and 30 of glebe, or clerical, land. In addition, there were about 2,000 acres of common land, called the "forest," 20 of which, called a "break," were enclosed in lieu of tithes by agreement between the tithe tenant and the parish. The farmers' use of the break for tillage and the common for keeping sheep was seen as compensation for the tithes they had to pay for their open fields and enclosures.[19] The quantity of land at Arnold and the amounts given over to different uses were imprecisely known, since there had been no survey. Proceeding from incomplete information, Revill made proposals to the proprietors about what share of the common fields and the forest Lord Charles Cavendish should receive in return for giving up his tithes.

Revill's proposals were ill received by the proprietors of Arnold, whose spokesman called repeatedly on Lord Charles Cavendish, bringing their objections to him in person. Cavendish wanted them to deal with Revill instead, but they objected to Revill even more than to his proposals.

Cavendish was told that "there was such animosity between /Revill/ & the people of Arnold" that the proprietors believed any agreement with him was impossible.[20] Revill was at fault, Cavendish concluded, by asking for more than was "just," and by regarding his proposals as absolute demands, a "peremptory" manner certain to create enemies. Instead of high-handed practice, reason and negotiation should be used, Cavendish urged; Revill should talk with the proprietors.[21] The matter of the Arnold enclosure languished, but several years later, in 1782, it came up again, this time in the form of a petition for a bill. Having just taken charge of his father's farms, Henry Cavendish faced a local history of bad feeling.[22]

The recent enclosures had been "attended with great detriment and injury to the estate," the new steward Gould told Henry Cavendish, by which he meant not the unavoidable "great sums that have been expended on those inclosures and the buildings upon them" but the avoidable, absolute loss in the value of the estate.[23] That was what Cavendish was determined to avoid at Arnold if enclosure should come to pass. He received hereditary wealth in the form of income off the land, and in return he was responsible for maintaining the income for the term of his life. It was his duty, really a point of honor, to secure the value of his estate, the measure of which was rent. To this end Cavendish entered into a long dispute with the proprietors at Arnold about the amount of land he was entitled to receive in lieu of tithes. In principle, it was land equivalent in rental value to the tithes he would have received from the improved land after enclosure, but the comparison

---

[18]W. Gould to Henry Cavendish, 25 Mar. 1784, Devon. Coll., L/34/7. Chambers, *Nottinghamshire*, 178, 199–200.

[19]W. Gould to Henry Cavendish, 7 and 28 Sep. 1782, 25 Mar. and 24 Nov. 1784, Devon. Coll., L/34/7.

[20]Lord Charles Cavendish to Thomas Revill, draft, 3 Dec. 1776, Devon. Coll., L/34/5.

[21]Lord Charles Cavendish to Thomas Revill, drafts, 19 Sep. and 12 Dec. 1776, Devon. Coll., L/34/5.

[22]The animosity was clearly generated by Revill's manner. His proposals were not unreasonable, even if Lord Charles Cavendish believed them to be. Henry Cavendish's steward asked for the same share of the forest as Revill had, one seventh, which Lord Charles Cavendish thought was too much, and he asked for a greater share of the fields, one fifth, than Cavendish thought was right, one seventh. Lord Charles Cavendish to Thomas Revill, 8/9/ Dec. 1776. W. Gould to Henry Cavendish, 31 Dec. 1784, Devon. Coll., L/34/7. Gould forwarded the petition from Arnold in a letter to Cavendish, 28 Sep. 1782.

[23]Gould to Cavendish, 28 Sep. 1782.

of values was not straightforward. Depending on how it was figured, the farmers benefited more or Cavendish more.

After a meeting of the proprietors at Arnold on parliamentary enclosure in 1784, their spokesman, William Sherbrooke, wrote to Cavendish to convey their offer of a specified allotment of land to compensate him for the loss of his tithes.[24] Gould calculated the rent Cavendish would receive on this offer, using current rents and deducting the interest he would pay for fences and buildings and the vicarial tithes he would go on paying, as we discuss below. It came to £169 per year, far below the £250 Gould estimated Cavendish's tithes would bring. Cavendish should accept an allotment of yearly value no less than £360, to be laid out by the commissioners. That value recognized the expenses Cavendish would be put to; it was fair, Gould said, but he felt certain the proprietors would not like it.[25] But neither did Cavendish, who explained to his steward that if a value, 360 pounds or whatever, were proposed, he would come out a "loser," because the commissioners routinely overvalued land. He wanted the allotment decided Sherbrooke's way (but not at his value), which was for the commissioners to allot him a certain "proportion" of the land. That, Cavendish believed, was a surer measure of the value of the land than money.[26] Gould, of course, accepted his master's wish, and he advised him accordingly on the proportion of land to ask for. Gould wanted to select the location of the allotment on the forest, but Cavendish thought he was being overly zealous, making unnecessary trouble for the commissioners, who might then be "less disposed to do me justice." Otherwise, Cavendish accepted the proportions Gould had calculated for him. Cavendish did not want enclosure, but he was resigned to it as long as he received his just due.[27]

The Arnold proprietors rejected Cavendish's counter proposals. The land Cavendish would receive, Sherbrooke said, would rent for £500, and he knew a man who would pay it. Sherbrooke complained not just about the proposals but about Cavendish's steward as well. Cavendish was told of Gould's refusal to answer letters, to attend the parish meeting, or even to receive a delegation of "very respectable men," thereby exhibiting "all the insolence of delegated authority."[28] Gould, that is, was behaving just like Revill. Cavendish did not

mention to Gould the proprietors' complaint, which in any event could hardly have been news to him, nor did he advise him on his behavior relative to the proprietors. Cavendish, it would seem, had come to accept confrontation as inevitable, and he paid his steward to defend his interests and bear the abuse. He wanted Gould to get more exact information on acreage, rents, and tithes at Arnold, for only then could they "prove" that their proposals were not "unreasonable." Justice in this issue was a simple matter of arithmetic even though the quantities involved could be no firmer than estimates: Cavendish told Gould that justice all around would be served only if his "estate should be improved in the same proportion as that of the land owners." His duty to his estate was to insure that it received this proportion. His letters to his steward began to look like laboratory notes.[29]

The "affair of Arnold," as Cavendish called it, dragged on for years.[30] Early in 1789 Gould informed Cavendish that enclosure was likely, but a little later he informed Cavendish that it was unlikely because the vicar, a hard bargainer, wanted more for his tithes on turnips and lambs than the proprietors offered him. Then on 11 March 1789, Gould told Cavendish that the landholders intended to go to parliament without the vicar, leaving the old enclosure and the new allotments still subject to vicarial tithes. Gould had arrived at an agreement for Cavendish's allotment of land, which excluded it

---

[24]The offer was one eighth of the enclosed land, one seventh of the open fields, and one tenth of the forest subject to a deduction, to be determined by the commissioners, for the small vicarial tithes. Sherbrooke acknowledged that the proportions they offered were not as large as those granted in some other parishes. W. Sherbrooke to Henry Cavendish, 10 Nov. 1784, Devon. Coll., L/34/7.

[25]W. Gould to Henry Cavendish, 24 Nov. 1784, Devon. Coll., L/34/7.

[26]Henry Cavendish to W. Gould, drafts, Dec. and 24 Dec. 1784, Devon. Coll., L/34/7.

[27]W. Gould to Henry Cavendish, 31 Dec. 1784; Henry Cavendish to W. Gould, draft, 6 Jan. 1985 and 2 Dec. 1787, Devon. Coll., L/34/7.

[28]Henry Cavendish to W. Sherbrooke, draft, 6 Jan. 1785; W. Sherbrooke to Henry Cavendish, 3 and 18 Feb. 1785. Cavendish also received an anonymous letter from a landholder in Arnold complaining of Gould, Mar. 1785, Devon. Coll., L/34/7.

[29]Henry Cavendish to W. Gould, drafts, 23 Feb. 1785 and n.d. /after 28 Feb./ 1785; Henry Cavendish to W. Sherbrooke, 16 Feb. 1785, draft, Devon. Coll., L/34/7. From Gould's earlier rough estimates, Cavendish calculated that by the terms he requested, he would get £266 annually, which was slightly more than the £233 he calculated for his tithes and rent of breack should an enclosure not take place. He wanted better information to refine this calculation. Henry Cavendish to W. Gould, draft, 20 Feb. 1785, ibid.

[30]Cavendish to Gould, draft, 2 Dec. 1787.

from vicarial tithes. Cavendish had then to be given additional land equal to the tithes he must pay the vicar. The amount was around £15 a year for Cavendish.[31]

Characteristically, Cavendish pressed Gould for facts on the vicar's turnip tithes.[32] It was quite complicated to know what "part of the turnips are tithable," and Cavendish felt acute discomfort if he lacked sufficient reason in making decisions about his estate, even if the amount of money involved was insignificant, as it was in this case. Concerning the vicar's turnip tithes, Cavendish wrote sternly to Gould that he wished Gould had "explained the matter to me clearly." Gould had given Cavendish his recommendations about the turnip tithes without at the same time giving him his "reasons." Henceforth Gould was always to give Cavendish his "reasons."[33]

In its own good time, the Arnold affair came to a close. On 20 March 1789, Gould sent Cavendish a draft of the Arnold enclosure bill, which was soon law.[34] News from Arnold would be bad before it was good again: in the following summer, Gould told Cavendish that he had collected the rents from all but two of Cavendish's tenants, but he was not remitting them. The entire money was expended in the Arnold enclosure, going for fences, to the stone getters, and to the masons who were building the barn and stables. None of this was surprising.[35]

At Arnold and elsewhere, as an administrator of farm property in a time of enclosure, Cavendish was a party to the politics of local proprietors, in itself an activity that came with the family. We give one more example of an enclosure on his properties to illustrate how it could also entangle him in the politics of parliament. As at Arnold, at Doveridge in Derbyshire, Cavendish owned tithes, which he rented to a man whose country seat neighbored on Doveridge, the colorful Irish-born parliamentarian Sir Henry Cavendish. The same age as our Henry Cavendish, Sir Henry was distantly related by blood and by wealth.[36] ("If you were poor, & I rich, instead of the contrary," Sir Henry Cavendish wrote to his landlord, the Right Honorable Henry Cavendish, proposing an exchange of property.[37]) Like his namesake, though in his case through politics rather than through science, Sir Henry Cavendish was a man of quantity: from Doveridge, writing to Matthew Bolton, who ran an alternative

mint to the Tower of London at his Soho works in Birmingham, Sir Henry said that he was going to propose in parliament an "Irish Mint," and he asked Bolton to recommend a man "acquainted with the Mathematicks, & arithmetick" to assist him in this project as an amanuensis.[38] At Doveridge, as at Arnold, Cavendish was confronted by an enclosure bill, which in its original form entailed a loss of tithes for him, rational grounds for his opposition to it.[39] This bill stumbled over the same practical difficulty as the bill at Arnold, that of getting consent from owners to allocate land in lieu of tithes. The final bill, which Cavendish did not oppose, took no notice of the tithes, and the two Henrys entered into a separate agreement on setting the value of the tithes upon enclosure.

---

[31]W. Gould to Henry Cavendish, 9 and 21 Feb., 11 and 19 Mar. 1789, Devon. Coll., L/34/12.

[32]Henry Cavendish to W. Gould, draft, n.d./reply to letter of 21 Feb. 1789/, Devon. Coll., L/34/12.

[33]Cavendish to Gould, draft, n.d. /reply to letter of 21 Feb. 1789/; W. Gould to Henry Cavendish, 19 Mar. 1789.

[34]W. Gould to Henry Cavendish, 30 Mar. 1789, Devon. Coll., L/34/12. Following the preliminary agreements, in which Cavendish was involved, came the elaborate parliamentary procedure leading to the act. The petition was presented; a bill was ordered, presented, and read; a committee was appointed and reported; the king's consent was signified; the bill was passed by the Commons; it was then passed by the Lords with amendments; the amendments were agreed to; and, finally, the royal assent was granted. Altogether it took over four months, from March 2 to July 13, 1789.

A Petition of William Coape Sherbrooke, John Need, Robert Fauley, Edward Jones, and others, Lords of the Manor of Arnold, in the County of Nottingham, and likewise, with others, are Owners and Proprietors of Lands in the Open Common Fields and Meadows, and entitled to Right of Common in and upon the Commons and Waste Lands within the said Manor, was presented to the House, and read; Setting forth, That the Lands of the Petitioners in the said Fields and Meadows lie intermixed and dispersed, and, in their present Situation. . . .
With the exception of one proprietor of fifty acres and another of twelve acres, all parties gave their assent to the bill. The whole of the property affected was 2,000 acres. No one came before the committee to oppose the bill. 2 Mar., 13 May, and 12 June 1789, *Journal of the House of Commons* 44:138, 361, 454, and 456.

[35]W. Gould to Henry Cavendish, 5 June 1790, Devon. Coll., L/34/12.

[36]Sir Henry Cavendish was descended from an illegitimate son of a brother of the first duke of Devonshire. Historians of British politics are indebted to him for the shorthand notes he kept of debates in parliament. His contemporaries had to listen to hotheaded speeches by him; beside his name on a government list in 1783 is the observation: "A good shorthand writer but a tiresome speaker." L. B. Namier and John Brooke, *The House of Commons 1754–1790*, 3 vols. (London: Her Majesty's Stationary Office, 1964) 2:201–3.

[37]Sir Henry Cavendish to Henry Cavendish, 22 Nov. 1785, Devon. Coll., L/34/7.

[38]Sir Henry Cavendish to Matthew Boulton, 14 Aug. 1788, Birmingham University Library.

[39]Henry Cavendish to W. Gould, draft, 2 and 3 Dec. 1790, Devon. Coll., L/34/12.

During the course of the bill, Cavendish had defended his property, proposing a clause to the bill, considering hiring someone to keep him informed about it, and drawing on the parliamentary offices of Lord George Cavendish.[40]

We might wonder why Cavendish bothered about his farms at all. After all he had a busy life in London with absorbing interests of his own choosing. His farms in northern England did not even give him the satisfaction a city man might feel from time to time by standing on land that was his and surveying a good harvest brought forth from it by his industrious tenants. From the questions Cavendish asked of his steward, we get the distinct impression that he never saw his farms. He was burdened with landed property on which he never lived and which gave him endless trouble for a relatively small income he did not need after the first year. His steward sent him enclosure bills to study, and because he owned so many properties, these bills demanded his attention all too often for his taste. With regard to an enclosure that had been pending for two years, Cavendish wrote irritably to Gould: "You ought to have informed me of it at the time instead of delaying it till lately & then representing it to me as brought in by surprise & without your knowledge /./ I am very sorry to find that you could act in this manner & hope I shall never see another instance of any thing of the kind."[41] Cavendish suffered endless irritations like this because they came with his life, and he probably never questioned their need as he never relaxed his vigilance over his property to ensure that it was not injured. He managed his property as a family duty, which if joyless nevertheless was for a man like him a source of satisfaction. No matter how far from his family his activities in science took him, in his occupation with landed property he was at one with it.

Less compatible with Cavendish's instincts than political issues was personal confrontation, but he could not avoid that either in the farm business. Throughout the time he was occupied with the Arnold enclosure, he was also dealing with the consequences of an earlier, completed enclosure at the parish of Hilton in Derbyshire. The Hilton enclosure was a "terrible business," Gould said, and Cavendish agreed,[42] citing his father's experience there as evidence that the enclosure commissioners

overvalued land. Upon consulting a commissioner at Hilton about the value of Lord Charles's allotment, Revill had set far too high a rent on it. Nevertheless it had been taken at that rent, which might seem an error to Cavendish's advantage, but it was not. Rather it was the beginning of a long saga of the imprudent tenant and of Cavendish and Gould, who had to deal with him.[43]

To a man named Rose, Lord Charles Cavendish had rented the Marston tithes together with the new farm at Hilton created after its enclosure in 1780. When Henry Cavendish took over the management of the estate in 1782, the first problem he addressed was Hilton. To make Hilton a "compleat farm," there had been mutual commitments between Lord Charles Cavendish and Rose, which included putting up buildings at Cavendish's expense. Henry Cavendish told Gould to go see what had actually been done in the meantime.[44] Gould reported that the buildings were in bad shape, with four feet of water standing in the cellar, but given the excessive rent that Rose was paying, Gould doubted that he could keep up Cavendish's property.[45]

Soon afterwards, Rose called on Cavendish to complain about the value that had been placed on the land, for the rent was way too much. Cavendish assured Rose that he would make allowances for him if he took "good care of the farm."[46] Rose told Gould that Cavendish had "ordered" him immediately to build a drain in the cellar.[47] In dismay, Cavendish wrote to Gould:

I never gave him any directions to get the drain done. . . . I am so much displeased with his

---

[40]George Bramwell to Thomas Dunn, n.d., enclosed in a letter from Thomas Dunn to Henry Cavendish, 14 Dec. 1790; Edward Barwell to Henry Cavendish, 3 Dec. 1790; J. Clementson to Henry Cavendish, 13 Dec. 1790; Lord George Cavendish to Henry Cavendish, 14 Dec. 1790; Henry Cavendish to Lord George Cavendish, draft, n.d. /reply to letter of 14 Dec. 1790/, Devon. Coll., L/34/10.
[41]Henry Cavendish to W. Gould, draft, 12 May 1789, Devon. Coll., L/34/12. Gould defended himself against Cavendish's "severe reprimand" and gave his reasons. W. Gould to Henry Cavendish, 20 May 1789, Devon. Coll., L/34/12.
[42]W. Gould to Henry Cavendish, 8 Dec. 1788, Devon. Coll., L/34/12.
[43]Henry Cavendish to W. Gould, drafts, n.d. /reply to letter of 28 Feb. 1785/, Devon. Coll., L/34/7.
[44]Henry Cavendish to W. Gould, draft, 28 and 31 Aug. 1782, Devon. Coll., L/34/7.
[45]Gould to Cavendish, 28 Sep. 1782.
[46]Henry Cavendish to W. Gould, draft, 12 Dec. 1782, Devon. Coll., L/34/7.
[47]W. Gould to Henry Cavendish, 11 Jan. 1783, Devon. Coll., L/34/7.

behaviour that if it can be done without inconvenience I should wish to get rid of him as there seems great reason to expect both from this & from his offering to take the farm at so much more than its true value that he will make a very bad tenant.[48]

When Gould wrote to him next but did not discuss Rose, Cavendish noted this omission in the index of his correspondence. When Gould wrote again but still did not mention Rose,[49] Cavendish wrote to remind him he was waiting:

I have the more reason too to be dissatisfied with him /Rose/ as I find he is the only one who has not paid his rent /./ I must desire therefore that you will let me know what you think of him & whether he will make a good tenant & if he will not whether I can remove him without inconvenience/./ I desire also that you will let me know what you have done about the drain.[50]

Gould came to see Cavendish in person. Rose's drain was finished, but there remained much to be done on the house. Rose had paid the rent according to his own valuation, and Gould thought that Rose might just do as a tenant. Besides it might prove hard to find another.[51]

Gould was to change his mind about Rose, who was Cavendish's one tenant who always fell behind in his rent. The more dealings he had with Rose, the more he came to regard him as untrustworthy. There came a point when Gould wanted to give notice to Rose and moreover to "make a distress on his effects," and he gave Cavendish a list of Rose's cattle and an evaluation. Cavendish agreed that Rose would never be a good tenant and the sooner he was gone the better. Rose was not the only, or the first, tenant Cavendish had considered giving notice to; there had been several dismissals soon after he took charge of the estate following Gould's advice. But from the beginning Cavendish and Gould had disagreed on how tenants were to be treated. Because the tenants had grown fat off Cavendish's tithes, Gould reasoned, they could hardly complain of being ill treated if they were required to quit promptly. Cavendish, however, was "unwilling to turn out tenants who have not behaved ill on such short notice" as Gould wanted, and "a ½ year though a sufficient legal notice would hardly afford them time enough to provide themselves."[52] In the particular case of Rose, Cavendish again cautioned Gould in the same vein:

I would wish to do it /turn him out/ in a manner as little distressing to him as I can & as I suppose distraining his effects will besides the expense oblige him to part with them to great loss I should be glad if you could avoid that though at the expense of ¼ or even more of what is due to me.[53]

Having been so often deceived, Gould brought the bailiff with him when he went to see Rose, intending to make a distress after all. But Rose gave him apologies and Gould backed down, agreeing that Rose's son should give security for the rent due.[54]

After six years of trouble with Rose, Cavendish still did not know why he was always so much in arrears, whether it was extravagance or poor management. Gould thought it was both, but he did not know much about Rose either.[55] Repeatedly, Cavendish resolved that Rose must go, and as often he resolved to do him as little harm as possible, charging his steward with restraint. "It is in vain to think of continuing Rose as tenant any longer," but Cavendish did "not mean to act hardly by him," and he regarded it was only "reasonable" to forgive part of the arrears.[56] Cavendish disliked "violent measures" and "harsh methods,"[57] so that although he wanted to recover what arrears from Rose he could, he told Gould that "if gentle methods will not do I wish you to send me word before you have recourse to others."[58] But when Rose would not vacate the farm even after Cavendish had rebated part of his arrears ("though

---

[48]Henry Cavendish to W. Gould, draft, 15 Jan. 1783, Devon. Coll., L/34/7.
[49]W. Gould to Henry Cavendish, 22 Jan. 1783, Devon. Coll., L/34/7.
[50]Henry Cavendish to W. Gould, draft, 11 Aug. 1783, Devon. Coll., L/34/7.
[51]Cavendish's notes of his conversation with Gould in London, 11 Sep. 1783, Devon. Coll., L/34/7.
[52]Cavendish to Gould, 16 Sep. 1782.
[53]W. Gould to Henry Cavendish, 23 Jan. 1785; Henry Cavendish to W. Gould, draft, 6 Feb. 1785, Devon. Coll., L/34/7.
[54]W. Gould to Henry Cavendish, 13 Mar. 1785, Devon. Coll., L/34/7.
[55]If the problem had turned out to be that Rose had debts, Cavendish was willing to buy Rose's land adjacent to his own to enable him to continue. But if Rose was an incompetent farmer, he had to be got rid of. Henry Cavendish to W. Gould, draft, 1 Dec. 1788; W. Gould to Henry Cavendish, 8 Dec. 1788, Devon. Coll., L/34/12.
[56]Henry Cavendish to W. Gould, draft, 21 Jan. 1790, Devon. Coll., L/34/12.
[57]Henry Cavendish to W. Gould, drafts, Mar. 1790 and 7 Mar. 1791, Devon. Coll., L/34/12.
[58]Henry Cavendish to W. Gould, draft, 8 Feb. 1790, Devon. Coll., L/34/12.

if he has hurt the farm so much, as you say, he does not deserve any thing"), Cavendish told Gould to take measures to distrain Rose if necessary. Eventually Rose left the farm, protesting the expenses he had been out.[59]

Whatever the circumstances, Rose provided ample evidence that he was a poor manager and adept at making excuses, playing off Gould and Cavendish, at least twice coming to London to see Cavendish. Rose's name turns up in the correspondence more often than any other, and Cavendish as always was jealous of his time. Moreover, like Gould, Cavendish came to see Rose as devious. Because Cavendish placed high value on straightforwardness in dealing with people, and because Rose fell short in this as well as in his rent payments, from early on Cavendish wanted to be rid of him. Yet he put up with Rose's evasions for ten years while he kept after his steward for more facts and advice. There may have been practical considerations, but clearly the main reason Cavendish took no action for so long was his sense of justice, which translated into indecision. Explaining to Gould why he was ready to forego part of Rose's arrears, Cavendish said that "it perhaps would hardly have been worth his /Rose's/ while to have taken the farm had he known it would have been taken from him so soon."[60] And that was eight years after Rose had become his tenant.

Most of Cavendish's tenants gave him little occasion for direct involvement. By and large, they took care of his property and paid him on time. Their demands or derelictions were occasional and minor, and as these came up, they were handled routinely by Cavendish's steward with Cavendish's advice and approval. From the smooth operation of most of the properties, little is to be learned about Cavendish. Fortunately, for what they tell us about Cavendish, there were the troublesome enclosures and the troublesome tenant Rose.

Cavendish's early correspondence concerning his farms reveals him to be new to the business. His father clearly had handled it by himself until then. Once the farms were his responsibility, Cavendish approached their management in the same spirit with which he approached science. He set out to acquire a total familiarity with the facts, and he reasoned from them on the basis of general principles, including principles of justice, to conclusions about the actions to take.

Hampstead

Lord Charles Cavendish appears on the rate books for his house on Great Marlborough Street to 1782, the year before his death. He is followed by Henry Cavendish for two years, to 1784. Henry leased the house for many years to Joshua Brookes, who continued its scientific tradition in a bizarre fashion. Brookes held a "Theatre of Anatomy" in Cavendish's house in 1786–98, in which he lectured and exhibited bodies of notorious criminals, and in the garden behind the house, where Lord Charles and Henry Cavendish had measured the earth and the atmosphere with their delicate instruments, he built a vivarium out of huge rocks, and there he chained wild animals.[61]

Hampstead was the location of Cavendish's first house of his own. It was no doubt the prospect of financial independence that prompted and made feasible his move. His first appearance in the Hampstead rate books was on 3 January 1782, which was about the time he prepared to take over the management of his father's estate and to receive the rents from it. His last appearance in the rate books was on 19 September, 1785.[62]

William Thornton's contemporary guide to London and the countryside surrounding it, published in 1784, describes Hampstead as follows: this village located about four miles on the north-west side of London

was once very small, but by the increase of buildings is now of considerable extent. Many of the citizens of London have fine houses here, because the situation is not only delightful, but the air is esteemed exceeding wholesome. . . . At the north extremity of the village is a heath or common, which is adorned with many handsome buildings, and is so elevated, as to command one of the most extensive prospects of the kingdom.[63]

[59]Henry Cavendish to W. Gould, draft, Sep. 1790. "When Rose quitted the farm he petitioned for an abatement on account of extraordinary expenses he had been at. . . ." Henry Cavendish to W. Gould, draft, 4 Feb. 1794, Devon. Coll., L/34/12.

[60]Henry Cavendish to W. Gould, draft, 21 Jan. 1790, Devon. Coll., L/34/12.

[61]"Henry Cavendish to Mr. Joshua Brookes. Counterpart Lease of a Messuage or Tenement with the Apperts No. in Marlborough Street in the Parish of St James Westminster County Middlesex," 1788, Devon. Coll., L/38/35. London County Council, *Survey of London.* Vol. 31: *The Parish of St. James Westminster. Part 2: North of Piccadilly.* General editor F. H. W. Sheppard (London: Athlone Press, 1963), 256.

[62]"Hampstead Vestry. Poor Rate," Holborn Public Library, London.

[63]William Thornton, ed., *New, Complete, and Universal History, Description, and Survey of the Cities of London and Westminster. . .*

Then, as today, Hampstead was fashionable and expensive, a draw for Londoners who wanted a vista and an escape from city stench and squalor.

Hampstead had already begun to change from a rural to an urban village in the late seventeenth century, when a mineral springs was opened there. Hampstead acquired a reputation for healthiness and a good income from its waters, which were recommended by physicians who drank it in quantity. Bottled, the waters were sold in shops in London, while people traveled to Hampstead for the cure. Hampstead was a popular spa early in the eighteenth century, but it could not compete with more exclusive spas such as Bath and Epsom. It remained a resort while its continuing growth owed to prosperous Londoners, such as Cavendish, taking up residence there.[64]

Befitting a convenient, healthy, and handsomely situated village, Hampstead hosted its share of prominent people. The actors Barton Booth, Robert Wilks, and Colley Cibber stayed there during the summers to plan for the next season. Among writers, Alexander Pope, Mark Akenside, Richard Steele, John Gay, and John Arbuthnot lived or visited there.[65] But the popular association of Hampstead with artists stems from the time of John Keats and Leigh Hunt in the next century. Eighteenth-century Hampstead attracted a more substantial society: physicians, lawyers, bankers, publishers, booksellers, and West and East Indian merchants. Cavendish, the aristocrat, chose to live among people of business and the professions.[66]

There was the occasional Hampstead resident with interests overlapping Cavendish's. One was the great Shakespeare scholar George Steevens, who was also a Fellow and sometime council member of the Royal Society and a common guest at Joseph Banks's *conversaziones*.[67] Before Cavendish moved to Hampstead, the famous clock-maker John Harrison lived there.[68] Residing only a few doors from Cavendish was, we suppose, his favorite instrument-maker Edward Nairne,[69] from whom Cavendish may have learned of the house he took.

Cavendish's house was number 34, Church Row. Church Row was the street of choice in Hampstead, where the important residents and visitors congregated and persons of "quality" promenaded. The street has not much changed since the eighteenth century: the houses today are three-storey, complete with attic and basement, with a uniform terraced appearance. In the gardens behind the houses, there was never stabling, which suggests that the residents did not go daily to London by private carriage.[70]

The Hampstead house was Cavendish's second house. For a time after his father died, he kept the Great Marlborough Street house as his townhouse, where he was as apt to be found as in his new house.[71] At least some of his scientific work he moved to Hampstead. Blagden helped Cavendish with experiments and instruments connected with freezing mercury at Hampstead during his first winter there.[72] Nairne helped him compare the clean air of Hampstead with the foul air of the city.[73] Cavendish determined the error of the time given by the meridian line by comparing the times of rocket explosions observed at Hampstead with those at Greenwich and at Loam Pit Hill.[74] The brick, plainly attractive Hampstead parish church at the end of Church Row, rebuilt in the 1740s, and standing as a symbol of the growth and prosperity of Hampstead, served Cavendish as the prominent, nearby object for determining the bearings of his

Likewise the Towns, Villages, Palaces, Seats, and Country, to the Extent of Above Twenty Miles Round, rev. ed. (London, 1784), 482.

[64]Alex J. Philip, *Hampstead, Then and Now. An Historical Topography* (London: George Routledge, 1912), 45–46. F. M. L. Thompson, *Hampstead: Building a Borough, 1650–1964* (London: Routledge & Kegan Paul, 1974), 20–22, 24.

[65]Daniel Lysons, *Environs of London; Being an Historical Account of the Towns, Villages, and Hamlets, within Twelve Miles of That Capital*, vol 2: *County of Middlesex* (London, 1795), 535–36.

[66]Thompson, *Hampstead*, 27–30.

[67]"Biographical Anecdotes of George Steevens, Esq," *Gentlemen's Magazine*, Feb. 1800, pp. 178–80, on p. 180.

[68]Thomas J. Barrett, *The Annals of Hampstead*, 3 vols. (London: Adam & Charles Black, 1912) 2:67–68.

[69]We are assuming that it was *the* Edward Nairne who was one of three persons in the rate books listed at number 21, Church Row. Cavendish lived in number 34; see below. "Hampstead Vestry. Poor Rate." A few years before, a paper by Nairne was headed "Hampstead": "Experiments on Water . . . from the Melted Ice of Sea-Water . . .," *PT* 66 (1776): 249–56. Later Cavendish and Nairne did experiments together at Hampstead; see below.

[70]Stabling could be had elsewhere in the village, and coach service into London was very convenient, there being between fourteen and eighteen return trips a day. Barrett, *Annals of Hampstead* 1: 279–80. Thompson, *Hampstead*, 25, 56. "Hampstead Vestry. Poor Rate."

[71]Blagden, wanting to see Cavendish, left a message for him at his "town house," believing him to be at his Hampstead house. Charles Blagden to Joseph Banks, 24 Dec. 1783, BM(NH), DTC 3:176.

[72]Entries for 17 Dec. 1782 and 15 Jan. 1783, Blagden Diary, Royal Society, 1.

[73]Henry Cavendish, minutes of experiments on air, 15 and 16 Mar. 1782, Cavendish Mss II, 5:189.

[74]Cavendish began these observations by stating the distance between his townhouse and his country house: "Hampstead is 182 miles or 10.2 seconds of time west of Marlborough street & Marlborough street is 31" west of Greenwich & Greenwich is 5."4 east of Loam pit hill & therefore Hampstead is 25."8 west of Loam pit hill." Cavendish Mss, unclassified.

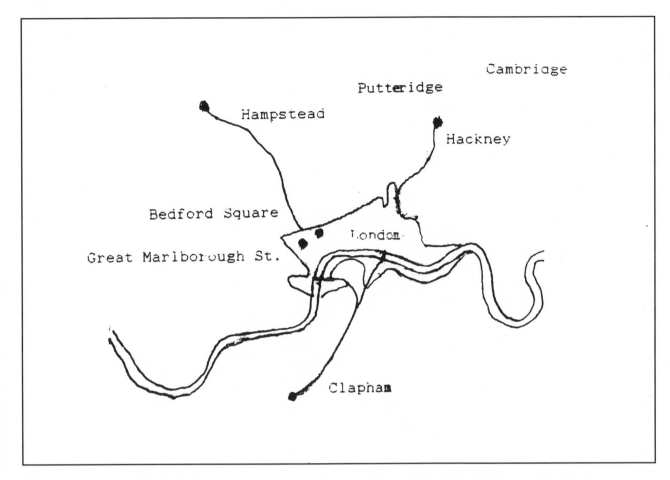

PLATE VII. Map of Henry Cavendish's Homes. The places where Cavendish is known to have lived are shown on this map of London and its suburbs. To the north, off the map at the top, are Cambridge, fifty-odd miles from London, and Putteridge, about half as far.

new location, no doubt in connection with William Roy's great trigonometrical survey at just this time. From his house on Church Row, Cavendish took measures, using a theodolite and two stations in his garden, of the distance and bearing of the closest, the kitchen, window to the church. He sighted on the church's weathercock, and from the steeple, he or an associate took angles with a quadrant of conspicuous objects in the surroundings. So commanding was the view from Hampstead's hill that Cavendish was able to take in much of London and its outlying villages with his instrument. He could look down on the properties of his family, the duke of Devonshire's palladian house at Chiswick and the Bentinck chapel, and on a variety of temples, gazebos, and pagodas, and on the steeples of Walton, Battersea, Hammersmith, Stretham, Acton, Paddington, Chelsea, and Ealing, and even on the steeple of the church at Clapham Common, on the far side of London, where Cavendish would soon own his next country house.[75]

Bedford Square

But for his Cambridge years, Cavendish lived all of his life in London. His move to Clapham Common in the summer of 1785, like his move to Hampstead a few years earlier, was a move not away from London but to a convenient suburb. He always kept a townhouse as well. Sometime after 1784 he rented out the house on Great Marlborough Street[76] and bought a new townhouse not many blocks away, on Bedford Square.

Cavendish was not a man who changed addresses easily. Evidence that his moves in mid life were attended by turmoil can be read into the fate of his assistant, Charles Cullen, son of the

---

[75]Cavendish had help with the observations taken from the Hampstead church steeple, as the angles were written in another's hand; dated 23 and 25 July 1783. There are a great many sheets of observations of bearings, with dates falling between 1770 and 1792, among the unclassified papers in the Cavendish Mss.

[76]*Survey of London*, vol. 31, Part 2, p. 256.

famous Edinburgh professor of medicine, William Cullen. We have pointed out that Cullen had been Blagden's teacher, and it is no doubt through this connection that Cullen's son came to be employed by Cavendish. (Cavendish was accustomed to having assistants in his researches, as he was accustomed to having servants in his life, and no doubt sometimes they were one and the same. In memoranda on his earlier electrical researches, he referred to an assistant named "Richard.") William Cullen's son had "unluckily fallen" into needy circumstances, financial it sounds like, and Blagden was helping him.[77] In June 1784 Blagden wrote to Cullen that his son was working out well, though there is a hint in the letter that he was not, which was probably the reason for the letter. Blagden mentioned that the young man had been totally unfamiliar with a certain book and with Cavendish's studies. Cullen had told Blagden of his "utmost respect for the character of Mr. Cavendish," but he clearly had had no direct contact with him, and perhaps to reassure Cullen that his son was in good hands, Blagden said that Cullen's respect for Cavendish was "no more than his due" and that Cavendish was a person not only of great scientific ability but one who in private life was distinguished for "the strictest integrity, the most amiable candour & a truly philosophical simplicity of manners."[78] In November we hear that Charles Cullen was considering resigning because Cavendish was dissatisfied with his skill and knowledge of books. He accepted the criticism, but he also had an excuse, which he hoped would earn him a reprieve: "the moving from Marlboro Street to Bedford Square" had distracted him from his regular work, which he had put off until "after the house was a little more settled."[79]

Located in the west end of London, Bedford Square is one of the many squares that were laid out in the seventeenth and early eighteenth centuries, imparting a measure of order to the urban sprawl. These squares were the joint venture of the owner of a large estate and builders, who were granted long-term leases and low ground rent. Typically, the houses had to be of a certain kind and value; they were expensive, which is why they tended to be the addresses of aristocrats and gentry.[80]

The duke of Bedford's 112-acre Bloomsbury estate was converted into several large gardens and squares, one of which was Bedford Square, a rectangular development measuring 520 by 320 feet between houses. The duke granted Henry Cavendish a ninety-nine-year lease beginning in 1775, eleven years of which had expired, which meant that in eighty-eight years the land would be returned to the heirs of the duke. In 1786 Cavendish entered the rate books, which show that the immediate predecessor in his house, number 11 Bedford Square, was his first cousin, the parliamentary leader Lord John Cavendish. The house came with obvious family connections, with the Cavendishes and, through the duke of Bedford, with the Russells. Bedford Square, the most ambitious example of town planning in eighteenth-century London, is intact today, and on each side of it, one can still see the original block of nearly uniform, three-storey, brick houses, built of specified materials, dimensions, and design. The middle of each block of houses is distinguished by a prominent, stuccoed facade, ornamented with pediments and pilasters, and the entrance doors of the houses are crowned with varied, rounded fanlights.[81] In style, Cavendish's house is the same as that of the blocks of houses, but it does not physically join them. It is an end-of-row house on the northeast corner of the square, on Gower Street, with its entrance on Montague Place. The house, since taken over for offices by the nearby University of London, carries a plaque identifying it as having once belonged to the chemist Henry Cavendish.

"I have scarce ever met with a more substantial or better built House, and the whole Edifice is finished with the best materials," an appraiser wrote of Cavendish's house on Bedford Square.[82] Cavendish appreciated value. The floors of the two

[77]William Cullen to Charles Blagden, 8 May 1784, Blagden Letters, Royal Society, C70.
[78]Charles Blagden to William Cullen, 17 June 1784, draft, Blagden Letterbook, Yale.
[79]Charles Cullen to Charles Blagden, 7 Nov.1784 and "Monday" /1784/, Blagden Letters, Royal Society, C.62 and C.63. Perhaps it did work out; there is one more letter from Charles Cullen to Charles Blagden, n.d., ibid., C.64, which says that Cavendish finds that Macquer's chemical dictionary with Bergman's notes is almost out of print, and Cullen wonders if he might bring out a new edition. He says he has been asked to do a translation of this kind.
[80]George Rudé, *Hanoverian London, 1714–1808* (Berkeley: University of California Press, 1971), 11–14. London County Council, *Survey of London*, vol. 5: *The Parish of St. Giles-in-the-Fields*, part 2 (London: 1914), 150.
[81]*Survey of London*, vol 5, part 2, p. 150. Rudé, *London*, 14.
[82]"Mr. Willock's Valuation of House & Stables in Bedford Square," a letter from John Willock to John Heaton, 30 Dec. 1813, Devon. Coll., L/34/10.

main storeys of the house were of Norway oak and the hall and staircase of Portland stone. All three storeys and the attic for the servants had bowed windows to the back, which, like the veranda, overlooked a deep garden. Detached from the house and located at the bottom of the garden were a double coach house and stabling for five horses. These outer buildings had been converted to another use, their entrance on Montague Place walled up, and new, equivalent coach houses and stabling built opposite them opening onto Keppel Mews.[83]

Cavendish's Bedford Square house is best described as a green, live-in scientific facility. The color scheme of the furnishings was consistent: green moreen window curtains, green transparent canvas-lined mahogany blinds, green chair covers, and fire screens covered with green silk. The furniture was mahogany.[84] By far the greatest part of the house was given over to books and such fixtures as book users require.[85] The house may also have been used to display Cavendish's mineral collection.[86] With the exception of the dining and back parlor rooms, all of the main rooms had bookshelves. So altered was the house that, according to an estimate after Cavendish's death, a sum equal to a quarter of the value of the house would have been required to restore it to a condition "fit for the residence of a family."[87]

Elsewhere we discuss the nature of Cavendish's books and the use of the Bedford Square house as a semi-public library; here we limit our account to a physical description of the altered house. The main entrance to the house opens onto a large hall, to the left of which is the dining parlor, which was used as intended. To the right of the hall is a room called the lower library with bookshelves consisting of 90 sliding shelves mounted on 20 uprights. The uprights, fitted with plinth and cornice, no doubt extended from floor to ceiling. Off of this library to the right is an adjoining room where a copying machine was located, a double-roller apparatus by Watt & Co., and here there were bookshelves consisting of 14 uprights and 93 sliding shelves. From this room, to the left, is an adjoining room, which had 10 uprights, sliding shelves, and a cupboard for maps. The floor plan shows curved stairs opposite the entrance hall leading from the ground floor to the principal floor, which Cavendish evidently gave over entirely to library use. It is

here that the main library room was located, with its 28 uprights, 268 sliding shelves, Wedgwood ink stands, high and low steps, cushioned chairs, desks and table, and a table clock. The next floor, the two-pair floor, also had rooms for books, but they were not equipped with tables and chairs for readers. This private floor held what was called the upper library, which was fitted with 18 uprights and 121 sliding shelves. The room adjoining it had 10 uprights, more than 40 sliding shelves, and a set of bookshelves with six folding doors. There was also a small room to the front of the house containing 5 uprights and 15 sliding shelves. Even Cavendish's bedroom on this floor had a bookcase with a glass door and bookshelves with 3 uprights and 16 sliding shelves.[88] This enumeration of uprights and shelves is intended to convey a correct notion of what was essential about the Bedford Square house: it was a house of books, with little room for anything else. Its owner was a bookish man, who not only collected books, as rich men then did, but also read them. The Bedford Square house was a material expression of Cavendish's single-minded quest for a scientific understanding of the world.

If it were not the embodiment of a rare intellectual force, the Bedford Square house might seem to be nothing but so many yards of occupied shelving, a place of utmost *im*personality. This impression is reinforced by the use of the house as a public place, where books were checked out to qualified users by a salaried librarian.[89] Yet in the selection of books, as we will see, the Bedford

[83]*The Particulars of a Capital Leasehold House and Offices Situate at the North East Corner of Bedford Square . . . Sold by Auction, by Mr. Willock . . . The Twenty-ninth of April, 1814* . . . Willock to Heaton, 30 Dec. 1814.

[84]"Inventory of Sundry Fixtures, Household Furniture, Plate, Linen etc etc. the Property of the Late Henry Cavendish Esquire at His Late Residence in Bedford Square. Taken the 2nd Day of April 1810," Devon. Coll., L/114/74.

[85]Of Cavendish's Bedford Square house, George Wilson says that "books and apparatus formed its chief furniture": *The Life of the Honourable Henry Cavendish* (London, 1851), 163. At first Cavendish kept considerable apparatus in this house, but at the end of his life there was almost none.

[86]That is the likely meaning of "museums," the word appearing in the appraiser's report. The rooms of Cavendish's house, he wrote, "have been many years used as Libraries, and Museums, and are at present in that state. . . ." Willock to Heaton, 30 Dec. 1813.

[87]After Cavendish's death, the house in its present state was appraised at £4,000. The cost of making it fit for human habitation was estimated at £1,000 to £1,200. Willock to Heaton, 30 Dec. 1813.

[88]"Inventory of Sundry Fixtures, Household Furniture, Plate, Linen etc etc."

[89]Cavendish's last librarian, who did not live in the Bedford Square house but on the Strand, received a yearly salary of £13. "Collingwood, the Librarian, One Years Salary Due Xtmas 1811," Devon. Coll.

Square library expressed the personality of its owner; it was not a gentleman's library meant to impress the outside world but a library to serve its owner. Limited as were the other contents of the Bedford Square house, they too revealed Cavendish's personality. The inventory of the house included a category "Paintings." Cavendish was not an art collector like his grandfathers; he hung paintings in his house not because they were art but because of their subject. His paintings included four three-quarter portraits of members of the Cavendish family and one small portrait of an earl of Devonshire. In addition, in storage he kept ten damaged family portraits. The paintings in the Bedford Square house, otherwise devoted to scientific books, expressed the other side of Cavendish's identity: as well as a man of science, he was a Cavendish.[90]

Apart from seeing to it that the books were cared for, Cavendish had few needs at Bedford Square, and he kept only three servants there, a porter, a housemaid, and a cook.[91] He sometimes stayed in the city at his Bedford Square house, which was just around the corner from the British Museum and convenient to the Royal Society. He kept appointments at the house, too.

For the last twenty-five years of his life, Cavendish's scientific establishment consisted of two houses, one at Bedford Square and one at Clapham Common (which we will get to). In certain ways they duplicated one another: in their valuations, the furnishings of the Bedford Square house and those of the Clapham Common house were almost identical.[92] There was a good deal of plate, linen, and china at both houses, though there was more at Bedford than at Clapham, which might be expected of a townhouse.[93] Cavendish devoted to them the familiar aristocrat's attention to his houses, though their function was unfamiliar. His houses were, in their own terms, "great" houses, only not in the sense of "piles" but of their arrangements. They were houses of science, which have to be seen together to be properly appreciated.

To keep order in his life in two houses, Cavendish drew up a list of keys under various headings, including under "instruments." He kept a small but choice selection of instruments at Bedford Square, made by John Bird, Jeremiah Sisson, and Edward Nairne, among others. They were the kinds of instruments to be expected: microscopes, presumably for the minerals kept at

Bedford Square, and instruments for taking measurements at a fixed location: astronomical telescopes, quadrants, and clocks, and magnetic dipping needles.[94] Cavendish kept most of his large collection of instruments at Clapham Common, where he made most of his observations and experiments.

Just as Cavendish made some observations at Bedford Square, at Clapham Common he kept a small library; the division of functions of his two houses was not absolute, but at the end of his life, it was nearly so. Bedford Square then had clocks by John Shelton and Richard Graham and a couple of thermometers and a barometer, but these were instruments that might be found in any gentleman's house. In the valuations of the two houses, only at Clapham Common were scientific instruments listed.[95] Cavendish's investment in books was far greater than in instruments. The value of his books at Bedford Square was truly enormous, over twice the combined value of the total contents of both houses and twice the value of the Bedford Square house itself.[96] Scientific books were very expensive. Cavendish's Bedford Square house stood for scientific knowledge already attained, as recorded in books and journals, and his Clapham Common house stood for knowledge in progress,

---

[90] "Inventory of Sundry Fixtures." He had one painting that was not a family portrait, a landscape.

[91] "Wages Due to the Servants at Clapham and Bedford Square," Devon Coll.

[92] The household furniture at the Clapham Common house was valued at £645.10.6, at the Bedford Square house at £633.13.1. "Extracts from Valuations of Furniture etc.," Devon. Coll.

[93] The value of the plate, linen, and china at Bedford Square was four times the value of the same at Clapham Common, £699.16.8 vs. £168.4.0. "Extracts."

[94] The keys are listed under headings L.1 through L.6, which might stand for "London," and "Clapham No. 1" followed by Nos. 2 through 4. The Clapham No. 1 keys were, he noted, "carried about me," some or all of which fit Bedford Square locks. The other "N" keys may have been for Bedford Square or they could have been duplicates for Clapham Common. There is a key for "Observatory," which we know Cavendish had at Clapham Common but which he probably also had at Bedford Square. In any case, the instruments under lock and "N" keys are of the same type: microscopes and astronomical instruments by excellent instrument-makers, such as Jesse Ramsden, John Dolland, and John Hadley. There were two instruments that do not fit the above description: an air pump and an electrical machine. "Keys at London," Cavendish Mss., unclassified.

[95] Under the category of philosophical and astronomical instruments, Clapham Common was listed at £544.19.0 and Bedford Square at nothing. "Extracts."

[96] Cavendish's books at Bedford Square were valued at £7,000. Thomas Payne to John Heaton, 6 Sep. 1810. After Cavendish's death, his Bedford Square house brought £3,530. "29 April etc. 1814 Account Respecting the Sale of a Leasehold House at the North East Corner of Bedford Square," Devon. Coll.

experiment and observation. Dedicated totally to scientific pursuits, Cavendish's two houses complemented one another.

The Library

Practitioners of science in the eighteenth century rarely could afford to buy or subscribe to many scientific books and journals. Large scientific libraries were a luxury of the rich. Like Hans Sloane, Joseph Banks, and other collectors, Henry Cavendish, and probably his father before him,[97] made his library available upon application. This private man allowed the library in his house on Bedford Square to be used as a public institution.[98] He ran a tight ship. There was a catalogue of all the books and a take-out register and a librarian to watch over both and, as well, over the books, the patrons, and, most important, his master's wishes. When the twenty-one year old Alexander Humboldt traveled to London in 1790, he applied for permission to use Cavendish's library, which he received together with the advice that under no circumstances was he to talk to Cavendish if he should see him there.[99] (Later Cavendish took an interest in Humboldt's measurements with a eudiometer, which Cavendish thought were wrong due to a faulty method;[100] and Humboldt took satisfaction at succeeding to this haughty aristocrat's place in the Paris Institute.) The request from another reader was communicated through Blagden, who explained the official policy. "Wishing to promote science by every measure in his power," Cavendish made his library accessible "at all seasons of the year." Blagden made it clear that what was accessible was the library and not its owner: Cavendish did not want people even to sit in his library but to "borrow such books as they wish & take them home for a limited time."[101] To further this policy books would even be sent to borrowers.[102] Even with these rules in effect, ordinarily it was not Cavendish but his librarian who met the public.[103] In addition to aiding persons in their researches, the librarian acted as the lion at the gate, guarding Cavendish's privacy, if imperfectly. One who got by him was Pahin de La Blancherie, who was in London on a visit. La Blancherie complained to Cavendish about the treatment he received from his librarian. Having requested a history of astronomy (shelved on the ground floor, just to the left of the entrance), he

was told by Cavendish's librarian that Cavendish had just taken that book to Clapham Common. He then asked for a biographical dictionary; the librarian told him that Cavendish had taken it too. The librarian told him to come back, which he did, whereupon the librarian told him that Cavendish still had the books and moreover had great need for them. La Blancherie had been thwarted at the British Museum and now at Cavendish's library, and he thought the British nation owed him damages. He knew that Cavendish would not authorize this conduct by his librarian but would condemn it.[104] We are not so sure.

One of the rare stories of Cavendish's largesse concerns his librarian, who lived in his

---

[97]At least we know that Lord Charles Cavendish lent books to friends; e.g., he lent Thomas Birch the latest book by the metaphysician Dobbs, an enquiry into being, A Miscellaneous Metaphysical Essay. Birch to "Dear Sir," 18 Oct. 1748, draft, British Museum, Add. Mss. 4324 A, f. 1.

[98]There is some question about the location of Cavendish's library. Wilson says that for his library, "Cavendish set apart a separate mansion in Dean Street, Soho." For this information, he cites Cavendish's early biographers Cuvier and Biot. But all that Biot says is that Cavendish located his library two leagues, or five English miles, from his residence so as not to be disturbed by readers consulting it, and five miles is roughly the distance from Clapham to the center of London. Since neither Biot nor Cuvier mentions Dean Street, Wilson supplied this address from unknown sources. Georges Cuvier, "Henry Cavendish," in *Great Chemists*, ed. E. Faber (New York: Interscience Publishers, 1961), 227–38, on 237; J. B. Biot, "Cavendish (Henri)," *Biographie Universelle*, vol. 7 (Paris, 1813), 272–73, on 273; Wilson, *Cavendish*, 163. We have found no other record of Cavendish at Dean Street. At the end of his life, Cavendish's library was in his house on Bedford Square, and we are inclined to think that Wilson's source got the location wrong.

[99]Humboldt's irrepressible talkativeness may have had something to do with the advice that in Cavendish's library "he was on no account to presume so far as to speak to, or even greet, the proud and aristocratic owner should he happen to meet him." This anecdote from Bruhn's biography is quoted in James Thorne, *Environs of London* (London, 1876) 1: 111.

[100]Henry Cavendish to Charles Blagden, 18 Dec., Blagden Papers, Royal Society.

[101]Charles Blagden to Thomas Beddoes, 12 Mar. 1788, draft, Blagden Letters, Royal Society, 7:129.

[102]Blagden told Herschel that Cavendish had the books he wanted to borrow and that Herschel could either look at them in his library or have the books sent to him at Slough. Charles Blagden to William Herschel, 19 May 1786, draft, Blagden Letters, Royal Society, 7:762.

[103]Thomas Young said that after Cavendish's librarian died, Cavendish himself devoted one day a week to checking books in and out of his library. Thomas Young, "Life of Cavendish," originally published in the supplement to the *Encyclopaedia Britannica* for 1818–1824; it was reprinted in Cavendish, *Sci. Pap.* 1: 435–47, on 445. Cavendish had a librarian at the time he died, but given the small salary he was paid, he might not have been expected to check books in and out among his other duties. "29th May 1812. Taxes etc. for House in Bedford Square," Devon. Coll.

[104]Pahin de La Blancherie to Henry Cavendish, 23 Feb. 1794, Cavendish Mss, New Correspondence.

house but who eventually left Cavendish's employment to live in the country. At his club Cavendish was told that his former librarian was in poor health. Cavendish was sorry to hear that. It was then suggested that Cavendish might help him out with an annuity. "Well, well, well, a check for ten thousand pounds, would that do?"[105] Truth or tall tale, there is reason to think that Cavendish had got satisfactory service from this librarian. Despite Cavendish's reputation for clockwork routine, he was not particularly good at keeping order in his affairs and his things, including his books, which were described as being in a "bad state of arrangement."[106] He needed help. The librarian made a catalogue of his and his father's big library and entered it in a great, heavy volume of blank pages (the entries are in more than one hand, none Cavendish's), and he physically arranged and dispensed the items listed in it. He was also Cavendish's live-in linguist, a German[107] by the name of Heidinger, evidently.[108] Cavendish did his part to preserve the system created by his librarian, signing for every book he borrowed like any stranger off the street.[109]

With the exception of about 450 books in their original paper covers,[110] Henry Cavendish's books are now bound in leather and dispersed among the other books of the great ducal library at Chatsworth,[111] most of them shelved in the beautiful, old Long Gallery. Cavendish's books are identifiable both by his book stamp, a simple HC, and by his separate catalogue number. The catalogue of Cavendish's library is incomplete, since it includes new entries only into the early 1790s, which is probably when his German left, and we know that Cavendish continued to buy books after that time. For this reason we can speak with greater accuracy of the contents of his catalogue than of his library.[112] The catalogue lists about 9,000 titles, representing some 12,000 volumes.[113] Cavendish's library was large but not immense for the time. Sloane's library was four times as large, and even Cavendish's sea-going friend Alexander Dalrymple had a library larger than his. (Dalrymple was unusual; not a rich man, he had a great library, which may be why he was often in debt and borrowed money from Cavendish.)[114] Many of Cavendish's colleagues had substantial libraries though of an order of magnitude smaller than his. Nevil Maskelyne's in

1811 contained 757 lots; John Playfair's in 1820, 1421 lots; Charles Hutton's in 1816, 1854 lots. Notable libraries by professional persons tended to be libraries of physicians; William Cullen's, for example, contained 3010 lots.[115] Cavendish's library was intermediate in size; that it was not even larger was because it was selective. Although it was open to a qualified public, its contents were not selected for the public. The works it contained were works that interested the Cavendishes.[116] The largest category of his collection is natural philosophy with nearly two thousand titles.

---

[105]Wilson, *Cavendish*, 174.

[106]Ibid.

[107]Thomas Young, "Life of Cavendish," *Encyclopaedia Britannica*, Supplement, 1816–24; in Cavendish, *Sci. Pap.* 1:435–47, on 445.

[108]Cavendish did not read German fluently if at all, and he certainly did not read German script. Blagden, who did read it, was out of town when a letter from the German chemist Lorenz Crell arrived. "I hope you got Mr. Heydinger to read Crell's letter," Blagden wrote to Cavendish. Letter of 23 Sep. 1787, Cavendish Mss X(b), 14.

[109]Georges Cuvier, "Henry Cavendish," translated from the French by D. S. Faber, in E. Faber, ed., *Great Chemists* (New York: Interscience Publishers, 1961), 227–38, on 237.

[110]Listed as "Cavendish Tracts Draft Catalogue 1966." These books may have been bound and shelved with the others by now.

[111]Five years after Henry Cavendish's death, the sixth duke of Devonshire brought together the books from his several houses to make the great Chatsworth library, and Henry Cavendish's books were included, a gift from his heir, Lord George Cavendish. Historical notice by J. P. Lacaita, July 1879, on p. xvii of vol. 1 of *Catalogue of the Library at Chatsworth*, 4 vols. (London, 1879). Henry Cavendish's books constitute about one quarter of the ducal library.

[112]The catalogue is not identified as Henry Cavendish's, but an inspection of books owned by Cavendish in the Chatsworth library confirms that this catalogue lists those books; penciled in the books are numbers that correspond to the numbers of the catalogue.

[113]This count is given in R. A. Harvey, "The Private Library of Henry Cavendish (1731–1810)," *The Library* 2 (1980): 281–92, on 284.

[114]We have only "Part I" of the catalogue of Dalrymple's library, and it contains 7190 entries. Part II, containing books on navigation and travel, his specialty, might be even longer. *A Catalogue of the Extensive and Valuable Library of Books; Part I. Late the Property of Alex. Dalrymple, Esq. F.R.S. (Deceased). Hydrographer to the Board of Admiralty, and the Hon. East India Company, Which Will Be Sold by Auction, by Messrs. King & Lochee, . . . on Monday, May 29, 1809, and Twenty-three Following Days, at Twelve O'Clock* (London, 1809).

[115]Ellen B. Wells, "Scientists' Libraries: A Handlist of Printed Sources," *Annals of Science* 40 (1983): 317–89, on 338, 354, 362, and 370.

[116]Harvey has tallied books in Cavendish's catalogue by subject according to whether they were published before or after 1752, the year Henry finished his university education. The results are not meaningful in the way they are intended. The appropriate division for assessing Henry Cavendish's interests from the entries in the catalogue is 1783, when Lord Charles Cavendish died. The very different approaches to the library of father and son are illustrated by the books they bought by subscription. By a recent count, Lord Charles subscribed to 50 books over the course of his life. (His 50 subscriptions were a large number. Only one of his contemporaries had substantially more, Richard Mead with 210. William Stukeley had 60, William Jones 52, John Freind 50, Thomas Coke, earl of Leicester 50, and George Parker, earl of Macclesfield 49.) By subject Lord Charles's subscriptions

Chemical books are not listed under a separate category but under natural philosophy, as are books on most of Cavendish's other main interests, mechanics, instruments, meteorology, and mineralogy. In this same category are many books on medicine, anatomy, and animal economy, but very few of these books were published after Lord Charles Cavendish died. Mathematics, the second largest category, includes in addition to books on mathematics, books on natural philosophy in which mathematics is used, such as Newton's *Principia* (all editions) and *Opticks* (all editions) and Robert Smith's *System of Opticks*. Astronomy is well represented. Lord Charles and Henry Cavendish were lovers of rare books; they owned first editions of the classic works of science by Copernicus, Brahe, Kepler, and others. In natural history, as opposed to natural philosophy, Cavendish had only a slight interest;[117] what works he added in this category are generally on mineralogy and geology. Not all books in the catalogue are scientific. Editions of the classics with Richard Bentley's signature are in the collection.[118] A category as large as mathematics is poetry and plays, eleven hundred volumes, a subject on which father and son evidently parted company. The catalogue lists the works of Shakespeare, Dryden, Congreve, Pope, Swift, Gray, Goldsmith, Gay, Johnson, Sheridan, and other authors one would expect to find in a literary library; there are some works of poetry from the 1750s, but in the 1760s and 1770s, the entries are of plays only,[119] and after Lord Charles's death in 1783, only one book was added to this category, an Indian drama, published in 1790, two years before Cavendish published his paper on the civil year of the Hindoos.[120] After Lord Charles's death, when Henry alone added to the library, there was no more poetry, theater, or fiction, nor editions of classics, books of antiquities, or works on architecture.[121] Henry had at most a passing interest in history, and he did not keep this section of his library current. By contrast, he had great interest in books on voyages and travels, which he used in his scientific work. The catalogue, we note, begins with astronomy, mathematics, and natural philosophy, the subjects that came first in Cavendish's life.

Often libraries are revealing of their owners because of marginalia in their books. Cavendish, however, rarely put a mark in a book; in the third edition of Newton's *Principia*, he penciled in some corrections of numbers, and that is about all we have

found. Holding few surprises, Cavendish's library is confirming, not revealing. It tells us that he was not interested in literature and languages,[122] but that he was interested in the physical sciences and mathematics.

Clapham Common

In the years 1782 to 1785, Cavendish was pretty much constantly engaged in "removing my house," as he told Joseph Priestley to excuse his poor record as a correspondent. There is substance behind this excuse, as suggested by the episode of Charles Cullen. Within the space of three or four years, Cavendish moved out of his father's house on Great Marlborough Street, into and out of a

---

correspond to his very broad range of interests: about 20 of them could be regarded as historical, including antiquities, state papers, and religious history; 15 of them were mathematical and scientific, including natural history, and including editions of Bacon's and Boyle's works. The remaining subscriptions are to books of travels, maps, law, poetry, plays, and of miscellaneous other categories. Lord Charles's subscriptions agree with the content of the Cavendish library in general, according to his son's catalogue. Henry Cavendish subscribed to 10 books, 9 of which were on science, mathematics, and travels. The exceptional book to which Cavendish gave a double subscription would seem to have been an instance of charity: Benjamin Clement, *Sermons on Several Subjects and Occasions* (Wolverhampton, 1774), "for author's widow." The one book to which both Henry and his father subscribed was about science: Priestley's *History of Vision*, in 1772. R. V. and P. J. Wallis, *Biobibliography of British Mathematics and Its Applications*, part 2: *1701–1760* (Newcastle upon Tyne: PHIBB, 1986): *Index of British Mathematicians*, part 3: *1701–1800* (Newcastle upon Tyne: PHIBB, 1993). F. J. G. Robinson and P. J. Wallis, *Book Subscription Lists. A Revised Guide* (Newcastle upon Tyne, 1975). P. J. Wallis, completed and edited by Ruth Wallis, *Book Subscription Lists, Extended Supplement to the Revised Guide* (Newcastle upon Tyne: PHIBB, 1996).

[117]But Linneaus was there, in nine volumes, the last two added by Henry, in or after 1785. The last book to which Henry Cavendish subscribed was too late to enter the catalogue of his library: it was by the late Thomas Garnett, with whom Cavendish had associated at the Royal Institution, *Popular Lectures on Zoonomia: or, The Laws of Animal Life, in Health and Disease* (London: published by the press of the Royal Institution, 1802). There is the suggestion that in his later years, Cavendish took an interest in the life sciences.

[118]Lacaita, *Catalogue of the Library at Chatsworth* :xvii.

[119]With the one exception, Thomas Rowley, *Poems, with a Commentary by Jer. Milles* (London, 1782).

[120]Cálidás, *Sacontula, or the Fatal Ring, an Indian Drama* (London, 1790). Not entered in the catalogue (it was too late) under poetry and plays but found in the Chatsworth library, with Henry Cavendish's stamp, is the related work, *The Loves of Cámarúpa and Cámaluta, An Ancient Indian Tale*, trans. W. Franklin (London, 1793).

[121]Two works on architecture bought by Henry Cavendish might well have gone under different headings: John Smeaton's *A Narrative of the Building and Description of the Construction of Eddystone Lighthouse* and a translation of Vitruvius's *Architecture*.

[122]There are a few dictionaries of translation, but not the reference works of a person who loves languages for their own sake. Latin is as common as English in the books in Cavendish's library, but that was a working language still, not an interest. Cavendish, of course, read Latin, and undoubtedly with ease. To keep up to date in the sciences in which he worked, Cavendish bought books and subscribed to journals in the modern European languages, especially French, which he read and copied notes in.

house at Hampstead, and into houses on Bedford Square and on Clapham Common.

Clapham, Cavendish's new suburban address, was similar to his old, Hampstead, and to a good many other villages at about the same distance from London, inhabited by well-to-do professional people with ties to London. He could see them from his elevated perch at Hampstead, villages such as Chelsea, Fulham, Putney, Hammersmith, and Wandsworth. He chose Clapham or, to locate him precisely, Clapham Common.[123]

The move to Clapham Common was a particularly upsetting event in Cavendish's well-ordered life, but it could have been much worse. Cavendish, who in his daily life always had help and depended on it, now had as his associate Blagden, who like his librarian was the soul of order. Blagden relieved Cavendish of a great many of the details of his moves, as we learn from Blagden's financial records. We find there, for example, a bill from the summer of 1785 for carpenter work on his, *Blagden's*, house at Clapham Common, and also one for metal work there; these misdirected bills can only mean that Blagden was acting as Cavendish's agent.[124] Other bills for the winter of 1784 and the fall of 1785 are for household furnishing for a large house, again evidently Cavendish's. Items include enormous yardages of green fabrics, damask, moreen, and silk lace for the windows, chairs, and beds.[125] Like his house on Bedford Square, Cavendish's house at Clapham Common was decorated in the color green.

Despite Blagden's considerable help, Cavendish's move to Clapham Common left his scientific work in disarray. Because of the need for repairs on the new house, Cavendish and Blagden's planned scientific journey to Wales had to be postponed by three weeks in June 1785.[126] That September, Cavendish refused an invitation to visit Yorkshire, as Blagden explained to the host, John Michell: Cavendish "promises himself that pleasure sometime or other, yet he cannot spare time for another journey this year, as it will give him full employment till winter to bring his new country-house of Clapham into order. He is but just removed thither: & all his pursuits are interrupted till his books, instruments etc can be brought out of the confusion in which they lie at present."[127] The interruptions continued. In November, Blagden wrote to Laplace that "Mr. Cavendish will not soon have another paper ready, his apparatus having

been deranged by moving to another house, where, however, he has /illegible/ conveniences for carrying on his experiments to still greater perfection."[128] Cavendish had to bide his time while his new house was arranged as a house of science. He was fifty-three at the time of his move to Clapham, and it was to be the place of his scientific researches to the end of his life.

With his father's generous inheritance, Cavendish had the wherewithal to build a great house or buy one or several and to live in a grand style, but of course he did none of these things. Not lavish estates with large households, for which he had no use, but a well-built, ample but still modest house (vacated by a failed banker, we are told) met his needs. To buy it he needed only a tiny portion of his inheritance. Clapham Common was not a retreat for the aristocracy; no other Cavendishes lived there, no Russells, no Manners. According to a contemporary map identifying the seventy-four houses on Clapham Common by their occupants, only Cavendish was addressed as the "Rt. Hon.," and only one other person had a title, a Lady Tibbs; the others were simply "Mrs." or "Esq."[129] Cavendish stood out for his rank and his wealth, but his house, household, and expenditure were in line with that of the neighborhood.

---

[123]Henry Cavendish to Joseph Priestley, 20 Dec. 1784, draft, Cavendish Mss, New Correspondence; in Joseph Priestley, *A Scientific Autobiography of Joseph Priestley (1733–1804)*, ed. R. E. Schofield (Cambridge, Mass.: MIT Press, 1966), 239–40, on 239. Villages comparable to Hampstead included Greenwich, Stoke Newington, Highgate, Camberwell, Dulwich, and Twickenham. Thompson, *Hampstead*, 26. From his new location, Clapham Common, Cavendish used some of these villages for taking bearings: the Observatory at Greenwich, a church in Highgate, a house on Camberwell. Henry Cavendish, "Bearings," Cavendish Mss.

[124]"Carpenters Work Done for Dr Blagden at His House at Clapham," submitted by the firm Hanscomb & Fothergill. The dates of this work fall between August and November 1785. There is another bill from the same period for metal work on the house, submitted by Thomas Charles. Gloucestershire Record Office, D 1086, F 153.

[125]Bills submitted by Quinton Kay for purchases and repairs in October and November 1784 and in September, October, and November 1785. Gloucestershire Record Office, D 1086, F 153. Blagden himself was moving, from King's Road to Gower Street, so the bills for his expenses and those for Cavendish's are mixed together in Blagden's papers and could be confused for one another.

[126]Charles Blagden to Mr. Lewis, draft, 20 June 1785, Blagden Letterbook, Yale.

[127]Charles Blagden to John Michell, draft, 13 Sep. 1785, Blagden Letterbook, Yale.

[128]Charles Blagden to P. S. Laplace, draft, 16 Nov. 1785, Blagden Letterbook, Royal Society.

[129]"Perambulation of Clapham Common 1800. From C. Smith's 'Actual Survey of the Road from London to Brighthelmston.'" British Library.

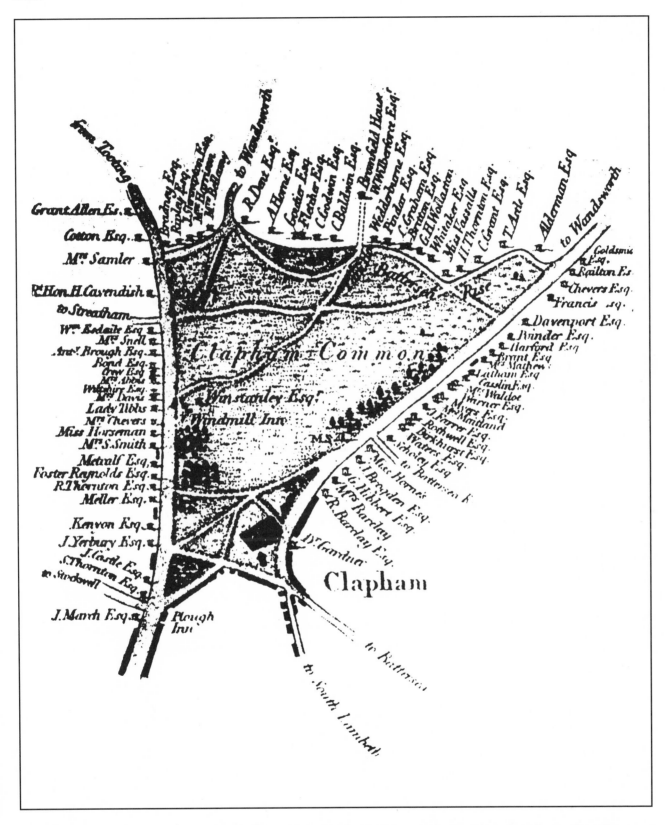

PLATE VIII. Map of Clapham Common. Cavendish's house is on the left side of the common, fourth house from the top. "Perambulation of Clapham Common 1800. From C. Smith's 'Actual Survey on the Road from London to Brighthelmston.'" *The Chronicles of Clapham/Clapham Common/. Being a Selection from the Reminiscences of Thomas Parsons. Sometime Member of the Clapham Antiquarian Society* (London: printed privately by A.V. Huckle & Son, Ltd., The Ramsdan Press, 1929), opposite page 112. Reproduced by permission of the Bodleian Library.

Clapham Common was described in a survey of 1784 as "a very large straggling village," "pleasantly situated," and containing "many country seats belonging to the gentry and citizens of London." South of London, Clapham Common stood on a low hill overlooking the Thames, four miles from Westminster Bridge, with daily coach service into the metropolis. Good roads made it possible for Clapham inhabitants to go to London by way of London Bridge, do business from one end of the city to the other, and "without being any further from home" return by Westminster Bridge," completing a triangle.[130] Lysons, in his survey published a few years after Cavendish's move, said that the population of Clapham had increased faster than that of any other parish he had examined. In 1788 the population was 2,477; four years later it was about 2,700 with an average of ten new houses going up each year.[131] Clapham's draw was its magnificent common, which was described to Cavendish as "the most beautiful, the most healthy and highly improved spot of land, not only round the metropolis, but perhaps in the kingdom."[132] This was an interested developer's hyperbole, but the appeal of the common to city dwellers like Cavendish was strong. Bankers, merchants, and other well-to-do Londoners built big houses, often second houses, facing the common. The feel of the common is captured in a print from the time, 1784. Evoking pastoral calm and quiet, in the foreground it shows footpaths, a man with his dog, a cow, and in the distance across the Long Pond, the new parish church and several substantial houses. (The cow in the print illustrates the only story to have come down in which Cavendish appears as a man of spontaneous action, a hero. He is said to have saved a woman who lived at Clapham from the attack of a mad cow, causing a sensation at Clapham where Cavendish was known to go to lengths to avoid female encounters.[133])

Clapham Common had not always been that attractive. Not many years before Cavendish arrived there, this triangular piece of ground of over two hundred acres had been a morass with impassable roads. By means of a subscription from the inhabitants, the wilderness had been transformed into highly desirable residential property. Drains were installed, paths were laid, and a great many trees, English and exotic, were set out. The energy and vision behind the public works were provided in considerable measure by the Clapham Common developer and resident Christopher Baldwin, with whom, as we will see, Cavendish was to have relentless and unpleasant business dealings. Baldwin was justice of the peace, an office he used together with personal influence to pursue his schemes for Clapham.[134] The result was what Cavendish saw from his house, a pleasant vista of ponds, mounds, groves of horse-chestnuts, poplars, gorse thickets, pasture, and cows.

Clapham Common would become a park, but when Cavendish moved there, the parish still paid a bounty on hedgehogs and polecats. If in ways Clapham was still countrified, it was nonetheless thoroughly civilized. The men who went daily to work in the city or Westminster could leave their families and possessions behind, confident of their safety,[135] and at night they could sleep in peace owing to the lighting and the watch. Although there had long been lighting and a watch at Clapham, it was only in 1784, just at the time Cavendish moved there, that trustees were appointed by an act of parliament to organize the lighting and watch of the streets of Clapham and of the roads leading to it. Cavendish and his neighbors were protected by a dozen or so armed men, who from dusk to dawn manned watchboxes when they were not patrolling the roads between them. Misdeeds at Clapham Common were few and usually minor: lead was stolen or a duck or a pig but rarely was anyone robbed by a highwayman.[136] Other aspects of civilized life at Clapham, such as buying land for widening a road, examining sewers, and regulating fines in lieu of serving a church office, were taken up in vestry meetings.[137]

---

[130]Christopher Baldwin to Henry Cavendish, 3 May 1784, "1784–1786. H. Cavendish & C. Baldwin. Correspondence re Sale of Land," Devon. Coll., 86/comp. 1.

[131]Daniel Lysons, *The Environs of London: Being an Historical Account of the Towns, Villages, and Hamlets, within Twelve Miles of That Capital*, vol 1: *County of Surrey* (London, 1792), 169.

[132]Baldwin to Cavendish, 3 May 1784.

[133]This story came down secondhand to Wilson from Mrs. William Herbert, the then occupant of Cavendish's former house at Clapham Common. The rescued woman was said to be Mrs. Keer, who was no longer living. Wilson, *Cavendish*, 178. There is possibly more to this story; the cow could have belonged to Cavendish, who had three at the time of his death. "Mr Cavendish's Executorship Agenda," Devon. Coll.

[134]Lysons, *Environs of London* 1:159.

[135]E. M. Forster, *Battersea Rise* (New York: Harcourt, Brace, 1956), 5.

[136]Cavendish is listed among the householders but not among the trustees in "Watching and Lighting Trust," P/C/11, "The Minutes of the Trustees for Watching and Lighting the Village of Clapham & Certain Roads Leading Thereto," 1786–1802, Minet Library, London.

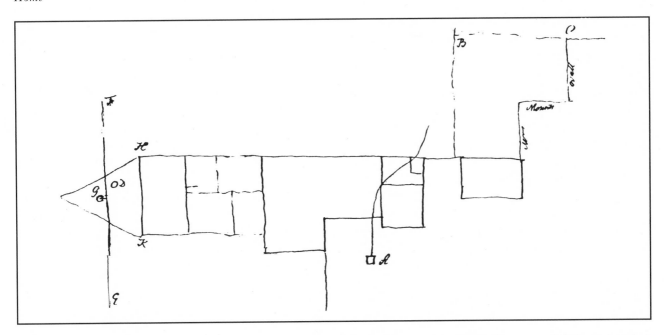

PLATE IX. Plan of Drains at Clapham. Cavendish's house faces the Common at the bottom of the diagram. The separate building to the right is evidently a greenhouse, formerly containing an outhouse, which Cavendish refers to in his notes on experiments on air. To the left is a basin that becomes a pond, 7 1/2 feet deep, into which the drains from H and K run, and which is filled from the pipe EF, which probably comes from the pond across the road in the Common. G is the valve for letting water into the pond. The other letters stand for: A, a drain sink; B, the gate to the kitchen garden; BC, a drain running from Mrs. Mount's house to the right of what Cavendish has labelled Mrs. Mount's wall; D, a well formerly supplying the pantry or dairy. Water from A eventually runs into a ditch in the field behind the house, and from there it is conducted to the "lane," presumably Dragmire Lane, which bounds Cavendish's property. Next to the pond is a sundial, which Cavendish used as a marker in taking measurements of the basin. Cavendish refers to his walled "court yard," but he does not indicate its location. This diagram was probably drawn up in connection with renovations Cavendish made before moving into the house. "Plan of Drains at Clapham & Measures Relating to Bason," Cavendish Mss, Misc.

In 1905 Cavendish's house at Clapham Common—it had come to be called "the Cavendish House"—was pulled down and the estate sold to be replaced by rows of red-brick villas. At a sale near the end of its life, the house was described as "a capital family residence with a suite of well-proportioned reception rooms, elegant drawing room, noble dining room, handsome library, morning room and billiard room, a large conservatory and 17 bedrooms." The grounds were "enriched with stately timber of oak, cedar, beech, fir and cypress, laid out with a terrace walk, lake and summerhouse." In addition there were a kitchen garden, greenhouse, orchid house, aloe-house, and vineries. Cavendish would have been hard-pressed to recognize this showy, sprawling, stuck-on structure as having once been his. Its subsequent owners had had very different taste and had put the house to very different purposes. In 1833 it was bought by a developer, who added a big reception room, another servants' wing, and the terrace fronting the garden. Thirty years later it was bought by an art patron, who enlarged it to hold a splendid collection of contemporary paintings. By imagining these accretions

gone and the white stucco laid over the original red brick removed, the central block can just be made out in late photographs of the house. This well-proportioned eighteenth-century country house was the house that Cavendish bought.[138]

Cavendish's house was located near the southeast corner of the common, a good ways from Clapham village. We get an idea of the shape and arrangement of the house from a rough sketch in Cavendish's hand of the layout of the drains. The house faced northwest with its long dimension

---

These minutes give a good idea of the measures taken for the security of life and property at Clapham, as do, in detail, "The Minutes of the Sub-Committee for Watching & Lighting of the Village of Clapham & Certain Roads Leading Thereto," 1786–1802, Minet Library, London. Extracts from the latter are published in R. de M. Rudolf, "The Clapham Sect," in *Clapham and the Clapham Sect*, ed. E. Baldwin (London: Clapham Antiquarian Society, 1927), 89–142.

[137]The minutes of these meetings show that Cavendish did not take an active part. His one appearance in the minutes was his nomination and appointment for a year as "headborough." Entry for 9 Apr. 1798, "Clapham Vestry Minutes 1752 to 1798," Greater London Record Office, P 95/TRI 1/6.

[138]Cavendish was the second owner of the house; the first, Henton Brown, was a banker whose business failed, according to Eric E. F. Smith, *Clapham* (London: London Borough of Lambeth, 1976), 78.

parallel to the road bounding the common, and access to it was by a circular drive from the road.

Cavendish made alterations in his Clapham house for privacy and for science, if the two can meaningfully be separated. He is said to have had a back stairs built because he was annoyed by encountering a maid with a broom and pail on the existing stairs.[139] The conversion of a conventional eighteenth-century house into Cavendish's work-place left a memorable impression on his contemporaries. Little of the house was reserved for comfort, as the rooms were given new functions; for example, upstairs, Cavendish outfitted rooms for an astronomical observatory, complete with a "transit-room,"[140] and downstairs, he made over the drawing room into a laboratory and an adjacent room into a forge. The lawn had a wooden platform from which Cavendish climbed a large tree to make scientific measurements.[141] "The whole of the house at Clapham was occupied as workshops and laboratory," the noted London instrument-maker John Newman recalled.[142] Another recalled that "it was stuck about with thermometers, rain-gauges, etc."[143]

People who entered Cavendish's house at Clapham Common reacted to "its desolate appearance, and its scanty and mean-looking furniture,"[144] according to Cavendish's younger contemporary John Barrow. A house so given over to scientific purposes no doubt could leave a chilling impression with some people, but Barrow's hearsay needs qualification. It may be impossible now to know if Cavendish's house was scantily furnished by the standards of the day, but it definitely was not meanly furnished. Before moving in, Cavendish bought a costly drawing-room suite that included ten inlaid satinwood cabriole elbow chairs, a cabriole sofa to match, and a pair of inlaid satinwood pier tables with leather covers.[145] This furniture along with some of the other contents of the house were listed by an auctioneer as "modern" furnishings of a "professional gentleman," containing "rich cut glass and china, in table and tea services, bronze chimney ornaments, paintings and prints, elegantly framed . . . Grecian sofas and lounging chairs, French and festoon window curtains . . . Brussells and Kidderminster carpets."[146]

To take care of these furnishings and to do all the other tasks of running a house, Cavendish employed a staff of seven domestic servants: a housekeeper, a housemaid, a cook, a gardener, a coachman, and two footmen. Because his house was not ordinary but a place for doing science, Cavendish had an additional servant who was not ordinary, a mathematical instrument-maker, whom he paid much more than the others, sixty-five pounds a year. As Cavendish's way of life did not change over the twenty-five years he lived in the Clapham house, neither did the complement of servants.[147]

Land Developer

In his survey of London in 1792, Lysons said that the improvement of Clapham Common owed to the "good taste and exertions of Christopher Baldwin Esquire, who has resided many years in the spot." Proof of the improvement, Lysons said, was Baldwin's recent sale of fourteen

[139] Wilson, *Cavendish*, 170.
[140] "Transit-room" at Cavendish's Clapham Common house appears on the map in William Roy, "An Account of the Trigonometrical Operation, Whereby the Distance between the Meridians or the Royal Observatories of Greenwich and Paris Has Been Determined," *PT* 80 (1790): 111–270, on 261.
[141] These details were collected by Wilson from Mrs. William Herbert and from another Clapham resident, Dr. Sylvester. Wilson, *Cavendish*, 164.
[142] Ibid., 164.
[143] This quotation was from a Fellow of the Royal Society . Ibid., 164.
[144] John Barrow, *Sketches of the Royal Society and Royal Society Club* (London, 1849), 150.
[145] "About Purchase of House & Furn at Clapham," 1785, Devon. Coll., 86/comp. 1. This packet contains a list of the satinwood chairs and related furnishings, "Sundry Drawing Room Furniture etc. of Wm. Robertson's Esqr. Appraised to Cavendish Esqr. 11th June 1785."
[146] The catalogue lists six four-poster beds and two of the sofa type. The beds and related furniture were covered in green, and the Venetian blinds were evidently green, too. (The prevalent color green reinforces our belief that the bills for furnishings in Blagden's papers refer to Cavendish's house at Clapham.) The catalogue also lists over fifty cushioned chairs made of a variety of woods: rosewood, satinwood, and mahogany, and covered with red and yellow morocco (a departure from monotone green). Throughout the house, the wood was predominantly mahogany. *A Catalogue of an Assortment of Modern Household Furniture . . . which Will Be Sold by Auction by Mr. Squibb, at His Great Room Saville Passage, Saville Row, on Wednesday, December 5, 1810, and Two Following Days, at Twelve O'clock.* This catalogue is incomplete, since only part of the contents of Cavendish's house at Clapham was taken to the place of this auction, Saville Row, part being taken to Swift's Auction Room. "Mr. Swift's Account with the Executor of Henry Cavendish Esq. Deceased," 26 Jan. 1811. In the packet "About Purchase of House & Furn. at Clapham," 1785, is "An Inventory," with notations by Cavendish, "of Fixtures Belonging to Messr Collinson and Tritton of Clapham in Surry to Be Valued to the Purchaser of the Estate, May 13th, 1732," Devon. Coll., 86/comp. 1.
[147] "Account of the Number of Persons Residing in the Parish of Clapham . . . Dtd 18 Feb. 1788," Greater London Record Office, P 95/TRI 1/72. "Wages Due to the Servants at Clapham and in Bedford Square," 1810, Devon. Coll.

acres of land close to his house for the steep price of £5,000.[148] Lysons gave the amount of land incorrectly—it was fifteen acres, not fourteen—but the price was right. The unnamed buyer of this piece of real estate was, we know, Henry Cavendish.

Baldwin was a merchant and West Indian landowner who was interested in some of the same things Cavendish was. Baldwin was well known to the "amateurs of agriculture as a zealous promoter" of agricultural science.[149] Beyond that, Baldwin had a general curiosity about science. Shortly before doing business with Cavendish, he had assisted Benjamin Franklin in experiments on stilling waves on a pond at Clapham Common. Baldwin was a member of the Monday Club,[150] as were many men of science, including Cavendish, who was a member at the time he bought the property. Perhaps it was through this scientifically oriented club that Cavendish learned of Baldwin's undeveloped land at Clapham Common in the first place. An early letter of Baldwin to Cavendish began with a cordial reminder of their connection. With reference to the experiments on air that Cavendish was currently making, Baldwin wished that "among your other learned & very curious investigations in our atmosphere, you would tell me when I may safely begin hay-making, since you are interested in the attempt."[151] This familiarity was a disastrous tack to take with Cavendish. The business dealings of the two men were to prove long, difficult, and acrimonious.

Well over a year before moving to his new villa at Clapham Common, Cavendish had approached Baldwin about the land, letting him know of his interest in buying fifteen or twenty acres from him. At first Baldwin was not tempted and suggested to Cavendish other landowners in the area he might approach. For a time Cavendish considered buying a farm, but then he came back to Baldwin. The land in question was three fields, totaling fifteen acres, bordering on Clapham Common, next to Baldwin's house and extending behind it. Baldwin, now agreeable, began to speak of the "*market price*" of his prime real estate, a piece of the diminishing "front land" on the common. His was not just any land, and it could no more be sold by the acre than could land in London and Westminster.[152].

Among Cavendish's scientific manuscripts is a mathematical study of musical intervals, on the back of which is the draft of a letter. Although the letter is undated and unaddressed, the year is clearly 1784 and the recipient clearly Baldwin: "I forgot to ask you yesterday where you would have me return the plans you sent me. I would have told you yesterday how much I would give for the estate had it not been that it is so much less than what you said you had refused that I thought it to no purpose. If however you have a mind I will let you know what I think it worth & at the same time as I hate hagling will tell you the utmost I will give for it but in that case you may depend upon it that I shall not offer any more."[153] Being uncertain of the value of the land, Cavendish wrote to Baldwin again that all he could say was that "if you are willing to take 5,000 £ for it I will give it though I shall be almost ashamed to own how much it cost me but I cannot by any means think of giving more than that."[154] Baldwin asked for £5,650, which he claimed was £1,280 below the market value as established by what builders had offered him for the land in the past. Rich as Cavendish was, Baldwin implied, it would be nothing for him to come up with the difference, only a few hundred pounds. Trying flattery again, Baldwin said that Cavendish's offer, even though it was insufficient, expressed the "gentleman and the noble blood of a Cavendish."[155] Having told Baldwin that he did not haggle, Cavendish now proved it: "I did not make you the offer of £5,000 without due consideration & a resolut. not to give more than that & therefore cannot consent to make any addit. to my former proposal." Upon this note of finality, Baldwin stepped down, agreeing to the £5,000, Cavendish's original offer.[156]

Given that there was an agreement in writing between buyer and seller, the closing of the deal

[148]Lysons, *Environs of London* 1:159–60.

[149]Ibid., 159.

[150]Verner W. Crane, "The Club of Honest Whigs: Friends of Science and Liberty," *William and Mary Quarterly* 23 (1966), 210–33, on 215.

[151]Christopher Baldwin to Henry Cavendish, 15 June 1784, Devon Coll., 86/comp. 1.

[152]Baldwin to Cavendish, 3 May 1784.

[153]Henry Cavendish to "Sir," draft, on the back cover of Henry Cavendish, "Musical Intervals," Cavendish Mss VI(a): 28.

[154]Henry Cavendish to Christopher Baldwin, draft, nd. /reply to letter of 3 May 1784/, Devon. Coll., 86/comp. 1.

[155]Christopher Baldwin to Henry Cavendish, 2 June 1784, Devon Coll., 86/comp. 1.

[156]Henry Cavendish to Christopher Baldwin, draft, n.d.; Christopher Baldwin to Henry Cavendish, 7 June 1784, Devon. Coll., 86/comp. 1.

should have been straightforward, but it was not. Three weeks later Cavendish had not yet received Baldwin's deed of purchase and documentation of title. "It is so very inconv. to me to wait so long," Cavendish complained, and he told Baldwin to get after his lawyer. Baldwin responded that it was Cavendish's lawyer, Thomas Dunn, who was causing the delay, besides which, the "dilitaryness of the gentᵐ of the law is proverbial." For himself, Baldwin had plenty of "patience." Baldwin's wordiness did not help matters. "I know you dont like long letters," Baldwin wrote in a postscript to Cavendish.[157]

In his twenty years of residence at Clapham Common, Baldwin never knew of anyone having difficulty selling land there—"til now." Dunn believed that Baldwin was causing the difficulty by not being forthright with the people holding mortgages on his land,[158] and on his own he proceeded to get releases of claims on the land by parties who had court judgments against Baldwin. As it turned out, the purchase money of £5,000 was exhausted in paying off the mortgages and encumbrances on the land, Baldwin receiving a mere residue of £166 for his land and his trouble. On 2 November 1784, Cavendish agreed with Baldwin for the absolute purchase of the land on Clapham Common.[159]

For a year after the sale, there was a break in Cavendish and Baldwin's correspondence. Then a new conflict arose concerning a half acre, a narrow strip at the edge of the land Cavendish had just bought. It was where Baldwin had extended his property a little way into a lane leading off the common. Cavendish wanted to settle this business with Baldwin promptly, but he could not; when Cavendish returned from a trip into the country, Dunn told him that Baldwin wanted £60 for the legal expenses he was out. Dunn told Baldwin's lawyer, who had advised Baldwin to accept a lower figure of £40, that Cavendish would never pay him £60 but that he might take him to court to force him to convey the property. "I hope I shall never have any business to transact with such another man as long as I live,"[160] Dunn told Cavendish. Baldwin complained to Cavendish that Dunn did not mind damaging Baldwin to save "a little matter to you." Baldwin claimed he was actually out £120 for the closing arrangements, but if Dunn was to be believed, Cavendish would file a bill in Chancery against him if he would not take £40, requiring Baldwin in turn to file an action against Cavendish

to try to recover the rest of his expenses. Baldwin could not believe that Cavendish wanted to "go through all this" for a "slip of land."[161]

The dispute over the £40 was not yet settled when another arose. Dunn had heard that the people of Clapham planned to pull down all fences on the common. Baldwin, he said, knew of the plan. If this was so, Cavendish "must not give him a farthing for the piece of ground," which encroached on the common. Hearing of this, Baldwin wrote to Cavendish: "In my whole life I never was so heartily tired of any thing as I am of the unmeaning correspondence into which I have been drawn by you and your attorney. . . . I am buried in letters founded in error and ignorance." Baldwin was not going to accept £40, and it was not true that the people of Clapham were going to pull down the fences. It was true, Cavendish said, and he told Baldwin that he was informed that the people of Battersea, the parish neighboring Clapham, planned to tear down the fences on *their* common unless the owners paid them a composition. Cavendish said he was "so confident" of the information he had received—its source, whom he did not name, was an owner of land next to Cavendish's—that he was no longer prepared to pay Baldwin the £40, but only £40 less the composition. It was up to Baldwin to discover the composition the vestry would demand. Baldwin warned Cavendish not to stir up the people of Clapham by spreading the idea of tearing up the fences or else he could lose part of the garden of his new house there. Cavendish replied that if Baldwin did not accept his offer, £40 less composition, and make over the rights to the property in two or three days, he would take it as refusal and act accordingly.[162]

---

[156]Henry Cavendish to Christopher Baldwin, draft, n.d.; Christopher Baldwin to Henry Cavendish, 7 June 1784, Devon. Coll., 86/comp. 1.

[157]Henry Cavendish to Christopher Baldwin, draft, n.d.; Christopher Baldwin to Henry Cavendish, 3 July 1784, Devon. Coll., 86/comp. 1.

[158]Baldwin to Cavendish, 3 July 1784; Thomas Dunn to Henry Cavendish, 7 July and 27 Aug. 1784 and "Friday," Devon. Coll., 86/comp. 1.

[159]"Abstract of the Title . . .," Devon. Coll., L/38/78.

[160]Christopher Baldwin to Henry Cavendish, 7 July /1785/; Henry Cavendish to Christopher Baldwin, draft, n.d. /July 1785/; Thomas Dunn to Henry Cavendish, 6 Sep. 1785, Devon. Coll., 86/comp. 1.

[161]Christopher Baldwin to Henry Cavendish, 19 Sept. 1785, Devon. Coll., 86/comp. 1.

[162]Thomas Dunn to Henry Cavendish, 6 Feb. 1786; Christopher Baldwin to Henry Cavendish, 22 Feb. 1786; Henry Cavendish to

Cavendish asked for a "direct answer," but Baldwin's answer was anything but direct. He asked a question, which was about Cavendish's intention to build a fence between their properties. Even before Cavendish had bought the fifteen acres, Baldwin had sent him "Hints for Consideration," advice to Cavendish about building fences and foundations.[163] Cavendish had not responded. Later, after Cavendish had bought the land, Baldwin told him that his fences were ruined, allowing cattle to break in from the common and enter Baldwin's garden from Cavendish's fields. Baldwin ordered Cavendish immediately to put up the fence between their properties, as Cavendish had proposed to do. He would have put it up long before, Cavendish said, if he had not waited to settle the dispute about the piece of land taken from the common.[164] "I shall observe my agreement about the fence but will not be prescribed to about it nor bear your delays or cavils." Baldwin was to come to Dunn's on Wednesday or Thursday, when Cavendish would be there to execute the deed; otherwise, it would be too late and Cavendish would give him nothing for the land. When Baldwin wrote back asking Cavendish what he meant by saying he would observe his agreement about the fence, Cavendish was driven to the limit. The correspondence between Cavendish and Baldwin came to an end with a flurry of letters, four letters passing between them on one day, the first Saturday in April 1786. Cavendish wrote: "I can not at all conceive what is the cause of this behavior whether you have any private reason for wishing to delay the agreement or whether you distrust my honour about the pailing & wish to make some further conditions about it. If the latter is the true cause you may assure yourself that I will never submit to make any such conditions or explanation with a person who distrusts my honour."[165] The papers were signed a few days later, legally conveying the property to Cavendish.[166] The whole transaction had taken two years.

Baldwin had tried to lighten his negotiations with Cavendish with a learned quotation. He gave up, making a chemical pun of his defeat: "attick salt does not easily unite with matters of business."[167] Doing business with Cavendish was so straightforward that Baldwin never grasped it. Cavendish did not bargain, which would have required social skills he lacked or chose not to use. His way of doing business was to inform himself of value and make a fair offer, which the seller was then to take or leave.

Cavendish's way was not Baldwin's, which was to try to gain advantage by bargaining, pleading, and bluffing. All of this Cavendish simply took to be Baldwin's evasions, with which he had no patience, and yet over the whole course of the transaction, Cavendish was patient. He did not break off negotiations, even when, as he saw it, there was nothing to negotiate. He persevered despite their disagreement over price, their disagreement over lawyer fees, his lawyer's doubts about Baldwin's honesty in dealing with his creditors, his lawyer's suspicions that Baldwin was concealing knowledge of Clapham's plans to tear down fences, their argument over the fences to be built, and Baldwin's delays. He waited out Baldwin. He told Baldwin what he wanted, and if Baldwin complained about it, he did not argue but said what he wanted again, this time more firmly. It worked; for in the end, Cavendish got what he wanted, the land, with clear title, and he got it at his price.

Baldwin misjudged Cavendish from the start, and because he did, he provoked Cavendish into exposing a side of his personality. Baldwin thought that money was the issue throughout, and for him no doubt it was, especially given his large debts. But for Cavendish, the difference between £40 and £60 or the cost of a fence was of no financial consequence. The point was correct procedure. Property transactions were to be conducted fairly, in accordance with property law, business customs, and knowledge of local conditions, without relation to what one privileged party could afford and one needy party might wish for. After an agreement was reached, keeping one's word was a point of

Christopher Baldwin, draft, n.d. /after 22 Feb. 1786/; Christopher Baldwin to Henry Cavendish, 27 Feb. 1786; Henry Cavendish to Christopher Baldwin, draft, n.d. /after 27 Feb. 1786/, Devon. Coll., 86/comp. 1.

[163]Christopher Baldwin to Henry Cavendish, Midsummer's Day, 1784, Devon Coll., 86/comp. 1.

[164]Christopher Baldwin to Henry Cavendish, 8 Feb. /1786/; Henry Cavendish to Christopher Baldwin, draft, n.d. /on or after 8 Feb. 1786/, Devon. Coll., 86/comp. 1.

[165]Christopher Baldwin to Henry Cavendish, 3 Mar. 1786, Saturday /1 Apr. 1786/, Saturday /1 Apr. 1786/; Henry Cavendish to Christopher Baldwin, drafts, 1 Apr. /1786/, n.d. /1 Apr. 1786/, Devon. Coll., 86/comp. 1.

[166]Christopher Baldwin to Henry Cavendish, "Lease for a Year," 5 Apr 1786; "Release of a Piece of Land on Clapham Common," 6 Apr. 1786. At the same time, Baldwin gave up all claim to the original fifteen acres. Christopher Baldwin to Henry Cavendish, "General Release," 6 Apr. 1786. Devon. Coll., L/38/78.

[167]Baldwin to Cavendish, 3 July 1784.

honor. Baldwin's single worst mistake was to doubt the word of Cavendish.

In his correspondence with Baldwin, Cavendish said nothing of his reasons for buying the land. Baldwin thought that Cavendish intended to build on it for himself, and perhaps at first he did, but in the middle of their dealings, Cavendish moved into an existing house on another part of the common. Later Baldwin thought Cavendish intended to rent the land, in which case he asked to be the renter, but Cavendish turned him down.[168] Cavendish had bought an extensive, expensive parcel of land, making him a dominant property owner at Clapham Common. He had made a good investment: at the time of his death twenty-five years later, land on Clapham Common was selling for £500 an acre, a price fifty percent above what he had paid.[169] But land was not where Cavendish chose to invest his money, and it was not primarily as an investment that he bought Baldwin's fields at Clapham Common. Clapham Common was to be his main residence, the place of his scientific researches. By owning a sizable piece of land fronting onto the common, he could conceivably exert local influence if he needed to. But that was probably a side benefit if it was a consideration at all. After Lord Charles's death, Henry Cavendish had a legal analysis made of his parents' marriage settlement. He was told that he could "suffer recoveries" and thereby obtain absolute power of disposal of the land or stocks in question. We do not have the documents that followed from this legal opinion, but we know that Henry Cavendish did pursue recoveries, and the purchase of land was one possible route.[170]

Whatever his motivation, Cavendish arrived on Clapham Common as a developer. He promptly rented Baldwin's former land to three builders at £200 a year each. By the terms of their lease, they were to spend at least £4,000 within four years to build "good & substantial dwelling houses with convenient stables coach houses" and to spend another £6,000 within eight years for the same purpose. When the buildings were "compleated to the satisfaction" of Cavendish, the builders and Cavendish would join in granting separate leases for the houses provided that the rent was payable to

Cavendish and that it was not below a certain amount. The separate leases were to prohibit the building of a brick kiln—which made a terrible stench—on the premises and the use of any buildings as public houses or shops "for carrying on any noisome or offensive trade or business."[171] There would be a proper tone, and the new residents living across the corner of the common from Cavendish would not disturb the quiet of his studies. Five long-term leases agreeable to his conditions were granted, which brought him a total yearly rent of £200.[172]

Ultimately, the money that Cavendish paid Baldwin came from other Cavendishes, and like everything he owned, the Clapham Common property was one day to be returned to other Cavendishes. He assured his Cavendish patrimony and his science by naming as trustees of his Clapham Common estate his closest scientific colleagues in London, Charles Blagden, Alexander Dalrymple, and Alexander Aubert. They were parties to the purchase of the land with the responsibility, which would pass to their heirs, of protecting the inheritance. That is what happened; in due time, in 1827, the heirs of Cavendish's trustees discharged their responsibility by transferring their trusteeships to other persons, who held the Clapham Common estate in trust for the biggest landowning Cavendish of them all, the then current duke of Devonshire.[173]

---

[168]Baldwin to Cavendish, 3 May 1784 and 8 Feb. 1786; Cavendish to Baldwin, draft, n.d. /on or after 8 Feb. 1786/.

[169]In 1810 Robert Thornton sold his land on the common for this price. T. C. Dale, "History of Clapham," in *Clapham and the Clapham Sect*, pp. 1–28, on p. 1.

[170]Henry Cavendish's legal analysis of his parents' marriage settlement, Devon. Coll., L/114/74. From a list, "Deeds and Writings Belonging to the Honble Henry Cavendish," we have the title of a document concerning recoveries but we have not been able to locate the document: "Bargain and Sale Inrolled in Chancery from Henry Cavendish Esq. to Mr. Wilmot for Leading the Uses of Recoveries," 22 Apr. 1784. Ibid.

[171]"Henry Cavendish Esquire and Messrs Hanscomb, Fothergill and Poynder Articles of Agreement for a Building Lease," 2 May 1791, Devon. Coll., L/31/45.

[172]Four leases for buildings and land were signed in 1795, the fifth, to two of the builders themselves, in 1805. A sixth lease, in 1805, was for land only, and it went to the third builder. "Statement of Leases Granted by the Honourable Henry Cavendish of Messuages and Land at Clapham in Surry," Devon. Coll., L/34/10.

[173]"Abstract of the Title . . . ." Henry Cavendish's brother, Frederick, and after him the duke of Devonshire received rents from the Clapham Common estates until they were sold in 1827. Devon. Coll., L/16/20.

CHAPTER 2

Politics

Political fervor, like religious fervor, was unwelcome at the meetings of the Royal Society. The president Sir Joseph Banks took pride in keeping a personal distance from all things having to do with political faction: "I have never entered the doors of the House of Commons," he told Benjamin Franklin at the time of the American Revolution, "& I will tell you that I have escaped a Million of unpleasant hours & preserved no small proportion of Friends of both parties by that fortunate conduct."[1] But within every group, however disinterested in politics in principle, power can become an issue, a truth that would be brought home to Banks the year after his letter to Franklin on the subject of his political innocence.

The inevitability of politics in life would not have been news to Lord Charles Cavendish. When he changed the focus of his work from the House of Commons to the Royal Society, he did not move from a political life to one outside politics. Rather, he moved to a social setting in which he had more control: from a back bench committeeman in parliament, he had become an almost permanent member of the ruling council and a frequent vice-president of the Royal Society. Henry Cavendish did not directly participate in national politics, but he found himself in the middle of a political fight in the Royal Society that reflected the political divisions of the nation at large. The parallels between the Royal Society and the monarch, court, ministers, and parliamentary parties were perfectly obvious to the scientific participants, who liked to point them out.

The Royal Society

In his *History of the Royal Society*, Charles Richard Weld wrote that it was "painful" for him to turn to the events of 1783 and 1784, and he would rather have passed over them in "silence," but duty forbade it. He then proceeded to give what he regarded as an impartial account of the events of the so-called "dissensions," which "turned the hall of science into an arena of angry debate, to the great and manifest detriment of the Society."[2]

The dissensions originated, Weld explained, in a widespread resentment of Joseph Banks, who since the end of 1778 had been the elected president of the Royal Society. A certain faction of the membership was particularly unhappy with Banks's conduct in the election of new members to the Society, which took the following form. Fellows wishing to elect a new member usually brought him to one of Banks's Thursday morning breakfasts. If Banks approved of him, the candidate would then be invited as a guest to a dinner of the Royal Society Club, at which Banks also presided, where he would meet influential members. But if Banks disapproved of the candidate, he would urge individual members to blackball him at balloting time.[3]

For the good of the Society, Banks believed, the members should bring in two kinds of persons: men of science and men of rank. Like the membership at large, the ruling council of the Society contained men of both kinds, and here again in the elections Banks made clear his likes and dislikes, exposing himself to the charge of packing the council with pliant friends. The result of Banks's forceful interference in elections revealed a pattern, so certain members thought, which was a bias against men of science,

---

[1]Joseph Banks to Benjamin Franklin, 9 Aug. 1782, quoted in A Hunter Dupree, *Sir Joseph Banks and the Origins of Science Policy* (Minneapolis: Associates of the James Ford Bell Library, University of Minnesota, 1984), 15.

[2]Charles Richard Weld, *A History of the Royal Society*, 2 vols. (London, 1848) 2:151. This discussion of the Royal Society's dissensions is taken from Russell McCormmach, "Henry Cavendish on the Proper Method of Rectifying Abuses," in *Beyond History of Science: Essays in Honor of Robert E. Schofield*, ed. E. Garber (Bethlehem, Lehigh Univ. Press, 1990), 35–51. We acknowledge permission by the Associated University Presses to use material from this article.

[3]Weld, *History* 2:152–54.

particularly men of the mathematical sciences, and in favor of men of rank. Their dissatisfaction with Banks came to a head in, as Weld termed it, the "violent dissentions, foreign to matters of science," of 1783 and 1784.[4]

In Weld's account and in other historical accounts of the dissensions, Henry Cavendish receives only one brief mention, if any at all. Passages from violent speeches are quoted at greater or lesser length, but Cavendish is recalled only for his seconding of a motion of approval of Banks as president of the Society.[5] This, to be sure, was the only time Cavendish entered the public record of the dissensions, but there was much more to Cavendish's involvement than this, as there almost had to be given the stakes and the eminence of Cavendish in the Society. At the height of the dissensions, Charles Blagden, who at the time was both a scientific assistant to Cavendish and personal assistant to Banks, wrote daily letters to Banks, which afford us a detailed account of Cavendish's thoughts and actions.

To understand Cavendish's part in the dissensions, we need to recall some of the characteristics of the Cavendishes in politics with which we began this biography. A contemporary historian writes of the Cavendishes:

> Much was heard of the "great Revolution families"—of whom some of the proudest, as Sir Lewis Namier has pointed out, were in fact descended from Charles II's bastards. These families—above all, perhaps, the Cavendishes—could not forget that their ancestors had, as it were, conferred the crown upon the king's ancestors, and they did not mean to let him forget it either, for they alluded to it in season and out of season. They looked upon themselves as his creators rather than his creation: one would almost say that they had forgotten that the dukedom of Devonshire itself had been established, less than a century earlier, by the merely human agency of a king.[6]

Edmund Burke observed in 1771 that "No wise king of Great Britain would think it for his credit to let it go abroad that he considered himself, or was considered by others, as personally at variance with . . . the families of the Cavendishes."[7]

George III, Burke also believed, was no wise king. Whereas the first two Georges had had to conciliate the families of, and to reconcile themselves to the principles of, the Glorious Revolution, George III could take for granted the security of the dynasty. Upon acceding to the throne in 1760, he immediately set about to break the power of the old whig families. In fact, although it was not entirely obvious at the time, the whig ascendancy had come to an end. Marking this historic turn was the resignation in 1762 of the fourth duke of Devonshire; never again could the Devonshires assume that high office was their birthright. At just this time, Henry Cavendish entered the world of science; *if* he had desired a life in politics, and *if* he had been adept at politics as he was at science, he might well have turned against his wishes and wisely chosen a life in science all the same. We have an idea of the kind of politician Henry Cavendish would have been from his part in the dissensions of the Royal Society. He would have been a politician of a very recognizable Cavendish variety.

Devonshire House, the Piccadilly mansion of the dukes of Devonshire, was the London headquarters of the whigs.[8] The whigs of the 1780s, the so-called New Whigs, were libertarian, passionately opposed to George III's policy on the American colonies, and admiring of Charles James Fox, the most implacable of George III's personal enemies.[9] This whig leader and his king were in fundamental disagreement about power: Fox believed that power was properly exercised only through the king's ministers, whereas George III believed that his ministers were bound by loyalty to uphold his policy. George III found unintelligible Fox's doctrine that the king was to enjoy no personal power, that he was merely to sit on the throne, not to rule from it. In the ensuing constitutional struggle between George III and Fox and his allies, the government of the kingdom was brought to a standstill. The person of George III was *the* political issue, as John Dunning's famous resolution of 1780, which was favored by a

---

[4] Ibid., 2:153, 170. Henry Lyons, *The Royal Society, 1660–1940: A History of Its Administration under Its Charters* (New York: Greenwood, 1968), 198–99.

[5] Weld, *History* 2:162. Lyons, *Royal Society*, 213.

[6] Richard Pares, *King George III and the Politicians* (Oxford: Clarendon, 1953), 58–59.

[7] The plural "families" was used by Burke because there was more than one politically influential Cavendish family. In the sentence quoted, Burke referred to several political leaders in addition to the Cavendishes. Pares, *King George III and the Politicians*, 59.

[8] Whigs are the subject of Hugh Stokes, *The Devonshire House Circle* (London: Herbert Jenkins, 1917).

[9] John Pearson, *The Serpent and the Stag: the Saga of England's Powerful and Glamourous Cavendish Family from the Age of Henry the Eighth to the Present* (New York: Holt, Rinehart and Winston, 1983), 128–29.

parliamentary majority, asserted: "That the influence of the Crown has increased, is increasing, and ought to be diminished."[10] The years 1783–84, it has been argued, witnessed the greatest political crisis in Britain since the Revolution of 1688.[11]

It was these same years, 1783–84, that witnessed the dissensions of the Royal Society, in which the president, Joseph Banks, was accused, like George III, of desiring personal rule. The regular business of the Society was brought to a standstill. While Henry Cavendish's relatives, above all his first cousin and chancellor of the exchequer Lord John Cavendish, were actively concerned with the constitutional crisis, Henry himself was actively concerned with the crisis in the Royal Society. Henry was, according to a relative who was in a position to know, "very proud of his family name,"[12] and the nature of his activity in the political affairs of the Royal Society was as characteristically "Cavendish" as his slouching gait. Just what this means we will take up later after first discussing the dissensions of the Royal Society and Cavendish's place in them.

The political crisis in the Royal Society began with a disagreement between the president and his council on the one hand and the foreign secretary, the mathematician Charles Hutton, on the other. Unlike the two regular secretaries of the Society, the foreign secretary was not necessarily on the ruling council. When Hutton was elected to his office in 1779, he happened also to be an elected member of the council, but after 1780, when the dissensions occurred, he was no longer. The first indication of the disagreement was recorded at a meeting of the council on 24 January 1782, at which time Hutton's responsibility and performance were taken up. The one was judged onerous, the other inadequate: Hutton, it was decided, had not dealt punctually with the foreign correspondence, his first obligation; he was also overworked and underpaid, which seemed a likely reason for the tardiness. The council resolved that in the future, Hutton should not be expected also to translate foreign articles and extracts from foreign books, and in return he was not to fall behind in the foreign correspondence. Hutton agreed to continue on as foreign secretary with this new understanding. Nothing more was heard of the matter publicly until nearly two years later when, at a meeting of the council on 20 November 1783, it was resolved

that the foreign secretary of the Society had to live permanently in London. Hutton was professor of mathematics at the Royal Military Academy of Woolwich and so could not live in London. Two members of the council, the astronomer royal, Maskelyne, and one of the regular secretaries of the Society Paul Maty, dissented from this move, which was obviously directed against Hutton. Hutton promptly resigned. At the ordinary meeting of the Society on 11 December 1783, it was moved that Hutton be formally thanked for his services as secretary for foreign correspondence. Banks opposed the motion, which was vigorously debated. The motion passed by a narrow margin, and Banks duly thanked Hutton. At the following meeting, on 18 December, Hutton delivered, and a secretary read aloud, a written defense of his handling of the foreign correspondence. Afterwards, a motion was made and carried that Hutton had justified himself, which again was attended by a vigorous debate. The mathematician Samuel Horsley attacked Banks, accusing him of infringing upon the chartered rights of the Society. Horsley said he knew of enough wrongs to keep the Society "in debate the whole winter . . . perhaps beyond the winter."[13]

The prospect of a winter of discontent, spent in acrimonious debate, was abhorrent to Cavendish, who regarded the serious scientific purpose of the Society as inviolable. At this point he became actively—if invisibly to all but a handful of members—engaged in shaping the outcome of the dissensions. His activity is reported in letters Blagden wrote daily from London to Banks at his country house.

It quickly became apparent that the person of Joseph Banks was *the* issue. The debates, highly personal in tone, turned on a scientific judgment. The question the members had to answer was this: had the Society been seriously damaged scientifically by its president, Banks? To inform Banks, Blagden delicately inquired into Cavendish's position on the question. Naturally, Banks needed to know where the Society's *scientifically* most eminent member stood.

---

[10]Pares, *King George III and the Politicians*, 119–25, 134–35.
[11]John Cannon, *The Fox-North Coalition: Crisis of the Constitution, 1782–4* (Cambridge: Cambridge University Press, 1969), x–xi.
[12]Lady Sarah Spencer quoted in Stokes, *Devonshire House Circle*, 315.
[13]Weld, *History* 2:154–60.

On Monday, four days after the stormy meeting of the Royal Society, after dining at their scientific club, Cavendish went with Blagden to his home, where they discussed the troubles of the Society.[14] That morning Cavendish had gone to see William Heberden, and the two of them had arrived at a common position. Blagden reported that Cavendish and Heberden would support Banks, but "just." While Cavendish did not "absolutely refuse a vote of approbation" of Banks, he would absolutely reject any resolution that, by its wording, would seem to pass censure on Horsley and his friends for what they had done in the past. They had given no evidence of acting out of any motive other than the good of the Society, Cavendish said. Furthermore, the good of the Society required of its members just such vigilant scrutiny of their president and council. But Cavendish did not mean for this watch to take the form of debates during regular meetings, which disrupted the scientific business of the Society. To put a stop to the debates without denying the members their rights, Cavendish proposed a resolution, which he believed would be passed by a very large majority. From dictation Blagden wrote down the resolution and then read it back, to make sure of the wording:

> That the proper method of rectifying any abuses which may arise in the society is, by choosing into the council such persons as it is supposed will exert themselves in removing the abuses and not by interrupting the ordinary meetings of the society with debates.

Blagden did not think that this resolution would have the result Cavendish expected of it. Horsley would agree that it was the task of a new council to remedy the abuses, but he would argue that for the Society to be made aware of the abuses, the debates must continue. Cavendish thought that such an argument from Horsley would carry weight, but there was an effective answer to it. For example, the Society could inform itself of any abuses by holding special meetings for the purpose. Then if Horsley persisted with his interruptions, the Society would be within its rights to censure him. Blagden gave Banks his opinion after this conference with Cavendish: the resolution Cavendish proposed was probably the best of any proposed so far, and if to it was added another resolution to the effect that any motion had to be announced at the meeting before it was

to be debated, the whole affair might be brought to a speedy and favorable conclusion.[15]

But Cavendish's resolution omitted all mention of support for the incumbent president, Banks, which was something less than Blagden and Banks had hoped from him. Cavendish did not even want to talk to Banks about past councils because he found it awkward. With the help of Blagden's prompting, however, Cavendish recalled past presidents he had served under. Banks's predecessor, the physician John Pringle, Cavendish said, had acted like Banks and had given rise to the same complaint about ineffective councils.[16] Pringle's predecessor, the antiquary James West, was "King Log" (of Aesop's fable of the frogs who desired a king to watch over their morals and were thrown an incipid log instead). But West's predecessor, the astronomer and mathematician Lord Morton, handled the affairs of the Society in an unexceptional way. Cavendish allowed that Banks's method of choosing the candidates for council was fair; but he blamed Banks for not doing as Morton did, which was to "put in people who would have an opinion of their own, without agreeing implicitly with the President in every thing." Cavendish believed that if his resolution carried, it would mean that on election day there would be a contest. He wanted Blagden to reassure Banks that he would support the "House list" on election day unless it was "very exceptionable." He also wanted Blagden to tell Banks that he did not want to be consulted on the list beforehand, as Banks hoped he would (for it would have tended to forestall further criticism of Banks concerning the scientific respectability of the council).[17]

The day after he talked to Cavendish, Blagden went to see Heberden. Heberden had not only talked with Cavendish but also with Banks

[14]On Monday evenings, Cavendish and Blagden generally dined together at their club meeting at the George & Vulture, which we assume is what brought them together on that Monday, 22 December 1783.

[15]Charles Blagden to Sir Joseph Banks, 22 December 1783; original letter in Fitzwilliam Museum Library; copy in BM(NH), DTC 3 171–72.

[16]Yet Banks's opponents professed to admire Pringle, at least in certain respects, and wished Banks were more like him. Personality and political temper, not consistency of argument, gave the dissensions of 1783–84 their impetus. Weld, *History* 2:160–61.

[17]Charles Blagden to Sir Joseph Banks, 22 December 1783. Charles Blagden to Sir Joseph Banks, Wednesday morning, 24 December 1783; original letter in Fitzwilliam Museum Library; copy in BM(NH), DTC 3:176.

and with one of Banks's opponents, no doubt Horsley, and his opinion was settled. His opinion was the same as Cavendish's: the proper method of correcting abuses was to choose the proper council, and Banks was fit for his office. To Blagden's proposal of a vote of approval of Banks, Heberden said that he would vote for it and that if it should pass almost unanimously, the disturbances would die down, but he objected to it on the grounds that it would prompt a debate about Banks's conduct and inflame the passions it was intended to quiet. No "method," he believed, would prevent Horsley from bringing motions from time to time. So from Cavendish and Heberden, two highly respected, senior members of the Society, Banks received the same advice: let the Society affirm that power was invested in the elected council and not in the Society acting as a body any time it should choose, nor, it went without saying, in the person of the president, whoever he happened to be.[18]

Blagden wrote to Banks twice the next day, 24 December. In the morning he wrote to say that Cavendish was probably at his country house at Hampstead. He did not want to go there, since it would appear "too solicitous," and instead he intended to go to Cavendish's townhouse.[19] Later in the day Blagden wrote again, this time to say that he had left a note for Cavendish telling of his meeting with Heberden and conveying Banks's wish that Cavendish would come to his house the next day. Cavendish, finding the note, had then called on Blagden to tell him that he could not go to Banks's house. To this, Blagden wrote to Banks that it was "possible" that Cavendish had set aside the following day for doing experiments, but most likely he wanted to avoid an "embarrassing conversation" with Banks. Banks was to be reassured that Cavendish was not "hostile" toward him and wanted to remain on good terms with him. It was only necessary that Banks allow Cavendish to differ with him in opinion at any time "without an open quarrel," which was to repeat what Cavendish wanted of Banks in his dealings with the council.[20]

Blagden then turned their conversation to the principal disrupter of the meetings of the Society, Banks's enemy, Horsley. Blagden put their conversation in quotation marks so that Banks would have Cavendish's exact meaning. (Being the only recorded spoken words by the reserved Henry Cavendish, these quotations hold an interest of their own.)

CAVENDISH: I did not expect any success from the Drs negotiations [Dr. Heberden and, no doubt, Dr. Horsley's]. But whatever violence *they* may express, that is no reason against proceeding with all moderation, as by such conduct the sense of the Society will be ensured against them.

BLAGDEN: I wish you would see Dr. H[orsley] & learn from himself the implacable temper expressed; as I think you would then change the opinion to which you seemed inclined when we conversed last, that those gentlemen might have nothing in view but the good of the Society.

CAVENDISH: I did not say they had nothing else in view, but only that no proof yet appeared of other motives.

At the end of their conversation, Cavendish came around to Blagden's position: he, like Heberden, would approve a vote of confidence in Banks, but only if its wording gave no offense. With this, Blagden declared himself highly satisfied with the results of his mediation.[21] What remained to be done was to bring the right members together to determine a course of action.

The next day was a Thursday, ordinarily a day on which the Society met, but this Thursday was Christmas. Blagden did not take a holiday from his politicking but made plans that day to see Banks.[22] On Friday, Banks wrote to Blagden that since his meeting with Heberden, at which he learned that Heberden would not support any motion that would suppress debate in the slightest, he was forced to change his "plan" somewhat. Lest his supporters think him cold-blooded and abandon the cause, Banks intended to come to town on Monday with a modified plan. Blagden was to summon certain persons to meet with him. He would "strike while the iron is hot."[23]

---

[18]Charles Blagden to Sir Joseph Banks, 23 December 1783, Fitzwilliam Museum Library, Perceval H. 199.

[19]Blagden to Banks, Wednesday morning, 24 December 1783.

[20]Charles Blagden to Sir Joseph Banks, 24 December 1783; original letter in Fitzwilliam Museum Library; copy in BM(NH), DTC 3:177–79.

[21]Throughout the dissensions, Banks's supporters usually advised, as Cavendish did here, moderation. Banks's opponents would either become moderate or by their violence turn the Society away from them and into Banks's camp; they were, that is, to be offered the rope to hang themselves. Some of them accepted.

[22]Blagden to Banks, 24 December 1783.

[23]Sir Joseph Banks to Charles Blagden, 26 December 1783, Blagden Letters, Royal Society, B.25.

In anticipation of a crucial vote to come, some members of the Society were busy canvassing against Banks. On Saturday Blagden, who was canvassing for Banks, reported to Banks his findings to date. He named several persons who would definitely support Banks, but some of them would oppose any motion that would limit debate, which meant they would oppose Cavendish's resolution. Their compromise proposal would grant the Society both its usual hour for the reading of scientific papers and conducting other normal business and also time for unlimited free debate. Every member would have the right to make a motion and the president would have to remain in his chair for as long after the hour as the debate went on. Blagden thought that the great majority of the Society wanted Banks to remain president, but on the question of free debate he did not know how the Society would come down.[24]

In his Saturday letter and in another letter on Sunday, Blagden alerted Banks to the serious trouble he was in. "Great opposition is making against you," Blagden said, and he named some members who were "decidedly against [Banks] even on the subject of the Presidency." So far as he could learn, Blagden said, they intended to put Lord Mahon in Banks's place. The alleged injustice done to Hutton as foreign secretary was only the occasion of the dissensions; their real cause was a "grudge of very long standing," backed by many grievances.[25] For example, Banks's opponents charged him with excluding deserving men from the Society because they were not of sufficient social rank. The able mathematician Henry Clark, they said, was kept out because he was merely a schoolmaster. And the membership of the last council they held in derision. The battle line, as they drew it, was between Banks's fancy gentlemen, or "Maccaronis," and the "men of Science."[26]

When Banks came to town on Monday, he held a meeting at his house. Cavendish, who already had stayed away from one earlier meeting at Banks's, may have stayed away from this one, too. But whether or not he was there, he entered centrally into the planning done there. To a letter to Banks, Blagden attached a postscript dated Monday, 29 December, which read:

> Resolved, That this Society approve of Sir Jos: Banks as their President, and mean to support him in that office.

"Such, my dear friend," Blagden wrote to Banks, "is the resolution Mr. C. has just approved at my house." In Blagden's view, the vote on this resolution would sort out Banks's friends from his foes. Cavendish, he added, still thought that the resolution he first proposed would prove necessary, since the Society would not agree that under the present statutes they are forbidden to debate except at the day of elections.[27]

The next day Blagden wrote to Banks that Horsley was busy telling his friends that Banks was going to try to expel him at the next meeting, in that way insuring an ample turnout of Horsley's friends.[28] To ensure that his own friends turned out, Banks sent a card to all members of the Society requesting their attendance at the next meeting. When the meeting took place, on 8 January 1784, some 170 members came, fewer than half of whom attended regularly. From the president's chair, facing the massed assembly, Banks watched as "each side took their station and looked as important as if matters of the utmost consequence to the State were the subject of their deliberation."[29] As planned, the accountant general of the Society T. Anguish rose to make the motion. The previous two meetings of the Society, he reminded his audience, had been

---

[24]Charles Blagden to Sir Joseph Banks, 27 December 1783; original letter in Fitzwilliam Museum Library; copy in BM(NH), DTC 3:180–81.

[25]Blagden to Banks, 23 and 27 December 1783. *Supplement* to Friend to Dr. Hutton, *An Appeal to the Fellows of the Royal Society, Concerning the Measures Taken by Sir Joseph Banks, Their President, to Compel Dr. Hutton to Resign the Office of Secretary to the Society for Their Correspondence* (London, 1784), 11,15. Charles Stanhope, Lord Mahon, the gifted electrician and inventor, at the close of the meeting of the Royal Society on 8 January, discussed below, moved that in the future no motion should be made in the ordinary course of business without giving notice two weeks in advance. This motion, which was supposed to discourage spontaneous agitation at the meetings, was seconded and passed unanimously. Lord Mahon, who was also active in parliament at the time of the dissensions, would go on to become one of the founders of the Revolution Society in 1788. For a time he was in harmony with the whig opposition led by Fox. Later he became increasingly isolated, and reviled, because of his persistent championing of the ideals of the French Revolution. F. M. Beatty, "The Scientific Work of the Third Earl Stanhope," *Notes and Records of the Royal Society* 11 (1955): 217-19.

[26]Blagden to Banks, 27 December 1783. Charles Blagden to Sir Joseph Banks, 28 December 1783, Fitzwilliam Museum Library, Perceval H 202.

[27]Postscript dated 29 December 1783, Blagden to Banks, 28 December 1783.

[28]Charles Blagden to Sir Joseph Banks, 30 December 1783, Fitzwilliam Museum Library, Perceval H 203.

[29]Notes of the meeting taken by Banks, quoted in Hector Charles Cameron, *Sir Joseph Banks, K B., P. R. S.: The Autocrat of the Philosophers* (London: Batchworth, 1952), 134.

disrupted by debates, and at the second of these, Horsley had threatened to keep the Society debating the rest of the winter, the obvious intent of which was to unseat Banks. The motion Anguish put to the members was the resolution approving of Banks, which Cavendish had earlier approved. Cavendish now seconded the resolution before the Society. Cavendish said nothing in support of it, and there is no evidence that he said anything else during this long night of angry speeches.[30]

The first speech was made by E. Poore, a barrister at law in Lincoln's Inn, who called the motion a dishonorable attempt to evade scrutiny of Banks's conduct by praising it. The attempt would not succeed, he said; it would not stop debate (and did not, as Cavendish and Heberden had predicted). Francis Maseres, cursitor baron of the exchequer, said that for the Society to exercise its power of election of president and council, the Society had first to discuss the question of Banks's "abuse of power." Horsley said that the "abuses are enormous," and he went on about them at such length that Banks's supporters clamored for the question, almost drowning him out with their cries and with a clattering of sticks. As a last resort, Horsley said, "the scientific part of the Society" would secede, which would leave Banks leading his "feeble *amateurs*," his mace standing for the "ghost of that Society in which philosophy once reigned and Newton presided as her minister." Maskelyne said that if it proved necessary to secede, the "*best* Society would be the *Royal* Society in fact, though not in name." The mathematician James Glenie was interrupted before he could finish what he had to say, which was that the present council was incapable of understanding mathematics, mechanics, astronomy, optics, and chemistry, and that the Society as led by Banks, a natural historian, was degenerating into a "cabinet of trifling curiosities," a "virtuoso's closet decorated with plants and shells." When late in the evening the motion was finally put to a vote, it carried 119 to 42. By a three to one margin, the Society wished Banks to continue as their president.[31] This, then, was the outcome of the meetings, letters, maneuverings, and canvassing. The safest course had been taken by Banks's supporters. The resolution contained no detail; it said nothing about limiting debates, nothing about abuses, nothing about reforms, nothing, that is, that might divide the majority.

The opponents of Banks as well as his supporters claimed that they longed for a return of "tranquility, order, harmony, and accord" and the "instructive business of these weekly meetings, *the reading of the learned papers presented to the Society*."[32] For three consecutive meetings, however, the debates had prevented the reading of all new scientific papers. Only John Michell's great paper on the distance and other measures of the fixed stars, which Cavendish had communicated to the Royal Society, continued to be read at two of these meetings, on 11 and 18 December, while at the third meeting, on 8 January, no papers at all were read.[33]

The main new paper read together with Michell's at the next, the January 15, meeting was no run-of-the-mill paper. It was a paper by Cavendish, destined to be his most famous, "Experiments on Air," containing his discovery of the production of water from the explosion of gases. Coming after three meetings in which the members had listened to speeches contrasting the present, feeble state of the Royal Society with what it had been in Newton's day, and coming one week after Cavendish had seconded the successful motion approving of Banks's presidency, the reading of Cavendish's work at the first opportunity was clearly a power move, and if by any chance it was not calculated, the effect was the same.[34]

----

[30][Paul Maty], *An Authentic Narrative of the Dissensions and Debates in the Royal Society, Containing the Speeches at Large of Dr. Horsley, Dr. Maskelyne, Mr. Maseres, Mr. Poore, Mr. Glenie, Mr. Watson, and Mr. Maty* (London, 1784), 24–25. *Supplement to the Appeal to the Fellows of the Royal Society; Being Letters Taken from the Public Advertiser and Morning Post* (London, 1784), 9.

[31]*Narrative*, 26–77. *Supplement*, 9. Royal Society, JB 31 (1782–85): 270–71. Despite charges to the contrary, in the Royal Society at this time, the physical sciences looked to be flourishing and appreciated. At the St. Andrew's Day meeting for elections on 1 December 1783, Banks gave a discourse on two Copley Medals, one awarded to John Goodricke for his paper on the variation of the star Algol, the other to Thomas Hutchins for his experiments, which Cavendish took part in, on freezing mercury. Entry for 1 December 1783, Royal Society, JB.

[32]*Narrative*, 30, 70.

[33]Blagden to Claude Louis Berthollet, 13 January 1784, draft, Blagden Letterbook, Yale. Royal Society, JB 31:265, 268–71. On 27 November 1783, the reading began of the paper by John Michell, "On the Means of Discovering the Distance, Magnitude, etc. of the Fixed Stars, in Consequence of the Diminution of the Velocity of Their Light, in Case Such a Diminution Should Be Found to Take Place in Any of Them, and Such Other Data Should Be Procured from Observations, as Would Be Farther Necessary for that Purpose," *PT* 74 (1784): 35–57.

[34]Henry Cavendish, "Experiments on Air," *PT* 74 (1784): 119–69: reprinted in *The Scientific Papers of the Honourable Henry Cavendish, F. R. S.*, vol. 2: *Chemical and Dynamical*, E. Thorpe, ed. (Cambridge: Cambridge University Press, 1921), 161–81. The juxtaposition is reflected in a letter Banks received from abroad at the time. Its author begins by saying that the Royal Society's dissensions "have made a good deal of noise on the Continent," that the opposition

This business-as-usual, the quiet reading of the papers, was not to last. The new statute requiring all motions to be announced in advance did not produce the desired calm. Duly announced was a motion to reinstate Hutton in his office, and it and motions to restrain Banks's interference with elections led predictably to renewed debates in late January and February.[35] At a meeting in March, Maty gave a speech and then went on to read papers, as was his duty. Horsley was at that meeting but few of his supporters came. Banks took hope, writing to Blagden that there was now peace at the Society and that it was likely to remain.[36] This was not to be.

The printing of the *Philosophical Transactions* had been held up because of the dissensions, and in general the affairs of the Society remained in turmoil.[37] Maty, who had "distinguished himself by his violence against Sir Jos. Banks," in Blagden's words, resigned as secretary of the Society.[38] Banks sent another card to all members of the Society on 29 March, this one to tell them of the vacancy left by Maty and that, "at his desire," Blagden had declared himself a candidate for the office and that Blagden would make an admirable secretary. Banks's opponents took fresh offense and referred to Banks's card as the "President's Congé d'Elire."[39]

The row over the election of Maty's replacement alarmed Cavendish. New contingency plans were laid with Cavendish again taking part and for the same reason. On Monday, 5 April, Blagden told Banks that Cavendish and his friend Alexander Dalrymple had accompanied him home that evening to determine the "proper measures for preventing a few turbulent individuals from continuing to interrupt the peace of the R. S." Cavendish was willing to join a committee or to call a meeting to form a plan of action and draft appropriate resolutions. The general idea was that the committee would present the resolutions to the much larger meeting of members, the composition of which was to be decided by the committee. If the resolutions were acceptable to these members, they would be expected to vote for them at such times when the dissensions again interrupted the scientific work of the Society. From a list of members, Cavendish selected seven who would draft the resolutions. Heberden was one of them, and when Blagden said that Heberden probably would not join them, Cavendish offered to go to

Heberden the next morning to try to persuade him. Cavendish had nothing against taking the lead except for his general "unfitness for active exertions."[40] That evening Cavendish wrote to Blagden: "It is determined that Mr Aubert & I shall go to Dr H[eberden] & see what we can do. If it is to no purpose a larger meeting will be called & very likely some resolution similar to what you mentioned proposed to them."[41]

Despite his general disclaimer, Cavendish took an "active part," Blagden wrote to tell Banks the next day, to "render the R. S. more peaceable." Cavendish had called not only on Heberden but also on Francis Wollaston and Alexander Aubert, and he was going to write to William Watson, all of whom were on Cavendish's list of seven, and he had even called for the meeting to take place in his house and had settled on a time for it.[42]

That is the last we hear of Cavendish's efforts to restore peace to the Royal Society. One month later the Society voted for the secretary to replace Maty. Hutton, the deposed foreign secretary and still the primary rallying cause for Banks's opponents, ran against Banks's man, Blagden. The vote was again not close, 139 to 39, in favor of Blagden. Banks in effect had made the election of the secretary a vote of confidence in him, since he had endorsed Blagden who had served throughout the stormy times as Banks's proxy.[43] Banks's victory was conclusive. Blagden wrote to a foreign correspondent that the disaffected members of the Society had not only

to Banks seems to have acted with "extraordinary animosity," and that Banks's report that the troubles are "nearly quelled" is welcomed news. The author's next observation is that Cavendish's discovery of the production of water from air is "one of the greatest steps that have been made" towards understanding the elements. T. A. Mann to Banks, 4 June 1784, published in Henry Ellis, ed., *Original Letters of Eminent Literary Men of the Sixteenth, Seventeenth, and Eighteenth Centuries* (London, 1843), 426–29, on 426–27.

[35] Weld, *History* 2:162–64. *Narrative*, 79–134.
[36] Sir Joseph Banks to Charles Blagden, 6 March 1784, Blagden Letters, Royal Society, B.26.
[37] Charles Blagden to le comte de C., 2 April 1784, draft, Blagden Letterbook, Yale.
[38] Charles Blagden to le comte de C., 14 May 1784, draft, Blagden Letterbook, Yale.
[39] Weld, *History* 2:165. *Supplement*, 12.
[40] Charles Blagden to Sir Joseph Banks, 5 April 1784, BM(NH), DTC 3:20–21.
[41] Henry Cavendish to Charles Blagden, Monday evening [5 April 1784,] Blagden Papers, Royal Society, c 26.
[42] Blagden to Banks, 5 April 1784. Charles Blagden to Sir Joseph Banks, 6 April 1784, BM(NH), DTC 3:22–23.
[43] Weld, *History* 2:165–66.

failed in their plan to unseat Banks but in the end had planted him in his seat more firmly than ever.[44] After the event, the dissensions seemed hardly more than a tempest in a teapot to Blagden, who was surprised that foreigners took such interest in that "foolish & trifling affair, as it really was with us."[45] The most important evidence for this was that science had not stopped: to a friend, Blagden wrote that "notwithstanding the interruption given to our business in the Royal Society by some turbulent members . . . several valuable papers have been read, and some discoveries of the first magnitude announced," adding that "of these, the most remarkable was made by Mr Cavendish."[46]

During the dissensions, Cavendish was not on the council of the Royal Society, so he had no direct part in the Hutton affair, which had brought them on. (If he had been on the council, the case against Banks would have been substantially weakened. Banks would not be exposed this way again. Before Banks became president of the Royal Society in 1778, Cavendish had frequently sat on the council, but in the years following, 1778–84, he was on it only *once*. In 1785, the year after the dissensions, Cavendish was elected to the council, as he was *every* year after that through 1809, just before his death.) As an ordinary member without office, Cavendish attended all of the meetings of the Society at which the great debates took place. Insofar as we have record, he made no public speeches at any of them. He seconded, undoubtedly by prearrangement, the motion approving Banks's presidency, but nothing more. That was all that was needed, for Cavendish was not simply another member of the Society. First of all, he was a *Cavendish*, a name which carried an authority of its own. He owed nothing to, and needed nothing from, Banks, and for him to act out of personal gain or personal loyalty or disloyalty would have been seen as acting out of character. Second, he was universally respected for his achievements in physical science, not natural history, and he was also known to be a good mathematician. If Cavendish had sided with Horsley and his friends, mathematicians who styled themselves as the genuine scientific element of the Society, Banks's credibility would have been shaken and the voting conceivably could have gone differently. Blagden fully understood this, which is why Cavendish was

the key to his stratagems to save Banks's presidency, as his letters to Banks reveal. Cavendish's endorsement of Banks by seconding the crucial motion was a *scientific* answer to Horsley's characterization of Banks's men as feeble amateurs.

Blagden, in a letter of 2 April 1784 in which he referred to the dissensions at the Royal Society, also spoke of "our internal operations in politics, & the consequent general election, [which] have set the whole kingdom in a ferment; it is a very interesting scene which the wisest & steadiest among us contemplate not without emotion."[47] Scientific and general politics were constantly being compared in the course of the dissensions. The one side spoke of the "ruins of liberty," the other side of Englishmen "apt to be mad with ideas of liberty, ill understood."[48] Again, the one side spoke of the "leveling spirit and impatience of all government which infects the present age," the other side of the Royal Society as a "republic," according to which all laws decided by the council are to be debated by the entire membership whenever a mover and a seconder wish it.[49] Or

[44]Blagden to le comte de C., 2 April 1784.
[45]Charles Blagden to Sir Joseph Banks, 9 August 1788, BL Add Mss 33272, pp. 50–51. Blagden believed that the affair was behind them. While it is true that the dissensions did not flare up again, smoldering resentments continued to the end of Banks's long presidency, in 1820. David Philip Miller, "Sir Joseph Banks: An Historiographical Perspective," *History of Science* 19 (1981): 284–92, on 289. Some dozen years after his dismissal as foreign secretary, Charles Hutton gave an embittered description of the Royal Society in his *Mathematical and Philosophical Dictionary*. The entry "Royal Society of London" begins: "This once illustrious body . . ." The meeting hour of the Society had been adjusted to the convenience of "gentlemen of fashion." The *Philosophical Transactions* "were, till lately, very respectable. . . . Indeed this once very respectable society, now consisting of a great proportion of honorary members, who do not usually communicate papers; and many scientific members being discouraged from making their usual communications, by what is deemed the arbitrary government of the society, the *Philosophical Transactions* have badly deteriorated." Charles Hutton, *A Mathematical and Philosophical Dictionary*, 2 vols. (London, 1795–96) 2:399–400.
[46]Charles Blagden to Charles Grey, 3 June 1784, draft, Blagden Letterbook, Yale .
[47]Blagden to le comte de C., 2 April 1784. Writing to Banks three days later, on 5 April, about the dissensions, Blagden added a postscript concerning the elections in London.
[48]J. Glenie's speech on 8 January, quoted in *Narrative*, 70. Blagden to Berthollet, 13 January 1784.
[49]Blagden to Banks, 28 December 1783. Letter written by Michael Lort to Lord Percy, 14 February 1784, at the height of the dissensions, quoted in Weld, *History* 2:169. Lort was a friend of Cavendish, who brought him as a guest to the Royal Society before he was elected. Lort elaborated his view of the connection between the politics of the Royal Society and that of the country: at the Royal Society "every fortnight a set of orators get up and fatigue themselves, and much the greater part of the Society with virulent

again the one side urged a democratic solution to the abuses of the Society, while the other warned of an illegal "democratic infringement on the principles of the constitution," which was "very much like what was passing in another place."[50] The analogy between scientific debates and those "passing in another place," parliament, was made explicit. When speakers against Banks were shouted down and the question was demanded, Maskelyne said that he had been at other meetings that modeled their debates after the example of parliament, and there the question was not put until everyone had had a chance to speak.[51] The favorite analogy was between Banks as president of the Royal Society and the king or some official in government. Horsley described Banks's call upon the members to elect Blagden as their secretary as a "nomination by the president, *as their sovereign*, of the person he would have them chuse; which is exactly similar to the proceeding of the king in the nomination of a new bishop."[52] Horsley's colleague Maty said that his view of the presidency of the Royal Society is of a "presidency of bare order, like that of the Speaker of the House of Commons, and in Council the President ought not to lead more than any other person."[53] Banks's opponents talked of his despotism, of his dictatorial ways, of his wish for dominion. The age of absolute monarchs was over, but Banks seemed not to have noticed, they said. But the supporters of Banks did not wish for an absolute monarch any more than his detractors did, and none was more definite on this subject than Henry Cavendish.

In explaining Cavendish's behavior to Banks, Blagden drew the appropriate parallel between Cavendish's position in science and that of his relatives in politics. "The sum is," Blagden wrote to Banks, "that like his namesakes elsewhere, he is so far loyal as to prefer you to any other King, but chooses to load the crown with such shackles, that it shall scarcely be worth a gentleman's wearing."[54] With regard to Cavendish's "grievance" against Banks, Blagden wrote again to Banks, "It is exactly the old story of an absolute Monarchy, whereas he [Cavendish] thinks the Sovereign cannot be too much limited."[55] In a more reassuring voice, Blagden wrote to Banks after a meeting with Cavendish, "The utmost consequence will be, some diminution of power, but none of dignity."[56]

The Nation

Although the arena in which Henry Cavendish acted upon his political views was the Royal Society, in his manner of acting he resembled the Cavendishes in parliament. An appropriate Cavendish to bring up for comparison is William Cavendish, the fourth duke and older first cousin to Henry. The fourth duke held high positions in government including, briefly, the position of prime minister in 1756–57. In the political diary he kept, the fourth duke revealed, his editors write, his "complete self-assurance as to his place in the order of the world. He sits in [Privy] Council as naturally as at his dining-room table. Devonshire's assumption was that Great Britain should be governed by an aristocracy, with himself a principal. . . . [His] main concern was always to preserve harmony amongst His Majesty's servants." The fourth duke had no intimate friends in political life. "This detachment was natural to him and inevitably confirmed his exalted station. Here however lay the key to Devonshire's usefulness, recognized by everyone. He was the supremely objective man, never led away by passion, completely reliable and so the ideal receiver of confidences." Devoted to work and

---

and illiberal charges against the President. Horsley, Maskelyne, Maty, Maseres, and Poore are the leaders of this band, who are joined by all those turbulent spirits that are impatient of all government and subordination, which is indeed the great evil and disease of the times. I believe I have prolonged and increased my complaints by going out twice to vote against these innovators, who kept the society talking and disputing and balloting till near eleven and twelve o'clock, though they have been baffled in almost every question by near three to one. I will say nothing of our politics; our newspapers contain scarce anything else." Michael Lort to Bishop Percy, 24 February 1784, published in *Literary Anecdotes of the Eighteenth Century*, 9 vols., John Nichols, ed. (London, 1812–16) 7:461.

[50]The accountant general Anguish's speech on 12 February, quoted in *Narrative*, 112.

[51]Maskelyne's speech on 8 January, quoted in *Narrative*, 62. The Royal Society and parliament occasionally came together in the same person. C. J. Phipps, Lord Mulgrave, for example, was active both in the debates of the House of Commons and in those of the Royal Society. When Blagden came to see him on the subject of the dissensions, Lord Mulgrave talked to him as much as "his present political agitation would allow." Lord Mulgrave strongly urged Banks and his supporters against temporizing, since discontented men were "never made quiet by coaxing." Blagden, who used the analogy himself, thought that Lord Mulgrave carried the analogy of "H [ouse] of C [ommons] ideas to our Society" farther than was justified. Blagden to Banks, 23 December 1783.

[52]Horsley's speech on 1 April, quoted in *Supplement*, 12.

[53]Maty's speech on 12 February, quoted in *Narrative*, 99.

[54]Blagden to Banks, 22 December 1783.

[55]Blagden to Banks, morning, 24 December 1783.

[56]Blagden to Banks, 24 December 1783.

duty, everything the fourth duke did he did well.[57] These characteristics of the fourth duke—self-assured, conscientious, cautious, withdrawn, competent, and supremely objective—were those, by and large, of the Cavendish family and, in particular, of that member who distanced himself farthest from the active political life of the nation, Henry Cavendish.[58]

Like the fourth duke and like other politicians of his family, Henry Cavendish preferred to work in committees, to exercise power behind the scenes rather than to come forward as a leader. That behavior agreed with his understanding that power should be exercised by councils of serious men of independent judgment. He did not want to be president of the Royal Society, nor did he want to make or depose presidents, but he was always ready to advise presidents and others, as a call of duty, and always in the interest of stability and harmony.

Like his namesakes in government, whatever Henry Cavendish did, he did well. Whatever he did not do well—which included delivering speeches, inspiring men to follow him into political battle, his special "unfitness"—he did not do at all. He acted constantly in society, only his was not the given society of high fashion and politics, his birthright, but that of his own choosing, the society of scientific men. He acted from his strengths, which were his intelligence, his sense of fairness, his impartiality, and his ability to work with groups of equals to arrive at decisions for common action. His strengths also included, as his participation in the events of 1783–84 show, an understanding of political behavior; he was a close observer of men just as he was of natural phenomena.

In drawing comparisons between Henry Cavendish's political views and those of his namesakes, Blagden knew his subject well. He was a frequent caller at Devonshire House, where the Cavendishes came together with Fox and like-minded whigs to talk about politics, and, of course, he was an intimate of Henry Cavendish, whose views on politics were a private matter. And Blagden was well informed on and greatly interested in national politics.

In his capacity as secretary to the Royal Society Blagden wrote to correspondents in 1789 to say that there was no science to report, that "everybody's attention seems turned to politics."[59]

The next year he wrote that science throughout Europe was languishing and that the Royal Society had heard nothing important since William Herschel's paper on the rotation of Saturn's ring, "the minds of men being turned to greater interests."[60] Two years later Blagden on a visit to France was mobbed and nearly hanged. Banks wrote to him that in England their "minds are much heated" by the dreadful state of France and that he trusted that the English people would learn a lesson from it.[61]

It seemed to Blagden that Cavendish too was caught up in the current distractions and malaise. He wrote to Richard Kirwan in 1790 that "Mr Cavendish does not seem to be very busy."[62] From someone, perhaps Blagden, Kirwan had heard that "Mr. Cavendish talks politics." He was surprised because Cavendish had been silent during "Ld North's Rump Parliament, in wh his family were so much engaged."[63] Then came the wars with France, and at the George & Vulture, Cavendish was "freer than usual," saying that "minister & measures" had to be changed and that they "should have confidence in Fox."[64] Henry Cavendish stood by his family in politics, by the brilliant and flawed Charles Fox, whose public address was, in effect, Devonshire House in London. Present during a conversation about war the sooner the better, Cavendish "said he could scarcely refrain from bursting out."[65] Blagden recorded a good many of Cavendish's observations

---

[57] *The Devonshire Diary: William Cavendish, Fourth Duke of Devonshire, Memoranda on State of Affairs, 1759–1762*, ed. P. D. Brown and K. W. Schweizer, Camden Fourth Series, vol. 27 (London: Royal Historical Society, 1982) 27:19–21.

[58] Caution has been singled out by other writers on Henry Cavendish as a characteristic common to him and to the Cavendishes in general. The family motto *Cavendo tutus*, a play on words meaning "Safe by being cautious," was Cavendish's guide throughout his life according to his main biographer George Wilson, *The Life of the Honourable Henry Cavendish* (London, 1851), 190.

[59] Charles Blagden to William Farr, 24 Jan. 1789, draft, Blagden Letterbook, Royal Society, 7:206. Charles Blagden to M. A. Pictet, 9 Apr. 1789, draft, ibid., 7:223.

[60] Charles Blagden to William Farr, 31 July 1790, draft, Blagden Letterbook, Royal Society, 7:429.

[61] Charles Blagden to Sir Joseph Banks, 5 Sep. 1792, BL Add Mss 33272, pp. 107–8. Sir Joseph Banks to Charles Blagden, 19 Feb. 1793, Blagden Letters, Royal Society, B.41.

[62] Charles Blagden to Richard Kirwan, 20 Mar. 1790, draft, Blagden Letterbook, Royal Society, 7:322.

[63] Richard Kirwan to Sir Joseph Banks, 10 Jan. 1789, copy, BM(NH), DTC, 6:122–24.

[64] 16 Mar. 1795, Blagden Diary, Royal Society, 3:back p. 50.

[65] 20 Dec. 1795, Blagden Diary, Royal Society, 3:back p. 82.

about the ongoing wars, though in each instance the note is so brief that only the tenor of Cavendish's opinion can be got. But that is sufficient for us to get an idea of Cavendish's view of nations in conflict, France, Prussia, Russia, Austria, and Britain. The conversations took place at the George & Vulture and the Crown & Anchor and Banks's house. Blagden, a great admirer of Napoleon, would set out theses of Realpolitik. He presented Cavendish with the arguments for setting on Prussia while holding out peace. "Never was a nation so mad," Cavendish responded.[66] The only possibility of a combined resistance to the French was by a "fair intelligence" between Prussia and Austria, Cavendish said, to which Blagden replied "impossible," since Austria's goal was to swallow up Prussia.[67] On the report of a new war with America, Cavendish said that the Americans were "now more moderate than their predecessors." Blagden rejected that opinion on the grounds that Americans would hold onto their places at any cost, to which Cavendish "assented & looked in agitation." Blagden said that England had best turn into a nest of pirates and war against all the world, and that England was likely to be at war soon with Russia: "to all this /Cavendish/ sadly assented."[68] On two major points Cavendish and Blagden agreed. In the making of a new ministry,

in which Cavendish's "family took an active part," Blagden said he was for the old opposition, Fox. To Blagden's remark that all of mankind had gone mad together, Cavendish "thought there was a great diminution of common sense in the world."[69] Taken together these and other comments by Cavendish point to a man who looked to reason in human affairs and who was dejected because he did not find much there.

If one looks at the dissensions of the Royal Society as a kind of experiment of the Enlightenment, a test in real life of its characterizing beliefs, the outcome is subject to interpretation. But it seems clear that through it all, Cavendish acted consistently upon certain of these beliefs. He trusted that disputes can and ought to be settled by discussion between men who are fair, moderate, informed, and willing to exercise their reason. In the eighteenth century, as in any other, anyone who held that expectation of human nature was set up for disillusionment.

----

[66] Ibid.
[67] 30 Nov. 1804, Blagden Diary, Royal Society, 4:286.
[68] 15 May 1806, Blagden Diary, Royal Society, 4:442.
[69] 3 Apr. 1804, Blagden Diary, Royal Society, 4:217. This exchange on the unreason of people may not have had to do with politics, but it would apply.

CHAPTER 3

꧁ ❦ ꧂

Air and Water

Good Air

"Chemistry is the *rage* in London at present," John Playfair noted in his journal on a visit in 1782.[1] This observation sets the stage for the next researches of Henry Cavendish.

In our account of Cavendish's earliest work, we discussed the role of phlogiston in chemistry. The period was the 1760s, a relatively confident time for the followers of phlogiston. In the period we now take up, the 1780s, phlogiston was questioned, and before the end of the century chemists will have renounced it. The opponents of phlogiston were called "anti-phlogistonists," and because phlogiston is absent from the chemistry we learn today, we are all anti-phlogistonists; and for that reason, we may have difficulty following the arguments of the early chemists. In this chapter we will be concerned primarily with the chemistry of the components of common air, "dephlogisticated air" (our oxygen) and "phlogisticated air" (our nitrogen mainly), and with two other distinct gases, "nitrous air" (nitric oxide) and "inflammable air" (hydrogen). The meanings, though not the chemistry, of "dephlogisticated" and "phlogisticated" air were possibly straightforward, referring to the absence and presence of phlogiston.

Upon combining different kinds of air, chemists observed a large change in volume, the basic understanding of which did not come until the very end of Cavendish's life, long after the end of his work in chemistry. To look ahead: in 1808 Joseph Louis Gay-Lussac reported that gases combine in simple proportions and that their contraction upon combining bears a simple proportion to their original volume; in 1811 this law of combining volumes received a molecular interpretation by Amadeo Avogadro. In Cavendish's period, the major accomplishment of chemistry was the distinction between various kinds of airs, the first step in the chemistry of the gaseous state of matter. That came about through the chemistry of phlogiston and through the invention of subtle techniques in the laboratory. Unless one takes the ahistorical position that all once good science becomes wrongheaded once it is superseded, phlogiston chemistry was good chemistry up to a point.

Cavendish's second publication in chemistry came in 1783, seventeen years after his first, in 1766; both were about air. Having occupied himself in the meantime with researches on electricity and tasks for the Royal Society, in 1778 he began a new series of researches that would continue for eight years. The stimulus was a new instrument for studying air, the eudiometer.

The eudiometer incorporated a fundamental process, the "phlogistication" of air, which was itself a central problem of chemistry, so that the eudiometer was at the same time an instrument of meteorology, an instrument for the study of gases, and a physical process that needed clarification. Its inventor was Joseph Priestley.

Priestley, a dissenting minister in Birmingham, was approximately the same age as Cavendish and had scientific interests parallel to those of Cavendish. Priestley had preceded Cavendish in electricity; as we have noted, his book on electricity in 1767 had been a stimulus to Cavendish's researches. In pneumatic chemistry, the order was reversed. In 1772, in a long paper in the *Philosophical Transactions*, Priestley reviewed the territory already explored in pneumatic chemistry and added to it a new gas, nitrous air (nitric oxide), the first of his many new gases.[2] Priestley was led to this discovery, he said, by a conversation with Cavendish about experiments done by Hales.[3] In technique, too, Priestley learned from Cavendish and went beyond him;

---

[1]John Playfair, *The Works of John Playfair*, ed. J. G. Playfair, 4 vols. (Edinburgh, 1822) 1:xxxv.

[2]Joseph Priestley, "Observations on Different Kinds of Air," *PT* 62 (1772): 147–264. Priestley had already published a pamphlet on artificial sparkling water, made by impregnating water with fixed air.

[3]Ibid., 210.

Cavendish had stored water-soluble gas over mercury, a decisive innovation for the further development of pneumatic chemistry, and Priestley made the mercury trough a tool of discovery. Priestley's work on gases in turn stimulated Cavendish to return to the subject, at first in connection with Priestley's new gas, nitrous air, the agent of Priestley's new instrument.

The eudiometer is based upon a striking property of nitrous air: "I hardly know any experiment that is more adapted to amaze and surprise than this is," Priestley wrote, "which exhibits a quantity of air, which, as it were, devours a quantity of another kind of air half as large as itself, and yet is so far from gaining any addition to its bulk, that it is diminished by it."[4] Nitrous air was another means in addition to breathing, burning, and putrefaction of consuming "good" air. Moreover, this new way of phlogisticating air promised a new exactness in the study of air; the decrease in the volume of the mixture of a measured quantity of common air and a measured quantity of nitrous air over water (the products of the reaction being absorbed in the water) measured the goodness of the common air, a better test, Priestley said, that putting mice in it to see how they fared. The "eudiometer," measurer of goodness, was an addition to the tools of science and of public health. Bad air caused bad health.[5]

In his first experiments on gases, Cavendish had estimated the combustible portion of common air by the loudness of the explosion when it was detonated with inflammable air; he had, in effect, invented a crude sort of eudiometer.[6] The new, potentially exact instrument Cavendish described in 1783 in the *Philosophical Transactions*: "Dr. Priestley's discovery of the method of determining the degree of phlogistication of air by means of nitrous air, has occasioned many instruments to be contrived . . . ."[7] The variant of the instrument that Cavendish preferred, as did several other eudiometrists such as Tiberius Cavallo and Jan Ingen-Housz, was the "more accurate" eudiometer invented by the Florentine Felice Fontana in 1775. Fontana pursued the study of airs in Cavendish's way by determining their specific gravities with great exactness. With his eudiometer Fontana tested the air in different locations in Europe and in London, publishing two papers on the subject in the *Philosophical Transactions* for 1779. With his instrument, Fontana had come to the conclusion that the air in different places and at different times was almost the same and that the large differences other observers measured arose from errors in their methods.[8] Cavendish agreed, but the agreement was by no means general among chemists. At about the time Cavendish took up the subject, Cavallo wrote in his treatise on air that the laws of the differences in the purity of common air in different parts of the world was "perhaps the most interesting part of the study of elastic fluids."[9] The problem was interesting to Cavendish, but the solution lay not in the differences of samples of common air but in their uniformity.

Fontana's eudiometer was essentially a container for mixing nitrous and common airs. By Cavendish's modified instrument[10] and method, the quantities of the gases before and after mixing were determined by weight rather than by volume. The weighing, which Cavendish did under water, determined the decrease in the common air, which was the measure of the pure, or good, air. For this measure, or "test" of the air, Cavendish introduced a "standard" and a scale of measurement, which assumed (as Cavendish had determined) that the composition of the atmosphere is constant: the upper fixed point of the scale was the "standard" 1, which stood for the goodness of common air; the lower fixed point was the "standard" 0 of perfectly phlogisticated air (nitrogen). According to this scale, the "standard" of any sample of air was

―――――

[4]Ibid., 212.

[5]Tiberius Cavallo, *A Treatise on the Nature and Properties of Air, and Other Permanently Elastic Fluids. To Which Is Prefixed, an Introduction to Chemistry* (London, 1781), 453–57.

[6]George Wilson said this technique might be called an "Acoustic Eudiometer." *The Life of the Honourable Henry Cavendish* (London, 1851), 41.

[7]Henry Cavendish, "An Account of a New Eudiometer," *PT* 73 (1783): 106–35; *Sci. Pap.* 2:127–44, on 127.

[8]Felice Fontana, "Account of the Airs Extracted from Different Kinds of Waters; With Thoughts on the Salubrity of the Air at Different Places," *PT* 69 (1779): 432–53. Rembert Watermann, "Eudiometrie (1772–1805)," *Technik-Geschichte* 35 (1968): 293–319, on 302–3.

[9]Cavallo, *A Treatise on the Nature and Properties of Air*, 477.

[10]The eudiometer Cavendish described in his paper of 1783 was not what later became known as the "Cavendish Eudiometer," which the Cavendish Society adopted as its emblem in the early nineteenth century. The so-called Cavendish eudiometer was an electrically detonated eudiometer invented by Volta. Cavendish used such an apparatus in his experiments on the condensation of water, but he never referred to it as a eudiometer. Wilson, *Cavendish*, 42–43. Kathleen R. Farrar, "A Note on a Eudiometer Supposed to Have Belonged to Henry Cavendish," *British Journal for the History of Science* 1 (1963): 375–80.

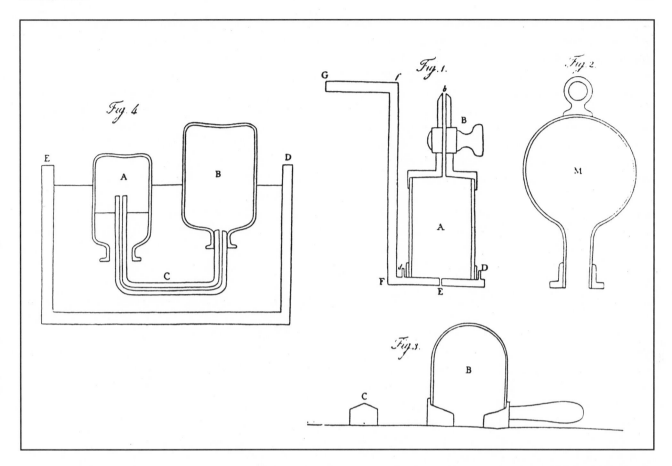

PLATE X. Eudiometer. Figure 1 shows the main apparatus, a glass cylinder A with brass cap and a cock at the top and an open brass cap at the bottom fitted into a socket of a bent brass holder as "a bayonet is on a musquet." The whole is submerged in a tub of water. Figure 2 is an inverted bottle for holding air, and Figure 3 is a standard measure of air. Cavendish's method is to put a certain measure of nitrous air (nitric oxide) into the inverted bottle and a certain measure of respirable air (oxygen) into the glass cylinder. The cylinder is then set on the socket and the bottle over the cock, and the two kinds of air are mixed in the bottle. Cavendish determines the quantities of air used and the diminution upon mixing the two kinds of air by weighing the vessels containing the air under water with a balance. "An Account of a New Eudiometer," *Philosophical Transactions* 73 (1783): 134.

proportional to the quantity of deplogisticated air (oxygen) in it. The standard of pure dephlogisticated air (pure oxygen) Cavendish found to be 4.8, later adjusted to 5. It was not known then that the airs reacting in the eudiometer, our nitric oxide and oxygen, combine in different proportions, the reason for the vastly different purities of air reported from different places. What was known, certainly to Cavendish, was that the only way to achieve uniform results was by laying down a uniform procedure, and that was the burden of Cavendish's publication.[11] He also gave results from sixty days of trials with the instrument, on clear, soggy, and wet days, early in the day and late, from which he concluded that within the error of the measurement, there was no difference in the degree of phlogistication of the air from place to place and time to time. With these measurements,

which he made with the utmost accuracy (with "superhuman care," as they have been described), he arrived at a result which subsequent chemists have translated into terms and quantities corresponding to our understanding of the atmosphere: the concentration of oxygen in the atmosphere is, according to Cavendish, 20.83 percent, which is remarkably near the currently accepted value of 20.95 percent. In making this comparison, however, Cavendish is credited with a somewhat greater precision that he would likely have claimed.[12]

---

[11]Edward Thorpe, "Introduction," Henry Cavendish, *The Scientific Papers of the Honourable Henry Cavendish, F.R.S.*, 2 vols. (Cambridge: Cambridge University Press, 1921) 2:18.

[12]Separated off from his "Experiments on Air" is another manuscript of fourteen pages on eudiometer tests made in Kensington and London (Great Marlborough Street) and reported in Cavendish's paper of 1783, "Miscellaneous Data on Eudiometer Experiments, 1780–81" (not Cavendish's label), Cavendish Mss II, 8. The experi-

Cavendish advocated his standard and common scale because eudiometers "differ so much, that at present it is almost impossible to compare the observations of one person with those of another."[13] (Like Fontana, Cavendish was unable to persuade his fellow chemists to adopt his demanding procedure.[14]) In this regard, Cavendish's paper on the eudiometer can be seen as a continuation of his paper on the meteorological instruments of the Royal Society and their uniform usage. Only the Royal Society did not need to include this instrument among the other meteorological instruments it used for its daily record of the weather, since, as Cavendish showed with it, there was no significant variation in the goodness of the air to record.

At the end of his account of the eudiometer, Cavendish compared its action with the sense of smell. The eudiometer was not like the telescope, an instrument that extended one of the human senses. On the contrary, by their sense of smell people could detect "infinitely smaller" quantities of impure air than they could detect using the eudiometer; for example, they could detect a ten-ounce measure of nitrous air released into a twelve-by-twelve-foot room, an immeasurably small quantity that would not alter the eudiometer test by more than 1/47,000 part. The nitrous test showed the degree of phlogistication "and that only," but this limitation did not diminish the usefulness of the test in experiments; for our smell is no "test," Cavendish said, of phlogistication, and there are ways of phlogisticating air that do not impart a smell to it as there are ways of imparting a smell that do not phlogisticate.[15] In the last analysis, Cavendish's conclusion was an affirmation of instruments of measurement in science.

At the time Cavendish published his work on the composition of air, the atmosphere became a medium of human transport. The balloon was invented, and with it a new kind of man appeared in the world, the "aronaut." Much about this earliest human flight was empirical and derring-do, but there was also an element of science, both in the principles of flight and in the use of flight for meteorology. Cavendish took an immediate interest in both. There was born a new field of applied pneumatic chemistry.

In fact Cavendish was regarded at the time as a kind of founding father of balloon flight, which went back to his first publication on air, in 1766. From Cavendish's description of inflammable air, it was self-evident to Black that balloons filled with this lighter-than-common air were a practical possibility. Black spoke about it with friends and in his lectures, but he did not bother to do the experiment.[16] "Theoretical flying," Blagden said, "has been a topic of conversation among our philosophers as long as I can remember, at least ever since Mr Cavendish discovered the great lightness of inflammable air."[17]

In 1782 the French brothers Joseph and Étienne de Montgolfier experimented with balloons filled with inflammable air and with hot air, and in the following year, they gave a public demonstration of a hot-air balloon.[18] Soon people began going up in balloons, fulfilling an age-old dream. Balloons created a sensation in France and mixed feelings in Britain. Not without a touch of national envy, the British spoke of "Balloon madness" or else of missed opportunity: the

---

ments continued after Cavendish's move to Hampstead in 1782, where he recorded tests of air in "Register of Test Air," and "Eudiometer Results of Air Taken by Dr. Jeffries" (not Cavendish's label), in Cavendish Mss, Misc. and II, 9, respectively. There is another untitled manuscript comparing his, Fontana's, and Ingen-Housz's methods, in the miscellany of his papers. A hundred years later, in admiration, William Ramsay compared Cavendish's measurements with the latest results, 79.04 percent nitrogen and 20.46 percent oxygen. Ramsay, *Gases of the Atmosphere*, 125–26. Cavendish's result is even closer to the more recent value of 20.95 percent: Peter Brimblecombe, "Earliest Atmospheric Profile," *New Scientist* 76 (1977): 364–65. Bent Soren Jorgensen, however, cautions that in extolling Cavendish's accuracy in his atmospheric determinations, modern chemists have overlooked a remark by Cavendish in a publication a year after his paper on the eudiometer; in this subsequent paper, in 1784, Cavendish noted that his dephlogisticated air contained impurities amounting to one thirtieth its volume, which led him to suspect that common air contains one fifth part dephlogisticated air (that is, closer to 20 percent than to 20.83 percent). Even if Cavendish's value for the proportion of oxygen in the atmosphere may not be quite as close to our value today as the histories of chemistry maintain, Jorgensen says, Cavendish was much closer than Scheele, Lavoisier, and Priestley, whose values were between twenty-five and thirty percent. "On a Text-Book Error: The Accuracy of Cavendish's Determination of the Oxygen Content of the Atmosphere," *Centaurus* 12 (1968): 132–34.

[13]Cavendish, "Account of a New Eudiometer," 141.

[14]Jan Golinski, *Science as Public Culture: Chemistry and Enlightenment in Britain, 1760–1820* (Cambridge: Cambridge University Press, 1992), 124.

[15]Cavendish, "Account of a New Eudiometer," 144.

[16]In a letter from Joseph Black to James Lind, in William Ramsay, *The Life and Letters of Joseph Black, M.D.* (London: Constable, 1918), 77–78.

[17]Charles Blagden to le Comte de C., 2 Apr. 1783, draft, Blagden Letterbook, Yale.

[18]W. A. Smeaton, "Montgolfier, Étienne Jacques de; Montgolfier, Michel Joseph de," *DSB* 9:492–94. The early experimentation in France with balloons filled with inflammable air and hot air is discussed in Charles C. Gillispie, *The Montgolfier Brothers and the Invention of Aviation 1783–1784* (Princeton: Princeton University Press, 1983), 15–31.

French made no scientific observations from their balloons, Banks complained.[19] It was to be hoped, Banks said, that the English would "not rise to the absurd height we have seen in France."[20]

Cavendish appreciated the French achievement in his way.[21] Since the principle of the inflammable-air balloon was fully understood on the basis of weight, Cavendish's interest was directed to the hot-air balloon. Evidently to decide if the hot air alone caused the balloon to rise or if the balloon also depended on a substance lighter than common air given off by the burning material, Cavendish and Blagden collected the air from burning straw and leather and tested it with a eudiometer. Finding it to be a mixture of gases heavier, not lighter, than common air,[22] they concluded that hot-air balloons ascend solely because of the rarefaction of air.[23] In practical terms, the hot-air balloons were extremely dangerous and clumsy; Blagden expected nothing of them, but he thought that inflammable-air balloons could bring about an "important revolution in human affairs."[24]

Not immediately but before long, balloons appeared in the sky over England too. The first balloon to carry a person there was that of the Italian Vincenzo Lunardi; the second that of the Frenchman Jean Pierre Blanchard, who was joined by the first English aeronaut, John Sheldon, professor of anatomy at the Royal Academy; and the third another balloon of Blanchard, who went up more times than anyone,[25] this time accompanied by the American physician John Jefferies.[26] Cavendish was there to observe these multinational adventures. He and his friends—Alexander Aubert, Alexander Dalrymple, Charles Blagden, William Herschel, Nevil Maskelyne, William Heberden, William Roy, and Jesse Ramsden—observed the balloons from Putney Heath, Aubert's observatory in Austin Friar's, and elsewhere.[27] With theodolite and clock, they recorded the position and time every minute or two while the balloon was in sight. Cavendish calculated the course of the balloon as if it were a low-flying comet.[28] Cavendish took much interest in the science of flying, but unfortunately his manuscripts on this subject have been lost.[29]

Balloons offered their passengers "scenes of majestic grandeur," raising them to an "unknown degree of enthusiastic rapture and pleasure."[30] But

to Cavendish, balloons were a means of elevating the scientific laboratory thousands of feet above the earth. He could now extend his measurements of the composition of the air to great heights. Through Blagden, Cavendish asked Jefferies to sample the air during his flight with Blanchard on 30 November 1784. Jefferies took with him five glass phials filled with distilled water, and at various heights he emptied the phials and bottled the air. With the eudiometer, Cavendish tested these samples and compared them with air taken on the ground at Hampstead, establishing that there is little systematic variation in the concentration of dephlogisticated air (oxygen) in the lower atmosphere. He did not publish this finding; the credit is given to Gay-Lussac for his research twenty years later.[31] We note that

----

[19]Joseph Banks to Charles Blagden, 22 Sep. and 12 Oct. 1783, Blagden Letters, Royal Society, B.29–30.

[20]Sir Joseph Banks to Charles Blagden, 22 Sep. 1784, Blagden Letters, Royal Society, B.29.

[21]In Cavendish's papers is a testimonial signed by Benjamin Franklin among others of a Montgolfier experiment on 21 July 1783 and also an extract, in Blagden's hand, about Montgolfier from the *Journal Encyclopédique.*

[22]Notations in both Blagden's and Cavendish's hand, beginning "Smoke of Straw," Cavendish Mss, Misc.

[23]Letter from Charles Blagden 5 Dec. 1783, draft, Blagden Letterbook, Yale.

[24]Charles Blagden to Claude Louis Berthollet, 19 Dec. 1783, draft, Blagden Letterbook, Yale.

[25]Blanchard went up in balloons in many places, such as in Philadelphia in an inflammable-air balloon, in which he made medical observations. Jean Pierre Blanchard, *Journal of My Forty-Fifth Ascension* (Philadelphia, 1793).

[26]Charles Hutton, "Aerology," in *Mathematical and Philosophical Dictionary*, vol. 1 (London, 1795), 38–40.

[27]Charles Blagden to Sir Joseph Banks, 17 and 24 Oct. 1784, copy, Banks Correspondence, BM(NH), DTC, 4:75–78.

[28]Alexander Aubert to William Herschel, 13 Sep. 1784, Royal Astronomical Society, Herschel M 1/13. Charles Blagden to Sir Joseph Banks, 16 Sep., 1784, Banks Correspondence, Kew, l:173. "Path of Balloon," for an ascent on 16 Oct. 1784, Cavendish Mss VIII, 24. In Cavendish's hand, "Result of Observations of Balloons," Blagden Collection, Royal Society, Misc. Notes. Archibald and Nan L. Clow, *The Chemical Revolution: A Contribution to Social Technology* (London: Batchworth Press, 1952), 156.

[29]For his sketch of Cavendish in 1845, Lord Brougham borrowed two manuscripts that are now lost: "Theory of Kites" and "On Flying." Their existence and loan to Brougham are noted in Cavendish's manuscripts at Chatsworth.

[30]Thomas Baldwin, *Aeropaidia: Containing the Narrative of a Balloon Excursion from Chester, the Eighth of September, 1785* (London, 1785), 2.

[31]"Eudiometer Results of Air Taken by Dr. Jefferies," and "Test of Air from Blanchard's Balloon," Cavendish Mss II, 9 and 10. Thorpe, in *Cavendish, Sci. Pap.* 2:22. Jefferies' air samples were numbered, but the explanation of the numbers is not in Cavendish's Mss, and it was believed lost. However, recently it was located in Jefferies' account of his flight, from which the earliest atmospheric profile, the "Cavendish-Jefferies profile," has been reconstructed, showing that at the various sampling elevations, between one and

Cavendish himself had no more inclination to travel above the earth than across it, but he did have use for people who went up in balloons.

Water

Pneumatic chemistry was recognized as an indispensable part of chemistry, at least from Cavendish's publication on factitious air in 1766. In 1771 the industrial chemist James Keir brought out an English translation of Macquer's *Dictionary of Chemistry*, originally published in 1766, and to ensure that the dictionary reflected the "present state of chemical knowledge," Keir added material from Black, MacBride, and Cavendish.[32]

By 1773 the president of the Royal Society, John Pringle, could give a discourse on the *history* of pneumatic chemistry.[33] The field of pneumatic chemistry at the time Cavendish returned to it was summarized by Tiberius Cavallo, in his *Treatise on . . . Air* in 1781. This book of over eight hundred pages was about a subject, distinct airs, that can hardly be said to have existed before Cavendish's work just fifteen years before.

In his paper in the *Philosophical Transactions* for 1784, "Experiments on Air," Cavendish reported his experiments on the production of water from the explosion of common air with inflammable air. We might expect that just as Black and Cavendish showed that the ancient element air consisted of distinct airs, Cavendish would show that the ancient element water is another combination of airs, but that is not what Cavendish did. He did not bring into question the elemental notion of water, even as his experiments laid the factual basis for our modern understanding of water as a chemical combination of gases. His way of talking about water was ambiguous as to its elemental or compound nature, but that question was beside the point. His purpose was to explain the phlogistication of common air, and his discussion of water in this connection was unambiguous. Because of the subsequent importance of water in this work, we refer to Cavendish's paper of 1784 on the phlogistication of air as his paper on the "condensation" of water, his term (alternative terms used by his contemporaries include "composition" of water and "decomposition" of air); at the same time we recognize that the condensation of water was incidental. Several paths led to Cavendish's experiments on the condensation of

water from exploding gases. The obvious one was his previous work on gases, in particular, his recognition of inflammable air as a distinct air in 1766. Another was his study of latent and specific heats, another his study of electricity, and yet another was his experiments on common air using the eudiometer, which led directly to the experiments in his paper of 1784. The wider setting was the investigations from the late 1770s of the air lost during phlogistication by Priestley, Lavoisier, and Carl Wilhelm Scheele. Cavendish's immediate stimulus was the work of Priestley together with his fellow experimenter John Warltire.

Cavendish's purpose in "Experiments on Air" was "to find out the cause of the diminution which common air is well known to suffer by all the various ways in which it is phlogisticated . . . ."[34] It was a question as important as it was difficult; Priestley had varied opinions on it, and other chemists had other opinions.[35] Cavendish's answer went back to an experiment he performed in late June or early July 1781 labeled: "Explosion of Inflam. Air by El. in Glass Globe to Determine Mr Warltires Experiment."[36] Warltire, as reported by Priestley, electrically fired a mixture of inflammable and common air in a closed vessel, noting the generation of heat and light and a loss of weight, which Warltire attributed to the escape of a ponderable matter of heat. Warltire and Priestley also noted a deposit of dew inside the vessel, to which they did not attribute a fundamental significance.[37] Cavendish repeated Warltire's experiment, obtaining dew and heat but not a loss of weight. The latter fact could not have surprised him, since he believed that heat is motion not ponderable matter. Given that he found dew, he could not have been

---

three kilometers, the amount of oxygen in the air over London was virtually constant. Brimblecombe, "Earliest Atmospheric Profile," 365.

[32]Pierre Joseph Macquer, *A Dictionary of Chemistry Containing the Theory and Practice of That Science . . .* , trans. J. Keir, 2 vols. (London, 1771) 1:i, iv.

[33]John Pringle, "A Discourse on the Different Kinds of Air, Delivered at the Anniversary Meeting of the Royal Society, November 30, 1773," *PT* 64 (1774): 1–31, Supplement at the end of the volume.

[34]Henry Cavendish, "Experiments on Air," *PT* 74 (1784): 119–69; *Sci. Pap.*2:161–81, on 161.

[35]Cavallo, *Treatise*, 419–20.

[36]Cavendish, "Experiments on Air," Cavendish Mss, II, 5: 115. In the same year, 1781, Cavallo too took notice of Warltire's experiment, which he thought elegant and the outcome of which he thought very remarkable. Cavallo, *Treatise*, 666.

[37]Joseph Priestley, *Experiments and Observations Relating to Various Branches of Natural Philosophy . . .* (London, 1781) 2:395–98.

surprised by the heat, since he had found that condensation, the change from a gas to a liquid, always generated heat, though what was involved here was more than a simple change of state.[38] He would probably have been surprised by the dew itself; in any event he recognized its significance. He repeated the experiment, observing that all of the first and about one-fifth part of the common air lost their "elasticity" and "condensed" into the dew lining the vessel. This dew had no color, taste, or smell; "in short, it seemed pure water."[39] Cavendish determined that the lost fifth part of the common air was the new air Priestley had announced in 1774, and which was discovered independently by Scheele, "dephlogisticated air," our oxygen. He inferred from the experiments on the condensation of water that dephlogisticated air is "in reality nothing but dephlogisticated water, or water deprived of its phlogiston," and that inflammable air is in all probability "phlogisticated water" or "water united to phlogiston." When the two airs combine with the help of an electric spark, their water condenses out.[40] In this explanation, phlogiston is treated as elemental and dephlogisticated and inflammable airs as compounded. To the question of what causes the decrease in common air when it is phlogisticated, Cavendish's answer was that the dephlogisticated part of common air combines with inflammable air and is then no longer air but pure liquid water.

To be complete, Cavendish identified the other part of atmospheric air, the already phlogisticated air, our nitrogen: phlogisticated air, he said, is nitrous acid united to phlogiston.[41] These several relationships between phlogiston, dephlogisticated air, phlogisticated air, and water constitute Cavendish's understanding of air.

By giving essentially his theory of chemistry, Cavendish was now in open disagreement with formidable adversaries, Priestley, Kirwan, Watt, and Lavoisier. Having abandoned his earlier probable identification of phlogiston with inflammable air, Cavendish was at variance with the chemists who had adopted the same interpretation, Priestley and Kirwan. Finding no role for fixed air in the phlogistication of common air, Cavendish contradicted Kirwan, from whom Cavendish would soon hear. His differences with Watt and Lavoisier were more fundamental. Watt, in a paper read before the Royal Society, proposed that water was a union of dephlogisticated air and inflammable air or phlogiston, deprived of their latent heat. In his paper the year before on the freezing of mercury, Cavendish had given his differences with Black on the subject of latent heat. Now it came up again in chemistry, and Cavendish again rejected latent heat because he did not believe that heat was a kind of matter instead of motion; even the use of the term "latent" led to "false ideas" in chemistry. He rejected Watt's theory in chemistry because he rejected latent heat.[42] He was circumspectly opposed to Lavoisier's proposal to eliminate phlogiston from chemistry and to introduce in its stead oxygen (Cavendish's dephlogisticated air). Conceding that nature seemed to be about as well explained on Lavoisier's phlogistonless chemistry as on his own, Cavendish said that there was a circumstance that persuaded him that phlogiston still held the advantage. On the phlogiston theory, plants gave off phlogiston when they were burned, and it seemed obvious to Cavendish that plants were more compounded than their ash; on Lavoisier's theory, the ash, containing oxygen, was the more compounded. But Cavendish thought it would be "very difficult to determine by experiment which of these opinions is the truest."[43] So this otherwise strong paper by Cavendish ended with equivocation and an admittedly weak defense of the advantage of phlogiston over phlogistonless chemistry.

Over the next four years, Cavendish published three more papers on chemistry. The first was in reply to Kirwan, who accepted that Cavendish had succeeded in showing that dephlogisticated air was turned into water by its combination with phlogiston, but who thought that Cavendish had gone too far in claiming that in the phlogistication of air, water was *always* generated and fixed air *never*. Cavendish had ignored all the proofs Kirwan had given of the involvement of fixed air, which played the role of a universal acid in Kirwan's theory of chemistry. The importance Kirwan attributed to fixed air was a common idea at the time, and Cavendish had taken pains at the

---

[38]This analysis draws on Russell McCormmach, "Henry Cavendish: A Study of Rational Empiricism in Eighteenth-Century Natural Philosophy," *Isis* 60 (1969): 293–306, on 305.

[39]Cavendish, "Experiments on Air," 166–67.

[40]Cavendish, "Experiments on Air," 171–73.

[41]Ibid., 170–72.

[42]Ibid., 173–74.

[43]Ibid., 179–80.

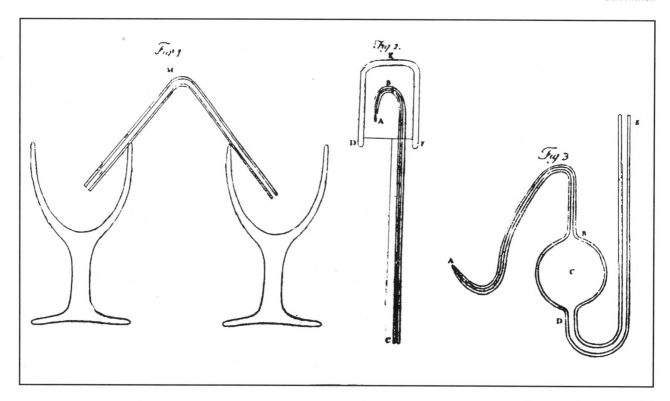

PLATE XI. Apparatus for Experiments on Air. For converting phlogisticated air (nitrogen) into nitrous (nitric) acid. Cavendish passes a spark through air trapped in the bent tube shown in Figure 1. The tube, first filled with mercury, is inverted into two glasses containing mercury. Figures 2 and 3 show small-bore tubes used to insert the nitrous air into the bent tube. "Experiments on Air," *Philosophical Transactions* 75 (1785): 384.

beginning of his paper on the condensation of water to show that fixed air was not involved; Cavendish would hear from others on this point.[44] Cavendish responded; Kirwan answered back, but Cavendish let it pass this time.[45]

Nitrous Acid

In 1785, in a paper of the same title, "Experiments on Air," Cavendish made a thorough examination of a point from the first paper: if a trace of phlogisticated air was admitted into a mixture of inflammable and dephlogisticated air and detonated, dilute nitrous acid rather than pure water was deposited. In a new series of experiments he showed that the inflammable air was unnecessary for this result. When fired by electricity, phlogisticated air and dephlogisticated air alone yielded nitrous acid, and if they were mixed in the right proportions, the gases were entirely condensed into nitrous acid.[46] This research exactly paralleled Cavendish's research on the condensation of water from dephlogisticated air and another air, inflammable air.

Lavoisier with two colleagues tried in vain to repeat Cavendish's experiment on the con-

version of the two airs into nitrous acid by means of the electric spark; Cavendish could not imagine why they failed except for "want of patience." Martin van Marum wrote to Cavendish in 1785— the year of van Marum's great electrical machine, the largest in existence—about his similar failure to obtain Cavendish's result with the electric spark. Cavendish did not know why van Marum failed either, though he thought that the apparatus might be faulty.[47] Instead of guessing what went wrong in

[44]Jean Senebrier, writing to Cavendish about his paper on the condensation of water, brought up a single experiment that seemed to show that fixed air results from the phlogistication of the pure part of common air. Letter to Cavendish, 1 Nov. 1785, Cavendish Mss, New Correspondence.

[45]Henry Cavendish, "Answer to Mr. Kirwan's Remarks upon the Experiments on Air," *PT* 74 (1784): 170–77; *Sci. Pap.* 2:182–86. Cavendish's papers contain an extract, in Blagden's hand, of a letter from Kirwan to Crell that appeared in Crell's journal discussing the whole unresolved dispute. "Extract of a Letter from Mr. Kirwan in London to Professor Crell (Chem. Annals. no. VI p. 523. June 1784)," Cavendish Mss X(b), 10.

[46]Henry Cavendish, "Experiments on Air," *PT* 75 (1785): 372–84; *Sci. Pap.* 2:187–94, on 191.

[47]Martin van Marum to Henry Cavendish, 6 Jan. 1785; Cavendish to van Marum, undated, draft, Cavendish Mss, New Correspondence. Cavendish published this correspondence in his paper, "On the Conversion of a Mixture of Dephlogisticated and Phlogisticated Air into Nitrous Acid by the Electric Spark," *PT* 78 (1788): 261–76; *Sci. Pap.* 2:224–32, on 231–32.

experiments by others, Cavendish again demonstrated what was right in his own. He asked the clerk of the Royal Society, George Gilpin, to repeat the experiment before some persons who were familiar with the subject. On several days in late 1787 and early 1788, the witnesses gathered, ten at least, most of whom came to each part of the experiment: Banks, Blagden, Heberden, Watson, John Hunter, George Fordyce, J. L. Macie, and Johann Casper Dollfuss; William Higgins and Richard Brockelsby came on a day when an "accident" happened, and Cavendish did not list them in his paper.[48] Gilpin worked Nairne's patent electrical machine a half hour at a stretch, obtaining two or three hundred sparks a minute, whereas Cavendish had only worked his machine for ten minutes at a time. Details of method aside, Gilpin's experiments confirmed Cavendish's. They were the substance of Cavendish's last publication in chemistry.

Cavendish's contributions to chemistry were widely separated, the first in 1766 and the second almost twenty years later, in 1783–85. The earlier work, on factitious air, was fundamental to the development of chemistry as a science: it opened up a field of discovery of new airs, and it demonstrated a rigorously quantitative approach, essential for keeping track of these elastic fluids, the nature of which is to escape. The later work, on the condensation of water and nitrous acid, was only one, if important, contribution at a time of rapid advances by many contributors. The field by then had clear objectives, established techniques, and a theoretical direction (or directions, Lavoisier's being opposed to the phlogistic chemistry Cavendish worked within). The production of water from airs was observed by several chemists at about the same time. From the point of view of the chemists involved, what was important was who did it first. What was important for chemistry was the model—a repeat for Cavendish—of experimental research in the chemistry of airs. To have read and grasped Cavendish's paper of 1785 was to have taken a master class in the art of experiment. Jean Senebrier, an experimentalist who wrote penetrating works on the experimental method, wrote to Cavendish after reading his recent papers on airs that he admired Cavendish's "exactitude": "You are a master and a great master in the difficult art of making experiments."[49]

Atmosphere

If we look at Cavendish's later work as a kind of chemical meteorology, we see that it takes on an additional significance. The title Cavendish gave to his two major chemical papers in 1784 and 1785, "Experiments on Air," did not refer to a single, universal air, because he did not believe in one. Rather it referred to common air, that of the atmosphere. He, along with other leading chemists, understood that this air consisted of two "distinct substances," dephlogisticated air and phlogisticated air (we continue to use the terminology of phlogistic chemistry), neither of which was understood when Cavendish took up his researches with the eudiometer. He intended his paper of 1784 to "throw great light on the constitution and manner of production of dephlogisticated air."[50] In his paper of 1785, he wrote that "we scarcely know more of the nature of the phlogisticated part of our atmosphere, than that it is not diminished by lime-water, caustic alkalies, or nitrous air; that it is unfit to support fire, or maintain life in animals; and that its specific gravity is not much less than that of common air"; we do not know if there are "in reality many different substances confounded together by us under the name of phlogisticated air." By experiment Cavendish showed that the phlogisticated air of the atmosphere was only one substance.[51] Joining together his knowledge of pneumatic chemistry, affinity, heat, and electricity, Cavendish clarified the understanding of the atmosphere. In 1785 Blagden sent his brother three papers by Cavendish and Watt, which taken together seemed to Blagden "fully to explain the nature of our atmosphere."[52] Blagden noted that the most important of the three papers was Cavendish's on the origin of nitrous acid (and not the one on the condensation of water), for it showed that the greatest part of the atmosphere "is nothing but that acid in aerial form." Blagden's

[48]Higgins and Brockelsby came on 23 Jan. 1788; Cavendish refers to the "accident" of that day but not to the people attending. T. S. Wheeler and J. R. Partington, *The Life and Work of William Higgins, Chemist (1763–1825)* (New York: Pergamon, 1960), 33, 66.
[49]Senebrier to Cavendish, 1 Nov. 1785.
[50]Cavendish, "Experiments on Air," 161.
[51]Cavendish, "Experiments on Air," 192–93.
[52]Charles Blagden to Thomas Blagden, 8 Dec. 1785, Blagden Letterbook, Yale.

view of Cavendish's work was usually Cavendish's own. Priestley wrote to Cavendish that his experimental work on phlogisticated air was "one of the greatest, perhaps the very greatest, and most important, relating to the doctrine of air."[53]

Phlogisticated air was examined first by Cavendish, but he did not publish on the subject. Daniel Rutherford, Black's and Cullen's student, wrote his medical dissertation in 1772 at the University of Edinburgh on Black's fixed air, which Rutherford called "mephitic air." In the course of his experiments, Rutherford isolated another similar air, phlogisticated air, which we call nitrogen. Rutherford's dissertation was published, and so, properly, he is given credit for discovering nitrogen, but many years earlier Cavendish had studied this air. In a paper written for a correspondent, "you," who had shown him a letter from Priestley on what Priestley called "mephitic air," by which Cavendish understood Priestley to mean air that "suffocates animals," Cavendish said that "in all probability there are many kinds of air which possess this property." Cavendish knew of at least two airs of this kind, Black's fixed air and common air in which something has burned, or "burnt air." Cavendish gave his correspondent the results of an earlier experiment of his, in which he had determined by specific gravity and other characteristics that a sample of burnt air was not fixed air. This paper by Cavendish is undated, but Priestley gave a version of it in his paper of 1772.[54]

There was an extraordinary follow-up of Cavendish's study. In his experiments on phlogisticated air, Cavendish was unable to eliminate a tiny "bubble" in his apparatus, 1/120th of the whole. This minuscule residue, which Cavendish described as an experimental error, was consequently, and consequentially, noticed by William Ramsay. The occasion was the "water controversy," which had resulted in George Wilson's biography of Henry Cavendish, a secondhand copy of which Ramsay had bought when he was a student. Years later, in the 1890s, Ramsay recalled the pertinent passage and drew it to the attention of Lord Rayleigh. Ramsay and Rayleigh were working on the same problem, a third-decimal difference in density of the nitrogen in the atmosphere and the nitrogen produced chemically. Together they determined that Cavendish's residue was a new gas of the atmosphere, the chemically inert gas argon. Nitrogen, they found, was actually a mixture of nitrogen and argon, which finding opened up a new epoch in the study of the atmosphere. The discovery of argon inspired Ramsay to write a history of the gases of the atmosphere, in which he observed that of all the experimenters in this field, Cavendish was "undoubtedly the greatest."[55]

As we have seen, Cavendish was guided in his experimental study of the atmosphere by the phlogiston theory, to which he gave his own twist. His interlocked interpretations of phlogiston, phlogisticated air, dephlogisticated air, nitrous acid, and water provided a satisfactory understanding of the atmosphere, which we can look upon as a late triumph of the phlogiston theory.

New Chemistry

The progressive development of exact techniques in chemistry, as in other parts of natural philosophy, would have happened even if there had been no "chemical revolution." Cavendish's most important work in chemistry had been to advance the methods of examining airs, in workaday chemistry. But there was a chemical revolution—that is accepted by most historians of chemistry even as they disagree about what it was, what its boundaries were, and what place the overthrow of phlogiston had in it[56]—and consequently the historical interest in Cavendish's work has been largely in relation to that event. Cavendish's contribution to chemistry was substantial, though it was not among the conceptual changes that mark the chemical revolution. By contrast Lavoisier set a course for himself that required a break with the chemistry he learned, which was what every chemist then learned, phlogistic chemistry. From

[53]Joseph Priestley to Henry Cavendish, 30 Dec. 1784, Cavendish Mss, New Correspondence. Priestley's letter was in reply to Cavendish's, written late in 1784, which summarized the main points of what would become the published paper of the following year. Henry Cavendish to Joseph Priestley, 20 Dec. 1784, draft, Cavendish Mss, New Correspondence. These letters are published in *Scientific Autobiography of Joseph Priestley*, 239–42, quotation on 241.

[54]Henry Cavendish, "Paper Communicated to Dr. Priestley," Cavendish Mss, Misc. Scheele too studied this gas, perhaps as early as 1771, but he did not publish on it until 1777. E. L. Scott, "Rutherford, Daniel," *DSB* 12:24–25.

[55]Ramsay, *The Gases of the Atmosphere*, 143. Bruno Kisch, *Scales and Weights: A Historical Outline* (New Haven: Yale University Press, 1965), 8.

[56]Arthur L. Donovan, "Introduction," in *The Chemical Revolution: Essays in Reinterpretation*, ed. A. Donovan, ser. 2, vol. 4 of *Osiris*, published in 1988 by the History of Science Society, 5–12, on 5–6. Robert Siegfried, "The Chemical Revolution in the History of Chemistry," ibid., 34–50, on 34–35.

the early 1770s he consciously worked to make a revolution in physics and chemistry. Twenty years later he had done nothing less, or, depending upon one's interpretation, he had completed the first part of that revolution. For a change of this magnitude to have taken place in chemistry, a number of developments were needed. The most obvious of these was pneumatic chemistry, which replaced the ancient idea of elementary air by chemically active, distinct gases, or the gaseous state. Lavoisier's chemistry was built upon the new understanding of gases. Cavendish's production of water from airs, or gases, was particularly important for Lavoisier, who saw immediately that Cavendish's experiments implied that water was a compound. That gave him the answer to the critical question of what happens when metals were dissolved in acids: the inflammable air, or hydrogen, that was released did not come from the metals, as the phlogiston theory taught, but from the dissociated water. This was the understanding he needed to bring about his reconstruction of chemistry. The same experiments did not, and could not, lead Cavendish to the new chemistry, since he had a perfectly satisfactory explanation of them in the phlogiston theory. Other developments leading to the revolution in chemistry Cavendish did not participate in. For example, he did not accept at face value the increase in weight of burned and calcined bodies. The bizarre phlogistic explanations of this increase gave Lavoisier strong arguments for the absurdity of phlogiston. In order to build as well as destroy, Lavoisier had to work out a new understanding of chemical compounds and a new nomenclature to express it, and he had to win disciples. These things, of course, he did. His *Traité élémentaire de chemie* in 1789 would instruct the next generation of chemists in the new chemistry.[57]

Cavendish had strong feelings about the changes Lavoisier was bringing about. We know this because of private remarks in a correspondence between Blagden and Cavendish when Blagden was away from London on the French and English triangulation project in 1787. The French crossed the Channel bearing anti-phlogistic chemical publications for Cavendish and other English scientists, and these included a copy of the *Méthode de nomenclature chimique* written by Lavoisier and his colleagues, just out. From Dover Blagden wrote to Cavendish in London that he had the book and

would hold it if Cavendish planned to join him or forward it to Banks's where Cavendish could pick it up.[58] Because of foul weather, Cavendish did not go to Dover, with the result that he and Blagden discussed the nomenclature by letter. Cavendish understood that the proposal for the systematic renaming of the substances of chemistry was a move to impress the new theory on chemistry. The language and the theory could not be separated and could even be seen as one and the same thing. Nothing, Cavendish said, serves "more to rivet a theory in the minds of learners than to form all the names which they are to use upon that theory." If this precedent were to succeed, every chemist with a new theory could present it together with a new language, and no one could understand what was being said without learning the theory. Moreover, every experimental advance in chemical composition would be followed by renaming. A systematic nomenclature did not lead to clarity, as the proposers believed, but to "confusion," which was a "great mischief." Cavendish, however, had no opposition to naming uncommon neutral salts by the names of their components because there were so many of them. Apologizing to Blagden for this uncharacteristic "long sermon" on the "present rage of name-making," Cavendish said that he did not believe that the nomenclature would take hold in any case.[59] Blagden's reaction was much the same. The authors of the chemical nomenclature had been seduced by the Linnean natural history, Blagden wrote to Cavendish, and the analogy was false. The objects studied by natural history remained the same over long periods, but in chemistry, discoveries came so rapidly that names would have to change constantly. Like Cavendish, Blagden saw "little danger that the systematic names will be adopted."[60] Cavendish and Blagden were typical of British

---

[57]Changes that underlay the chemical revolution are summarized in William H. Brock, *The Fontana History of Chemistry* (London: Fontana, 1992), 84–85.

[58]Berthollet's memoirs were delivered to Blagden at Dover by Legendre, but the *Nomenclature chimique* was brought to him in London, and he had already left London for Dover. So it appears that the copy Blagden had in Dover was meant for Banks. None of this matters since Cavendish received a copy from Lavoisier. Charles Blagden to Henry Cavendish, 16 Sep. 1787, Cavendish Mss X(b), 13. Charles Blagden to Claude Louis Berthollet, 17 Nov. 1787, draft, Blagden Letterbook, Royal Society, 7:85. Henry Cavendish, n.d. /Sep. 1787/, draft, Cavendish Mss, Misc., *Sci. Pap.* 2:324–26.

[59]Cavendish to Blagden, /Sep. 1787/, draft.

[60]Charles Blagden to Henry Cavendish, 23 Sep. 1787, Cavendish Mss X(b), 14.

scientists in their response to the nomenclature. There was a kind of British bluffness about their belief in common-language chemistry. Soon after the nomenclature, another good idea, the French metric system, was proposed, which prompted Cavendish's scientific friend George Shuckburgh to appeal to British "good sense" and "preserve, with the measures, the language of their fore-fathers": he would "call a yard a yard and a pound a pound."[61]

What is striking about the exchange between Cavendish and Blagden over the nomenclature is that the dissatisfaction it conveys was directed solely at systematic naming and not at all at the content of the theory it expressed. Cavendish not only did not oppose systematic chemistry, he insisted on it; a chemistry that was not regularly connected would have held no interest for him. To his chemical researches as to all of his scientific undertakings, he brought a strong theoretical need and competence. That phlogistic chemistry was systematic was evident to the chemists working within it, as it was to one who had just abandoned it in favor of Lavoisier's new system, L. B. Guyton de Morveau. To the upholder of phlogiston Kirwan, Guyton wrote that until now, Kirwan's phlogistic "system" was "without doubt both the most scientific and the most ingenious that has been proposed."[62] The kind of system that Cavendish did oppose was systematic naming, where it seemed to prejudice the theoretical questions. Other proposals of chemical nomenclature and shorthands around this same time were met with skepticism by Blagden.[63] The fate of phlogistic chemistry did not seem to be the issue with Cavendish. Blagden told Cavendish that Lavoisier had "ably combated the arguments of the phlogistic chemists,"[64] as if Blagden excluded Cavendish from the phlogistic chemists, as perhaps he did. Blagden and Berthollet had been in regular correspondence as representatives of their national societies, and by 1785 Berthollet was an anti-phlogistonist. That year Blagden wrote to Berthollet that the English had not given up on phlogiston; he mentioned its warm advocacy by Kirwan, "but with Mr. Cavendish it is a doubtful point."[65] Whether the "old hypothesis of p" is right or Lavoisier's that dephlogisticated air is a "simple substance," Blagden told Berthollet, is a "question which I think cannot remain long undecided."[66] To William Cullen, Blagden wrote about the

"question now warmly agitated relative to the existence of phlogiston"; whichever system, Stahl's or Lavoisier's, was adopted, however, Cavendish's work was of equal importance in either.[67] Two years later, in 1787, in the same letter in which he acknowledged receipt of the *Nomenclature chimique*, Blagden told Berthollet that his memoirs had answered the "principal objections made by the supporters of the old doctrine of phlogiston." The arguments of the new chemistry were so much clearer than those of phlogistic chemistry that the "combat must soon be at an end."[68] In these letters written at the turning point of the chemical revolution Blagden was expressing his own opin-ion, but we wonder to what degree, if any, it was in opposition to the opinion of the chemist he worked with daily, Cavendish.

If Kirwan is to be believed, by the time of the new chemical nomenclature, Cavendish had already given up on the old chemistry. In a postscript to a letter to one of the authors of the *Nomenclature chimique*, Guyton de Morveau, Kirwan wrote: "Mr Cavendish has renounced phlogiston." Kirwan did not give his source or elaborate, but what he said is consistent with what Blagden had been saying to and about Cavendish. The date was 2 April 1787, only a few weeks after van Marum had told Lavoisier that he had rejected phlogiston. Cavendish and van Marum were evidently the first two scientists outside of France to abandon the old

———————

[61]George Shuckburgh is quoted from his paper on weights and measures in the *Philosophical Transactions* for 1798 in Kisch, *Scales and Weights*, 19.

[62]This passage from Guyton's letter is translated by the editors of *A Scientific Correspondence During the Chemical Revolution: Louis-Bernard Guyton de Morveau and Richard Kirwan, 1782–1802*, ed. E. Grison, M. Sadoun-Goupil, and P. Bret (Berkeley: Office for History of Science and Technology, University of California at Berkeley, 1994), 33.

[63]"Dr. Black has just made a new chl nomenclature: I think he might have been better employed"; J.-H. Hassenfratz's chemical shorthand was thought to serve no "useful purpose" in England; and James Watt risked his reputation with his chemical algebra. Charles Blagden to M.-A. Pictet, 12 Feb. 1790, draft, and James Watt, 6 Dec. 1788, draft, Blagden Letterbook, Royal Society, 7:402 and 7:185.

[64]Blagden to Cavendish, 23 Sep. 1787.

[65]Charles Blagden to Claude Louis Berthollet, 21 May 1785, draft, Blagden Letterbook, Yale.

[66]Charles Blagden to Claude Louis Berthollet, 24 May 1785, draft, Blagden Letterbook, Yale.

[67]Charles Blagden to William Cullen, 5 July 1785, draft, Blagden Letterbook, Yale.

[68]Charles Blagden to Claude Louis Berthollet, 17 Nov. 1787, draft, Blagden Letterbook, Royal Society, 7:85.

chemistry.[69] There would soon be many. For example, the Jacksonian professor at Cambridge, Isaac Milner, who lectured on chemistry as well as on natural philosophy, saw the handwriting on the wall; in his final lecture, in 1788, he discussed Lavoisier's experiments and commented that the "antient hypothesis of Phlogiston seems overturned at one Stroke, and a new and simple theory substituted in its place—a Theory founded on direct and satisfactory Experiments."[70]

In 1788 an English translation of the new nomenclature came out, but its adoption by users of that language was relatively slow, given their reluctance to use French words or their anglicized versions and, in some cases, to parting with phlogiston. Priestley never adopted the new language nor gave up phlogiston. Black soon gave up phlogiston, but he accepted the new language only selectively and made up a partially new one of his own. In the 1790s, however, the French nomenclature was commonly used in Edinburgh as in London.[71] (In a letter in 1794 Blagden spoke of Thomas Beddoe's apparatus and the "dephlogisticated dog" inside it; he crossed out "dephlogisticated" and wrote instead "oxygenated." Scientifically correct speech had to be practiced.[72]) Cavendish, late in life, used Lavoisier's new names on occasion.[73]

Water Controversy

The "water controversy" arose from the following events. In 1781, as we have just seen, Cavendish repeated Warltire's experiment on the electrical sparking of inflammable and dephlogisticated air, determining that the resulting dew was pure water. He informed Priestley, who repeated the experiments and reported them to Watt. In a letter that circulated among members of the Royal Society, Watt concluded that water is a compound of inflammable and deplogisticated airs. Hearing about Cavendish's experiments and Watt's conclusions from Blagden on a trip to Paris in 1783, Lavoisier promptly did experiments of his own and wrote up an account of them.[74] Then, in 1784, Cavendish's paper on the condensation of water appeared. Cavendish, Watt, and Lavoisier, the principals in the water controversy, all had different interpretations of the meaning of the experiments, and from the point of view of the history of chemistry, that is all that matters. Cavendish's and Watt's differing phlogistic interpretations we have

already given; Lavoisier's was the modern interpretation: water is produced by the combination of hydrogen and oxygen. If the water controversy had been about these different interpretations, it would have been a controversy of the usual kind in science, but this one was about character. It began with the Swiss scientist Jean André Deluc, who had been living in England for ten years. This expert on meteorological instruments, whose work Cavendish respected and with whom he did experiments, was away in Paris at the time Cavendish's paper on the condensation of water was read in London, but he heard about it, and when he returned he asked Blagden for a copy of the manuscript to read. Deluc then wrote to his friend Watt that Cavendish had put forward Watt's discovery "word for word" without mentioning Watt. Watt, who believed the worst of Lavoisier, was prepared to believe that Cavendish had stolen his discovery as well. Blagden, who had carried the news about water to Lavoisier, was appalled by Lavoisier's claim, and he took a variety of measures, public and private, to set matters straight. Lavoisier stood corrected; Lavoisier after

---

[69]If, as Kirwan said, Cavendish gave up phlogiston, we still do not know his views on Lavoisier's theory. We do, however, know van Marum's. To Lavoisier on 26 Feb. 1787, Van Marum wrote that he had "adopted almost entirely your theory, having rejected phlogiston, which I regard at present as an insufficient and useless hypothesis . . ." To Kirwan on 13 Dec. 1787, Guyton de Morveau wrote: "You know that M. Van Marum has decomposed water by electricity, repeated the experiment with nitrous acid of M. Cavendish, and that he has also abandoned phlogiston." Van Marum's letter to Lavoisier of 26 Feb. 1787 is quoted, p. 175, n. 8, and Kirwan's letter to Guyton of 2 Apr. 1787 and Guyton's to Kirwan of 13 Dec. 1787 are published, pp. 165–67 and 171–77, in *A Scientific Correspondence During the Chemical Revolution.*

[70]L. J. M. Coleby, 'Isaac Milner and the Jacksonian Chair of Natural Philosophy," *Annals of Science* 10 (1954): 234–57, on 256.

[71]Maurice Crosland, *Historical Studies in the Language of Chemistry* (London: Heinemann, 1962), 193–206.

[72]Charles Blagden to Georgiana, duchess of Devonshire, 4 Jan. 1794, Devon. Coll.

[73]In computations made probably around 1800, Cavendish used "hydrogen" and "oxygen": Henry Cavendish, "Experiments on Air," Cavendish Mss II, 5:390. Blagden and Cavendish discussed a paper by Humboldt on the eudiometer, and Cavendish wrote to Blagden with his second thoughts about it. In this letter Cavendish uses Lavoisier's name for phlogisticated air (our nitrogen) "azote." This would have been at the end of the 1790s; some ten years had passed since his fulminations against Lavoisier's new chemical nomenclature. Henry Cavendish to Charles Blagden, 18 Dec. /no year/, Blagden Papers, Royal Society.

[74]The day after Lavoisier had repeated Cavendish's experiment, Blagden wrote to Banks that Lavoisier made the experiment after Blagden's account of it from Priestley's paper and Cavendish's verbal information. Letter of 25 June 1783, copy, BM(NH), DTC 3:184–86. It seems that word of Priestley's experiments had already reached Paris. Henry Guerlac, "Lavoisier, Antoine-Laurent," *DSB* 8:66–91, on 78.

all did not covet a discovery so much as all of chemistry, and the experiments on water had told him how to get it.[75]

The passion behind the water controversy was decidedly Watt's. He was an inventor and engineer for whom a stolen idea was stolen income, and he took pride in his scientific understanding. He told his informer Deluc that he did not depend on the favor of "Mr. C: or his friends; and could despise the united power of *the illustrious house of Cavendish*, as Mr. Fox calls them."[76] Cavendish was a rich man with a mean spirit, was how Watt put it.[77] Watt's outrage was fueled by a resentment of privilege that was not uncommon in England at the time (nor in France, which was only five years away from its political revolution). He began to cool down when he got hold of Cavendish's paper and saw that his and Cavendish's conclusions were not the same after all, and he and Cavendish later met on friendly terms, in Birmingham, where Watt not Cavendish was king, to examine steam engines. The trouble-maker in all this was Deluc, whose motives are unclear, though resentment over Cavendish's rejection of his ideas in a committee of the Royal Society may have been one of them. It may have been a case of bad conscience too, since at just this time Deluc allegedly was appropriating Joseph Black's discoveries in latent heat as his own, with Watt's unwitting help;[78] he had reason to ingratiate himself with Watt, and it might also have helped for him to believe that Cavendish was the true blackguard of science. Blagden's complicity in the water controversy was built into his relationship with Cavendish; intimacy with him was his scientific passport, while at the same time his zealous regard for the reputation of Cavendish made him vulnerable. Latter-day champions of Watt made Blagden a scapegoat, but he was guilty not of the unfairness and venality he was charged with but only of neglect of his own better interest. Nor was Cavendish guilty of exploiting Blagden's dependent position to get him to commit fraud on his behalf. Priestley comes off as the almost completely innocent party. But with the remote exception of Deluc, there was no malice on the part of anyone. When the steps leading to the dispute are examined one by one, this conclusion seems inescapable: the basic cause of this "controversy," as opposed to the scientific debate, was the casual way scientific information was communi-

cated in the eighteenth century. The discovery of the nature of water was timely, and the stakes were high, so that otherwise tolerable exchanges by letters, conversations, visits, meetings, with their indifferent datings, could, with proper incitement, seem darkly suspicious. As it turned out, precisely because there was also controversy of the usual kind, different interpretations of the same experiments, there was glory to go around. A second water controversy occurred long after the participants of the first were dead. The revival was prompted by the secretary of the French Academy D. F. J. Arago's éloge of Watt with its revisionist history of the discovery of water. This controversy was fueled by passion of another kind, familiar in the nineteenth century, nationalism. It was the occasion for Cavendish's unpublished scientific work to begin to be made public, and so it had that value if probably no other.

Keeping Up with Chemistry

In 1784 the German chemist Lorenz Crell launched the *Chemische Annalen*, a monthly journal that replaced the quarterly one he had been editing. Cavendish took great interest in this journal, which had the support of German chemists and favored, as he still did, the phlogiston approach to chemistry. Cavendish was soon in touch with the editor about subscriptions. It was no simple matter to obtain foreign journals in England in the eighteenth century, as Cavendish's negotiations with Crell bear out.

The water controversy had begun, and as a result Cavendish and the *Chemische Annalen* had gotten off on the wrong foot. In his new journal Crell had published two accounts of the discovery

[75]Our main source here is George Wilson, *The Life of the Honourable Henry Cavendish* (London, 1846), which is primarily about the water controversy. James Watt to Jean André Deluc, 6 Mar. 1784, in *Correspondence of the Late James Watt on His Discovery of the Theory of the Composition of Water*, ed. J. P. Muirhead (London, 1846), 48–49.

[76]Jean André Deluc to James Watt, 1 Mar. 1784, in *Correspondence of the Late James Watt*, 48–49.

[77]Still fuming, Watt again identified Cavendish as "a member of the illustrious house of Cavendish, worth above £ 100,000, and does not spend £ 1000 per year. Rich men may do mean actions . . ." James Watt to Mr. Fry of Bristol, 15 May 1784, *Correspondence of the Late James Watt*, 61.

[78]According to an account of the controversy between Black and Deluc in the *Edinburgh Review* in 1803, as quoted in Paul A. Tunbridge, "Jean André De Luc," *Notes and Records of the Royal Society of London* 26 (1971): 15–33, on 27–28.

concerning air and water in which Lavoisier was named the discoverer and Cavendish the confirmer. Crell wrote to Banks for more information about Cavendish's work. Banks passed the letter to Blagden, who replied to Crell with a "short history of the discovery," setting Crell straight by correcting the claims of Lavoisier, who had "suppressed part of the truth." Blagden complimented Crell on the quick publication of translated extracts from Cavendish's paper containing the true discovery and for Crell's correct dating of the paper, 1784, instead of 1783, as the separately printed cover of the paper had erroneously put it. This first letter from Blagden to Crell included the latest scientific news from Britain, meant to entice Crell to join in a regular scientific exchange between the two countries.[79]

Crell proposed to publish Blagden's short history of Cavendish's discovery. Although Blagden had not intended it for the public, he had no objection, since it was "strictly true." He only hoped that Crell's German translation of it would rather "soften than strengthen the expressions," since however poorly Lavoisier had behaved in this affair, he was "upon the whole a very respectable character & eminent as a philosopher." Again Blagden enclosed scientific news, in keeping with his invitation to Crell. The news had to do with "Mr Cavendish, whose name I shall so often have occasion to mention in this correspondence," but this time it had to do with Cavendish's new work on the freezing of mercury rather than the history of his old. Definitely from this point on, and no doubt from the beginning, the guiding hand behind Blagden's correspondence with Crell was Cavendish's.[80]

The German chemist knew of Cavendish's rank but little of English titles. "The Honourable Henry Cavendish (not My Lord)," Blagden corrected him. The Honourable Henry Cavendish—and this was the point of Blagden's writing in this instance—"desires to become one of your subscribers." To this end, Blagden said, Cavendish had given directions to the post office to ensure that he received the journals promptly.[81] It proved a futile hope.

Six months later, on 4 July 1786, Blagden wrote to Crell that the postmaster at Amsterdam had told him that some of the packets Crell had sent were held up at Amsterdam because of their large size and were probably irrecoverable. Crell

had sent them not by post but by stagecoach or wagon, conveyances which were not "connected with but in opposition to the Post." By post Cavendish succeeded in receiving a few issues of the *Chemische Annalen* and its supplement, the *Beiträge*, and Blagden instructed Crell to send Cavendish the rest by post as well. When after three months the issues had not yet arrived in London, Blagden complained to the post office and then to Crell: "Mr Cavendish pays many times the original value of the work to have it in this manner quick by the post; but the various delays have entirely frustrated that object."[82] The post office proved not to be a better way. Two years later, at last, the business of delivery was settled and the correspondence on it ended: "Mr Cavendish finds it more convenient to get the Ch. Annalen," Blagden wrote to Crell, "in the common way, tho' a little later, than to be perplexed with the post office; he . . . will not give you any further trouble on the subject."[83]

But complications continued. There was the matter of payment for the subscription, of how much and to whom. Blagden told Crell to send directions and to appoint some person to collect Cavendish's money. In addition to Cavendish there were others in Britain who wanted to subscribe, for example, the chemist Kirwan, and Banks, who wanted to subscribe both for his own library and for the king's, and the journal could not be sent to everyone "through the same channel under one cover." Then, in addition to Crell's journal, there were other publications by Crell that Cavendish wanted: from his German bookseller, Cavendish had ordered Crell's *Auswahl aus den neuen Entdeckungen*, but the bookseller had disappointed

[79]Charles Blagden to Lorenz Crell, 28 Apr. 1785, draft, Blagden Letterbook, Yale.

[80]Charles Blagden to Lorenz Crell, 2 Dec. 1785, draft, Blagden Letterbook, Royal Society, 7:738. The historical part of Blagden's letter was translated in Crell's journal in 1786. It was translated back into English by Muirhead, *Correspondence of the Late James Watt*, 71–74, and reprinted in Wilson, *Cavendish*, 362–63. Wilson dates the letter 1786, p. 144, but it was written in early 1785.

[81]Charles Blagden to Lorenz Crell, 20 Jan. 1786, draft, Blagden Letterbook, Royal Society, 7:742.

[82]Charles Blagden to Lorenz Crell, 4 July, 12 Aug., and 13 Oct. 1786, drafts; Charles Blagden to Charles Jackson at the post office, 10 Oct. 1786, Blagden Letterbook, Royal Society, 7:7, 26, 44, and 45. By July 4, Cavendish had received the first and second issues of the *Annalen* and the fourth issue of volume 1 of the *Beiträge*. On 13 October, he was still waiting for the third through sixth issues of the *Annalen* and the first through third issues of the *Beiträge*.

[83]Charles Blagden to Lorenz Crell, 4 Apr. 1788, draft, Blagden Letterbook, Royal Society, 7:137.

him. Crell offered to copy out the material Cavendish wanted, but instead Cavendish asked Crell to send the entire volumes directly.[84]

To send scientific publications from Britain to Germany was no simpler than the reverse. Blagden sent a copy of Cavendish's latest paper to Crell in a packet, which he gave to William Herschel, who was going to Göttingen to erect one of his telescopes as a present from the king. From Göttingen, Herschel was to forward the packet by the nearest conveyance to Helmstadt, where Crell would receive it. Blagden apologized to Crell: "It is extremely difficult to get an opportunity of sending you any thing from England, otherwise you should be furnished sooner with such publications."[85]

Blagden and Crell corresponded about the science of the day while struggling with the slow business of getting scientific publications from one country to the next. Blagden wrote to Cavendish about his last letter from Crell, which mixed scientific news and subscription delays: "I hope you got Mr. Heydinger to read Crell's letter; there was something about your subscription from his journal which he allows to have been already paid, & an account of the freezing of /mercury/ by natural cold in Russia, perfectly conformable to Mr. Hutchins's experiments. . . Be so good as to open & read or get read any letters that you think may contain news."[86] Correspondence was the surest and quickest way of exchanging scientific news, but it was not a substitute for complete publications. Cavendish's protracted exchange with Crell, through Blagden, shows his determination to keep posted (and as promptly as possible) on developments in the subject of his researches.

Exactitude

We have suggested that Henry Cavendish's early chemical correspondent was John Hadley, the fourth professor of chemistry at Cambridge. Hadley had taken his teaching seriously, but since the chair was not endowed, he received no salary and had to depend on student fees, a problematic source since chemistry was not a subject students needed for the examinations. Hadley left Cambridge to practice medicine in London in 1760, but he did not give up his chair, perhaps intending to return. He died unexpectedly in 1764, whereupon the chair again became available. The person elected to it that year was Robert Smith's protégé Richard

Watson, second wrangler in 1759 and now fellow of Trinity. His main qualification was his willingness to take the impecunious position, since he readily conceded that he knew nothing about chemistry. But he worked hard to learn it, and he was soon giving experimental lectures, teaching students privately, and working in his own laboratory. His lecturing began in the same year as Cavendish's first published paper, on factitious air, in 1766, and his approach to chemistry was clearly based on the precise quantitative experimental work reported in that paper. His *Plan of a Course of Chemical Lectures*, published in 1771, makes that connection explicit. To a bright young person like Watson taking up chemistry in the 1760s, the promising direction could be seen, correctly; it was the chemistry of Cavendish, and of Black and Lavoisier, that of quantitative exactness.[87]

For its logogram, the Cavendish Society, a nineteenth-century chemists' publishing club, picked the glass vessel in which Cavendish detonated gases to obtain water. This apparatus, which appeared on the title page of Wilson's biography of Cavendish, was a kind of eudiometer, and it was fitting, but the Society might have chosen another apparatus or instrument just as well. Although it lacked the urn-like simple beauty (or the controversial relevance) of the water vessel, the air pump might have stood for "Cavendish"; or just the pump's pear-shaped glass bulb for holding mercury would have been sufficient. In his experiments on phlogisticated air and nitrous acid—experiments of the same kind as those on water—Cavendish needed the best vacuum he could get, and so a good air pump. As with all the

---

[84] Blagden to Crell, 4 July and 12 Aug. 1786.

[85] Blagden to Crell, 4 July 1786.

[86] Charles Blagden to Henry Cavendish, 23 Sep. 1787, Cavendish Mss X(b), 14. As Crell knew, Cavendish would have been interested in the confirmation of Hutchins's experiments, which he had directed. Cavendish evidently could not read Crell's script and relied on Blagden's account of the letters.

[87] Through political connections, Watson got a 100 pound grant from the king for his chemical teaching, but when the well-endowed regius professorship of divinity was vacated by Thomas Rutherforth, Watson preferred it and was appointed to it in 1771. He published several papers in the *Philosophical Transactions*. His paper of 1770 is a good example of his method, a quantitative study of specific gravities: "Experiments and Observations on Various Phaenomena Attending the Solution of Salts," *PT* 60 (1770): 325–54. Between 1781 and 1787, he published five popular, elementary volumes on chemistry, entitled *Chemical Essays*. L. J. M. Coleby, "Richard Watson, Professor of Chemistry in the University of Cambridge, 1764–71," *Annals of Science* 9 (1953): 101–23, on 102–7, 121–22.

instruments he used, his success with the air pump was based on his grasp of the physical principles, as we now illustrate. With his greatly improved air pump of the 1750s, John Smeaton claimed a rarefaction of air of 1000 or 2000 times instead of the previous limit of less than 150. Implicit confidence was placed in his claim until the instrument-maker Edward Nairne discovered a fallacy, to which he was led after obtaining incredible rarefactions of 100,000. By making comparisons with other standard gauges, Nairne saw that the error lay in Smeaton's new gauge, the pear-shaped bulb, but Nairne did not know the reason for it. He showed an experiment with the air pump to Smeaton and other Fellows of the Royal Society. Cavendish, one of the Fellows, explained that the discrepancy was due to water vapor. To get the gauges to agree, he said, the pump must be as free as possible of all traces of water, since Smeaton's gauge did not measure vapor pressure in addition to the air pressure as other gauges did. When Nairne took this precaution, the gauges agreed and the rarefaction turned out to be a believable 600. Cavendish's explanation rested on his father's experiments, which showed that whenever the pressure of the atmosphere on water is reduced to a certain degree (which depends on temperature), the water is immediately turned into vapor and is as immediately turned back into water on restoring the pressure.[88] This change of state affected Smeaton's gauge but not the others. Or the Cavendish Society might have picked for its logogram the thermometer, the instrument to which Cavendish devoted more attention to than to any other. But, we think, the logogram best typifying Cavendish's technique in chemistry would have been the instrument of weighing, the balance. Cavendish owned the first of the great precision balances of the eighteenth century.[89] Built to Cavendish's plan, the balance is housed in a rough wooden case standing about ten feet. Made of sheet iron 19½ inches long, the beam is supported by steel knife edges rotating on steel planes, and suspended from its ends by brass universal joints are the weighing pans, measuring about a foot across and placed about two feet beneath the beam. The balance is capable of weighing to an accuracy of 5 milligrams.[90] It is not dated but the instrument-maker's name is known to be Harrison. This is not the John Harrison of the chronometers nor his only

surviving son, William. He is very likely another William Harrison, whom Cavendish employed as his private instrument-maker in his later years.[91] Cavendish's weighings were persuasive. Blagden said it with clarity in a letter at the time to his counterpart in the French Academy, Berthollet: upon exploding the two elastic fluids, Cavendish found the *weight* of the two fluids to be equal to the *weight* of the resulting water, and that settled it for him; all that remained was for him to show that the water was just that, pure water.[92]

Lavoisier was usually a meticulous weigher too, and like Cavendish he knew how to make weighing effective in scientific arguments.[93] When Lavoisier learned of Cavendish's experiments on water, he made his own with the assistance of the great mathematical astronomer P. S. Laplace. So caught up did Laplace become in chemistry that Blagden inquired if what he was told was true, that Laplace "had renounced his mathematical studies, & was applying himself solidly to chemistry."[94] Thanks to the balance, chemistry was becoming a

----

[88]This clarification of the air pump occurred in 1776. It was described by Nairne in a paper and by Charles Hutton in his entry "Air" in *Mathematical and Philosophical Dictionary*, vol. 1 (London, 1795), 56–57.

[89]After Cavendish's balance, Jesse Ramsden made the next great balance, for the Royal Society The next after that were the ones made for Lavoisier by P. Mégnié and J. N. Fortin. The innovations in Cavendish's balance included the knife edges of the beam, the form of the beam, the kind of suspension used for the pans, the lift for the beam, the regulation of the sensitivity of the balance, and the index. Maurice Daumas, *Scientific Instruments of the Seventeenth and Eighteenth Centuries*, trans. M. Holbrook (New York: Praeger, 1972), 134–35, 221–23.

[90]Ernest Child, *The Tools of the Chemist* (New York: Reinhold, 1940), 79.

[91]From Lord George Cavendish's list of Henry Cavendish's servants at his death in 1810, we know that his instrument-maker's name was William Harrison. At that time this William Harrison was sixty-one. Earlier he had worked for Ramsden, and so we can assume that he was highly skilled. He was a source of one of the accounts of Cavendish's death, in Wilson, *Cavendish*, 183.

[92]Charles Blagden to Claude Louis Berthollet, 24 Oct. 1783, draft, Blagden Letterbook, Yale.

[93]Lavoisier could be cavalier with weights too. When he and Laplace burned oxygen and hydrogen to obtain water, they did not keep track of the exact quantities of the gases, but they thought it was safe to assume that the weights of the gases and of the water formed from them were equal. According to Blagden, who witnessed it, Lavoisier and Laplace's first experiment on the production of water was "good for nothing as to determining the proportions of air & water," and their only dependable result was the test of the purity of water; they intended to repeat the experiment with the "necessary precision," but the account of this first experiment was read before the Academy of Sciences anyway. Charles Blagden to Joseph Banks, 25 June 1783, BM(NH), DTC 3.56–58. Henry Guerlac, "Lavoisier, Antoine-Laurent," *DSB* 8:66–91, on 78.

[94]Charles Blagden to Claude Louis Berthollet, 8 Dec. 1789, draft, Blagden Letterbook, Royal Society, 7:377.

science exact enough to win over an astronomer. When he read Cavendish's paper on water, Laplace wrote to Blagden that Cavendish's experiments were "infinitely important" and made with the "precision and finesse that distinguish that excellent physicist."[95] This may be taken as a tribute from one astronomer to another, both of whom were working in chemistry. In the combination of skills Cavendish brought to chemistry, he was, in effect, Laplace and Lavoisier in one. What Laplace said of Cavendish's work everyone else who commented on it said too: it was work of exemplary precision. This way in which Cavendish's work was distinguished was the direction chemistry was taking in the late eighteenth century, at which time already about a third of all chemical publications were quantitative. Cavendish's work, all quantitative (at the very least, he measured what went in and what came out) was widely read; of British authors in chemistry, his and Priestley's were cited most often at home, and in France his came only after Priestley's.[96] It was appreciated that to communicate productively with Cavendish it was good to deal in quantities, if possible. The only letter containing a quantitative table in Priestley's correspondence is Priestley's first letter to Cavendish, sent with the hope of beginning an exchange.[97] Cavendish's lasting work in chemistry was the impetus he gave to the increasing precision of that science (far removed from the misunderstandings of the original water controversy and from the theater put on by the schoolish resurrectors of the water controversy in the nineteenth century).

We conclude our discussion with an example of precision in Cavendish's chemistry. The meaningful recording of natural events in numbers presupposes standards, whereby tests can be made, allowing the numbers obtained by experiment or observation to be compared. In all parts of science in which he worked, Cavendish introduced standards; since agreed-upon international standards of science did not yet exist, he had to define his own. Typical of Cavendish's practice is his weighings of acids and alkalies, in which he used the concept of "equivalent weights." This concept gained power with the atomic theory of chemistry, but before then it served Cavendish very well, as before Cavendish it had served others. The concept goes back to the turn of the eighteenth century, to Wilhelm Homberg, who is remembered for

introducing scientific chemistry into the French Academy. Homberg's most important work was to provide a way to arrange acids by their relative strengths in neutralizing alkalies, which provided the foundation of the understanding of neutral salts.[98] Working quantitatively, Homberg determined the weights of various acids required to neutralize an equivalent weight of an alkali, salt of tartar.[99] His method was deficient in one respect: it ignored the weight of gases absorbed and given off, as Black pointed out in his work on magnesia alba.[100] James Keir, the translator of Macquer's *Dictionary of Chemistry* in 1771, said that most of Macquer's errors "proceeded from the author not having been acquainted with some very late discoveries, especially those important ones concerning *fixable air*." Keir corrected Homberg's table of the equivalent weights of four acids referred to salt of tartar with numbers he took from Cavendish's 1766 paper on factitious air.[101] From the start of his chemical researches, Cavendish recorded equivalent weights and was evidently the first to use the word "equivalent."[102] The substance Cavendish began with, tartar, would seem to relate his direction in chemistry to Homberg's quantitative equivalents.[103] In his first publication, on factitious air, Cavendish compared the weights of different alkalis required to saturate a given quantity of acid to 1000 grains of marble, his standard; by this measure, he ranked alkalis by the quantities of fixed air they contained, the subject of his research.[104] By the use of the balance, Cavendish gave to chemistry an ordering, which was one by quantity instead of by nomenclature. His equivalent weights prefigured the

---

[95]Pierre Simon Laplace to Charles Blagden, 7 May 1785, Blagden Letters, Royal Society, L.181.

[96]H. Gilman McCann, *Chemistry Transformed: The Paradigmatic Shift from Phlogiston to Oxygen* (Norwood: Ablex, 1978), 143–46.

[97]Joseph Priestley to Henry Cavendish, 31 May 1784, Cavendish Mss, New Correspondence; published in *Scientific Autobiography of Joseph Priestley*, 231–32.

[98]Marie Boas Hall, "Homberg, Wilhelm or Guillaume," *DSB* 6:477–78.

[99]J. R. Partington, *A History of Chemistry*, vol. 3 (London: Macmillan, 1962), 44–45.

[100]Joseph Black, *Experiments upon Magnesia Alba, Quicklime, and Some Other Alkaline Substances*, 1755 (Edinburgh: Alembic Club Reprints, No. 1, 1898), 17–18.

[101]Entry "Acid" in Macquer's *Dictionary of Chemistry*.

[102]Partington, *History of Chemistry* 3:320.

[103]Henry Cavendish, "New Experiments on Tartar," Cavendish Mss II, 2(b):13.

[104]Henry Cavendish, "Three Papers, Containing Experiments on Factitious Air," in *Sci. Pap.* 2:92–94, 96.

quantitative laws of chemistry, such as the laws of combining proportions, which were the next stage in the development of chemistry. In chemistry, as in other parts of natural philosophy, Cavendish's insistence on standards gave to his work its characteristic stamp of exactitude.

CHAPTER 4

⚜

✍Mercury

Cold

In the 1780s Cavendish returned to his researches on heat at the same time that he returned to those on chemistry, two fields which for him always had a large overlap. He published three papers dealing specifically with experiments on cold; they rested on the totality of his understanding of heat.

In the 1770s Pyotr Simon Pallas, a member of the St. Petersburg Academy of Sciences, published the results of his scientific explorations of Siberia,[1] where he recorded a temperature of minus 70 degrees Fahrenheit. The mercury of Pallas's thermometer froze to the glass stem, and Pallas noted, as did Cavendish, that when the mercury began to melt the thermometer stood at minus 45 degrees.[2] Pallas's discussion was perceptive; by this time some, but by no means full, clarification had been brought to the subject of extreme cold.

Temperatures down to forty degrees below zero had been achieved artificially by Fahrenheit, using a mixture of spirit of nitre and ice.[3] That, as it turned out, was nothing compared to subsequent accounts of artificial cold produced by freezing mixtures and to other accounts of the extremes of natural cold in the frozen parts of the earth, such as the natural historian Johann Georg Gmelin's readings with the mercury thermometer in Siberia of 120 degrees below zero.[4] (We can surmise why Lord Charles Cavendish entertained his dinner guests with experiments on the production of artificial cold in 1750, for it was the year after the publication of Gmelin's travels with his report of the incredible cold of Siberia. William Watson, who reported on Gmelin's observations, was one of the guests at Charles Cavendish's dinner-demonstration.[5])

At the beginning of his researches on heat, in 1765, having just shown that cold is produced by a change of state of substances, such as from ice to liquid water, Cavendish examined the cold produced by mixtures of snow and chemical reagents, record-ing temperatures of around 20 degrees Fahrenheit. He seems to have done nothing more with artificial cold until ten years later, in January 1776, when with a mixture of snow and aqua fortis he reached 25 degrees *below* zero. That still was not equal to the natural cold that had frozen the mercury in Pallas's thermometer in Siberia, but that was not Cavendish's object either, since the experiments he wanted done on the freezing of mercury had already begun at Albany Fort, in Hudson's Bay.

The first clear evidence of the freezing of mercury—the substance once regarded as the essence of fluidity—was already fifteen years old. In St. Petersburgh in December 1759, J. A. Braun especially but also Aepinus and other academicians witnessed mercury cold enough to be hammered and drawn like any other metal. In the *Philosophical Transactions* for 1761, William Watson published an enthusiastic account of Braun's work on this "intirely new" subject.[6] In a paper he gave to the St. Petersburgh Academy—Cavendish made a long extract of this paper—Braun told of repeating Fahrenheit's experiments with snow and spirit of nitre and being surprised when the mercury in the thermometer fell hundreds of degrees below zero.

---

[1]Pyotr Simon Pallas, *Reise durch verschiedenen Provinzen des russischen Reiches in den Jahren 1768–1773*, 2 vols. (St Petersburg, 1771–76).

[2]"Account of Freezing of /mercury/ from Pallas Journey into Siberia," extract in Cavendish's hand, Cavendish Mss III(a), 15.

[3]This experiment by Fahrenheit was reported in Boerhaave's *Chemistry*. Cromwell Mortimer, "A Discourse Concerning the Usefulness of Thermometers in Chemical Experiments . . .," *PT* 46 (1746–47): 672–95, on 682.

[4]Earlier, in our discussion of science at the time Henry Cavendish was studying at the university, we quoted Gmelin on his finding of 120 degrees below zero on the Fahrenheit scale and Watson's acceptance of this remarkable cold. John Fothergill, "An Account of Some Observations and Experiments Made in Siberia, Extracted from the Preface to the Flora Siberica . . . /by/ Gmelin . . .," *PT* 45 (1748): 248–62, on 258–60. William Watson, "A Comparison of Different Thermometrical Observations in Siberia," *PT* 48 (1753): 108–9.

[5]Thomas Birch to Philip Yorke, 18 Aug. 1750, BL Add Mss 35397, f. 277.

[6]William Watson, "An Account of a Treatise in Latin, Presented to the Royal Society, Intitled, De admirando frigore artificiali, quo mercurius est congelatus, dissertatio, &," *PT* 52 (1761): 156–72.

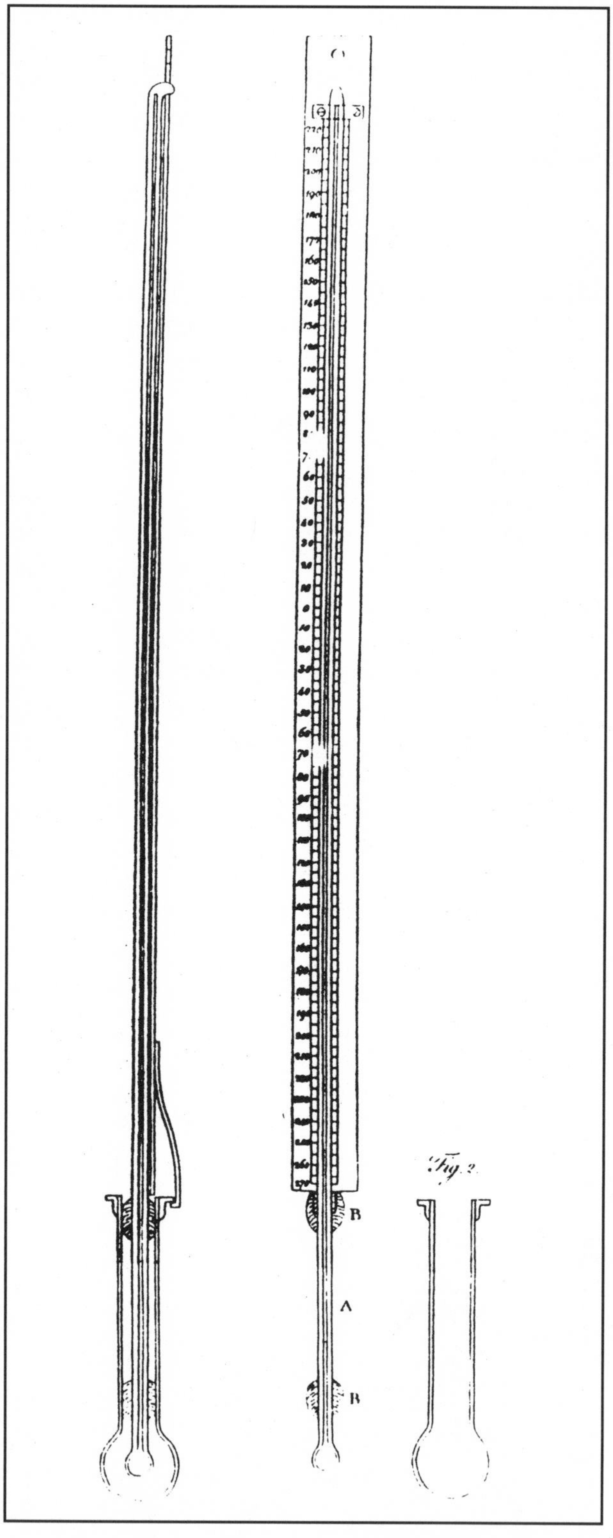

PLATE XII. Hudson's Bay Thermometers. Figure 1 shows the thermometer with the stem and bulb extending below the scale. Figure 3 gives a side view of the thermometer with the extended stem and bulb inserted into a cylinder holding the mercury to be frozen. Thomas Hutchins, "Experiments for Ascertaining the Point of Mercurial Congelation," *Philosophical Transactions* 73 (1783): *370.

Braun could arrive at no consistent freezing point of mercury.[7]

Braun's experiments were repeated by Thomas Hutchins, governor of Albany Fort, in Hudson's Bay, using the instruments and the instructions sent to him by the Royal Society. In the winter of 1774, Hutchins arrived at what Braun had, frozen mercury, and the same inconclusiveness about the freezing temperature. There seemed to be no instant of freezing, for without changing appearance the mercury continued to fall to below minus 400 degrees. Hutchins asked the Royal Society for more tubes of mercury capable of graduation to *1000 degrees below zero*.[8] The reason why Hutchins's experiments had got no further than Braun's was evident to the two persons who had clarified for themselves the principles of latent heat, Joseph Black and Cavendish. In a letter in 1779 about Braun's and Hutchins's experiments, Black said that frozen mercury could not record its own freezing temperature. To get around that difficulty he proposed a new experimental arrangement, which was to surround the thermometer bulb containing mercury with a mercury bath. Since metals solidify slowly from the outside inward, when the mercury in the bath is frozen but that in the bulb is still liquid, the thermometer can record the freezing temperature. Hutchins informed the Royal Society of Black's proposal, which he made the basis of his next series of experiments. Cavendish had already proposed the same apparatus. To Cavendish the apparatus had suggested itself, since the experiment on mercury was a repeat of his many experiments on the freezing of metals. The reason why a mercury thermometer cannot of its own measure the freezing point of mercury is that, as Braun's and Hutchins's experiments made clear, mercury contracts upon freezing and thereby registers a heat far below its freezing temperature. Black did not publish on this subject, but this time Cavendish did.[9]

---

[7]This extract, in Cavendish's hand, in Cavendish Mss, Misc, is an account of the experiments by several Petersburg academicians following Braun's discovery; in English translation from the French by James Parsons, "An Account of Artificial Cold Produced at Petersburg: By Dr. Himsel. In a Letter to Dr. De Castro, F.R.S.," *PT* 51 (1760): 670–76.

[8]Thomas Hutchins, "An Account of Some Attempts to Freeze Quicksilver, at Albany Fort, in Hudson's Bay, in the Year 1775: with Observations on the Dipping-needle," *PT* 66 (1776): 174–81.

[9]Joseph Black to Andrew Graham on 5 Oct. 1779; letter published by Thomas Hutchins in "Experiments for Ascertaining the Point of Mercurial Congelation," *PT* 73 (1783): *303–*370, on

The reason for delegating the experiments on cold to the Hudson's Bay Company was that it was located in a cold climate, a better place than (relatively) warm London. Cavendish drew up lists of experiments on the freezing of mercury and the expansion with heat of some other fluids and showed them to the president of the Royal Society, Sir Joseph Banks.[10] He then supplied Hutchins with apparatus, with which Hutchins froze mercury by exposing it both to freezing mixtures and to natural cold, determining the freezing point both ways. Hutchins's experiments were "very accurate," Cavendish told John Michell.[11] In his next paper on the freezing of mercury, in 1783, Hutchins said that his "excellent instructions" left him with "nothing to do but to follow them."[12]

Hutchins's paper in the *Philosophical Transactions* was followed directly by a paper by Cavendish. Cavendish's "observations" on Hutchins's experiments confirmed Cavendish's hypothesis, which was that the great sinking of mercury in thermometers in extreme cold is owing to the great contraction of mercury. The earlier reports of the great cold produced by freezing mixtures would, if true, have been "really astonishing," but these were actually reports about the contraction of mercury. Submerged in freezing mixtures, Hutchins's thermometer fell to 450 degrees below zero, but the cold of the freezing mixture was never less than 46 degrees below zero. Referring to the results of his much earlier, unpublished experiments on freezing lead and tin, Cavendish said that he had "no reason to doubt that the same thing would obtain in quicksilver." He referred also to his experiments on the latent heat of water, presenting the investigation into the freezing of mercury as a direct continuation of his work from the 1760s.[13]

The only kind of instrument used in these experiments was the thermometer. Although in the experiments there were subsidiary considerations—these were the burden of Cavendish's "observations"—the essential point was clearly and simply demonstrated. The thermometer placed in the container of mercury fell to minus 40 degrees where it stayed, while another thermometer placed in the freezing mixture of snow and spirit of nitre continued to fall. The only interpretation could be that mercury freezes at minus 40 degrees. Hutchins returned to England, meeting with Cavendish and Blagden at Cavendish's house in Hampstead to demonstrate the apparatus.[14] Hutchins then returned them to the Royal Society, where in the best practice of the time, in the presence of witnesses—in addition to Cavendish, they were Banks, Hutchins, Nairne (who made them), and Charles Blagden—they were examined according to the procedure recommended by the boiling-point committee of 1777. By making corrections for the boiling point on Hutchins's thermometers, the adjusted freezing temperature of mercury was declared to be minus 38⅔ degrees or, in round numbers, minus 39 degrees, in remarkably close agreement with the modern value, minus 38.87 degrees. Mercury, upon freezing, Cavendish concluded, shrinks by almost ⅟₂₃rd of its bulk, which is also close to modern measurements.[15]

In 1789 Cavendish received a letter from Richard Walker, who told of freezing mercury in the presence of some Oxford professors. Walker thought it was the first time it had been done in Britain, and there is no reason he should have thought otherwise.[16] Cavendish himself had frozen mercury six years before at Hampstead, and at the time he had shown it to Blagden and told friends about it, but he did not publish the fact.[17] Cavendish had simply been doing experiments in parallel to the more accurate ones done under his direction in the Canadian cold by Hutchins.

---

on *305–*306. Black did not give his "reasons" for the inability of a mercury thermometer to measure the freezing temperature of mercury, but they obviously included the contraction of mercury. Cavendish said that he had recommended the apparatus to the president of the Royal Society, Joseph Banks, who had approved it. Black had not known what Cavendish had done. Henry Cavendish, "Observations on Mr. Hutchins's Experiments for Determining the Degree of Cold at Which Quicksilver Freezes," *PT* 73 (1783):303–28; *Sci. Pap.* 2: 145–60, on 149.

[10] There are many related drafts in Cavendish's papers, most collected in Cavendish Mss III(a), 4 and 14. The first group is mainly concerned with Hutchins's experiments published in 1783, though it contains some subsequent instructions sent in 1784. The second group is concerned with the next series of experiments at Hudson's Bay Company, conducted by John McNab, published in 1786 and 1788. In addition, there are unclassified papers on the Hudson's Bay experiments in the miscellany of Cavendish's manuscripts.

[11] Henry Cavendish to John Michell, 27 May 1783, draft, Cavendish Mss, New Correspondence.

[12] Hutchins, "Experiments for Ascertaining the Point of Mercurial Congelation," *304.

[13] Cavendish, "Observations," 146, 150–51.

[14] Thomas Hutchins to Charles Blagden, n.d., "Monday Morning," Blagden Letters, Royal Society, H.59.

[15] Cavendish, "Observations," 148, 157.

[16] Richard Walker to Henry Cavendish, 4 Jan. 1789, Cavendish Mss, New Correspondence.

[17] Cavendish to Michell, 27 May 1783.

Cavendish was not done with artificial cold. In 1783 he built an apparatus to produce cold by rarefying air mechanically,[18] and over the next few years Adair Crawford and Erasmus Darwin did experiments with the same goal.[19] Wanting to know the greatest cold that could be produced by a freezing mixture of snow and various chemical solutions, Cavendish requested more experiments at Hudson's Bay, and these too he published, in 1786 and 1788. This time his experimenter-at-a-distance was John McNab, master at Henley's House, Hudson's Bay.

Cavendish was fortunate in his Hudson's Bay experimenters, first Hutchins and then McNab, who earned rare praise from Cavendish for their "utmost attention and accuracy" and "great judgement." They also showed extraordinary endurance; McNab did his experiments in weather that reached fifty degrees below zero. The new experiments provided these results: cold "greatly superior" to any yet produced (as opposed to claimed), and insight into the "remarkable" way nitrous and vitriolic acids freeze.[20]

In a field, heat, which had only just begun to be quantitative, Cavendish introduced the "standard" measures he had first used in his experiments on gases, specifying the strength of acids in the freezing mixtures by the weight of marble they could dissolve. He made a table of specific gravities of the acids corresponding to a range of strengths of the acids at a temperature of sixty degrees; this table corresponds with modern, theoretical values to the third decimal.[21] In his attempt to determine the strength of acid that required the least degree of cold to freeze, he made a discovery: there were several "points of easiest freezing" of acids, points of "inflexion" (corresponding to various hydrates).[22] Cavendish asked McNab to do another set of experiments on the freezing of acids of varying strengths, which became the subject of Cavendish's last paper on heat, in 1788.[23]

Heat

In 1810 Blagden was selected by Lord George Cavendish and, presumably, by William, duke of Devonshire, to write the obituary of Cavendish for the "papers." Blagden began it with the observation that Cavendish had made himself master of "every part of Sir Isaac Newton's philosophy." It is odd that in what follows Blagden

failed to mention Cavendish's work on heat, although he made note of all of his other major works. Odd, we say, because in none of his other work was Cavendish known to have declared himself publicly a more decided follower of Newton than in his work on heat, and also because Blagden assisted Cavendish in this work. If there is a circumstance that might bear on Blagden's neglect or forgetfulness in his obituary of his late friend and colleague, it is that Blagden subscribed to the popular material theory of heat, of which, as we will see, Cavendish held a low, almost contemptuous, opinion.[24]

In 1783 Cavendish determined the freezing point of mercury with the help of the concept of latent heat, but he did not use the word *latent*, deliberately not, because it "relates to an hypothesis depending on the supposition, that the heat of bodies is owing to their containing more or less of a substance called the matter of heat; and as I think

---

*   [18] The accounts of these experiments are published in Henry Cavendish, *The Scientific Papers of the Honourable Henry Cavendish*, ed. E. Thorpe, 2 vols. (Cambridge: Cambridge University Press, 1921) 2:384–89.

[19] Charles Blagden to Erasmus Darwin, 14 Sep. 1786, draft, Blagden Letterbook, Royal Society, 7:34. Charles Blagden to Mrs. Grey, 30 Jan. 1788, ibid., 7:111.

[20] Henry Cavendish, "An Account of Experiments Made by John McNab, at Henly House, Hudson's Bay, Relating to Freezing Mixtures," *PT* 76 (1786): 241–72; in *Sci Pap.* 2: 195–213, on 195.

[21] The comparison was made by Thorpe, in Cavendish, *Sci. Pap.* 2:59–60.

[22] Ibid., 62.

[23] Henry Cavendish, "An Account of Experiments Made by Mr. John McNab, at Albany Fort, Hudson's Bay, Relative to the Freezing of Nitrous and Vitriolic Acids," *PT* 78 (1788): 166–81; in *Sci. Pap.* 2: 214–23.

[24] The complete draft of Blagden's obituary of Cavendish, Blagden Collection, Royal Society, Misc Notes, No. 225. The obituary was published in *Gentleman's Magazine* (Mar. 1810), 292. Publicly, Blagden did not commit himself on the theory of heat: latent heat, "be it a matter or motion," he wrote in "Experiments on the Cooling of Water Below Its Freezing Point," *PT* 78 (1788): 125–46, on 140. Even in correspondence with colleagues, he was noncommittal, cautioning Berthollet against speaking of the "matter" of heat instead of its effects, since the "matter" had not been proven: Charles Blagden to C. L. Berthollet, 5 June 1786, draft, Blagden Letters, Royal Society, 5. Privately, however, he was an advocate of the material theory. An undated draft of a paper by Blagden, obviously addressed to Cavendish, begins by recalling experiments on the freezing point of mercury that Blagden carried out under Cavendish's direction and goes on to discuss subsequent experiments of Blagden's own on liquids cooled below their freezing points. In his explanation of this phenomenon Blagden said that the particles of bodies have attracting surfaces, a sort of polarity, and that interposed between the particles, lessening the power of their attraction, is latent heat, which is an "elastic fluid": Charles Blagden Papers, Yale, box 2, folder 23. The discussion of heat in this section draws on Russell McCormmach, "Henry Cavendish on the Theory of Heat," *Isis* 79 (1988): 37–67. We acknowledge permission to use material: University of Chicago Press: copyright 1988 by the History of Science Society, Inc., all rights reserved.

Sir Isaac Newton's opinion, that heat consists in the internal motion of the particles of bodies, much the most probable, I chose to use the expression, heat is generated."[25] He rejected Black's "latent heat" in this his first public mention of the motion theory of heat. This theory was then a contested, even dubious theory, and his grounds for saying that it was "much the most probable" he did not give, not here nor elsewhere in print, though he did make one more public pronouncement on the theory of heat, which again was to object to the expression and hypothesis of "latent heat." It occurred in his paper on the condensation of water, which appeared the following year, in 1784. Cavendish remarked on a recent paper by James Watt concerning the production of water, but Cavendish's point was again the relationship between words and reality in describing the phenomena of heat. In the passage in question, now remembered not for its content so much as for its part in the priority dispute, the water controversy, Cavendish gave his reasons for avoiding Watt's "language," Watt's "form of speaking": "Now I have chosen to avoid this form of speaking, both because I think it more likely that there is no such thing as elementary heat, and because saying so in this instance, without using similar expressions in speaking of other chemical unions, would be improper, and would lead to false ideas; and it may even admit of doubt, whether the doing it in general would not cause more trouble and perplexity than it is worth."[26] So, in Cavendish's judgment, the use of the expression "elementary heat," referring to the material view of heat, would lead only to false ideas, trouble, and perplexity.

The passage on Watt in 1784 and the footnote on Joseph Black the year before were all that Cavendish in his lifetime was to tell his readers about the nature of heat. The scientific manuscripts he left at his death were found to contain two more references to Newton's theory of heat, which we have pointed out earlier. One was buried in a corollary to a theorem in a paper on the theory of motion, a mechanical formulation of Newton's theory that concluded with reasons why the theory was "insufficient" in itself; the other was in an experimental paper on latent and specific heats that concluded with the observation that certain of his experiments at first seemed to him "very difficult to reconcile with Newton's theory of heat, but on further consideration they seem by no means to be

so. But to understand this you must read the following proposition."[27] Unfortunately, there the paper ends, abruptly, without the promised proposition. Until recently these references, one published and two unpublished, were the only known explicit statements by Cavendish on Newton's theory of heat. Since it can be shown that Cavendish's understanding of the nature of heat entered fundamentally into his researches on factitious airs, the production of water, and electricity, as well as his researches on the freezing of mercury and on freezing mixtures in general,[28] what was missing was a fully developed theory of heat, one comparable to his fully developed theory of electricity.

In 1969 Lord Chesham, a direct descendant of Henry Cavendish's heir Lord George Cavendish, put up for sale several manuscripts by Henry Cavendish, including a theoretical paper, "Heat." This paper was written in two drafts, one a revised, nearly fair, copy with some crossings out. It gives, as we would say, a rigorously mathematical, mechanical theory of heat complete with the principle of conservation of energy, the concept of the mechanical equivalent of heat, and applications of the theory to the principal branches of physical science.[29] By any reading, this paper must be seen as the culmination of Cavendish's experimental and theoretical researches. More than any of his other writings, "Heat" testifies to Cavendish's concern with the foundations of natural philosophy.

The idea of heat as motion had received many formulations by Cavendish's time. To the question of what it is that moves, a variety of

---

[25]Cavendish, "Observations," 150–51.

[26]Henry Cavendish, "Experiments on Air," *PT* 74 (1784): 119–53; *Sci Pap.* 2:161–81, on 173–74.

[27]Henry Cavendish, "Remarks on the Theory of Motion," Henry Cavendish Mss VI(b), 7; *Sci Pap.* 2:415–30, corollary 2 on 425–26. Henry Cavendish, "Experiments on Heat," ibid., Misc.; *Sci. Pap.* 2:327–51, on 351 (the title is not Cavendish's). .

[28]Russell McCormmach, "Henry Cavendish: A Study of Rational Empiricism in Eighteenth-Century Natural Philosophy," *Isis* 60 (1969): 293–306.

[29]The expressions "conservation of energy" and "mechanical theory of heat" are, of course, anachronistic and were not used by Cavendish. The revised draft of "Heat" consists of forty-three pages of text and notes, one page of diagrams with an accompanying page of explanation, and one page of additions and alterations. Both drafts of "Heat," along with several other Cavendish manuscripts, were auctioned in London. With the exception of "Heat," they were bought by the duke of Devonshire and added to Henry Cavendish's scientific papers at Chatsworth. The original manuscripts of both versions of "Heat" are located, under the reference M G 23, L 6, in the Manuscript Division, Pre-Confederation Archives, Public Archives of Canada, Ottawa.

answers had been proposed. The vibrating object might be the ordinary particles of bodies, the air and acid sulfur in bodies, the subtle ether, the subtle fluid of fire or something else, or some combination. Newton's authority was invoked in support of more than one of these options, but to Cavendish, Newton's theory meant the vibrations of the ordinary particles of bodies. Many of the examples in the queries of Newton's *Opticks* invoked this view of heat, contributing to the coherence of Newton's natural philosophy as it did to that of Cavendish.[30]

This, "Newton's," theory had a good many arguments in its favor. The hypothesis of the internal vibrations of the parts of bodies offered plausible explanations of, for example, the heat produced by chemical operations, hammering, friction, and the absorption of light. But there were also a good many well-known objections to the theory. The heat and cold produced by dissolutions and fermentations were seen as a challenging difficulty long before Cavendish singled them out in the "Remarks." Another, and to some a fatal, difficulty was that the heat capacities of bodies were found not to be proportional to their densities, as the motion theory was understood to require. Further difficulties were discussed by the first Jacksonian professor of natural philosophy at Cambridge, Isaac Milner, in his lectures delivered in 1784–88, at the same time as Cavendish's work on heat. One objection, according to Milner, was that the vibrations of particles alleged to constitute heat had not been proven to exist, and even if they had, they would not correspond with the phenomena. Another objection was that heat was not observed to be proportional to motion, as it would be if heat were motion. Another was that when oil and grease were used to eliminate friction, heat seemed to be eliminated too, although motion was communicated to their particles. Milner listed still more objections. Heat was observed to pass slowly through bodies, as a liquid might, rather than rapidly, as motion does. The motion theory of heat implied that heat should not spread at all, since the quantity of motion of a system of particles is unaffected by their mutual actions and collisions. It was said that the observed passage of heat across a vacuum could not be explained by motion since there are no intervening particles to be set in vibration. And it was said that the

liberation of heat during the solidification of a liquid was inconceivable if heat were motion. Milner had answers to all of these objections, for he happened to be a believer in the motion theory and a critic of the opposing material theories. "The arguments against this [motion] Theory have of late Years been esteemed so numerous and weighty that it has almost been given up by Philosophers," he said. It had been given up "a little too precipitately," and he wished that "somebody else had endeavoured to shew the truth" of it by contrasting it with the fashionable material fluid theories of heat.[31]

The difficulties of the motion theory could be grouped together as one general difficulty: new mechanical ideas for the motion theory did not keep pace with the rapid experimental development of the science of heat in the late eighteenth century. By contrast, the material theory of heat had developed together with the experimental state of the science, so that to many investigators, heat, as an experimentally measurable quantity, appeared better understood by the material theory than by the motion theory.[32]

Heat, according to the material theory, was one of a number of imponderable fluids, which, as we remarked in our discussion of Cavendish's electrical theory, had come to characterize British speculative natural philosophy from about the middle of the eighteenth century. Newton's ideas about a subtle, elastic ether were a principal inspiration for such fluids, though Newton was not their creator. Cavendish contrasted "Newton's" theory of heat with the theory of heat as a fluid.[33]

The fluid of heat was usually taken to be imponderable, subtle, and closely associated with

---

[30] Robert E Schofield, *Mechanism and Materialism: British Natural Philosophy in an Age of Reason* (Princeton: Princeton University Press, 1970), 13, 37, 48, 77–78, 84–85, 139, 160, 179, 183. Schofield points out, p. 183, that Newton "confuses the issue" in query 18, where he speaks of the contribution of the vibrations of the ether to the heat of bodies. To be cautious we should say that the theory of heat as the vibration of the parts of bodies contributes to the coherence of Newton's natural philosophy as presented in query 31. Newton, *Opticks* (New York: Dover reprint, 1952), 348–49, 375–406.

[31] L. J. M. Coleby, "Isaac Milner and the Jacksonian Chair of Natural Philosophy," *Annals of Science* 10 (1954): 234–57, on 242–52, quotation on 244. The theory of heat that Milner preferred was this: "*Heat* consists in a vibrating motion of the parts of bodies, and *Fire* is a body so heated as to emit light copiously"; ibid.

[32] Robert Fox, *The Caloric Theory of Gases from Lavoisier to Regnault* (Oxford: Clarendon, 1971), 19, 22–23.

[33] The imponderable fluid of heat drew on a variety of views about ether, fire, repulsive forces, factitious airs, and the imponderable fluids of electricity and magnetism. The proponents of

fire, and its particles were usually assumed to repel one another while they were attracted to the particles of ordinary substances. This subtle, repellent fluid had a single quantifiable property, its amount, which accounted for most experiments involving the transfer of heat. The fluid theory was readily grasped, easy to apply, plausible, predictive, and supported by the leading authorities of the day. Black was thought to hold the fluid theory, as were his students William Cleghorn, William Irvine, and Adair Crawford, all of whom worked on the subject. Cleghorn's dissertation, *De igne*, of 1779, which drew on the work of Black and his other students, was particularly important for its early advocacy and systematic presentation of the material theory.[34] Crawford, in his treatise *Animal Heat*, also of 1779, advanced similar views, and although his approval of the material theory was tentative, he argued that it explained latent heat better than did the motion theory. Shortly before, in 1777, Lavoisier had published views on fire similar to Cleghorn's. While it was still common then for authors not to commit themselves in print to any particular theory of heat, most would have agreed with Crawford that latent heat is better accounted for by the material theory. It was within this climate of thought that the new language of heat was successfully introduced.[35]

Researchers rarely needed to declare themselves for one theory of heat or the other, since they could get on with their experiments very well without doing so. The classic case in point is Lavoisier and Laplace's joint paper in 1783. In this fundamental study in the emerging science of calorimetry, the authors described both theories of heat, side by side, without deciding between them. Lavoisier almost certainly held the material theory of heat. What Laplace thought is uncertain, and he was later to hold the material theory, but in any event it was he who described the motion theory in their joint paper. Unlike the standard statement of the motion theory of the past, which did little more than assert the identity of heat and motion, Laplace's was mechanically precise. He pointed out that just as in the material theory, in which the quantity of fluid is conserved, in the motion theory there is also a conserved quantity, *vis viva*: by appeal to the law of conservation of *vis viva*, he said, the communication of heat from one body to another can be understood. When two

bodies of unequal temperatures are brought into contact, the *vis viva* of the warmer body diminishes while that of the cooler body increases until their temperatures are equalized, at which time the *vis viva* exchanged in each direction is identical.[36] This is the same insight as Cavendish's in his early "Remarks on the Theory of Motion." In the context of his later "Heat," the coincidence was not only of ideas but also of timing: in May 1783 Cavendish's paper on the freezing point of mercury, with its assertion of Newton's theory of heat, was read before the Royal Society, and in June Lavoisier and Laplace's paper on calorimetry was presented to the Royal Academy of Sciences. Cavendish's papers on heat were routinely sent to Lavoisier and others in Paris through Blagden, and on trips to Paris Blagden reported to Cavendish on

---

the imponderable fluid of heat, as of other imponderables, it should be noted, also regarded their theories as "Newtonian"; Schofield, *Mechanism and Materialism*, 157–90; P. M. Heimann, "Ether and Imponderables," in *Conceptions of Ether: Studies in the History of Ether Theories, 1740–1900*, ed. G. N. Cantor and M. J. S. Hodge (Cambridge: Cambridge University Press, 1981), 61–83, on 67–73. Arthur Quinn, "Repulsive Force in England, 1706–1744," *Historical Studies in the Physical Sciences* 13 (1982): 109–28, on 127; and Fox, *Caloric Theory*, 19.

[34] For a number of reasons Cleghorn rejected the motion theory of heat. Nevertheless he followed "Newtonian principles closely" in developing the mechanical consequences of a conserved fluid of "fire," the particles of which repel one another and are attracted to the particles of ordinary matter with a force that is different for different bodies. He did not know the law of force or how to find it, but he regarded its discovery as important. Although he gave a few simple equations, he did not give the theory a mathematical development; Douglas McKie and Niels H. de V. Heathcote, "William Cleghorn's *De igne* (1779)," *Annals of Science* 14 (1958): 1–82. On the fluid theory of heat and those who held it: Fox, *Caloric Theory*, 19–20, 22, 25; and Schofield, *Mechanism and Materialism*, 185.

[35] There were some rejections of the motion theory; e.g., by Jean Hyacinth de Magellan in 1780 and by Tiberius Cavallo in 1781; Fox, *Caloric Theory*, 11, 28. Although Magellan accepted the material theory, he rejected Black's terms "latent heat" and "heat capacity" and introduced the neutral sounding term "specific heat" for heat capacity and also the term "sensible heat" for the heat of the thermometer. "Caloric," standing for the matter of heat, appeared in 1787 in L. B. Guyton de Morveau et al., *Méthode de nomenclature chimique*, the language of Lavoisier's new system of chemistry; Fox, *Caloric Theory*, 6, 26.

[36] The original publication of the often reprinted paper by Lavoisier and Laplace is *Mémoire sur la chaleur, lu à l'Académie Royale des Sciences, le 28 juin 1783 . . .* (Paris, 1783). Our discussion is based on Henry Guerlac, "Chemistry as a Branch of Physics: Laplace's Collaboration with Lavoisier," *Historical Studies in the Physical Sciences* 7 (1976): 193–76, on 244–50. Guerlac asks, p. 246, "how Laplace, who of course used the principle of the conservation of *vis viva* in treating the dynamics of the solar system, came to apply this approach to the study of heat." He suggests that the idea came from Daniel Bernoulli's *Hydrodynamica* of 1738, in which heat is associated with the motion of particles of an aeriform fluid and the pressure of the fluid with their *vis viva*. If Laplace did not read it there, Guerlac thinks, he probably read the summary of it in J. A. Deluc's *Recherches sur les modifications de l'atmosphère* of 1772. Larmor referred Cavendish to the same early source, Daniel Bernoulli's *Hydrodynamica*.

the latest experiments on heat there.[37] We know that Cavendish read Lavoisier and Laplace's paper—as we would expect, given the subject and the authors—and in it he found Laplace's statement of the motion theory of heat, a reflection of his own reasoning, if perhaps reasoning without the same theoretical commitment.[38]

It was from about the time of Cavendish's and Lavoisier and Laplace's papers that the material theory acquired its great following, which would continue well into the next century. The arguments about heat would usually be carried on among the followers of the material theory themselves rather than between them and upholders of the motion theory. By the end of the eighteenth century in Britain, the material theory was all but universally accepted.[39] The motion theory of heat would seem to be going in the same direction as the phlogiston theory of chemistry, into the collection of historical curiosities of science.

Cavendish, exacting measurer of heat, was naturally interested in any promising quantitative ideas about heat.[40] At the time of his "Experiments on Heat," as we have seen, he believed that changes in specific heats are responsible for the heats observed during changes of state. Among his miscellaneous unpublished papers are derivations of formulas for the absolute heat in a body and the absolute zero of temperature, but why he made them he did not say. In another miscellaneous paper he gave an experimental disproof of the idea that the absolute heats in bodies are proportional to their specific heats.[41] He was not alone in this criticism,[42] but this or any other criticism of contemporary views on heat was not what was wanting, which was a positive case for the most probable theory. "Heat," the recently unearthed manuscript, was to be it.

Cavendish knew what a persuasive case for the motion theory required. He knew what Black knew: Black had the common difficulty of being unable to form an idea of the internal motions of bodies that could account for the phenomena of heat, but his main complaint against the motion theory was that none of its supporters had shown how to apply it to the entirety of heat phenomena. The same complaint could not have been made about the fluid theory, at least not after Cleghorn's work.[43] With "Heat," Cavendish intended to supply what was missing from the side of the motion theory.

"Heat" is a systematic presentation of Newton's theory of heat together with comprehensive supporting evidence drawn from diverse fields. With this, so far as we know his last, fundamental

---

[37]Cavendish's paper on the freezing of mercury, for example, was sent by Blagden to Berthollet in multiple copies for Lavoisier and other friends. Charles Blagden to Claude Louis Berthollet, 27 Apr. 1784, draft, Blagden Letterbook, Yale. From Paris, Blagden sent news of experiments on the latent heat of water to Banks, with instructions to pass the news along to Cavendish. Charles Blagden to Sir Joseph Banks, 27 June 1783, draft, Blagden Letters, Royal Society, B.166a.

[38]In a letter to Lavoisier, Blagden included a comment written out by Cavendish on Lavoisier and Laplace's memoir on heat: Charles Blagden to Antoine Laurent Lavoisier (draft), 15 Sept. 1783, Blagden Letterbook, Yale.

[39]Fox, *Caloric Theory*, 19–20, 23, 104–5. There are well-known exceptions, critics of the material theory of heat at the turn of the century, Humphry Davy, Thomas Young, and Benjamin Thompson, Count Rumford: ibid., 104, 115–16, and Schofield, *Mechanism and Materialism*, 290–95.

[40]For example, Cavendish was interested in certain quantitative ideas advanced by Black's students. These included the ideas that the heat or cold accompanying a change of state or a chemical reaction is a consequence solely of a change in the heat capacities of the bodies concerned; that the absolute quantities of heat in bodies are proportional to their specific heats; and that from specific heats the absolute zero of temperature can be calculated. Despite scant experimental evidence, these views enjoyed a relatively long life owing to the still rudimentary stage of calorimetry. Fox, *Caloric Theory*, 26–27.

[41]The first miscellaneous sheet is headed: "That all the heat which appears in bodies either by its being absorbed or united to them or in its being again set loose from them whether it be by their combinations or separation from each other or by any other change in their nature depends intirely on the specific heat of each body & the change of it": Cavendish Mss, Misc. This sheet contains formulas for the absolute quantity of loose heat in a body and for the absolute zero of temperature. The formulas assume that the absolute heat of a body is proportional to its specific heat, an assumption which Cavendish brought into question: the second miscellaneous sheet bears the heading: "A compleat proof that the quantity of heat in different bodies at a given temperature is not in proportion to their specific heats." The proof, using Cavendish's experimental data, begins with the statement: "The mixing of sp. wine and water affords a compleat proof that the absolute quantity of heat in different bodies of a given temperature is not in proportion to their specific heat for if it was the nearer the heat of 2 bodies approach to absolute cold the less should be the heat or cold produced by their mixture whereas the heat produced by mixing spirit of wine & water is greater when they are cold than hot"; Cavendish Mss, Misc. Cavendish drew a line through the heading of this sheet; however, there is a version of this same proof in nearly identical wording, in Cavendish's hand, among Blagden's papers: Blagden Collection, Royal Society, Misc. Notes.

[42]Using their recent measurements of specific and latent heats, Laplace and Lavoisier in 1783 publicly criticized the rule for calculating the absolute zero of temperature and the doctrine that the quantities of heat in bodies are proportional to their specific heats; Fox, *Caloric Theory*, 31.

[43]For Black's difficulty: John Robison's edition in 1803 of Black's *Lectures on the Elements of Chemistry*, discussed in Schofield, *Mechanism and Materialism*, 186–87. Cleghorn, after stating two principles from which all of the effects of fire can be deduced, took up in turn the principal "effects" of fire, eight in number: fluidity and evaporation, inflammability, animal heat, heat from electric fluid, heat from fermentation, friction, heat from mixtures, and heat of sun's rays; McKie and Heathcote, "William Cleghorn's *De igne*."

theory, Cavendish brought the mechanical understanding of heat to a level that would not be surpassed for over a half century.[44]

Cavendish's paper starts out as a purely mechanical investigation.[45] Cavendish divided *vis viva*, defined as the mechanical effect of a body in motion, into two kinds, "visible" and "invisible." The visible *vis viva* is that of the center of mass of a body undergoing progressive motion or of the body undergoing rotation or both; the invisible *vis viva* is that of the particles of the body moving among themselves; the total *vis viva* of the body is the sum of both. Cavendish further divided the invisible *vis viva* into two parts, one "active," the other inactive, the potential for becoming active. His symbol s, standing for the active, is the actual *vis viva* of all of the particles constituting the body; his symbol S stands for one half the sum of the *vis viva* that each particle would acquire by the attraction or repulsion of every other particle in falling from infinity to its actual position within the body. Upon the understanding that the attractions and repulsions between particles are always the same at the same separations and different at different separations, Cavendish derived the generalized law of conservation of *vis viva*, active and inactive; the quantity $s - S$ cannot change as a result of the motions of the particles among one another.

Cavendish identified the mechanical quantities occurring in the propositions concerning *vis viva* with the quantities occurring in heat. The connection between the two is made through the fundamental "hypothesis" of the theory: "Heat," Cavendish supposed, "consists in the internal motion of the particles of which bodies are composed." This internal motion is to be regarded as vibratory, the particles being bound close to their place by attracting and repelling forces. Cavendish identified the "active heat" of the body with the active, actual *vis viva* s and the "latent heat" with the potential *vis viva* - S and consequently the "total heat" with $s - S$, the conserved quantity. "Sensible heat" is what Cavendish called the heat of a body as given by a thermometer, and it is related to the active and latent heats through the constitution of the body. With these terms, Cavendish had a complete technical vocabulary for developing the science of heat.[46]

It was then necessary to show that the theory accounted for the facts of heat. Cavendish first applied the theory to the communication of heat and to specific heats. When two bodies, isolated and unequally heated, are brought into contact, one gives up heat and the other acquires it until the sensible heat of each is the same. In the exchange the total heat given up must be the same as the total heat received, but just how this heat is divided between the active and latent heats in the two bodies depends on the weights of the bodies and on "some function either of the size of their particles or of any other quality in them," for example, the frequency of vibration of the particles.[47] There are two reasons why one substance requires a greater increment of total heat than another substance to produce the same increment of sensible heat:

> First that some bodies may require a greater addition of active heat than others in order to produce the same increase of sensible heat; & 2ndly because in all bodies an alteration of sensible heat can hardly help being attended with an alteration of the quantity of latent heat. For as the bulk of all or at least almost all bodies is increased by heat, the distance of their particles must be alterd; which can hardly fail of being attended by an alteration of the value of S, that is of their latent heat; & that alteration can hardly fail of being greater in some bodies than others.[48]

The distinctions, based on experimental knowledge, between sensible, total, active, and latent heats provided Cavendish with the concepts he needed to analyze complex heat processes in terms of precise mechanical analogues.

---

[44]In "Heat," Cavendish showed that the "effects" of internal vibrations of bodies agree with seven classes of phenomena, which are largely the same as Cleghorn's in *De igne*.

[45]The mechanical propositions in "Heat" parallel those in the "Remarks on the Theory of Motion," but the arguments are developed with greater thoroughness. E.g., whereas in the "Remarks" Cavendish considered the interaction of only two particles in detail, in "Heat" he did it for four particles before generalizing the result to any number of particles: Cavendish, "Heat," 7–11.

[46]Cavendish, "Heat," 11–12. Cavendish did not formally introduce a word for specific heat, though he mentioned the "capacities for heat" of bodies (24, 41). His distinction between active and latent heat in a body parallels the common distinction made in the material theory between free heat in a body and heat that is combined with it, or latent heat.

[47] Cavendish, "Heat," 14–16. The explanation, which draws on the mechanical propositions, is that different substances require different quantities of active heats to raise their sensible heats by a given amount; further, that the changes in sensible heats are accompanied by changes in bulk, which translate into changes in the separations of the particles and therefore into changes in latent heats in ways that depend on the nature of the substances.

[48]Cavendish, "Heat," 16.

With his new theory, Cavendish no longer saw his experimental findings on latent heat and on chemical operations as possible difficulties for Newton's theory but presented them as consequences of it. He explained that when a body changes from a solid to a liquid or from a liquid to an elastic fluid, or when two bodies unite by their chemical affinity, the particles undergo rearrangement, and with it the latent heat and the active heat required to produce a given sensible heat change; since the total heat remains constant, the sensible heat has to change. In addition, Cavendish had the beginnings of a fundamental understanding of chemical reactions using measurements of heat.[49]

Having secured Newton's vibrational theory within the subject of heat, Cavendish applied it to other subjects, to optics first. "There can be no doubt," Cavendish said, that light is a body consisting of extremely small particles emitted from luminous bodies with extremely high velocity. When these particles are reflected from a body, they are not reflected by a single particle or by a few particles of that body but by a great quantity of its matter, so that, by mechanical principles, no perceptible *vis viva* is communicated to the body. The same explanation applies to the case of refracted light. But where light is absorbed, its particles are reflected back and forth within the body until their velocity is no greater than that of the particles of the body, "so that their vis viva will be equally distributed between the body & them" and the absorbing body will thereby acquire sensible heat.[50]

The theory of heat is a theory about *vis viva*, so that if the heating effect of light is to be calculated theoretically, its *vis viva* must first be known. For this purpose Cavendish turned to an experiment by John Michell, which was widely regarded as proof that light really consists of streaming material particles.[51] In this experiment, inside a box with a window to the sun, a thin sheet of copper was fastened to one end of a horizontal wire, which was balanced by a weight at the other end. Rays of the sun were concentrated and directed by a concave mirror so that they struck the copper plate perpendicularly, resulting in a rotation of the wire.[52] From the observed speed of rotation and other details of the experiment, and from the ideal assumption that the light was perfectly reflected

from the copper, Cavendish calculated the momentum and *vis viva* of the sunlight falling each second on 1½ square feet of surface. To translate this result into its mechanical effect, Cavendish calculated the rate of *vis viva* of sunlight falling on that surface, an enormous quantity, exceeding the work done by two horses, that is, over two horsepower.[53]

It was well known that a plate of glass is heated more than a plate of polished metal when exposed to a fire and probably when exposed to the sun as well. But since the metal absorbs more light than the glass, according to Cavendish's theory, it rather than the glass ought to be heated

---

[49]Ibid., 16–17. Recognizing the complexity of the problem of chemical heats, Cavendish could only suggest how the concepts of active and latent heats might be applied. He was seeking an understanding, in terms of the heats involved, of why different substances should mix and combine. Before this goal could be realized, additional concepts had to be created, as they later would be within the science of thermodynamics. That the heats of chemical reactions were still the least understood of the phenomena of heat is clear from Cavendish's long discussion of them, which he relegated to a footnote, since the "reasoning is too hypothetical" and also not central to the main purpose of the paper. The note reads: "when 2 substances which have a chymical affinity unite, it seems likely that heat & not cold should commonly ensue; for unless the attracting particles approach nearer together or the repelling particles recede further, so as to increase the value of *S*, one does not easily see why the 2 bodies should mix. But if *S* is increased, the quantity of active heat must be equally increased; & consequently the sensible heat will in all probability be increased. This agrees with observation; for except where one of the bodies is changed by the mixture from a solid to a fluid form, or from either of those forms to that of an elastic fluid, I do not know a single instance of cold being produced by any chymical mixture. But in mixtures in which this change of form takes place, it is well known that cold is frequently produced. But if this increase of sensible cold proceeds from an increase of latent heat, one does not well see as was before said why the mixture should take place; which might incline one to think that the cold which always attends this change of form proceeded from the latter of the abovementiond causes, or to more active heat being necessary to produce a given sensible heat when the body is in a fluid than a solid form": ibid., 17–19.

[50]Ibid., 18–20.

[51]G. N. Cantor, *Optics after Newton: Theories of Light in Britain and Ireland, 1704–1840* (Manchester: Manchester University Press, 1983), 57.

[52]This experiment was described by Priestley, who said that there was no question but that the rotation was to be "ascribed to the impulse of the rays of light": Joseph Priestley, *The History and Present State of Discoveries Relating to Vision, Light and Colours* (London, 1772), 387–89. It would be a long time before the cause of this rotation was properly understood: S. G. Brush and C. W. F. Everitt, "Maxwell, Osborne Reynolds, and the Radiometer," *Historical Studies in the Physical Sciences* 1 (1969): 103–25.

[53]Since Michell's experiment was done under glass, which admits light rays but not heat rays, Cavendish pointed out that his calculation of the total *vis viva* of the sun's rays was below the actual total: Cavendish, "Heat," 24–25. For the value of 1 horsepower, Cavendish assumed the work of a horse in a mill lifting 100 pounds at the speed of 3 miles per hour: ibid., 22. This value is equivalent to 26,400 foot pounds of work per minute, which is somewhat lower than our accepted value of 33,000 foot pounds per minute, as it was defined by James Watt and Matthew Boulton.

most by the light. To resolve this apparent conflict with the theory, Cavendish referred to recent experiments by Carl Wilhelm Scheele and Horace Bénédict de Saussure on the newly discovered "heat rays." Cavendish believed that heat rays, like light rays with which they commingle in various proportions, are material particles emitted by hot bodies, and although their velocity is not known, they too must communicate *vis viva*. But heat rays differ from light rays too; not only do they not excite the sensation of vision, but they are absorbed by glass and are efficiently reflected by polished metals, which is just the reverse of the behavior of light. It is the heat rays, then, and not the accompanying light rays, that warm the glass preferentially. These new, invisible rays enabled Cavendish to reconcile the facts with his theory of heat; if the rays did not exist, the theory would fail.[54]

According to Newton's theory, bodies are warmed when they emit light and heat, but since the repulsion by bodies of the particles of light and radiant heat is accomplished by a relatively great amount of matter, the *vis viva* of recoil in the bodies is too small to detect. But the theory agrees well with the familiar observation that as a body grows hotter, it emits more light and heat. By Cavendish's hypothesis, the particles of light and radiant heat are bound to their natural places in a body by the forces of attraction and repulsion of the particles of the body, and when the particles of the body are set in brisk vibration, the particles of light and radiant heat are moved into positions where they experience violent repulsion, flying off from the body as free light and radiant heat.[55]

Heat can be produced mechanically—for example, by friction and hammering—and Cavendish showed how this effect too agrees with the theory. Since a violent force is required to produce heat, the particles of the heated body must be displaced or even torn away at its surface, and that in turn alters the latent heat of the body, giving rise to sensible heat. The same displacement or tearing away of particles is responsible for the loss of elasticity in the collision of two bodies or in the bending of a body. Cavendish's analysis here of the forces of particles was more problematic than in some other applications of the theory, but on the basic point he was "certain": if any visible *vis viva* is lost by the rubbing, striking, or bending of bodies, these bodies must acquire an "augmentation

of total heat equivalent thereto."[56]

Electricity is the science Cavendish had worked over with the greatest theoretical and experimental thoroughness, devoting the labor of a decade to it without, however, having closely examined the heat produced by electricity in motion. Now, he said, he was going to "argue upon the principles laid down in my paper concerning the cause of electricity," his paper of 1771, to derive a formula for the *vis viva* of electric fluid discharged by an electric jar through a wire. He doubted that the particles of the electric fluid, because of their extreme lightness, could communicate sufficient *vis viva* to the particles of the wire to account for the violent heat of the wire. His explanation of the heat is that the electric discharge displaces the particles of the wire, greatly diminishing the latent heat. The heat caused by electric discharge is consistent with the theory, "though," Cavendish said, "it is an effect which I should not have expected."[57]

As the final application of his theory Cavendish discussed the expansion and change of state of bodies with heat. When a body is heated, he reasoned, the increased vibrations of its particles alter their mutual attractions and repulsions, which in turn alter the size of the body. When the vibrations become great enough, the attractions and repulsions of the particles vary sufficiently for the body to change its form and properties entirely, which is what happens in evaporation and in melting: the increased vibrations of the particles diminish their adhesion, making bodies more fluid. By the same reasoning Cavendish explained why chemical decomposition and combination are promoted by heat.[58]

Experiment, for Cavendish, was never distant from theory, and in three places in "Heat" he made a note to himself to do an experiment suggested by the theory, and in the rough draft he

---

[54]Ibid., 23–24.
[55]Ibid., 25–26.
[56]Ibid., 26–31, on 31.
[57]Ibid., 32–38, on 41.
[58]Ibid., 38–39. Because of the increase of the vibrations of the particles of a body when it is heated, "even their mean attraction & repulsion can hardly be the same as if they were at rest in their mean position." With a change in the arrangement and distance of the particles, the size of the body changes. Although the observed change is always an increase in the size of the heated body, Cavendish could see no theoretical reason why it could not just as well be a decrease.

noted another experiment to try. In one place he said that he wanted to determine if "friction is as much diminished by oil & grease as the heat is" (recall here one of Milner's objections to the motion theory of heat). In another, he said that he was concerned about the diminution of the latent heat of a wire during an electric discharge. In another, he said that he intended to expose various equally dark bodies to sunlight to determine that the total heat acquired by different bodies from the sun's rays is the same. In the rough draft of "Heat" he commented on this last experiment:

> If it should prove that different bodies do not receive the same total heat from the [sun]s light it would be difficult to reconcile with this hypothesis. But then it seems as difficult to reconcile it with the supposition of heat being a material substance except that as those hypotheses are less capable of being brought to the test of strict reasoning it is easier for those gentlemen to find loop holes to escape by.[59]

The experiments Cavendish planned all bore on "this hypothesis," the fundamental, contested hypothesis of Newton's theory of heat. His intention is especially clear from another proposed experiment, which appears in the discussion of the heat caused by the impulse of light and Michell's experiment to determine the momentum of sunlight: "Exper. to determine the vis viva necessary to give a given increase of sensible heat to a given body by alternately exposing a thermometer in the [sun] & shading."[60]

Whether or not Cavendish performed an experiment like this, or any other experiments with the same goal, we do not know. In any event, the proposed experiment involved the calculation of a mechanical equivalent of sensible heat for a given substance.[61] Cavendish's interest in the experiment did not end with this calculation. It was the hypothesis of the theory of heat, the reality of the vibrations constituting heat, that most interested him, as he revealed in the rough draft of "Heat," where he gave a fuller statement of the experiment. From the determination of the *vis viva* equivalent to an increase of sensible heat in a body, and by making a supposition about the variation of the total heat in a body with its temperature, he could "give a guess at the velocity with which the particles of a body vibrate."[62]

At the end of "Heat" Cavendish provided a "Conclusion," which begins: "It has been shewn therefore by as strict reasoning as can be expected in subjects not purely mathematical, that if heat consists in the vibrations of the particles of bodies, the effects will be strikingly analogous, & as far as our experiments yet go, in no case contradictory to the phenomena." By showing that it is fully sufficient to explain the phenomena, Cavendish made a strong case for the hypothesis that the vibrations of the particles of bodies constitute heat. The hypothesis was not only sufficient, Cavendish argued, but necessary. "To put the matter in a stronger light," he said, it "seems certain that the action of such rays of light as are absorbed by a body must produce a motion & vibration of its particles; so that it seems certain that the particles of bodies must actually be in motion." Given, then, that the vibrations certainly exist, there must be effects corresponding to them, and these are "analogous to most of the phenomena of heat and disagree with none." The hypothesis is demanded.[63]

With these remarks Cavendish let rest the case for Newton's theory of heat, having answered, implicitly, the main criticisms of it. He showed that the hypothetical vibrations can account not only for the heat of friction, for example, for which a motion theory would seem to be well suited, but also for heats, such as those accompanying changes of state, for which the material theory seems especially well suited; the motion theory is a theory for all of heat. In each application of the theory Cavendish gave a picture of the motions and configurations responsible, intended to show that, unlike earlier motion theories, his theory could not be faulted for lack of clear ideas of the mechanism. By logical and, where possible, mathematical arguments Cavendish proceeded from a precise hypothesis and from accepted mechanical principles

---

[59]Cavendish, "Heat," rough draft, 15. The experiment on exposing dark bodies to sunlight is proposed in "Heat," 24.

[60]Cavendish, "Heat," 22.

[61]Distantly related determinations of the equivalence of heat and work would be made systematically by others, using experiments of different kinds, much later, in the nineteenth century, when they would provide the foundation for the development of the mechanical theory of heat.

[62]Cavendish, "Heat," rough draft, 12. To make the calculation, Cavendish would suppose "that the total heat of a body heated to 1,000° is double its heat at 0°." It is easy to arrive at this supposition, as we imagine Cavendish did, by assuming that the total heat of a body is proportional to its specific heat and that the absolute zero of temperature is -1,000° F, which is the order of magnitude of the widely varying calculations of absolute zero made around this time. Cavendish's goal was, and could be, no more than a "guess at the velocity.".

[63]Cavendish, "Heat," 40, 43.

to a demonstration of the "striking" analogy between the effects of invisible vibrations and the phenomena of heat. He judged his theory to be a strong, good theory, not "of that pliable nature as to be easily adapted to any appearances."[64]

Cavendish was not finished yet. In the fair copy of "Heat" he had not said a word about one of its obvious motivations, the material theory, which for Cavendish failed the criteria of a strong, good theory. He reserved his judgment of the material theory to the end of the "conclusion": given the evidence for the existence of internal vibrations, he wrote, there was no reason to "have recourse to the hypothesis of a fluid, which nothing proves the existence of." Moreover, not only was the material theory superfluous, it was insufficiently testable and therefore a weak theory:

> The various hypotheses which have been formed for explaining the phenomena of heat by a fluid seem to shew that none of them are very satisfactory; & though it does not seem impossible that the fluid might exist endued with such properties as to produce the effects of heat; yet any hypothesis of such kind must be of that unprecise nature, as not to admit of being reduced to strict reasoning, so as to suffer one to examine whether it will really explain the phenomena or whether it will not rather be attended with numberless inconsistencies & absurdities. So that though it might be natural for philosophers to adopt such an hypothesis when no better offerd itself; yet when a theory has been proposed by Sr I.N. which, as may be shewn by strict reasoning, must produce effects strongly analogous to those observed to take place, & which seems no ways inconsistent with any, there can no longer be any reason for adhering to the former hypothesis.[65]

Cavendish did not criticize the material theory in general, nor any of its variants in particular, for specific failures; he criticized it only for the kind of theory it was. All material theories were burdened with possible inconsistencies; all were weak by comparison with the motion theory. The already-tried hypotheses of the material theory were unsatisfactory, but even if a hypothesis were found that agreed with the facts, it would still be unsatisfactory because it would be imprecise.

Three times in the conclusion of "Heat" Cavendish used the expression "strict reasoning." The phrase epitomizes the spirit in which Cavendish studied physical nature. He had used it before in his other great theoretical work: "The method I propose to follow," he wrote in the introduction of his published electrical theory of 1771, "is, first, to lay down the hypothesis; next, to examine by strict mathematical reasoning, or at least, as strict reasoning as the nature of the subject will admit of, what consequences will flow from thence"; and, finally, to compare these consequences with experiment.[66] The method he used in the heat theory was the same. It was to compare a fundamental hypothesis about the nature of heat with the results of experiment using mathematical reasoning and, where that proved impossible, strict verbal reasoning. His conclusion in "Heat" was that Newton's theory of heat was the best theory because of its high probability and its strict reasoning.

"Heat" carries no date,[67] but the pattern of Cavendish's researches suggests that "Heat" was not only later than "Remarks on the Theory of Motion" but much later, falling in the late 1780s. During the years 1783–88 Cavendish worked most intently on heat and on the closely related subject of pneumatic chemistry. With the exception of his first publication, in 1766, all of his publications on pneumatic chemistry appeared then, as did all of his publications on heat. These experimental publications bore on the fundamentals of heat theory, as is

[64]Ibid., 41–42.

[65]Ibid., 42.

[66]Henry Cavendish, "An Attempt to Explain Some of the Principal Phaenomena of Electricity, by Means of an Elastic Fluid," *PT* 61 (1771): 584–677, on 584.

[67]At recent sales it was assigned first to the decade 1795–1805 and then to around 1780, but both of these datings are probably off, the truth lying somewhere in between. Cavendish certainly wrote this paper after "Remarks on the Theory of Motion," which mentions only some of the phenomena discussed in "Heat." Also, in "Remarks" Cavendish regarded the cold produced by chemical mixtures as a difficulty for the theory, whereas in "Heat" he no longer did. Most important for this comparison is that in "Heat" Cavendish drew on his knowledge of specific and latent heats and developed the mechanical theory accordingly, whereas in "Remarks" he did not mention them. The connection between "Heat" and Cavendish's experiments on specific and latent heats is direct: e.g., the numbered paragraph 7 on p. 16 of "Heat," concerning the heats of chemical mixtures, states in general terms the conclusion on p. 39 of the experimental notes on heat, Cavendish Mss III(a), 9. Christie's sales catalogue assigned the first dating primarily on the basis of the watermarks of the paper, in which the name J. Cripps alternates with Britannia in a crowned circle. The assumption was that the earliest recorded mark of James Cripps was in 1792. Cavendish did use the J. Cripps stationery several times in the 1790s and 1800s, but he also used it earlier, in the 1780s (the earliest appearance being manuscript pages A3 through A5 of "Experiments on Air," Cavendish Mss II, 10, published in the *Philosophical Transactions* in 1785). "Heat" came up again at Dawsons of Pall Mall; James Cripps, father and son, made paper from 1753 to 1803, it was noted, and based on references to other authors in the manuscript, a dating of around 1780 was proposed.

shown by Cavendish's note on Newton's theory in his 1783 publication.

As we have seen, in 1783 Cavendish rejected Black's term "latent heat" because of the theory of heat it implied, and four years later, in 1787, he rejected another terminology for the same kind of reason. The terminology proposed in the *Méthode de nomenclature chimique* implied Lavoisier's theory of chemistry, and moreover it listed among the elements of chemistry the matter of heat, "caloric." Upon receiving a copy of the treatise, Cavendish wrote his "long sermon" to Blagden about the "present rage of namemaking," which sermon Cavendish took to heart when writing "Heat." He now used the standard terminology of mechanics, "*vis viva*," rather than his own "mechanical momentum." By the same token, little as he liked Black's terminology, he used it because it was now standard. In his early writings on heat he used expressions such as "heat is generated"; in "Heat" he systematically used "latent heat," while giving it an interpretation within the Newtonian heat theory. "Heat" was certainly written after 1783.

That conclusion is firmed by Cavendish's mention of other authors in "Heat." He cited Joseph Priestley's book on the history of optics, but that appeared early, in 1772. He cited the names, but not the publications, of Scheele and Saussure for their researches on radiant heat. Cavendish closely followed Scheele's work—which, like his own, joined the sciences of heat and pneumatic chemistry—and the reference in "Heat" shows his familiarity with Scheele's only book, which appeared in English translation in 1780.[68] Cavendish's mention of Saussure no doubt refers to the second volume of his travels in the Alps, which came out in 1786.[69] He cited no other authors in "Heat," and the absence of citations to work done in the 1790s may be taken as indirect evidence for an upper limit for the dating.[70]

For these several reasons we would place "Heat" in or very close to 1787. As to the immediate stimulus for writing the paper, Cavendish said nothing. Researches on heat by others could have provided it. In 1785, for example, George Fordyce published an experimental paper in the *Philosophical Transactions* demonstrating the loss of weight by ice upon melting. Since the ice lost weight as it gained heat, he speculated that heat might be a body possessing absolute levity. He was inclined to

believe that heat was a completely general quality like attraction, only its opposite. Because any change of weight of a body with heat was thought to be an argument against the motion theory, Fordyce's experiments had a fundamental significance.[71] If Fordyce's—and Crawford's too—were proven right, Blagden told Laplace, they would work an "extraordinary revolution in our ideas."[72] That was recognized by Benjamin Thompson, who was later to try to establish experimentally the motion theory of heat. In 1787 Thompson repeated Fordyce's experiments, convincing himself that they were wrong and that heat could not be a material substance.[73] Cavendish had earlier witnessed experiments like Fordyce's, and although he did none himself and never discussed the question in print,[74] he was interested and was kept informed on pertinent researches in Paris.[75] We do not believe, however, that Fordyce's paper on heat or any other

---

[68] It is an indication of Cavendish's interest in Scheele's work around the time of "Heat" that he, together with a helper, wrote out a 24-page extract of Scheele's "New Observations on Air and Fire, and the Generation of Water" from Crell's *Chemische Annalen* in 1785: Cavendish Mss X(c), 4. Cavendish wrote that Scheele "proved that hot bodies emit not only rays of light, but also other particles, which though not capable of exciting the sensation of light in our eyes are yet able to produce heat, & which may therefore be called rays of heat; he has shewn too that these rays of heat are reflected by polished metals, but are neither reflected nor transmitted by glass": Cavendish, "Heat," 23. Cavendish's source is undoubtedly the experiments on "heat rays" and light using polished metal and glass discussed in Carl Wilhelm Scheele, *Chemical Observations and Experiments on Air and Fire* (1777), trans. J. R. Forster, with notes by Richard Kirwan (London, 1780), 72–74, 92–98.

[69] Saussure, Cavendish said, "found that bodies emit rays of heat though not near hot enough to emit rays of light": Cavendish, "Heat," 23. Saussure described experiments he did with M. A. Pictet on the reflection of "obscure heat" emitted by hot, but not red-hot, bodies in *Voyages dans les Alps*, vol. 2 (Geneva, 1786), 354–55. Cavendish saw this volume soon after it appeared; in a letter to Blagden, in response to the latter's of 16 Sept. 1787, Cavendish wrote, "I do not know whether you have seen the sequel of Saussures journey," and he gave some information from it: Cavendish, *Sci. Pap.* 2:324–25.

[70] For example, Pierre Prevost's experiments on heat rays and Count Rumford's on the mechanical production of heat, belonging to the 1790s, would have been relevant to Cavendish's argument.

[71] George Fordyce, "An Account of Some Experiments on the Loss of Weight in Bodies on Being Melted or Heated," *PT* 75 (1785): 361–65, on 364; Coleby, "Isaac Milner," 245.

[72] Charles Blagden to Lorenz Crell, 28 Apr. 1785, draft, Blagden Letterbook, Yale. Charles Blagden to Pierre Simon Laplace, 5 Apr. 1785, ibid.

[73] Sanborn C. Brown, *Benjamin Thompson, Count Rumford* (Cambridge, Mass.: M.I.T. Press, 1979), 219–220. Fordyce himself in 1787 declared against the view that heat is a "substance." He did not go so far as to say that it is motion but called it a "quality": George Fordyce, "An Account of an Experiment on Heat," *PT* 77 (1787): 310–17, on 316.

[74] John Roebuck, "Experiments on Ignited Bodies," *PT* 66 (1776): 509–12. These experiments, witnessed by Cavendish among others, showed an increase of weight in iron and silver upon cooling, a result in agreement with Fordyce's later experiments.

theoretical or experimental paper on heat around 1787 was the occasion for Cavendish to write "Heat." If it had been, he would have discussed it. Nor, we believe, was the occasion any new theoretical work of his own. "Heat" was not based on a new understanding of his; the central idea, the identification of heat with *vis viva*, had come to him long before, at the time of the "Remarks." Nor was the stimulus his own heat experiments, since the experiments crucial to the refinement of the theory, those on specific and latent heats, he had done much earlier.

Another possible stimulus was the practical applications of heat, which were abundant, the time being the "industrial revolution." For several years, in the mid-1780s, Cavendish and Blagden made journeys to various parts of Britain, visiting industrial works wherever they went and making close observations of power machinery, of water wheels and steam engines, for example. The late 1780s were just the years of Cavendish's concentrated researches on heat, including, if our dating is right, the theoretical study "Heat." But any stimulus Cavendish received from his industrial tours was, at most, of a general nature. "Heat" contains no practical discussions. On his tours Cavendish took a keen interest in mechanical forces in practice, but in "Heat" he treated the subject philosophically. An example will bear this out. To the text, immediately following his calculation of the horsepower of light and his proposed experiment to determine the *vis viva* required to produce a given increase of sensible heat in a body, he added this footnote:

> If it was possible to make a wheel with float boards like those of a water wheel which should move with ½ the velocity of light without suffering any resistance from friction & the resistance of the air, & as much of the [sun]s light as falls on a surface of 1½ sq. feet was thrown on one side of this wheel, it would actually do more work for any mechanical purpose than 2 horses.[76]

Implications for the conversion of forces for practical purposes might be read into this, but the example, taken at face value, is a thought experiment.

The principal reason why Cavendish wrote "Heat," we believe, is that he had recently been doing extensive experimental work on heat and now wanted to clarify for himself, anew, the theoretical foundations of the subject. His way of clarification was by the systematic, rigorous development of the consequences of the fundamental hypothesis and the comparison of these consequences with experimental results. This interpretation is supported by two pages among the unnumbered sheets at the end of the rough draft of "Heat." These pages are evidently notes Cavendish made before writing the draft, for they list and briefly comment on the phenomena he would discuss there. Some notes are straightforward headings, such as "Heat from action of [sun]s light" leading to the "calculation of vis viva of [sun]s rays & of D° required to commun. given quant. heat." Other notes are tentative, as if Cavendish were posing questions to answer. "Heat by friction & hammering. Whether they can give suffic. vis viva," to which Cavendish added a footnote suggesting a possible answer to the question: "Perhaps may where much force is concentrated in small space as in boring holes etc but as friction is not produced without tearing the greatest part of heat produced thereby is likely to be owing to other cause." To the note "Heat by emission of light, the light commonly impelled by repulsion of large particles of matter," he added a footnote, "but quere whether this can be the case in flame." He raised other questions. "Whether all kinds of force applied should give any vis viva to a body or only suffic. quick motions." "What is the cause of friction & want of elasticity whether it is not always owing to tearing off of particles or altering their arrangement," which question was followed up by a proposed experiment on friction. "Cannot explain why the motion of the particles should cause a body to expand," which is followed by a suggestion about the altered interactions and therefore positions of particles in motion.[77] There is nothing in Cavendish's wording to suggest that he was in any doubt about the truth of the hypothesis that heat is the vibration of particles. What it does strongly suggest is that he had genuine questions about the explanations, based on this hypothesis, of some principal phenomena of heat. The working through of the theory of heat was an effort of understanding.

---

[75]Charles Blagden to Henry Cavendish, n.d., /1785/, Cavendish Mss X(b), 4.

[76]Cavendish, "Heat," 22.

[77]Cavendish, "Heat," rough draft, two sequential, unnumbered pages, the first beginning "heat from action of [sun]s light . . ."

Important as it was, Cavendish's need to satisfy his own curiosity was, of course, not his only motivation in writing "Heat." He was part of the larger scientific world, and he was writing for it, in intent if not in deed. He had much that he wanted to say about the directions that that world was taking. By the late 1780s, he saw the general understanding of physical reality that had guided his researches for twenty years everywhere under attack or ignored. Cavendish's electrical theory was regarded by his British colleagues as mathematically beyond them and remote from the experimental problems they were addressing; abroad his theory remained all but unknown.[78] The late eighteenth century was a time when electrical researchers were commonly interested in the connections between electricity and the ether, chemical action, air, sound, light, and heat, whereas Cavendish's theory was exclusively electrical, concerned solely with the implications of a hypothetical electric fluid together with the law of electric force. At the same time, the old phlogiston theory of chemistry was under attack. By 1783, when Cavendish publicly defended the phlogiston theory, Lavoisier's new understanding of combustion was well advanced, and over the next few years chemists began converting to it. By the time it was first publicly taught in Britain, in 1787, the arguments over the foundations of chemistry were running decidedly in Lavoisier's favor. Pneumatic chemistry, the science which owed greatly to Cavendish's work, was just then acquiring a caloric theory of gases, according to which the particles of gases are surrounded by a repellent fiery matter. Elsewhere, too, the Newtonian theory of heat was largely ignored, as we have seen: the number of its remaining proponents was dwindling, while writings on the material theory of heat were growing.[79] The beleaguered Newtonian theory of heat was a demonstrable physical truth to Cavendish. It was supported by his researches not only in the science of heat proper but also in the two other sciences in which he had done his most important work, chemistry and electricity. The ether and the imponderable fluids were now widely understood to have provided the basis of a new, unified natural philosophy replacing the older one subscribed to by Cavendish and a few other British interpreters of Newton. Cavendish's goal was to quantify the forces of attraction and

repulsion between the particles of matter, retaining so far as possible Newton's unity of matter; it was the program that Newton had laid down in query 31 of the *Opticks*. Cavendish demonstrated in "Heat" that the older natural philosophy was not outmoded, that it was more than adequate to the task of accommodating recent experimental advances. These considerations underlie the unusually forceful wording of "Heat." This theoretical work conveys a feeling of urgency that we find in no other writing by Cavendish.

It is easier to understand the circumstances of Cavendish's writing "Heat" than to say why he dropped it. First, it has to be remembered that Cavendish did many original researches that he did not see through publication. Yet he did publish his most important researches, if only in part, so the question remains why he apparently did no more with "Heat." It is instructive to compare "Heat" with Cavendish's manuscript "Thoughts Concerning Electricity" and the mathematical propositions belonging to it. Together they comprise thirty-five manuscript pages, which is roughly the length of "Heat." They are the preliminary version of the long article containing a complete electrical theory that Cavendish published in the *Philosophical Transactions* in 1771.[80] He did not, so far as we know, write the comparable, fuller version of the theoretical work "Heat." Yet Cavendish might be expected to have amplified and perfected "Heat" for eventual publication in the *Philosophical Transactions*, given the importance of the subject for him and for science and given that "Heat," even as it stood, answered the main mechanical objections to the motion theory.

[78]For example, Blagden, upon delivering to Cavendish a gift of René-Just Haüy's new treatise on electricity and magnetism, which contained an electrical hypothesis similar to Cavendish's, observed that the author seemed unaware of Cavendish's fundamental paper of 1771: Blagden to C. L. Berthollet, draft, 11 Sept. 1787, Blagden Letterbook, Royal Society, 7:69. The reception of Cavendish's electrical theory in light of contemporary directions of electrical experimentation and speculation is discussed in McCormmach, "Electrical Researches of Henry Cavendish," 476–97.

[79]In 1786 Bryan Higgins gave a "true caloric theory of gases" in his *Experiments and Observations Relating to Acetous Acid*; Fox, *Caloric Theory*, 11, 21, 22.

[80]Henry Cavendish, "Thoughts Concerning Electricity" and "Cavendish's First Mathematical Theory," Cavendish Mss I, 17 and 18, and his published paper of 1771, "An Attempt to Explain Some of the Principal Phaenomena of Electricity, by Means of an Elastic Fluid," reprinted in *The Electrical Researches of the Honourable Henry Cavendish*, ed. J. C. Maxwell (Cambridge: Cambridge University Press, 1879), 94–103, 411–17, and 1–63, respectively.

Blagden, in advising Lord George about Cavendish's unpublished papers, said that Cavendish was "always ready to publish" what was good. Moreover, Cavendish was acutely aware that if good work is withheld, it will likely be forestalled by someone else.[81] This unhappy outcome, however, was not likely in the case of "Heat," nor was rivalry with its disagreeable consequences. No one had come forward with a work like Cavendish's, nor would anyone soon. The paper would draw criticism, but Cavendish knew that when he wrote it.

A possible reason for abandoning work on the theory is the new experiments that occurred to Cavendish in the writing of "Heat," but we doubt that they have any bearing on the question. He did not need more experimental proof: he was, he said, as fully convinced of the theory of heat as he was of anything in science this side of pure mathematics. In a footnote in "Heat" he referred to the "text," and he drafted the whole twice and planned yet another writing in which certain paragraphs would be reordered. There can be little doubt that it was with publication in mind that Cavendish wrote the preliminary drafts of "Heat."

It may be that when Cavendish began "Heat" he expected more from it. Founded on the principles of mechanics, Cavendish's theory of heat was mathematically rigorous, but at the stage he left it, with the manuscript "Heat," he had not yet shown it capable of predicting new, quantitatively determinable phenomena. In that important respect its development was inferior to that of his electrical theory, which had impressive predictive powers.

Referring to Cavendish's papers that went unpublished, Blagden said that "it is to be supposed that he afterwards discovered some weakness or imperfection in them." But if the ideas in "Heat" were not good enough for Cavendish, given his standards, the question is only pushed back. What were his standards and what was their source? "When a theory has been proposed by Sr I.N." and agrees with the facts, Cavendish said of Newton's theory of heat, it is to be accepted. Cavendish spoke of "Newton's" theory; and though in reality it was his own theory, to his way of thinking they were one and the same. Cavendish had written up his electrical researches as an intended treatise on the universal force of electricity, an electrical system of the world, in

form and substance the electrical sequel of Newton's universal gravitational system of the world. Heat was an equally fundamental subject, its phenomena even more universal than those of electricity and gravitation, since heat is produced by every kind of force. Its proper treatment would have required yet another treatise, another chapter in the final treatise on the one, encompassing system of the world of particles and forces. It is against the standards established by Newton that Cavendish's individual mix of assertion and caution must be viewed.

The Natural Philosopher

In *The Life of the Honourable Henry Cavendish*, George Wilson defined Cavendish's universe as consisting "*solely* of a multitude of objects which could be weighed, numbered, and measured." Wilson came to this understanding of what he called Cavendish's "Theory of the Universe" after examining his chemical papers closely and his papers on heat cursorily. These papers contained experimental researches in which weighings, thermometer readings, and like numbers occurred throughout. They were, Wilson believed, the restricted language of a man whose elected vocation was to "weigh, number, and measure as many of those objects as his allotted three-score years and ten would permit." A "calculating engine" was Wilson's characterization of Cavendish.[82] Wilson's judgment has been uncritically repeated ever since, but he was fundamentally in error about his subject.

In all three of Cavendish's major original lines of research, chemistry, electricity, and heat, he did a series of experiments *after* he had sketched out the basic theory. Cavendish's chemical researches were guided by the phlogiston theory, which he discussed in his earliest, unpublished chemical writings and more fully in his published ones. The starting point of his electrical researches was the unpublished "Thoughts Concerning Electricity" and their elaboration and refinement in the published theoretical paper of 1771. Cavendish's researches in heat, as we have seen, began in an unpublished paper on mechanics,

[81]Cavendish to Michell, 27 May 1783.
[82]Wilson, *Cavendish*, 185–86.

"Remarks on the Theory of Motion." All of these earliest theoretical writings belong to the 1760s, when Cavendish was in his thirties and just setting out as a researcher. For the rest of his life he worked from these theoretical ideas, modifying them as needed, perfecting them, and studying the phenomena in question experimentally.

Cavendish's goal was the understanding of nature, not calculation for its own sake. That much is clear from "Heat," though the manuscript contains calculations. Following the mechanical theorems governing vibrating particles, Cavendish carried through a long calculation for the example of electric discharge and another for Michell's experiment. But for the most part the subject of heat did not yet lend itself to extended mathematical and quantitative treatment. The persuasiveness of Cavendish's paper derived from another source, its coherence, comprehensiveness, and strict reasoning, which included mathematical reasoning where it applied. Passing from one branch of natural philosophy to another, he argued that the phenomena were explained by Newton's theory. From beginning to end, "Heat" gave testimony that heat consists of the invisible vibrations of bodies; it gave *understanding*.

In developing his case for Newton's theory, which is a theory about nature at the level of the particles of matter, Cavendish repeatedly called on a general standpoint. Elsewhere in his writings he called on it, too, but only in "Heat" did he make explicit his fundamental beliefs about the ultimate constituents, his "Theory of the Universe." The discussion occurs in a footnote to the discussion of friction, which in the rough draft is motivated by an observation omitted from the fair copy: "The nature of friction & imperfect elasticity deserves to be considered more accurately." The fair copy continues:

> According to Father Boscovich & Mr. Michell matter does not consist of solid impenetrable particles as commonly supposed, but only of certain degrees of attraction & repulsion directed towards central points. They also suppose that the action of 2 of these central points on each other alternately varies from repulsion to attraction numberless times as the distance increases. There is the utmost reason to think that both these suppositions are true; & they serve to account for many phenomena of nature which would otherwise be inexplicable. But even if it is otherwise, & if it must be admitted that there are

solid impenetrable particles, still there seems sufficient reason to think that those particles do not touch each other, but are kept from ever coming in contact by their repulsive force.[83]

This is what Cavendish thought the world was made of. He believed that Boscovich and Michell were likely to be right about particles, but it would change nothing if Newton was right. In either case, the force of repulsion keeps particles from touching and losing *vis viva*, which is the point.[84]

John Michell's views were made public through Priestley's account of them in 1772 in his history of optics.[85] Roger Joseph Boscovich's were known directly, principally through his treatise *Theoria philosophiae naturalis*, which appeared just as Cavendish was setting out as a researcher.[86] The Leibnizian and Newtonian elements in Boscovich's theory, such as Leibniz's law of continuity and Newton's attractive and repulsive forces, made his theory compatible with, and useful for understanding, Newton's theory of heat in the form Cavendish gave to it. In Boscovich's world of point masses interacting through central forces, there could be no friction or inelastic collisions, which destroy *vis viva*. At close separations, particles experience infinite repulsion, at large separations gravitational attraction, and in between the attractions and repulsions responsible for cohesion, vaporization, and a great variety of other chemical and physical phenomena. Boscovich represented his universal "law of forces" by a continuous curve: above the axis the force is repulsive, and below it

---

[83]Cavendish, "Heat," rough draft, 17–18; and Cavendish, "Heat," 28–29. Cavendish's questioning of the existence of solid, impenetrable particles in the context of a conservation law belongs to a long debate, which is the subject of Wilson L. Scott, *The Conflict between Atomism and Conservation Theory, 1644–1860* (New York: Elsevier, 1970).

[84]With this statement by Cavendish, a puzzle is solved. In a number of places in his writings he spoke of particles as if he thought of them as Newtonian solid bodies, while in other places he spoke of them as if he did not. In "Heat" he explained that either view was acceptable to him.

[85]Priestley, *History* 1:392–93, 311. Priestley not only gave Michell's views on matter and forces but also his application of them to Newton's observations of the colors of thin plates and to the immense force with which light is emitted from bodies: ibid., 309–11, 392–93, 786–91. In his electrical researches Cavendish used Michell's explanation of colored plates as an analogy for the motion of electricity within glass plates: "Further Experiments on Charges of Plates. . . ," Cavendish Mss III(a), 5; *Sci. Pap.* 2:354–62, on 361–62.

[86]Priestley also discussed Boscovich's views in his *History*, but Cavendish had got them directly from their author in his first edition of 1758 of the *Theoria*. We note too that Cavendish and Michell met Boscovich on his tour of England, both dining with him at the Royal Society Club on 5 June 1760 and Cavendish with him again on 26 June 1760: Royal Society Club Minute Book, Royal Society.

attractive, and the points where it passes from repulsion to attraction mark limit points of cohesion. Particles vibrate about these points when disturbed, and the vibrations continue indefinitely until the particles are again disturbed. The area between the curve and the axis is proportional to *vis viva*, since it measures the action of a force across a distance. Boscovich's theory, with its implied possibility of perpetually vibrating particles accounting for combustion, dissolution, and fermentation, and with its implied conservation law, provided support for Newton's theory of heat, which is why Cavendish introduced it in "Heat."[87]

Cavendish, as we know, accepted as the first task of natural philosophy the determination of forces, but the forces responsible for the phenomena of heat act over minute distances and are otherwise inaccessible. It is problematic that they can be known in the way that gravitation is known, in detail, in the form of a mathematical law.[88] Nevertheless, as Cavendish showed, the phenomena of heat can be deduced from a knowledge only of the general nature of the acting forces. Boscovich's law of forces encompasses forces that depend on the distance and are directed to central points, and so these forces satisfy the assumptions of Cavendish's derivation of the conservation law. It is conceivable that Cavendish's reading of Boscovich gave him his original direction, but for someone as widely read as Cavendish we doubt that the impetus was so straightforward.[89] It is clear that early on, Cavendish mastered Newton's science, but he needed more than Newton could give him to develop "Newton's" theory of heat, and important as Leibnizian *vis viva* was for Cavendish's purposes, that did not give it to him either. Neither did Michell's and Boscovich's views on the nature of matter and force. Rather Cavendish drew on all of these sources and on his and others' experimental investigations of heat, and by strict reasoning, he brought them together to make the theory he presented in "Heat."

Cavendish was not one to speculate on the unity of nature. He developed mathematical theories and followed them with experimental measurements, carefully delimiting the phenomena under review. For work of this kind it was important to make distinctions, not assert unities. Yet he held to a theoretical view by which the disparate phenomena of nature are seen to have a uniform cause in attractive and repulsive, centrally acting forces.[90] This understanding, together with the mechanical theorems about *vis viva*, permitted Cavendish to display a connectedness, through an analogy with heat, between the several major domains of delimited phenomena constituting the broad field of natural philosophy.

---

[87] It makes no difference here that Boscovich himself believed in the matter of fire; Roger Joseph Boscovich, *A Theory of Natural Philosophy*, trans J. M. Child from the 2d edition of 1763 (Cambridge, Mass.: MIT Press, 1966), 22–23, 43, 73, 76–96. Boscovich did not have a conservation law and generally regarded *vis viva* as having little significance; it may be surprising given his theory's ready explanation of the conservation of *vis viva*. Thomas L. Hankins, "Eighteenth-Century Attempts to Resolve the *Vis viva* Controversy," *Isis* 56 (1965): 281–97, on 294, and on Boscovich, 291–97; on Michell and Boscovich, Schofield, *Mechanism and Materialism*, 236–49.

[88] To the time of Cavendish's "Heat," the search for the laws of the forces acting over minute distances had proven unsuccessful. The law of force of light particles eluded Newton's followers as it had Newton, and no "universal synthesis of short-range forces" had been established: Cantor, *Optics after Newton*, 87. There was a way of retaining, in part, Newton's understanding of the future of natural philosophy: it was not to wait until the laws of force were known but to "compute the forces" in ignorance of them, using *vis viva*. That was Cavendish's way, one suggested by Boscovich's law of forces.

[89] Michell arrived independently at views similar to Boscovich's, and Cavendish may have done so, too, given the theoretical problems he was working on. It has been pointed out that there was a British tradition paralleling Boscovich's views; ibid., 71–72; Schofield, *Mechanism and Materialism*. 237–38; and P. M. Heimann and J. E. McGuire, "Newtonian Forces and Lockean Powers: Concepts of Matter in Eighteenth-Century Thought," *Historical Studies in the Physical Sciences* 3 (1971): 233–306.

[90] In view of the incompleteness of Cavendish's manuscripts, it is hazardous to speak confidently of what he did not accomplish. That has been done by Yukitoshi Matsuo, who asserts Cavendish's "failure to unify a variety of heat phenomena in terms of dynamics and his subsequent abandonment of a systematic consideration of them." Equally hazardous is his consequent assertion that Cavendish never "gave any special consideration to systematic thought in chemistry": Yukitoshi Matsuo, "Henry Cavendish: A Scientist in the Age of the *Révolution chimique*," *Japanese Studies in the History of Science* 14 (1975): 83–94, on 93–94.

CHAPTER 5

Sky

The astronomical observations that Henry Cavendish made with his father probably gave him his start in science. He went on to do work on nearly every astronomical subject: instruments, atmospheric refraction, tides, earth, moon, planets, comets, sun, and stars. His astronomical papers constitute the largest single group of manuscripts. These papers, part observational and larger part mathematical and theoretical, often begin as carefully drafted studies with a clear objective and then trail off into calculations of unclear significance, but in a number of instances they have a finished quality and are meant to be shown to someone. Although he did not single out any one central problem in astronomy, here as in other areas of science, he took a painstaking interest in instruments and in methods and errors of observation. He did not make systematic observations of the heavens like Nevil Maskelyne or William Herschel—he did not have that kind of observatory and he did not spend his life that way—but he made observations from time to time to test techniques, such as taking transits, and he looked at things that other astronomers were looking at, a planet, a comet, a variable star, or volcanoes on the moon.[1]

In the vicinity of London there was a series of observatories roughly following the course of the Thames. Cavendish's observatory at Clapham Common was directly south of London, and on a line with it to the east were Aubert's observatory at Loam Pit and just beyond that the Royal Observatory at Greenwich, where Maskelyne worked. Considerably to the west of this group was Herschel's observatory near Windsor Castle. From 1788 Aubert had a new observatory, built for him by Smeaton at Islington, directly north of London.[2] The astronomers were in the practice of paying visits to one another's observatories[3] and to collaborating, as we show by example.

Collaborators

The 1780s were a time of discovery in astronomy, and the greatest discoverer was William Herschel. He was the first person known to have discovered a new major planet, in 1782, which he astutely named after George III (it was renamed Uranus), who rewarded him with a royal pension, freeing him from his original profession, music. Herschel settled near Windsor Castle, where he spent the rest of his life making observations at night and, by day, telescopes, which he either sold to supplement his pension or used himself to see ever deeper into space. In 1783 he began his systematic "sweeps" of the sky, and at the same time he worked on a telescope of (for that time) gigantic proportions, four feet across and forty feet in length. Blagden walked through the iron tube of this telescope hardly having to stoop.[4] Herschel never got this telescope to work satisfactorily, but its size was a proper measure of his ambition, which was to see to the ends of the universe and to determine the configuration of all of its contents. In these years he made his single most important contribution, his theory of the structure of the visible universe based on a great mass of observations he had made.[5] His addition to astronomical knowledge was prodigious. This imaginative and industrious observer

---

[1]Herschel observed what he regarded as an eruption on the moon, shining with a fiery light, and he observed two "extinct" volcanos as well, concluding they were volcanos "by analogy, or with the eye of reason." William Herschel, "An Account of Three Volcanos in the Moon," *PT* 77 (1787): 229–32, quotation on 229. To see Herschel's volcanos, Cavendish and Blagden used a very good achromatic telescope, owned by Cavendish. With it they saw the unusual light in the dark part of the moon's surface where Herschel had located the big volcano. Charles Blagden to Mrs. Grey, 14 June 1787, draft, Blagden Letterbook, Royal Society, 7:324.

[2]These observatories were all used as corners of triangles in the great trigonometrical operation of the 1780s. They are shown in the plates at the end of William Roy, "An Account of the Trigonometrical Operation. Whereby the Distance Between the Meridians of the Royal Observatories of Greenwich and Paris Has Been Determined," *PT* 80 (1790): 111–270.

[3]For instance, Aubert planned a dinner at Loam Pit for Cavendish, Herschel, Michell, Smeaton, Blagden, and Lord Palmerston. Alexander Aubert to William Herschel, 19 June 1786, Royal Astronomical Society, Herschel W1/13, A3.

[4]Charles Blagden to John Michell, 31 Oct. 1786, draft, Blagden Letterbook, Royal Society, 7:49.

[5]Michael A. Hoskin, *William Herschel and the Construction of the Heavens* (New York: American Elsevier, 1963), 17–18, 62–64.

lived near Cavendish, who naturally took the greatest interest in his work.

As a guest of the Royal Society Club one day, John Playfair noticed that the members paid no attention to their guests, who included several foreigners. There was one exception, Alexander Aubert, whom Playfair found "a very polite man, and a great consolation to a stranger."[6] This detail captures a truth about Aubert: he was observant and helpful. Aubert seemed to have had no personal ambition in astronomy but only a passion for it and a standard of excellence. Equipping his observatories with instruments by the leading instrument-makers, Jesse Ramsden, Peter Dolland, John Bird, and James Short, he was reputed to have the best astronomical establishment of any private person in the country.[7] Because of the quality of his instruments, Herschel appealed to Aubert to confirm his own observations so that they would be taken seriously.[8] Wealthy (needless to say), Aubert was a director and from 1787 governor of the London Assurance Company. He brought his administrative skills to his learned side pursuits. A Fellow of the Royal Society since 1772, he was elected to the council and appointed to committees for astronomy and meteorology, on which he served regularly with, and almost as often as, Cavendish. When John Pringle stepped down as president of the Royal Society in 1778, the council considered two members to replace him, Aubert and Banks, and after long deliberation they made their fateful choice of Banks.[9] In the Society of Antiquaries, Aubert served as vice-president. He combined an observant nature with a daring streak: as chairman of the Harbour Board, he descended to the bottom of Ramsgate Harbour in a diving bell to examine a pier.[10] His avoidance of controversy was made easier by his avoidance of publication.[11] He and Cavendish were the same age and had similar interests, and they saw each other constantly at their clubs. As he did in the case of Blagden and Dalrymple, Cavendish brought Aubert into his financial affairs as a trustee of his property at Clapham Common.[12]

Cavendish saw Maskelyne as often and in the same places, at the Royal Society and at their clubs. Maskelyne brought to Cavendish something that Herschel and Aubert did not; he was not only a man of observation and instruments but, like Cavendish, he was a mathematician as well, and the memoranda that passed between Maskelyne and

Cavendish reflected that uncommon ability. Like Herschel, Maskelyne was hard working and prolific, but there the resemblance ends. Maskelyne did not engage in Herschel's flights of theorizing, which in any case would not have been invited by his position at Greenwich, but it was not in his nature to do so either. Playfair made an apt observation: Maskelyne "is slow in apprehending new truths, but his mind takes a very firm hold of them at last."[13] Maskelyne could be defensive and short- tempered, and he could even be rude to Cavendish,[14] but his methodic exactness and his devotion to astronomy suited Cavendish, and their two difficult temperaments were compatible.

Remote from his colleagues in London, from his home at Thornhill, Yorkshire, John Michell kept up an astronomical exchange as best he could. Of what sort of observatory he had, if any, there is no record, but of his intentions we know a good deal. Michell would have liked to succeed James Bradley as astronomer royal, but he did not have the connections or, it would seem, proof of observational competence.[15] Also standing in his way of high ambition was Michell's behavior as an independent whig at Cambridge, offending the influential John Pringle, for example.[16] Throughout

---

[6]Playfair quoted in Archibald Geikie, *Annals of the Royal Society Club* (London: Macmillan, 1917), 160.

[7]"Aubert, Alexander," *DNB* 1:715.

[8]William Herschel to Alexander Aubert, 9 Jan. 1782, copy, Royal Astronomical Society, Herschel W1/1, pp. 21–24; published in Constance A. Lubbock, *The Herschel Chronicle. The Life-Story of William Herschel and His Sister Caroline Herschel* (Cambridge: Cambridge University Press, 1933), 102–3.

[9]Henry Lyons, *The Royal Society, 1660–1940: A History of Its Administration under Its Charters* (New York: Greenwood, 1968), 197.

[10]Bernard Drew, *The London Assurance, a Second Chronicle* (London: printed for The London Assurance at the Curwen Press, Plaistow, 1949), 159.

[11]Aubert published very little during his long activity in astronomy: there were some observations of the transit of Venus in 1769, a new method of finding time by equal altitudes in 1776, and an account of meteors in 1783, all appearing in the *Philosophical Transactions*.

[12]In a bundle of papers concerning Cavendish's Clapham Common property are extracts from Aubert's and Aubert's heirs' wills. These materials were assembled to transfer the property to the duke of Devonshire after Cavendish's death. Devon. Coll., L/38/78.

[13]John Playfair, *The Works of John Playfair*, ed. J. G. Playfair, 4 vols. (Edinburgh, 1822), 1: "Appendix," no. 1: "Journal," lxxviii.

[14]Charles Blagden to Joseph Banks, 16 Oct. 1783, Fitzwilliam Museum Library, Percival H190.

[15]Thomas Birch to Philip Yorke, 17 July 1762, BL Add Mss 35399, ff. 298–301.

[16]Alexander Small to Benjamin Franklin, 1 Dec. 1764, *Papers of Benjamin Franklin*, ed. L. W. Labaree, vol. 11 (New Haven: Yale University Press, 1967), 479–83. Also involved in the politics of this appointment to astronomer royal was Michell's vote on John Harrison's chronometer. For voting against it, Michell further

the 1780s Michell worked on a reflecting telescope that was second only to Herschel's. Its main mirror was two and a half feet across, ground, polished (and broken) by Michell, and acquired by Herschel after Michell's death.[17] We do not know what Michell planned to do with his telescope once he had perfected it, for his publications in astronomy were—by default, it would seem—theoretical. In speculative verve he was Herschel's equal, and since he had mathematical skills equal to Maskelyne's and Cavendish's, he could develop his theoretical ideas farther. In breadth of scientific knowledge, Michell resembled William Watson, who was now near the end of his life: like Watson, Michell was knowledgeable in natural history as well as in natural philosophy. Michell lived in the vicinity of Priestley, allowing visits; the two did not regularly correspond, and[18] Michell wrote only one letter to Herschel.[19] For his personal contact with men of science, Michell regularly made the long journey from Yorkshire to London. An historian notes that for the English middle class in the eighteenth century, travel "was too irksome or expensive for most to pay more than one or two visits to the great world of London, and such visits rarely repaid them."[20] That could not be said of Michell. His one sustained correspondence with Cavendish was a continuation of a conversation on astronomy from his last visit to London. This exchange had ramifications, as we will see.

Weighing the Stars

Newton wrote in the *Principia* that all bodies are to be regarded as subject to the principle of gravitation.[21] Insofar as ordinary matter was concerned (excluding the imponderable fluids), this postulated universality of mutual attraction was, for followers of Newton, an untested article of faith for nearly a century. During this time the evidence for attraction continued to be drawn from the motions of the earth, moon, planets, comets, and falling bodies, and recently from the attraction of mountains, phenomena which span an intermediate range of masses, sizes, and distances. In three domains of experience, involving the greatest and the smallest bodies, the action of gravity had not yet been observed: the gravity of the "fixed" stars; the mutual attraction of hand-held sized bodies; and the gravitation of the particles of light. The task of deducing observable consequences from

each of these supposed instances of universal gravitation fell to Michell, and his friend Cavendish encouraged him in these researches and became involved in the resulting observational and experimental questions.

Michell and Cavendish received a body of opinions on the nature of stars, which included the understanding that stars shine by their own and not by reflected light, and that their light and the sun's are of the same kind. It was understood that stars are physical bodies, suns, each with its gravitationally bound family of planets and comets, each supplying its world with warmth and light and life. Stars were known to be immensely distant from earth and from one another, which explained why their planets were invisible.

The exact distance of the stars was the great problem of the astronomy of stars. From expeditions, astronomers had determined the earth's measures and the measures of the solar system—the worldwide observations the transits of Venus had been directed to this end—but the measures of the stellar universe remained unknown. Lord Charles Cavendish, as we have noted, got his start as a practicing scientist by helping Bradley look for the distance of the stars. Henry Cavendish carried on the search, as we will see, working with astronomers Herschel and Michell as they looked for the same thing by other means.

Bradley's failure to detect any parallax had led him to remove the stars to a distance of at least 400,000 times that of the sun; this lower bound on stellar distances was cited often through the century. Herschel made surveys of double stars with the hope of finding the parallax by a well-

offended Pringle. James Short, who also was in the running for the job, voted the other way on Harrison, thereby offending another influential person, Lord Morton. Ibid.

[17]Henry C. King, *History of the Telescope* (Cambridge, Mass: Sky Publisher, 1955), 91.

[18]Joseph Priestley to William Herschel, 12 Aug. 1780, in Joseph Priestley, *A Scientific Autobiography of Joseph Priestley (1733–1804)*, ed. R. E. Schofield (Cambridge, Mass: M.I.T. Press, 1966), 186.

[19]John Michell to William Herschel, 12 Apr. 1781, in William Herschel, *The Scientific Papers of Sir William Herschel*, ed. J. L. E. Dreyer, 2 vols. (London: The Royal Society and the Royal Astronomical Society, 1912) 1:xxxii.

[20]Basil Williams, *The Whig Supremacy, 1714–1760*, 2d rev. ed., ed. C. H. Stuart (Oxford: Clarendon Press, 1962), 144.

[21]The following discussion is taken from Russell McCormmach, "John Michell and Henry Cavendish: Weighing the Stars," *British Journal for the History of Science* 4 (1968): 126–55. For material used from that article, we acknowledge permission by the Council of the British Society for the History of Science.

known indirect method. If two stars that looked close were actually at very different distances and were only lined up with the earth, the fainter of the two stars could be considered sufficiently distant as to be fixed, and the apparent displacement of the brighter star as viewed from the orbit of the earth could be measured with reference to it.

Herschel's method of finding the distances of stars was useless, of course, if nearby stars were actually neighboring ones. Michell had reason to believe that they were often indeed neighbors: in his two major papers on astronomy, in 1767 and 1784, he regarded close-lying stars as clusters, their members removed the same distance from the earth. In the first of his papers, he made an original application of the doctrine of chances to astronomy, arguing that the great number of observed nearby stars could not be the result of accident. He assumed that most stars that looked close were physically bound by mutual gravitation. Given certain hypothetical data, the distances and sizes of these companion stars could be estimated on photometric principles.[22] Not convinced by Michell's probabilistic reasoning, as he later would be by observational evidence that most double stars were companions, in 1782 Herschel published a great catalogue containing 269 double stars, most of which he had discovered himself.[23] It was this publication of Herschel that prompted Michell to write his second paper dealing with double stars. Michell had had no idea that there were so many of them. Encouraged by the observational possibilities, he proposed a new method of determining the measures of stars, their distances, sizes, and weights. He sent a paper on the subject to Cavendish to communicate to the Royal Society, accompanied by two letters, one to introduce the paper, and the other to remind Cavendish of the conversation they had on the subject and to say that no one else was as suited as he to judge the paper.[24]

Michell's method depended upon the assumption that the light emitted by stars was attracted back to them. The gravitational motions of the particles of light were not ordinarily observed because of their great velocity, but still, Michell reasoned, an extraordinarily massive body such as a star might attract its own light with sufficient strength to cause a measurable reduction in its velocity. Michell, in fact, had calculated the gravitational retardation of the sun's light for

Priestley's *History of Optics* in 1772, and he followed this line of reasoning in the paper he sent Cavendish in 1783.[25]

Michell calculated that if a star of the same density as the sun had a radius 497 times greater than the sun's, it would attract back to itself all of the light it emitted; thus, at great distances it would be invisible, though its existence might be inferred by a visible star rotating about it. The light from a smaller star would continue to infinity though with a retarded velocity, and it was this retardation that Michell hoped to detect. Based upon Newton's view that the faster light travels, the less it is turned from its course by a refracting medium like glass, Michell's plan was to point a narrow-angled prism at a double star with the leading edge of the prism at right angles to the line joining the stars. The observer would then rotate the prism, directing the light from the stars first at one face and then at the other. Because the retarded light from the central star would be refracted more than the light from the smaller star rotating around it, the pair would be seen to have a slightly different angular separation in the two prism positions. The difference was necessarily small, but Michell thought that John Dolland's achromatic prisms could reveal it if the central star were, say, of the sun's density and at least twenty-two times its size.[26]

To draw conclusions about the distance, size, and weight of a central star from the change in the refrangibility of its light, it was necessary also to know its angular diameter and the period of the star revolving around it. Neither was known for any stars, but Michell thought that it was not out of the question that this information could be found for

[22]John Michell, "An Inquiry into the Probable Parallax, and Magnitude of the Fixed Stars, from the Quantity of Light Which They Afford Us, and the Particular Circumstances of Their Situation," *PT* 57 (1767): 234–64.

[23]William Herschel, "Catalogue of Double Stars," *PT* 72 (1782): 112–62.

[24]John Michell to Henry Cavendish, 26 May 1783, Cavendish Mss, New Correspondence. Michell's paper was published, "On the Means of Discovering the Distance, Magnitude, etc. of the Fixed Stars, in Consequence of the Diminution of the Velocity of Their Light, in Case Such a Diminution Should Be Found to Take Place in Any of Them, and Such Other Data Should Be Procured from Observations, as Would Be Farther Necessary for That Purpose," *PT* 74 (1784): 35–57.

[25]Joseph Priestley, *The History and Present State of Discoveries Relating to Vision, Light, and Colours* (London, 1772), 787–91.

[26]Michell, "On the Means of Discovering the Distance," 51, 53.

some stars somewhere in the "infinite variety" of creation, though it might take "many years, or perhaps some ages."[27] Whatever the future held for attempts to observe the dimensions and motions of double stars, the method stood or fell by the measurement of the decrease in the speed of the light from the stars. This measurement could be made independently of observations of stellar diameters and motions and might succeed immediately, a prospect which drew the attention of astronomers in London, who wanted to try the measurement as a fundamental experiment. If it worked, they had in mind an application that did not have to be deferred for years or ages. If the solar system had a preferred direction in space, the light coming from stars in that direction would, by a simple addition of velocities, strike the earth with greater speed than would the light coming from the opposite direction of the sky.[28] Michell's method could measure the speed with which the solar system was moving toward or away from given stars. (In 1783, using another method, Herschel concluded that the solar system was "moving very fast," Cavendish wrote to Michell. "I forget the direction."[29])

Michell's proposal fell on prepared ground for another reason. In London the year before, and earlier in Paris, there had been much discussion of a scheme for deciding if light really does move, as Newton said it did, with greater velocity in a more refracting medium. Patrick Wilson, assistant to Alexander Wilson, professor of practical astronomy at Glasgow University, proposed an experiment using a telescope filled with water. If the prediction was confirmed, he said, it would be "very strong additional evidence" for Newton's optical principles.[30] There was a small dispute over the priority of this discovery, and when it came up at a dinner of the Royal Society Club, "Mr Cavendish put in, that he did not think it a matter of any consequence to either of them, as nothing seemed likely to be determined by that method."[31]

Michell's method was another matter. Upon receiving Michell's paper, Cavendish wrote that he was "glad you put your thoughts on this subject upon paper."[32] He pointed out a mathematical slip, and he came to disagree with Michell on the best apparatus for detecting the retarded light, but he did not criticize the basic idea of the paper. That the matter of the stars should exert a gravitational

pull upon the particles of light and affect their velocity was for him a correct physical assumption.[33] It was not for everyone.[34]

Michell asked Cavendish to communicate his paper, but if that could not be done before the recess, he wanted Cavendish "not to let the principle of it go abroad, till the paper itself can come before the Society, for reasons, that will be sufficiently obvious."[35] If the reasons were obvious

---

[27]Michell, "On the Means of Discovering the Distance," 48, 57.

[28]There was general interest in this use of the principle of retarded light; e.g., Charles Blagden to Claude Louis Berthollet, 24 Oct. 1783, draft, Blagden Letterbook, Yale; Charles Blagden to Sir Joseph Banks, 25 Oct. 1783, Fitzwilliam Museum Library, Perceval H194.

[29]Henry Cavendish to John Michell, 27 May 1783, draft, Cavendish Mss, New Correspondence. Herschel concluded that the direction was toward the constellation Hercules; discussed in M. A. Hoskin, "Herschel, William," *DSB* 6: 328–36, on 331.

[30]Patrick Wilson, "An Experiment Proposed for Determining, by the Aberration of the Fixed Stars, Whether Rays of Light, in Pervading Different Media, Change Their Velocity According to the Law Which Results from Sir Isaac Newton's Ideas Concerning the Cause of Refraction; and for Ascertaining Their Velocity in Every Medium Whose Refractive Density is Known," *PT* 72 (1782): 58–70.

[31]Charles Blagden to Sir Joseph Banks, 16 Oct. 1783, Fitzwilliam Museum Library, Perceval H190. This is the second letter Blagden wrote to Banks that day, a Thursday. In the earlier letter (Perceval H189) he said that the night before he had read in J. J. de Lalande's latest volume of *Astronomy* the same idea as Wilson's for testing the velocity of light. Lalande's work came out in 1781, the year before Wilson's paper, and moreover, Lalande said that Boscovich had proposed the method in 1766. Blagden was mortified that Wilson's paper was allowed to be published in the *Philosophical Transactions*. Maskelyne was to blame, he thought, and that evening he brought it up; Maskelyne became defensive. Blagden described the testy conversation he had provoked in his second letter to Banks that night.

[32]Cavendish to Michell, 27 May 1783.

[33]Cavendish made a calculation like Michell's on the other effect of gravity on light, bending it rather than slowing it. There is no date, but it is very late; the watermark on the sheet reads "1802." It may have been inspired by Michell's paper and perhaps the failed attempts it led to. It also might have come out of his study of the orbits of comets, since it is inserted loosely in a packet of papers on that subject. Henry Cavendish, "To Find the Bending of a Ray of Light Which Passes Near the Surface of Any Body by the Attraction of That Body," Cavendish Mss VIII, 52; in Cavendish, *Sci. Pap.* 2: 437. Clifford M. Will, "Henry Cavendish, Johann von Soldner, and the Deflection of Light," *American Journal of Physics* 56 (1988): 413–15. J. Eisenstaedt, "De l'influence de la gravitation sur la propagation de la lumière en théorie newtonienne. L'archéologie des trous noirs," *Archive for History of the Exact Sciences* 42 (1991): 315–86.

[34]Light might be regarded as one of the imponderable fluids. Bryan Higgins, for example, in his *Philosophical Essay Concerning Light* in 1776, described light as an expansive, atomic fluid that does not gravitate. His views are discussed in J. R. Partington and D. McKie, "Historical Studies on the Phlogiston Theory.— III. Light and Heat in Combustion," *Annals of Science* 3 (1938): 337–71. Or light might be regarded as possessing negative weight; for example, P. D. Leslie, *A Philosophical Inquiry into the Cause of Animal Heat: With Incidental Observations on Several Phisiological and Chymical Questions, Connected with the Subject* (London, 1778), 121.

[35]John Michell to Henry Cavendish, 26 May 1783, Cavendish Mss, New Correspondence.

to Cavendish, he did not accept them. Before giving Cavendish's response, we need to point out that Michell believed that a great injustice had been done to him in the past. His first publication, on magnetism, is remembered for the first correct and complete statement of the mathematical properties of the magnetic force, but for Michell the importance of this publication was its practical value for seamen, who were interested not in philosophy but in compass needles. Michell believed that his method for making artificial magnets was as good as that of Gowin Knight, who made the best magnets at that time.[36] Knight had kept his method secret, since artificial magnets were a subject of practical as well as scientific interest, allied to patents. John Canton also had a secret method, with which he intended to make money. When Michell published his method in 1750, then so did Canton the next year.[37] Michell believed that Canton had taken the method from him. Michell never forgot or forgave, and Canton was unhappy about the allegation to his dying day, in 1772; in 1785 the controversy, long pursued privately, became public. The *Biographia Britannica* published a life of Canton in which his paper on magnets was said to have been read in January 1750, one year before it was, the error arising from the old-style dating. There followed a notice in the *Monthly Review*, to which Michell sent a letter protesting its printing and pressing his claim that Canton's experiments were "borrowed."[38] In response, William Canton, son of John, collected testimonials for publication. The man in the middle, Joseph Priestley, friend of both Michell and Canton, tried without success to get Michell to retract. Resigned as he was to the imperfections of the world, Priestley told Canton's son that the dispute was "one of the inconveniences attending *secrets*, of which your father sincerely repented."[39]

Cavendish thought as Priestley did: the lesson he drew from the dispute was opposite to the one Michell did. Whereas Michell wanted more secrecy, Cavendish wanted none. Cavendish was happy to receive Michell's paper, but he was

sorry however that you wish to have the principle kept secret. The surest way of securing the merit to the author is to let it be known as soon as possible and those who act otherwise commonly find themselves forestalled by others. But in the present case I can not conceive why you should wish to have it kept secret for when you was last in town you made no secret of the principle but mention'd it openly at our Mondays meeting and if I mistake not at other places and I have frequently heard it talked of since then. As to the method you propose for determining whether the vel. light is diminished (which seems a very good one) I do not remember that you did mention that but as I do not imagine that you are likely soon to make any exper. of that kind yourself I see no reason why you should wish to keep that secret. On the whole I think that instead of you desiring me to keep the princ. of the paper secret you ought rather to wish me to show the paper to as many of your friends as are desirous of reading it.[40]

In reply Michell said that the prism was an afterthought and that it could not, therefore, have been revealed on his last visit to London. He remembered having been more discreet and elliptic than Cavendish gave him credit for. "I thought I had given some obscure hints," he said, "about the principle of my paper, to other friends, when I was last in London, yet except what I had said to yourself, I apprehended they were too obscure to have the drift of them fully understood." But on the main point, he yielded: "upon farther consideration, I believe you are right, and shall therefore have no objections to your permitting any one, you think proper to read it; indeed the more people see it the better, if it is divulged at all."[41]

Cavendish promptly showed Michell's paper to Maskelyne, Herschel, and others. Cavendish came to believe that a telescopic lens—Michell's first thought on the matter—was a better instrument than a prism for measuring the diminution of light, and he told Michell that Maskelyne was now of the same opinion.[42] Cavendish made a calculation to show what could be expected from a lens: if the

[36]John Michell, *A Treatise of Artificial Magnets; in Which Is Shewn an Easy and Expeditious Method of Making Them, Superior to the Best Natural Ones* . . . (Cambridge, 1750), 2, 8, 10, 17–20.
[37]John Canton, "A Method of Making Artificial Magnets Without the Use of Natural Ones," *PT* 47 (1751): 31–38 .
[38]John Michell, letter of 17 May 1785, *Monthly Review* 72 (1785): 478–80.
[39]Michell and Canton's well-known antagonism long antedated the controversy in 1785. "I am very sorry for the difference between you and him /Michell/," Priestley wrote to John Canton on 11 Aug. 1768; in Priestley, *A Scientific Autobiography*, 69–70, on 70. In a letter to the son William Canton, 20 Aug. 1785, Priestley said that he had tried to get Michell to take back his accusations. This letter along with several letters of testimony on Canton's behalf, solicited by his son, are in the Canton Papers, Royal Society.
[40]Cavendish to Michell, 27 May 1783.
[41]John Michell to Henry Cavendish, 2 July 1783, Cavendish Mss, New Correspondence.
[42]Henry Cavendish to John Michell, 12 Aug. 1783, draft, Cavendish Mss, New Correspondence.

velocity of light from a star was decreased by as small a fraction as 1 in 1000, the focal length of an achromatic lens would be reduced by 17 parts in 10,000. Maskelyne, he reported, supposed that even a much smaller reduction in focal length would be detectable: the alteration of the focus was 5/3rd the alteration of the velocity of light, and therefore a star with a diameter of only 7 times that of the sun would, Maskelyne calculated, diminish the velocity of its light by 1/10,000, which would be detectable by a good achromatic telescope.[43]

These calculations were promising, but Cavendish had to inform Michell that Maskelyne had looked at some likely stars with an achromatic lens without success, and that Herschel had done the same on a "great many stars." Herschel was now grinding a prism to try the experiment Michell's way. From these negative findings, Cavendish concluded that "there is not much likelyhood of finding any stars whose light is sensibly diminished."[44] That was in August 1783; two months later Blagden reported that the astronomers had not given up but were having instruments made to continue the search.[45] Three years later he reported on an instrument "formed like a hook with achromatic prisms fit all round . . . ."[46] Blagden added that no such instrument had actually been built. Twenty years later, in 1804, Herschel reported on an experiment on the "velocity of differently colour'd light" with his forty-foot telescope, on which subject he had had a conversation with Cavendish at the Royal Society.[47] The variable velocity of light was a meaningful concept and a potentially useful principle in the design of astronomical instruments until the early twentieth century, when a new physics was founded on the absoluteness of the velocity of light.

Michell may have been discouraged by Cavendish's report. Three months later he still had not replied to it, and Cavendish sent him a reminder that he had written a "good while ago."[48] He had forwarded a list of errata compiled by Maskelyne, and now that the meetings of the Society were about to begin he wanted to know what Michell would have him do. Michell sent instructions concerning the errata,[49] but he did not answer Cavendish's letter for some time. Eight months passed before he replied to the negative findings that Cavendish had conveyed. He referred to his languidness and to other vague reasons for the long delay, and he spoke of his method in a disheartened vein. Because he had never held sanguine hopes for the experiment, he would not be "greatly disappointed in case nothing should come of it." He went on to acknowledge Cavendish's verdict that there might be no stars out there big enough.[50]

It happened that at just this time an astronomical discovery was made that held out hope for Michell's method. Regular variations in the brightness of the star Algol were observed by John Goodricke, a deaf-and-dumb prodigy (who would die at age twenty-one), whom Michell had never heard of. In May 1783, the month when Michell sent his paper to Cavendish, Goodricke submitted his paper on Algol, for which he was awarded the Copley Medal of the Royal Society.[51] Goodricke guessed (correctly) that the reason for the variation of Algol was that it was a double star; a second body revolved around the bright star, periodically cutting off its light. Michell contrived a theory of its variations, confessing that it required the "concurrence of so many circumstances" that it was improbable.[52] By assuming that Algol was a double star and that the central star was both larger and duller than the other, and by inventing hypotheses about the eccentricity and orientation of the orbit, Michell accounted for the regularities that Goodricke had observed in the variation of the light from Algol. He thought that if his explanation was correct, his prism test would "almost with

[43]Maskelyne's calculations, in his hand, are on a sheet enclosed in Cavendish's draft of his letter to Michell, 27 May 1783.
[44]Cavendish to Michell, 12 Aug. 1783.
[45]Charles Blagden to Claude Louis Berthollet, 24 Oct. 1783, draft, Blagden Letterbook, Yale.
[46]Charles Blagden to Pierre Simon Laplace, 31 May 1786, draft, Blagden Letterbook, Royal Society, 7:1.
[47]William Herschel to Patrick Wilson, 26 Dec. 1804, copy, Royal Astronomical Society, Herschel Mss, W1/1, pp. 255–56. Cavendish asked Herschel if he had seen a recent article on the velocity of heat rays in the *Philosophical Magazine*. This new journal Cavendish subscribed to and read.
[48]Henry Cavendish to John Michell, 4 Nov. 1783, draft, Cavendish Mss, New Correspondence.
[49]John Michell to Henry Cavendish, 10 Nov. 1783, Cavendish Mss, New Correspondence.
[50]John Michell to Henry Cavendish, 20 Apr. 1784, Cavendish Mss, New Correspondence.
[51]John Goodricke, "On the Periods of the Changes of Light in the Star Algol," and "A Series of Observations on, and a Discovery of, the Period of the Variation of the Light of the Bright Star in the Head of Medusa, Called Algol," *PT* 73 (1783): 474–82, and 74 (1784): 287–92.
[52]Michell to Cavendish, 2 July 1783.

certainty" confirm it. Cavendish was again deflating: "I imagine you rather wish than think it to be likely."[53]

Algol held an interest for Cavendish apart from Michell's method, though this too was connected with Michell. In their correspondence about his method, Michell told Cavendish of an instrument he had invented for measuring the comparative brightness of stars. Michell proposed calling his instrument an "astrophotometer," since a "hard name adds much to the dignity of a thing."[54] "I like your Astrophotomer very well," Cavendish replied. He too wished that observations of that kind were made, and he went on to describe a contrivance for the same purpose he had earlier designed. His photometer employed the reflection from a speculum to bring the brightness of one star into equality with that of another.[55] Cavendish and Aubert both measured the light from Algol,[56] and with a photometer made to his design, Cavendish and Blagden observed Algol together. Cavendish's photometer did not work very well.[57]

Cavendish's involvement in Michell's work was immediate. The subject belonged to the far-reaching implications of the unity of the Newtonian world, and Michell developed a dynamics of stars based upon the pervasive action of forces. The members of multiple systems of stars orbit about each other by reason of their mutual gravitation. They expel and accelerate light by enormous forces, as Michell had calculated for Priestley's *History of Optics*, and they attract it back by the almost infinitely weaker but infinitely extended force of gravity. The particles of starlight are once again accelerated by strong forces in glass prisms when they are received on earth. The forces of the light, the glass, and the stars determine a unique, calculable path of light in the prism. It together with the motions and apparent dimensions (if observable) of the multiple stars determine the crucial magnitudes of sidereal astronomy: the distances, sizes, and masses of the stars. Michell's method brought together the two exact sciences of planetary theory and optics, one the science of the greatest bodies of the universe and the other the science of the minutest bodies. Just as Newton had used his gravitational mechanics to determine the local motions of the solar system, Michell sought the motions and measures of the universe beyond the solar system by the same methods. Michell and Cavendish's collabora-

tion was an affirmation of the tradition of the mathematical physics of forces.

Aerial Telescope

No sooner had Cavendish settled into his new house at Clapham Common than he took the first step toward erecting a large telescope on the premises. Given the timing, the suggestion is that Cavendish had wanted to try this telescope and was only waiting until he had a place for it. Christiaan Huygens, the builder of the telescope, had described its needs: "In a large area every way open to the view of the heavens, let a long pole or mast be fixt upright in the earth."[58] Cavendish followed directions.

The telescope had been given to the Royal Society in 1691 by Constantine Huygens, then secretary to King William III. Constantine was a telescope-builder like his brother Christiaan, though it is Christiaan who is generally credited with introducing telescopes of this sort, the so-called "aerial." The telescope in question is usually (and slightly inaccurately) referred to as Huygens' 123-foot telescope.[59] The incentive to develop telescopes of such extraordinarily long focal lengths in the first place was to reduce aberrations and also to achieve high magnifications.[60] Not until John

---

[53]Cavendish to Michell, 12 Aug. 1783.

[54]Michell to Cavendish, 2 July 1783. Michell's instrument was a variant of one proposed in 1700 by R. P. François-Marie, as reported in Pierre Bouguer, *Optical Treatise on the Gradation of Light*, 1760, trans. with notes by W. E. Knowles Middleton (Toronto: University of Toronto Press, 1961). Bouguer's principles appear throughout Michell's astronomical writings.

[55]Cavendish to Michell, 12 Aug. 1783.

[56]Charles Blagden to Charles Le Roy, 15 Sep. 1783, draft, Blagden Letterbook, Yale.

[57]Charles Blagden to Sir Joseph Banks, 16, 23, and 30 Oct. 1783, Fitzwilliam Museum Library, Percival H190, H193, and H195.

[58]Robert Smith, *A Compleat System of Opticks in Four Books, viz a Popular, a Mathematical, a Mechanical, and a Philosophical Treatise. To Which Are Added Remarks upon the Whole*, 2 vols. (Cambridge, 1738) 2:355.

[59]The accurate dimensions of this telescope are: focal length 122 feet and aperture 7 7/8 inches. Constantine Huygens also gave the Royal Society two other object-glasses of even greater focal length, 170 feet and 210 feet, and Cavendish evidently borrowed them too. R. A. Sampson and A. E. Conrady, "On Three Huygens Lenses in the Possession of the Royal Society of London," *Proceedings of the Royal Society of Edinburgh* 49 (1929): 289–99, on 289–92.

[60]The 123-foot Huygens telescope has a magnification of 218. William Kitchener, *The Economy of the Eyes*. Part 2: *Of Telescopes: Being the Result of Thirty Years' Experiments with Fifty–One Telescopes, of from One to Nine Inches in Diameter* (London, 1825), 22. The very slight curvature of the long focal-length lens greatly reduces spherical aberration. Chromatic aberration is also practically eliminated for the following reason. The telescope consists of two lenses, neither of

Hadley developed the Newtonian reflecting telescope did astronomers know of any way to improve their telescopes other than by lengthening the tubes, which was a deadend, for the length increased faster than the magnification: to double the magnification, the length had to be quadrupled, to triple it, the length had to be increased ninefold, etc. Huygens showed astronomers that they could dispense with the unwieldly rigid tubes for mounting the object-glass and eye-glass; this in turn made possible much longer telescopes.

With Huygens' aerial telescope, the object-glass was fixed to the top of a tall pole, and the observer aligned the eye-glass with the help of a taut thread.[61] This telescope was as hard to use as it sounds. The Royal Society considered fixing the telescope to a tall, solid building, but they could not settle on any tall enough or solid enough. Halley was ordered to consider the scaffolding of St. Paul's Church. James Pound mounted the telescope on a maypole, removed from the Strand and relocated in Wanstead Park. Pound made improvements on the "furniture and Apparatus," but the pole broke, as his collaborator Bradley explained when he returned the telescope to the Society in 1728. The main improvement was a micrometer, which gave Huygens' telescope its one advantage over the Newtonian; the longer the telescope, the larger the image, and the micrometer measures a large image more accurately than a small image. The telescope was borrowed again by William Derham, who explained why he was returning it in 1741: "The chief inconvenience is the want of a long pole of 100 or more feet, to raise my long glass to such a height as to see the heavenly bodies above the thick vapours," and he was told that this would cost him eighty or ninety pounds, which was beyond his means. Next, in 1748, Lord Macclesfield borrowed the telescope for mounting at Shirburn Castle,[62] and Lord Charles Cavendish was one of the Fellows who conveyed it from the Royal Society to Shirburn Castle.[63] A visitor wrote of going to Shirburn to "look at Jupiter through one of Mr. Huygens' long telescopes," which revealed "that bright planet in perfection."[64] In 1778 Nevil Maskelyne borrowed the long, 210-foot Huygens telescope.[65]

At this juncture, Henry Cavendish enters the history of Huygens' telescopes. In November 1785 the council of the Royal Society gave Cavendish permission to borrow the 123-foot telescope and other object-glasses. He brought the telescopes to Clapham Common, where he kept them for three years,[66] and where he built a proper mount. Huygens had told how to prepare the mast, secure it in the ground, and make it climbable, and how to lengthen or shorten the thread by a peg that turned, as on a musical stringed instrument. Among Cavendish's manuscripts is a study of a ship's mast, which we take to be the mount for the Huygens telescope. It begins with fundamentals: "According to Newton the resistance of wind to a globe is equal to . . . and therefore if wind is 60 miles per hour . . . ." In this vein Cavendish determined the pressure of wind on two cylinders of unequal diameters each forty feet in length. To judge from his calculations, the Huygens telescope was erected on a wooden mast 80 feet high and tapered from 23 inches in diameter at the bottom to 13½ inches at the top. It was supported by 20-foot struts planted 11 feet from the base. A horizontal piece was fixed to the mast.[67] The mast towered above Cavendish's house as if it were the home of a nostalgic man of the sea. To the

---

which is achromatic, but if the two lenses are made of glass of the same dispersion and the telescope is focused at infinitely distant objects, such as stars, the angular magnification for any given color depends only on the curvature of the lenses and not on the refractive index. The workmanship on the Huygens lenses was of high quality but not the glass, which compares poorly with today's cheapest bottle or window glass. The tangle of fine veins in the glass made the refraction irregular. The glass available to Huygens resulted in poor definition of images, as Cavendish no doubt determined; this bore on his and Herschel's interest in indistinct images. Sampson and Conrady, "On Three Huygens Lenses," 298–99.

[61]Smith, *A System of Opticks*, 354. Christiaan Huygens' explanation of the working of the aerial telescope is quoted in Sampson and Conrady, "On Three Huygens Lenses," 298. The observer stood, resting his arms on a light frame or hurdle, and holding the eyepiece (concentric, adjustable metal tubes containing the eye-glass) by the handle. A cord connected it with a short board, upon which the objective was mounted at one end and a counterpoise at the other. By tension on the cord the observer could bring the two lenses into parallel.

[62]Smith, *Opticks*, 354, 440. R. S. Rigaud, "Memoirs of Dr. James Bradley," James Bradley, *Miscellaneous Works and Correspondence of the Rev. James Bradley, D.D., F.R.S.*, ed. S. P. Rigaud (Oxford, 1832), ix, lx, lxxxiv. Royal Society, JB 13:237 (20 June 1728). Royal Society, Minutes of Council 4:5–8 (10 and 29 Aug. 1748). King, *History of the Telescope*, 63.

[63]Charles Yorke to Philip Yorke, 23 Aug. 1748, BL Add Mss 35360, f. 185.

[64]Catherine Talbot to Elizabeth Carter, 10 Oct. 1748, in *A Series of Letters Between Mrs. Elizabeth Carter and Miss Catherine Talbot from the Year 1741 to 1770 etc.*, vol. 1 (London, 1809). 293–94.

[65]Royal Society, Minutes of Council 5:369 (10 Dec. 1778).

[66]Royal Society, Minutes of Council 7:134 (17 Nov. 1785). Cavendish returned the telescope on 13 Nov. 1788.

[67]The computations for the mast are in Cavendish Mss, Misc.

neighborhood it was the most conspicuous sign of Cavendish's scientific vocation. Well built, the mast remained in place after Cavendish had returned the Huygens telescopes and long after his death. A much later description of Cavendish's property reads: "In a paddock at the back of the house is a mast of a ship, erected for the purpose of making philosophical experiments."[68]

A half year after borrowing the Huygens lenses, Cavendish still had not tried them on objects on the land, Aubert told Herschel, but he was busy on an apparatus (the mast) for trying them on celestial objects.[69] Then, in June 1786, Blagden told Berthollet that Cavendish was ready to "make a trial of the old aerial telescopes." Herschel looked forward to the trial for "comparing the effect with that of his large reflectors."[70] Blagden told Benjamin Thompson that 200-plus-foot telescopes would probably be found inferior to Herschel's big reflectors, but still it was "desirable to form a just estimate of the tools with which our ancestors worked."[71] That does not mean that Cavendish acted out of historical curiosity or out of a desire to resurrect the aerial telescope in practice, since it was unwieldly and the art of telescopes had advanced. Cavendish went to trouble and expense because of fundamental questions about optics and telescopes. Herschel came to Clapham Common to participate in the trials, as did the instrument-maker Peter Dolland, whose father, John, had shown how to eliminate one of the major aberrations (chromatic) of telescopes. There was a party of scientific witnesses. Dolland found that his forty-six-inch triple-lens, achromatic refractor, his "Dwarf," was "fairly a match for the [123-foot] Giant."[72] Cavendish evidently was the last person to mount Huygens' telescopes for celestial observations, though the "Giant" continued to draw interest.[73] Cavendish's experiments with Huygens' object-glasses of the Royal Society undoubtedly were connected with, and help date, a large body of mathematical studies of his on the aberration of lenses.

Indistinct Vision

John Herschel told an anecdote about his father, William, and Henry Cavendish. The year was 1786, and the setting was a dinner given by Aubert at which Herschel and Cavendish sat together. Cavendish was his usual silent self until suddenly he said to his table companion, "I am

told that you see the stars round, Dr. Herschel." "Round as a button," Herschel replied. Cavendish relapsed into silence until toward the end of dinner he asked in a doubtful voice, "Round as a button?" "Exactly, round as a button," and with that Herschel brought the conversation to an end.[74] It was a story about Cavendish's legendary taciturnity, told at his expense, but the year and the subject can be given an historical reference: in 1786, in the year of the dinner at Aubert's and likely as a result of that dinner, Cavendish entered into Herschel's scientific work on optical images.

When Herschel took up astronomy, it was almost unthinkable that stars seen in telescopes would not show tails and rays. Herschel's claim that with his high-power telescopes stars appeared round and well defined, like buttons, was met with raised eyebrows, and not just Cavendish's. Four years before the dinner at Aubert's, in 1782, Dr. William Watson wrote to Herschel that Aubert and Maskelyne had never seen stars without aberration and that they doubted that Herschel saw them "round and well defined." Herschel wrote back that he was "surprized" that Aubert and Maskelyne had not seen stars as he did, which was not without aberration but *"round and well-defined"* nonetheless.

[68]J. H. Michael Burgess, *The Chronicles of Clapham [Clapham Common]. Being a Selection from the Reminiscences of Thomas Parsons, Sometime Member of the Clapham Antiquarian Society* (London: Ramsden, 1929), 57.

[69]Alexander Aubert to William Herschel, 23 Mar. 1786, Royal Astronomical Society Mss. Herschel W.l/13, A23.

[70]Charles Blagden to C. L. Berthollet, draft, 5 June 1786, Blagden Letterbook, Royal Society, 7:2.

[71]Charles Blagden to Benjamin Thompson, draft, 7 July 1786, Blagden Letterbook, Royal Society, 7.

[72]This is what Dolland told William Kitchner, *The Economy of the Eyes*, 22.

[73]Out of historical curiosity, the astronomer W. H. Smyth considered setting up the telescope again, around 1835: "I was so puzzled to know how they contrived to get the eye and object-glasses of these unwieldly machines *married*, or brought parallel to each other for perfect vision, and so desirous of comparing the performance of one of them, that I was about to ask the Royal Society's permission to erect the aerial 123-foot telescope in their possession. The trouble, however, promised to be so much greater than the object appeared to justify, that I laid the project aside." Quoted in Charles Richard Weld, *A History of the Royal Society*. 2 vols. in 1, 1848 (New York: Arno Press, 1975), 331. In 1929 Sampson and Conrady examined the two Huygens lenses of longer focal lengths but not the 123-foot lens. To determine the focal lengths, they used an interferometer. To determine the radii of curvature, they also relied on interference phenomena, since the extreme shallowness of the curvature of the long focal-length lenses precluded the use of a spherometer. Sampson and Conrady, "On Three Huygens Lenses," pp. 294–97.

[74]John Herschel's recollection in Lubbock, *The Herschel Chronicle*, 102.

Herschel's mirrors were polished so accurately that the aberration was symmetrical, the images round.[75]

The question of the indistinctness of vision prompted a kind of collaboration between Herschel and Cavendish in 1786. When Herschel had begun observing the heavens with his Newtonian telescope using high powers of magnification, he had come across statements by authorities that would discourage this practice. There was one by Huygens, for example, quoted in Smith's *System of Opticks*, and there was another closer to home by Michell, reported in Priestley's *History of Optics*. Priestley wrote of the "remarkable indistinctness of vision" that occurs when the pencils of light that form the image of an object are very small, contrary to expectation. Unable to find an account of this fact in his sources, Priestley turned to Michell, who told him that the best way to observe the indistinctness was by narrowing the aperture of a telescope. Michell carried out some experiments along that line: by viewing a flame and the sun through tiny but measurable perforations in a card, Michell calculated that the indistinctness was present with pencils less than 1/30th of an inch across. There was "very little, if anything, gained by increasing the magnifying power of telescopes" if it meant reducing the pencil below this limit, even if there was sufficient light to see by; to Michell the explanation of indistinctness lay not in the telescope but in "some unknown peculiarity in the structure of the eye."[76]

If Michell was right, Herschel was wasting his time observing with high magnifying powers. But both parts of Michell's conclusion, the anatomical cause of indistinct vision and the consequent absolute limitation on the perfectibility of telescopes, conflicted with Herschel's experience with his telescopes. In 1778 he had done experiments to confirm his doubts about the alleged limitation of telescopes, and in a paper in 1781 on the parallax of the fixed stars, he brought forward his doubts. Theories about telescopes take too much "for granted": they tell us that "we gain nothing by magnifying *too* much," but until we can see better with lower magnifications, we should not condemn "too much" magnification. "I see no reason," Herschel concluded, "why we should limit the powers of our instruments by any theory."[77] Herschel urged other astronomers not to be

deterred from joining him in his laborious but promising study of double stars, for their telescopes should give, as his did, images of stars "perfectly round and well-defined." With regard to indistinct vision, theories conflicted not only with Herschel's experience with telescopes but also with experiments done with microscopes made of single-lens globules. These microscopes were notable both for their distinctness of image and for their high powers of magnification, of the order of 10,000, from which it followed that their the optic pencils at the eye were not greater than 1/2,500th of an inch in diameter. Distinctness, for Herschel, was determined by the perfection of the lens or speculum and not by the eye.

"Late conversation with some of my highly esteemed and learned friends," who certainly included Cavendish, in 1786 prompted Herschel to write up his old experiments in the form of a paper for the *Philosophical Transactions*.[78] For this paper Herschel wanted to know exactly what the authorities had said about indistinct vision, and through Blagden he borrowed books from Cavendish to look it up.[79] Blagden spread word of Herschel's new work weeks before his paper was read to the Royal Society.[80]

Herschel looked with the naked eye through minute holes in a brass plate at printed letters, which he could read even though the pencils were much less than 1/40th or 1/50th part of an inch, only 1/244th part. Then with a two-lens microscope, he produced pencils no greater than 1/2,173rd part of an inch, with which he could see the bristles on the edge of the wing of a fly. Finally, he varied the aperture of the object lens of the

[75]Herschel's correspondent was the son of William Watson, the electrician who was awarded the Copley Medal. Dr. William Watson to William Herschel, 4 Jan. /1782/, quoted in J. B. Sidgwick, *William Herschel. Explorer of the Heavens* (London: Faber and Faber, 1953), 80. William Herschel to Dr. William Watson, 7 Jan. 1782, quoted in Lubbock, *The Hershel Chronicle*, 101. "Herschel, Sir William," *DNB* 9:719-25, on 724.

[76]Priestley, *The History and Present State of Discoveries Relating to Vision* 2:784-85.

[77]William Herschel, "Investigation of the Cause of that Indistinctness of Vision Which Has Been Ascribed to the Smallness of the Optic Pencil," *PT* 76 (1786): 500-507, on 500-501; "On the Parallax of the Fixed Stars," *PT* 72 (1782): 82-111, on 92, 96.

[78]Herschel, "Investigation of the Cause," 501.

[79]Herschel, "Investigation of the Cause," 501. Blagden to Herschel, draft, 19 May 1786, Blagden Letterbook, Royal Society, 7:762.

[80]Blagden to Berthollet, draft, 5 June 1786, Blagden Letterbook, Royal Society, 7:2.

microscope until it was very small in proportion to the focal length. Indistinctness resulted from the smallness of that proportion, not from the smallness of pencils, Herschel concluded. Herschel wrote up this conclusion, but before his paper was read to the Royal Society, he wanted Cavendish to read it.

Although Cavendish found that Herschel's experiments with the microscope were "curious & very well deserve attending," he found in them an indistinctness of a kind unacceptable to him; namely, an unthorough investigation and an incomplete description of what was done. Cavendish's optical manuscripts contain calculations testifying to his efforts to make intelligible Herschel's paper. He found an error in the diameter of the optic pencil in the eighth experiment but that was incidental. He had two major criticisms. First, he could not judge the "degree of force" of the experiments because Herschel had not given the proportion of aperture to focal length in experiments with *distinct* vision as well as those with indistinct. Herschel accepted this criticism and asked William Watson, jun., to give back the microscope with which he had made his original experiments so that he could determine this proportion exactly. The measures appeared in the published version of the paper. Second, Herschel had done no more than to describe his experiments; there were, after all, well-known causes of indistinctness of optical images. (In the case of refracting telescopes, they were discussed, for example, by John Dolland, who showed how to eliminate one of the causes, chromatic aberration, and how to reduce the other, spherical aberration, in eye glasses.[81]) Cavendish wrote to Herschel:

It deserves to be considered that though what Huygens supposed about the smallness of the pencils is difficult to account for yet yours is much more so as his may depend on the manner in which the sensation of the retina is affected by light which is a subject we know very little of whereas in your supposition I think only the refraction of light through glass can be concerned which is a subject we know much more of. For this reason it can not be expected that anyone should assent to your hypothesis without good proof & accordingly we will wish to examine whether the appearances you observed may not depend on some other cause. For this reason I think it would be much more satisfactory if you would set down in all the experiments not only the diameter of the pencil & proportion of the aperture to the focal length but also the

magnifying power & the degree of indistinctness which ought to arise from the aberration & difference of refrangibility in the object glass & any other circumstances which may be supposed to influence the exper.

Herschel acknowledged that he did not assign a "*Physical* cause" to indistinctness but only gave a hint as to the existence of one, but even if "we should never know the *physical* cause," the experimental connection between indistinctness and lens proportions had a practical value. He told Cavendish that he would conclude his paper with his "wish that what I had said might be looked upon etc," as he did.[82] He was kept from doing more experiments with a view to "submitting this cause of optical imperfection to theory" because of his work on his forty-foot reflecting telescope. In any case, his intention was only to give the experiments and leave the rest to the "theoretical optician."[83] Herschel's interest was, after all, primarily in telescopes and in his work with them, the determination of the contents, size, and structure of the universe. Herschel was finished with this side investigation for now, but Cavendish was not, it would seem. Cavendish left a number of undated, theoretical papers in manuscript on the aberration in reflecting and refracting telescopes. Several of them are carefully drafted, with corrections, evidently written to be shown to someone. One of them is titled "On the Aberration in Reflecting Telescope Used in Herschels Manner."[84] Cavendish rarely spoke in company but when he did, it was precisely to the point. "Round as a button?" stuck with Herschel.

We leave the subject of indistinct vision where it began for Herschel, with John Michell. Blagden sent Herschel's paper to Michell, who then wrote to Cavendish about it. Herschel was wrong, he said, to think that his distinct images

[81]John Dolland, "A Letter . . . Concerning an Improvement of Refracting Telescopes," *PT* 48 (1753): 103.
[82]Cavendish to Herschel, draft, n.d. /after 12 June 1786/; Herschel to Cavendish, 12 June 1786, Cavendish Mss, New Correspondence. Henry Cavendish, "Relating to Herschels Exper on Indistinct Vision in Telescopes," Cavendish Mss V, 13.
[83]Herschel, "Investigation of the Cause," 507.
[84]Henry Cavendish, "Of the Figure of Glasses Necessary to Bring Rays to a Focus & of the Aberration of Rays"; "Aberration in Reflecting Telescope Pointed to Near Object When the Figure of the Specula Are Adapted to Distant Ones"; "On the Aberration in Reflecting Telescope Used in Herschels Manner"; "On the Aberration of Rays Passing Through Spherical Lens," Cavendish Mss V, 7, 8, 10, 11.

contradicted Huygens, and he reminded Cavendish of the explanation he gave him at the Royal Society for the images. Herschel's findings were of great value to the "optical world" but not because of what they taught about telescopes but for what they implied for the "natural history of the eye."[85]

Comets

From the 1780s Cavendish devoted a large body of work to the orbits of comets, beginning, it seems, with the "comet" discovered by Herschel in 1781; Cavendish made computations from observations made of it by Maskelyne and Thomas Hornsby, who rejected the fashion of calling it a "planet" since it was a comet (it was, in fact, Uranus).[86] The next dated work we come upon in Cavendish's papers is his own method for computing the orbits of comets. Herschel was again the instigator, only this time it was Herschel brother and sister. Caroline Herschel worked with her brother at the observatory, and when he was away she made sweeps of the sky herself, in the course of which she became renowned as a discoverer of comets, eight in all. Blagden at the Royal Society was informed directly by her of her first comet, in 1786, and also by Aubert.[87] When she discovered another comet in 1788, Cavendish observed it himself.[88]

Newton had laid down that comets moved on a parabolic path, which in the case of a returning comet coincided with a highly eccentric ellipse. In principle, three observations would determine the elements of the path; in practice it was a difficult problem, a challenge to mathematical astronomers. A forty-year-old method by Boscovich had recently been rejected by Laplace, leading to an acrimonious dispute, and capturing the attention of calculators. As a test of their methods and their skill, astronomers eagerly looked forward to the return of a comet in late 1788.[89] The mathematical problem was to find the distortion of the path of the comet by the great planets Jupiter and Saturn as the comet left the solar system, since this would affect the exact timing of its return. The French Academy announced a prize for the best solution. Maskelyne published a paper "in order to assist astronomers in looking out for this comet," and Cavendish corresponded with Maskelyne about the method of it.[90]

Cavendish now immersed himself in the general problem of determining the paths of comets.[91] Finding Laplace's method wanting,[92] he devised one of his own, with which he planned to determine the orbit of Caroline Herschel's comet. Cavendish's method, which entailed covering a globe with white paper, proved tedious in practice, and he told Maskelyne that he planned to hire someone to draw up the tables for it.[93] Ten years later Cavendish and Maskelyne collaborated on computing the path of another comet; by this time Cavendish was using Boscovich's method, which he thought was very accurate.[94] The immense labor Cavendish devoted to the paths of comets is to be understood only partly in terms of the technical challenge of the problems astronomers were grappling with at the time. Once regarded as transient phenomena of the atmosphere, comets were one of the triumphs of the Newtonian world

---

[85] John Michell to Henry Cavendish, 8 Nov. 1786, Cavendish Mss, New Correspondence.

[86] Hornsby, too, supported by Cavendish's computations, thought that Herschel's observations were off. Herschel thought otherwise. Thomas Hornsby to William Herschel, 26 Feb. 1782; William Herschel, "Memorandum for Mr Cavendish," in Lubbock, *Herschel Chronicle*, 106-7.

[87] Blagden announced the discovery to the astronomers at Greenwich on the recent visitation. On the coming Sunday, he said, if the weather was clear, he, Banks, and others were going to Caroline Herschel's to look at the comet themselves. Charles Blagden to Claude Louis Berthollet and Benjamin Thompson, 4 Aug. 1786, drafts, and to Caroline Herschel, 5 Aug. 1786, draft, Blagden Letterbook, Royal Society, 7:18-20. "In consequence of the friendship which I know to exist between you and my brother," she wrote to Blagden, in the introduction to her paper she sent him: Caroline Herschel, "An Account of a New Comet," *PT* 77 (1786): 1-3. She asked Blagden to communicate her discovery to her brother's other friends, and he did.

[88] "Miss Herschels Comet," Cavendish Mss VIII, 37.

[89] Charles Coulston Gillispie, "Laplace, Pierre- Simon, Marquis de," *DSB* 15:273–356, on 309–10.

[90] We assume that Maskelyne was the "you" referred to in Henry Cavendish, "In Order to Compute the Return of a Comet," Cavendish Mss, VIII, 39. Nevil Maskelyne, "Advertisement of the Expected Return of the Comet of 1532 and 1661 in the Year 1788," *PT* 76 (1786): 426–31, on 429.

[91] Charles Blagden to Mrs. Grey, 5 Oct. 1786, draft, Blagden Letterbook, Royal Society, 7:39.

[92] "La Places Method," Cavendish Mss VIII, 41.

[93] Henry Cavendish, "Method of Finding Comets Orbits Fair," Cavendish Mss, III, 43. This paper of 37 pages, written in fair copy, was given to Maskelyne and returned. In another bundle of comet calculations is the draft of Cavendish's reply to Maskelyne, unaddressed and undated: Cavendish Mss VIII, 54.

[94] This exchange begins with observations of a comet sent by Maskelyne to Cavendish together with a request for Cavendish to compute its elements. Nevil Maskelyne to Henry Cavendish, 4, 8, and 9 Oct. 1799; there is an undated draft of a reply from Cavendish that begins, "Since my letter of last Thursday . . ." Cavendish Mss VIII, 46. Henry Cavendish, "Example of Computing Orbit on Bosc. Principle Without Graphical Operat."; "Comet of 1799 Computed by the Table for Boscovic's Sagitta"; "Comet of 1799"; "Computation of Comet of 1799 by Fluxional Process"; "Boscovic's Method of Finding the Orbit of a Comet," Cavendish Mss VIII, 42, 44, 46, 47, 50.

system; these seemingly capricious objects were found to be subject to the force of gravitation and so to theoretical calculation.[95] We recall the earliest record we have of Cavendish's thoughts, the poem from his Cambridge years: nature mocks, but "She does lay bare hidden causes/ And the wandering paths of the stars." Cavendish's study of comets in his later years can be seen as a vindication of that thought (and, perhaps, of his calling).

Published Work

None of the examples we have given so far of Cavendish's work in astronomy was published. We now turn to what he did publish; his last five papers in the *Philosophical Transactions*. They all had to do directly or indirectly with astronomy, though only one of them was a major work, his continuation of Michell's experiment of weighing the world, which we discuss separately. Another of these papers was a note on the aurora borealis, a subject which by method and practitioner belonged equally to astronomy and to meteorology. Still another was a note about a method in nautical astronomy, a comment on a recent paper by Mendez y Rios (a highly technical point, which led nowhere and which we will pass by).[96] Two others are more substantial, a study of the Hindoo civil year and a method of dividing astronomical instruments.

Although meteors were regarded by some as terrestrial comets,[97] they had not been subjected to calculation in the way comets in the sky had. One of Aubert's very few publications was on two meteors he saw in 1783. So little was known about them, Aubert said, that as many accounts as possible of them should be collected "to enable us to form some idea of their nature, path, magnitude, and distance from the earth."[98] In that same year, 1783, Blagden and Maskelyne, independently, sent out queries about meteors.[99] In his query, Blagden recommended a standard practice for observers of meteors, much as Jurin had early in the century for observers of the weather. An obvious problem for observers was the speed with which meteors moved; Blagden gave calculations by Herschel, Aubert, and Watson that suggested twenty miles per second, or ninety times the speed of sound. In principle, the pocket watch was an all-important instrument for observers of meteors, but the "emotion felt by the spectator" usually rendered the watch useless, and other points of reference

were needed. To know their height and velocity, observations needed to be made by "different persons in concert at distant stations."[100] Blagden thought that meteors were masses of electric fluids attracted to or repelled from the earth's poles, and he anticipated that observations of them would lead to the laws of motion of the electric fluid in empty spaces, laws which could not be learned from "our small experiments" in the laboratory. The aurora borealis, Blagden believed, was an electrical phenomenon of the same nature only higher in the sky.[101]

In the eighteenth century, "meteors" included the aurora borealis; "meteors of the aurora kind," as Cavendish called them.[102] Auroras borealis were observed by Cavendish with "much attention," his brother, Frederick, noted in 1780.[103] By then Cavendish was already computing their coronas.[104] In 1790 Cavendish published an account of an aurora that had been observed six years earlier by three persons, one of whom was the Cambridge scientist Francis John Hyde Wollaston (whom we will meet in our discussion of the experiment of weighing the world). Their accounts were communicated to the Royal Society

---

[95]A. Wolf, *A History of Science, Technology & Philosophy in the 16th & 17th Centuries*, vol. 1 (New York: Harper & Brothers, 1959), 159–60.

[96]Mendoza y Rios's object was to give general formulas from which the different methods of nautical astronomy can be deduced and compared. He said that Cavendish gave him this method and permission to publish an extract from his letter (probably arising from the committee of papers). It is printed at the end of Josef de Mendoza y Rios, "Recherches sur les principaux problèms de l'astronomie nautique," *PT* 87 (1797): 43–122: "Addition. Contenant une méthode pour réduire les distances lunaires," 119–22; "Extract of a Letter . . . to Mr. Mendoza y Rios, January, 1795," in Cavendish, *Sci. Pap.* 2:246–48.

[97]That was John Pringle's theory, for example .

[98]Alexander Aubert, "An Account of the Meteors of the 18th of August and 4th of October,1783," *PT* 74 (1784): 112–15, on 112.

[99]Charles Blagden to Joseph Banks, 16 Oct. 1783, Fitzwilliam Museum Library, Percival H190.

[100]Charles Blagden, "An Account of Some Late Fiery Meteors; with Observations," *PT* 74 (1784): 201–32, on 217–18, 224.

[101]Ibid., 224, 231.

[102]Henry Cavendish, "On the Height of the Luminous Arch Which Was Seen on Feb. 23, 1784," *PT* 80 (1790): 101–5; *Sci. Pap.* 2: 233–35, on 233.

[103]From Market Street, north of London, where he lived, Frederick Cavendish wrote to his brother, Henry, at their father's house in Great Marlborough Street. The night before, Frederick had seen an aurora borealis, the most remarkable he had ever seen. "It had the most perfect Corona I ever beheld, with Radii streaming down on all sides, and over-spreading *the whole* Hemisphere." Frederick gave a clear and precise description of it, consulting his atlas of the stars to locate it. Letter of 1 Mar. 1780, Cavendish Mss X(b), 9; *Sci. Pap.* 2:69.

[104]Henry Cavendish, "Computation of Corona of Aurora Borealis on Feb. 26. 1778," Cavendish Mss, Misc.

in 1786 and published in the *Philosophical Transactions* in 1790. Cavendish's purpose in drawing attention to them was to encourage "people to attend to these arches" in order to test his "hypothesis," which was that the aurora consisted of parallel rays of light shooting skyward. Should this hypothesis be confirmed, it would then be a proper "theory."[105] At the same time that he was studying the aurora borealis, Cavendish was requesting information about the other sort of meteor, the terrestrial comet or whatever it was.[106]

At the time of his paper in 1792 on the civil year of the Hindoos, Cavendish was a subscriber to the *Asiatick Researches*, three volumes of which had come out; the footnotes in his paper show that he read this new journal with profit. Its publisher, the Asiatic Society in Calcutta, was modeled after the Royal Society in London. Its founder was the Orientalist William Jones, the youngest son of the mathematician by that name, who had proposed Lord Charles Cavendish for fellowship in the Royal Society. The younger William Jones was said to have understood Newton's *Principia*, and he was in any case a Fellow of the Royal Society and a good friend of Banks, Blagden, Phipps, and other scientific men close to Cavendish.[107] Jones, who himself had studied the Hindoo lunar year and chronology,[108] formed his "opinions of men and things from *evidence*, which is the only solid basis of *civil*, as *experiment* is of *natural*, knowledge."[109]

There was a widespread interest in Hindoo astronomy when Cavendish took up the subject. William Marsden was an Oriental scholar who published his researches in the journals of all of the learned societies he belonged to, in the *Asiatick Researches*, the *Archaeologia*, and the *Philosophical Transactions*. In the latter, in 1790, he published a paper on the Hindoo year and calendar, in which he remarked that Sanskrit scholars were making possible "considerable discoveries in regard to the scientific attainments of this ancient and celebrated people," and that French astronomers too had recently done important work on the subject. Marsden attributed the attention to Hindoo astronomy to its originality and probable influence on the Greeks.[110] Samuel Davis, a civil servant in Benares and one of the more scientifically oriented members of the Asiatick Society, published papers on Hindoo astronomy in the early

volumes of the *Asiatick Researches*. It was probably through Davis that Cavendish came to make a study of Hindoo almanacs. Davis had asked Banks to show one of his papers to Cavendish, who made comments on it and queried the author in 1791.[111] Hindoo months depended solely on the motions of the sun and moon, and so they had no definite number of days and were not ordered by any cycle, and moreover the month began on different days at different latitudes and longitudes. This state of affairs seemed chaotic to Cavendish, but Davis assured him that three almanacs were commonly used by the Hindoos and that they usually worked fine for them.[112] Cavendish asked the Sanskrit scholar Charles Wilkins, F.R.S., to lend him three almanacs, which he then proceeded to work through to decipher how the learned men of India knew the date. Banks mentioned a possible membership in the Royal Society to Davis, and in 1792, the year of Cavendish's paper, Davis was elected; Cavendish's name appears first on Davis's certificate.[113] The underlying reason for Cavendish's curiosity about Hindoo astronomy was, we believe, the meaning it held for his chosen life. On the other side of the world, there were people like him who ordered their existence according to the ways of nature.

In 1809 Cavendish published his last paper. He was seventy-eight, and he had not published anything for the past ten years. The subject in question was close to his heart, astronomical instruments.

Instrument-makers had watchmakers to thank for their dividing engines, the basis of

---

[105]Henry Cavendish, "On the Height," 235.

[106]In 1790, clearly in response to a request by Cavendish, Herschel sent him his observations on two meteors in 1784: William Herschel to Henry Cavendish, 1 Feb. 1790, Cavendish Mss, New Correspondence.

[107]Garland Cannon, "Sir William Jones, Sir Joseph Banks, and the Royal Society," *Notes and Records of the Royal Society* 29 (1975): 205–30, on 207–8.

[108]B. V. Subbarayappa, "Western Science in India up to the End of the Nineteenth Century A.D.," in *A Concise History of Science in India*, ed. D. M. Bose (New Delhi: Indian National Science Academy, 1971), 484–97, on 495–96.

[109]Hans Aarsleff, *The Study of Language in England, 1780–1860* (Minneapolis: University of Minnesota Press, 1983), 135.

[110]William Marsden, "On the Chronology of the Hindoos," *PT* 80 (1790): 560–84, on 560 .

[111]Samuel Davis to Joseph Banks, 10 Mar. 1791, Banks Correspondence, Kew, l.38.

[112]Blagden forwarded to Cavendish Davis's answers to his questions. Charles Blagden to Henry Cavendish, 7 Nov. 1791, draft, Blagden Letterbook, Royal Society, 7:579. Cavendish, "On the Civil Year," 242.

[113]Royal Society, Certificates, 5 (28 June 1792).

precision in eighteenth-century science.[114] Nothing was so important to the success of instrument-makers as the accurate division into equal parts of the circles and parts of circles and straight lines of their measuring instruments. Up to about 1740 the divisions were always done by hand, a most delicate procedure. John Bird, the master of hand dividing, never let more than one other person into the room when he was working, since the heat could spoil his divisions. Reporting on the performance of a mural quadrant divided by his method, Bird gave what was the faith of an instrument-maker: "a mean of several observations, made by good observers with accurate instruments, properly adjusted, will always lead us either to the truth itself, or extremely near to it."[115] Jesse Ramsden made an excellent dividing machine in the early 1770s using an endless screw to turn a wheel under a cutting point, six revolutions of the screw translating into one degree; the Board of Longitude paid him to publish a description of this engine.[116] When Ramsden completed his mural quadrant for Milan in 1790, he invited Cavendish, Aubert, Smeaton, who was another divider of instruments, and others to see and try it. Ramsden told them that "any common man in his workshop, with good eyes and hands, could, on the same principles, have divided it to equal perfection."[117] Ramsden made it sound easy, but dividing was the hardest part of the instrument-maker's work. The instrument-maker Edward Troughton stimulated Cavendish to invent and publish his own method of dividing.

Edward Troughton and his older brother, John, were renowned for their dividing instruments, which were used by other instrument-makers, the ultimate compliment. By the beginning of the nineteenth century, Edward Troughton, who now conducted the business alone, had succeeded Ramsden as the foremost instrument-maker in England. In 1807 Cavendish was one of a visitation committee from the Royal Society who agreed with the astronomer royal, Maskelyne, that greater accuracy would be obtained if observations were made with a circular instrument as well as with the existing mural quadrant. The committee invited Troughton to give a recommendation, which he did, a circle six feet in diameter. The committee and the council of the Royal Society approved the recommendation, which was sent to the Board of

Ordnance.[118] In the following year, Troughton delivered a paper to the Royal Society on his method of dividing, for which he was awarded a Copley Medal in 1809.[119] These events are the setting of Cavendish's paper of that year.

Cavendish's purpose was to ease the "great inconvenience and difficulty" of the common method of dividing, which bruised the divisions by laying the point of the beam compass in them. Troughton had just published an alternative "ingenious method," Cavendish said. By Cavendish's method, the need to set the compass point in the divisions was eliminated, and the "great objection to the old method of dividing is entirely removed." It was now up to instrument-makers to decide if his or Troughton's method was best.[120] Cavendish's method does not seem to have been adopted, but it nonetheless holds an interest for a biography of Cavendish. This last publication of his was about a method for improving the method of making the most precise instruments of science; it was about the tools for making the tools of science. Besides Troughton, the only other instrument-maker named by Cavendish in the paper was Bird, with whose observation (above) he would have agreed: with accurate instruments an accurate observer could arrive at the truth or the closest thing to it. Cavendish's last paper acknowledged the direction of science, to which his earlier work had given such impetus.

----

[114]Maurice Daumas, "Precision of Measurement and Physical and Chemical Research in the Eighteenth Century," in *Scientific Change…*, ed. A. C. Crombie (New York: Basic Books, 1963), 418–30, on 422.

[115]John Bird, *The Method of Dividing Astronomical Instruments* (London, 1767), 13.

[116]Jesse Ramsden, *Description of an Engine for Dividing Mathematical Instruments* (London, 1777).

[117]These are Blagden's words in reporting the inspection of Ramsden's quadrant to Sir Joseph Banks. Letter of 23 Sep. 1790, BL Add Mss 33272, pp. 89–90.

[118]Meeting of the committee on 22 Jan. and report of the meeting of the council of the Royal Society on 28 May 1807, "Visitations of Greenwich Observatory 1763 to 1815," Royal Society, Ms. 600, XIV.d.11, ff. 59–62.

[119]A. W. Skempton and Joyce Brown, "John and Edward Troughton, Mathematical Instrument Makers," *Notes and Records of the Royal Society* 27 (1973): 233–49, on 246. Roderick S. Webster, "Troughton, Edward," *DSB* 13: 470–71. Edward Troughton, "An Account of a Method of Dividing Astronomical and Other Instruments by Ocular Inspection, in Which the Usual Tools for Graduating Are Not Employed, etc.," *PT* 99 (1809): 105–45.

[120]Henry Cavendish, "On an Improvement in the Manner of Dividing Astronomical Instruments," *PT* 99 (1809): 221–45; *Sci. Pap.* 2:287–93, on 287.

CHAPTER 6

&arth

Triangulation

In 1783, Cavendish participated in an international survey, proposed by the French: a joint determination of the relative positions of the national observatories in Paris and Greenwich (there was an error of ten seconds in their longitudes). Asked by the British government for his opinion of the French proposal, Banks replied proudly that the Royal Society had "people enough . . . capable and willing." One of them was Cavendish, a skilled surveyor and a conscientious servant of the Royal Society, who could not have stayed away. The survey touched on a number of Cavendish's favorite interests: e.g., the measurement of the heights of mountains using a barometer;[1] precision of technique; and coordination of distant observers, an aspect of standardization.

William Roy, a Fellow of the Royal Society, was assigned responsibility for laying down the triangles for the British half of the project.[2] Roy brought considerable experience to this job: he had made a military map of Scotland after the Jacobite rebellion in 1745, and after the Seven Years War he had been involved in proposals to make a map of all of Britain, but nothing came of it. Then in 1783, after the American War, on his own he began to make triangles in and around London.[3] His chance to realize his goal of a national survey came later that year with the French proposal.

The initial step was to measure a base-line, after which only angles needed to be taken to determine the triangles. On 16 April 1784 Roy began observations along a five-mile stretch of Hounslow-Heath, near Greenwich, assisted by Banks, Blagden, and Cavendish. Banks was enthusiastic; there morning to night, he opened his tents and offered refreshments to all comers. Even the king came to look at what was going on. By the end of the summer this first phase of the triangulation was finished.[4]

The next phase was to build triangles twelve to eighteen miles on a side on a southward course to the coast, to Dover, there to connect up with the French triangulation from across the channel. The ideal route would have been a straight chain of equilateral triangles but the terrain dictated a snake-like progression.[5] A French party came to England, and Blagden crossed to France to oversee the hookup of the triangles. Since at one point Blagden spoke of Cavendish's plans to come to Dover, Cavendish may have participated at the end of the project as well as at the beginning. In any event, it was finished in late 1787.[6]

Cavendish's own locations at Hampstead and Clapham Common were used as corners in the triangulation. He took bearings with respect to every steeple and elevation in sight. His address now had an astronomical reference.

The accuracy of the triangulation was a point of honor, both professional and national. The French had devised a method of repeated mea-

---

[1]Theodore S. Feldman, "Applied Mathematics and the Quantification of Experimental Physics: The Example of Barometric Hypsometry," *Historical Studies in the Physical Sciences* 15:2 (1988): 127–97, on 162.

[2]Joseph Banks to Charles Blagden, 13 Oct. 1783, draft, Blagden Letters, Royal Society, B.19. Charles Coulston Gillispie, *Science and Polity in France at the End of the Old Regime* (Princeton: Princeton University Press, 1980), 122–23.

[3]William Roy, "An Account of the Measurement of a Base on Hounslow-Heath," *PT* 75 (1785): 385–480, on 385–88. This earlier work of Roy, beginning in 1783, involved Banks, Hutton, and Deluc, and it entailed measuring the heights of mountains (Shooter's Hill) either by the barometer or by geometry. Joseph Banks to Charles Hutton, n.d. /early 1784/, Wellcome Institute, MS 5270.

[4]Charles Blagden to Joseph Banks, 12 July and "Tuesday" 1784, Banks Correspondence, Kew, nos. 167, 171. Roy, "An Account of the Measurement of a Base," 391, 425–26.

[5]William Roy, "An Account of the Mode Proposed to Be Followed in Determining the Relative Situation of the Royal Observatories of Greenwich and Paris," *PT* 77 (1787): 188–228.

[6]Charles Blagden to Benjamin Thompson, 22 May 1787, draft, Blagden Letterbook, Royal Society, 7:55. Charles Blagden to Henry Cavendish, 16 Sep. 1787, Cavendish Mss X(b), 13. Charles Blagden to William Watson, 27 Oct. 1787, draft, Blagden Letterbook, Royal Society, 7:76.

surements that enabled them to achieve high accuracy with a modest instrument, a circle a foot across.[7] The English achieved comparable accuracy with a theodolite with a three-foot circle made by Ramsden and paid for by the king. Blagden described it as an "astonishing piece of workmanship, accurate to a degree hitherto wholly unexampled."[8] Roy carted this giant weighing two hundred pounds into the field, where it stood, a monument to the instrument-maker's precision.

Errors

Precision, however, is not only in the instrument but also in the eye of the user and in the hand of the calculator. Roy, a military engineer, took great pride in his art, the supreme aim of which was accuracy and precision.[9] Unforgiving when it came to errors in calculations, in his 1787 paper on the planned trigonometrical operation in Britain, he said that after bestowing "much care" on the computations, he trusted that "no error of any consequence will be found." That much any self-respecting calculator might say, but Roy went further, citing an error of his own, which he hoped not to repeat: "Here it is proper that I should mention a typical *erratum* in one of the tables of Transactions, for 1777. It is Tab. VI . . . instead of 27.714 read 27.214."[10] This venial error, a 2 in place of a 7, was no doubt made in transcribing or typesetting. Roy concluded his paper with a few corrections in the tables, in a brief section of *Errata*.[11]

But there were more errors in Roy's tables, as he noted in his next paper on the subject, in 1790: "it is become necessary to take notice of some mistakes that, through inadvertency, were fallen into in the computed lengths of the arcs." There were, in fact, "three kinds" of mistakes, and at this stage all he could do was append a correction slip to be pasted over the erroneous part of the previous paper.[12] Roy had a reputation for painstaking work in a field that had no tolerance for error: he regarded the triangulation project under his direction as "infallible."[13] It would seem to be a case of the gods striking down one whom they love. Roy's troubles had just begun. While preparing sheets of Roy's paper for the *Philosophical Transactions*, Blagden discovered numerical "blunders," which he pointed out to Roy, who proceeded to find more on his own. The paper in which he corrected errors of his previous paper was itself full

of errors. Roy's health was now poor, and while he was absorbed in the melancholy task of discovering and correcting his errors, on 1 July 1790 he suddenly died at his house in London.[14]

There were probably more errors buried in the paper, and no doubt they would be (triumphantly) discovered by the French commissioners, especially P.F.A. Méchain, who was bound to read the paper carefully. That was the issue. Had Roy's errors been limited to the first paper they would not have been damaging, since that paper was only a sketch of the operation to come. Errors in the paper of 1790 were another matter, for that paper was the final report of the operation as carried out, an official undertaking of the Royal Society. Blagden turned to the Royal Society's learned member on the subject of errors. "Conversing a few days ago on this subject with Mr. Cavendish," Blagden told Banks, "he suggested, that the best way of preventing any disgrace which might fall upon the Society on this account would be, to get the paper well examined here, and print such errors as might be discovered in the *errata* to the present volume of the Transactions, thereby anticipating, as far as possible, the remarks of foreigners."[15]

Cavendish's proposal was one Roy himself would have endorsed. At the time when the French triangulation had been condemned as "extremely erroneous," Roy had expressed confidence that the Paris Academy of Sciences would, "no doubt, vindicate the credit of their own operations."[16] To vindicate its own, the Royal Society did what Cavendish recommended. Roy's assistant, Isaac Dalby—in Roy's words, "an able

[7]Charles Blagden to Joseph Banks, 24 Sep. 1787, BL Add Mss 33272, pp. 45–46.

[8]Charles Blagden to William Watson, 22 Aug. 1787, draft, Blagden Letterbook, Royal Society, 7:347.

[9]Sven Widmalm, "Accuracy, Rhetoric, and Technology: The Paris-Greenwich Triangulation, 1784–88," in *The Quantifying Spirit in the Eighteenth Century*, eds. T. Frangsmyr, J.L. Heilbron, and R.E. Rider (Berkeley: University of California Press, 1990), 179–206, on 199.

[10]Roy, "An Account of the Mode Proposed," 222.

[11]Ibid., 226.

[12]William Roy, "An Account of the Trigonometrical Operation, whereby the Distance between the Meridians of the Royal Observatories of Greenwich and Paris Has Been Determined," *PT* (1790): 111–270, on 201. Errata sheet follows p. 270.

[13]Roy, "Account of the Mode Proposed," 214.

[14]"Roy, William," *DNB* 17:371–73, on 373.

[15]Charles Blagden to Sir Joseph Banks, draft, 31 Aug. 1790, BL Add Mss 33272.

[16]Roy, "An Account of the Mode Proposed," 211.

and indefatigable calculator"—was selected to examine the paper for errors. Blagden reported to Banks: "I have seen Mr Dalby, for the first time this morning. He said there were to his knowledge very many blunders retained by the General, though clearly pointed out to him. Mr. Dalby seemed doubtful whether it would look well in him to be the detector; but I desired him to put himself in the place of a foreigner, whose object it might be to criticize as severely as possible, & that we would then take care to present the result to the public in the tenderest manner for the General's reputation, consistent with our duty to the Society. He then undertook it . . . "[17] Roy's paper of 1790 was corrected this way: in addition to Roy's own errata for his previous paper of 1787, this paper contained a second table of errata applying to itself, as assembled by Dalby. To this now posthumous paper, Blagden also appended a brief personal account of Roy, which offered a partial excuse for Roy's lapses. Roy had finished the triangulation in September 1788, and he had spent the next winter in Lisbon because of poor health. He had hurriedly finished writing his paper on the results of the triangulation before going to Lisbon, and in the same month that he returned, in April 1790, his paper went to press. He died before the paper was completely printed, and although he had corrected the sheets, he had not compared the manuscript with the original observations. Errors were found, with the result, Blagden said, that the "General's friends, members of the Royal Society," had the whole paper revised by Dalby.[18] Blagden presented his appendix as an introduction to another appendix by Dalby, in which Dalby went through Roy's paper page by page, noting where corrections belonged.[19] Errors haunted the project; Dalby, in a paper the next year on measures deducible from Roy's triangulation, noted yet another error in Roy's 1790 paper, "which should have been corrected in the Appendix."[20] Cavendish's house on Clapham Common had been the corner of one of Roy's secondary triangles, and in Roy's paper of 1790 its bearing eastward from the meridian of the dome of St. Paul's was printed—incorrectly. Dalby naturally wrote to Cavendish about this error and corrected it in his appendix.[21] The error might not seem like much: instead of 26 degrees, 29 minutes, and 56.1 seconds, it should have been 26 degrees, 29 minutes, and 52

seconds. But given the instruments, methods, and abilities involved in the triangulation, it was an inexcusable error. Ramsden's theodolite was accurate to nearly one second, which was accordingly the measure of scientific reputation and national honor. To extricate the Royal Society from the errors made in its name, Cavendish played his familiar behind-the-scenes role as advisor. His recommendation was candor: admit that mistakes were made, find and fix them, and cut losses. In the process of salvaging the reputation of the Society, the reputation of Roy was protected as well; for what was important about Roy's work was used and saved, his *observations*.[22]

Journeys

Active as he was in the planning of voyages and expeditions approved by the Royal Society, Cavendish, we have noted, never went on one of these himself. He did, however, make a number of journeys by carriage, within Britain, always in the summer when conditions of travel were at their best. The first journey of which we have record was in late August 1778, which took Cavendish through Oxford to Birmingham and back by way of Towcester. At each stop he made a trial of Nairne's dipping needle, which is all we know about the trip and which may have been the whole point. For it came soon after Cavendish's report on the meteorological instruments of the Royal Society, which included its earth-magnetic instruments, and he was still very much involved in the testing of meteorological instruments.[23] Beginning in 1785 Cavendish became a regular and more rounded

---

[17]Blagden to Banks, 31 Aug. 1790.

[18]Charles Blagden, "Appendix," to Roy, "An Account of the Trigonometrical Operation," 591–92.

[19]Isaac Dalby, "Remarks on Major–General Roy's Account of the Trigonometrical Operation, from Page 111 to Page 270. of This Volume," *PT* 80 (1790): 593–614.

[20]Isaac Dalby, "The Longitudes of Dunkirk and Paris from Greenwich, Deduced from the Triangular Measurement in 1787, 1788, Supposing the Earth to Be an Ellipsoid," *PT* 81 (1791): 236–45, on 245, note.

[21]Letter from Isaac Dalby, undated, presumably to Cavendish, in Cavendish Mss, Misc.

[22]Roy's errors were unimportant relative to his observations, according to John Playfair, in his review of William Mudge's collection of memoirs on the triangulation begun by Roy, in *The Works of John Playfair*, ed. J. G. Playfair, 4 vols. (Edinburgh, 1822) 4:181–220, on 198–201.

[23]Henry Cavendish, "Trials of Nairne's Needle in Different Parts of England," Cavendish Mss IX, ll:45–54. The usual place for taking the trial was a garden. Dates in the second half of August 1778 are scattered through this record of observations.

scientific tourist. This fiftyish man of fixed, settled habits had recently befriended Charles Blagden, who had much to do with Cavendish's adventurous turn.

Blagden was an inveterate traveler. He was also a compulsive note-taker and saver, who left us a record, in the form of letters, of the journey he took from London to Scotland, where he went to study at age seventeen. The first letter begins: "As I have often heard you mention how very agreeable the acct of a journey is to you."[24] Next we have his report of a visit to Wales, when he was twenty-three and an impressionable if conventional tourist. He was a follower of Rousseau,[25] drawn to abbeys and vistas but also to mines and iron works and "philosophical curiosities." His early observations also reveal the accurate, scientific note-taker he was to become in Cavendish's company. Blagden yearned to know the world, yet wherever he traveled he felt frustrated because people could not answer his straightforward questions about what lay a mile around them, places, routes, departures, and the like. He was astonished at the "stupidity of the people," who were entirely satisfied with their "little world."[26] (In this early journal, a trait comes through, which would endure and bring Blagden enemies: an air of superiority.) For several years while a surgeon in the British army, he observed as well as served in the New World. So it was as a seasoned traveler that soon after his return to Britain, he toured Devonshire, where he found the coves and rocks "beautiful" and "romantic," but where he also observed mileages, weather, slate, and clay.[27] His most memorable journey, as it turned out, was from Plymouth to London, where he would make his life in science.[28] In the summer of 1783 Blagden visited France, but by then he was already in the service of Cavendish.[29]

Blagden urged Cavendish to take up traveling with him. In the first of his many letters to John Michell, in 1785, Blagden wrote that he "endeavoured to persuade our friend Mr Cavendish to make you a visit at Thornhill," so far in vain.[30] Blagden told Michell that he did not want to come alone but he hoped that he and Cavendish could come next year,[31] which they did. For this year they were going in another direction, to south Wales, and Blagden had made advance arrangements: the plans were set; Blagden wanted to see the industrial landscape, and so did Cavendish. Blagden wrote to William Lewis that he had

proposed to Cavendish that they visit his iron works in Glamorganshire and that Cavendish was "very curious." Lewis wrote back that they could stay at his house or if the "Hammers should be too noisy" at another, distant house.[32] They left on a three-week trip, Cavendish taking with him one servant.[33] Along the way they talked to the owners of works, engineers, agents, and workmen, who told them things no one else could. At Glamorganshire Cavendish visited not only the iron works but a spring that gave off bubbles, which he tested.[34] Midway into their journey Blagden could tell Banks that Cavendish "bears the journey remarkably well."[35] In Wales they visited the iron and the cloth manufacturers. Lewis became another scientific outpost for Cavendish; for years after this visit, Lewis sent him specimens, especially of kish (a kind of graphite that separates from iron in smelting), for Cavendish to examine.[36] The sixty-two-page journal kept of this trip shows that the main purpose of it was to learn about industry.

Their tour was by no means original. That same year, for example, the London chemist William Higgins visited the English factories.[37]

---

[24]Charles Blagden to Sarah Nelmes, 1 Nov. 1765, Blagden Letters, Royal Society, B.159. The next letter, B.160, continues the account of that journey. In other letters in 1767 Blagden gave Nelmes accounts of shorter journeys in Scotland. Nelmes, who lived in Bristol, and Blagden were distant relatives. "Accounts, Bills, Insurance, and Copy of Will of S. Nelmes," Blagden Mss, Royal Society.

[25]To a friend Blagden recommended that he read Rousseau, "the most eloquent & feeling of men." Charles Blagden to Thomas Curtis, 26 July 1771, Blagden Letters, Royal Society, B.162.

[26]Charles Blagden, "Memorandum of a Tour Taken for Four Days Beginning Aug. 18 1771," Blagden Papers, Yale, box 1, folder 3.

[27]Charles Blagden, "Tour of the South Hams of Devonshire," 1780, Blagden Diaries, Yale, Osborne Shelves f c 16.

[28]Charles Blagden, "Journey from Plymouth to London 1781," Yale, Osborne Shelves f c 16.

[29]Charles Blagden, memoranda of his trip to France in 1783, Blagden Papers, Yale, box 1, folder 3.

[30]Charles Blagden to John Michell, 25 Apr. 1785, draft, Blagden Letterbook, Yale.

[31]Charles Blagden to John Michell, 13 Sep. 1785, draft, Blagden Letterbook, Yale.

[32]Charles Blagden to William Lewis, 20 June 1785, draft, Blagden Letterbook, Yale. William Lewis to Charles Blagden, 25 June 1785, draft, Blagden Letters, Royal Society, L.46.

[33]Blagden was undecided if he would bring his servant too. Bladgen to Lewis, 20 June 1785.

[34]Charles Blagden to Joseph Banks, 9 Oct. 1785, Banks Correspondence, Kew, l.210.

[35]Charles Blagden to Joseph Banks, 31 July 1785, Blagden Correspondence, Kew, l.199.

[36]Charles Blagden to William Lewis, 10 Nov. 1786, 6 Nov. 1787, drafts, Blagden Letterbook, Royal Society, 7:53 and 7:83.

[37]A.E. Musson and E. Robinson, *Science and Technology in the Industrial Revolution* (Toronto: University of Toronto Press, 1969), 122.

This kind of sightseeing had been going on; fifteen years earlier, Benjamin Franklin had visited the manufacturing towns of England. At the Soho Works outside Birmingham, Matthew Boulton showed machines to scientists and manufacturers, even ambassadors and princes.[38] The conventional beginning of the British industrial revolution is 1760, the year Cavendish entered the Royal Society. His scientific work was carried out in the time of this great technical and social transformation, which could not fail to interest him. By the time of his journeys with Blagden, twenty-five years later, an extraordinary industrial landscape was coming into being. Cavendish ventured into it with all the curiosity he brought to his studies in heat and air. In the same period, science in Britain had begun to flourish in the industrial provinces and was no longer primarily located in the metropolis. On this first journey, after Wales, Cavendish went to Birmingham, where the Lunar Society had been meeting since the late 1760s. This scientific and technical society included James Watt, Joseph Priestley, Joseph Black, James Keir, Josiah Wedgwood, and other prominent scientific and industrial men. Manchester and other provincial towns were acquiring their scientific and literary societies. Cavendish might seem to be carrying coals to Newcastle, but his purpose in touring the industrial provinces was to learn firsthand about this new way of mastering nature.

Cavendish and Blagden observed quarries, cloth manufacture, especially dying, coal mining, coal-tar manufacture, lime kilns, coke-making, copper-casting, brass-drawing, and, above all, iron-making. They saw iron and steel being made for buttons, needles, nails, and ship bolts. They saw slitting and flatting mills, hammers, rollers, cranes, pincers, and other heavy machinery, and enormous iron furnaces, standing as high as forty-five feet. It was spectacular: the scenes at the forges were violent with their intense heat and fireworks, and coal pits burned. Yet there was an unmistakable similarity between this landscape and Cavendish's serene laboratory. The manufacturers used the same chemicals he did, such as spirit of salt, only they used them in vast quantity. The hearth, the bellows, the concern with impurities, and the bringing together of materials by proportionate weights were all familiar to Cavendish. He and Blagden brought with them a collection of instruments including chemical equipment, and they even tried their own little experiment on tin in acid.[39]

In Birmingham, they saw Watt and the industrialist John Wilkinson. Watt had made his greatest improvement in the steam engine, the separate condenser, in the 1760s, but he had made another important one in 1782, just three years before Cavendish's visit. This one converted the linear motion of the piston's drive to a rotary motion, useful in mills, and Cavendish saw this latest improvement. Early that year, when Watt was in London, he dined with Cavendish at the Royal Society Club.[40] In Birmingham Cavendish called on Watt, now just over a year after the water controversy and Watt's private denunciations of Cavendish. The journal gives no hint that there was any barrier between the two men or that they talked about the composition of water. They surely talked about machines. Watt showed them a machine for making plate, invented and patented by another man but claimed by Watt as his original idea. Watt described scientific experiments he had done with the steam engine on the condensation of steam, complete with an explanation of the "latent" heat evolved: the latent heat of steam was 948 degrees Fahrenheit, he told Cavendish (who had found 982 degrees). Watt showed them a furnace he had contrived for burning smoke, which he intended to apply to the steam engine. At other iron works, Cavendish and Blagden came across more of Watt's steam engines in use.[41] Cavendish was intrigued by Watt's inventions; in the journal of the visit, there is a drawing by him of the rotative mechanism for the steam engine, and in his papers there is a drawing of Watt's smoke-burning furnace.[42] That fall Watt came to London to Albion Mills at Black Friars Bridge, where his new smoke-burning furnaces were to be installed, and we can be sure that Cavendish was on hand.[43]

---

[38]Robert E. Schofield, *The Lunar Society of Birmingham: A Social History of Provincial Science and Industry in Eighteenth-Century England* (Oxford: Oxford University Press, 1963), 26–27, 113.

[39]The journal is in a wrapper labeled in Cavendish's hand, "Computations & Observations in Journey 1785," Cavendish Mss X(a), 4. The journal itself is in another hand.

[40]It was on 24 Feb. 1785. Archibald Geikie, *Annals of the Royal Society Club* (London: Macmillan, 1917), 174.

[41]"Computations & Observations in Journey 1785."

[42]Henry Cavendish, "Watts Fire Place for Burning Smoke," Cavendish Mss, Misc.

[43]Charles Blagden to Sir Joseph Banks, 23 Oct. 1785, Banks Correspondence, Kew, l.212.

On this their first journey together, Cavendish and Blagden carried out studies in Cavendish's well established interests: heats of wells, heights of mountains by the barometer, and measures of tides. There is also a new active interest, geology. Cavendish and Blagden made regular observations of strata and the rocks on the surface and the pebbles surfacing the roads, noting color, texture, and lay. They saw blue, red, and white clay and limestone, granite, sand, slate, and so on. They drew no conclusions but no discouragement either; they continued to make geological observations on all of their subsequent journeys.[44]

In the early summer of the following year, 1786, Blagden's brother, John Blagden Hale, invited Cavendish to join Blagden on a visit. Blagden told his brother that he had "every reason to believe that he /Cavendish/ will not find it convenient to go from home." Blagden conveyed the invitation, but he knew his friend. A week later he wrote to his brother to confirm that Cavendish did "not find it convenient to leave home . . . "[45] He added "at this time": two months later Cavendish and Blagden set out again on a roughly three-week trip, this one much longer than the first, over eight hundred miles to the north of England and back. It was the trip Blagden had wanted to make the year before, to see John Michell at Thornhill, near Wakefield. They went directly to Michell's,[46] then to John Phipps, now Lord Mulgrave (to whom Cavendish gave scientific instructions on his voyage to the north), then to the Lake District, and then back to Michell's where they stayed six days.[47] In the journal of this trip, there is no mention of Michell's experiment on weighing the world, which he still had not got around to doing. The main attraction was Michell's great telescope, which was spectacular but disappointing, since Michell had cracked the speculum; although he had ground and polished it again, it was imperfect.[48] In his diary, Blagden wrote:

> At Mr Michell's took some altitudes & looked over his fossils . . . At night looked thro' his telescope: tho' much false light & confused images yet obs'd /Saturn/ with it well: could see the belt plainly; & obs'd an emersion of the 3 sat. much better than it appeared thro' the 2 feet reflector.[49]

Blagden went to Michell's sermon on Sunday, which he had heard or read before. Most of his and Cavendish's time seemed to have been spent making—rather wanting to make, since the weather was foul—excursions up mountains with Cavendish's barometer, "a main object" of their tour.[50] They came away from Michell's with one treasure: Michell's table of strata, their depths measured to the inch, down to 221 feet.[51] Cavendish's account of this journey is mostly about strata.[52] He discussed geology with Michell, Michell's particular field, and after this visit he corresponded with Michell about geology.[53] Michell was a stimulus to Cavendish in geology as he was in other subjects. Michell was one of the new geologists who brought together theory and field work, which had been separated in the past. Cavendish was one of the new geologists too by virtue of his journeys; in Britain the main spur to geology in the late eighteenth century was precisely what he was doing, crossing large tracks of country making observations of strata.[54]

Cavendish and Blagden took in other things on this trip. They toured an alum works near Lord Mulgrave's.[55] They went to an iron works in Rotheram, from which Cavendish brought home a chunk of kishy iron to examine. In Sheffield they observed file-making and other manufactures

[44]"Computations & Observations in Journey 1785." Cavendish Mss, Misc. contain many pages of data from this trip. Cavendish and Blagden used a Hadley's quadrant borrowed from Aubert, and they made a long series of elevations taken by the barometer and corrected by the thermometer. They brought their journey to an end with readings in Cavendish's library at Bedford Square on their return to London on August 8.

[45]Charles Blagden to his brother, John Blagden Hale, 13 and 20 June 1786, drafts, Blagden Letterbook, Royal Society, 7:4 and 8.

[46]Charles Blagden to Lord Mulgrave, 2 Aug. 1786, draft, Blagden Letterbook, Royal Society, 7:17. Charles Blagden to John Michell, 5 Aug. 1786, draft, ibid., 7:21.

[47]Charles Blagden to his brother, 14 Sep. 1786, draft, Blagden Letterbook, Royal Society, 7:33.

[48]Charles Blagden to Sir Joseph Banks, 19 Aug. 1786, BL Add Mss 33272.

[49]Entry for 2 Sep. 1786, Blagden Diary, Yale, Osborn Shelves f c 16.

[50]Charles Blagden to Sir Joseph Banks, 13 Aug. 1786, BL Add Mss 33272, p. 1.

[51]Henry Cavendish, "Strata Which Michell Dug Through for Coal," in Cavendish's journal of the 1786 trip, Cavendish Mss X(a), 3:13–14. In Michell's table there are thirty levels, coal alternating with various other matter. Down to 77 feet it gave Michell's own knowledge; the rest came from pits.

[52]Cavendish's journal of the journey of 1786, Cavendish Mss X(a), 3.

[53]Henry Cavendish to John Michell, n.d. /1787/, draft, Cavendish Mss, Misc. John Michell to Henry Cavendish, 14 Aug. 1788, Cavendish Mss X(b), 15.

[54]Roy Porter, *The Making of Geology: Earth Science in Britain, 1660–1815* (Cambridge: Cambridge University Press, 1977), 119.

[55]"Computations & Observations in Journey 1786," Cavendish Mss X(a), 5. The wrapper is labeled in Cavendish's hand, the narrative in another.

"pretty much in detail," and they stayed at an inn recommended by Michell ("the vilest house," Blagden complained to Michell, "at which I had ever the misfortune to put up").[56] In Chesterfield they went down the mines; Blagden found the ladders "fatiguing" and his legs too short, but he said nothing of Cavendish's discomfort, if any. Cavendish was interested in the mine and the evidence of violence in it, which led him to think that there had been an explosion.[57] "Tempestuous" wind and rain frustrated their plans to climb mountains in the Lake District, and they left sooner than they had planned, but not before Blagden had caught a glimpse of the "magnificent & beautiful" scene.[58] What Cavendish thought of it he did not say or Blagden did not record. (The closest Blagden came to a criticism of Cavendish was in connection with this trip to the Lake District; to a friend fifteen years later, Blagden wrote, "When I went to the lakes it was in company with Mr Cavendish, who had no curiosity for several things which it would have given me great pleasure to have seen."[59]) A month after their return to London, Blagden wrote to Banks that Cavendish was "making experiments upon the stones we brought home," especially specimens from the iron and alum works.[60]

For the third straight year, in 1787, Cavendish and Blagden set off on a journey of about three weeks, now to the southwestern corner of England, Cornwall. As before, long in advance Blagden made arrangements for them to be met and shown the sights along the way. Their route was planned so that Cavendish always saw something new by traveling a new road.[61] Blagden had solicited letters of recommendation identifying them and giving their purpose, "a philosophical tour."[62] James Watt and his partner Matthew Boulton supplied them with letters to admit them to mines, for example.[63] The famous mines of Cornwall being new to both Cavendish and Blagden,[64] they went down one, a tin mine a hundred fathoms deep. Blagden found the descent troublesome and uninteresting because he could not see anything, and Cavendish may have too, since on the rest of the trip they contented themselves with seeing what was above ground.[65] This included tin and copper mines and Josiah Wedgwood's clay pits for his porcelain manufacture. The travelers were already in touch

with Wedgwood, who in the previous winter had sent Blagden a number of specimens of minerals with the request that he show them to Cavendish and Kirwan. They were mainly specimens of feldspar (he called it feltspat), which of course were of interest to him as a manufacturer of pottery (clay originating mainly in the decomposition of felspathic rocks). Wedgwood was an industrialist who looked to experimental chemistry and heat to advance technology, in his case ceramic; he was exactly the kind of person Cavendish liked to associate with, and these journey gave him plenty of opportunity.[66] Cavendish and Blagden observed the smelters with their strong smell of arsenic and the workmen covered with red dust. They saw the great stampers driven by waterwheels, crushing the ore, and steam engines everywhere, emptying the mine shafts of water and hauling up the ore.[67] They saw the pumping machinery improved by Watt, to whom, Blagden thought, the Cornish were indebted to be able to "work their copper mines at all."[68] As before, Cavendish returned home with specimens of all kinds of ore to subject to "chemical analysis," which Blagden expected would "shew

[56]Charles Blagden to John Michell, 19 Sep. 1786, draft, Blagden Letterbook, Royal Society, 7:37.

[57]Charles Blagden to Sir Joseph Banks, 17 Sep. 1786, BL Add Mss 33272, pp. 9–10.

[58]Charles Blagden to Sir Joseph Banks, 4 Sep. 1786, BL Add Mss 33272, pp. 7–8.

[59]Charles Blagden to Lord Palmerston, 25 Nov. 1800, Blagden Letters, Yale.

[60]Charles Blagden to Joseph Banks, 8 Oct. 1786, BM Add Mss 33272.

[61]Blagden explained that they would take a route to Cornwall along the sea because of "particular experiments" to be done there, and they would probably not accept an invitation from Bristol because Cavendish had been there and would "wish to return by a new road." Charles Blagden to William Lewis, 11 July 1787, draft, Blagden Letterbook, Royal Society, 7:338.

[62]Two letters from George Hunt /?/, 23 Jan. 1787, who was asked to write letters of introduction by his nephew R Wilbraham, "The bearer of this are Mr Cavendish . . ." Blagden Papers, Yale, box 1, folder 4. Along the way, too, Blagden solicited letters, such as James Rennell to Rev. Burington, 18 Aug. 1787, "The bearer, Dr Blagden, is my particular friend . . ." Blagden Letters, Royal Society, R.5.

[63]Charles Blagden to James Watt, 23 Aug. 1787, Blagden Letterbook, Royal Society, 7:349.

[64]Charles Blagden to Mrs. Grey, 14 June 1787, Blagden Letterbook, Royal Society, 7:324.

[65]Charles Blagden to William Watson, 22 Aug. 1787, Blagden Letterbook, Royal Society, 7:347.

[66]Josiah Wedgwood to Charles Blagden, 30 Dec. 1786, Gloucestershire Record Office, D 1086, F 158.

[67]Thirty-page journal of the 1787 journey in another's handwriting but with many insertions in Cavendish's hand. Cavendish Mss X(a), 6.

[68]Charles Blagden to Mrs. Grey, 28 Aug. 1787, draft, Blagden Letterbook, Royal Society, 7:351.

some more light upon their origin."[69] Their industrial tour was at the same time a geological and mineralogical tour; Cavendish's own notes on the journey between industrial sites were mainly of observations of strata.[70] The weather favored them on this journey, enabling them to go up mountains with their barometer to measure heights.[71] They kept busy and happy, and Blagden thought that Cavendish looked "the better for his journey."[72]

Independently of their industrial sightseeing in Cornwall, Cavendish and Blagden made a side trip to Dartmoor, there to carry out an elaborate experiment on the heights of mountains, planned long in advance. Ever since Pascal sent his brother-in-law up a mountain with a barometer in 1648, the prospect of measuring the heights of scalable mountains barometrically was recognized as an alternative to trigonometrical methods. During his first year in the Royal Society, Lord Charles Cavendish, for example, heard a report on a method for finding heights by the barometer.[73] Henry Cavendish's associates had recently gone to Mont Blanc to make measurements by a combination of barometry and trigonometry. In the 1770s, first Jean André Deluc and then George Shuckburgh, a specialist in instruments and weights and measures, published the observations they had taken on Mont Blanc; they made a case for Mont Blanc being Europe's highest peak, and they also disagreed about heights.[74] Traveling through the Alps with his "portable philosophical cabinet," Shuckburgh repeated Deluc's experiments using Deluc's "rule" for correcting the barometer for temperature, and he got yet different results. In that decade, other of Cavendish's associates, Nevil Maskelyne, Samuel Horsley, and William Roy, still published on the heights of mountains as measured by barometers. Shuckburgh and Roy devised variant "rules" of their own in the belief that if the right rule were found, the method would be accurate enough to become practical; as Shuckburgh said in 1777, the long-known and rarely practiced method of taking heights with the barometer had been "capable of but little precision till within these few years."[75] With the new researches from the 1770s, stimulated especially by Deluc, the method did become both reasonably practical and exact.[76] Cavendish's work on it was a continuation of his work in meteorology; he compared the competing rules for correcting the barometer for temperature,

drawing on his father's experiments.[77] He assisted Roy in experiments on the expansion of mercury in connection with measuring the heights of mountains, again drawing on his father's work.[78] Like Roy, Cavendish did not go to that three-mile high mountain, Mont Blanc, but was satisfied to do computations on it at home, using the barometer and thermometer readings taken by Deluc and Shuckburgh;[79] Cavendish, too, arrived at different results for the height.[80] At just about this time, Mont Blanc was scaled for the first time, in 1786, by Michel Gabriel Paccard. It was a bold climb, made with only one porter, and since many attempts by others had failed, this one was especially stirring. Paccard had taken a barometer with him, not to advance science but his nation; he wanted to prove that his mountain was the highest in Europe.[81] The next year, 1787, his ambitious countryman Horace Bénédict de Saussure led a party of twenty up the mountain to return with a treasure of scientific observations. The results of Saussure's barometric readings on that climb were published only in 1796, in a volume of his *Voyages dans les Alpes*,[82] but the feat was widely publicized

---

[69]Charles Blagden to John Michell, 11 Sep. 1787, draft, Blagden Letterbook, Royal Society, 7:354.

[70]Henry Cavendish's journal of the 1787 trip, Cavendish Mss X(a), 7.

[71]There are several large sheets of observations taken with the barometer on the 1787 trip in Cavendish Mss, Misc.

[72]Charles Blagden to Sir Joseph Banks, 14 Aug. 1787, BL Add Mss 33272.

[73]J. G. Scheuchzer's paper on the subject was read on 8 Feb. 1727/28, Royal Society, JB 13:173.

[74]Gavin de Beer, "The History of the Altimetry of Mont Blanc," *Annals of Science* 12 (1956): 3–29, on 3–4.

[75]George Shuckburgh, *Observations Made in Savoy, in Order to Ascertain the Height of Mountains by Means of the Barometer; Being an Examination of Mr De Luc's Rules, Delivered in His Recherches sur les Modifications de l'Atmosphère. Read at the Royal Society, May 8 and 15, 1777* (London, 1777), 1–2, 12–13.

[76]Feldman, "Applied Mathematics and the Quantification of Experimental Physics," 151, 177–78.

[77]Comparing rules by Deluc, Bouguer, and Maskelyne, Cavendish referred to his father's experiments on the specific gravity of air at given temperatures and pressures. Henry Cavendish, "Rule for Taking Heights of Barometers," Cavendish Mss VIII, 12.

[78]William Roy, "Experiments and Observations Made in Britain, in Order to Obtain a Rule for Measuring Heights with the Barometer," *PT* 67 (1778): 653–788, on 673.

[79]Henry Cavendish, "Observations of Thermom on Mont Blanc," in Cavendish Mss, Misc.

[80]Charles Blagden to Sir Joseph Banks, 5 Oct. 1786, BL Add Mss 33272, pp. 19–20. Cavendish's calculation of the summit of Mont Blanc, Blagden reported, came out lower than Shuckburgh's by 700 feet.

[81]Charles Blagden to Mrs. Grey, 5 Oct. 1786, draft, Blagden Letterbook, Royal Society, 7:39. T. Graham Brown and Gavin de Beer, *The First Ascent of Mont Blanc* (London: Oxford University Press, 1957), v, 3.

[82]De Beer, "History," 22.

at the time. That was the year of Cavendish and Blagden's journey to Dartmoor, to Cavendish's mountain, only a few hundred feet high.

In an earlier volume of Saussure's *Voyages*, published in 1786,[83] he gave observations on Mont Blanc but not yet from the top. It was this account that suggested to Cavendish the idea for the experiment on Dartmoor. Twice, two days apart, Saussure measured the elevation of one station on the mountain over another and obtained different results, a discrepancy of nearly two percent. Even more puzzling was the effect of the temperature correction on the barometer reading: instead of making the two measurements more consistent, it made them less so. Saussure concluded that an important consideration was being overlooked in the measurement of mountains; namely, variations of the barometer over time were proportionately less on the mountain than they were on the plain. There was no known reason why they should not be proportional, but there it was, and it pointed to the need for a correction to a (temperature) correction in the barometric measurement of heights. To show what he meant, Saussure gave an example: high up on a mountain where the mean reading of the barometer was only 7/8 or 3/4 of what it was at sea level, the barometric variations about the mean reading should also be 7/8 or 3/4 of the variations at sea level, but experiment showed that the variations were proportionately much less above than below. Daniel Bernoulli had observed this fact long before and had postulated heavy exhalations in the air that did not rise to higher elevations. Deluc had recognized irregularities in the variations, but he did not consider any corrections other than those for heat and humidity. Saussure proposed the existence of a correction of an "absolutely different genre." The solution to the problem of determining heights by the barometer was not the construction of corrective scales and tables but research into the "law of variations." It was "in effect one of the most interesting problems of meteorology," Saussure wrote, and he called for new observations at different heights and in very different states of the atmosphere.[84] The barometric measurement of the heights of mountains pointed to a fundamental problem of the atmosphere.

Cavendish responded by arranging for a long series of observations using barometers, ther-

mometers, and rain gauges at the top and bottom of Dartmoor. The project was conceived, planned, and funded by Cavendish.

Dartmoor was close to Plymouth, where Blagden had lived before coming to London. He made the local arrangements, which called for three men to assist in the experiment.[85] The one in charge at the site was William Farr, a long-time friend of Blagden and physician at the royal naval hospital near Plymouth.[86] Farr was a graduate of Edinburgh, where he wrote his dissertation on the uses of mathematics and natural philosophy in the study of medicine. A Fellow of the Royal Society, Farr regularly published his meteorological journals from Plymouth in the *Philosophical Transactions*. These journals recorded that he took readings twice a day, *precisely* at 9 a.m. and 11 p.m.; he was an observer who could be counted on.[87] The lower of the two meteorological stations on Dartmoor was Thomas Vivian's house. The higher station had to be built by Vivian and Farr, who made it solid enough to be secure "both from storms & ill-disposed persons." Cavendish ordered instruments for Vivian's house and the new building and sent them ahead with instructions. He hired a third helper, R. Wilson, to read the "small very sensitive ther." and other instruments three times a day.[88] The setting-up of the experiment was to be done by Cavendish himself, and on 15 July 1787 Cavendish and Blagden left London for Plymouth to arrive at about the same time as the instruments. The exact difference in elevation of the two stations had to be known (it was roughly a thousand feet), and to this end, in a heavy rain, the party struggled up the moor with their leveling instruments.[89]

---

[83]Charles Blagden to John Michell, 11 Sep. 1787, draft, Blagden Letterbook, Royal Society, 7:354.

[84]Horace Bénédict de Saussure, *Voyages dans les Alpes, précédés d'un essai sur l'histoire naturelle des environs de Genève* (Geneva, 1786), 575–78, 581–82.

[85]Blagden also traveled in the region around Dartmoor. Relative to an observation near Dartmoor, Cavendish wrote in his account in 1787 that "Dr Bl. in a former journey was informed . . . " Cavendish's journal of his 1787 trip, Cavendish Mss X(a), 7.

[86]Letters about family and work from William Farr to Blagden, 27 Apr. 1781 and 3 Nov. 1782, Blagden Letters, Royal Society, F.2 and F.3.

[87]William Farr, "Observations on the Barometer and Thermometer, and Account of the Whole Rain in Every Month of the Year 1767, Taken at the Royal Hospital Near Plymouth," *PT* 58 (1769): 136–39; "Abstract from a Meteorological Register Kept at the Royal Hospital Near Plymouth, During the Year 1768," *PT* 59 (1769): 81–85.

[88]Charles Blagden to William Farr, 12 June and 3 July 1787, drafts, Blagden Letterbook, Royal Society, 7:67 and 7:335.

[89]Charles Blagden to William Farr, 3 July 1787. From the bottom of the sill of Vivian's door to a pencil mark on the post of the

It soon became clear that their effort had been in vain. On the point raised by Saussure, the experiment proved inconclusive, probably because Dartmoor was not Mont Blanc: the difference in elevation of the two stations was too small to register the effect. Blagden described to Michell their meager consolation: the experiment showed something about the value of comparing barometers and of comparing rain at the top and the bottom of a hill,[90] and Cavendish had estimated the height of the highest part of the local hills.[91] Correspondence passed between Plymouth and London about the readings with the rain gauge,[92] and then the correspondence turned to practical matters of bringing the experiment to a close.[93] In early 1789, a year and a half after the experiment had begun, Blagden wrote to Farr in Plymouth mentioning the king's madness but nothing about the experiment.[94] But the experiment had been carefully executed, and it had theoretical significance. Through it Cavendish revealed his administrative skills as a scientific director with Blagden's indispensable help. This scientific expedition into the wet and windy moors had taken the coordinated efforts of four men, in addition to Cavendish's own.

On Dartmoor Cavendish had his scientific staff, but for most of his other distant geological information, he relied solely upon Blagden, who for three years in succession, 1787–89, journeyed without Cavendish to France. In the same year as the experiment on Dartmoor, Blagden sent Cavendish observations from France on strata with the clear intention of connecting them with their observations of English strata.[95] In the summer of 1788, Blagden observed that the soils in France were similar to England's.[96] In the fall of 1789 Blagden was back in France, from where he made an extended trip into western Germany, making notes of strata all the way.[97]

Cavendish made one more journey, this time on his own, in 1793, when he was nearly sixty-two. Blagden was then living in Europe and in correspondence with Cavendish.[98] Cavendish traveled north from London as far as Derbyshire and Lincolnshire, stopping at quarries and collieries, and noting the strata. The purpose of this trip would seem to be Watt. Using his steam engine as a scientific instrument, Watt measured the specific gravity of steam, an experiment which Cavendish

entered in his journal of the trip. Cavendish witnessed trials of Watt and Boulton's steam engines in Birmingham, and it seems that Banks took Blagden's place in encouraging Cavendish to be there, as he himself intended to be.[99]

Such were Cavendish's purposes in his journeys outside London. These journeys were active. He examined industrial processes and their materials and products; he determined the heights of mountains; he collected "stones," noting their physical descriptions, and, often, dissolving them in acids;[100] and he observed the "order of the strata."[101]

Cavendish had the same interests as his geological colleagues: mountains, strata, and minerals. Saussure said of his alpine voyages that once he had enough facts about high mountains, he would have the foundation for some general

---

meteorological hut on top of Dartmoor, they measured 958 63/100 feet. The distances from the bottom of the sill to the bottom of the cistern of Vivian's barometer, and from the pencil mark on the post to the bottom of the cistern of the barometer in the hut, they left for Wilson to measure. Charles Blagden to William Farr, 22 Aug. 1787, draft, Blagden Letterbook, Royal Society, 7:346.

[90] Blagden to Michell, 11 Sep. 1787.

[91] Blagden to Watson, 22 Aug. 1787. Charles Blagden to Mrs. Grey, 28 Aug. 1787, draft, Blagden Letterbook, Royal Society, 7:351.

[92] Judging from Farr's observations, Cavendish suspected an irregularity in Sisson's glass rain tube. Charles Blagden to William Farr, 5 Dec. 1787 and 8 Jan. 1788, drafts, Blagden Letterbook, Royal Society, 7:93 and 7:103. Farr promised to correct any mistake in the register. William Farr to Henry Cavendish, Mar. 2 /1788/, Cavendish Mss, New Correspondence.

[93] Cavendish offered to let Vivian keep the instruments at his house. He told Farr to give the instruments in the hut to anyone who could use them or else to return them. Cavendish had intended for Wilson to keep the register only until the end of 1787, but he continued on at Cavendish's expense and under Farr's direction. Charles Blagden to William Farr, 25 Oct. 1788, draft, Blagden Letterbook, Royal Society, 7:168. Vivian thanked Cavendish for the instruments and for the expense and trouble in "promoting philosophical knowledge by experiments in the neighborhood." Thomas Vivian to Henry Cavendish, 26 Nov. 1788, Cavendish Mss, New Correspondence.

[94] Charles Blagden to William Farr, 24 Jan. 1789, draft, Blagden Letterbook, Royal Society, 7:206.

[95] The notes of Blagden's journey in France in 1787 are in Cavendish's handwriting. Cavendish Mss X(a), 1.

[96] Charles Blagden to Joseph Banks, 13 July 1788, .BL Add Mss 33272.

[97] This ten-page account by Blagden is in Cavendish's hand. Cavendish Mss X(a), 8.

[98] Charles Blagden to Sir Joseph Banks, 11 May 1793, BL Add Mss 33272, 119–20. Henry Cavendish to Sir Joseph Banks, 23 Sep. 1793, copy, BM(NH), DTC, 8:257.

[99] Sir Joseph Banks to Matthew Boulton, 6 and 10 July, 10 Aug. 1793, Birmingham Assay Office.

[100] Henry Cavendish, "List of Stones With Their Examination," Cavendish Mss, Misc.

[101] This twenty-one page paper on strata in Cavendish's hand does not have a group number, but it is kept with the travel journals in the Cavendish Mss.

[102] Saussure, *Voyages dans les Alpes* 2:i.

"truths" if not "a complete system of geology."[102] Deluc said that Saussure's *Voyages* marked an epoch in geology by showing that mountains are not masses of rock but successively formed strata. As Deluc now understood the task of geology, it was to study mountains, hills, valleys, plains, and coasts to learn the origin of the "mineral strata."[103] The geologist should draw on chemistry and mineralogy, Deluc said, the point Saussure had made. At the time of writing, 1786, Saussure said that he had studied the analysts Bergman, Scheele, Kirwan, and others and that he too was now occupied with the chemical analyses of minerals; he dedicated himself not to the study of valuable metals in their matrices but "principally to the study of rocks, a study which by the confession of mineralogists and to the detriment of their art, has been too much neglected."[104] Kirwan, Cavendish's fellow chemist, published a book on mineralogy in 1784 and later one on geology, which explained "how to read the huge and mysterious volume of inanimate nature, of which mineralogy supplies the alphabet."[105] The interests Cavendish had in common with Saussure, Deluc, Kirwan, and others gave scientific meaning and coherence to his activities on his several journeys.

The only geological author Cavendish referred to in his notes on his journeys was John Whitehurst, who like Michell was at the same time an observer and a theorist. He was also what one might call a local geologist, who studied the strata of Derbyshire, which was close to home for Cavendish. Whitehurst's book in 1778 laid out a section of the strata underlying the great Cavendish house in Derbyshire, Chatsworth. Henry Cavendish subscribed to this book as did some other Cavendishes and their relatives. Despite the limited range of his observations, Whitehurst's goal was a "system" of geology, of which Derbyshire strata were just an illustration. There was, Whitehurst believed, a constant order beneath the apparent chaos of strata, and it could be inferred from the impressions of vegetable and animals and from the minerals. His natural history of the earth began with Newton's law of gravitation, which showed that the earth had a certain shape. Its composition depended on attractions of other kinds, the chemical affinities; Whitehurst cited Macquer. Its mountainous surface had arisen from the expansive force of steam; he cited Michell. Whitehurst listed the order and thicknesses of the strata of Derbyshire,

the most puzzling constituent of which was toadstone, which Whitehurst concluded was volcanic in origin, lava.[106] It was in connection with toadstone that Cavendish mentioned Whitehurst, to disagree with him. Cavendish, with Michell, believed that toadstone was clay (as it happens Whitehurst was right and Michell and Cavendish wrong).[107] Cavendish made a close study of toadstone in connection with this question of geological strata.

The journeys began at the same time that Cavendish's chemistry changed direction. For several years he had pursued a certain kind of research, pneumatic chemistry, which, in effect, came to an end with his paper on phlogisticated air in 1785, the year he made his first journey with Blagden. In 1786 he began keeping a new record of chemical experiments, an indexed, bound book, which he labeled "White Book No. 1."[108] It was a transcription from his laboratory "minutes," some of which (bearing telltale chemical stains) are inserted loosely and not yet transcribed. The experiments recorded in it, which go on to 1806, might be called geological and industrial chemistry, but the simpler name mineralogical chemistry would not be misleading, given the often undifferentiated eighteenth-century usage of "mineralogy," encompassing both ores and stones.[109] In light of Cavendish's previous work in chemistry, this next stage seems almost inevitable.

The four elements of the Greeks were still

---

[103] Jean André Deluc, *An Elementary Treatise on Geology: Determining Fundamental Points in That Science, … and Particularly of the Huttonian Theory of the Earth*, trans H. de la Fite (London, 1809), 41, 368.

[104] Saussure, *Voyages dans les Alpes* 2:ii, 120.

[105] Richard Kirwan, *Geological Essays* (London, 1799), iii.

[106] John Whitehurst, *An Inquiry into the Original State and Formation of the Earth; Deduced from Facts and the Laws of Nature. To Which Is Added an Appendix, Containing Some General Observations on the Strata in Derbyshire* . . . (London, 1778), ii, 2, 19–22, 94, 162, and plate 6.

[107] Cavendish's 21-page summary of his observations on strata, p. 14.

[108] This book has 138 numbered pages, and 90 loose sheets are laid between the bound ones. Large blank spaces are left in the book for cross-referencing and later additions. It is a copy book for preserving results of experiments in narrative form. "White Book," Cavendish Mss. On p. 59 Cavendish referred to "2d book," which suggests that there once was a "White Book No. 2." We note that Cavendish was still using chemicals belonging to Charles Cavendish: on pp. 61–62 of "White Book No. 1," Cavendish took a measure of tincal (an Asiatic crude borax) "of my fathers."

[109] V. A. Eyles, "The Extent of Geological Knowledge in the Eighteenth Century, and Methods by Which It Was Diffused," in *Toward a History of Geology*, ed. C. J. Schneer (Cambridge, Mass.: M.I.T. Press, 1969), 175.

[110] Robert Siegfried and Betty Jo Dobbs, "Composition, a Neglected Aspect of the Chemical Revolution," *Annals of Science* 24 (1968): 275–93, on 276.

credible when Cavendish took up chemistry.[110] Macquer wrote in his *Dictionary of Chemistry* that the "most probable opinion is, that as only one kind of fire, of air, and of water, so only one kind of simple elementary earth, exists."[111] In his way Cavendish had acquired an understanding of three of these elements, only one of which, water, was perhaps elementary. Fire was not a substance for Cavendish; the contemporary embodiment of it, the elementary matter of heat, he rejected for the motion theory of heat. Air was not an element either, as Cavendish's work on the discrimination of different gases helped to demonstrate. There remained earth, a term which bore on the objects of enquiry of his geological and industrial journeys from 1785. Earth was not an element either. Black, in his chemical lectures, taught that there were at least six earths,[112] and Cavendish distinguished at least that many.[113] Earths belonged to the mineral kingdom and were the least studied of the classes of minerals. Stones began to be studied as composites of minerals, mainly earths, and the preferred mode of study came to be chemical. The Swedish chemist Axel Cronstedt proved that there was no chemical difference between earths and stones.[114] In an influential book on mineralogy in 1758, translated into English in 1770, Cronstedt said that to make a "complete system" of mineralogy, it was necessary to add chemical experiments to the physical examination of mineral specimens, and the "compleat tribunal" for settling mineralogical disputes was the "institution of a laboratory."[115] In 1771, in the English version of Macquer's *Dictionary*, the translator, James Keir, added the chemical properties of a number of minerals, which he learned from Cronstedt and the work of several other chemists including his own. The "most intelligent mineralogists agree," Keir wrote, that the classification of minerals ought to be based on an examination "chiefly of the chemical properties, and not of external forms."[116] To Cronstedt's compatriot Torbern Bergman, the need for chemistry in mineralogy was obvious from the unreliability of the external properties of minerals (this before crystallography), their color, size, hardness, texture, and form. These externals were not exactly despicable, Bergman said, or even dispensable, but their use was largely limited to field identification. Bergman followed in Cronstedt's path, but he was even more rigorously the chemist:

Cronstedt, like other writers, put "volcanoes" in their books, but Bergman did not: all that mattered in mineralogy was what the minerals were made of, not their history. That was consistent with Bergman's understanding that the main purpose of mineralogy was to make minerals useful to man.[117] Bergman was the first to give a standard procedure for the chemical analysis of minerals.[118] Cavendish turned to this new domain of chemistry and informed himself thoroughly, buying many books on mineralogy. Though Cavendish published no work of his own on minerals and strata, he left ample record that he made this a serious study in the last quarter of his life.

Contemporary mineralogists such as Bergman put forward nomenclatures for mineralogy, but this aspect of the science did not interest Cavendish. This is the case even though classification in mineralogy had a quantitative direction, which might have interested him.[119] His indifference is perhaps expected given his antipathy to what he called the "present rage of name-making," which was not limited to chemistry and botany. Cavendish forbore using neologisms (except for his occasional own), and in mineralogy with perhaps better reason, since the mineral earth was an even greater terra incognita than the reagents and reactants on the chemists' shelves.

On his journeys Cavendish picked up stones from the roadside and from gravel pits and lime kilns and the like. Sometimes he did a quick chemical test on the spot and a thorough one when

---

[111]Article "Earths" in vol. 1 of Pierre Joseph Macquer, *A Dictionary of Chemistry . . .*, trans. J. Kier (London, 1771).

[112]Siegfried and Dobbs, "Composition," 278–79.

[113]In the "White Book," Cavendish worked with a number of distinct earths, vitrifiable earth, calcareous earth, siliceous earth, argillaceous earth, earth of alum, and others.

[114]Rachel Laudan, *From Mineralogy to Geology: The Foundations of a Science, 1650–1830* (Chicago: University of Chicago Press, 1987), 56–57, 63, 68.

[115]Axel Fredric Cronstedt, *An Essay Towards a System of Mineralogy*, trans. G. von Engestrom, rev. E. M. Da Costa (London, 1770), vii, x. His mineralogy distinguished between simple minerals and stones containing a variety of minerals, the latter of which he excluded from his system.

[116]Translator's preface to Macquer, *Dictionary of Chemistry*, iv.

[117]Torbern Bergman, *Outlines of Mineralogy*, trans. W. Withering (Birmingham, 1783), 6–11, 127–28.

[118]Thomas Thomson, *History of Chemistry*, 2 vols. (London, 1830–31) 2:190–91.

[119]Anders Lundgren, "The Changing Role of Numbers in 18th-Century Chemistry," in *The Quantifying Spirit in the 18th Century*, eds. T. Frangsmyr, J. L. Heilbron, and R. E. Rider (Berkeley: University of California Press, 1990), 243–66, on 255.

he got home. He also brought home samples of ores and products from the mines and furnaces, which he subjected to the same kind of analysis. Industry and nature produced complex substances, which were equally grist for Cavendish's chemical mill. The tremendous heat of industrial processes was like the earth's interior and like Cavendish's forges and furnaces at home, and their vats of chemicals were like his bottles of chemicals from the pharmacist. Mines and manufacturers were great suppliers of substances of interest. They had potential geological significance as well as meaning for industrial operations.

British mining included tin and copper in Cornwall and lead in Derbyshire (the dukes of Devonshire owned lead mines there) but the main direction was in stratiform deposits like coal; in either case, there were technical processes, often deep secrets of the trade, and in most cases they were incompletely understood on the grounds of science. The same can be said of manufacturing processes. Unlike Continentals, the British did not have mining academies and government jobs waiting for their graduates. Owners, managers, and engineers learned mining and metallurgy on the job; their extensive knowledge was rooted in practical experience and tradition.[120] There was less incentive for systematic teaching and development of mineralogy and geology in Britain than abroad; at the same time, there was added incentive for scientifically curious persons of means like Cavendish to cultivate these sciences by field and laboratory investigations. In pursuing a general chemistry of minerals, encompassing rocks, earths, kish, slag, slams, and refinery cinders, Cavendish furthered his understanding of strata and provided practical men with results of his chemical analyses. Just as in his earlier studies of air, heat, and electricity, in this late stage of his scientific work, Cavendish was widely connected with other persons; these connections he established by leaving London on journeys, and it was to be expected that they would be located in the industrial provinces. As always, Cavendish's work even when it was not published was not private but a possession of science.

In his new work, Cavendish typically proceeded by first giving a physical description of a specimen and where it came from, then heating it or grinding it or doing whatever else was needed to

help it dissolve in acid, and then often adding an alkali to form a precipitate and then examining the solution and the residue. The connection of Cavendish's experiments on minerals with his earlier work in chemistry is obvious through the collection and weighings of gases; he could not have done this work on minerals without his skills in pneumatic chemistry as well as in analytic chemistry. It would seem that several of Cavendish's later experiments related to Lavoisier's chemistry, but in only one place did he refer to it. In connection with coal and iron ore, in a paper he gave to the engineer James Cockshutt, he said that cast iron gives up less inflammable air than hammered iron when dissolved in acid, "from which Bergman & the partizans of phlogiston conclude that . . . it contains less phlogiston than the latter & for the same reason the favourers of the new system say that /it/ contains some dephlogisticated air . . ."[121] Here as in his paper on the condensation of water Cavendish withheld judgment on the competing theories, identifying himself neither with the partisans of phlogiston nor with Lavoisier's favorers. He did a number of experiments on iron that Lavoisier would have considered a confirmation of his theory but which had phlogistic explanations too; Cavendish did not comment.[122] Independently of the question of phlogiston, the makeup of rocks and earths posed

---

[120]Laudan, *From Mineralogy to Geology*, 55–56.

[121]The paper used here has a watermark that does not appear on paper Cavendish used before 1785. Given the subject of the chemical analysis, the time would undoubtedly be 1785 or later, when Cavendish made his industrial and geological journeys. James Cockshutt was a civil engineer instructed and sometimes employed by John Smeaton, of Wortley Iron Works near Sheffield, whom Cavendish recommended for fellowship in the Royal Society on 26 Apr. 1804. Royal Society Certificates, 6. "Paper Given to Cockshutt" is a loose insert between pp. 117 and 118 of Cavendish's "White Book."

[122]Cavendish recognized that iron absorbed dephlogisticated air, turning it into calx or finery cinder. "To Judge of the Dephlog. of Iron," ibid. He did an experiment, "Iron contained in calx of iron," concluding that the calx was 1.72 times the weight of the iron. "White Book," p. 63. "On the Absorption of Deph. Air by Grass in Drying," on pp. 121–24 of the "White Book," might be related to the reason Cavendish gave for preferring the phlogiston theory over Lavoiser's in his 1784 paper, namely, the constitution of plants. Cavendish followed the work reported in the new French journal created in 1789 to disseminate the new antiphlogistic chemistry, *Annales de chemie*. He cited it in connection with an experiment on diamonds; from a report in the journal he calculated how much dephlogisticated air diamond consumes in burning and how much fixed air it gives off; and he concluded with his own experiments on this point. "Comput. of Result of Burning of Diamond," Cavendish Mss, Misc.

great difficulties for chemists; the new anti-phlogistic chemistry did not eliminate them and, in some respects, complicated them further.[123]

Whitehurst's proposal that there was a worldwide deposition of strata[124] (which Michell believed too, apparently) would seem to have been Cavendish's hypothesis. Despite Cavendish's wide-ranging geological observations, he knew that he had arrived at nothing worth publishing. In one place he acknowledged that he was only scratching the surface and that only superficial knowledge could come of it.[125] He would surely have said the same of his knowledge of industrial machinery. His knowledge of the constitution of minerals was extensive but largely happenstance, and again he published nothing of it and showed no inclination even to organize his experiments. The scientific observations Cavendish made during and following his journeys are easily associated with important directions in the science of that time, as we have seen, but there is a sense in which his journeys were summer vacations too, justified by his active curiosity about the natural and the manmade landscapes outside London. A great reader of travels by others, as we know from his library holdings, he was prepared to be enticed out of his study by Blagden. His journals do not differ from travel journals commonly kept at the time except perhaps in their spareness. They have much in common with the geological journals of the chemist William Lewis, Saussure, and Deluc and with the journal of observations on strata and steam engines by Cavendish's colleague Charles Hatchett.[126] It is hard to think of Cavendish enjoying himself, but it seems that he did on these journeys, in his active way. As his traveling companion, Blagden, observed, Cavendish held up well on the journeys and looked better for them.

Bristol Harbor

Blagden and Cavendish together, probably through Blagden, who had local knowledge and connections, became involved in the problems of Bristol Harbor in the 1790s. The problems by that time had a long history. This busy harbor was plagued by huge tides, which left ships stranded in the mud, as Alexander Pope described: the scene was a "long street, full of ships in the middle and houses on both sides, /looking/ like a dream."[127] The engineer John Smeaton had been brought in

in the early 1760s; Blagden's papers contain a sketch by Smeaton of the rivers Avon and Frome, a dam, a canal, and sluices. Plans for making one or both rivers into a floating harbor were considered. Time passed, the problems remained, and in 1791 the city's Society of Merchant Venturers resolved that to make its port competitive with other ports, a dam needed to be built across the Avon, with locks on the river below its confluence with the Frome.[128] The greater part of the house sewers of Bristol discharged into these waters, which posed the problem that was presented to Cavendish: would the proposed dam cause Bristol to suffer smells from the sewage? Smeaton still and several men of science were brought in as high-level consultants, Adair Crawford, Bryan Higgins, and Cavendish and Blagden. Benjamin Vaughan, who had scientific connections with Cavendish,[129] sent Cavendish papers about the project and asked for his opinion.[130] Cavendish declined to answer the questions put to him on the grounds that only physicians could answer some of them and that the others were better answered by the engineers. The data were too incomplete anyway for him to make any determination.[131] Vaughan did not take no for an answer.[132] Cavendish made some calculations about the flows,[133] but it does not seem that he helped Bristol with its sewage. There was no

[123]Siegfried and Dobbs, "Composition," 275–76.

[124]John Challinor, "Whitehurst, John," *DSB* 14:311–12.

[125]Archibald Geikie, "Note on Cavendish as a Geologist," Cavendish, *Sci Pap.* 2:432.

[126]Saussure's *Voyages.* Deluc, *Geological Travels.* Charles Hatchett, *The Hatchett Diary. A Tour Through the Counties of England and Scotland in 1796 Visiting Their Mines and Manufactures,* ed. A. Raistrick (Truro: D. Bradford Barton, 1967). F. W. Gibbs, "A Notebook of William Lewis and Alexander Chisholm," *Annals of Science* 8 (1952): 202–20, on 211.

[127]Pope quoted in Margaret C. Jacob, *The Cultural Meaning of the Scientific Revolution* (Philadelphia: Temple University Press, 1988), 226.

[128]Patrick McGrath, *The Merchant Adventurers of Bristol* (Bristol: The Society of Merchant Adventurers, 1975), 159.

[129]Benjamin Vaughan to Thomas Jefferson, 2 Aug. 1788, in *The Papers of Thomas Jefferson,* ed. J. P. Boyd, vol. 13 (Princeton: Princeton University Press, 1956), 459–61, on 460.

[130]Benjamin Vaughan to Richard Bright, 21 and 29 Oct. 1791, Bristol Record Office, 11168(3)r and 11168(3)s. Benjamin Vaughan to Henry Cavendish, 25 and 29 Oct. 1791, Cavendish Mss, New Correspondence.

[131]Henry Cavendish to Benjamin Vaughan, n.d., draft, Cavendish Mss, New Correspondence. The mailed letter is dated 1 Nov. /1791/, Bristol Record Office, 11168(3)t.

[132]Benjamin Vaughan to Richard Bright, 2 and 30 Nov. 1791, Bristol Record Office, 11168(6)r and 11168(3)k. Richard Bright to Benjamin Vaughan, 7 Dec. 1791, Blagden Letters, Royal Society, B.325.

[133]Henry Cavendish, "Data Extracted from Queries about Bristol Intended Harbour," Cavendish Mss, Misc.

urgency, as more than ten years would pass before there was any construction. With Bristol Harbor Cavendish had a brush with practical science of a civic kind that would become commoner in the next century.

Banks, Blagden, and Cavendish

Joseph Banks was a unique force in English science in the second half of the eighteenth century, though it was not for any significant research he did, for he did none. He was an administrator who directed a substantial part of the scientific energies of a nation without an official scientific establishment. On familiar terms with government ministers and other useful persons, he moved in society as president of the Royal Society and, through sheer force of personality, as the embodiment of science. He was a social creature of inexhaustible determination, who began his day with a formidable breakfast by invitation at his house, and before the day was finished he had spoken with dozens of persons on as many subjects and corresponded with as many more. No one activity can sum up Banks's way of working, but he may have shown himself to best advantage as host of a regular Sunday salon in his house.

Cavendish was a faithful attender of these Sundays at Banks's house. Since they were not formal meetings, Cavendish could not know everyone who would be there, and that was unnerving. He was seen to hesitate on the landing of Banks's house, evidently undecided if he could bear the eyes of strangers on him, and would go in only when someone came up behind him.[134] But he did go in: Banks attracted the kinds of people Cavendish liked, men of science and men of action, world voyagers, and foreign travelers who happened to be in London. One of the attenders of Banks's Sunday gatherings compared and contrasted them with gatherings at the homes of aristocrats who had an interest in science.[135] In the associations he formed, Banks liked to think that he did not favor the aristocracy, but he had a proper appreciation of its importance. From Banks's perspective, Cavendish, aristocrat and scientist at once, was a welcome guest at the sober (tea-drinking only) social gatherings of scientists and patrons in a civilized setting (Banks's library), which Banks called his "conversaziones," an elegant word for an English at-home.

Banks and Cavendish, more than any of their contemporaries, put their hearts and souls into the Royal Society. They had that in common, which enabled them to maintain a working relationship for the thirty-two years Cavendish served the Society under Banks's presidency. Theirs was at the same time a wary relationship, which could never become a friendship. Too much was at stake for both men, for Banks his authority within the Society, for Cavendish the correct working of the Society in his understanding of it.

The relationship between Cavendish and Blagden began in 1782 and changed in some way in 1789. Someone said it did not "suit."[136] However, the break, as we have pointed out, was in the first instance between Blagden and Banks, with Cavendish the affected third party. Blagden's services to the Royal Society and to Banks could not easily be distinguished. Banks so identified himself with the Society that a good measure of personal loyalty was an inevitable part of the job of a secretary of the Society. Blagden recognized and accepted that, but after a few years, he wanted out of what he perceived as a one-way relationship. In early 1788 he wrote to Banks that he intended to resign as secretary, and on the same day he sent a copy of that letter to Cavendish, explaining that he was taking this step to prevent him and Banks from becoming a "violent mixture."[137] Three days later Blagden wrote to Watson, who evidently had intervened to make peace, that he would sacrifice himself no longer.[138] He told Banks that his secretaryship of the Royal Society was the "great misfortune" of his life, and that this had to do with his "connexion" with Banks.[139] Banks replied that he had no idea what Blagden was talking about, whether Blagden's complaints were leveled at him

[134]George Wilson, *The Life of the Honourable Henry Cavendish* (London, 1851), 169.
[135]Sometime after 1805, the young anatomist and surgeon Benjamin Brodie was invited by Banks to his Sunday meetings, where he saw Cavendish together with scientists, distinguished foreigners, and noblemen whom Banks regarded as patrons. By their intimacy and regularity, Banks's Sunday meetings were distinguished by Brodie from those held three or four times a season by the duke of Sussex, the marquis of Northampton, and Lord Rosse. Timothy Holmes, *Sir Benjamin Collins Brodie* (London, 1898), 46, 68.
[136]Wilson, *Cavendish*, 129.
[137]Letters from Charles Blagden to Sir Joseph Banks, 2 Feb. 1788, draft, and to Henry Cavendish, 2 Feb. 1788, Blagden Letters, Royal Society, B.38–39.
[138]Charles Blagden to William Watson, 5 Feb. 1788, draft, Blagden Letterbook, Royal Society, 7:115.
[139]Charles Blagden to Sir Joseph Banks, 27 Mar. 1789, BL, Add Mss 33272, pp. 56–57.

or at the world in general. He had thought they were friends but now he feared they were enemies.[140] Banks said he was taken by complete surprise.

Blagden's misery was exacerbated by Banks's assignment to him of a problem that he had accepted in the name of the Royal Society: to find a way to determine the correct excise duty on alcoholic beverages. The Swiss chemist Johann Caspar Dollfuss, then in London, had started work on the problem by establishing a "standard" for the specific gravity of pure alcohol at sixty degrees of heat. Dollfuss left London, and his experiments were repeated by George Gilpin, clerk of the Royal Society, who then recommended other experiments for Blagden to make. Cavendish gave Blagden assistance by developing a rule for figuring duty; the distillers objected to it, but Blagden adopted it for the reason Cavendish gave, of preventing fraud.[141] The determination of the specific gravity of a mixture of pure alcohol and water was not straightforward, owing to the mutual penetration of alcohol and water and to the different expandabilities of the two liquids with heat. The experiments on varying proportions of alcohol and water were done by weighing, the most accurate way. Blagden recommended that the government set duty strictly by specific gravity, not by the old "proof." He prepared tables calculated to five places but due to the error of the experiments, only three places could be counted on, the number of places Blagden accordingly proposed for practical tables at excise. He published a paper on these experiments in this "so material a branch of the revenue" in the *Philosophical Transactions* in 1790.[142] It undoubtedly had cost him a lot of time.

Blagden thought he should have been paid for this tedious business of the excise duties, which was Banks's business in any case; the literary reward, a publication, did not begin to compensate. Banks replied that he had done many jobs for the government and never thought of reward, but he would look into the possibility of payment if Blagden would tell him what he expected. Blagden's resentment of Banks had been building, and now it all came out. From the time he returned from America, Blagden believed, Banks had taken him for granted, and deceived him, and made him a "tool of his ambition." When Blagden took the job of secretary to the Royal Society, he believed that Banks would advance him in society and

improve his fortune. Banks did nothing of the kind but instead, Blagden believed, discouraged him from pursuing his profession, medicine, and even from marrying, Banks's purpose being to keep Blagden dependent on him. Banks defended his character and conduct.[143] Blagden's rancor at Banks continued and so did their correspondence until it became tedious.[144]

It has been said that Cavendish made Blagden his associate on the condition that he give up medicine and devote himself to science.[145] The contrary would seem to be the truth. Blagden reminded Banks that in 1784, some two years after Blagden had become Cavendish's associate, he had told him that "Mr Cavendish wished me to prosecute seriously the profession of physic," but that Banks had discouraged him.[146] Blagden seemed to have abandoned the idea of returning to medicine at about this time, writing plaintively to people about "being now quite out of the practice

---

[140]Sir Joseph Banks to Charles Blagden, n.d. /after 28 Mar. 1789/, BL Add Mss 33272, p. 58.

[141]"Remarks by Mr. Cavendish," Blagden Collection, Misc Notes, Royal Society, No. 65. Charles Blagden to Henry Cavendish, 12 and 26 Mar. 1790, draft, Blagden Letterbook, Royal Society, 7:317 and 7:695. Once again Cavendish made available experimental results of his father, this time a table of the expansion of water with heat. "From the Experiments of Lord Charles Cavendish, Communicated by Mr Henry Cavendish. March 1790," Blagden Collection, Misc. Notes, Royal Society, No. 99.

[142]Charles Blagden, "Report on the Best Method of Proportioning the Excise on Spirituous Liquors," *PT* 80 (1790): 321–45, quotation on 345. Jesse Ramsden published a pamphlet criticizing the report, *An Account of Experiments to Determine the Specific Gravity of Fluids* (London, 1792). Blagden did the experiments all over again to eliminate a source of error, publishing the results in a second paper, "Supplementary Report on the Best Method of Proportioning the Excise upon Spirituous Liquors," *PT* 82 (1792): 425–38. George Gilpin published an immense series of tables, in small print, based on the experiments reported by Blagden: "Tables for Reducing the Quantities by Weight, in Any Mixture of Pure Spirit and Water, to Those by Measure; and for Determining the Proportion, by Measure, of Each of the Two Substances in Such Mixtures," *PT* 84 (1794): 275–382.

[143]Charles Blagden to Sir Joseph Banks, 28 Mar. 1789, BL, Add Mss 33272, pp. 56-57. Sir Joseph Banks to Charles Blagden, 15 July 1789, Blagden Letters, Royal Society, B.39. Charles Blagden to Sir Joseph Banks, 25 July 1789, Blagden Collection, Royal Society, Misc. Matter—Unclassified. Sir Joseph Banks to Charles Blagden, 31 July 1789, Blagden Letters, Royal Society, B.40.

[144]Charles Blagden to Sir Joseph Banks, 27 Mar. 1790, BL, Add Mss 33272, p. 73. Sir Joseph Banks to Charles Blagden, n.d., draft, ibid., 73-74. Charles Blagden to Sir Joseph Banks, 28 and 29 Mar. 1790, 3 Apr. 1790, ibid., 75, 79. Sir Joseph Banks to Charles Blagden, n.d., draft, ibid., 80. Charles Blagden to Sir Joseph Banks, 8 Apr. 1790, ibid., 81.

[145]Henry, Lord Brougham, "Cavendish," in *Lives of Men of Letters and Science Who Flourished in the Time of George III*, vol. 1 (Philadelphia, 1845), 250-59, on 258.

[146]Blagden to Banks, 8 Apr. 1790.

of physic" and therefore unable to advise on remedies,[147] and being as little familiar with inoculation and other topics of medicine "as if I had never been of the profession."[148] Blagden now blamed Banks for encouraging him to abandon his profession and then not compensating him.

There is a draft of a letter in Blagden's papers that may have been addressed to Cavendish but we suspect that it was addressed to their common friend, the always helpful physician William Heberden. It reads: to make Banks's "ungenerous, (if not treacherous) conduct the more evident, let me contrast it with your own. You, to whom I had not had any opportunity of being serviceable, seeing how unwisely I neglected my profession had the goodness not only to advise me to resume it, but likewise to offer that you would bear all the pecuniary risk attending the pursuit, so that my private fortune should at all events remain unimpaired. I am sensible how imprudently I acted in not following your advice; but at that time I had still the weakness to believe Sir J.B.'s professions sincere."[149] Blagden wrote of the "generosity of your conduct in your original offer, in your subsequent present of this house, in your late confirmation of that present, and especially in your further offer when I expected to marry last year." Blagden expected to marry in 1789. The house he lived in, from 1784, was on Gower Street, just a few doors from Cavendish's house on Bedford Square.[150] The reason we think that the benefactor in question is Heberden is the timing and message of a letter from Blagden to Banks in late 1783. In this letter, Blagden spoke of "Heberden's proposal," and he felt out Banks, asking his advice on how to decline the proposal. The proposal had to do with Blagden's practice of medicine; if he did decline, Blagden said, he probably would never have another chance to practice.[151] There is another letter, however, that may have been addressed to Cavendish, in which Blagden spoke of the "liberal offer" the recipient had just made on a house.[152]

This much is clear: in 1789 Blagden was on good terms with Cavendish and bad terms with Banks. That summer, to free himself from his servitude to Banks, as he saw it, Blagden contemplated going abroad with friends, Henry Temple, second viscount Palmerston and his wife, Lady Mary, and staying away all the coming winter.

His concern with that plan was Cavendish, who raised one objection: it would interfere with what Blagden had "more at heart than any object in life," his return to medicine (and possibly marriage too). Blagden thought his chances of practicing medicine at the resorts abroad were as good as in London. But if by being away he would hold up Cavendish in any of his pursuits, he would stay home.[153] Cavendish gave his blessing, and Blagden left with the Palmerstons. Before he did, he sold his house and its furnishings on Gower Street, with the thought that he would never again have a permanent address in England. Persons with messages for him were to be directed to Cavendish's house on Bedford Square. His bureau containing private papers was left in Cavendish's bedroom, and Cavendish was given the key and instructed to open the bureau and keep or burn the papers if Blagden should suffer an accident.[154] Blagden had recently turned forty and his life seemed headed nowhere, as he set out on yet another Continental

---

[147]Charles Blagden to William Farr, 14 Nov. 1785, draft, Blagden Letterbook, Yale.

[148]Charles Blagden to Françoise Delaroche, 1 Dec. 1786, draft, Blagden Letterbook, Yale.

[149]Draft of letter in Blagden Collection, Misc. Notes, Royal Society, No. 224. This letter is after 28 Mar. 1789, and because of the similarity of content and wording to a letter from Blagden to Banks on 8 Apr. 1790, it is probably around the latter date.

[150]Charles Blagden to his brother, John Blagden Hale, /Oct. or Nov. 1784/, draft, Blagden Letterbook, Yale.

[151]Charles Blagden to Sir Joseph Banks, 16 Oct. 1783, BM(NH), DTC 3:127-31.

[152]The letter reads: "Just after you were gone Mr. Hanscombe called here with the inclosed note, & opened it; he had /undeciphered/ before at your house, but having been informed you were gone by to Hampstead came to shew it to me. I am extremely obliged to you for the liberal offer you have made; but as, were I so rich that the sum would be no object to me I should still think it too much for the house, & sho^d probably refuse to give it. I cannot but consider it as totally inequitable that you sho^d give it for me. I therefore do most seriously request that you would refuse to comply with the terms proposed, & wait till an opportunity offers of making a fairer purchase; and in the mean time I will use every means in my power to become reconciled to my present situation." Charles Blagden to /Henry Cavendish?/, n.d., draft, Blagden Collection, Royal Society, Misc. Matter—Unclassified. In 1784 Cavendish still had his country house at Hampstead, the place referred to in the letter above.

[153]Charles Blagden to Henry Cavendish, Aug. 1789, draft, Blagden Letters, Royal Society, 7:694.

[154]Charles Blagden to John Blagden Hale, 17 Sep. 1784; "An Inventory of Furniture etc. Taken September 3.1789 at Dr. Blagden's House in Gower Street Appraised & Sold to Hill Esqr.," Gloucestershire Record Office, D 1086, F 155 and F 157. Charles Blagden to Mr. Lewis, 15 Sep. 1789, Blagden Letterbook, Royal Society, 7:306. Blagden to his brother, 16 Sep. 1789, ibid., 7:309. Blagden to Henry Cavendish, 16 Sep. 1789, Blagden Letters, Royal Society, B.166b.

journey, evidently with gloomy premonitions.

When Blagden's marriage was in prospect, Cavendish entered into his plans in an essential way. In 1789 the potential wife was picked out, and in November of that year Blagden asked his brother to inform him about her. Would she enjoy Blagden's kind of company and "particularly would so far enter into the pursuits of my friend Mr. C. as not to think some portion of time spent in his company tedious? This would be a matter of the utmost consequence to us both. You will easily suppose I do not mean that she should enter into our studies, but simply that she should not find it disagreeable to be present when such matters were the subject of conversation, or when any experiment which had nothing offensive in it, was going on."[155] Blagden contemplated the three of them together, Cavendish, he, and his wife. He was not worried about Cavendish's reaction but hers. Blagden knew Cavendish very well, and his plans to continue his work with Cavendish in the presence of his wife bring into serious doubt the anecdotal absolute misogyny of Cavendish. In one of his letters of reproach, Blagden told Banks that he "had great reason to believe Mr. Cavendish would assist me in making such a settlement as the family could not properly object to."[156] From the letters of 1789 and 1790 we see that Cavendish was a friend to Blagden in need. Blagden did not resume his profession, and the marriage did not happen either. Lord Palmerston did not go on to Italy to spend the winter, as planned, and in the late fall Blagden returned to resume his job as secretary of the Royal Society. In time Blagden's relations with Banks settled down. Out of all that emotional turmoil, nothing much changed, which might be how Blagden wanted it to come out. On the day Cavendish died, Blagden told Banks that Cavendish always knew "what was right for him," that Cavendish was a "true anchor."[157] Blagden admired in Cavendish what he himself lacked.

As Blagden saw it, Cavendish encouraged him in the direction of independence, whereas Banks used him. From Banks's point of view, Blagden had got what he seemed to want, with Banks's help; Banks deserved no blame at all, if anything credit. If Blagden did not know or say what he wanted, there was nothing Banks could do about it. Blagden placed all blame for his unhappiness on Banks, and Banks saw himself as entirely blameless. Neither man showed any insight into their relationship, though Blagden, who experienced what we might call a breakdown, might hardly be expected to.

Blagden made himself easily available, ever offering himself to Banks, with Banks ever accepting. After their quarrel, they resumed their friendship, but it had an edge to it. Banks could be wounding, as he was when Blagden considered stepping down as secretary of the Royal Society. He had been elected to that job for fourteen successive years, and in his opinion he had burned his eyes out for it. It had got so bad that he could no longer read papers at the meetings (with the aid of candle light). But he wanted to leave open the possibility of resuming the job later, and Banks told him, in effect, to forget it. Blagden's "enemies" would bring up his absences on his travels, and they would accuse him of "not cultivating science with the same ardor as you have formerly done, owing to the habits you have lately adopted of mixing much in the gay circles of the more elevated ranks of society."[158] Blagden replied with indignation: he had "never performed the office so well" as he had last winter.[159] Blagden resigned for good in the winter of 1797.[160]

One thing did change at the time of Blagden's charges against Banks, and probably because of them. The relationship between Blagden and Cavendish was less close afterwards. Like their original understanding, their new one, whatever it was, was evidently not written down. We can safely assume that Cavendish did not want to quarrel with Banks, and it might have seemed to him prudent to keep an impartial distance from both parties. We assume that the distancing was desired by Blagden too.

As with Banks, with Cavendish Blagden

---

[155]Charles Blagden to his brother, John Blagden Hale, 13 Nov. 1789, draft, Blagden Papers, Royal Society, box 5, folder 49.

[156]Charles Blagden to Sir Joseph Banks, 8 Apr. 1790, BL Add Mss 33272, p. 81.

[157]24 Feb. 1810, Blagden Diary, Royal Society, 5:426.

[158]Joseph Banks to Charles Blagden, 27 Apr. 1797, Blagden Letters, Royal Society, B.44.

[159]Charles Blagden to Joseph Banks, 17 Apr. 1797, BL Add Mss 33272, pp. 158-59.

[160]He resigned on 30 Nov. 1797. The letter of resignation is in his papers, undated and without address. It begins: "The inflammation of my eyes . . ." Blagden Collection, Royal Society, Misc. Matter—Unclassified.

continued to have a close association. Blagden never doubted that in the case of his friend Cavendish, he was in the presence of greatness. Writing to Banks from Paris in 1802, Blagden compared Cavendish and Laplace: "Laplace, who is as much superior among them here as Mr Cavendish is with us."[161] On Cavendish's death eight years later, Blagden wrote to a correspondent in Paris that Cavendish was "by much the best philosopher in my opinion that we have, or have had, in my time, at the R.S."[162]

[161]Sir Charles Blagden to Sir Joseph Banks, 1 Apr. 1802, BL Add Mss 33272, pp. 172-73.
[162]Sir Charles Blagden to B Delessert, 20 Mar. 1810, Blagden Letters, Royal Society, D 44g.

CHAPTER 7

❦

Weighing the World

Cavendish lived all of his adult life in and around London in solid houses with servants to protect his privacy. These houses he turned into places of science, where the drama of his life was staged, unseen, internal, and profound.[1]

In 1810, an anonymous biographical notice of Cavendish was published in the *Gentleman's Magazine*.[2] The author was Blagden, we know, because his papers contain an otherwise unidentified fragment of the notice in his handwriting. The circumstances are explained in two letters to Blagden from Lord George Cavendish, Henry Cavendish's main heir and in entries in Blagden's diary. Evidently, Lord George had written a sketch of Cavendish's character to go in the papers when Cavendish's remains were removed from Clapham, and at dinner with Banks and Blagden, he asked Blagden to "fill it up."[3] Blagden wrote his sketch then and showed it to Banks and Lord George the next day.[4] Lord George wished that Blagden had altered the part about Cavendish's character, which probably referred to what he himself had written, and he said he would consult with the duke of Devonshire about this family matter.[5] Lord George next wrote to Blagden that the duke of Devonshire had approved his sketch of Cavendish's "character" for the "Publick Papers." In a second letter, written the next day, Lord George informed Blagden that some corrections Blagden meanwhile had sent him had arrived too late (they had not, as it turned out), since being concerned that nothing about Cavendish should appear in print before Blagden's notice, he had already sent the notice to press. At the bottom of Lord George's letter, Blagden wrote out again the three corrections he had requested, two of which are of no consequence here. The third correction says that Blagden wanted Cavendish's habits to be called not "retired" but "secluded."[6] "Retired" and "secluded" each conveyed much the same impression, but there was a nuance. "Retired" suggested withdrawn or inactive, "secluded" shut up.[7] The second word, Blagden (and perhaps Lord George) decided, was the better (and more forceful) word for Cavendish.

The best word for characterizing Cavendish's biographers is *bewilderment*. Cavendish's scientific manuscripts confront them with studies on every topic in the physical sciences, carried out independently of one another, without rhyme or reason other than with the implicit goal of totality of understanding. That is a first impression. If the biographers persist, they see that the studies fall into groups, connected by large goals, which belong to the goals of the science of Cavendish's time. One extended group of papers has to do with his researches on the earth, including its gaseous envelope and its location and orientation in the solar system. Researches on the earth that were most significant for eighteenth-century science tended to involve numbers of investigators working together, in contrast to researches on general laws of nature, which tended to be done by individuals working on their own, at least in the first instance. In the several organized researches on the earth that Cavendish took part in, he worked with others while preserving his measure of essential privacy. In his last published experiment, the determination of the mean density of the earth, he worked in seclusion in the ordinary sense of the word. He brought the earth into his place of seclusion, his home, where he experimented on it virtually alone.

---

[1]The discussion in this chapter is taken from Russell McCormmach, "The Last Experiment of Henry Cavendish," in *'No Truth Except in Details': Essays in Honor of Martin J. Klein*, eds. A. J. Kox and D. M. Siegel (Dordrecht: Kluwer Academic Publishers, 1995), 1–30. We acknowledge permission to use material from this chapter: Copyright Kluwer Academic Publishers 1995: reprinted by permission of Kluwer Academic Publishers.

[2]*Gentleman's Magazine*, March 1810, 292.

[3]If we get the sense of the entry right: 6 Mar. 1810, Blagden diary, 5:back p. 431.

[4]7 Mar. 1810, Blagden diary, 5:431.

[5]8 Mar. 1810, Blagden diary, 5:back p. 431 and p. 432.

[6]Lord George Cavendish to Sir Charles Blagden, 9 and 10 Mr. 1810, Blagden Letters, Royal Society, G.17 and G.19.

[7]"Shut up apart" is an eighteenth-century meaning of "seclude." *Oxford Universal Dictionary*, 3rd rev. ed., 1935, p. 1825.

Then because it was science he was doing, he communicated his results. The experiment of weighing the world came to be known to scientists as *the Cavendish experiment*. It was well named.

The Density of the Earth

Cavendish's interest in weighing the world is on record in a letter he wrote to John Michell in 1783. He knew that Michell was already in trouble with the telescope he was building because of its tremendous scale. He wrote: "if your health does not allow you to go on with that /the telescope/ I hope it may at least permit the easier and less laborious employment of weighing the world."[8] This letter of 1783 contains the earliest mention of Michell's "weighing the world." "Experiments to Determine the Density of the Earth," Cavendish's paper in the *Philosophical Transactions* for 1798, opens with an explanation of his and Michell's connection.

> Many years ago, the late Rev. John Michell, of this Society, contrived a method of determining the density of the earth, by rendering sensible the attraction of small quantities of matter; but, as he was engaged in other pursuits, he did not complete the apparatus till a short time before his death, and did not live to make any experiments with it. After his death the apparatus came to the Rev. Francis John Hyde Wollaston, Jacksonian Professor at Cambridge, who, not having conveniences for making experiments with it, in the manner he could wish, was so good as to give it to me.[9]

Michell died in 1793, and he had not finished building his apparatus until shortly before then. Michell's instruments and, probably, some apparatus were left to his former college at Cambridge, Queen's.[10] Just how the apparatus came into Wollaston's hands Cavendish does not say, nor does he say who initiated the gift of the apparatus from Wollaston to Cavendish, though from all that passed before, it was almost surely Cavendish. In any event, Michell, Cavendish, and Wollaston were all on familiar terms. Wollaston belonged to a dynasty of men of science and the Church, all of whom, like all of the principals in weighing the world—Cavendish, Maskelyne, and Michell—were Cambridge men. The educational, scientific, and personal connections between the Wollastons, Michell, and Cavendish are hard to keep in mind, given the large number of Wollastons and the family parsimony in assigning first and middle

names.[11] It is—this is the point—entirely reasonable that Michell's apparatus should end up in Cambridge with one of the Wollastons, and that Cavendish knew its whereabouts, coveted it, and was given it to use.

Cavendish was nearly sixty-seven when he weighed the world. His most recent publication of experiments had been on chemistry ten years before, and it would have been his last if it had not been for Michell's work, which Cavendish finished for him. Cavendish's experiment was, in reality, several "experiments," seventeen in number, each consisting of many trials. The first experiment was done on 5 August 1797, and the first eight were done a few days apart through the rest of August up to the last week in September. The remaining nine experiments were done the following year, from the end of April to the end of May. The paper reporting the experiments was read to the Royal Society on 21 June 1798, just three weeks after the last experiment. The long paper with its lengthy calculations must have been largely written by the end.

---

[8]Cavendish added: "for my own part I do not know whether I had not rather hear that you had given the exper. /of weighing the world/ a fair trial than that you had finished the great telescope." Henry Cavendish to John Michell, 27 May 1783, draft, Cavendish Mss, New Correspondence.

[9]Henry Cavendish, "Experiments to Determine the Density of the Earth," *PT* 88 (1798): 469–526; in Cavendish, *Sci. Pap.* 2: 249-86, on 249.

[10]"Michell, John," *DNB* 13:333-34, on 334.

[11]Wollaston's father, Francis, born the same year as Cavendish, took his degree in law but entered the Church instead. He had a passion for astronomy, and he had his own observatory with first-class instruments. With at least that much in common, in 1768 Cavendish brought Francis Wollaston as a guest to a meeting of the Royal Society on 8 Dec. 1768; Wollaston's certificate is dated 12 Jan. 1769 and signed by Cavendish along with Maskelyne and several other prominent members; Wollaston was elected that year. Royal Society, JB26:1767–1770; Royal Society, Certificates, 3:65; "Wollaston, Francis," *DSB* 21:778–79. One of Francis Wollaston's sons, William Hyde Wollaston, was an eminent chemist. Cavendish proposed him, as he had his father, as a member of the Royal Society, and he too was elected: Royal Society, Certificates, 5 (9 May 1793); "Wollaston, William Hyde," *DNB* 21: 782–87, on 782. Another of Francis's sons, George Hyde Wollaston, was one of Cavendish's neighbors at Clapham Common, where Cavendish performed his experiment on the density of the earth. "Wollaston of Shenton," *Burke's Genealogical and Heraldic History of the Landed Gentry* (London, 1939), 2479. George Hyde Wollaston's house as well as Cavendish's are on the map of Clapham Common, "Perambulation of Clapham Common 1800," from C. Smith, *Actual Survey of the Road from London to Brighthelmston*. Yet another of Francis's sons was Francis John Hyde Wollaston, Jacksonian Professor of Chemistry, from whom Cavendish received Michell's apparatus. Michell's association with the Wollastons went back as far as Cavendish's. To give but one indication: as a recently elected Fellow of the Royal Society, Michell's first recommendation for a new member, in 1762, was for Francis's youngest brother, George Wollaston, Fellow and Mathematical Lecturer of Sidney-Sussex College, Cambridge. "Wollaston, Francis," 779.

Cavendish began the report of his work proper with what in an experimental paper is a promising beginning: "The apparatus is very simple." The apparatus, which Cavendish largely remade, is in truth easily described. Its moving part was a six-foot wooden rod suspended horizontally by a slender wire attached to its center, and suspended from each end of the rod was a lead ball two inches across. The whole was enclosed in a narrow wooden case to protect it from wind. Toward the ends of the case and on opposite sides of it were two massive lead balls, or "weights," each weighing about 350 pounds. The weights could be swung to either side of the case to approach the lead balls inside, and in the course of the experiment this was regularly done. The gravitational attraction between the weights and the balls was able to draw the rod sensibly aside. From the angle of twist of the rod, the density of the earth could be deduced; but for this to be done, the force needed to turn the rod against the force of the twisted wire had to be known, and for this it was necessary to set the rod moving freely as a horizontal pendulum and to observe the time of its vibrations.

To the modern reader the way Cavendish got from the mutual attraction of the lead "weights" and balls to the density of the earth seems roundabout, which is to be expected. Cavendish did not write equations, and he did not distinguish between weight and mass, and so no gravitational constant appears. He introduced an artifice, a simple pendulum, the length of which was one half the length of the beam of his apparatus. The simple pendulum, which was not part of the experiment but only of the analysis, oscillates in a vertical plane under the action of the earth's gravity. It does not look at all like Cavendish's horizontal beam oscillating freely as a horizontal pendulum, but the two pendulums are described mathematically the same way; they are both "pendulums" performing simple harmonic motion. By combining and manipulating the formulas that relate the forces on the two pendulums, certain proportionalities result, which include the wanted expression for the density of the earth in terms of the measures of the apparatus and two things observed in the experiment, the period of the torsion balance and the displacement of the beam when the weights were swung from one side to the other. The reason why the earth enters this expres-

sion is that the "weights" have weight owing to the attraction of the earth, which is proportional to the matter of the earth. Using modern terminology and notation, this derivation can be done with a few lines of equations, but they would not correspond to Cavendish's reasoning.[12]

In the earlier experiment of the Royal Society on the attraction of mountains, it was an open question whether or not a mass the size of a mountain was sufficient to cause a detectable effect. In Cavendish's experiment, the detectable effect was readily achieved by weights small enough to fit into an apparatus. The lead balls were what he "weighed" with his apparatus, thereby weighing, indirectly, the world. This was not an obvious weighing like the chemist's weighing with his balance (Cavendish, the chemist, was renowned for his weighings of this sort).[13] Rather it measured the attraction of lead spheres, which led by a chain of theoretical arguments to the weight, or density, of the world.

Cavendish's experiment was a precision measurement of a seemingly inaccessible magnitude. Newton had made the calculation of the attraction of two one-foot spheres of earth matter placed one-quarter inch apart to show that the force was too feeble to produce a sensible motion; he thought it would take a month for the spheres to cross the quarter inch separating them.[14] The force between the spheres in Cavendish's experiment was only

---

[12]The modern analysis of Cavendish's experiment is simpler than Cavendish's. But what modern accounts usually say Cavendish did, he did not do. The universal gravitational constant he did not derive, though it can be readily derived from the results of his experiment. This is the point of B. E. Clotfelter, "The Cavendish Experiment as Cavendish Knew It," *American Journal of Physics* 55 (1987): 210-13. Cavendish's object was to determine the density of the earth, and there is nothing in his analysis to require the gravitational constant, nor is there any reason why, at that time, he should have regarded it as desirable. Although it is not necessary to derive the gravitational constant, the unit of force suggests it, and the unit of force did not yet exist for expressing $F = GM_1M_2/r^2$, the attraction between two masses, M_1 and M_2, separated by distance r.

[13]The chemist's balance *was* used to determine the earth's density, but later, in attempts to improve upon Cavendish's experiment; notably by P. J. G. von Jolly in 1878-80, J. H. Poynting in 1890, and F. Richarz and O. Krigar–Menzel in 1898. Edward Thorpe, "Introduction," Cavendish *Sci. Pap.* 2:1-74, on 72-73.

[14]In his *System of the World*, Newton asked why, since all bodies attract, we do not see them do it on earth. His answer was that "experiments in terrestrial bodies do not count," and the reason they do not he showed by a calculation: "a sphere of one foot in diameter, and of a like nature to the earth, would attract a small body placed near its surface with a force 20000000 times less than the earth would

PLATE XIII. Apparatus for Weighing the World. In Cavendish's modification of John Michell's apparatus, the large spheres R are the weights that attract the small spheres, which are suspended from the arm, which in turn is suspended by the fine wire gl. The room in which the apparatus is housed is also shown and as well as the arrangements for viewing it from outside the room. "Experiments to Determine the Density of the Earth." *Philosophical Transactions* 88 (1798): 526.

1/50,000,000 part of their weight, so that the minutest disturbance could destroy the accuracy of it. To guard against any disturbance, Cavendish placed the apparatus in a small, closed "room," about ten feet high and as many feet across. From outside the room, he observed the deflection and vibration of the rod by means of telescopes installed at each end. Verniers at the ends of the rod enabled him to read its position to within 1/100th of an inch. The only light admitted into the room was provided by a lamp near each telescope, which was focused by a convex lens onto the vernier. The rod and weights were manipulated from outside the room. In doing the experiment, Cavendish brought the massive weights close to the case, setting the rod in motion. Then peering through the telescope into the semi-dark room, he took readings from the illuminated vernier at the turning points of the motion, and he timed the passing of the rod past two close-lying, predetermined divisions. The experiment was a trial of the observer's patience: depending on the stiffness of the suspension wire, a single vibration could take up to a half hour, and a single experiment might take two and one half hours.

Much of the time Cavendish spent on the experiment was devoted to errors and corrections. He traced a minute irregular motion of the rod to a difference of temperature between the case and the weights, which gave rise to air currents. One entirely negligible correction he published as an appendix to his paper. This was the attraction on the rod and balls of the mahogany case that enclosed them, the counterpart of Cavendish's previous calculation of the attraction of ideal mountains: it amounted to an exhaustive summing of the attractions of the box on the movable part of the apparatus, only instead of the cones and other figures he had used to represent mountains, here he used rectangular planes to represent the regular boards of the wooden case. It is fitting that

---

do if placed near its surface; but so small a force could produce no sensible effect. If two such spheres were distant but by $1/4$ of an inch, they would not, even in spaces void of resistance, come together by the force of their mutual attraction in less than a month's time." Isaac Newton, *Sir Isaac Newton's Mathematical Principles of Natural Philosophy and His System of the World*, trans. A. Motte, rev. F. Cajori, 2 vols. (Berkeley and Los Angeles: University of California Press, 1962) 2:569-70.

Cavendish's paper should read like a dissertation on errors. Errors were, after all, the point at which he had entered the subject: the first evidence of his interest in the density of the earth was his criticism of astronomical observations that ignored the attraction of mountains.

"To great exactness," Cavendish concluded, the mean density of the earth is 5.48 times the density of water.[15] The number was the object of Cavendish's last experiment, the work of ten months near the end of his life and the reward for twenty-five years of tenacity.

In addition to the precision of the technique and to the knowledge of the earth's interior it offered, there was another reason, we believe, why Cavendish did this last major experiment. He had long since completed the principal researches of his middle years: his fundamental researches in electricity, chemistry, and heat, for which he is famous. By the end of the eighteenth century, in all of these fields scientific opinion had moved away from his. But his experiment on gravity was not subject to the vagaries of scientific opinion in the same way. This is not to say that he did not expect criticism. In any case, he got it.

Despite and, in part, because of his last experiment, Cavendish had not freed himself from the claims of the earlier preferred method of determining the density of the earth. His paper brought a prompt response from Charles Hutton, who had done the calculations on the mountain Shiehallien. The paper in manuscript had been given to him by Maskelyne, and it had not given him pleasure. Just a year or so before Cavendish's paper, Hutton had called attention to his calculation of the density of the earth from the Royal Society's experiment. In the article "Earth" in his *Mathematical and Philosophical Dictionary*, Hutton wrote of the density of the earth: "This I have calculated and deduced from the observations made by Dr. Maskelyne, Astronomer Royal, at the mountain Shehallien, in the years 1774, 5, and 6." In this work he took pride, and then came Cavendish's paper. On the same day that Hutton received a second copy of Cavendish's paper from the Royal Society, he wrote to Cavendish from the Royal Military Academy in Woolwich where he worked. He went straight to the point: Cavendish's "ingenious" paper, which made the density of the

earth 5.48 that of water, concluded with a paragraph that called attention to the earlier, much lower value of $4\frac{1}{2}$, in the "calculation of which" he, Hutton, had borne "so great a share." Anyone who has looked at Hutton's calculations can sympathize with the plaintive note. Hutton thought that Cavendish's wording hinted at inaccuracies in his calculations and seemed to disparage the Royal Society's experiment. That experiment, Hutton reminded Cavendish, had determined not the density of the earth but only the ratio of that density to the density of the mountain, 9 to 5. Hutton had supposed that the density of the mountain is the density of ordinary stone, $2\frac{1}{2}$ times that of water, but the actual density of the mountain was unknown, as Hutton had pointed out at the time. All that was known was that Shiehallien was a "mass of stone." Hutton now believed that the mountain's density was higher, 3 or even $3\frac{1}{2}$, which would then make the density of the earth "between 5 and 6"—or exactly where Cavendish had put it—and "probably nearer the latter number." The Royal Society had not finished its experiment because it had not determined the density of stone, Hutton said. Even now, he hoped that the Society would finish it, so that "an accurate conclusion, as to the density of the earth, may be thence obtained."[16]

Cavendish believed that he had just drawn that accurate conclusion and that it was 5.48. Hutton wanted the density of the earth to depend on what could never be made precise, the density of "stone." At the bottom of Hutton's letter to him, Cavendish drafted a brief response. Without referring to Hutton's guesswork or excuses, it read: "According to the experiments made by Dr. Maskelyne on the attraction of the hill Shiehallien the density of the earth is $4\frac{1}{2}$ times that of water." As to which density, his or the Society's, was better, Cavendish did not commit himself, since the Society's determination was "affected by irregularities whose quantity I cannot measure."[17]

It would have been known to Cavendish that Hutton had not let go of the problem of

[15]Cavendish, "Experiments to Determine the Density of the Earth," 284.

[16]Charles Hutton to Henry Cavendish, 17 Nov. 1798, Cavendish Mss, New Correspondence.

[17]Ibid. Cavendish, "Experiments to Determine the Density of the Earth," 284.

determining the earth's density by the attraction of mountains. In 1780, two years after his calculation of the density of the earth, Hutton had published another paper following up "the great success of the experiment" on Shiehallien to "determine the universal attraction of matter," in which he repeated his wish that more experiments of the same kind would be made.[18] Hutton was to have his wish but not his way. In 1811 he got John Playfair to do an investigation of the structure of the rocks of Shiehallien, and Playfair found the density of the rocks to be between 2.7 and 2.8. Since Hutton had guessed 2.5, Playfair's result raised his calculated density of the earth, but only slightly, to 4.7. Cavendish's density, 5.48, is much closer to, within one percent of, the accepted value today, 5.52. Recall that the Charles Hutton of the attraction of mountains is the Charles Hutton who had lost his job as foreign secretary at the Royal Society in the early 1780s, precipitating a bitter feud known as the Society's "dissensions." Maskelyne, who had brought Hutton into the experiment on the attraction of mountains, had earlier been a vigorous supporter of Hutton's losing side in the dissensions. By contrast Cavendish had given decisive support to Hutton's nemesis, the Society's president, Joseph Banks. If this unhappy experience of Hutton at the Royal Society and the now suspected opposition of Cavendish had anything to do with his continuing efforts to keep alive the method of the attraction of mountains as an alternative to Michell and Cavendish's method, it is impossible to say now. Hutton had a vested interest in the earlier method, after all. Hutton lived to 1823, long enough to know of the high regard in which Cavendish's experiment was held, though not long enough for him to know that it was *the* Cavendish experiment.

The Cavendish Experiment

From Paris Cavendish was asked to repeat his own experiment on the density of the earth. Blagden wrote to Banks in 1802, telling him of a conversation with Laplace about Cavendish's experiment. He thought that Banks might want to pass along what Laplace had said, which was that the attraction Cavendish measured might involve electricity as well as gravity. Laplace also expressed the wish that "Mr. Cav. would repeat it /the experiment/ with another body of greater specific

gravity than lead."[19] So far as we know, if Cavendish got the message he never repeated the experiment, but there was no need to; others would do it, and many times, ever with the desire to achieve greater accuracy and perfection. Experiments on the attraction of mountains ceased to be regarded as a precise way to determine the earth's density, though the attraction of mountains remained a consideration as a source of error in astronomical measurements of location and distance.[20]

The Cavendish experiment outlived the problem of the density of the earth, and that it did so has to do not only with its precision but as well with its subject, a fundamental and still enigmatic force of nature, gravity, with its characteristic universal constant. It became the experiment to determine "big *G*," as C. V. Boys explained in 1892:

> Owing to the universal character of the constant G, it seems to me to be descending from the sublime to the ridiculous to describe the object of this / Cavendish's and now Boys's/ experiment as finding the mass of the earth or the mean density of the earth, or less accurately the weight of the earth.[21]

Still today, three hundred years after Newton and two hundred after Cavendish, gravity is at the center of physical research. To quote from a recent publication by contemporary researchers in gravity: The

> most important advance in experiments on gravitation and other delicate measurements was the introduction of the torsion balance by Michell and its use by Cavendish. . . .

---

[18]Charles Hutton, "Calculations to Determine at What Point in the Side of a Hill Its Attraction Will be the Greatest, etc," *PT* 70 (1780): 1-14, on 3.

[19]Charles Blagden to Joseph Banks, 1 Apr. 1802, BL Add Mss 33272, pp. 172-73. Notable repetitions include R. Reich, *Versuche über die Mittlere Dichtigkeit der Erde mittelst der Drehwage* (Freiburg, 1838); Francis Baily, *Memoirs of the /Royal/ Astronomical Society of London* 14 (1843): 1-120; C. V. Boys, "On the Newtonian Constant of Gravitation," *PT* 186 (1895): 1-72.

[20]For example, John Henry Pratt's criticism of the observations taken in the Great Indian Survey in the middle of the nineteenth century owing to the neglect of the attraction of the Himalayas and his own calculation of their attraction: Mott T. Greene, *Geology in the Nineteenth Century: Changing Views of a Changing World* (Ithaca and London: Cornell University Press, 1982), 238- 43.

[21]Boys is quoted by Clotfelter on the shift in interest in Cavendish's experiment: "The Cavendish Experiment as Cavendish Knew It," 211. Boys first calculated *G* from the Cavendish experiment, and then from it he calculated the mean density of the earth. Conversely to obtain *G* from the density of the earth, Boys said he could have recalculated the attraction of the earth by viewing it as an ellipsoid of similar shells of equal density, which is the way J. H. Poynting had calculated it in 1892. Boys recommended using a room with a more uniform temperature than Oxford's, a detail that will be appreciated by anyone who knows Oxford and the uniform chill of its rooms. His accuracy was very great, despite his room; he believed that his *G* had an accuracy of 1 in 10,000.

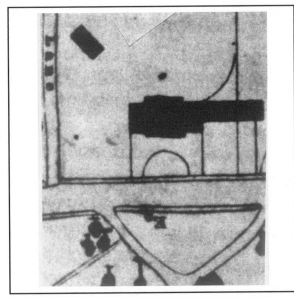

PLATE XIV. Plan of Clapham. This detail from "Batten's Plan of Clapham" of 1827 shows the shape of Cavendish's house seventeen years after his death and twenty-nine years after his experiment on the density of the earth. To the right of the house, it shows an outbuilding about 58 by 26 feet, the long dimension of which is oriented in the east-west direction. Cavendish refers to the arm of his apparatus aligned in the magnetic east-west, which suggests that this outbuilding is where Cavendish performed the experiment. This reasoning is given, and this detail from Batten's plan is reproduced, in P. F. Titchmarsh, "The Michell-Cavendish Experiment," *The School Science Review*, no. 162 (March 1966): 321–22.

It has been the basis of all the most significant experiments on gravitation ever since.[22]

That is why Cavendish's experiment became *the* Cavendish experiment.

Cavendish initiated no more ambitious programs of research. His only publication after his paper on the density of the earth came some ten years later, a short paper on a typical concern, a way to improve the accuracy of astronomical instruments.[23] Except for going regularly to meetings of the Royal Society and to other meetings of scientific men, he stayed home, which is where he had done his experiment on the density of the earth. Long after Cavendish's death, Clapham Common neighbors would point to the house and tell their children that that was where the world was weighed. Although Cavendish was not the first owner of that house, after his death it was known as *the Cavendish house*.[24]

The world of science has changed. John Henry Poynting, for his repetition of the Cavendish experiment a hundred years later, received a grant from the Royal Society, and he was given a workplace in an institute, in the laboratory at Cambridge named after Henry Cavendish. Clerk Maxwell, the first

director of the Cavendish Laboratory, gave Poynting permission to do the experiment.[25] Poynting's repetition of the Cavendish experiment belongs to physics after it had become an established discipline with its principal home in places of higher learning, complete with institutes, directors, and grants. Cavendish did his experiment at home.

In connection with the determination of the density of the earth, Cavendish brought into his home one person from the outside, George Gilpin, not a member of the Royal Society but its clerk. Replacing Cavendish at the telescope, Gilpin made the last two experiments. He was no doubt cast by Cavendish as a detector of error as well as a confirming witness.

Cavendish's weighing of the world had a precedent in William Gilbert's experiments on magnetism two hundred years earlier, reported in his *De magnete*, the classic work of early experimental physics. "By forming a little load-stone into the shape of the earth," Gilbert "found the properties of the whole earth, in that little body," on which he could experiment at will.[26] Mountains high on the earth and open to the sky could deflect weights, and the earth could be weighed that way,

[22]A. H. Cook, "Experiments on Gravitation," in *Three Hundred Years of Gravitation*, ed. S. W. Hawking and W. Israel (Cambridge: Cambridge University Press, 1987), 51-79, on 52. Appropriately, Cook talks of the Cavendish experiment only in connection with G and not with the density of the earth. Only recently, he says, has the accuracy of G been improved upon over what can be obtained from Cavendish's own experiment, and although in the study of materials we can achieve an accuracy of 1 part in 10^{12}, we still know G only to about 1 part in 10^3. Cook speaks of the use of the torsion balance in electrostatics as well as in gravitation. In a footnote in his paper of 1798, on p. 250, Cavendish too referred to Coulomb, who had used an apparatus of the same kind for measuring small electric and magnetic attractions. Cavendish said that "Mr. Michell informed me of his intention of making this experiment, and of the method he intended to use, before the publication of any of Mr. Coulomb's experiments." From what Cavendish knew of Michell, the torsion balance was independently invented by him and by Coulomb. Coulomb's biographer C. Stewart Gillmor discusses the question of priority in *Coulomb and the Evolution of Physics and Engineering in Eighteenth-Century France* (Princeton, 1971), 163-65.
[23]Henry Cavendish, "On an Improvement in the Manner of Dividing Astronomical Instruments," *PT* 99 (1809): 221-31.
[24]According to hearsay, Cavendish weighed the world not in his house proper but in an outbuilding in his garden. For our discussion, it does not really matter; Cavendish weighed the world at home.
[25]J. H. Poynting, "On a Determination of the Mean Density of the Earth and the Gravitation Constant by Means of the Common Balance," *PT* 182 (1892): 565–656, on 565–66. It all comes together: Poynting did this experiment in Cavendish's spirit, to improve upon Cavendish's accuracy, in the Cavendish Laboratory directed by Maxwell, who edited Henry Cavendish's electrical paper and whose edition is reprinted as the first volume of Cavendish's *Scientific Papers*.
[26]Kenelm Digby, 1645, quoted in the "Biographical Memoir," in William Gilbert, *De magnete*, 1600, trans P. Fleury Mottelay (1893; New York: Dover reprint, 1958), xviii.

and Cavendish had worked with the astronomers who weighed it that way, but his own experiment was better suited to his temperament. With it he did not need to go out into the world to know it; he could know it and know it more precisely by staying home and manipulating his apparatus and reasoning from universal principles. The world came to Cavendish. (Another way of viewing it is that Henry Cavendish was a *Cavendish*, and the Cavendishes liked to stay home and let the world come to them.) Cavendish stayed at home, inside of a building, looking inside of a room and through a slit in a case inside of which was the world—his world, on his terms.

It has been noted that while there is much talk about the effect of the scientist's personality on science, there is little of the other, perhaps more profound, effect of science on the personality.[27] In Cavendish we see both effects, mutually reinforcing. From the beginning Cavendish turned away from what he found difficult, ordinary society, and toward nature and its understanding through science, and through science he came into a society he found, if not comfortable, to his liking. Those traits that in his casual contact with people gave rise to anecdotes about his eccentricities were precisely the traits that in his scientific work made him extraordinary. To do science, Cavendish did not have to overcome his extreme diffidence; he had only to adapt it to science. The experiment on the density of the earth is arguably not Cavendish's most important experiment, but if it is looked at for what it reveals about the experimenter—as if it were a diary, which he did not keep, or a formal portrait, which he did not allow—it is the most expressive of his experiments.

No preliminary manuscripts connected with the experiment on the earth's density have survived or, anyway, surfaced.[28] That cannot be said of any other important experiment by Cavendish. The quirky history of his papers after his death enabled Cavendish this time to exclude not only his contemporaries but his biographers as well. With his paper of 1798, he appeared before the world finished, complete.

The man who weighed the world was a secluded figure and yet a constant companion of men of science, posing and symbolizing the historian's problem of the relationship of the individual person or event to collective actions. Through the experiment on the density of the earth, Cavendish worked

out his private destiny, and at the same time he was the able representative of a general development in science, the drive for precision, which began in his time and which has gathered force ever since.[29] Cavendish worked secluded at Clapham Common, but his experiment belonged to a public world of established scientific problems, instrumental possibilities, and interested, qualified parties.[30]

The Cavendish experiment did more than provide precise information about the earth; it became an ideal of scientific practice. Cavendish was not a "geophysicist" or a "physicist" but a universal natural philosopher in a time when the discipline of physics was just emerging. In Germany, for example, the early physics journal was the *Annalen der Physik und Chemie*. When after eight years of operation its founder, F. A. C. Gren, died—this was in 1798, the year of Cavendish's experiment—its new editor, L. W. Gilbert, wrote a foreword to the new beginning under him, and under the new, restricted title, *Annalen der Physik*. Explaining that the richest vein of material for his journal would continue to be mined from foreign sources, Gilbert trusted that in his journal, work by the best physicists in Germany would stand side by side with the best work from abroad, such as Cavendish's experiment on the density of the earth with its wonderful "exactness."[31] Cavendish's

[27]Philip J. Hilts, Scientific Temperaments: Three Lives in Contemporary Science (New York: Simon and Schuster, 1982), 11.

[28]One manuscript should be mentioned nevertheless. Cavendish experimentally determined what we would call the moduli of bend and twist of wires and glass tubes by comparing the vibrations of his twisting apparatus with the vibrations of a simple seconds pendulum. He tried wires of different materials, iron, copper, silver, and brass, suspending from them rods of wood, brass, and zinc. His undated experiments on twist show Cavendish's interest in torsion, but they are not necessary for his experiment with Michell's torsion balance. "Exper. on Twisting of Wire Tried by the Time of Vibration," Henry Cavendish Mss VI(b), 22.

[29]It was only at the end of the eighteenth century that precision measurement "becomes a really essential factor in scientific progress." Maurice Daumas, "Precision of Measurement and Physical and Chemical Research in the Eighteenth Century," in A. C. Crombie, ed., *Scientific Change...* (New York: Basic Books, 1963), 418–30, on 429.

[30]The interested parties were experimenters, instrument-makers, astronomers, mathematicians, and the practical "lesser" men whose collaboration is the subject of E. G. R. Taylor, *The Mathematical Practitioners of Hanoverian England, 1714–1840* (Cambridge, 1966).

[31]L. W. Gilbert, "Vorrede," *Annalen der Physik* 1 (1799): unnumbered page in the three-page foreword. This quotation connects Henry Cavendish with the starting point of Christa Jungnickel and Russell McCormmach, *Intellectual Mastery of Nature*, 2 vols. (Chicago: Chicago University Press, 1986) 1: 35.

experiment, in this sense, belongs to the history of physics of the nineteenth and twentieth centuries.

In the usual biographical sense, of course, Cavendish's experiment belonged exactly to the time when it was made. The experiment made history, but there was no history in it. We will explain. Cavendish always kept a number of clocks going. He compared them, used them in his researches, and consulted them in his daily life (and, by the standard portrait, was ruled by them). Time for him was a measure of events, but it was not a generator of events, a point of view which more than his phlogistic ideas or anything else places him within a certain framework. The nature of his interest in time is shown by his study of the Hindoo civil year; based on astronomical periodicities, the civil year implied nothing new in the world. In his work on heat, Cavendish arrived at the first law of thermodynamics, but he did not state the second, which implies the physical directionality of time. He rarely dated his experiments, nor was there need to, given the kind of questions he asked of nature. His observations in the field led him to the chemistry of minerals but not to ideas about an earth evolving in time. His last published experiment, the subject of this chapter, replaced the static chemical balance with the torsion balance, but it was a balance all the same. The secular changes in his readings during the weighing of the world were not a datum but an erratum. This last experiment of the master experimenter was one of the great dynamic experiments of the passing age, and it was in the vanguard of the emerging physics of precision, but it did not point in the direction of the new history of the earth with its dynamic idea of time. The experiment had been conceived in the period of Cavendish's work, the 1760s to the 1780s. That work was complete unto itself, and it was only by chance that the experiment had had to wait until the end of the century.[32] It was then, just as Cavendish was doing the experiment, that scientists working in the physical and life sciences began fully to appreciate the scale of time and the related significance of development over time. From the middle of the eighteenth century, of course, Buffon, Kant, and other scientific thinkers had proposed impressive, comprehensive conceptions of nature in which the world evolved over eons in concordance with Newtonian principles, but it

would be the scientists who came after Cavendish who would work so intensively within a new world view strongly imprinted by history.[33] The Cavendish experiment was a replication in the laboratory of the workings of the solar system, and as such it belonged to the classical harmony of a certain Newtonian world view. The system of weights that Cavendish observed was dynamic but it was stable too. The same could be said of the Cavendish ideal of the social and political world, which was also passing into history.[34]

In one other respect, Cavendish's last experiment might seem to place him in an age of science about to be superseded. A leading theme of the physical sciences of the nineteenth century was the interconversion of forces. This, however, unlike the historical perspective, would probably have fitted into Cavendish's view of nature. We have had occasion to point out Cavendish's understanding of forces, which seems to have been fairly widely held in Britain in the second half of the eighteenth century. With this understanding, according to which the forces surrounding force-centers alternate between regions of repulsion and regions of attraction, Cavendish rescued his theory of electricity from experimental contradiction, as we have shown. He invoked it again, as we have also shown, to bring his theory of heat into agreement with experience. In his theory of the construction of the magnetic dipping needle, he analyzed the error of the instrument by assuming that the "axis /of the needle/ & plane on which it rolls do not actually touch but are kept from one /another/ by a repulsive force."[35] He incorporated

---

[32]Cavendish's late weighing of the world was a reflection and comment on the whole of his work. By then new tools and concepts for directing the energies of experimental science had arrived or were imminent. The electrical battery was one year away, the wave theory of light was two years away, and the atomic theory of chemistry was only a few years in the future. The relationships between the forces of nature were established by experiments of a new kind (exact but not in the first instance inspired by the ideal of maximum precision). The mathematical development of these relationships led up to the work of Maxwell, our other marker after Newton for placing Cavendish in the history of science.

[33]Stephen Toulmin and June Goldfield, *The Discovery of Time* (New York: Harper & Row, 1965), 125, 266.

[34]Historians of science today are inclined to regard the Newtonian world view as a reflection and rationale of the British monarchy after the Glorious Revolution. Margaret C. Jacob, *The Cultural Meaning of the Scientific Revolution* (Philadelphia: Temple University Press, 1988), 109, 112, 123.

[35]Henry Cavendish, "On the Different Construction of Dipping Needles," Cavendish Mss IX, 40:12–14.

his understanding of forces in his weighing of the world by anticipating the objection that over the small distances of his apparatus the gravitational force might follow a different law. Experience suggested that this possibility could only occur at "very minute distances," where the attraction of cohesion comes into play; he did experiments in which the lead balls of the apparatus were brought to rest as close as possible to the sides of the case, and he found no difference "to be depended on."[36] He examined experimentally the role of heat in magnetism,[37] electricity,[38] and in nearly every other part of natural philosophy. His theoretical work on heat led him to a fully general law of the conservation of force, or energy, the great unifying law of the doctrine of the interconversion of forces.

One of the earliest of the interconversions to be discovered was between electricity and chemistry, and we know that Cavendish took a great interest in this and came often to the laboratory of the Royal Institution to witness the work of that avid developer of electrochemistry, Davy. The pity is that Cavendish did not live another ten years to learn of Hans Christian Oersted's discovery of a fundamental connection between electricity and magnetism and to tell us what he made of it.

---

[36]Cavendish, "Experiments to Determine the Density of the Earth," 284.

[37]Henry Cavendish, "Effect of Heat on Magnets," Cavendish Mss IX, 3.

[38]Henry Cavendish, "Experiments on Electricity," in *The Electrical Researches of the Honourable Henry Cavendish*, ed. J. C. Maxwell (Cambridge: Cambridge University Press, 1879), 104–93, on 180–81.

CHAPTER 8

❧

Last Years

The Duchess and the Philosopher

For most of Henry Cavendish's adult life, the head of the Cavendish family was the fifth duke of Devonshire, the first of the dukes of Devonshire to turn his back on politics. He had that much in common with Henry Cavendish, as he did these traits: he was intelligent, withdrawn, reclusive, long lived, and, perhaps, he "had something of the questioning way of Mr /Henry/ Cavendish."[1] He understood that his distinction was not at all personal but hereditary, and therefore—here he departed from Henry—no individual exertion was required of him. Told he was going to receive the blue ribbon of the Garter, he said he would rather have a blue greatcoat. His way of dealing with the world was to avoid it; he stayed in bed until the middle of the afternoon, when he got up to go to his club, Brooks's, to gamble all night. He was dissolute, unfaithful, and, in his dedicated passivity, fascinating.[2] He disapproved of Henry Cavendish because *he works.*[3] When Henry Cavendish died, the duke took a passing interest in the inheritance. The duke lived only one year beyond this working second cousin of his, Henry.

The fifth duke married Georgiana Spencer. Since the marriage was dynastic, to be eligible they did not need to be compatible, and they were not, although they did have one thing in common: like their great friend Fox, they were both prodigal gamblers.[4] Otherwise the duchess was the duke's temperamental opposite, vivacious, enthusiastic, charming; "her animal spirits were excessive," it was said of her. The duke, by contrast, was said to be a simile for winter.[5]

Like the Cavendishes, Georgiana Spencer's family had sided with the victorious party in the Glorious Revolution. Far more interested in politics than the duke was, the duchess actively supported the (lost) cause of Fox and his followers, the old whigs, who opposed Pitt's power and the new democratizing whigs. She was known as the queen of London fashion, and at the same time she had an avid if unfocused interest in music, literature, history, and science. Like Henry Cavendish she studied music under Giardini, who composed a (somewhat too difficult) piece for her to play.[6] She had a tutor to teach her astronomy using the globes[7] and another to lecture her on chemistry and mineralogy.[8] She and Blagden wrote to one another with scientific news.[9] From abroad she asked Blagden about "any chemical, mineralogical, or philosophical novelty," and she asked him to give her compliments to Cavendish.[10] When she and Blagden happened both to be abroad and meet, they spent an evening with "much talk about chemistry & mineralogy." At another meeting on that trip, they talked with Gibbon about geography, chemistry, and experiments on nerves: "Dss of Devonshire said she was quite wild with studies of that nature: asked much about Mr Cavendish & his pursuits." At yet another meeting: "much talk with the Dss about Sir Jos. Banks's meetings, Mr Cavendish, etc."[11] The

---

[1] The full quotation is: "Talk with D about Dss. 10h: had something of the questioning way of Mr Cavendish." This comparison, we realize, could as easily refer to the duchess as to the duke. 4 Sep. 1794, Blagden Diary, Royal Society, 3:15.

[2] John Pearson, *The Serpent and the Stag: The Saga of England's Powerful and Glamourous Cavendish Family from the Age of Henry the Eighth to the Present* (New York: Holt, Reinhart & Winston, 1983), 122–23.

[3] Francis Bickley, *The Cavendish Family* (London: Constable, 1911), 202.

[4] Hugh Stokes, *The Devonshire House Circle* (London: Herbert Jenkins, 1917), 283–88.

[5] Mary Robinson, *Beaux & Belles of England* (London: Grolier Society, n.d.), 301.

[6] Bickley, *The Cavendish Family*, 241.

[7] Duchess of Devonshire to Countess Spencer, 11 Jan. 1783, Devon. Coll., no. 483.

[8] Charles Blagden to Lord Palmerston, 21 Feb. 1794, draft, Yale, Osborn Collection, box 63/43.

[9] Charles Blagden to the duchess of Devonshire, 4 Jan. and 6 Mar. 1794, Devon. Coll.

[10] Duchess of Devonshire to Charles Blagden, 4 Mar. 1794, Blagden Letters, Royal Society, D.61.

[11] "The Diary of Sir Charles Blagden," ed. Gavin De Beer, *Notes and Records of the Royal Society of London* 8 (1950): 65–89, on 76, 80, 83.

duchess was not just making small talk with Blagden: she called on Cavendish at his house,[12] and Cavendish called on her. When Blagden came to see her at Devonshire House, he found Cavendish there engaged in scientific talk.[13] The duchess and the philosopher were friends.

Coinage of the Realm

In his *Sentimental Journey Through France and Italy*, Laurence Sterne wrote that he had in his pocket "a few king William's shillings as smooth as glass," as he explained: "by jingling and rubbing one against another for seventy years together in one body's pocket or another's, they are become so much alike you can scarce distinguish one shilling from another."[14] That accurate description was made in 1768, just five years before a large recall and recoinage of smooth gold coins.

In 1787 Charles Jenkinson, first earl of Liverpool, had a committee of the privy council look into the state of the coins of the kingdom. Liverpool was president of the committee, and all the principal secretaries of state were members plus one man of science, Banks. For years the committee collected information. In 1796 Banks gave Liverpool a long list of questions about the "extravagant waste" of gold in the wear of coins.[15] Two years later, in 1798, the committee appointed Henry Cavendish and Charles Hatchett to make the necessary experiments, essentially to answer Banks's questions. Soon after this, the engineer John Rennie was brought in to make a complete investigation of the mint. Rennie had worked with Matthew Boulton, who had applied the steam engine to coin-making in Birmingham. Boulton had, in fact, set up a mint, which began by making coins on commission from British territories and from foreign nations and ended up, in 1797, making all of the copper coins for Britain. The London mint lacked steam among other things, and Rennie's report on it was scathing.[16].

Money was the *standard* of the realm: the "standard coin of every country is the measure of property in it," Liverpool said.[17] The most energetic of the masters of the mint up to that time had been Newton, and the connection of the mint with the Royal Society had remained substantial: most of the masters of the mint after Newton had been Fellows of the Royal Society. Cavendish's work for the mint belonged to a tradition of scientific service in the government.

Matthew Boulton and Charles Hatchett both wrote reports on the coinage, which were given to Rennie and then to Banks and to Cavendish for comment. Boulton's report was found useless, Hatchett's useful,[18] and Cavendish recommended that the necessary experiments on coins be done by Hatchett.[19] Cavendish was asked to assist, and if it would help to persuade him (it was not needed), the king would appoint him a privy councillor.[20]

The wider setting of the problem of coinage was the war. The prospect of a Napoleonic invasion in 1797 caused a run on the Bank of England, which suspended payment of its notes in gold. Up to then paper money had been of high denomination only, and traders and wage-earners rarely used it, but now one and two pound notes were introduced. Although as it turned out, the last year that new coinage was minted on any scale was 1798,[21] it was thought important to know how to make gold coins so that they would not wear away so fast.[22]

---

[12]Once when she called on Cavendish, his servant told her he was not well, and she asked Blagden to find out how he was. Sir Charles Blagden to Sir Joseph Banks, 1 Aug. 1795, BL Add Mss 33,272, p. 143. It was not an excuse; Blagden called on Cavendish later that month and found him "decaying: his forehead healing not kindly." 27 Aug. 1795, Blagden Diary, Royal Society, 3:67.

[13]1 Sep. 1794, Blagden Diary, Royal Society, 3:14. The duchess proposed that Cavendish "shew extracts from Js de Physique." On 27 Nov. 1794, Blagden again came across Cavendish at the duchess's: ibid., back p. 33.

[14]Laurence Sterne, *A Sentimental Journey Through France and Italy*, first published in 1768; introduction by V. Woolf (London: Milford, 1951), 165–66.

[15]Unsigned memorandum by Sir Joseph Banks to the second earl of Liverpool, /1796/, in Liverpool Papers, BL Add Mss 38422, vol. 233, ff. 320–24, on 321–22.

[16]J. C. Chaston, "Wear Resistance of Gold Alloys for Coinage: An Early Example of Contract Research," *Gold Bulletin* 7 (1974): 108–12, on 108. John Craig, "The Royal Society and the Royal Mint," *Notes and Records of the Royal Society* 19 (1964): 156–67, on 161–63. Beginning in 1807 Boulton installed steam power in a new mint in London.

[17]"Heads of So Much of Lord Liverpool's Speech at the Council Board . . . Respecting the Coins and Mint of this Kingdom . . .," Liverpool Papers, BL Add Mss 38423, vol. 234, ff. 402–3.

[18]Lord Liverpool to Sir Joseph Banks, 10 May 1798, copy, BM(NH), DTC 3 279–80.

[19]Henry Cavendish to Sir Joseph Banks, 28 July and 6 Aug. 1798, copy, BM(NH), DTC 3. 19–20, 29. Lord Liverpool to Sir Joseph Banks, 13 Feb. 1799, copy, ibid., 195–96. A report was also given, on Cavendish's urging, by A. Robertson, an Oxford scholar who did research on coinage; Robertson's report was delivered and read by Cavendish, to whom Liverpool gave his thanks on 12 Apr. 1799: Liverpool Papers, BL Add Mss, 38424, vol. 235, f. 55.

[20]Lord Liverpool to Joseph Banks, 7 July 1798, copy, BM(NH), DTC 3 19–20.

[21]John Clapham, *The Bank of England. A History*, 2 vols. (Cambridge: Cambridge University Press, 1945) 2:2–4, 7–9.

[22]Banks's list of questions about coinage to Lord Liverpool, f. 321.

PLATE XV. Coinage Apparatus. This drawing shows the apparatus designed by Cavendish for examining the wear of coins; it was built for him by John Cuthbertson. In it twenty-eight pairs of coins are pressed and rubbed together by turning the crank. Each pair of coins is separately weighted, and the frames holding the top and bottom coins vibrate at different rates to reduce grooving. Charles Hatchett, "Experiments and Observations on the Various Alloys, on the Specific Gravity, and on the Comparative Wear of Gold. Being the Substance of a Report Made to the Right Honourable the Lords of the Committee of Privy Council...," *Philosophical Transactions* 93 (1803): end of volume.

Newton and Folkes had understood that silver was the standard coinage, coins made of other metal or notes having only conventional value, but for most of the eighteenth century gold had been the de facto standard.[23] The experiments Cavendish laid out were to decide what kind of gold coin would best resist wear. They were lengthy, since they had to replicate the wearing down of coins in Laurence Sterne's pocket. The punishing machines were designed by Cavendish and built by the instrument-maker John Cuthbertson, in whose house the experiments were carried out. One machine was a rotating oak container in which a large number of pieces of gold of different ductility were agitated.[24] Another, more complex machine, pressed coins together and moved them laterally across one another. To Cavendish the weigher, it was obvious that the measure of wear was the loss of weight of the coins. In another part of the experiment, thirteen gold alloys were hammered and rolled.

Hatchett wrote the report for the privy council committee on coins, confirming the "practice of the moneyers" and also bringing forward "many points very interesting to Science that are quite new."[25] Cavendish prefaced the report with a letter explaining that Hatchett was the sole author because he had done the experiments and was best able to give an account of them. The experiments were done with "great judgement & accuracy, & in the manner which to both of us seemed best adapted to the object proposed," Cavendish said.[26] He then

---

[23] "Heads of So Much of Lord Liverpool's Speech," ff. 402–9.

[24] Charles Hatchett to Sir Joseph Banks, 14 Mar. 1800, BL Add Mss 33,980, f. 225.

[25] Sir Joseph Banks to Charles Jenkinson, 11 May 1801, BL Add Mss 38424, ff. 158–59. The report, addressed to Lord Liverpool and the select committee for coins, signed by Hatchett, 28 Apr. 1801: BL Add Mss 38426. The title of the report of the experiments, beginning on f. 25, is "Experiments and Observations on the Various Alloys, on the Specific Gravity, and on the Comparative Wear of Gold."

[26] Cavendish to the Privy Council Committee for Coins, prefacing Hatchett's report signed 28 Apr. 1801, BL Add Mss 38426, f. 1.

made an appeal to the government to let Hatchett publish his results and not keep them a government secret. Nothing in these experiments, he explained, "requires to be kept secret" and no "bad effect" could come of their publication.[27] Hatchett's abridged paper was read to the Royal Society and published in the *Philosophical Transactions*. "At the request of Mr. Cavendish," Hatchett wrote, " I have written the following account; but I should be highly unjust and ungrateful to that gentleman, did I not here publicly acknowledge how great a portion truly belongs to him." The machines and dies were "entirely contrived" by him.[28]

Then in his early thirties, Hatchett had published chemical analyses in the *Philosophical Transactions*, and he would go on to discover a new element. He was using Lavoisier's new nomenclature of "oxyde,"[29] and the giants of the recent great past of British chemistry looked ancient to him. On a journey in England and Scotland in 1796, he met Black, "a thin old man," and Brownrigg, "the oldest pupil of Boerhaave now living,"[30] and soon after he collaborated with Cavendish, who probably seemed another (albeit very vigorous) ancient. Hatchett was elected to the Royal Society in 1797, and Cavendish took an interest in his election to the Society's dining club in 1802. They were both managers of the Royal Institution, where they saw one another frequently. Hatchett's field was chemistry and mineralogy, which was the basis of his friendship with Cavendish and their collaboration on experiments.[31] Hatchett was one of a number of young chemists and natural philosophers with whom Cavendish was scientifically close toward the end of his life.

The experiment on coins dragged on for two or three years, and when it was done, the results turned out not to be particularly useful to the government.[32] It was superb science all the same. Hatchett said correctly that knowledge of metal alloys had not "kept pace with the rapid progress of modern chemistry" and had hardly gone beyond what Pliny and the ancients knew.[33] According to a recent commentator, "the grasp shown by Cavendish of the complex nature of wear was masterly; it could have been studied with advantage by investigators a century later."[34]

Weighing and coinage had been inseparable over the ages; traditionally the main interest of governments in reliable weights was coinage, as the names of currency indicate, the British "pound," for example.[35] It was self-evident that Britain's most celebrated weigher, the man who had just weighed the world, would be chosen as the weigher of gold coins. For Cavendish, it was public service as usual.

Royal Institution

For decades Cavendish served two institutions, the Royal Society and the British Museum, and in the last decade of his life, for several years, he served a third, the Royal Institution. This latter was the brain child of a soldier of fortune born in America, Benjamin Thompson, or as he was then better known, Count Rumford. Having served on the losing side in the American Revolution, Rumford retired from the British army to become a Massachusetts Yankee at the court of the elector of Bavaria, where he rose to the head of the army and acquired his title, count. His Yankee ingenuity found ample outlet in feeding, clothing, and warming the army of Bavaria and the poor of Munich. There in addition to making mechanical inventions, he did experiments on the principles of heat and conceived of the idea of an institution of mechanics and heat in London, which became the Royal Institution. In 1798 Rumford came to London, where his ideas on

---

[27]Henry Cavendish to Charles Hatchett, 15 Oct. 1802; this letter was enclosed in one to Banks by Hatchett, in which Hatchett said that Lord Liverpool was satisfied with Cavendish's opinion on the publishable nature of the material. Banks gave his approval too, which he sent to Lord Liverpool: Charles Hatchett to Sir Joseph Banks, 24 Oct. 1802. Hatchett and Cavendish's desire to see the experiments published was first put to Lord Liverpool by Sir Joseph Banks on 21 Aug. 1801, BL Add Mss 38424, f. 160.

[28]Charles Hatchett, "Experiments and Observations on the Various Alloys, on the Specific Gravity, and on the Comparative Wear of Gold. Being the Substance of a Report Made to the Right Honourable the Lords of the Committee of Privy Council . . .," *PT* 93 (1803): 43–194, on 45.

[29]Charles Hatchett, *The Hatchett Diary: A Tour Through the Counties of England and Scotland in 1796 Visiting Their Mines and Manufacture*, ed. A Raistrick (Truro: D. Bradford Barton, 1967), 41.

[30]Ibid, 84, 104.

[31]They collaborated on platina, evidently in 1799, as recorded in Cavendish's "White Book," p. 129, and in a letter from Cavendish to Hatchett enclosed between pp. 65 and 66, thanking Hatchett for experiments he made on platina.

[32]The experiments showed that there was really nothing much to be gained by substituting smooth coins for embossed ones or a harder or softer alloy for the standard twenty–two carat gold. Chaston, "Wear Resistance," 112.

[33]Hatchett, "Experiments and Observations," 193.

[34]Chaston, "Wear Resistance," 112.

[35]Bruno Kisch, *Scales and Weights: A Historical Outline* (New Haven: Yale University Press, 1965), 6, 9.

kitchens and heating had preceded him, put in place at the Foundling Hospital by the professional philanthropist Thomas Bernard. Bernard and the recently formed Bettering Society asked Rumford to draw up a plan for an institution to teach applications of science and spread knowledge of inventions. Another variant on the Baconian plan, Rumford's scheme nearly came off. He organized a subscription whereby a person who gave fifty guineas or more became a perpetual proprietor, and one who gave less received a lesser title. There was a quick response, and in 1799 the Royal Institution was launched.[36]

The original proprietors were not men of science, with the major exception of Banks. The meeting at which the new institution was founded was held at Banks's house, which gave it an unofficial imprimatur of the Royal Society. The second man of science was Cavendish,[37] who paid his fifty guineas almost a year later, in early 1800. The duke of Devonshire paid at the same time, the Cavendishes joining only when the institution was clearly respectable. Their relative the earl of Bessborough, who was already a member, had just become a manager of the Institution. It was just about this time that the first lecture was given in a house on Albemarle Street; the Royal Institution was off and running.[38]

Cavendish had long been a subscriber to the Society of Arts, which like the Royal Institution fostered invention. Cavendish took no part in the affairs of the Society of Arts, but in those of the Royal Institution he became fully involved. The obvious difference between the two institutions was the strong connection with science in the Royal Institution. The month after Cavendish subscribed, a standing committee of science was established to oversee the syllabus and the philosophical experiments and to communicate worthy experiments to the sister institution, the Royal Society. Cavendish was an original member of this committee along with Maskelyne, Blagden, Hatchett, and several others, all Fellows of the Royal Society.[39] The governing body of the institution was nine managers, elected from the proprietors initially, and Cavendish promptly became a manager as well.[40] The meetings of the managers were irregular but frequent; as a rule only three or four managers turned up along with the secretary and treasurer. Banks, Hatchett, and two or three others came often, but Cavendish

with his typical all-or-nothing commitment became the most faithful attender. The first years of the institution were chaotic owing to Rumford's dictatorial methods. When the first scientific lecturer, Thomas Garnett, acted independently, Rumford got the managers to appoint a committee of three to supervise the syllabus in the future: the triumvirate was Rumford, Cavendish, and Banks.[41] In this and other ways, Rumford leaned on Cavendish and Banks to establish his authority and get what he wanted.

But Rumford did not get the practical institution he wanted. His plans for instructing the lower classes were opposed by the managers, and his plans for an exhibition of inventions were opposed by the manufacturers. But because of Rumford's drive, the institution existed in the first place, and it began functioning even as the workmen were expanding its house to make it suited for lectures and experiments. Important changes of staff were made in 1801. On Banks's recommendation, the original senior lecturer, Garnett, was replaced by Thomas Young, and on Rumford's recommendation, Humphry Davy was hired as assistant lecturer in chemistry. Davy, more than anyone, insured the scientific eminence of the institution by attracting fashionable London to his public lectures on science and by doing outstanding chemical research.[42] Rumford's presence at the institution was erratic, and in 1802 this restless man

---

[36] K. D. C. Vernon, *The Foundation and Early Years of the Royal Institution* (London: Royal Institution, 1963), 1–4. W. J. Sparrow, *Knight of the White Eagle* (London: Hutchinson, 1964), 109–10. Sanborn C. Brown, "Thompson, Benjamin (Count Rumford)," *DSB* 13:350–52.

[37] Vernon, *Foundation*, 4.

[38] Cavendish became a proprietor on 10 Feb. 1800. The managers, at their meeting on 17 Feb., said that the Royal Institution was "now established on a Basis so firm & respectable, that no Doubt can be entertained of its Success." The first lecture at the Royal Institution was announced for 4 Mar. 1800: Royal Institution of Great Britain, *The Archives of the Royal Institution of Great Britain in Facsimile. Minutes of Managers' Meetings 1799–1900*, vols. 1 and 2 (in one volume), ed. F. Greenaway (Ilkley, Yorkshire: published in association with the Royal Institution of Great Britain by the Scolar Press Limited, 1971).

[39] Entry for 31 Mar. 1800, Minutes of the Meetings of Managers, Royal Institution Archive, pp. 39–41. The other six members were Major Rennell, Joseph Planta, E. Whitaker Gray, J. Vince, and William Farish; the last two were professors of experimental philosophy and of chemistry at Cambridge. Maskelyne turned down the appointment because he was too busy.

[40] He was elected at the annual meeting of proprietors on 1 May 1800. Entry for 5 May 1800, Minutes of the Meetings of Managers, Royal Institution, p. 70.

[41] Entry for 31 Mar. 1800, Minutes of the Meetings of Managers, Royal Institution. Vernon, *Foundation*, 18.

[42] Vernon, *Foundation*, 24, 29.

left it for good. The soon-to-appear movement for mechanics institutes would take up the cause of technical education; the Royal Institution was set on its course of scientific achievement.

The year after Rumford left, in 1803, the scientific committee was reappointed, with Cavendish, Banks, and Hatchett on it again.[43] Later in the year the committee recommended Thomas Young's successor, John Dalton.[44] Cavendish did not live quite long enough to see the arrival of the greatest of all the scientists to work in the Royal Institution, Michael Faraday.[45]

We have no idea what Cavendish thought of the practical plans for the Royal Institution, but we do know that he wanted the closest possible cooperation between it and the Royal Society. It was he who seconded Rumford's motion to direct the secretaries of the two institutions to keep one another regularly informed.[46] Cavendish took an interest in the scientific lectures, as was required of him by his appointment to the scientific committee; among his papers is a letter from Thomas Young asking his opinion on something about gearwork he intended to put in his syllabus, and in his lectures he gives an explanation of halos around the sun that Cavendish suggested to him.[47] Cavendish's main interest, however, was not in the lectures but in the experiments at the Institution. He, Banks, and Hatchett were in charge of the scientific research in the laboratory,[48] and through the last year of his life Cavendish witnessed experiments and assisted in them.[49]

The Royal Institution was, in particular, an institution of heat, the field in which Rumford was scientifically preeminent. He had been publishing his researches on heat in the *Philosophical Transactions* since 1786, and in a paper read before the Royal Society in 1798, the year he moved to London, he wrote: "The effects produced in the world by the agency of Heat are probably *just as extensive*, and quite as important, as those which are owing to the tendency of the particles of matter towards each other; and there is no doubt but its operations are, in all cases, determined by laws equally immutable."[50] One of Rumford's readers was Cavendish, who did not need to be told that heat is as ubiquitous and important as gravity. Rumford started out believing that heat is a fluid but had since corrected his error.[51] It was fortunate that he did, for his view of heat as motion was responsible for his far-sighted

selection of Humphry Davy as chemical lecturer. In 1799 the twenty-one year-old Davy published a tract[52] that came to Rumford's notice; Rumford recognized ideas similar to his on the nature of heat, and their author was offered the job.[53] Garnett had studied under Black at Edinburgh University, and in his lectures at the Royal Institution he gave full treatment to Black's theory of "latent heat" and used the word "caloric" throughout. This was just after Rumford believed he had proven that there is no such thing as caloric and that heat is motion. Rumford and Garnett had a falling out when Garnett published his syllabuses without approval, but Rumford may have been dissatisfied with the contents of Garnett's lectures as well.[54] Like Davy,

[43]Entry for 26 May 1803, Minutes of the Meetings of Managers, Royal Institution, pp 137–38.

[44]Entry for 5 Sep. 1803, Minutes of the Meetings of Managers, Royal Institution, p. 151.

[45]Three years after Cavendish's death, in 1813, Davy received from Faraday a copy of the notes Faraday took of Davy's lectures at the Royal Institution. This was the start of Faraday's association with the Institution.

[46]The Royal Institution began its own journal. The motion that Cavendish seconded called for the Royal Society to inform the Royal Institution of papers read at its meetings that were suitable for the Royal Institution's journal. It also required that an earlier resolution of the Royal Institution be communicated to the Royal Society; this resolution concerned the duty of the scientific committee to communicate discoveries to the Royal Society. Entry for 5 Apr. 1802, Minutes of the Meetings of Managers, Royal Institution, p. 260.

[47]Thomas Young to Henry Cavendish, 3 Sep. 1801, enclosed in a paper, "On the Shape of the Teeth in Rack Work," Cavendish Mss, VI(b), 31. In Thomas Young's *A Syllabus of a Course of Lectures on Natural and Experimental Philosophy* (London, 1802), paragraph 179, Young acknowledged Cavendish for the demonstration. Joseph Larmor's comment in Cavendish, *Sci. Pap.* 2: 410. Thomas Young, *A Course of Lectures on Natural Philosophy and the Mechanical Arts*, 2 vols. (London, 1807) 2:308.

[48]Vernon, *Foundation*, 27.

[49]John Davy, *Memoirs of the Life of Sir Humphry Davy, Bart.*, 2 vols. (London, 1836) 1:222.

[50]Count Rumford, "An Inquiry Concerning the Source of the Heat Which Is Excited by Friction," *PT* 88 (1798): 80–102; in Benjamin Thompson, Count Rumford, *The Complete Works of Count Rumford*, vol. 1 (Boston, 1870), 469–92, on 491.

[51]Count Rumford, "An Inquiry Concerning the Weight Ascribed to Heat," *PT* 89 (1799): 179–94.

[52]Davy was working in Thomas Beddoes's Pneumatic Institution at the time. Beddoes included Davy's "Essay on Heat, Light, and the Combinations of Light" in a collection in 1799, *Contributions to Physical and Medical Knowledge, Principally from the West of England.* David M. Knight, "Davy, Humphry," *DSB* 3:598–604, on 599.

[53]George E. Ellis, *Memoir of Sir Benjamin Thompson, Count Rumford...* (Philadelphia, 1871), 486.

[54]Thomas Garnett, *Outlines of a Course of Lectures on Chemistry: Delivered at the Royal Institution of Great Britain, 1801* (London, 1801), 15–16, 30–31. He published at the same time *Outlines of a Course of Lectures on Natural and Experimental Philosophy, Delivered at the Royal Institution of Great Britain, 1801* (London, 1801). On his studies at Edinburgh, "The Life of the Author," in Thomas Garnett, *Popular Lectures on Zoonomia, or The Laws of Animal Life, in Health and Disease* (London, 1804), vi–vii.

Thomas Young, Garnett's replacement, held a view of heat similar to Rumford's. Davy and Young, in their lectures at the institution, did not make Garnett's mistake; they made clear their preference for the vibratory theory of heat. For a time at the Royal Institution, there was an extraordinary concentration of upholders of a view of heat that most practicing scientists believed had long since been discarded: Rumford, at the head of the institution, the two science lecturers, Davy and Young, and the experimentalist of Rumford's inner circle, Cavendish. Whatever else might be made of this, it is noteworthy that near the end of his life, Cavendish was placed in the company of scientists who broadly agreed with him on the nature of heat, the subject Cavendish cared most about then.[55]

The Royal Institution offered Cavendish a chance both to serve science publicly and to come together with gifted young scientists. Two of the most perceptive biographical accounts of Cavendish were written by Davy and Young, who knew him especially from the Royal Institution. "He was reserved to strangers," Davy said of Cavendish, "but, when he was familiar, his conversation was lively, and full of varied information. Upon all subjects of science he was luminous and profound; and in discussion wonderfully acute. Even to the very last week of his life, when he was nearly seventy-nine, he retained his activity of body, and all his energy and sagacity of intellect. He was warmly interested in all new subjects of science." The exchange, by this account, was not all one way. Cavendish was invigorated by Davy's work, and Davy, fifty years his junior, benefitted.[56]

Cavendish's presence at the Royal Institution outlived him. When Davy arrived there in 1801, he was received by Rumford, Cavendish, and Banks, who promised him any apparatus he wanted for his experiments.[57] When Cavendish died, his proprietorship in the Institution was inherited by Lord George Cavendish, and from him Davy obtained some of Cavendish's choice chemical apparatus. Five months after Cavendish's death, Davy received permission from the managers to bring this apparatus to the Royal Institution to use in experiments and lectures.[58] In his chemical treatise published two years after Cavendish's death, Davy made this observation: Cavendish "carried into his chemical researches a delicacy and precision, which have never been exceeded."[59]

Institute of France

When the Institute of France succeeded the Academy of Sciences of the old regime, the question of foreign members necessarily came up. Each of the several classes of the institute proposed candidates, who were then balloted for at a general meeting. In foreign scientific circles there was intense interest in this election, just as there was a frenzy of lobbying among the French. Foreign scientists were ranked like race horses, since the number to be admitted was fixed, at twenty-four. From Paris in late 1801, Rumford confidentially informed Banks that he headed the list of ten foreigners put up by the class of mathematics and physics. Following him, in order, came Maskelyne, Cavendish, Herschel, Priestley, Pyotr Simon Pallas, Alessandro Volta, and three others. Rumford was himself proposed but in another class.[60] Charles Blagden, who was in Paris as the election grew near in 1802, wrote to Banks that he was pressing Cavendish's claims with the scientists he knew in the Institute, and that he fully expected Cavendish to be the first elected after the Institute had elected all its former associates from the Academy.[61]

[55]If the theory of heat had a larger role at the Royal Institution, it vanished with Rumford. John Dalton, Young's replacement in 1803, was known to hold the fluid theory of heat. G. N. Cantor has noted the agreement on heat between Rumford, Davy, and Young, in "Thomas Young's Lectures at the Royal Institution," *Notes and Records of the Royal Society* 25 (1970): 87–112, on 90. In contrast to Garnett, Young in his lectures at the Royal Institution argued by analogy with sound to the truth of the vibration theory of heat, "Newton's opinion." Thomas Young, *A Course of Lectures on Natural Philosophy and the Mechanical Arts* 2 vols. (London, 1807) 1:148–49, 656. Davy and Young both were particularly concerned to impart in their lectures the new understanding of radiant heat. With praise for Rumford's experiments, Davy explained that vibrating particles of bodies give rise to vibrations in the ether, which in turn communicate vibrations to particles of bodies. Humphry Davy, *A Syllabus of a Course of Lectures on Chemistry Delivered at the Royal Institution of Great Britain* (London, 1802), 50–54. Davy's first publication in science, in 1799, which Rumford saw, reported experiments on the conversion of ice to water by friction. Davy said: "It has then been experimentally demonstrated that caloric, or the matter of heat, does not exist," and that heat is a "peculiar motion, probably a vibration, of the corpuscles of bodies." *The Collected Works of Sir Humphry Davy, Bart.*, ed. J. Davy, 4 vols. (London, 1839) 2:13–14. Arnold Thackray, "Dalton, John," *DSB* 3:537–47, on 541.
[56]John Davy, *Memoirs of the Life of Sir Humphry Davy*, 1:222.
[57]Humphry Davy to Davies Gilbert, 8 Mar. 1801, in John Ayrton Paris, *The Life of Sir Humphry Davy* (London, 1831), 78.
[58]*The Archives of the Royal Institution* 5 (1975): 47, 62 126, 160.
[59]Humphry Davy, *Elements of Chemical Philosophy*, vol. 1 (London, 1812), 37.
[60]Count Rumford to Sir Joseph Banks, 22 Nov. 1801, BL Add Mss 8099.
[61]Sir Charles Blagden to Sir Joseph Banks, 19 June 1802, copy, BM(NH), DTC 3.170–74.

His next letter was less certain. Pallas and Cavendish were tied on the first ballot, and on the second Pallas came off one vote ahead, as might be expected, since Pallas was a former associate of the Academy, and it was understood that the foreign members of the old Academy would be reelected to the new Institute. Watt, Volta, and Martin Heinrich Klaproth were highly regarded too, which meant that while Cavendish might be chosen at the next election, there was "no certainty." In his favor, Blagden thought, was Napoleon's high esteem for Cavendish.[62] (Blagden, who talked with Napoleon, was much impressed by his knowledge and promotion of science.) In his next report, Blagden said that at the coming election, the mathematics and physics class intended to present, first, Cavendish, then Watt, "who ran him pretty hard," and third Paolo Mascagni, and Volta was not in the running.[63] This time Blagden was proved right: Cavendish was elected.[64] That was not the end of it, however: among those elected there was yet another ranking, this one by the French government. The Institute listed the foreign members according to their merits in science: Banks came first, Maskelyne came next because of his lunar tables for determining longitude,[65] and then came Cavendish.

Wealth

Henry Cavendish had big houses, which if they had been used for conventional purposes would have incurred big expenses. But Cavendish did not entertain at home often, and when he did the company was usually scientific. What his guests were served was meager and invariable, according to the stories, one leg of mutton, and that was it. On one occasion several guests were expected, and Cavendish's housekeeper complained to him that one leg of mutton would be insufficient. Cavendish is supposed to have said, "Well, then, get two." This incident has been taken as an indication of Cavendish's indifference to hospitality,[66] but we have another interpretation. Cavendish formed his social preferences early in life, never changing them, and that applies, in particular, to his idea of hospitality. We do not know what Lord Charles provided at home, but we do know that at Cambridge, Henry Cavendish ate mutton five days of the week. Mutton was common fare for invited guests; Peter Collinson

asked Martin Folkes, president of the Royal Society, and his daughter to visit him and "take a piece of Mutton with me."[67] It has been observed that from the 1760s, under French influence, the composition of English meals changed. Henry Cavendish continued what he had known as the usual hospitality from his early years, but now his guests were perhaps used to more diverse meals and disappointed if faced with mutton as the only meat course. Cavendish's hospitality was probably never that inflexible, in any case. We have the butcher's and fishmonger's bills from the very end of his life, and at that time, although leg of mutton would seem to have been the favorite selection, Cavendish's housekeeper ordered beef, loin pork, cod, and oysters, too.[68] However that may be, Cavendish did not entertain lavishly, which is one reason why his wealth was not squandered.

The reason why Henry Cavendish's wealth existed in the first place was that his father was wealthy. The great wealth of Lord Charles and then of Henry Cavendish had three sources: the family settlements and legacies, without which there would have been no wealth at all; financial prudence; and the public debt of the kingdom.

In addition to the two revolutions we have discussed, the political and the scientific, Lord Charles and Henry Cavendish were beneficiaries of a third, contemporary so-called "revolution," this one commercial. Certainly one of the major outcomes of the political revolution was a change in the relationship between business and government. In the past, most government borrowing had been on the king's word, which had proven untrustworthy. Parliament took over the responsibility for guaranteeing loans in 1793, from which time we can properly speak of a "public debt." The public now had sufficient confidence in the financial stability of the country to deposit its

[62]Sir Charles Blagden to Sir Joseph Banks, 15 Oct. 1802, BM Add Mss 33272, pp. 204–5.

[63]Sir Charles Blagden to Sir Joseph Banks, 26 Nov. and 6 Dec. 1802, BL Add Mss 33,272, pp. 210–13.

[64]Sir Charles Blagden to Sir Joseph Banks, 29 Jan. 1803. Fitzwilliam Museum Library, Perceval H205.

[65]Sir Charles Blagden to Sir Joseph Banks, 1 Feb. 1803, Fitzwilliam Museum Library, Percival H206.

[66]Wilson, *Cavendish*, 164.

[67]Peter Collinson to Martin Folkes, n.d., Folkes Correspondence, Royal Society, Mss 250, vol. 3, No. 55.

[68]Devon. Coll., box 31: "Vouchers to Mrs Stewarts Household," at Clapham Common.

money in the Bank of England, which was designated to handle the public debt in part.[69] As good land was becoming scarce, public loans appealed as an alternative source of income, and there were several to choose from. Two were offered by trading companies and the rest by the Bank of England: an enormous loan from the South Sea Company and a smaller one from the East India Company; and a substantial loan from the Bank of England, which also issued a group of annuities. The latter contained so-called perpetual annuities, or annuities requiring the government to pay a fixed rate of interest in perpetuity; and over the course of the century, most of the public debt—and most of our Cavendishes' wealth—came to be held in annuities of this kind.[70]

The perpetual annuities owned by the Cavendishes were controlled by a new policy introduced in 1751 (on the eve of Henry Cavendish's majority). The outstanding loans paying three percent, some through the Bank of England and some through the exchequer, were consolidated into a single fund, which was named the "3 per cent Consolidated Annuities," or "consols" for short. Other annuities paying more than three percent were united in another fund now paying only three percent, which were named "3 per cent Reduced Annuities." Both of these funds were managed by the Bank of England, which paid out interest, or "dividends," since these annuities were called "stock." The dividends were paid twice yearly; in other words, three percent annuities paid six percent annually, though there were fluctuations. On stated days the dividends were drawn and signed for; if the owner of the stock was not present—of course, the Cavendishes were never present—through power of attorney the dividends were deposited with the Bank or the trading companies.[71]

Most of the owners of Bank of England stock lived in and around London. They were a varied lot, with many migrants, Huguenots and Spanish and Portuguese Jews, a good many gentry, gentlemen, and peers, especially dowagers and ladies, and corporate bodies such as the colleges of Cambridge. Increasingly, Bank of England stock was used to support spinsters and widows and to meet the demands of marriage settlements. The number of investors in the eighteenth century was small, and the majority of these were small investors; most of the stock was held by a few persons, such as the Cavendishes. And like the Cavendishes, most investors bought stock and kept it, regarding it as gilt-edged, and withdrawing only dividends or else reinvesting them.[72]

The foundations of Lord Charles Cavendish's wealth were modest, his inheritance and his due according to the marriage settlement, which took the now familiar form of Bank of England and South Sea stock. He sold the stock to buy property, but when he sold the property after his wife's death he invested in and stayed with the same kind of investment. By the time of his death fifty-five years later, by accretion, his investments had turned into a reasonable fortune. He held what we would now call a diversified portfolio: between his South Sea annuities, new and old, and his Bank of England stock, consols, and reduced three percent annuities, he was worth 159,200 pounds. This amount Henry Cavendish inherited in 1783. It did not contain Elizabeth Cavendish's legacy, which only appeared in 1784, as an addition to Henry Cavendish's account. This legacy nearly doubled his wealth, bringing him 48,000 pounds in mortgages and 97,100 pounds in consols and reduced three percent annuities. In addition, before his father died, Henry Cavendish held stocks in his own name, and although by comparison their value was not a great deal, it was not negligible either, and it shows that he was independently well off: as of 1776 he had 1,100 pounds in South Sea annuities, and as of 1781 he had 14,000 pounds in reduced three percent annuities. Thus, in the year after his father's death, Henry Cavendish held 48,000 pounds in mortgages and 272,800 in securities (plus possibly a few other small holdings).[73]

---

[69]The Glorious Revolution had been quickly followed by a burst of business initiatives, including a great many joint-stock companies, usually organized around patents. Hanoverian London was inventive, prosperous, and full of entrepreneurial energy. John Carswell, *The South Sea Bubble*, rev. ed. (London: Alan Sutton, 1993), 8, 12, 18–20.

[70]Alice Clare Carter, *The English Public Debt in the Eighteenth Century* (London: The Historical Association, 1968), 2–9.

[71]Eugen von Philippovich, *History of the Bank of England, and Its Financial Services to the State*, 2d ed., trans C. Meredith (Washington, D.C.: Government Printing Office, 1911), 135. John Clapham, *The Bank of England, A History*, 2 vols. (Cambridge: Cambridge University Press, 1945) 2:77, 97–98. Carter, *English Public Debt*, 10.

[72]Carter, *English Public Debt*, 18–19. Clapham, *Bank of England* 1:280–88.

[73]Lord Charles Cavendish's stock at the time of his death consisted of: Bank of England stock, 25,815 pounds; New South Seas Annuities, 47,000; Reduced 3% Annuities, 18,285; Consolidated 3%

Wilson gives an anecdote about Cavendish and his bankers. A large sum of cash, perhaps 80,000 pounds, had accumulated in Cavendish's account, prompting a banker to call on him to ask what to do with it. The banker overheard the following conversation between Cavendish and his servant:

"Who is he? Who is he? What does he want with me?"

"He says he is your banker, and must speak to you."

When the banker was admitted, Cavendish cried,

"What do you come here for? What do you want with me?"

The banker explained, and Cavendish responded,

"If it is any trouble to you, I will take it out of your hands. Do not come here to plague me."

"Not the least trouble to us, Sir, not the least; but we thought you might like some of it to be invested."

"Well! well! What do you want to do?"

"Perhaps you would like to have forty thousand pounds invested." "Do so! Do so, and don't come here and trouble me, or I will remove it."[74]

This story might be taken to illustrate Cavendish's indifference to practical matters like money in the bank, and it has been. It as easily illustrates his annoyance with interruptions. He gave orders about what to do with his dividends to his bankers, Messrs. Denne and Co., and in particular to Robert Snow, who worked there. He was not indifferent to money, but he did not want to be bothered about it either. His directions would seem to have been straightforward and consistent: his dividends were reinvested alternately in four stocks: new and old South Sea annuities and consols and reduced three percent annuities.[75] His farm rents went directly to his bankers, and all of his business was transacted through them, and he expected them to know his wishes and carry them out to the letter. He did not like to have to repeat himself, especially in person. He had enough wealth that he did not have to think about it, an ideal life that he did not want disturbed.

Cavendish paid bankers to do his banking. When occasionally he himself acted as a banker-in-need to his friends and family, who turned to him for loans, he took little trouble over the business and gave it even less thought. He did not, for example, remember if he had received interest on some money he had lent to a friend; the reason he

gave for his uncertainty was that "I am not very regular in my accounts."[76]

To the world, Cavendish's vast wealth has proven as intriguing as his discoveries, as Biot's well-known epigram testifies: Cavendish was "the richest of the wise and the wisest of the rich." The source of his wealth and how and when he came by it have been stated variously, but that it happened "suddenly," as Biot said, has been generally assumed. He made it precise: his uncle, a general overseas, returned to England in 1773 to find his nephew neglected by his family, and to make it aright he left his entire fortune to Henry Cavendish.[77] We have not found a general from India, who is in any case unnecessary, since Cavendish's wealth can be explained otherwise. In 1784, as we have pointed out, his wealth was already very considerable. A millionaire when he died twenty-six years later, Henry Cavendish was already one third of the way there. From the beginning Blagden tried to control

---

Annuities, 62,100; and Old South Sea Annuities, 6,000; which made a total of 159,200 pounds The next year, 1784, Henry Cavendish's bank account was augmented by Elizabeth Cavendish's legacy to Lord Charles Cavendish, which consisted of: Reduced 3 % Annuities, 22,100 pounds; Consolidated 3% Annuities, 50,000; and another group of the latter, 25,000; which made a total of 97,100 pounds. The earl of Hardwicke deposited 916 pounds in his account in 1783. So to start with, Henry Cavendish had 272,800 pounds from these sources, and he had several thousand pounds in securities in his own name. The above information is from the ledgers of the Bank of England Archive: South Sea Annuities 1776–1793, vol. 154, p. 65; Bank Stock, 1783–1798, No. 59, p. 389, and 1798–1815, No. 64, p. 439; Reduced 3% Annuities, Supplement Ledger, 1781–1785, p. 10614, and 1785–1793, pp. 1505, 2242, and 1793–1801, pp. 1727, 1801, and 1803–1807, p. 1937, and 1807–1817, p. 6001; Consolidated 3% Annuities, 1782–1788, pp. 3449–50, 3854, 3927, and 1788–1792, pp. 8000, 8619, and 1792–1798, pp. 8000, 8730, and 1799–1804, pp. 8001, 9012, and 1804–1812, p. 8001; South Sea Old Annuities, vol. 79, 1776–1786, p. 90, and vol. 90, 1794–1815, p. 648.

[74]George Wilson, *The Life of the Honourable Henry Cavendish* (London, 1851), 175–76.

[75]There is correspondence from his bankers in Devon. Coll., 86/comp 3.

[76]Cavendish's undated draft of a letter to Alexander Dalrymple's administrator: Devon. Coll., L/34/64.

[77]In literal translation, Biot's epigram is wordier: Cavendish was "the richest of all the learned and probably also the most learned of all the rich." J. B. Biot, "Cavendish (Henri)," *Biographie Universelle* vol. 7 (Paris, 1813), 272–73, on 273. The alleged uncle who left his fortune to Henry Cavendish in 1773 was repeated in biographical dictionaries including the most important of them all for scientists: "Cavendish, Henry," in J. C. Poggendorff, *Biographisch-Literarisches Handwörterbuch zur Geschichte der exacten Wissenschaften*, vol. 1 (Leipzig, 1863), 406. In a variant explanation, this one closer to the mark, Thomas Thomson said that besides Cavendish's father, an aunt left him a great deal of money after his father's death: *History of Chemistry*, vol. 1 (London, 1830): 336–49, on 336. The different accounts are discussed by Wilson, who regarded as unimportant the source of Cavendish's wealth but not the timing, which he placed no later than 1783: *Cavendish*, 158–60.

the mistaken assumptions about his late friend's finances. For his éloge of Cavendish, Georges Cuvier went directly to Blagden, but he also took details from Biot's biography, which was filled with errors. Blagden let Cuvier know this and, in particular, that he had the origin of Cavendish's fortune wrong. Blagden believed it was Cavendish's father, and he was right.[78]

Henry Cavendish once again followed his father's course, investing in gilt-edged securities and not touching them. Shortly before his father's death, when he was establishing an independent life, Cavendish sold a small part of his securities, 8,500 pounds worth, but that was the exception. From the ledgers of the Bank of England, we see that Henry Cavendish's account increased steadily and by modest increments. During the Napoleonic Wars, the government offered a higher return on loans and very substantial bonuses as a percentage of capital on top of the half-yearly dividends, and so in these latter years Cavendish's account rose much faster than before. Pitt's great experiment with an income tax in 1800 excluded dividends. If the figure of 80,000 pounds in the story about Cavendish and his banker is at all close, the time would have been the Napoleonic, when money poured in, and it would have been easy to lose track; toward the end Cavendish's securities earned him, in effect, ten percent on his investment, which came to around 80,000 pounds per year, the figure quoted in the anecdote of Cavendish and his banker.[79] When Cavendish died in 1810 most of his stocks were selling below par, which was usual. On paper their value was well over a million pounds; their discounted value was about 821,000 pounds for stocks in his own name and about 18,000 pounds for stocks in trust. Cavendish owned some of every kind of security, but the bulk of his investment was in only two, consols and reduced three percent annuities. He still owned the 48,000 pounds in mortgages given to his father by Elizabeth Cavendish. And his banker had about 11,000 pounds cash in hand.[80] Henry Cavendish's fortune compared favorably with some large fortunes in the late eighteenth century: Lady Bute's 800,000 pounds, Lord Bath's 1,200,000 pounds, and Sir Samuel Fludyer's 900,000 pounds.[81]

As Biot said, Cavendish was the richest of the wise, and insofar as his investments were concerned, he was at least one of the wiser of the rich; over the long run, during the years in which he amassed his fortune, he could hardly have done better than to buy into Bank of England stocks, especially since he was a man who had other things to do with his days than to spend them in his counting house.

End of Life

The Devonshire estate papers contain several letters between Henry Cavendish and his brother, Frederick, saved perhaps because they mention their banker along with a couple of small sums. The letters, falling in 1806 to 1810, give us a glimpse into the brothers' relationship near the end of their lives.

The brain damage Frederick suffered from an accident at age twenty-one did not otherwise affect his health. In their letters the brothers showed equal and largely unnecessary concern for one another's health. Henry had heard that Frederick was ill, and Frederick reassured him that he had never felt better other than for the gout that cramped his handwriting. He lived still in Hertfordshire, just across the border from Bedfordshire, in Market Street, a quiet village near the Benedictine Monastery of St. Albans.[82] He liked to walk, which he did in old age with his carriage ordered to follow behind him. He spent his time visiting in the neighborhood, where he was regarded as a harmless eccentric and a soft touch. He gave to all needy comers, the poor, the out of luck, the church. People came to him from considerable distances, since they had reason to expect that they would not go away empty handed. Bookish, whiggish, intelligent, unfashionable, in several respects Frederick resembled his brother.

[78]Blagden's correspondent Madame D. Gautier was acquainted with Cuvier's wife. On 30 April 1811 Gautier communicated Cuvier's thanks to Blagden, and on 20 April 1812 Blagden wrote back after seeing Cuvier's éloge. Blagden Letters, Royal Society, G.11 and G.11a. Georges Cuvier, "Henry Cavendish," translated by D. S. Faber, in *Great Chemists*, ed. E. Faber (New York: Interscience Publishers, 1961), 229–38.
[79]Clapham, *Bank of England* 2:39–40, 46.
[80]Mess. Snow & Co., "Valuation of Property in the Funds," 24 Feb. 1810. Devon. Coll., L/114/74. Cavendish's mortgages were from the duke of Devonshire and Knight Mitchell, and the trust was under the names of Lord Hardwicke, Lord George Cavendish, and Lord Frederick Cavendish.
[81]L B. Namier, *Structure of Politics at the Accession of George III*, 2d ed. (London: Macmillan, 1957), 164.
[82]Herbert W. Tompkins, *Highways and Byways in Hertfordshire* (London: Macmillan, 1902), 113–14, 139.

He had a huge library, though of classics and literature and not of science. He had the remarkable memory of the Cavendishes; his he devoted to poetry, which he could recite with such accuracy that he was called a "living edition." He was fond of modern poets, such as Thomson, Akenside, Gray, and Mason; it was thought that his selection of favorites was influenced by their politics. For Frederick was at one with his family, a staunch whig of the old school. Extremely proud of his family, he was given to quoting the epitaph of the first duke of Devonshire, friend of good princes and enemy of tyrants. The outward appearances of these bachelor brothers were fixed in their youth; with his bag wig, cocked hat, and deep ruffles, Frederick in his later years was a quaint relic, like Henry with his much commented-on way of dressing. In his later years Frederick was not as well as he let on, but his way of life was unaffected.[83] He continued his charity to one and all. One of his last letters to his brother is about a young married man who was just getting started and needed 150 pounds to pay off his upholsterer's bill. Frederick asked Henry for this amount, since he did not have it. Henry obliged his brother, who was "confident /it/ will do a great deal of good."[84] Henry received a thank-you letter from the young man.[85] (Typical of Henry was his response about this time to a man with fourteen children and as many literary projects, asking Cavendish to give him 2000 pounds a year for the next five years while he completed them; Henry wrote him that he "must decline."[86]) Frederick's income came from two sources, annuities in his own name, and funds in trust, in about equal amounts; he had a comfortable income, but he exceeded it and had to ask Henry for money.[87] He needed help with his property taxes, which were (then as now) baffling. Henry was sympathetic: "The printed forms sent both by the comissioners of Income & assessed taxes are intricate & not clearly expressed."[88] Frederick was mindful of his brother's interests: "As I believe you attend a good deal to the observation of the barometer," he sent Henry a careful account of the reading by his barometer that morning. He said he had read in the paper that Herschel predicted a wet end-of-summer, and Henry, who had read this in the paper too, told his brother that Herschel could have said no such thing since he had "too much sense to make

predictions of the weather."[89] Such was the last existing correspondence between the brothers. Frederick was two years younger than Henry, and he outlived him by two years.

Life span in this branch of the Cavendish's was remarkably constant. In this respect, as in so many others, Henry (like Frederick) was like his father: they lived to seventy-nine. Up to the end, Henry Cavendish was vigorous, physically and mentally.[90] Blagden, though a physician, was not Cavendish's physician, for among perhaps other reasons he had stopped practicing. Cavendish's choice was his good friend, John Hunter. The first we hear of him as Cavendish's physician was in 1792, when Cavendish was sixty. Blagden went to Clapham Common only to be told, to his surprise, that Cavendish was ill. Blagden responded with sympathy (and perhaps hurt): "If you had chosen that I should wait upon you, I cannot doubt but you would have sent to me."[91] That same day he learned that Cavendish was being seen by Dr. Hunter, and he wrote again to Cavendish saying that he "could not do better" and asked only if he

[83] "Memoirs of the Late Frederick Cavendish, Esq," *Gentleman's Magazine* 82 (1812): 289–91.
[84] Frederick Cavendish to Henry Cavendish, 5 and 12 Feb. 1810, Devon. Coll., 86/comp. 1.
[85] George Marriott to /Henry Cavendish/, 15 Feb. 1810, Devon. Coll., 86/comp. 2.
[86] John Sinclair to Henry Cavendish, 1 July 1809; Henry Cavendish to John Sinclair, n.d., draft, Devon. Coll., 86/comp. 2.
[87] Frederick Cavendish to Henry Cavendish, 9 Feb. 1810, Devon. Coll., 86/ comp. 1. At the beginning of 1810 Frederick's assets were his estate in Market Street, where he lived, and his funds, which were invested primarily in three-percent reduced Bank of England annuities, old South Sea annuities, and new South Sea annuities, totaling a little over 47,000 pounds. That year Henry died, leaving Frederick his farms and his Clapham freehold estate, which added about 3500 pounds to Frederick's income, otherwise derived solely from his funds. Devon. Coll., L/114/74.
[88] Frederick Cavendish to Henry Cavendish, 28 Oct. 1806; Henry Cavendish to Frederick Cavendish, n.d., draft, Devon. Coll., 86/comp. 1.
[89] Frederick Cavendish to Henry Cavendish, 10 Sep. and 18 Dec. 1809; Henry to Frederick, n.d., draft, Devon. Coll., 86/comp. 1.
[90] There is an unexplained entry in the inventory of papers Henry Cavendish made sometime after his father's death. Labeled "Mine," i.e., Henry Cavendish's papers and not his father's or other family papers, the entry reads: "Receipts from hospitals." It is unlikely that Henry Cavendish would have received treatment at a hospital. The receipts may be for donations. Charles Cavendish's will left 1000 pounds to charity, to be dispersed at the discretion of his executor, who was Henry Cavendish. Hospitals would have been a convenient choice for Henry and one consistent with his scientific outlook, and as executor he would have kept receipts. Henry Cavendish, "List of Papers Classed," Cavendish Mss. Misc. Charles Cavendish's will, Devon. Coll., L/69/12.
[91] Charles Blagden to Henry Cavendish, 12 Mar. 1792, draft, Blagden Letterbook, Royal Society, 7:624.

could visit shim "as a friend."⁹² Cavendish invited Blagden, who told Banks the next day that he was "engaged to be with Mr Cavendish (who is much disposed) at Clapham."⁹³ In his discomfort, whatever it was, Cavendish was with two friends, Blagden and Hunter.

Since there was a famous contemporary surgeon and anatomist named John Hunter, we need to point out that Cavendish's doctor was not that John Hunter. He is not well known today but at the time he was highly regarded for his scientific as well as medical skills. He was proposed for membership in the Royal Society in 1785, and his certificate was signed by twenty-five Fellows of the Royal Society,⁹⁴ which was the same number Captain Cook received ten years before in an extraordinary expression of support. Cavendish was one of the signers, along with all of Cavendish's good friends, Dalrymple, Aubert, Heberden, Blagden, Nairne, Smeaton, Maskelyne, and others including the other John Hunter. Hunter was then a physician to the army who was, his certificate read, "well versed in various branches of natural knowledge."

At the time of his election to the Royal Society Hunter was thirty-one. He was a graduate of the University of Edinburgh, and his writings on medicine show that he followed the teachings of William Cullen. His dissertation of 1775 was remarkable for its subject, anthropology, but just as he has been eclipsed by his namesake, his dissertation has been eclipsed by a more famous work on the subject appearing in the same year by J. F. Blumenbach.⁹⁵

Hunter regarded humans as a species and the differences among them as varieties, just as with plants, butterflies, and shell creatures, which natural history took more interest in than in man. He looked into the natural causes of differences of color, stature, parts, and minds of men. One of the main causes of differences was "heat," which is where his path crossed Cavendish's.⁹⁶ Before Hunter went to Jamaica in 1780 to superintend the military hospitals, Cavendish suggested that he observe the heat of springs and wells while he was there. His paper on the subject appearing in the *Philosophical Transactions* for 1788 referred not only to Cavendish's stimulus but also to mean temperatures taken by Lord Charles Cavendish and Heberden (who had helped secure his military

appointment). Hunter gave a full account of the purpose of the observations, which was Cavendish's hypothesis: the heat of the earth now comes solely from the sun, not the earth's interior, and so precise measurements of the temperature deep enough inside the earth to remain constant through the seasons should provide the mean temperature of any climate; in this way a few observations would teach as much as "meteorological observations of several years."⁹⁷ Hunter included these observations in his main publication, *Observations on the Diseases of the Army in Jamaica*.⁹⁸ Hunter's other publications were on medical topics in medical journals, and the judgment on his work is that it did not live up to its early promise. He died at the age of fifty-four, in 1809, the year before his famous patient Cavendish died, and he had not published any new work in over ten years.⁹⁹ In his will, Cavendish left a legacy for Hunter along with his other scientific friends, Blagden and Dalrymple.

The next illness of Cavendish we learn about again from Blagden. Cavendish was a faithful attender of Banks's open houses, so that when Cavendish was absent one Sunday in 1804, Blagden made note of it.¹⁰⁰ A few days later Blagden was informed that Cavendish was ill.¹⁰¹

⁹²Charles Blagden to Henry Cavendish, 12 Mar. 1792, draft, Blagden Letterbook, Royal Society, 7:625.

⁹³Charles Blagden to Joseph Banks, 13 Mar. 1792, draft, Blagden Letterbook, Royal Society, 7:626.

⁹⁴12 Jan. 1786, Royal Society, Certificates, 5.

⁹⁵Hunter's dissertation is rightly eclipsed by the other, though it has an interest of its own. Blumenbach's *De generis humani varietate nativa* was translated by T. Bendyshe and published together with a translation of Hunter's *Disputatio inauguralis quaedam de Hominum varietatibus, et harem causis exponens . . .*(Edinburgh, 1775) in *The Anthropological Treatises of Johann Friedrich Blumenbach . . . and the Inaugural Dissertation of John Hunter, MD. On the Varieties of Man* (London, 1865).

⁹⁶Hunter, *On the Varieties of Man*, 365–68, 378.

⁹⁷John Hunter, "Some Observations on the Heat of Wells and Springs in the Island of Jamaica, and on the Temperature of the Earth Below the Surface in Different Climates," *PT* 78 (1788): 53–65, on 53, 58, 65. Charles Blagden to William Farr, 21 Jan. 1788, draft, Blagden Letterbook, Royal Society, 7:107.

⁹⁸Hunter included the paper from the *Philosophical Transactions* as an appendix to the second edition of his *Observations on the Diseases of the Army in Jamaica* (London, 1796). The first edition was in the same year as the paper, 1788.

⁹⁹Lise Wilkinson, "'The Other' John Hunter, M.D., F.R.S. (1754–1809): His Contributions to the Medical Literature, and to the Introduction of Animal Experiments into Infectious Disease Research," *Notes and Records of the Royal Society* 36 (1982): 227–41, on 235–36.

¹⁰⁰12 Feb. 1804, Blagden Diary, Royal Society, 4:201.

¹⁰¹16 Feb. 1804, Blagden Diary, Royal Society, 4:back 202.

Cavendish was attended by Everard Home, F.R.S., anatomist, and surgeon at St. George's. From Home, Blagden learned that Cavendish had a rupture, nothing more serious; he would need a truss, that was all. Home was about the same age as Hunter, and at the same time as Hunter he had served with the army in Jamaica; the two were well acquainted, both active members of a medical club founded in 1783, which met at Slaughter's Coffee House.[102] In 1804, when Cavendish called on his services, Home was a famous surgeon, having succeeded *the* John Hunter as surgeon to St. George's, and he was a prolific writer on surgical and anatomical subjects. He was well known to Cavendish at the Royal Society, where he repeatedly was chosen to give the physiological Croonian lectures.[103] As he had with his previous physician, the "other" John Hunter, with Home Cavendish had a scientific connection; in response to a paper by Home, Cavendish did an optical experiment on the cornea.[104] Unlike some of the young scientists Cavendish was now around, such as Davy and Hatchett, Home was "no great master of the art of conversation," which may have struck a chord with his silent patient.[105] Home would attend Cavendish at the time of his death.

When Cavendish had his rupture, in 1804, Home told Blagden that the disorder began with a swelling of the legs: "as if old the first time," Blagden wrote in his diary that day.[106] Cavendish was ill on 16 and 17 February, and Blagden went to see him on the 18th. On the 18th Cavendish made out his final will, though it seems that he did not show it to Blagden.[107] Either Home or Blagden, or both, had a true insight. Cavendish was seventy-two, and he had an intimation of—perhaps a brush with—death. But otherwise, outwardly, there was no indication that Cavendish felt old.

With one exception, which we will get to, Cavendish's formal scientific associations remained of the same general nature to the end of his life. So far as we know, he was not drawn to specialized scientific clubs and societies, though these had been in existence even before his father's time. At the end of the seventeenth century, the Temple Coffee House Botanic Club was formed, and Hans Sloane and good number of eminent natural historians belonged.[108] In chemistry, a field close to Cavendish's heart, there was the Chapter Coffee

House Society, formed in 1780, and characterized at the time as a chemical society, though its interests were probably broader than chemistry. There was Bryan Higgin's short-lived Society for Philosophical Experiments and Conversations, an extension of Higgin's chemical lectures, which in the mid 1790s taught Lavoisier's new chemical nomenclature; Cavendish's friend Thomas Young was one of the subscribers. At the very end of Cavendish's life, a number of small, private chemical societies were founded in and around London: the London Chemical Society, announced in 1807 by Friedrich Accum, a chemical teacher and briefly Davy's assistant at the Royal Institution; the Lambeth Chemical Society, launched around 1809; and a group of young physicians and chemists with an interest in organic chemistry who met as a dining club, the Society for the Improvement of Animal Chemistry.[109] The latter society had a close connection with the Royal Society, as is made clear by the founding resolution at a meeting of the council of the Royal Society in April 1809, which designated the new society as an "assistant society" that was in no sense in competition with the original. To underscore the continuity with the old society, and to add prestige to the new, at the same meeting the council resolved "that Mr Cavendish be requested to allow his name to be added to those of the members of

---

[102]It was the Society for the Improvement of Medical and Chirurgical Knowledge, which brought out a short-lived *Transactions*. The leading spirit behind this society, or club, was *the* (other) John Hunter. Wilkinson, "John Hunter," 234.

[103]William LeFanu, "Home, Everard," *DSB* 6:478–79.

[104]In 1795 Blagden sent Cavendish a paper by Home, which we assume was Home's account of what would have been in John Hunter's Croonian Lecture if he had not died before he could give it. Hunter believed that the cornea could adjust itself by its own internal actions to focus the eye at different distances. Everard Home, "Some Facts Relative to the Late Mr. John Hunter's Preparation for the Croonian Lecture," *PT* 84 (1794): 21–27. Blagden then assisted Cavendish in his experiment to detect changes in the convexity of the cornea accompanying changes in the focus, using a divided object-glass micrometer. Entries for 8, 11, and 16 Nov. 1795, Blagden Diary, Royal Society, pp. 75 (back), 76, and 77 (back).

[105]Benjamin Collins Brodie, *Autobiography of the Late Sir Benjamin C. Brodie, Bart..* 2d ed. (London, 1865), 92.

[106]17 Feb. 1804, Blagden Diary, Royal Society, 4: back 202, and 203.

[107]"Copy of the Will of Henry Cavendish Esq," in the "Account of the Executor of Henry Cavendish Esq. as to Money in the Funds," Devon. Coll., L/31/65.

[108]David Elliston Allen, *The Naturalist In Britain: A Social History* (London: Allen Lane, 1976), 10.

[109]Gwen Averley, "The `Social Chemists': English Chemical Societies in the Eighteenth and Early Nineteenth Century," *Ambix* 33 (1986): 99–128, on 102, 107–9, 113.

this new society."[110] The meetings took the form of dinners and conversation every three months held alternately at the house of Cavendish's doctor, Home, and at the house of his collaborator Hatchett. Other members included their friends Davy, William Thomas Brande (who would succeed Davy as professor of chemistry at the Royal Institution), the physician William Babington (one of the founders of the Geological Society), and the physician Benjamin Collins Brodie (who was the outstanding pupil of Home).[111] Later the Society turned into a mere dinner club, but at the beginning it was given to serious scientific discussion. If Cavendish came to any of the few meetings held before his death, he would have been an interested party to these discussions and not a monument from the past; in 1806, at least, Cavendish was still doing experiments in chemistry, such as a long series on platina,[112] and we know that he came around to the Royal Institution to observe Davy's experiments. In 1809, the year of its founding, the Society sponsored two papers printed in the *Philosophical Transactions*, one by Home and one by Brande, both electrochemical. Home's paper continued the discussion of the electric eel or torpedo, Cavendish's subject; it is revealing of the changed state of science that Cavendish heard Home describe the torpedo as a "Voltaic battery" instead of Cavendish's battery of Leyden jars. The torpedo was now a problem of chemistry rather than of electricity.[113] Cavendish's membership in the society specializing in animal chemistry was unique; as he did not join the large, public specialized societies that began to appear at this time, such as the Linnaean Society in 1788, the Mineralogical Society in 1799, and the Geological Society in 1807. His age might explain it, but he was vigorous, and the suggestion was even made that he add to his social obligations in science: in 1805 Banks proposed to enlarge the Board of Longitude and to include Cavendish.[114] The fuller explanation is, we think, that the great national societies, which would eventually include the Chemical Society of London in 1841, belong to a different era of science than Cavendish's. They emerged with the professional identity of the scientific expert; Cavendish would no more have been at home in a professional scientific society than he would have been in one of the Inns of Court.

To the end Cavendish was fully active in the work of the Royal Society, as visitor to the Royal

Observatory, as member of the committee of papers, and so on. His last attendance at a council meeting was on 21 December 1809. He missed only one meeting, that of 15 February 1810. When he died on 24 February 1810, he still had work for the Society in progress, which brought him back to his starting point. He had agreed to superintend the construction of an apparatus for measuring the temperature in the depths of the sea. His father had recommended this use for the thermometer he invented over fifty years before, and Henry Cavendish had made apparatus for this purpose. He did not have time to do the experiment once more.[115]

When George Wilson came to write about the end of Cavendish's life, he found, to his regret, an apparent absence of any spirituality in his subject.[116] The Cavendish family had extensive connections with the Church: the duke of Devonshire had the second largest patronage empire, holding twenty-nine and a half livings,[117] but this had to do with temporal power, not spiritual inclinations. Lord Charles Cavendish might have had an interest in religion; at least he was willing to give to an endowment for the Fairchild Sermon, which was overseen by the Royal Society.[118] But if there was any religion in the family, there was no fervor. That absence would not have shocked Cavendish's doctor, Home, as it did Wilson; Home was a materialist who regarded the mind as an arrangement of matter and denied any difference between man

---

[110] 27 Apr. 1809, Royal Society, Minutes of Council, 7:527–31.

[111] *Autobiography of the Late Sir Benjamin Brodie*, 88–92 .

[112] In January 1806, e.g., on platina: "White Book," Cavendish Mss, p. 68.

[113] Everard Home, "Hints on the Subject of Animal Secretions," *PT* 99 (1809): 385–91, on 386.

[114] 23 Feb. 1805, Blagden Diary, Royal Society, 4:313.

[115] The clerk of the Royal Society, Gilpin, died right after Cavendish; Gilpin was going to oversee the actual construction of the apparatus. Banks wrote to the person it was intended for that Cavendish's "unexpected" death and Gilpin's death prevented him from procuring it. Joseph Banks to William Scoresby, Jun., 8 Sep. 1810, copy, Whitby Literary & Philosophical Society.

[116] Wilson, *Cavendish*, 180–82.

[117] John Cannon, *Aristocratic Century: The Peerage of Eighteenth-Century England* (Cambridge: Cambridge University Press, 1984), 64.

[118] Lord Charles Cavendish was one of several Fellows of the Royal Society who subscribed to increase the fund to pay a lecturer to preach on Whitson at a certain church on the theme "The Wonderful Works of God" or the "Certainty of the Resurrection of the Dead." From 1746 the president and council of the Royal Society chose the lecturer for this Fairchild Sermon. Henry Lyons, *The Royal Society, 1660–1940: A History of Its Administration under Its Charters* (New York: Greenwood, 1968), 175–76.

and animal other than in the arrangement of matter. Many other eighteenth-century scientists had a similar outlook; Martin Folkes, for example, when presiding over the Royal Society, scoffed at the mention of anything religious.[119] Cavendish's thinking belonged to the rational, secular current of thought of his time, which together with his extreme privacy guaranteed that his religiosity, if he had any, would not be evident to strangers or to his biographers.

The several accounts of Cavendish's last days vary but agree in this particular: Cavendish was fully alert and resigned to the imminent end. The account most at variance with the others was given by Home to John Barrow, who published it long after the event. It is also the most likely. When one of Cavendish's servants came to Home's house to say that Cavendish was dying, Home went directly to Clapham Common, finding Cavendish "rather surprised" to see him there. His servant should not have bothered Home, Cavendish said, since he was dying, and there was no point in prolonging the misery. Home stayed all night at Cavendish's bedside. Through it all Cavendish was calm, and shortly after dawn he died.[120]

Be that account as it may, Home was certainly there, we know from an entry in Blagden's diary from the time. In fact, Home and Heberden were both there, as we know from Home's account to Blagden and from Lord George Cavendish, who as Cavendish's executor paid their fees.[121] This Heberden was William Heberden, son of Charles and Henry Cavendish's old friend, who had died in 1801. The younger Heberden was as distinguished as his father, at the time physician in ordinary to the king and the queen. Home gave Blagden an "affecting account" of Cavendish's death the previous day. There was a "shortness of questionings," Home said; Cavendish "seemed to have nothing to say, nor to think of any one with request." He told Home "it is all over, with unusual cheerfulness, & at parting wished Home good by with uncommon mildness." Cavendish ordered that his main heir, Lord George Cavendish, "be sent for as soon as the breath was out of his body, but not before."[122] Home, who had treated Cavendish's rupture six years earlier, as we have seen, told Blagden that that the rupture had had nothing to do with Cavendish's death, even though he evidently had refused to wear a truss.

Cavendish had an "inflammation of the colon," which for the past year had caused diarrhea but which in the end obstructed the passage of food.[123] On the day Cavendish died, Blagden heard about it at Banks's house. Banks lamented the loss to science, but that was all, "felt nothing." Blagden, by contrast, was moved, noting in his diary that he "continued all day to feel the effect of this event on my spirits." He also noted that it was a cloudy, threatening day, as if a mirror to his spirits.[124] Two weeks later Blagden watched from his window the "funeral procession of my late friend . . . with much emotion."[125]

We now pass to another, all-too-human emotion. Cavendish's fortune was on everyone's mind, including Home's. The morning Cavendish died, Home got a servant to give him the keys, and he prowled through the house opening drawers, trunks, and cupboards looking for treasures, which he found and noted.[126] In a few days word was out that no will had been found. Blagden had seen the will but not "since the time I was intimate with him," twenty-one years before, in 1789. Blagden knew he had been in the will then and thought, correctly, that Cavendish had probably changed it since then.[127] The scientific men speculated and questioned Blagden, who had known Cavendish best. Blagden told them that Cavendish got 40,000 pounds a year. Cavendish was known to be not a "person who gave the 40,000 pounds to hospitals," and since Cavendish did not spend more than 5,000 pounds a year (so Blagden told them), he had to have left a fortune.[128]

---

[119]Keith Thomas, *Man and the Natural World: A History of the Modern Sensibility* (New York: Pantheon, 1983), 124.

[120]John Barrow, *Sketches of the Royal Society and Royal Society Club* (London, 1849), 153–54.

[121]Heberden prescribed neutral salts (as it happened, the subject of Cavendish's first chemical experiments), which he could not keep down. 25 Feb. 1810, Blagden Diary, Royal Society, 5:back p. 426 and p. 427.Home's fee was 105 pounds, Heberden's 21 pounds. Lord George Cavendish, "Mr Cavendish's Executorship Agenda," Devon. Coll.

[122]25 Feb. 1810, Blagden Diary, Royal Society, 5:back p. 426 and p. 427.

[123]4 Mar. 1810, Blagden Diary, Royal Society, 5:back p. 429 and p. 430.

[124]24 Feb. 1810, Blagden Diary, Royal Society, 5:p. 426 and back p. 426.

[125]8 Mar. 1810, Blagden Diary, Royal Society, 5:back p. 431 and p. 432.

[126]Barrow, *Sketches*, 154–55.

[127]1 Mar. 1810, Blagden Diary, Royal Society, 5:back p. 428.

[128]1 and 2 Mar. 1810, Blagden Diary, Royal Society, 5:back p. 428 and p. 429.

In time the will was found, and Blagden was informed that he was left 15,000 pounds. Dalrymple and Hunter were each left 5,000 pounds, though both of them had died since 1804. These were trifling sums, relatively speaking. Cavendish's wealth came from the family, and now it went back to its source. His landed property was entailed to his brother, Frederick; his personal property was left to Lord George (Augustus Henry) Cavendish, his executor. As for the funds—over 800,000 pounds—one sixth went to Frederick Ponsonby, the third earl of Bessborough[129] and five sixths to Lord George Cavendish and his family; the latter was portioned into two sixths for Lord George and one sixth each for Lord George's three sons, William and, still minors, the namesakes of our branch of the family, Henry and Charles. Both Lord Charles and Henry Cavendish had a history of dealing with Lord George over property,[130] and Henry had decided on Lord George as his principal heir long before he died. Lord George had married sensibly and so was rich, even by Cavendish standards; Henry Cavendish's legacy had nothing to do with need but only with loyalty, fairness, and duty. The dukedom would eventually revert to Lord George's descendants, an eventuality Henry Cavendish might have considered. The present (fifth) duke of Devonshire, brother of Lord George, was "quite convinced" that Cavendish would leave him nothing, and he was right.[131] Resigned to nothing, the duke was delighted to learn that Cavendish had left his money to the family, specifically to the earl of Bessborough. The duke however was "disgusted to see the disposal of so vast a property in a few lines, as if to save trouble . . . "[132] We have seen many wills from the time and none briefer (or clearer) than Henry Cavendish's.

By the way he disposed of his wealth, Cavendish gives us a view of how he saw his family relationships. Apart from his brother, he had outlived his own generation of Cavendishes. Of the next generation, there were five prospective male heirs, only two of whom Henry named in his will, Lord George Cavendish and Frederick, earl of Bessborough (son of Lady Carolina Cavendish, daughter of the third duke of Devonshire). It was said that Cavendish enriched Bessborough because he was pleased by his conversation at the Royal Society Club.[133] That reason seems unlikely and is certainly insufficient, since not only was Cavendish

not a conversationalist, but Bessborough was not a member of the Royal Society nor of its club. (That is not to deny that Cavendish was closely associated with the Bessboroughs. Cavendish and Bessborough's father, the second earl, saw one another constantly, as both were active trustees and members of the standing committee of the British Museum. But this Bessborough, whose house at Roehampton was filled with valuable Italian and Flemish paintings, gave the Museum objects of art, not of science.[134] Frederick, the third earl and Cavendish's heir, met regularly with Cavendish at the Museum, where they were both managers). The more likely principal reason for Cavendish's bequest is family connections of the usual kind. Bessborough's father was secretary to the duke of Devonshire when he was lord lieutenant of Ireland. This duke borrowed money from Lord Charles Cavendish for the portion of his sister Elizabeth upon her marriage to the second earl of Bessborough.[135] The third earl of Bessborough was married to Lady Henrietta-Frances Spencer, sister of Georgiana, duchess of Devonshire and friend of Henry Cavendish. Henry Cavendish was involved with Bessborough over property.[136] Cavendish probably liked Bessborough too, but friendship would have been only one of the considerations. With his principal heir, Lord George, Cavendish seems to have had only a formal relationship, meeting with him once a year for a half hour.[137] The

---

[129]This was Frederick Ponsonby, third earl of Bessborough, and second cousin to Henry Cavendish. His father was married to Henry Cavendish's first cousin Carolina Cavendish.

[130]For example: schedule of deeds delivered by Lord Charles Cavendish to Lord George Cavendish in 1780: Devon Coll., comp. 3.

[131]Letter from the fifth duke's second wife, Elizabeth Foster, to Augustus Foster, 1 Mar. 1810, in *The Two Duchesses. Georgiana Duchess of Devonshire. Elizabeth Duchess of Devonshire. Family Correspondence*, ed. V. Foster (London, 1898), 345.

[132]Quotation from the "Journal" kept by the duchess of Devonshire, in Dorothy Margaret Stuart, *Dearest Bess: The Life and Times of Lady Elizabeth Foster, Afterwards Duchess of Devonshire* (London: Methuen, 1955), 174.

[133]This piece of information is from George Wilson, who also said that Cavendish "was not, I believe," related to Bessborough. Wilson missed their family connection, though it was close. Wilson, *Cavendish*, 190.

[134]Entry for 2 June 1775, "Diary & Occurrence-Book of the British Museum, Ap. 2nd 1773 to April 1782 (Signed Dan. Solander.") BL Add Mss 45875, p. 76.

[135]"Bond from His Grace the Duke of Devonshire to the Rt. Honble Lord Charles Cavendish," 22 Sep. 1743, Devon. Coll., L/44/12.

[136]Henry Cavendish and the duke of Devonshire to the earl of Bessborough, lease for a year, 1 Nov. 1805: Devon. Coll., L/35/22.

[137]Wilson, *Cavendish*, 173.

one obvious Cavendish who was not in Henry Cavendish's will was, formally speaking, the first and most expectant Cavendish of them all, the tenant for life of the vast family estate, the fifth duke of Devonshire. Lady Sarah Spencer, Georgiana's niece, speculated on why Henry Cavendish forgot the duke's existence in his will: perhaps Cavendish "thought that said existence was something of a *disgrace* to the noble name of Cavendish,"[138] as well he might have. The Cavendishes, including Henry, were a family of achievement, with the notable exception of the fifth duke. The last two male Cavendishes of the next generation were Horatio Walpole, second earl of Orford, and George Walpole, sons of Rachel Cavendish. For the name Walpole to appear with the name of Cavendish might be regarded as the final legacy of the second duke of Devonshire to his family. His career had been inseparable from that of Robert Walpole, and the Cavendish in-law Walpoles were relatives of the prime minister. But we have no idea if Henry Cavendish associated with them in any way. From the Grey side of his family, there were three living members of Cavendish's generation, John William and Francis Henry Egerton, the seventh and eighth earls of Bridgewater, and John, second earl of Ashburnham, and in the next generation there was George, the future third earl of Ashburnham. The two earls of Bridgewater were Fellows of the Royal Society, and Francis Henry, the eighth earl, is well known to historians of science as the founder of the *Bridgewater Treatises*, the authors of which were selected by the president of the Royal Society and the Bishop of London to demonstrate the "Power, Wisdom, and Goodness of God, as manifested in the Creation."[139] This clergyman was strongly interested in science but not in a way that would have brought him and Henry Cavendish together. Lord Charles Cavendish kept a correspondence with his sister-in-law Lady Ashburnham, Jemima de Grey,[140] but we have come upon no record of contact between Henry Cavendish and the Ashburnham or Bridgewater families. The second and third earls of Ashburnham were tories, but that would not have been a main consideration. Henry Cavendish saw to it that his wealth remained within the Cavendish family; his will made perfect sense, its surprises merely minor variations on the standard theme.

Lady Sarah Spencer did not regret that the duke of Devonshire gained nothing from Cavendish's death, since he and his heir, Hartington, were "*pretty well* off."[141] The duke's complaint about Cavendish's will had to do with ritual. The scientists, however, believed that they had a substantial complaint. Cavendish received more criticism in death than he had in life, in particular for not leaving money to Davy.[142] Davy himself had expected it, Blagden thought:.

> Davy said, Mr. C. has at least remembered one man of science /i.e., Blagden/, in a tone of voice which expressed much: & added that at the time when Mr. C. made Hatchett much distressed & much with him, so wondered he had not then remembered him, to this I answered, it was not likely that he shd leave to a man of Hatchett's expectations /Hatchett would become rich/. Wollaston's countenance was unchanged.[143]

There were rumors that even Blagden was disappointed, that he had higher expectations,[144] but there is no evidence of this in anything he wrote including his diary. Amidst the disappointments in the days following Cavendish's death, Blagden staunchly defended his old friend.

The funeral procession that Blagden watched from his window set out with the body from Clapham Common at seven in the morning on March 8th. The train of carriages carrying members of the family proceeded northward through London on their way to Derby,[145] where Cavendish was to be buried in the family vault under the Church of All Saints. Before that the procession would be met at the gates of the city by twenty-four burghers and twenty-four constables and a retinue of city officials (all of whom were paid to do this) dressed in black. The pomp and ceremony were invariable for the Cavendish dead,

---

[138]Lady Sarah Spencer quoted in Hugh Stokes, *The Devonshire House Circle* (London: Herbert Jenkins, 1917), 315.

[139]Charles C. Gillispie, *Genesis and Geology: A Study in the Relations of Scientific Thought, Natural Theology, and Social Opinion in Great Britain, 1790–1850* (New York: Harper & Row, 1959), 209.

[140]Henry Cavendish, "Papers in Walnut Cabinet," Cavendish Mss, Misc.

[141]Stokes, *Devonshire House Circle*, 315.

[142]5 and 6 Mar. 1810, Blagden Diary, Royal Society, 5:back p. 430 and p. 431.

[143]8 Mar. 1810, Blagden Diary, Royal Society, 5:back p. 431 and p. 432.

[144]Henry, Lord Brougham, *Lives of Men of Letters and Science Who Flourished in the Time of George III* (Philadelphia, 1845), 250–59, on 258.

[145]Lord Bessborough to Charles Blagden, 7 Mar. 1810, Blagden Letters, Royal Society, B.149.

and it was elaborate and expensive. The pace of the procession was appropriately funereal, nine days to and from Derby. Everything had to be rented for that period, the hearse and coach ornamented with black ostrich feathers and drawn by six horses, eight men on horses, and on and on. There were five private carriages belonging to the duke of Devonshire and to Henry Cavendish's heirs, Lord George Cavendish, Lord Bessborough, and Lord George's oldest son, William Cavendish. The bill for nine days came to about 750 pounds.[146]

One of Lord George's minor expenses was the inscription on Cavendish's tomb. He might have followed the example of Archimedes, whose tomb, at his request, was inscribed with a sphere inside a cylinder, whose proportions he had determined. Cavendish's tomb would then have had a sphere and a circular plate of the same diameter, the electrical charges of which Cavendish determined were in the proportion of 1 to 1.57, to the wonder of later scientists.[147] But nothing so scientifically fitting was done. What went onto Cavendish's tomb was traditional and otherwise fitting, composed, we think, by Blagden for the family:

Henry Cavendish Esq. F.S.A. Son of the late Lord Charles Cavendish, one of the old Council and a Fellow of the Royal Society and an elected trustee of the British Museum. Born the 10th of October 1731. Died February 24th 1810.[148]

The scientific colleagues who gathered at Banks's house in the weeks following Cavendish's death had concerns other than his will, about which nothing could be done. For one thing, there was Cavendish's great library, which passed along with all of his other personal possessions to Lord George. Blagden knew that Cavendish wanted it not to be dispersed but to be kept accessible, as it had been in his lifetime.[149] There was no doubt talk about Cavendish's instruments, for Davy was soon to be given his pick of them, while others went to the instrument-maker John Newman of Regent Street, son of the maker of Cavendish's wind measurer.[150].

Of great importance to Cavendish's colleagues were his scientific papers, and with this subject we come around to our starting point; for if Cavendish's papers had not been preserved, we, his biographers, would not have got far. From the first days there was talk of an edition of Cavendish's published works, but just what to do

about his unpublished papers was an open question.[151] Blagden thought that these papers would be found in a state unfit for publication. Lord George wanted Blagden to look over the papers anyway, and so on 6 April Blagden, Banks, and evidently other interested colleagues met with Lord George at Cavendish's house at Clapham Common to inspect the manuscripts. After spending about four hours on them they decided that the papers were, for the most part, "only mathematics." Blagden returned to Cavendish's house, and for the next two weeks he was kept busy with the papers, after which he reported to Lord George:

We have now finished the search which your Lordship desired us to make, in the hope of finding, among the papers of the late Mr Henry Cavendish, something which he had prepared & thought fit for printing. Our search has in this respect been fruitless; a result for which we are sorry, though we must confess that it was not unexpected to us; because we knew that Mr Cavendish was always ready to publish whatever he had made out to his full satisfaction. There are some few small scraps, which are transcribed nearly fair, as if he had thought of communicating them to the R.S.: but as it is apparent that they have been laid by, in that state, for a considerable time, it is to be supposed that he afterwards discovered some weakness or imperfection in them, or that they had been anticipated in a manner of which he was not aware when he composed them; in short, that he had some good reason for not giving them to the public. In truth,

---

[146] "Mr Swift's Bill for Expenses Att⁸ the Funeral of Hen: Cavendish Esq.," 29 Aug. 1810, Devon. Coll., L/114/74.

[147] The inscription could have been globe and cylinder, exactly like Archimedes', since Cavendish measured their relative capacities too. For the circular plate and sphere, Cavendish did several experimental determinations, obtaining a value between 1.50 and 1.57. The latter value he preferred, since he entered it in the paper he intended for publication. William Thomson came across the value 1.57 in Cavendish's papers in 1849 and remarked: "a most valuable mine of results. I find already that the capacity of a disc (circular) was determined experimentally by Cavendish as 1/1.57 of that of a sphere of same radius. Now we have capacity of disc = $2/\pi$ a = $a/1.571$!" Quoted in *The Electrical Researches of the Honourable Henry Cavendish*, ed. James Clerk Maxwell (Cambridge, 1879), xxxix. In 1832 George Green had derived the modern theoretical value for the ratio: $1/2$ π, or 1.57. Cavendish, *Sci. Pap.* 1: 433.

[148] "H. Cavendish Esq. Inscription for the Plate on the Coffin. Died 24 Feb. 1810," Devon. Coll.

[149] 3 and 4 Mar. 1810, Blagden Diary, Royal Society, 5:429, back p. 429, and p. 430.

[150] Wilson, *Cavendish*, 475.

[151] This discussion of Cavendish's papers is taken from Russell McCormmach, "Henry Cavendish on the Theory of Heat," *Isis* 79 (1988): 37–67, on 37–38.

Mr Cavendish's fame stands so high already in the scientific world, that no papers but of the most perfect kind could be expected to increase it, whilst it might be lowered by anything of an inferior nature.[152]

Blagden and his colleagues firmly recommended against including any of the unpublished papers in the proposed edition of Cavendish's papers, but they expected that dates and circumstances of his discoveries might be found among them that would be useful for the introduction. Since the papers were in "great disorder," some qualified person with time to spare would have to be found to go through them. They could think of only one person, the man whom Cavendish sometimes employed, the clerk of the Royal Society, George Gilpin, but they decided that he was probably too ill to take on the task. They supposed that Lord George might ask around. Three months after Cavendish's death, Blagden and Banks, between themselves, agreed to postpone plans for an edition of Cavendish's works.

Blagden, Banks, and the others recognized the perils of trying to improve a reputation posthumously, but they were mistaken about the worth of Cavendish's papers. That could hardly have been otherwise, since the papers contained much that was original, and much more than the work of a few hours or a few days was required to appreciate this. Blagden was right in thinking that Cavendish's fame was then so great that no unfinished papers could increase it, but he was wrong about the future. Today Cavendish is nearly as well known for what he did not publish as for what he did. One eminent scientist after another has studied his manuscripts and has come away in wonder at what he achieved with the instruments and concepts available to him. To them it has seemed as if Cavendish were not of his own century, but of the next.[153]

---

[152]Charles Blagden to "My Lord" /Lord George Cavendish/, n.d., draft, Blagden Collection, Royal Society, Misc. Matter—Unclassified.

[153]For example: one hundred years after Cavendish had done his experiments on electrical capacity, in 1874, Maxwell wrote to W. Garnett, his future biographer, that Cavendish's "measures of capacity will give us some work at the Cavendish Laboratory, before we work up to the point where he left it." Quoted in Joseph Larmor's preface to vol. 1 of the 1921 edition of Cavendish's *Sci. Pap.*

IN CONCLUSION

Cavendish

Henry Cavendish was the outstanding mathematical and experimental scientist in Britain between Newton and Maxwell. The first part of this estimate was often made soon after Cavendish died, as we have pointed out. The second half we make with hindsight.

But what of Cavendish the *complete* man? Is that question a contradiction in terms? In the introduction to a course in chemistry in 1855, the lecturer warned his students: "It may be fairly asked, why bring such a character forward for examination? . . . Is it enough *not* to be a villain, a debauchee, a murderer? Or rather is it not our duty to be *something* that shall create for *positive good* on our fellow-men? To this the answer must be made, that the character of Cavendish is not introduced as a subject of admiration, or for imitation, but rather as a warning to all men who cultivate the intellect, that they do not neglect the social portion of their nature . . ."[1] This lecturer had read a book published four years before, George Wilson's *The Life of the Honourable Henry Cavendish*.

Wilson's Cavendish is a vivid portrait of Victorian negations, of a man lacking in piety, family, philanthropy, and poetry. What Wilson made of this moral negativism cannot be improved upon, a perfect portrait of its kind. Concerned with the individual soul, Wilson looked deeply into his subject with his probe, morality, and rendered a judgment, which was pitiless. The anecdotes testifying to Cavendish's cold eccentricity can be looked at another way, however, as evidence of withdrawal and a desperate dependence on external regularity. They are good anecdotes, but they do not of themselves offer us an understanding of the complete man. This is perhaps to say the obvious: Wilson's *Life of Cavendish* cannot satisfy our age as it did his.

We have presented Cavendish's life from the perspective of science; according to our understanding, a life of science in the eighteenth century could be a complete life for one as gifted and directed as Cavendish. Moreover, it could be a rich life, not an impoverished one. We have brought forward not what is absent in our subject but what is there, and what is there, within our subject, is in part drawn from what is there outside it. The familial, political, and scientific mansions that Cavendish inhabited provided him with the choices by which he gave shape and meaning to his life. We have written this biography primarily from the perspective of the social world of our subject.

Yet if any one scientist of the past invites our psychological wonder, surely he is Cavendish. Lest our biography appear incomplete in this respect, we here briefly discuss a psychological perspective, that of personality.

Consider one of the standard personality traits used in psychological questionnaires today, openness. Cavendish, a man of profoundly secluded habits, was an outspoken champion of openness, one who placed the utmost value on public knowledge and the ideas of others.[2] The Royal Society with its profession of openness was a congenial second home for him. Between societies. too, he stood for openness: he urged that as policy the Royal Society and the Royal institution should exchange materials presented to them. Famous, after his lifetime, for his reluctance to publish his work, Cavendish had rather, to put it provocatively, a fever to publish. When he held back from publication, which he often did, he did so not from a desire for secrecy. He saw the damage secrecy did to his friends, Michell, Canton, and Knight. He refused Michell's request that he keep a discovery secret and instead persuaded Michell to let him announce it to the world. He persuaded the government to lift the official cloak of secrecy on

---

[1]The introductory lecture to a course on chemistry at the National Medical College by Lewis H. Steiner, *Henry Cavendish and the Discovery of the Chemical Composition of Water* (New York, 1855), 6.

[2]Robert R. McCrea and Paul T. Costa, Jr.,*Personality in Adulthood* (New York and London: Guilford Press, 1990), 44.

Hatchett's experiments carried out under his direction. When asked his opinion on the author of a scientific pamphlet who wanted to remain anonymous, Cavendish "answered at once & decisively that the only way to make it produce any useful effect was for the author to sign his name"; Cavendish's "opinion, so decisively against its being anonymous," caused the author to change his mind and sign his name to it.[3] When he took over his father's farms—to give an example from outside science—he told his steward that the condition of his job was complete openness. Openness is a significant trait of Cavendish.

Let us consider another standard trait, neuroticism. There is ample evidence that Cavendish suffered from intense anxiety. His voice was excited, feeble, and hesitating, and at meetings of scientists, he could be heard to utter a "shrill cry . . . as he shuffled quickly from room to room." In reaction to the stress of the outside world, he lived as a solitary, "secluded," as Blagden said.

The term most often used to describe Cavendish's personality by persons who knew him was "shyness."[4] His shyness was extreme, a disposition which—like its opposite in another person, total lack of shyness—was and is regarded as anti-social. Extreme shyness does not preclude a public life and it is compatible with good social skills, but it does make that life uncomfortable, as Cavendish certainly found it to be. His anxiety was greatest when he was in the presence of strangers, especially those of the opposite sex. He was observed to be awkward, show embarrassment, fall silent, and if he had a chance, run. He was also observed to approach strangers, revealing a mix of interest and avoidance that is typical of excessively shy persons.[5] Upon seeing Cavendish for the first time, a visitor at Banks's house noticed that Cavendish was listening attentively to what he was saying: "When I caught his eye he retired in great haste, but I soon found he was again listening near me."[6] Morbid shyness is correlated with obsessive-compulsive behavior, the subject of many Cavendish anecdotes. Another way of looking at it is that by intelligently ordering his life in science, Cavendish escaped a common outcome of shyness, a delayed and poor career.[7] Thomas Young observed Cavendish's "painful preminence":[8] the pain and the eminence were inseparable. In the complete absence of records for Cavendish's early life, we

can only mention common causes of shyness, which might have been present in his case. Even if parents are considerate, children can be bullied by caretakers into fearful shyness, or if children are kept in isolation, their earliest fears of strangers may never leave them.[9] That is compatible with the modern finding that the onset of intense, irrational fears of strangers and scrutiny is adolescence, followed by a lifelong disability. It would seem likely in any case that Cavendish's shyness had a hereditary component. The taciturnity of the Cavendishes was legendary, and of all the traits of personality, shyness has the strongest genetic basis.[10] In prevalence, among mental disorders,

---

[3]Charles Blagden to Joseph Banks, 24 and 26 Oct. 1784, BM(NH), DTC 3: 83–86.

[4]For example: John Barrow spoke of Cavendish's "extreme shyness," confirmed by "all his habits": Cavendish seemed "to consider himself as a solitary being in the world, and to feel himself unfit for society": *Sketches of the Royal Society and Royal Society Club* (London, 1849), 144. Another example: Henry Brougham spoke of Cavendish's "peculiarly shy habits" and his "morbid shyness": *Lives of Men of Letters and Science Who Flourished in the Time of George III*, vol. 1 (London, 1845), 446.

[5]Jonathan M. Cheek and Stephen R. Briggs, "Shyness as a Personality Trait," in *Shyness and Embarrassment: Perspectives from Social Psychology*, ed. W. Ray Crozier (Cambridge: Cambridge University Press, 1990), 315–37, on 316, 319, 322. Carroll E. Izard and Marion C. Hyson, "Shyness as a Discrete Emotion," In *Shyness: Perspectives on Research and Treatment*, eds. W. H. Jones, J. M. Cheek, and S. R. Briggs (New York and London: Plenum Press, 1968), 147–60, on 151, 153.

[6]George Wilson, *The Life of the Honourable Henry Cavendish* (London, 1851), 168.

[7]Cheek and Briggs, "Shyness," 328–29.

[8]Thomas Young, "Life of Cavendish," reprinted in Henry Cavendish, *The Scientific Papers of the Honourable Henry Cavendish*, vol. 1, ed. E. Thorpe (Cambridge: Cambridge University Press, 1921), 435–47, on 445.

[9]Arnold H. Buss, "A Theory of Shyness," in *Shyness: Perspectives on Research and Treatment*, 39–46, on 44–45. Buss thinks that fearful shyness and self–conscious shyness are distinct; if so, both behaviors were evident in Cavendish.

[10]Cheek and Briggs, "Shyness," 329. Jerome Kagan, J. Steven Reznick, and Nancy Snidman, "Biological Bases of Childhood Shyness," *Science* 240 (1988): 167–71. Debate about personality traits goes through cycles, and some social and experimental psychologists deny them entirely. There would seem, however, to be little doubt that certain enduring emotional aspects of personality such as fearfulness, so conspicuous in Cavendish, agree with an interpretation relying on traits. Psychologists who work with traits have more than one model from which to choose. According to one in common use, five traits are sufficient to describe empirically the configuration of any personality. Another uses seven traits grouped into four traits of "temperament" and three of "character." Temperamental traits, according to the latter model, are moderately heritable and unchanging from infancy to adulthood; those of character are only weakly heritable and are largely learned and continue to develop through life. As this biography goes to press, we note the first confirmed demonstration of a "specific genetic locus involved in neurotransmission and a normal personality trait." The trait in question is one of temperament, "novelty seeking," on which Cavendish would rank exceedingly low. (Although Cavendish enters

social phobia comes only after alcoholism and depression.[11]

We have noted that Cavendish would be seen to freeze in front of the door at Banks's Sunday open houses, unable to go inside until other guests approached him from behind. Cavendish was not only a man of extreme social phobia but at the same time a man of considerable courage, for courage is required of one to perform the most ordinary motions in society if one is afflicted as he was. It was because of his courage that he did science instead of pursue a reclusive hobby, since doing science implies coming into the world.

Depression is a disorder of mood commonly found in extremely shy people;[12] from that disorder, we may speculate, Cavendish suffered all his life. Concerning its causes, there is a range of medical opinion, but on its symptoms there is good agreement: lowering of vital activity, loss of interest, absence of sexual desire, emotional unresponsiveness, irritability, and anxiety, among others.[13] Cavendish showed most of these symptoms. After an evening spent in Cavendish's company, Blagden normally noted one word in his diary to sum up Cavendish's behavior. "Secluded," his word for his character sketch of Cavendish, is not a word found in his diary, nor would preferred it have been fitting, since Cavendish was in Blagden's company. The words Blagden used in his diary did, however, suggest a desire for seclusion. They were harsh words: melancholy, forbidding, dry, sulky. Occasionally, and far less often, he used words of relief: civil, civiler, and pleasant to talk with. *Odd*: peculiar, eccentric, that which stands alone, solitary, singular. *Dry*: showing no emotion, uncommunicative, cold, distant. *Sulky*: obdurately out of humor, aloof, passive and silent in fending off approaches. "Dry" and "sulky" are the words Blagden used most often, and although he occasionally applied them to Joseph Banks and other companions, he applied them consistently only to Cavendish.

After a social gathering, Blagden wrote in his diary, "talk about Mr Cavendish, & explanation of character,"[14] but he did not record what that explanation was. On another occasion, after Cavendish had left his party at the Monday Club, Blagden and Aubert talked about Cavendish and agreed that he had "no affections, but always meant well."[15] In a moment of truth, Blagden confided in his diary: "made nothing of C cannot understand him."[16] In

one respect biographers have it easier than do the friends of the subject, since they do not have to adapt to the living reality. But they have it harder, too, in that they must come to an understanding of their subject, however ambiguous and limited the evidence. In the case of Cavendish, we, his biographers, must try to understand a man who could be characterized by his *friends* as a man without affections. Depression is commonly described as an inability to feel affections; although they would seem to have more reason to, depressed people cry less than others, for the affect is suppressed.[17]

In response to a correspondence begun by Priestley, Cavendish said that he would send an account of his experiments in the future, "but I am so far from possessing any of your activity that I am afraid I shall not make any very soon."[18] Compared to Priestley, any person might feel inactive, but for Cavendish inactivity was self-characterizing. For six months Priestley's second letter went unanswered by Cavendish, who apologized:

---

the standard histories of science as a "discoverer" of new truths of nature, he did not seek novelty as psychologists understand the term; there is no contradiction here, as is clarified in Thomas S. Kuhn's *Structure of Scientific Revolutions*.) The stories about Cavendish's strange behavior all relate to heritable traits of temperament; his life in science relates as well to the more plastic traits of character. We would not be surprised if future biographers of Cavendish were to give even greater attention than we have to his familial background. The rapidly expanding understanding of personality on a fundamental scientific level promises useful insights in this regard. C. Robert Cloninger, "Temperament and Personality," *Current Biology* 4 (1994): 266–73. C. Robert Cloninger, Rolf Adolfsson, and Nenad M. Svrakic, "Mapping Genes for Human Personality," *Nature Genetics* 12 (1996): 3–4. Richard P. Ebstein et al., "Dopamine D4 Receptor (D4DR) Exon III Polymorphism Associated with the Human Personality Trait of Novelty Seeking," ibid., pp. 78–80. Jonathan Benjamin et al., "Population and Familial Association between the D4 Dopamine Receptor Gene and Measures of Novelty Seeking," ibid., pp. 81–84.

[11] From a summary of a symposium on social phobia held on 18 Nov. 1993 in San Diego: "Practical Approaches of to the Treatment of Social Phobia," *Journal of Clinical Psychiatry* 55 (1994): 367–74.

[12] McCrae and Costa, *Personality in Adulthood*, 29.

[13] Max Hamilton, "Symptoms and Assessment of Depression," in *Handbook of Affective Disorders*, ed. E. S. Paykel (New York: Guilford Press, 1982), 3–11.

[14] 14 July 1795, Blagden Diary, Royal Society, 3:back p. 65.

[15] 15 Sep. 1794, Blagden Diary, Royal Society, 3:back p. 16.

[16] 27 Aug. 1795, Blagden Diary, Royal Society, 3:67.

[17] Carol Zisowitz Stearns, "Sadness," in *Handbook of Emotions*. eds. M. Lewis and J. M. Haviland (New York: Guilford Press, 1993) 547–61, on 559.

[18] Henry Cavendish to Joseph Priestley, n.d. /May or June 1784/, draft, Cavendish Mss. New Correspondence; published in *A Scientific Autobiography of Joseph Priestley (1733–1804): Selected Scientific Correspondence*, ed. R.E. Schofield (Cambridge, Mass.: MIT Press, 1966), 232–33.

as I make not a tenth part of the exper that you do & as my facility in writing falls short of yours in a still greater proportion I am afraid you will think me a bad correspondent & that the advantage lies intirely on my side. . .[19]

During the dissensions of the Royal Society, Blagden wrote to Banks that "Mr. Cavendish said he had no other objection to taking the lead than his unfitness for active exertion."[20]. Repeatedly Cavendish abandoned promising researches, and there were spells when he did no research at all but only followed routine, the substitute for undependable initiative.

Depression is fully compatible with scientific work of the highest order, even if it is seriously interrupted; examples are Cavendish's contemporary Joseph Louis Lagrange, and our Salvador Luria, who has written movingly about it.[21] The earlier standard image of the scholar as unequal to polite society, contentious and melancholy, has counterparts in real life throughout history.[22] Newton was secluded and morose, and so have been many other good scientists.

It is, of course, conceivable that Cavendish suffered from an affective disorder of a far less familiar kind, one which today might readily be identified with this or that one-in-a thousand syndrome. His habitual profound withdrawal led one contemporary to characterize him as the "coldest and most indifferent of mortals."[22a] The last few years have seen the publication of a number of neurological and psychological interpretations of historical figures including scientists such as Newton and Einstein; Cavendish, too, with his singular drive to understand the universe, may well one day invite such interpretation. Like everyone, his neurological makeup together with his life experiences imbued him with a select view of the world; his, we know, was inhabited by, among other things, demons that he could subdue only by imposing a vigilant orderliness on all phases of his life. By following in his father's footsteps, he brought his world together with that of science, with its discoverable orderliness, the calming paths of wandering stars, laid bare by nature, from which demons are strictly excluded. How did he come to make this choice? What did it mean to him? Cavendish left no "inside narrative" of his life telling us why science attracted him, nor would we expect one from him, but other scientists have done so, and their accounts may suggest questions that could lead to a deeper understand of our subject.[22b]

We have deferred these observations on Cavendish's personality to the end of this biography, for we did not write it beginning with them. In the Introduction, we discuss our direction and why we take it. Here we will make only one further point. Other than for both being studious, Lord Charles and Henry Cavendish do not seem to have had similar personalities. Lord Charles was well rounded, drawn to sports, races, and hunting.[23] Comfortable in society, Lord Charles was a man who confidently assumed the chair at meetings. By contrast, ordinary company caused Henry acute

[19]Henry Cavendish to Joseph Priestley, 20 Dec. 1784, draft, Cavendish Mss, New Correspondence; published in *A Scientific Autobiography of Joseph Priestley*, 239–40, on 240.

[20]Charles Blagden to Joseph Banks, 5 Apr. 1784, BM(NH), DTC 3:20–21.

[21]S. E. Luria, *A Slot Machine, a Broken Test Tube: An Autobiography* (New York: Harper & Row, 1984), 215–16.

[22]Steven, Shapin, " 'A Scholar and a Gentleman': The Problematic Identity of the Scientific Practitioner in Early Modern England," *Hist. Sci.* 29 (1991): 279–327, on 290, 292.

[22a]Wilson, *Cavendish*, 173. A poignant, if ambiguous, entry in Blagden's diary reads: "Conversation about Monday Club. Mr. C/avendish/ knew not what to do. Said some men without certain feelings." 12 Nov. 1795, Blagden diary, RS, 3:76. If we are right about Cavendish's interest in music, he had a means of expressing feeling independently of companionship. The main task of music, as it was understood in the eighteenth century, was not to imitate nature but to imitate the feelings, and of all of the arts, music was understood to be the art that related most directly to the feelings. *Music and Aesthetics in the Eighteenth Century and Early Nineteenth Centuries*, ed. P. le Huray and J. Day (Cambridge: Cambridge University Press, 1981), 3, 5.

[22b]Until ten years ago, when Temple Grandin published an autobiography, *Emergence: Labeled Autistic*, it was believed that an inside narrative could not be written by an autistic person. Regarding herself as a "totally logical and scientific person" and her autism as a disorder of affect and empathy, she recalls Cavendish in certain ways. (We observe in Cavendish a number of autisticlike traits: single-mindedness, apparent inability to feel certain emotions, secludedness, rigidities of behavior, odd gait, harsh voice, strange vocalizations, panic attacks, self-acknowledged social unfitness.) Grandin does not have feelings associated with personal relations, as a result of which she misses those social signals that are the basis of humanity's "magical communication." To deal with her "primary emotion," fear, she has looked to "logic, science, and intellect": she has found the language of science to be relatively free of implicit social assumptions, inviting her to "make science her whole life." She regards her relatively mild, high-functioning form of autism not only as a deprivation but also as a positive gift, endowing her with a singlemindedness that enables her to excel. Holding the prevalent view that there is a genetic component to autism, she believes that the persistence of autistic traits has an evolutionary significance and that persons with bits of them might be geniuses. Whatever the neuropsychological basis of Cavendish's fears, he like Grandin overcame them to achieve a productive, fulfilling life within science. Temple Grandin, *Thinking in Pictures and Other Reports from My Life with Autism* (New York: Doubleday, 1995), 60, 172, 185–89. Oliver Sacks, *An Anthropologist on Mars* (New York: Vintage, 1995), 165–65, 272–73, 277, 291–92.

[23]Duke of Newcastle to the duke of Devonshire, 21 Nov. 1745. Lord Hartington to the duke of Devonshire, 23 Dec. 1746. Lord Charles Cavendish to John Manners, 18 June 1772, draft, Devon. Coll., Nos. 182.32, 260.65, and L/114/32.

discomfort, and he would rather have been lashed to the mast than outwardly to take charge. Yet in their dedication to science and tireless attention to the affairs of the Royal Society, they were very much alike. Factors in addition to individual personality were decisive in their choice of a common path.

Lord Charles and Henry Cavendish gave themselves to science with the intensity that their forebears, the early dukes of Devonshire, had given themselves to politics. We have made the case that in a certain sense their lives in science began in English dukedoms. We return to this connection, to the qualification English. In England the power of the nobility did not derive from legal rights and royal favors but from ownership of land. Land could be kept in the family by marriage settlements, which in turn kept the family intact with an identity that passed from generation to generation.[24] Lord Charles Cavendish and after him Henry had landed property, and although the income from it was trifling in the end—the great wealth of Charles and Henry Cavendish was the same as that of rich people in the city, not land but stocks—the meaning of this land was not trifling, since it derived from the source of the family's place in society, its estate. The landowner and the man of science had this in common, an authority that resided in something normally regarded as outside politics, and so outside time, as eternal.

The English aristocracy escaped the fate of their Continental counterparts, overthrown by revolution, because they themselves had proved ready to carry out revolution to protect their property. The repeated rejections by the aristocracy of attempts by the crown to increase its power culminated in the Glorious Revolution at the end of the seventeenth century, making the state subservient to the landed interest.[25] In eighteenth-century England, a contented aristocracy acted responsibly, ensuring its survival, and establishing, as one commentator has put it, "the tradition of public duty."[26] That tradition contained within it, if implicitly, the direction that Charles and Henry Cavendish gave to their lives; in so doing they extended the idea of public service.

Younger sons of the aristocracy, if not totally dissolute, ordinarily went into the established professions, especially politics and the military.

That brought them a supplementary income, however small. Lord Charles Cavendish had a good income from his family, which gave him some choice, which he exercised by entering first politics and then science. The professions in England had greatly expanded in the fifty years before Lord Charles Cavendish, but the new ones were largely improvised and without formal training or standards of entry, and science as not yet truly recognized as an occupation. At around the time Lord Charles Cavendish came of age, in the 1720s and 1730s, the professions in Britain were harder to define than before, and an experience of what we would call professional solidarity was rare indeed, though esprit de corps could be found here and there.[27] For the Cavendishes, the ambiguous character of science was fortunate, since if it had been regarded as a profession equivalent to law or medicine, it would have been foreclosed to them. Science instead was open to interpretation, and like art or gaming or amateur architecture or any kind of public service bridging status and income, it could be embraced by an aristocrat like Cavendish as a freely chosen outlet for his energies. Cavendish's redirection did not take social courage so much as intelligence and imagination in thinking about the possibilities of his social world.

In time Lord Charles Cavendish came to recognize in science a complete sphere of action, a world in becoming; in his son Henry's time, it was a realized world, only one waiting to be generally recognized. Henry Cavendish went beyond his father's activity to the one that has come to be valued highest in modern science, the advancement of the knowledge of nature through published research. (But we will have written this book in vain if we have not made the point that in the eighteenth-century, publication was only one and

---

[24]H. J. Habakkuk, "England," in *The European Nobility in the Eighteenth Century*, ed. A. Goodwin (London: Adam and Charles Black, 1953), 1–21, on 2.

[25]M.L. Bush, *The English Aristocracy: A Comparative Synthesis* (Manchester: Manchester University Press, 1984), 12.

[26]Edward John B. D. S., Lord Montagu of Beaulieu, *More Equal Than Others: The Changing Fortunes of the British and European Aristocracies* (London: Michael Joseph, 1970), 156–57.

[27]Geoffrey Holmes, *Augustan England. Professions, State and Society, 1680–1730* (London: George Allen & Unwin, 1982), 4, 9. We agree generally with Holmes's point, though when a physician was proposed for fellowship in the Royal Society, the proposal was usually by another physician, which suggests an element of association.

not necessarily the most important indication of a scientist's direct contributions.)[28]

The eighteenth century was the age of aristocracy in Britain. Stirring speeches were made in parliament and bold actions were taken in the field by men who came from that segment of society. But Walpole and Nelson did not come from it, nor did the leaders of industry and commerce, nor did the poets, artists, and inventors. A case might be made that the aristocracy knew its finest hour when Henry Cavendish delicately laid his standard weights in the pan of his precision chemical balance. We conclude our biography by returning to the beginning, the "Problem." Although Henry Cavendish left a treasure-hoard of written words on scientific subjects for posterity, he spoke few of them to his contemporaries. Lord Brougham, who knew him, thought that he "uttered fewer words in the course of his life than any man who ever lived to fourscore years, not at all excepting the monks of La Trappe."[29] Johnson said that "words are the daughters of the earth, and . . . things are the sons of heaven," and "language is only the instrument of science, and words are but the signs of ideas."[30] The scientists' credo was the Royal Society's *Nullius in verba*, their insistence that the facts of nature are not bound by any dogma.[31] Pronouncements of the new philosophy, however, do not help distinguish Cavendish from his voluble individualistic colleagues. Poverty of language was certainly not at issue, for Cavendish wrote as he worked, with precision and with complete command of word and expression. Neither was disinterest in communicating; that can be ruled out by everything Cavendish stood for. Neither, we believe, was Cavendish's station in society, though a case has been made that it was.[32] His acute social anxiety is obvious and certainly contributed to his silent way as did, perhaps, the family's "hereditary tactiurnity."[33] But Cavendish's silence had other or additional origins: we believe that like the Trappists' vow, there was something chosen about it. Two considerations have weight with us. We have given a number of examples of Cavendish's wariness of words, of their use as instruments of deception. His understanding of language was in agreement with linguistic thought in England in the late eighteenth century, when the object was no longer to reform language, to make it perfect, as it had been with the founders of the Royal Society, but to study it as it was used,

as custom[34]. The scientific revolution had revealed a new world and with it the need for a language of measurements and abstract mathematical relations, and in part, we think, Cavendish's silence was an acknowledgment of the inadequacy of customary spoken language to represent that world. The pains he took always to define his quantitative terms before beginning to reason with them is an indication of what we mean here. When Cavendish did speak, as Playfair noted, his speech was always

––––––––––

[28]There were different opinions on the weight to be given to publication in the eighteenth century, the differences having much to do with the scientists' occupations and status. When Cavendish said to Priestley that he did not have a tenth of Priestley's industry in experimenting and in writing, Priestley took offense. He lectured Cavendish: "You greatly overrate both my readiness in making them /experiments/, and my facility in writing; and may not perhaps consider that my time is likewise much engaged in things of a very different nature." Priestley may have had Cavendish, among others, in mind in the preface to *Experiments and Observations on Different Kinds of Air*, "When, for the sake of a little more reputation, men can keep brooding over a new fact, in the discovery of which they might, possibly, have very little real merit, till they think they can astonish the world with a system as complete as it is new, and give mankind a prodigious idea of their judgment and penetration; they are justly punished for their ingratitude to the fountain of all knowledge, and for their want of a genuine love of science and of mankind, in finding their boasted discoveries anticipated . . . ." Priestley was probably right in thinking that Cavendish did not know how he spent his time; by the same token, Priestley did not how Cavendish spent his. Apart for their regard for one another's work in science, which was very high, Priestley and Cavendish probably had little understanding and appreciation of one another's way of living and thinking. The social gulf between them was too great. Henry Cavendish to Joseph Priestley, 20 Dec. 1784, draft; Joseph Priestley to Henry Cavendish, 30 Dec. 1784; published in *A Scientific Autobiography of Joseph Priestley*, 239–42; quotation of Priestley on 240. The quotation from Priestley's *Experiments and Observations* is taken from Edward Thorpe's introduction to vol. 2 of *The Scientific Papers of the Honourable Henry Cavendish*, F.R.S., ed. E. Thorpe (Cambridge: Cambridge University Press, 1921), 6.

[29]Henry, Lord Brougham, "Cavendish," in *Lives of Men and Letters and Science Who Flourished in the Time of George III* (Philadelphia, 1845), 250–59, on 259.

[30]Quoted in Hans Aarsleff, *The Study of Language in England, 1780–1860* (Minneapolis: University of Minnesota Press, 1983), 122.

[31]Larry Stewart, *The Rise of Public Science: Rhetoric, Technology. and Natural Philosophy in Newtonian Britain, 1660–1750* (Cambridge: Cambridge University Press, 1992), 3.

[32]James Gerald Crowther attributes Cavendish's failure to publish much of his best work to his class and wealth, which isolated him from the scientists of the industrial age who would otherwise have encouraged him. Crowther's analysis is provocative, but it is too schematic to be very convincing or helpful. Class and wealth *were* important to Cavendish and in *many* ways, as we have argued. Lord Charles and Henry Cavendish, for instance, derived stimulus from their class to enter public work in science, just as, say, James Watt derived scientific stimulus from his class. "Henry Cavendish," in *Scientists of the Industrial Revolution: Joseph Black, James Watt, Joseph Priestley. Henry Cavendish* (London: Crescent Press, 1962), 271–340.

[33]Expression used by Henry Holland, quoted in Gwendy Caroe, *The Royal Institution: An informal History* (London: John Murray, 1985), 39.

[34]Murray Cohen, *Sensible Words: Linguistic Practice in England 1640–1785* (Baltimore: The Johns Hopkins University Press, 1977), 78, 88–96. The vogue of books on prescriptive English grammar in the late eighteenth century does not invalidate the point made here.

"exceedingly to the purpose, and either brings some excellent information, or draws some important conclusion."[35] Davy put it forcefully: when Cavendish did choose to speak, what he said was "luminous and profound."[36] On the subjects he cared to speak about, Cavendish spoke precisely and sparingly as a point of conscience. This leads us to our second consideration: silence can be positive.[37] Young recognized this in his observation that Cavendish's hesitancy of speech was not a physical defect but an expression of the "constitution of his mind."[38]

Cavendish's wonderfully concentrated inner life was directed to nature, as we have seen, but if we are right about his music, it was not entirely so directed. The main task of music, as it was understood in the eighteenth century, was not to imitate nature but to imitate the feelings, and of all of the arts, music was understood to be the art that spoke most directly to the feelings.[39] Together with many of his colleagues, through music Cavendish had access to an expression of feeling that was at once mathematically precise and distinct from the mathematics of natural description, one that could stand in for the (for him so difficult) spoken and otherwise conventionally acted out expression of feeling. This is not to say that the work of science lies outside the world of feelings, far from it, but only to suggest the clearly *limited* domain of social experience in which Cavendish might be characterized, as his colleagues did characterize him, as a man without affections.

This silent man is an endlessly fascinating figure. Despite the length of this biography, when all is said and done, the person of Cavendish remains in large part in shadow. At the heart of the problem of Cavendish lies the mystery of human communication.

35John Playfair quoted in Wilson, Cavendish, 166.

36John Davy, *Memoirs of the Life of Sir Humphry Davy. Bart.*, vol. 1 (London, 1836), 222.

37Susan Sontag, "The Aesthetics of Silence," in *Styles of Radical Will* (New York: Farrar, Straus and Giroux, 1969), 19–20, 26. Maurice Merleau-Ponty, *The Prose of the World* (Evanston: Northwestern University Press, 1973), 4-6.

38"Thomas Young, "Life of Cavendish," in Cavendish, *Sci. Pap.* 1:435–47, on 444.

39*Music and Aesthetics in the Eighteenth and Early-Nineteenth Centuries*, ed. P. le Huray and J. Day (Cambridge: Cambridge University Press, 1981), 3, p. passim.

ACKNOWLEDGMENTS

We express our special gratitude to Peter Day, Keeper of the Devonshire Collections, and to his associate Michael Pearman for their valuable and courteous assistance.

In the captions we acknowledge permission to reproduce illustrations, and in footnotes we acknowledge permission to use published material. Here we acknowledge permission to quote from unpublished material in archives: Society of Antiquaries of London; Bedfordshire Record Office; Trustees of the Natural History Museum, London; Trustees of the Chatsworth Settlement; syndics of the Fitzwilliam Museum; Trustees of the Royal Botanic Gardens, Kew; Beinecke Library, Yale University (the James Marshall and Marie-Louise Osborn Collection).

APPENDIX

Officers of the Royal Society

Presidents:

1703.	Sir Isaac Newton
1727.	Sir Hans Sloane
1741.	Martin Folkes
1752.	George, Earl of Macclesfield
1764.	James, Earl of Morton
1768.	James West
1772.	Sir John Pringle
1778.	Sir Joseph Banks

Treasurers:

1700.	Alexander Pitfield
1728.	Roger Gale
1736.	James West
1768.	Samuel Wegg
1802.	William Marsden

Secretaries (two):

1718–47.	John Machin
1721–27.	James Jurin
1727–30.	William Rutty
1730–52.	Cromwell Mortimer
1747–59.	Peter Davall
1752–65.	Thomas Birch
1759–73.	Charles Morton
1765–76.	Matthew Maty
1773–78.	Samuel Horsley
1776–1804.	Joseph Planta
1778–84.	Paul Henry Maty
1784–97.	Charles Blagden
1797–1807.	Edward Whitaker Gray
1804–16.	William Hyde Wollaston
1807–12.	Sir Humphry Davy.

Foreign Secretaries:

1723.	Philip Henry Zollman
1728.	Dr. Dillenius and Dr. Schuchzer
1748.	Thomas Stack
1751.	James Parson
1762.	Matthew Maty
1766.	John Bevis
1772.	Paul Henry Maty
1774.	Joseph Planta
1779.	Charles Hutton
1784.	Charles Peter Layard
1804.	Thomas Young

Clerks and Assistant Secretaries:

1723.	Francis Hawksbee
1763.	Emanuel Mendez da Costa
1768.	John Robertson
1777.	John Robertson (son of above)
1785.	George Gilpin

Source: Charles Richard Weld, A History of the Royal Society.

BIBLIOGRAPHY

Archives

Bank of England
Bedfordshire Record Office
Birmingham Assay Office
Birmingham University Library
Bristol Record Office
British Library, Department of Manuscripts
British Museum (Natural History), Department of Botany
Cambridge University Library
Cumbria County Record Office
Devonshire Collections, Chatsworth
Fitzwilliam Museum, Cambridge
Gloucester Record Office
Greater London Record Office
Holborn Public Library
Lancashire Record Office
Minet Library
Public Record Office, Chancery Lane
Royal Astronomical Society
Royal Botanic Gardens, Kew
Royal Greenwich Observatory
Royal Institution of Great Britain
Royal Society of London
Royal Society of Arts
Scheffield Central Library
Society of Antiquaries
Wellcome Historical Medical Library
Whitby Literary and Philosophical Society
Westminster City
Yale University Library

Note on the Cavendish and Grey family trees printed on the end papers. The duke of Kent liked the nobiliary particle *de*, and we oblige him. We refer to him not as Henry Grey, as he is commonly known, but as Henry de Grey, and we do the same for his children. Put together from many sources, our family trees are liable to inaccuracy and uncertainty, we realize. Omitted, for example, is a mysterious Lady Rachel Cavendish, identified as the youngest daughter of the duke of Devonshire in an obituary in the October 1735 issue of *London Magazine*. At the risk of angering a few ghosts, we include the charts as a reasonably reliable aid to readers who wish to keep track of the relationships between the principal family members referred to in the biography.

Printed sources

Note: Because of their large number, scientific articles are not given in this bibliography but only in the notes.

Aarsleff, Hans. *The Study of Language in England, 1780–1860*. Minneapolis: University of Minnesota Press, 1983.

Adams, George, Jr. *An Essay on Electricity*. 2d ed. London, 1785.

Aepinus, Franz Ulrich Theodorius. *Aepinus's Essay on the Theory of electricity and Magnetism*. Notes and Introduction by R. W. Home. Translated by P. J. Connor. Princeton: Princeton University Press, 1979.

Albert, William. *The Turnpike Road System in England 1663–1840*. Cambridge: Cambridge University Press, 1972.

Allan, D. G. C., and Robert E. Schofield. *Stephen Hales: Scientist and Philanthropist*. London: Scolar Press, 1980.

Allen, David Elliston. *The Naturalist in Britain: A Social History*. London: Allen Lane, 1976.

Allibone, T. E. *The Royal Society and Its Dining Clubs*. Oxford: Pergamon Press, 1976.

————. "The Thursday's Club Called the Club of the Royal Philosophers, and Its Relation to the Royal Society Club." *Notes and Records of the Royal Society London* 26 (1971): 73–80.

Antoine, Michel. "La cour de Lorraine dans l'Europe des lumières." In *La Lorraine dans l'Europe des lumières. Actes du colloque organisé par la Faculté des lettres et des sciences humaines de l'Université de Nancy, Nancy, 24–27 octobre 1966*, 69–76. Series *Annales de l'Est*. Memoire 34. Nancy: Faculté des lettres et sciences humaines de l'Université, 1968.

Ashton, T. S. *The Industrial Revolution, 1760–1830*. London: Oxford University Press, 1977.

"Aubert, Alexander." *DNB* 1: 715.

Austen Leigh, R. A. *Eton College Lists 1678–1790*. Eton College: Spottiswoode, 1907.

Austin, Jilian F., and Anita McConnell. "James Six, F.R.S.: Two Hundred Years of the Six's

Self-Registering Thermometer." *Notes and Records of the Royal Society London* 35 (1980): 49–65.

Averley, Gwen. "The `Social Chemists': English Chemical Societies in the Eighteenth and Early Nineteenth Century." *Ambix* 33 (1986): 99–128.

Badcock, A. W. "Physical Optics at the Royal Society, 1600–1800." *British Journal for the History of Science* 1 (1962) 99–116.

————. "Physics at the Royal Society, 1660–1800. 1. Change of State." *Annals of Science* 16 (1960): 95–115.

Baker, C. H. Collins, and Muriel I. Baker. *The Life and Circumstances of James Brydges, First Duke of Chandos, Patron of the Liberal Arts.* Oxford: Clarendon Press, 1949.

"Baker, Sir George." *DNB* 1:927–29.

Baker, John R. *Abraham Trembley of Geneva: Scientist and Philosopher, 1710–1784.* London: Edward Arnold, 1952.

Baker, Thomas. *History of the College of St. John the Evangelist, Cambridge.* Cambridge, 1869.

Ball, W. W. Rouse. *History of the Study of Mathematics at Cambridge.* Cambridge, 1889.

Barker, T. C., and M. Robbins. *A History of London Transport, Passenger Travel and the Development of the Metropolis.* Vol. 1. London: Allen & Unwin, 1963.

Barrett, Thomas J. *The Annals of Hampstead.* 3 vols. London: Adam & Charles Black, 1912.

Barrow, John. *Sketches of the Royal Society and Royal Society Club.* London, 1849.

Baumé, Antoine. *Manual de chymie, ou exposé des opérations et des produits d'un cours de chymie. Ouvrage utile aux personnes qui veulent suivre un cours de cette science, ou qui ont dessein de se former un cabinet de chymie.* Paris, 1763.

Baxandall, David. "The Circular Dividing Engine of Edward Troughton, 1793." *Transactions of the Optical Society* 25 (1923–24): 135–40.

Baxter, Stephen B. *William III and the Defense of European Liberty 1650–1702.* New York: Harcourt, Brace & World, 1966.

Beaglehole, J. C. "Cook, James." *DSB* 3: 396–97.

Beale, Catherine Hutton. *Reminiscences of a Gentlewoman of the Last Century: Letters of Catherine Hutton.* Birmingham, 1891.

Beattie, John M. *The English Court in the Reign of George I.* Cambridge: Cambridge University Press, 1967.

Beatty, F. M. "The Scientific Work of the Third Earl Stanhope," *Notes and Records of the Royal Society of London* 11 (1955): 217–19.

Beckett, J. V. *The Aristocracy in England, 1660–1914.* Oxford: Basil Blackwell, 1986.

————. "Dr William Brownrigg, F.R.S.: Physician, Chemist and Country Gentleman." *Notes and Records of the Royal Society of London* 31 (1977): 255–71.

————. "The Lowthers at Holker: Marriage, Inheritance and Debt in the Fortunes of an Eighteenth–Century Landowning Family." *Transactions of the Historic Society of Lancashire and Cheshire* 127 (1977): 47–64.

Beddoes, Thomas, ed. *Contributions to Physical and Medical Knowledge, Principally from the West of England.* Bristol, 1799.

————, and James Watt. *Considerations on the Medicinal Use of Factitious Airs, and on the Manner of Obtaining Them in Large Quantities.* Bristol, 1794.

"Bentley, Richard." *DNB* 2: 306–14.

Bergman, Torbern Olaf. *Outlines of Mineralogy.* Translated by W. Withering. Birmingham, 1783.

————. *Physical and Chemical Essays; . . . To Which Are Added Notes and Illustrations, by the Translator.* Translated by E. Cullen. 3 vols. London, 1784–91.

Berman, Morris. "The Early Years of the Royal Institution, 1799–1810: A Re-Evaluation." *Science Studies* 2 (1972): 205–40.

Berry, A. J. *Henry Cavendish: His Life and Scientific Work.* London: Hutchinson, 1960.

Berry, Mary. *Some Account of the Life of Rachael Wriothesley Lady Russell . . . Followed by a Series of Letters . . .* London, 1819.

Besant, Walter. *London in the Eighteenth Century.* London: Adean & Charles Black, 1902.

Bickley Francis. *The Cavendish Family.* London: Constable, 1911.

Biddle, Sheila. *Bolingbroke and Harley.* New York: Knopf, 1974.

A Bill Intitled an Act for the Encouragement of the British White Herring Industry. London, 1750.

Bingham, Hiram. *Elihu Yale: The American Nabob of Queen Square.* New York: Dodd, Mead, 1939.

"Biographical Anecdotes of George Steevens, Esq." *Gentleman's Magazine.* Feb. 1800, pp. 178–80.

Biot, J. B. "Cavendish (Henri)." *Biographie Universelle.* Vol. 7, pp. 272–73. Paris, 1813.

Birch, Thomas. *The History of the Royal Society of London for Improving of Natural Knowledge, from Its First Rise* . . . . Vol. 1. London, 1756.

————. *The Life of the Honourable Robert Boyle.* London, 1744.

Bird, John. *A Method of Constructing Mural Quadrants.* London, 1768.

————. *The Method of Dividing Astronomical Instruments.* London, 1767.

Bishop, John. *Considerations upon the Expediency of Making, and the Manner of Conducting the Late Regulations at Cambridge.* London, 1751.

Black, Joseph. *Experiments up on Magnesia Alba, Quicklime, and Some Other Alcaline Substances.* Edinburgh: Alembic Club Reprints, No. 1, 1898.

————. *Experiments upon Magnesia Alba, Quick-lime, and Other Alkaline Substances; by Joseph Black. To Which Is Annexed, an Essay on the Cold Produced by Evaporating Fluids, and of Some Other Means of Producing Cold; by William Cullen.* Edinburgh, 1777.

————. *Lectures on the Elements of Chemistry.* 2 vols. Edited by J. Robison. Edinburgh, 1803.

————. *Notes from Doctor Black's Lectures on Chemistry 1767/8.* Edited by D. McKie. Cheshire: Imperial Chemical Industries, 1966.

————. See Thomas Cochrane.

————. See James Watt.

Blagden, Charles. "The Diary of Sir Charles Blagden." Edited by Gavin De Beer in *Notes and Records of the Royal Society of London* 8 (1950): 65–89.

————. "Some Letters of Sir Charles Blagden." Edited by Gavin De Beer. *Notes and Records of the Royal Society of London* 8 (1951): 253–60.

Blanchard, Jean Pierre. *Journal of My Forty-Fifth Ascension.* Philadelphia, 1793.

Bloomfield, Paul. *Uncommon People: A Study of England's Elite.* London: Hamish Hamilton, 1955.

Boerhaave, Hermann. *Elements of Chemistry: Being the Annual Lectures of Herman Boerhaave.* . . . Translated by T. Dallow. 2 vols. in 1. London, 1735.

————. *A New Method of Chemistry; Including the Theory and Practice of That Art; Laid Down on Mechanical Principles, and Accommodated to the Uses of Life. The Whole Making a Clear and Rational System of Chemistry* . . . . Translated by P. Shaw and E. Chambers. 2 vols. London, 1727.

Borgeaud, Charles. *Histoire de l'Université de Genève. L'Académie de Calvin 1559–1798.* Genève: Georg, 1900.

Boscovich, Roger Joseph. *A Theory of Natural Philosophy.* Translated from the 2d edition of 1763 by J. M. Child. Cambridge, Mass.: M.I.T. Press, 1966.

Boswell, James. *The Life of Samuel Johnson LL.D.* 3 vols. New York: Heritage, 1963.

Bouguer, Pierre. *Le figure de la terre, determinée par les observations de Messieures De la Condamine et Bouguer, de l'Académie Royale des Sciences, envoyés par order du Roy au Pérou pour observer aux environs de l'équateur* . . . . Paris, 1749.

Bouguer, Pierre. *Pierre Bouguer's Optical Treatise on the Gradation of Light.* Translated with notes by W. E. Knowles Middleton. Toronto: University of Toronto Press, 1961.

Boyé, Pierre. *Les Chateaux du Roi Stanislas en Lorraine.* Marseille: Lafitte Reprints, 1980.

Boyer, Carl B. *A History of Mathematics.* New York: Wiley, 1968.

Bradley, James. *Miscellaneous Works and Correspondence of the Rev. James Bradley, D.D., F.R.S.* Edited by S. P. Rigaud. Oxford: Oxford University Press, 1832.

Brewster, David. *Memoirs of the Life, Writings, and Discoveries of Isaac Newton.* 2 vols. Edinburgh, 1855.

Briggs, Stephen R. See Jonathan M. Cheek.

Brimblecombe, Peter. "Earliest Atmospheric Profile." *New Scientist* 76 (1977): 364–65.

Brock, William. H. *The Fontana History of Chemistry.* London: Fontana, 1992.

————. "The Society for the Perpetuation of Gmelin: The Cavendish Society, 1846–1872." *Annals of Science* 35 (1978): 599–617.

Brodie, Sir Benjamin Collins. *Autobiography of the Late Sir Benjamin C. Brodie, Bart..* 2d ed. London, 1865.

Brooke, John, and L. B. Brooke. *The House of Commons 1754–1780.* 3 vols. London: Her Majesty's Stationary Office, 1964.

Brooke, L. B. See John Brooke.

Brooks, William Eric St. John. *Sir Hans Sloane, the Great Collector and His Circle.* London: Batchworth Press, 1954.

Brougham, Henry, Lord. *Lives of Men of Letters and Science Who Flourished in the Time of George III.* 2 vols. London, 1845–46. Vol. 1. Philadelphia, 1845.

Brown, Joyce. See A. W. Skempton.

Brown, Sanborn C. *Benjamin Thompson, Count Rumford.* Cambridge, Mass.: M.I.T. Press, 1979.

———. "Thompson, Benjamin (Count Rumford)." *DSB* 13: 350–52.

Brown, T. Graham, and Gavin de Beer. *The First Ascent of Mont Blanc.* London: Oxford University Press, 1957.

Bullen, Keith Edward. *The Earth's Density.* New York: Wiley, 1974.

Buller, Audley Cecil. *The Life and Works of Heberden.* London, 1879.

Burgess, J. H. Michael. *The Chronicles of Clapham[Clapham Common]. Being a Selection from the Reminiscences of Thomas Parsons, Sometime Member of the Clapham Antiquarian Society.* London: Ramsden, 1929.

Burke's Genealogical and Heraldic History of the Landed Gentry. London: Burke's Peerage Limited, 1939.

Burrow, John. *Sketches of the Royal Society and Royal Society Club.* London, 1849.

Bush, M. L. *The English Aristocracy: A Comparative Synthesis.* Manchester: Manchester University Press, 1984.

Buss, Arnold H. "A Theory of Shyness." In *Shyness: Perspectives on Research and Treatment*, edited by Warren H. Jones et al., 39–46. New York: Plenum Press, 1986.

Bynum, W. F. "Health, Disease and Medical Care." In *Ferment of Knowledge: Studies in the Historiography of Eighteenth Century Science*, edited by G. S. Rousseau and R. Porter, 221–53. Cambridge: Cambridge University Press, 1980.

Byrom, John. *The Private Journal and Literary Remains of John Byrom.* 2 vols. in 4 parts. Edited by R. Parkinson. Manchester, 1854–57.

Cambridge University. *Academiae Cantabrigiensis Luctus in Obitum Frederici celsissimi Walliae Principis.* Cambridge, 1751.

Cameron, Hector Charles. *Sir Joseph Banks, K. B., P.R.S. The Autocrat of the Philosophers.* London: Batchworth, 1952.

Canini, Gerard. See Michel Parisse.

Cannon, Garland. "Sir William Jones, Sir Joseph Banks, and the Royal Society." *Notes and Records of the Royal Society of London* 29 (1975): 205–30.

Cannon, John. *Aristocratic Century. The Peerage of Eighteenth-Century England.* Cambridge: Cambridge University Press, 1984.

———. *The Fox-North Coalition: Crisis of the Constitution, 1782–4.* Cambridge: Cambridge University Press, 1969.

Cantor, G. N. *Optics After Newton: Theories of Light in Britain and Ireland, 1704–1840.* Manchester: Manchester University Press, 1983.

———. "Thomas Young's Lectures at the Royal Institution." *Notes and Records of the Royal Society of London* 25 (1970): 87–112.

———, and M. J. S. Hodges, eds. *Conceptions of Ether: Studies in the History of the Ether Théories, 1740–1900.* Cambridge: Cambridge University Press, 1981.

Caroe, Gwendy. *The Royal Institution: An Informal History.* London: John Murray, 1985.

Carswell, John. *The South Sea Bubble.* Rev. ed. London: Alan Sutton, 1993.

Carter, Alice Clare. *The English Public Debt in the Eighteenth Century.* London: The Historical Association, 1968.

Carter, Edmund. *The History of the University of Cambridge, from Its Original, to the Year 1753.* London, 1753.

Carter, Elizabeth, and Catherine Talbot. *A Series of Letters Between Mrs. Elizabeth Carter and Miss Catherine Talbot from the Year 1741 to 1770 etc.* Vol. 1. London, 1809.

Cavello, Tiberius. *A Complete Treatise on Electricity.…* 2d ed. London, 1782.

———. *A Treatise on the Nature and Properties of Air, and Other Permanently Elastic Fluids. To Which Is Prefixed, an Introduction to Chemistry.* London, 1781.

Cavendish, Elizabeth, Duchess of Devonshire, and Georgiana Cavendish, Duchess of Devonshire. *The Two Duchesses. Georgiana Duchess of Devonshire. Elizabeth Duchess of Devonshire. Family Correspondence.* Edited by V. Foster. London, 1898.

Cavendish, Georgiana, Duchess of Devonshire. *Georgiana: Extracts from the Correspondence of Georgiana, Duchess of Devonshire.* Edited by the Earl of Bessborough. London: John Murray, 1955.

_____. See Elizabeth Cavendish, Duchess of Devonshire.

Cavendish, Henry. *The Electrical Researches of the Honourable Henry Cavendish, F.R.S. . . .* Edited by J. C. Maxwell. Cambridge, 1879; London: Frank Cass Reprint, 1967.

_____. *The Scientific Papers of the Honourable Henry Cavendish, F.R.S.* Vol. I: *The Electrical Researches.* Edited with notes by James Clerk Maxwell. Revised with notes by Sir Joseph Larmor. Cambridge: Cambridge University Press, 1921. Vol. II: *Chemical and Dynamical.* Edited with notes by Sir Edward Thorpe. Contributions by Charles Chree, Sir Frank Watson Dyson, Sir Archibald Geikie, Sir Joseph Larmor. Cambridge: Cambridge University Press, 1921.

Cavendish, William, Fourth Duke of Devonshire. *The Devonshire Diary: William Cavendish, Fourth Duke of Devonshire, Memoranda on State of Affairs, 1759–1762.* Camden Fourth Series, Vol. 27. Edited by Peter D. Brown and Karl W. Schweizer. London: Royal Historical Society, 1982.

Chaldecott, J. A. *Handbook of the King George III Collection of Scientific Instruments.* London: His Majesty's Stationary Office, 1951.

Challinor, John. "Whitehurst, John," *DSB* 14: 311–12.

Chambers, J. D. *Nottinghamshire in the Eighteenth Century: A Study of Life and Labour Under the Squirearchy.* 2d ed. London: Frank Cass, 1966.

Chaston, J. C. "Wear Resistance of Gold Alloys for Coinage: An Early Example of Contract Research." *Gold Bulletin* 7 (1974): 108–12.

Cheek, Jonathan M., and Stephen R. Briggs, "Shyness as a Personality Trait." In *Shyness and Embarrassment: Perspectives from Social Psychology,* edited by W. Ray Crozier, 315–37. Cambridge: Cambridge University Press, 1990.

The Chemical Revolution: Essays in Reinterpretation. Vol. 4, new series of *Osiris.* Edited by A. Donovan. Published by the History of Science Society in 1988.

Child, Ernest. *The Tools of the Chemist.* New York: Reinhold, 1940.

Clapham, John. *The Bank of England. A History.* 2 vols. Cambridge: Cambridge University Press, 1945.

Clare, Martin. *The Motion of Fluids, Natural and Artificial. . . .* 3d ed. London, 1747.

Clark, George N. *A History of the Royal College of Physicians of London.* 3 vols. Oxford: Clarendon Press, 1964–72.

Cleghorn, William. "William Cleghorn's *De igne* (1779)." Edited, annotated, and translated by Douglas McKie and Niels N. de V. Heathcote in *Annals of Science* 14 (1958): 1–82.

Cloninger, C. Robert. "Temperament and Personality," *Current Biology* 4 (1994):266–73.

Clotfelter, B. E. "The Cavendish Experiment As Cavendish Knew It." *American Journal of Physics* 55 (1987): 210–13.

Clow, Archibald. "Some Notes on William Walker's 'Distinguished Men of Science.'" *Proceedings of the Royal Institution* 35 (1954): 890–94.

_____, and Nan L. Clow, *The Chemical Revolution: A Contribution to Social Technology.* London: Batchworth Press, 1952.

Cobbett's Parliamentary History of England. From the Norman Conquest, in 1066, to the Year 1803. Vol. 6: *Comprising the Period from the Accession of Queen Anne in 1702, to the Accession of King George the First in 1714.* London, 1810.

Cochrane, Thomas. *Notes from Dr. Black's Lectures on Chemistry, 1767/8.* Edited with an introduction by Douglas McKie. Wilmslow, England: Imperial Chemical Industries Ltd., Pharmaceuticals Division, 1966.

Cohen, I. B. "The Eighteenth-Century Origins of the Concept of Scientific Revolution." *Journal of the History of Ideas* 37 (1976): 257–88.

_____. *Franklin and Newton: An Inquiry into Speculative Newtonian Experimental Science and Franklin's Work in Electricity As an Example Thereof.* Philadelphia: American Philosophical Society, 1956.

_____. *Introduction to Newton's Principia.* Cambridge: Cambridge University Press, 1971.

_____. "Newton, Isaac." *DSB* 10: 42–101.

_____. *The Newtonian Revolution.* Cambridge: Cambridge University Press, 1980.

Cohen, Murray. *Sensible Words: Linguistic Practice in England 1640–1785.* Baltimore: The Johns Hopkins University Press, 1977.

Cokayne George Edward. *The Complete Peerage of England, Scotland, Ireland, Great Britain and the United Kingdom: Extant, Extinct, or Dormant.* Vols. 1–3. Gloucester: A. Sutton, 1982.

Coleby, L. J. M. "Isaac Milner and the Jacksonian Chair of Natural Philosophy." *Annals of Science* 10 (1954): 234–57.

———. "John Francis Vigani." *Annals of Science* 8 (1952): 46–60.

———. "John Hadley, Fourth Professor of Chemistry in the University of Cambridge." *Annals of Science* 8 (1952): 293–301.

———. "John Mickleburgh, Professor of Chemistry in the University of Cambridge, 1718–56." *Annals of Science* 8 (1952): 165–74.

———. "Richard Watson, Professor of Chemistry in the University of Cambridge, 1764–71." *Annals of Science* 9 (1953): 101–23.

Collins, A. S. *Authorship in the Days of Johnson, Being a Study of the Relation Between Author, Patron, Publisher and Public, 1726–1780.* New York: E. P. Dutton, 1929.

Collins's Peerage of England; Geneological, Biographical, and Historical. 9 vols. Edited by E. Brydges. London, 1812.

Collot, Claude. "La faculté de droit de l'Université de Pont-à-Mousson et de Nancy au XVIIIe siècle." In *La Lorraine dans l'Europe des lumières. Actes du colloque organisé par la Faculté des lettres et des sciences humaines de l'Université de Nancy, Nancy, 24–27 octobre 1966,* 215–26. Series *Annales de l'Est.* Memoire 34. Nancy: Faculté des lettres et sciences humaines de l'Université, 1968.

"Colson, John." *DNB* 4: 801–2.

Colvin, Howard Montagu. *A Biographical Dictionary of British Architects, 1600–1840.* Rev. ed. London: J. Murray, 1978.

Conant, James Bryant. *The Overthrow of the Phlogiston Theory.* Cambridge: Harvard University Press, 1950.

A Concise and Accurate Description of the University, Town, and County of Cambridge. New ed. Cambridge, n.d. (prob. 1784).

Conrady, A. E. See R. A. Sampson.

Cook, A. H. "Experiments on Gravitation." In *Three Hundred Years of Gravitation.* Edited by S. W. Hawking and W. Israel, 51–79. Cambridge: Cambridge University Press, 1987.

Cooper, W. Durrant, ed. *Lists of Foreign Protestants, and Aliens, Resident in England 1618–1688.* London, 1862.

Copenhaver, Brian P. "Natural Magic, Hermeticism, and Occultism in Early Modern Science." In *Reappraisals of the Scientific Revolution,* edited by D. C. Lindberg and R. S. Westman, 261–301. Cambridge: Cambridge University Press, 1990.

Cornell, E. S. "Early Studies in Radiant Heat." *Annals of Science* 1 (1936): 217–25.

Costa, Paul T., and Robert R. McCrea. "Set Like Plaster? Evidence for the Stability of Adult Personality," 21–40. In *Can Personality Change?* Edited by T. F. Heatherton and J. L. Weinberger. Washington, D.C.: American Psychological Association, 1994.

Costamagna, Henri. "Nice au XVIIIe siècle: présentation historique et géographique." *Annales de la Faculté des Lettres et Sciences Humaines de Nice,* no. 19, 1973, pp. 7–28.

Cotes, Roger. *Harmonia Mensurarum, sive Analysis & Synthesis per Rationum & Angulorum Mensuras Promotae: Accedunt alia Opuscula Mathematica.* Edited by Roger Smith. London, 1722.

———. *Hydrostatical and Pneumatical Lectures.* Edited by Robert Smith. London, 1738. 2d ed., Cambridge, 1747.

Cowper, Mary Clavering Cowper, Countess. *Diary of Mary Countess Cowper, Lady of the Bedchamber to the Princess of Wales 1714–1720.* Edited by C. S. Cowper. London, 1864. 2d ed. London, 1865.

Cowper, Spencer. *Letters of Spencer Cowper, Dean of Durham, 1746–74.* Edited by E. Hughes. Durham: Surtees Society, 1956.

Cox, R. T. "Electric Fish." *American Journal of Physics* 11 (1943): 13–22.

Coxe, William. *Memoirs of the Life and Administration of Sir Robert Walpole, Earl of Orford.* 3 vols. London, 1798.

Craig, John. "The Royal Society and the Royal Mint." *Notes and Records of the Royal Society of London* 19 (1964): 156–67.

Crane, Verner W. "The Club of Honest Whigs: Friends of Science and Liberty." *William and Mary Quarterly* 23 (1966): 210–33.

Crawford, Adair. *Experiments and Observations on Animal Heat, and the Inflammation of Combustible*

Bodies; Being an Attempt to Resolve These Phaenomena into a General Law of Nature. London, 1779.

Creighton, Charles. *A History of Epidemics in Britain.* Vol. 2: *From the Extinction of the Plague to the Present Time.* 2d ed. London: Frank Cass, 1965.

Crombie, A. C., ed. *Scientific Change; Historical Studies in the Intellectual, Social, and Technical Conditions for Scientific Discovery and Technical Invention, from Antiquity to the Present.* New York: Basic Books, 1963.

Cronstedt, Axel Fredric. *An Essay Towards a System of Mineralogy.* Translated by G. von Engestrom. Revised by E. M. Da Costa. London, 1770.

Crosland, Maurice. "The Development of Chemistry in the Eighteenth Century." *Studies on Voltaire* 24 (1963): 369–41.

Crosland, Maurice. *Historical Studies in the Language of Chemistry.* London: Heinemann, 1962.

Crowther, James Gerald. *Scientists of the Industrial Revolution: Joseph Black, James Watt, Joseph Priestley, Henry Cavendish.* London: Crescent Press, 1962.

Cullen, William. See Joseph Black.

Cuthbertson, John. *Description of an Improved Air-Pump, and an Account of Some Experiments Made with It . . .* London, c. 1795.

Cuvier, Georges. "Henry Cavendish," 1812. Translated by D. S. Faber. In *Great Chemists*, edited by E. Faber, 227–38. New York: Interscience Publishers, 1961.

Dale, T. C. "History of Clapham." In *Clapham and the Clapham Sect*, edited by E. Baldwin, 1–28. Clapham, England: Clapham Antiquarian Society, 1927.

Dalrymple. Alexander. *A Collection of Charts and Memoirs.* London, 1772.

Darby, H. C. "The Draining of the Fens, A.D. 1600–1800." In *An Historical Geography of England Before A.D. 1800*, edited by H. C. Darby, 444–64. Cambridge: Cambridge University Press, 1936.

Daston, Lorraine. *Classical Probability in the Enlightenment.* Princeton: Princeton University Press, 1988.

Daumas, Maurice. "Precision of Measurement and Physical and Chemical Research in the Eighteenth Century." In *Scientific Change; Historical Studies in the Intellectual, Social, and*

Technical Conditions for Scientific Discovery and Technical Invention, from Antiquity to the Present. Edited by A. C. Crombie, 418–30. New York: Basic Books, 1963.

————. *Scientific Instruments of the Seventeenth and Eighteenth Centuries.* Translated by M. Holbrook. New York: Praeger, 1972.

Davies, J. D. Griffith. "The Banks Family." *Notes and Records of the Royal Society of London* 1 (1938): 85–87.

Davy, Humphry. *The Collected Works of Sir Humphry Davy, Bart.* Edited by J. Davy. Vol. 2. London, 1839.

————. *A Discourse Introductory to a Course of Lectures on Chemistry . . . .* London, 1802.

————. *Elements of Chemical Philosophy.* Vol. l. London, 1812.

————. *A Syllabus of a Course of Lectures on Chemistry Delivered at the Royal Institution of Great Britain.* London, 1802.

Davy, John. *Memoirs of the Life of Sir Humphry Davy, Bart.* 2 vols. London, 1836.

Day, Archibald. *The Admiralty Hydrographic Service 1795–1919.* London: Her Majesty's Stationary Office, 1967.

DeBeery, Gavin. "The History of the Altimetry of Mont Blanc." *Annals of Science* 12 (1956): 3–29.

————. *Sir Hans Sloane and the British Museum.* London: Oxford University Press, 1953.

————. See Charles Blagden.

————. See T. Graham Brown.

————, and Max. H. Hey. "The First Ascent of Mont Blanc." *Notes and Records of the Royal Society of London* 11 (1955): 236–55.

"Delaval, Edward Hussey." *DNB* 5:766–67.

Delorme, Edmond. *Lunéville et son arrondissement.* Marseille: Lafitte Reprints, 1977.

Deluc, Jean André. *An Elementary Treatise on Geology: Determining Fundamental Points in That Science, and Containing an Examination of Some Modern Geological Systems, and Particularly of the Huttonian Theory of the Earth.* Translated by H. de la Fite. London, 1809.

————. *Idées sur la météorologie.* Paris, 1786–87.

————. *Geological Travels in the North of Europe and in England.* 3 vols. Translated by H. de la Fite. London, 1810–11.

Deluc, Jean André. *Recherches sur les modifications de l'atmosphère . . .* 2 vols. Geneva, 1772.

Desaguliers, J. T. *A Course of Experimental Philosophy.* 2 vols. London, 1734–44.

————. *Physico–Mechanical Lectures.* London, 1717.

————. *A System of Experimental Philosophy, Prov'd by Mechanicks . . . .* London, 1719.

Deutsch, Otto Erich. *Handel: A Documentary Biography.* New York: DaCapo Press, 1974.

Dickinson, H. T. *Bolingbroke.* London: Constable, 1970.

Dickson, P. G. M. *The Financial Revolution in England: A Study in the Development of Public Credit 1688–1756.* London: Macmillan, 1967.

Dictionary of National Biography. Edited by L. Stephen and S. Lee. 22 vols. New York: Macmillan, 1908–9.

Dictionary of Scientific Biography. Edited by C. C. Gillispie. 16 vols. New York: Charles Scribner's Sons, 1970–80.

Dobbs, Betty Jo. See Robert Siegfried.

Dodson, James. *The Anti–Logarithmic Canon. Being a Table of Numbers Consisting of Eleven Places of Figures, Corresponding to All Logarithms under 100000.* London, 1742.

————. *The Mathematical Repository. Containing Analytical Solutions of Five Hundred Questions, Mostly Selected from Scarce and Valuable Authors. Designed to Conduct Beginners to the More Difficult Properties of Numbers.* 3 vols. London, 1748–55.

Dollond, Peter. *On Hadley's Quadrant & Sextant.* London, 1766.

————. *Some Account of the Discovery Made by the Late Mr. John Dollond, F.R.S. Which Led to the Grand Improvement of Refracting Telescopes . . . .* London, 1789.

Donovan, Arthur L. *Philosophical Chemistry in the Scottish Enlightenment: The Doctrines and Discoveries of William Cullen and Joseph Black.* Edinburgh: Edinburgh University Press, 1975.

Dorling, Jon. "Henry Cavendish's Deduction of the Electrostatic Inverse Square Law from the Result of a Single Experiment," *Studies in the History and Philosophy of Science* 4 (1974): 327–48.

"Douglas, James, Fourteenth Earl of Morton," *DNB* 5:1236–37.

Drew, Bernard. *The London Assurance, a Second Chronicle.* London: Printed for The London Assurance at the Curwen Press, Plaistow, 1949.

Dubbey, J. M. "Cotes, Roger." *DSB* 3: 430–33.

Duncan, A. M. "The Functions of Affinity Tables and Lavoisier's List of Elements," *Ambix* 17 (1970): 26–42.

————. "Some Theoretical Aspects of Eighteenth-Century Tables of Affinity." Parts I and II. *Annals of Science* 18 (1962): 177–94, 217–32.

Dupree, A. Hunter. *Sir Joseph Banks and the Origins of Science Policy.* Minneapolis: The Associates of the James Ford Bell Library, University of Minnesota, 1984.

Dyment, S. A. "Some Eighteenth Century Ideas Concerning Aqueous Vapour and Evaporation." *Annals of Science* 2 (1937): 465–73.

Edwards, Edward. *Libraries and Founders of Libraries, from Ancient Times to the Beginning of the Nineteenth Century.* Amsterdam: G. T. van Heusdan, 1968.

————. *Lives of the Founders of the British Museum; with Notices of Its Chief Augmentors and Other Benefactors, 1570–1870.* London, 1870.

Eisenstaedt, J. "De l'influence de la gravitation sur la propagation de la lumière en théorie newtonienne. L'archéologie des trous noirs," *Archive for History of Exact Sciences* 42 (1991): 315–86.

Eklund, Jon. *The Incompleat Chymist. Being an Essay on the Eighteenth-Century Chemist in His Laboratory, with a Dictionary of Absolute Chemical Terms of the Period.* Washington, DC: Smithsonian Institution, 1975.

Ellis, Aytoun. *The Penny Universities: A History of the Coffee Houses.* London: Secker & Warburg, 1956.

Ellis, George E. *Memoir of Sir Benjamin Thompson, Count Rumford. With Notices of His Daughter.* Boston, 1871.

Ellis, Henry, ed. *Original Letters of Eminent Literary Men of the Sixteenth, Seventeenth, and Eighteenth Centuries.* London, 1843.

Emerson, William. *The Doctrine of Fluxions: Not Only Explaining the Elements Thereof, But Also Its Application and Use in the Several Parts of Mathematics and Natural Philosophy.* London, 1768.

Emerson, William. *The Elements of Trigonometry*. 2d ed. London, 1764.

Esdaile, Arundell. *The British Museum Library: A Short History and a Survey*. London: George Allen & Unwin, 1946.

Evans, Joan. *A History of the Society of Antiquaries*. Oxford: Oxford University Press, 1956.

Everitt, C. W. F. "Gravitation, Relativity and Precise Experimentation." In *Proceedings of the First Marcel Grossmann Meeting on General Relativity*, edited by R. Ruffini, 545–615. Amsterdam: North-Holland, 1977.

Eyles, V. A. "The Extent of Geological Knowledge in the Eighteenth Century, and the Methods by Which It Was Diffused." In *Toward a History of Geology*, edited by Cecil J. Schneer, 159–83. Cambridge, Mass.: M.I.T. Press, 1969.

Farrar, Kathleen R. "A Note on a Eudiometer Supposed to Have Belonged to Henry Cavendish." *British Journal for the History of Science* 1 (1963): 375–80.

Farrell, Maureen. *William Whiston*. New York: Arno, 1981.

Feigenbaum, L. "Brook Taylor and the Method of Increments." *Archive for History of Exact Sciences* 34 (1985): 1–140.

Feldman, Theodore S. "Applied Mathematics and the Quantification of Experimental Physics: The Example of Barometric Hypsometry." *Historical Studies in the Physical Sciences* 15, no. 2 (1988): 127–97.

Feldman, Theodore S. "Late Enlightenment Meteorology." In *The Quantifying Spirit in the Eighteenth Century*, edited by T. Frangsmyr, J. L. Heilbron, and R. E. Rider, 143–77. Berkeley: University of California Press, 1990.

Féliciangeli, Daniel. "Le développement de Nice au cours de la seconde moitié de XVIIIe siècle. Les anglais à Nice." *Annales de la Faculté des Lettres et Sciences Humaines de Nice*, no. 19, 1973, pp. 45–67.

Ferguson, Donald N. *A History of Musical Thought*. 2d ed. New York and London: Appleton, Century, Crofts, 1935.

Ferguson, James. *An Introduction to Electricity . . . .* London, 1778.

Fiske, Roger. *English Theatre Music in the Eighteenth Century*. London: Oxford University Press, 1973.

"Fitzroy, August Henry, Third Duke of Grafton." *DNB* 7: 198–201.

Folkes, Martin. *A Table of English Silver Coins from the Norman Conquest to the Present Time. With Their Weights, Intrinsic Values, and Some Remarks upon the Several Pieces*. London, 1745.

Forbes, Eric G. "The Origin and Development of the Marine Chronometer." *Annals of Science* 22 (1966): 1–25.

Forster, E. M. *Battersea Rise*. New York: Harcourt, Brace, 1956.

Foster, Joseph. *Alumni Oxonienses: The Members of the University of Oxford, 1715–1886 . . .* 4 vols. London, 1891.

Fothergill, Brian. *Sir William Hamilton, Envoy Extraordinary*. New York: Harcourt, Brace & World, 1969.

Fox, Robert. *The Caloric Theory of Gases from Lavoisier to Regnault*. Oxford: Clarendon Press, 1971.

Franklin, Benjamin. *Benjamin Franklin's Experiments. A New Edition of Franklin's Experiments and Observations on Electricity*. Edited with an historical introduction by I. B. Cohen. Cambridge, Mass.: Harvard University Press, 1941.

————. *Philosophical & Miscellaneous Papers*. London, 1787.

————. *The Papers of Benjamin Franklin*. New Haven: Yale University Press, 1959–. Edited by L. W. Labaree (through vol. 14), W. R. Wilcox (through vol. 26), C. A. Lopez (vol. 27), and B. B. Oberg (from vol. 28).

Freke, John. *An Essay to Shew the Cause of Electricity; and Why Some Things Are Non-Electricable*. London, 1746.

Freshfield, Douglas W. and H. F. Montagnier. *The Life of Horace Bénédict De Saussure*. London: Edward Arnold, 1920.

Fry, Howard T. *Alexander Dalrymple (1737–1808) and the Expansion of British Trade.* London: Frank Cass, 1970.

Gaber, Stephane. See Michel Parisse.

Garnett, Thomas. *Outlines of a Course of Lectures on Chemistry: Delivered at the Royal Institution of Great Britain, 1801.* London, 1801.

———. *Outlines of a Course of Lectures on Natural and Experimental Philosophy, Delivered at the Royal Institution of Great Britain, 1801.* London, 1801.

———. *Popular Lectures on Zoonomia, or the Laws of Animal Life, in Health and Disease.* London, 1804.

Garraty, John A., *The Nature of Biography.* New York: Knopf, 1957.

Gascoigne, John. *Cambridge in the Age of the Enlightenment: Science, Religion and Politics from the Restoration to the French Revolution.* Cambridge: Cambridge University Press, 1989.

———. *Joseph Banks and the English Enlightenment: Useful Knowledge and Polite Culture.* Cambridge: Cambridge University Press, 1994.

———. "Mathematics and Meritocracy: The Emergence of the Cambridge Mathematical Tripos." *Social Studies of Science* 14 (1984): 547–84.

Geikie, Archibald. *Annals of the Royal Society Club: The Record of a London Dining–Club in the Eighteenth & Nineteenth Centuries.* London: Macmillan, 1917.

———. *Founders of Geology.* 2d ed. London: Macmillan, 1905.

———. *Memoir of John Michell.* Cambridge: Cambridge University Press, 1918.

George, Dorothy. *London Life in the Eighteenth Century.* Harmondsworth: Penguin Books, 1966.

George III, King of Great Britain. *The Later Correspondence of George III.* Vol. 1: *December 1783 to January 1793.* Edited by A. Aspinall. Cambridge: Cambridge University Press, 1962.

Getman, Frederick H. "Sir Charles Blagden, F.R.S." *Osiris* 3 (1937): 69–87.

Gibbon, Edward. *The Autobiography of Edward Gibbon.* Edited by John Murray. London, 1896.

Gibbs, F. W. *Joseph Priestley: Adventurer in Science and Champion of Truth.* London: T. Nelson, 1965.

———. "A Notebook of William Lewis and Alexander Chisholm." *Annals of Science* 8 (1952): 202–20.

———. "Peter Shaw and the Revival of Chemistry." *Annals of Science* 7 (1951): 211–37.

Gilbert, L. F. "W. H. Wollaston Mss. at Cambridge." *Notes and Records of the Royal Society of London* 9 (1952): 311–32.

Gilbert, William. *De Magnete*, 1600. Translated by P. Fleury Mottelay. New York: Dover, 1958.

Gillespie, Richard. "Ballooning in France and Britain, 1783–1786: Aerostation and Adventurism." *Isis* 75 (1984): 249–68.

Gillispie, Charles Coulston. "Laplace, Pierre–Simon, Marquis de." *DSB* 15: 273–356.

———. The *Montgolfier Brothers and the Invention of Aviation, 1783–1784.* Princeton: Princeton University Press, 1983.

———. *Science and Polity in France at the End of the Old Regime.* Princeton: Princeton University Press, 1980.

Gillmor, C. Stewart. *Coulomb and the Evolution of Physics and Engineering in Eighteenth-Century France.* Princeton: Princeton University Press, 1971.

Godber, Joyce. *The Marchioness Grey of Wrest Park.* Vol. 47. Bedford: Bedfordshire Historical Record Society, 1968.

———. *Wrest Park and the Duke of Kent. Henry Grey (1671–1740).* 4th ed. Elstow Moot Hall: Bedfordshire County Council Arts and Recreation Department, 1982.

Golinski, Jan. *Science as Public Culture in Britain, 1760–1820.* Cambridge: Cambridge University Press, 1992.

Gooch, G. P. *Life of Charles, 3rd Earl Stanhope.* London: Longmans, 1914.

Goodfield, June. See Stephen Toulmin.

Gosse, Edmund William. *Gray.* New ed. London: Macmillan, 1906.

Gough, J. B. "Réaumur, René–Antione Ferchault de." *DSB* 11: 327–35.

Gower, Leveson, Lord Granville. *Lord Granville Leveson Gower (First Earl Granville) Private Correspondence 1781 to 1821.* Edited by Castalia Countess Granville. 2 vols. London: John Murray, 1916.

Gowing, Ronald. *Roger Cotes, Natural Philosopher*. Cambridge: Cambridge University Press, 1983.

Grant, Francis. *A Letter to a Member of Parliament, Concerning the Free British Fisheries*. London, 1750.

'sGravesande, Willem Jacob van. *An Explanation of the Newtonian Philosophy, in Lectures Read to the Youth of the University of Leyden*. Translated by E. Stone. 2d edition. London, 1741.

Great Britain. Historical Manuscripts Commission. *Calendar of the Stuart Papers Belonging to His Majesty the King Preserved at Windsor Castle*. Vol. 6. London: His Majesty's Stationery Office, 1916.

————. *The Manuscripts of the House of Lords*. Vol. 4: *1699–1702*. Vol. 7: *1706–1708*. London: His Majesty's Stationery Office, 1908, 1921.

————. *Report on Manuscripts in Various Collections*. Vol. 8: *The Manuscripts of the Hon. Frederick Lindley Wood; M. L. S. Clements, Esq.; Philip Unwin, Esq.* London: His Majesty's Stationery Office, 1913.

————. *Report on the Laing Manuscripts Preserved in the University of Edinburgh*. Vol. 2. London: His Majesty's Stationery Office, 1925.

————. *Report on the Manuscripts of J. B. Fortescue, Esq., Preserved at Dropmore*. Vol. 8. London: His Majesty's Stationery Office, 1912.

————. *Report on the Manuscripts of Lord Polwarth, Preserved at Mertoun House, Berwickshire*. Vols. 2 and 3. London: His Majesty's Stationary Office, 1916, 1931.

————. *Report on the Manuscripts of Sir William Fitzherbert, Bart., and Others*. London, 1893.

————. *Report on the Manuscripts of the Earl of Egmont. Diary of Viscount Percival Afterwards First Earl of Egmont*. Vols. 1–3. London: His Majesty's Stationery Office, 1920–23.

————. *Report on the Manuscripts of the Late Reginald Rawden Hastings, Esq., of the Manor House, Ashby de la Zouche*. 4 vols. London: His Majesty's Stationery Office, 1928–47.

————. *Report on the Manuscripts of the Marquess of Downshire, Preserved at Easthampstead Park, Berks*. Vol. 1: *Papers of Sir William Trumbull*. Parts 1 and 2. London: His Majesty's Stationery Office, 1924.

Great Britain, Parliament. *House of Commons. Journals, 1547–1900*. New York: Readex Microprint, 1966.

Green, Frederick Charles. *Eighteenth– Century France: Six Essays*. New York: D. Appleton, 1931.

Green, George. *An Essay on the Application of Mathematical Analysis to the Theories of Electricity and Magnetism*. Nottingham, 1828.

Greene, Mott T. *Geology in the Nineteenth Century: Changing Views of a Changing World*. Ithaca and London: Cornell University Press, 1982.

Gregory, David. *The Elements of Astronomy, Physical and Geometrical*. 2 vols. London, 1715.

Guerlac, Henry. "Black, Joseph." *DSB* 2: 173–83.

————. "Chemistry As a Branch of Physics: Laplace's Collaboration with Lavoisier." *Historical Studies in the Physical Sciences* 7 (1976): 193–276.

————. "Joseph Black and Fixed Air: A Bicentenary Retrospective, with Some New or Little Known Material." *Isis* 48 (1957): 124–51.

————. "Newton's Changing Reputation in the Eighteenth Century." In *Carl Becker's "Heavenly City" Revisited*, edited by Raymond O. Rockwood, 3–26. Ithaca: Cornell University Press, 1958.

————. "Quantification in Chemistry." *Isis* 52 (1961): 194–214.

————. "Where the Statue Stood: Divergent Loyalties to Newton in the Eighteenth Century." In *Aspects of the Eighteenth Century*. Edited by Earl R. Wasserman, 317–34. Baltimore: The Johns Hopkins University Press, 1965.

Gunther, A. E. *The Founders of Science at the British Museum, 1753–1900*. Halesworth: Halesworth Press, 1980.

————. *An Introduction to the Life of the Rev. Thomas Birch D.D., F.R.S., 1705–1766*. Halesworth: Halesworth Press, 1984.

————. "The Royal Society and the Foundation of the British Museum, 1753–1781." *Notes and Records of the Royal Society of London* 33 (1979): 207–16.

Gunther, Robert W. T. *Early Science in Cambridge*. London: Dawsons, 1937.

Guyton de Morveau, Louis-Bernard, et al. *Method of Chymical Nomenclature*. Translated from the French edition of 1787 by James St. John. London, 1788.

Guyton de Morveau, Louis-Bernard, and Richard Kirwan. *A Scientific Correspondence During the Chemical Revolution: Louis-Bernard Guyton de Morveau and Richard Kirwan, 1782–1802.* Edited by E. Grison, M. Sadoun-Goupil, and P. Bret. Berkeley: Office for the History of Science and Technology, University of California at Berkeley, 1994.

Habakkuk, H. J. "England." In *The European Nobility in the Eighteenth Century*, edited by A. Goodwin, 1–21. London: Adam & Charles Black, 1953.

_____. "Marriage Settlements in the Eighteenth Century." *Transactions of the Royal Historical Society* 32 (1950): 15–30.

Hacking, Ian. "Moivre, Abraham de." *DSB* 9: 452–55.

Hackmann, W. D. *Electricity from Glass: The History of the Frictional Electricity Machine 1600–1850.* Alphen aan den Rijn: Sijthoff & Nordhoff, 1978.

Hadley, John. *A Plan of a Course of Chemical Lectures.* Cambridge, 1758.

"Hadley, John." *DNB* 8: 879–80.

Hales, Stephen. *Vegetable Statics: Or, an Account of Some Statical Experiments on the Sap in Vegetables . . . Also, a Speciment of an Attempt to Analyze the Air . . .* London, 1727; London: Macdonald, 1969.

Hall, A. Rupert. " 'sGravesande, Willem Jacob." *DSB* 5:509–11.

_____. "Vigani, John Francis." *DSB* 14: 26–27.

Hall, H., and F. T. J. Nicholas, eds. *Select Tracts and Table Books Relating to English Weights and Measures (1100–1742).* Camden Miscellany, Vol. 15. London: Office of the Society, 1929.

Hall, Marie Boas. "Homberg, Wilhelm or Guillaume." *DSB* 6: 477–78.

Hamilton, Hugh. *Four Introductory Lectures in Natural Philosophy.* London, 1774.

_____. *A Geometrical Treatise of the Conic Sections.* London, 1773.

Hamilton, Max. "Symptoms and Assessment of Depression." In *Handbook of Affective Disorders*, edited by E. S. Paykel, 3–11. New York: Gilford, 1982.

Hankins, Thomas L. "Eighteenth-Century Attempts to Resolve the *Vis Viva* Controversy." *Isis* 56 (1965): 281–97.

_____. *Science and the Enlightenment.* Cambridge: Cambridge University Press, 1985.

Hans, Nicholas. *New Trends in Education in the Eighteenth Century.* London: Routledge & Kegan Paul, 1951.

Harcourt, W. Vernon. "Address," 3–45, with "Appendix," 45–68, followed by sixty pages of lithographed facsimiles of Cavendish's papers. *British Association Report*, 1839.

Hardin, Clyde L. "The Scientific Work of the Reverend John Michell." *Annals of Science* 22 (1966): 27–47.

Hardinge, George. *Biographical Anecdotes of Daniel Wray.* London, 1815.

Harrington, Robert. *A New System on Fire and Planetary Life . . . Also, an Elucidation of the Phaenomena of Electricity and Magnetism.* London, 1796.

Harris, John. *Lexicon Technicum; or, An Universal English Dictionary of Arts and Sciences . . .* Re-edited with a Supplement by a Society of Gentlemen. London, 1744.

Harrison, John. *An Account of the Proceedings, in Order to the Discovery of the Longitude.* London, 1763.

_____. *The Principles of Mr. Harrison's Time-Keeper.* London, 1767.

Harvey, R. A. "The Private Library of Henry Cavendish (1731–1810)." *The Library* 2 (1980): 281–92.

Hatchett, Charles. *The Hatchett Diary: A Tour Through the Counties of England and Scotland in 1796 Visiting Their Mines and Manufactures.* Edited by Arthur Raistrick. Truro: D. Bradford Burton, 1967.

Hatton, Ragnhild. *George I, Elector and King.* Cambridge, Mass.: Harvard University Press, 1978.

Hauksbee, Francis. *Physico-Mechanical Experiments in Various Subjects . . . .* 2d ed. London, 1719.

Haydn, Joseph Timothy. *The Book of Dignities: Continued to the Present Time (1894) . . .*, 3d ed., edited by N. and R. McWhirter. Baltimore: Geneological Publishing Pub. Co., 1970.

Heathcote, Niels N. de V. See Douglas McKie.

_____. See William Cleghorn.

Heberden, Ernest. "Correspondence of William Heberden, F.R.S. with the Reverend Stephen Hales and Sir Charles Blagden." *Notes and Records of the Royal Society of London* 39 (1985): 179–89.

Heberden, William. *Commentaries on the History and Cure of Diseases.* 2d edition. London, 1803.

Heilbron, John L. *Electricity in the 17th and Eighteenth Centuries: A Study of Early Modern Physics.* Berkeley: University of California Press, 1979.

_____. *Physics at the Royal Society During Newton's Presidency.* Los Angeles: William Andrews Clark Memorial Library, 1983.

_____. *Weighing the Imponderables and Other Quantitative Science Around 1800.* Supplement to vol. 24, part 1 of *Historical Studies in the Physical and Biological Sciences,* 1993.

Heimann, P. M. "Ether and Imponderables." In *Conceptions of Ether: Studies in the History of Ether Theories, 1740–1900,* edited by G. N. Cantor and M. J. S. Hodge, 61–83. Cambridge: Cambridge University Press, 1981.

_____. "Geometry and Nature: Leibniz and Johann Bernoulli's Theory of Motion." *Centaurus* 21 (1977): 1–26.

_____. "'Nature Is a Perpetual Worker': Newton's Aether and Eighteenth-Century Natural Philosophy." *Ambix* 20 (1973): 1–26.

_____. "Newtonian Natural Philosophy and the Scientific Revolution." *History of Science* 11 (1973): 1–7.

_____, and J. E. McGuire. "Cavendish and the *Vis Viva* Controversy: A Leibnizian Postscript." *Isis* 62 (1970): 225–27.

_____, and J. E. McGuire. "Newtonian Forces and Lockean Powers: Concepts of Matter in Eighteenth-Century Thought." *Historical Studies in the Physical Sciences* 3 (1971): 233–306.

Helsham, Richard. *A Course of Lectures in Natural Philosophy.* Edited by Bryan Robinson. 7th ed. Philadelphia, 1802.

Henderson, Alfred James. *London and the National Government, 1721–1742. A Study of City Politics and the Walpole Administration.* Durham: Duke University Press, 1945.

Herschel, William. *The Scientific Papers of Sir William Herschel . . . .* 2 vols. Edited by J. L. E.

Dreyer. London: Royal Society and Royal Astronomical Society, 1912.

Hervey, Lord John. *Memoirs of the Reign of George the Second from His Accession to the Death of Queen Caroline,* edited by J. W. Croker. 2. vols., London, 1848. 3 vols., London, 1884.

Hey, Max H. See Gavin De Beer.

Heyd, Michael. *Between Orthodoxy and the Enlightenment. Jean-Robert Chouet and the Introduction of Cartesian Science in the Academy of Geneva.* Boston: Martinus Nijhoff, 1982.

Hiebert, Erwin N. *Historical Roots of the Principle of Energy Conservation.* Madison: State Historical Society of Wisconsin, 1962.

Higgins, Bryan. *Experiments and Observations Relating to Acetous Acid, Fixable Air . . . & Other Subjects of Chemical Philosophy.* London, 1786.

_____. *A Philosophical Essay Concerning Light.* London, 1776.

Hill, J. W. F. *The Letters and Papers of the Banks Family of Revesby Abbey, 1704–1760.* Hereford, England: Lincoln Record Society, 1952.

Hilts, Philip J. *Scientific Temperaments: Three Lives in Contemporary Science.* New York: Simon and Schuster, 1982.

Hobhouse, Hermione. *Lost London.* New York: Weathervane Books, 1971.

Hodges, M. J. S. See G. N. Cantor.

Holmes, Geoffrey. *Augustan England: Professions, State and Society, 1680–1730.* London: George Allen & Unwin, 1982.

_____. *Britain After the Glorious Revolution 1689–1714.* New York: Macmillan, 1982.

_____. *British Politics in the Age of Anne.* London: Macmillan, 1967.

_____. *The Trial of Doctor Sacheverell.* London: Eyre Methuen, 1973.

_____, and W. A. Speck, eds. *The Divided Society. Parties and Politics in England 1694–1716.* Documents of Modern History. New York: St. Martin's Press, 1968.

Holmes, Timothy. *Sir Benjamin Collins Brodie.* London, 1898.

Home, Roderick W. "Aepinus and the British Electricians: The Dissemination of a Scientific Theory." *Isis* 63 (1972): 190–204.

Home, Roderick W. "Out of a Newtonian Straitjacket: Alternative Approaches to Eighteenth-Century Physical Science." In *Studies in the Eighteenth Century. IV. Papers Presented at the Fourth David Nichol Smith Memorial Seminar, Canberra 1976*. Edited by R. F. Brissenden and J. C. Eade, 235–49. Canberra: Australian National University Press, 1979.

——. "The Third Law in Newton's Mechanics." *British Journal for the History of Science* 4 (1968): 39–51.

Horwitz, Henry. *Parliament, Policy and Politics in the Reign of William III*. Newark: University of Delaware Press, 1977.

——. *Revolution Politicks. The Career of Daniel Finch, Second Earl of Nottingham, 1647–1730*. Cambridge: Cambridge University Press, 1968.

Hoskin, Michael A. "Herschel, William," *DSB* 6:328–36.

——. *William Herschel and the Construction of the Heavens*. New York: American Elsevier, 1963.

——. *William Herschel. Pioneer of Sidereal Astronomy*. New York: Sheed & Hand, 1959.

Howse, Derek. "The Greenwich List of Observatories: A World List of Astronomical Observatories, Instruments and Clocks, 1670–1850," *Journal for the History of Astronomy* 17, pt. 4 (1986): 1–100.

——. *Greenwich Observatory*. Vol. 3: *The Buildings and Instruments*. London: Taylor & Francis, 1975.

——. *Nevil Maskelyne: The Seaman's Astronomer*. Cambridge: Cambridge University Press, 1989.

Hudson, Derek, and Kenneth U. Luckhurst. *The Royal Society of Arts, 1754–1954*. London: John Murray, 1954.

Hughes, Edward. "The Early Journal of Thomas Wright of Durham," *Annals of Science* 7 (1951): 1–24.

Hunt, L. B. "William Lewis on Gold: The First Methodical Account of Its Chemical and Physical Properties." *Gold Bulletin* 14 (1981): 36–40.

Hunter, John. *The Anthropological Treatises of Johann Friedrich Blumenbach . . . and the Inaugural Dissertation of John Hunter, MD. On the Varieties of Man*. Translated by T. Bendysche. London, 1865.

——. *Observations on the Diseases of the Army in Jamaica*. 2d ed. London, 1796.

Hutton, Charles. *A Mathematical and Philosophical Dictionary*. 2 vols. London, 1795–96.

Hutton, James. *A Dissertation upon the Philosophy of Light, Heat, and Fire*. Edinburgh, 1794.

Irwin, Raymond. *The Origins of the English Library: Sources and History*. London: George Allen & Unwin, 1958.

Izard, Carroll E., and Marion C. Hyson. "Shyness as a Discrete Emotion." In *Shyness: Perspectives on Research and Treatment*, edited by W. H. Jones, T. M. Cheek, and S. R. Briggs, 147–60. New York: Plenum Press, 1986.

Jackman, W. T. *The Development of Transportation in Modern England*. 2 vols. Cambridge: Cambridge University Press, 1916.

Jacob, Margaret C. *The Cultural Meaning of the Scientific Revolution*. Philadelphia: Temple University Press, 1988.

——. *The Newtonians and the English Revolution 1689–1720*. Ithaca: Cornell University Press, 1976.

Jacquot, Jean. "Sir Charles Cavendish and His Learned Friends. A Contribution to the History of Scientific Relations between England and the Continent in the Earlier Part of the 17th Century. I. Before the Civil War. II. The Years of Exile," *Annals of Science* 8 (1952): 13–27, 175–91.

Janssens, Uta. *Matthieu Maty and the Journal Britannique, 1750–1755* Amsterdam: Holland University Press, 1975.

Jefferson, Thomas. *The Papers of Thomas Jefferson*. Vol. 3. Edited by Julian P. Boyd. Princeton: Princeton University Press, 1956.

Jones, Henry Bence. *The Royal Institution: Its Founder and Its First Professors*. London, 1871.

Jones, Phillip S. "Cramer, Gabriel." *DSB* 3: 459–62.

——. "Taylor, Brook." *DSB* 13: 265–68.

Jones, William. *An Essay on the First Principles of Natural Philosophy . . ..* Oxford, 1762.

"Jones, William." *DNB* 10: 1061–62.

Jorgensen, Bent Søren. "On a Text-Book Error: The Accuracy of Cavendish's Determination of the Oxygen Content of the Atmosphere." *Centaurus* 12 (1968): 132–34.

Jurin, James. "An Essay upon Distinct and Indistinct Vision." In Robert Smith, *Opticks*, at the end of vol. 2, pp. 115–170.

"Jurin, James." *DNB* 10:1117–18.

Kagan, Jerome, J. Steven Reznick, and Nancy Snidman. "Biological Bases of Childhood Shyness." *Science* 240 (1988): 167–71.

Kaye, I. "Captain James Cook and the Royal Society." *Notes and Records of the Royal Society of London* 24 (1969): 7–18.

"Keene, Edmund." *DNB* 10: 1191–92.

Kendrick, T. D. *The Lisbon Earthquake.* London: Methuen, 1956.

Kenyon, J. P. *Robert Spencer, Earl of Sunderland, 1641–1702.* London: Longmans, Green, 1958.

Kerridge, Eric. *The Agricultural Revolution.* London: Allen & Unwin, 1967.

Ketton-Cremer, Robert Wyndham. *Thomas Gray: A Biography.* Cambridge: Cambridge University Press, 1955.

King, Henry C. *The History of the Telescope.* Cambridge, Mass.: Sky Publisher, 1955.

King-Hele, Desmond. *Doctor of Revolution: The Life and Genius of Erasmus Darwin.* London: Faber and Faber, 1977.

Kippis, Andrew. See John Pringle.

Kirwan, Richard. *An Estimate of the Temperature of Different Latitudes.* London, 1787.

―――――. *Geological Essays.* London, 1799.

―――――. See Louis-Bernard Guyton de Morveau.

Kisch, Bruno. *Scales and Weights: A Historical Outline.* New Haven: Yale University Press, 1965.

Kitchiner, William. *The Economy of the Eyes.* Pt. 2: *Of Telescopes; Being the Result of Thirty Years' Experiments with Fifty-One Telescopes, of from One to Nine Inches in Diameter.* London, 1825.

Kline, Morris. *Mathematical Thought from Ancient to Modern Times.* New York: Oxford University Press, 1972.

Knight, David M. "Davy, Humphry," *DSB* 3:598–604.

Knight, Gowin. *An Attempt to Demonstrate, That All the Phaenomena in Nature May Be Explained by Two Simple Active Principles, Attraction and Repulsion: Wherein the Attractions of Cohesion, Gravity and Magnetism, Are Shewn to Be One and the Same; and the Phaenomena of the Latter Are More Particularly Explained.* London, 1748.

Koyré, Alexander. *Newtonian Studies.* London: Chapman & Hall, 1965.

Kuhn, Thomas S. "Mathematical Versus Experimental Traditions in the Development of Physical Science," 31–65. In Kuhn, *The Essential Tension: Selected Studies in Scientific Tradition and Change.* Chicago: Chicago University Press, 1977.

Kula, Witold. *Measures and Men.* Translated by R. Szreter. Princeton: Princeton University Press, 1986.

Labelye, Charles. *A Description of Westminster Bridge.* London, 1751.

―――――. *The Present State of Westminster Bridge.* London, 1743.

Larmor, Joseph. *Mathematical and Physical Papers.* 2 vols. Cambridge: Cambridge University Press, 1929.

Laudan, Rachel. *From Mineralogy to Geology: The Foundations of a Science, 1630–1830.* Chicago: University of Chicago Press, 1987.

Lavoisier, Antoine Laurent. *Elements of Chemistry, in a New Systematic Order, Containing All the Modern Discoveries.* Translated from the French by R. Kerr. Edinburgh, 1790.

LeFanu, William. "Home, Everard," *DSB* 6:478–79.

Leigh, R. A. Austen. *Eton College Lists, 1678–1790.* Eton College: Spottiswoode, 1907.

Leslie, John. *An Experimental Inquiry into the Nature and Propagation of Heat.* London, 1804.

Leslie, Peter Dugud. *A Philosophical Inquiry into the Cause of Animal Heat . . .* London, 1778.

Lewis, William. *Commercium Philosophico—Technicum; or, The Philosophical Commerce of Arts: Designed as an Attempt to Improve Arts, Trades, and Manufactures.* London, 1763.

Lillywhite, Bryant. *London Coffee Houses. A Reference Book of Coffee Houses of the Seventeenth, Eighteenth, and Nineteenth Centuries.* London: George Allen & Unwin, 1963.

Lindeboom, G. A. *Boerhaave and Great Britain.* Leyden: Brill, 1974.

London and the Advancement of Science. London: British Association for the Advancement of Science, 1931.

London County Council. *Survey of London.* Vol. 3l: *The Parish of St. James Westminster.* Part 1: *South of Piccadilly.* Part 2: *North of Picadilly.* General editor F. H. W. Sheppard. London: Athlone, 1960 and 1963.

————. *Survey of London.* Vol. 5: *The Parish of St. Giles-in-the-Fields.* Part 2. London, 1914.

Long, Roger. *Astronomy, In Five Books.* 2 vols. Cambridge, 1742, 1764.

"Long, Roger, D.D." *DNB* 12: 109.

Lovett, Richard. *The Electrical Philosopher. Containing a New System of Physics Founded upon the Principle of an Universal Plenum of Elementary Fire . . . .* Worcester, 1774.

————. *Philosophical Essay, in Three Parts.* Worcester, 1766.

"Lowther, James, Earl of Lonsdale." *DNB* 12: 217–20.

Lubbock, Constance A. *The Herschel Chronicle. The Life-Story of William Herschel and His Sister, Caroline Herschel.* Cambridge: Cambridge University Press, 1933.

Luckhurst, Kenneth W. See Derek Hudson.

Ludlam, William. *Astronomical Observations Made in St. John's College, Cambridge in the Years 1767 and 1768: With an Account of Several Astronomical Instruments.* London, 1769.

————. *The Rudiments of Mathematics; Designed for the Use of Students at the Universities . . .* Cambridge, 1785.

Lundgren, Anders. "The Changing Role of Numbers in 18th-Century Chemistry." In *The Quantifying Spirit in the 18th Century,* edited by T. Frangsmyr, J. L. Heilbron, and R. E. Rider, 245–66. Berkeley: University of California Press, 1990.

Luria, Salvador Edward. *A Slot Machine, a Broken Test Tube: an Autobiography.* New York: Harper & Row, 1984.

Luttrell, Narcissus. *A Brief Historical Relation of State Affairs from September 1678 to 1714.* 6 vols. Oxford, 1857.

Lyon, John. *Experiments and Observations Made with a View to Point Out the Errors of the Present Received Theory of Electricity . . . .* London, 1780.

Lyons, Henry. "The Officers of the Royal Society (1662–1860)." *Notes and Records of the Royal Society of London* 3 (1941): 116–40.

————. *The Royal Society, 1660–1940: A History of Its Administration under Its Charters.* Cambridge: Cambridge University Press, 1944. New York: Greenwood, 1968.

Lysons, Daniel. *Environs of London; Being an Historical Account of the Towns, Villages, and Hamlets, within Twelve Miles of That Capital.* Vol. 1: *County of Surrey.* London, 1792. Vol. 2: *County of Middlesex.* London, 1795.

Lyte, H. C. Maxwell. *A History of Eton College 1440–1884.* London, 1889. Fourth edition, London: Macmillan, 1911.

Maclaurin, Colin. *An Account of Sir Isaac Newton's Philosophical Discoveries ....* London, 1748.

————. *The Collected Letters of Colin Maclaurin.* Edited by S. Mills. Nanturch, Cheshire: Shiva, 1982.

Macquer, Pierre Joseph. *A Dictionary of Chemistry. Containing the Theory and Practice of That Science; Its Applications to Natural Philosophy, Natural History, Medicine, and Animal Economy. . .* Translated by J. Keir. 2 vols. London, 1771. 2d ed., 3 vols. London, 1777.

————. *Elements of the Theory and Practice of Chemistry.* Translated from the French edition of 1756 by A. Reid. 2 vols. London, 1758.

Magellan, J. D. de. *Essai sur la nouvelle théorie du feu élémentaire, et de la chaleur des corps . . . .* London, 1780.

Marlborough, Sarah, Duchess of. *Letters of a Grandmother 1732–1735....* Edited by G. S. Thomson. London: Jonathan Cape, 1943.

————. *The Marlborough-Godolphin Correspondence.* Edited by H. L. Snyder. 3 vols. Oxford: Clarendon Press, 1975.

Marshall, Dorothy. *Dr. Johnson's London.* New York: John Wiley & Sons, 1968.

Martin, Benjamin. *A Course of Lectures in Natural and Experimental Philosophy, Geography and Astronomy . . . Exhibited and Explain'd on the Principles of the Newtonian Philosophy.* Reading, 1743.

————. *A Description of the Nature, Construction, and Use of the Torricellian, or Simple Barometer. With a Scale of Rectification.* London, 1778.

Martin, Benjamin. *An Essay on Electricity: Being an Enquiry into the Nature, Cause and Properties Thereof on the Principles of Sir Isaac Newton's Theory of Vibrating Motion, Light and Fire*. Bath, 1746.

———. *A New and Comprehensive System of Mathematical Institutions, Agreeable to the Present State of the Newtonian Mathesis*. 2 vols. London, 1759–64.

———. *The New Art of Surveying by the Goniometer*. London, 1766.

———. *Philosophia Britannica: Or a New and Comprehensive System of the Newtonian Philosophy, Astronomy, and Geography, in a Course of Twelve Lectures*. 2 vols. London, 1747.

———. *A Plain and Familiar Introduction to the Newtonian Philosophy*. London, 1751.

Martin, D. C. "Former Homes of the Royal Society." *Notes and Records of the Royal Society of London* 22 (1967): 12–19.

Martin, Thomas. "Origins of the Royal Institution." *British Journal for the History of Science* 1 (1962): 49–63.

Martine, George. *Essays and Observations on the Construction and Graduation of Thermometers, and on the Heating & Cooling of Bodies*. 2d ed. Edinburgh, 1772.

Martine, George. *Essays Medical and Philosophical*. London, 1740.

Matsuo, Yukitoshi. "Henry Cavendish: A Scientist in the Age of the *Révolution chimique*." *Japanese Studies in the History of Science* 14 (1975): 83–94.

Maty, Matthew. *Mémoire sur la vie et sur les écrits de Mr. Abraham de Moivre*. The Hague, 1760.

Maty, Paul. *An Authentic Narrative of the Dissentions and Debates in the Royal Society. Containing the Speeches at Large of Dr. Horsley, Dr. Maskelyne, Mr. Maseres, Mr. Poore, Mr. Glenie, Mr. Watson, and Mr. Maty*. London, 1784.

Maxwell, James Clerk. "On the Unpublished Electrical Papers of the Hon. Henry Cavendish." *Proc. Camb. Phil. Soc.* 3 (1877): 86–89.

McCann, H. Gilman. *Chemistry Transformed: The Paradigmatic Shift from Phlogiston to Oxygen*. Norwood: Ablex, 1978.

McClellan, James E., III. *Science Reorganized: Scientific Societies in the Eighteenth Century*. New York: Columbia University Press, 1985.

McClure, Ruth K. *Coram's Children: The London Foundling Hospital in the Eighteenth Century*. New Haven: Yale University Press, 1981.

McCormmach, Russell. "Cavendish, Henry." *DSB* 3 (1971): 155–59.

———. "The Electrical Researches of Henry Cavendish." Ph.D. diss., Case Institute of Technology, 1967.

———. "Henry Cavendish: A Study of Rational Empiricism in Eighteenth-Century Natural Philosophy." *Isis* 60 (1969): 293–306.

———. "Henry Cavendish on the Proper Method of Rectifying Abuses." In *Beyond History of Science: Essays in Honor of Robert E. Schofield*, ed. by E. Garber, 35–51. Bethlehem, PA: Lehigh University Press, 1990.

———. "Henry Cavendish on the Theory of Heat." *Isis* 79 (1988): 37–67.

———. "John Michell and Henry Cavendish: Weighing the Stars." *British Journal for the History of Science*. 4 (1968): 126–55.

———. "The Last Experiment of Henry Cavendish." *'No Truth Except in Details': Essays in Honor of Martin J. Klein*. Edited by A. J. Kox and Daniel M. Siegel, 1–30. Dordrecht: Kluwer Academic Publishers, 1995.

McCrae, Robert R., and Paul T. Costa, Jr. *Personality in Adulthood*. New York and London: The Guilford Press, 1990.

———. See Paul T. Costa, Jr.

McEvoy, John G. "Continuity and Discontinuity in the Chemical Revolution." In *The Chemical Revolution: Essays in Reinterpretation*. Vol. 4, new series of *Osiris*. Edited by A. L. Donovan, 195–213. Published by the History of Science Society, 1988.

———, and J. E. McGuire. "God and Nature: Priestley's Way of Rational Dissent." *Historical Studies in the Physical Sciences* 6 (1975); 325–404.

McGrath, Patrick. *The Merchant Adventurers of Bristol*. Bristol: The Society of Merchant Adventurers, 1975.

McGuire, J. E. See P.M. Heimann.

———. See John G. McEvoy.

McKie, Douglas. "On Thos. Cochrane's MS. Notes of Black's Chemical Lectures, 1767–8." *Annals of Science* 1 (1936): 101–10.

———. "Priestley's Laboratory and Library and Other of His Effects." *Notes and Records of the Royal Society of London* 12 (1956): 114–36.

_____, and Niels H. de V. Heathcote. *The Discovery of Specific and Latent Heats.* London: Arnold, 1935.

McKie, Douglas. See William Cleghorn.

McNeill, William H. *Plagues and Peoples.* New York: History Book Club, 1993.

"Memoirs of the Late Frederick Cavendish, Esq." *Gentleman's Magazine* 82 (1812): 289–91.

Metzger, Héléne. *Newton, Stahl, Boerhaave et la doctrine chimique.* Paris: Librairie Felix Alcan, 1930.

Meyer, Gerald Dennis. *The Scientific Lady in England, 1650–1760.* . .Berkeley: University of California Press, 1955.

Michell, John. *A Treatise of Artificial Magnets, in Which Is Shewn an Easy and Expeditious Method of Making Them Superior to the Best Natural Ones . . . .* London, 1750.

"Michell, John," *DNB* 13:333–34.

Middleton, William E. Knowles. *The History of the Barometer.* Baltimore: The Johns Hopkins University Press, 1964.

_____. *A History of the Thermometer and Its Use in Meteorology.* Baltimore: The Johns Hopkins University Press, 1966.

_____. *Invention of the Meteorological Instruments.* Baltimore: The Johns Hopkins University Press, 1969.

Milhous, Judith, and Robert D. Hume. *Vice Chamberlain Coke's Theatrical Papers 1706–1715.* Edited from the Manuscripts in the Harvard Theatre Collection and Elsewhere. Carbondale and Edwardsville: Southern Illinois University Press, 1982.

Milhous, Judith. "New Light on Vanbrugh's Haymarket Theatre Project." *Theatre Survey* 17 (1976): 143–61.

Millburn, John R. "Benjamin Martin and the Royal Society." *Notes and Records of the Royal Society of London* 28 (1973): 15–23.

_____. *Benjamin Martin: Author, Instrument-Maker, and "Country Showman."* Leyden: Noordhoff, 1976.

Miller, David Philip. "'Into the Valley of Darkness': Reflections on the Royal Society in the Eighteenth Century," *History of Science* 27 (1989): 155–66.

_____. "Sir Joseph Banks: An Historiographical Perspective." *History of Science* 19 (1981): 289–92.

Miller, Edward. *That Noble Cabinet: A History of the British Museum.* London: Deutsch, 1973. Athens, Ohio: Ohio University Press, 1974.

Mintz, Samuel I. "Hobbes, Thomas," *DSB* 6:444–51.

Moivre, Abraham de. *The Doctrine of Chances: Or, a Method of Calculating the Probably of Events in Play.* London, 1718.

_____. *Miscellanea analytica de seriebus et quadraturis.* London, 1730.

_____. *A Treatise of Annuities on Lives.* London, 1725.

Monk, James Henry. *The Life of Richard Bentley, D.D..* 2d ed. 2 vols. London, 1833.

Montagnier, H. F. See Douglas W. Freshfield.

Montagu of Beaulier, Edward John B. D. S., Lord. *More Equal Than Others: The Changing Fortunes of the British and European Aristocracies.* London: Michael Joseph, 1970.

Morgan, Augustus de. "Dr. Johnson and Dr. Maty." *Notes and Queries* 4 (1857): 341.

Morse, E. W. "Smith, Robert." *DSB* 12: 477–78.

"Morton, Charles." *DNB* 13: 1047–48.

Munk, W. *The Roll of the Royal College of Physicians of London. Comprising Biographical Sketches of All the Eminent Physicians Whose Names Are Recorded in the Annals.* 2d ed., 4 vols. London, 1878.

Musschenbroek, Petrus van. *The Elements of Natural Philosophy. Chiefly Intended for the Use of Students in Universities.* Translated by J. Colson. 2 vols. London, 1744.

Musson, A. E., and E. Robinson. *Science and Technology in the Industrial Revolution.* Toronto: University of Toronto Press, 1969.

Nairne, Edward. *Directions for Using the Electrical Machine, As Made and Sold by Edward Nairne . . . .* London, 1764.

Nalbach, Daniel. *The King's Theatre 1704–1867: London's First Italian Opera House.* London: Society for Theatre Research, 1972.

Namier, L. B. *Crossroads of Power: Essays on Eighteenth-Century England.* London: H. Hamilton, 1962.

_____. *The Structure of Politics at the Accession of George III.* 2 vols. London: Macmillan, 1929. 2d ed. London: Macmillan, 1957.

Namier, L. B. and John Brooke. *The House of Commons 1754–1790.* 3 vols. London: Her Majesty's Stationary Office, 1964.

Neumann, Caspar. *The Chemical Works . . . Abridged and Methodized. With Large Additions, Containing the Later Discoveries and Improvements Made in Chemistry and the Arts Depending Thereon.* Translated by W. Lewis. London, 1759.

Newton, Isaac. *The Correspondence of Isaac Newton.* Vols. 2 and 3. Edited by H. W. Turnbull. Cambridge: Cambridge University Press, 1960, 1961. Vol. 6. Edited by A. R. Hall and L. Tilling. Cambridge: Cambridge University Press, 1976.

_____. *Mathematical Papers of Isaac Newton.* Edited by D. T. Whiteside. 8 vols. Cambridge: Cambridge University Press, 1967–81.

_____. *Opticks; or a Treatise of the Reflections, Refractions, Inflections & Colours of Light.* Based on the 4th ed. (1730). New York: Dover Publications, 1952.

_____. *Sir Isaac Newton's Mathematical Principles of Natural Philosophy and His System of the World.* Translated by Andrew Motte in 1729 from the 3d ed. (1726). Revised translation and notes by Florian Cajori. 2 vols. Berkeley and Los Angeles: University of California Press, 1962.

_____. *Universal Arithmetick; or, A Treatise of Arithmetical Composition and Resolution . . . .* Edited by William Whiston. Translated by Joseph Ralphson. London, 1720.

Nichols, John. *Literary Anecdotes of the Eighteenth Century.* 9 vols. London, 1812–16.

_____. *Illustrations of the Literary History of the Eighteenth Century....* 8 vols. London, 1817–58.

Nichols, R. H., and F. A. Wray. *The History of the Foundling Hospital.* London: Oxford University Press, 1935.

Nicholson, William. *An Introduction to Natural Philosophy.* 2 vols. London, 1781.

_____. *The London Diaries of William Nicolson, Bishop of Carlisle 1702–1718.* Edited by C. Jones and G. Holmes. Oxford: Clarendon Press, 1985.

O'Donoghue, Yolande. *William Roy 1726–1790. Pioneer of the Ordnance Survey.* London: British Museum, 1977.

Oldroyd, David R. "Some 18th-Century Methods for the Chemical Analysis of Minerals." *Journal of Chemical Education* 50 (1973): 337–40.

Oliver, J. "William Borlase's Contributions to Eighteenth-Century Meteorology and Climatology." *Annals of Science* 25 (1969): 275–317.

Pallas, Pyotr Simon. *Reise durch verschiedenen Provinzen des russischen Reiches in den Jahren 1768–1773.* 2 vols. St. Petersburg, 1771–76.

Pares, Richard. *King George III and the Politicians.* Oxford: Clarendon Press, 1953.

Paris, John Ayrton. *The Life of Sir Humphry Davy.* London, 1831.

Parisse, Michel, Stéphane Gaber, and Gérard Canini. *Grandes Dates de L'Histoire Lorraine.* Nancy, France: Service des Publications de l'Université de Nancy II, 1982.

"Parker, George, Second Earl of Macclesfield." *DNB* 15: 234–35.

"Parker, Thomas, First Earl of Macclesfield." *DNB* 15: 278–82.

Parsons, F. G. *The History of St. Thomas's Hospital.* Vol. 2: *From 1600 to 1800.* London: Methuen, 1934.

Partington, J. R. *A History of Chemistry.* Vols. 2 and 3. London: Macmillan; New York: St. Martin's Press, 1961–62.

_____. *A Short History of Chemistry.* 2d edition. London: Macmillan, 1951. 3d edition. New York: Harper & Brothers, 1960.

_____, and Douglas McKie. "Historical Studies on the Phlogiston Theory. 1. The Levity of Phlogiston; 2. The Negative Weight of Phlogiston; 3. Light and Heat in Combustion; 4. Last Phases of the Theory." *Annals of Science* 2 (1937): 361–404; 3 (1938): 1–58, 337–71; 4 (1939): 113–49.

_____. See T. S. Wheeler.

Peacock, George. *Life of Thomas Young, M.D., F.R.S. . . .* London, 1855.

Pearson, John. *The Serpent and the Stag: The Saga of England's Powerful and Glamourous Cavendish Family from the Age of Henry the Eighth to the Present.* New York: Holt, Reinhart & Winston, 1983.

Pemberton, Henry. *A Course of Chemistry, Divided into Twenty- Four Lectures.* London, 1771.

_____. *A View of Sir Isaac Newton's Philosophy.* London, 1728.

Perkins, James Breck. *France under the Regency with a Review of the Administration of Louis XIV.* Boston and New York, 1892.

Perrin, Carleton E. "Joseph Black and the Absolute Levity of Phlogiston." *Annals of Science* 40 (1983): 109–37.

Petty, Frederick C. *Italian Opera in London 1760–1800.* Ann Arbor: Umi Research Press, 1980.

Pfister, Christian. *Histoire de Nancy.* Tome III. Paris and Nancy: Berger-Levrault, 1908.

Philip, Alex J. *Hampstead, Then and Now. An Historical Topography.* London: George Routledge, 1912.

Philippovich, Eugen von. *History of the Bank of England, and Its Financial Services to the State.* 2d ed. Translated by C. Meredith. Washington, DC: Government Printing Office, 1911.

Philosophical Magazine. Natural Philosophy Through the Eighteenth Century and Allied Topics. Commemoration number to mark the 150th anniversary of the foundation of the magazine. Edited by Allen Ferguson. London: Taylor & Francis, 1948.

Phipps, Constantine John. *A Voyage Towards the North Pole, Undertaken by His Majesty's Command, 1773.* London, 1774.

Playfair, John. *Outlines of Natural Philosophy, Being Heads of Lectures Delivered in the University of Edinburgh.* 2 vols. Edinburgh, 1812, 1814.

_____. *The Works of John Playfair.* Edited by J. G. Playfair. 4 vols. Edinburgh, 1822.

Plumb, J. H. *Men and Centuries.* Boston: Houghton Mifflin, 1963.

_____. *Sir Robert Walpole.* Vol. 1: *The Making of a Statesman.* London: Cresset, 1956. Vol. 2: *The King's Minister.* London: Cresset, 1960.

Poggendorff, J. C. *Biographisch-Literarisches Handwörterbuch zur Geschichte der exacten Wissenschaften.* 2 vols. Leipzig, 1863.

Porter, Roy. *The Making of Geology: Earth Science in Britain, 1660–1815.* Cambridge: Cambridge University Press, 1977.

_____. "Science, Provincial Culture, and Public Opinion in Enlightenment England." *Brit. J. 18th-Cent. Stud.* 3 (1980): 20–46.

_____. See George S. Rousseau.

Porter, Theodore M. "The Promotion of Mining and the Advancement of Science: The

Chemical Revolution of Mineralogy." *Annals of Science* 38 (1981): 543–70.

Poynting, J. H. *The Mean Density of the Earth.* London, 1894.

Priestley, Joseph. *Experiments and Observations Relating to Various Branches of Natural Philosophy . . . .* London, 1781.

_____. *The History and Present State of Discoveries Relating to Vision, Light, and Colours.* 2 vols. London, 1772.

_____. *The History and Present State of Electricity, with Original Experiments.* London, 1767.

_____. *A Scientific Autobiography of Joseph Priestley (1733–1804).* Edited by Robert E. Schofield. Cambridge, Mass.: M.I.T. Press, 1966.

Pringle, John. *A Discourse on the Attraction of Mountains, Delivered at the Anniversary Meeting of the Royal Society, November 30, 1775.* London, 1775.

_____. *A Discourse on the Torpedo Delivered at the Anniversary Meeting of the Royal Society, November 30, 1774.* London, 1775.

_____. *Six Discourses, Delivered by Sir John Pringle, Bart. When President of the Royal Society; on Occasion of Six Annual Assignments of Sir Godfrey Copley's Medal. To Which Is Prefixed the Life of the Author. By Andrew Kippis, D.D. F.R.S. and S.A.* London, 1783.

"Pringle, Sir John." *DNB* 16:386–88.

Quill, Humphrey. "John Harrison, Copley Medallist, and the Twenty Thousand Pound Longitude Prize." *Notes and Records of the Royal Society of London* 18 (1963): 146–60.

_____. *John Harrison: The Man Who Found Longitude.* London: Baker, 1966.

_____. *The Life and Letters of Joseph Black, M.D.* London: Constable, 1918.

Ramsden, Jesse. *An Account of Experiments to Determine the Specific Gravity of Fluids.* London, 1792.

_____. *Description of an Engine for Dividing Mathematical Instruments.* London, 1771.

Ravetz, J. "The Representation of Physical Quantities in Eighteenth-Century Mathematical Physics." *Isis* 52 (1961): 7–20.

Read, John. *A Summary View of Spontaneous Electricity of the Earth and Atmosphere . . . .* London, 1793.

Reich, R. *Versuche über die Mittlere Dichtigkeit der Erde mittelst der Drehwage*. Freiburg, 1838.

Rigaud, Stephen Jordan, ed. *Correspondence of Scientific Men of the Seventeenth Century*. Vol. 1. Hildesheim: Georg Olms reprint, 1965.

Robins, Benjamin. *Mathematical Tracts of the Late Benjamin Robins*. Edited by James Wilson. 2 vols. London, 1761.

Robinson, Bryan. *A Dissertation on the Aether of Sir Isaac Newton*. Dublin, 1743.

Robinson, Eric. "James Watt, Engineer and Man of Science." *Notes and Records of the Royal Society of London* 24 (1969): 221–32.

Robinson, Eric. See Musson, A. E.

Robinson, Mary. *Beaux & Belles of England*. London: Grolier Society, n.d.

Robison, John. *A System of Mechanical Philosophy* . . . Edited with notes by David Brewster. 4 vols. Edinburgh, 1822.

Roger, Jacques. "Whiston, William." *DSB* 14: 295–96.

Rolleston, Humphry. "The Two Heberdens." *Annals of Medical History* 5 (1933): 409–24, 566–83.

Ronan, Colin A. "Halley, Edmond." *DSB* 6: 67–72.

_____. *Edmond Halley*. New York: Doubleday, 1969.

"Ross or Rosse, John." *DNB* 17:266–67.

Rouse Ball, W. W. *A History of the Study of Mathematics at Cambridge*. Cambridge, 1889.

Rousseau, George S., and Roy Porter, eds. *The Ferment of Knowledge: Studies in the Historiography of 18th-Century Science*. Cambridge: Cambridge University Press, 1980.

Rowning, John. *A Compendious System of Natural Philosophy. With Notes Containing Mathematical Demonstrations, and Some Occasional Remarks*. 4th ed. London, 1745.

"Rowning, John." *DNB* 17: 367.

"Roy, William." *DNB* 17:371–73.

Royal Institution of Great Britain. *The Archives of the Royal Institution of Great Britain in Facsimile. Minutes of Managers' Meetings 1799–1900*. Vols. 1 and 2 (in one volume). Edited by F. Greenaway. Ilkley, Yorkshire: Published in association with the Royal Institution of Great Britain by the Scolar Press Limited, 1971.

Royal Society of London. *The Record of the Royal Society at London for the Promotion of Natural knowledge*. 4th ed. London: Royal Society of London, 1940.

Rubini, Dennis. *Court and Country 1688–1702*. London: Rupert Hart-Davis, 1967.

Rudé, George. *Hanoverian London 1714–1808*. Berkeley: University of California Press, 1971.

Rudolf, R. de M. "The Clapham Sect." In *Clapham and the Clapham Sect*, edited by E. Baldwin, 89–142. Clapham, England: Clapham Antiquarian Society, 1927.

Ruestow, Edward G. *Physics at Seventeenth and Eighteenth–Century Leiden: Philosophy and the New Science in the University*. The Hague: Martinus Nijhoff, 1973.

Russell, Lady Rachel. *Letters of Lady Rachel Russell; from the Manuscript in the Library at Woburn Abbey*. 5th ed. London, 1793.

Russell, Lord John, Fourth Duke of Bedford. *Correspondence of John, 4th Duke of Bedford. . . .* 3 vols. Edited by Lord John Russell. London, 1842, 1843, 1846.

Russell-Wood, J. "The Scientific Work of William Brownrigg, M.D., F.R.S. (1711–1800)—I." *Annals of Science* 6 (1950): 436–47.

Rutherforth, Thomas. *A System of Natural Philosophy, Being a Course of Lectures in Mechanics, Optics, Hydrostatics, and Astronomy; Which Are Read in St Johns College Cambridge . . . .* 2 vols. Cambridge, 1748.

"Rutherforth, Thomas." *DNB* 17: 499–500.

Sachse, William L. *Lord Somers: A Political Portrait*. Manchester: Manchester University Press, 1975.

Salmon. *A Short View of the Families of the Present Nobility*, 3d ed. London, 1761.

Sampson, R. A., and A. E. Conrady. "On Three Huygens Lenses in the Possession of the Royal Society of London." *Proceedings of the Royal Society of Edinburgh* 49 (1928–29): 289–99.

Saunderson, Nicholas. *Elements of Algebra*. 2 vols. London, 1740.

_____. *The Method of Fluxions Applied to a Select Number of Useful Problems; . . . and an Explanation of the Principal Propositions of Sir Isaac Newton's Philosophy*. London, 1756.

"Saunderson or Sanderson, Nicholas." *DNB* 17: 821–22.

Saussure, Horace Bénédict de. *Voyages dans les Alpes, précédés d'un essai sur l'histoire naturelle des environs de Genève.* 4 vols. Neuchâtel-Genève, 1779–96.

Schaffer, Simon. "Natural Philosophy and Public Spectacle in the 18th Century." *History of Science* 21 (1983): 1–43.

Scheele, Karl Wilhelm. *The Chemical Essays of Charles-William Scheele.* Translated with additions by T. Beddoes. London, 1786.

_____. *Chemical Observations and Experiments on Air and Fire.* Translated by J. R. Forster, with notes by Richard Kirwan. London, 1780.

Schneider, Ivo. "Der Mathematiker Abraham de Moivre (1667–1754)." *Archive for History of Exact Sciences* 5 (1968): 177–317.

Schofield, Robert E. "The Counter-Reformation in 18th-Century Science, Last Phase." *Perspectives in the History of Science and Technology*, edited by Duane H. D. Roller, 39–54. Norman: University of Oklahoma Press, 1971.

_____. "Electrical Researches of Joseph Priestley." *Archives Internationales d'Histoire des Sciences* 16 (1963): 277–86.

_____. "Joseph Priestley, Natural Philosopher." *Ambix* 14 (1967): 1–15.

_____. "Joseph Priestley, the Nature of Oxidation and the Nature of Matter." *Journal of the History of Ideas* 25 (1964): 285–94.

_____. *The Lunar Society of Birmingham. A Social History of Provincial Science and Industry in Eighteenth-Century England.* Oxford: Clarendon Press, 1963.

_____. *Mechanism and Materialism: British Natural Philosophy in an Age of Reason.* Princeton: Princeton University Press, 1970.

_____. See D. G. C. Allan.

_____. See Joseph Priestley.

Schwoerer, Lois G. *Lady Rachel Russell. "One of the Best of Women."* Baltimore: The Johns Hopkins University Press, 1988.

Scott, E. L. "The 'Macbridean Doctrine' of Air; an Eighteenth-Century Explanation of Some Biochemical Processes Including Photosynthesis." *Ambix* 17 (1970): 43–57.

_____. "Richard Kirwan, J. H. de Magellan, and the Early History of Specific Heat." *Annals of Science* 38 (1981): 141–53.

_____. "Rutherford, Daniel." *DSB* 12:24–25.

"Scott, George Lewis." *DNB* 17: 961–62.

Scott, Wilson L. *The Conflict Between Atomism and Conservation Theory, 1644–1860.* New York: Elsevier, 1970.

Sedgwick, Romney. *The House of Commons 1715–1754.* 2 vols. New York: Oxford University Press, 1970.

Shapin, Steven. "The House of Experiment in Seventeenth-Century England." *Isis* 79 (1988): 373–404.

_____. "'A Scholar and a Gentleman': The Problematic Identity of the Scientific Practitioner in Early Modern England." *History of Science* 29 (1991): 279–327.

Shaw, Peter. *Chemical Lectures. . . . .* 2d ed. London, 1755.

Sheets-Pyenson, Susan. "New Directions for Scientific Biography: The Case of Sir William Dawson," *History of Science* 28 (1990): 399–410.

Shepperd, James A., and Robert M. Arkin. "Shyness as a Personality Trait." In *Shyness and Embarrassment: Perspectives from Social Psychology*, edited by W. Ray Crozier, 315–37. Cambridge: Cambridge University Press, 1990.

Sheynin, O. B. "Newton and the Classical Theory of Probability." *Archive for History of Exact Sciences* 7 (1970–71): 217–43.

Shuckburgh, George. *Observations Made in Savoy, in Order to Ascertain the Height of Mountains by Means of the Barometer; Being an Examination of Mr. De Luc's Rules, Delivered in His Recherches sur les Modifications de l'Atmosphère. Read at the Royal Society, May 18 and 15, 1777.* London, 1777.

Sichel, Walter. *Bolingbroke and His Times. The Sequel.* New York: Greenwood, 1968.

Sidgwick, J. B. *William Herschel: Explorer of the Heavens.* London: Faber and Faber, 1953.

Siegfried, Robert. "The Chemical Revolution in the History of Chemistry," 34–50. In *The Chemical Revolution: Essays in Reinterpretation.* Edited by A. L. Donovan. Vol. 4, new series of *Osiris.* Published by the History of Science Society in 1988.

_____. "Lavoisier's View of the Gaseous State and Its Early Application to Pneumatic Chemistry." *Isis* 63 (1972): 59–78.

_____, and Betty Jo Dobbs. "Composition, a Neglected Aspect of the Chemical Revolution." *Annals of Science* 24 (1968): 275–93.

Sime, James. *William Herschel and His Work*. New York: Charles Scribner's Sons, 1900.

Simpson, Thomas. *The Doctrine and Application of Fluxions*. 2 vols. London, 1750.

————. *Miscellaneous Tracts on Some Curious and Very Interesting Subjects in Mechanics, Physical Astronomy, and Speculative Mathematics, Wherein the Precession of the Equinox, the Nutation of the Earth's Axis, and the Motion of the Moon in Her Orbit Are Determined*. London, 1757.

————. *The Nature and Doctrine of Chance*. London, 1740.

Singer, Dorothea Waley. "Sir John Pringle and His Circle—Part I. Life." ". . .—Part III. Copley Discourses." *Annals of Science* 6 (1949): 127–80 and 6 (1950): 248–61.

Sivin, Nathan. "William Lewis (1708–1781) as a Chemist." *Chymia* 8 (1962): 63–88.

Six, James. *Construction and Use of a Thermometer for Shewing the Extremes of Temperature in the Atmosphere, During the Observer's Absence . . . .* London, 1794.

Skempton, A. W., and Joyce Brown. "John and Edward Troughton, Mathematical Instrument Makers." *Notes and Records of the Royal Society of London* 27 (1973): 233–49.

————., ed. *John Smeaton, FRS*. London: Telford, 1981.

Sloan, W. R. "Sir Hans Sloan, F.R.S.: Legend and Lineage." *Notes and Records of the Royal Society of London* 35 (1980): 125–33.

Smeaton, John. *Experimental Enquiry Concerning the Natural Powers of Wind and Water*. London, 1794.

Smeaton, W. A. "Macquer, Pierre Joseph." *DSB* 8: 618–24.

————. "Montgolfier, Étienne Jacques de; Montgolfier, Michel Joseph de," *DSB* 9: 492–94.

Smiles, Samuel. *The Huguenots: Their Settlements, Churches, and Industries in England and Ireland*. New York, 1868.

Smith, Eric E. F. *Clapham*. London: London Borough of Lambeth, 1976.

Smith, John Edward and W. Parkinson Smith. *The Parliamentary Representation of Westminster from the Thirteenth Century to the Present Day*. Vol. 2. London: Wightman, 1923.

Smith, Robert. *A Compleat System of Opticks in Four Books, viz. a Popular, a Mathematical, a Mechanical, and a Philosophical Treatise. To Which Are Added Remarks upon the Whole*. 2 vols. Cambridge, 1738.

————. *Harmonics, or the Philosophy of Musical Sounds*. 2d ed. Cambridge, 1759.

"Smith, Robert." *DNB* 18: 517–19.

Snyder, Henry L. "The Defeat of the Occasional Conformity Bill and the Tack: A Study in the Techniques of Parliamentary Management in the Reign of Queen Anne," In *Peers, Politics and Power: The House of Lords, 1603–1911*. Edited by C. and D. L. Jones, 111–31. London and Ronceverte: The Hambledon Press, 1986.

Sparrow, W. J. *Knight of the White Eagle*. London: Hutchinson, 1964.

Speck, W. A. *Tory & Whig. The Struggle in the Constituencies 1701–1715*. New York: St. Martin's Press, 1970.

Spray, W. A. "Alexander Dalrymple, Hydrographer." *American Neptune* 30 (1970): 200–16.

Stanhope, Charles, Lord Mahon. *Principles of Electricity, Containing Diverse New Theorems and Experiments . . .* London, 1779.

Stanhope, Philip Dormer, Earl of Chesterfield. *Letters Written by the Late Right Honourable Philip Dormer Stanhope, Earl of Chesterfield, to His Son, Philip Stanhope, Esq; Late Envoy Extraordinary at the Court of Dresden: Together with Several Other Pieces on Various Subjects*. Edited by E. Stanhope. Vol. 2. Dublin, 1774.

Stansfield, Dorothy A. *Thomas Beddoes, M.D., 1760–1808: Chemist, Physician, Democrat*. Dordrecht: Reidel, 1984.

Stearns, Carol Zisowitz. "Sadness." In *Handbook of Emotions*. Edited by M. Lewis and J. M. Haviland, 547–61. New York: Guilford, 1993.

Stearns, Raymond Phineas. *Science in the British Colonies of America*. Urbana: University of Illinois Press, 1970.

Steffens, Henry John. *The Development of Newtonian Optics in England*. New York: Science History Publications, 1977.

Steiner, Lewis H. *Henry Cavendish and the Discovery of the Chemical Composition of Water*. New York, 1855.

Stelling–Michaud, Sven, and Suzanne Stelling–Michaud, eds. *Le Livre du Recteur de l'Académie de Genève*. Vols. 1–3. Geneva: Droz, 1959–72.

Stephenson, R. J. "The Electrical Researches of the Hon. Henry Cavendish, F.R.S." *The American Physics Teacher* 6 (1938): 55–58.

Sterne, Laurence. *A Sentimental Journey Through France and Italy.* Originally published in 1768. Introduction by V. Woolf. London: Milford, 1951.

Stewart, Larry. "Public Lectures and Private Patronage in Newtonian England." *Isis* 77 (1986): 47–58.

———. *The Rise of Public Science: Rhetoric, Technology, and Natural Philosophy in Newtonian Britain, 1660–1750.* Cambridge: Cambridge University Press, 1992.

Stimson, Dorothy. *Scientists and Amateurs. A History of the Royal Society.* New York: Schuman, 1948.

Stirling, James. *The Differential Method: or, a Treatise Concerning Summation and Interpolation of Infinite Series.* London, 1749.

Stokes, Hugh. *The Devonshire House Circle.* London: Herbert Jenkins, 1917.

Stone, Edmund. *The Construction and Principal Uses of Mathematical Instruments. Translated from the French of M. Bion, Chief Instrument-Maker to the French King . . .* London, 1723.

Stone, Lawrence. *The Family, Sex and Marriage in England 1500–1800.* Abr. ed. Harmondsworth: Penguin Books, 1982.

Struik, D. J. "Musschenbroek, Petrus van." *DSB* 9:594–97.

Stuart, Dorothy Margaret. *Dearest Bess: The Life and Times of Lady Elizabeth Foster, Afterwards Duchess of Devonshire.* London: Methuen, 1955.

Subbarayappa, B. V. "Western Science in India up to the End of the Nineteenth Century A.D." In *A Concise History of Science in India,* edited by D. M. Bose, 484–97. New Delhi: Indian National Science Academy, 1971.

Summerson, John. *Georgian London.* Rev. ed. Harmondsworth: Penguin Books, 1978.

Supplement to Friend to Dr. Hutton. *An Appeal to the Fellows of the Royal Society, Concerning the Measures Taken by Sir Joseph Banks, Their President, to Compel Dr. Hutton to Resign the Office of Secretary to the Society for Their Correspondence.* London, 1784.

Supplement to the Appeal to the Fellows of the Royal Society: Being Letters Taken from the Public Advertiser and Morning Post. London, 1784.

Susskind, Charles. "Henry Cavendish, Electrician." *Journal of the Franklin Institute* 249 (1950): 181–87.

Sykes, Norman. *Church and State in England in the XVIIIth Century.* Cambridge: Cambridge University Press, 1934.

Talbot, Catherine, See Elzabeth Carter.

Taylor, Brook. *Contemplatio Philosophica: A Posthumous Work of the Late Brook Taylor, L.L.D. F.R.S. Some Time Secretary of the Royal Society to Which Is Prefixed a Life of the Author by His Grandson, Sir William Young, Bart., F.R.S. A.S.S. . . .* London, 1793.

Taylor, E. G. R. *The Mathematical Practitioners of Hanoverian England, 1714–1840.* Cambridge: Cambridge University Press, 1966.

———. *The Mathematical Practitioners of Tudor and Stuart England.* Cambridge: Cambridge University Press, 1954.

Thackray, Arnold W. *Atoms and Powers: An Essay on Newtonian Matter-Theory and the Development of Chemistry.* Cambridge, Mass.: Harvard University Press, 1970.

———. "Dalton, John." *DSB* 3: 537–47.

———. "Natural Knowledge in Cultural Context: The Manchester Model." *American Historical Review* 79 (1974): 672–709.

Thomas, Keith. *Man and the Natural World: A History of the Modern Sensibility.* New York: Pantheon, 1983.

Thomas, Lewis. *The Medusa and the Snail: More Notes of a Biology Watcher.* New York: Bantam, 1980.

———. *The Youngest Science: Notes of a Medicine-Watcher.* New York: Viking, 1983.

Thomas, P. D. G. *The House of Commons in the Eighteenth Century.* Oxford: Clarendon Press, 1971.

Thompson, Benjamin, Count Rumford. *The Complete Works of Count Rumford.* 4 vols. Boston, 1870–75.

Thompson, F. M. L. *Hampstead: Building a Borough, 1650–1964.* London: Routledge & Kegan Paul, 1974.

Thomson, Gladys Scott. *Life in a Noble Household, 1641–1700.* London: Jonathan Cape, 1937.

Thomson, John. *An Account of the Life, Lectures, and Writings of William Cullen, M.D.,*

Professor of the Practice of Physic in the University of Edinburgh. 2 vols. Edinburgh, 1859.

Thomson, A.T. *Memoirs of Viscountess Sundon, Mistress of the Robes to Queen Caroline.* Vol. 1, 2d ed. London, 1848.

Thomson, Thomas. *The History of Chemistry.* 2 vols. London, 1830–31.

————. *History of the Royal Society from Its Institution to the End of the Eighteenth Century.* London, 1812.

Thornton, William. *The New, Complete, and Universal History, Description, and Survey of the Cities of London and Westminster . . . Likewise the Towns, Villages, Palaces, Seats, and Country, to the Extent of Above Twenty Miles Round.* Rev. ed. London, 1784.

Titchmarsh, P. F. "The Michell-Cavendish Experiment." *The School Science Review,* no. 162 (Mar.1966): 320–30.

Titchmarsh, P. F. "Temperature Effects in the Michell-Cavendish Experiment." *The School Science Review,* no. 163 (June 1966): 678–93.

Todhunter, Isaac. *A History of the Mathematical Theories of Attraction and the Figure of the Earth, from the Time of Newton to That of Laplace.* London, 1873.

Todhunter, Isaac. *A History of the Mathematical Theory of Probability from the Time of Pascal to That of Laplace.* Cambridge, 1865.

Tompkins, Herbert W. *Highways and Byways in Hertfordshire.* London: Macmillan, 1902.

Toulmin, Stephen, and June Goodfield. *The Discovery of Time.* New York: Harper & Row, 1965.

Treasures from Chatsworth. The Devonshire Inheritance. A Loan Exhibition from the Devonshire Collection, by Permission of the Duke of Devonshire and the Trustees of the Chatsworth Settlement. Organized and Circulated by the International Exhibitions Foundation, 1979–1980.

Trengove, Leonard. "Chemistry at the Royal Society of London in the 18th Century." *Annals of Science* 19 (1963): 183–237; 20 (1964): 1–57; 21 (1965): 81–130, 75–201; 26 (1970): 331–53.

Trent, Christopher. *The Russells.* New York: Barnes & Noble, 1966.

Truesdell, Clifford. "A Program Toward Rediscovering the Rational Mechanics of the Age of Reason." *Archive for History of Exact Sciences* 1 (1960): 1–36.

Trevelyan, George Macauley. *England under Queen Anne: Blenheim.* London: Longmans, Green, 1930.

Trumbach, Randolph. *The Rise of the Egalitarian Family: Aristocratic Kinship and Domestic Relations in Eighteenth-Century England.* New York: Academic Press, 1978.

Tunbridge, Paul A. "Jean André De Luc, F.R.S. (1727–1817)." *Notes and Records of the Royal Society of London* 26 (1971): 15–33.

Turberville, A. S., ed. *Johnson's England: An Account of the Life & Manners of His Age.* Vol. 2. Oxford: Clarendon Press, 1933.

Turner, A. J. "Mathematical Instruments and the Education of Gentlemen." *Annals of Science* 30 (1973): 51–88.

Turner, G. l'E. "The Auction Sale of the Earl of Bute's Instruments, 1793." *Annals of Science* 23 (1967): 213–42.

Tweedie, Charles. *James Stirling. A Sketch of His Life and Works Along with His Scientific Correspondence.* Oxford: Clarendon Press, 1922.

Twigg, John. *A History of Queens' College, Cambridge, 1448–1986.* Woodbridge, Suffolk: Boydell Press, 1987.

Venn, John and J. A. Venn. *Alumni Cantabrigienses . . . Part 1. From the Earliest Times to 1751.* 4 vols. Cambridge: Cambridge University Press, 1922–1954.

Vernon, Kenneth D. C. *The Foundation and Early Years of the Royal Institution.* London: Royal Institution, 1963. Reprinted from *Proc. Roy. Inst.* 39 (1962): 364–402.

The Victoria History of the Counties of England. Cambridge and the Isle of Ely. London: Published for the University of London, Institute of Historical Research by Dawsons of Pall Mall, 1967. Reprinted from the original edition of 1948.

The Victoria History of the Counties of England. Derbyshire. London: Published for the University of London, Institute of Historical Research by Dawsons of Pall Mall, 1970. 2 vols. Reprinted from the original edition of 1905.

The Victoria History of the County of Hertford. Vol. 2. Folkestone and London: Published for the University of London, Institute of Historical Research by Dawsons of Pall Mall, 1971. Reprinted from the original edition of 1902.

The Victoria History of the County of Lancaster. Edited by W. Farrer and J. Brownbill. Vol. 8. London: Constable, 1914.

Walker, R. J. B. *Old Westminster Bridge: The Bridge of Fools.* Newton Abbot: David and Charles, 1979.

Walker, Thomas Alfred. *Admissions to Peterhouse or S. Peter's College in the University of Cambridge. A Biographical Register.* Cambridge: Cambridge University Press, 1912.

———. *Peterhouse.* Cambridge: W. Heffer, 1935.

Walker, W. Cameron. "Animal Electricity Before Galvani." *Annals of Science* 2 (1937): 84–113.

Wallis, P. J. "The MacLaurin 'Circle': The Evidence of Subscription Lists." *Bibliotheck* 11 (1982): 38–54.

———. "Stirling, James." *DSB* 13: 67–70.

Wallis, R. V., and P. J. Wallis. *Biobibliography of British Mathematics and Its Applications.* Part 2: *1701–1760.* Newcastle upon Tyne: Epsilon Press, 1986.

Walpole, Horace. *Horace Walpole's Correspondence.* Edited by W. S. Lewis. 48 vols. New Haven: Yale University Press, 1937–83.

———. *Memoirs of King George II.* Vol. 1: *January 1751–March 1754.* Edited by John Brooke. New Haven: Yale University Press, 1985.

"Walsh, John." *DNB* 20: 671–72.

Ward, W. R. *Georgian Oxford: University Politics in the Eighteenth Century.* Oxford: Clarendon, 1958.

Watermann, Rembert. "Eudiometrie (1772–1805)." *Technik-Geschichte* 35 (1968): 293–319.

Watson, John Steven. *Reign of George III, 1760–1815.* Oxford: Clarendon Press, 1960.

Watson, Richard. *Anecdotes of the Life of Richard Watson, Bishop of Landaff; Written by Himself at Different Intervals, and Revised in 1814.* 2d ed., vol. 1. London, 1818.

"Watson, Sir William." *DNB* 20:956–58.

Watson, William. *An Account of a Series of Experiments Instituted with a View of Ascertaining the Most Successful Method of Inoculating the Smallpox.* London, 1768.

Watt, James. *Correspondence of the Late James Watt on His Discovery of the Theory of the Composition of Water.* Edited by James Patrick Muirhead. London, 1846.

———, and Joseph Black. *Partners of Science: Letters of James Watt and Joseph Black.* Edited by Eric Robinson and Douglas McKie. Cambridge, Mass.: Harvard University Press, 1970.

———. See Thomas Beddoes.

Webb, Sidney, and Beatrice Webb. *English Local Government: The Story of the King's Highway.* London: Longmans, Green, 1920.

Webster, Roderick S. "Troughton, Edward." *DSB* 13: 470–71.

Weiss, Leonard. *Watch-Making in England, 1760–1820.* London: Robert Hale, 1982.

Weld, Charles Richard. *A History of the Royal Society,* . . . 2 vols. London, 1848. New York: Arno Press, 1975.

Wells, Ellen B. "Scientists' Libraries: A Handlist of Printed Sources," *Annals of Science* 40 (1983): 317–89.

Wells, Samuel. *The History of the Drainage of the Great Level of the Fens, Called Bedford Level: With the Constitution and Laws of the Bedford Level Corporation.* 2 vols. London, 1830.

Wentworth, Thomas. *The Wentworth Papers 1705–1739. Selected from the Private and Family Correspondence of Thomas Wentworth, Lord Raby, Created in 1711 Earl of Strafford, of Stainborough, Co. York.* Edited by James J. Cartwright. London, 1883.

Westfall, Richard. *Never at Rest. A Biography of Isaac Newton.* Cambridge: Cambridge University Press, 1980.

Wheatley, Henry B. *London, Past and Present. A Dictionary of Its History, Associations, and Traditions.* 3 vols. London, 1891.

Wheeler T. S., and J. R. Partington. *The Life and Work of William Higgins, Chemist (1763–1825).* New York: Pergamon, 1960.

Whiston, William. *Astronomical Lectures, Read in the Publick Schools of Cambridge* . . . . English translation from the Latin edition of 1707. London, 1715. 2d ed. London, 1728.

———. *Memoirs of the Life and Writings of Mr. William Whiston.* London, 1749.

———. *A New Theory of the Earth* . . . 5th ed. London, 1737.

———. *Sir Isaac Newton's Mathematic Philosophy More Easily Demonstrated.* Translated from the Latin edition of 1710. London, 1716.

Whitehurst, John. *An Inquiry into the Original State and Formation of the Earth; Deduced from Facts and the Laws of Nature. To Which Is Added an Appendix, Containing Some General Observations on the Strata in Derbyshire....* London, 1778.

Whittaker, Sir Edmund. *A History of the Théories of Aether and Electricity.* Vol. I: *The Classical Théories.* New York: Harper & Bros., 1960.

Widmalm, Sven. "Accuracy, Rhetoric, and Technology: The Paris-Greenwich Triangulation, 1784–88." In *The Quantifying Spirit in the Eighteenth Century*, edited by T. Frangsmyr, J. L. Heilbron, and R. E. Rider, 179–206. Berkeley: University of California Press, 1990.

Wightman, William P. D. "The Copley Medal and the Work of Some of the Early Recipients." *Physis* 3 (1961): 344–55.

Wilkinson, Lise. "'The Other' John Hunter, M.D., F.R.S. (1754–1809): His Contributions to the Medical Literature, and to the Introduction of Animal Experiments into Infectious Disease Research." *Notes and Records of the Royal Society of London* 36 (1982): 227–41.

Will, Clifford M. "Henry Cavendish, Johann von Soldner, and the Deflection of Light." *American Journal of Physics* 56 (1988): 413–15.

Willey, Basil. *The Eighteenth Century Background: Studies on the Idea of Nature in the Thought of the Period.* Boston: Beacon, 1940.

————. *The Whig Supremacy, 1714– 1760.* 2d rev. ed. Edited by C. H. Stuart. Oxford: Clarendon Press, 1962.

Willis, Robert, and John Willis Clark. *Architectural History of the University of Cambridge, and of the Colleges of Cambridge and Eton.* Cambridge, 1886.

Wilson, Benjamin. *An Essay Towards an Explication of the Phaenomena of Electricity, Deduced from the Aether of Sir Isaac Newton.* London, 1746.

Wilson, George. *The Life of the Honourable Henry Cavendish, Including Abstracts of His More Important Scientific Papers, and a Critical Inquiry into the Claims of All the Alleged Discoverers of the Composition of Water.* London, 1851.

Wilson, Jessie Aitken. *Memoir of George Wilson.* London & Cambridge, 1862.

Wilson, Joseph. *Memorabilia Cantabrigiae: Or, an Account of the Different Colleges in Cambridge ...* London, 1803.

Winstanley, Denys Arthur. *Unreformed Cambridge.* Cambridge: Cambridge University Press, 1935.

Wolf, A. *A History of Science, Technology, & Philosophy in the 16th & 17th Centuries.* 2d ed. Edited by D. McKie. 2 vols. New York: Harper & Bros., 1961.

————. *A History of Science, Technology, & Philosophy in the 18th Century.* 2d ed. Edited by D. McKie. 2 vols. New York: Harper & Bros., 1961.

"Wollaston, Francis." *DNB* 21: 778–79.

Wood, Alexander, and Frank Oldham. *Thomas Young, Natural Philosopher, 1773–1829.* Cambridge: Cambridge University Press, 1954.

Woolf, Harry. "Theories of the Universe in the Late Eighteenth Century." In *Biology, History, and Natural Philosophy*, edited by Allen D. Breck and Wolfgang Youngrau, 263–89. New York: Plenum, 1972.

————. *The Transits of Venus: A Study of Eighteenth-Century Science.* London: Oxford University Press, 1959.

Woolley, Richard. "Captain Cook and the Transit of Venus of 1769." *Notes and Records of the Royal Society of London* 24 (1969): 19–32.

Wordsworth, Christopher. *Scholae Academicae: Some Account of the Studies at the English Universities in the Eighteenth Century.* Cambridge, 1877. London: Frank Cass, 1968.

Worster, Benjamin. *A Compendious and Methodical Account of the Principles of Natural Philosophy.* 2d ed. London, 1730.

Wray, R. A. See R. H. Nichols.

Wright, Thomas. *An Original Theory or New Hypothesis of the Universe, Founded upon the Laws of Nature....* London, 1750.

Yorke, Philip Chasney. *The Life and Correspondence of Philip Yorke, Earl of Hardwicke, Lord High Chancellor of Great Britain.* 3 vols. Cambridge: Cambridge University Press, 1913.

Young, Thomas. *A Course of Lectures on Natural Philosophy and the Mechanical Arts.* 2 vols. London, 1807.

————. "Life of Cavendish." *Encyclopaedia Britannica*, Supplement (1816–24); reprinted in Henry Cavendish, *The Scientific Papers of the Honourable Henry Cavendish* 1:435–47.

————. *A Syllabus of a Course of Lectures on Natural and Experimental Philosophy.* London, 1802.

Name Index

Adams, George, 163
Aepinus, F. U. T., 279:
    electrical theory, 179–80
    reception in Britain, 180–81
Akenside, Mark, 72n.46
Alexander, William:
    portrait of Henry Cavendish, 8–9
Anguish, T., 252–53
Anne, Queen:
    second Duke of Devonshire at the court of, 23
    Duke of Kent at the court of, 24–28
Arago, D. F. J., 272
Arbuthnot, John, 56, 90
Arderon, William, 141
Arnold, John, 204
Aubert, Alexander, 213, 217, 263:
    Royal Society, 165, 195–96, 254
    friendship with Henry Cavendish, 246, 300
    astronomy, 299–300, 300n.11, 308, 311
    meteors, 312
Avogadro, Amadeo, 259
Ayloffe, Joseph, 91

Babington, William, 359
Bacon, Francis, 57–58
Baker, George, 72
Baldwin, Christopher, 242–46
Banks, Sir Joseph, 203, 206, 235, 281, 346:
    Royal Society, 191n.41, 192, 267, 300, 315, 329
    and Charles Blagden, 213–15, 329–32
    political dissentions at the Royal Society, 247–56
    Royal Institution, 349–50
Barker, Robert, 202
Barrington, Daines, 200n.26, 206
Barrow, John, 366n.4
Bayley, William, 167n.52
Bentinck, Margaret Cavendish, Duchess of Portland:
    scientific interests, 2–3
Bentley, Richard, 118–19, 237
Bergman, Torbern:
    mineral water, 155
    mineralogy, 326
Bernard, Thomas, 349
Bernoulli, Daniel, 183, 323
Bernoulli, Johann I, 50
Berry, A. J.:
    view of Henry Cavendish, 8
Berthollet, Claude Louis, 270
Bevis, John, 137
Bickley, Francis:
    view of Henry Cavendish, 8
Biot, J. B.:
    opinion of Henry Cavendish, 1, 354:
Birch, Thomas, 70–74, 88, 109:
    at Wrest Park, 16
    patronized by the first and second Earls of Hardwicke, 68
    becoming friends with Lord Charles Cavendish, 70
    Royal Society, 72–73, 94, 108
    on Robert Boyle, 73
    recommended Henry Cavendish for F.R.S., 130
Bird, John, 101, 163, 168, 234, 300, 314
Black, Joseph, 212, 319:
    fixed air, 151–52
    latent and specific heats, 157–58, 160, 280, 280n.9, 283
    lectures, 160
    on phlogiston, 271
Blagden, Sir Charles, 349:
    Royal Society, 191, 191n.41, 195, 267, 309, 332

friendship with Henry Cavendish, 212–17, 246, 356–58, 360, 362, 367
    student and friend of William Cullen, 212, 232
    opinion of Henry Cavendish, 232, 333, 335
    moving Henry Cavendish's house, 238, 238nn.124,125
    part in the Royal Society dissentions, 248–56
    on national politics, 256–58
    assistant to Cavendish, 214–16, 263, 267–68, 281, 308
    view of chemical nomenclature, 269
    water controversy, 271–73
    heat, 282, 282n.24
    meteors, 312
    triangulation, 315–17
    journeys with Cavendish, 318–25
    Bristol Harbor, 328
    excise duty on alcohol, 330, 330n.142
    Cavendish's death, 354–55, 363–64
Blake, Francis, 101–2, 101nn.89,93
Blanchard, Jean Pierre, 263
Blunt, Thomas, 161–63
Boerhaave, Hermann, 148, 158, 175:
    consulted by Lord Charles and Lady Anne Cavendish, 66
Bonaparte, Napoleon:
    opinion on Henry Cavendish, 352
Borlase, William, 164
Boscovich, Roger Joseph, 133
    attraction of mountains, 199n.22
    on particles and forces, 296–97, 297n.87
    comets, 311
Bouger, Pierre, 198
Boulton, Matthew, 319, 321, 346
Boyle, Charles, Earl of Orrey (son of Anne Cavendish, sister of the first Duke of Devonshire):
    orrery, 3
Boyle, Robert, 73, 112, 148:
    related to the Cavendishes, 3, 78
    experiments on air, 120, 152
    Boyle's law, 177
Boys, C. V., 340–41, 340n.21
Bradley, James:
    Royal Society, 56, 75, 95, 99, 103
    aberration of light, 61, 121
    observations with Lord Charles Cavendish, 61
    collaboration with Lord Macclesfield, 61
    supported by Lord Charles Cavendish for Astronomer Royal, 61
    proposed Henry Cavendish for F.R.S., 129
    nutation, 135–36
    distance of the stars, 301
Braikenridge, William, 168
Brande, William Thomas, 359
Braun, J. A., 279
Brice, Alexander, 162
Brockelsby, Richard, 267
Brodie, Sir Benjamin, 329n.135, 359
Brougham, Henry Peter, Baron:
    on scientific biographies, 7
    on Henry Cavendish's silence, 369
Brownrigg, William, 141:
    coal damps, 155–56
    connections with Sir James Lowther and Henry Cavendish, 155–56
    mineral water, and Copley Medal, 155–56
Burke, Edmund, 248
Burrow, Sir James, 75, 95, 134, 195–96, 200, 206, 207n.81
Burrow, Reuben, 200
Bussiere, Paul, 56
Byrom, John, 60

Subject Index

fire:
    as element, 152, 326
    doctrine of elementary fire, 175, 285
fluids, imponderable, 175:
    relations between, 192, 294
    electrical, 176
    heat, caloric, 284-85
forces:
    science of, 4
    attracting and repelling, 172, (plate) 172, 186, 296-97, 297nn.88,89, 306
    interconversion of, 344-45
Foundling Hospital, 127, (figure 27):
    smallpox inoculations, 58
    establishment of, 85-86

Geological Society, 359
geology, 116:
    earthquakes, 60, 134, 138-40
    journeys, 317-28
    heights of mountains, 320
    strata, 320, 324-25, 328
    and chemistry, 325
    and mineralogy, 325
Giardini Academy, 126-28
Glorious Revolution:
    Cavendishes, descendants of, and participants in, 3
    character of, 3
    and Cambridge, 114
government administration:
    as a profession, 49-50
Great Marlborough Street, (figure 14):
    purchase and description of house, 66-67
    as laboratory, 144, 186
    as double home, 130-31
    lease of, 229
    Henry Cavendish's townhouse, 230, 237
Greenwich Observatory, Royal, 168:
    longitude at sea, 59
    Royal Society's visitations, 96-97, 96n.77
Grey family, (figure 5):
    in politics, 14, 24-30
    characteristics, relationships, 14-16, 68-69
    scientific connections and interests, 15-16, 69
    dukedom, 27
    music, love of, 27, 126-27

Hackney Academy, 107-8
Hampstead, 229-31, 263, 315:
    Church Row, (figure 15)
Hardwick Hall, 2, 33, 222
Haymarket:
    and Kent, 28
Heat:
    freezing solutions, 70
    Lord Charles Cavendish's thermometers, (plate) 98, 99, 164, 203, 203n.49, 359
    expansion of water and steam with heat, 103
    expansion of mercury with heat, 103
    as motion, and mathematical theory of, 115, 170, 172-74, 264, 282-95
    and earthquakes, 140
    extreme natural and artificial cold, 140, 214, 279-82, 213
    latent and specific, 156-60, 173-74, 265, 279-83, 287-89, 287n.46, 292, 319
    quantitative science of, 156
    experimental technique of, 158-59
    standard, water, 159
    equivalent weight, 159
    boiling, theory of, 170
    and the human body, 213
    mercury, freezing of, 279-81

cold by rarefaction of air, 282
freezing mixtures, 281-82
nomenclature, 282-83, 87, 292
mechanical theory of heat, 282, 283n.29, 290, 290n.61, 293
from fermentations and dissolutions, 173, 284
difficulties of the theory of heat as motion, 284
material, fluid, caloric theory of heat, 284-86, 290, 294
absolute heat, 286
and light, 172, 288-90
and chemical reactions, 288-89, 288n.49
heat rays, 289
and friction and hammering, 289-90, 293
and electricity, 289-90
velocity of vibrating particles in a heated body, 290
unsatisfactoriness of the material theory of heat, 291
weight of, 292
caloric theory of gases, 294
active, 287, 287n.46
sensible, 287, 287n.47
see mechanics
Heytesbury:
    parliamentary seats, 40
Holker Hall, 80-81, 81n.117
Homes of Henry Cavendish, (map) 231:
    Putteridge, 64-67
    Great Marlborough Street, 66-67
    Hampstead, 229-31
    Bedford Square, 231-35
    Clapham Common, 237-46
House of Commons:
    in session, (figure 23)
    power of, 18-19, 30
    Cavendishes in, 18-23, 39-46
    business of, 40
    committee work, 40-42
    and Fellows of the Royal Society, 45-46, 45n.74
House of Lords:
    Devonshires in, 22-24
    Kent in, 24-25
Huguenots:
    and the Cavendishes, 35, 50-51, 71
    De Moivre, 49-56
Hudson's Bay Company, 204-5:
    experiments on cold, 280, 282

industry:
    iron and steel, 37, 44, 318-21
    textiles, 35, 44-45, 318-19
    and heat, 293
    journeys, 317-28
    industrial revolution, 319
    quarries, 319
    coal and coke, 319
    coal damps, 59, 140, 155-56
    kilns, 319
    copper, tin, and brass, 319, 321
    chemicals, 319
    alum, 321
    clay pits, 321
    lead mines, 34, 37, 327
instrument-makers, London, 121, 125, 161-62, 164, 168, 313-14
Institute of France, 351-52
instruments and apparatus:
    scientific revolution, 3
    marine chronometers, 59, 96, 99-100, 204
    telescopes, 121, 132, 162, 299, 301, 306-11, 320
    musical, 122-24
    planetarium, 124
    accuracy, and calibration, of, 133, 136, 158, 161, 163-64, 166, 315-16
    drawings, 135
    pyrometer, 135

Grey Family

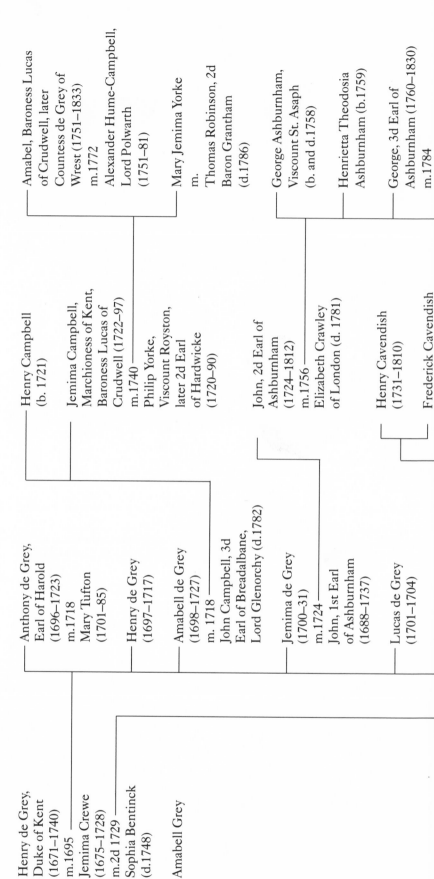

Henry de Grey,
Duke of Kent
(1671–1740)
m.1695
Jemima Crewe
(1675–1728)
m.2d 1729
Sophia Bentinck
(d.1748)

Amabell Grey

Anthony de Grey,
Earl of Harold
(1696–1723)
m.1718
Mary Tufton
(1701–85)

Henry de Grey
(1697–1717)

Amabell de Grey
(1698–1727)
m. 1718
John Campbell, 3d
Earl of Breadalbane,
Lord Glenorchy (d.1782)

Jemima de Grey
(1700–31)
m.1724
John, 1st Earl
of Ashburnham
(1688–1737)

Lucas de Grey
(1701–1704)

Henry Campbell
(b. 1721)

Jemima Campbell,
Marchioness of Kent,
Baroness Lucas of
Crudwell (1722–97)
m.1740
Philip Yorke,
Viscount Royston,
later 2d Earl
of Hardwicke
(1720–90)

John, 2d Earl of
Ashburnham
(1724–1812)
m.1756
Elizabeth Crawley
of London (d. 1781)

Henry Cavendish
(1731–1810)

Frederick Cavendish

Amabel, Baroness Lucas
of Crudwell, later
Countess de Grey of
Wrest (1751–1833)
m.1772
Alexander Hume-Campbell,
Lord Polwarth
(1751–81)

Mary Jemima Yorke
m.
Thomas Robinson, 2d
Baron Grantham
(d.1786)

George Ashburnham,
Viscount St. Asaph
(b. and d.1758)

Henrietta Theodosia
Ashburnham (b.1759)

George, 3d Earl of
Ashburnham (1760–1830)
m.1784